P9-BJG-211

12 EDITION

Accounting for Governmental and Nonprofit Entities

Earl R. Wilson, Ph.D., CPA
KPMG/Joseph A. Silvoso
Distinguished Professor
University of Missouri–Columbia

Susan C. Kattelus, Ph.D., CPA, CGFM
Associate Professor
Eastern Michigan University

Leon E. Hay, Ph.D., CPA, CGFM
Distinguished Professor Emeritus
University of Arkansas–Fayetteville

Boston Burr Ridge, IL Dubuque, IA Madison, WI New York San Francisco St. Louis
Bangkok Bogotá Caracas Lisbon London Madrid
Mexico City Milan New Delhi Seoul Singapore Sydney Taipei Toronto

McGraw-Hill Higher Education

A Division of The **McGraw-Hill** *Companies*

ACCOUNTING FOR GOVERNMENTAL AND NONPROFIT ENTITIES

This book is printed on acid-free paper.

2 3 4 5 6 7 8 9 0 DOC/DOC 0 9 8 7 6 5 4 3 2 1

ISBN 0072410264

Senior vice president and editorial director: *Robin J. Zwettler*
Publisher: *Jeffrey J. Shelstad*
Sponsoring editor: *Steve Hazelwood*
Editorial assistant: *Angela Jacobs*
Marketing manager: *Richard Kolasa*
Project manager: *Scott Scheidt*
Production supervisor: *Rose Hepburn*
Senior supplement coordinator: *Cathy L. Tepper*
Media technology producer: *Ed Przyzycki*
Cover design: *Kiera Cunningham*
Interior design: *Kiera Cunningham*
Compositor: *GAC Indianapolis*
Typeface: *10.5/12 Goudy*
Printer: *R. R. Donnelley & Sons Company/Crawfordsville*

Library of Congress Cataloging-in-Publication Data

Wilson, Earl Ray (date)
Accounting for governmental and nonprofit entities / Earl R. Wilson, Susan C. Kattelus, Leon E. Hay — 12th ed.
p. cm.
ISBN 0-07-241026-4 (alk. paper)
Includes bibliographical references and index.
1. Finance, Public — Accounting. 2. Nonprofit organizations — Accounting. 3. Nonprofit organizations — United States — Accounting. I. Kattelus, Susan Convery. II. Hay, Leon Edwards, 1923-
HJ9733.W48 2001
657'.95dc—21 00-037003

www.mhhe.com

Preface

Honoring this book's tradition as the oldest and most comprehensive text on governmental and nonprofit accounting, we offer this revision as the first to fully integrate the GASB's new financial reporting models (GASB *Statement Nos. 34* and 35, 1999). Educators and professionals have made this the leading text on the subject since 1951 because they can rely on it to be accurate and thorough and to incorporate the most effective pedagogy in teaching this complex topic. In this edition, we use "dual-track" accounting throughout the book to capture information necessary to prepare both government-wide and fund financial statements.

Professor R. M. Mikesell of Indiana University–Bloomington set the standard of excellence with the first two editions (1951, 1956). Dr. Leon E. Hay, then at Indiana University and later at the University of Arkansas–Fayetteville, joined Professor Mikesell in 1961 and continues through this edition to ensure that the text is the most accurate in the field. Dr. Earl R. Wilson of the University of Missouri–Columbia joined Dr. Hay with the ninth edition (1992). As a former member of the Governmental Accounting Standards Advisory Council and several task forces of the GASB and other professional organizations, he provides insight for the most up-to-date coverage in the field. Dr. Susan C. Kattelus of Eastern Michigan University joined with the 11th edition (1999) and adds her expertise in the area of nonprofit accounting as well as pedagogical tools, such as cases and Internet resources.

This edition incorporates changes in FASB, GASB, FASAB, AICPA, OMB, GAO, and other authoritative sources through the spring of 2000. The authors will continue the service of issuing to adopters of this text Update Bulletins that describe changes after the book is in print. These bulletins can be downloaded from Dr. Wilson's website, http://www.missouri.edu/~accterw. The authors welcome technical inquiries about the text, preferably by e-mail.

Many professors who were thanked by name in the Prefaces to earlier editions have continued to give generously of their time and effort in improving explanations in chapters of the text and improving the wording of questions, exercises, problems, and solutions. The authors gratefully acknowledge the following individuals who were particularly helpful with this edition of the text: Dr. Kenneth W. Brown of Southwest Missouri State University for Chapter 10 on the evaluation of financial performance; Robert Bramlett and Dr. James Patton of the Federal Accounting Standards Advisory Board, Bruce K. Michelson of the U.S. General Accounting Office, and J. Thomas Luter, formerly of the U.S. Department of the Treasury, for Chapter 12 on federal government accounting; and Dr. Mary L. Fischer of the University of Texas at Tyler and David Smarr of the University of Missouri–Columbia for Chapter 16 on colleges and universities. We gratefully acknowledge the support of our spouses, Florence J. Wilson, John T. Kattelus, and Bobbye S. Hay, CPA, who have contributed greatly to this and previous editions, both technically and personally.

The authors appreciate the courtesy of the Governmental Accounting Standards Board in giving permission to quote their pronouncements and reproduce illustrations from their publications. We are grateful to the Government Finance Officers Association, American Institute of Certified Public Accountants, and International City/County Management Association who granted permission for use of their materials.

Ancillary materials that accompany this text (also available on CD-ROM) include:

- Instructor's Guide and Solutions Manual (including teaching and case analysis tips)
- Power Point lecture presentations (which include 20 to 60 slides for each chapter)
- Test Bank (including a computerized version)
- City of Smithville Computerized Continuous Problem

Although we are extremely careful in checking the text and end-of-chapter material, it is probable that errors, inconsistencies, and ambiguities remain in this edition. As readers encounter errors of omission or commission in this text, we urge them to let us know so that corrections can be made. Additionally, every user of this edition who has suggestions or comments about the material in the chapters is invited to share them with either of the following two coauthors, either by regular mail or e-mail.

Dr. Earl R. Wilson
School of Accountancy
University of Missouri–Columbia
Columbia, MO 65211
wilsonea@missouri.edu
http://www.missouri.edu/~accterw

Dr. Susan C. Kattelus
Department of Accounting
Eastern Michigan University
Ypsilanti, MI 48197
susan.kattelus@emich.edu
http://www.online.emich.edu/~acc_kattelus

Brief Contents

Contents

Accounting for Governmental and Nonprofit Entities

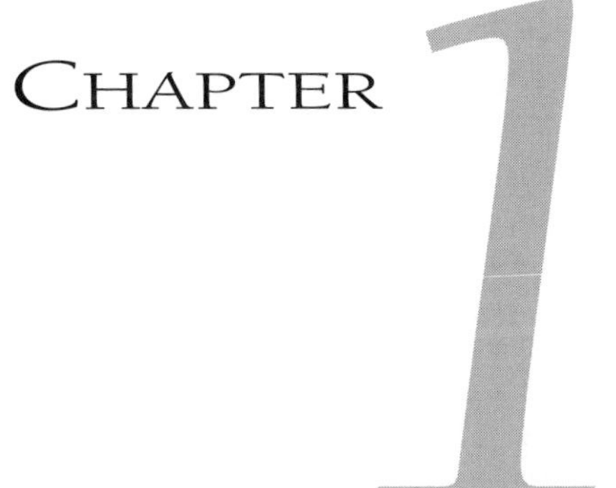

Financial Reporting for Governmental and Not-for-Profit Entities

Learning Objectives

After studying this chapter, you should be able to:

- Identify and explain the characteristics that distinguish governmental and not-for-profit entities from for-profit entities.
- Identify the authoritative bodies responsible for setting financial reporting standards for (1) state and local governments, (2) the federal government, and (3) not-for-profit organizations.
- Contrast and compare the objectives of financial reporting for (1) state and local governments, (2) the federal government, and (3) not-for-profit organizations.
- Distinguish management's discussion and analysis (MD&A), basic financial statements, and required supplementary information of state and local governments from their comprehensive annual financial reports.
- Explain the different objectives, measurement focus, and basis of accounting of the government-wide financial statements and fund financial statements of state and local governments.
- Explain why analysis of the financial performance of governmental and not-for-profit entities differs from that of for-profit entities.

What Are Governmental and Not-for-Profit Organizations?

Governmental and not-for-profit organizations are vast in number and diversity. In the United States, governments exist at the federal, state, and local levels and serve a wide variety of functions. The most recent census of governments reports 87,453 local governmental units, in addition to the federal government and 50 state governments. These 87,453 local governments consist of 3,043 counties, 19,372 municipalities, 16,629 towns and townships, 13,726 independent school districts, and 34,683 special district governments.[1]

States, counties, municipalities (for example, cities and villages), and townships are **general purpose governments**—governments that provide many categories of services to their residents (such as police and fire protection; sanitation; construction and maintenance of streets, roads, and bridges; and health and welfare). Independent school districts, public colleges and universities, and special districts are **limited or special purpose governments**—governments that provide only a single function, or a limited number of functions (such as education, drainage and flood control, irrigation, soil and water conservation, fire protection, and water supply). Special purpose governments have the power to levy and collect taxes and to raise revenues from other sources as provided by state laws to finance the services they provide.

Not-for-profit organizations also exist in many forms and serve many different functions. Estimates of the number of not-for-profit organizations range from several hundred thousand to more than 1 million.[2] These include private colleges and universities, various kinds of health care entities, some libraries, museums, professional and trade associations, fraternal and social organizations, and religious organizations.

Distinguishing Characteristics of Governmental and Not-for-Profit Entities

Governmental and not-for-profit organizations differ in important ways from business organizations. Moreover, as you will soon learn, accounting and financial reporting for governmental and not-for-profit organizations are markedly different from accounting and financial reporting for businesses. An understanding of how governmental and not-for-profit organizations differ from business organizations is

[1]U.S. Department of Commerce, Bureau of the Census, *1997 Census of Governments*, vol. 1, no. 1 (Washington, DC: U.S. Government Printing Office), p. v.

[2]The U.S. Bureau of the Census (1992 *Census of Service Industries*, SC92-S-1, Table 1b) reports that in 1992 there were 208,911 tax-exempt service organizations. This does not include, however, numerous other not-for-profit organizations such as religious organizations, labor unions, and political organizations. The total of tax-exempt not-for-profits numbers more than 1 million (*1996–97 Nonprofit Almanac: Dimensions of the Independent Sector*, Washington, DC).

essential to understanding the unique accounting and financial reporting principles that have evolved for governmental and not-for-profit organizations.

In its *Statement of Financial Accounting Concepts No. 4*, the **Financial Accounting Standards Board (FASB)** noted the following characteristics that it felt distinguished governmental and not-for-profit entities from business organizations:

a. Receipts of significant amounts of resources from resource providers who do not expect to receive either repayment or economic benefits proportionate to the resources provided.

b. Operating purposes that are other than to provide goods or services at a profit or profit equivalent.

c. Absence of defined ownership interests that can be sold, transferred, or redeemed, or that convey entitlement to a share of a residual distribution of resources in the event of liquidation of the organization.[3]

The **Governmental Accounting Standards Board (GASB)** further distinguishes governmental entities in the United States from not-for-profit entities and from businesses by stressing that governments exist in an environment in which the power ultimately rests in the hands of the people. Voters delegate that power to public officials through the election process; the power is divided among the executive, legislative, and judicial branches of the government so that the actions, financial and otherwise, of governmental executives are constrained by legislative actions; and executive and legislative actions are subject to judicial review. Further constraints are imposed on state and local governments by the existence of the federal system in which higher levels of government encourage or dictate activities by lower levels and finance the activities (partially, at least) by an extensive system of intergovernmental grants and subsidies that require the lower levels to be accountable to the entity providing the resources, as well as to the citizenry. Revenues raised by each level of government come, ultimately, from taxpayers. Taxpayers are required to serve as providers of resources to governments even though they often have very little choice about which governmental services they receive and the extent to which they receive them.

Since governments may have a monopoly on the services they provide to the public, the lack of a competitive marketplace makes it difficult to measure efficiency in the provision of the services. It is also extremely difficult to measure optimal quantity or quality for many of the services rendered by government—for example, how many police are "enough"? The Governmental Accounting Standards Board notes the determination of optimal quantity or quality of government services is complicated by the involuntary nature of the resources provided. "A consumer purchasing a commercial product can determine how much to purchase

[3]Financial Accounting Standards Board, *Statement of Financial Accounting Concepts No. 4*, "Objectives of Financial Reporting by Nonbusiness Organizations" (Norwalk, CT, 1980), p. 3. In 1985 the FASB decided to replace the term *nonbusiness* with the term *not-for-profit*. Other organizations use the term *nonprofit* as a synonym for not-for-profit. The terms are used interchangeably in this text.

Illustration 1–1 Primary Sources of Accounting and Financial Reporting Standards for Business, Governmental, and Not-for-Profit Organizations

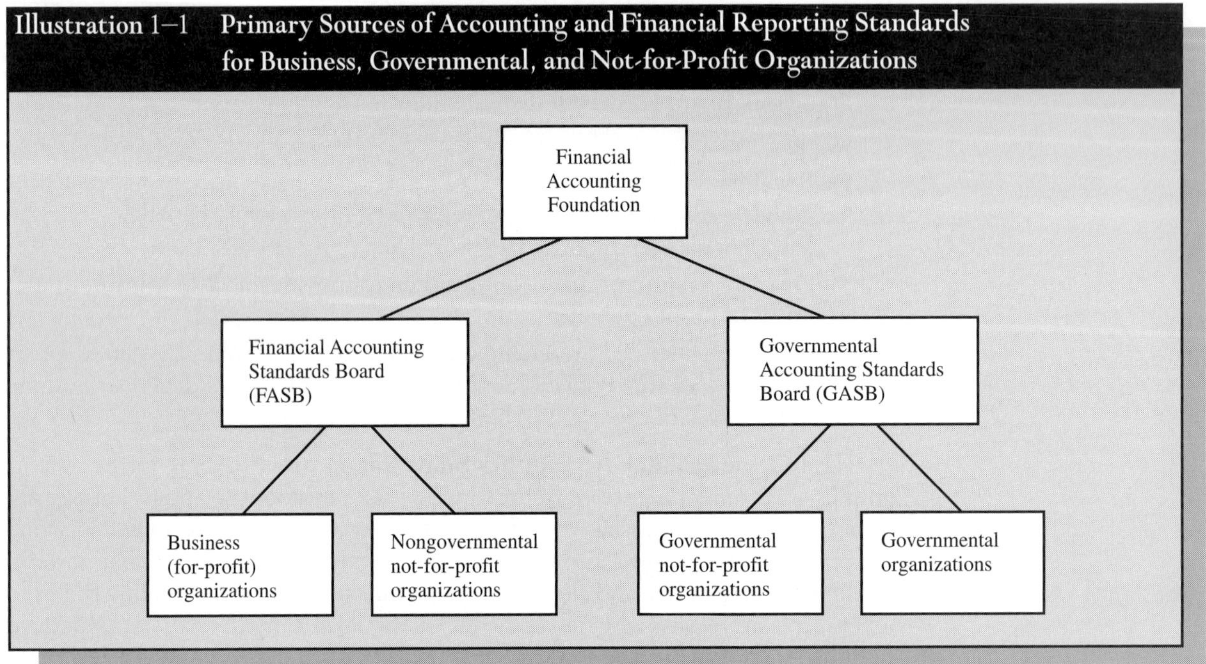

and may choose among 'good,' 'better,' or 'best' quality and pay accordingly. A group of individuals paying for governmental services (and paying in different proportions for services that some of them may not use or desire) presents a far more complex situation."[4]

Sources of Financial Reporting Standards

Illustration 1–1 shows the primary sources of accounting and financial reporting standards for business, governmental, and not-for-profit organizations. As shown, the FASB establishes accounting and financial reporting standards for business (for-profit) organizations; the GASB establishes standards for governmental organizations.

Authority to establish accounting principles (accounting and financial reporting standards) for not-for-profit organizations is split between the GASB and the FASB because a sizable number of not-for-profit organizations (particularly colleges and universities, and hospitals) are governmentally related, but many others are

[4]Governmental Accounting Standards Board, *Codification of Governmental Accounting and Financial Reporting Standards as of June 30, 1999* (Norwalk, CT, 1999), Appendix B, par. 17e.

independent of governmental units. Accordingly, the GASB has the responsibility for establishing accounting and financial reporting standards for not-for-profit organizations that are considered to be governmental in character. The FASB has the responsibility for establishing accounting and financial reporting standards for nongovernmental not-for-profit organizations.

The GASB and the FASB are parallel bodies under the oversight of the Financial Accounting Foundation. The Financial Accounting Foundation appoints the members of the two boards and supports the operating expenses of the boards by obtaining contributions from business corporations; professional organizations of accountants, financial analysts, and other groups concerned with financial reporting; CPA firms; debt-rating agencies; and state and local governments (for support of the GASB). Because of the breadth of support and the lack of ties to any single organization or governmental unit, the GASB and the FASB are referred to as "independent standards-setting boards in the private sector." Before the creation of the GASB and the FASB, financial reporting standards were set by groups sponsored by professional organizations: The forerunners of the GASB (formed in 1984) were the National Council on Governmental Accounting (1973–84), the National Committee on Governmental Accounting (1948–73), and the National Committee on Municipal Accounting (1934–41). The forerunners of the FASB (formed in 1973) were the Accounting Principles Board (1959–73) and the Committee on Accounting Procedure (1938–59) of the American Institute of Certified Public Accountants.

Federal statutes assign responsibility for establishing and maintaining a sound financial structure for the federal government to three officials: the Comptroller General, the Director of the Office of Management and Budget, and the Secretary of the Treasury. In 1990, these three officials created the **Federal Accounting Standards Advisory Board (FASAB)** to recommend accounting principles and standards for the federal government and its agencies. It is understood that, to the maximum extent possible, federal accounting and financial reporting standards should be consistent with those established by the GASB and, where applicable, by the FASB.

In Rule 203 of its Code of Professional Conduct, the American Institute of Certified Public Accountants (AICPA) has formally designated the GASB, the FASAB, and the FASB as the authoritative bodies to establish accounting principles for state and local governments, for the federal government, and for business organizations and nongovernmental not-for-profit organizations, respectively. "Authority to establish accounting principles" is interpreted in practice to mean "authority to establish accounting and financial reporting standards."

Determining Whether a Not-for-Profit Organization Is Governmental

Illustration 1–1 suggests that the kinds of organizations for which the FASB and GASB are responsible for setting standards are clearcut. Unfortunately, this is sometimes not the case. In practice, it may be difficult to determine whether some types of not-for-profits are governmental in nature or not, and thus which standards-setting body to look to for authoritative guidance.

The U.S. Bureau of the Census defines a *government* as:

> An organized entity which, in addition to having governmental character, has sufficient discretion in the management of its own affairs to distinguish it as separate from the administrative structure of any other governmental unit.[5]

This definition, though helpful, provides insufficient guidance because it fails to explain the meaning of "having governmental character." In order to provide additional guidance for auditors on this issue, two audit and accounting guides of the AICPA, with the tacit approval of both the FASB and the GASB, state:

> Public corporations and bodies corporate and politic are governmental organizations. Other organizations are governmental organizations if they have one or more of the following characteristics:
>
> *a.* Popular election of officers or appointment (or approval) of a controlling majority of the members of the organization's governing body by officials of one or more state or local governments,
>
> *b.* the potential for unilateral dissolution by a government with the net assets reverting to a government, or
>
> *c.* the power to enact *and* enforce a tax levy.[6]

Furthermore, organizations are presumed to be governmental if they have the ability to issue directly (rather than through a state or municipal authority) debt that pays interest exempt from federal taxation. However, organizations possessing only that ability (to issue tax-exempt debt) and none of the other governmental characteristics may rebut the presumption that they are governmental if their determination is supported by compelling, relevant evidence.

Objectives of Financial Reporting

In its *Concepts Statement No. 1*, "Objectives of Financial Reporting," the Governmental Accounting Standards Board stated that "**Accountability** is the cornerstone of all financial reporting in government . . . Accountability requires governments to answer to the citizenry—to justify the raising of public resources and the purposes for which they are used."[7] The board elaborated:

> Governmental accountability is based on the belief that the citizenry has a "right to know," a right to receive openly declared facts that may lead to public debate by the citizens and their elected representatives. Financial reporting plays a major role in fulfilling government's duty to be publicly accountable in a democratic society.[8]

---

[5]U.S. Department of Commerce, Bureau of the Census, *1997 Census of Governments*, vol. 1, no. 1 (Washington, DC: U.S. Government Printing Office), p. ix.

[6]American Institute of Certified Public Accountants, Audit and Accounting Guide, *Health Care Organizations* (New York, 1999), par. 1.02(c); and American Institute of Certified Public Accountants, Audit and Accounting Guide, *Not-for Profit Organizations* (New York, 1999), par. 1.03.

[7]GASB, *Codification*, Appendix B, *Concepts Statement No. 1*, par. 56.

[8]Ibid.

Financial reports of state and local governments, according to the GASB, are used primarily to (1) compare actual financial results with the legally adopted budget; (2) assess financial condition and results of operations; (3) assist in determining compliance with finance-related laws, rules, and regulations; and (4) assist in evaluating efficiency and effectiveness.

Closely related to the concept of accountability as the cornerstone of governmental financial reporting is the concept the GASB refers to as **interperiod equity.** The concept and its importance are explained as follows:

> The Board believes that interperiod equity is a significant part of accountability and is fundamental to public administration. It therefore needs to be considered when establishing financial reporting objectives. In short, *financial reporting should help users assess whether current-year revenues are sufficient to pay for services provided that year and whether future taxpayers will be required to assume burdens for services previously provided.* (Emphasis added.)[9]

Accountability is also the foundation for the financial reporting objectives the Federal Accounting Standards Advisory Board (FASAB) has developed for the federal government. The FASAB's *Statement of Accounting and Reporting Concepts Statement No. 1* identifies four objectives of federal financial reporting. In brief, the objectives are to assist report users in evaluating budgetary integrity, operating performance, stewardship, and adequacy of systems and controls.

Unlike the FASB and the GASB, which focus their standards on external financial reporting, the FASAB and its sponsors in the federal government are concerned with both internal and external financial reporting. Accordingly, the FASAB has identified four major groups of users of federal financial reports: citizens, Congress, executives, and program managers. Given the broad role the FASAB has been assigned, its standards focus on cost accounting and service efforts and accomplishment measures, as well as on financial accounting and reporting.

Financial reports of not-for-profit organizations—voluntary health and welfare organizations, private colleges and universities, private hospitals, religious organizations, and others—have similar uses. However, in recognition of the fact that the financial operations of not-for-profit organizations are generally not subject to as detailed legal restrictions as are those of governments, the Financial Accounting Standards Board believes the financial reports for not-for-profit organizations should provide: (1) information useful in making resource allocation decisions; (2) information useful in assessing services and ability to provide services; (3) information useful in assessing management stewardship and performance; and (4) information about economic resources, obligations, net resources, and changes in them.[10]

Note the objectives of financial reporting for governments and not-for-profit entities stress the need for the public to understand and evaluate the financial

---

[9]Ibid., par. 61.

[10]FASB, *Statement of Financial Accounting Concepts No. 4*, pp. 19–23.

activities and management of these organizations. All readers must already be aware of the impact on their lives, and on their bank accounts, of the activities of the layers of government they are obligated to support and of the not-for-profit organizations they voluntarily support. Since each of us is vitally affected, it is important that we be able to read intelligently the financial reports of governmental and not-for-profit entities. In order to understand the content of the financial reports it is necessary for the reader to make the effort to learn the accounting and financial reporting standards developed by authoritative bodies. The standards are explained and illustrated in Chapters 2 through 17 of this text. This chapter is intended to set forth the distinguishing characteristics of governmental and not-for-profit entities and to provide an overview of the objectives of accounting and financial reporting for these entities.

Financial Reporting of State and Local Governments

Like the FASB, the GASB has issued concepts statements that communicate the framework within which the Board strives to establish consistent financial reporting standards for entities within their jurisdiction. The GASB, as well as the FASB, is concerned with establishing standards for financial reporting to external users—those who lack the authority to prescribe the information they want and who must rely on the information management communicates to them. The Board does not intend to set standards for reporting to managers and administrators or others deemed to have the ability to enforce their demands for information.

Illustration 1–2 displays the minimum requirements for general purpose external financial statements under the governmental financial reporting model specified by GASB *Statement No. 34*.[11] Central to the new model is the **management's discussion and analysis (MD&A).** The MD&A is **required supplementary information (RSI)** designed to communicate in narrative, easily readable form the purpose of the basic financial statements and the government's current financial position and results of financial activities compared with those of the prior year.

As shown in Illustration 1–2, *Statement No. 34* prescribes two categories of **basic financial statements,** government-wide and fund. **Government-wide financial statements** are intended to provide a highly aggregated overview of a government's net assets and results of financial activities. The government-wide financial

[11]GASB *Statement No. 34*, "Basic Financial Statements—and Management's Discussion and Analysis—for State and Local Governments" (Norwalk, CT, 1999). Mandatory implementation of *Statement No. 34* is for fiscal periods beginning after June 15, 2001, for phase 1 governments (those with total annual revenues of $100 million or more); June 15, 2002, for phase 2 governments (total revenues of $10 million but less than $100 million; and June 15, 2003, for phase 3 governments (total revenues less than $10 million). Early implementation is encouraged, however. Where appropriate, the text will point out current accounting and reporting requirements that are being superseded by GASB *Statement No. 34*, but that continue to be used until a government decides to implement *Statement No. 34*, or its provisions become mandatory for that size government.

Illustration 1–2 Minimum Requirements for General Purpose External Financial Reporting— GASB *Statement No. 34* Reporting Model

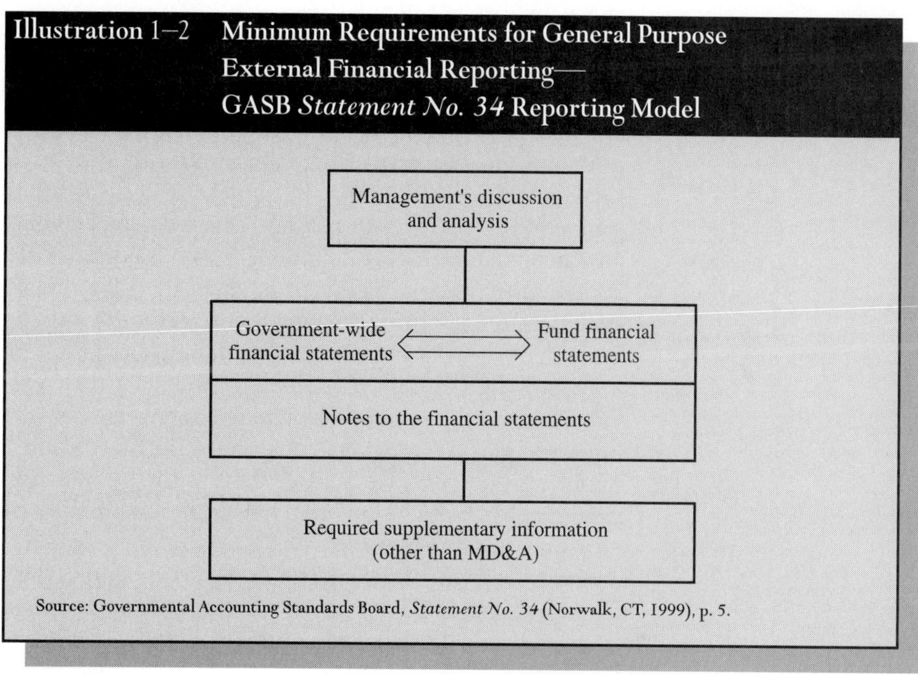

Source: Governmental Accounting Standards Board, *Statement No. 34* (Norwalk, CT, 1999), p. 5.

statements report on the government as a whole and assist in assessing ***operational* accountability**—whether the government has used its resources efficiently and effectively in meeting operating objectives. The GASB concluded that reporting on operational accountability is best achieved by using essentially the same basis of accounting and measurement focus used by business organizations: the accrual basis and flow of economic resources measurement focus.

Fund financial statements, the other category of basic financial statements prescribed by the new reporting model, assist in assessing ***fiscal* accountability**—whether the government has raised and spent financial resources in accordance with budget plans and in compliance with pertinent laws and regulations. The fund financial statements of the new reporting model are similar to those reported in the fund accounting model being replaced. Certain funds, referred to as governmental funds, continue to focus on the short-term flow of financial resources rather than on the flow of economic resources. Other funds, referred to as proprietary and fiduciary funds, account for the business-type and certain trust activities of the government. These funds continue to follow accounting and reporting principles similar to those of business organizations, although a number of GASB standards applicable to these funds differ substantially from FASB standards applicable to business organizations.

As shown in Illustration 1–2, the notes to the financial statements are considered integral to the statements. In addition, governments are required to disclose certain RSI (other than the MD&A). These additional information disclosures are discussed in several of the following chapters.

General purpose financial reporting includes not only financial statements but also all other means of communicating information that relate directly or indirectly to the information provided by the accounting system. In addition to the minimum financial information shown in Illustration 1–2, GASB standards state: "Every governmental entity should publish, as a matter of public record, a comprehensive annual financial report (CAFR)."[12] As discussed in the next section, a CAFR includes introductory information about the government, individual fund financial statements, combining financial statements for nonmajor funds, schedules that assist in demonstrating fiscal accountability, and multiple-year statistical data.

Although GASB standards recommend that each government prepare a CAFR, the minimum reporting requirements to meet **generally accepted accounting principles (GAAP)** are those shown in Illustration 1–2: the MD&A, the basic financial statements (including notes to the financial statements), and RSI (other than the MD&A). The basic financial statements of a governmental reporting entity are the statements that an independent certified public accountant typically audits and on which the auditor expresses an opinion about whether the statements fairly present financial position and results of operations in conformity with GAAP.

Some governments also publish highly condensed popular reports. These reports usually contain selected data from the audited financial statements, statistical data, graphic displays, and narrative explanations, but the reports themselves are not audited. In addition, many state and local governments have begun to identify and report nonfinancial performance measures. For several years, GASB has encouraged state and local governments to experiment with reporting **service efforts and accomplishments (SEA)** measures to provide more complete information about a governmental entity's performance than can be provided by basic financial statements, budgetary comparison statements, and schedules. Indicators of service efforts include inputs of nonmonetary resources as well as inputs of dollars. Indicators of service accomplishments include both outputs and outcomes; outputs are quantitative measures of work done, such as the number of juvenile cases handled, and outcomes are the impacts of outputs on program objectives, such as a reduction in the high school dropout rate or incidence of juvenile crime.

Comprehensive Annual Financial Report

Serious users of governmental financial information need much more detail than is found in the MD&A, basic financial statements, and RSI (other than MD&A). For state and local governments, much of that detail is found in the governmental reporting entity's **comprehensive annual financial report (CAFR)**, which is considered the entity's official annual report published as a matter of public record. Standards for the content of the CAFR are found in the GASB's *Codification of Governmental Accounting and Financial Reporting Standards*. Each CAFR should contain the following sections:

[12]GASB, *Codification*, Sec. 2200.101.

Introductory Section. Introductory material includes such items as title page and contents page, the letter of transmittal, and other material deemed appropriate by management. The letter of transmittal may be literally that—a letter from the chief finance officer addressed to the chief executive and governing body of the governmental unit—or it may be a narrative over the signature of the chief executive. In either event, the letter or narrative material should cite legal and policy requirements for the report.

Financial Section. The financial section of a comprehensive annual financial report should include: (1) an auditor's report, (2) management's discussion and analysis, (3) basic financial statements, (4) required supplementary information (other than MD&A), and (5) combining and individual fund statements and schedules. Laws regarding the audit of governmental units vary markedly from state to state. In some states, state law requires that all state agencies and all local governments be audited by an audit agency of the state government. In other states, local governments are audited by independent certified public accountants. In still other states, some local governments are audited by the state audit agency and some by independent certified public accountants. In any event, the auditor's opinion should accompany the financial statements reproduced in the report.

The financial section should contain sufficient information to disclose fully and present fairly the financial position and results of financial operations during the fiscal year. As noted previously, the financial operations of governmental units are constrained in considerable detail by laws of higher jurisdictions and by the actions of the legislative branch of the governmental unit itself. In addition, agreements with creditors and others provide constraints over financial activities and introduce financial reporting requirements.

To determine and demonstrate compliance with laws, regulations, and agreements, governmental units use **fund accounting.** The technical definition of *fund* is given in Chapter 2; the nature of each fund type as provided in GASB standards is also explained in Chapter 2.

The government-wide financial statements present financial information in separate columns for the governmental and business-type activities of the primary government and its discretely presented component units (units for which the primary government is deemed financially accountable). The fund financial statements present the financial position and results of operations separately for the governmental, proprietary, and fiduciary activities, and for each type of activity columns are provided for each major fund. Proprietary funds also present a statement of cash flows. Transactions between the governmental activities and business-type activities, or between those activities and component units, are not eliminated in the government-wide financial statements. Similarly, the effects of interfund transactions are not eliminated in the fund statements; therefore, unlike business entities, the basic financial statements of a state or local government are not properly referred to as *consolidated*.

Several basic financial statements of a reporting entity should be included in the financial section of a CAFR.

Government-wide financial statements:

1. Statement of Net Assets (see Illustration 2–1).
2. Statement of Activities (see Illustration 2–2).

Fund financial statements:

1. Balance Sheet—Governmental Funds (see Illustration 2–3).
2. Statement of Revenues, Expenditures, and Changes in Fund Balances—Governmental Funds (see Illustration 2–4).
3. Statement of Net Assets—Proprietary Funds (see Illustration 2–6).
4. Statement of Revenues, Expenses, and Changes in Fund Net Assets—Proprietary Funds (see Illustration 2–7).
5. Statement of Cash Flows—Proprietary Funds (see Illustration 2–8).
6. Statement of Fiduciary Net Assets (see Illustration 2–9).
7. Statement of Changes in Fiduciary Net Assets (see Illustration 2–10).

Governments may have many different funds within each fund type. GASB *Statement No. 34* requires a separate column in fund financial statements for each *major fund* (see Chapter 2 for the criteria for classifying a fund as major). Reporting by major fund is expected to meet the information needs of citizens and other report users having a specific depth of interest in the financial condition and financial operations of a particular fund. To meet the needs of individuals having an interest in *nonmajor* funds, governments also should provide separate combining financial statements for nonmajor governmental, proprietary, and fiduciary funds, as well as for nonmajor discretely presented component units. Illustration 4–8 presents an example of a combining financial statement for nonmajor governmental funds. When a reporting entity maintains only one fund within a given fund type, it should be obvious that the financial data for that fund would be presented in a basic fund financial statement if it is major and in an individual fund statement if it is nonmajor, rather than in a combining statement. Individual fund statements may be presented for one or more funds included in a combining fund statement where necessary to present compliance with finance-related legal and contractual requirements. Combining and individual fund statements are not ordinarily audited, but if the reporting entity has need for an auditor's opinion on those statements, the audit can be extended to cover the necessary additional work. Unaudited information often presented in the financial section of the CAFR following the combining and individual fund statements includes schedules necessary to demonstrate compliance with finance-related legal and contractual provisions; schedules to present comparative data on such items as tax collections, long-term debt, and so on; and schedules to provide greater detail for information reported in the statements.

Statistical Section. In addition to the introductory and financial sections of the CAFR, which were described above, a CAFR should contain a statistical section.

The statistical section typically presents tables and charts showing social and economic data, financial trends and the fiscal capacity of the government in detail needed by readers who are more than casually interested in the activities of the governmental unit. The GASB Codification suggests the content of the statistical tables usually considered necessary for inclusion in a CAFR. The statistical section is discussed at greater length in Chapter 9 of this text.

Current Financial Reporting Requirements Being Superseded by GASB Statement No. 34

As discussed previously, the mandatory implementation date for GASB *Statement No. 34* depends on the size of the government (fiscal years beginning after June 15, 2001, for the large governments, one year later for medium-size governments, and two years later for small governments). Although governments are encouraged to implement the standard early, many may continue to use current GAAP until the fiscal year in which they implement the new reporting model.

Governments that continue to follow current accounting and reporting standards for some time will have fund structure and financial statements quite different from the minimum external financial reporting requirements discussed previously. The primary differences are:

1. No MD&A is required under the current reporting model.
2. Only fund financial statements are required; government-wide financial statements are not required in the current model.
3. The required financial statements that constitute minimum GAAP under the current model are referred to as **general purpose financial statements.** These statements contain separate columns for the totals of each fund type. A single combined balance sheet is provided for all funds and account groups. Separate combined operating statements are provided for governmental funds and proprietary and similar fiduciary funds. A budget and actual comparison statement is required in the current model for all governmental funds for which a budget was adopted, whereas this comparison can be reported as part of RSI under the new model. A combined statement of cash flows is required for proprietary funds.
4. As no government-wide financial statements are required under the current model, that model provides for two account groups, a General Fixed Assets Account Group (GFAAG) to record fixed assets acquired from governmental fund resources and a General Long-Term Debt Account Group (GLTDAG) to record long-term liabilities arising from activities of governmental funds. Account groups are not needed in the new reporting model as general capital assets and general long-term liabilities are reported in the government-wide statement of net assets.

Chapter 9 presents a comprehensive review of the current financial reporting model and current fund structure that are being superseded.

Analysis of Governmental Financial Statements; Independent Auditors' Reports

The characteristics that distinguish governmental and not-for-profit entities from business entities are identified in the section of this chapter headed "Distinguishing Characteristics of Governmental and Not-for-Profit Entities." Consideration of those characteristics should make it obvious that the majority of the ratios used in the analysis of the financial statements of business organizations have no relevance to the analysis of the financial statements of a governmental reporting entity or a not-for-profit entity. Similarly, the section on distinguishing characteristics and the section headed "Objectives of Financial Reporting" should indicate that the objectives of independent audits of governmental financial statements are broader than the objectives of independent audits of profit-seeking businesses. Governmental auditing objectives include reviews of the economy and efficiency with which governmental agencies manage and utilize resources, determination of whether results intended by those who authorized programs or activities are being achieved, as well as audits (similar to those of businesses) to determine whether financial statement presentations are in conformity with generally accepted accounting principles. In all cases auditors of governmental entities should ascertain that the entity has complied with relevant laws and regulations. Chapter 10 discusses financial ratios useful for the analysis of governmental financial statements. Chapter 11 explains government auditing standards established by the Comptroller General of the United States and related publications issued by the AICPA for the guidance of auditors of governmental and not-for-profit entities.

GASB Statement No. 34 *Principles and Standards*

The principles that underlie GASB accounting and financial reporting standards are introduced and discussed briefly in Chapter 2. Chapters 3 through 9 explain and illustrate in depth the standards applicable to general purpose external financial reporting of state and local governments, including the measurement focus and basis of accounting utilized for the government-wide and fund financial statements. Chapter 2 also identifies the types of funds and characteristics of each fund type, and distinguishes between major and nonmajor funds. Chapter 9 provides an extensive discussion of the financial reporting entity and GASB *Statement No. 34* financial reporting requirements, in addition to a review of the current fund accounting requirements that are being superseded by *Statement No. 34*.

Financial Reporting of the Federal Government and Not-for-Profit Organizations

Accounting and financial reporting standards for the federal government differ significantly from those for state and local governments. An introduction to accounting and reporting standards for the federal government and illustrative financial statements for federal departments or agencies is provided in Chapter 12. Similarly, accounting and financial reporting standards for not-for-profit organizations differ from those for both state and local governments and the federal government. Although logic would suggest that similar entities, such as public and private colleges and universities, should follow similar accounting and reporting practices, the fact is that their practices are quite different. The reason, of course, is the different standards-setting bodies for governmental and nongovernmental not-for-profit organizations, as discussed previously and depicted in Illustration 1–1. Chapters 14 and 15 discuss accounting for not-for-profit organizations and related regulatory and taxation issues. Specific accounting and reporting requirements applicable to colleges and universities and health care organizations are discussed in Chapters 16 and 17.

A Caveat

The first edition of this text was written by the late Professor R. M. Mikesell. Some words of his bear thoughtful rereading from time to time by teachers and students in all fields, not just those concerned with accounting and financial reporting for governmental and not-for-profit entities:

> Even when developed to the ultimate stage of perfection, governmental accounting cannot become a guaranty of good government. At best, it can never be more than a valuable tool for promotion of sound financial management. It does not offer a panacea for all the ills that beset representative government; nor will it fully overcome the influence of disinterested, uninformed citizens. It cannot be substituted for honesty and moral integrity on the part of public officials; it can help in resisting but cannot eliminate the demands of selfish interests, whether in the form of individual citizens, corporations, or the pressure groups which always abound to influence government at all levels.

It is difficult to strike a balance between the pursuit of perfection in a given field in isolation and the effort to improve the total system within which we live (which often involves settling for less than perfection in the elements of the system). The reader is urged to keep in mind the ultimate goal of improving the system in which we live during the time the text is being studied—and thereafter.

Key Terms*

Accountability, 6
Basic financial statements, 8
Comprehensive annual financial report (CAFR), 10
Federal Accounting Standards Advisory Board (FASAB), 5
Financial Accounting Standards Board (FASB), 3
Fiscal accountability 9
Fund accounting, 11
Fund financial statements, 9
General purpose financial statements (GPFS), 13
General purpose governments, 2
Generally accepted accounting principles (GAAP), 10
Governmental Accounting Standards Board (GASB), 3
Government-wide financial statements, 8
Interperiod equity, 7

*See the glossary at the back of the text for a definition of each term and concept.

Management's discussion and analysis (MD&A), 8
Operational accountability, 9
Required supplementary information (RSI), 8
Service efforts and accomplishments (SEA), 10
Special purpose governments, 2

Questions

1–1. Explain the essential differences between general purpose and special purpose governments and give several examples of each.

1–2. What are the principal characteristics that distinguish governmental and not-for-profit organizations from business enterprises?

1–3. Explain which standard-setting bodies have responsibility for establishing accounting and financial reporting standards for: (1) governmental organizations, (2) business organizations, and (3) not-for-profit organizations.

1–4. Explain what distinguishes governmental not-for-profit organizations from nongovernmental not-for-profit organizations. Why is such a distinction necessary?

1–5. GASB and FASB standards are concerned only with *external* financial reporting whereas FASAB standards are concerned with both internal and external financial reporting. Do you agree with this statement? Why or why not?

1–6. Why should persons interested in reading financial reports of governmental and not-for-profit entities be familiar with standards set by the GASB and FASB?

1–7. Explain in your own words why accountability is the cornerstone of all financial reporting in government.

1–8. Why is it more difficult to determine the optimal quantity or quality of services rendered by a government than it is to determine the optimal quantity or quality of the goods or services of a business enterprise?

1–9. In your own words state the primary uses the GASB believes external users have for financial reports of state and local governments. Contrast and compare these with the uses the FASB believes external users have for the financial reports of not-for-profit organizations.

1–10. What material should be included in the introductory section of a Comprehensive Annual Financial Report (CAFR)?

1–11. What material should be included in the financial section of a CAFR? List the financial statements that should be included in this section.

1–12. What material should be included in the statistical section of a CAFR?

1–13. What information is the Management's Discussion and Analysis (MD&A) intended to provide?

1–14. Describe some differences between the new financial reporting model prescribed in GASB *Statement No. 34* and the current model.

1–15. What should the government-wide financial statements report on and why?

1–16. What should the fund financial statements report on and why?

Cases

1–1. Governmental or Not-for-Profit Entity. Vinson Pioneer Museum is located in Dodge Valley, a small western city. The museum is open to the general public at no charge; however, signs at the information desk in the entry lobby encourage gifts of $3.00 for adults and $1.00 for children, 12 and under. Many visitors make the recommended contribution, some contribute larger amounts, and some do not contribute at all. Such contributions comprise 40 percent of the museum's total annual revenues, with net proceeds from fund-raising events and governmental grants comprising the remaining 60 percent. The museum shares a building with the local post office, for which it pays fair rental. Except for a part-time director, the museum is staffed exclusively by unpaid volunteers. Duly organized as a tax-exempt not-for-profit organization, the museum is governed by a six-member board of trustees, each appointed for a three-year term. Four of the trustees are appointed by the Dodge Valley City Council, one is appointed by the Dodge County Commission, and one is appointed by the Dodge Arts Commission. The museum's original charter provides that in the event the museum ceases to operate, two-thirds of its net assets will revert to the city and the remaining one-third will revert equally to the county and the Arts Commission.

Although the museum has never been audited, the board of trustees has decided to initiate annual audits. The board wishes to receive an unqualified (clean) audit opinion stating that the museum's financial statements present fairly in conformity with generally accepted accounting principles.

Required

Assume you have been engaged to conduct this audit. To which standards-setting body (or bodies) would you look for accounting and financial reporting standards to assist you in determining whether the museum's financial statements are in conformity with generally accepted accounting principles? Explain how you arrived at this conclusion.

1–2. Implementing GASB *Statement* No. 34. You are the finance director for a city that has population of 50,000, total assets of $110 million, and total revenues of $15 million, not including other financing sources, for the fiscal year ending June 30, 2002. Earlier in the year, you made a presentation to the City Council explaining the new financial reporting model described in GASB *Statement No. 34*. You made the necessary changes to the accounting information system to produce the required government-wide and fund-based financial statements. At the most recent City Council meeting, a council member asked whether it was really necessary to change the way the financial statements are presented. This person felt that he and the public at large understood the old financial statements and did not want to relearn a new system.

Required

Prepare remarks to present at the next City Council meeting about the required implementation date of GASB *Statement No. 34* and the rationale for implementing the statements early.

1–3. Internet Case. Use your favorite Internet browser to search for the term "GASB." Browse some of the selected sites as necessary to prepare a brief report about the GASB's mission and structure, its current technical projects, and its current and proposed due-process documents (such as discussion memoranda and exposure drafts). Which organizations are represented on the Governmental Accounting Standards Advisory Council? [Note: As of March 2000, the preceding information can be obtained at http://www.gasb.org]

Exercises and Problems

1–1. Examine the CAFR. Obtain a copy of a recent comprehensive annual financial report (CAFR) of a governmental reporting entity (city, town, or county) and, if possible, the related budget.* Familiarize yourself with the organization of the comprehensive annual financial report—reread Chapter 1 of this text, particularly the section headed "Financial Reporting of State and Local Governments." Note particularly the items suggested below.

a. Introductory Section.

Read the *letter of transmittal* or any narrative that accompanies the financial statements. Does this material define the governmental reporting entity and name the primary government and all related component units included in the report? (If the reporting entity is not discussed in the *introductory section*, you should find this information in the Notes to the Financial Statements.) Is the explanation of the reporting entity understandable to you at this time? Does the introductory section discuss the financial condition of the reporting entity at the balance sheet date? Does it discuss the most significant changes in financial condition that occurred during the year? Does it alert the reader to forthcoming changes in financial condition that are not as yet reflected in the financial statements? Do the amounts reported in the letter of transmittal or other narrative agree with amounts in the statements and schedules in the financial section? (Specify any exceptions.) Does the introductory section define the major fund types included in the CAFR? Does the introductory section include a list of principal officials? An organization chart? Is a reproduction of a Certificate of Achievement for Excellence in Financial Reporting from the Government Finance Officers Association (GFOA) included in the

*These may be obtained from the chief financial officer of the city, town, or county. If you do not know the exact title and address, you should write "Director of Finance, City of _____," and address it to the City Hall in the city and state of your choice. It is also acceptable, if you prefer, to obtain a copy of the comprehensive annual financial report of a state government. If you plan on studying Chapter 13 of this text, it would be convenient to request a copy of the most recent available operating budget document as well as the most recent available comprehensive annual financial report. Because some governmental units may not have any report available to send at the time of your request, it may be necessary to write a second or even a third request. The instructor may wish to obtain the reports and budgets before the term starts, or at least approve the selection of governmental units, so that every member of the class has a different report.

introductory section?[†] Does the introductory section mention that the CAFR has been submitted to the GFOA for consideration for an award of the Certificate of Achievement?

b. Financial Section.

(1) *Audit Report*. Are the financial statements in the report audited? By an independent CPA? By state auditors? By an auditor employed by the governmental unit being audited? Does the auditor express an opinion that the statements are (*a*) "in conformity with generally accepted accounting principles," (*b*) "in conformity with generally accepted accounting principles applicable to governmental entities," or (*c*) "in compliance with state laws"? Is the opinion qualified in some manner or disclaimed? Does the auditor clearly indicate the extent of any responsibility taken for other financial section contents? Does the auditor indicate specific responsibility for the basic or general purpose financial statements?

(2) *Basic Financial Statements*. If the entity has implemented GASB *Statement No. 34*, does the CAFR contain the two government-wide financial statements and seven fund statements?

(3) *General Purpose Financial Statements*. If the entity has not yet implemented GASB *Statement No. 34*, does the CAFR contain the five combined statements that must be included?

(4) *Notes to the Financial Statements*. Does the report contain Notes to the Financial Statements? Notes are an integral part of the statements and are intended to be read with the statements.

(5) *Individual Fund and Combining Financial Statements*. Following the notes to the financial statements, does the CAFR provide combining and individual fund statements? The combining statements should aggregate all the funds of a given fund type or for all nonmajor funds. For the general fund and other fund types containing one fund, individual fund statements should be provided.

(6) *Management's Discussion and Analysis (MD&A)*. Does the CAFR contain an MD&A? If so, where is it located and what does it contain?

c. Statistical Tables.

Become familiar with the material presented in the statistical tables so that you can refer to these tables as needed in subsequent weeks.

[†]The Certificate of Achievement for Excellence in Financial Reporting (Certificate of Achievement) is recognized as the highest award in government financial reporting. The Government Finance Officers Association (GFOA) established the Certificate of Achievement Program in 1945 to encourage government units to publish excellent comprehensive annual financial reports (CAFRs) and to provide peer recognition and educational assistance for the officials preparing CAFRs. (Source: Government Finance Officers Association, 1999.)

CHAPTER 2

Principles of Accounting and Financial Reporting for State and Local Governments

Learning Objectives

After studying this chapter, you should be able to:

- Explain the nature of the three major activity categories of a state or local government: governmental activities, business-type activities, and fiduciary activities.
- Describe the 13 principles of accounting and financial reporting, including
  - Definition of a *fund*.
  - Identification of the various fund types and the three categories of funds.
  - Accounting treatment for capital assets and long-term liabilities.
  - Measurement focus and basis of accounting for each fund type.
  - Definition of a major fund.
  - Integration of budgetary control into accounting and financial reporting.
  - Annual financial reporting requirements.
- Explain the distinguishing accounting characteristics of governmental, proprietary, and fiduciary fund types.

Activities of Government

Chapter 1 showed that the characteristics of governmental organizations differ from those of for-profit business organizations. One key difference is that governments are not profit seeking. Rather governments exist to meet citizens' demand for services, consistent with the availability of resources to provide those services. Although the types and levels of services vary from government to government, certain core services are provided by most general purpose governments—those related to protection of life and property (e.g., police and fire protection), public works (e.g., streets and highways, bridges, and public buildings), parks and recreation facilities and programs, and cultural and social services. Governments must also incur costs for general administrative support such as data processing, finance, and personnel. Core governmental services, together with general administrative support, comprise the major part of what GASB *Concepts Statement No. 1* refers to as governmental-type activities.[1] In more recent documents, GASB refers to these activities as simply **governmental activities.** Chapters 3 through 6 of the text focus on various aspects of accounting for governmental activities.

Some readers may be surprised to learn that governments also engage in a variety of **business-type activities**. These include, among others, public utilities (for example, electric, water, gas, and sewer utilities), transportation systems, toll roads and toll bridges, airports, hospitals, parking garages and lots, liquor stores, golf courses, and swimming pools. Many of these activities are intended to be self-supporting by charging users for the services they receive. Operating subsidies from general revenues are not uncommon, however, particularly for transportation systems. Accounting for business-type activities is covered in Chapter 7 of the text.

A final category of activity in which governments are involved is **fiduciary activities.** Governments often act in a fiduciary capacity, either as an agent or trustee, for parties outside the government. For example, a government may serve as agent for other governments in the administering and collecting of taxes. Governments serve also as trustees for amounts placed in trust from private citizens for parks and other purposes, for **escheat properties** that revert to the government when there are no legal claimants or heirs to a deceased individual's estate, and for assets being held for employee pension plans. Under currently effective standards, all fiduciary activities, both those that benefit parties outside of government and those that benefit the government's own programs, are reported in fiduciary funds. The GASB *Statement No. 34* reporting standards significantly change accounting and reporting for fiduciary activities, however.[2] *Under Statement No. 34*, only

---

[1]Governmental Accounting Standards Board, *Codification of Governmental Accounting and Financial Reporting Standards as of June 30, 1999* (Norwalk, CT, 1999); and GASB *Concepts Statement No. 1*, Appendix B, par. 10.

[2]As discussed in Chapter 1, the mandatory implementation date for GASB *Statement No. 34* occurs in three phases, depending on a government's total revenues. Phase 1 governments must implement the standards not later than their fiscal period beginning June 15, 2001. Phase 2 and phase 3 governments have one and two additional years, respectively, to implement the new

private-purpose fiduciary activities, those that benefit individuals, private organizations, and other governments, are reported as fiduciary activities. Public-purpose fiduciary activities that primarily benefit the government's own programs are treated as governmental activities in the new reporting standards. Accounting for private-purpose fiduciary activities is covered in Chapter 8 of the text.

Accounting and financial reporting principles for the *governmental activities* category described above have evolved to meet the legal budgetary and financial compliance needs of government—what was termed *fiscal accountability* in Chapter 1. Generally, these principles involve segregating the accounting for the receipt and expenditures of restricted use resources from general use resources. Emphasis is placed on reporting the inflows and outflows of current financial resources. **Current financial resources** are cash or items expected to be converted into cash during the current period, or soon enough thereafter to pay current period liabilities.

Accounting and financial reporting principles for the *business-type activities* of a government are quite similar to those for commercial business entities. As in business, if a government intends to charge users for the goods or services they receive, it needs to know the full cost of those goods and services in order to determine appropriate prices. Knowing the full cost is also essential in deciding whether the government should continue to produce or provide particular goods or services, or contract for them with an outside vendor. Thus, as in commercial business accounting, accrual accounting is essential to measuring the full cost of providing governmental business-type services, and reporting on the extent to which each business-type activity is self-sufficient or has to be subsidized. In short, the principles of accounting for business-type activities are intended to measure and report on *operational accountability*, as the term was defined in Chapter 1.

Accounting and reporting for the *fiduciary activities* of a government use principles similar to those of business-type activities. Certain fiduciary activities, those related to defined benefit pension plans and similar postemployment health care plans, use unique recognition standards prescribed by GASB, as explained in Chapter 8 of the text.

GASB *Statement No. 34* reporting standards reflect the GASB's view that users such as citizens, legislative and oversight bodies, and investors and creditors have diverse information needs. In particular, users want and need information about the medium- to long-term financial performance of government as well as information about short-term financial compliance with budget and finance-related laws and regulations. To achieve *operational accountability* reporting for the government as a whole, *Statement No. 34* requires highly aggregated financial statements (called government-wide financial statements) that report both governmental activities

---

standards. As encouraged by *Statement No. 34*, however, many governments are implementing the new standards early. For those who wish to review the currently effective (as of April 2000) governmental accounting and reporting standards, many of which are being superseded by *Statement No. 34*, we have provided a comprehensive review of those standards as an appendix to Chapter 9 of the text.

and business-type activities on the accrual basis (the accounting basis used by business organizations), in addition to the traditional disaggregated financial statements (called fund financial statements). As discussed previously, the traditional fund financial statements focus on fiscal accountability for governmental activities and operational accountability for business-type activities.

The preceding overview provides a good foundation for better understanding the principles of governmental accounting and financial reporting provided in the GASB's *Codification of Governmental Accounting and Financial Reporting Standards*, as modified by GASB *Statement No. 34*. The principles are discussed in brief in this chapter, and in greater detail in Chapters 3 through 9.

Summary Statement of Principles

At its inception in 1984, the GASB adopted 12 accounting and financial reporting principles for state and local governments that had been established by its predecessor standards-setting body, the National Council on Governmental Accounting (NCGA). The standards prescribed by GASB *Statement No. 34* retain, with certain modifications, the original NCGA principles. A separate principle has been articulated for long-term liabilities, bringing the total now to 13 principles. The following overview of these principles, including those changed or added by *Statement No. 34*, should afford the reader an understanding of the unique nature and complexity of governmental accounting and financial reporting.[3, 4]

1. **Accounting and Reporting Capabilities**
   A governmental accounting system must make it possible both: (a) to present fairly and with full disclosure the funds and activities of the government in conformity with generally accepted accounting principles, and (b) to determine and demonstrate compliance with finance-related legal and contractual provisions.

Adherence to generally accepted accounting principles (GAAP) is essential to ensuring a reasonable degree of comparability among the general purpose financial reports of state and local governmental units. The American Institute of Certified Public Accountants (AICPA) recognizes the GASB as the designated body to

[3]These principles are excerpted from GASB, *Codification*, Sections 1100–2100, and GASB *Statement No. 34*, Appendix D, Section 1100.101–114. Boldface type or other emphases added by the authors are noted as such. Explanatory notes within cited text are included in brackets. We add explanatory text following certain of the principles.

[4]It is assumed the reader of this text is familiar with principles of accounting for business entities, and therefore the text is focused on the differences between accounting for governmental and not-for-profit entities and accounting for business enterprises rather than on the many similarities. Readers who are not familiar with basic accounting should study any contemporary introductory accounting text before attempting to understand the more technical portions of Chapters 3 through 17. Particular attention should be given to the discussion in the introductory text of financial statements and to the explanation of double-entry methodology and the accounting cycle.

establish accounting principles for state and local governments under the AICPA Ethics Rule 203, *Accounting Principles*.[5]

In some states, however, laws require the state government and the local governments within the state to follow practices (such as cash basis accounting) not consistent with GAAP. In those cases, financial statements and reports prepared in compliance with state law are considered "special reports" or "supplemental schedules" and are *not* the basic financial statements discussed in Chapter 1. Governmental units may prepare two sets of financial statements: one set in compliance with legal requirements and one set in conformity with GAAP.

2. **Fund Accounting Systems**
   Governmental accounting systems should be organized and operated on a fund basis. A **fund** is defined as a fiscal and accounting entity with a self-balancing set of accounts recording cash and other financial resources, together with all related liabilities and residual equities or balances, and changes therein, which are segregated for the purpose of carrying on specific activities or attaining certain objectives in accordance with special regulations, restrictions, or limitations. Fund financial statements should be used to report detailed information about the primary government, including its blended component units. The focus of governmental and proprietary fund financial statements is on **major funds.**[6] [Boldface font added by authors to denote key terms.]

The definition of *fund* given above is mentioned in Chapter 1. The principle quoted below defines and categorizes the various fund types that should be used, as needed, by state and local governments, both general purpose and special purpose such as public school systems.

3. **Types of Funds**[7]
   The following types of funds should be used by state and local governments to the extent that they have activities that meet the criteria for using those funds.
   a. **Governmental Funds**
      (1) *The General Fund*—to account for all financial resources except those required to be accounted for in another fund.
      (2) *Special Revenue Funds*—to account for the proceeds of specific revenue sources (other than private-purpose trusts or for major capital projects) that are legally restricted to use for specified purposes.

---

[5]American Institute of Certified Public Accountants, *Statement on Auditing Standards No. 69*, "The Meaning of 'Present Fairly in Conformity with Generally Accepted Accounting Principles' in the Independent Auditor's Report" (New York, 1991), par. 12.

[6]In relation to each fund category or type shown in the next principle, a fund is classified as *major* if (a) total assets, liabilities, revenues, or expenditures/expenses of the individual governmental or enterprise fund are at least 10 percent of the corresponding total of assets, liabilities, revenues, or expenditures/expenses for all funds of that category or type (total governmental or total enterprise funds), and (b) total assets, liabilities, revenues, or expenditures/expenses of the individual governmental fund or enterprise fund are at least 5 percent of the corresponding total for all governmental and enterprise funds combined.

[7]GASB *Codification*, Sec. 1300.102, as modified by GASB *Statement No. 34*, par. 63. For governmental and enterprise funds, the focus is on *major* funds (see footnote 6 for definition). Major fund reporting does not apply to internal service funds.

(3) *Capital Projects Funds*—to account for financial resources to be used for the acquisition or construction of major capital facilities (other than those financed by proprietary funds and trust funds).
(4) *Debt Service Funds*—to account for the accumulation of resources for, and the payment of, general long-term debt principal and interest.
(5) *Permanent Funds*—to account for legally restricted resources provided by trust in which the earnings but not the principal may be used for purposes that support the primary government's programs (those that benefit the government or its citizenry). [Note: Similar permanent trusts that benefit private individuals, organizations, or other governments—that is, private-purpose trust funds—are classified as fiduciary funds, as shown below.]

b. **Proprietary Funds**

(6) *Enterprise Funds*—to account for operations (*a*) that are financed and operated in a manner similar to private business enterprises—where the intent of the governing body is that the costs (expenses, including depreciation) of providing goods or services to the general public on a continuing basis be financed or recovered primarily through user charges; or (*b*) where the governing body has decided that periodic determination of revenues earned, expenses incurred, and/or net income is appropriate for capital maintenance, public policy, management control, accountability, or other purposes.
(7) *Internal Service Funds*—to account for the financing of goods or services provided by one department or agency to other departments or agencies of the governmental unit, or to other governmental units, on a cost-reimbursement basis.

c. **Fiduciary Funds** (and similar component units). These are *trust and agency funds* that are used to account for assets held by a governmental unit in a trustee capacity or as an agent for individuals, private organizations, and other governmental units. These include:

(8) Agency funds.
(9) Pension (and other employee benefit) trust funds.
(10) Investment trust funds.
(11) Private-purpose trust funds.

These fund types correspond to the types of activities in which governments engage: Governmental funds are used to account for governmental activities, proprietary funds are used to account for business-type activities, and fiduciary funds are used to account for fiduciary activities. Both the definition of *fund* and the description of each governmental fund type emphasize the segregation of accounting for restricted current financial resources to facilitate reporting on fiscal accountability. Creating a separate self-balancing set of accounts (fund) for each business-type activity permits those activities to be accounted for using accounting principles similar to those of commercial business rather than using the principles for governmental funds. Finally, as mentioned earlier in this chapter, accounting for fiduciary funds follows the principles of accounting for business-type activities.

Accounting for each of the fund types defined above is explained and illustrated in Chapters 3 through 9. Accounting characteristics common to each of the three categories of fund types—governmental funds, proprietary funds, and fiduciary funds—are set forth in the final section of this chapter.

4. **Number of Funds**
   Governmental units should establish and maintain those funds required by law and sound financial administration. Only the minimum number of funds consistent with legal and operating requirements should be established, however, because unnecessary funds result in inflexibility, undue complexity, and inefficient financial administration.

The importance of the Number of Funds Principle is sometimes overlooked by academicians and, even, independent auditors. *The fund types defined in the Types of Funds Principle are to be used if needed by a governmental unit to demonstrate compliance with legal requirements or if needed to facilitate sound financial administration.* In rare instances GASB standards require the use of a certain fund type. If legal requirements, GASB standards, or sound financial administration do not require the use of a given fund type, it should not be used. In the simplest possible situation, a governmental unit could be in conformity with GAAP if it used a single fund, the General Fund, to account for all events and transactions.

5. **Reporting Capital Assets**
   A clear distinction should be made between general capital assets and capital assets of proprietary and fiduciary funds. Capital assets of proprietary funds should be reported in both the government-wide and fund financial statements. Capital assets of fiduciary funds should be reported in only the statement of fiduciary net assets. All other capital assets of the governmental unit are general capital assets. They should not be reported as assets in governmental funds but should be reported in the governmental activities column in the governmental-wide statement of net assets.

General capital assets include land, buildings, improvements other than buildings, and equipment used by activities accounted for by the fund types classified as governmental funds. The following two principles establish requirements that relate to general capital asset accounting.

6. **Valuation of Capital Assets**
   Capital assets should be reported at historical cost. The cost of a capital asset should include capitalized interest and ancillary charges necessary to place the asset into its intended location and condition for use. Donated capital assets should be reported at their estimated fair value at the time of the acquisition plus ancillary charges, if any.
7. **Depreciation of Capital Assets**
   Capital assets should be depreciated over their estimated useful lives unless they are either inexhaustible or are infrastructure assets using the modified approach as set forth in GASB *Statement No. 34*, pars. 23–26. Inexhaustible assets such as land and land improvements should not be depreciated. Depreciation expense should be reported in the government-wide statement of activities; the proprietary fund statement of revenues, expenses, and changes in fund net assets; and the statement of changes in fiduciary net assets.
8. **Reporting Long-Term Liabilities**
   A clear distinction should be made between fund long-term liabilities and general long-term liabilities. Long-term liabilities directly related to and expected to be paid from proprietary funds should be reported in the proprietary fund statement of net

assets and in the government-wide statement of net assets. Long-term liabilities directly related to and expected to be paid from fiduciary funds should be reported in the statement of fiduciary net assets. All other unmatured general long-term liabilities of the governmental unit should not be reported in governmental funds but should be reported in the governmental activities column in the government-wide statement of net assets. [Note: Application of the preceding capital assets and long-term liabilities principles in the context of both fund accounting and reporting and government-wide accounting and reporting is explained in Chapters 5 and 6, respectively.]

9. **Measurement Focus and Basis of Accounting in the Basic Financial Statements**
   a. Government-wide Financial Statements
   The government-wide statement of net assets and statement of activities should be prepared using the **economic resources measurement focus** and the **accrual basis** of accounting. **Revenues, expenses, gains, losses, assets,** and **liabilities** resulting from the **exchange and exchange-like transactions** should be recognized when the exchange takes place. Revenues, expenses, assets, and liabilities resulting from **nonexchange transactions** should be recognized in accordance with [*Codification*] Section N50, "Nonexchange Transactions."[8]
   b. Fund Financial Statements
   In fund financial statements, the **modified accrual** or accrual basis of accounting, as appropriate, should be used in measuring financial position and operating results.
   (1) Financial statements for governmental funds should be presented using the current financial resources measurement focus and the modified accrual basis of accounting. Revenues should be recognized in the accounting period in which they become available and measurable. **Expenditures** should be recognized in the accounting period in which the fund liability is incurred, if measurable, except for unmatured interest on general long-term liabilities, which should be recognized when due.
   (2) Proprietary fund statements of net assets and revenues, expenses, and changes in fund net assets should be presented using the economic resources measurement focus and the accrual basis of accounting.
   (3) Financial statements of fiduciary funds should be reported using the economic resources measurement focus and the accrual basis of accounting, except for the recognition of certain liabilities of defined benefit pension plans and certain postemployment healthcare plans. [Note: defined benefit pension plans and similar postemployment health care plans are discussed in Chapter 8 of the text.]
   (4) Transfers [between funds] should be reported in the accounting period in which the interfund receivable and payable arise.

The principle quoted above is not difficult to read, but its importance becomes evident to most students only after they have studied the chapters dealing with each fund type. Briefly, accrual accounting means that (1) revenues should be

---

[8]GASB, *Codification*, Sec. N50, codifies GASB *Statement No. 33*, "Accounting and Financial Reporting for Nonexchange Transactions" (Norwalk, CT, 1998), the provisions of which are effective for fiscal periods beginning after June 15, 2000. Chapters 3 and 4 of this text provide an overview of these provisions.

recorded in the period in which the service is given, although payment is received in a prior or subsequent period, and (2) expenses should be recorded in the period in which the benefit is received, although payment is made in a prior or subsequent period. In business organization accounting, the accrual basis is employed to obtain a matching of costs against the revenue flowing from those costs, thereby producing a more useful income statement. In governmental entities, however, even for government-wide financial reporting and those funds that attempt to determine net income, the objective is to provide services to the public, not to maximize economic gain or profit. Rather the government as a whole and the funds that use the economic resources measurement focus and accrual basis of accounting make use of revenue and expense accounts to assist in assessing operational accountability and to guard against impairment of ability to render the services desired. For these reasons, the government-wide operating statement is called a statement of activities and those of proprietary funds are called statements of revenues and expenses rather than income statements.

Most of the governmental fund types (general funds, special revenue funds, capital projects funds, and debt service funds) are not concerned with income determination. As explained in Chapter 3, these funds are concerned with matching expenditures of legal appropriations, or legal authorizations, with revenues available to finance expenditures. Although permanent funds are concerned with income determination and capital maintenance, GASB *Statement No. 34* notes that because financial resources are the dominant assets of permanent funds, earnings measurement is, in most cases, substantially the same under modified accrual and accrual accounting. Accordingly, even for permanent funds, GASB standards require that governmental fund types use the modified accrual basis. The modified accrual basis requires recognition of revenues in the period in which they become available and measurable. **Measurable** means capable of being expressed in monetary terms; **available** *is* defined as "collectible within the current period or soon enough thereafter to be used to pay liabilities of the current period."[9] GASB standards require the accrual of revenue from property taxes in the period for which the taxes are levied. For other categories of nonexchange revenue transactions, except when certain time requirements and eligibility requirements have not been met, revenues should be accrued if both measurable and available.[10] In respect to expenditure recognition, the modified accrual basis is almost identical to the accrual basis when the only assets of a fund are financial resources.

10. **Budgeting, Budgetary Control, and Budgetary Reporting**
    a. An annual budget(s) should be adopted by every governmental unit.
    b. The accounting system should provide the basis for appropriate budgetary control.
    c. Budgetary comparison schedules should be presented as **required supplementary information** (RSI) for the general fund and each major special revenue fund that has a legally adopted annual budget. The budgetary comparison

[9]GASB, *Codification*, Sec. 1600.106.
[10]GASB, *Codification*, Sec. N50, pars. 105–107; Sec. P70, pars. 103–105.

schedule should present both (a) the original and (b) the final appropriated budgets for the reporting period as well as (c) actual inflows, outflows, and balances, stated on the government's budgetary basis.

Part *a* above is not an accounting or financial reporting principle, but it is a necessary precondition to parts *b* and *c*. A budget, when adopted according to procedures specified in state laws, is binding on the administrators of a governmental unit. Accordingly, a distinctive characteristic of governmental accounting resulting from the need to demonstrate compliance with laws governing the sources of revenues available to governmental units, and laws governing the utilization of those revenues, is the formal recording of the legally approved budget in the accounts of funds operated on an annual basis. Chapter 3 explains in appropriate detail the nature and operation of **budgetary accounts.** Briefly, budgetary accounts are opened as of the beginning of each fiscal year and closed as of the end of each fiscal year; therefore, they have no balances at year-end. During the year, however, the budgetary accounts of a fund are integrated with its proprietary (balance sheet and operating statement) accounts. Budgetary accounting and budgetary reporting are explained in Chapter 3.

11. **Transfer, Revenue, Expenditure, and Expense Account Classification**
    a. Transfers should be classified separately from revenues and expenditures or expenses in the basic financial statements.
    b. Proceeds of general long-term debt issues should be classified separately from revenues and expenditures in the governmental fund financial statements.
    c. Governmental fund revenues should be classified by fund and source. Expenditures should be classified by fund, function (or program), organization unit, activity, character, and principal classes of objects.
    d. Proprietary fund revenues should be reported by major sources, and expenses should be classified in essentially the same manner as those of similar business organizations, functions, or activities.
    e. The statement of activities should present *governmental* activities at least at the level of detail required in the governmental fund statement of revenues, expenditures, and changes in fund balances—at a minimum by *function*. Governments should present *business-type* activities at least by *segment*. [Chapter 7 of the text discusses required segment disclosures by enterprise funds.]

The preceding principle is intended to ensure that account classifications provide for separate financial statement reporting of transfers from revenues and expenditures (or expenses) and for appropriate levels of detail in the basic financial statements. Subsequent chapters provide illustrations of applications of this principle.

12. **Common Terminology and Classification**
    A common terminology and classification should be used consistently throughout the budget, the accounts, and the financial reports of each fund.

The Common Terminology and Classification Principle is simply a statement of the commonsense proposition that if the Budgeting, Budgetary Control, and Budgetary Reporting Principle is to be implemented, persons responsible for preparing the budgets and persons responsible for preparing the financial statements and financial reports should work with the persons responsible for designing and operating the accounting system. Agreement on a common terminology and classification scheme is needed to make sure the accounting system produces the information needed for budget preparation and for financial statement and report preparation.

13. **Annual Financial Reports**
    a. A **comprehensive annual financial report** (CAFR) should be prepared and published, covering all activities of the primary government (including its blended component units) and providing an overview of all discretely presented component units of the reporting entity—including introductory section, management's discussion and analysis (MD&A), basic financial statements, required supplementary information other than MD&A, combining and individual fund statements, schedules, narrative explanations, and statistical section. The reporting entity is the primary government (including its blended component units) and all discretely presented component units presented in accordance with [*Codification*] Section 2100, "Defining the Financial Reporting Entity."
    b. The minimum requirements for MD&A, basic financial statements, and required supplementary information other than MD&A are:
    (1) Management's discussion and analysis.
    (2) Basic financial statements. The basic financial statements should include:
    (a) Government-wide financial statements.
    (b) Fund financial statements.
    (c) Notes to the financial statements.
    (3) Required supplementary information other than MD&A.
    c. As discussed in [*Codification*] Section 2100, the financial **reporting entity** consists of (1) the primary government, (2) organizations for which the primary government is financially accountable, and (3) other organizations for which the nature and significance of their relationship with the primary government are such that exclusion would cause the reporting entity's basic financial statements to be misleading or incomplete. The reporting entity's government-wide financial statements should display information about the reporting government as a whole distinguishing between the total primary government and its discretely presented component units as well as between the primary government's governmental and business-type activities. The reporting entity's fund financial statements should present the primary government's (including its blended component units, which are, in substance, part of the primary government) major funds individually and nonmajor funds in the aggregate. Funds and component units that are fiduciary in nature should be reported only in the statements of fiduciary net assets and changes in fiduciary net assets.
    d. The nucleus of a financial reporting entity usually is a primary government. However, a governmental organization other than a primary government (such as a component unit, joint venture, jointly governed organization, or other stand-alone government) serves as the nucleus for its own reporting entity when it issues separate financial statements. For all of these entities, the provisions of [*Codification*] Section 2100 should be applied in layers "from the bottom up." At each layer, the definition and display provisions should be applied before the layer is included in the financial statements of the next level of the reporting government.

Chapter 1 provides an overview of the content of a comprehensive annual financial report and the basic financial statements and MD&A. A more detailed discussion is given in Chapter 9 as well as other chapters where appropriate. In Illustrations 2–1 through 2–10 we depict two government-wide financial statements and seven fund financial statements specified by GASB *Statement No. 34*. Illustration 2–5 presents an example of the required reconciliation of governmental fund information to the information reported at the government-wide level, and thus is not a financial statement. General purpose financial statements (GPFS) under the current model being superseded by GASB *Statement No. 34* are illustrated in the appendix to Chapter 9.

The following section contains explanations of financial reporting concepts and terminology that readers of this text will encounter in state and local government financial reports. Additional terms used in governmental and not-for-profit accounting are defined in the glossary at the end of the book.

Governmental Financial Reporting Entity

A governmental reporting entity consists of (*a*) the primary government, (*b*) organizations for which the primary government is financially accountable, and (*c*) other organizations for which the nature and significance of their relationship with the primary government are such that exclusion would cause the reporting entity's financial statements to be misleading or incomplete.[11]

A **primary government** is defined as "a state government or general purpose local government. Also, a special purpose government that has a separately elected governing body, is legally separate, and is fiscally independent of other state or local governments." **Component units** are legally separate organizations for which the elected officials of the primary government are financially accountable. In addition, a component unit can be another organization for which the nature and significance of its relationship with the primary government is such that exclusion would cause the reporting entity's financial statements to be misleading or incomplete. Reporting financial data of component units in the manner shown in Illustration 2–1 is called a **discrete presentation.** Discrete presentation should be used unless the financial activities of a component unit are so intertwined with those of the primary government that they are, in substance, the same as the primary government. In such cases the component unit's balances and transactions should be reported in a manner similar to the balances and transactions of the primary government itself; this method of inclusion is known as **blending.** Blending is accomplished by adding financial totals for the component unit's General Fund and special revenue funds to the financial totals for the primary government's special revenue funds, and adding the financial totals for other fund types of the component unit to the same fund type of the primary government.[12]

Notes to the financial statements should contain a brief description of the component units of the financial reporting entity and their relationships to the

[11]GASB, *Codification*, Sec. 2100.111.

[12]All definitions in this paragraph are quoted or paraphrased from GASB *Codification*, Sec. 2100.501.

Illustration 2–1

SAMPLE CITY
STATEMENT OF NET ASSETS
DECEMBER 31, 2002

	Primary Government			
	Governmental Activities	*Business-type Activities*	*Total*	*Component Units*
ASSETS				
Cash and cash equivalents	$ 13,597,899	$ 10,279,143	$ 23,877,042	$ 303,935
Investments	27,365,221	—	27,365,221	7,428,952
Receivables (net)	12,833,132	3,609,615	16,442,747	4,042,290
Internal balances	175,000	(175,000)	—	—
Inventories	322,149	126,674	448,823	83,697
Capital assets, net	170,022,760	151,388,751	321,411,511	37,744,786
Total assets	224,316,161	165,229,183	389,545,344	49,603,660
LIABILITIES				
Accounts payable	6,783,310	751,430	7,534,740	1,803,332
Deferred revenue	1,435,599	—	1,435,599	38,911
Noncurrent liabilities				
Due within one year	9,236,000	4,426,286	13,662,286	1,426,639
Due in more than one year	83,302,378	74,482,273	157,784,651	27,106,151
Total liabilities	100,757,287	79,659,989	180,417,276	30,375,033
NET ASSETS				
Invested in capital assets, net of related debt	103,711,386	73,088,574	176,799,960	15,906,392
Restricted for:				
Capital projects	11,705,864	—	11,705,864	492,445
Debt service	3,020,708	1,451,996	4,472,704	—
Community development projects	4,811,043	—	4,811,043	—
Other purposes	3,214,302	—	3,214,302	—
Unrestricted (deficit)	(2,904,429)	11,028,624	8,124,195	2,829,790
Total net assets	$123,558,874	$ 85,569,194	$209,128,068	$19,228,627

Source: GASB *Statement No. 34* (GASB: Norwalk, CT, 1999), Exhibit A–1.

primary government. This disclosure should include a brief discussion of the criteria for including the component units and how the component units are reported. Information about individual component units may be presented in condensed financial statements within the notes, or in combining statements. The notes also should include information about how separate financial statements for the individual component units may be obtained.

Illustration 2–2

SAMPLE CITY
STATEMENT OF ACTIVITIES
FOR THE YEAR ENDED DECEMBER 31, 2002

		Program Revenues		
Functions/Programs	*Expenses*	*Charges for Services*	*Operating Grants and Contributions*	*Capital Grants and Contributions*
Primary government:				
Governmental activities:				
General government	$ 9,571,410	$ 3,146,915	$ 843,617	$ —
Public safety	34,844,749	1,198,855	1,307,693	62,300
Public works	10,128,538	850,000	—	2,252,615
Engineering services	1,299,645	704,793	—	—
Health and sanitation	6,738,672	5,612,267	575,000	—
Cemetery	735,866	212,496	—	—
Culture and recreation	11,532,350	3,995,199	2,450,000	—
Community development	2,994,389	—	—	2,580,000
Education (payment to school district)	21,893,273	—	—	—
Interest on long-term debt	6,068,121	—	—	—
Total governmental activities	105,807,013	15,720,525	5,176,310	4,894,915
Business-type activities:				
Water	3,595,733	4,159,350	—	1,159,909
Sewer	4,912,853	7,170,533	—	486,010
Parking facilities	2,796,283	1,344,087	—	—
Total business-type activities	11,304,869	12,673,970	—	1,645,919
Total primary government	$117,111,882	$28,394,495	$5,176,310	$6,540,834
Component units:				
Landfill	$ 3,382,157	$ 3,857,858	$ —	$ 11,397
Public school system	31,186,498	705,765	3,937,083	—
Total component units	$ 34,568,655	$ 4,563,623	$3,937,083	$ 11,397

General revenues:
Taxes:
Property taxes, levied for general purposes
Property taxes, levied for debt service
Franchise taxes
Public service taxes
Payment from Sample City
Grants and contributions not restricted to specific programs
Investment earnings
Miscellaneous
Special item—Gain on sale of park land
Transfers
Total general revenues, special items, and transfers
Change in net assets
Net assets—beginning
Net assets—ending

Source: GASB *Statement No. 34* (GASB: Norwalk, CT, 1999), Exhibit B–1.

Net (Expense) Revenue and Changes in Net Assets			
Primary Government			
Governmental Activities	*Business-type Activities*	*Total*	*Component Units*
$ (5,580,878)	$ —	$ (5,580,878)	$ —
(32,275,901)	—	(32,275,901)	—
(7,025,923)	—	(7,025,923)	—
(594,852)	—	(594,852)	—
(551,405)	—	(551,405)	—
(523,370)	—	(523,370)	—
(5,087,151)	—	(5,087,151)	—
(414,389)	—	(414,389)	—
(21,893,273)	—	(21,893,273)	—
(6,068,121)	—	(6,068,121)	—
(80,015,263)	—	(80,015,263)	—
—	1,723,526	1,723,526	—
—	2,743,690	2,743,690	—
—	(1,452,196)	(1,452,196)	—
—	3,015,020	3,015,020	—
(80,015,263)	3,015,020	(77,000,243)	—
—	—	—	487,098
—	—	—	(26,543,650)
—	—	—	(26,056,552)
51,693,573	—	51,693,573	—
4,726,244	—	4,726,244	—
4,055,505	—	4,055,505	—
8,969,887	—	8,969,887	—
—	—	—	21,893,273
1,457,820	—	1,457,820	6,461,708
1,958,144	601,349	2,559,493	881,763
884,907	104,925	989,832	22,464
2,653,488	—	2,653,488	—
501,409	(501,409)	—	—
76,900,977	204,865	77,105,842	29,259,208
(3,114,286)	3,219,885	105,599	3,202,656
126,673,160	82,349,309	209,022,469	16,025,971
$123,558,874	$85,569,194	$209,128,068	$19,228,627

Illustration 2–3

SAMPLE CITY
BALANCE SHEET
GOVERNMENTAL FUNDS
DECEMBER 31, 2002

	General	*HUD Programs*	*Community Redevelopment*
ASSETS			
Cash and cash equivalents	$3,418,485	$1,236,523	$ —
Investments	—	—	13,262,695
Receivables, net	3,644,561	2,953,438	353,340
Due from other funds	1,370,757	—	—
Receivables from other governments	—	119,059	—
Liens receivable	791,926	3,195,745	—
Inventories	182,821	—	—
Total assets	$9,408,550	$7,504,765	$13,616,035
LIABILITIES AND FUND BALANCES			
Liabilities:			
Accounts payable	$3,408,680	$ 129,975	$ 190,548
Due to other funds	—	25,369	—
Payable to other governments	94,074	—	—
Deferred revenue	4,250,430	6,273,045	250,000
Total liabilities	7,753,184	6,428,389	440,548
Fund balances:			
Reserved for:			
Inventories	182,821	—	—
Liens receivable	791,926	—	—
Encumbrances	40,292	41,034	119,314
Debt service	—		
Other purposes	—		
Unreserved, reported in:			
General fund	640,327	—	—
Special revenue funds	—	1,035,342	—
Capital projects funds	—	—	13,056,173
Total fund balances	1,655,366	1,076,376	13,175,487
Total liabilities and fund balances	$9,408,550	$7,504,765	$13,616,035

Source: GASB *Statement No. 34* (GASB: Norwalk, CT, 1999), Exhibit C–1.

The notion of financial accountability is basic to the definition of a governmental financial reporting entity. A primary government is, of course, financially accountable for the organizations that make up its legal entity. It is also financially accountable for legally separate organizations if its officials appoint a voting majority of an organization's governing body and either it is able to impose its will on that organization or there is a potential for the organization to provide specific financial benefits to, or to impose specific financial burdens on, the primary government. A primary government also may be financially accountable for governmental organizations that are fiscally dependent on it.

Route 7 Construction	Other Governmental Funds	Total Governmental Funds
$ —	$ 5,606,792	$ 10,261,800
10,467,037	3,485,252	27,214,984
11,000	10,221	6,972,560
—	—	1,370,757
—	1,596,038	1,715,097
—	—	3,987,671
—	—	182,821
$10,478,037	$10,698,303	$ 51,705,690
$ 1,104,632	$ 1,074,831	$ 5,908,666
—	—	25,369
—	—	94,074
11,000	—	10,784,475
1,115,632	1,074,831	16,812,584
—	—	182,821
—	—	791,926
5,792,587	1,814,122	7,807,349
	3,832,062	3,832,062
	1,405,300	1,405,300
—	—	640,327
—	1,330,718	2,366,060
3,569,818	1,241,270	17,867,261
9,362,405	9,623,472	34,893,106
$10,478,037	$10,698,303	

Amounts reported for *governmental activities* in the statement of net assets (Illustration 2–1) are different because:	
Capital assets used in governmental activities are not financial resources and therefore are not reported in the funds.	161,082,708
Other long-term assets are not available to pay for current-period expenditures and therefore are deferred in the funds.	9,348,876
Internal service funds are used by management to charge the costs of certain activities, such as insurance and telecommunications, to individual funds. The assets and liabilities of the internal service funds are included in governmental activities in the statement of net assets (Illustration 2–6).	2,994,691
Long-term liabilities, including bonds payable, are not due and payable in the current period and therefore are not reported in the funds.	(84,760,507)
Net assets of governmental activities	$123,558,874

Illustration 2–4

SAMPLE CITY
STATEMENT OF REVENUES, EXPENDITURES, AND CHANGES IN FUND BALANCES
GOVERNMENTAL FUNDS
FOR THE YEAR ENDED DECEMBER 31, 2002

	General	*HUD Programs*	*Community Redevelopment*
REVENUES			
Property taxes	$51,173,436	$ —	$ —
Franchise taxes	4,055,505	—	—
Public service taxes	8,969,887	—	—
Fees and fines	606,946	—	—
Licenses and permits	2,287,794	—	—
Intergovernmental	6,119,938	2,578,191	—
Charges for services	11,374,460	—	—
Investment earnings	552,325	87,106	549,489
Miscellaneous	881,874	66,176	—
Total revenues	86,022,165	2,731,473	549,489
EXPENDITURES			
Current:			
General government	8,630,835	—	417,814
Public safety	33,729,623	—	—
Public works	4,975,775	—	—
Engineering services	1,299,645	—	—
Health and sanitation	6,070,032	—	—
Cemetery	706,305	—	—
Culture and recreation	11,411,685	—	—
Community development	—	2,954,389	—
Education—payment to school district	21,893,273	—	—
Debt service:			
Principal	—	—	—
Interest and other charges	—	—	—
Capital outlay	—	—	2,246,671
Total expenditures	88,717,173	2,954,389	2,664,485
Excess (deficiency) of revenues over expenditures	(2,695,008)	(222,916)	(2,114,996)
OTHER FINANCING SOURCES (USES)			
Proceeds of refunding bonds	—	—	—
Proceeds of long-term capital-related debt	—	—	17,529,560
Payment to bond refunding escrow agent	—	—	—
Transfers in	129,323	—	—
Transfers out	(2,163,759)	(348,046)	(2,273,187)
Total other financing sources and uses	(2,034,436)	(348,046)	15,256,373
SPECIAL ITEM			
Proceeds from sale of park land	3,476,488	—	—
Net change in fund balances	(1,252,956)	(570,962)	13,141,377
Fund balances—beginning	2,908,322	1,647,338	34,110
Fund balances—ending	$ 1,655,366	$1,076,376	$13,175,487

Source: GASB *Statement No. 34* (GASB: Norwalk, CT, 1999), Exhibit C–2.

	Route 7 Construction	Other Governmental Funds	Total Governmental Funds
	$ —	$ 4,680,192	$ 55,853,628
	—	—	4,055,505
	—	—	8,969,887
	—	—	606,946
	—	—	2,287,794
	—	2,830,916	11,529,045
	—	30,708	11,405,168
	270,161	364,330	1,823,411
	2,939	94	951,083
	273,100	7,906,240	97,482,467
	16,700	121,052	9,186,401
	—	—	33,729,623
	—	3,721,542	8,697,317
	—	—	1,299,645
	—	—	6,070,032
	—	—	706,305
	—	—	11,411,685
	—	—	2,954,389
	—	—	21,893,273
	—	3,450,000	3,450,000
	—	5,215,151	5,215,151
	11,281,769	3,190,209	16,718,649
	11,298,469	15,697,954	121,332,470
	(11,025,369)	(7,791,714)	(23,850,003)
	—	38,045,000	38,045,000
	—	1,300,000	18,829,560
	—	(37,284,144)	(37,284,144)
	—	5,551,187	5,680,510
	—	(219,076)	(5,004,068)
	—	7,392,967	20,266,858
	—	—	3,476,488
	(11,025,369)	(398,747)	(106,657)
	20,387,774	10,022,219	34,999,763
	$ 9,362,405	$ 9,623,472	$ 34,893,106

Illustration 2–5

SAMPLE CITY
RECONCILIATION OF THE STATEMENT OF REVENUES, EXPENDITURES, AND CHANGES IN FUND BALANCES OF GOVERNMENTAL FUNDS TO THE STATEMENT OF ACTIVITIES
FOR THE YEAR ENDED DECEMBER 31, 2002

Net change in fund balances—total governmental funds	$ (106,657)
Amounts reported for *governmental activities* in the statement of activities (Illustration 2–2) are different because:	
Governmental funds report capital outlays as expenditures. However, in the statement of activities, the cost of those assets is allocated over their estimated useful lives as depreciation expense. This is the amount by which capital outlays exceeded depreciation in the current period.	14,039,717
In the statement of activities, only the *gain* on the sale of the park land is reported, whereas in the governmental funds, the proceeds from the sale increase financial resources. Thus, the change in net assets differs from the change in fund balance by the cost of the land sold.	(823,000)
Revenues in the statement of activities that do not provide current financial resources are not reported as revenues in the funds.	1,920,630
Bond proceeds provide current financial resources to governmental funds, but issuing debt increases long-term liabilities in the statement of net assets. Repayment of bond principal is an expenditure in the governmental funds, but the repayment reduces long-term liabilities in the statement of net assets. This is the amount by which proceeds exceeded repayments.	(16,140,416)
Some expenses reported in the statement of activities do not require the use of current financial resources and therefore are not reported as expenditures in governmental funds.	(1,245,752)
Internal service funds are used by management to charge the costs of certain activities, such as insurance and telecommunications, to individual funds. The net revenue (expense) of the internal service funds is reported with governmental activities.	(758,808)
Change in net assets of governmental activities.	$(3,114,286)

Source: GASB *Statement No. 34* (GASB: Norwalk, CT, 1999), Exhibit C–3.

A primary government has the ability to impose its will on an organization if it can significantly influence the programs, projects, or activities of, or the level of services performed or provided by, the organization. A financial benefit or burden relationship exists if the primary government (a) is entitled to the organization's resources; (b) is legally obligated or has otherwise assumed the obligation to finance the deficits of, or provide financial support to, the organization; or (c) is obligated in some manner for the debt of the organization.

Some organizations are included as component units because of their fiscal dependency on the primary government. An organization is fiscally dependent on the primary government if it is unable to adopt its budget, levy taxes or set rates or charges, or issue bonded debt without approval by the primary government.

Illustration 2–6

SAMPLE CITY
STATEMENT OF NET ASSETS
PROPRIETARY FUNDS
DECEMBER 31, 2002

	Business-type Activities—Enterprise Funds			Governmental Activities—
	Water and Sewer	*Parking Facilities*	*Totals*	*Internal Service Funds*
ASSETS				
Current assets:				
Cash and cash equivalents	$ 8,416,653	$ 369,168	$ 8,785,821	$ 3,336,099
Investments	—	—	—	150,237
Receivables, net	3,564,586	3,535	3,568,121	157,804
Due from other governments	41,494	—	41,494	—
Inventories	126,674	—	126,674	139,328
Total current assets	12,149,407	372,703	12,522,110	3,783,468
Noncurrent assets:				
Restricted cash and cash equivalents	—	1,493,322	1,493,322	—
Capital assets:				
Land	813,513	3,021,637	3,835,150	—
Distribution and collection systems	39,504,183	—	39,504,183	—
Buildings and equipment	106,135,666	23,029,166	129,164,832	14,721,786
Less accumulated depreciation	(15,328,911)	(5,786,503)	(21,115,414)	(5,781,734)
Total noncurrent assets	131,124,451	21,757,622	152,882,073	8,940,052
Total assets	143,273,858	22,130,325	165,404,183	12,723,520
LIABILITIES				
Current liabilities:				
Accounts payable	447,427	304,003	751,430	780,570
Due to other funds	175,000	—	175,000	1,170,388
Compensated absences	112,850	8,827	121,677	237,690
Claims and judgments	—	—	—	1,687,975
Bonds, notes, and loans payable	3,944,609	360,000	4,304,609	249,306
Total current liabilities	4,679,886	672,830	5,352,716	4,125,929
Noncurrent liabilities:				
Compensated absences	451,399	35,306	486,705	—
Claims and judgments	—	—	—	5,602,900
Bonds, notes, and loans payable	54,451,549	19,544,019	73,995,568	—
Total noncurrent liabilities	54,902,948	19,579,325	74,482,273	5,602,900
Total liabilities	59,582,834	20,252,155	79,834,989	9,728,829
NET ASSETS				
Invested in capital assets, net of related debt	72,728,293	360,281	73,088,574	8,690,746
Restricted for debt service	—	1,451,996	1,451,996	—
Unrestricted	10,962,731	65,893	11,028,624	(5,696,055)
Total net assets	$ 83,691,024	$ 1,878,170	$ 85,569,194	$ 2,994,691

Source: GASB *Statement No. 34* (GASB: Norwalk, CT, 1999), Exhibit D–1.

Illustration 2–7

SAMPLE CITY
STATEMENT OF REVENUES, EXPENSES,
AND CHANGES IN FUND NET ASSETS
PROPRIETARY FUNDS
FOR THE YEAR ENDED DECEMBER 31, 2002

	Business-type Activities—Enterprise Funds			Governmental Activities—Internal Service Funds
	Water and Sewer	*Parking Facilities*	*Totals*	
Operating revenues:				
Charges for services	$11,329,883	$1,340,261	$12,670,144	$15,256,164
Miscellaneous	—	3,826	3,826	1,066,761
Total operating revenues	11,329,883	1,344,087	12,673,970	16,322,925
Operating expenses:				
Personal services	3,400,559	762,348	4,162,907	4,157,156
Contractual services	344,422	96,032	440,454	584,396
Utilities	754,107	100,726	854,833	214,812
Repairs and maintenance	747,315	64,617	811,932	1,960,490
Other supplies and expenses	498,213	17,119	515,332	234,445
Insurance claims and expenses	—	—	—	8,004,286
Depreciation	1,163,140	542,049	1,705,189	1,707,872
Total operating expenses	6,907,756	1,582,891	8,490,647	16,863,457
Operating income (loss)	4,422,127	(238,804)	4,183,323	(540,532)
Nonoperating revenues (expenses):				
Interest and investment revenue	454,793	146,556	601,349	134,733
Miscellaneous revenue	—	104,925	104,925	20,855
Interest expense	(1,600,830)	(1,166,546)	(2,767,376)	(41,616)
Miscellanaous expense	—	(46,846)	(46,846)	(176,003)
Total nonoperating revenue (expenses)	(1,146,037)	(961,911)	(2,107,948)	(62,031)
Income (loss) before contributions and transfers	3,276,090	(1,200,715)	2,075,375	(602,563)
Capital contributions	1,645,919	—	1,645,919	18,788
Transfers out	(290,000)	(211,409)	(501,409)	(175,033)
Change in net assets	4,632,009	(1,412,124)	3,219,885	(758,808)
Total net assets—beginning	79,059,015	3,290,294	82,349,309	3,753,499
Total net assets—ending	$83,691,024	$1,878,170	$85,569,194	$2,994,691

Source: GASB *Statement No. 34* (GASB: Norwalk, CT, 1999), Exhibit D–3.

A Summary of Accounting Characteristics of Fund Types

Information pertaining to accounting and financial reporting for governmental funds is given in a number of different contexts in the principles discussed in the preceding section of this chapter. The same is true of information pertaining to accounting and financial reporting for proprietary funds and for fiduciary funds. Chapters following this one deal with individual fund types as well as with government-wide accounting and financial reporting. In order to provide a framework for the student to keep the detailed discussion of fund types in perspective, this section presents the accounting characteristics common to each category of fund types: governmental, proprietary, and fiduciary. Illustration 2–11 provides a summary of these characteristics.

Accounting Characteristics Common to Governmental Funds

All funds in any of the five types of funds classified by the GASB as governmental funds (the General Fund, special revenue funds, capital projects funds, debt service funds, and permanent funds) have certain accounting characteristics that differentiate them from proprietary funds and fiduciary funds:

1. Governmental funds are created in accord with legal requirements. Each fund has only those resources allowed by law—a local governmental unit may choose not to use a resource authorized by state law, but it may *not* choose to utilize an unauthorized resource. The resources may be expended only for purposes and in amounts approved by the legislative branch in accord with procedures detailed in laws of component jurisdictions. Therefore, the measurement focus of governmental fund accounting is on the flow of current financial resources (as distinguished from a business organization's focus on the determination of net income). Governmental funds are said to be *expendable;* that is, resources are received and expended, with no expectation that they will be returned through user or departmental charges. Revenues and expenditures (*not* expenses) of governmental funds are recognized on the modified accrual basis of accounting. The meaning of the term *modified accrual* is explained further in Chapter 3.
2. Legal constraints on the raising of revenue and the expenditure of revenue are, in most jurisdictions, set forth in a legally adopted budget. Accordingly, it is a recognized principle of accounting and financial reporting for state and local governmental units that accounting systems of governmental funds should provide the basis for appropriate budgetary control. The nature and operation of budgetary accounts recommended for use by each of the fund types in the governmental funds category is explained in following chapters.
3. Governmental funds account only for current financial resources: cash, receivables, marketable securities, and, if material, prepaid items and supplies inventories. They do not account for plant and equipment.

Illustration 2–8

SAMPLE CITY
STATEMENT OF CASH FLOWS
PROPRIETARY FUNDS
FOR THE YEAR ENDED DECEMBER 31, 2002

CASH FLOWS FROM OPERATING ACTIVITIES

Receipts from customers
Payments to suppliers
Payments to employees
Internal activity—payments to other funds
Claims paid
Other receipts (payments)
Net cash provided by operating activities

CASH FLOWS FROM NONCAPITAL FINANCING ACTIVITIES

Operating subsidies and transfers to other funds

CASH FLOWS FROM CAPITAL AND RELATED FINANCING ACTIVITIES

Proceeds from capital debt
Capital contributions
Purchases of capital assets
Principal paid on capital debt
Interest paid on capital debt
Other receipts (payments)
Net cash (used) by capital and related financing activities

CASH FLOWS FROM INVESTING ACTIVITIES

Proceeds from sales and maturities of investments
Interest and dividends
Net cash provided by investing activities
Net (decrease) in cash and cash equivalents
Balances—beginning of the year
Balances—end of the year

Reconciliation of operating income (loss) to net cash provided (used) by operating activities:

Operating income (loss)
Adjustment to reconcile operating income to net cash provided (used) by operating activities:
Depreciation expense
Change in assets and liabilities:
Receivables, net
Inventories
Accounts and other payables
Accrued expenses
Net cash provided by operating activities

Source: GASB *Statement No. 34* (GASB: Norwalk, CT, 1999), Exhibit D–4.

Business-type Activities— Enterprise Funds			Governmental Activities—
Water and Sewer	*Parking Facilities*	*Totals*	*Internal Service Funds*
$11,400,200	$ 1,345,292	$12,745,492	$15,326,343
(2,725,349)	(365,137)	(3,090,486)	(2,812,238)
(3,360,055)	(750,828)	(4,110,883)	(4,209,688)
(1,296,768)	—	(1,296,768)	—
—	—	—	(8,482,451)
(2,325,483)	—	(2,325,483)	1,061,118
1,692,545	229,327	1,921,872	883,084
(290,000)	(211,409)	(501,409)	(175,033)
4,041,322	8,660,778	12,702,100	—
1,645,919	—	1,645,919	—
(4,194,035)	(144,716)	(4,338,751)	(400,086)
(2,178,491)	(8,895,000)	(11,073,491)	(954,137)
(1,479,708)	(1,166,546)	(2,646,254)	41,616
—	19,174	19,174	131,416
(2,164,993)	(1,526,310)	(3,691,303)	(1,264,423)
—	—	—	15,684
454,793	143,747	598,540	129,550
454,793	143,747	598,540	145,234
(307,655)	(1,364,645)	(1,672,300)	(411,138)
8,724,308	3,227,135	11,951,443	3,747,237
$ 8,416,653	$ 1,862,490	$10,279,143	$ 3,336,099
$ 4,422,127	$ (238,804)	$ 4,183,323	$ (540,532)
1,163,140	542,049	1,705,189	1,707,872
653,264	1,205	654,469	31,941
2,829	—	2,829	39,790
(297,446)	(86,643)	(384,089)	475,212
(4,251,369)	11,520	(4,239,849)	(831,199)
$ 1,692,545	$ 229,327	$ 1,921,872	$ 883,084

Illustration 2–9

SAMPLE CITY
STATEMENT OF FIDUCIARY NET ASSETS
FIDUCIARY FUNDS
DECEMBER 31, 2002

	Employee Retirement Plan	*Private-Purpose Trusts*	*Agency Funds*
ASSETS			
Cash and cash equivalents	$ 1,973	$ 1,250	$ 44,889
Receivables:			
Interest and dividends	508,475	760	—
Other receivables	6,826	—	183,161
Total receivables	515,301	760	183,161
Investments, at fair value:			
U.S. government obligations	13,056,037	80,000	—
Municipal bonds	6,528,019	—	—
Corporate bonds	16,320,047	—	—
Corporate stocks	26,112,075	—	—
Other investments	3,264,009	—	—
Total investments	65,280,187	80,000	—
Total assets	65,797,461	82,010	$228,050
LIABILITIES			
Accounts payable	—	1,234	$ —
Refunds payable and others	1,358	—	228,050
Total liabilities	1,358	1,234	$228,050
NET ASSETS			
Held in trust for pension benefits and other purposes	$65,796,103	$80,776	

Source: GASB *Statement No. 34* (GASB: Norwalk, CT, 1999), Exhibit E–1.

4. Funds in the governmental category account for only those liabilities to be paid from fund assets.
5. The arithmetic difference between fund assets and fund liabilities is called the **Fund Equity.** Fund Equity may be reserved for reasons discussed in following chapters; the portion of Fund Equity that is not reserved is called **Fund Balance.** Residents of the governmental unit have no legal claim on any portion of the Fund Equity, so it is not equivalent to the capital section of an investor-owned entity.

Illustration 2–10

SAMPLE CITY
STATEMENT OF CHANGES IN FIDUCIARY NET ASSETS
FIDUCIARY FUNDS
FOR THE YEAR ENDED DECEMBER 31, 2002

	Employee Retirement Plan	*Private-Purpose Trusts*
ADDITIONS		
Contributions:		
Employer	$ 2,721,341	$ —
Plan members	1,421,233	—
Total contributions	4,142,574	—
Investment earnings:		
Net (decrease) in fair value of investments	(272,522)	—
Interest	2,460,871	4,560
Dividends	1,445,273	—
Total investment earnings	3,633,622	4,560
Less investment expense	216,428	—
Net investment earnings	3,417,194	4,560
Total additions	7,559,768	4,560
DEDUCTIONS		
Benefits	2,453,047	3,800
Refunds of contributions	464,691	—
Administrative expenses	87,532	678
Total deductions	3,005,270	4,478
Change in net assets	4,554,498	82
Net assets—beginning of the year	61,241,605	80,694
Net assets—end of the year	$65,796,103	$80,776

Source: GASB *Statement No. 34* (GASB: Norwalk, CT, 1999), Exhibit E–2.

Accounting Characteristics Common to Proprietary Funds

The definition of *internal service funds*, given in the Types of Funds Principle, states that these funds provide services to users on a "cost-reimbursement basis." The definition of *enterprise funds*, given in the same principle, states that they are "operated in manner similar to a private business enterprise," and that they are used in the event that the governmental body desires to compute revenues earned, costs incurred, or net income of certain activities. Proprietary funds are not subject to income taxation, nor do they have owners in the sense that business entities do, but in all other respects it follows that funds properly classified as proprietary funds should adhere to accounting practices deemed appropriate for business organizations:

Illustration 2–11 Summary of Characteristics of Fund Types

Activities* of government

- Governmental activities
- Business-type activities
- Fiduciary activities

Governmental Fund Types (General, special revenue, capital projects, debt service, and permanent)

Characteristics:

- Focus on fiscal accountability
- Measure and report current (expendable) financial resources
- Use modified accrual basis of accounting
- Account for and report revenues and expenditures
- No capital assets or long-term liabilities accounted for in funds; no depreciation reported in funds
- Budgetary accounts integrated into the funds to achieve legal budgetary control

Proprietary Fund Types (Enterprise and internal service)†

Characteristics:

- Focus on operational accountability
- Measure and report economic resources (as in business accounting)
- Use full accrual basis of accounting
- Account for and report revenues and expenses
- Account for capital assets and long-term liabilities within the funds; report depreciation
- Budgetary accounts ordinarily not integrated into the funds; should use budgeting for planning and control

Fiduciary Fund Types (Agency, private-purpose trust, investment trust, and pension trust)

Characteristics:

- Trust funds use principles similar to proprietary fund types
- GASB standards prescribe certain unique liability recognition rules for pension trust funds
- Agency funds have only asset and liability accounts; have no net assets

*Governmental activities of the primary government also are reported in aggregate as a separate column in the government-wide financial statements using the economic resources measurement focus and accrual basis of accounting.

†Under the GASB *Statement No. 34* reporting model requirements, internal service funds are usually reported as part of the governmental activities in the government-wide financial statements and identified as governmental activities in the proprietary fund financial statements (see Illustrations 2–6 and 2–7).

1. Proprietary funds are established in accord with enabling legislation, and their operations and policies are subject to legislative oversight. Ordinarily, however, the purposes of legislative oversight are served by proprietary fund accounting and financial reporting that focuses on the matching of revenues and expenses (*not* expenditures) on the full accrual basis recommended for business organizations.
2. Funds classified as proprietary should prepare budgets as an essential element in the management planning and control processes. It is generally true, however, that proprietary funds do not have to adopt budgetary documents by law as governmental funds do. Therefore, standards established by the GASB state that accounting systems of proprietary funds do not need to provide for the integration of budgetary accounts.
3. Proprietary funds account for all assets used in fund operations—current assets, plant and equipment, and any other assets considered as belonging to the fund.
4. Proprietary funds account for current and long-term liabilities to be serviced from fund operations and/or to be repaid from fund assets.

Accounting Characteristics Common to Fiduciary Funds

Since the four types of fiduciary funds (agency funds, private-purpose trust funds, investment trust funds, and pension trust funds) all are used to account for assets held by a governmental unit as a trustee or agent for others, they have that characteristic in common. The manner in which trust funds are created and operated leads the GASB to conclude that these types of fiduciary funds should be accounted for in essentially the same manner as the two types of proprietary funds.

Key Terms

Accrual basis, 28
Assets, 28
Available, 29
Blending, 32
Budgetary accounts, 30
Business-type activities, 22
Component unit, 32
Comprehensive annual financial report (CAFR), 31
Current financial resources, 23
Discrete presentation, 32
Economic resources measurement focus, 28
Escheat properties, 22
Exchange transactions, 28
Exchange-like transactions, 28
Expenditure, 28
Expense, 28
Fiduciary activities, 22
Fiduciary funds, 26
Fund, 25
Fund Balance, 46
Fund Equity, 46
Gains, 28
Governmental activities, 22
Governmental funds, 25
Liabilities, 28
Losses, 28
Major funds, 25
Measurable, 29
Modified accrual basis, 28
Nonexchange transactions, 28

Selected References

Governmental Accounting Standards Board. *Codification of Governmental Accounting and Financial Reporting Standards as of June 30, 1999*. Norwalk, CT, 1999.
Governmental Accounting Standards Board, *Statement No. 34*, Norwalk, CT, 1999.

Questions

2–1. Describe the governmental activities of a state or local government and explain the focus of accounting and financial reporting for these activities.

2–2. Describe the business-type activities of a state or local government and explain the focus of accounting and financial reporting for these activities.

2–3. Describe the fiduciary activities of a state or local government and explain the focus of accounting and financial reporting for these activities.

2–4. "The primary purpose of an accounting system for a state or a local governmental unit is to make it possible for financial statements to demonstrate compliance with finance-related legal and contractual provisions." Explain why you believe this statement to be correct or incorrect.

2–5. What is the technical meaning of the term *fund* in governmental accounting?

2–6. "Capital assets of a governmental unit should always be reported on the same basis as a business—depreciated historical cost." Do you agree? Why or why not?

2–7. "Proprietary funds have as their objective to make a profit; therefore, proprietary funds should use the same accounting principles as a business enterprise." Do you agree or disagree? Why?

2–8. "Because budgetary accounts are used by governmental units, their financial statements can never be said to be in accord with generally accepted accounting principles." Comment.

2–9. What is the distinction between fund long-term liabilities and general long-term liabilities?

2–10. Describe the purpose of the "new financial reporting model" prescribed by GASB *Statement No. 34* in your own words.

2–11. What are the two government-wide financial statements required by GASB *Statement No. 34* and what are the measurement focus and basis of accounting that should be used in preparing these statements?

2–12. List the seven fund financial statements that are required in the general purpose financial statements by GASB *Statement No. 34*. What are the measurement focus and basis of accounting that should be used in preparing these statements?

2–13. When must governments implement the new financial reporting model described in GASB *Statement No. 34*?

2–14. Explain in your own words what the term *governmental financial reporting entity* means.

2–15. "If a discrete presentation is used for the financial data of a component unit in the statement of net assets of a governmental financial reporting entity, there is no need for the component unit to issue a separate financial report." Is this statement true or false? In your answer explain what is meant by the term *discrete presentation*.

Exercises and Problems

2–1. Examine the CAFR. Utilizing the CAFR obtained for Exercise 1–1, examine the financial statements included in the financial section and answer the following questions.

a. General Fund. What title is given to the fund that functions as the General Fund of the reporting entity? Does the report specify that the General Fund of the reporting entity is the General Fund of the primary government? Does the report state the basis of accounting used for the General Fund? If so, is the financial statement presentation consistent with the stated basis (i.e., some reports claim the modified accrual basis was used but show no receivables in the balance sheet or any other evidence that measurable and available revenues are accrued)? If the basis of accounting is not stated, analyze the statements to determine what basis is used. Is the same basis used for both revenues and expenditures? Is the basis used consistent with GASB standards?

b. Special Revenue Funds. What special revenue funds are included in the report? Are they described as special revenue funds, or only by a title such as "Library Fund," "School Fund," or "Street Fund"? Does the report specify why each special revenue fund was created (is there a reference to a state statute, local government ordinance, or other legislative or administrative action)? Is the basis of accounting for these funds stated, or must it be determined by analysis of the statements? Is the same basis used for all special revenue funds? Is it the same basis as used for the General Fund? If not, does the report explain why each basis is used? Is the basis of accounting for special revenue funds in conformity with GASB standards?

c. Other Governmental Fund Types. List the names of governmental fund types, in addition to the General Fund and special revenue funds, that are included in the combined balance sheet of the reporting entity or the balance sheet for the governmental funds if the government has implemented GASB *Statement No. 34*. Are any governmental fund types included in other statements but not included in the balance sheet? If so, determine why.

d. Proprietary Funds. List the names of the proprietary fund types included in the financial statements. Do the balance sheet accounts provide evidence that all proprietary funds are accounted for on the full accrual basis?

e. Fiduciary Funds. List the names of fiduciary fund types included in the financial statements. (You may have to refer to a combining balance sheet for fiduciary funds to determine the types of fiduciary funds used by this reporting entity.) For each fiduciary fund type identify the basis of accounting used.

f. *General Capital Assets*. If the government has not yet implemented GASB *Statement No. 34*, does the combined balance sheet include a column for financial data of the General Fixed Assets Account Group? For the General Long-Term Debt Account Group? If the government has implemented GASB *Statement No. 34*, where are capital assets reported?

g. *Notes to the Financial Statements*. Read through the notes to the financial statements in order to become generally familiar with their content so that you can refer to the notes as needed in subsequent weeks. At this time determine whether the notes include a summary of significant accounting policies. Do the notes describe the criteria used in determining the scope of the entity for financial reporting purposes? Do the notes disclose which component units were included in the reporting entity and the key decision criteria considered? If there is a component unit disclosed in a separate column as a discrete presentation of the combined financial statements of the reporting entity, do the notes clearly disclose the accounting policies of the component unit and the relationship of the component unit to the primary government? Are there notes that disclose: (1) any material violations of legal provisions, (2) any deficit fund balance or net assets, or retained earnings of individual funds, or (3) any excess of expenditures over appropriations in individual funds, explanations for the excess, and remedial action planned?

2–2. Multiple Choice. Choose the best answer.

1. Which of the following is *not* one of the activity categories of government, as described in this chapter?
   a. Fiduciary.
   b. Business-type.
   c. Profit-seeking.
   d. Governmental.
2. An accounting system for a state or local governmental unit must make it possible:
   a. To prepare consolidated statements for the governmental reporting entity in conformity with FASB standards.
   b. To present fairly the financial position and results of financial operations of the government in conformity with GAAP and to demonstrate compliance with finance-related legal and contractual provisions.
   c. To prepare financial statements as required by relevant laws.
   d. To demonstrate service efforts and accomplishments.
3. A fund is a (an):
   a. Legal entity created only when authorized or required by law.
   b. Self-balancing set of accounts recording cash and other financial resources, together with all related liabilities and residual equities or balances, and changes therein.
   c. Accounting but not a fiscal entity.
   d. All of the above.

4. The governmental funds category under GASB *Statement No. 34* is made up of:
   a. The General Fund, special revenue funds, capital projects funds, and debt service funds.
   b. The General Fund, special revenue funds, capital projects funds, debt service funds, and the internal service fund.
   c. The General Fund, special revenue funds, and permanent funds.
   d. The General Fund, special revenue funds, capital projects funds, debt service funds, and permanent funds.
5. Self-supporting activities that provide goods or services to the public on a user-charge basis should be accounted for in what fund category?
   a. Governmental.
   b. Governmental Business-Type Fund.
   c. Fiduciary.
   d. Proprietary.
6. Under currently effective GASB standards, governmental funds should recognize revenues and expenditures on the:
   a. Cash basis.
   b. Full accrual basis.
   c. Modified accrual basis.
   d. There is no specific requirement; each government may choose whatever basis it wants, as long as it uses that basis consistently.
7. The proprietary funds category is made up of:
   a. Enterprise funds, nonexpendable trust funds, pension trust funds, and internal service funds.
   b. Internal service funds, special revenue funds, and enterprise funds.
   c. Enterprise funds and internal service funds.
   d. Any of the above, depending on management intent.
8. Currently effective GASB standards require proprietary funds to recognize revenues and expenses on the:
   a. Cash basis.
   b. Full accrual basis.
   c. Modified accrual basis.
   d. There is no specific requirement; each government may choose whatever basis it wants, as long as it uses that basis consistently.
9. The fiduciary funds category is made up of:
   a. Agency funds, internal service funds, and general funds.
   b. Agency funds, investment trust funds, and debt service funds.
   c. Private-purpose trust funds, agency funds, and special revenue funds.
   d. Private-purpose trust funds, investment trust funds, agency funds, and pension trust funds.

10. Fiduciary funds use which of the following bases of accounting?

	Full Accrual	Modified Accrual
a.	Yes	Yes
b.	Yes	No
c.	No	Yes
d.	No	No

2–3. Multiple Choice. *GASB Statement* No. 34. Choose the best answer.

1. Which of the following is *not* a government-wide financial statement?
   a. Statement of Net Assets.
   b. Statement of Revenues, Expenditures, and Changes in Fund Balances.
   c. Statement of Activities.
   d. All of the above are required government-wide financial statements.
2. If a government has total annual revenues of $90 million and a June 30 fiscal year end, it must implement GASB *Statement No. 34* for [Note: FY2001 means fiscal year ending June 30, 2001]
   a. FY2001.
   b. FY2002.
   c. FY2003.
   d. FY2004.
3. Government-wide financial statements are designed to demonstrate
   a. Fiscal accountability.
   b. Operational accountability.
   c. Liquidity.
   d. Compliance with the budget.
4. A major fund is one in which
   a. Total assets, liabilities, revenues, or expenditures/expenses are at least 10 percent of the corresponding total for all funds of that category or type (i.e., governmental or enterprise funds).
   b. Total assets, liabilities, revenues, or expenditures/expenses are at least 5 percent of the corresponding total for all funds combined (i.e., both governmental and enterprise funds).
   c. Neither *a* nor *b* is true.
   d. Both *a* and *b* are true.
5. Permanent funds are used to account for legally restricted resources provided by trust in which the earnings but not the principal may be used for purposes that support the
   a. Primary government's programs.
   b. Private individuals.
   c. Other governments.
   d. Other nonprofit organizations.
6. Which of the following is *not* properly classified as a fiduciary fund?
   a. Pension and other employee benefit fund.
   b. Investment trust fund.
   c. Permanent fund.
   d. Private-purpose trust fund.

7. Capital assets of proprietary funds should be reported in
   a. Government-wide financial statements only.
   b. Proprietary fund financial statements only.
   c. General long-term debt account group.
   d. Both the government-wide and proprietary fund financial statements.
8. Inexhaustible assets, such as land and land improvements, should
   a. Be depreciated over their estimated useful lives.
   b. Not be depreciated.
   c. Be depreciated over their useful lives using a modified approach.
   d. Be depreciated and reported in the government-wide financial statements.
9. Liabilities that are directly related to and expected to be paid from proprietary funds are called
   a. Fund long-term liabilities.
   b. General long-term liabilities.
   c. Noncurrent liabilities.
   d. None of the above.
10. The measurement focus and basis of accounting that should be used in the government-wide basic financial statements are

	Measurement Focus	Basis of Accounting
a.	Current financial resources	Modified accrual
b.	Current financial resources	Accrual
c.	Economic resources	Modified accrual
d.	Economic resources	Accrual

2–4. True or False. Write F if the corresponding statement is false. If the statement is false, state what changes should be made to make it true.

1. The General Fund, capital projects funds, and debt service funds are the only fund types that are classified as governmental funds.
2. The measurement focus of governmental funds should be on the flow of current financial resources, rather than on income determination.
3. The accounting system of the General Fund of a governmental reporting entity should incorporate budgetary accounts to assist administrators to achieve budgetary control.
4. The accounting system for proprietary funds should provide for integration of budgetary accounts.
5. Depreciation should be recorded for capital assets accounted for in the General Fund and reported in the fund statements.
6. A governmental fund accounts for only liabilities to be paid from currently available fund assets.
7. Interfund transfers should be recognized in the period in which the interfund receivable and payable arise.
8. Interfund transfers and proceeds of general long-term debt need not be distinguished from a fund's revenues and expenditures or expenses for financial reporting purposes.
9. Revenues of a proprietary fund type are recognized when earned and measurable.

10. Bonds issued to double the capacity of a city's electric utility (an enterprise fund) and that will be repaid from revenues of the electric utility should be accounted for in the enterprise fund.

2–5. True or False. GASB *Statement* No. 34. If the statement is false, state what changes should be made to make it true.

1. Internal service funds usually are reported as part of the governmental activities column in the government-wide financial statements.
2. Business-type activities measure and report current (expendable) financial resources and expenditures.
3. Budgetary accounts are integrated into the funds to achieve legal budgetary control for governmental fund-types, but not into proprietary fund-types.
4. The fiduciary fund-type includes agency, private-purpose trust, investment trust, pension trust, and permanent trust funds.
5. Financial reporting for fiduciary funds includes a statement of changes in fiduciary net assets and a statement of fiduciary net assets in the fund financial statements, and no reporting in the government-wide financial statements.
6. A reconciliation is required between the statement of net assets and the statement of revenues, expenditures, and changes in fund balances of governmental funds.
7. Component units of the reporting entity may be shown on the government-wide financial statements, but would not appear on the fund financial statements.
8. A special revenue fund and debt service fund always are considered "major funds."
9. Large governments have more time to implement GASB *Statement No. 34* than small governments.
10. GASB *Statement No. 34* added one more principle about long-term liabilities and modified many of the original 12 principles prescribed by the National Council on Governmental Accounting.

2–6. Reporting Entity. Garden City is financially accountable, as defined in GASB standards, for the Garden City Water Utility, although the administrators of the utility report to the Garden City Water Board.

Required

a. Name the primary government of the Garden City financial reporting entity. Explain your answer.

b. Should the balances of the Garden City Water Utility be blended with the balances of the city, or should the balances of the utility be shown in a discrete presentation? Explain your answer.

c. Should the capital assets of the utility be reported at cost, or at depreciated cost? Explain.

Continuous Problem

Note: Chapters 3 through 9 of this text deal with specific knowledge needed to understand the accounting for the funds recommended for use by state and local governmental units and with specific aspects of financial management. In order to help the student keep the entire accounting and financial management area in perspective, a series of related problems are presented. This series covers representative activities of the City of Bingham; the problems in this series relate to all funds and the government as a whole; they are designated 2–B, 3–B, 4–B, and so on.

At the option of the instructor, students may be required to solve the City of Bingham problems manually, using journal paper and ledger paper available from college bookstores and from office supply stores, or students can develop computer programs to maintain accounting records and produce financial statements. The instructions accompanying the B problems at the end of this chapter and the following chapters are presented on the assumption that the student is required to prepare solutions manually.

2–B. **1.** The City of Bingham has the following funds in addition to its General Fund; you are required to classify each in accordance with the types described in the GASB Types of Funds Principle quoted in this chapter.

City Hall Annex Construction Fund. This fund was created to account for the proceeds of the sale of serial bonds issued for the construction and equipping of an annex to the city hall.

Debt Service Fund. Nonactuarially determined contributions and earnings thereon, for the purpose of the payment of interest on and redemption of tax-supported and special assessment long-term debt issued by the City, are accounted for by this fund.

Stores and Services Fund. This fund was established to account for centralized purchasing and management of inventories used by a number of departments of the city government.

Water Utility Fund. The water utility serving the City of Bingham was originally constructed and operated by a private corporation. It was subsequently sold to the City, but it is still operated on a self-supporting basis under the regulations of the State Public Service Commission.

Pass-Through Agency Fund. This fund is used to account for grants, entitlements, and shared revenues that the City of Bingham receives as the primary recipient, and that it must transmit in whole or in part to other governmental units or organizations.

Employees' Retirement Fund. This fund was established to account for actuarially determined retirement contributions and earnings thereon, and for the payment of retirement annuities.

2. For each of its funds and the government as a whole, the City of Bingham maintains separate, manually kept books of original entry and ledgers.

Required

a. Open a *general journal* for the General Fund. Allow seven pages of 8½-by-11-inch loose-leaf journal paper, or its equivalent. (Do not open general journals for other funds or for governmental activities at the government-wide level until instructed to do so in subsequent B problems.) The form you use must allow for entry of subsidiary ledger accounts as well as general ledger accounts, and for entry of adequate explanations for each journal entry. (The form in which journal entries are illustrated in Chapter 3 is appropriate.) You will use the journal as your only posting medium; it should be complete.

b. Open a *general ledger* for the General Fund. Allow three pages of 8½-by-11-inch loose-leaf ledger paper, or its equivalent. On each page allow the number of lines shown below for each account.

Account No.	*Title*	*Lines*
1110	Cash	12
1111	Petty Cash	5
1130	Taxes Receivable—Current	5
1131	Estimated Uncollectible Current Taxes	5
1132	Taxes Receivable—Delinquent	5
1133	Estimated Uncollectible Delinquent Taxes	5
1134	Interest and Penalties Receivable on Taxes	5
1135	Estimated Uncollectible Interest and Penalties	5
1140	Advance to Stores and Services Fund	5
1210	Vouchers Payable	10
1211	Tax Anticipation Notes Payable	5
1212	Due to Federal Government	5
1213	Due to Other Funds	5
1300	Estimated Revenues	5
1400	Revenues	8
1500	Appropriations	5
1600	Expenditures—2002	15
1650	Expenditures—2001	5
1700	Encumbrances—2002	5
1800	Reserve for Encumbrances—2002	5
1801	Reserve for Encumbrances—2001	5
1802	Reserve for Advance to Stores and Services Fund	5
1900	Fund Balance	8

c. The trial balance of the General Fund of the City of Bingham as of June 30, 2001, the last day of the fiscal year prior to the year with which the B problems are concerned, is shown below.

(1) Prepare an entry in general journal form to enter the amounts shown in the trial balance in the proper general ledger accounts. Date the entry "July 1, 2001." Note that no subsidiary ledger accounts are affected by this entry.

(2) Post the journal entry to the proper general ledger accounts opened in part *b* of this problem; each of the amounts entered should be dated "July 1, 2001."

CITY OF BINGHAM
GENERAL FUND TRIAL BALANCE
AS OF JUNE 30, 2001

		General Ledger	
Account No.	*Title*	*Debits*	*Credits*
1110	Cash	$ 45,000	
1132	Taxes Receivable—Delinquent	244,000	
1133	Estimated Uncollectible Delinquent Taxes		$ 24,400
1134	Interest and Penalties Receivable on Taxes	13,376	
1135	Estimated Uncollectible Interest and Penalties		662
1210	Vouchers Payable		187,000
1213	Due to Other Funds		7,000
1801	Reserve for Encumbrances—2001		14,000
1900	Fund Balance		69,314
		$302,376	$302,376

CHAPTER 3

Governmental Operating Statement Accounts; Budgetary Accounting

Learning Objectives

After studying this chapter, you should be able to:

- Distinguish between exchange and nonexchange operating transactions.
- Explain the rules for recognition of nonexchange revenues and expenses/expenditures.
- Explain how operating revenues and expenses related to governmental activities are classified and reported in the government-wide financial statements.
- Distinguish, at the fund level, between Revenues and Other Financing Sources and between Expenditures and Other Financing Uses.
- Explain how budgetary accounting contributes to achieving budgetary control over revenues and expenditures, including such aspects as:
  - Recording the annual budget.
  - Accounting for revenues.
  - Accounting for encumbrances and expenditures.
  - Accounting for allotments.
  - Reconciling GAAP and budgetary amounts.
- Describe computerized accounting systems.
- Explain the classification of revenues and expenditures of a public school system.

As discussed in Chapters 1 and 2, the GASB *Statement No. 34* financial reporting model is designed to meet the diverse needs of financial statement users and achieve the broad reporting objectives set forth in GASB *Concepts Statement No. 1*. The fund-based reporting model used for decades by state and local governments meets reasonably well the *fiscal accountability* needs of users for information about the current financial position and flows of current financial resources through the governmental funds. But that model falls far short of meeting users' needs for information about the medium- to long-term impacts of the government's current operating and capital decisions, as well as information about the costs of conducting the government's functions and programs.

To meet users' broader needs for *operational accountability* information, the new reporting model requires—in addition to traditional fund-based financial statements—a management's discussion and analysis (MD&A) and two government-wide financial statements: a statement of net assets (a statement of financial position) and a statement of activities (an operating statement).[1] This chapter focuses on the latter statement as well as on the operating statements prepared for the governmental fund-types.

Concepts and Rules for Recognition of Revenues and Expenses (or Expenditures)

Exchange Transactions

Current GASB standards provide guidance for the accounting recognition of revenues and expenses on the accrual basis in the government-wide financial statements and revenues and expenditures on the modified accrual basis in the governmental fund financial statements.[2] Recognition rules for **exchange transactions** and **exchange-like transactions,** those in which each party receives value essentially equal to the value given, are generally straightforward; for operating transactions, the party selling goods or services recognizes an asset (for example, a receivable or cash) and a revenue when the transaction occurs and the revenue has been earned. The party purchasing goods or services recognizes an expense or expenditure and liability (or reduction in cash). As discussed in Chapter 2, under the *modified accrual* basis of accounting, if a governmental fund provides goods or services to another party or fund, it should recognize an asset (receivable or cash) and a revenue if the assets (financial resources) are deemed *measurable* and *available*. If a governmental fund *receives* goods or services from another party or fund, it should recognize expenditures (not expense) when the fund liability has been incurred. In most cases, exchange transactions of governmental funds result in

[1]See Chapters 1 and 2 for the definition and discussions of operational accountability.

[2]GASB *Codification of Governmental Accounting and Financial Reporting Standards as of June 30, 1999* (Norwalk, CT, 1999), Sec. 1600, and GASB *Statement No. 33*, "Accounting and Financial Reporting for Nonexchange Transactions" (Norwalk, CT, 1998).

measurable and available assets being received or a fund liability being incurred when the transaction occurs, and thus result in immediate recognition of revenues and expenditures. For example, the General Fund should recognize a revenue immediately when a citizen is charged a fee for a building permit and an expenditure when a purchase order for supplies has been filled.

Nonexchange Transactions

Nonexchange transactions are defined as external events in which a government gives or receives value without directly receiving or giving equal value in exchange.[3] Accounting for nonexchange transactions raises a number of conceptual issues, some of which are explored in this chapter and some in later chapters. Two key concepts that affect a resource recipient's recognition of revenues (or a resource provider's recognition of expenses/expenditures) are *time requirements* and *purpose restrictions*.[4]

Time requirements relate either to the period when resources are required to be used or when use *may* begin. Thus, time requirements determine the *timing* of revenue or expense (expenditure) recognition—that is, whether these elements should be recognized (recorded in the accounts) in the current period or deferred to a future period. **Purpose restrictions** refer to specifications by resource providers of the purpose or purposes for which resources are required to be used. For example, a grant may specify that resources can be used only to provide transportation for senior citizens. The *timing* of revenue recognition is unaffected by purpose restrictions. Rather, the purpose restrictions should be clearly reported as restrictions of net assets in the government-wide statement of net assets or as reservations of fund balance in the governmental funds' balance sheet (see Illustrations 2–1 and 2–3 in Chapter 2 for examples).

For certain classes of nonexchange transactions, discussed later in this section, revenue and expense recognition may be delayed until program **eligibility requirements** are met. Eligibility requirements may include, in addition to time requirements, specified characteristics that program recipients must possess or reimbursement provisions and contingencies tied to required actions by the recipient. GASB *Statement No. 33*, Appendix C, provides the example of state-provided reimbursements to school districts for special education. To meet the specified eligibility requirements, (1) the recipient must be a school district, (2) the applicable school year must have started, and (3) the district must have incurred allowable costs. Only when all three conditions are met can a school district record a revenue and the state record an expense. The school district would record an asset and deferred revenue if the resources are received in advance of meeting eligibility requirements. Otherwise the school district would not record an asset nor would the state record a liability to provide the resources until all the eligibility requirements have been met.

[3] GASB *Statement No. 33*, par. 7.
[4] Ibid., par. 12.

Nonexchange transactions are subdivided into four classes: (1) **derived tax revenues** (e.g., income and sales taxes), (2) **imposed nonexchange revenues** (e.g., property taxes and fines and penalties), (3) **government-mandated nonexchange transactions** (e.g., certain education, social welfare, and transportation services mandated and funded by a higher level of government), and (4) **voluntary nonexchange transactions** (e.g., grants and entitlements from higher levels of government and certain private donations).[5]

Recognition of Nonexchange Transactions

Illustration 3–1 provides a summary of the recognition criteria applicable to each class of nonexchange transactions, both for the accrual basis of accounting and for modified accrual. Assets and revenues in the *derived tax revenues* category are generally recognized in the period in which the underlying exchange occurs—the period in which income is earned for income taxes and when sales have occurred for sales taxes.

For *imposed nonexchange revenues*, an asset (receivable or cash) is recognized when there is an enforceable legal claim or when cash is received, whichever is first. Revenues should be recognized in the period in which the resources are required to be used or the first period when their use is permitted. For property taxes, revenues usually are recognized in the period for which the taxes are levied. In governmental funds, the additional criterion of availability for use must be met. Current standards, as interpreted, define *available* in the context of property taxes as meaning "collected within the current period or expected to be collected soon enough thereafter to be used to pay liabilities of the current period."[6] *Soon enough thereafter* means not later than sixty days after the end of the current period.[7]

A common set of recognition rules applies to the remaining two classes of nonexchange transactions: *government-mandated* and *voluntary exchange*. An asset (a receivable or cash) is recognized when all eligibility requirements have been met or when cash is received, whichever occurs first. For example, although cash has not been received from a grantor, when a program recipient meets matching requirements imposed by the grantor agency in order to become eligible for a social services grant, a receivable (Due from [Grantor])would be recorded. Revenues should be recognized only when all eligibility criteria have been met. If cash is received in the period prior to intended use (that is, there is a time restriction) or before eligibility requirements have been met, deferred revenues should be reported rather than revenues. In the period when the time restriction expires, the account Deferred Revenues will be debited and Revenues will be credited.

It should be apparent that a particular nonexchange transaction may lead to recognition of revenues in one period in the government-wide statement of activities, but be reported as deferred revenues in a governmental fund because it is deemed not to be *available* to pay current period obligations. These recognition

---

[5]Ibid., par. 7.

[6]GASB, *Codification*, Sec. P70.103.

[7]Ibid.

Illustration 3–1 Summary Chart—Classes and Timing of Recognition of Nonexchange Transactions

Class	*Recognition*
Derived tax revenues Examples: sales taxes, personal and corporate income taxes, motor fuel taxes, and similar taxes on earnings or consumption	**Assets*** Period when *underlying exchange has occurred* or when resources are received, whichever is first. **Revenues** Period when *underlying exchange has occurred*. (Report advance receipts as deferred revenues.) When modified accrual accounting is used, resources *also* should be "available."
Imposed nonexchange revenues Examples: property taxes, most fines and forfeitures	**Assets*** Period when an *enforceable legal claim has arisen* or when resources are received, whichever is first. **Revenues** Period when *resources are required to be used* or first period that use is permitted (for example, for property taxes, the *period for which levied*). When modified accrual accounting is used, resources *also* should be "available." (For property taxes, apply NCGA Interpretation 3, as amended.)
Government-mandated nonexchange transactions Examples: federal government mandates on state and local governments **Voluntary nonexchange transactions** Examples: certain grants and entitlements, most donations	**Assets* and Liabilities** Period when *all eligibility requirements have been met* or (for asset recognition) when resources are received, whichever is first. **Revenues and expenses or expenditures** Period when *all eligibility requirements have been met*. (Report advance receipts or payments for use in the following period as deferred revenues or advances, respectively. However, when a provider precludes the sale, disbursement, or consumption of resources for a specified number of years, until a specified event has occurred, or permanently [for example, permanent and term endowments], report revenues and expenses or expenditures when the resources are, respectively, received or paid and report resulting net assets, equity, or fund balance as restricted.) When modified accrual accounting is used for revenue recognition, resources *also* should be "available."

*If there are purpose restrictions, report restricted net assets (or equity or fund balance) or, for governmental funds, a reservation of fund balance.

Source: GASB *Statement No. 33* (Norwalk, CT, 1998), Appendix C.

timing differences are illustrated in later chapters. The following sections discuss classification and reporting of revenues and expenses/expenditures at the government-wide level and at the fund level, and explain the budgetary accounting process applicable to governmental funds.

Classification and Reporting of Revenues and Expenses at the Government-wide Level

The format prescribed for the government-wide statement of activities (see Illustration 2–2) displays the net expense or revenue of each function or program comprising the governmental activities of the government. As shown in Illustration 2–2, the net expense (reported in parentheses if net expense) or net revenue of each business-type segment and discretely presented component unit is reported separately from the functions (programs) of the governmental activities. (Governmental and business-type activities were described in depth in Chapter 2.) According to the GASB, reporting in the net expense or revenue format "identifies the extent to which each function of the government draws from the general revenues of the government or is self-financing through fees and intergovernmental aid."[8]

Functions and programs are discussed in greater detail in this chapter. Generally, governments should report *at a minimum* major functions such as those depicted in Illustration 2–2. The GASB encourages governments to provide additional information for more detailed programs if such information is useful and does not detract from readers' understanding of the statement.

Reporting Direct and Indirect Expenses

Except for extraordinary or special expenses, described later in this section, expenses should be reported by function or program (see Illustration 2–2). **Direct expenses**—those that are specifically associated with a function or program—should be reported on the line for that function or program. **Indirect expenses**—those that are not directly linked to an identifiable function or program—can be reported in a variety of ways. A typical indirect expense is interest on general long-term liabilities. In most cases, interest on general long-term liabilities should be reported as a separate line item, rather than being allocated to functions or programs (observe, for example, how it is reported as the last line of governmental activities in Illustration 2–2).

Some readers might find it surprising that depreciation expense often is reported as a direct expense. For capital assets that are clearly identified with a function or program, depreciation expense for those assets should be included in the expenses of that function or program. Similarly, depreciation expense for infrastructure assets should be reported as a direct expense of the function responsible for the infrastructure assets (for example, public works or transportation). Depreciation expense for shared assets should be allocated to functions on an appropriate basis (for example, square footage of building use). If a government opts to report unallocated depreciation expense as a separate line item, it should indicate that the amount reported on that line does not include depreciation expense reported as part of direct expense of functions or programs.[9]

[8]GASB *Statement No. 34*, par. 38.

[9]Ibid., par. 44.

To achieve full costing, some governments allocate to other functions or programs certain central administrative costs that other governments may report in the general government function. If such expenses are allocated to other functions, the allocated expenses should be reported in a separate column from the direct expenses, so the direct expenses will be more comparable with the direct expenses of similar functions of other governments. On the other hand, if a government regularly assigns administrative overhead costs to functions through an internal service fund or other billings, it is not required to eliminate these costs from the direct expenses of functions or to report them in a separate column. Rather, the government should disclose in the notes to the financial statements that such overhead charges are included as part of function/program direct expenses.[10]

The foregoing discussion should make it clear that governments will be required to allocate a variety of depreciation and other expenses to particular functions or programs. Allocation methods are discussed in Chapters 13 and 14 of this text and, of course, in most managerial accounting texts. Governmental accounting computer systems typically provide for a variety of classifications of expenses/expenditures, in addition to classification by function or program. These classifications are discussed later in this chapter.

Program Revenues and General Revenues

Reporting in the net (expense) revenue format requires a government to distinguish carefully between **program revenues** and **general revenues.** As shown in Illustration 2–2, *program revenues* are reported in the functions/programs section of the statement of activities, where they reduce the net expense of each function or program or produce a net revenue. *General revenues* are not directly linked to any specific function or program and thus are reported in a separate section at the bottom of the statement.

Three categories of *program revenues* are reported in the statement of activities (see Illustration 2–2): charges for services, operating grants and contributions, and capital grants and contributions. Charges for services include charges to customers or others for both governmental and business-type activities. Charges for services, within the governmental activities category, are exchange transactions and include fees charged for such items as licenses and permits (for example, business licenses and building permits) and operating special assessments sometimes charged for services provided outside the normal service area or beyond the normal level of services. A typical example of the latter is snow removal for or maintenance of private lanes or roads that connect with public roads normally maintained by the government. Charges to other governments for services such as incarceration of prisoners also are reported in the charges for services column.

Grants and contributions and other nonexchange revenues restricted by other governments, organizations, or individuals for the *operating* purposes of a particular function or program should be reported in a separate column from those restricted for *capital* purposes, as shown in Illustration 2–2. GASB requires that multipurpose grants and contributions be reported as *program revenues* if "the amounts restricted

[10]Ibid., pars. 42–43.

to each program are specifically identified in either the grant award or grant application."[11] Otherwise, multipurpose grants and contributions should be reported as *general revenue*.

Earnings from endowments, permanent funds, or other investments that are restricted for a specific purpose in the endowment or permanent fund contract or agreement should be reported as program revenue in the appropriate grants and contributions category. Unrestricted earnings from such sources should be reported as general revenue. In addition, all taxes, even those specified by law for a particular use (for example, motor vehicle fuel taxes that can only be used for road and bridge purposes), should be reported as general revenue.

Reporting Special Items and Transfers

In the *Statement No. 34* reporting model, extraordinary items and special items must be reported as separate line items below General Revenue in the statement of activities to distinguish these nonrecurring items from normal recurring general revenues. Separate reporting of such items serves to inform citizens and other report users when governments engage in the unusual practice of balancing their budget by selling government assets, or other similar practices. **Extraordinary items** are defined in the same manner as in business accounting: "transactions or other events that are both unusual in nature and infrequent in occurrence."[12] Special items are items *within management's control* that may be either unusual in nature or infrequent in occurrence but not both. An example would be one-shot revenues from the sale of a significant governmental asset. Extraordinary items should be reported as the last item on the statement of activity; special items should be reported before extraordinary items. Special items that are beyond management's control (such as a loss due to civil riot) should be disclosed in the notes to the financial statements.

Other items that should be reported on separate lines below General Revenue (see Illustration 2–2) are contributions to the principal amounts of endowments and permanent funds and transfers between funds reported as part of governmental activities and funds reported as part of business-type activities. Interfund transactions between governmental and business-type activities that involve the sale of goods or services (such as the sale of water from a water utility enterprise fund to the General Fund) are reported as program revenue and expenses, not as transfers. The reader should note that when transfers are reported, as shown in Illustration 2–2, they are reported as an inflow in one activities column and as an outflow in the other activities column, and thus are eliminated from the Total Primary Government column.

The foregoing discussion covers the major points relating to the government-wide operating statement—the statement of activities. Some of the unique aspects of governmental fund accounting are discussed next, focusing on the General Fund.

---

[11]Ibid., par. 50.
[12]Ibid., par. 55.

Structure and Characteristics of the General Fund; Classification and Description of Operating Statement Accounts

The General Fund has long been the accounting entity of a state or local government that accounts for current financial resources raised and expended for the core governmental services provided to the people. General Funds are sometimes known as operating funds or current funds; the purpose, not the name, is the true test of identity. The typical governmental unit now engages in many activities that for legal and historical reasons are financed by sources other than those available to the General Fund. Whenever a tax or other revenue source is authorized by a legislative body to be used for a specified purpose only, a governmental unit availing itself of that source may create a special revenue fund in order to be able to demonstrate that all revenue from that source was used for the specified purpose only. A common example of a special revenue fund is one used to account for state gasoline tax receipts distributed to a local government; in many states, the use of this money is restricted to the construction and maintenance of streets, highways, and bridges. The accounting structure specified for special revenue funds by GASB standards is identical with that specified for general funds.

For sake of simplicity and to avoid excessive repetition, the term *General Fund* will be used in the remainder of this chapter and Chapter 4 to denote all *revenue funds*, a generic name sometimes used to describe the General Fund and special revenue funds. According to the GASB Types of Funds principle discussed in Chapter 2, there are three other fund types besides the General Fund and special revenue funds that are classified as governmental funds. Those other fund types are debt service funds, capital projects funds, and permanent funds. The essential characteristics of all governmental fund types were presented in brief in Chapter 2. This chapter illustrates in greater depth the manner in which generally accepted accounting principles (GAAP) are applied to the General Fund and special revenue funds. Although permanent funds obtain their revenues from permanent investments in financial securities rather than taxes and other typical sources of governmental revenues, these funds are accounted for in essentially the same manner as the General Fund and special revenue funds. Illustrative accounting transactions for a permanent fund are provided in Chapter 4. Accounting and reporting for capital projects funds and debt service funds are discussed in Chapters 5 and 6, respectively.

Governmental Fund Balance Sheet and Operating Statement Accounts

It should be emphasized that the General Fund, special revenue funds, and all other funds classified as governmental funds account for only financial resources (cash, receivables, marketable securities, and, if material, prepaid items and inventories). Economic resources, such as land, buildings, and equipment utilized in fund operations, are not accounted for by these funds because they are not normally converted into cash. Similarly, these categories of funds account for only those liabilities incurred for normal operations that will be liquidated by use of fund assets. As discussed in Chapter 2, however, general capital assets and general long-term liabilities are reported in the statement of net assets at the government-wide level.

The arithmetic difference between the amount of financial resources and the amount of liabilities recorded in the fund is the Fund Equity. Residents of the governmental unit have no legal claim on any excess of liquid assets over current liabilities; therefore, the Fund Equity is not analogous to the capital accounts of an investor-owned entity. Accounts in the fund equity category of general funds and special revenue funds consist of reserve accounts established to disclose that portions of the equity are, for reasons explained later, not available for appropriation; the portion of equity available for appropriation is disclosed in an account called *Fund Balance* (also referred to as Unreserved Fund Balance).

In addition to the balance sheet accounts described above, the General Fund and special revenue funds account for financial activities during a fiscal year in operating statement accounts classified as Revenues, Other Financing Sources, Expenditures, and Other Financing Uses. *Revenue* is defined as increases in fund financial resources other than from interfund transfers and debt issue proceeds. Transfers into a fund and debt issue proceeds received by a fund are classified as **Other Financing Sources** of the fund. Accounting standards specify that the revenues of all governmental fund types be recognized on the *modified accrual* basis. Because the operations of governmental funds are subject to rather detailed legal restrictions, governmental fund revenues should be recognized in the fiscal year in which they are available to finance expenditures. In a few jurisdictions laws require that taxes be collected in the year before the year in which they are available to finance expenditures. In such jurisdictions, tax collections should be credited to Deferred Revenues when cash is debited; in the following year Deferred Revenues should be debited and Revenues should be credited.

Expenditure is a term that replaces both the terms *costs* and *expenses* used in accounting for profit-seeking entities. Expenditures are defined as decreases in fund financial resources other than through interfund transfers. Interfund transfers out of a fund are classified as **Other Financing Uses.** As noted earlier in this chapter, under the modified accrual basis an expenditure is recognized when a liability to be met from fund assets is incurred. It is important to note that an appropriation is considered to be expended in the amount of a liability incurred whether the liability is for salaries (an expense), for supplies (a current asset), or for land, buildings, or equipment (long-lived capital assets). Of course, at the government-wide levels such items as salaries and utilities are recorded as expenses rather than expenditures; items such as supplies may be recorded either as expenses or assets when purchased as long as material unused balances are reported as an asset at year-end. Capital assets are recorded as assets when acquired and are expensed as the capital assets are depreciated.

An example of the use of transfer accounts occurs in those jurisdictions where a portion of the taxes recognized as revenue by the General Fund of a unit is transferred to a debt service fund that will record expenditures for payment of interest and principal of general obligation debt. The General Fund would record the amounts transferred as Interfund Transfers Out; the debt service fund would record the amount received as Interfund Transfers In. Thus, use of the transfer accounts achieves the desired objective that revenues be recognized in the fund that levied the taxes, and expenditures be recognized in the fund that expends the revenue. Other Financing Sources accounts and Other Financing Uses accounts are closed to Fund Balance in a manner identical with the closing of Revenues and Expenditures, but are disclosed separately in the Statement of Revenues, Expenditures, and Changes in Fund Balances, as shown in Illustration 2–4.

Budgetary Accounts

The fact that budgets are legally binding upon administrators has led to the incorporation of budgetary accounts in the General Fund, and in special revenue funds and all other funds required by state laws to adopt a budget. GASB *Statement No. 34* requires that a budget to actual comparison schedule be provided for the General Fund and for each *major* special revenue fund for which a budget is legally adopted.[13] *Statement No. 34* recommends that these schedules be provided as required supplementary information (RSI), which should be placed immediately following the notes to the financial statements. *Statement No. 34* provides the option, however, for governments to report the budgetary comparison information in a budgetary comparison *statement,* a statement of revenues, expenditures, and changes in fund balances—budget and actual, which would then be part of the basic financial statements.[14] This is also the current practice under the reporting model being superseded by *Statement No. 34*.

Illustration 3–2 presents an example of a budgetary comparison schedule for the General Fund. The budgetary comparison schedule must present, at a minimum, separate columns for both the originally adopted and final amended budgets and for actual amounts of inflow, outflows, and balances. The variance column shown in Illustration 3–2 is encouraged but not required by GASB standards.

In order to achieve meaningful budgetary comparisons the *actual* amounts in the schedule should be reported using the government's budgetary basis. Some governments, for example, budget their revenues on the cash basis. If the Actual column of the budgetary comparison schedule (or statement) uses a non-GAAP budgetary basis, such as the cash basis, the column heading should so indicate, as in Illustration 3–2.

Budgetary practices of a government may differ from GAAP accounting practices in respects other than basis. GASB standards identify timing, entity, and perspective differences. Discussion of these differences is beyond the scope of this text; it is sufficient to emphasize that GASB standards require that the amounts shown in the Actual column of the budgetary comparison schedule conform in all respects

[13]Ibid., par. 130. Recall from Chapter 2 that a major fund is defined as one for which total assets, liabilities, revenues, or expenditures/expenses of the individual governmental fund is at least 10 percent of the corresponding total for all governmental funds, or for which any of these elements of the fund are at least 5 percent of the corresponding total for all governmental and enterprise funds combined. (See the Glossary also for a definition.)

[14]Ibid., footnote 53.

Illustration 3–2 Budgetary Comparison Schedule

SAMPLE CITY
BUDGETARY COMPARISON SCHEDULE
GENERAL FUND
FOR THE YEAR ENDED DECEMBER 31, 2002

	Budgeted Amounts		Actual Amounts (Budgetary Basis)	Variance with Final Budget Positive (Negative)
	Original	*Final*		
Budgetary fund balance, January 1	$ 3,528,750	$ 2,742,799	$ 2,742,799	$ —
Resources (inflows):				
Property taxes	52,017,833	51,853,018	51,173,436	(679,582)
Franchise taxes	4,546,209	4,528,750	4,055,505	(473,245)
Public service taxes	8,295,000	8,307,274	8,969,887	662,613
Licenses and permits	2,126,600	2,126,600	2,287,794	161,194
Fines and forfeitures	718,800	718,800	606,946	(111,854)
Charges for services	12,392,972	11,202,150	11,374,460	172,310
Grants	6,905,898	6,571,360	6,119,938	(451,422)
Sale of land	1,355,250	3,500,000	3,476,488	(23,512)
Miscellaneous	3,024,292	1,220,991	881,874	(339,117)
Interest received	1,015,945	550,000	552,325	2,325
Transfers from other funds	939,525	130,000	129,323	(677)
Amounts available for appropriation	96,867,074	93,451,742	92,370,775	(1,080,967)
Charges to appropriations (outflows)				
General government:				
Legal	665,275	663,677	632,719	30,958
Mayor, legislative, city manager	3,058,750	3,192,910	2,658,264	534,646
Finance and accounting	1,932,500	1,912,702	1,852,687	60,015
City clerk and elections	345,860	354,237	341,206	13,031
Employee relations	1,315,500	1,300,498	1,234,232	66,266
Planning and economic development	1,975,600	1,784,314	1,642,575	141,739
Public safety:				
Police	19,576,820	20,367,917	20,246,496	121,421
Fire department	9,565,280	9,559,967	9,559,967	—
Emergency medical services	2,323,171	2,470,127	2,459,866	10,261
Inspections	1,585,695	1,585,695	1,533,380	52,315
Public works:				
Public works administration	388,500	385,013	383,397	1,616
Street maintenance	2,152,750	2,233,362	2,233,362	—
Street lighting	762,750	759,832	759,832	—
Traffic operations	385,945	374,945	360,509	14,436
Mechanical maintenance	1,525,685	1,272,696	1,256,087	16,609

(continued)

with practices used to develop the amounts shown in the Budget columns of the schedule, so there is a true comparison. Standards further require that either on the face of the budgetary comparison schedule or on a separate schedule the amounts reported in the Actual column of the budgetary comparison schedule must be

Illustration 3–2 (Continued)

	Budgeted Amounts		Actual Amounts	Variance with Final Budget
	Original	*Final*	*(Budgetary Basis)*	*Positive (Negative)*
Engineering services:				
Engineering administration	1,170,650	1,158,023	1,158,023	—
Geographical information system	125,625	138,967	138,967	—
Health and sanitation:				
Garbage pickup	5,756,250	6,174,653	6,174,653	—
Cemetery:				
Personal services	425,000	425,000	422,562	2,438
Purchases of goods and services	299,500	299,500	283,743	15,757
Culture and recreation:				
Library	985,230	1,023,465	1,022,167	1,298
Parks and recreation	9,521,560	9,786,397	9,756,618	29,779
Community communications	552,350	558,208	510,361	47,847
Nondepartmental:				
Miscellaneous	—	259,817	259,817	—
Contingency	2,544,049	—	—	—
Transfers to other funds	2,970,256	2,163,759	2,163,759	—
Funding for school district	22,000,000	22,000,000	21,893,273	106,727
Total charges to appropriations	93,910,551	92,205,681	90,938,522	1,267,159
Budgetary fund balance, December 31	$ 2,956,523	$ 1,246,061	$ 1,432,253	$ 186,192

Source: GASB *Codification, Appendix A, Statement No. 34* (GASB: Norwalk, CT, 1999), Illustration G–1.

reconciled with the GAAP amounts shown in the statement of revenues, expenditures, and changes in fund balances (see Illustration 2–4). Such a reconciliation is discussed and illustrated in a later section of this chapter.

In order to provide the information needed to prepare budgets and the budgetary comparison schedules (or statements), accounting systems of funds for which budgets are legally adopted include **budgetary accounts,** in addition to the normal balance sheet and operating statement accounts. Only three general ledger budgetary control accounts are needed in the General Fund (and other funds for which a budget is adopted) to provide adequate budgetary control: **Estimated Revenues, Appropriations,** and **Encumbrances.** Subsidiary ledger accounts should be provided in whatever detail is required by law or for sound financial administration to support each of the three control accounts. Budgeted interfund transfers and debt proceeds may be recorded in two additional budgetary control accounts: **Estimated Other Financing Sources** and **Estimated Other Financing Uses.** Again, these control accounts should be supported by subsidiary detail accounts as needed.

Illustration 3–3 shows the relationship between the typical balance sheet and operating statement accounts of a governmental fund and the budgetary accounts. The budgetary accounts are all *temporary* subfund balance accounts and like the operating statement accounts are closed to Fund Balance at year-end. The discerning reader may surmise that comparing the actual Revenues account balance to the corresponding Estimated Revenues account balance provides budgetary control over revenues. Similarly, comparing the actual Expenditures account balance plus the Encumbrances account balance (estimated budgetary amounts for goods on order) to the Appropriations account balance (legal authorization to incur expenditures) provides for budgetary control over expenditures. Budgetary control procedures for both revenues and expenditures are discussed later in this chapter.

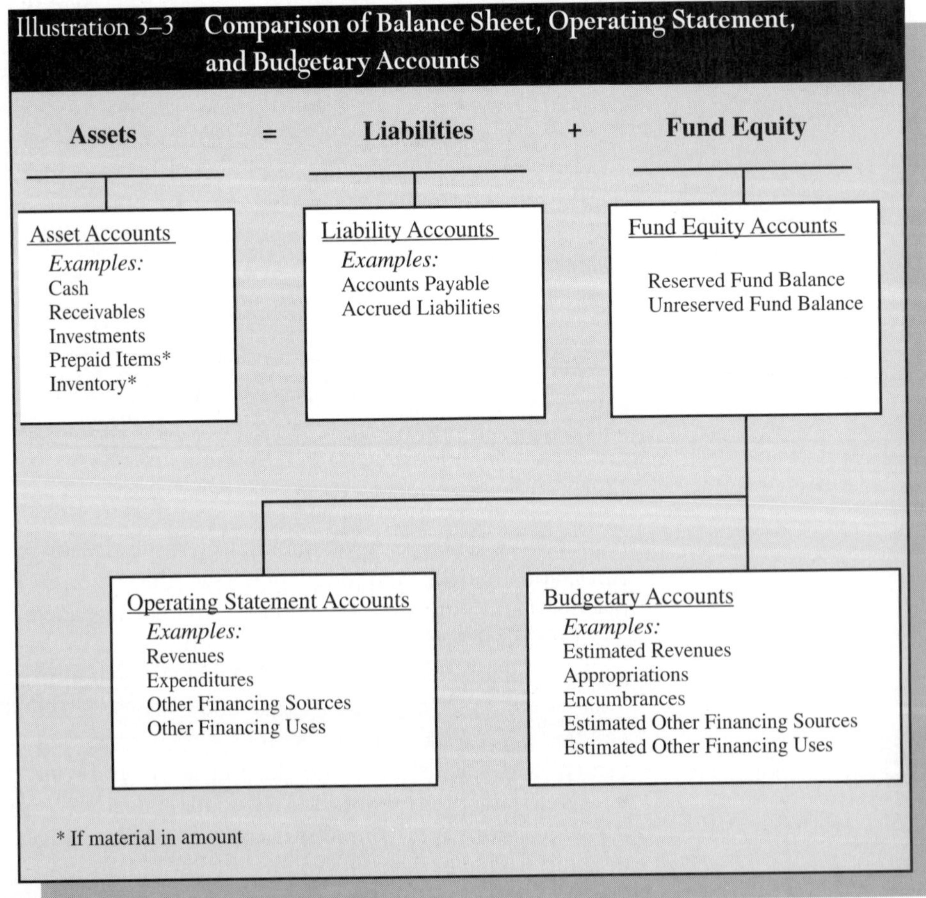

Terminology and Classification for Governmental Fund Budgets and Accounts

Budgets as they are incorporated in legal documents and in financial reports required for conformity with GAAP may be described as legally approved plans of financial operations embodying the authorization of expenditures for specified purposes to be made during the budget period and the proposed means of financing them. The sequence of budget preparation in practice is often the same as the sequence in the preceding sentence: Expenditures are planned first; then plans are made to finance the expenditures. For that reason, the discussion in this chapter follows the same sequence. Governmental budgeting is discussed in more detail in Chapter 13.

Classification of Appropriations and Expenditures

Recall that an appropriation, when enacted into law, is an authorization to incur on behalf of the governmental unit liabilities for goods, services, and facilities to be used for purposes specified in the appropriation ordinance, or statute, in amounts not in excess of those specified for each purpose. When liabilities authorized by an appropriation have been incurred, the appropriation is said to be expended. Thus budgeted appropriations are often called *estimated expenditures*, and the appropriation budget is called the **Expenditures budget**. According to the GASB Transfer, Revenue, Expenditure, and Expense Account Classifications Principle (see Chapter 2), expenditures should be classified by (1) fund, (2) function or program, (3) organization unit, (4) activity, (5) character, and (6) object. The GASB Common Terminology and Classification Principle should also be recalled at this time. It provides that a common terminology and classification should be used consistently throughout the budget, the accounts, and the financial reports of each fund.

Classification by Fund. *The primary classification of governmental expenditures is by fund*, since funds are the basic fiscal and accounting entity of a governmental unit. Within each fund, the other five classifications itemized in the preceding paragraph are used to facilitate the aggregation and analysis of data to meet the objectives of financial reporting set forth in Chapter 1.

Classification by Function or Program. The GASB distinguishes between functions and programs in the following manner:

> **Functions** group related activities that are aimed at accomplishing a major service or regulatory responsibility. **Programs** group activities, operations, or organizational units that are directed to the attainment of specific purposes or objectives.[15] [Emphasis added.]

[15]GASB, *Codification*, Sec. 1800.117.

Examples of functional classifications commonly found are:

General government	Health and welfare
Public safety	Culture and recreation
Highways and streets	

In one city in New England, the budget is summarized according to the following program classification:

Policy formulation and administration	Environmental protection
	Transportation
Protection of persons and property	Social enrichment opportunities
	Physical resource development

Classification by Organization Unit. Classification of expenditures by **organization unit** is considered essential to management control, assuming the organizational structure of a given governmental unit provides clear lines of responsibility and authority. Some examples of organization units that might be found in a city are:

Police Department	City Clerk
Fire Department	Personnel Department
Building Safety Department	Parks and Recreation Department
Public Works Department	
City Attorney	

The key distinction between classification of expenditures by organization unit and classification by program or function is that responsibility for a department is fixed, whereas a number of departments may be involved in the performance of a program or a function. Management control within a department, and rational allocation of resources within the governmental unit, both require much more specific identification of expenditures (and costs and expenses) than is provided by the major classifications illustrated thus far. The next step needed is classification by activity.

Classification by Activity. An **activity** is a specific and distinguishable line of work performed by an organization unit. For example, within the Public Works Department, activities such as the following may be performed:

Solid waste collection—residential.
Solid waste collection—commercial.
Solid waste disposal—landfill.
Solid waste disposal—incineration.

Activity classification is more meaningful if responsibility for the performance of each activity is fixed, performance standards are established, and a good management accounting system is installed to measure input of resources (dollars, personnel time, equipment and facilities used) versus output of services. Such information is useful to those interested in assessing the efficiency of government operations.

The GASB recommends that expenditures also be classified by character.

Classification by Character. Classification by **character,** as defined by the GASB, is based on the fiscal period that benefits from a particular expenditure. A common classification of expenditures by character recognizes three groups:

Current expenditures
Capital outlays
Debt service

Current expenditures are expected to benefit the period in which the expenditure is made. Capital outlays are expected to benefit not only the period in which the capital assets are acquired but as many future periods as the assets provide service. Debt service includes payment of interest on debt and payment of debt principal; if the debt was wisely incurred, residents received benefits in prior periods from the assets acquired by use of debt financing, are receiving benefits currently, and will continue to receive benefits until the service lives of the assets expire.

Character classification of expenditures is potentially of great significance to taxpayers and other citizens. Properly used, it could give them valuable information for appraising the cost of government during a given period. Generally speaking, expenditures for debt service relate to actions incurred by previous administrations. Capital outlays are current expenditures expected to provide benefits in future periods; but the present statement of governmental accounting "principles" does not allow depreciation expense to be recorded in governmental funds although, as discussed earlier in this chapter, depreciation expense on general capital assets is reported in the government-wide statement of activities (see GASB, "Depreciation of Capital Assets Principle" in Chapter 2). It appears that expenditures in the current expenditures class are the most influential on the public mind, strongly influencing popular attitudes toward responsible officials.

A fourth character class, *intergovernmental*, is suggested by the GASB for use by governmental units that act as an intermediary in federally financed programs or that transfer "shared revenues" to other governmental units.

Classification by Object. The **object** of an expenditure is the thing for which the expenditure was made. Object classes may be viewed as subdivisions of character classifications. One scheme of object classification includes the following major classes:

Personal services
Supplies
Other services and charges
Capital outlays
Debt service

Many other object classifications are encountered in practice, generally more detailed than that listed above. Greater detail can, of course, be achieved by the utilization of subclasses under the major titles. Thus personal services may be subdivided on the basis of permanence and regularity of employment of the persons represented; and each subclass may be further subdivided to show whether the services performed were regular, overtime, or temporary. Employee benefits may be recorded in as much detail as desired as subclasses of the personal services class. "Other services and charges" obviously must be subdivided if the class is to provide any useful budgeting and control information. Professional Services, Communication, Transportation, Advertising, Printing and Binding, Insurance, Public Utility Services, Repairs and Maintenance, Rentals, Aid to Other Governments, and Miscellaneous are possible subdivisions.

Debt service, also listed as both an object of expenditure and a character class, should be subdivided in as much detail as needed to provide evidence that all interest payments and principal payments that should have been made in a certain fiscal period were actually made (or the appropriate liability recorded).

Classification of Estimated Revenues and Revenues

In order for administrators to determine that proposed expenditures presented in the Appropriations budget can be financed by resources available under the laws of the budgeting jurisdiction and higher jurisdictions, a Revenues budget should be prepared. *Revenue*, in the sense in which it is customarily used in governmental budgeting, includes all financial resource inflows—all amounts that increase the net assets of a fund—interfund transfers and debt issue proceeds, as well as taxes, licenses and permit fees, fines, forfeits, and other revenue sources described in following sections of this chapter.

It should be emphasized that a governmental unit, and the funds thereof, may raise revenues only from sources available to them by law. Often, the law that authorizes a governmental unit to utilize a given revenue source to finance general governmental activities, or specific activities, also establishes the maximum rate that may be applied to a specified base in utilizing the source, or establishes the maximum amount that may be raised from the source during the budget period.

The primary classification of governmental revenue is by *fund*. Within each fund, the major classification is by *source*. Within each major source class, it is desirable to have as many secondary classes as needed to facilitate revenue budgeting and accounting. Secondary classes relating to each major source are discussed below under each source caption. Major revenue source classes commonly used are:

- Taxes
- Special Assessments
- Licenses and Permits
- Intergovernmental Revenues
- Charges for Services
- Fines and Forfeits
- Miscellaneous Revenues

The Revenues budget and the accounting system for each governmental fund should include all revenue sources available to finance activities of that fund. The General Fund of most governmental units will ordinarily need all seven major classes itemized above; in some units, additional major classes may be needed. Each special revenue fund will need to budget and account for only those revenues legally mandated for use in achieving the purpose for which the special revenue fund was created. Similarly, debt service funds budget and account for those sources of revenue that are to be used for payment of interest and principal of tax-supported and special assessment long-term debt. Revenues and other financing sources earmarked for construction or acquisition of general capital assets are reported as being budgeted and accounted for by capital projects funds.

In order to determine during a fiscal year that revenues are being realized from each budgeted source in amounts consistent with the budget, actual revenues should be accounted for on the same classification system as used in the Estimated Revenues budget.

Taxes. Taxes are of particular importance because (1) they provide a very large portion of the revenue of governmental units on all levels and (2) they are compulsory contributions to the cost of government, whether the affected taxpayer approves or disapproves of the levy.

Ad valorem (based on value) **property taxes** are a mainstay of financing for many units of local government but are not used as a source of revenue by many state governments or by the federal government. Ad valorem taxes may be levied against real property and personal property. Some property taxes are levied on a basis other than property values, one illustration being the tax on some kinds of financial institutions in relation to the deposits at a specified date. Other kinds of taxes are sales taxes, income taxes, gross receipts taxes, death and gift taxes, and interest and penalties on delinquent taxes.

The valuation of each parcel of taxable real property, and of the taxable personal property owned by each taxpayer, is assigned by a process known as **property assessment**. The assessment process differs state by state, and in some states by jurisdictions within the state. The tax rate is set by one of two widely different procedures: (1) the governmental body simply multiplies the assessed valuation of property in its jurisdiction by a flat rate—either the maximum rate allowable under state law or a rate determined by policy—or (2) the property tax is treated as a residual source of revenue. In the latter event, revenues to be recognized from all sources other than property taxes must be budgeted; the total of those sources must be compared with the total proposed appropriations in order to determine the amount to be raised from property taxes. Illustration 3–4 shows the computation of the total amount of revenues to be raised from property taxes under the assumption that property taxes are a residual source of revenues. The heading of Illustration 3–4 indicates that it is for the Town of Merrill's General Fund. A similar computation would be made for each other fund for which property taxes are levied. It is common for an elected county official to serve as collector for all property taxes levied for all the funds of all of the governmental units within the county (and, of course, for all the funds of the county government itself). As discussed in Chapter 8, in such cases the county official serves as an agent for all funds for which property taxes have been levied; the Taxes Receivable are properly accounted for as assets of the funds for which they are levied, and those funds recognize revenues from the taxes to the extent that the taxes are expected to be collectible.

Note that Illustration 3–4 is a computation of the amount of revenue to be raised from property taxes, which is one step in determining the tax levy for the year. A second step is the determination from historical data and economic forecasts of the percentage of the tax levy expected to be collectible. (Even though property taxes are a lien against the property, personal property may be removed from the taxing jurisdiction and some parcels of real property may not be salable enough for the taxing jurisdiction to recover accumulated taxes against the property.) Therefore, the levy must be large enough to allow for estimated uncollectible taxes. For example, assume the Town of Merrill can reasonably expect to collect only 96 percent of the year 2002 property tax levy for its General Fund. Thus, if tax revenue is to be $3,582,000 (per Illustration 3–4), the gross levy must be $3,582,000 ÷ .96, or $3,731,250.

When the gross levy is known, the tax rate may be computed on the basis of the assessed valuation of taxable property lying within the taxing jurisdiction. The term **taxable property** is used in the preceding sentence in recognition of the fact that property owned by governmental units and property used by religious and charitable organizations are often not taxable by the local government. In addition, senior citizens, war veterans, and others may have statutory exemption from

Illustration 3–4

TOWN OF MERRILL
GENERAL FUND
STATEMENT OF AMOUNT TO BE RAISED
BY PROPERTY TAXES FOR 2002
JULY 31, 2001

Requirements:		
Estimated expenditures, August 1–December 31, 2001		$ 4,200,000
Proposed appropriations for 2002		8,460,000
Estimated working balance required for beginning of 2003		510,000
Estimated total requirements		13,170,000
Resources other than tax levy for 2002:		
Actual balance, July 31, 2001	$ 654,000	
Amount to be received from second installment of 2001 taxes	2,430,000	
Miscellaneous receipts expected during balance of 2001	1,960,000	
Revenue expected from sources other than property taxes during 2002	4,544,000	
Estimated total resources other than property tax levy		9,588,000
Amount required from property taxes in 2002		$ 3,582,000

taxation for a limited portion of the assessed valuation of property. Continuing the example, assume the net assessed valuation of property taxable by the General Fund of the Town of Merrill is $214,348,000. In that case, the gross property tax levy ($3,731,250) is divided by the net assessed valuation ($214,348,000) to determine the property tax rate. The rate would be expressed as "$1.75 per $100 assessed valuation," or "$17.41 per $1,000 assessed valuation"—rounding up the actual decimal fraction (.017407) to two places to the right of the decimal, as is customary.

Interest and Penalties on Delinquent Taxes. A **penalty** is a legally mandated addition to a tax on the day it becomes delinquent (generally, the day after the day the tax is due). Penalties should be recognized as revenue when they are assessed. *Interest* at a legally specified rate also must be added to delinquent taxes for the length of time between the day the tax becomes delinquent until the day it is ultimately paid or otherwise discharged; interest revenue should be accrued at the time financial statements are to be prepared.

Sales Taxes, Income Taxes, and Gross Receipts Taxes. GASB *Statement No. 33* provides that revenue from sales taxes, income taxes, and gross receipts taxes be recognized, net of estimated refunds, in the accounting period in which underlying transactions occur.

Special Assessments. Special assessments differ from ad valorem real property taxes in that the latter are levied against all taxable property within the geographic boundaries of the government levying the taxes, whereas the former are levied against certain properties to defray part or all of the cost of a specific improvement or service that is presumed to be of particular benefit to the properties against which the special assessments are levied. Briefly, when routine services (street cleaning, snow plowing, and so on) are extended to property owners outside the normal service area of the government, or are provided at a higher level or at more frequent intervals than for the general public, "service-type" special assessments are levied. Service-type special assessments are accounted for by the fund that accounts for similar services rendered to the general public—usually the General Fund or a special revenue fund. Special assessments for capital improvements should be accounted for by a capital projects fund during the construction phase, and by a debt service fund during the debt service phase.

Licenses and Permits. Licenses and Permits include those revenues collected by a governmental unit from individuals or business concerns for various rights or privileges granted by the government. Some licenses and permits are primarily regulatory in nature, with minor consideration to revenue derived, whereas others are not only regulatory but provide large amounts of revenue as well, and some are almost exclusively revenue producers. Licenses and permits may relate to the privilege of carrying on business for a stipulated period, the right to do a certain thing that may affect the public welfare, or the right to use certain public property. Vehicle and alcoholic beverage licenses are found extensively on the state level and serve both regulatory and revenue functions. States make widespread use of professional and occupational licenses for purposes of control. Local governments make extensive use of licenses and permits to control the activities of their citizens; and from some they derive substantial amounts of revenue. Commonly found among licenses and permits are building permits, vehicle licenses, amusement licenses, business and occupational licenses, animal licenses, and street and curb permits.

Regardless of the governmental level or the purpose of a license or permit, the revenue it produces is ordinarily accounted for on a cash basis. Applicable rates or schedules of charges for a future period may be established well in advance, and fairly reliable information may be available as to the number of licenses or permits to be issued, but the probable degree of fluctuation in the latter factor is so great as to prevent satisfactory use of the accrual basis.

Intergovernmental Revenue. Intergovernmental Revenues include grants and other financial assistance. Grants are usually intended for either operating or capital purposes. GASB standards provide the following definitions.

1. *Grants and other financial assistance* are defined as transactions in which one governmental entity transfers cash or other items of value to [or incurs a liability for] another governmental entity, an individual, or an organization as a means of sharing program costs, subsidizing other governments or entities, or otherwise reallocating resources to the recipients.
2. A *capital grant* is a contribution or gift of cash or other assets restricted by the grantor for the acquisition or construction of fixed (capital) assets.
3. An *operating grant* is one that is intended to finance operations or that may be used for either operations or for capital outlays at the discretion of the grantee.[16]

Revenue recognition rules for intergovernmental revenues were discussed earlier in this chapter in the discussion on government-mandated and voluntary nonexchange transactions. Governmental funds generally should recognize such revenues when all time restrictions and eligibility requirements have been met and the resources are available to pay current period obligations. If a state or federal agency notifies a local governmental unit that a grant of a specified amount will be received at a specified date, and the preceding recognition rules are met, the local government should record the accrual of the revenue by debiting Due from State Government or similar title and crediting Revenues. In other cases, recognition is not possible until cash is received.

Charges for Services As discussed earlier in this chapter, Charges for Services of the governmental funds (and governmental activities at the government-wide level) include all charges for goods and services provided by a governmental fund

[16]GASB *Statement No. 33*, pars. 503–511.

to enterprise funds, individuals and organizations, and other governments. A few of the many revenue items included in this category are court costs; special police service; solid waste collection charges (unless accounted for in an enterprise fund); street, sidewalk, and curb repairs; receipts from parking meters; library use fees (but not fines); and tuition.

Classification of expenditures by function is discussed earlier in this chapter. The grouping of Charges for Services revenue may be correlated with the functional classification of expenditures. For example, one functional group of expenditures is named General Government, another Public Safety, and so on. A governmental unit, in connection with providing general government service, collects some revenue such as court cost charges, fees for recording legal documents, and zoning and subdivision fees, and should relate the revenues to the expenditures. Charges for Services should be recognized as revenue when earned, if that is prior to the collection of cash.

Fines and Forfeits. Revenue from Fines and Forfeits includes fines and penalties for commission of statutory offenses and for neglect of official duty; forfeitures of amounts held as security against loss or damage, or collections from bonds or sureties placed with the government for the same purpose; and penalties of any sort, except those levied on delinquent taxes. Library fines are included in this category. If desired, Fines and Forfeits may be the titles of two accounts within this revenue class, or they may be subgroup headings for more detailed breakdowns.

Revenues of this classification should be accrued to the extent practicable. In direct contrast with general property taxes, neither rates nor base or volume may be predetermined with any reasonable degree of accuracy for this type of revenue. Because of these uncertainties, it is often difficult to determine whether all amounts paid by transgressors have been accounted for; therefore, revenues from fines and forfeits may be recognized on the cash basis if accrual is not practicable.

Miscellaneous Revenues. Although the word *miscellaneous* is not informative and should be used sparingly, its use as the title of a revenue category is necessary. It (1) substitutes for other possible source classes that might have rather slight and infrequent usage and (2) minimizes the need for forcing some kinds of revenue into source classifications in which they do not generically belong. While Miscellaneous Revenues in itself represents a compromise, its existence aids in sharpening the meanings of other source classes. The heterogeneous nature of items served by the title is indicated by the following listing: interest earnings (other than on delinquent taxes); rents and royalties; sales of, and compensation for loss of, capital assets; contributions from public enterprises (utilities, airports, etc.); escheats (taking of property in default of legally qualified claimants); contributions and donations from private sources; and "other."

Some items of Miscellaneous Revenues, such as interest earnings on investments, might well be accrued, but mostly they are accounted for on the cash basis.

Budgetary Accounting

Budgetary accounts were defined earlier in this chapter. Their use in journal entries and ledgers is described here. At the beginning of the budget period, the Estimated Revenues control account is debited for the total amount of revenues expected to be recognized, as provided in the Revenues budget. The amount of revenue expected from each source specified in the Revenues budget is recorded in a subsidiary ledger account, so that the total of subsidiary ledger detail agrees with the debit to the control account, and both agree with the adopted budget. If a separate entry is to be made to record the Revenues budget, the general ledger debit to the Estimated Revenues control account is offset by a credit to Fund Balance. Recall that the Fund Balance account, before the budget is recorded, would normally have a credit balance representing the excess of fund assets over the total of liabilities and reserved Fund Equity. (If fund liabilities and reserved Fund Equity exceed fund assets, the Fund Balance account would have a debit balance—referred to as a *deficit.*) After the revenues budget is recorded, Fund Balance represents the excess of fund assets *plus* the estimated revenues and other financing sources for the budget period over liabilities and reserves.[17] The credit balance of the Fund Balance account, therefore, is the total amount available to finance appropriations. Consequently, the accounting entry to record the legally approved appropriations budget is a debit to Fund Balance and a credit to Appropriations for the total amount appropriated for the activities accounted for by the fund. The Appropriations control account is supported by a subsidiary ledger kept in the same detail as provided in the appropriations ordinance, so that the total of the subsidiary ledger detail agrees with the credit to the Appropriations control account, and both agree with the adopted budget. The use of the Encumbrances account is explained in a later section of this chapter.

As explained in the preceding section, the use of budgetary accounts permits comparison of actual revenues and expenditures to budgeted amounts. Budgetary control is further enhanced by clear and logical classification of revenues and expenditures, and by formally recording the budget in the accounts of the General Fund and other funds for which a budget is approved. The use of subsidiary ledgers, which permit recording revenues and expenditures—both actual and budgeted amounts—in the same level of detail as the budget, also helps to achieve sound budgetary control. Each of these topics is discussed in the remainder of this chapter.

Recording the Budget

The use of budgetary accounts is described earlier in this chapter. In order to illustrate entries in journal form to record a budget, assume the amounts shown below are the amounts that have been legally approved as the budget for the General

[17]For simplicity, we assume that a single Fund Balance account is used to record both budgetary (estimated) and actual amounts. In practice, many governments utilize a separate Budgetary Fund Balance account to record the credit amount of estimated revenues and the debit amount of appropriations.

Fund of a certain governmental unit for the fiscal year ending December 31, 2001. As of January 1, 2001, the first day of the fiscal year, the total Estimated Revenues should be recorded in the General Fund general ledger control account, and the amounts expected to be recognized during 2001 from each revenue source specified in the budget should be recorded in subsidiary ledger accounts. An appropriate entry would be:

	General Ledger		Subsidiary Ledger	
	Debits	*Credits*	*Debits*	*Credits*
1. Estimated Revenues	1,277,500			
Fund Balance		1,277,500		
Revenues Ledger:				
Taxes			882,500	
Intergovernmental Revenues			200,000	
Licenses and Permits			195,000	

The total Appropriations and Other Financing Uses legally budgeted for 2001 for the General Fund of the same governmental unit should also be recorded in the General Fund general ledger control accounts, and the amounts appropriated for each function itemized in the budget should be recorded in subsidiary ledger accounts. An appropriate entry using assumed budget amounts would be:

	General Ledger		Subsidiary Ledger	
	Debits	*Credits*	*Debits*	*Credits*
2. Fund Balance	1,636,500			
Appropriations		1,362,000		
Estimated Other Financing Uses		274,500		
Appropriations Ledger:				
General Government				1,150,000
Public Safety				212,000
Other Financing Uses Ledger:				
Interfund Transfers Out to Other Funds				74,500
Interfund Transfers Out to Component Units				200,000

It would, of course, be acceptable to combine the two entries illustrated above and make one General Fund entry to record Estimated Revenues, Appropriations, and Estimated Other Financing Uses; in this case there would be a debit to Fund Balance for $359,000 (the amount by which Appropriations and Estimated Other Financing Uses exceed Estimated Revenues). Even if a single combined entry is made in the General Fund general ledger accounts, that entry must provide for entry of the budgeted amounts in each individual subsidiary ledger account as shown in the illustrations of the two separate entries.

Budgetary Control of Revenues

In the preceding section, entries to record the budget in general ledger accounts and in subsidiary ledger accounts are illustrated. During a fiscal year, actual revenues should be recognized in the general ledger accounts of governmental funds by credits to the Revenues account (offset by debits to receivable accounts for revenues that are accrued or by debits to Cash for revenues recognized on the cash basis). The general ledger Revenues account is a control account supported by Revenues subsidiary ledger accounts kept in exactly the same detail as kept for the Estimated Revenues subsidiary ledger accounts. For example, assume the General Fund of the governmental unit for which budgetary entries are illustrated in the preceding section collected revenues in cash during the month of January from Licenses and Permits, $13,200, and Intergovernmental Revenues, $61,900. In an actual case, entries should be made on a current basis and cash receipts should be deposited each working day; however, for the purpose of this chapter, the following entry illustrates the effect on the General Fund accounts of collections during the month of January 2001:

	General Ledger		Subsidiary Ledger	
	Debits	*Credits*	*Debits*	*Credits*
3. Cash	75,100			
Revenues		75,100		
Revenues Ledger:				
Licenses and Permits				13,200
Intergovernmental Revenues				61,900

Comparability between Estimated Revenues subsidiary accounts and Revenues subsidiary accounts is necessary so that periodically throughout the fiscal year actual revenues from each source can be compared with estimated revenues from that source. Material differences between estimated and actual revenues should be investigated by administrators to determine whether (1) estimates were made on the basis of assumptions that may have appeared realistic when the budget was prepared but are no longer realistic (in that event, the budget needs to be revised so that administrators and legislators have better knowledge of revenues to be realized during the remainder of the fiscal year), or (2) action needs to be taken so that revenues estimated with reasonable accuracy are actually realized (i.e., one or more employees may have failed to understand that certain revenue items are to be collected). Illustration 3–5 shows a form of Revenues subsidiary ledger in which the debit column is subsidiary to the Estimated Revenues general ledger control account and the credit column is subsidiary to the Revenues general ledger control account.

A Statement of Actual and Estimated Revenues is illustrated in Chapter 4. Normally, during a fiscal year, the amount of revenue budgeted from each source will exceed the amount of revenue from that source realized to date; consequently, the Balance column will have a debit balance and may be headed Estimated Revenues Not Yet Realized. This amount is a *resource* of the governmental unit—legally and realistically budgeted revenues that will be recognized as assets before the end of the fiscal year.

Budgetary Control of Encumbrances and Expenditures

When enacted into law, an appropriation is an authorization for administrators to incur on behalf of the governmental unit liabilities in the amounts specified in the appropriation ordinance or statute, for the purposes set forth in that ordinance or

Illustration 3–5

NAME OF GOVERNMENTAL UNIT
REVENUES LEDGER
GENERAL FUND

Class: Licenses and Permits — Number: 351.1
Subclass: — Title:

Date	Item	Reference	Estimated Revenues DR.	Revenues CR.	Balance DR. (CR.)
2001					
January 1	Budget estimate	J1	$195,000		$195,000
31	Collections	CR6		$13,200	181,800

statute, during the period of time specified. An appropriation is considered *expended* when the authorized liabilities have been incurred. Because penalties are imposed by law on an administrator who incurs liabilities for any amount in excess of that appropriated, or for any purpose not covered by an appropriation, or who incurs liabilities after the authority to do so has expired, prudence dictates that each purchase order and each contract be reviewed before it is signed to determine that a valid and sufficient appropriation exists to which the expenditure can be charged when goods or services are received. If the review indicates that a valid appropriation exists and it has an available balance in excess of the amount of the purchase order or contract being reviewed, the purchase order or contract legally may be issued. When a purchase order or contract has been issued it is important to record the fact that the appropriation has been *encumbered* in the amount of the purchase order or contract. The word *encumbered* is used, rather than the word *expended*, because the amount is only an estimate of the liability that will be incurred when the purchase order is filled or the contract executed. (It is reasonably common for quantities of goods received to differ from quantities ordered, and it is not uncommon for invoice prices to differ from unit prices shown on purchase orders.) The use of appropriation authority is also somewhat tentative inasmuch as some suppliers are unable to fill orders or to perform as stipulated in a contract; in such cases, related purchase orders or contracts must be canceled.

Notice the issuance of purchase orders and/or contracts has two effects: (1) the encumbrance of the appropriation(s) that gave the governmental unit the authority to order goods or services and (2) the starting of a chain of events that will result in the government incurring a liability when the purchase orders are filled and the contracts executed. Both effects should be recorded in order to assist administrators to avoid overexpending appropriations and to plan to be able to pay liabilities on a timely basis. The accounting procedure used to record the two effects is illustrated by Entry 4. The first effect is recorded by the debit to the general ledger account

Encumbrances. Encumbrances is a control account that is related to the *Appropriations* control account discussed previously and to the *Expenditures* control account discussed in relation to Entries 5a and 5b. In order to accomplish the matching of Appropriations, Expenditures, and Encumbrances necessary for budgetary control, subsidiary account classifications of all three must correspond exactly (see Illustration 3–6). The general ledger account credited in Entry 4, *Reserve for Encumbrances*, is used to record the second effect of issuing purchase orders and contracts—the creation of an expected liability. Reserve for Encumbrances, sometimes called *Outstanding Encumbrances*, is not a control account; the balance of the account at the balance sheet date is reported as a reservation of Fund Equity, as illustrated in Chapter 4.

Entries 4, 5a, and 5b illustrate accounting for Encumbrances and Expenditures for the General Fund of the governmental unit for which entries are illustrated in previous sections of this chapter. Entry 4 is made on the assumption that early in January purchase orders are issued pursuant to the authority contained in the General Fund appropriations; assumed amounts chargeable to each function for which purchase orders are issued on this date are shown in the debits to the Encumbrances subsidiary accounts.

	General Ledger		**Subsidiary Ledger**	
	Debits	*Credits*	*Debits*	*Credits*
4. Encumbrances—2001	45,400			
Reserve for Encumbrances—2001		45,400		
Encumbrances Ledger:				
General Government			38,000	
Public Safety			7,400	

Illustration 3–6

NAME OF GOVERNMENT UNIT
APPROPRIATIONS, EXPENDITURES, AND ENCUMBRANCES LEDGER

Code No.: 0607-03
Fund: General
Function: General Government

Year: 2001

Month and Day	Reference	Encumbrances			Expenditures		Appropriations	
		Debits	Credits	Open	Debits	Cumulative Total	Credits	Available Balance
Jan. 2	Budget (Entry 2)						$1,150,000	$1,150,000
3	Purchase orders issued (Entry 4)	$38,000		$38,000				1,112,000
17	Invoices approved for payment (Entries 5a, 5b)		$35,000	3,000	$35,100	$35,100		1,111,900

When goods or services for which encumbrances have been recorded are received and the suppliers' invoices are approved for payment, the accounts should record the fact that appropriations have been *expended*, not merely encumbered, and that an actual liability, not merely an expected liability, exists. Entry 5a reverses Entry 4 to the extent that purchase orders are filled (ordinarily some of the purchase orders recorded in one encumbrance entry will be filled in one time period, and some in other time periods); it is important to note that since estimated amounts were used when encumbrances were recorded, the reversing entry must also use the estimated amounts. Thus the balance remaining in the Encumbrances control account, and in the Reserve for Encumbrances account, is the *total* estimated dollar amount of purchase orders and contracts outstanding. The estimated dollar amount of purchase orders outstanding against each appropriation is disclosed by the subsidiary accounts, as shown in Illustration 3–5.

5a. Reserve for Encumbrances—2001	42,000			
Encumbrances—2001		42,000		
Encumbrances Ledger:				
General Government				35,000
Public Safety				7,000
5b. Expenditures—2001	42,400			
Vouchers Payable		42,400		
Expenditures Ledger:				
General Government			35,100	
Public Safety			7,300	

Expenditures and the liability account must both be recorded at the actual amount the governmental unit agrees to pay the vendors who have filled the purchase orders (see Entry 5b). The fact that estimated and actual amounts differ causes no accounting difficulties as long as goods or services are received in the same fiscal period as ordered. The accounting treatment required when encumbrances outstanding at year-end are filled, or canceled, in a following year is illustrated in Chapter 4.

The encumbrance procedure is not always needed to make sure that appropriations are not overexpended. For example, although salaries and wages of governmental employees must be chargeable against valid and sufficient appropriations in order to give rise to legal expenditures, many governmental units do not find it necessary to encumber the departmental personal services appropriations for estimated payrolls of recurring, relatively constant amounts. Departments having payrolls that fluctuate greatly from one season to another may follow the encumbrance procedure to make sure the personal service appropriation is not overexpended.

From the foregoing discussion and illustrative journal entries, it should be apparent that administrators of governmental units need accounting systems designed to provide at any given date during a fiscal year comparisons for each item in the legal Appropriations budget of (1) the amount appropriated, (2) the amount of outstanding encumbrances, and (3) the cumulative amount of expenditures to this date. The net of the three items is accurately described as "Unencumbered

Unexpended Appropriations" but can be labeled more simply as "Available Appropriations" or "Available Balance." Classification of appropriations, expenditures, and encumbrances was discussed in a preceding section of this chapter. In order to provide needed comparisons, classification of expenditures and encumbrances must agree with the classifications of appropriations mandated by law. In many jurisdictions, good financial management may dictate all three elements be classified in greater detail than required by law.

Illustration 3–6 shows a form of subsidiary ledger that supports all three general ledger control accounts: Appropriations, Expenditures, and Encumbrances.

At intervals during the fiscal year, a Statement of Budgeted and Actual Expenditures and Encumbrances should be prepared to inform administrators and members of the legislative branch of the data contained in the subsidiary ledger records. An example of such a statement is illustrated in Chapter 4 (see Illustration 4–4). Also in Chapter 4, the entry needed at year-end to close budgetary and nominal accounts is illustrated (Entry 27, Chapter 4).

Accounting for Allotments

In some jurisdictions, it is necessary to regulate the use of appropriations so only specified amounts may be used from month to month or from quarter to quarter. The purpose of such control is to prevent expenditure of all or most of the authorized amount early in the year, without providing for unexpected requirements arising later in the year. A common device for regulating expenditures is the use of allotments. An **allotment** may be described as an internal allocation of funds on a periodic basis usually agreed upon by the department heads and the chief executive.

Allotments may be formally recorded in ledger accounts. This procedure might begin with the budgetary entry, in which Unallotted Appropriations would replace Appropriations. If this is desired, a combined entry to record the budget would be (using the numbers given in Entries 1 and 2, omitting entries in subsidiary accounts—which would be as illustrated previously, except the subsidiary ledger credits in Entry 2 would be designated as Unallotted Appropriations instead of Appropriations):

	General Ledger		Subsidiary Ledger	
	Debits	*Credits*	*Debits*	*Credits*
Estimated Revenues	1,277,500			
Fund Balance	359,000			
Unallotted Appropriations		1,362,000		
Estimated Other Financing Uses		274,500		

If it is assumed that $342,000 is the amount formally allotted for the first period, the following entry could be made (amounts allotted for each function are shown in the subsidiary ledger entries):

Unallotted Appropriations	342,000			
Allotments		342,000		
Allotments Ledger:				
General Government				289,000
Public Safety				53,000

Expenditures can be recorded periodically as reports are received from using departments or divisions. Under this procedure, Expenditures, Allotments, and Unallotted Appropriations are all closed to Fund Balance at year-end, usually in one combined entry.

Reconciliation of Differences between GAAP and Budgetary Amounts

As previously noted in this chapter, GASB *Statement No. 34* requires that differences between amounts reported in the GAAP basis operating statement (Illustration 2–4) and those reported in the budgetary comparison schedule (Illustration 3–2) be reconciled either on the face of the budgetary comparison schedule or on a separate page, as in Illustration 3–7. Because Illustration 3–2 presented a budgetary

Illustration 3–7 Budgetary Comparison Schedule Budget-to-GAAP Reconciliation

Explanation of Differences between Budgetary Inflows and Outflows and GAAP Revenues and Expenditures

	General Fund
Sources/Inflows of Resources	
Actual amounts (budgetary basis) "available for appropriation" from the budgetary schedule (Illustration 3–2)	$92,370,775
Differences—budget to GAAP:	
The fund balance at the beginning of the year is a budgetary resource but is not a current-year revenue under GAAP.	(2,742,799)
Transfers from other funds are inflows of budgetary resources but are not revenues under GAAP.	(129,323)
The proceeds from the sale of park land are budgetary resources but are regarded as a *special item* rather than revenues under GAAP.	(3,476,488)
Total general fund revenues as reported on the statement of revenues, expenditures, and changes in fund balances—governmental funds.	$86,022,165
Uses/Outflows of Resources	
Actual amounts (budgetary basis) "total charges to appropriations" from the budgetary comparison schedule (Illustration 3–2)	$90,938,522
Differences—budget to GAAP:	
The city budgets for claims and compensated absences only to the extent expected to be paid, rather than on the modified accrual basis.	129,100
Encumbrances for supplies and equipment ordered but not received is reported in the year the order is placed for *budgetary* purposes, but in the year the supplies are received for *financial reporting* purposes.	(186,690)
Transfers to other funds are outflows of budgetary resources but are not expenditures under GAAP.	(2,163,759)
Total General Fund expenditures as reported in the statement of revenues, expenditures, and changes in fund balances—governmental funds (Illustration 2–4)	$88,717,173

Source: Adapted from GASB *Statement No. 34*, Appendix C (GASB: Norwalk, CT, 1999), Exhibit G–3.

comparison for only the General Fund, that is the only fund included in the reconciliation shown in Illustration 3–7.

Readers will note that both actual revenues on the budget basis and actual expenditures on the budget basis differ from the actual revenues and expenditures reported in the GAAP operating statement shown in Illustration 2–4 for the General Fund. The reasons for those differences and the corresponding amounts are explained in the reconciliation. These differences, of course, apply only to Sample City. Other governments are free to choose their own ways of recognizing revenues and expenditures for budget purposes. Thus the reconciliation schedule must be tailored to explain the budget-to-GAAP differences applicable to a particular government.

Computerized Accounting Systems

If a computerized accounting system is used, which is typically the case, an account number structure provides for appropriate classification of revenues and expenditures, as well as for the desired classification of assets, liabilities, and fund equities. Many alternative fund accounting software systems are available. Because current information technology makes it feasible to handle large numbers of files and a high transaction volume, the general ledger module of most systems can easily accommodate all the revenue and expenditure detail accounts needed for effective budgetary control. Thus, computerized systems often do not use general ledger control accounts and subsidiary ledgers in the manner of the manual system described in this section.

Instead of using general ledger control accounts and related subsidiary ledgers, computerized systems typically use separate files or ledgers for proprietary and budgetary reporting. For example, the general ledger module of one leading fund accounting software system includes both a general ledger and a budget ledger. Actual revenues and expenditures are posted to the general ledger and budget amounts are posted to the budget ledger. Of course, the same account numbers and titles used in the budget ledger are used in the general ledger to permit budgetary comparison reporting. In addition, the system provides a separate encumbrance ledger to record encumbered amounts and monitor budgetary compliance. Selecting the type of transaction from a menu on the screen determines in which ledger (or ledgers) a particular transaction is posted. All such systems must provide transaction detail reports and other documentation of entries and postings in order to provide an adequate "audit trail."

In a computerized system, the account number structure is an important design feature—one that affects the ease of operation and the ability to prepare useful financial reports. Most account number structures provide for the multiple expenditure classification categories recommended by the GASB, or similar classification. Consider, for example, the following eight-segment account number structure for one eastern city:

XXXX -	XXXX -	XXX -	XXXX -	XX -	X -	XX -	XXXX
(1)	(2)	(3)	(4)	(5)	(6)	(7)	(8)

The eight segments of numbers represent the following classifications:

Segment	*Represents*
1	Fund or Account Group
2	Department/Division (or Function)
3	Office/Bureau (or Program)
4	Activity
5	Report Group
6	Account Type
7	Object (Major Object)
8	Line Item (Detailed Object)

Even though these segment names do not agree completely with the classification categories recommended by the GASB and described in this section, their similarity should be apparent. Moreover, it appears that the segments used in this account number provide for at least as much detail as that recommended by GASB.

To illustrate how this account structure appears in practice, an example screen display is presented below for one particular account: an expenditures account for part-time salaries in the Aquatics (swimming pools, etc.) activity of the Customer Relations Program within the Leisure Services Division, accounted for in the General Fund.

```
                    City of Sample
              Display Account Segments
Fund . . . . . . . . . . :0001 General Fund
Dept/Div (Function) . . :0253 Leisure Services
Office/Bureau (Prog.) . :205 Customer Relations
Activity (Location) . . :2531 Aquatics
Report Group . . . . . :43 Cultural, Parks, & Rec.
Account Type . . . . . :2 Recreation
Object (Major Obj.) . . :10 Salaries
Line Item (Detl. Obj.)  :1201 Part-Time
```

All segments of the account number are used for expenditure transactions, but not all segments are needed for revenue and some balance sheet transactions. Segments not needed to record a transaction are left blank. The menu-driven program used by the system makes it relatively simple to move around within the account classification structure. Further, information can be aggregated within any given segment, or groups of segments, to provide a wide variety of custom financial reports, in addition to the financial statements.

Accounting for Government-wide Operating Activities

The illustrative journal entries shown in this chapter to record the budget have no impact on the government-wide statement of activities. Revenue and expenditure transactions, however, may be treated differently at the government-wide level than in the General Fund. Because the illustrative transactions presented in this chapter were intended to illustrate budgetary control over revenues and expenditures, the possible effects of those transactions at the government-wide level were ignored. In Chapter 4, the dual effects of accounting transactions are analyzed and appropriate journal entries are made in both the general journal for the General Fund and the general journal used to record government activities at the government- wide level.

Finally, the discussion of computerized accounting systems in this chapter focused on the systems that have evolved to meet the *fund* accounting needs of government. Governments now face the challenge of redesigning their existing systems or acquiring new systems that will accommodate government-wide accounting and financial reporting requirements, as well as preparing the new fund financial statements required by GASB *Statement No. 34*. Many governments may continue for an extended period to use their present fund accounting computer systems, supplemented perhaps by spreadsheet interfaces that permit the reclassifications of fund-based information needed to prepare government-wide financial statements.

Appendix
Accounting for Public School Systems

As mentioned in Chapter 1, there are nearly 14,000 independent public school systems in the United States. Although they are classified as special purpose governments, these school systems follow the same generally accepted accounting principles as state and local governments—the accounting and reporting standards issued by GASB. The approximately 1,500 "dependent" school systems are accounted for as part of their parent general purpose government, either a state, county, municipality, or township. Public school systems, both independent and dependent, often follow specialized accounting and reporting procedures prescribed by a state oversight department or agency. Further, all state oversight departments or agencies collect revenues and expenditures data for all prekindergarten through grade 12 public schools in their state and provide these data to the National Center for Educational Statistics (NCES) so the NCES can prepare the annual "National Public Education Financial Survey."[18] For sake of uniformity, most school systems follow the system of classification for revenues and expenditures recommended by the NCES. This system of classification is discussed next. In addition, of course, they must prepare the MD&A and basic financial statements required by GASB *Statement No. 34*.

Classification of Expenditures of Public School Systems

The NCES system of expenditure classification combines several of the GASB classifications discussed in this chapter. In NCES terminology, a combination of classifications is called a *dimension*. Two groups of dimensions are provided in the expenditure classification system: (1) dimensions essential to meet reporting requirements at the federal level and (2) dimensions optionally available for management use. The dimensions essential to meet federal (and most state) reporting requirements are Program, Function, Object, and Project/Reporting. In the optional group are Level of Instruction, Operational Unit, Subject Matter, Job Classification, and Special Cost Center.

Essential Dimensions. *Program* dimensions provided in the NCES publication include Special Programs (such as Mentally Retarded, Physically Handicapped, or Gifted and Talented), Vocational Programs, Other Instructional Programs—Elementary/Secondary, Nonpublic School Programs, Adult/Continuing Education Programs, Community/Junior College Programs, Community Services Programs, and Enterprise Programs (Food Services, etc.). The *Function* dimension includes Instruction, Support Services such as Guidance Services, Health Services, Psychological Services, Support Services—Instructional Staff, Support Services—General Administration, Support Services—School Administration, Support Services—Business, Operation and Maintenance of Plant Services, Student Transportation Services, Support Services—Central, Other Support Services, Operation of Non-Instructional Services (Food Services, Other Enterprise Services, Community Services), Facilities Acquisition and Construction Services, and Other Outlays. *Object* classifications of a public school system are Personal Services—Salaries, Personal Services—Employee

---

[18]An extensive list of NCES reports and resources is available on the Internet at http://NCES.ed.gov.

Benefits, Purchased Professional and Technical Services, Purchased Property Services, Other Purchased Services, Supplies and Materials, Property, Other Objects (Dues and Fees, Judgments, Interest, etc.), and Other Uses of Funds (Redemption of Principal, Housing Authority Obligations, and Fund Transfers). The *Project/Reporting* code permits school systems to accumulate expenditures to meet a variety of specialized reporting requirements, such as Local Projects, State Projects, and Federal Projects.

Optional Dimensions. The optional dimensions are: Level of Instruction (Elementary, Middle, Secondary, Post-Secondary, and Districtwide); Operational Unit (possibly attendance centers, budgetary units, buildings, or location code for paycheck distribution); Subject Matter (Agriculture, Arts, Business, etc.); Job Classification (this dimension may be used to [1] classify payroll costs for personnel purposes, such as Official, Professional, Technical, Clerical, and [2] segregate certified and noncertified salaries and benefits or accumulate payroll costs by bargaining unit for purposes of labor negotiations); and Special Cost Centers such as Term, Course, Work Order, Bus Route or Vehicle, State Accounting Number, or Federal Common Accounting Number.

Classification of Revenues of Public School Systems

Revenues of public school systems, both those dependent upon a general purpose government and those independent entities, should be classified in the manner prescribed by the National Center for Education Statistics. As is true of the NCES expenditure classification, the NCES revenue classification system provides for a combination of classifications known as a *dimension*. Generally, public school revenues should be classified by fund, source, and project/reporting code. The NCES suggests the following revenue classification:

- 1000 Revenue from Local Sources
  - 1100 Taxes levied/assessed by the school system
  - 1200 Revenue from local governmental units other than the school system
  - 1300 Tuition
  - 1400 Transportation fees
  - 1500 Earnings on investments
  - 1600 Food services
  - 1700 Student activities
  - 1800 Community services activities
  - 1900 Other revenue from local sources
- 2000 Revenue from Intermediate Sources
  - 2100 Unrestricted grants-in-aid
  - 2200 Restricted grants-in-aid
  - 2800 Revenue in lieu of taxes
  - 2900 Revenue for/on behalf of the school system
- 3000 Revenue from State Sources
  - 3100 Unrestricted grants-in-aid
  - 3200 Restricted grants-in-aid
  - 3800 Revenue in lieu of taxes
  - 3900 Revenue for/on behalf of the school system

4000 Revenue from Federal Sources
- 4100 Unrestricted grants-in-aid received directly
- 4200 Unrestricted grants-in-aid received through state
- 4300 Restricted grants-in-aid received directly
- 4500 Restricted grants-in-aid received through state
- 4700 Grants-in-aid received through other agencies
- 4800 Revenue in lieu of taxes
- 4900 Revenue for/on behalf of the school system

5000 Other Sources
- 5100 Sale of bonds
- 5200 Interfund transfers
- 5300 Sale or compensation for loss of fixed assets

An additional level of detail provided in the NCES revenue source classification system is not illustrated above. The nature of the detail is readily apparent; for example, revenue account 1100, Taxes, comprehends account 1110, Ad Valorem Taxes levied by local school system; account 1120, Sales and Use Taxes; account 1130, Income Taxes; account 1140, Penalties and Interest on Taxes; and account 1190, other taxes.

"Intermediate" sources of revenue are administrative units or political subdivisions between the local school system and the state. "Grants-in-aid" from intermediate, state, or federal governments are contributions from general revenue sources of those governments, or, if related to specific revenue sources of those units, are distributed on a flat grant or equalization basis. "Revenue in lieu of taxes" analogous to payment from an enterprise fund to the General Fund discussed in Chapter 7 are payments made out of general revenues of intermediate, state, or federal governments to a local school system because the higher governmental units own property located within the geographical boundaries of the local unit that is not subject to taxation. "Revenue for/on behalf of the local school system" includes all payments made by intermediate, state, or federal governments for the benefit of the local system; payments to pension funds, or a contribution of fixed assets, are examples.

Key Terms

Activity, 76
Ad valorem property taxes, 79
Allotment, 90
Appropriations, 73
Budgetary accounts, 73
Character, 77
Derived tax revenues, 64
Direct expenses, 66
Eligibility requirements, 63
Encumbrances, 73
Estimated other financing sources, 74
Estimated other financing uses, 74
Estimated revenues, 73
Exchange transactions, 62
Exchange-like transactions, 62
Expenditures budget, 75
Extraordinary items, 68
Functions, 75
General revenues, 67
Government-mandated nonexchange transactions, 64
Imposed nonexchange revenues, 64
Indirect expenses, 66
Nonexchange revenues, 64
Nonexchange transactions, 63
Object, 77

Selected References

American Institute of Certified Public Accountants. *Audit and Accounting Guide. Audits of State and Local Governmental Units*. Revised. New York, 1999.

Governmental Accounting Standards Board. *Codification of Governmental Accounting and Financial Reporting Standards as of June 30, 1999*. Norwalk, CT, 1999.

National Center for Education Statistics. *Financial Accounting for Local and State School Systems*. State Educational Records and Reports Series: Handbook II, Revision. Washington, DC: U.S. Government Printing Office, 1990. Reprinted 1995.

Questions

3–1. Define *nonexchange transactions* and describe the four classes of nonexchange transactions. Give an example of each class.

3–2. When does a city recognize revenue from an exchange transaction? What factors must be considered in recognizing revenue from nonexchange transactions?

3–3. Distinguish between direct and indirect expenses. Under what circumstances might depreciation expense be considered a direct expense?

3–4. Indicate whether the following sources of revenue would most likely be classified as program revenues or general revenues on the government-wide statement of activities.

a. Charges for services.
b. Operating grants that can be used for many discretionary purposes.
c. Special assessment for snow removal.
d. Unrestricted investment earnings on permanent funds.
e. Motor vehicle fuel taxes restricted for road repair.
f. Capital grants restricted for public safety.
g. Building permits.

3–5. Describe the form and content of the government-wide statement of activities.

3–6. How should one determine whether the routine activities of a city's Street Department ought to be accounted for in the General Fund or in a special revenue fund?

3–7. Define *fund equity* and explain the kinds of accounts that comprise the fund equity category. How does fund equity compare to net assets?

3–8. Distinguish between:

a. Expenditures and Encumbrances.
b. Revenues and Estimated Revenues.

c. Reserve for Encumbrances and Encumbrances.

d. Reserve for Encumbrances and Fund Balance.

e. Appropriations and Expenditures.

f. Expenditures and Expenses.

3–9. Explain the potential usefulness of each of the following expenditure classification categories:

a. By function or program.

b. By organization unit.

c. By activity.

d. By character.

e. By object.

3–10. Indicate whether each expenditure item should be classified as a function, program, organization unit, activity, character, or object.

a. County Treasurer's Office.

b. Welfare.

c. Solid waste disposal—landfill.

d. Accident investigation.

e. Supplies.

f. Debt service.

g. Environmental protection.

h. Health.

i. Department of Health.

j. Personal services.

3–11. State whether each item should be classified as Taxes, Licenses and Permits, Intergovernmental Revenue, Charges for Services, Fines and Forfeits, or Miscellaneous Revenue.

a. Sales taxes levied by the governmental units.

b. Receipts from county in payment for rural library service.

c. Dog licenses.

d. Traffic violation penalties.

e. Federal grant for housing rehabilitation.

f. Royalties from oil wells on city property.

g. Charges for solid waste collection and disposal.

h. Plumbers' registration fees.

i. City's share of state severance tax.

j. Charges for pumping basements.

3–12. Governmental accounting gives substantial recognition to budgets, with those budgets being recorded in the accounts of the governmental unit.

a. What is the purpose of a governmental accounting system, and why is the budget recorded in the accounts of a governmental unit? Include in your discussion the purpose and significance of appropriations.

b. Describe when and how a governmental unit records its budget and closes it out.

(AICPA)

3–13. Why do GASB standards specify that the amounts in the Actual column of a budgetary comparison statement be reported on the basis required by law for budget preparation—even if that basis differs from GAAP?

3–14. If Estimated Revenues and Estimated Other Financing Sources exceed Appropriations and Estimated Other Financing Uses when the budget of a special revenue fund is recorded, would you expect the balance of Fund Balance to increase, or to decrease, with respect to the balance displayed in the balance sheet of the special revenue fund prepared as of the end of the year preceding the budget year? Explain your answer.

3–15. Explain how expenditure and revenue classifications for public school systems differ from those for state and local governments.

Cases

3–1. Budgetary accounting and GAAP. Sara Smith, chief accountant for the Town of Woolridge, has several years of experience in corporate accounting, but only recently began her current position. Sara found the manner in which the town had previously used budgetary accounts to achieve budgetary control as being confusing and stated her opinion that "there are too many accounts to keep up with." Accordingly, for the current year, she prepared a "budgetary spreadsheet" that lists all budgeted revenues and appropriations for the year. Sara explained to the town administrator that her budgetary accounting procedures are much simpler than those previously used and will work just as well. At the end of the fiscal year, she will simply compare actual revenues and expenditures to the budgeted amounts and then manually prepare the required budgetary comparison schedule.

Required

Evaluate the appropriateness of the chief accountant's new budgetary accounting procedures. Do these procedures conform to GAAP?

3–2. Chart of Accounts. The City of Belmont utilizes a 10-digit account number as part of its computerized accounting system. Its 10-digit account number is organized as follows:

XX-XX-XX-XXXX

The first two positions represent a particular fund, the second two positions represent the organization unit (for example, department), the third two positions represent organization subunit, and the final four positions represent either object class for an expenditure entry or source class for a revenue transaction. (These four positions are also used to represent other transactions such as capital assets, long-term liabilities, and other financing sources and uses.) Among the several ledgers in the city's accounting system are a general ledger for proprietary accounts, a budget ledger for budgetary accounts, and an encumbrances ledger. There are no subsidiary ledgers per se. Rather, the first two positions of the final four positions in the account number represent a major expenditure/expense or revenue category. For example, the following accounts are found in the City of Belmont's general ledger for the General Fund, Street Department, Supplies and Maintenance (01 represents General Fund, 08 represents Street Department, 0200 represents Supplies, and 0300 represents Maintenance).

Account Number	*Account Description*
01-08-00-0210	Chemical Supplies
01-08-00-0220	Clothing Supplies
01-08-00-0260	General Office Supplies
01-08-00-0270	Janitorial Supplies
01-08-00-0285	Fuel and Vehicle Supplies
01-08-00-0290	Other Supplies
01-08-00-0302	Building Maintenance
01-08-00-0304	Street Maintenance
01-08-00-0306	Sidewalk Maintenance
01-08-00-0307	Street Sweeping

These same account numbers are utilized in the general ledger, the budget ledger, and the encumbrances ledger, as appropriate. Actual revenues and expenditures are posted from a general journal or special journals to the general ledger accounts, budgeted estimated revenues and appropriations are posted to the budget ledger, and purchase orders placed for goods are posted to the encumbrances ledger.

Required

a. Discuss whether a system such as that used by the City of Belmont, which does not use the system of general ledger control accounts and subsidiary ledgers discussed in Chapter 3, can achieve the desired level of budgetary control over revenues and expenditures.

b. What improvements would you recommend in the City of Belmont's system?

3–3. Property Taxes and GAAP. In auditing the Town of Appleton you become aware that the town's accounting procedures for property taxes may not be in conformity with GAAP. This is the first year Appleton has engaged your firm as auditor. Consistent with options allowed under state law, Appleton levies taxes in December. These taxes are due in two equal installments on January 31 and July 31. The fiscal year ends on June 30. The town controller has for several years recorded the total levy as revenues in the fiscal year of the levy. The controller argues that since the second installment is receivable within 60 days of fiscal year-end, it is properly recognized as revenues of the current fiscal year. Based on an audit of another municipality located in the same state as Appleton, you know that in the same circumstances your previous client recorded the second installment of the current year levy as deferred revenue in the year of the levy and as revenue of the following year. You believe that if the second installment is not legally due until the next fiscal year, it cannot be recognized as a revenue of the current period. The controller is strongly opposed to changing the accounting procedures for these taxes.

Required

a. Who is correct in this situation, you or the client? Explain your answer fully. Base your response on analysis of applicable GASB standards.

b. Assuming that the two property tax installments are due on March 31 and September 30, and the levy date and fiscal year-end are unchanged, what effect would this have on the recognition of revenue for the second installment of property taxes? Explain fully.

3–4. Internet Case. You are an accountant in a state that has recently allowed charter schools, or public school academies, to educate kindergarten through 12th grade students and receive public funds to do so. A group of parents and teachers is forming such a school and has asked for your help in establishing an accounting system. Use the Internet to identify resources that may help you in this task. For example, use your favorite search engine to look for information on "charter schools" and "accounting systems." Would you expect an accounting system for this type of school to be any different than that used by traditional public schools? Should you incorporate budgetary accounting? [Hint: try http://www.uscharterschools.org/tech_assist/ta_finance.htm and look for Budgets and Fiscal Management.]

Exercises and Problems

3–1. Examine the CAFR. Utilizing the CAFR obtained for Exercise 1–1, review the governmental fund financial statements and related data and government-wide financial statements if the entity has implemented GASB *Statement No. 34*. Note particularly the items suggested below:

a. **Statement of Revenues, Expenditures, and Changes in Fund Balances for Governmental Funds.**

(1) *Revenues and Other Financing Sources*. What system of classification of revenues is used in the combined, combining, and individual fund statements? Do the major classes used agree with the source classes listed in Chapter 3? If there are differences, are they minor differences of terminology, or major differences in system of classification? Are transfers, proceeds of debt issues, and assets acquired under capital lease agreements identified as described in Chapter 3?

List the three most important sources of General Fund revenues, and list the most important source of revenue of each special revenue fund. Is the reporting entity dependent upon any single source for as much as one-third of its General Fund revenue? What proportion of revenues is derived from property taxes? Do the notes clearly indicate recognition criteria for primary revenue sources? Do the notes disclose details of the property tax calendar, including lien dates, levy (assessment) dates, due dates, and collection dates?

Are charts, graphs, or tables included that show the changes over time in reliance on each revenue source? Are there any interfund transfers? Are interfund transfers in reported in the same section of the statement as Revenues, or are they reported in an Other Financing Sources (Uses) section following the Expenditures section? Are proceeds of debt issues and general capital assets acquired under capital lease agreements, if any, reported in the same section as interfund transfers in?

(2) *Expenditures and Other Financing Uses.* What system of classification of expenditures is used in the combined, combining, and individual fund statements? If the system of classification is not one discussed in Chapter 3, does it appear to be more or less informative than any of those discussed in the chapter? Are interfund transfers out shown in the same section of the statement as expenditures, or are they reported in an Other Financing Sources (Uses) section following the Expenditures section? List the three categories that caused the largest General Fund expenditures; list the category of the largest expenditure of each of the special revenue funds.

Does the report contain, perhaps in the Introductory Section, any information that would enable the reader to determine what results were achieved for the expenditures?

Are charts, tables, or graphs presented to show the trend of General Fund expenditures, by category, for a period of 10 years? Is expenditure data related to population of the governmental unit, square miles within the governmental unit, or workload statistics (such as tons of solid waste removed and number of miles of street constructed)?

b. **Budgetary comparison schedule or statement.** What name is given to this schedule or statement? Read the following before analyzing the budgetary comparisons in the CAFR you are using: The Budget versus Actual schedule or statement should include budgetary comparisons for the General Fund and major special revenues funds for which budgets have been legally adopted. If the entity has not yet implemented GASB *Statement No. 34*, other special revenue funds and the debt service funds(s) may be included.

(1) Actual data presented in budgetary comparison statements should be prepared on the same basis as the budgetary data (which may include encumbrances along with expenditures). If basis, timing, perspective, or entity differences, defined in GASB *Codification*, Sec. 2400.114–121, exist between budgetary data and actual data reported in conformity with GAAP, the "actual" data reported in the budgetary comparison statement should be reconciled with the actual data reported in conformity with GAAP; the reconciliation may be made as a part of the budgetary comparison statement or in the Notes to the Financial Statements. If the data reported in the Actual column of the budgetary comparison statement are not in conformity with GAAP, the heading of the statement should make clear that the data are "Non-GAAP."

(2) Are any fund types in addition to the General Fund and major special revenue funds included in the budgetary comparison statement? If so, list the additional fund types included and attempt to determine whether the inclusion is mandated by state law, local ordinance, or custom.

(3) Is the budgetary comparison presented only as required supplementary information, or are there also budgetary comparisons in the combining statements and individual fund statements? Do budgetary comparison statements show only the budget as originally enacted, the original budget plus or minus budget amendments made during the year, or only the budget

as it existed at balance sheet date; or is the report unclear as to which budget is presented? If amendments to the budget are not shown in the financial statement are they shown in the notes to the financial statements, or elsewhere in the CAFR? Is the legal procedure for budget adoption and budget amendment explained in the notes or elsewhere in the CAFR?

(4) Do the notes state whether or not appropriations lapse at year-end? Do the notes disclose the level of control for each budget for which data are presented (the level at which expenditures may not legally exceed appropriations)?

(5) Are the amounts in the Actual column clearly labeled (either in the heading of the statement or in the column heading) as being on the budgetary basis, or does the statement disclose that the budget is on the GAAP basis, or are the bases unclear? Are differences between budgeted amounts and actual amounts shown only in dollars, or are percentage differences shown? Is there any explanation in the notes to the financial statements, the introductory section, or elsewhere in the CAFR, of material differences between budget and actual?

(6) If the budget differs from the GAAP reporting model as to *basis*, *timing*, *perspective*, or *entity*, are the amounts in the Actual column reconciled with the amounts reported in the combined statement of revenues, expenditures, and changes in fund balances (the statement you analyzed in part *a* of this Exercise)? Do reconciling items include encumbrances outstanding at year-end not considered as expenditures in GAAP-based statements, or expenditures made during one year that were authorized by appropriations (sometimes called *budgetary expenditures*) of a preceding year? Are these and other reconciling items disclosed within the budgetary comparison statement, within the notes to the financial statements, or elsewhere in the CAFR? Is the reconciliation clear and understandable to you, or is it merely confusing?

(7) Do all blended component units use the same budgetary practices as the primary government of the reporting entity? Does the CAFR state this explicitly, or does it indicate that budgetary practices differ by disclosures in the headings of statements, the headings of columns within statements, or by narrative and schedules within the notes to the financial statements?

3–2. Multiple Choice. Choose the best answer.

1. Which of the following is *not* a budgetary account?
   a. Appropriations.
   b. Encumbrances.
   c. Reserve for Encumbrances.
   d. Estimated Revenues.
2. Which of the following terms refers to an actual cost rather than an estimate?
   a. Expenditure.
   b. Appropriation.
   c. Budget.
   d. Encumbrance.

3. Which of the following steps in the acquisition of goods and services occurs first?
   a. Appropriation.
   b. Encumbrance.
   c. Disbursement.
   d. Expenditure.
4. An Expenditures account appears in:
   a. A pension trust fund.
   b. An enterprise fund.
   c. A special revenue fund.
   d. An internal service fund.
5. The Appropriations Control account of a governmental unit is debited when:
   a. Supplies are purchased.
   b. Expenditures are recorded.
   c. The budgetary accounts are closed.
   d. The budget is recorded.
6. Equipment repairs that have been made for a governmental unit, and for which a bill has been received, should be recorded in the General Fund as a debit to an:
   a. Expenditure.
   b. Encumbrance.
   c. Expense.
   d. Appropriation.
7. The City of Hinton incurred $150,000 of salaries and wages for the month ended May 31. To record this transaction the City of Hinton should debit:
   a. Encumbrances.
   b. Expenditures.
   c. Reserve for Encumbrances.
   d. Both Expenditures and Reserve for Encumbrances.
8. The following balances are included in the subsidiary records of Burwood Village's Parks and Recreation Department at March 31:

Appropriations—Supplies	$7,500
Expenditures—Supplies	4,500
Encumbrances—Supplies Orders	750

   How much does the Parks and Recreation Department have available for additional purchases of supplies?
   a. $0.
   b. $2,250.
   c. $3,000.
   d. $6,750.

9. The Board of Commissioners of the City of Fulton adopted its budget for the year ending July 31, which indicated revenues of $1,000,000 and appropriations of $900,000. If the budget is formally integrated into the accounting records, what is the required journal entry?

	Debits	Credits
a. Memorandum entry only		
b. Appropriations	900,000	
General Fund	100,000	
Estimated Revenues		1,000,000
c. Estimated Revenues	1,000,000	
Appropriations		900,000
Fund Balance		100,000
d. Revenues Receivable	1,000,000	
Expenditures Payable		900,000
Fund Balance		100,000

10. Which of the following will decrease the Fund Balance of a governmental unit at the end of the fiscal year?
    a. Appropriations are more than Expenditures and Reserve for Encumbrances—Prior Year.
    b. Appropriations are less than Expenditures and Encumbrances.
    c. Appropriations are more than Estimated Revenues.
    d. Appropriations are more than Expenditures and Encumbrances.

(AICPA, adapted)

3–3. Multiple Choice. GASB *Statement* No. 34. Choose the best answer.

1. Revenue from sales tax is classified as a:
   a. Derived tax revenue.
   b. Imposed nonexchange revenue.
   c. Government-mandated nonexchange transaction.
   d. Voluntary nonexchange transaction.
2. Revenue from nonexchange transactions is recognized:
   a. When the transaction occurs and the revenue has been earned.
   b. When the cash is received.
   c. When the underlying transaction has occurred and the resources are available.
   d. It depends upon the classification of the nonexchange transaction.
3. Expenses that are specifically associated with a function or program should be:
   a. Reported as a separate line item in the statement of activities.
   b. Reported on the line for that function or program in the statement of activities.
   c. Combined with indirect expenses in the statement of activities.
   d. Classified as extraordinary or special expenses in the statement of activities.
4. Which of the following statements is *not* true about program revenues?
   a. They reduce the net expense of each function or program or produce net revenue.

b. They include charges for services, operating grants and contributions, and capital grants and contributions.

c. They are reported in a separate section at the bottom of the statement of activities.

d. Examples include building permits, special assessments, grants restricted to programs.

5. The statement of activities in the government-wide financial statements includes:

   a. Net expense or revenue of each function or program comprising the governmental activities of the government.

   b. Separate columns for governmental activities, business-type activities, and discretely presented component units.

   c. A separate section at the bottom of the statement that shows general revenues that subsidize the net expense of programs or functions.

   d. All of the above are important components of the statement of activities.

6. The statement of activities in the government-wide financial statements is designed to provide information to assess:

   a. Fiscal accountability.

   b. Operational accountability.

   c. Functional accountability.

   d. Financial position.

7. Which of the following is a true statement about reporting special items and transfers on the statement of activities?

   a. Special items are reported separately so users can clearly see if a significant, unusual, or infrequent transaction or event has occurred.

   b. Special items and transfers are reported as separate line items in the program revenues section.

   c. Extraordinary items are defined much differently than they are in business accounting.

   d. Transfers between funds are reported only as business-type activities.

8. GASB *Statement No. 34* requires which of the following regarding the budget?

   a. A budget to actual comparison for all funds: governmental, proprietary, and fiduciary.

   b. A budget to actual comparison schedule for the General Fund and each major special revenue fund for which a budget is legally adopted.

   c. A budgetary comparison statement that is part of the basic financial statements.

   d. The same type of budget to actual comparisons that were required under the current reporting model being superseded by GASB *Statement No. 34*.

9. The budgetary comparison schedule required by GASB *Statement No. 34*:

   a. Must include a variance column showing the difference between budget and actual numbers.

   b. Will ensure that government officials are not spending more than what was legally authorized in the appropriations budget.

c. Must present separate columns for both the originally adopted and final amended budgets.

d. Will always report the cash-based budget in the Budgeted Amounts column.

10. One of the significant benefits of financial reporting under GASB *Statement No. 34* that is not available under the previous model is:

a. Government-wide statements that allow users to assess operational accountability.

b. Comparison of budgeted revenues and expenditures to actual.

c. Segregation of other financing sources and uses from revenues and expenditures.

d. There is little difference between the GASB *Statement No. 34* financial reporting model and the previous GASB model.

3–4. Budgets. King City has budgeted the following General Fund revenues and appropriations for the fiscal year 2002.

Estimated Revenues:	
Taxes	$6,000,000
Licenses and Permits	1,200,000
Fines and Forfeits	400,000
Intergovernmental Revenues	2,000,000
Total Estimated Revenues	$9,600,000
Appropriations:	
General Administration	$1,700,000
Police	2,000,000
Fire	2,300,000
Health and Welfare	1,800,000
Public Works	1,900,000
Total Appropriations	$9,700,000

a. Assuming a reasonably responsible level of financial management, what is the minimum figure the administration of King City expects to have as the General Fund Balance at the conclusion of fiscal year 2001? Explain.

b. Show in general journal form the entry, or entries, that would be necessary to record the budget, assuming it is legally approved, at the beginning of the budget year, 2002. Show entries in subsidiary ledger accounts as well as general ledger accounts.

3–5. Appropriations. Assume purchase orders and contracts in the following estimated amounts were issued by King City (Problem 3–4), chargeable against the 2002 appropriations shown below:

General Administration	$100,000
Police	180,000
Fire	200,000
Public Works	135,000
Total	$615,000

a. Show the necessary entry in general journal form to record the issuance of purchase orders and contracts. (Show entries in subsidiary ledger accounts as well as general ledger accounts.)

b. Explain why GASB standards for state and local governmental units require that the estimated amount of purchase orders issued be recorded in the accounts of governmental fund types, whereas FASB standards for business organizations do not have a similar requirement.

3–6. Allotments. The common council of the City of Dexter adopted for the City General Fund a budget that is shown below in summary form:

Estimated Revenues:	
Taxes	$11,420,000
Licenses and Permits	2,740,000
Fines and Forfeits	3,790,000
Intergovernmental Revenue	3,010,000
Charges for Services	2,400,000
Total Estimated Revenues	$23,360,000
Appropriations:	
Personal Services	$10,540,000
Contractual Services	2,560,000
Commodities	5,435,000
Capital Outlays	4,639,000
Total Appropriations	$23,174,000

a. Assume that the City of Dexter employs a system of quarterly allotments to enhance expenditure control. Show in general journal form the entry to record the complete budget as of January 1, the first day of the fiscal year, in general ledger and subsidiary ledger accounts.

b. Assume allotments for the first quarter were as follows; make the journal entry as of January 1 to record the allotments in general ledger and subsidiary ledger accounts. Show subsidiary ledger accounts for both unallotted appropriations and allotments.

Personal Services	$2,660,000
Contractual Services	640,000
Commodities	1,350,000
Capital Outlays	1,400,000
Total	$6,050,000

3–7. **Subsidiary Ledgers.** The printout of the Estimated Revenues and Revenues subsidiary ledger accounts for the General Fund of the City of Salem as of February 28, 2002 appeared as follows:

Property Taxes

Date	*Tracer*	*Estimated Revenues*	*Revenues*	*Balance*
01 01	45 1	9,600,000		9,600,000
02 28	45 6	(20,000)	9,580,000	–0–

Licenses and Permits

Date	*Tracer*	*Estimated Revenues*	*Revenues*	*Balance*
01 01	45 1	1,600,000		1,600,000
01 31	27 4		640,000	960,000
02 27	27 7		200,000	760,000

Intergovernmental Revenue

Date	*Tracer*	*Estimated Revenues*	*Revenues*	*Balance*
01 01	45 1	3,200,000		3,200,000
02 28	27 7		1,500,000	1,700,000

Charges for Services

Date	*Tracer*	*Estimated Revenues*	*Revenues*	*Balance*
01 01	45 1	600,000		600,000
02 28	27 7		160,000	440,000

Assuming the above printout is correct in all details and that there are no other General Fund revenue classifications, you are to answer the following questions. *Show all necessary computations in good form.*

a. What should be the balance of the Estimated Revenues control account?

b. What was the original approved budget for Estimated Revenues for 2002?

c. (1) Was the FY2002 Estimated Revenues budget adjusted during the year?
(2) If so, when?
(3) If so, how much?
(4) If so, was the original budget increased or decreased?

d. What should be the balance of the Revenues control account?

e. If in the Tracer column of the accounts the numerals 45 stand for General Journal and the numerals 27 stand for Cash Receipts Journal, what is the most likely reason that revenues from Property Taxes are first recognized in a general journal entry, whereas revenues from the other three sources are first recognized in cash receipts journal entries?

3–8. Appropriations, Encumbrances, Expenditures. The Director of Finance of the Town of Liberty has asked you to determine whether the appropriation, expenditures, and encumbrances comparison for Office Supplies for a certain year (reproduced on page 112) presents the information correctly.

You determine that the General Fund manual of accounts describes Office Supplies as "tangible items of relatively short life to be used in a business office." You also determine that the transfer of stationery, at cost, to the town water utility was properly authorized; the Water Utility Fund is to pay the General Fund $330 for the supplies. The transfer of $46,000 from Office Supplies to Personal Services was made by an accounting clerk without knowledge of superiors to avoid reporting that the Personal Services appropriation had been overexpended.

Required

In order to determine whether the comparison shown below is correct you are required to compute each of the following. Organize and label your computations so the director of finance can understand them.

a. The final amended amount of the appropriation for Office Supplies for the year.

b. The valid amount of encumbrances outstanding against this appropriation at the end of the year.

c. The net amount of expenditures made during the year that were properly chargeable to this appropriation.

d. The unencumbered unexpended balance of this appropriation.

TOWN OF LIBERTY
GENERAL FUND
APPROPRIATION, EXPENDITURES, AND ENCUMBRANCES
OFFICE SUPPLIES

Purchase No.	Explanation	Appropriations	Encumbrances		Expenditures	Available Balance
			Debits	Credits		
	Budget legally approved	62,200				62,200
350	Purchase order—computer paper		600			61,600
356	Purchase order—stationery			420		62,020
	Refund of prior year expenditure	30				62,050
370	Purchase order—filing supplies		400			61,650
350	Invoice			605	605	61,045
378	Purchase order—microcomputer		3,160			57,885
380	Contract for washing office windows		2,000			55,885
356	Invoice			420	420	55,885
	Cost of stationery issued to town's water utility	330				56,215
	Refund on P.O. 350	10				56,225
370	Invoice			400	425	55,800
380	Invoice				2,000	53,000
385	Purchase order—furniture		7,000			46,000
	Transfer to Personal Services appropriation	(46,000)				–0–

Continuous Problem

3–B. The following budget for the General Fund of the City of Bingham (see Problem 2–B) was legally adopted for the fiscal year ending June 30, 2002.

Estimated Revenues:	
Property Taxes	$3,104,000
Interest and Penalties on Taxes	29,000
Licenses and Permits	443,000
Fines and Forfeits	376,000
Intergovernmental Revenue	531,000
Charges for Services	110,000
Miscellaneous Revenues	70,000
Total Estimated Revenues	$4,663,000

Appropriations:	
General Government	$ 780,000
Public Safety	1,650,000
Public Works	710,000
Health	200,000
Public Welfare	250,000
Recreation	375,000
Contributions to Retirement Funds	344,000
Miscellaneous Appropriations	66,000
Total Appropriations	$4,375,000

Required

a. Record the budget in the general journal of the General Fund. Include the general ledger accounts, subsidiary ledger accounts, and adequate explanations for each entry (and for all journal entries in all B problems).

b. Post the entries to *general ledger* accounts.

c. (1) Open *revenues ledger* accounts for the seven sources of Estimated Revenues listed in the budget for the City of Bingham General Fund. (An appropriate form is illustrated in Chapter 3.) Allow five lines for each account.

(2) Post to the appropriate revenues ledger accounts the amounts shown in the general journal entry.

d. (1) Open *appropriations ledger* accounts for the eight classifications of appropriations shown in the budget for the General Fund. (An appropriate form is illustrated in Chapter 3.) Allow 10 lines for each account.

(2) Post the amounts shown in the general journal entry to the proper accounts in the appropriations ledger.

CHAPTER 4

Accounting for Governmental Operating Activities—Illustrative Transactions and Financial Statements

Learning Objectives

After studying this chapter, you should be able to:

- Recognize typical operating transactions for governmental activities and prepare appropriate journal entries at both the government-wide and fund levels.
- Account for expense recognition at the government-wide level and expenditures at the fund level for goods encumbered in the prior year.
- Explain the contents of interim balance sheets and budgetary comparison schedules.
- Explain and make entries for internal exchange transactions.
- Prepare adjusting entries, including reclassification of property taxes to delinquent status, accrual of interest and penalties for property taxes, and adjustment for inventories.
- Prepare a pre-closing trial balance for the General Fund.
- Prepare closing journal entries.
- Prepare year-end General Fund financial statements.
- Account for operating grants and other financial assistance using special revenue funds.
- Account for interfund transactions; distinguish between intra- and inter-activity transactions; and explain accounting for intra-entity transactions.
- Account for transactions of a permanent fund.

In Chapter 3, the use of general ledger budgetary control accounts (Estimated Revenues, Estimated Other Financing Sources, Appropriations, Estimated Other Financing Uses, and Encumbrances) and related operating statement accounts (Revenues, Other Financing Sources, Expenditures, and Other Financing Uses) was discussed and illustrated. The necessity for subsidiary ledgers, or equivalent computer files or ledgers, supporting the budgetary control accounts and related operating statement accounts was also discussed. In this chapter, common transactions and events arising from the operating activities of a hypothetical local governmental unit, the Town of Brighton, are discussed, and appropriate accounting entries and financial statements are illustrated.

Operating transactions and events affect, of course, the Town's government-wide accounting records and financial statements as well as those of its General Fund. Thus, transactions are recorded, where appropriate, in both the general journal used to collect financial information for government-wide financial reporting and the general journal for the General Fund. We call this a "dual-track" accounting system similar to that used to account for federal government agencies (see Chapter 12). In addition, for the sake of completeness, subsidiary ledger accounts as well as general ledger accounts are illustrated for the General Fund. The accounting structure illustrated in this chapter for the General Fund is also applicable to special revenue funds of state and local governmental units.

Illustrative Case

The Town of Brighton's [partial] government-wide Statement of Net Assets, showing only the governmental activities, and its General Fund Balance Sheet, both at the end of the 2001 fiscal year, are presented in Illustration 4–1. Because this chapter focuses on *governmental* operating activities, only the financial information for the governmental activities column is presented at this time. The Town of Brighton does have business-type activities, but those activities will be discussed in Chapter 7 of the text. Although the Town has no discretely presented component units, the column is shown in the statement of net assets simply to illustrate the recommended financial statement format.

Measurement Focus and Basis of Accounting

As discussed at several points in the earlier chapters, the government-wide statement of net assets reports financial position using the economic resources measurement focus and the accrual basis of accounting—in short, using accounting principles similar to accounting for business entities. In contrast, the General Fund Balance Sheet reports financial position using the current financial resources measurement focus and the modified accrual basis of accounting. Although both of these statements represent financial position at the same point in time, even a casual comparison reveals dramatic differences. A brief examination of those differences might be useful.

Perhaps the most striking difference between the two statements is that the Statement of Net Assets reports both capital assets and long-term liabilities, whereas the General Fund Balance Sheet reports only current financial resources

Illustration 4–1

TOWN OF BRIGHTON
STATEMENT OF NET ASSETS
DECEMBER 31, 2001

	Primary Government			
	Governmental Activities	*Business-Type Activities*	*Total*	*Component Units (None)*
Assets				
Cash	$ 477,500	(Omitted intentionally)		
Investments	1,339,040			
Receivables (net)	653,338			
Capital assets (net)	19,330,018			
Total Assets	21,799,896			
Liabilities				
Vouchers payable	320,000			
Accrued interest payable	50,000			
Due to federal government	90,000			
Current portion of long-term debt	200,000			
Bonds payable	3,300,000			
Total Liabilities	3,960,000			
Net Assets				
Invested in capital assets, net of related debt	15,830,018			
Restricted for:				
Debt service	1,659,978			
Unrestricted	349,900			
Total Net Assets	$17,839,896			

TOWN OF BRIGHTON
GENERAL FUND BALANCE SHEET
DECEMBER 31, 2001

Assets

Cash		$190,000
Taxes receivable—delinquent	$660,000	
Less: Estimated uncollectible delinquent taxes	50,000	610,000
Interest and penalties receivable on taxes	13,200	
Less: Estimated uncollectible interest and penalties	3,300	9,900
Total Assets		$809,900

Liabilities and Fund Equity

Liabilities:		
Vouchers payable		$320,000
Due to federal government		90,000
Total liabilities		410,000
Fund Equity:		
Reserve for encumbrances—2001	$127,000	
Fund balance	272,900	
Total Fund Equity		399,900
Total Liabilities and Fund Equity		$809,900

and current liabilities to be paid from current financial resources. *Current financial resources* include cash and items (such as marketable securities and receivables) expected to be converted into cash in the current period or soon enough thereafter to pay current period obligations. Prepaid items and inventories of supplies, if material, are also included in current financial resources.

Another major difference is that the information reported in the governmental activities column of the Statement of Net Assets includes financial information for *all* governmental activities, not just for the General Fund. For example, the Town of Brighton also has debt service funds whose cash and receivables are combined with those of the General Fund in the assets section of the Statement of Net Assets. The investments reported in the Statement of Net Assets belong to the debt service funds. In fact, it will be noted that $1,659,978 of net assets are restricted for purposes of paying debt service (principal and interest) on long-term debt. [Note: the debt service funds are discussed in Chapter 6.]

There are some other less important but still noteworthy differences. One noteworthy difference involves format. The Town's Statement of Net Assets is in the GASB-recommended net assets format (that is, assets minus liabilities equals net assets) rather than the traditional balance sheet format (assets equals liabilities plus fund equity). This is not a *necessary* condition, however, as GASB *Statement No. 34* permits governments the option of preparing a government-wide *balance sheet* rather than statement of net assets, if they prefer.

An alert reader may have noted that the Statement of Net Assets reports financial information in a more condensed manner than does the General Fund Balance Sheet. The primary reason for reporting more aggregated financial information is that the government-wide financial statements, along with the required management's discussion and analysis (MD&A), are intended to provide a broad overview of the government's financial position. Additional detail is provided in the notes to the financial statements (not provided in this chapter for sake of brevity), as well as in the fund financial statements.

In the case of the Town of Brighton the $349,900 amount reported for unrestricted net assets in the Statement of Net Assets is only $50,000 less than the $399,900 reported as the total fund equity of the General Fund. In practice these amounts may be markedly different as many governments will have unreserved net assets in other governmental fund types that will be reported as part of the governmental activities unrestricted net assets. At any rate, neither the Net Assets at the government-wide level nor the Fund Equity at the fund level are analogous to the Stockholders' Equity of an investor-owned entity. Residents have no legal claim on any net assets or fund equity of the government.

A few final points should be noted about the General Fund Balance Sheet before we move on to recording the budget and operating transactions. The arithmetic difference between total financial resources and total liabilities of the fund is the Fund Equity. The Town of Brighton's General Fund Balance Sheet illustrates that at December 31, 2001, a portion of Fund Equity is reserved because not all of the purchase orders issued in fiscal year 2001 were filled by the end of that year. The liability that will result when goods or services are received in fulfillment of purchase orders outstanding on December 31, 2001, is estimated to total $127,000, as shown by the Reserve for Encumbrances—2001 in the balance sheet. The portion of Fund Equity not reserved is shown as Fund Balance in the balance sheet. An alternate and more descriptive designation would be "Available for Appropriation" because this amount ($272,900 in the Town of Brighton General Fund Balance Sheet) is the excess of financial resources over actual liabilities and amounts expected to become liabilities when goods and services on order at the balance sheet date are received.

Illustrative Journal Entries

Typical journal entries related to governmental activities are illustrated in the following pages. Some of these activities, for example those relating to the General Fund budget, have no effect on the government-wide financial statements. Other activities or transactions affect both the General Fund financial statements and the governmental activities column of the government-wide financial statements. Still other activities, such as recording depreciation expense or accrual of interest on long-term debt, affect only the government-wide financial statements and have no effect on the General Fund's or any other governmental fund's statements. Examples of the latter journal entries are provided in Chapters 6 and 9.

For the illustrative journal entries that follow, *separate* journal entries are illustrated for the General Fund general journal and governmental activities general journal (government-wide level) if the account titles or amounts differ in any respect. For activities or transactions in which the entries in the General Fund and governmental activities journals are identical, only a single journal entry is provided. In these cases, the heading for the entry indicates that the entry applies to both journals.

Recording the Budget

As discussed in detail in Chapter 3, the budget should be recorded in the accounts of each fund for which a budget is legally adopted. Entry 1, below, illustrates an entry to record the budget in the general journal for the General Fund of the Town of Brighton for fiscal year 2002. (The entry is shown in combined form to illustrate that format. The detail shown is assumed to be the detail needed to comply with laws applicable to the Town of Brighton. Since both Estimated Revenues and Appropriations accounts refer only to the fiscal year 2002 budget and will be closed at the end of the year, it is not necessary to incorporate "2002" in the title of either.)

	General Ledger		Subsidiary Ledger	
	Debits	*Credits*	*Debits*	*Credits*
General Fund:				
1. Estimated Revenues	3,986,000			
Fund Balance	194,000			
Appropriations		4,180,000		
Revenues Ledger:				
Property Taxes			2,600,000	
Interest and Penalties on Delinquent Taxes			13,000	
Sales Taxes			480,000	
Licenses and Permits			220,000	
Fines and Forfeits			308,000	
Intergovernmental Revenue			280,000	
Charges for Services			70,000	
Miscellaneous Revenues			15,000	
Appropriations Ledger:				
General Government				660,000
Public Safety				1,240,000
Public Works				910,000
Health and Welfare				860,000
Parks and Recreation				315,000
Contributions to Retirement and Other Postemployment Benefits Plans				180,000
Miscellaneous Appropriations				15,000

Tax Anticipation Notes Payable

In the December 31, 2001, Statement of Net Assets and General Fund Balance Sheet of the Town of Brighton, two items, Vouchers Payable and Due to Federal Government, are current liabilities. Assuming there will be a need to pay these in full within 30 days after the date of the Balance Sheet, the Town Treasurer will be forced to do some cash forecasting because the balance of Cash in the General Fund is not large enough to pay the $410,000 debt. In addition to this immediate problem, the Treasurer, and most governmental treasurers, face the problem that cash disbursements during a fiscal year tend to be approximately level month by month, whereas cash receipts from major revenue sources are concentrated in just a few months. For example, property tax collections are concentrated in two separate months, such as May and November, when the installments are due; collections by a local government from the state or federal government of revenues collected by superior jurisdictions for distribution to a local government are also usually concentrated in one or two months of the year.

Knowing these relationships, the Treasurer of the Town of Brighton may forecast the need to disburse approximately one-fourth of the budgeted appropriations before major items of revenue are received; one-fourth of $4,180,000 is $1,045,000. This amount plus current liabilities at the beginning of the year, $410,000, equals $1,455,000 expected cash disbursements in the period for which the forecast is made. Experience may indicate that a conservative forecast of collections of delinquent taxes and interest and penalties thereon during the forecast period will amount to $425,000. Further, assume the Treasurer's review of the items in the Estimated Revenues budget indicates that at least $140,000 will be collected in the forecast period. Therefore, total cash available to meet the $1,455,000 disbursements is $755,000 ($190,000 cash as of the beginning of the period, plus the $425,000 and $140,000 items just described), leaving a deficiency of $700,000 to be met by borrowing. The taxing power of the government is ample security for short-term debt; local banks customarily meet the working capital needs of a governmental unit by accepting a **tax anticipation note** from the unit. Additional discussion of cash budgeting is provided in Chapter 13. If the amount of $700,000 is borrowed at this time, the necessary entries are:

	General Ledger		Subsidiary Ledger	
General Fund and Governmental Activities:	*Debits*	*Credits*	*Debits*	*Credits*
2. Cash	700,000			
Tax Anticipation Notes Payable		700,000		

[Note: Journal entries with the heading *Governmental Activities* refer to the general journal for governmental activities at the government-wide level. As stated previously, entries at the government-wide level reflect the economic resources measurement focus and accrual basis of accounting.]

Encumbrance Entry

Purchase orders for materials and supplies were issued in the total amount of $306,450; amounts chargeable against the appropriations for 2002 are shown as debits to Encumbrance Ledger accounts. (Since some encumbrance documents issued in 2002 will likely not be filled until the following year, it is convenient in General Fund entries to incorporate "2002" in each general ledger account title.) The entry to record the encumbrance for the purchase orders follows. [Recall that budgetary entries affect only funds for which a budget is legally adopted; they have no effect at the government-wide level.]

	General Ledger		Subsidiary Ledger	
General Fund:	*Debits*	*Credits*	*Debits*	*Credits*
3. Encumbrances—2002	306,450			
Reserve for Encumbrances—2002		306,450		
Encumbrances Ledger:				
General Government			28,000	
Public Safety			72,000	
Public Works			160,000	
Parks and Recreation			36,000	
Health and Welfare			10,000	
Miscellaneous Appropriations			450	

Payment of Liabilities as Recorded

Checks were drawn to pay the vouchers payable and the amount due to the federal government as of the end of 2001. The following entry would be made in the general journals for both the General Fund and governmental activities:

	General Ledger		Subsidiary Ledger	
General Fund and Governmental Activities:	*Debits*	*Credits*	*Debits*	*Credits*
4. Vouchers Payable	320,000			
Due to Federal Government	90,000			
Cash		410,000		

Note that it is not necessary in the above entry for the General Fund to know which appropriations were affected at the time goods and services giving rise to the liabilities were received, because under the modified accrual basis applicable to the General Fund, the appropriations were considered expended in the prior year, 2001, when the goods and services were received.

Payrolls and Payroll Taxes

The gross pay of employees of General Fund departments for the month of January 2002 amounted to $252,000. The Town does not use the encumbrance procedure for payrolls. Deductions from gross pay for the period amount to $19,278 for employees' share of FICA tax; $25,200, employees' federal withholding tax; and $5,040, employees' state withholding tax—the first two will, of course, have to be remitted by the Town to the federal government, and the last item will have to be remitted to the state government. The gross pay is chargeable to the appropriations in the General Fund as indicated by the Expenditures Ledger debits. Assuming the liability for net pay is vouchered, the entry in the General Fund is:

	General Ledger		Subsidiary Ledger	
General Fund:	*Debits*	*Credits*	*Debits*	*Credits*
5a. Expenditures—2002	252,000			
Vouchers Payable		202,482		
Due to Federal Government		44,478		
Due to State Government		5,040		
Expenditures Ledger:				
General Government			35,040	
Public Safety			156,120	
Public Works			29,160	
Health and Welfare			19,080	
Parks and Recreation			12,600	

In addition, the following entry would be required to record the payroll transaction in the governmental activities general journal at the government-wide level, using the accrual basis (expenses rather than expenditures):

	Debits	Credits
Governmental Activities:		
5b. Expenses—General Government	35,040	
Expenses—Public Safety	156,120	
Expenses—Public Works	29,160	
Expenses—Health and Welfare	19,080	
Expenses—Parks and Recreation	12,600	
Vouchers Payable		202,482
Due to Federal Government		44,478
Due to State Government		5,040

Recording the salaries and wages expenses in the manner shown in Entry 5b permits reporting direct expenses by function, as shown in Illustration 2–2 and as discussed in Chapter 3 in the discussion on expense classification in the government-wide statement of activities. If a government prefers to also record the expenses by natural classification (that is, as salaries and wages expense), it will be necessary to add additional classification detail; for example, Expenses—General Government—Salaries and Wages.

Payment of the vouchers for the net pay results in the following entry in both the General Fund and governmental activities journals:

	General Ledger		Subsidiary Ledger	
General Fund and Governmental Activities:	*Debits*	*Credits*	*Debits*	*Credits*
6. Vouchers Payable	202,482			
Cash		202,482		

Inasmuch as the Town is liable for the employer's share of FICA taxes ($19,278) and for contributions to additional retirement plans established by state law (assumed to amount to $5,400 for the pay period ended), it is necessary that the Town's liabilities for its contributions be recorded, as shown in Entry 7a. These obligations were provided for in the Appropriations budget under the account "Contributions to Retirement Plans."

	Debits	Credits	Debits	Credits
General Fund:				
7a. Expenditures—2002	24,678			
Due to Federal Government		19,278		
Due to State Government		5,400		
Expenditures Ledger:				
Contributions to Retirement Plans			24,678	

Entry 7b is also required to record the payroll expense on the accrual basis at the government-wide level.

	Debits	Credits	Debits	Credits
Governmental Activities:				
7b. Expenses—General Government	3,430			
Expenses—Public Safety	15,289			
Expenses—Public Works	2,856			
Expenses—Health and Welfare	1,869			
Expenses—Parks and Recreation	1,234			
Due to Federal Government		19,278		
Due to State Government		5,400		

The expenses in Entry 7b relate directly to payroll; hence it is assumed that a pro rata allocation of these items to functions is appropriate. For each function, that function's pro rata share is multiplied by the $24,678 total expense to obtain the amount of allocated expense. For example, the share allocated to General Government is $35,040/$252,000, or 13.9 percent, multiplied by $24,678, yielding an allocated expense of $3,430 (rounded to nearest whole dollar).

Recording Property Tax Levy

Entry 1 of this chapter shows that the estimated revenue for fiscal year 2002 from property taxes levied for the Town of Brighton General Fund is $2,600,000. If records of property tax collections in recent years, adjusted for any expected changes in tax collection policy and changes in local economic conditions, indicate that approximately 4 percent of the gross tax levy will never be collected, the **gross tax levy** must be large enough so that the collectible portion of the levy, 96 percent, equals the needed revenue from this source, $2,600,000. Therefore, the gross levy of property taxes for the General Fund of the Town of Brighton must be $2,708,333 ($2,600,000 ÷ .96). In an actual situation, property situated in the Town of Brighton also would be taxed for other funds of that Town; for various funds of other general purpose governmental units, such as the township and the county in which the property in the Town of Brighton is located; the various funds of special purpose governmental units that have the right to tax the same property, such as one or more independent school districts or a hospital district; and perhaps the state in which the Town is located.

The gross property tax levies for each fund of the Town of Brighton, and for each other general purpose and special purpose governmental unit, must be aggregated, and the aggregate levy for that unit divided by the assessed valuation of property within the geographical limits of that unit, in order to determine the **tax rate** applicable to property within the unit. In many states, a county official prepares bills for all taxes levied on property within the county; the same official, or another, acts as collector of all property taxes levied for the county and all governmental units within the county. Although the billing and collecting functions may be centralized, the taxes levied for each fund must be recorded as an asset of that fund. If the accounts are to be kept in conformity with generally accepted accounting principles, the portion of the taxes expected to be collectible (.96 of the total levy, in this example) must be recorded as revenues of that fund, and the portion expected to be uncollectible (.04 of the total levy, in this example) recorded in a "contra-asset" account, as illustrated by Entries 8a and 8b.

	General Ledger		Subsidiary Ledger	
General Fund:	*Debits*	*Credits*	*Debits*	*Credits*
8a. Taxes Receivable—Current	2,708,333			
Estimated Uncollectible Current Taxes		108,333		
Revenues		2,600,000		
Revenues Ledger:				
Property Taxes				2,600,000
Governmental Activities:				
8b. Taxes Receivable—Current	2,708,333			
Estimated Uncollectible Current Taxes		108,333		
General Revenues—Property Taxes		2,600,000		

As Entry 8a shows, since in the General Fund the general ledger control account, Revenues, is credited, an entry must also be made in the Revenues subsidiary ledger. Taxes Receivable—Current is also a control account, just as is the Accounts Receivable account of a business entity; each is supported by a subsidiary ledger that shows how much is owed by each taxpayer or customer. Ordinarily, the subsidiary ledger supporting the real property taxes receivable control is organized by parcels of property according to their legal descriptions, since unpaid taxes are liens against the property regardless of changes in ownership. Because of its conceptual similarity to accounting for business receivables, taxes receivable subsidiary ledger accounting is not illustrated in this text.

Recognition of Expenditures/ Expenses for Encumbered Items

When supplies and services ordered during the current year have been received and found to be acceptable, the suppliers' or contractors' invoices should be checked for agreement with purchase orders or contracts as to prices and terms, and for clerical accuracy. If everything is in order, the invoices are approved for payment. If, as is probable, the estimated liability for purchase orders and contracts was recorded in the General Fund in the Encumbrances account and in the appropriate subsidiary accounts, the encumbrance entry must be reversed, and expenditures must be recorded in the control account and appropriate subsidiary accounts in the amount of the actual liability for goods or services received. In addition, expenses and/or assets must be recorded at the government-wide level, as appropriate.

Assume goods and services ordered during 2002 by departments accounted for by the Town of Brighton General Fund (see Entry 3) are received. Invoices for the items received totaled $269,450; related purchase orders totaled $269,775. (The appropriations assumed to be affected are shown in Entries 9 and 10a for the General Fund.)

	General Ledger		Subsidiary Ledger	
General Fund:	*Debits*	*Credits*	*Debits*	*Credits*
9. Reserve for Encumbrances—2002	269,775			
Encumbrances—2002		269,775		
Encumbrances Ledger:				
General Government				12,250
Public Safety				72,000
Public Works				150,900
Parks and Recreation				30,000
Health and Welfare				4,175
Miscellaneous Appropriations				450
10a. Expenditures—2002	269,450			
Vouchers Payable		269,450		
Expenditures Ledger:				
General Government			12,300	
Public Safety			72,000	
Public Works			150,600	
Parks and Recreation			30,000	
Health and Welfare			4,100	
Miscellaneous Appropriations			450	

Assuming that the Town of Brighton uses periodic inventory methods and does not capitalize its inventory of supplies unless they are material, it would record purchases of supplies initially as direct expenses of the functions acquiring the items, as shown in Entry 10b. (Note: After discussion with the appropriate officials, the Town Accountant decided that the $450 expenditure charged to Miscellaneous Appropriations would most appropriately be considered a direct expense of the General Government function.)

	General Ledger		Subsidiary Ledger	
Governmental Activities:	*Debits*	*Credits*	*Debits*	*Credits*
10b. Expenses—General Government	12,750			
Expenses—Public Safety	72,000			
Expenses—Public Works	150,600			
Expenses—Parks and Recreation	30,000			
Expenses—Health and Welfare	4,100			
Vouchers Payable		269,450		

In practice, departments accounted for in the General Fund also make various equipment and perhaps other general capital asset acquisitions that are accounted for as "capital outlay" expenditures. Although capital outlay expenditures are not illustrated in this chapter, they would be accounted for in the General Fund in the same manner as were materials and supplies in Entries 3, 9, and 10a. At the government-wide level only an entry similar to Entry 10b would be required, except that the debit would be to equipment (or other capital asset category as appropriate).

Revenues Recognized on Cash Basis

Revenues from licenses and permits, fines and forfeits, and other sources not previously accrued are usually recognized on the cash basis. Collections to date in 2002 are assumed to be as shown in Entry 11a:

	General Ledger		Subsidiary Ledger	
General Fund:	*Debits*	*Credits*	*Debits*	*Credits*
11a. Cash	259,200			
Revenues		259,200		
Revenues Ledger:				
Licenses and Permits				100,000
Fines and Forfeits				151,000
Charges for Services				7,000
Miscellaneous Revenues				1,200

Of the above revenues, Licenses and Permits and Charges for Services are deemed by the Town of Brighton to be *program revenues* at the government-wide level. Licenses and Permits are attributed to the General Government function and Charges for Services were received from customers of the Parks and Recreation Department. Both Fines and Forfeits and Miscellaneous Revenues are recorded as *general revenues* at the government-wide level. Based on this information, the entry that should be made in the journal for governmental activities is shown in Entry 11b.

Governmental Activities:	General Ledger Debits	General Ledger Credits	Subsidiary Ledger Debits	Subsidiary Ledger Credits
11b. Cash	259,200			
Program Revenues—Charges for Services—General Government		100,000		
Program Revenues—Charges for Services—Parks and Recreation		7,000		
General Revenues—Fines and Forfeits		151,000		
General Revenues—Miscellaneous		1,200		

Collection of Delinquent Taxes

Delinquent taxes are subject to interest and penalties that must be paid at the time the tax bill is paid. It is possible for a government to record the amount of penalties at the time the taxes become delinquent. Interest may be computed and recorded periodically to keep the account on the accrual basis; it must also be computed and recorded for the period from the date of last recording to the date when a taxpayer pays delinquent taxes. Assume taxpayers of the Town of Brighton have paid delinquent taxes totaling $440,000, on which interest and penalties of $8,800 had been recorded as receivable at the end of 2001; further assume $600 additional interest was paid for the period from the first day of 2002 to the dates on which the delinquent taxes were paid. Since it is common for the cashier receiving the collections to be permitted to originate source documents that result only in credits to Taxes Receivable—Current, Taxes Receivable—Delinquent, or Interest and Penalties Receivable on Taxes, it is necessary to record the $600 interest earned in 2002 in a separate entry, such as the following:

General Fund:				
12a. Interest and Penalties Receivable on Taxes	600			
Revenues		600		
Revenues Ledger:				
Interest and Penalties on Delinquent Taxes				600

The corresponding entry at the government-wide level is:

Governmental Activities:		
12b. Interest and Penalties Receivable on Taxes	600	
General Revenues—Interest and Penalties on Delinquent Taxes		600

Collection of the delinquent taxes and interest and penalties is summarized in Entry 13, which is the entry that would be made in both the General Fund and governmental activities journals.

General Fund and Governmental Activities:		
13. Cash	449,400	
Taxes Receivable—Delinquent		440,000
Interest and Penalties Receivable on Taxes		9,400

Correction of Errors

No problems arise in the collection of current taxes if they are collected as billed; the collections are debited to Cash and credited to Taxes Receivable—Current. Sometimes, even in a well-designed and well-operated system, errors occur and must be corrected. If, for example, the assessed valuation of a parcel of property were legally reduced but the tax bill erroneously issued at the higher valuation, the following correcting entry would be made when the error was discovered, assuming the corrected bill to be $364 smaller than the original bill. (The error also caused a slight overstatement of the credit to Estimated Uncollectible Current Taxes in Entry 8, but the error in that account is not considered material and, for that reason, does not require correction.)

	General Ledger		Subsidiary Ledger	
General Fund:	*Debits*	*Credits*	*Debits*	*Credits*
14. Revenues	364			
Taxes Receivable—Current		364		
Revenues Ledger:				
Property Taxes			364	

An entry similar to Entry 14 would also be made at the government-wide level to correct the overstatement of General Revenues and Taxes Receivable—Current.

Postaudit may disclose errors in the recording of expenditures during the current year, or during a prior year. If the error occurred during the current year, the Expenditures account and the proper Expenditures subsidiary account can be debited or credited as needed to correct them. If the error occurred in a prior year, however, the Expenditures account in error has been closed to Fund Balance, so logically the correcting entry should be made to the Fund Balance account. The "all-inclusive income statement" practice that is considered appropriate for profit-seeking entities does not have equal acceptance in governmental accounting because of the greater importance of legal constraints on governmental actions. For example, if a governmental unit collects from a supplier an amount that was erroneously paid in a preceding year, the appropriation for the year of the collection is not increased by the amount collected; it remains as originally budgeted. As a practical matter, collections from suppliers of prior years' overpayments may be budgeted as Miscellaneous Revenues and recorded as credits to the Revenues account.

Receipt of Goods Ordered in Prior Year

As noted earlier in this chapter under the heading "Measurement Focus and Basis of Accounting," purchase orders and other commitment documents issued in 2001 and not filled or canceled by the end of that year total $127,000. This amount is designated as Reserve for Encumbrances—2001 in the December 31, 2001, General Fund Balance Sheet of the Town of Brighton. As stated previously, budgetary accounting has no effect on the government-wide financial statements, thus no encumbrance is recorded at the government-wide level when goods or services are ordered or contracted for. When the goods on order at the end of fiscal year 2001 are received in 2002 their actual cost is considered an Expenditure of the 2001 Appropriations to the extent of the amount encumbered in 2001; any additional amount must be charged to the 2002 Appropriations. The Appropriations account for 2001, however, was closed at the end of that year to Fund Balance, as were the other budgetary accounts for that year.

Although other procedures may be used, the authors prefer to reestablish the Encumbrances account at the beginning of fiscal year 2002, as shown in Entry 15 below, assuming that the goods were ordered by the Parks and Recreation function.[1] When goods or services ordered in 2001 are received in 2002 it is convenient to debit the Expenditures—2001 account when the liability account is credited and eliminate the encumbrance in the normal manner. At year-end, the Expenditures—2001 account is closed to Fund Balance, along with Expenditures—2002 and all other operating statement and budgetary accounts.

	General Ledger		Subsidiary Ledger	
General Fund:	*Debits*	*Credits*	*Debits*	*Credits*
15. Encumbrances—2001	127,000			
Fund Balance		127,000		
Encumbrances Ledger:				
Parks and Recreation—2001			127,000	

Assuming that all goods and services for which encumbrances were outstanding at the end of 2001 were received in 2002 at a total invoice cost of $127,250, Entries 16 and 17a are necessary in the General Fund and Entry 17b is made in the governmental activities journal. Notice that only the estimated amount, $127,000, is be charged to Expenditures—2001 since this was the amount of the encumbrance against the 2001 appropriation; the difference between the amount encumbered in 2001 and the amount approved for payment in 2002 must be charged against the 2002 appropriation for Parks and Recreation.

General Fund:				
16. Reserve for Encumbrances—2001	127,000			
Encumbrances—2001		127,000		
Encumbrances Ledger:				
Parks and Recreation—2001				127,000
17a. Expenditures—2001	127,000			
Expenditures—2002	250			
Vouchers Payable		127,250		
Expenditures Ledger:				
Parks and Recreation—2001			127,000	
Parks and Recreation—2002			250	
Governmental Activities:				
17b. Expenses—Parks and Recreation	127,250			
Vouchers Payable		127,250		

[1]State laws vary considerably regarding the treatment of appropriations and encumbrances at year-end. In some states, appropriations do not lapse at year-end. In others, appropriations lapse and goods encumbered at year-end require a new appropriation in the next year's budget, or else must be charged to the next year's normal appropriation. Discussion of the methods of accounting for the various alternative laws and practices is beyond the scope of this text.

Interim Financial Statements

Periodically during a year it is desirable to prepare financial statements for the information of administrators and members of the legislative branch of the governmental unit. Illustration 4–2 shows how a Balance Sheet would look for the Town of Brighton if it were prepared in 2002 after the entries numbered 1 through 17a and additional payroll entries not shown were made; the date is assumed to be March 31, 2002.

The Interim Balance Sheet, Illustration 4–2, reflects the balances of both actual and budgetary accounts. Instead of Assets, which those familiar with accounting for profit-seeking entities would expect, the caption must be Assets and Resources, because the excess of Estimated Revenues over Revenues is not an asset as of balance sheet date but does indicate the amount that will be added to assets when legally budgeted revenues are recognized. Similarly, the caption is not Equities, or Liabilities and Capital, or another title commonly found in financial reports of profit-seeking entities, but Liabilities and Fund Equity. The Liabilities section is consistent with that of profit-seeking entities, but the next section discloses the three subdivisions of the Fund Equity. The first presents the amount appropriated for the year, less the amount of appropriations that have been expended during the year to date, and less the amount of appropriations that have been encumbered by purchase orders and contracts outstanding at balance sheet date; the net is the amount that legally may be expended or encumbered during the remainder of the budget year. In Illustration 4–2 only one item, Reserve for Encumbrances, is shown in the second subdivision. This subdivision discloses the portion of net assets and resources that is not available for appropriation because expected liabilities exist (or because, as discussed later in the Town of Brighton example, certain assets will not be converted into cash in the normal operations of the fund). The remaining subdivision, Fund Balance, discloses that portion of the taxpayers' equity available for appropriation. Accordingly, in financial statement presentation, the word *Unreserved*, or the phrase *Available for Appropriation*, is sometimes used in place of *Fund Balance*. Fund Balance, it should be emphasized, is the excess of the sum of actual assets and budgeted resources over the sum of actual liabilities, available appropriations, and reserves for assets not available for appropriation; in short, it has both actual operating and budgetary aspects.

Interim statements and schedules should be prepared to accompany the interim balance sheet to disclose other information needed by administrators and members of the legislative body; a statement comparing the detail of budgeted and actual revenues is shown as Illustration 4–3, and a statement comparing appropriations, expenditures, and encumbrances in detail is shown as Illustration 4–4. Interim budget and actual comparison statements or schedules, such as those shown in Illustrations 4–3 and 4–4, are essential to sound budgetary control, and are more commonly used than is the interim balance sheet.

Illustration of Events Subsequent to Date of First Quarter Interim Statements

Transactions and events such as the collection of revenue and receivables, and the encumbering and expenditure of appropriations, would obviously occur frequently

Illustration 4–2 Interim Balance Sheet

TOWN OF BRIGHTON
GENERAL FUND BALANCE SHEET
AS OF MARCH 31, 2002

Assets and Resources			
Assets:			
Cash			$ 513,660
Taxes receivable—current		$2,707,969	
Less: Estimated uncollectible current taxes		108,333	2,599,636
Taxes receivable—delinquent		220,000	
Less: Estimated uncollectible delinquent taxes		50,000	170,000
Interest and penalties receivable on taxes		4,400	
Less: Estimated uncollectible interest and penalties		3,300	1,100
Total Assets			3,284,396
Resources:			
Estimated revenues		3,986,000	
Less: Revenues		2,859,436	1,126,564
Total Assets and Resources			$4,410,960
Liabilities and Fund Equity			
Liabilities:			
Vouchers payable			$ 581,450
Due to federal government			51,520
Due to state government			10,800
Tax anticipation notes payable			700,000
Total Liabilities			1,343,770
Fund Equity:			
Appropriations		$4,180,000	
Less: Expenditures—2002	$1,191,710		
Encumbrances—2002	36,675	1,228,385	
Available appropriations		2,951,615	
Reserve for encumbrances—2002		36,675	
Fund balance		78,900	
Total Fund Equity			3,067,190
Total Liabilities and Fund Equity			$4,410,960

Note: Expenditures—2001 (see Entry 17a) were closed in worksheet form to Fund Balance since these expenditures are not charged to current year (2002) appropriations and, from a management perspective, have already reduced the amount of Fund Balance available for appropriation. Expenditures—2001 are closed formally to Fund Balance as part of the closing entries illustrated later in this chapter.

in a governmental unit of any appreciable size. Since entries for the recurring events would be similar to the entries illustrated above, it seems unnecessary to present entries for these events in the portion of fiscal year 2002 subsequent to the date of the Interim Balance Sheet shown as Illustration 4–2. Entries for common General Fund transactions and events not previously illustrated are shown in the following sections.

Illustration 4–3

TOWN OF BRIGHTON
GENERAL FUND
STATEMENT OF ACTUAL AND ESTIMATED REVENUES
FOR THE THREE MONTHS ENDED MARCH 31, 2002

Sources of Revenues	*Estimated*	*Actual*	*Estimated Revenues Not Yet Realized*
Taxes:			
Property taxes	$2,600,000	$2,599,636	$ 364
Interest and penalties on taxes	13,000	600	12,400
Sales taxes	480,000	—	480,000
Total taxes	3,093,000	2,600,236	492,764
Licenses and permits	220,000	100,000	120,000
Fines and forfeits	308,000	151,000	157,000
Intergovernmental revenue	280,000	—	280,000
Charges for services	70,000	7,000	63,000
Miscellaneous revenues	15,000	1,200	13,800
Total General Fund Revenue	$3,986,000	$2,859,436	$1,126,564

Illustration 4–4

TOWN OF BRIGHTON
GENERAL FUND
STATEMENT OF BUDGETED
AND ACTUAL EXPENDITURES AND ENCUMBRANCES
FOR THE THREE MONTHS ENDED MARCH 31, 2002

Function	*Appropriations*	*Expenditures of 2002 Appropriations*	*Outstanding Encumbrances*	*Available Appropriations*
General government	$ 660,000	$ 129,100	$15,750	$ 515,150
Public safety	1,240,000	592,400	—	647,600
Public works	910,000	247,800	9,100	653,100
Health and welfare	860,000	67,700	5,825	786,475
Parks and recreation	315,000	72,000	6,000	237,000
Contributions to retirement plans	180,000	82,260	—	97,740
Miscellaneous appropriations	15,000	450	—	14,550
Total General Fund	$4,180,000	$1,191,710	$36,675	$2,951,615

Revision of the General Fund Budget

Comparisons of budgeted and actual revenues, by sources, and comparisons of departmental or program appropriations with expenditures and encumbrances, as well as interpretation of information that was not available at the time the budgets were originally adopted, may indicate the desirability or necessity of legally amending the budget during the fiscal year. For example, the Statement of Actual and Estimated Revenues for the three months ended March 31, 2002 (Illustration 4–3), shows that over 70 percent of the revenues budgeted for the General Fund of the Town of Brighton for 2002 have already been realized—almost entirely because revenue from property taxes is recognized on the accrual basis, whereas in this illustrative case revenues from all other sources have been recognized on the cash basis during the three-month period for which entries are illustrated. Consequently, administrators of the Town must review the information shown in Illustration 4–3 and determine whether the budget that was legally approved before the beginning of 2002 appears realistic or whether changes should be made in the Revenues budget in light of current information about local economic conditions; possible changes in state or federal laws relating to grants, entitlements, or shared revenues; or other changes relating to license and permit fees, fines, forfeits, and charges for services. Similarly, revenue collection procedures and revenue recognition policies should be reviewed to determine if changes should be made in the remaining months of the year. Assume the Town of Brighton's General Fund Revenues budget for 2002 has been reviewed as described and the budget is legally amended to reflect that revenues from Charges for Services are expected to be $5,000 more than originally budgeted, and Miscellaneous Revenues are expected to be $10,000 more than originally budgeted; revenues from other sources are not expected to be materially different from the original 2002 budget. Entry 18 records the amendment of the Revenues budget, as well as the amendment of the Appropriations budget, as discussed below.

Information shown in Illustration 4–4 should be reviewed by administrators of the Town of Brighton to determine if the appropriations legally approved before the beginning of 2002 appear realistic in light of expenditures of the 2002 budget incurred in the first three months of 2002 and encumbrances outstanding on March 31 of that year. Illustration 4–4 shows that total cumulative expenditures and outstanding encumbrances exceed 29 percent of the total appropriations for 2002, which can be related to the fact that as of March 31, the year is almost 25 percent over. By function, however, cumulative expenditures and outstanding encumbrances range from 3 percent of the Miscellaneous appropriation to almost 48 percent of the Public Safety appropriation. Therefore, each appropriation should be reviewed carefully in whatever detail is available, in light of current information about expenditures needed to accomplish planned services during the remainder of 2002. Assume the Town of Brighton's General Fund appropriations for 2002 have been reviewed and are legally amended to reflect a $50,000 decrease in the appropriation for Public Works and an $80,000 increase in the appropriation for Public Safety. Entry 18 reflects the legal amendment of appropriations for 2002, as well as the amendment of the Revenues budget. Note the net increase in Appropriations ($30,000) is larger than the net increase in Estimated Revenues ($15,000), requiring a decrease in Fund Balance.

	General Ledger		Subsidiary Ledger	
General Fund:	*Debits*	*Credits*	*Debits*	*Credits*
18. Estimated Revenues	15,000			
Fund Balance	15,000			
Appropriations		30,000		
Revenues Ledger:				
Charges for Services			5,000	
Miscellaneous Revenues			10,000	
Appropriations Ledger:				
Public Works			50,000	
Public Safety				80,000

Comparisons of Budget and Actual should be made periodically during each fiscal year. Generally, monthly comparisons are appropriate. In the Town of Brighton case, it is assumed that comparisons subsequent to the ones illustrated disclosed no further need to amend either the Revenues budget or the Appropriations budget for 2002.

Collection of Current Taxes

Collections of property taxes levied in 2002 for the General Fund of the Town of Brighton amount to $2,041,668. Since the revenue was recognized at the time the levy was recorded (see Entry 8), the following entry is made in both the General Fund and governmental activities journals.

General Fund and Governmental Activities:				
19. Cash	2,041,668			
Taxes Receivable—Current		2,041,668		

Repayment of Tax Anticipation Notes

As tax collections begin to exceed current disbursements, it becomes possible for the Town of Brighton to repay the local bank for the money borrowed on tax anticipation notes. Just as borrowing the money did not involve the recognition of revenue, the repayment of the principal is merely the extinguishment of debt of the General Fund and is not an expenditure. Payment of interest, however, must be recognized as the expenditure of an appropriation because it requires a reduction in the net assets of the fund. Assuming the interest to be $13,500, and the amount is properly chargeable to Miscellaneous Appropriations, the entry is:

General Fund:				
20a. Tax Anticipation Notes Payable	700,000			
Expenditures—2002	13,500			
Cash		713,500		
Expenditures Ledger:				
Miscellaneous Appropriations			13,500	

Procedures of some governmental units would require the interest expenditures to have been recorded as an encumbrance against Miscellaneous Appropriations at the time the notes were issued, and the liability for the principal and interest to have been vouchered before payment. Even if these procedures were followed by the Town of Brighton, the net result of all entries is achieved by Entry 20a.

A similar entry, shown as Entry 20b below, is made at the government-wide level, except that an expense rather than expenditure is recorded for the interest charged on the note. This expense is deemed to be an indirect expense that benefits no single function.

	General Ledger		Subsidiary Ledger	
Governmental Activities:	*Debits*	*Credits*	*Debits*	*Credits*
20b. Tax Anticipation Notes Payable	700,000			
Expenses— Interest on Tax Anticipation Notes	13,500			
Cash		713,500		

Internal Exchange Transactions

Water utilities ordinarily provide fire hydrants and water service for fire protection at a flat annual charge. A governmentally owned water utility accounted for by an enterprise fund should be expected to support the cost of its operations by user charges. Fire protection is logically budgeted for as an activity of the fire department, a General Fund department. Assuming the amount charged by the water utility to the General Fund for hydrants and water service is $30,000, and the fire department budget is a part of the Public Safety category in the Town of Brighton example, the General Fund should record its liability as:

General Fund:				
21a. Expenditures—2002	30,000			
Due to Other Funds		30,000		
Expenditures Ledger:				
Public Safety			30,000	

The corresponding entry to record the inter-activities transaction (between the governmental activities and business-type activities) at the government-wide level is given as Entry 21b.

Governmental Activities:				
21b. Expenses—Public Works	30,000			
Due to Business-Type Activities		30,000		

Governmental utility property is not assessed for property tax purposes, but it is common for governmental utilities to make an annual "in lieu of taxes" contribution to the General Fund in recognition of the fact the utility does receive police and fire protection and other services. In fact, an amount in lieu of taxes is sometimes billed to the utility's customers; the aggregate amount so collected is simply passed on to the General Fund.

If the water utility of the Town of Brighton agrees to contribute $25,000 to the General Fund in lieu of taxes, and that amount fairly represents the value of services received from the general government, the required journal entries for the General Fund and governmental activities are:

	General Ledger		Subsidiary Ledger	
General Fund:	*Debits*	*Credits*	*Debits*	*Credits*
22a. Due from Other Funds	25,000			
Revenues		25,000		
Revenues Ledger:				
Miscellaneous Revenues				25,000
Governmental Activities:				
22b. Due from Business-Type Activities	25,000			
General Revenues—Payments in lieu of taxes		25,000		

Internal exchange transactions of the nature illustrated by Entries 21 and 22 were called quasi-external transactions under the GASB standards being superseded by GASB *Statement No. 34*. Given that such transactions now affect both the government-wide and fund financial statements, the term *quasi-external transactions* is being eliminated, but no comparable term is provided in the standards. *Internal exchange transactions* captures both the inter-fund and inter-activity nature of these transactions, as well as reflecting the fact they are reciprocal exchange transactions; that is, transactions in which the parties to the transaction give and receive essentially equal value. Thus, it is appropriate for these transactions to recognize revenues and expenditures (or expenses at the government-wide level or in proprietary funds) in the funds involved, just as if each fund was transacting with an external entity. Other types of internal transactions between funds, between governmental and business-type activities, and between the primary government and its discretely presented component units are discussed in a later section of this chapter.

Adjusting Entries

Physical Inventories. If a governmental unit is large enough to have sizable inventories of supplies that are used by a number of departments and funds, it is generally recommended that the purchasing function be centralized and the supply activity be accounted for by an internal service fund. For one reason or another, some governments have not created the appropriate internal service fund and account for the supply activity as a part of the General Fund. In either case, accountants would feel better control was provided if perpetual inventory accounts were kept; this procedure is illustrated in Chapter 7. Many small cities, such as the Town of Brighton, not only account for supply activity in the General Fund but do so only on the basis of periodic physical inventories. (If only minor amounts are involved, no accounting records at all may be kept.)

The purchase of supplies must be authorized by an appropriation; therefore, when supplies are received the Expenditures account is debited. If the dollar amount of the physical inventory at the end of a fiscal year is larger than the dollar amount of the inventory at the end of the preceding fiscal year, it is obvious that the amount of inventory consumed or used during the year was less than the amount purchased (expended) during the year. Therefore, the Inventory of Supplies account should be debited to reflect the increase in inventory during the year and the Expenditures account should be credited by the corresponding amount, reflecting that the amount consumed was less than the amount purchased. (If the dollar amount of the physical inventory at year-end is smaller than the dollar amount of the inventory at the end of the prior year, the Expenditures account should be debited, and the Inventory of Supplies account credited, for the amount of the decrease in inventory.) This procedure is called the **consumption method** of accounting for inventory.

Since the inventory ordinarily will not be converted into cash in the normal operations of a governmental fund, it is not a financial asset whose carrying cost should be reflected in the Fund Balance as being available for appropriation. Consequently, the authors recommend that the Inventory account should be offset by a Reserve for Inventory account that is classified for balance sheet purposes in the same manner as discussed for Reserve for Encumbrances under the heading "Interim Financial Statements" earlier in this chapter—both represent elements of Fund Equity not available for appropriation. If a governmental unit uses the consumption method of inventory accounting, the Reserve for Inventory account is credited, and the Fund Balance account is debited, for the increase in the dollar amount of the physical inventory at the time the entries are made in the Inventory and Expenditures accounts. (If the dollar amount of the physical inventory has decreased, Reserve for Inventory should be debited and Fund Balance credited for the amount of the decrease.)[2]

Assuming that the dollar amount of the physical inventory of the Town of Brighton General Fund, as of the end of 2002, is $61,500, and that the inventory at the end of 2001 was such a small amount that it was not recorded, the increase in both the Inventory account and the Reserve for Inventory Account is $61,500. Entries 23a and 23b illustrate the consumption method of accounting for inventories in the General Fund and at the government-wide level, assuming, for the sake of simplicity, that all items in ending inventory were acquired by the Public Works appropriation:[3]

	General Ledger		Subsidiary Ledger	
General Fund:	*Debits*	*Credits*	*Debits*	*Credits*
23a. Inventory of Supplies	61,500			
Fund Balance	61,500			
Expenditures—2002		61,500		
Reserve for Inventory of Supplies		61,500		
Expenditures Ledger:				
Public Works				61,500
Governmental Activities:				
23b. Inventory of Supplies	61,500			
Expenses—Public Works		61,500		

[2]Apparently under the theory that the inventory could be liquidated or else that the government can avoid having to appropriate financial resources for inventory in the next period, GASB standards allow an option of not establishing a fund balance reserve for inventory unless an established minimum amount must be maintained. GASB *Codification*, Sec. 1800.903.

[3]If perpetual inventories are used, Inventory of Supplies should be debited as inventory is purchased. In this case, Expenditures/Expenses is debited and Inventory of Supplies is credited as supplies are consumed or used.

As with several earlier entries, modified accrual accounting appears to require more complex journal entries than does accrual accounting. In this case, however, the added complexity of Entry 23a is attributable to the emphasis on budgetary accounting, which makes it necessary to record increases or decreases in Reserve for Inventory of Supplies and make detail entries in the Expenditures subsidiary ledger.

An alternative method of accounting for inventories of governmental funds—acceptable under GASB standards at the fund level—is known as the **purchases method.** In fact, this is the method most commonly used in governmental fund accounting. The purchases method is conceptually inconsistent with the accrual basis of accounting and therefore should not be used for accounting at the government-wide level or for proprietary funds. Under the purchases method the Expenditures account is not credited for the increase in the dollar amount of the physical inventory, nor is the Fund Balance account debited. The only entry required is the debit to the asset account, Inventory, with offsetting credit to the Reserve for Inventory account, for the amount of the increase in the dollar amount of the physical inventory (or the reverse in the event that the dollar amount of the physical inventory decreased). At the government-wide level, the entry in the governmental activities general journal would be a debit to Inventory of Supplies and credits to Expenses—(functions), where the functions (General Government, Public Safety, etc.) would be those whose supplies inventories have increased. In the case of the Town of Brighton, the government-wide entry would be identical to Entry 23b.

Write-Off of Uncollectible Delinquent Taxes. Just as officers of profit-seeking entities should review aged trial balances of receivables periodically in order to determine the adequacy of allowance accounts and authorize the write-off of items judged uncollectible, so should officers of a governmental unit review aged trial balances of taxes receivable and other receivables. Although the levy of property taxes creates a lien against the underlying property in the amount of the tax, accumulated taxes may exceed the market value of the property, or, in the case of personal property, the property may have been removed from the jurisdiction of the governmental unit. When delinquent taxes are deemed uncollectible, the related interest and penalties must also be written off. If the Treasurer of the Town of Brighton receives approval to write off delinquent taxes totaling $26,300 and related interest and penalties of $1,315, the entry in both the General Fund and governmental activities would be:

	General Ledger		Subsidiary Ledger	
General Fund and Governmental Activities:	*Debits*	*Credits*	*Debits*	*Credits*
24. Estimated Uncollectible Delinquent Taxes	26,300			
Estimated Uncollectible Interest and Penalties	1,315			
Taxes Receivable—Delinquent		26,300		
Interest and Penalties Receivable on Taxes		1,315		

When delinquent taxes are written off, the tax bills are retained in the files, although no longer subject to general ledger control, because changes in conditions may make it possible to collect the amounts in the future. If collections of written-off taxes are made, it is highly desirable to return the tax bills to general ledger control by making an entry that is the reverse of the write-off entry, so that the procedures described in connection with Entries 12 and 13 may be followed.

Reclassification of Current Taxes. Assuming all property taxes levied by the Town of Brighton in 2002 were to have been paid before the end of the year, any balance of taxes receivable at year-end is properly classified as **delinquent taxes** rather than *current*. The related allowance for estimated uncollectible taxes should also be transferred to the delinquent classification. An entry to accomplish this, using amounts assumed to exist in the accounts at year-end, is:

	General Ledger		Subsidiary Ledger	
General Fund and Governmental Activities:	*Debits*	*Credits*	*Debits*	*Credits*
25. Taxes Receivable—Delinquent	666,301			
Estimated Uncollectible Current Taxes	108,333			
Taxes Receivable—Current		666,301		
Estimated Uncollectible Delinquent Taxes		108,333		

Accrual of Interest and Penalties. Delinquent taxes are subject to interest and penalties, as discussed previously. If the amount of interest and penalties earned in 2002 by the General Fund of the Town of Brighton and not yet recognized is $13,320, but it is expected that only $10,800 of that can be collected, the following entry is necessary:

	General Ledger		Subsidiary Ledger	
General Fund:				
26a. Interest and Penalties Receivable on Taxes	13,320			
Estimated Uncollectible Interest and Penalties		2,520		
Revenues		10,800		
Revenues Ledger:				
Interest and Penalties on Delinquent Taxes				10,800
Governmental Activities:				
26b. Interest and Penalties Receivable on Taxes ...	13,320			
Estimated Uncollectible Interest and Penalties		2,520		
General Revenues—Interest and Penalties on Delinquent Taxes		10,800		

Pre-Closing Trial Balance

Assuming the illustrated entries for the transactions and events pertaining to the year 2002 for the Town of Brighton have been made and posted, and a number of other entries—not illustrated because they pertain to similar transactions and events—have been made and posted, the trial balance below shows the General Fund general ledger accounts before closing entries:

TOWN OF BRIGHTON
GENERAL FUND
PRE-CLOSING TRIAL BALANCE
AS OF DECEMBER 31, 2002

	Debits	*Credits*
Cash	$ 145,800	
Taxes Receivable—Delinquent	666,300	
Estimated Uncollectible Delinquent Taxes		$ 88,000
Interest and Penalties Receivable on Taxes	3,085	
Estimated Uncollectible Interest and Penalties		1,985
Due from Other Funds	25,000	
Inventory of Supplies	61,500	
Estimated Revenues	4,001,000	
Revenues		4,015,000
Vouchers Payable		396,800
Due to Federal Government		126,520
Due to State Government		39,740
Due to Other Funds		30,000
Expenditures—2001	127,000	
Appropriations		4,210,000
Expenditures—2002	4,069,260	
Encumbrances—2002	70,240	
Reserve for Encumbrances—2002		70,240
Reserve for Inventory of Supplies		61,500
Fund Balance		129,400
	$9,169,185	$9,169,185

Closing Entries

The essence of the closing process for a governmental fund is the transfer of the balances of the operating statement accounts and the balances of the budgetary accounts for the year to the Fund Balance account. Individual accountants have preferences as to the sequence in which this is done, and as to the combinations of accounts in each closing entry. Any sequence and any combination, however, should yield the same result that closing entries for a profit-seeking entity do: All financial events in the history of the organization are summarized in the balance sheet accounts. Entry 27 shows the entry needed to close the accounts at year-end to fund balance of the General Fund. A closing entry is also made at this time to close the governmental activity operating statement accounts at the government-wide level. That entry is shown in Chapter 9 rather than this chapter since the governmental activities also include operating activities of the capital projects fund and debt service funds, two fund types discussed in Chapters 5 and 6, respectively.

General Fund:	General Ledger Debits	General Ledger Credits	Subsidiary Ledger Debits	Subsidiary Ledger Credits
27. Revenues	4,015,000			
Appropriations	4,210,000			
Fund Balance	42,500			
Estimated Revenues		4,001,000		
Expenditures—2002		4,069,260		
Expenditures—2001		127,000		
Encumbrances—2002		70,240		

Although Entry 27 affects five General Fund general ledger control accounts, it is not considered necessary to make closing entries in their subsidiary ledger accounts because in a manual system separate subsidiary ledgers are kept for each budget year.

It is important to notice the closing entry has the effect of reversing the entry made to record the budget (Entry 1) and the entry made to amend the budget (Entry 18). Therefore, after the closing entry is posted, the Fund Balance account is purely a balance sheet account and not one in which historical and expected effects are mixed, as is true during a year. That is, it again represents the net amount of financial resources available for appropriation for fund purposes.[4]

Year-End Financial Statements

The Balance Sheet for the General Fund of the Town of Brighton as of the end of 2002 is shown as Illustration 4–5. Since only balance sheet accounts are open, the captions "Assets" and "Liabilities and Fund Equity" are used instead of the captions in the Interim Balance Sheet, Illustration 4–2. The amount due from the Water Utility Fund is offset against the amount due to the same fund, and only the net liability is shown in the balance sheet, in conformity with GASB standards. It should be emphasized that it is *not* acceptable to offset a receivable from one fund against a payable to a different fund. The General Fund balance sheet would be presented in columnar form in the Balance Sheet—Governmental Funds, one of the several basic financial statements required for conformity with generally accepted accounting principles (see Illustrations 2–3 through 2–10). In addition, GASB standards require disclosures in the notes to the financial statements of a number of details regarding deposits with financial institutions, investments, property taxes, receivables, and other assets.

[4]As noted in Chapter 3, many governments record the difference between Estimated Revenues and Appropriations in a *Budgetary Fund Balance* account. In that case, the budgetary control accounts, Estimated Revenues and Appropriations, are closed to Budgetary Fund Balance and the remaining accounts are closed to an account called *Unreserved Fund Balance*. For sake of simplicity, in this text we use a single Fund Balance account that combines the preceding two accounts.

Illustration 4–5

TOWN OF BRIGHTON
GENERAL FUND BALANCE SHEET
AS OF DECEMBER 31, 2002

Assets		
Cash		$145,800
Taxes receivable—delinquent	$666,300	
Less: Estimated uncollectible delinquent taxes	88,000	578,300
Interest and penalties receivable on taxes	3,085	
Less: Estimated uncollectible interest and penalties	1,985	1,100
Inventory of supplies		61,500
Total Assets		$786,700
Liabilities and Fund Equity		
Liabilities:		
Vouchers payable	$396,800	
Due to federal government	126,520	
Due to state government	39,740	
Due to other funds	5,000	
Total Liabilities		$568,060
Fund Equity:		
Reserve for encumbrances—2002	70,240	
Reserve for inventory of supplies	61,500	
Fund balance	86,900	
Total Fund Equity		218,640
Total Liabilities and Fund Equity		$786,700

A second financial statement should be presented for the General Fund in the year-end comprehensive annual financial report, a Statement of Revenues, Expenditures, and Changes in Fund Balance (see Illustration 4–6). Illustration 4–6 presents the actual revenues and actual expenditures that resulted from transactions illustrated in this chapter and other transactions not illustrated because they were similar in nature. If the General Fund of the Town of Brighton had had any financial inflows or outflows resulting from interfund transfers, the receipt of debt issue proceeds, or other transactions not strictly defined as resulting in revenues or expenditures, their effects should be reported as Other Financing Sources or Other Financing Uses.

The Other Financing Sources (Uses) section in Illustration 4–6 shows a common means of disclosure of nonrevenue financial inflows and nonexpenditure financial outflows. Information shown here as Illustration 4–6 would be presented in columnar form in the Statement of Revenues, Expenditures, and Changes in Fund Balances—Governmental Funds (see Illustration 2–4).

Illustration 4–6

TOWN OF BRIGHTON
GENERAL FUND
STATEMENT OF REVENUES, EXPENDITURES, AND CHANGES IN FUND BALANCE
FOR THE YEAR ENDED DECEMBER 31, 2002

Revenues:		
Property taxes	$2,599,636	
Interest and penalties on delinquent taxes	11,400	
Sales taxes	485,000	
Licenses and permits	213,200	
Fines and forfeits	310,800	
Intergovernmental revenue	284,100	
Charges for services	82,464	
Miscellaneous revenues	28,400	
Total Revenues		$4,015,000
Expenditures:		
2002:		
General government	649,400	
Public safety	1,305,435	
Public works	778,300	
Health and welfare	850,325	
Parks and recreation	292,500	
Contributions to retirement plans	179,100	
Miscellaneous appropriations	14,200	
Expenditures—2002	4,069,260	
2001:		
Parks and recreation	127,000	
Total Expenditures		4,196,260
Excess of Expenditures over Revenues		(181,260)
Other Financing Sources (Uses):		
Interfund transfers in	–0–	
Interfund transfers out	–0–	
Total Other Financing Sources		–0–
Excess of Expenditures and Other Uses over Revenues and Other Sources		(181,260)
Increase in Reserve for Inventory of Supplies		(61,500)
Decrease in Reserve for Encumbrances during 2002		56,760
Change (Decrease) in Fund Balance for Year		(186,000)
Fund Balance, January 1, 2002		272,900
Fund Balance, December 31, 2002		$ 86,900

GASB *Statement No. 34* requires a Budgetary Comparison Schedule, as shown previously in Illustration 3–2, or, alternatively, a Statement of Revenues, Expenditures, and Changes in Fund Balance—Budget and Actual for the General Fund, as well as for each *major* special revenue fund for which a budget is legally adopted. Illustration 4–7 presents a budgetary comparison for the Town of Brighton General Fund prepared in the alternative Statement of Revenues, Expenditures, and Changes in Fund Balances—Budget and Actual format. Note that columns must be provided for both the legally adopted budget amounts as well as final amended amounts.

The amounts in the Revenues section of the Actual column in Illustration 4–7 present the same information as shown in the Revenues section of Illustration 4–6 because in the Town of Brighton example the General Fund revenues budget is on a GAAP basis, the same as actual Revenues. However, the amounts in the Expenditures section of the Actual column of the budgetary comparison statement (Illustration 4–7) differ from the Expenditures shown in Illustration 4–6 because under GAAP Expenditures chargeable to 2001 appropriations ($127,000) as well as Expenditures of the 2002 appropriations ($4,069,260) are reported in Illustration 4–6. Also, in the GAAP operating statement, Illustration 4–6, Encumbrances are not reported in the Expenditures section of the statement. In contrast, GASB standards require the amounts in the Actual column of Illustration 4–7 to conform with budgetary practices; therefore, in that statement Encumbrances outstanding at the end of fiscal 2002 are added to 2002 Expenditures because both are uses of the 2002 appropriation authority.

Note that in the budgetary comparison statement, Illustration 4–7, Expenditures (Public Works) is not adjusted for the inventory of supplies at year-end because the purchase of supplies was a use of 2002 appropriation authority, whether or not the supplies were used in 2002. Expenditures for 2001 are excluded from the Budget and Actual statement because that statement relates only to the 2002 budget. GASB standards require differences between the amounts reported in the two statements (Illustrations 4–6 and 4–7) to be reconciled in a separate schedule or in the notes to the required supplementary information. For example, the notes to the budgetary comparison statement for the Town of Brighton might include the following reconciliation of General Fund Expenditures reported in the two operating statements illustrated:

Expenditures for 2002, budgetary basis	$4,201,000
Less: Reserve for Encumbrances as of December 31, 2002	(70,240)
Reserve for Inventory of Supplies as of December 31, 2002	(61,500)
Expenditures for 2002, GAAP basis	$4,069,260

The presentation of Reserve for Encumbrances in Illustrations 4–5, 4–6, and 4–7, and in the illustrative reconciliation, is based on the assumption that amounts encumbered at year-end do not need to be appropriated for the following year. The amounts shown in Illustration 4–7 in the Expenditures section in the Actual Over

Illustration 4–7

TOWN OF BRIGHTON
GENERAL FUND
STATEMENT OF REVENUES, EXPENDITURES, AND
CHANGES IN FUND BALANCE—BUDGET AND ACTUAL
(NON-GAAP PRESENTATION)
FOR THE YEAR ENDED DECEMBER 31, 2002

	Budgeted Amounts			
	Original	*Final*	*Actual Amounts Budgetary Basis*	*Variance with Final Budget Over (Under)*
Revenues:				
Taxes:				
Property taxes	$2,600,000	$2,600,000	$2,599,636	$ (364)
Interest and penalties on taxes	13,000	13,000	11,400	(1,600)
Sales taxes	480,000	480,000	485,000	5,000
Total Taxes	3,093,000	3,093,000	3,096,036	3,036
Licenses and permits	220,000	220,000	213,200	(6,800)
Fines and forfeits	308,000	308,000	310,800	2,800
Intergovernmental revenue	280,000	280,000	284,100	4,100
Charges for services	70,000	75,000	82,464	7,464
Miscellaneous revenues	15,000	25,000	28,400	3,400
Total Revenues	3,986,000	4,001,000	4,015,000	14,000
Expenditures and Encumbrances:				
General government	660,000	660,000	658,850	(1,150)
Public safety	1,240,000	1,320,000	1,318,500	(1,500)
Public works	910,000	860,000	859,200	(800)
Health and welfare	860,000	860,000	858,650	(1,350)
Parks and recreation	315,000	315,000	312,500	(2,500)
Contributions to retirement plans	180,000	180,000	179,100	(900)
Miscellaneous appropriations	15,000	15,000	14,200	(800)
Total Expenditures	4,180,000	4,210,000	4,201,000	(9,000)
Excess of Expenditures over Revenues	194,000	209,000	186,000	(23,000)
Other Financing Sources (Uses)	–0–	–0–	–0–	–0–
Decrease in Fund Balance for Year	(194,000)	(209,000)	(186,000)	(23,000)
Fund Balance, January 1, 2002	272,900	272,900	272,900	–0–
Fund Balance, December 31, 2002	$ 78,900	$ 63,900	$ 86,900	$ 23,000

(Under) Budget column, however, disclose the portion of each appropriation for 2002 that was neither expended nor encumbered during that year; those amounts, totaling $9,000, are said to *lapse*, that is, become unavailable for expenditure or encumbrance, in the year following 2002.

Special Revenue Funds

As noted in Chapters 2 and 3, special revenue funds are needed when legal or policy considerations require separate funds to be created for current purposes other than those served by proprietary or fiduciary funds. An example of a special revenue fund created to demonstrate legal compliance is a Street Fund, which is largely financed by a local government's share of the motor fuel tax levied by the state to be used only for maintenance and construction of streets, roads, and bridges. A second example of a special revenue fund is a Library Operating Fund created to account for a special tax levy or simply the desire of the governing board to have a separate fund to account for an activity that differs from other governmental activities: A third example is a fund to account for grants received from a higher jurisdiction, such as a federal Community Development Block Grant (CDBG). Grant accounting is discussed briefly in the following paragraph. A final example, for governments that have implemented the GASB *Statement No. 34* reporting model, is a trust fund in which both the investment principal and the investment earnings are available to support a government program or the citizenry. A common example of the latter is a gift received under a trust agreement that can only be used to purchase works of art for public buildings. Under the current reporting model being superseded, such trusts are accounted for in expendable trust funds in the fiduciary category.

Accounting for Operating Grants

Grants received by a local government from the state or federal government—or received by a state from the federal government—are often restricted for specified operating purposes. Consequently, revenues of such grants are frequently accounted for by use of a special revenue fund. A number of grants provide that the grantor will pay the grantee on a reimbursement basis. In such instances, GASB standards require that the grant revenue not be recognized until the expenditure has taken place.[5] As an example of appropriate accounting procedures, assume a local government has been awarded a state grant to finance a fine arts program, but the state will provide reimbursement only after the grantee has made expenditures related to the fine arts program. As discussed in Chapter 3, this is an example of a voluntary nonexchange transaction in which an eligibility requirement (incurrence of allowable costs) must be met before the local government can recognize an asset and revenue. Assuming the grantee government creates a special revenue fund to account for the fine arts program, and has incurred qualifying expenditures or expense at the government-wide level, the required entries in both the special revenue fund and the governmental activities journals would be:

---

[5]GASB *Codification*, Appendix A; GASB *Statement No. 33*, par. 30.d.

Special Revenue Fund and Governmental Activities:	*Debits*	*Credits*
Expenditures (or expense)	50,000	
Vouchers Payable (or Cash)		50,000
Cash	50,000	
Revenues		50,000

The latter entry, of course, records the reimbursement, which presumably would be a short time after the expenditures are incurred. If the grant provided instead that a specified amount would be available for the current accounting period, regardless of whether qualifying expenditures are incurred, there would be no eligibility requirement (except that the grantee be an authorized recipient). In this case, it would be appropriate for the special revenue fund to recognize an asset (Grants Receivable) and Revenues upon notification by the state grantor agency. If the grant should specify that the amount is intended for a future accounting period, a liability account, Deferred Revenues, would be credited upon notification of the grant rather than Revenues. In the period for which the grant is intended, an entry would be made in the special revenue fund and governmental activities journals to debit Deferred Revenues and credit Revenues.

Financial Reporting

Special revenue fund accounting and financial reporting are essentially the same as for the General Fund, as described in depth in this chapter. Along with the General Fund, amounts for *major* special revenue funds would be included in the Balance Sheet and Statement of Revenues, Expenditures, and Changes in Fund Balances prepared for the governmental funds. A budgetary comparison schedule is also provided as required supplementary information (RSI) for each major special revenue fund. Elsewhere in the financial section of the government's CAFR, a combining balance sheet and combining operating statement should be provided for all *nonmajor* governmental funds, including nonmajor special revenue funds. An example of a Combining Statement of Revenues, Expenditures, and Changes in Fund Balances for nonmajor governmental funds is presented in Illustration 4–8.

Interfund Activity

Reciprocal Interfund Activity

Internal exchange transactions—those involving the sales and purchases of goods and services in a reciprocal exchange transaction between two funds—were discussed earlier in this chapter. These transactions are termed *interfund services provided and used* in GASB *Statement No. 34*. Other transactions between funds are discussed in this section.

Interfund Loans. **Interfund loans** are sometimes made from one fund to another with the intent that the amount be repaid. If the loan must be repaid

Illustration 4–8

SAMPLE CITY
COMBINING STATEMENT OF REVENUES,
EXPENDITURES, AND CHANGES IN FUND BALANCES
NONMAJOR GOVERNMENT FUNDS
FOR THE YEAR ENDED DECEMBER 31, 2002

	Special Revenue Funds			
	Impact Fees	*Local Gas Tax*	*Historic District*	*Total*
REVENUES				
Property taxes	$ —	$ —	$ —	$ —
Intergovernmental	—	1,312,670	60,426	1,373,096
Charges for services	30,708	—	—	30,708
Investment earnings	4,543	123,329	226	128,098
Miscellaneous	—	94	—	94
Total revenues	35,251	1,436,093	60,652	1,531,996
EXPENDITURES				
Current:				
General government	50,000	3,622	—	53,622
Public works	705,487	2,968,283	47,772	3,721,542
Debt service:				
Principal	—	—	—	—
Interest and other charges	—	—	—	—
Capital outlay	—	—	—	—
Total expenditures	755,487	2,971,905	47,772	3,775,164
Excess (deficiency) of revenues over expenditures	(720,236)	(1,535,812)	12,880	(2,243,168)
OTHER FINANCING SOURCES (USES)				
Proceeds of long-term debt	—	—	—	—
Payment to bond refunding escrow agent	—	—	—	—
Transfers in	—	—	177,000	177,000
Transfers out	—	(42,500)	—	(42,500)
Total other financing sources and uses	—	(42,500)	177,000	134,500
Net change in fund balances	(720,236)	(1,578,312)	189,880	(2,108,668)
Fund balances—beginning	1,030,484	3,547,620	—	4,578,104
Fund balances—ending	$ 310,248	$1,969,308	$189,880	$2,469,436

Source: GASB *Statement No. 34*, Appendix C, Exhibit H–2.

during the current year or soon thereafter, the lending fund should record a current receivable and the borrowing fund should record a current liability. This is

Debt Service Funds			Capital Projects Funds			Permanent Fund	
Central City Development	*Community Redevelopment*	*Total*	*Culvert Project*	*Bridge*	*Total*	*Cemetery Care*	*Total Nonmajor Governmental Funds*
$ 4,680,192	$ —	$ 4,680,192	$ —	$ —	$ —	$ —	$ 4,680,192
—	—	—	1,457,820	—	1,457,820	—	2,830,916
—	—	—	—	—	—	—	30,708
103,631	42,973	146,604	13,878	3,061	16,939	72,689	364,330
—	—	—	—	—	—	—	94
4,783,823	42,973	4,826,796	1,471,698	3,061	1,474,759	72,689	7,906,240
8,920	2,900	11,820	13,460	42,150	55,610	—	121,052
—	—	—	—	—	—	—	3,721,542
2,910,000	540,000	3,450,000	—	—	—	—	3,450,000
3,885,191	1,329,960	5,215,151	—	—	—	—	5,215,151
—	—	—	1,961,440	1,228,769	3,190,209	—	3,190,209
6,804,111	1,872,860	8,676,971	1,974,900	1,270,919	3,245,819	—	15,697,954
(2,020,288)	(1,829,887)	(3,850,175)	(503,202)	(1,267,858)	(1,771,060)	72,689	(7,791,714)
38,045,000	—	38,045,000	—	1,300,000	1,300,000	—	39,345,000
(37,284,144)	—	(37,284,144)	—	—	—	—	(37,284,144)
1,604,149	2,387,149	3,991,298	—	1,382,889	1,382,889	—	5,551,187
—	—	—	(113,167)	—	(113,167)	(63,409)	(219,076)
2,365,005	2,387,149	4,752,154	(113,167)	2,682,889	2,569,722	(63,409)	7,392,967
344,717	557,262	901,979	(616,369)	1,415,031	798,662	9,280	(398,747)
1,122,014	1,808,069	2,930,083	616,369	501,643	1,118,012	1,396,020	10,022,219
$ 1,466,731	$2,365,331	$ 3,832,062	$ 0	$1,916,674	$ 1,916,674	$1,405,300	$ 9,623,472

illustrated by the following journal entries assuming the General Fund makes a short-term loan in the amount of $100,000 to the Central Stores Fund, an internal service fund.

General Fund:	General Ledger Debits	General Ledger Credits	Subsidiary Ledger Debits	Subsidiary Ledger Credits
Interfund Loans Receivable—Current	100,000			
Cash		100,000		
Internal Service Fund:				
Cash	100,000			
Interfund Loans Payable—Current		100,000		

If this interfund loan did not require repayment for two (or more) years, the suffix "Noncurrent" should be used rather than "Current" to signify the noncurrent nature of the loan. As shown in the following entries, *Noncurrent is* added to each of the interfund loan receivable/payable accounts to indicate that the loan is not payable during the current year or soon thereafter.

General Fund:	General Ledger Debits	General Ledger Credits	Subsidiary Ledger Debits	Subsidiary Ledger Credits
Interfund Loans Receivable—Noncurrent	100,000			
Cash		100,000		
Internal Service Fund:				
Cash	100,000			
Interfund Loans Payable—Noncurrent		100,000		

Because the noncurrent receivable interfund loan receivable represents assets that are not available for current year appropriation in the General Fund, the Fund Balance account should be reserved for this amount, as was done for encumbered amounts and ending inventories of materials and supplies.

General Fund:		
Fund Balance	100,000	
Reserve for Noncurrent Interfund Loans Receivable		100,000

An interesting question is whether the illustrated interfund loans require journal entries at the government-wide level. The answer is no since GASB *Statement No. 34* requires that internal service fund amounts be reported in the governmental activities column of the government-wide financial statements. Interfund receivables and payables between two funds that are both included in governmental activities have no effect on the amounts reported in the government-wide Statement of Net Assets.

Nonreciprocal Interfund Activity

Interfund Transfers. The current reporting model being superseded identified two types of interfund transfers: *operating transfers* and *residual equity transfers*, which were reported in two different ways in governmental fund operating statements. Under GASB *Statement No. 34*, both types of transfers are described simply as **interfund transfers** and reported in the same manner—as other financing sources by the receiving fund and as other financing uses by the transferring funds.

Some interfund transfers, those formerly referred to as operating transfers, are generally periodic, routine transfers. For example, state laws may require that taxes be levied by a General Fund or a special revenue fund to finance an expenditure to be made from another fund (such as a debt service fund). Since the general rule is that revenues should be recorded as such only once, the transfer of tax revenue to the expending fund is recorded by the transferor as an Interfund Transfer Out and by the transferee as an Interfund Transfer In. As mentioned above, the transferee fund should recognize the transfer as an Other Financing Source not as Revenues.

Other interfund transfers, those formerly called residual equity transfers, are nonroutine transactions often made to establish or liquidate a fund. The creation of a fund by transfer of assets and/or resources from an existing fund to a new fund, or transfers of residual balances of discontinued funds to another fund, results in the recognition of an other financing source rather than as revenue by the new fund and an other financing use rather than an expenditure by the transferor fund. In the current model being superseded by *Statement No. 34*, residual equity transfers are reported in the Changes in Fund Balances section of the Statement of Revenues, Expenditures, and Changes in Fund Balances, rather than in the Other Financing Sources/Uses section.

Reimbursements. Internal exchange transactions for interfund services provided and used, described earlier in this chapter, are the only form of interfund transactions that result in the recognition of revenue by the receiving fund. In certain instances, one fund may record as an expenditure an item that should have been recorded as an expenditure by another fund. Often this is the result of an accounting error. When the second fund reimburses the first fund, the first fund should recognize the reimbursement as a reduction of its Expenditures account, not as an item of revenue. The second fund should debit Expenditures and credit Cash, as should have been done when the transaction initially occurred. Reimbursements are not reported in the financial statements, except for reporting expenditures/expenses in the correct fund.

Intra- Versus Inter-Activity Transactions (Government-wide Level)

In all the preceding examples, if the interfund transaction occurs between two governmental funds (or between a governmental fund and an internal service fund) or between two enterprise funds, that is, an **intra-activity transaction,** then neither governmental activities nor business-type activities is affected at the government-wide level. Interfund loans or transfers between a governmental fund (or internal service fund) and an enterprise fund results in an **inter-activity transaction.** These transactions are reported as "Internal Balances" on the government-wide Statement of Net Assets (see Illustration 2–1) and "Transfers" in the Statement of Activities (see Illustration 2–2). Except for internal exchange transactions between governmental funds and internal service funds, which are eliminated prior to preparing the government-wide financial statements, other internal exchange transactions should be reported as Revenues and Expenses in the Statement of Activity.

Intra-Entity Transactions

Intra-entity transactions are exchange or nonexchange transactions between the primary government and its blended or discretely presented component units. Transactions between the primary government and *blended* component units follow the same standards as for reciprocal and nonreciprocal interfund activity discussed in preceding paragraphs. Transactions between the primary government and *discretely presented* component units are treated as if the component units are external entities, and thus should be reported as revenues and expenses in the Statement of Activities. Amounts receivable and payable resulting from these transactions should be reported on a separate line in the Statement of Net Assets.

Permanent Funds

In the current reporting model, all fiduciary activities relating to trust and agency agreements are accounted for in trust and agency funds. GASB *Statement No. 34* makes significant changes in the accounting and financial reporting for such activities. Trust activities are particularly affected by these changes. In the reporting model being superseded, contributions received under trust agreements in which the principal amount is not expendable, but earnings are, are accounted for in nonexpendable trust funds. Most of these trusts, however, are established to benefit a government program or function, or the citizenry, rather than an external individual, organization, or government. Trusts of the first type are now called **public-purpose trusts;** trusts of the second type are **private-purpose trusts.**

The *Statement No. 34* model requires that public-purpose trusts for which the earnings are expendable for a specified purpose, but the principal amount is not expendable (also referred to as endowments), must be accounted for in a governmental fund called a **permanent fund.** Thus, accounting for these funds has been shifted from a fiduciary fund type (nonexpendable trust fund) to a governmental fund type. Public-purpose trusts for which both principal and earnings thereon can be expended for a specified purpose are accounted for in the current model as expendable trust funds, a fiduciary fund type. The *Statement No. 34* reporting model requires these expendable trusts to be accounted for in a special revenue fund, again a governmental fund type. Because most government trust funds hold only financial assets, neither of these changes has much practical impact, other than changing the financial statements in which they are reported. Accounting issues involving trusts are discussed in Chapter 8.

Budgetary Accounts

Budgetary accounts generally should not be needed for permanent funds because transactions of the fund result in changes in the fund principal only incidentally; by definition, the principal cannot be appropriated or expended. Public-purpose expendable trust funds accounted for in special revenue funds, however, may be required by law to use the appropriation procedure to ensure adequate budgetary control over the expenditure of fund assets. If the appropriation procedure is required, the use of the other budgetary accounts discussed earlier in this chapter is also recommended. The following paragraphs illustrate a public-purpose nonexpendable trust that is accounted for as a permanent fund.

Illustrative Case

As an illustration of the nature of accounting for permanent fund trust principal and expendable trust revenue, assume on November 1, 2001, James Smith died, having made a valid will that provided for the gift of various securities to the City of Columbia to be held as a nonexpendable trust; the net income from the securities for distribution purposes is to be computed on the full accrual basis, but does not include increases or decreases in the fair value of investments. Income, so measured, is to be transferred to the City's Library Operating Fund, a special revenue fund. Accounting for the Library Operating Fund is not illustrated here because it would be very similar to General Fund accounting already covered in depth in this chapter. For sake of brevity, corresponding entries in the general journal for governmental activities at the government-wide level are also omitted.

The gift was accepted by the City of Columbia and the Library Endowment Fund (a permanent fund) was established to account for the nonexpendable trust. The following securities were received by the Library Endowment Fund:

	Interest Rate per Year	*Maturity Date*	*Face Value*	*Fair Value as of 11/1/01*
Bonds:				
AB Company	10%	1/1/06	$330,000	$340,000
C&D Company	9%	7/1/03	110,000	112,000
D&G Company	9%	1/1/25	200,000	200,000
Total			$640,000	$652,000

	Number of Shares	*Fair Value as of 11/1/01*
Stocks:		
M Company, common	2,400	$126,000
S Company, common	10,000	96,000
K Company, common	3,000	129,000
GF Company, common	2,000	145,000
Total		$496,000

Journal Entries—Permanent Fund

The receipt of the securities by the Library Endowment Fund is properly recorded at the fair value of the securities as of the date of the gift because this is the amount for which the trustees are responsible. Although the face value of the bonds will be received at maturity (if the bonds are held until maturity), GASB Standards require that investments in bonds maturing more than one year from receipt be reported at fair value on the balance sheet date.[6] Thus the entry in the Library

[6]GASB *Codification*, Sec. I50.105.

Endowment Fund to record the receipt of the securities at initiation of the trust on November 1, 2001, is:

Permanent Fund:	*Debits*	*Credits*
1. Investment in Bonds	652,000	
Investment in Stocks	496,000	
Accrued Interest Receivable	20,300	
Revenues—Contributions for Endowment		1,168,300

[Interest accrued is AB ($330,000 × 10% × 4/12 = $11,000), C&D ($110,000 × 9% × 4/12 = $3,300), and D&G ($200,000 × 9% × 4/12 = $6,000)]

As of January 1, 2002, interest is received on all bonds—$16,500 from AB Company; $4,950 from C&D Company; and $9,000 from D&G Company; however, only two months of this interest (one-third of the total received) is earned investment revenue that can be transferred to the Library Operating Fund. The entry for the receipt of bond interest on January 1, 2002, and the revenue earned for transfer to the Library Operating Fund is:

Permanent Fund:		
2. Cash	30,450	
Accrued Interest Receivable		20,300
Revenues—Investment Earnings		10,150

Dividends on stock do not accrue. They become a receivable only when declared by the corporation issuing the stock. Ordinarily the receivable is not recorded because it is followed in a reasonably short time by issuance of a dividend check. Assuming dividends on the stock held by the Library Endowment Fund were received early in January 2002 in the amount of $9,800, Entry 3 is appropriate:

Permanent Fund:		
3. Cash	9,800	
Revenues—Investment Earnings		9,800

The Library Endowment Fund has sufficient cash to pay the amount owed to the Library Operating Fund for bond interest during the two months since the bond interest and dividends were received in cash. Assuming cash is transferred as of January 3, 2002, Entry 4 is:

Permanent Fund:		
4. Interfund Transfers Out	19,950	
Cash		19,950

On the advice of an investment manager, 1,000 shares of GF Company stock were sold for $78,750; this amount and cash of $19,000 were invested in 2,000 shares of LH Company common stock. The GF Company stock sold was half the number of shares received when the trust was established; therefore, it was recorded at its fair value then of $72,500; the difference between its book value and the proceeds is considered in this trust to belong to the corpus and does not give rise to gain or loss that would adjust the net income to be transferred to the Library Operating Fund. Therefore, the sale of GF Company stock and the purchase of

LH Company stock should be recorded in the Library Endowment Fund as shown in Entries 5a and 5b:

Permanent Fund:	*Debits*	*Credits*
5a. Cash	78,750	
Investment in Stocks		72,500
Revenues—Change in Fair Value of Investents		6,250
5b. Investment in Stocks	97,750	
Cash		97,750

Assuming there were no further purchases or sales of stock and that dividends received on April 1, 2002, amounted to $9,920, Entry 6a is necessary, as well as Entry 6b to make the required operating transfer to the Library Operating Fund.

Permanent Fund:		
6a. Cash	9,920	
Revenues—Investment Earnings		9,920
6b. Interfund Transfers Out	9,920	
Cash		9,920

Interest accrued on June 30, 2002, amounted to $30,450, the same amount received early in January 2002. The fair value of the Library Endowment Fund investments as of June 30, 2002, the last day of the City of Columbia's fiscal year, is given below.

		Fair Value as of 11/1/01	*Fair Value as of 6/30/02*	*Change in Fair Value*
Bonds:				
AB Company		$340,000	$360,000	$20,000
C&D Company		112,000	108,000	(4,000)
D&G Company		200,000	206,000	6,000
Total		$652,000	$674,000	$22,000
Stocks:	*No. of Shares*			
M Company	2,400	$126,000	$132,000	$6,000
S Company	10,000	96,000	98,000	2,000
K Company	3,000	129,000	122,000	(7,000)
GF Company	1,000	72,500	75,500	3,000
LH Company	2,000	97,750*	96,450	(1,300)
Total		$521,250	$523,950	$2,700

*As of date of transaction 5 for LH Company.

Entry 7a records the accrual of interest earned for transfer to the Library Operating Fund. Entry 7b records the adjusting entry to record the change in fair value of investments at the end of the fiscal year, compared with the prior fair value recorded for the investments. Entry 7c records the liability to the Library Operating Fund.

Permanent Fund:	*Debits*	*Credits*
7a. Accrued Interest Receivable	30,450	
Revenues—Investment Earnings		30,450
7b. Investment in Bonds	22,000	
Investment in Stocks	2,700	
Revenues—Change in Fair Value of Investments		24,700
7c. Interfund Transfers Out	30,450	
Due to Library Operating Fund		30,450

The closing entry at the end of the fiscal year, June 30, 2002, is shown in Entry 8.

Permanent Fund:		
8. Revenues—Contributions to Endowment	1,168,300	
Revenues—Investments Earnings	60,320	
Revenues—Change in Fair Value of Investments	30,950	
Interfund Transfers Out		60,320
Fund Balance—Reserved for Endowment		1,199,250

In Entry 8, one can see that the total interest earned on bonds and dividends received on investments in stocks in the amount of $60,320 was transferred during the year to the Library Operating Fund; the net change (increase) in fair value of investments, $30,950 and the orginal contributions are added to the Fund Balance. If the net increase in the value of investments was permitted under the trust agreement to be used for Library operating purposes, the entire $91,270 (sum of earnings and increase in fair value) would have been transferred out, and the addition to Fund Balance would have been just for the $1,168,300 original contribution.

At year-end, financial statements for the Library Endowment Fund would be presented in essentially the same formats as the General Fund Balance Sheet and General Fund Statement of Revenues, Expenditures, and Changes in Fund Balance shown in Illustrations 4–5 and 4–6. If the Library Endowment Fund meets the criteria for a major fund, its balance sheet and operating statement information would be included as a column in the Balance Sheet—Governmental Funds and Statement of Revenues, Expenditures, and Changes in Fund Balances—Governmental Funds, examples of which are presented in Illustrations 2–3 and 2–4 in Chapter 2. If the fund is determined to be a nonmajor fund, it would be reported in the combining balance sheet and operating statement presented in the CAFR for the nonmajor governmental funds (see Illustration 4–8 for an example of the latter type financial statement).

As indicated previously, entries in the Library Operating Fund are omitted for sake of brevity because special revenue funds are accounted for in a manner similar to the General Fund. Thus, at the beginning of the 2002 fiscal year (at July 1, 2001) a budgetary entry would have been recorded; that entry would have been amended on November 1, 2001, the date the Library Endowment Fund was created, to reflect the Estimated Other Financing Sources (interfund transfers in) expected from the endowment and to authorize expenditures of all or a portion of those resources in the Library Operating Fund. Each time Interfund Transfers Out are recorded in the Library Endowment Fund, Interfund Transfers In would be recorded in the same amount in the Library Operating Fund.

Chapters 3 and 4 focus on Governmental Activities relating to operations that are recorded in the General Fund, Special Revenue Funds, and Permanent Funds. Chapter 5 discusses accounting for capital assets and the Capital Projects Fund, while the Debt Service Fund and long-term financing are discussed in Chapter 6.

Key Terms

Consumption method, 137
Delinquent taxes, 139
Gross tax levy, 124
Inter-activity transactions, 151
Interfund loans, 147
Interfund transfers, 150
Intra-activity transactions, 151
Intra-entity transactions, 152
Internal exchange transactions, 136
Permanent fund, 152
Private-purpose trusts, 152
Public-purpose trusts, 152
Purchases method, 138
Tax anticipation note, 121
Tax rate, 124

Selected References

American Institute of Certified Public Accountants. Audit and Accounting Guide. *Audits of State and Local Governmental Units*. Revised. New York, 1999.

Governmental Accounting Standards Board. *Codification of Governmental Accounting and Financial Reporting Standards as of June 30, 1999*. Norwalk, CT, 1999.

Questions

4–1. Why do certain transactions of a government require an entry in the general journal of the General Fund as well as an entry in the general journal of governmental activities at the government-wide level? Give some examples.

4–2. Explain why it is often necessary to reserve a portion of the fund equity of the General Fund or a special revenue fund.

4–3. Explain why a city, even a well-managed one, may find it necessary to issue "tax anticipation notes."

4–4. Identify some of the key differences between the government-wide Statement of Net Assets and the Balance Sheet for governmental funds.

4–5. If the General Fund of a certain city needs $5,760,000 revenue from property taxes to finance estimated expenditures of the forthcoming year, and historical experience and forecasts indicate 4 percent of the gross levy will not be collected, how much should the gross levy of General Fund property taxes for the forthcoming year be? Show all computations in good form.

4–6. Is it ever permissible to write off uncollectible delinquent property taxes? If so, explain the accounting procedures involved.

4–7. "If the actual liability for goods or services received in one fiscal year but ordered in a prior fiscal year differs from the estimated liability recorded in the prior year, the actual liability should be reported as an Expenditure of the prior year." Do you agree? Why or why not?

4–8. In late 2001 Cato City ordered goods estimated to cost $300. At year-end these goods had not been received and thus were reported as Reserve for Encumbrances—2001 on the City's balance sheet. In early fiscal year 2002 these goods were received at an actual cost of $320. What total amount of expenditures should be reported for these goods on the City's Statement of Revenues, Expenditures, and Changes in Fund Balances for the year 2002? What amount of expenditures is chargeable to the year 2002 appropriation?

4–9. Explain the relationship between financial statement accounts showing actual amounts and budgetary amounts in an interim balance sheet prepared for the General Fund.

4–10. "If a budget is prepared on the cash basis, in order to comply with state law, it should be adjusted to the modified accrual basis in order that the budget and actual statement may be prepared in conformity with generally accepted accounting principles." Do you agree? Why or why not?

4–11. Give some examples of types of revenue that should be accounted for in a special revenue fund. Are these funds accounted for any differently than the General Fund?

4–12. Grant A from the federal government will reimburse the city for allowable costs incurred for authorized operating purposes; grant B is also restricted for a specified operating purpose, but the full amount under the grant is provided to the city at the beginning of the fiscal year in which the grant monies will be used. Explain the difference in revenue recognition procedures for these two grants.

4–13. Since all funds of a governmental unit are part of the same reporting entity, why are certain interfund transactions recorded as Expenditures and liabilities of one fund, and as assets and Revenues of another fund?

4–14. A governmental fund may charge materials and supplies to Expenditures when the items are purchased (the purchases method) or when the items are used (the consumption method). In either case, significant amounts of inventories should be reported in the balance sheet. If administrators are interested in computing and reporting the cost of services rendered, would you recommend the purchases method or the consumption method?

4–15. Describe some of the reasons why one fund of a government might transfer money to another fund. How are each of these transactions recorded in the general journal?

4–16. The city received an endowment under the terms of a trust agreement that indicates the principal of the gift should be held in perpetuity and the investment income spent to benefit the Parks Department, an activity of the General Fund. Should this transaction be reported in a fiduciary fund or a permanent fund? Why?

Exercises and Problems

4–1. Examine the CAFR. Utilizing the comprehensive annual financial report obtained for Exercise 1–1, follow the instructions below:

a. **General Fund.** What statements and schedules pertaining to the General Fund are presented? In what respects (headings, arrangements, items included, etc.) do they seem similar to the year-end statements illustrated or described in the text? In what respects do they differ?

What purpose is each statement and schedule intended to serve? How well, in your reasoned opinion, does each statement and schedule accomplish its intended purpose? (After reading the first four chapters of this text carefully and solving assigned problems, you have a much greater understanding of the purposes of General Fund accounting and reporting than most other citizens, and even than nonaccountants in elective or appointive governmental positions.)

Are any noncurrent or nonliquid assets included in the General Fund balance sheet? If so, are they offset by "Reserve" accounts in the Fund Equity section? Are any noncurrent liabilities included in the General Fund balance sheet? If so, describe them.

b. **Special Revenue Funds.** What statements and schedules pertaining to the special revenue funds are presented? Are these only combining statements, or are there also statements for individual special revenue funds?

Refer to *a* above—answer questions from the perspective of the special revenue funds. Review your answers to Exercises 1–1, 2–1, and 3–1 in light of your study of Chapter 4. If you feel your earlier answers were not entirely correct, change them to conform with your present understanding of GASB financial reporting standards.

4–2. Multiple Choice. Choose the best answer.

1. Oro County's Expenditures control account at December 31 had a balance of $9,000,000. When Oro's books were closed, this $9,000,000 Expenditures control balance should have:
   a. Been credited.
   b. Been debited.
   c. Remained open.
   d. Appeared as a contra account.
2. If a city legally adopts its annual General Fund budget on the modified accrual basis of accounting, its estimated revenues should be:
   a. Reported as current assets in the General Fund Balance Sheet.
   b. Reported as noncurrent assets in the General Fund Balance Sheet.
   c. Reported on the modified accrual basis of accounting in the General Fund Statement of Revenues, Expenditures, and Changes in Fund Balance—Budget and Actual.
   d. Converted to the cash basis of accounting and reported in the General Fund Statement of Revenues, Expenditures, and Other Changes in Fund Balance—Budget and Actual.
3. At December 31, 2002, Alto Township's encumbered appropriations that had not been expended in 2002 totaled $10,000. Encumbered appropriations do not

lapse at year-end. Alto reports on a calendar-year basis. On its December 31, 2002, balance sheet, the $10,000 should be reported as:

a. Fund Balance Reserved for Encumbrances.

b. Budgetary Fund Balance—Encumbrances.

c. Vouchers Payable—Prior Year.

d. Deferred Expenditures.

4. When Rolan County adopted its budget for the year ending June 30, $20,000,000 was recorded in Estimated Revenues. Actual revenues for the year amounted to $17,000,000. In closing the budgetary accounts at June 30:

   a. Estimated Revenues should be debited for $3,000,000.

   b. Revenues should be debited for $3,000,000.

   c. Estimated Revenues should be credited for $20,000,000.

   d. Revenues should be credited for $20,000,000.

5. When equipment was purchased with General Fund resources, which of the following accounts would have been increased in the General Fund?

   a. Appropriations.

   b. Expenditures.

   c. Due from Capital Projects Fund.

   d. No entry should be made in the General Fund.

6. Property taxes levied in fiscal year 2002 to finance the General Fund budget of fiscal year 2002 should be reported as general fund revenues in 2002:

   a. Regardless of the fiscal year in which collected.

   b. For the amount collected in fiscal year 2002 only.

   c. For the amount collected before the end of fiscal year 2002 or within one year thereafter.

   d. For the amount collected before the end of fiscal year 2002 or within 60 days thereafter.

7. Goods costing $62,000 were received early in 2002. The estimated liability for these goods had been recorded in 2001 as $60,000. The journal entry to record these goods in 2002 will include a:

   a. Debit to Expenditures—2001 in the amount of $62,000.

   b. Debit to Expenditures—2001 in the amount of $60,000.

   c. Debit to Expenditures—2002 in the amount of $62,000.

   d. Debit to Expenditures—2002 in the amount of $60,000.

8. The City of Thomasboro uses the consumption method for recording its inventory of supplies in the General Fund. Physical inventories of supplies were $100,000 and $85,000 at December 31, 2001, and December 31, 2002, respectively. The adjusting journal entry on December 31, 2002, will include a:

   a. Debit to Inventory of Supplies in the amount of $15,000.

   b. Credit to Reserve for Inventory of Supplies in the amount of $85,000.

   c. Debit to Expenditures in the amount of $15,000.

   d. Credit to Expenditures in the amount of $15,000.

9. Gold County received goods that had been approved for purchase but for which payment had not been made. Should the accounts listed below be increased?

	Encumbrances	*Expenditures*
a.	No	No
b.	No	Yes
c.	Yes	No
d.	Yes	Yes

10. In which of the following fund types of a city government are revenues and expenditures recognized on the same basis of accounting as the General Fund?
    a. Enterprise.
    b. Internal service.
    c. Special revenue.
    d. Agency.

(AICPA, adapted)

4–3. Multiple Choice. GASB *Statement* No. 34. Choose the best answer.

1. The Statement of Net Assets may contain columns for all of the following except:
   a. Governmental activities.
   b. Business-type activities.
   c. Fiduciary activities.
   d. Component units.
2. The format of the government-wide Statement of Net Assets must be:
   a. Assets minus liabilities equal net assets.
   b. Assets equal liabilities plus fund equity.
   c. Assets equal liabilities plus net assets.
   d. None of the above. Governments have considerable discretion in presenting assets, liabilities, and net assets.
3. The measurement focus and basis of accounting for government-wide financial statements are

	Measurement Focus	*Basis of Accounting*
a.	Economic resources	Modified accrual
b.	Economic resources	Accrual
c.	Current financial resources	Modified accrual
d.	Current financial resources	Accrual

4. Which of the following is *not* a classification of net assets in the government-wide Statement of Net Assets?
   a. Reserved for encumbrances.
   b. Investment in capital assets, net of related debt.
   c. Restricted for debt service.
   d. Unrestricted.
5. When property taxes are levied and an appropriate allowance is established for uncollectible taxes, an entry is necessary in the general journal of:
   a. The General Fund only.
   b. Governmental activities only.

   c. Both General Fund and governmental activities.
   d. Neither General Fund nor governmental activities.
6. When materials and supplies are ordered with a purchase order, an entry is necessary in the general journal of:
   a. The General Fund only.
   b. Governmental activities only.
   c. Both General Fund and governmental activities.
   d. Neither General Fund nor governmental activities.
7. The expenditure or expense and liability for payroll and payroll taxes should be recorded in the general journal of:
   a. The General Fund only.
   b. Governmental activities only.
   c. Both General Fund and governmental activities.
   d. Neither General Fund nor governmental activities.
8. If a city charges fees for services at its municipal airport, an entry should be recorded in the general journal of:
   a. The General Fund only.
   b. Governmental activities only.
   c. Both General Fund and governmental activities.
   d. Neither General Fund nor governmental activities.
9. Internal exchange transactions between governmental funds and internal service funds are:
   a. Reported as Revenues and Expenses in the Statement of Activities.
   b. Eliminated prior to preparing the government-wide financial statements.
   c. Reported as revenues and expenses in the business-type activities column of the government-wide financial statements.
   d. Both *b* and *c* are true.
10. Gifts of endowments restricted to serve public purposes should be recorded in a:
   a. Permanent fund.
   b. Fiduciary fund.
   c. Agency fund.
   d. Any of these funds are appropriate.

4–4. Interim Balance Sheet. The following is a list of the ledger accounts of the General Fund of Brentwood as of June 30, 2001 (the fiscal year ends on December 31):

Accounts Payable	$ 372,600
Appropriations	2,665,000
Cash	304,600
Encumbrances	120,000
Estimated Revenues	2,700,000
Estimated Uncollectible Current Taxes	75,000
Expenditures—2001	1,398,400

Reserve for Encumbrances—2001	120,000
Revenues	1,480,000
Tax Anticipation Notes Payable	540,000
Taxes Receivable—Current	908,700
Fund Balance	?

Required

a. Determine the balance of the Fund Balance account as of June 30, 2001, without preparing a balance sheet or closing entries. Show computations.

b. Prepare in good form an Interim Balance Sheet as of June 30, 2001.

c. If the only entry recorded in the Fund Balance account during the first six months of 2001 was to record the original budget for the year, compute the balance of the Fund Balance account that would have been reported in the General Fund Balance Sheet as of December 31, 2000.

4–5. Interfund Transactions. The following transactions affected more than one fund in Brady City.

1. The Fire Department, a governmental activity, purchased $100,000 of water from the Water Utility Fund, a business-type activity.
2. The General Fund made a long-term loan in the amount of $50,000 to the Central Stores Fund, an internal service fund.
3. The Municipal Golf Course Fund, an enterprise fund, reimbursed the General Fund $1,000 for office supplies that the General Fund purchased on its behalf.
4. The General Fund made its annual contribution of $100,000 to the Debt Service Fund for the payment of interest and principal on general obligation bonds.
5. The $4,000 balance in a Capital Projects Fund at the completion of construction of a new City Hall was transferred to the General Fund.

Required

a. Make the required journal entries in the general journal of the General Fund and any other fund affected for the interfund transactions described above. Do not make entries in the general journal for governmental activities at the government-wide level, nor in the subsidiary ledgers.

b. Describe the effect, if any, of each of the transactions on the government-wide financial statements.

4–6. Closing journal entries. At the end of a fiscal year, budgetary and operating statement control accounts in the general ledger of the General Fund of the City of Adams had the following balances: Appropriations, $5,224,000; Estimated Other Financing Uses, $2,776,000; Estimated Revenues, $7,997,000; Encumbrances, $0; Expenditures, $5,182,000; Other Financing Uses, $2,780,000; and Revenues. $8,022,000. Appropriations included an authorization to order a certain item at a cost not to exceed $64,700; this was not ordered during the year because it will not be available until late in the following year. Show in general journal form the entry needed to close all of the accounts listed above that should be closed as of the end of the fiscal year.

4–7. Budget versus Actual. For budgetary purposes the City of Rockton reports encumbrances in the Expenditures section of its Statement of Revenues, Expenditures, and Changes in Fund Balance—Budget and Actual. Expenditures chargeable to a prior year's appropriation are excluded from the current year budgetary comparison statements. From the following information prepare:

a. Entries in general journal form to record the transactions for fiscal year 2001 given below in both the General Fund and Governmental Activities General Journal, if appropriate.

b. A Statement of Revenues, Expenditures, and Changes in Fund Balance—Budget and Actual for the General Fund of the City of Rockton for the fiscal year ending December 31, 2001. Do not prepare a government-wide Statement of Activities since other governmental funds would affect that statement.

(1) The budget prepared for the fiscal year 2001 was as follows:

Estimated Revenues:	
Taxes	$1,943,000
Licenses and Permits	372,000
Intergovernmental Revenue	297,000
Miscellaneous Revenues	62,000
Total Estimated Revenues	$2,674,000
Appropriations:	
General Government	$ 471,000
Public Safety	786,000
Public Works	650,000
Health and Welfare	600,000
Miscellaneous Appropriations	86,000
Total Appropriations	$2,593,000
Budgeted Increase in Fund Balance	$ 81,000

(2) Encumbrances issued against the appropriations during the year were as follows:

General Government	$ 58,000
Public Safety	201,000
Public Works	392,000
Health and Welfare	160,000
Miscellaneous Appropriations	71,000
Total	$882,000

(3) A current-year tax levy of $2,005,000 was recorded; uncollectibles were estimated as $62,000.

(4) Tax collections from prior years' levies totaled $132,000; collections of the current year's levy totaled $1,459,000.

(5) Personnel costs during the year were charged to the appropriations shown below in the amounts indicated. Encumbrances were not recorded for personnel costs.

General Government	$411,000
Public Safety	584,000
Public Works	254,000
Health and Welfare	439,000
Miscellaneous Appropriations	11,100
Credit to Vouchers Payable	$1,699,100

(6) Invoices for all items ordered during the prior year were received and approved for payment in the amount of $14,470. Encumbrances had been recorded in the prior year for these items in the amount of $14,000. The amount chargeable to each year's appropriations should be charged to the Public Safety appropriation.

(7) Invoices were received and approved for payment for items ordered in documents recorded as encumbrances in transaction 2 of this problem. The following appropriations were affected:

	Actual Liability	*Estimated Liability*
General Government	$ 52,700	$ 52,200
Public Safety	187,800	189,700
Public Works	360,000	357,000
Health and Safety	130,600	130,100
Miscellaneous Appropriations	71,000	71,000
	$802,100	$800,000

(8) Revenue other than taxes collected during the year consisted of: licenses and permits, $373,000; intergovernmental revenue, $299,000; and $66,000 of miscellaneous revenues.

(9) Payments on Vouchers Payable totaled $2,475,000.

The General Fund Fund Balance account had a credit balance of $62,700 as of December 31, 2000; no entries other than the entry at the beginning of 2001 to record the budgeted increase have been made in the Fund Balance account during 2001.

4–8. Interim Balance Sheet. The City of Warren's General Fund had the following after-closing trial balance at April 30, 2001, the end of its fiscal year:

	Debits	Credits
Cash	$ 93,000	
Taxes Receivable—Delinquent	583,000	
Estimated Uncollectible Delinquent Taxes		$189,000
Interest and Penalties Receivable	26,280	
Estimated Uncollectible Interest and Penalties		11,160
Inventory of Supplies	16,100	
Vouchers Payable		148,500
Due to Federal Government		59,490
Reserve for Inventory of Supplies		16,100
Fund Balance		294,130
	$718,380	$718,380

During the six months ended October 31, 2001, the first six months of fiscal year 2002, the following transactions, in summary form, with subsidiary ledger detail omitted, occurred:

1. The budget for fiscal 2002 provided for General Fund estimated revenues totaling $3,170,000 and appropriations totaling $3,100,000.
2. The City Council authorized a temporary loan of $300,000 in the form of a 120-day tax anticipation note. The loan was obtained from a local bank at a discount of 6 percent per annum (debit Expenditures for discount).
3. The property tax levy for fiscal 2002 was recorded. Net assessed valuation of taxable property for the year was $43,000,000, and the tax rate was $5.00 per hundred. It was estimated that 4 percent of the levy would be uncollectible. Classify this tax levy as current.
4. Purchase orders, contracts, and so on, in the amount of $1,027,000 were issued to vendors and others.
5. $1,034,000 of current taxes, $340,000 of delinquent taxes, and interest and penalties of $13,240 were collected. Because of taxpayers' delinquencies in payment of the first installment of taxes, additional penalties of $15,230 were levied but not yet collected.
6. Total payroll during the first six months was $481,070. Of that amount, $36,800 was withheld for employees' FICA tax liability, $61,200 for employees' federal income tax liability, and $20,000 for state taxes; the balance was paid in cash.
7. The employer's FICA tax liability amounted to $36,800.
8. Revenues from sources other than taxes were collected in the amount of $339,000.

9. Amounts due the federal government as of April 30, and amounts due for FICA taxes and state and federal withholding taxes during the first six months of fiscal 2002, were vouchered.
10. Purchase orders and contracts encumbered in the amount of $890,800 were filled at a net cost of $894,900, which was vouchered.
11. $1,099,060 cash was paid on vouchers payable and credit for purchases discount earned was $8,030 (credit Expenditures).
12. The tax anticipation note of $300,000 was repaid.

Required

a. Record in general journal form the effect on the General Fund and governmental activities of the transactions for the six months ended October 31. You need not record subsidiary ledger debits and credits.

b. Prepare a City of Warren General Fund Interim Balance Sheet as of October 31, 2001.

4–9. General Fund Financial Statements. This problem continues Problem 4–8. During the second six months of fiscal 2002, the following transactions that affected the City of Warren's General Fund occurred:

1. Because of a change in a state law, the City is informed it will receive $100,000 less revenue from the state than was budgeted. Make the entry to amend the Estimated Revenues account accordingly. Do not amend the Appropriations account.
2. Purchase orders and other commitment documents in the amount of $1,032,000 were issued during the six months ended April 30, 2002.
3. Property taxes of $6,500 and interest and penalties receivable of $1,340, which had been written off in prior years, were collected. Additional interest of $270 that had accrued since the write-off was collected at the same time.
4. Personnel costs, excluding the employer's share of the FICA tax, totaled $338,420 for the second six months. Withholdings amounted to $25,890 for FICA; $42,510 for employee's federal income tax liability, and $14,400 for state withholding tax; the balance was paid in cash.
5. The employer's FICA tax of $25,890 was recorded as a liability.
6. The County Board of Review discovered unassessed properties of a total taxable value of $500,000 located within the City boundaries. The owners of these properties were charged with taxes at the City General Fund rate of $5.00 per hundred dollars assessed value. (Do not adjust the Estimated Uncollectible Current Taxes Account.)
7. The following were collected in cash: Current taxes of $927,000; delinquent taxes of $43,270; interest and penalties of $7,330, and revenues of $593,700 from a number of sources. (No part of any of these amounts is included in any other transaction given above.)
8. Accrued interest and penalties, estimated to be 30 percent uncollectible, was recorded in the amount of $23,200.
9. All unpaid current year's taxes became delinquent. The current taxes and related estimated uncollectibles were transferred to the delinquent classification.
10. All amounts due to the federal government and state government were vouchered.

11. Invoices and bills for goods and services that had been encumbered at $1,097,240 were received in the amount of $1,092,670 and were vouchered.
12. Personal property taxes of $39,940 and interest and penalties of $4,180 were written off because of inability to locate the property owners.
13. A physical inventory of materials and supplies at April 30, 2002, showed a total of $19,100. Inventory is recorded on the consumption method.
14. Payments made on vouchers during the second half-year totaled $1,202,600.

Required

a. Record in general journal form transactions in both the General Fund and Governmental Activities for the second half of fiscal 2002.

b. Record in general journal form entries to close the budgetary accounts and operating statement accounts.

c. Prepare a Balance Sheet as of April 30, 2002, for the City of Warren General Fund.

d. Prepare a Statement of Revenues, Expenditures, and Changes in Fund Balance for the fiscal year ended April 30, 2002, in as much detail as is possible from the data given in Problems 4–8 and 4–9. Do not prepare a government-wide Statement of Net Assets or Statements of Activities.

4–10. Statements of Net Assets and Activities. The trial balance for Sanilac City as of June 30, 2002, is provided below (rounded to the nearest dollar):

	Debits	*Credits*
Cash and Investments	$ 2,967,134	
Receivables	383,231	
Internal Receivables	5,550	
Due from Other Governmental Units	181,126	
Inventory	12,456	
Capital Assets	2,123,998	
Accounts Payable		$ 46,453
Accrued and Other Liabilities		59,877
Internal Payables		85,471
Long-term Debt		461,333
Net Assets—Invested in Capital Assets (net of debt)		1,795,685
Net Assets—Restricted for Debt Service		252,873
Net Assets—Unrestricted		3,261,221
Program Revenues:		
General Government—Charges for Services		1,373,662
General Government—Operating Grants		232,295
Police—Charges for Services		142,351
Police —Capital Grants		646,837
Cemetery—Charges for Services		35,653
Roads and Bridges—Charges for Services		42,443
General Revenues:		
Property Taxes		1,666,862
State Shared Revenue		622,683
Investment Income		197,751

	Debits	Credits
Expenses:		
General Government	2,665,568	
Police and Fire	1,512,564	
Cemetery	30,098	
Roads and Bridges	542,256	
Interest on Long-term Debt	289,469	
Depreciation on Capital Assets	210,000	
Total	$10,923,450	$10,923,450

Additional information:

1. Depreciation expense should be allocated to the different functions the capital assets relate to as follows: General Government, 40 percent; Police and Fire, 30 percent; Cemetery, 10 percent; and Roads and Bridges, 20 percent.
2. The change in net assets is due in part to the increase to "Invested in Capital Assets" arising from the capital grant, with the balance attributed to unrestricted net assets.
3. For the sake of simplicity, assume that this city does not have any business-type activities or component units.

Required

a. Prepare a government-wide Statement of Net Assets for the year ended June 30, 2002.

b. Prepare a government-wide Statement of Activities for the year ended June 30, 2002.

Continuous Problem

4–B. Presented below are a number of transactions of the General Fund of the City of Bingham that occurred during the first six months of fiscal year 2002 for which the budget given in Problem 3–B was prepared, that is, July 1, 2001, through December 31, 2001. You are required to:

a. Open a general journal for Governmental Activities at the government-wide level. Record in the general journal of the General Fund and Governmental Activities, where appropriate, the transactions given below. Make any computations to the nearest dollar. For each entry affecting budgetary accounts or operating statement accounts, show subsidiary account titles and amounts as well as general ledger control account titles and amounts.

(1) A general tax levy in the amount of $3,200,000 was made. It is estimated that 3 percent of the tax will be uncollectible.

(2) Tax anticipation notes in the amount of $250,000 were issued.

(3) Purchase orders, contracts, and other commitment documents were issued against appropriations in the following amounts:

General Government	$120,000
Public Safety	162,000
Public Works	342,000
Health	112,000
Public Welfare	105,000
Recreation	114,000
Miscellaneous Appropriations	24,000
Total	$979,000

(4) The General Fund collected the following in cash: Delinquent Taxes, $212,000; Interest and Penalties Receivable on Taxes, $10,720; Licenses and Permits, $188,000; Fines and Forfeits, $163,000; Charges for Services, $24,500; and Miscellaneous Revenues, $30,000.

(5) A petty cash fund was established for general operating purposes in the amount of $6,000.

(6) General Fund payrolls totaled $1,033,000. Of that amount, $147,450 was withheld for employees' income taxes and $79,000 was withheld for employees' FICA tax liability; the balance was paid in cash. The encumbrance system is not used for payrolls. The payrolls were for the following departments:

General Government	$ 316,233
Public Safety	467,771
Public Works	111,732
Health	22,066
Public Welfare	33,653
Recreation	81,545
Total	$1,033,000

(7) The liability for the City's share of FICA taxes, $79,000, was recorded. The amount was budgeted as part of the Contributions to Retirement Funds appropriation.

(8) Invoices for some of the services and supplies ordered in transaction (3) were received and approved for payment; departments affected are shown below:

	Actual	*Estimated*
General Government	$113,500	$113,100
Public Safety	146,375	140,500

Public Works	300,000	298,500
Health	111,700	112,000
Public Welfare	103,100	102,800
Recreation	97,125	99,000
Miscellaneous Appropriations	20,400	20,000
Totals	$892,200	$885,900

(9) Delinquent taxes receivable in the amount of $12,000 were written off as uncollectible. Interest and penalties accrued on these taxes amounting to $600 were also written off.

(10) Collections of the first installment of the current year's taxes totaled $1,632,000.

(11) Payments on General Fund vouchers amounted to $1,060,000.

(12) Collections on delinquent taxes written off in a prior year amounted to $438. Interest and penalties on the taxes written off amounted to $30. Interest accrued since the date of write-off amounted to $14 (this is Revenue of fiscal year 2002). All interest and penalties were collected at the time delinquent taxes were collected.

(13) The General Fund vouchered its required contributions to the Employees' Retirement Fund, $56,490, its liability for employees' income taxes withheld; the total amount of FICA tax liability; and the amount due other funds on July 1. Checks were drawn for all these vouchers.

b. Post each entry to the general ledger accounts and to all subsidiary ledger accounts required. (Do not post to governmental activities general ledger until instructed to do so in Chapter 9.) (If you used the subsidiary ledger forms illustrated in Chapter 3, the Revenues ledger debit column supports the Estimated Revenues control account in the general ledger and the credit column supports the Revenues general ledger control account. Similarly, Chapter 3 illustrates how a single account in a subsidiary ledger can support three general ledger control accounts: Appropriations, Encumbrances, and Expenditures. Note the subsidiary ledger form provides only a debit column for Expenditures, so if a general journal entry indicates a credit to Expenditures, the amount must be entered in the subsidiary ledger account as a negative item in the Expenditures debit column. Since only a credit column is provided for Appropriations, if a general journal entry indicates a debit to Appropriations, the amount must be entered as a negative item in the Appropriations credit column of the subsidiary ledger account.)

c. Prepare a trial balance of the General Fund general ledger as of December 31, 2001, the end of the first six months of the fiscal year.

d. Prepare in good form an Interim Balance Sheet for the General Fund as of December 31, 2001. (See Illustration 4–2.) Do not prepare the government-wide statement.

e. Prepare in good form a Statement of Actual and Estimated Revenues for the six months ended December 31, 2001. (See Illustration 4–3.) Make sure the total

Estimated Revenues and total Revenues shown on this statement agree with the same items shown on the December 31 Balance Sheet.

f. Prepare in good form a Statement of Budgeted and Actual Expenditures and Encumbrances for the six months ended December 31, 2001. (See Illustration 4–4.) Make sure the total Appropriations, Expenditures, and Encumbrances shown on this statement agree with the same items shown on the December 31 Balance Sheet.

g. Below are described the transactions during January 1–June 30, 2002, the second six months of the fiscal year. Record each in the general journal for the General Fund and governmental activities. For each entry affecting budgetary accounts or operating statement accounts, show subsidiary ledger account titles and amounts as well as general ledger control account titles and amounts.

(1) In view of the information shown in the Statement of Actual and Estimated Revenues and the Statement of Budgeted and Actual Expenditures and Encumbrances, each for the first six months of the fiscal year, the City Council revised the budgets for the current year as shown below:

	Budget Adjustments Inc. (Dec.)
Estimated Revenues:	
Taxes	$ –0–
Licenses and Permits	3,000
Fines and Forfeits	4,000
Intergovernmental Revenue	(11,000)
Charges for Services	–0–
Miscellaneous Revenue	5,000
Appropriations:	
General Government	60,000
Public Safety	–0–
Public Works	–0–
Health	–0–
Public Welfare	40,000
Recreation	(22,000)
Contributions to Retirement Funds	–0–
Miscellaneous Appropriations	(6,000)

(2) Purchase orders, contracts, and other commitment documents totaling $842,000 were issued against the following appropriations:

General Government	$ 87,490
Public Safety	416,000

Public Works	120,710
Health	40,000
Public Welfare	104,800
Recreation	52,000
Miscellaneous Appropriations	21,000

(3) Invoices for services and supplies were received and approved for payment: Actual, $938,730; and Estimated, $918,000.

	Expenditure	*Encumbrance*
General Government	$ 96,470	$ 94,390
Public Safety	460,450	435,800
Public Works	161,810	160,310
Health	40,000	40,000
Public Welfare	102,000	106,000
Recreation	53,000	56,500
Miscellaneous Appropriations	25,000	25,000

(4) Payrolls were computed, liabilities for withholdings were recorded, and the net paid in cash, as follows: General Fund—Gross Pay, $1,157,500; Income Tax Withheld, $170,800; and FICA Tax Withheld, $88,500. Payrolls are not encumbered. The distribution was:

General Government	$301,800
Public Safety	551,700
Public Works	132,000
Health	26,000
Public Welfare	50,000
Recreation	96,000

(5) The City's liability for FICA tax, $88,500, was recorded as an expenditure of the Contributions to Retirement Funds appropriation.

(6) Collections of the second installment of the current year's taxes were $1,300,000.

(7) The General Fund collected the following revenue in cash: Licenses and Permits, $259,000; Fines and Forfeits, $220,000; Intergovernmental Revenues, $520,000; Charges for Services, $84,000; and Miscellaneous Revenues, $49,500.

(8) A taxpayer who had been classified as delinquent proved he had paid general taxes of $8,440 when due. Audit disclosed that a former employee had embezzled $8,440—through oversight of the Treasurer, the employee had not been bonded. Interest and penalties in the amount of $845 had been recorded as receivable on the $8,440 "delinquent" tax bill at the end of the prior year. Since neither the $8,440 taxes nor the $845 interest and penalties are actually receivable, the total of the two, $9,285, was by resolution of the City Council charged as an expenditure of the current year's Miscellaneous Appropriations.

The audit also disclosed that tax bills totaling $2,586 on several pieces of property had been sent to both the present and the prior owner, and no tax bills at all had been prepared for several pieces of property—general taxes of $2,250 should have been charged. (Correct all accounts affected; do not adjust the Estimated Uncollectible Taxes account.)

(9) Tax anticipation notes issued by the General Fund were paid at maturity at face amount plus interest of $5,000. (Charge Miscellaneous Appropriations for the expenditure.)

(10) Invoices for all items encumbered in the prior year were received and approved for payment in the amount of $14,180. (Charge the amount encumbered in 2001 to Expenditures of Public Works Appropriation. Charge the excess of the amount approved for payment over the Reserve for Encumbrances—2001 balance to Expenditures of the fiscal year 2002 Public Works Appropriation.)

(11) The petty cash fund was reimbursed for $4,810. (Charge General Government for the entire expenditure.)

(12) The General Fund vouchered and paid its liability for employees' income taxes withheld, the total liability for FICA taxes, and the required contribution to the Employees' Retirement Fund, $119,900.

(13) The General Fund recorded its liabilities to other funds for services received during the year, $20,000. ($15,300 should be charged to the Public Safety appropriation and $4,700 to the General Government appropriation.)

(14) The General Fund paid vouchers in the amount of $870,000.

(15) The General Fund made a long-term interfund loan of $30,000 cash to the Stores and Services Fund.

(16) Current taxes receivable and related estimated uncollectibles were transferred to the delinquent category. Interest and penalties accrued on delinquent taxes amounted to $31,240; of this amount it is estimated that $9,360 is uncollectible.

h. Post to the general ledger and prepare a trial balance before adjustment of the accounts of the General Fund. Post to the subsidiary ledgers and make sure the totals of the subsidiary ledger columns agree with the balances of their respective control accounts.

i. Prepare and post the necessary closing entries for the General Fund.

j. Prepare in good form a Balance Sheet as of the end of the fiscal year, June 30, 2002.

k. Prepare in good form a Statement of Revenues, Expenditures, and Changes in Fund Balance for the General Fund for the year ended June 30, 2002. (See Illustration 4–6. Classify 2001 expenditures as Public Works.) Do not prepare the government-wide statements.

l. Prepare in good form a Statement of Revenues, Expenditures, and Changes in Fund Balance—Budget and Actual for the year ended June 30, 2002. Use the final adjusted budget figures. (See Illustration 4–7.)

CHAPTER 5

Accounting for General Capital Assets and Capital Projects

Learning Objectives

After studying this chapter, you should be able to:

- Describe the nature and characteristics of general capital assets.
- Account for the acquisition of general capital assets, including infrastructure assets.
- Account for the maintenance and disposition of general capital assets.
- Account for depreciation of general capital assets, including the modified approach for infrastructure assets.
- Explain the purpose and characteristics of a capital projects fund.
- Explain the typical sources of financing for capital projects.
- Prepare journal entries for a typical capital project, both within the capital projects fund and within the governmental activities category at the government-wide level.
- Explain and prepare journal entries for special cases such as:
    - Alternative treatments of project surpluses or deficits at completion.
    - Original issue premiums or discounts and accrued interest on bonds issued.
- Explain the concepts and accounting procedures for special assessment capital projects.
- Prepare financial statements for capital projects funds.

Chapters 3 and 4 illustrate that long-lived assets such as office equipment, police cruisers, and other items may be acquired by a governmental unit by expenditure of appropriations of the General Fund or one or more of its special revenue funds. Long-lived assets used by activities accounted for by governmental fund types are called **general capital assets.** General capital assets should be distinguished from capital assets that are specifically associated with activities reported in proprietary and fiduciary funds. Capital assets acquired by proprietary and fiduciary funds are accounted for in those funds.

Acquisitions of general capital assets that require major amounts of money ordinarily cannot be financed from General Fund or special revenue fund appropriations. Major acquisitions of general capital assets are commonly financed by issuance of long-term debt to be repaid from tax revenues, or by special assessments against property deemed to be particularly benefited by the long-lived asset. Other sources of financing the acquisition of long-lived assets include grants from other governmental units, transfers from other funds, gifts from individuals or organizations, or a combination of several of these sources. If money received from these sources is restricted, legally or morally, to the purchase or construction of specified capital assets, it is recommended that a **capital projects fund** be created to account for resources to be used for such projects. Where deemed useful, capital projects funds may also be used to account for the acquisition by a governmental unit of major general capital assets, such as buildings, under a capital lease agreement. Leases involving equipment are more commonly accounted for in the General Fund.

Illustration 5–1 summarizes the interrelationships among fund types and activities at the government-wide level, as they relate to capital asset acquisition. It shows that general capital assets may be acquired from expenditures of the General Fund, special revenue funds, or capital projects funds. The cost or other carrying value of general capital assets, and long-term debt related to general capital assets acquisition, is accounted for in the general ledger for the governmental activities category at the government-wide level.[1] This chapter focuses on capital projects funds accounting and financial reporting. Chapters 3 and 4 discuss accounting and financial reporting for the General Fund, special revenue funds, and permanent funds. Subsequent chapters discuss accounting and financial reporting of the other governmental fund types and governmental activities as shown in Illustration 5–1.

---

[1]Under the financial reporting model being superseded by the GASB *Statement No. 34* reporting model, general capital assets are accounted for in a set of accounting records called the General Fixed Assets Account Group and general long-term liabilities are accounted for in a second set of accounting records called the General Long-Term Debt Account Group. Both account groups are being eliminated by the *Statement No. 34* model, but many governments may continue to use these records for several more years until their accounting systems have been redesigned. The appendix to Chapter 9 explains the function of account groups.

Illustration 5–1 General Capital Asset Acquisition: Governmental Funds and Government-wide Governmental Activities

General Fund and/or Special Revenue Funds	*Capital Projects Funds*	*Government-wide Governmental Activities*
Account for capital outlay expenditures from annual budget appropriations. General capital assets acquired are accounted for in the governmental activities general ledger at the government-wide level.	Account for construction or other major capital expenditures from debt proceeds, capital grants, special assessments, and other sources restricted for capital asset acquisition. General capital assets acquired and related long-term debt to be serviced from tax revenues, or from special assessments, are recorded in the governmental activities general ledger at the government-wide level.	Account for the cost and depreciation of general capital assets (GCA) acquired by expenditures of the General Fund, Special Revenue Funds, and Capital Projects Funds. Also account for GCA acquired under capital leases and for GCA acquired by gift. Account for all unmatured long-term debt except debt being repaid from revenues of Enterprise Funds.

Accounting for General Capital Assets

Only enterprise and internal service funds routinely account for capital assets (property, plant, and equipment) used in their operations. The relatively few governmental trust funds that use capital assets for the production of income also account for property, plant, and equipment. All other funds account only for financial resources. Capital assets acquired by those funds cannot be accounted for in the funds. Rather, general capital assets purchased or constructed with governmental fund resources are accounted for in the governmental activities general ledger at the government-wide level (See Footnote 1 for a related discussion.)

As indicated in most intermediate financial accounting texts, records of individual assets that exceed the minimum value threshold established for capitalization, or groups of related assets of lesser unit value, should include all information needed for planning an effective maintenance program, preparing budget requests for replacements and additions, providing an adequate insurance coverage, and fixing the responsibility for custody of the assets.

In conformity with generally accepted accounting principles, general capital assets are recorded at historical cost or fair value at time of receipt if assets are received by donation. **Historical cost** includes acquisition cost plus ancillary costs necessary to put the asset into use. Ancillary costs may include items such as freight and transportation charges, site preparation costs, set-up costs, and, for assets acquired through construction projects, capitalized interest.[2] If the cost of capital

[2]GASB *Statement No. 34*, par. 106.

assets was not recorded when the assets were acquired and is unknown when accounting control over the assets is established, it is acceptable to record them at estimated cost.

Until implementation of GASB *Statement No. 34* depreciation was not recorded on general capital assets in any governmental fund, but accumulated depreciation could optionally be reported in the General Fixed Assets Account Group. Few governments opted to report depreciation since it was not required.

As mentioned in Footnote 1, the General Fixed Assets Account Group is not used in the *Statement No. 34* reporting model. General capital assets are recorded instead in the governmental activities ledger at the government-wide level and reported in the governmental activities column of the Statement of Net Assets, net of accumulated depreciation, where appropriate. Depreciation is not reported for inexhaustible assets such as land and land improvements, noncapitalized collections of works of art or historical treasures, and infrastructure assets that are accounted for using the **modified approach.**[3] The modified approach is explained later in this chapter. Even though general capital assets are acquired for the production of general governmental services rather than for the production of services that are sold, reporting depreciation on general capital assets may provide significant benefits to users and managers alike. Reporting depreciation expense as part of the direct expenses of functions and programs in the governmental activities column of the government-wide Statement of Activities (see Illustration 2–2) helps to determine the full cost of providing each function or program. Depreciation expense on capital assets used in the operations of a government grant–financed program is often an allowable cost under the terms of a grant. In addition, depreciation expense may provide useful information to administrators and legislators concerned with the allocation of resources to programs, departments, and activities. To a limited extent, a comparison of the accumulated depreciation on an asset with the cost of the asset may assist in budgeting outlays for replacement of capital assets. For these reasons, some observers view the *Statement No. 34* requirement to report depreciation on general capital assets in the government-wide financial statements as a significant improvement in governmental financial reporting.

Required Disclosures about Capital Assets

GASB standards require certain disclosures about capital assets in the notes to the basic financial statements, both the general capital assets reported in the governmental activities column and those reported in the business-type activities column of the government-wide financial statements.[4] In addition to disclosure of their general policy for capitalizing assets and for estimating the useful lives of depreciable assets, governments should provide certain other disclosures in the notes to the financial statements. These disclosures should be divided into major classes of capital assets (as discussed in the following section) and should distinguish between general capital assets and those reported in business-type activities. Capital assets

[3]Ibid., par. 107.
[4]Ibid., pars. 116–118.

that are not being depreciated should be disclosed separately from those assets that are being depreciated. Required disclosures about each major class of capital assets include:

1. Beginning of year and end of year balances, showing accumulated depreciation separate from historical cost.
2. Capital acquisitions during the year.
3. Sales or other dispositions during the year.
4. Depreciation expense for the current period, with disclosure of the amounts charged to each function in the statement of activities.
5. For collections of works of art or historical treasures that are not capitalized, disclosures should describe the collections and explain why they are not capitalized.[5] If collections are capitalized, they should be included in the disclosures described in items 1 through 4.

Illustration 5–2 presents capital asset note disclosures for the hypothetical City of Smallville. Note that the schedule presented includes all the required disclosures listed in items 1–4 above. The City of Smallville is assumed to not have any valuable collections.

Classification of General Capital Assets

The asset accounts shown in Illustration 5–2 are those commonly used to classify capital assets. Additional or substitute accounts may be used as needed to present information relating to capital assets of a given governmental unit. As discussed previously in this chapter, general capital assets typically are those acquired using the financial resources of a governmental fund. Many of these assets, however, are not used exclusively in the operations of any one fund nor do they belong to a fund. Consider, for example, that general capital assets include courthouses and city halls, public buildings in general, the land on which they are situated, highways, streets, sidewalks, storm drainage systems, equipment, and other tangible assets with a life longer than one fiscal year. The following paragraphs present a brief review of generally accepted principles of accounting for each category of capital assets, based on applicable GASB and FASB standards.

Land. The cost of land acquired by a governmental unit through purchase should include not only the contract price but also such other related costs as taxes and other liens assumed, title search costs, legal fees, surveying, filling, grading, drainage, and other costs of preparation for the use intended. Governments are

[5]Even though the GASB encourages capitalization of all collections of works of art or historical treasures, governments can opt *not* to capitalize if the collection is: (1) held for public exhibition, education, or research in furtherance of public service, rather than for financial gain; (2) protected, kept unencumbered, cared for, and preserved; and (3) subject to an organizational policy that requires the proceeds from sales of collection items to be used to acquire other items for collections (GASB *Statement No. 34*, pars. 116–118). These criteria, all of which must be met in order not to capitalize, are identical to those in FASB *Statement No. 116* for nongovernmental nonprofit organizations (see Chapter 14 for discussion).

Illustration 5–2 Illustrative Capital Assets Disclosures for City of Smallville

	Primary Government			
	Beginning Balance	*Additions*	*Retirements*	*Ending Balance*
Governmental Activities:				
Land	$ 2,410,231	$ 243,600	$(198,798)	$ 2,455,033
Buildings	3,559,826	347,568	(359,620)	3,547,774
Improvements	896,459	84,665	(41,598)	939,526
Equipment	2,298,988	260,976	(203,730)	2,356,234
Infrastructure	6,253,248	503,736	–0–	6,756,984
Totals, at historical cost	15,418,752	1,440,545	(803,746)	16,055,551
Less: Accumulated depreciation:				
Buildings	(854,358)	(88,996)	90,379	(852,975)
Improvements	(112,857)	(12,916)	4,647	(121,126)
Equipment	(748,922)	(197,118)	155,724	(790,316)
Infrastructure	(1,011,694)	(75,039)	–0–	(1,086,733)
Total accumulated depreciation	(2,727,831)	(374,069)*	250,750	(2,851,150)
Governmental activities capital assets, net	$12,690,921	$1,066,476	$(552,996)	$13,204,401
Business-type activities:				
Land	$1,958,690	$ –0–	$ –0–	$ 1,958,690
Buildings	4,638,563	759,284	–0–	5,397,847
Equipment	2,798,468	427,516	(271,329)	2,954,655
Totals, at historical cost	9,395,721	1,186,800	(271,329)	10,311,192
Less: Accumulated depreciation:				
Buildings	(1,064,863)	(118,352)	–0–	(1,183,215)
Equipment	(1,257,963)	(349,875)	85,342	(1,522,496)
Business-type activities capital assets, net	$ 7,072,895	$ 718,573	$(185,987)	$ 7,605,481

*Depreciation expense was charged to governmental functions as follows:

General government	$ 59,806
Public safety	80,738
Public works, including depreciation on general infrastructure assets	158,767
Parks and recreation	41,864
Culture	20,933
Mosquito abatement	11,961
Total depreciation expense	$374,069

Source: Prepared by authors in the format shown in GASB *Statement No. 34*. GASB *Statement No. 34*, "Appendix C, Notes to the Financial Statements, Note I" (Norwalk, CT, 1999), p. 245.

frequently subject to damage suits in connection with land acquisition, and the amounts of judgments levied are considered capital costs of the property acquired. Land acquired through forfeiture should be capitalized at the total amount of all taxes, liens, and other claims surrendered, plus all other costs incidental to acquiring ownership and perfecting title. Land acquired through donation should be recorded on the basis of appraised value at the date of acquisition; the cost of the appraisal itself should not be capitalized, however.

Buildings and Improvements Other than Buildings. The nature of assets to be classified as buildings is a matter of common knowledge; but if a definition is needed, they may be said to consist of those structures erected above ground for the purpose of sheltering persons or property. "Improvements Other than Buildings" consists of land attachments of a permanent nature, other than buildings, and includes, among other things, roads, bridges, tunnels, walks, walls, and parking lots.

The determination of the cost of buildings and improvements acquired by purchase is relatively simple, although some peripheral costs may be of doubtful classification. The price paid for the assets constitutes most of the cost of purchased items; but legal and other costs, plus expenditures necessary to put the property into acceptable condition for its intended use, are proper additions. The same generalizations may be applied to acquisitions by construction under contract; that is, purchase or contract price, plus positively identified incidentals, should be capitalized. The determination of the cost of buildings and improvements obtained through construction by some agency of the governmental unit (sometimes called **force account construction**) poses slightly more difficulty. In these cases, costs should include not only all the direct and indirect expenditures (including net interest during the period of construction on debt incurred for the purpose of financing construction of capital assets) of the fund providing the construction but also materials and services furnished by other funds as well.

The valuation of buildings and improvements acquired by donation should be established by appraisal. As in the case of land, one reason for setting a value on donated buildings and improvements is to aid in determining the total value of capital assets used by the government, and for reports and comparisons. However, more compelling reasons exist for setting a value on buildings and certain improvements: the need for obtaining proper insurance coverage and the need for being able to substantiate the insurance claim if loss should occur. Lastly, of course, one should not lose sight of the fact that the cost of general capital assets is also required to be reported in the governmental activities column of the government-wide financial statements.

Equipment, or Machinery and Equipment. Machinery and equipment are usually acquired by purchase. Occasionally, however, machinery and equipment may be constructed by the government, perhaps financed by an internal service fund. In such cases, the same rules will apply as for buildings and improvements constructed by governmental employees. The cost of machinery and equipment purchased should include items conventional under business accounting practice: purchase price, transportation costs if not included in purchase price, installation cost, and other direct costs of readying for use. Cash discounts on machinery and equipment purchased should be treated as a reduction of costs. Donated equipment should be accounted for in the same manner, and for the same reasons, as donated buildings and improvements.

Construction Work in Progress. Construction Work in Progress, as an account classification of an enterprise fund, is discussed in Chapter 7. As a general capital asset classification, it is needed to account for construction expenditures accumulated to balance sheet date on projects financed by capital projects funds. As described later in this chapter, construction expenditures by capital projects funds are ordinarily closed to Fund Balance at the end of each year, but the amounts are not capitalized in the funds doing the construction. Instead the amounts to be capitalized are debited to the account Construction Work in Progress in the governmental activities general journal at the government-wide level of accounting.

Infrastructure Assets. **Infrastructure Assets** are capital assets such as highways, streets, sidewalks, storm drainage systems, and lighting systems, that are stationary in nature and normally can be preserved for a greater number of years than most other capital assets. The GASB *Statement No. 34* reporting model ushers in a new era in infrastructure accounting and reporting by requiring that all state and local governments report the cost of their infrastructure assets in the government-wide statement of net assets. Unless a government adopts the so-called *modified approach* discussed below, it also must report depreciation expense for infrastructure assets in its government-wide statement of activities. Under the previous standards, most governments opted not to report their investment in infrastructure assets because they believed the immovable and nontransferable nature of such assets made financial information about them of limited value for stewardship or decision-making purposes. In its *basis for conclusions* in *Statement No. 34*, the GASB argues that failure to recognize the benefits in the statement of net assets associated with investment in capital assets (including infrastructure), while recognizing the long-term debt incurred to acquire the capital assets, would result in a misleading net assets deficit.[6] Moreover, the cost of using capital assets (in the form of a depreciation) should properly be included in determining the full costs of conducting governmental programs.

Modified Approach. Under the *modified approach*, a government can elect not to depreciate certain *eligible* infrastructure assets, provided that two requirements are met.[7] The two requirements that must be met to avoid depreciation reporting are that

(1) the government manages the eligible infrastructure assets using an asset management system that includes (a) an up-to-date inventory of eligible assets, (b) condition assessments of the assets and summary of results using a measurement scale,

---

[6]GASB *Statement No. 34*, Appendix B, Part I, pars. 274–276.

[7]Eligible assets are those that are part of network of infrastructure assets or a subsystem of a network. For example, all roadways in a state might be considered a network, and interstate highways and state highways could be considered subsystems of that network.

and (c) estimates each year of the annual amount needed to maintain and preserve the eligible assets at the condition level established and disclosed by the government, and

(2) the government documents that the eligible infrastructure assets are being preserved approximately at (or above) the condition level established and disclosed (see item 1, (c) above).

What constitutes adequate documentation requires professional judgment. At a minimum, the government must provide documentation that (1) complete condition assessments are done at least every three years, and that (2) the three most recent condition assessments provide reasonable assurance that the eligible infrastructure assets are being preserved at or above the established condition level.

If the preceding requirements are met and adequate documentation is maintained, all expenditures incurred to preserve the eligible infrastructure assets should be expensed in the period incurred. Additions and improvements to the eligible assets should be capitalized. As long as the conditions are met, there is evidence that the eligible assets have an indefinite useful life and thus do not need to be depreciated. If the government subsequently fails to maintain the assets at or above the established and disclosed condition level, then it must revert to reporting depreciation for its infrastructure assets and discontinue its use of the modified approach.

Transition Reporting of Infrastructure Assets. As mentioned previously, as they implement the GASB *Statement No. 34* reporting model, most governments do not have a comprehensive inventory of infrastructure assets. *Statement No. 34* permits governments considerable time to develop an inventory of infrastructure assets and determine applicable costs during the transition to the new model. Governments must report all infrastructure assets acquired subsequent to their implementation of *Statement No. 34*. In addition to this *prospective* reporting, governments must begin *retroactive* reporting of all *major* infrastructure assets,[8] with the amount of time allowed for retroactive reporting depending on the size of the government. Retroactive reporting of *nonmajor* infrastructure assets is encouraged but not required. The amount initially capitalized for retroactive reporting should be based on historical cost. However, if inadequate records make it infeasible to determine historical cost, then estimated historical cost can be used. GASB *Statement No. 34* provides examples of methods that can be used to estimate historical costs.

Statement No. 34 allows governments considerable time to begin retroactive reporting of major infrastructure assets. Phase 1 and 2 governments (see Chapter 1, Footnote 11, for definitions of Phase 1, 2, and 3 governments) have until fiscal years beginning after June 15, 2005 and 2006, respectively, to begin retroactive

[8]*Major* infrastructure assets are determined at the network or subsystem (see Footnote 7) level and consist of those in which (1) the cost or estimated cost of the subsystem is expected to be at least 5 percent of the total cost of general capital assets reported in the first fiscal year ending after June 15, 1999, or (2) the cost or estimated cost of the network is expected to be at least 10 percent of the total cost of all general capital assets reported in the first fiscal year ending after June 15, 1999.

reporting of all major infrastructure assets. Phase 3 governments, because of their relatively small size, are exempted from retroactive reporting of major general infrastructure assets.

General Capital Assets Acquired under Capital Lease Agreements

As explained in some detail in Chapter 6, state and local governmental units generally are subject to constitutional or statutory limits on the amount of long-term debt they may issue. Consequently, it has been customary for governmental units that have reached their legal debt limit, or nearly done so, to acquire the use of capital assets through a lease agreement. A brief example is given below of the computation of the amount to be recorded in a governmental fund under the provisions of GASB standards if a general capital asset is acquired under a capital lease. For equipment leases an entry is made in the General Fund or other appropriate governmental fund to debit an Expenditure offset by a credit to Other Financing Sources, in the amount of the present value at the inception of the lease of the stream of lease payments.[9] That amount (or the fair value of the leased property, if less) is also recorded in the governmental activities ledger at the government-wide level as the cost of the leased property.

FASB *SFAS No. 13* defines and establishes accounting and financial reporting standards for a number of forms of leases, only two of which, operating leases and capital leases, are of importance in governmental accounting. GASB standards accept the *SFAS No. 13* definitions of these two forms of leases and prescribe accounting and financial reporting for lease agreements of state and local governmental units.[10] If a particular lease meets any one of the following classification criteria, it is a **capital lease.**

1. The lease transfers ownership of the property to the lessee by the end of the lease term.
2. The lease contains an option to purchase the leased property at a bargain price.
3. The lease term is equal to or greater than 75 percent of the estimated economic life of the leased property.
4. The present value of rental or other minimum lease payments equals or exceeds 90 percent of the fair value of the leased property less any investment tax credit retained by the lessor.

If no criterion is met, the lease is classified as an **operating lease** by the lessee. Rental payments under an operating lease for assets used by governmental funds are recorded by the using fund as expenditures of the period. In many states, statutes prohibit governments from entering into obligations extending beyond the current budget year. Because of this legal technicality, governmental lease agreements typically contain a "fiscal funding clause," or cancellation clause, which permits

---

[9]Intermediate accounting texts generally discuss at length the computation of amounts to be capitalized under capital lease agreements.

[10]GASB *Codification*, Sec. L20.107.

governmental lessees to terminate the agreement on an annual basis if funds are not appropriated to make required payments. GASB standards specify that lease agreements containing fiscal funding or cancellation clauses should be evaluated. If the possibility of cancellation is judged remote, the lease should be disclosed in financial statements and accounts in the manner specified for capital leases.[11]

As an example of accounting for the acquisition of general capital assets under a capital lease agreement, assume a governmental unit signs a capital lease agreement to pay $10,000 on January 1, 2001, the scheduled date of delivery of certain equipment to be used by an activity accounted for by a special revenue fund. The lease calls for annual payments of $10,000 at the beginning of each year thereafter; that is, January 1, 2002, January 1, 2003, and so on, through January 1, 2010. There are 10 payments of $10,000 each, for a total of $100,000, but GASB standards require entry in the accounts of the present value of the stream of annual payments, not their total. Since the initial payment of $10,000 is paid at the inception of the lease, its present value is $10,000. The present value of the remaining nine payments must be calculated using the borrowing rate the lessee would have incurred to obtain a similar loan over a similar term to purchase the leased asset. Assuming the rate to be 10 percent, the present value of payments 2 through 10 is $57,590. The present value of the 10 payments is, therefore, $67,590. GASB standards require a governmental fund (including, if appropriate, a capital projects fund) to record the following entry at the inception of the capital lease:

Special Revenue Fund.		
Expenditures	67,590	
Other Financing Sources—Capital Lease Agreements		67,590

The corresponding entry in the governmental activities general journal at the government-wide level to record the equipment and long-term liability under the capital lease is:

Governmental Activities:		
Equipment	67,590	
Capital Lease Obligations Payable		67,590

Costs Incurred after Acquisition

Governmental accounting procedures should include clear-cut provisions for classifying cost incurred in connection with capital assets after the acquisition cost has been established. Outlays closely associated with capital assets will regularly occur in amounts of varying size, and responsible persons will be charged with deciding whether these should be recorded as additions to assets. In general, any outlay that definitely adds to the utility or function of a capital asset or enhances the value of an integral part of it may be capitalized as part of the asset. Thus, drainage of land, addition of a room to a building, and changes in equipment that increase its output or reduce its cost of operation are clearly recognizable as additions to assets. Special difficulty arises in the case of large-scale outlays that are partly replacements and partly additions or betterments. An example would be replacement of a composition-type

[11]Ibid., pars. 119–122.

roof with a roof of some more durable material. To the extent that the project replaces the old roof, outlays should not be capitalized unless cost of the old roof is removed from the accounts; and to the extent that the project provides a better roof, outlays should be capitalized. The distribution of the total cost in such a case is largely a matter for managerial determination. Consistent with policy in recording original acquisition costs, some outlays unquestionably representing increases in permanent values may not be capitalized if the amount is less than some specified minimum or on the basis of any other criterion previously decided on.

Outlays that are partly replacements and partly additions or betterments occasion some accounting difficulty. The distribution of the outlay having been decided on, the estimated amount of addition or betterment might be added to the asset. Perhaps better results might be obtained by crediting the appropriate asset account for the cost of the replaced part, thus removing the amount, and then debiting the asset account for the total cost of the replacing item.

Reduction of Cost

Reductions in the cost of capital assets may relate to the elimination of the total amount expended for a given item or items, or they may consist only of removing the cost applicable to a specific part. Thus, if an entire building is demolished, the total cost of the structure should be removed from the appropriate accounts; but if the separation applies only to a wing or some other definitely identifiable portion, the cost eliminated should be the amount estimated as applying thereto. Reductions in the recorded cost of capital assets may be brought about by sale, retirement from use, destruction by fire or other casualty, replacement of a major part, theft or loss from some other cause, and possibly other changes. The cost of capital assets recorded in the governmental activities ledger may sometimes be reduced by the transfer of a unit to an enterprise fund, or vice versa.

Accounting for cost reductions consisting of entire units is a relatively simple matter if adequate asset records have been kept. If the reduction is only partial, the cost as shown by the capital assets record must be modified to reflect the change, with a complete description of what brought about the change.

Since depreciation is now recorded on general capital assets, the removal of a capital asset from the governmental activities general ledger may be accomplished by crediting the ledger account recording its cost and debiting Accumulated Depreciation and Cash, if the item was sold. Gains or losses should be recognized if the value received differs from the book value of the assets removed. The gains and losses are reported on the government-wide statement of activities.

Governments sometimes trade used capital assets for new items. In the governmental activities general ledger, the total cost of the old item should be removed and the total cost (not merely the cash payment) of the new one set up.

Illustrative Entries

Acquisition of general capital assets requires a debit to the appropriate governmental activities asset account and a credit to Cash or a liability account. Thus, if office equipment is purchased for the treasurer's office from General Fund resources, the following journal entries would be made in the general journals for the General Fund (ignoring encumbrances) and governmental activities at the government-wide level:

General Fund:		
Expenditures	450	
Vouchers Payable		450
Governmental Activities:		
Equipment	450	
Vouchers Payable		450

Assuming the Vouchers Payable is paid shortly after the equipment acquisition, Vouchers Payable will be debited and Cash will be credited, both in the General Fund and the governmental activities journal at the government-wide level. General capital assets acquired by use of Capital Projects Fund resources would be recorded in essentially the same manner as if acquired from the General Fund. If construction of a general capital asset is in progress at the end of a fiscal year, Construction Expenditures to the date of the financial report should be capitalized in the governmental activities ledger. These capital asset entries will be illustrated later in this chapter in the discussion of capital projects fund transactions.

Accounting for the disposal of general capital assets is relatively simple unless cash or others assets are involved in the liquidation. Accounting for an asset disposal requires elimination of the capital asset and accumulated depreciation accounts and recognition of a gain or loss, as appropriate. Assuming a building that cost $100,000, and with $80,000 of accumulated depreciation, is retired without revenue or expenditure to the General Fund, the following entry in the governmental activities general journal would be required:

Governmental Activities:		
Loss on Disposal of Building	20,000	
Accumulated Depreciation—Buildings	80,000	
Buildings		100,000

Property records for the building should receive appropriate notations about the transaction and thereafter be transferred to an inactive file.

In the event cash is disbursed or received in connection with the disposal of general capital assets, the Cash Account would be debited or credited as part of the entry to remove the book value of the capital asset, and a gain or loss would be recorded, as appropriate. Assuming that in the preceding example the General Fund incurred $3,000 for the demolition of the building, an entry in the following form should be made on the General Fund books:

General Fund:		
Expenditures	3,000	
Vouchers Payable		3,000

The corresponding entry at the government-wide level is:

	Debits	Credits
Governmental Activities:		
Loss on Disposal of Building	23,000	
Accumulated Depreciation—Buildings	80,000	
Buildings		100,000
Vouchers Payable		3,000

If cash is received from the disposal of a general capital asset, some question may arise as to its disposition. Theoretically, it should be directed to the fund that provided the asset; but this may not always be practicable. If the asset was provided by a capital projects fund, the contributing fund may have been liquidated before the sale occurs. Unless otherwise prescribed by law, disposition of the results of a sale will be handled as decided by the legislative body having jurisdiction over the asset and will be accounted for in the manner required by the accounting system of the recipient fund. Commonly, proceeds of sales of general capital assets are budgeted as Estimated Other Financing Sources in the General Fund. In such cases, when sales actually occur, the General Fund debits Cash (or a receivable) for the selling price and credits Other Financing Sources—Proceeds of Sales of Assets.

Accounting for Capital Projects

The reason for creating a fund to account for capital projects is the same as the reason for creating special revenue funds: to provide a formal mechanism to enable administrators to ensure revenues and other financing sources dedicated to a certain purpose are used for that purpose and no other, and to enable administrators to report to creditors and other grantors of capital projects fund resources that their requirements regarding the use of the resources were met.

Capital projects funds differ from general and special revenue funds in that the latter categories have a year-to-year life, whereas capital projects funds have a project-life focus. In some jurisdictions governments are allowed to account for all capital projects within a single capital projects fund. In other jurisdictions laws are construed as requiring each project to be accounted for by a separate capital projects fund. Even in jurisdictions that permit the use of a single fund, managers may prefer to use separate funds in order to enhance control over each project. In such cases a fund is created when a capital project or a series of related projects is legally authorized; it is closed when the project or series is completed. Budgetary accounts need not be used because the legal authorization to engage in the project is in itself an appropriation of the total amount that may be obligated for the construction or acquisition of the capital asset specified in the project authorization. Estimated revenues need not be recorded because few contractors will start work on a project until financing is ensured through the sale of bonds or the receipt of grants or gifts. To provide control over the issuance of contracts and purchase orders, which may be numerous and which may be outstanding for several years in construction projects, it is recommended that the encumbrance procedure described in Chapter 3 be used. Since the purpose of the capital projects fund is to account for the acquisition and disposition of revenues for a specific purpose, it (as is true for general and special revenue funds) contains balance sheet accounts for only financial resources and for the liabilities to be liquidated by those resources. Neither the capital assets acquired nor any long-term debt incurred for the acquisition is accounted for by a capital projects fund; these items are accounted for in the governmental activities general ledger at the government-wide level, as discussed earlier in this chapter and in Chapter 6.

In some jurisdictions, annual revenues are raised for the expressed purpose of financing major repairs to existing capital assets, or for replacement of components of those assets (e.g., furnaces, air conditioning systems, roofs). Revenues of the nature described are accounted for by a **capital improvements fund,** sometimes called a *cumulative building fund*. The specific repairs and replacements to be undertaken in a given year are not necessarily known at the time the revenues are budgeted. The appropriation process described in previous chapters is used to authorize expenditures from capital improvement funds when the nature and approximate cost of needed repairs and replacements become known. Necessary expenditures that cannot be financed by appropriation of the Fund Balance of a capital improvement fund, nor from the General Fund or special revenue funds, may occasion the establishment of a capital projects fund.

Legal Requirements

Since a governmental unit's power to issue bonds constitutes an ever-present hazard to the welfare of its property owners in particular,[12] and its taxpayers in general, the authority is ordinarily closely regulated by legislation. The purpose of legislative regulation is to obtain a prudent balance between public welfare and the rights of individual citizens. In some jurisdictions, most bond issues must be approved by referendum; in others, by petition of a specified percentage of taxpayers. Not only must bond issues be approved according to law but other provisions, such as method and timing of payments from the proceeds, and determination of validity of claims for payment, must be complied with. A knowledge of all details related to a bond issue is prerequisite to the avoidance of difficulties and complications that might otherwise occur.

Participation of state and federal agencies in financing capital acquisitions by local government adds further complications to the process. Strict control of how such grants are used is imperative for ensuring proper use of the funds. This necessitates more or less dictation of accounting and reporting procedures to provide information necessary for proving or disproving compliance with terms of the grants. Details of the fund structure and operation should provide for producing all the required information when it is needed, in the form in which it is needed.

---

[12]An issue of bonds to be repaid from tax revenues in essence places a lien on all taxable property within a governmental unit's jurisdiction. Responsibility for payments of principal and interest on general bonded debt provides for no consideration of a property owner's financial condition, and ability or inability to pay.

Accomplishment of a capital acquisition project may be brought about in one or more of the following ways:

1. Outright purchase from fund cash.
2. By construction, utilizing the governmental unit's own working force.
3. By construction, utilizing the services of private contractors.
4. By capital lease agreement.

Illustrative Transactions—Capital Projects Funds

GASB standards require use of the same basis of accounting for capital projects funds as for the other governmental fund types. Proceeds of debt issues should be recognized by a capital projects fund at the time the issue is sold, rather than the time it is authorized, because authorization of an issue does not guarantee its sale. Proceeds of debt issues should be recorded as Proceeds of Bonds or Proceeds of Long-Term Notes rather than as Revenues, and they should be reported in the Other Financing Sources section of the Statement of Revenues, Expenditures, and Changes in Fund Balance. Similarly, tax revenues raised by the General Fund, or a special revenue fund, and transferred to a capital projects fund are recorded as Interfund Transfers In and reported in the Other Financing Sources section of the operating statement.

Taxes raised specifically for a capital projects fund would be recorded as Revenues of that fund, as would special assessments to be used for the construction of assets deemed to be of particular benefit to certain property owners. Grants, entitlements, or shared revenues received by a capital projects fund from another governmental unit are considered Revenues of the capital projects fund, as would be interest earned on temporary investments of the capital projects fund if the interest is available for expenditure by the capital projects fund (if, by law, the interest must be used for service of long-term capital debt the interest should be transferred to the appropriate debt service fund).

In the following illustration of accounting for representative transactions of a capital projects fund, it is assumed the Town Council of the Town of Brighton authorized an issue of $1,200,000 of 6 percent bonds as partial financing of a fire station expected to cost approximately $1,500,000; the $300,000 additional was to be contributed by other governments. The project, to utilize land already owned by the Town, was done partly by a private contractor and partly by the Town's own workforce. Completion of the project was expected within the current year. Transactions and entries were as shown below, all of which are assumed to occur in fiscal year 2002. For economy of time and space, vouchering of liabilities will be omitted, as will entries in subsidiary ledger accounts.

The $1,200,000 bond issue, which had been approved by voter referendum, was officially approved by the Town Council. No formal entry is required to record voter and Town Council approval. A memorandum entry may be made to identify the approved project and the means of financing it.

The sum of $50,000 was borrowed on a short-term basis from the National Bank for defraying engineering and other preliminary expenses. Because this transaction affects both the Fire Station Capital Projects Fund and the governmental activities at the government-wide level, the following entry is made in both journals:

Fire Station Capital Projects Fund and Governmental Activities:		
1. Cash	50,000	
Short-term Notes Payable		50,000

The receivable from the other governments was recorded both at the fund and government-wide levels:

Fire Station Capital Projects Fund:		
2a. Due from Other Governmental Units	300,000	
Revenues		300,000
Governmental Activities:		
2b. Due from Other Governmental Units	300,000	
Program Revenues—Capital Grants and Contributions—Public Safety		300,000

Total purchase orders and other commitment documents issued for supplies, materials, items of minor equipment, and labor required for the part of the project to be performed by the Town's employees amounted to $443,000. (Since the authorization is for the project, not for a budget year, it is unnecessary to include 2002, or any other year, in the account titles.) The following budgetary control entry is made in the capital projects fund but is not recorded at the government-wide level.

Fire Station Capital Projects Fund:		
3. Encumbrances	443,000	
Reserve for Encumbrances		443,000

A contract was let for certain work to be done by a private contractor in the amount of $1,005,000. As with Entry 3, only the capital projects fund is affected.

Fire Station Capital Projects Fund:		
4. Encumbrances	1,005,000	
Reserve for Encumbrances		1,005,000

Special engineering and miscellaneous costs that had not been encumbered were paid in the amount of $48,000. These costs are deemed to be properly capitalized as part of the fire station.

Fire Station Capital Projects Fund:		
5a. Construction Expenditures	48,000	
Cash		48,000
Governmental Activities:		
5b. Construction Work in Progress	48,000	
Cash		48,000

Entries 5a and 5b highlight a major difference between accounting for a governmental fund and governmental activities at the government-wide level. Accounting for a governmental fund focuses on the inflows and outflows of current financial resources, on the modified accrual basis; accounting for governmental activities focuses on the inflows and outflows of economic resources, including capital assets, on the accrual basis used in accounting for business organizations.

When the project was approximately half finished, the contractor submitted a billing requesting payment of $495,000.

Fire Station Capital Projects Fund:

	Debit	Credit
6a. Reserve for Encumbrances	495,000	
Encumbrances		495,000
6b. Construction Expenditures	495,000	
Contracts Payable		495,000

Governmental Activities:

	Debit	Credit
6c. Construction Work in Progress	495,000	
Contracts Payable		495,000

Entries 6a and 6b record conversion of an estimated liability to a firm liability, eligible for payment upon proper authentication. Contracts Payable records the status of a claim under a contract between the time of presentation and verification for vouchering or payment.

Payment in full was received from the other governmental units that had agreed to pay part of the cost of the new fire station.

Fire Station Capital Projects Fund and Governmental Activities:

	Debit	Credit
7. Cash	300,000	
Due from Other Governmental Units		300,000

The National Bank loan was repaid with interest amounting to $1,000.

Fire Station Capital Projects Fund:

	Debit	Credit
8a. Construction Expenditures	1,000	
Short-term Notes Payable	50,000	
Cash		51,000

Governmental Activities:

	Debit	Credit
8b. Construction Work in Progress	1,000	
Short-term Notes Payable	50,000	
Cash		51,000

The reader will note that the $1,000 of interest expenditure (expense) is treated in Entries 8a and 8b as an item to be capitalized as part of the total cost of the new fire station. Capitalization of interest incurred during construction, in the manner required by FASB standards for business organizations, is now required by GASB *Statement No. 34*. Capitalization of interest incurred during construction was optional under previous GASB standards. Additional discussion is provided on this topic later in this chapter.

The bond issue was sold at par on June 15, 2002, which is also the date of the bonds—the date from which interest begins to accrue. Entries 9a and 9b below show the sharp contrast in accounting for this transaction in the capital projects fund and in the governmental activities ledger at the government-wide level. Again, in the capital projects fund, the focus is on the inflow of current financial resources that increases the fund balance, whereas at the government-wide level, the focus is on the change in economic resources. In this case, the inflow of cash produces no change in net assets since the cash inflow is offset by a long-term liability.

	Debit	Credit
Fire Station Capital Projects Fund:		
9a. Cash	1,200,000	
Other Financing Sources—Proceeds of Bonds		1,200,000
Governmental Activities:		
9b. Cash	1,200,000	
Bonds Payable		1,200,000

The contractor's initial claim was fully verified and paid (see Entries 6b and 6c).

	Debit	Credit
Fire Station Capital Projects Fund and Governmental Activities:		
10. Contracts Payable	495,000	
Cash		495,000

Total disbursements for all costs encumbered in Transaction 3 amounted to $440,000. Although the encumbrances entry only affects the capital projects fund, the disbursement affects both the capital projects fund and governmental activities at the government-wide level.

	Debit	Credit
Fire Station Capital Projects Fund:		
11a. Reserve for Encumbrances	443,000	
Encumbrances		443,000
11b. Construction Expenditures	440,000	
Cash		440,000
Governmental Activities:		
11c. Construction Work in Progress	440,000	
Cash		440,000

Billing for the balance owed on the construction contract was received from the contractor.

	Debit	Credit
Fire Station Capital Projects Fund:		
12a. Reserve for Encumbrances	510,000	
Encumbrances		510,000
12b. Construction Expenditures	510,000	
Contracts Payable		510,000
Governmental Activities:		
12c. Construction Work in Progress	510,000	
Contracts Payable		510,000

Inspection revealed only minor imperfections in the contractor's performance, and on correction of these, the liability to the contractor was paid.

Fire Station Capital Projects Fund and Governmental Activities:

	Debit	Credit
13. Contracts Payable	510,000	
Cash		510,000

All requirements and obligations related to the project having been fulfilled, the operating statement accounts were closed in the capital projects fund and governmental activities general ledgers.

Fire Station Capital Projects Fund:

	Debit	Credit
14a. Revenues	300,000	
Other Financing Sources—Proceeds of Bonds	1,200,000	
Construction Expenditures		1,494,000
Fund Balance		6,000

Governmental Activities:

	Debit	Credit
14b. Program Revenues—Capital Grants and Contributions—Public Safety	300,000	
Net Assets—Invested in Capital Assets, Net of Related Debt		300,000

(Note: If the $300,000 had not yet been expended for the project, the account credited would have been Net Assets—Restricted for Capital Projects. If only part of the resources had been expended, appropriate amounts would have been credited to both accounts.)

Since the project has been completed, it is appropriate to close the Capital Projects Fund. The only asset of the fund remaining after the 14 transactions illustrated is Cash in the amount of $6,000. State laws often require that assets no longer needed in a capital projects fund be transferred to the fund that will service the debt incurred for this project, a debt service fund. Transfers of this nature are called **interfund transfers** and are reported as other financing uses by the transferor fund and other financing sources by the transferee fund in their Statement of Revenues, Expenditures, and Changes in Fund Balance (see Illustration 5–3) The entries to record the transfer and the closing of the Capital Projects Fund accounts are:

Fire Station Capital Projects Fund:

	Debit	Credit
15a. Other Financing Uses—Interfund Transfers Out	6,000	
Cash	6,000	
15b. Fund Balance	6,000	
Other Financing Uses—Interfund Transfers Out		6,000

Similar entries would be required to record the Interfund Transfers In by the debt service fund. No entry is required at the government-wide level since the transfer occurs *within* the governmental activities category.

The cost of the fire station constructed by the Town of Brighton is recorded in the governmental activities general journal at the government-wide level. Because all capitalizable costs have previously been recorded as Construction Work in Progress during the period of construction, the only entry required is to reclassify the amount in that account to the Buildings account, as shown in the following entry.

Governmental Activities:

	Debit	Credit
16. Buildings	1,494,000	
Construction Work in Progress		1,494,000

Illustration 5–3

TOWN OF BRIGHTON
FIRE STATION CAPITAL PROJECTS FUND
STATEMENT OF REVENUES, EXPENDITURES,
AND CHANGES IN FUND BALANCE
FOR THE YEAR ENDED DECEMBER 31, 2002

Revenues:		
From other governmental units		$ 300,000
Expenditures:		
Construction		1,494,000
Excess of Revenues over (under) Expenditures		(1,194,000)
Other Financing Sources (Uses):		
Proceeds of bonds	$1,200,000	
Interfund transfer out	(6,000)	1,194,000
Excess of Revenues and Other Financing Sources/ Uses over Expenditures		–0–
Fund Balance, January 1, 2002		–0–
Fund Balance, December 31, 2002		$ –0–

Illustrative Financial Statements for a Capital Projects Fund

Inasmuch as all balance sheet accounts of the Town of Brighton Fire Station Capital Projects Fund are closed in the case illustrated in the preceding section of this chapter, there are no assets, liabilities, or fund equity to report in a balance sheet. The operations of the year, however, should be reported in a Statement of Revenues, Expenditures, and Changes in Fund Balance, as shown in Illustration 5–3. Since it is assumed the Town of Brighton is not required to adopt a legal budget for its capital projects funds, there is no need to prepare a budgetary comparison schedule or statement for the capital projects fund type.

At the government-wide level, the completed fire station is reported as a capital asset, net of accumulated depreciation (if any depreciation expense is recorded in the first year in which the asset is placed into service), in the governmental activities column of the Statement of Net Assets (see Illustration 2–1). The $1,200,000 of tax-supported bonds issued for the project is reported as a long-term liability in the governmental activities column of the Statement of Net Assets. If any depreciation expense is recorded for the portion of a year the fire station has been in service, it would be reported as a direct expense of the Public Safety function in the Statement of Activities (see Illustration 2–2).

Alternative Treatment of Residual Equity or Deficits

In the example presented above, a modest amount of cash remained in the Capital Projects Fund after the project had been completed and all liabilities of the fund were liquidated. If necessary expenditures and other financing uses are planned carefully, and controlled carefully so that actual does not exceed plans, revenues and other financing sources of the Capital Projects Fund should equal, or slightly exceed, the expenditures and other financing uses, leaving a residual fund equity.

If, as in the example presented above, long-term debt had been incurred for the purposes of the Capital Projects Fund, the residual equity is ordinarily transferred to the fund that is to service the debt. If the residual equity were deemed to have come from grants or shared revenues restricted for capital acquisitions or construction, legal advice may indicate that any residual equity must be returned to the source(s) of the restricted grants or restricted shared revenues.

In some situations, in spite of careful planning and cost control, expenditures and other financing uses of a Capital Projects Fund may exceed its revenues and other financing sources, resulting in a negative Fund Balance, or deficit. If the deficit is a relatively small amount, the legislative body of the governmental unit may be able to authorize transfers from one or more other funds to cover the deficit in the Capital Projects Fund. If the deficit is relatively large, and/or if intended transfers are not feasible, the governmental unit may seek additional grants or shared revenues from other governmental units to cover the deficit. If no other alternative is available, the governmental units would need to finance the deficit by issuing debt in whatever form is legally possible and salable under market conditions then existing.

Bond Premium, Discount, and Accrued Interest on Bonds Sold

Governments that issue bonds, or long-term notes, to finance the acquisition of capital assets commonly sell the entire issue to an underwriter, or a syndicate of underwriters, on the basis of bids. The underwriters then "retail" the bonds or notes to institutions or individuals, who often have agreed in advance to purchase a specified amount of bonds should the underwriters be successful in tendering the winning bid. Statutes in many states prohibit the initial sale of an issue of local government bonds at a discount. Accordingly, it is usual to set the interest rate high enough to enable the underwriters to pay the issuer at least the par, or face, value of the bonds; it is not unusual for underwriters to pay issuers an amount in excess of par, known as a premium. State statutes, local ordinances, or bond indentures often require that initial issue premiums be used for debt service. In such cases only the par value of the bonds is considered as an Other Financing Source of the Capital Projects Fund; the premium is considered as an Other Financing Source of the Debt Service Fund. Therefore, the sale of bonds at a premium would require an entry in the Capital Projects Fund for the face of the bonds (as shown in Entry 9 of this chapter) and an entry in the Debt Service Fund for the premium. At the government-wide level, a premium would be recorded as an additional component of the general long-term liability for the bonds, as in accounting for business organizations. The premium should be amortized, using the effective-interest method, over the life of the bonds, the amount of amortization being the difference between the actual cash paid for interest and the calculated amount of effective interest expense for the period.

Similarly, when bonds are sold between interest payment dates the party buying the bonds must pay up front the amount of interest accrued from the date of the bonds (the starting date for purposes of calculating interest) to the date the bonds are actually sold, as part of the total price of the bonds. Thus, assuming two months of interest have already accrued by the sale date, the two months of interest that bondholders pay at the sale date yields the equitable result that they earn a *net* four months of interest, although they will receive a full six months of interest only four months after the sale date. Conceptually in a governmental fund, accrued interest sold should be credited to Interest Expenditure and be offset against the six-month interest expenditure recorded on the first interest payment date following the sale of the bonds. In practice, however, accrued interest sold is generally recorded as a Revenue of the Debt Service Fund. This practice simplifies budgetary control by permitting the government to budget appropriations for and record an expenditure for the full six months of interest that must be paid on the first interest payment date. At the government-wide level, however, cash received on the sale date for accrued interest would be credited either as Accrued Interest Payable or Interest Expense, as in business accounting.

It may happen that the issuing government receives one check from the underwriters for the total amount of the par plus the premium. If procedures of that government indicate that it is desirable to record the entire amount in the Capital Projects Fund, the following entries are appropriate (using assumed amounts):

Capital Projects Fund:		
Cash	1,509,000	
Other Financing Sources—Proceeds of Bonds		1,500,000
Due to Other Funds		9,000

This entry accounts for the bond premium as a liability of the Capital Projects Fund because it must be remitted to the Debt Service Fund. In the Debt Service Fund, an entry would be made to debit Due from Other Funds and credit Other Financing Sources—Premium on Bonds Sold. Some accountants credit Premium on Bonds rather than Due to Other Funds in the Capital Projects Fund, particularly if the disposition of the premium is still to be determined on the sale date. Some accountants also include the amount of the premium as part of the credit to Other Financing Sources—Proceeds of Bonds in the Capital Projects Fund. If this latter procedure is used, it is necessary to make a second entry debiting Other Financing Uses—Interfund Transfers Out and crediting Due to Other Funds.

In those jurisdictions in which it is legal for bonds to be sold initially at a discount, using the amounts assumed in the entry above, except the debt proceeds are less than the face amount of the bonds, the entry might be:

Capital Projects Fund:		
Cash	1,491,000	
Discount on Bonds	9,000	
Other Financing Sources—Proceeds of Bonds		1,500,000

Crediting Other Financing Sources—Proceeds of Bonds for $1,500,000 carries the implication that, if necessary, the discount is expected to be counterbalanced at a future date by receipt of money from another source. When money from another source has been provided, or it has been determined that no money from another source will be provided, the discount would be written off against Proceeds of Bonds. When the money from another source is received, the Capital Projects Fund should debit Cash and credit either Revenues or another financing source, depending on the source of the money. When it is known in advance that the discount will not be made up by transfers from other sources, an entry debiting Cash and crediting Other Financing Sources—Proceeds of Bonds, each for par value less discount, should be made.

Retained Percentages

It is common to require contractors on large-scale contracts to give performance bonds, providing for indemnity to the governmental unit for any failure on the contractor's part to comply with terms and specifications of the agreement. Before final inspection of a project can be completed, the contractor firm may have moved its working force and equipment to another location, thus making it difficult to remedy possible objections to the firm's performance. Also, the shortcoming alleged by the governmental unit may be of a controversial nature, with the contractor unwilling to accede to the demands of the governmental unit; and results of legal action in such disagreements are not predictable with certainty.

To provide more prompt adjustment on shortcomings not large or convincing enough to justify legal action, and not recoverable under contractor's bond, as well as those the contractor may admit but not be in a position to rectify, it is common practice to withhold a portion of the contractor's remuneration until final inspection and acceptance have come about. The withheld portion is normally a contractual percentage of the amount due on each segment of the contract.

In the Town of Brighton illustration, the contractor submitted a bill for $495,000, which, on preliminary approval, was recorded previously in Entry 6b in the Capital Projects Fund as:

Construction Expenditures	495,000	
Contracts Payable		495,000

Assuming the contract provided for retention of 5 percent, current settlement on the billing would be recorded as follows:

Contracts Payable	495,000	
Cash		470,250
Contracts Payable—Retained Percentage		24,750

This same entry would also be made in the governmental activities general journal at the government-wide level. Alternatively, the intention of the government to retain the percentage stipulated in the contract could be recorded at the time the progress billing receives preliminary approval. In that event, the credit to Contracts Payable in the first entry in this section would be $470,250, and the credit to Contracts Payable—Retained Percentage in the amount of $24,750 is made at that time. The second entry, therefore, would be a debit to Contracts Payable and a credit to Cash for $470,250.

On final acceptance of the project, the retained percentage is liquidated by a payment of cash. In the event the governmental unit that made the retention finds it necessary to spend money on correction of deficiencies in the contractor's performance, the payment is charged to Contracts Payable—Retained Percentage. If the cost of correcting deficiencies exceeds the balance in the Contracts Payable—

Retained Percentage Account, the excess amount is debited to Construction Expenditures in the Capital Projects Fund and to Buildings (or other appropriate capital asset account) in the governmental activities general journal.

Claims and Judgments Payable

Claims and judgments often, although not always, relate to construction activities of a government. If a claim has been litigated and a judicial decision adverse to the governmental unit has been rendered, there is no question as to the amount of the liability that should be recorded. If claims have not been litigated, or judgments have not been made, as of balance sheet date, liabilities may be estimated through a case-by-case review of all claims, or the application of historical experience to the outstanding claims, or a combination of these methods.[13]

GASB standards specify that the amount of claims and judgments recognized as expenditures and liabilities of governmental funds is limited to the amount that would normally be liquidated with expendable resources then in the fund; however, the full known or estimated liability should be reported in the governmental activities column of the government-wide Statement of Net Assets.

Bond Anticipation Notes Payable and the Problem of Interest Expenditures

Bond Anticipation Notes Payable is a liability resulting from the borrowing of money for temporary financing before issuance of bonds. Delay in perfecting all details connected with issuance of bonds and postponement of the sale until a large portion of the proceeds is needed are the prevailing reasons for preliminary financing by use of **bond anticipation notes.** The "bond anticipation" description of the debt signifies an obligation to retire the notes from proceeds of a proposed bond issue. If two conditions specified in FASB *Statement No.* 6 are met, then the liability for bond anticipation notes should be treated as a long-term liability:[14]

1. All legal steps have been taken to refinance the bond anticipation notes.
2. The intent is supported by an ability to consummate refinancing the short-term notes on a long-term basis.

In most cases in which the bond anticipation notes are secured by approved but unissued bonds, and the intent is to repay the notes from the proceeds of the bond issue, it would appear the two criteria would be met and thus most bond anticipation note issues would be reported as a long-term liability in the governmental activities column of the government-wide Statement of Net Assets and as an other financing source (proceeds of bond anticipation notes) in the Capital Projects Fund.

As an example of a bond anticipation note that meets the two criteria provided above, assume a particular city issued $500,000 of 6% bond anticipation notes,

---

[13]GASB standards (GASB *Codification*, Sec. C50.110–.111) require governmental units to use the criteria of FASB *SFAS No. 5* as guidelines for recognizing a loss liability. That is, if information available prior to issuance of the financial statements indicates it is probable that an asset has been impaired or a liability has been incurred at the date of the financial statements and the amount of the loss can be estimated with a reasonable degree of accuracy, the liability should be recognized.

[14]GASB *Codification*, Sec. B50.101.

under a written agreement that the notes will be retired within six months from the proceeds of a previously approved $5,000,000 bond issue. When the bond anticipation notes are issued, the journal entries for the Capital Projects Fund and governmental activities would be as follows:

Capital Projects Fund:		
Cash	500,000	
Other Financing Sources—Proceeds of Bond Anticipation Notes		500,000
Governmental Activities:		
Cash	500,000	
Bond Anticipation Notes Payable		500,000

Six months later, the bonds are issued at par and the bond anticipation notes are retired from a portion of the bond proceeds. Cash from other sources is assumed to be used to pay interest on the bond anticipation notes. The required journal entries are:

Capital Projects Fund:		
Cash	5,000,000	
Other Financing Sources—Proceeds of Bonds		5,000,000
Other Financing Uses—Retirement of Bond Anticipation Notes	500,000	
Construction Expenditures	15,000	
Cash		515,000
Governmental Activities:		
Cash	5,000,000	
Bonds Payable		5,000,000
Bond Anticipation Notes Payable	500,000	
Construction Work in Progress	15,000	
Cash		515,000

(Note: Interest expense, presumed to be capitalized, is $500,000 × .06 × 6/12 = $15,000)

As indicated in the preceding example, interest almost always must be paid on Bond Anticipation Notes Payable. Both practical and theoretical problems are involved in the payment of interest on liabilities. Practically, payment of interest by the Capital Projects Fund reduces the amount available for construction or acquisition of the assets, so the administrators of the Capital Projects Fund would wish to pass the burden of interest payment to another fund. Logically, the Debt Service Fund set up for the bond issue should bear the burden of interest on bond anticipation notes, and possibly on judgments, but at the time this interest must be paid the Debt Service Fund may have no assets. It would also appeal to the Capital Projects Fund's administrators that interest on the bond anticipation notes and judgments should be paid by the General Fund (or any other fund with available cash). If such interest payments had been included in the appropriations budget by the General Fund (or other fund), the payment would be legal; if not, the legislative body might authorize the other fund to pay the interest.

If the Capital Projects Fund bears the interest on bond anticipation notes or other short-term debt, either initially or ultimately, an expenditure account must be debited. In Entry 8a in the series of Capital Projects Fund and Government Activities entries illustrated earlier in this chapter, interest paid on Bond Anticipation Notes was debited to Construction Expenditures rather than to an account such as Interest Expenditures. Entry 8b showed that the $1,000 paid for interest was capitalized as part of the Construction Work in Progress for the fire station project. As state and local governments implement the GASB *Statement No. 34* reporting model, they are required to prospectively capitalize interest payments made during the period of construction on self-constructed assets.[15] Previous GASB standards allowed each governmental unit to choose whether or not it wished to capitalize net interest incurred in the construction of general capital assets as a part of the cost of the asset, as long as the policy was consistently applied and was disclosed in the notes to the financial statements.

In most cases, it should be possible to associate specific bond issues with specific capital projects, in which case interest on those bonds is the interest that must be capitalized. The amount to be capitalized is the specific borrowing rate on the bonds issued to finance the project applied to the average construction cost for the period or the actual interest incurred, whichever is lower. In some cases, multiple bond issues may apply to multiple projects, making it difficult to directly associate a bond issue with a particular capital project. In this case, the weighted average interest rate from all borrowings is substituted for the specific interest rate. Most intermediate financial accounting texts provide detailed examples of how the FASB standards regarding interest capitalization are applied.

Although the completion date of the fire station in the illustrative transactions shown earlier in this chapter was not revealed, assume that the interest expense incurred between the issuance of the bonds on June 15, 2002, and the completion of construction was $30,000. The corresponding journal entry at the government-wide level to capitalize this interest is:

Governmental Activities:		
Building	30,000	
Interest Expense		30,000

(Note: The credit to Interest Expense assumes the Interest Expense had previously been recorded at the government-wide level and the entry shown above is treated as an adjusting entry.)

Investments

Interest rates payable by governmental units on general long-term debt have been lower than interest rates the governmental units can earn on temporary investments of high quality, such as U.S. Treasury bills and notes, bank certificates of deposit, and government bonds with short maturities. Consequently, there is considerable attraction to the practice of selling bonds as soon as possible after a capital project is legally authorized, and investing the proceeds to earn a net interest income. (This practice also avoids the problems and costs involved in financing by Bond Anticipation Notes Payable, described in the preceding section.) Arbitrage rules under the Internal Revenue Code, particularly after the Tax Reform Act of 1986 became effective, however, constrain the investment of bond proceeds to securities whose yield does not exceed that of the new debt. Application of these

[15]GASB *Statement No. 34*, par. 18.

rules to state and local governmental units is subject to continuing litigation and legislative action, so competent legal guidance must be sought by governmental units wishing to invest bond proceeds in a manner that will avoid incurring an **arbitrage rebate** and possible difficulties with the Internal Revenue Service.

Interest earned on temporary investments is available for use by the Capital Projects Fund in some jurisdictions; in others, laws or local practices require the interest income to be transferred to the Debt Service Fund or to the General Fund. If interest income is available to the Capital Projects Fund, it should be recognized on the modified accrual basis as a credit to Revenues. If it will be collected by the Capital Projects Fund but must be transferred, the credit for the income earned should be to Due to Other Funds; if the interest will be collected by the Debt Service Fund, or other fund that will recognize it as revenue, no entry by the Capital Projects Fund is necessary.

Multiple-Period and Multiple-Project Bond Funds

Thus far, discussion of capital projects fund accounting has proceeded on the tacit assumption that initiation and completion of projects occur in the same fiscal year. Many projects large enough to require a capital projects fund are started in one year and ended in another. Furthermore, a single comprehensive authorization may legalize two or more purchase or construction projects as segments of a master plan of improvements. Both multiple-period and multiple-project activities require some deviations from the accounting activities that suffice for one-period, one-project accounting.

The first difference appears in the budgeting procedure. Whereas for a one-period operation a single authorization might adequately cover the project from beginning to end, annual budgets, in one form or another, may be desirable or even required for those extending into two or more periods. This practice is resorted to as a means of keeping the project under the legislative body's control and preventing the unacceptable deviations that might result from lump-sum approval, in advance, of a long-term project. Likewise, a large bond issue, to be supplemented by grants from outside sources, may be authorized to cover a number of projects extending over a period of time but not planned in detail before initiation of the first project. Such an arrangement requires the fund administration to maintain control by giving final approval to the budget for each project only as it comes up for action.

For a multiple-projects fund, it is necessary to identify encumbrances and expenditures in a way that will indicate the project to which each encumbrance and expenditure applies, in order to check for compliance with the project budget. This can be accomplished by adding the project name or other designation (e.g., "City Hall," or "Project No. 75") to the encumbrance and expenditure account titles. This device is almost imperative for proper identification in the recording of transactions, and it facilitates preparation of cash and expenditure statements for multiproject operations.

In accounting for encumbrances for multiperiod projects, there is some difference of opinion as to the desirable procedure to follow in relation to encumbrances outstanding at the end of a period. In the management of a General Fund, for example, operations in terms of amounts of revenues and expenditures during a specified standard period of time (quarter, half year, etc.) provide measures of accomplishment. Because capital projects are rarely of the same size and may be started and ended at any time of year, periodic comparisons are of little significance. Furthermore, although the personnel of a legislative body may change at the beginning of a year during which a capital project is in progress, the change is unlikely to affect materially the project's progress. Although the operations of a capital projects fund are project-completion oriented, with slight reference to time, GASB standards require Encumbrances, Expenditures, Proceeds of Bonds, and Revenues accounts to be closed to Fund Balance at year-end in order to facilitate preparation of capital projects fund financial statements for inclusion in the governmental unit's annual report on a basis consistent with year-end statements of other funds.

The required procedure does produce year-end capital projects fund balance sheets that appear similar to those of general and special revenue funds illustrated in preceding chapters. The similarity of appearance and terminology may be misleading, however. The Fund Balance account of the General or a special revenue fund represents net financial resources available for appropriation, whereas the Fund Balance account of a multiple-period capital projects fund represents net assets already set aside for the acquisition of specified capital facilities. The Fund Balance of a multiple-period capital projects fund is comparable to the unexpended unencumbered appropriation item on an interim balance sheet of the General or a special revenue fund; it is not comparable to the year-end Fund Balance of such funds.

Reestablishment of Encumbrances

The year-end closing procedure required by GASB standards for use by capital projects funds artificially chops the Construction Expenditures pertaining to each continuing project into fiscal-year segments, rather than allowing the total cost of each project to be accumulated in a single Construction Expenditures account. Similarly, closing the Encumbrance account of each project to Fund Balance at year-end creates some procedural problems in accounting in the subsequent year. The procedure illustrated for general and special revenue funds (using separate Encumbrances, Reserve for Encumbrances, and Expenditures accounts for each year) could be followed. The procedure illustrated for general and special revenue funds is logical in that case because each appropriation expires at year-end, and yearly Expenditure and Encumbrance accounts are needed to match with the yearly Appropriations account. The authorization (appropriation) for a capital project, however, does not expire at the end of a fiscal year but continues for the life of the project. Accordingly, it is necessary to reestablish the Encumbrances account at the beginning of each year in order to facilitate accounting for expenditures for goods and services ordered in one year and received in a subsequent year. Reestablishment of the Encumbrances account may be accomplished as shown by the following entry in the Capital Projects Fund (amount assumed):

Encumbrances	210,000	
Fund Balance		210,000

If the Encumbrances account is reestablished, subsequent receipt of goods or services entered as encumbrances in a prior year may be accounted for in the same manner as if they had been ordered in the current year:

Reserve for Encumbrances	210,000	
Construction Expenditures	210,000	
Contracts Payable		210,000
Encumbrances		210,000

Capital Projects Financed by Special Assessments

In the second paragraph of this chapter it is noted that one common source of financing major acquisitions of general capital assets is by issuance of long-term debt to be repaid by special assessments. A **special assessment** is a compulsory levy made against certain property to defray part or all of the cost of a specific improvement or service that is presumed to be of general benefit to the public and of particular benefit to the property against which the special assessment is levied. Special assessment financing is allowed under the laws of many states. Generally, a majority of owners of the property that will be assessed must agree to the formation of a special assessment district, sometimes called a *local improvement district*. A special assessment district may be an independent special purpose governmental unit created under the laws of the state in which it is located; or it may be a component unit of a county, city, or other general governmental unit; or in some cases, special assessment transactions are administered directly by a general governmental unit.

If a special assessment district is an independent special purpose governmental unit, it will need to account for the construction phase of a capital project in the manner described in this chapter, the debt service phase of the project in the manner described in Chapter 6, and the resulting general capital assets and related long-term debt as described in this chapter and Chapter 6, respectively. The same observations apply to a special assessment district that is a component unit of a primary government, which should be reported in a discrete presentation in the basic financial statements of the governmental financial reporting entity, as discussed in relation to Illustration 2–1.

If the financial activities of a special assessment district are so intertwined with those of the primary government that the balances and transactions meet the criteria for blending (see discussion related to Illustration 2–1), it is logical that special assessment transactions be administered directly by the primary government. In that event the accounting and reporting standards set forth in this chapter apply to capital projects financed in whole, or in part, by special assessments, with the following modifications and additions.

The total dollar amount of a capital project to be financed by special assessments must be paid by owners of real property within the special assessment district. Accordingly, the portion of the total to be borne by each parcel of property within the district must be determined in whatever manner is specified by laws of the relevant jurisdiction. It is often true that the amount to be paid by each owner is large enough that laws will provide that the total special assessment against each parcel may be paid in equal installments over a specified period of years. Commonly, the first installment is due within a relatively short period of time (say, 60 days after the assessment is levied) and, if paid by the due date, is noninterest bearing. The remainder of the installments are due annually thereafter, and are interest bearing. Assume, for example, that the final installment is due five years after the levy of the special assessment. Contractors cannot be expected to wait five years to be paid for work done on the project; therefore, an issue of long-term debt is authorized in the amount of installments due in future years. The first installment and the proceeds of the long-term debt would be used to finance the capital project and would be accounted for by a capital projects fund. GASB standards provide that the first installment should be recognized as Revenue of the Capital Projects Fund and governmental activities at the government-wide level at the time of the levy—providing, of course, for any estimated uncollectibles. The deferred installments would be reported as Deferred Revenues, a liability account.

Long-term debt proceeds would be considered an Other Financing Source—Proceeds of Bonds (or Notes) of the capital projects fund, and as a long-term liability at the government-wide level, if the primary government has an obligation to assume debt service in the event that collections of remaining installments are insufficient. If the primary government has no obligation for debt service and the creditors are payable solely from collections of the special assessment installments and interest thereon, the proceeds of special assessment long-term debt should be credited to a capital projects fund equity account such as Contribution from Property Owners, rather than as Proceeds of Bonds (or Notes).

Installments of special assessments and interest thereon, which are to be used to service long-term debt, and are not available for expenditure by a Capital Projects Fund, should be accounted for as described in the discussion of Debt Service Funds in Chapter 6. General capital assets financed wholly or partially, through collections of special assessments are accounted for in the same manner as any other general capital assets, in the governmental activities category at the government-wide level.

Financial Reporting for Capital Projects Funds

Each capital projects fund that meets the definition of a *major fund* (see the Glossary for a definition) must be reported in a separate column of the Balance Sheet—Governmental Funds (see Illustration 2–3) and the Statement of Revenues, Expenditures, and Changes in Fund Balances—Governmental Funds (see Illustration 2–4). Nonmajor capital projects funds would be reported in the same column as other nonmajor governmental funds in these two basic financial statements.

Governments are also encouraged, but not required, to provide as supplementary information combining financial statements for all nonmajor funds. Combining financial statements present each nonmajor fund as a separate column. These statements usually would not be included within the scope of the auditor's examination, other than indirectly as part of the audit of the basic financial statements.

The required basic financial statements and notes thereto, along with the recommended combining financial statements, should meet most external report users' needs for information about capital projects funds. Internal management and those with oversight responsibility for capital projects may need additional information, however, of a more detailed nature. Additional information that may be useful for internal management or oversight purposes includes information about whether the amount and quality of work accomplished to date is commensurate with resources expended to date and project plans, and whether the remaining work can be accomplished within the established deadlines with remaining resources.

Key Terms

Arbitrage rebate, 204
Bond anticipation notes, 201
Capital improvements fund, 191
Capital leases, 186
Capital projects funds, 178
Force account construction, 183
General capital assets (GCA), 178
Historical cost, 179
Infrastructure assets, 184
Interfund transfers, 196
Modified approach, 180
Operating leases, 186
Special assessments, 206

Selected References

Financial Accounting Standards Board. *Statement of Financial Accounting Standards No. 5*, "Accounting for Contingencies." Norwalk, CT, 1975.

_________. *Statement of Financial Accounting Standards No. 13*, "Accounting for Leases as Amended and Interpreted through January 1990." Norwalk, CT, 1990.

Governmental Accounting Standards Board. *Codification of Governmental Accounting and Financial Reporting Standards as of June 30, 1999*. Norwalk, CT, 1999.

Questions

5–1. Explain how an accountant or administrator would be able to determine whether the cost of a certain piece of equipment purchased by a governmental unit should be accounted for in the government-wide governmental activities category or in an enterprise fund.

5–2. What sources are often used to finance the acquisition of general capital assets of governments?

5–3. Below are stated three major expenditures relating to the Town of Renton's general capital assets. Which expenditures should be debited to asset accounts of governmental activities in the government-wide ledgers? Which should not? Explain your answers.

a. Replaced an old boiler in the Town Hall with a new model having twice the capacity of the old model.

b. Added a new wing to the Town Hall.

c. Renovated the Town Council Chambers (replaced carpeting, painted walls, and upgraded the sound system).

5–4. Explain why the GASB in *Statement No. 34* departs from previous practice and now requires reporting of investment in infrastructure assets, such as highways, streets, sidewalks, storm drainage systems, and lighting systems.

5–5. "All infrastructure assets must be depreciated under GASB *Statement No. 34*." Do you agree with this statement? Explain.

5–6. Under what conditions should a state or local governmental unit utilize the capital projects fund type? If a unit does utilize the capital projects fund type, should it create a separate capital projects fund for each project? Why or why not?

5–7. How does an outlay for a capital *project* differ from a capital outlay of a general or special revenue fund? Give an example of a capital project and an example of a capital outlay.

5–8. How does a *capital projects* fund differ from *general* and *special revenue* funds?

5–9. Should interest expenditures during the period of construction be capitalized as a part of the cost of general capital assets? Explain your answer.

5–10. Why is encumbrance accounting recommended for capital projects funds even though it is not considered necessary to record Estimated Revenues or Appropriations?

5–11. If a capital project is incomplete at the end of a fiscal year, why is it considered desirable to close Encumbrances and all operating statement accounts at year-end? If these accounts are closed, why is it desirable to reestablish the Encumbrances account as of the first day of the following year?

5–12. "If general capital assets are acquired under a capital lease agreement, no entry at all needs to be made in any governmental fund at the inception of the lease." Do you agree or disagree? Explain.

5–13. If one capital projects fund is used to account for multiple capital projects, how can adequate control and accountability for individual projects be maintained?

5–14. "If all the capital projects funds of a governmental reporting entity have no assets, no liabilities, and no fund equity at balance sheet date, no columns need be provided for the capital projects fund type in any of the financial statements." Explain why you agree, or disagree, with this statement.

5–15. How should the residual equity or deficit existing at the completion of a capital project be treated?

Cases

5–1. Financing capital road improvements. The case described here illustrates how political factors can be as important as, or even more important than, economic factors in planning and financing major capital projects. Often the political dimension clouds the issues and makes it difficult for even knowledgeable citizens to determine the best course of action. After reading the case, you will be asked to "cast your vote" on the proposed financing plan and explain why you voted as you did. Although the names of the governments described in the case are fictitious, the case is adapted from an actual case that came to the authors' attention. Similar jurisdictional tax disputes are not uncommon.

Background. Brown County is a rural county with a well-diversified economy, mainly institutional (educational and medical), commercial and light manufacturing, and agricultural. The County has a population of about 125,000, which for the last decade has been growing at nearly 5 percent a year. The County's largest city and the County Seat is Brownville, with a population of about 75,000. The County is governed by three elected commissioners and most key County functions are managed by elected officials. The City has a Council-Manager form of government under which the Chief Executive Officer, the City Manager, is appointed by and serves at the pleasure of the City Council. The governments are "overlapping" in the sense that taxpayers who reside in Brownville pay property and sales taxes to both the City and County. However, except for the court system, the County mainly provides services for persons who live outside incorporated cities and towns. Historically, relationships between the County and City governments have been strained, with each government being suspicious of the motives of the other. As a result, regional planning has generally suffered and agreements, when they have occurred, have related to narrow issues or projects rather than long-range plans.

Situation and Facts. To cope with rapid population growth, the County has developed a five-year plan that includes paving and upgrading 55 miles of heavily traveled roads at a cost of $7,000,000; upgrading about 150 miles of substandard roads using "chip-and-seal overlay," $2,000,000; eliminating 10 "safety hazard areas," $210,000; and acquiring right of way, $500,000; for a total estimated cost of $9,710,000 over five years. Financing for the plan would come from the following sources:

Half-cent sales tax	$5,400,000
Increase in property tax of 5 cents per $100 of assessed valuation	400,000
Gasoline taxes	500,000
Motor vehicle sales tax	200,000
Annual Revenues	$6,500,000

The gasoline taxes and motor vehicle sales taxes are already being collected and distributed to localities by the state government. The property tax increase requires no special approval since the Road and Bridge property taxes are currently below the limit imposed by state statutes. The half-cent sales tax, however, requires approval by a simple majority of registered voters in the County, including those who reside in Brownville and other incorporated cities and towns. Accordingly, a special election has been called to schedule a vote on the proposed sales tax.

Even a casual look at the financing plan shows that $6,500,000 × 5 years will produce at least $32,500,000 in revenues (excluding probably investment earnings) whereas the required capital outlay will be only $9,710,000 over the five years. The remainder is intended to provide for expanded operations of the County Road and Bridge Department.

In the weeks before the special election, the Brownville City Council and Finance Director have strongly opposed the proposed sales tax on the grounds that it is unfair to expect taxpayers in the cities and towns to pay for road improvements that mainly benefit rural county residents. They argue that special assessment debt financing should be used, with the debt to be repaid by residents receiving the benefit. They further complain that the County's planning process was flawed and that joint planning with the City is needed to coordinate the five-year plan of both governments. City officials are also concerned that the County's proposed sales tax increase would eliminate the City's ability to raise sales taxes during the next five years if a need should arise. To mute some of the opposition, the County has amended the original plan and proposes to cut in half the Road and Bridge property taxes paid by taxpayers in the cities and towns. The property tax rollback would reduce revenues from $32,500,000 to about $27 million over the next five years. However, since property in that state is assessed at different levels for different classes of property (32 percent of market value for commercial and manufacturing property, 19 percent for residential property, and 12 percent for agricultural property), only the larger (mainly commercial and manufacturing) property owners stand to gain if the proposed sales tax increase is approved. For most taxpayers the sales tax increase will still be greater than the property tax decrease. Thus, while some large property owners might now support the sales tax, the majority of Brownville voters view the proposed rollback as regressive and only worsening the inequity for most property owners in the cities and towns.

Advocates for the sales tax argue that the cities and towns will benefit from improved transportation throughout the County. Further, nearly a quarter of the people who work in Brownville live in the unincorporated subdivisions surrounding the City. Advocates also point out that Brownville is a regional shopping center that draws shoppers from a 50-mile radius. Thus, one attractive feature of the proposed sales tax is that it would be borne, in part, by people who neither live nor work in the County.

Required

After weeks of heavy media coverage, both for and against the proposed sales tax, voters have become extremely interested in this issue but thoroughly confused. Election day has finally arrived and turnout is expected to be heavy. Imagine yourself as a voter in the City of Brownville and answer the following questions.

a. Would you vote *yes* for the proposed half-cent sales tax or *no* in opposition? Explain the rationale for your vote, being sure to analyze factors pertinent to your voting decision.

b. Would your vote have changed under different assumed scenarios (e.g., if you were a large commercial or manufacturing property owner versus a residential or agricultural property owner, or renter)?

c. Do you think special assessment financing would be more appropriate than general sales taxes for the proposed projects? Explain.

d. Are there any significant accounting issues related to the financing alternatives? Explain.

Exercises and Problems

5–1. Examine the CAFR. Utilizing the CAFR obtained for Exercise 1–1, follow the instructions below:

a. **General Capital Assets:**

(1) **Reporting of Capital Assets.** Are capital assets reported as a row in the government-wide Statement of Net Assets (post–GASB *Statement No. 34*) or in a column titled "General Fixed Assets Account Group" (pre–GASB *Statement No. 34*)? Is the term "capital assets" or "fixed assets" used? Is there a statement or schedule that discloses the function or activity that uses the assets? What categories of capital assets are shown in the statement? Are Improvements Other than Buildings separately disclosed and described? Do the Notes describe the accounting treatment accorded general capital assets? If donated capital assets are reported, are they stated at their fair value on the date donated? Are purchased capital assets stated at historical cost, if known, or estimated historical cost if actual cost is unknown? Has the government refrained from using terms like *appraised values* or *estimated values* without indicating whether they involve historical cost, replacement cost, or market value appraisals or estimates? Do the Notes specify capitalization policies for "public domain" (infrastructure) capital assets?

(2) **Sources of Capital Asset Financing.** Is there a statement that discloses the sources from which acquisitions or construction of capital assets were financed? If so, are the sources for all general capital assets disclosed, or only those assets acquired since a certain date? Do the source accounts agree with those discussed in Chapter 5? What three sources account for the major portion of capital asset acquisitions? What percentage of the total cost, or other carrying value, of capital assets is accounted for by each of the three major sources?

(3) **Changes in General Capital Assets.** Does the report contain a Schedule (or Statement) of Changes in General Capital Assets? If so, does the schedule disclose the sources from which capital asset acquisitions and construction were financed? Does the schedule disclose changes by function and activity, or merely by asset category?

(4) **Other.** Compare the general capital asset information disclosed in the report with related information disclosed in statements of general and special revenue funds, capital projects funds, or elsewhere in the report. Is the accumulated cost of construction work in progress recorded as an asset anywhere? If not, is the information disclosed adequately, in your opinion? Is net interest during the period of construction on debt incurred to finance construction capitalized? Is this true for just tax-supported debt, or for both tax-supported debt and special assessment debt? Which fund, or funds, account for cash received, or receivables created, from sales of general capital assets? Which fund, or funds, account for cash received, or receivables created, as a result of charging depreciation on general capital assets as a cost of grants?

b. **Capital Projects Funds:**

(1) **Title and Content.** What title is given the funds that function as capital projects funds, as described in Chapter 5? (Bond Funds and Capital Improvement Funds are common titles.) Does the report state the basis of accounting used for capital projects funds? If so, is the financial statement presentation consistent with the stated basis? (That is, the report may state that the modified accrual basis was used, but no receivables are shown, or there is a "Reserve for Receivables," or the report refers to "disbursements" rather than "expenditures.") If the basis of accounting is not stated, analyze the statements to determine which basis is used—full accrual, modified accrual, or cash basis. Is the same basis used for both revenues and expenditures? Is the basis used consistent with GASB standards discussed in Chapter 5? Are there separate capital projects funds for each project; or are there several funds, each of which accounts for related projects; or is only one fund used for all projects?

(2) **Statements and Schedules.** What statements and schedules pertaining to capital projects funds are presented? In what respects (headings, arrangement, items included, etc.) do they seem similar to statements illustrated or described in the text? In what respects do they differ? Are any differences merely a matter of terminology or arrangement, or do they represent significant deviations from GASB accounting and reporting standards for capital projects funds?

(3) **Financial Resource Inflows.** Describe the nature of the financial resource inflows utilized by the capital projects funds. If tax-supported bonds, or special assessment bonds, are a source, have any been sold at a premium? At a discount? If so, what was the accounting treatment of the bond premium or discount?

(4) **Fund Expenditures.** How much detail is given concerning capital projects fund expenditures? Is the detail sufficient to meet the information needs of administrators? Legislators? Creditors? Grantors? Interested residents? For projects that are incomplete at the date of the financial statement, does the report compare the percentage of total authorization for each project expended to date with the percentage of completion? For those projects completed during the fiscal year does the report compare the total expenditures for each project with the authorization for each project? For each cost overrun, how was the overrun financed?

(5) **Assets Acquired under Capital Leases.** Were any general capital assets acquired by the primary government or one or more component units under a capital lease agreement during the year for which you have statements? If so, was the present value of minimum lease rentals recorded as an Expenditure and as an Other Financing Source in a capital projects fund (or in any other governmental fund)? If the primary government or one or more component units leased assets from another

component unit, how are the assets, related liabilities, expenditures, and other financing sources reported in the general purpose financial statements, or in another section of the CAFR of the reporting entity?

5–2. Multiple Choice. Choose the best answer.

1. Capital assets donated to a governmental unit should be recorded:
   a. At estimated fair value when received.
   b. At the lower of donor's carrying amount or estimated fair value when received.
   c. At the donor's carrying amount.
   d. As a memorandum entry only.
2. General capital assets should be recorded at:
   a. Cost.
   b. Estimated cost, if cost is not practically determinable.
   c. Fair value, if the capital assets were donated.
   d. Either *a*, or *b*, or *c*, as appropriate.
3. One feature of state and local government accounting and financial reporting is that capital assets used for general government activities:
   a. Do not depreciate as a result of such use.
   b. Often are not expected to contribute to the generation of revenues.
   c. Are acquired only when direct contribution to revenues is expected.
   d. Should not be maintained at the same level as those of businesses so that current financial resources can be used for other government services.
4. General capital assets acquired under a capital lease:
   a. Should be capitalized under the same rules as proprietary fund capital assets acquired under an operating lease.
   b. Should be capitalized at the lesser of (1) the present value of rental and other minimum lease payments, or (2) the fair value of the leased property.
   c. Should not be capitalized.
   d. Should be capitalized at the lower of cost or market.
5. A capital projects fund of a municipality is an example of what type of fund?
   a. Fiduciary.
   b. Governmental.
   c. Internal Service.
   d. Proprietary.

Items 6 and 7 are based on the following:

On December 31, 2001, Vane City paid a contractor $3,000,000 for the total cost of a new municipal annex built in 2001 on city-owned land. Financing was provided by a $2,000,000 general obligation bond issue sold at face amount on December 31, 2001, with the remaining $1,000,000 transferred from the General Fund.

6. What account and amount should be reported in Vane's 2001 financial statements for the General Fund?

a. Other Financing Uses control, $1,000,000.

b. Other Financing Sources control, $2,000,000.

c. Expenditures control, $3,000,000.

d. Other Financing Sources control, $3,000,000.

7. What accounts and amounts should be reported in Vane's 2001 financial statements for the capital projects fund?

   a. Other Financing Sources control, $2,000,000; General Long-Term-Debt, $2,000,000.

   b. Revenues control, $2,000,000; Construction Expenditures control, $2,000,000.

   c. Other Financing Sources control, $3,000,000; Construction Expenditures control, $3,000,000.

   d. Revenues control, $3,000,000; Construction Expenditures control, $3,000,000.

8. In what fund type should the proceeds from special assessment bonds issued to finance construction of sidewalks in a new subdivision be reported? Assume that the city agreed to pay debt service if collections of assessments are insufficient.

   a. Agency fund.

   b. Capital projects fund.

   c. Enterprise fund.

   d. Special revenue fund.

9. As of the first day of a fiscal year it is normally desirable to enter in a capital projects fund account:

   a. The amounts of bonds expected to be sold during the year.

   b. The amount of grants expected to be received during the year.

   c. The reestablishment of Encumbrances closed to Fund Balance as of the end of the preceding year.

   d. All of the above.

10. Final inspection of a construction site revealed minor discrepancies that were corrected by employees of the Town of Quincy. An adequate amount had been retained from contractor billings to cover this contingency. The costs of correcting these discrepancies should be recorded in the capital projects fund as a debit to:

    a. Construction Expenditures.

    b. General Capital Assets.

    c. Reserve for Encumbrances.

    d. Contracts Payable—Retained Percentage.

Items 5, and 6 through 8 (AICPA, adapted)

5–3. Multiple Choice. GASB *Statement* No. 34. Choose the best answer.

1. A police vehicle purchased with property tax revenue is accounted for:

   a. As a capital asset in the General Fund.

   b. As a general capital asset reported in governmental activities on the government-wide statements.

   c. As an expenditure of a Capital Projects Fund.
   d. As an expense in an Enterprise Fund.
2. General capital assets would *not* be acquired by:
   a. Special assessment taxes.
   b. Donation.
   c. General obligation bonds.
   d. Revenue bonds.
3. General capital assets are:
   a. Capitalized in the General Fund.
   b. Recorded at fair value.
   c. Reported in the governmental activities column of the Statement of Net Assets, net of accumulated depreciation.
   d. Reported as long-term assets in both the Governmental Funds Balance Sheet and the government-wide Statement of Net Assets.
4. Depreciation is required for:
   a. Inexhaustible assets, such as land and land improvements.
   b. Collections of works of art.
   c. Infrastructure assets, unless the modified approach is elected.
   d. Historical treasures.
5. Which of the following is *not* a reason why depreciation on general capital assets is reported as part of the direct expenses of functions and programs on the government-wide Statement of Activities?
   a. Depreciation expense helps to measure the fair value of capital assets.
   b. Depreciation expense helps to determine the full cost of providing each function or program.
   c. Depreciation is often an allowable cost under the terms of a grant-financed program.
   d. Administrators and legislators are concerned with the allocation of resources to programs, departments, and activities.
6. All of the following are required disclosures about capital assets except:
   a. Capital acquisitions and dispositions during the year.
   b. Depreciation expense for the current period with the amount charged to each function in the government-wide Statement of Activities.
   c. Source of financing for each major class of asset.
   d. Reasons for not capitalizing works of art or historical treasures.
7. Infrastructure assets do *not* include:
   a. Highways.
   b. Storm drainage systems.
   c. Buildings used in the Highway Department.
   d. Street lighting systems.
8. If the modified approach is elected for use with infrastructure assets, then:
   a. No depreciation is taken on any infrastructure assets.
   b. Certain eligible infrastructure assets do not need to be depreciated.

c. Depreciation expense is recorded in the General Fund.

d. The government does not have to keep records on eligible assets.

9. When office equipment is purchased for use in the Mayor's office with General Fund resources, the complete entry(ies) to record this transaction is (are):

	Debit	*Credit*
a. General Fund:		
Expenditures	1,000	
Vouchers Payable		1,000
b. Governmental Activities:		
Equipment	1,000	
Vouchers Payable		1,000
c. General Fund:		
Expenditures	1,000	
Vouchers Payable		1,000
Governmental Activities:		
Equipment	1,000	
Vouchers Payable		1,000
d. General Fund:		
Expenditures	1,000	
Vouchers Payable		1,000
Governmental Activities:		
Expenses	1,000	
Vouchers Payable		1,000

10. Capital Projects Funds are *not* reported on the:

a. Balance Sheet for Governmental Funds.

b. Balance Sheet for Proprietary Funds.

c. Government-wide Statement of Net Assets.

d. Government-wide Statement of Activities.

5–4. General Capital Assets. Make an entry or entries for each transaction as it should be recorded in the government-wide governmental activities journal and journal of the appropriate governmental fund(s) for the current year.

1. During the year, a capital projects fund completed a building project initiated in the preceding year. The total cost of the project was $6,780,000, of which $4,130,000 had been expended in the two preceding years. Current-year expenditures on the project were reported to have consisted of $650,000 from a federal grant, with the balance coming from proceeds of a tax-supported bond issue.
2. A tract of land held for future development as a city park was, by resolution of the City Council, transferred to the City Water Utility. The Utility paid the City General Fund $200,000 for the land, which was carried at its estimated cost of $50,000. The land had been purchased from General Fund revenues.
3. An electric typewriter was traded in on a personal computer. List price of the personal computer was $3,500; $100 allowance was received for the old machine. The old typewriter had been purchased from General Fund revenue for $500 and it was fully depreciated. Cash for the new computer was furnished by a special revenue fund.

4. A piece of heavy equipment was purchased by the Street Fund, a special revenue fund. Catalog price of the equipment was $150,000. Terms of payment quoted by the manufacturer were 2/10, n/30. Payment for the equipment was made within the cash discount period.
5. The cost of remodeling of the interior of the City Hall was $514,700; $38,400 of this amount was classified as maintenance chargeable to the Public Works function rather than improvement. In the remodeling process, walls, partitions, floors, and so on, estimated to have cost $76,600 were removed and replaced. Cost of the remodeling was financed by a current appropriation of the General Fund. The original construction had been financed by a tax-supported bond issue accounted for by a capital projects fund.
6. A subdivision annexed by the City contained privately financed streets and sidewalks and a system of sewers. The best available information showed a cost of $1,400,000 for the sewer system and $1,550,000 for the streets and sidewalks, of which $150,000 was the estimated cost of the land. Both types of improvements were provided by the developers. In conformity with GASB *Statement No. 34*, the City records infrastructure assets.

5–5. Capital Asset Disclosures. Information in the CAFR of the Town of Centralia reported general fixed assets in the following amounts as of April 30, 2001.

	Cost	*Accumulated Depreciation*
Land	$1,326,780	$ –0–
Buildings	7,282,680	1,439,200
Improvements other than buildings	3,027,790	928,400
Equipment	1,733,820	837,500
Construction work in progress	401,130	–0–
Infrastructure assets	3,500,000	900,000

During fiscal year 2002 the following changes in general capital assets took place:

1. A project started during fiscal 2002 was being financed by a tax-supported bond issue of $3,000,000 sold at par during the year and a federal grant of $1,000,000, both accounted for through a capital projects fund. By the end of fiscal 2002, $80,000 of the federal grant had been received and expended for planning and engineering for a project in progress. Bond proceeds expended during the year totaled $900,000 ($300,000 for land and $600,000 for the building under construction).
2. Records of capital projects funds reported that construction work in progress at the end of fiscal 2001 was completed during fiscal 2002 at a total cost of $799,066, all financed from special assessment bonds. All of the construction resulted in additions to Improvements Other than Buildings.
3. Special revenue fund expenditures during the year added equipment costing $152,700.
4. General Fund expenditures during the year for equipment amounted to $416,000.

5. Annexation added buildings for which the estimated cost was $301,600, and land for which the estimated cost was $75,000.
6. Land having an appraised value of $750,000 was donated to the City, and additional land with an appraised value of $15,000 was received in settlement of delinquent General Fund property taxes.
7. Land acquired at an estimated cost of $12,000, on which an $80,000 building was located, was sold to the State Highway Department for a right-of-way at a price of $119,700.
8. Construction activities during fiscal 2002 required demolition of a building that had cost $33,600 and a bridge for which the estimated cost was $119,200. Equipment that had cost $19,300 could not be located and was presumed to have been stolen.
9. There were no additions or retirements to infrastructure assets this year.
10. Depreciation expense for the year was as follows: Buildings, $440,000; Improvements, $320,000; Equipment $210,000; and Infrastructure assets, $105,000. Accumulated depreciation related to retired assets was: Buildings, $51,000; Improvements, $102,000; Equipment, $5,000.

Required

Prepare in good form a Schedule of Capital Asset Disclosures similar to Illustration 5–2 for the fiscal year ended April 30, 2002. Ignore the related schedule showing how current depreciation expense is charged to governmental functions.

5–6. Allocation of Depreciation Expense. Depreciation expense for the Town of Centralia was as follows: Buildings, $440,000; Improvements, $320,000; Equipment, $210,000, and Infrastructure, $105,000, as shown in Problem 5–5. The accountant has determined that depreciation expense should be allocated to the functions/programs of the government according to the percentages in the following table.

	General Gov't	*Public Safety*	*Public Works*	*Parks and Recreation*	*Culture & Recreation*	*Total*
Buildings	30	20	30	10	10	100%
Improvements	10	10	60	10	10	100%
Equipment	30	20	30	10	10	100%
Infrastructure	0	0	100	0	0	100%

Required

Prepare a schedule in good form showing the amount of depreciation expense charged to government functions, similar to the schedule at the lower part of Illustration 5–2.

5–7. Statement of Revenues and Expenditures. The post-closing trial balance of the City of Pineville's Capital Projects Fund, as of December 31, 2001, listed Fund Balance in the amount of $1,500,000.

The project had been authorized early in 2001 in the total amount of $5,000,000, to be financed $800,000 by the federal government, $200,000 by the state government, and the remainder by a bond issue. Most of the work was to be done by various private contractors.

Cash from the state grant was received in full during 2001. The entire bond issue was sold at par early in 2001. The federal government is expected to pay its grant in full before March 1, 2002. Cash not disbursed during 2001 was invested on December 31, 2001.

a. Assuming GASB standards discussed in Chapter 5 were followed:
   (1) How much Revenue was recognized by the Capital Projects Fund in 2001? How much should this fund report as Other Financing Sources for 2001?
   (2) How much did 2001 expenditures total?
   (3) What was the balance of the Investments account on December 31, 2001, assuming all 2001 expenditures were paid in cash?

b. During 2002, the following events occurred:
   (1) Expenditures of the fund totaled $1,350,000 on construction contracts.
   (2) Interest on temporary investments totaled $16,000.

Prepare a Statement of Revenues, Expenditures, and Changes in Fund Balance for the City of Pineville's Capital Projects Fund for the year ended December 31, 2002.

5–8. Capital Projects Fund. The following information pertains to Eden Township's construction and financing of a new administration center:

Estimated total cost of project	$9,000,000
Project financing:	
State grant	3,000,000
General obligation bonds:	
Face amount	6,000,000
Stated interest rate	6%
Issue date	December 1, 2001
Maturity date	December 1, 2031

During Eden's year ended June 30, 2002, the following events occurred that affect the Capital Projects Fund established to account for this project:

July 1, 2001—The Capital Projects Fund borrowed $300,000 from the General Fund for preliminary engineering and planning costs.

July 9, 2001—Engineering and planning costs of $200,000, for which no encumbrance had been recorded, were paid to Napp Associates.

December 1, 2001—The bonds were sold at 101. Total proceeds were retained by the Capital Projects Fund. (The premium is available for expenditure for the project.)

December 1, 2001—The grant was formally approved by the state. The grant was to be used only for financing construction of the new administration center.

April 30, 2002—A $7,000,000 contract was executed with Caro Construction Corp., the general contractors, for the major portion of the project. The contract provides that Eden will withhold 4 percent of all billings pending satisfactory completion of the project.

May 9, 2002—$1,000,000 of the state grant was received.

June 10, 2002—The $300,000 borrowed from the General Fund was repaid.

June 30, 2002—Progress billing of $1,200,000 was received from Caro.

Eden uses encumbrance accounting for budgetary control.

Required

a. Prepare journal entries in the Administration Center Capital Projects Fund to record the foregoing transactions.

b. Prepare the June 30, 2002, closing entries for the Administration Center Capital Projects Fund.

c. Prepare the Administration Center Capital Projects Fund balance sheet at June 30, 2002.

(AICPA, adapted)

5–9. **Special Assessment Bonds.** The proceeds of the sale of special assessment bonds issued to finance the acquisition of capital facilities amounted to $5,080,000. The face amount of the bond issue was $5,000,000; $25,000 of the proceeds represented interest accrued on the bonds to date of sale.

a. Assuming both the premium on bonds sold and the interest accrued on the bonds to date of sale must be recorded directly in a debt service fund, show in general journal form the entries made by the capital projects fund and in the governmental activities journal for the receipt of the $5,000,000 face amount.

b. If several months are expected to elapse between receipt of bond proceeds and payment for the capital assets being acquired, what action should be taken by the governmental finance officer?

c. What are the accounting and financial implications of the course of action you recommended in part *b*?

5–10. **Construction Fund.** During fiscal year 2001, the voters of the Town of Winston approved the construction and equipping of a recreation center to be financed by tax-supported bonds in the amount of $3,000,000. During 2001, the following events and transactions occurred:

1. Preliminary planning and engineering expenses were incurred in the amount of $75,000. No money was immediately available for paying these costs (credit Vouchers Payable).
2. Supplies to be used by the town's own workforce in connection with the project were ordered in the amount of $30,000.
3. A contract was let under competitive bids for a major segment of the construction project in the amount of $2,500,000.
4. All the supplies referred to in item 2 were received at a net cost of $30,500. This amount was approved for payment.

5. An interfund invoice (not encumbered) was received from the Street Fund for work done on the project in the amount of $40,000. The invoice was approved for payment.
6. An invoice for $1,600,000 was received from a contractor for a portion of work that had been completed under the general contract.
7. The bond issue was sold at par plus accrued interest of $30,000 (the accrued interest was deposited in the fund that will service the bonded debt).
8. The amount due the Street Fund was paid.
9. The contractor's bill, less a 4 percent retention, was vouchered for payment.
10. All vouchers payable, except $1,300 (about which there was some controversy), were paid.
11. Cash in the amount of $1,300,000 was invested in short-term marketable securities.
12. Fiscal year-end closing entries were prepared.

Required

a. Prepare journal entries to record the above information in the general ledger accounts of the Recreation Construction Fund (you may omit subsidiary ledger accounts.) Omit entries in the government activities journal.

b. Prepare a Town of Winston Recreation Center Construction Fund Balance Sheet for the year ended December 31, 2001.

c. Prepare a Recreation Center Construction Fund Statement of Revenues, Expenditures, and Changes in Fund Balance for the year ended December 31, 2001.

5–11. Street Improvement Fund. In 2001, Wye City began the work of improving certain streets, to be financed by a bond issue supplemented by a federal grant. Estimated total cost of the project was $3,000,000; $2,500,000 was to come from the bond issue, and the balance from a federal grant. The capital projects fund to account for the project was designated as the Street Improvement Fund.

The following transactions occurred in 2001:

1. Issued $80,000 of 6 percent bond anticipation notes to be repaid from the proceeds of bonds in 180 days.
2. The federal grant was recorded as receivable; half of the grant is to be paid to Wye City in 2001, and the remainder late in 2002.
3. A contract was let to Rogers Construction Company for the major part of the project on a bid of $2,700,000.
4. An invoice received from the City's Stores and Services Fund for supplies provided to the Street Improvement Fund in the amount of $40,000 was approved for payment. (This amount had not been encumbered.)
5. Preliminary planning and engineering costs of $59,000 were paid to the Midwest Engineering Company. There had been no encumbrance for this cost.
6. A voucher payable was recorded for a $14,500 billing from the local telephone company for the cost of moving some of its underground properties necessitated by the street project.
7. An invoice in the amount of $1,000,000 was received from Rogers for progress to date on the project. The invoice was consistent with the terms of the contract and a liability was recorded in the amount of $1,000,000.

8. Cash received during 2001 was as follows:

From federal government	250,000
From sale of bonds at par	2,500,000

9. Repaid bond anticipation notes and interest thereon (see Transaction 1). Interest is an expenditure of the capital projects fund and will be capitalized as part of the cost of street improvements.
10. The amount billed by the contractor (see Transaction 7), less 5 percent retainage was paid.
11. Temporary investments were purchased at a cost of $1,700,000.
12. Closing entries were prepared as of December 31, 2001.

Required

a. Prepare journal entries to record the above information in the general ledger accounts of the Street Improvement Fund.

b. Prepare a Balance Sheet as of December 31, 2001.

c. Prepare a Statement of Revenues, Expenditures, and Changes in Fund Balance for the period, assuming the date of authorization was July 1, 2001.

Continuous Problem

5–B. The voters of the City of Bingham approved the issuance of 8 percent tax-supported bonds in the face amount of $3,000,000 for the construction and equipping of an annex to the City Hall. The bonds are to mature in blocks of $150,000 each year over a 20-year period commencing July 1, 2002.

a. Open a general journal for the City Hall Annex Construction Fund. Record the transactions below, as necessary, in both the Fund and Governmental Activities journals. Use account titles listed under requirement *b*.

(1) On the first day of the fiscal year (July 1, 2002), the bond issue was sold at 101. Cash in the face amount of the bonds, $3,000,000, was deposited in the City Hall Annex Construction Fund; the premium was deposited in the Debt Service Fund, as required by state law.

(2) The City Hall Annex Construction Fund purchased land needed for the site for the annex for $165,000; this amount was paid.

(3) Legal and other costs of the bond issue were paid in the amount of $40,000.

(4) Architects were engaged at a fee of 6 percent of the bid of the contractors. It is estimated that the architect's fee will be $150,000.

(5) Preliminary plans were received, and the architects were paid $10,000.

(6) The detailed plans and specifications were received, and a liability in the amount of $100,000 to the architects was recorded.

(7) Advertisements soliciting bids on the construction were run at a cost of $500. This amount was paid.
(8) Construction bids were opened and analyzed. A bid of $2,400,000 was accepted, and the contract let.
(9) The contractor requested a partial payment of $1,400,000. This amount was vouchered for payment.
(10) Vouchers payable to the contractor and to the architects were paid.
(11) Furniture and equipment for the annex were ordered at an estimated total cost of $247,000.
(12) The contractor completed the construction and requested payment of the balance due on the contract. After inspection of the work, the amount was vouchered and paid.
(13) Furniture and equipment were received at a total actual installed cost of $248,560. Invoices were approved for payment.
(14) The remainder of the architect's fee was approved for payment.
(15) The City Hall Annex Construction Fund paid all outstanding liabilities on June 30, 2002.

b. Open a general ledger for the City Hall Annex Construction Fund. Use the account titles shown below. Allow five lines unless otherwise indicated. Post the entries to the City Hall Annex Construction Fund general ledger.

Cash—12 lines
Proceeds of Bonds
Vouchers Payable—12 lines
Construction Expenditures—15 lines
Encumbrances—18 lines
Reserve for Encumbrances—18 lines
Interfund Transfers Out
Fund Balance

c. Prepare a City Hall Annex Construction Fund trial balance as of June 30, 2002.

d. The City Hall Annex Construction Fund was closed. Remaining assets were transferred to the debt service fund. Record the proper journal entries in the City Hall Annex Construction Fund and post to its general ledger. All transactions and events were as of June 30, 2002. Do not post entries to the governmental activities general ledger or prepare closing entries for the governmental activities until instructed to do so in Chapter 9.

e. Prepare a Statement of Revenues, Expenditures, and Changes in Fund Balance for the year ended June 30, 2002.

f. The capital asset account balances as of June 30, 2001, before the preceding entries in *a* (1) through *a*(15) were recorded, were

	Cost	Accumulated Depreciation
Land	$ 600,000	$ 0
Buildings	5,200,000	1,400,000
Improvements Other than Buildings	16,560,000	7,320,000
Equipment and Miscellaneous	3,930,000	1,943,000
Infrastructure	5,000,000	1,200,000
	$31,290,000	$11,863,000

Prepare a schedule similar to Illustration 5–2 showing the balances in each of these accounts as of June 30, 2002.

CHAPTER 6

Accounting for General Long-Term Liabilities and Debt Service

Learning Objectives

After reading this chapter you should be able to:

- Explain what kinds of liabilities are classified as general long-term liabilities.
- Make journal entries in the governmental activities general journal to record the issuance and repayment of general long-term liabilities.
- Make journal entries in the governmental activities general journal to record general long-term liabilities arising from capital lease agreements.
- Prepare a schedule summarizing changes in general long-term liabilities.
- Describe the reasons for and nature of statutory debt limits and explain the meaning of debt margin and overlapping debt.
- Explain the purpose and types of debt service funds.
- Describe the budgeting requirements for debt service funds.
- Make appropriate journal entries to account for debt service transactions.
- Describe the required fair value reporting of investments held by debt service funds.
- Describe the accounting procedures and make appropriate journal entries for special debt service transactions.

General Long-Term Liabilities

The use of long-term debt is a traditional part of the fiscal policy of state and local governments, particularly for financing the acquisition of general capital assets. Although some governments have issued taxable debt, the interest earned on most debt issued by state and local governments is exempt from federal taxation and, in some states, from state taxation. The tax-exempt feature enables governments to raise large amounts of capital at relatively low cost. For example, from 1997 to 1998 total long-term tax-exempt debt outstanding increased by 7.1 percent to $1.46 trillion.[1] Because of the relative ease with which governments can issue debt, most states have acted in the public interest to impose statutory limits on the debt that can be incurred by state and local governments. Consequently, effective management of state and local governmental debt requires good legal advice and a sound understanding of public finance.

This chapter describes the kinds of debt and other long-term liabilities that are termed "general long-term liabilities." **General long-term liabilities** are those that arise from activities of governmental funds and that are not accounted for as fund liabilities of a proprietary or fiduciary fund. General long-term liabilities are reported as liabilities in the governmental activities column of the government-wide Statement of Net Assets, but are not reported as liabilities of governmental funds. This chapter also discusses the concepts of direct and overlapping debt, statutory debt limit, and debt margin. It also provides illustrative journal entries at the government-wide level to record increases and decreases in general long-term liabilities. Finally, the chapter explains the nature and types of debt service funds and debt service accounting for various kinds of general long-term liabilities, as well as accounting for refunding of debt.

In studying this chapter, the reader should recall that the governmental fund types (General, special revenue, capital projects, debt service, and permanent funds) account for only short-term liabilities to be paid from fund assets.[2] Although, as described in Chapter 5, the proceeds of long-term debt may be placed in one of these fund types (usually a capital projects fund), the long-term liability itself must be recorded in the governmental activities accounting records at the government-wide level.[3] Enterprise funds and perhaps certain private-purpose trust

---

[1]Data reported in "News Briefs," *Government Finance Review*, August 1999, p. 7.

[2]Conceivably a permanent fund could have a long-term liability; for example, if a permanent fund consisted of a gift of income-producing real property that the government accepted subject to a long-term mortgage note. In establishing the permanent fund as a governmental fund type, the GASB cited its belief that the predominance of such funds hold only financial resources (for example, investments in financial securities and cash). Thus, it is not clear whether there are any permanent funds in practice that hold assets other than financial assets. If not, then the probability is low that any permanent funds have long-term liabilities. Moreover, GASB *Statement No. 34* provides no guidance on how income-producing real property and long-term liabilities could be accounted for as a governmental fund.

[3]As discussed in Chapter 5, the GASB *Statement No. 34* reporting model recently implemented by many governments or being implemented by others eliminates for external financial reporting

funds account for both long-term debt serviced by the fund and short-term debt to be repaid from fund assets.

As discussed in subsequent chapters, the liability of enterprise funds should be displayed on the face of the statement of the issuing fund, if that fund may realistically be expected to finance the debt service; however, if the liability also is secondarily backed by the full faith and credit of the governmental unit, the contingent general obligation liability of the government should be disclosed in a note to the financial statements. The contingent obligation to assume debt service of long-term debt backed primarily by special assessments is acknowledged by reporting such debt in the government-wide financial statement as "special assessment debt with governmental commitment."[4] Any portion of such debt that will be repaid directly by the government (for example, to finance the portion of a special assessment project deemed to have public benefit), should be reported like any other general long-term liabilities of the government.

Bonds and other debt of enterprise funds issued with covenants that give the debt the status, even contingently, of **tax-supported debt** may affect the governmental unit's ability to issue additional tax-supported debt. The reason for this is discussed under the heading "Debt Limit and Debt Margin" in this chapter. If the contingency clause becomes effective because resources of the enterprise fund are insufficient for debt service, the unpaid portion of the debt is recorded as a liability of the governmental activities at the government-wide level. The enterprise fund that is relieved of the liability then removes the unpaid debt from its liability accounts and recognizes an Other Financing Source, which is reported after the nonoperating revenues (expenses) section of the proprietary funds Statement of Revenues, Expenses, and Changes in Fund Net Assets, in the GASB *Statement No. 34* reporting model.

From the discussions earlier in this section and in Chapter 5, it should be evident that entries are ordinarily made in the governmental activities general journal at the government-wide level to reflect increases or decreases in general long-term liabilities that also require entries in the accounts of one or more governmental funds. As shown in illustrative entries 9a and 9b in Chapter 5, most increases in general long-term liabilities arising from debt issuances are recorded as an Other Financing Source in a governmental fund and as a general long-term liability at the government-wide level. Increases in long-term liabilities that arise from operating activities, such as estimated losses from long-term claims and judgments, for example, are recorded at the government-wide level by debiting an expense and crediting a liability. Except for certain defeasances, as discussed later in this chapter, most

---

purposes the General Long-Term Debt Account Group long used by state and local governments to account for their general long-term liabilities and the General Fixed Assets Account Group used to account for general capital assets. Both general long-term liabilities and general capital assets are now reported in the governmental activities column of the government-wide Statement of Net Assets (see Illustration 2–1 for an example of this statement).

[4]GASB *Codification*, Sec. 1500.108.

general long-term liabilities are settled by the payment of cash from a governmental fund. As one would expect, the entry in the governmental activities journal at the government-wide level to record the decrease in general long-term liabilities is straightforward: debit the liability account and credit Cash. At the same time the governmental fund paying the liability would debit Expenditures and credit Cash. Retirement of matured debt principal using a debt service fund is illustrated later in this chapter.

In any given year, it is common for new debt issues to be authorized, for previously authorized debt to be issued, and for older issues to be retired. When a combination of liability events takes place, a schedule detailing changes in long-term debt is needed to inform report users of the details of how long-term liabilities changed. The general long-term liability disclosures required by GASB *Statement No. 34* effectively meet these needs by providing detail of beginning of period long-term liabilities, additions to and reductions of those liabilities, ending liabilities, and the portion of the liabilities payable within one year. Illustration 6–1 presents this disclosure schedule for the hypothetical City of Sunnyville.

General Long-Term Liabilities Arising from Capital Lease Agreements

In Chapter 5, under the heading "Acquisition of General Capital Assets under Lease Agreements," a brief example is given of the computation of the present value of rentals under a capital lease agreement. The entry necessary in a governmental fund at the inception of the lease is illustrated in Chapter 5. The corresponding entry in the governmental activities general journal at the government-wide level is also given in Chapter 5 to show the capitalization of the asset acquired under the lease. That entry is reproduced here also in order to illustrate how the liability is recorded.

Governmental Activities:		
Equipment	67,590	
Capital Lease Obligations Payable		67,590

As shown in the preceding entry, at the inception of the lease an obligation is recognized at the government-wide level in an amount equal to the present value of the stream of annual payments. Although, the lease agreement calls for a $10,000 initial lease payment on January 1, 2001, the full present value should be recorded as the liability until the initial payment has been recorded. Accounting for the initial payment in the debt service fund is illustrated later in this chapter. When the initial payment is recorded in the debt service fund, it will be accompanied by the following entry at the government-wide level to record the reduction of the capital lease obligation.

Governmental Activities:		
Capital Lease Obligations Payable	10,000	
Cash		10,000

On January 1, 2002, the second lease rental payment of $10,000 is made. As the table given later in this chapter shows, only $4,241 of that payment applies to reduction of the principal of the lease obligation (the remaining $10,000 – $4,241,

Illustration 6–1 Illustrative Disclosures about Long-Term Liabilities, City of Sunnyville, September 30, 2002

NOTE 4—Long-Term Debt Liabilities

	Balance 10/1/2001	*Additions*	*Reductions*	*Balance 9/30/2002*	*Amounts Due Within One Year*
Governmental Activities					
General obligation bonds	$ 510,000	$ —	$ 140,000	$ 370,000	$ 35,000
Public improvement revenue certificates 1991	250,000	—	250,000	0	0
Public improvement revenue and refunding bonds 2000	9,940,000	—	580,000	9,360,000	505,000
State financing commission loan 2000	520,000	—	75,000	445,000	64,185
State financing commission loan 2001	410,000	—	410,000	0	0
State financing commission loan 2002	—	15,830,000	—	15,830,000	1,583,000
Promissory note	213,016	—	17,917	195,099	16,410
Capital leases	155,084	41,702	76,047	120,739	73,740
Compensated absences	1,296,122	77,864	—	1,373,986	0
Total general long-term liabilities	$ 13,294,222	$ 15,949,566	$ 1,548,964	$ 27,694,824	$ 2,277,335
Business-Type Activities					
Utility revenue bonds	$356,053,692	$134,920,000	$67,017,331	$423,956,361	$66,900,000
Utility notes	71,361,000	—	1,700,000	69,661,000	1,680,000
Total business-type long-term liabilities	$427,414,692	$134,920,000	$68,717,331	$493,617,361	$68,580,000

Source: Prepared by authors in the format shown in GASB *Statement No. 34*. GASB *Statement No. 34*, "Appendix C, Notes to the Financial Statements, Note 2" (Norwalk, CT, 1999), pp. 246–247.

or $5,759, represents interest on the lease). Thus, the following entry is required at the government-wide level to further reduce the balance of the lease principal and to recognize the related interest expense.

Governmental Activities:		
Capital Lease Obligations Payable	4,241	
Interest Expense on Capital Leases	5,759	
Cash		10,000

Schedule of Future Debt Service Requirements

In addition to the disclosures about long-term liabilities presented in Illustration 6–1, information about the amount of debt principal and interest falling due in future years is useful information to financial managers, bond analysts, and others

Illustration 6–2

CITY OF SUNNYVILLE
NOTES TO FINANCIAL STATEMENTS
SEPTEMBER 30, 2002

Aggregate annual debt service requirements (excluding the Commercial Paper Notes) including maturities of principal and payment of current interest are as follows:

	Debt Service Requirements			
Fiscal Year(s)	*General*	*Enterprise**	*Internal Service*	*Total*
2003	$ 2,815,299	$ 30,499,026	$22,273	$ 33,336,598
2004	2,838,305	34,499,804	22,273	37,360,382
2005	2,751,053	36,805,138	14,849	39,571,040
2006	2,693,201	39,340,417	—	42,033,618
2007	2,698,904	39,344,076	—	42,042,980
2008–2012	12,294,623	195,959,406	—	208,254,029
2013–2017	11,306,314	203,342,022	—	214,648,336
2018–2022	11,308,384	244,763,213	—	256,071,597
2023–2027	4,115,205	109,164,138	—	113,279,343
2028–2032	—	28,912,475	—	28,912,475
	52,821,288	962,629,715	59,395	1,015,510,398
Less Interest	26,500,450	538,673,354	5,285	565,179,089
Total Principal	$26,320,838	$423,956,361	$54,110	$ 450,331,309

*Excludes principal of $69,661,000 and undeterminable amount of interest. See prior description of the Utility System Commercial Paper Notes.

Included in the above tabulation are debt service requirements for the City's capital lease obligations as follows:

Fiscal year-end September 30:

2003	65,577
2004	64,016
2005	54,955
2006	15,632
Net minimum lease payments	$200,180
Less amount representing interest	(25,331)
Present value of net minimum lease payments	$174,849

having an interest in assessing a governmental unit's requirements for future debt service expenditures. One form of such a schedule, representing a disclosure from the notes to the financial statements for the City of Sunnyville, is shown in Illustration 6–2. The reader should note that the interest portion of the scheduled future debt service payments is *not* a present liability and should not be presented as such. To do so would not be in conformity with generally accepted accounting principles.

Debt Limit and Debt Margin

The debt schedules already illustrated in this chapter are primarily useful for the information of administrators, legislative bodies, and others concerned with the impact of long-term debt on the financial condition and activities of the governmental unit, particularly with reference to the resulting tax rates and taxes. Another matter of importance is the legal limit on the amount of long-term indebtedness that may be outstanding at a given time, in proportion to the assessed value of property within the jurisdiction represented. This type of restriction is of importance as a protection of taxpayers against possible confiscatory tax rates. Even though tax-rate limitation laws may be in effect for a governmental unit, the limitation on bonded indebtedness is usually needed because the prevailing practice is to exempt the claims of bondholders from the barrier of tax-rate restrictions. This is to say that, even though a law establishing maxima for tax rates is in the statutes, it will probably exclude debt service requirements from the restrictions of the law. This exclusion would be reiterated, in effect, in the bond indentures.

Before continuing a discussion of debt limitation, it seems well to clarify the meaning of the terms *debt limit* and *debt margin*. **Debt limit** means the total amount of indebtedness of specified kinds that is allowed by law to be outstanding at any one time. The limitation is likely to be in terms of a stipulated percentage of the assessed valuation of property within the government's jurisdiction. It may relate to either a gross or a net valuation. The latter is logical, but probably not prevalent, because debt limitation exists as a device for protecting property owners from confiscatory taxation. For that reason, tax-paying property *only* should be used in regulating maximum indebtedness. In many governmental jurisdictions, certain property is legally excluded even from *assessment*. This includes property owned by governments, churches, charitable organizations, and some others, depending on state laws. Exemptions, which apply to property subject to assessment, are based on homestead or mortgage exemption laws, military service, economic status, and possibly some others. Both exclusions and exemptions reduce the amount of tax-paying property.

Debt margin, sometimes referred to as *borrowing power,* is the difference between the amount of debt limit calculated as prescribed by law and the net amount of outstanding indebtedness subject to limitation. The net amount of outstanding indebtedness subject to limitation differs from total general long-term indebtedness because certain debt issues may be exempted by law from the limitation, and the amount available in debt service funds for debt repayment is deducted from the outstanding debt in order to determine the amount subject to the legal debt limit. Total general long-term indebtedness must, in some jurisdictions, include special assessment debt and debt serviced by enterprise funds if such debt was issued with covenants that give the debt tax-supported status in the event that collections of special assessments or enterprise fund revenues are insufficient to meet required interest or principal payments. Debt authorized but not issued as of the end of a fiscal year should be added to outstanding debt because it may be sold at any time. Although it would be in keeping with the purpose of establishing a legal debt limit to include the present value of capital lease obligations along with bonded debt in the computation of legal debt margin, state statutes at present generally do not specify

Illustration 6–3

CITY OF SUNNYVILLE
FY2002 COMPREHENSIVE ANNUAL FINANCIAL REPORT
STATISTICAL SECTION
LEGAL DEBT MARGIN AND
RATIO OF CITY'S GROSS BONDED DEBT TO TAXABLE VALUE
AND BONDED DEBT PER CAPITA

Legal Debt Margin
Taxable Value = $1,591,052,836
Legal Debt Limit = None (1)

NOTE: (1) Chapter 200.181, State Statutes, allows unrestricted Ad Valorem tax rate levies for debt service requirements for General Obligation Bonds approved by voter referendum.

Tax Roll Year	*Taxable Value (January 1)*	*Bonded Debt (September 30)*	*Bonded Debt Ratio*	*City Population (April 1)*	*Bonded Debt per Capita*
1993	$ 928,103,688	$1,885,000	0.20%	81,614	23.10
1994	1,003,863,526	1,305,000	0.13%	82,124	15.89
1995	1,068,009,730	1,210,000	0.11%	82,882	14.60
1996	1,190,125,000	1,110,000	0.09%	83,060	13.36
1997	1,256,295,392	1,005,000	0.07%	83,980	11.97
1998	1,281,612,508	890,000	0.06%	84,815	10.49
1999	1,307,412,913	770,000	0.06%	85,663	8.99
2000	1,349,653,947	645,000	0.05%	84,770	7.61
2001	1,345,552,130	510,000	0.04%	84,544	6.03
2002	1,591,052,836	370,000	0.02%	85,587	4.32

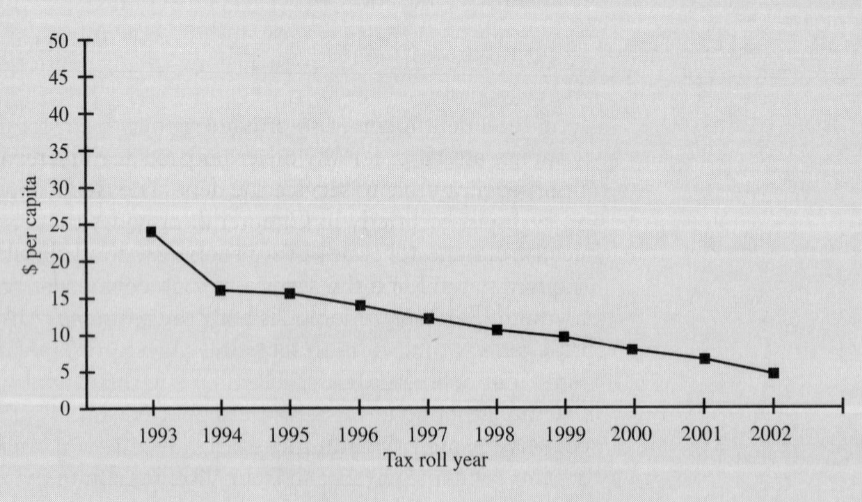

that the liability for capital lease obligations is subject to the legal debt limit. The computation of legal debt margin for the City of Sunnyville is shown in Illustration 6–3.

Overlapping Debt

Debt limitation laws ordinarily establish limits that may not be exceeded by each separate governmental unit affected by the laws. This means the county government may incur indebtedness to the legal limit, a township within that county may do likewise, and a city within the township may become indebted to the legal limit, with no restriction because of debt already owed by larger territorial units in which it is located. As a result, a given parcel of real estate or object of personal property may be the basis of debt beyond the so-called legal limit and also may be subject at a given time to assessments for the payment of taxes to retire bonds issued by two or more governmental units. When this situation exists, it is described as **overlapping debt.**

The extent to which debt may overlap depends on the number of units represented within an area that are authorized to incur long-term indebtedness. These may include the state, county, township, city, school board, library board, hospital board, and probably others. To show the total amount of fixed debt against property located within a given jurisdiction, a statement of direct and overlapping debt should be prepared. To this direct debt are added amounts owing by other units and authorities that levy taxes against the same property on which the direct debt is based. A Statement of Direct and Overlapping Debt is shown in Illustration 6–4. Notes included as a part of Illustration 6–4 disclose the relation of direct debt and overlapping debt to assessed valuation of real property within the City of Sunnyville.

Debt Service Funds

Long-term debt incurred to provide money to pay for the construction or purchase of capital assets, or for any other purposes, can be repaid only from revenue raised in subsequent years to service the debt. The Reporting Long-Term Liabilities Principle, discussed briefly in Chapter 2, provides that long-term liabilities to be serviced from the revenues of a proprietary fund should be accounted for by that proprietary fund and the service of such debt is also accounted for by the proprietary fund. *Debt service* includes both the payment of interest and the repayment of principal when due. Long-term debt serviced by tax levies, or by special assessments, however, is accounted for in the governmental activities category at the government-wide level. Revenue raised from taxes or from special assessments for debt service, and expenditures for debt service, are commonly accounted for by use of a *debt service fund*, the subject of this section of the chapter.

Types of Serial Bonds

Several decades ago, governmental issues of long-term debt commonly matured in total on a given date. In that era, bond indentures often required the establishment of a "sinking fund," sometimes operated on an actuarial basis. Some sinking fund

Illustration 6–4

CITY OF SUNNYVILLE
FY2002 COMPREHENSIVE ANNUAL FINANCIAL REPORT
STATISTICAL SECTION
STATEMENT OF DIRECT AND OVERLAPPING BONDED DEBT (5)

Taxing Authority	*Taxable Property Value (2)*	*General Obligation Bonded Debt (3)*	*Percent of Debt Applicable to City*	*City's Share of Debt (4)*
City of Sunnyville	$1,591,052,836	$ 370,000	100.00%	$ 370,000
Sunny County	3,478,806,917	16,930,000	45.74	7,743,782
Sunny County Schools	3,478,806,917	69,723,480	45.74	31,891,520
		$87,023,480	45.97%	$40,005,302

NOTES:

(1) The above information on Bonded Debt does not include Self-Supporting and Non-Self-Supporting Revenue Bonds, Certificates, and Notes as follows (Reserves and/or Sinking Fund balances have not been deducted).

(2) As of January 1, 1993, homestead property of certain qualified residents is eligible for up to $25,000 value exemption.

(3) Reserves and Sinking Fund Balances have *not* been deducted.

(4) Chapter 200.181, State Statutes, allows unrestricted Ad Valorem Tax rate levies for debt service for General Obligation Bonds approved by citizen referendum.

(5) Includes $14,735,000 in Sunny County Library District Serial & Term Bonds.

Taxing Authority	*Self-Supporting*	*Non-Self-Supporting*	*Totals*
Sunny County	$ 60,220,000	$ —	$ 60,220,000
Sunny County Schools	—	—	—
City of Sunnyville:			
Utilities	423,956,361	—	423,956,361
Other Than Utilities	—	16,275,000	16,275,000
	$484,176,361	$16,275,000	$500,451,361

term bond issues are still outstanding, but they are dwarfed in number and amount by serial bond issues, in which the principal matures in installments. Four types of serial bond issues are found in practice: regular, deferred, annuity, and irregular. If the total principal of an issue is repayable in a specified number of equal annual installments over the life of the issue, it is a **regular serial bond issue.** If the first installment is delayed for a period of more than one year after the date of the issue, but thereafter installments fall due on a regular basis, the bonds are known as **deferred serial bonds.** If the amount of annual principal repayments is scheduled to increase each year by approximately the same amount that interest payments decrease (interest decreases, of course, because the amount of outstanding bonds decreases) so that the total debt service remains reasonably level over the term of the issue, the bonds are called **annuity serial bonds. Irregular serial bonds** may have any pattern of repayment that does not fit the other three categories.

Budgeting for Debt Service

Whether or not additions to debt service funds are required by the bond indenture to be approximately equal year by year, good politics and good financial management suggest that the burden on the taxpayers be spread reasonably evenly rather than lumped in the years that issues or installments happen to mature. If taxes for payment of interest and principal on long-term debt are to be raised directly by the debt service fund, they are recognized as *Revenues* of the debt service fund. If the taxes are to be raised by another fund and transferred to the debt service fund, they must be included in the Revenues budget of the fund that will raise the revenue (often the General Fund) and also budgeted by that fund as *interfund transfers* to the debt service fund, and reported as an Other Financing Use by the General Fund. The transfers are reported as Other Financing Sources by the debt service fund. Since the debt service fund is a budgeting and accounting entity, it should prepare a Revenues and Other Financing Sources budget that includes interfund transfers from other funds as well as revenues it will raise directly or earn on its investments. Although the items may be difficult to budget accurately, debt service funds can often count on receiving premiums on debt issues sold and accrued interest on debt issues sold. Accrued interest on debt sold is commonly considered Revenues of the recipient debt service fund; premium on debt sold is an Other Financing Source. Similarly, as illustrated in Chapter 5, if capital projects are completed with expenditures less than revenues and other financing sources, the residual equity is ordinarily transferred to the appropriate debt service fund. Persons budgeting and accounting for debt service funds should seek competent legal advice on the permissible use of both premium on debt sold and residual equity interfund transfers. In some cases, one or both of these items must be held for eventual debt repayment and may not be used for interest payments; in other cases, both premiums and residual equity transfers-in may be used for interest payments.

The Appropriations budget of a debt service fund must provide for the payment of all interest on general long-term debt that will become legally due during the budget year, and for the payment of any principal amounts that will become legally due during the budget year. GASB standards currently require debt service fund accounting to be on the same basis as is required for general and special revenue funds. One peculiarity of the modified accrual basis used by governmental fund types (which is not discussed in Chapter 3 because it relates only to debt service funds) is that interest on long-term debt is not accrued in the debt service fund, but is accrued at the government-wide level. For example, if the fiscal year of a governmental unit ends on December 31, 2001, and the interest on its bonds is payable on January 1 and July 1 of each year, the amount payable on January 1, 2002, would not be considered a liability in the balance sheet of the debt service fund prepared as of December 31, 2001. The rationale for this recommendation is that the interest is not legally due until January 1, 2002. (See Illustration 6–5.) The same reasoning applies to principal amounts that mature on the first day of a fiscal year; they are not liabilities to be recognized in statements prepared as of the day

Illustration 6–5 **Modified Accrual Basis of Recognition of Expenditures for Long-Term Debt Interest and Principal**

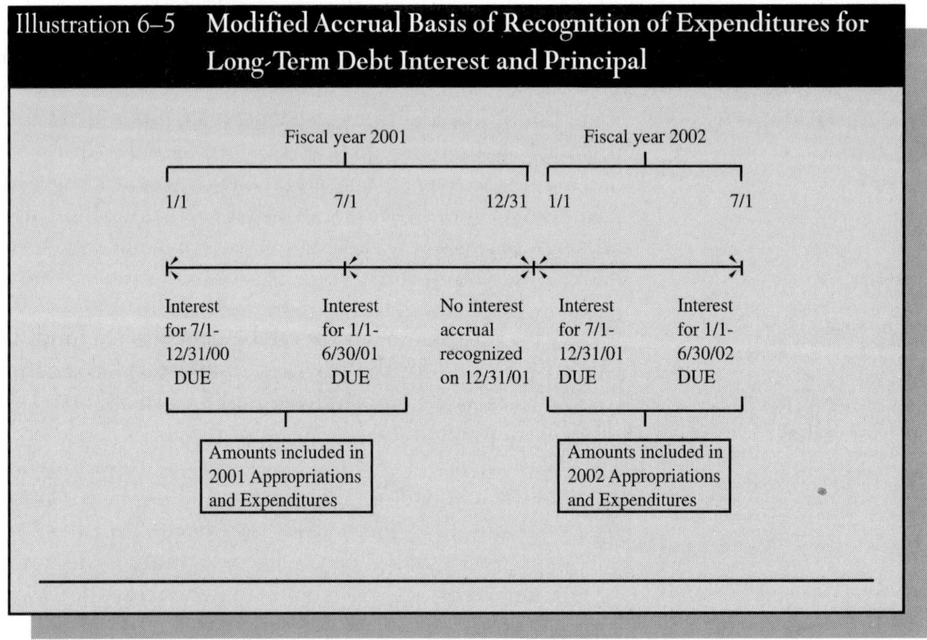

before. In the event 2001 appropriations include January 1, 2002, interest and/or principal payment, the appropriation and expenditures (and resulting liabilities) should be recognized in 2001.

Number of Debt Service Funds

In addition to term bonds and serial bonds, debt service funds may be required to service debt arising from the use of notes or warrants having a maturity more than one year after date of issue. In addition, debt service funds may be used to make periodic payments required by capital lease agreements. Although each issue of long-term or intermediate-term debt is a separate obligation and may have legal restrictions and servicing requirements that differ from other issues, GASB standards provide that, if legally permissible, a single debt service fund be used to account for the service of all issues of tax-supported and special assessment debt. Subsidiary records of that fund can provide needed assurance that restrictions and requirements relating to each issue are properly budgeted and accounted for. If legal restrictions do not allow the service of all issues of tax-supported and special assessment debt to be accounted for by a single debt service fund, as few additional debt service funds as is consistent with applicable laws should be created. In this chapter, a separate debt service fund for each bond issue is illustrated simply as a means for helping the reader focus on the different accounting procedures considered appropriate for each kind of bond issue encountered in practice.

Use of General Fund to Account for Debt Service

In some jurisdictions, laws do not require the debt service function to be accounted for by a debt service fund. Unless the debt service function is very simple, it may be argued that good financial management would dictate the establishment of a debt service fund even though not required by law. If neither law nor sound financial administration requires the use of debt service funds, the function may be performed within the accounting and budgeting framework of the General Fund. In such cases, the accounting and financial reporting standards discussed in this chapter should be followed for the debt service activities of the General Fund.

Debt Service Accounting for Regular Serial Bonds

Accounts recommended for use by debt service funds created to account for revenues to be used for the payment of interest and principal of serial bond issues are similar to those recommended for use by general and special revenue funds, but not exactly the same. Serial bond debt service funds should record the budget in Estimated Revenues and Appropriations control accounts and subsidiary accounts (and Estimated Other Financing Sources and Estimated Other Financing Uses control accounts and subsidiary accounts, if needed) just as General and special revenue funds should. However, because their operations do not involve the use of purchase orders and contracts for goods and services, the Encumbrances account is not needed. Proprietary accounts of a serial bond debt service fund include Revenues and Expenditures control and subsidiary accounts (and Other Financing Sources and Other Financing Uses control and subsidiary accounts, if needed); and liquid asset, current liability, and Fund Balance accounts. Liquid assets of a serial bond debt service fund are held for the purpose of paying interest on outstanding bonds and retiring the principal installments as they fall due; for the convenience of bondholders, the payment of interest and the redemption of matured bonds is ordinarily handled through the banking system. Usually the government designates a bank as Paying Agent or Fiscal Agent, to handle interest and principal payments for each issue whether the issue is in registered or bearer form. The assets of a debt service fund may, therefore, include "Cash with Paying Agent," and the appropriations, expenditures, and liabilities may include amounts for the service charges of paying agents. Investment management may be performed by governmental employees or by banks, brokers, or others who charge for the service; investment management fees are a legitimate charge against investment revenues.

Accounting for debt service of regular serial bonds furnishes the simplest illustration of recommended debt service fund accounting. Assume the bonds issued by the Town of Brighton as partial financing for the fire station construction project (discussed in Chapter 5, under the heading "Illustrative Transactions—Capital Projects Funds") are regular serial bonds maturing in equal annual amounts over 20 years and are registered as to interest and principal. The total face value of the issue was $1,200,000; all bonds in the issue bear interest of 6 percent per year, payable semiannually on June 15 and December 15. The bonds were dated June 15, 2002, and sold on that date at par. During 2002 the only expenditure the Debt Service Fund will be required to make will be the interest payment due December 15,

2002, in the amount of $36,000 ($1,200,000 × 0.06 × ½ year). Assuming revenues to pay the first installment of bonds due on June 15, 2003, and both interest payments due in 2003, will be raised in 2003, the budget for 2002 need only provide revenues in the amount of the 2002 interest expenditure. The entry to record the budget for the year ended December 31, 2002 is:

Regular Serial Bond Debt Service Fund:		
1. Estimated Revenues	36,000	
Appropriations		36,000

If revenues in the amount of $30,000 were collected in cash from various sources available for debt service, the entry is:

Regular Serial Bond Debt Service Fund:		
2a. Cash	30,000	
Revenues		30,000

The corresponding entry in the governmental activities general ledger at the government-wide level is (Note: Entry 1 had no effect at the government-wide level since budget entries are made only in governmental funds):

Governmental Activities:		
2b. Cash	30,000	
General Revenues—Miscellaneous—Restricted for Debt Service		30,000

As illustrated in Chapter 5, the $6,000 residual equity of the Fire Station Capital Projects Fund was transferred to the Debt Service Fund. The entry required in the latter fund is:

Regular Serial Bond Debt Service Fund:		
3. Cash	6,000	
Other Financing Sources—Interfund Transfers In		6,000

(Note: governmental activities at the government-wide level are unaffected since the transfers are between two funds within the governmental activities category.)

On December 15, 2002, when the first interest payment is legally due, the Debt Service Fund records the expenditure of the appropriation and the corresponding entry is made to record interest expense at the government-wide level:

Regular Serial Bond Debt Service Fund:		
4a. Expenditures—Bond Interest	36,000	
Interest Payable		36,000
Governmental Activities:		
4b. Interest Expense on Long-Term Debt	36,000	
Interest Payable		36,000

Checks totaling $36,000 are written to the registered owners of these bonds. The entries to record the payment in the debt service fund and governmental activities general journals are:

Regular Serial Bond Debt Service Fund and Governmental Activities:		
5. Interest Payable	36,000	
Cash		36,000

As of December 31, 2002, an adjusting entry would be made to accrue one-half of a month's interest expense on the accrual basis at the government-wide level, as would be the case in accounting for business organizations. As was discussed earlier, interest expenditure is recognized in the period when due in the debt service fund and is not accrued at the end of the accounting period.

Governmental Activities:		
6. Interest Expense on Long-term Debt	3,000	
Interest Payable		3,000

The Debt Service Fund has no assets and no liabilities, therefore has no need to prepare a balance sheet at year-end; however, the budgetary and operating statement accounts have balances, which are closed by the following entry:

Regular Serial Bond Debt Service Fund:		
7. Revenues	30,000	
Other Financing Sources—Interfund Transfers In	6,000	
Appropriations	36,000	
Estimated Revenues		36,000
Expenditures—Bond Interest		36,000

In addition, all temporary accounts of the governmental activities general ledger would be closed at year-end. Because that ledger has many temporary accounts besides those related to debt service, its closing entry is not illustrated here.

The Regular Serial Bonds Debt Service Fund Statement of Revenues, Expenditures, and Changes in Fund Balance for the year ended December 31, 2002, and a budgetary comparison statement for this fund for the year, both prepared for internal management use, are illustrated in combining statements for all debt service funds (Illustrations 6–6 and 6–7) that present all of the Town of Brighton's debt service funds, including those to be discussed in the following sections. Neither of these statements would be presented in the Town of Brighton's Comprehensive Annual Financial Report (CAFR). Rather, balance sheet and operating statement information for each debt service fund would be presented as a *major fund* column in the Balance Sheet—Governmental Funds and Statement of Revenues, Expenditures, and Changes in Fund Balances—Governmental Funds, if they meet the major fund criteria (see the Glossary for a definition of major fund). Each debt service fund that does *not* meet the major fund criteria would be included in a nonmajor funds combining Balance Sheet and combining Statement of Revenues, Expenditures, and Changes in Fund Balances, along with all other governmental nonmajor funds (not just debt service).

Debt Service Accounting for Deferred Serial Bonds

If a government issues bonds other than regular serial bonds, debt service fund accounting is somewhat more complex than that illustrated above. In the entries below, it is assumed the Town of Brighton issued a total of $2,000,000 face value of deferred serial bonds on January 1, 1992. Each installment is in the amount of $200,000. The first installment matures after 10 years on January 1, 2002; the final installment after 20 years on January 1, 2011. Interest is payable on January 1 and July 1 of each year at the nominal annual rate of 5 percent. Debt service is financed from taxes levied by the Debt Service Fund and from net earnings on Debt Service

Illustration 6–6

TOWN OF BRIGHTON
DEBT SERVICE FUNDS
COMBINING STATEMENT OF REVENUES, EXPENDITURES, AND CHANGES IN FUND BALANCES
FOR THE YEAR ENDED DECEMBER 31, 2002

	Regular Serial Bonds	Deferred Serial Bonds	Term Bonds	Total Debt Service Funds
Revenues:				
Taxes	$ –0–	$190,000	$117,000	$307,000
Miscellaneous sources	30,000	–0–	–0–	30,000
Interest on investments	–0–	104,100	3,145	107,245
Total Revenues	30,000	294,100	120,145	444,245
Expenditures:				
Interest on bonds	36,000	95,000	75,000	206,000
Redemption of matured bonds	–0–	200,000	–0–	200,000
Total expenditures	36,000	295,000	75,000	406,000
Excess of Revenues over (under) Expenditures	(6,000)	(900)	45,145	38,245
Other Financing Sources (Uses):				
Interfund transfers in	6,000	–0–	–0–	6,000
Increase in Fund Balance	–0–	(900)	45,145	44,245
Fund Balance, January 1, 2002	–0–	1,582,094	40,384	1,622,478
Fund Balance, December 31, 2002	$ –0–	$1,581,194	$ 85,529	$1,666,723

Fund investments. Taxes for this Debt Service Fund are levied in an amount equal to interest to be paid during the budget year, plus a level amount of $100,000 to be invested by the Debt Service Fund and used for principal repayment when the principal installments fall due. The trial balance of the Town of Brighton's Deferred Serial Bonds Debt Service Fund at the end of the 10th year (year ending December 31, 2001) following the date of the deferred serial bond issue showed:

	Debits	Credits
Cash	$ 250,000	
Investments	1,298,656	
Interest Receivable	33,438	
Fund Balance	—	$1,582,094
Totals	$1,582,094	$1,582,094

Illustration 6–7

TOWN OF BRIGHTON
DEBT SERVICE FUNDS
COMBINING STATEMENT OF REVENUES, EXPENDITURES,
AND CHANGES IN FUND BALANCES—BUDGET AND ACTUAL
FOR THE YEAR ENDED DECEMBER 31, 2002

	Regular Serial Bonds			Deferred Serial Bonds			Term Bonds			Total Debt Service Bonds		
	Budget	*Actual*	*Actual Over (Under) Budget*	*Budget*	*Actual*	*Actual Over (Under) Budget*	*Budget*	*Actual*	*Actual Over (Under) Budget*	*Budget*	*Actual*	*Actual Over (Under) Budget*
Revenues:												
Taxes	$ –0–	$ –0–	$–0–	$ 190,000	$ 190,000	$–0–	$114,787	$117,000	$2,213	$ 304,787	$ 307,000	$2,213
Miscellaneous sources	36,000	30,000	(6,000)	–0–	–0–	–0–	–0–	–0–	–0–	36,000	30,000	(6,000)
Interest on investments	–0–	–0–	–0–	103,900	104,100	200	3,056	3,145	89	106,956	107,245	289
Total Revenues	36,000	30,000	(6,000)	293,900	294,100	200	117,843	120,145	2,302	447,743	444,245	(3,498)
Expenditures:												
Interest on bonds	36,000	36,000	–0–	95,000	95,000	–0–	75,000	75,000	–0–	206,000	206,000	–0–
Redemption of matured bonds	–0–	–0–	–0–	200,000	200,000	–0–	–0–	–0–	–0–	200,000	200,000	–0–
Total expenditures	36,000	36,000	–0–	295,000	295,000	–0–	75,000	75,000	–0–	406,000	406,000	–0–
Excess of Revenues over (under) Expenditures	–0–	(6,000)	(6,000)	(1,100)	(900)	200	42,843	45,145	2,302	41,743	38,245	(3,498)
Other Financing Sources (Uses):												
Interfund transfers in	–0–	6,000	6,000	–0–	–0–	–0–	–0–	–0–	–0–	–0–	6,000	6,000
Increase in Fund Balance	–0–	–0–	–0–	(1,100)	(900)	200	42,843	45,145	2,302	41,743	44,245	2,502
Fund Balance, January 1, 2002	–0–	–0–	–0–	1,582,094	1,582,094	–0–	40,384	40,384	–0–	1,622,478	1,622,478	–0–
Fund Balance, December 31, 2002	$ –0–	$ –0–	$–0–	$1,580,994	$1,581,194	$200	$ 83,227	$ 85,529	$2,302	$1,664,221	$1,666,723	$2,502

Notice the trial balance shows Cash in the exact amount of interest on this bond issue due on January 1, 2002 ($2,000,000 × .05 × ½ year = $50,000), plus $200,000 for the bonds that mature on January 1, 2002. To ensure timely payment of interest and principal retirement, checks totaling $250,000, dated January 1, 2002, were written in late December and mailed to the registered bondholders; since the checks are dated the day after balance sheet date, they will not to be credited to Cash until that date. [Note: An alternative approach would be to debit an account such as Prepaid Interest and credit Cash when the checks are issued. Then, on January 1, 2002, Interest Expenditure would be debited in the debt service fund and Prepaid Interest would be credited. This approach may be necessary if the government's procedures require a journal entry before a payment can be vouchered.] Because the $250,000 liability does not legally exist until January 1, 2002, it is not reported in the December 31, 2001, balance sheet for the debt service fund. But the accrued liability is reported in the governmental activities column of the government-wide Statement of Net Assets presented at December 31, 2001, as "current portion of bonds payable," $200,000, and "interest payable," $50,000.

The budget for this fund for fiscal 2002 includes the appropriations for payment of the interest of $50,000 on January 1, the payment of matured bonds of $200,000 on January 1, and the payment of interest of $45,000 on bonds outstanding on July 1, 2002 ($1,800,000 × .05 × ½ year). It is assumed, for the sake of simplicity, that the Town will not incur any fees for paying agents or for investment management; therefore, the total of the Appropriations budget for 2002 is $295,000. As noted in the description of this deferred serial bond issue, taxes are levied each year to allow for collection of cash in the amount of interest checks to be written that year, plus an amount of $100,000 to be invested for use for bond principal payment; earnings on the investments are also accumulated for bond principal repayment. Therefore, the Revenues budget for 2002 for this fund for revenues from taxes totals $190,000 ($45,000 for the interest payment due July 1, 2002; $45,000 for the interest payment due January 1, 2003; and the $100,000 level amount to be invested); revenues from earnings on investments during 2002 are budgeted at $103,900. Total Estimated Revenues for 2002, therefore, amounts to $293,900. The entry to record the 2002 budget is:

Deferred Serial Bond Debt Service Fund:

	Debit	Credit
1. Estimated Revenues	293,900	
Fund Balance	1,100	
Appropriations		295,000

Subsidiary records, if needed, would be kept in the manner illustrated in Chapters 3 and 4. Since the records, and their use, are the same, they are omitted from this chapter.

Also, as of January 1, 2002, the bond payment and interest payment due on that date should be recognized as expenditures of 2002 appropriations (Entry 2a), and the fact that checks dated January 1, 2002, have been issued in payment of the interest and bond principal should be recorded (Entry 2b). In addition, Entry 2c would be made at the government-wide level to reduce the accrued liabilities that had been recorded on December 31, 2001, in the governmental activities general journal:

	Debit	Credit
Deferred Serial Bond Debt Service Fund:		
2a. Expenditures—Bond Principal	200,000	
Expenditures—Bond Interest	50,000	
Bonds Payable		200,000
Interest Payable		50,000
2b. Bonds Payable	200,000	
Interest Payable	50,000	
Cash		250,000
Governmental Activities:		
2c. Current Portion of Bonds Payable	200,000	
Accrued Interest Payable	50,000	
Cash		250,000

In an actual case it would, of course, simplify the accounting to make one entry for the net effect of Entries 2a and 2b: a debit to Expenditures and a credit to Cash. As shown in the basic GAAP operating statement presented in Illustration 2–4, as well as Illustrations 6–6 and 6–7 prepared for internal management use, the expenditures for bond interest and the expenditures for the redemption of matured bonds should be separately reported in the operating statements. Thus, the use of separate Expenditures accounts for principal repayment and interest, as shown in Entry 2a, should be used.

Taxes levied for debt service on the deferred serial bond issue are levied in the amount of $195,000; $5,000 of the levy is expected to be uncollectible:

	Debit	Credit
Deferred Serial Bond Debt Service Fund:		
3a. Taxes Receivable—Current	195,000	
Estimated Uncollectible Current Taxes		5,000
Revenues		190,000
Governmental Activities:		
3b. Taxes Receivable—Current	195,000	
Estimated Uncollectible Current Taxes		5,000
General Revenues—Property Taxes—Restricted for Debt Service		190,000

Entry 4a summarizes the collection of taxes during the first half-year (assumed to amount to $100,000), the collection of interest receivable as of December 31, 2001 ($33,438, per the trial balance), and the collection of $51,100 interest earned during the first half-year on investments of this fund. Entry 4b records the government-wide effect of the same transactions. Cash in the amount of $139,500 was promptly invested, as shown by Entry 4c; the entry being the same in both the debt service fund and the governmental activities category.

	Debit	Credit
Deferred Serial Bond Debt Service Fund:		
4a. Cash	184,538	
Taxes Receivable—Current		100,000
Interest Receivable		33,438
Revenues		51,100

Governmental Activities:

	Debit	Credit
4b. Cash	184,538	
Taxes Receivable—Current		100,000
Interest Receivable		33,438
General Revenues—Investment Earnings—Restricted for Debt Service		51,100

Deferred Serial Bond Debt Service Fund and Governmental Activities:

	Debit	Credit
4c. Investments	139,500	
Cash		139,500

Interest payable on July 1, 2002, is recorded as an expenditure, and checks are written and mailed in the amount of interest payable July 1:

Deferred Serial Bond Debt Service Fund:

	Debit	Credit
5a. Expenditures—Bond Interest	45,000	
Interest Payable		45,000
5b. Interest Payable	45,000	
Cash		45,000

Governmental Activities:

	Debit	Credit
5c. Interest Expense on Long-term Debt	45,000	
Cash		45,000

Tax collections during the second half of 2002 totaled $85,000; interest earnings received in cash during that period amounted to $32,500. Cash in the amount of $117,500 was invested:

Deferred Serial Bond Debt Service Fund:

	Debit	Credit
6a. Cash	117,500	
Taxes Receivable—Current		85,000
Revenues		32,500

Governmental Activities:

	Debit	Credit
6b. Cash	117,500	
Taxes Receivable—Current		85,000
General Revenues—Investment Earnings—Restricted for Debt Service		32,500

Deferred Serial Bond Debt Service Fund and Governmental Activities:

	Debit	Credit
6c. Investments	117,500	
Cash		117,500

Taxes not collected during 2002 must be classified as delinquent, as required by the laws of the state in which the Town of Brighton is located. Administrators estimate that $5,000 of taxes levied in 2002 will be collected before March 1, 2003, and the remainder of that levy, $5,000, will be uncollectible. Since the original estimate of uncollectible taxes was $5,000, no further adjustment to Revenues is required. Entry 7 accomplishes the necessary reclassifications for both the debt service fund and governmental activities:

Deferred Serial Bond Debt Service Fund and Governmental Activities:

	Debit	Credit
7. Taxes Receivable—Delinquent	10,000	
Estimated Uncollectible Current Taxes	5,000	
Taxes Receivable—Current		10,000
Estimated Uncollectible Delinquent Taxes		5,000

Bonds in the amount of $200,000 will mature on January 1, 2003, and interest in the amount of $45,000 will be payable on that date. Investments in the amount of $245,000 are converted to cash as of December 31, 2002, so that checks dated January 1, 2003, may be mailed. In addition, the bonds due on January 1, 2003, are reclassified as current and the interest due on January 1, 2003, is accrued at the government-wide level, in conformity with standard accrual accounting practices. The required entries on December 31, 2002, are given as:

	Debit	Credit
Deferred Serial Bond Debt Service Fund and Governmental Activities:		
8a. Cash	245,000	
Investments		245,000
Governmental Activities:		
8b. Bonds Payable	200,000	
Interest Expense on Long-term Debt	45,000	
Current Portion of Long-term Debt		200,000
Accrued Interest Payable		45,000

Interest receivable on investments accrued at year-end, December 31, 2002, amount to $20,500. This accrual is recorded both in the debt service fund and governmental activities:

	Debit	Credit
Deferred Serial Bond Debt Service Fund:		
9a. Interest Receivable on Investments	20,500	
Revenues		20,500
Governmental Activities:		
9b. Interest Receivable on Investments	20,500	
General Revenues—Investment Earnings—Restricted for Debt Service		20,500

Budgetary and operating statement accounts of the debt service fund for 2002 are closed (Entry 10a) on December 31, 2002. As noted previously, there are many additional operating statement accounts of the governmental activities besides debt service–related items that would need to be closed. A partial closing entry is presented here for illustrative purposes only:

	Debit	Credit
Deferred Serial Bond Debt Service Fund:		
10a. Revenues	294,100	
Appropriations	295,000	
Estimated Revenues		293,900
Expenditures—Bond Principal		200,000
Expenditures—Bond Interest		95,000
Fund Balance		200
Governmental Activities:		
10b. General Revenues—Property Taxes—Restricted for Debt Service	190,000	
General Revenues—Investment Earnings—Restricted for Debt Service	104,100	
Interest Expense		95,000
Net Assets—Restricted for Debt Service		199,100
10c. Net Assets—Restricted for Debt Service	200,000	
Net Assets—Invested in Capital Assets, Net of Related Debt		200,000

Entry 10c reflects the fact that net assets restricted for debt service were consumed on January 1, 2002, when the current portion of long-term debt was paid in the amount of $200,000. Presumably the $2,000,000 of deferred serial bonds were issued for a capital project that was long ago completed and for which general capital assets were recorded at the government-wide level. Thus, the credit to Net Assets—Invested in Capital Assets, Net of Related Debt would be appropriate to the extent the related debt has been retired. Recall also that Net Assets—Restricted for Debt Service would have an accumulated balance for the years 1992 through 2001 when taxes were levied and invested during the deferral period of the debt.

After recording the entries for 2002, the Town of Brighton Deferred Serial Bonds Debt Service Fund Balance Sheet would be as presented in Illustration 6–8, the combining balance sheet for all debt service funds of the Town of Brighton. (Recall that the Regular Serial Bond Debt Service Fund discussed in the preceding section would not be included in the combining balance sheet as it had no assets or liabilities at year-end.) In addition to the balance sheet, the revenues, expenditures, and changes in fund balance during the fiscal period should be reported for each debt service fund, as shown previously in Illustration 6–6 which presents the Combining Statement of Revenues, Expenditures, and Changes in Fund Balances for the Town of Brighton Deferred Serial Bonds Debt Service Fund for the year ended December 31, 2002, as well as the other debt service funds of the Town. Since the funds are assumed to operate under legally required budgets, a Combining Statement of Revenues, Expenditures, and Changes in Fund Balances—Budget and Actual for the year should also be prepared for internal management purposes. Illustration 6–7 presents a budgetary comparison for all debt service funds of the Town of Brighton.

Illustration 6–8

TOWN OF BRIGHTON
DEBT SERVICE FUNDS
COMBINING BALANCE SHEET
AS OF DECEMBER 31, 2002

	Deferred Serial Bonds	*Term Bonds*	*Total Debt Service Funds*
Assets			
Cash	$ 245,038	$ 613	$ 245,651
Investments	1,310,656	83,316	1,393,972
Taxes receivable, net	5,000	1,600	6,600
Interest receivable	20,500	0	20,500
Total Assets	$1,581,194	$85,529	$1,666,723
Fund Equity			
Fund Equity			
Fund Balance	$1,581,194	$85,529	$1,666,723
Total Fund Equity	$1,581,194	$85,529	$1,666,723

Debt Service Accounting for Term Bonds

Term bond issues mature in their entirety on a given date, in contrast to serial bonds, which mature in installments. Required revenues of term bond debt service funds may be determined on an "actuarial" basis or on less sophisticated bases designed to produce approximately level contributions during the life of the issue. If an actuarial basis is not used, accounting procedures and statements illustrated for the deferred serial bond issue of the Town of Brighton are appropriate for use by term bond debt service funds. In order to illustrate the differences that exist when an actuarial basis is used, the following example is based on the assumption that the Town of Brighton has a term bond issue amounting to $1,500,000 with a 20-year life. The term bonds bear semiannual interest coupons with a nominal (or stated) annual rate of 5 percent, payable on January 1 and July 1. Revenues and other financing sources of this particular debt service fund are assumed to be taxes levied directly for this debt service fund and earnings on investments of the debt service fund. The amount of the tax levy is computed in accord with annuity tables on the assumption that revenues for principal repayment will be invested and will earn 6 percent per year, compounded semiannually. (Actuaries are usually very conservative in their assumptions because they are concerned with a long time span.) Using either the annuity tables found in most intermediate accounting texts or a calculator, one will find that the future amount of $1 invested at the end of each period will amount to $75.4012597 at the end of 40 periods, if the periodic compound interest is 3 percent (as specified in the Town of Brighton example). Since the amount needed for bond repayment at the end of 40 six-month periods is $1,500,000, the tax levy for bond principal repayment must yield $1,500,000 divided by 75.4012597, or $19,893.57 at the end of each six-month period throughout the life of the bonds. Revenue for each bond interest payment must be $37,500 ($1,500,000, the face of the bonds, × 5 percent, the annual nominal interest rate, × ½ year).

Assuming the bonds were issued on January 1, 2001, and actual additions and actual earnings were both exactly as budgeted, the Term Bonds Debt Service Fund would have the following trial balance as of December 31, 2001.[5]

[5]The computation is:

Year	*Period*	*Addition at End of Period*	*3 Percent per Period*	*Balance at End of Period*
2001	1	$19,893.57	$ -0-	$19,893.57
	2	19,893.57	596.81	40,383.95
2002	3	19,893.57	1,211.52	61,489.04
	4	19,893.57	1,844.67	83,227.28

The balance at the end of period 2 is the total of Investments, and the total of Fund Balance, in this case since actuarial assumptions were met exactly in 2001. The sum of the interest for period 3 and period 4 is $3,056.19, the required earnings for the second year.

	Debits	*Credits*
Cash	$37,500.00	—
Investments	40,383.95	—
Fund Balance	—	$77,883.95
Totals	$77,883.95	$77,883.95

For every year of the life of the issue, the budget for the Term Bonds Debt Service Fund of the Town, reflecting the conditions described above, will include two required additions of $19,893.57 each for investment for eventual principal repayment, and two amounts of $37,500 each for interest payment, for a total of $114,787.14. The budget will also include earnings on debt service fund investments computed in accord with actuarial requirements. For 2002, the second year of the Term Bonds Debt Service Fund's operation, the actuarial assumption is that the fund will earn 6 percent per year, compounded semiannually; the required earnings for the year amount to $3,056.19 (see Footnote 5 for calculation). Therefore, Estimated Revenues is debited for $117,843.33 ($114,787.14 + $3,056.19). The Appropriations budget would include only the amounts becoming due during the budget year, $75,000 (two interest payments, each amounting to $37,500). The entry to record the budget for fiscal year 2002 is shown below. (Note: Entries at the government-wide level are omitted here as they would be essentially the same as illustrated for the deferred serial bond example provided in the preceding chapter.)

1. Estimated Revenues	117,843.33	
Fund Balance		42,843.33
Appropriations		75,000.00

If the debt service fund is to accumulate the amount needed to retire the term bond issue at maturity, both additions and earnings must be received, and invested, in accord with the actuarial assumptions. Therefore, the tax levy for this fund must yield collections in the first six months totaling $57,393.57, at least, so that $19,893.57 can be invested and $37,500 interest paid to bondholders, both as of the end of the first six-month period. Collections during the second six months must also total $57,393.57, for the same reason. In the real world it is unlikely that collections would ever total $57,393.57, to the penny, in either six-month period. If collections are less than that amount in either period, it should be obvious that this fund would have to borrow enough to make the required investments—there is no question that the interest would have to be paid when due, as discussed in an early section of this chapter. Assuming collection experience of the Town of Brighton indicates that a tax levy in the amount of $120,000 is needed in order to be reasonably certain that collections during each six-month period will equal the needed amount, the entry to record the levy and the expected uncollectibles amounting to $3,000 is:

		Debit	Credit
2.	Taxes Receivable—Current	120,000.00	
	Estimated Uncollectible Current Taxes		3,000.00
	Revenues		117,000.00

If actual collections during the first six months of 2002 were $57,400, Entry 3 records that fact.

		Debit	Credit
3.	Cash	57,400.00	
	Taxes Receivable—Current		57,400.00

Entry 4 records the investment of the required $19,893.57 and the payment of interest of $37,500.

		Debit	Credit
4.	Expenditures—Bond Interest	37,500.00	
	Investments	19,893.57	
	Cash		57,393.57

Entry 5 records the addition of interest on June 30 in the amount of $1,261.99 to the investments of $40,383.95 invested for the entire first six months of 2002. Note the actual interest for this period is $50.47 greater than the required earnings of $1,211.52 for the period, because the actual rate was slightly greater than the rate used in actuarial computations.

		Debit	Credit
5.	Investments	1,261.99	
	Interest Earnings		1,261.99

During the second six months, tax collections for the Term Bonds Debt Service Fund totaled $58,000 (Entry 6a). The required addition to the Investments account was made, and interest of $37,500 was paid, both actions as of December 31, 2002 (Entry 6b).

		Debit	Credit
6a.	Cash	58,000.00	
	Taxes Receivable—Current		58,000.00
6b.	Expenditures—Bond Interest	37,500.00	
	Investments	19,893.57	
	Cash		57,393.57

Interest earnings during the last six months on the $61,539.51 invested since July 1, 2002, totaled $1,883.10; this amount was added to the Investments account:

		Debit	Credit
7.	Investments	1,883.10	
	Interest Earnings		1,883.10

Taxes levied for 2002 but not collected during the year are recorded as delinquent; the amount in the related Estimated Uncollectible account is reviewed and determined to be reasonable.

		Debit	Credit
8.	Taxes Receivable—Delinquent	4,600.00	
	Estimated Uncollectible Current Taxes	3,000.00	
	Taxes Receivable—Current		4,600.00
	Estimated Uncollectible Delinquent Taxes		3,000.00

As of December 31, 2002, the budgetary accounts and operating statement accounts were closed.

9. Appropriations	75,000.00	
Revenues	117,000.00	
Interest Earnings	3,145.09	
Estimated Revenues		117,843.33
Expenditures—Bond Interest		75,000.00
Fund Balance		2,301.76

Assets, liabilities, and Fund Balance of the Term Bonds Debt Service Fund as of December 31, 2002 (all rounded to the nearest dollar), are shown in one column of the combining balance sheet of all debt service funds of the Town of Brighton, Illustration 6–8. Similarly, revenues, expenditures and changes in fund balance of the Term Bonds Debt Service Fund are shown in the Combining Statement of Revenues, Expenditures, and Changes in Fund Balances, Illustration 6–6, and the budget and actual comparison in Illustration 6–7.

Disclosures in Notes to the Financial Statements

Any information in addition to the financial statements shown as Illustrations 6–6, 6–7, and 6–8 that would be helpful to administrators, members of the legislative body, interested residents, creditors, or any other category of person who uses the financial reports of a governmental reporting entity should, of course, be provided. GASB standards require disclosure in the notes to the financial statements (the notes are an integral part of the basic financial statements and are covered by the auditor's report) of specific data about deposits with financial institutions and investments. Disclosures are required for the entity as a whole, not just for debt service funds. However, since the Town of Brighton's debt service funds hold over $1.6 million in cash and investments, it is appropriate to mention required note disclosures at this point.

GASB standards require disclosure in the notes of the types of deposits and investments authorized by legal and contractual provisions. Any significant violations during the period of legal or contractual provisions should, of course, be disclosed. If bank balances as of balance sheet date are entirely insured or collateralized with securities held by the entity or its agent in the entity's name, that fact should be mentioned. If not, the amount of the total bank balance should be classified and reported in the three categories of credit risk specified in the standards. Similarly, the fair value of investments as of balance sheet date should be disclosed in total and for each type of investment.[6] The disclosure of carrying amounts by type of investment should be classified in the three categories of credit risk specified in the standards.[7]

GASB standards apply to all state and local governmental reporting entities' financial reports that are intended to conform with generally accepted accounting

[6]GASB standards define **fair value** as "the amount at which an investment could be exchanged in a current transaction between willing parties, other than in a forced or liquidation sale." GASB, *Codification*, Sec. 150.105.

[7]GASB *Codification*, Sec. 150.125–132.

principles. A number of states have established by law reporting requirements for the state government itself and for local governments within the state. It is common for financial reports prepared in compliance with state laws to include a list of the amounts on deposit in named banks, a list of securities held, and their fair value as of the balance sheet date. Supplementary schedules presented in order to conform with laws, or presented because administrators feel the disclosures should be made, are not covered by the independent auditor's report unless the audit engagement specifically extends the scope of the audit to the supplementary schedules.

Debt Service Fund Investments

As shown in the Deferred Serial Bond Debt Service Fund and the Term Bond Debt Service Fund examples in this chapter, financial resources typically are accumulated in these types of debt service funds for eventual repayment of principal. Such resources should be invested prudently until they are needed for principal repayment. Interest earnings on investments in bonds and other securities purchased at a premium or discount generally would not be adjusted for amortization of any premiums or discounts. As noted in Footnote 6, current GASB standards require fair value accounting and reporting for most investments, except for certain money market investments with maturities of less than one year. The latter *may* be accounted for at amortized cost (interest earnings adjusted for amortization of premium or discount).[8] Often, however, premiums and discounts are not amortized for short-term investments. All long-term investments in debt and equity securities held for repayment of general long-term debt principal are reported at fair value in the debt service fund balance sheet. All *changes* in the fair value of investments during the period, both realized and unrealized, are reported as revenue in the Statement of Revenues, Expenditures, and Changes in Fund Balances.

Debt Service Accounting for Special Assessment Debt

Special assessment projects, as discussed in Chapter 5, typically follow the same pattern as transactions of other capital projects. Specifically, construction activities are usually completed in the first year or so, using either interim financing from the governmental unit or proceeds of special assessment debt issuances (bonds or notes) to pay construction costs to contractors. Either at the beginning of the project or, more commonly, when construction is completed, assessments for debt service are levied against property owners in the defined special benefit district. Annual assessment installments receivable, and interest on deferred installments, usually approximate the amount of debt principal and interest payable during the same year. If the governmental unit is obligated in some manner to make the debt service payments in the event amounts collected from benefited property owners

---

[8]The reader should note this discussion refers to amortization of premium and discount on investments purchased with the expectation of holding them until maturity. Premium or discount on bonds payable sold by a governmental unit is *not* amortized in the debt service fund, but should be amortized at the government-wide level, so that effective interest expense is reported in the Statement of Activities. Premium on bonds sold is considered as an Other Financing Source of the debt service fund if it must be used for debt service, as discussed in Chapter 5. Accrued interest sold should be recorded as revenue of the debt service fund.

are insufficient, the debt should be recorded in the governmental activities ledger at the government-wide level and a debt service fund should be used to account for debt service activities. If the governmental unit is not obligated in any manner for special assessment debt, the debt should *not* be recorded in any accounting records of the government. In the latter case, which is relatively rare, debt service transactions should be accounted for in an *agency fund*, as explained in Chapter 8.

Assume that special assessment bonds, secondarily backed by the general taxing authority of the City of X, were issued to complete a street-widening project. Upon completion of the project the City levied assessments amounting to $480,000, payable in 10 equal installments with 5 percent interest on deferred installments, on owners of properties fronting on the improved streets. As shown in Entry 1, all receivables are recorded at the time of the levy, but Revenues is credited only for the amount expected to be collected within one year from the date of the levy; Deferred Revenues is credited for the amount of deferred installments. Because the entries at the government-wide level would be similar, except that Interest Expense would be reported rather than Expenditures, those entries are omitted for the sake of brevity. Required budgetary entries, as shown earlier in this chapter for serial bond and term bond debt service funds, are omitted.

		Debit	Credit
1.	Assessments Receivable—Current	48,000	
	Assessments Receivable—Deferred	432,000	
	Revenues		48,000
	Deferred Revenues		432,000

All current assessments receivable, due at year-end, were collected along with interest of $24,000 (see Entry 2). Any amounts not collected by the due date should be reclassified by a debit to Assessments Receivable—Delinquent and a credit to Assessments Receivable—Current.

		Debit	Credit
2.	Cash	72,000	
	Assessments Receivable—Current		48,000
	Revenues		24,000

Matured special assessment bond principal in the amount of $48,000 and matured bond interest of $24,000 payable were recorded and paid on schedule.

		Debit	Credit
3a.	Expenditures—Bond Principal	48,000	
	Expenditures—Bond Interest	24,000	
	Bonds Payable		48,000
	Interest Payable		24,000
3b.	Bonds Payable	48,000	
	Interest Payable	24,000	
	Cash		72,000

The second installment of assessments receivable was reclassified from the Deferred category to the Current category. A corresponding amount of Deferred Revenues was reclassified as Revenues.

		Debit	Credit
4a.	Assessments Receivable—Current	48,000	
	Assessments Receivable—Deferred		48,000
4b.	Deferred Revenues	48,000	
	Revenues		48,000

This pattern of journal entries will be repeated during each of the remaining nine years until all special assessment bonds are retired.

Use of Debt Service Funds to Record Capital Lease Payments

In Chapter 5, under the heading "General Capital Assets Acquired under Capital Lease Agreements," an example is given of the computation of the amount to be recorded in a governmental fund at the inception of a capital lease. The example illustrates the entry required at the government-wide level when an asset is acquired by a capital lease agreement. The example presented in Chapter 5 specified that the first payment of $10,000 was due on January 1, 2001, the inception of the lease. Governmental units commonly use a Debt Service Fund to record capital lease payments because the annual payments are merely installment payments of general long-term debt. The first payment, since it is on the first day of the lease, is entirely a payment on the principal of the lease obligation. Accordingly, the payment would be recorded as:

Expenditures—Principal of Capital Lease Obligation	10,000	
Cash		10,000

The Expenditures detail record would show that the entire amount of the first payment was a payment on the principal. The payment due on January 1, 2002, and the payment due each year thereafter, however, must be considered a partial payment on the lease obligation and a payment of interest on the unpaid balance of the lease obligation. GASB standards are consistent with the FASB's *SFAS No. 13;* both specify that a constant periodic rate of interest must be used. In the example started in Chapter 5, the present value of the obligation is computed using the rate of 10 percent per year. It is reasonable to use the same interest rate to determine what part of the annual $10,000 payment is payment of interest, and what part is payment of principal. The following table shows the distribution of the annual lease rental payments:

Payment Date	*Amount of Payment*	*Interest on Unpaid Balance at 10 Percent*	*Payment on Principal*	*Unpaid Lease Obligation*
				$67,590
1/1/01	$10,000	$-0-	$10,000	57,590
1/1/02	10,000	5,759	4,241	53,349
1/1/03	10,000	5,335	4,665	48,684
1/1/04	10,000	4,868	5,132	43,552
1/1/05	10,000	4,355	5,645	37,907
1/1/06	10,000	3,791	6,209	31,698
1/1/07	10,000	3,170	6,830	24,868
1/1/08	10,000	2,487	7,513	17,355
1/1/09	10,000	1,736	8,264	9,091
1/1/10	10,000	909	9,091	-0-

As shown by the table above, although the total expenditure recorded each year, January 1, 2001, through January 1, 2010, is $10,000, the detail records for each year should show how much of the expenditure was for interest on the lease obligation and how much was payment on the obligation itself. As noted earlier in this chapter, the unpaid balance of the capital lease obligation is carried in the governmental activities general ledger at the government-wide level.

Accounting for Debt Refunding

If debt service fund assets accumulated for debt repayment are not sufficient to repay creditors when the debt matures, or if the interest rate on the debt is appreciably higher than the governmental unit would have to pay on a new bond issue, or if the covenants of the existing bonds are excessively burdensome, the governmental unit may issue refunding bonds.

The proceeds of refunding bonds issued at the maturity of the debt to be refunded are accounted for as Other Financing Sources of the debt service fund that is to repay the existing debt. The appropriation for debt repayment is accounted for as illustrated in the Town of Brighton Deferred Serial Bond Debt Service Fund example (see Entries 1, 2a, and 2b).

If a governmental unit has accumulated no assets at all for debt repayment, it is probable that no debt service fund exists. In such a case, a debt service fund should be created to account for the proceeds of the refunding bond issue and the repayment of the old debt. When the debt is completely repaid, the debt service fund relating to the liquidated issue should be closed, and a debt service fund for the refunding issue should be created and accounted for as described in this chapter. If the refunding bond issue is not sold but is merely given to the holders of the matured issue in an even exchange, the transaction would not require entries in a debt service fund or at the government-wide level but should be disclosed adequately in the Notes to the Financial Statements.

Advance Refunding of Debt

Advance refundings of tax-exempt debt are common during periods when interest rates are falling sharply. Complex accounting and reporting issues have surfaced relating to legal questions such as, "Are both issues still the debt of the issuer?" "If the proceeds of the new issue are to be held for the eventual retirement of the old issue, how can the proceeds be invested to avoid conflict with the Internal Revenue Service over the taxability of interest on the debt issue?" (Compliance with the arbitrage rules under the Internal Revenue Code Sec. 148 and related regulations is necessary for the interest to be exempt from federal income tax and, possibly, from state and local taxes.) Full consideration of the complexities of accounting for advance refundings resulting in defeasance of debt is presented in the GASB *Codification* Section D20. Defeasance of debt can be either "legal" or "in substance." **Legal defeasance** occurs when debt is legally satisfied based on certain provisions in the debt instrument even though the debt is not actually paid. **In-substance defeasance** occurs when debt is considered defeased for accounting and financial reporting purposes even though legal defeasance has not occurred. GASB *Codification* Section D20.103 sets forth in detail the circumstances for in-substance defeasance. Briefly, the debtor must irrevocably place cash or other assets in trust with an escrow agent to be used solely for satisfying scheduled payments of both interest and principal of the defeased debt. The amount placed in escrow must be sufficiently large so that there is only a remote possibility that the debtor will be required to make future payments on the defeased debt. The trust is restricted to owning only monetary assets that are essentially risk-free as to the amount, timing, and collection of interest and principal.

To illustrate accounting for advance refundings resulting in defeasance of debt reported in the governmental activities ledger at the government-wide level, assume the proceeds from the sale of the refunding issue amount to $2,000,000, and assume debt to be defeased amounted to $2,500,000. The proceeds are recorded in the fund receiving the proceeds (normally, a *debt service fund*) by an entry such as:

Cash	2,000,000	
Other Financing Source—Proceeds of Refunding Bonds		2,000,000

Payments to the escrow agent from resources provided by the new debt should be recorded in the debt service fund as an Other Financing Use; payments to the escrow agent from other resources are recorded as debt service expenditures. Therefore, assuming $500,000 has previously been accumulated in the debt service fund for payment of the $2,500,000 bond issue, the entry to record the payment to the escrow agent would be:

Other Financing Use—Payment to Refunded Bond Escrow Agent	2,000,000	
Expenditures—Payment to Refunded Bond Escrow Agent	500,000	
Cash		2,500,000

Disclosures about Advance Refundings

The *disclosure* guidance on debt refunding in GASB *Codification* Section D20 is applicable to state and local governments, public benefit corporations and authorities, public employee retirement systems, and governmental utilities, hospitals, colleges and universities, and to all funds of those entities.

Detailed disclosure guidance is set forth in Section D20.111–.114. Briefly, all entities subject to GASB jurisdiction are required to provide in the notes to the financial statements in the year of the refunding a general description of any advance refundings resulting in defeasance of debt. At a minimum the disclosures must include (1) the difference between the cash flows required to service the old debt and the cash flows required to service the new debt and complete the refundings and (2) the economic gain or loss resulting from the transaction. Economic gain or loss is the difference between the *present value* of the old debt service requirements and the *present value* of the new debt service requirements, discounted at the effective interest rate and adjusted for additional cash paid. Section D20.901–.915 provides examples of effective interest rate and economic gain calculations and of note disclosures.

Key Terms

Annuity serial bonds, 237
Debt limit, 233
Debt margin, 233
Deferred serial bonds, 236
Fair value, 252
General long-term liabilities, 228
In-substance defeasance, 256
Irregular serial bonds, 237

Selected References

American Institute of Certified Public Accountants. Audit and Accounting Guide. *Audits of State and Local Governmental Units*. Revised. New York, 1999.

Governmental Accounting Standards Board. *Codification of Governmental Accounting and Financial Reporting Standards as of June 30, 1999*. Norwalk, CT, 1999.

Questions

6–1. Describe the interrelationship between a debt service fund and governmental activities at the government-wide level. What is the relationship between a capital projects fund that receives the proceeds of tax-supported bonds and the governmental activities category at the government-wide level?

6–2. What are typical reasons why a government might incur general long-term liabilities?

6–3. *a.* When general obligation bonds are issued at a premium that is recorded in a debt service fund and is to be used for eventual retirement of that bond issue, what is the effect on the amount of liability to be shown in the Statement of Net Assets?

b. If a general obligation bond issue were sold at a premium that is required to be set aside for payment of bond interest, what is the effect upon the accounts in the Statement of Net Assets?

6–4. How does a government record a decrease in a general long-term liability; that is, what journal entry(ies) is required when a government makes a principal payment on general long-term liabilities?

6–5. If a bond ordinance provides for regular and recurring payments of interest and principal payments on a general obligation bond issue of a certain government to be made from earnings of an enterprise fund, and these payments are being made by the enterprise fund, how should the bond liability be disclosed in the comprehensive annual financial report of the government?

6–6. Why should a governmental annual report include disclosures about the types of long-term liabilities outstanding and additions and deletions from prior years?

6–7. The calculation of debt margin should take into account the amount of bonds authorized but not issued. This reduces borrowing power at a given date. What is the most logical reason for including authorized but unissued bonds?

6–8. "Debt service funds are established to account for all long-term debt issued by state or local governments and for assets held to pay interest and matured debt principal." Is this statement true or false? Explain.

6–9. What revenue sources and other financing sources are commonly utilized for service of types of debt discussed in this chapter?

6–10. What basis of accounting is used for expenditures of a debt service fund? What exception is usually followed in recognizing expenditures for matured bond principal and interest?

6–11. "If a certain city has six tax-supported bond issues and three special assessment bond issues outstanding, it would be preferable to operate nine separate debt service funds or, at a minimum, one debt service fund for tax-supported bonds and one for special assessment bonds." Do you agree? Explain.

6–12. It is conceivable that a debt service fund for an issue of regular serial bonds might have no assets or liabilities and, necessarily, no fund balance at the ends of some fiscal years. If this is true, why should the fund be created at all? Explain your answer.

6–13. What asset and liability accounts would you expect to find in the statements for a deferred serial bond debt service fund? Why would you expect deferred serial bonds to create a more complex accounting situation than regular serial bonds?

6–14. "Premiums and discounts on bond investments of the Debt Service Fund should not be amortized since the Debt Service Fund is not a profit-seeking entity." Do you agree or disagree? Explain your answer.

6–15. During periods of low interest rates, governmental units often refund outstanding bonds in advance of their maturity. Explain the different ways of treating advance refundings that will permit, under GASB standards, removal of the liability for the refunded bonds from the general long-term liabilities at the government-wide level.

Case

6–1. Purchase of G.O. Bonds. Northeast City is a medium-sized city with a population of 200,000. Because of the closing of the City's major employer, ACME Manufacturing Corporation, nearly 10 percent of the City's population has moved out of the City during the last two years to seek employment elsewhere. Northeast City's debt burden is quite heavy, with total debt amounting to 95 percent of the statutory debt limit. Moreover, the City's taxpayers are being taxed for the relatively heavy debt service of Northeast Township, Northeast Public Schools, and several other taxing authorities.

Northeast City's Debt Service Fund Combining Balance Sheet and Combining Statement of Revenues, Expenditures, and Changes in Fund Balances are shown on the following page. Study these statements and answer the following questions.

Required

a. Assume you are considering the purchase of $1 million of Northeast City's general obligation bonds from an existing bondholder. Do the City's combined debt service fund financial statements provide all the information you need to make your decision? If not, what additional information would you like to have in order to better assess the City's financial condition?

b. What is your assessment of the quality of the City's administration of debt service?

c. To date, the major bond rating services have not downgraded the City's bond ratings, but both agencies are actively reviewing the appropriateness of the investment grade rating currently assigned to the City's general obligation debt. What is your assessment of the probability that the City may have its rating downgraded? What is your assessment of the probability that the City may default on its general obligation debt? How does your assessment of the probability of a rating downgrade or default affect your decision regarding purchase of the City's bonds?

NORTHEAST CITY
COMBINING BALANCE SHEET—ALL DEBT SERVICE FUNDS
JUNE 30, 2002

	General Obligation Bonds	*Urban Renewal Tax Increment Notes*	Totals	
			June 30, 2002	*June 30, 2001*
Assets				
Cash and pooled cash investments	$ 12,000	$ 50,580	$ 62,580	$ 995,640
Taxes receivable	164,976	426,995	591,971	499,735
Total Assets	$176,976	$477,575	$654,551	$1,495,375
Liabilities and Fund Balances				
Liabilities:				
Warrants payable	$ —	$494,493	$494,493	$872,846
Matured bonds payable	5,000	—	5,000	50,000
Matured interest payable	167,171	—	167,171	167,034
Total Liabilities	172,171	494,493	666,664	1,089,880
Fund Balance:				
Unreserved:				
Designated for debt service	4,805	(16,918)	(12,113)	405,495
Total Fund Balance	4,805	(16,918)	(12,113)	405,495
Total Liabilities and Fund Balance	$176,976	$477,575	$654,551	$1,495,375

NORTHEAST CITY
COMBINING STATEMENT OF REVENUES, EXPENDITURES, AND CHANGES IN FUND BALANCES—BUDGET AND ACTUAL—ALL DEBT SERVICE FUNDS
FOR THE FISCAL YEAR ENDED JUNE 30, 2002

	General Obligation Bonds			Urban Renewal Tax Increment Notes			Totals Memorandum Only		
	Budget	*Actual*	*Variance—Favorable (Unfavorable)*	*Budget*	*Actual*	*Variance—Favorable (Unfavorable)*	*Budget*	*Actual*	*Variance—Favorable (Unfavorable)*
Revenues:									
Taxes	$6,216,292	$6,054,601	$(161,691)	$677,121	$573,170	$(103,951)	$6,893,413	$6,627,771	$(265,642)
Expenditures:									
Principal retirement	4,439,000	4,379,000	60,000	249,901	249,901	—	4,688,901	4,628,901	60,000
Interest and fiscal charges	2,025,292	1,989,258	36,034	427,220	427,220	—	2,452,512	2,416,478	36,034
Total Expenditures	6,464,292	6,368,258	96,034	677,121	677,121	—	7,141,413	7,045,379	96,034
Excess of Revenues over (under) Expenditures	(248,000)	(313,657)	(65,657)	—	(103,951)	(103,951)	(248,000)	(417,608)	(169,608)
Fund Balance—July 1, 2001	357,170	318,462	(38,708)	—	87,033	87,033	357,170	405,495	48,325
Fund Balance—June 30, 2002	$ 109,170	$ 4,805	$(104,365)	—	$(16,918)	$ (16,918)	$ 109,170	$ (12,113)	$(121,283)

Exercises and Problems

6–1. Examine the CAFR. Utilizing the CAFR obtained for Exercise 1–1, follow the instructions below:

a. **General Long-Term Liabilities.**

(1) *Disclosure of Long-Term Debt.* Does the report contain evidence that the governmental unit has General Long-Term Liabilities? What evidence is there? Does the report specify that no such debt is outstanding, or does the report include a list of outstanding tax-supported debt issues; capital lease obligations; claims, judgments, and compensated absence payments to be made in future years; and the unfunded pension obligations?

Refer to the Enterprise Funds balance sheets as well as a list of general debt outstanding: Are any enterprise debt issues backed by the full faith and credit of the general governmental unit? If so, how are the primary liability and the contingent liability disclosed?

(2) *Changes in Long-Term Liabilities.* How are changes in long-term liabilities during the year disclosed? If there is a schedule of changes, does the information in that schedule agree with the statements presented for capital projects funds and debt service funds?

Are interest payments and principal payments due in future years disclosed? If so, does the report relate these future payments with resources to be made available under existing debt service laws and covenants?

(3) *Debt Limitations.* Does the report contain information as to legal debt limit and legal debt margin? If so, is the information contained in the report explained in enough detail so that an intelligent reader (you) can understand how the limit is set, what debt is subject to it, and how much debt the governmental unit might legally issue in the year following the date of the report?

(4) *Overlapping Debt.* Does the report disclose direct debt and overlapping debt of the reporting entity? What disclosures are made of debt of the primary government in distinction to debt of component units? Is debt of component units reported as "direct" debt of the reporting entity or as "overlapping debt"?

b. **Debt Service Funds.**

(1) *Debt Service Function.* How is the debt service function for tax-supported debt and special assessment debt handled—by the General Fund, by a special revenue fund, or by one or more debt service funds? If there is more than one debt service fund, what kinds of bond issues or other debt instruments are serviced by each fund? Is debt service for bonds to be retired from enterprise revenues accounted for by enterprise funds?

Does the report state the basis of accounting used for debt service funds? If so, is the financial statement presentation consistent with the stated basis? If the basis of accounting is not stated, analyze the statements to determine which basis is used—full accrual, modified accrual, or cash basis. Is the basis used consistent with the standards discussed in Chapter 6?

(2) *Investment Activity.* Compare the net assets of each debt service fund at balance sheet date with the amount of interest and the amount of debt principal the fund will be required to pay early in the following year (you

may find debt service requirements in supplementary schedules following the individual fund statements in the Financial Section of the CAFR). If debt service funds have accumulated assets in excess of amounts needed within a few days after the end of the fiscal year, are the excess assets invested? Does the CAFR contain a schedule or list of investments of debt service funds? Does the report disclose increases or decreases in the fair value of investments realized during the year? Does the report disclose net earnings on investments during the year? What percentage of revenue of each debt service fund is derived from earnings on investments? What percentage of the revenue of each debt service fund is derived from taxes levied directly for the debt service fund? What percentage is derived from transfers from other funds? List any other sources of debt service revenue and other financing sources, and indicate the relative importance of each source.

Are estimated revenues for term bond debt service budgeted on an actuarial basis? If so, are revenues received as required by the actuarial computations?

(3) *Management*. Considering the debt maturity dates as well as the amount of debt, and apparent quality of debt service fund investments, does the debt service activity appear to be properly managed? Does the report disclose whether investments are managed by a corporate fiduciary, another outside investment manager, or governmental employees? If outside investment managers are employed, is the basis of their fees disclosed? Are the fees accounted for as additions to the cost of investments, or as expenditures?

Is one or more paying agents, or fiscal agents, employed? If so, does the report disclose if the agents keep track of the ownership of registered bonds, write checks to bondholders for interest payments and matured bonds or, in the case of coupon bonds, pay matured coupons and matured bonds presented through banking channels? If agents are employed, does the Balance Sheet, or Notes to the Financial Statements, disclose the amount of cash in their possession? If so, does this amount appear reasonable in relation to interest payable and matured bonds payable? Do the statements, schedules, or narratives disclose for how long a period of time debt service funds carry a liability for unpresented checks for interest on registered bonds, for matured but unpresented interest coupons, and for matured but unpresented bonds?

(4) *Capital Lease Rental Payments*. If general capital assets are being acquired under capital lease agreements, are periodic lease rental payments accounted for as expenditures of a debt service fund (or by another governmental fund)? If so, does the report disclose that the provisions of *SFAS No. 13* are being followed (see the "Use of Debt Service Funds to Record Capital Lease Payments" section of this chapter) to determine the portion of each capital lease payment considered as interest and the portion considered as payment on the principal.

6–2. Multiple Choice. Choose the best answer.

1. The following obligations were among those reported by Fern Village at December 31, 2001:

Vendor financing with a term of 10 months when incurred, in connection with a capital asset acquisition that is not part of a long-term financing plan	$ 150,000
Long-term bonds for financing of capital asset acquisition	3,000,000
Bond anticipation notes due in six months, issued as part of a long-term financing plan for capital purposes	400,000

   What aggregate amount should Fern report as general long-term liabilities at December 31, 2001?

   a. $3,000,000.

   b. $3,150,000.

   c. $3,400,000.

   d. $3,550,000.

   Items 2 through 4 are based on the following:

   On March 2, 2001, Finch City issued 10-year general obligation bonds at face amount, with interest payable March 1 and September 1. The proceeds were to be used to finance the construction of a civic center over the period April 1, 2001, to March 31, 2002. During the fiscal year ended June 30, 2001, no resources had been provided to the Debt Service Fund for the payment of principal and interest.

2. On June 30, 2001, Finch's Debt Service Fund should include interest payable on the general obligations bonds for:

   a. 0 month.

   b. 3 months.

   c. 4 months.

   d. 6 months.

3. Proceeds from the general obligation bonds should be recorded in the:

   a. General Fund.

   b. Capital Projects Fund.

   c. Special Revenue Fund.

   d. Debt Service Fund.

4. The liability for the general obligation bonds should be recorded in the:

   a. General Fund.

   b. Capital Projects Fund.

   c. Governmental activities journal.

   d. Debt Service Fund.

5. Which of the following liabilities are accounted for in the governmental activities category at the government-wide level?

   a. All tax-supported bonds and government-commitment special assessment bonds and notes not yet legally due; the noncurrent portion of claims, judgments, and compensated absences; and the unfunded liability for pensions.

   b. General obligation bonds and notes that will mature in more than one year from balance sheet date.
   c. All bonds and notes that will mature in more than one year from balance sheet date.
   d. General obligation bonds and notes not yet legally due.
6. Interest expenditures relating to tax-supported bonds payable should be recorded in a debt service fund:
   a. At the end of the fiscal period if the interest due date does *not* coincide with the end of the fiscal period.
   b. When bonds are issued.
   c. When the interest is legally payable.
   d. When the interest checks are written.
7. Debt service funds may be used to account for:
   a. Lease payments under capital lease agreements.
   b. Repayment of bond principal.
   c. The proceeds of refunding bond issues.
   d. All of the above.
8. Which of the following accounts is *least* likely to appear in a debt service fund?
   a. Estimated Revenues.
   b. Encumbrances.
   c. Appropriations.
   d. Matured Bonds Payable.
9. A debt service fund should be used to account for the payment of interest and principal on:
   a. Debt recorded in the government activities journal.
   b. Debt secured by the revenues of a governmentally owned enterprise.
   c. Debt recorded as a liability of the General Fund.
   d. All of the above.
10. Debt service funds would *not* appear on which of the following fund financial statements?
    a. Balance Sheet—Governmental Funds.
    b. Statement of Cash Flows.
    c. Statement of Revenues, Expenditures, and Changes in Fund Balances—Governmental-type Funds.
    d. Statement of Revenues, Expenditures, and Changes in Fund Balances—Governmental-type Funds—Budget and Actual.

6–3. Long-Term Liability Transactions. Below are stated a number of unrelated transactions for Culver County, some of which affect governmental activities at the government-wide level. None of the transactions has been recorded yet.

(1) The tax levy for the General Fund included $650,000 to be transferred to the debt service fund; $400,000 of this amount is designated for eventual retirement of outstanding serial bonds; the remainder is to be expended for interest on long-term debt. The transfer was made as planned, and the interest was paid.

(2) A $5,000,000 issue of serial bonds to finance a capital project was sold at 102, plus accrued interest in the amount of $50,000. The accrued interest was recorded as revenues of the debt service fund and the premium was recorded as an Other Financing Source. Accrued interest on bonds sold must be used for interest payments; premium is designated by state law for eventual payment of bond principal.

(3) A summary of debt service fund operations during the year showed receipt of interest on investments in the amount of $180,000; this amount is to be used for payment of interest on long-term debt.

(4) $2,800,000 par value of tax-supported serial bonds were issued in cash to permit partial refunding of a $3,500,000 par value issue of term bonds. The difference was settled with $700,000 that had been accumulated in prior years in a debt service fund.

Required

Prepare in general journal form the necessary entry in the governmental activities and appropriate fund journals for each transaction. Explanations may be omitted. For each entry you prepare name the fund or account group in which the entry should be made.

6–4. Capital Lease. The Town of Preston has agreed to acquire a new fire truck under a capital lease agreement. At the inception of the lease a payment of $50,000 is to be made; nine annual lease payments, each in the amount of $50,000, are to be made at the end of each year after the inception of the lease. The total amount to be paid under this lease, therefore, is $500,000. The Town could borrow this amount for 9 years at the annual rate of 8 percent; therefore, the present value of the lease at inception, including the initial payment, is $362,345. Assume that the fair value of the fire truck at the inception of the lease is $370,000.

a. Show the entry that should be made in a capital projects fund at the inception of the lease, after the initial payment has been made.

b. Show the entry that should be made at the inception of the lease in the government activities journal.

c. Show the entry that should be made in the debt service fund and governmental activities journal at the end of the first year after the inception of the lease.

6–5. Statement of Legal Debt Margin. In preparation for a proposed bond sale the city manager of the City of Collinsville requested you to prepare a statement of legal debt margin for the City as of December 31, 2001. You ascertain that the following bond issues are outstanding on that date:

Convention Center bonds	$3,600,000
Electric utility bonds	2,700,000
General obligation serial bonds	3,100,000
Tax increment bonds	2,500,000
Water utility bonds	1,900,000
Transit authority bonds	2,000,000

Other information obtained by you included the following items:

1. Assessed valuation of real and taxable personal property in the City totaled $240,000,000.
2. The rate of debt limitation applicable to the City of Collinsville was 8 percent of total real and taxable personal property valuation.
3. Electric utility, water utility, and transit authority bonds were all serviced by enterprise revenues, but each carries a full-faith-and-credit contingency provision and by law is subject to debt limitation.
4. The Convention Center bonds and tax increment bonds are subject to debt limitation.
5. The amount of assets segregated for debt retirement at December 31, 2001, is $1,800,000.

6–6. Direct and Overlapping Debt. At April 30, 2001, all property inside the limits of the City of Marksville was situated within four additional governmental units, each authorized to incur long-term debt. At that date, net long-term debt of the five was as follows:

Florence County	$40,000,000
Florence Library District	2,000,000
City of Marksville	8,000,000
Marksville School District	17,000,000
Marksville Hospital District	13,600,000

Assessed values of property at the same date were: County and Library District, $900,000,000; City, $360,000,000; School District, $450,000,000; and Hospital District, $720,000,000.

Required

a. Prepare a statement of direct and overlapping debt for the City of Marksville. (Carry percentages to tenths.)

b. Compute the actual ratio (in percent carried to tenths) of total debt applicable to the City of Marksville property to assessed value of property within the city limits.

c. Compute the share of the City's direct and overlapping debt that pertained to the Reliable Manufacturing Company, having assessed valuation of $3,600,000 at April 30, 2001.

6–7. Debt Service Fund Financial Statements. The Town of Shropshire Serial Bond Debt Service Fund Balance Sheet as of December 31, 2001, is presented:

TOWN OF SHROPSHIRE
SERIAL BOND DEBT SERVICE FUND—BALANCE SHEET
AS OF DECEMBER 31, 2001

Assets		Fund Equity	
Cash	$ 1,500	Fund Balance	$514,000
Investments	500,000		
Interest receivable on investments	12,500		
Total Assets	$514,000	Total Fund Equity	$514,000

Required

a. Prepare debt service fund entries in general journal form to reflect, as necessary, the following information:

(1) The Revenues budget for serial bond debt service for FY2002 consists of estimated revenues of $330,000 to be raised from a debt service tax levy, and estimated revenues of $30,000 from earnings on investments. The Appropriations budget consists of bond interest to be paid on January 1, $100,000, and bond interest to be paid on July 1, $100,000.

(2) Taxes receivable in the amount of $340,000 and estimated uncollectible taxes in the amount of $10,000 are recorded.

(3) Half of the gross levy of taxes is collected in cash.

(4) Checks are written and mailed for the interest payment due on January 1, 2002.

(5) Cash in the amount of $70,000 is invested.

(6) Interest receivable as of December 31, 2001, is collected and invested.

(7) Taxes in the amount of $160,000 are collected in cash.

(8) Checks are written and mailed for the interest payment due on July 1, 2002.

(9) Interest on investments is received in cash in the amount of $15,000; cash in the amount of $75,000 is invested.

(10) Accrued interest receivable on investments at year-end is computed as $13,000.

(11) Budgetary and operating statement accounts are closed, and Taxes Receivable and the related Estimated Uncollectible accounts are designated as Delinquent.

b. Prepare a Balance Sheet for the Town of Shropshire Serial Bond Debt Service Fund as of December 31, 2002.

c. Prepare a Statement of Revenues, Expenditures, and Changes in Fund Balance for the fund for the year ended December 31, 2002.

d. Prepare a Statement of Revenues, Expenditures, and Changes in Fund Balance—Budget and Actual for the year ended December 31, 2002.

6–8. DSF Financial Statements. The City of Hampton had outstanding 5 percent term bonds, scheduled to mature July 1, 2001, in the amount of $5,000,000. Early in 2001, only $1,000,000 had been accumulated in a Term Bonds Debt Service Fund to apply on retirement of the bonds so a proposal was made to refund the remainder with 6 percent serial bonds, to mature at the rate of $1,000,000 every year, beginning July 1, 2002. Interest on the new issue is to be paid semiannually—on January 1 and July 1. Present term bondholders are to accept the 6 percent serial bonds in exchange for $4,000,000 of term bonds. Enough of the present bondholders accepted the proposal to make it feasible, and the budget for the fiscal year ending June 30, 2002, was set up to pay all the semiannual interest due on July 1 and $1,000,000 to bondholders. The $1,000,000 in the Term Bonds Debt Service Fund was in a noninterest-bearing Cash account.

a. The following transactions occurred in the Term Bonds Debt Service Fund during the year ended June 30, 2002. Record them in general journal form in the Debt Service Fund.

(1) The Revenues budget for the year provided for an operating transfer from the General Fund in the amount of the interest due July 1 on the entire $5,000,000 worth of term bonds. The Appropriations budget authorized the July interest payment and the payment of $1,000,000 for bonds to be redeemed. Record the budget.

(2) The General Fund transferred enough cash to the Term Bonds Debt Service Fund to pay interest due July 1 on the entire $5,000,000 worth of term bonds.

(3) The $1,000,000 worth of bonds to be redeemed and the interest due on July 1 were recorded as liabilities.

(4) Interest for the year and the bond liability were paid.

(5) All remaining open accounts were closed.

b. A Serial Bond Debt Service Fund was created to account for debt service activities related to the new issue. During the year ended June 30, 2002, the following transactions occurred. Record them in general journal form:

(1) The budget for the year was recorded. Estimated revenues, to be raised from taxes levied directly for this fund, were in the amount of one year's interest payments and the first serial bond repayment. Appropriations were budgeted only for the interest legally due during the fiscal year.

(2) Taxes receivable were levied to yield the amount of estimated revenues, assuming 3 percent of the taxes would be uncollectible. Round computation of the levy to the nearest $10.

(3) Ninety percent of the gross levy of taxes was collected. The remainder of the taxes receivable and the related Estimated Uncollectible Current Taxes Account were classified as delinquent.

(4) Cash in the amount of the January 1, 2002, interest payment was paid to bondholders; remaining cash was invested.

(5) Interest on investments collected in cash during the year totaled $10,500; interest on investments accrued at year-end was $3,100. Interest and penalties receivable on taxes totaled $3,040, of which $600 is estimated to be uncollectible.

(6) Budgetary and operating statement accounts for the year were closed.

c. Prepare a Serial Bond Debt Service Fund Balance Sheet as of June 30, 2002.

d. Prepare a Serial Bond Debt Service Fund Statement of Revenues, Expenditures, and Changes in Fund Balance for the year ended June 30, 2002.

e. Prepare a Serial Bond Debt Service Fund Statement of Revenues, Expenditures, and Changes in Fund Balance—Budget and Actual for the year ended June 30, 2002.

6–9. Comprehensive Capital Assets/Capital Liabilities Problem. Following are transaction data for related capital assets and capital liabilities of the City of Stevens. Utilizing worksheets formatted as shown at the end of the problem, prepare all necessary journal entries for these transactions in the City's capital projects fund, debt service fund, and governmental activities category at the government-wide level. You may ignore related entries in the General Fund. Round all amounts to the nearest whole dollar.

a. On July 1, 2001, the first day of its 2002 fiscal year, the City of Stevens issued at par $2,000,000 of 6 percent term bonds to construct a new City office building. The bonds mature in five years on July 1, 2006. Interest is payable semiannually on January 1 and July 1. A sinking fund is to be established with equal semiannual additions made on June 30 and December 31, with the first addition to be made on December 31, 2001. Cash for the sinking fund additions and the semiannual interest payments will be transferred from the General Fund shortly before the due dates. Assume a yield on sinking fund investments of 6 percent per annum, compounded semiannually. Investment earnings are added to the investment principal. Based on this information:

(1) Prepare a schedule in good form showing the required additions to the sinking fund, the expected semiannual earnings, and the end-of-period balance in the sinking fund for each of the 10 semiannual periods. (Note: The future amount of an ordinary annuity of $1 for 10 periods at 3 percent per period is $11.4638793.)

(2) Record the issuance of the bonds. (Utilize worksheets formatted as shown at the end of the problem.)

(3) Create a Term Bond Debt Service Fund and record its budget for the fiscal year ended June 30, 2002. An appropriation should be provided only for the interest payment due on January 1, 2002. Also, record an accrual for all interfund transfers to be received from the General Fund during the year.

b. On July 17, 2001, the City entered into a construction contract with Jones Construction Company for $1,950,000 to construct the new City Office Building.

c. On December 28, 2001, the General Fund transferred $234,461.01 to the Debt Service Fund. The addition to the sinking fund was immediately invested in 6 percent certificates of deposit.

d. On December 28, 2001, the City issued checks to bondholders for the interest payment due on January 1, 2002.

e. On June 1, 2002, Jones Construction billed the City in the amount of $1,000,000 for construction work to date on the City office building project.

f. On June 15, 2002, the City paid the $1,000,000 partial billing from Jones Construction, except for 5 percent that was retained pending final inspection at the conclusion of the project.

g. On June 27, 2002, the General Fund transferred $234,461.01 to the Debt Service Fund. The addition for the sinking fund was invested immediately in 6 percent certificates of deposit.

h. Actual interest earned on sinking fund investments at year-end (June 30, 2002) was the same as the amount budgeted [see *a*(1) and *a*(3) above]. This interest adds to the sinking fund balance.

i. All appropriate closing entries were made at June 30, 2002.

j. On July 1, 2002, the City paid the interest payment due that date. (Note: As discussed in this chapter, it is important that all principal and interest be paid by the due date. Usually a City does not directly pay the bondholders but instead uses a paying (fiscal) agent to pay the bondholders of record. Further, the use of electronic funds transfer permits same day transfer of cash to the fiscal agent.)

k. On July 1, 2002, the encumbrances were reestablished in the Capital Projects Fund.

l. The budgetary entry for fiscal year 2003 was recorded on July 1, 2002.

m. On September 10, 2002, Jones Construction completed the City office building project and billed the City for the remaining $950,000 due on the contract.

n. On September 14, 2002, the City paid the $950,000 partial billing from Jones, except for 5 percent which was retained pending final inspection at the conclusion of the project.

o. Following final inspection, the City incurred $125,000 for additional exterior and interior refinishing and site cleanup. Public Works (General Fund) employees were used for the refinishing and cleanup, which was completed on October 1, 2002. On October 5, 2002, the $125,000 due to the City's General Fund was paid.

p. The balance of cash in the Capital Projects Fund was transferred to the Term Bond Debt Service Fund. This amount was deemed available for eventual repayment of the principal of the 6 percent term bonds and was invested immediately in 6 percent CDs. Record the transfer and close all accounts in the capital projects fund.

q. Ignoring all other transactions in fiscal years 2003 and those for 2004 and 2005, prepare the journal entries in the Term Bond Debt Service fund for the transfer of cash from the General Fund on June 27, 2006. None of this amount is invested.

r. On June 30, 2006, all sinking fund investments in the Term Bond Debt Service Fund were redeemed for cash in the amount of $1,825,538.99. Of this amount, $99,712.04 represented interest earned during fiscal 2006. $46,540.98 of the interest earned was previously recorded on December 31, 2005.

s. Prepare the closing entry for the Term Bond Debt Service Fund at the end of fiscal year 2006.

t. Prepare the budgetary entry for the Term Bond Debt Service Fund at July 1, 2006, the beginning of fiscal year 2007.

u. Record the payment of bond principal and interest on July 1, 2006. Close all accounts of the Term Bond Debt Service Fund.

Capital Projects Fund			*Capital Projects Fund*	*Governmental Activities*
Example:				
Cash	2,000,000			
OFS—Proceeds of Bonds		2,000,000		

Debt Service Fund	*Debt Service Fund*	*Debt Service Fund*

Governmental Activities	*Governmental Activities*	*(Label this column as needed)*

Continuous Problem

6–B. The City of Bingham utilizes a single debt service fund to account for the service of all issues of tax-supported and special assessment long-term debt. As of June 30, 2001, one issue of tax-supported serial bonds and one issue of special assessment term bonds were outstanding. The post-closing trial balance of the debt service fund as of June 30, 2001, is shown below.

The issue of tax-supported serial bonds outstanding on June 30, 2001, amounted to $6,000,000; bonds of this issue in the amount of $300,000 mature on July 1, 2001, and on each July 1 thereafter. This bond issue bears interest at the annual rate of 6 percent, payable on January 1 and July 1 of each year. The cash balance of the debt service fund on June 30, 2001, is to be used for the repayment of tax-supported bonds maturing on July 1, 2001, and for the interest on those bonds due on July 1, 2001.

The issue of special assessment term bonds outstanding on June 30, 2001, amounted to $600,000; it bears interest at the annual rate of 8 percent, payable on January 1 and July 1 of each year. The bonds will mature on July 1, 2011. As of June 30, 2001, investments in the amount of $260,000 are being held for payment of the special assessment bonds at maturity.

CITY OF BINGHAM
DEBT SERVICE FUND
TRIAL BALANCE
AS OF JUNE 30, 2001

	Debits	*Credits*
Cash	$505,000	
Taxes Receivable—Delinquent	42,000	
Estimated Uncollectible Delinquent Taxes		$ 38,000
Special Assessments Receivable—Current	66,000	
Special Assessments Receivable—Deferred	594,000	
Investments for Special Assessment Bond Payment	260,000	
Deferred Revenues		594,000
Fund Balance		835,000
Totals	$1,467,000	$1,467,000

In order to add to investments held to pay the bonds at maturity and to pay interest due in fiscal year 2002, the City of Bingham Debt Service Fund must budget revenues from special assessments during fiscal year 2002 in the amount of $66,000.

Capital lease obligations outstanding have a present value on June 30, 2001, of $1,020,000. Collections of delinquent taxes receivable plus revenues to be raised in fiscal year 2002 will be used to make required lease payments during fiscal year 2002.

On July 1, 2001, the City of Bingham sold an issue of tax-supported serial bonds to finance the construction and equipping of an annex to City Hall. As described in Problem 5–B, the total amount of bonds sold on that date was $3,000,000. The issue bears interest at the annual rate of 8 percent, payable on January 1 and July 1 of each year; bonds in the amount of $150,000 will mature on July 1, 2002, and each July 1 thereafter.

In addition to the accounts listed in the trial balance, general ledger accounts provided for the debt service fund are:

Investments—Temporary
Taxes Receivable—Current
Estimated Uncollectible Current Taxes
Interest and Penalties Receivable
Estimated Uncollectible Interest and Penalties
Estimated Revenues
Estimated Other Financing Sources
Revenues
Appropriations
Expenditures—2002

Subsidiary ledger accounts for the debt service fund are:

Revenues—Subsidiary Ledger Accounts
Property Taxes
Interest and Penalties on Taxes
Special Assessments
Interest on Investments

Other Financing Sources—Subsidiary Ledger Accounts
Proceeds of Bonds—Premium on Bonds Sold
Interfund transfers In

Appropriations and Expenditures—Subsidiary Ledger Accounts
Interest on Bonds Payable
Principal of Matured Bonds
Interest on Capital Lease Obligations
Principal of Capital Lease Obligations

Required

a. Prepare general journal entries to record the following transactions in the general ledger accounts and in subsidiary ledger accounts of the debt service fund and governmental activities journal.

(1) From the data given about the two bond issues outstanding on June 30, 2001, and the bond issue sold on July 1, 2001, record the adoption of the legal budget for the fiscal year ended June 30, 2002. (The budget provided estimated revenues or estimated other financing sources from property taxes, $1,182,000; from special assessments, $66,000; from premium on bonds sold, $30,000; and from earnings on investments, $28,000. Appropriations were provided for the payment of bonds maturing on July 1, 2001, for bond interest payments due on July 1, 2001, for bond interest payments due on January 1, 2002; $108,000, for interest payments on capital lease obligations, and $72,000 for payments on the principal of capital lease obligations.)

(2) Taxes were levied by the debt service fund in the amount of $1,218,000. Of this amount, $36,000 was expected to be uncollectible.

(3) Cash in the amount of the premium on the bonds sold on July 1, 2001 (see Problem 5–B, requirement *a*, Transaction 1) was received and deposited by the debt service fund. The premium is not to be amortized; credit Other Financing Sources—Proceeds of Bonds—Premiums on Bonds Sold for the entire $30,000.

(4) Temporary investments in the amount of $30,000 were purchased.

(5) Checks were written and mailed to pay holders of bonds maturing on July 1, 2001, and to pay all bond interest due that day.

(6) Delinquent taxes receivable were collected in the amount of $4,000. Taxes Receivable—Current were collected in the amount of $620,000. Special Assessments in the amount of $66,000 were collected.

(7) Investments to be held for repayment of special assessment bonds at maturity were purchased in the amount of $18,000. Temporary investments in the amount of $610,000 were purchased.

(8) Information was received that interest in the amount of $8,300 had been added to investments held for repayment of special assessment bonds. Interest on temporary investments was received in cash in the amount of $8,000.

(9) Temporary investments amounting to $425,000 were sold at par.

(10) Checks were written and mailed to holders of all three issues of bonds for the interest payments due January 1, 2002. Payments on capital lease obligations totaled $180,000—$108,000 interest and $72,000 on the principal.

(11) Current taxes receivable were collected in the amount of $550,000. The balance of taxes receivable, and the related estimated uncollectible account, were classified as delinquent.

(12) Information was received that interest in the amount of $8,800 had been added to investments held for repayment of special assessment bonds. Interest on temporary investments was received in cash in the amount of $4,600.

(13) Cash to close the City Hall Annex Construction Fund was received (see Problem 5–B, requirement *d*).

(14) Special assessments receivable in the amount of $66,000 were transferred from the deferred category to the current category; an equivalent amount was transferred from Deferred Revenues to Revenues.

(15) Interest and penalties on delinquent taxes as of year-end were computed as $9,200, of which $4,200 was expected to be uncollectible.

(16) All temporary investments were converted into cash.

(17) Budgetary and operating statement accounts for the Debt Service Fund for the year were closed.

b. Prepare a Balance Sheet for the Debt Service Fund as of June 30, 2002.

c. Prepare a Statement of Revenues, Expenditures, and Changes in Fund Balance for the Debt Service Fund for the year ended June 30, 2002.

d. Prepare a Statement of Revenues, Expenditures, and Changes in Fund Balance—Budget and Actual for the year ended June 30, 2002.

e. As of June 30, 2001, the City of Bingham had the following long-term liabilities:

Tax-Supported Serial Bonds Payable—6%	$6,000,000
Special Assessment Term Bonds Payable—8%	600,000
Capital Lease Obligations Payable	1,020,000

Prepare a schedule of general long-term liabilities as of June 30, 2002, similar to Illustration 6–1, after the entries in *a*(1) through *a*(17) have been made, that will appear in the government-wide Statement of Net Assets.

CHAPTER 7

Accounting for the Business-Type Activities of State and Local Governments

Learning Objectives

After reading this chapter, you should be able to:

- Distinguish between the purposes of internal service funds and enterprise funds.
- Describe the characteristics of proprietary funds.
- Explain the financial reporting requirements, including the differences between reporting of enterprise funds and internal service funds in the government-wide and fund financial statements.
- Explain the characteristics, accounting procedures, and termination of internal service funds.
- Prepare journal entries and describe financial reporting requirements for an internal service fund.
- Describe the characteristics and specialized accounting procedures for enterprise funds.
- Prepare journal entries and financial statements for an enterprise fund.

Proprietary Funds

The funds discussed in previous chapters (general, special revenue, capital projects, debt service funds, and permanent funds) owe their existence to legal constraints placed on the raising of revenue and/or the use of resources for the provision of services to the public or segments thereof, and for the acquisition of facilities to aid in the provision of services. As governmental units became more complex, it became apparent that efficiency should be improved if services used by several departments or funds, or even several governmental units, were combined in a single administrative unit. Purchasing is a common example, as is a motor pool. A logical name for a fiscal and accounting entity created to account for resources used for providing centralized services is *internal service fund*. Traditionally, the reason for the creation of funds in this category was to improve the management of resources. In recent years, large numbers of governmental units have experienced a shortfall of revenues with an increase in the demand for governmental services. Consequently, many governmental units have turned to user charges as a means of financing operations formerly financed by tax revenues and intergovernmental revenues. In order to determine whether user charges are commensurate with operating costs, and to improve the ability of administrators and governing bodies to determine that costs are reasonable in relation to benefits, it is desirable for the activities to be operated and accounted for on a business basis. Thus many activities formerly operated on a purely noncommercial basis and accounted for by governmental funds are now accounted for by proprietary funds: *enterprise funds* and *internal service funds*. Activities that produce goods or services to be sold to the general public are accounted for by enterprise funds. Activities that produce goods or services to be provided to departments or agencies of a governmental unit, or to other governmental units, on a cost-reimbursement basis are accounted for by internal service funds. (Internal service funds are sometimes called *intragovernmental service funds*, *working capital funds*, *revolving funds*, and other similar names.)

Activities accounted for in enterprise funds are referred to as *business-type activities* for purposes of financial reporting at the government-wide level (see Statement of Activities presented in Illustration 2–1). Although internal service funds are accounted for *internally* as business-type activities, their transactions predominantly involve sales of goods or services to, or interfund transactions with, the General Fund and other funds that comprise the governmental activities of a government. For this reason, GASB *Statement No. 34* requires that the financial balances of internal service funds be reported in the governmental activities category at the government-wide level. Nevertheless, internal service funds are properly classified as proprietary funds and are reported in a separate column of the proprietary fund financial statements (see Illustrations 2–6, 2–7, and 2–8 for examples).

Financial Reporting Requirements

Proprietary funds are accounted for in a manner similar to investor-owned business enterprises of the same type. An enterprise fund established to account for a government-owned electric utility, for example, should follow accounting principles similar to those of investor-owned electric utilities. Accordingly, proprietary funds focus on the flow of economic resources recognized on the accrual basis, both within the fund and at the government-wide level. Thus, these funds account for all capital assets used in their operations and for all long-term liabilities to be paid from the revenues generated from their operations, as well as for all current assets and current liabilities. Because proprietary funds follow business-type accounting principles, one should not be surprised that these funds prepare essentially the same financial statements that businesses do: a Balance Sheet (called either a Statement of Net Assets or a Balance Sheet); a Statement of Revenues, Expenses, and Changes in Fund Net Assets (equivalent to an income statement); and a Statement of Cash Flows. These statements are prepared according to GASB standards, however, which differ in some respects from the equivalent statements prescribed by FASB standards for business organizations. These differences are discussed at various points in this chapter. Illustrative financial statements for the Town of Brighton Supplies Fund (an internal service fund) are displayed in Illustrations 7–2, 7–3, and 7–4, later in this chapter. The corresponding financial statements for the Town of Brighton Water Utility Fund (an enterprise fund) are provided in Illustrations 7–6 through 7–8.

Unlike the General Fund and other major governmental funds for which a budget is legally adopted, proprietary funds are not required by GASB standards to record budgets in their accounting systems. Some governmental units do, however, require all funds to operate under legally adopted budgets. In such cases, GASB standards permit, but do not require, the integration of budgetary accounts in the manner described in Chapters 3 and 4 for general and special revenue funds.

Internal Service Funds

Although the reason for the establishment of an internal service fund is to improve financial management of scarce resources, it should be stressed that a fund is a fiscal entity as well as an accounting entity; consequently, establishment of a fund is ordinarily subject to legislative approval. The ordinance, or other legislative action, that authorizes the establishment of an internal service fund should also specify the source, or sources, of financial resources to be used for fund operations. The original allocation of resources to the fund may be derived from a transfer of assets of another fund, such as the General Fund or an Enterprise Fund, intended as a *contribution* not to be repaid, or a transfer in the nature of a long-term interfund loan to be repaid by the internal service fund over a period of years. Alternatively, or additionally, the resources initially allocated to an internal service fund may be acquired from the proceeds of a tax-supported bond issue or transfer from other governmental units that anticipate utilizing the services to be rendered by the internal service fund. Since internal service funds are established to improve the management of resources, it is generally considered that they should be operated, and accounted for, on a business basis. Application of this general truth to a specific case can lead to conflict between managers who wish the freedom to operate the fund in accord with their professional judgment, and legislators who wish to exercise considerable control over the decisions of the internal service fund managers.

For example, assume that administrators request the establishment of a fund for the purchasing, warehousing, and issuing of supplies used by a number of funds and departments. At the time of the request, since no internal service fund exists, each fund or department must include in its budget its requested appropriation for supplies, its requested appropriation for salaries and wages of personnel engaged in purchasing and handling the supplies, and its requested appropriation for any operating expense or facility costs associated with the supply function. Accordingly, legislators tend to feel that through their control over budgets they are controlling the investment in supplies and the use of supplies by each fund and department. Legislators may feel that if they approved the establishment of an internal service fund that had authority to generate operating revenues sufficient to perpetuate the fund without annual appropriations, the supply function would no longer be subjected to annual legislative budget review, and the legislature would "lose control" after the initial allocation of resources to the fund. Administrators are more likely to feel that if an internal service fund did not have authority to generate operating revenues sufficient to perpetuate the fund, and to spend those revenues at the discretion of fund management rather than at the discretion of persons possibly more concerned with reelection than with financial management, there would be little gained by establishment of the internal service fund.

The two opposing views should be somewhat balanced by the fact that, as shown in Illustration 7–1, the customers of an internal service fund are, by defini-

Illustration 7–1

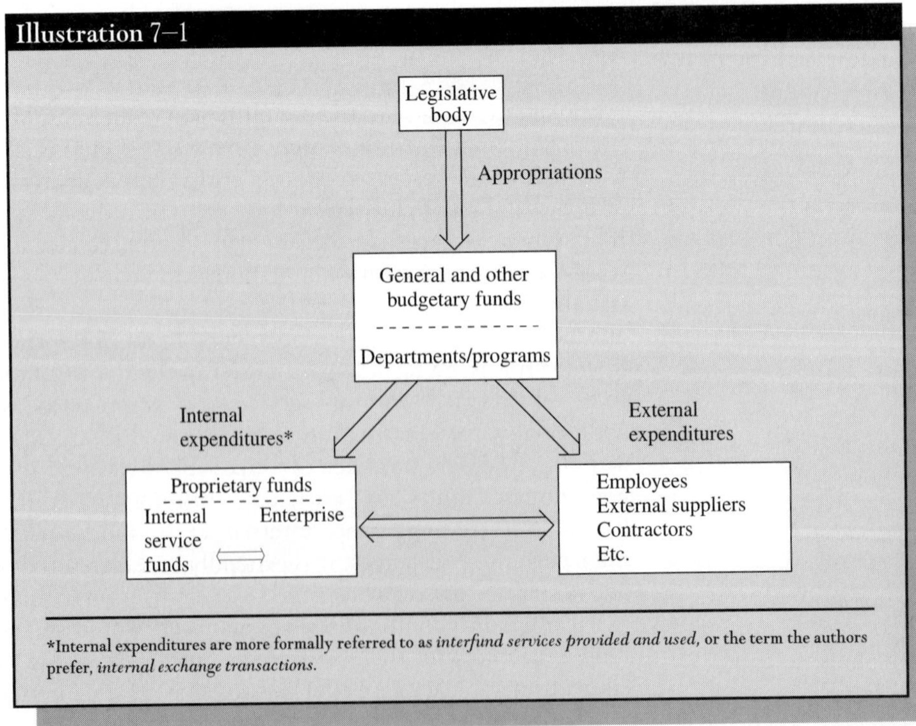

*Internal expenditures are more formally referred to as *interfund services provided and used,* or the term the authors prefer, *internal exchange transactions.*

tion, other funds and departments of the governmental entity, or of other governmental entities; therefore, each using fund and department must include in its Appropriations budget request justification for the amount to be spent (i.e., paid to the internal service fund) for supplies, so the legislative branch continues to exercise budgetary review over the amount each fund and department budgets for supplies. As shown in Illustration 7–1, departments and programs that require legislative appropriations to expend resources for goods and services should account for purchases of goods or services from internal suppliers (i.e., internal service funds or enterprise funds) in essentially the same manner as goods and services purchased from external suppliers. If the legislative branch were to set pricing policies for the internal service fund, and policies governing the use of current earnings, and retention of earnings, and require the submission of periodic financial statements to evidence that its policies were followed, the legislature would be able to maintain considerable control over the function performed by the internal service fund, yet leave the fund managers freedom to operate at their discretion within the policies set by the legislative branch.

One of the more difficult problems to resolve to the satisfaction of persons with opposing views is the establishment of a pricing policy. "Cost" is obviously an incomplete answer: Historical cost of the supplies themselves, whether defined as FIFO, LIFO, average, or specific identification, will not provide sufficient revenue to replace supplies issued if replacement prices have risen since the last purchase, or to increase the inventory quantities if the scale of governmental operations is growing. Payroll and other cash operating expenses of the internal service fund must be met; and if the internal service fund has received a loan from another fund or another governmental unit, prices must be set at a level that will generate cash needed for debt retirement. If the internal service fund is to be operated on a true business basis, it must also be able to finance from its operations replacement, modernization, and expansion of plant and equipment used in fund operations. Prices charged by the internal service fund, however, should be less than the using funds and departments would have to pay outside vendors for equivalent products and services, if the existence and continued operation of the internal service fund is to be justified.

Because of the considerations mentioned in preceding paragraphs, many different approaches to internal service fund operations may be found in practice. Since accounting systems should give appropriate recognition to operating policies, as well as to legal requirements, practices vary from those of profit-seeking businesses at one extreme, to those discussed in this text in the chapters relating to general and special revenue funds at the other extreme. In the illustrations given in following sections of this chapter, it is assumed the financial objective of an internal service fund is to recover from operating revenues the full cost of operations, with enough net income to allow for replacement of inventories in periods of rising prices, and enough increase in inventory quantities to meet the needs of using funds and departments whose scale of operations is increasing. Similarly, it is assumed net income should be sufficient to allow for replacement of capital assets used by the internal service fund, but expansion of the facilities must be financed through contributions from other funds authorized in their Appropriations budgets. Managers of internal service funds must prepare operating plans—budgets—as a management tool. In the illustrations it is assumed budgets of internal service funds are submitted to the legislative body, or bodies, and to the public for information but not for legal action, and therefore the budget is not formally recorded in internal service fund accounts. Similarly, managers of businesses must be kept informed of the status of outstanding purchase orders and contracts, but encumbrances need not be recorded in the accounts in order to accomplish this.

Accounting for an internal service fund concerned with the functions of purchasing, warehousing, and issuing supplies is illustrated in the following section.

Illustrative Case—Supplies Fund

Assume that the administrators of the Town of Brighton obtain approval from the Town Council to centralize the purchasing, storing, and issuing functions as of January 1, 2003, and to administer and account for these functions in a Supplies Fund. The town's General Fund is to transfer to the new fund its December 31, 2002, inventory of supplies ($61,500) and $30,000 in cash to be used for working capital; these transfers are intended as contributions to the Supplies Fund and are not to be repaid. Transfers of this nature are initially accounted for by the recipient fund as interfund transfers in, as shown in Entry 1. The Interfund Transfers In account is closed at the end of the fiscal period to Net Assets—Unrestricted. The interfund transfer is reported below the nonoperating revenues/expenses section of the Statement of Revenues, Expenses, and Changes in Net Assets.

	Debits	*Credits*
1. Cash	30,000	
Inventory of Supplies	61,500	
Interfund Transfers In		91,500

In order to provide cash to be used for acquisition of a building and equipment needed to handle the supply function efficiently, the town's Water Utility Fund is to provide a long-term interfund loan of $130,000 to the Supplies Fund. The loan is to be repaid by the Supplies Fund in 20 equal annual installments. Entry 2 illustrates the entry to be made by the Supplies Fund for the receipt of the interfund loan; Water Utility Fund entries for this transaction are illustrated later in this chapter.

2. Cash	130,000	
Interfund Loan from Water Utility Fund—Current		6,500
Interfund Loan from Water Utility Fund—Noncurrent		123,500

Assume that a satisfactory warehouse building is purchased for $95,000; $25,000 of the purchase price is considered a cost of the land. Necessary warehouse machinery and equipment is purchased for $25,000. Delivery equipment is purchased for $10,000. If the purchases are made for cash, the acquisition of the assets would be recorded in the books of the Supplies Fund as:

	Debits	*Credits*
3. Land	25,000	
Building	70,000	
Machinery and Equipment—Warehouse	25,000	
Equipment—Delivery	10,000	
Cash		130,000

Additional supplies would need to be ordered to maintain inventories at a level commensurate with expected usage. Encumbrances need not be recorded for purchase orders issued, and so information about the dollar value of purchase orders is omitted from this illustration. During 2003, it is assumed supplies are received and related invoices are approved for payment in the amount of $192,600; the entry needed to record the asset and the liability is:

4. Inventory of Supplies	192,600	
Vouchers Payable		192,600

The General Fund of the Town of Brighton (see Chapter 4) accounted for supplies on the periodic inventory basis. The Supplies Fund, however, should account for its inventories on the perpetual inventory basis since the information is needed for proper performance of its primary function. Accordingly, when supplies are issued, the inventory account must be credited for the cost of the supplies issued. Since the using fund will be charged an amount in excess of the inventory carrying value, the receivable and revenue accounts must reflect the selling price. The markup above cost should be determined on the basis of budgeted expenses and other items to be financed from net income, in relation to expected requisitions by using funds. If the budget for the Town of Brighton's Supplies Fund indicates a markup of 35 percent on cost is needed, issues to General Fund departments of supplies costing $185,000 would be recorded by the following entries:

5a. Cost of Supplies Issued	185,000	
Inventory of Supplies		185,000
5b. Due from General Fund	249,750	
Billings to Departments		249,750

If collections from the General Fund during 2003 totaled $231,000, the entry should be:

6. Cash	231,000	
Due from General Fund		231,000

Assuming that payrolls and fringe benefits during the year were all paid in cash and were distributed to the functional expense accounts in the amounts shown below, Entry 7 is appropriate.

7. Administrative Expenses	11,000	
Purchasing Expenses	19,000	
Warehousing Expenses	12,000	
Delivery Expenses	13,000	
Cash		55,000

If payments on vouchers during the year totaled $164,000, the entry is:

	Debits	Credits
8. Vouchers Payable	164,000	
Cash		164,000

The interfund loan from the Water Utility Fund is to be repaid in 20 equal annual installments; repayment of one installment at the end of 2003 and reclassification of the next installment are recorded as:

	Debits	Credits
9a. Interfund Loan from Water Utility Fund—Current	6,500	
Cash		6,500
9b. Interfund Loan from Water Utility Fund—Noncurrent	6,500	
Interfund Loan from Water Utility Fund—Current		6,500

It is assumed the building used as a warehouse was estimated at the time of purchase to have a remaining useful life of 20 years; the warehouse machinery and equipment was estimated to have a useful life of 10 years, and the delivery equipment to have a useful life of 5 years. If the administrative and clerical office space occupies 10 percent of the area of the warehouse, 10 percent of the depreciation of the warehouse, $350, may be considered administrative expense; similarly, if the purchasing office occupies 10 percent of the space in the warehouse building, 10 percent of the building depreciation, $350, may be considered purchasing expense. The remainder of the building is devoted to warehousing; therefore, 80 percent of the total building depreciation, $2,800, is to be charged to warehousing expense. The latter account is also charged $2,500 for machinery and equipment depreciation expense. Delivery expense is charged $2,000 for depreciation of equipment during the year.

	Debits	Credits
10. Administrative Expenses	350	
Purchasing Expenses	350	
Warehousing Expenses	5,300	
Delivery Expenses	2,000	
Allowance for Depreciation—Building		3,500
Allowance for Depreciation—Machinery and Equipment—Warehouse		2,500
Allowance for Depreciation—Equipment-Delivery		2,000

Organizations that keep perpetual inventory records must adjust the records periodically to reflect shortages, overages, or out-of-condition stock disclosed by physical inventories. Adjustments to the Inventory account are also considered adjustments to the warehousing expenses of the period. In this illustrative case, it is assumed no adjustments were found necessary at year-end.

Assuming all revenues and expenses applicable to 2003 have been properly recorded by the entries illustrated above, the operating statement accounts should be closed as of December 31, 2003:

	Debits	Credits
11. Billings to Departments	249,750	
Cost of Supplies Issued		185,000
Administrative Expenses		11,350
Purchasing Expenses		19,350
Warehousing Expenses		17,300
Delivery Expenses		15,000
Excess of Net Billings to Departments over Costs		1,750

Excess of Net Billings to Departments over Costs (or Excess of Costs over Net Billings to Departments, if operations resulted in a loss) is the account title generally considered more descriptive of the fund's results than Income Summary or Current Earnings—the titles commonly found in profit-seeking businesses. Whatever title is used for the account summarizing the results of operations for the period, the account should be closed at year-end. The title of the account that records earnings retained in an internal service fund, as well as contribution to equity, are recorded in the account Net Assets—Unrestricted.

12. Excess of Net Billings to Departments over Costs	1,750	
Net Assets—Unrestricted		1,750

The Interfund Transfers In account represents an other financing source and is closed to Net Assets—Unrestricted as shown in Entry 13:

13. Interfund Transfers In	91,500	
Net Assets—Unrestricted		91,500

Illustrative Statements

Statement of Net Assets. As one would expect of funds accounted for in a manner similar to profit-seeking businesses, the statement of net assets (or, alternatively, a traditional classified balance sheet) of proprietary funds is classified; that is, current assets are segregated from capital assets and other assets, and current liabilities are segregated from long-term debt. The statement of net assets for the Supplies Fund of the Town of Brighton as of December 31, 2003, is shown as Illustration 7–2.

GASB *Statement No. 34* requires that net assets be reported in three components, invested in capital assets, net of related debt; restricted; and unrestricted. As of December 31, 2003, the Supplies Fund investment in capital assets of $122,000 is less than the balance of the interfund loan of $123,500 ($117,000 long-term liability plus $6,500 current portion due within one year). Thus, there is no investment in capital assets to be reported. There also are no assets restricted as to use by external resource providers or legislative action. As a result, the Supplies Fund has only unrestricted net assets as of December 31, 2003.

Operating Statements. The results of operations of an Internal Service Fund for a period should be reported in a Statement of Revenues, Expenses, and Changes in Net Assets, which is the equivalent of an income statement for a profit-seeking

Illustration 7–2

TOWN OF BRIGHTON
SUPPLIES FUND
STATEMENT OF NET ASSETS
AS OF DECEMBER 31, 2003

ASSETS			
Current assets:			
Cash			$ 35,500
Due from General Fund			18,750
Inventory of supplies, at average cost			69,100
Total current assets			123,350
Capital assets:			
Land		$ 25,000	
Building	$70,000		
Less: Allowance for depreciation	3,500	66,500	
Machinery and equipment—warehouse	25,000		
Less: Allowance for depreciation	2,500	22,500	
Equipment—delivery	10,000		
Less: Allowance for depreciation	2,000	8,000	
Total capital assets			122,000
Total assets			$245,350
LIABILITIES			
Current liabilities:			
Vouchers payable			$ 28,600
Current portion of long-term liabilities			6,500
Total current liabilities			35,100
Long-term liabilities:			
Interfund loan from water utility			117,000
Total liabilities			152,100
NET ASSETS			
Unrestricted			$ 93,250

entity. In the reporting model being superseded by *Statement No. 34*, the statement is called a Statement of Revenues, Expenses, and Changes in Retained Earnings, since the fund equity (rather than net assets) under the previous model was reported in two components, contributed capital and retained earnings. Illustration 7–3 presents a Statement of Revenues, Expenses, and Changes in Net Assets for the year ended December 31, 2003, for the Town of Brighton Supplies Fund.

Statement of Cash Flows. GASB financial reporting standards require the preparation of a Statement of Cash Flows as a part of a full set of financial statements for

Illustration 7–3

TOWN OF BRIGHTON
SUPPLIES FUND
STATEMENT OF REVENUES, EXPENSES, AND CHANGES IN NET ASSETS
FOR THE YEAR ENDED DECEMBER 31, 2003

Operating revenues:		
Billings to departments		$249,750
Less: Cost of supplies issued		185,000
Gross Margin		64,750
Operating Expenses:		
Purchasing expenses	$19,350	
Administrative expenses	11,350	
Warehousing expenses	17,300	
Delivery expenses	15,000	
Total Operating Expenses		63,000
Operating Income		1,750
Interfund transfers in		91,500
Change in net assets		93,250
Net assets—January 1, 2003		-0-
Net assets—December 31, 2003		$ 93,250

all proprietary funds. Categories of cash flows provided by FASB *Statement No.* 95 were deemed insufficient to meet the needs of users of governmental financial reports. Consequently, GASB standards provide four categories of cash flows: Operating, Noncapital Financing, Capital and Related Financing, and Investing. In each category, the term *cash* also includes **cash equivalents** (defined as short-term, highly liquid investments).

Cash flows from operating activities include receipts from customers, receipts from sales to other funds, payments to suppliers of goods or services, payments to employees for services, payments for purchases from other funds (including payments in lieu of taxes), and other operating cash receipts and payments. The transactions of the Town of Brighton's Supplies Fund recorded in Entries 6, 7, and 8 are classified as operating activities and are reported in the first section of the Statement of Cash Flows (see Illustration 7–4). As required by GASB standards the Statement of Cash Flows is accompanied by a reconciliation of operating income with the net cash flow from operating activities.

Cash flows from *noncapital financing* activities include proceeds from debt not clearly attributable to acquisition, construction, or improvement of capital assets; receipts from grants, subsidies, or taxes other than those specifically restricted for capital purposes or those for specific operating activities; payment of interest on, and repayment of principal of, noncapital financing debt; grants or subsidies paid

Illustration 7–4

TOWN OF BRIGHTON
SUPPLIES FUND
STATEMENT OF CASH FLOWS
FOR THE YEAR ENDED DECEMBER 31, 2003

Cash flows from operating activities:		
Cash received from customers	$231,000	
Cash paid to employees for services	(55,000)	
Cash paid to suppliers	(164,000)	
Net cash provided by operating activities		$12,000
Cash flows from noncapital financing activities:		
Interfund transfer from General Fund	30,000	
Net cash provided by noncapital financing activities		30,000
Cash flows from capital and related financing activities:		
Advance from Water Utility Fund	130,000	
Partial repayment of advance from Water Utility Fund	(6,500)	
Acquisition of capital assets	(130,000)	
Net cash used for capital and related activities		(6,500)
Net Increase in Cash and Cash Equivalents		35,500
Cash and Cash Equivalents, 1/1/2003		–0–
Cash and Cash Equivalents, 12/31/2003		$35,500

Reconciliation of Operating Income to Net Cash Provided by Operating Activities

Operating income		$ 1,750
Adjustments:		
Depreciation expense		8,000
Increase in receivables from other funds		(18,750)
Increase in inventory	$ 69,100	
Less contributed inventory	61,500	(7,600)
Increase in vouchers payable		28,600
Net Cash Provided by Operating Activities		$12,000

to other governments, funds, or organizations, except payments for specific operating activities of the grantor government. The contribution from the General Fund to the Supplies Fund of the Town of Brighton (see Entry 1) is reported in the cash flows from noncapital financing activities section of the Statement of Cash Flows (Illustration 7–4).

Cash flows from *capital and related financing* activities include proceeds of debt and receipts from special assessments and taxes specifically attributable to acquisition, construction or improvement of capital assets; receipts from capital grants; receipts from the sale of capital assets; proceeds of insurance on capital assets that are stolen or destroyed; payments to acquire, construct, or improve capital assets; payment of interest on, and repayment or refunding of, capital and related financing debt. The transactions of the Town of Brighton's Supplies Fund recorded in Entries 2, 3, and 4 are classified as capital and related financing activities and are reported in that section of the Statement of Cash Flows (Illustration 7–4).

Cash flows from *investing* activities include receipts from collection of loans; interest and dividends received on loans, debt instruments of other entities, equity securities, and cash management and investment pools; receipts from the sales of debt or equity instruments; withdrawals from investment pools not used as demand accounts; disbursements for loans; payments to acquire debt or equity instruments; and deposits into investment pools not used as demand accounts. None of the transactions of the Town of Brighton's Supplies Fund during 2003 are in the nature of investing activities.

External Financial Reporting of Internal Service Funds. The financial statements presented in Illustrations 7–2, 7–3, and 7–4 should be prepared for internal management purposes. For *external* financial reporting purposes, the Supplies Fund financial information reported in each of those statements would be reported as a separate column of the Statement of Net Assets—Proprietary Funds; Statement of Revenues, Expenses, and Changes in Net Assets—Proprietary Funds; and Statement of Cash Flows—Proprietary Funds, each of which is prepared for all proprietary funds (see Illustrations 2–6, 2–7, and 2–8 for examples). In the government-wide Statement of Net Assets and Statement of Activities, internal service fund financial information is "collapsed" into the governmental activities and reported in that column of both government-wide financial statements. Various reclassifications, eliminations, and allocations may be required to avoid what *Statement No. 34* refers to as "doubling up"—that is, reporting internal service fund financial information once as part of the governmental activities and then again as part of internal service funds. As recommended by GASB *Statement No. 34*, the discussion that follows assumes that all internal service fund transactions occurred with governmental funds. Internal service fund financial information should be reported in the business-type activities column of the government-wide financial statements only if an enterprise fund is the predominant participant in the internal service fund.[1]

To permit reporting of the Town of Brighton's Supply Fund activities in the governmental activities category of the government-wide financial statements certain journal entries should be made in the governmental activities general journal, one that records the balance sheet effects and one that eliminates any net income recognized by the internal service fund.

The entry to record the balance sheet effects in the governmental activities general journal should record the *change* during the year in each internal service fund balance sheet account. Because this is the first year of operation of the Town of Brighton's Supplies Fund, the journal entry to record its balance sheet information (see Illustration 7–2) simply records the year-end amounts:

---

[1]GASB *Statement No. 34* (Norwalk, CT, 1999), par. 62.

	Debits	Credits
1. Cash	35,500	
Intra-activities Balance	18,750	
Inventory of Supplies	69,100	
Land	25,000	
Buildings	70,000	
Machinery and Equipment	35,000	
Allowance for Depreciation—Buildings		3,500
Allowance for Depreciation—Machinery and Equipment		4,500
Vouchers Payable		28,600
Intra-activities Balance		18,750
Current Portion of Long-term Liabilities		6,500
Interfund Loan from Business Activities		117,000
Net Assets—Unrestricted		74,500

In comparing Entry 1 to the Town of Brighton Supplies Fund Balance Sheet (Illustration 7–2), one will note that the amount shown as Due from General Fund in the balance sheet is debited to *Intra-activities Balance* in Entry 1, an amount that will be offset by credits in the same total amount to Inter-activities Balance at the government-wide level when expenses were recorded for prior billings from the internal service fund. This interfund receivable/liability has no net effect on the governmental activities column as both the General Fund and the Supplies Fund are part of the governmental activities category.

Although it may not be apparent, unless additional adjustments are made the balance of Cash and Inventory of Supplies will be overstated at the government-wide level. Why is this the case? The reason is that the interfund transfer from the General Fund to the Supplies Fund (see illustrative transaction Entry 1 earlier in this chapter) has no effect at the government-wide level since both funds are considered to be governmental activities. Thus, the interfund transfer did not result in a *net* reduction of Cash and Inventory of Supplies at the government-wide level. Accordingly, cash in the amount of $30,000 and supplies in the amount of $61,500 must be eliminated or else they will be counted twice at the government-wide level. Similarly, although the interfund transfer increased the unrestricted net assets of the Supplies Fund by $91,500, it had no effect on the net assets of *governmental activities* at the government-wide level. As shown in the Town of Brighton operating statement presented in Illustration 7–3, the Interfund Transfers In from the General Fund is also reported as a component of "net income" or, more formally, *change in net assets*. As just discussed, this component of change in net assets has no effect at the government-wide level. The required journal entry in the governmental activities general journal to eliminate the effects of the interfund transfer is:

	Debits	Credits
2. Net Assets—Unrestricted	91,500	
Inventory of Supplies		61,500
Cash		30,000

Another component of the change in net assets that must be eliminated is the operating income, shown as $1,750 in Illustration 7–3. Elimination of this component prevents double counting of net assets at the government-wide level. As governmental funds purchase supplies throughout the year from the internal service fund, the purchases are recorded as expenditures of the governmental funds and as direct expenses of the appropriate functions at the government-wide level. Because operating income results from billings that exceed the internal service fund's operating costs, the cost of functions (or programs) at the government-wide level would be overstated if the operating income were not eliminated from the amounts billed. In substance, the elimination of change in net assets adjusts the internal service fund information as if the governmental funds purchased their own supplies from external sources without using an internal service fund. Or, viewed alternatively, the elimination presents the internal service fund financial information as if the fund operated on a break-even basis, just covering its accrual basis operating costs. Entry 3 gives the journal entry needed to remove the operating income effect of the Town of Brighton's Supplies Fund, assuming a particular allocation to functions at the government-wide level:

	Debits	*Credits*
3. Net Assets—Unrestricted	1,750	
Expenses—General Government		175
Expenses—Public Safety		525
Expenses—Public Works		700
Expenses—Parks and Recreation		263
Expenses—Health and Welfare		87

Note that Entry 3 affects *only* the government-wide financial statements; expenditures would be reported in the governmental funds Statement of Revenues, Expenditures, and Changes in Fund Balances for the full amount billed by the Supplies Fund. The reader should also note that any internal service fund operating loss would have the opposite effect; it would increase the direct expenses of functions and net assets at the government-wide level.

After the eliminations in Entries 2 and 3 are recorded, only cash in the net amount of $5,500 and supplies in the net amount of $7,600 related to transactions of the internal service fund are reported as additions to those accounts at the government-wide level. Interestingly, during the 2003 fiscal year the operations of the Supplies Fund have no effect on net assets at the government-wide level. This is apparent from the fact that the $93,250 credit to Net Assets—Unrestricted in Entry 1 (as reported in the Supplies Fund Balance Sheet) is completely offset by the debits of $91,500 in Entry 2 and $1,750 in Entry 3.

If a portion of an internal service fund's operating income results from billings to enterprise funds, *Statement No. 34*'s requirement to report internal service fund financial information in the governmental activities category tends to understate unrestricted net assets in that category and overstate unrestricted net assets in the business-type category. Usually this effect should not be material, particularly if the internal service fund pricing is set to cover approximately the full cost of its operations.

Because internal service fund financial information is reported in most cases in the governmental activities column of the government-wide financial statements, the financial information reported in the business-type activities column will usually be that for enterprise funds only. If this is the case, there is no need to maintain a separate set of accounting records for the business-type activities at the government-wide level. Rather, the financial records of the enterprise funds can simply be added together for financial reporting purposes at the government-wide level. Any interfund transactions between enterprise funds would be eliminated as they would have no net effect on the overall business-type activities. Enterprise fund accounting and financial reporting are discussed later in this chapter.

Assets Acquired under Lease Agreements

The acquisition of general capital assets under lease agreements is discussed in Chapter 5. Assets for use by proprietary funds may also be acquired under lease agreements. The criteria set forth in FASB *SFAS No. 13* (these criteria are itemized in Chapter 5) are used to determine whether the lease is an operating lease or a capital lease.

Assets acquired under an operating lease belong to the lessor and not to the internal service fund; accordingly, the annual lease payment is recorded as a rental expense of the internal service fund,[2] and there is no depreciation expense on the assets acquired under an operating lease agreement. Assets acquired under a capital lease agreement by an internal service fund, or an enterprise fund, should be capitalized by that fund. The amount to be recorded by a proprietary fund as the *cost* of the asset acquired under a capital lease, and as the related liability, is the lesser of (*a*) the present value of the rental and other minimum lease payments or (*b*) the fair value of the leased property. The amount recorded as the cost of the asset is amortized in a manner consistent with the government's normal depreciation policy for owned assets of proprietary funds. The amortization period is restricted to the lease term, unless the lease (*a*) provides for transfer of title or (*b*) includes a bargain purchase option, in which case the economic life of the asset becomes the amortization period.

During the lease term, each minimum lease payment by an internal service fund is to be allocated between a reduction of the obligation under the lease and as interest expense in a manner that produces a constant periodic rate of interest on the remaining balance of the obligation. This allocation and other complexities that arise in certain events are described and illustrated in various paragraphs of *SFAS No. 13* and in many intermediate accounting texts. These complexities are beyond the scope of this text.

Internal Service Funds with Manufacturing Activities

The Supplies Fund of the Town of Brighton, for which journal entries and statements are illustrated in a preceding section of this chapter, is responsible for purchasing, storing, and issuing supplies used by other funds and departments of the

[2]GASB, *Codification*, Sec. L20.109–.112 establishes measurement criteria and recognition criteria for revenues and expenditures/expenses relating to operating leases with scheduled rent increases. This situation is beyond the scope of this text.

town. Many states and local governmental units have funds similar to that of the Town of Brighton. It is also common to find printing shops, asphalt plants, or other service units that produce a physical product to be used by funds and departments, or that facilitate the operations of the other funds and units by performing maintenance or repair jobs, or even perform a temporary financing function.

If an internal service fund performs a continuous process manufacturing operation, its accounting system should provide process cost accounts. If a service fund performs a manufacturing, maintenance, or repair operation on a job-order basis, the fund's accounting system should provide appropriate job-order cost accounts. To the extent that operations, processes, or activities are capable of being standardized, cost standards for materials, direct labor, and overhead should be established; in such cases, the accounting system should provide for the routine measurement and reporting of significant variances from the standards. Cost determination for governmental and nonprofit entities is discussed in Chapter 13 of this text.

Internal Service Funds as Financing Devices

Governmental units may utilize internal service funds as devices to finance risk management, equipment purchases and operations (including centralized computer operations), and other functions that are facilitated by generating revenues from user charges to cover costs and expenses computed on a full accrual basis. In the case of funds to finance equipment purchases and operations, including the operations of computers owned by the governmental unit, an internal service fund can include depreciation and, perhaps, expected increases in the cost of replacing assets, in the charge to the using funds—thus incorporating these costs in current appropriations of governmental funds, rather than budgeting the estimated cost of equipment expected to be replaced. If internal service funds are used to finance equipment purchases and operations, therefore, the appropriations and expenditures of governmental funds more nearly approximate costs that would be reported by entities using full accrual accounting than is true under the procedures discussed in Chapters 3 and 4.

GASB has issued accounting and financial reporting standards for risk financing and related insurance activities.[3] Government entities that use internal service funds to account for risk financing activities are required to recognize revenues and claims expenses and liabilities in essentially the same manner as public entity risk pools (cooperative groups of governmental entities joined together to finance risks of loss to property, workers' compensation, employee health care, and similar risks or exposures). Briefly, the internal service fund should recognize claims expense and liability when a claim is asserted, it is probable that an asset has been impaired or a liability has been incurred, and the amount of the loss is reasonably estimable; or if an estimable loss has been incurred and it is probable that a claim will be asserted. Reasonably possible (but not probable) loss contingencies,

---

[3]GASB, *Codification*, Sec. Po20.

probable losses that are not reasonably measurable, and loss exposure in excess of the accrued liability should be disclosed in the Notes to the Financial Statements. The disclosure should explain the nature of the contingency and an estimate of the possible loss or range of the loss, or a statement that the amount is not estimable.

Internal service fund charges to other funds for risk financing activities should be sufficient to recover the total amount of claim expenses recognized for the period or, alternatively, may be based on an actuarial method so that internal service fund revenues and expenses over time are approximately equal. Charges to other funds may also include a reasonable provision for expected future catastrophe losses. Internal service fund charges to other funds are recognized as revenues by the internal service fund and as expenditures by governmental funds or expenses by proprietary and nonexpendable trust funds. Internal service fund charges in excess of the full cost amount determined as above should be reported as an other financing source by the internal service fund and an other financing use by the other funds. If the internal service fund fails to recover the full cost of claims over a reasonable period of time, the accumulated fund deficit should be charged to the other funds and reported by the other funds as an expenditure or expense, as appropriate.

Dissolution of an Internal Service Fund

When an internal service fund has completed the mission for which it was established, or when its activity is terminated for any other reason, dissolution must be accomplished. Liquidation may be accomplished in any one of three ways or in combinations thereof. The three ways are: (1) transfer of the fund's assets to another fund that will continue the operation as a subsidiary activity, for example, a supply fund becoming a *department* of the General Fund; (2) distribution of the fund's assets in kind to another fund or to another governmental unit; (3) conversion of all its noncash assets to cash and distribution of the cash to another fund or other funds. Dissolution of an internal service fund, as for a private enterprise, would proceed by prior payments to outside creditors, followed by repayment of long-term interfund loans not previously amortized, and, finally, liquidation of remaining net assets. The entire process of dissolution should be conducted according to pertinent law and the discretion of the appropriate legislative body. Net assets contributed by another fund or governmental unit logically would revert to the contributor fund or governmental unit, but law or other regulations may dictate otherwise. If net assets have been built up out of charges in excess of costs, then liquidation will follow whatever regulations may govern the case; and if none exist, then the appropriate governing body must decide on the recipient or recipients.

Enterprise Funds

Enterprise funds and internal service funds are both classified by the GASB as proprietary funds, although as discussed previously, internal service fund financial information is reported as part of the governmental activities category at the government-wide level. Whereas internal service funds, discussed earlier in this chapter, are used primarily to account for services provided by one department or agency of a governmental unit to *other departments or agencies of the same government*, enterprise funds are used by governmental units to account for services provided to the *general public* on a user charge basis. Under the GASB *Statement No. 34* model, a governmental unit must report certain activities in an enterprise fund if the following criteria are met.[4]

1. The activity is financed with debt that is secured *solely* by a pledge of the revenues from fees and charges of an activity. [Emphasis added by authors.]
2. Laws or regulations require that the activity's costs of providing services, including capital costs (such as depreciation or debt service), be recovered with fees and charges, rather than with taxes or similar revenues.

These criteria are quite specific regarding when an enterprise fund *must* be used. For example, if debt is issued that is also backed by the full faith and credit of the governmental unit, even though it is intended to be repaid from revenues of a particular activity, that activity need not be reported in an enterprise fund. Similarly, if an activity is subsidized by a governmental unit's General Fund, rather than fully covering its costs of providing services with fees or charges, that activity need not be reported in an enterprise fund. In either of these examples, however, the governmental unit could opt to report the activities in an enterprise fund.

From this description, and from the fact that the word *enterprise* is often used as a synonym for "business-type activity," it is apparent that enterprise funds should use full accrual accounting and account for all assets used in the production of goods or services offered by the fund. Similarly, if long-term debt is to be serviced by the fund, it is accounted for by the fund.

The most common examples of governmental enterprises are public utilities, notably water and sewer utilities. Electric and gas utilities, transportation systems, airports, ports, hospitals, toll bridges, produce markets, parking lots, parking garages, liquor stores, and public housing projects are other examples frequently found. Services of the kinds mentioned are generally accounted for by enterprise funds because they are intended to be largely self-supporting. However, they are properly accounted for by a general or special revenue fund by those governments that support the activities largely from general or special revenue sources other than user charges and are not concerned with measuring the costs of the activities.

Almost every kind of enterprise operated by a government has its counterpart in the private sector. In order to take advantage of the work done by regulatory agencies and trade associations to develop useful accounting information systems for the investor-owned enterprises, *it is recommended that governmentally owned enterprises use the accounting structures developed for investor-owned enterprises of the*

---

[4]GASB *Statement No. 34*, par. 67.

same nature.[5] Budgetary accounts should be used only if required by law. Debt service and construction activities of a governmental enterprise are accounted for within the enterprise fund, rather than by separate debt service and capital projects funds. Thus, the financial statements of enterprise funds are self-contained; and creditors, legislators, or the general public can evaluate the performance of a governmental enterprise on the same bases as they can the performance of investor-owned enterprises in the same industry.

By far the most numerous and important enterprise services rendered by local governments are public utilities. In this chapter, therefore, the example used is that of a water utility fund.

Illustrative Case—Water Utility Fund

The Balance Sheet as of December 31, 2001, for the Town of Brighton Water Utility Fund is shown in Illustration 7–5. While the Balance Sheet appears fairly conventional, terminology peculiar to utilities warrants discussion prior to proceeding to the illustrative transactions for the year ending December 31, 2002.

Current and Accrued Assets

Cash and Materials and Supplies shown in Illustration 7–5 in the Current and Accrued Assets section are not peculiar to utilities and need not be discussed here. The other two asset accounts in this section—Customer Accounts Receivable and Accrued Utilities Revenues—are related. The former represents billings to customers that are outstanding at year-end (and are reduced, as one would expect, by an Accumulated Provision for Uncollectibles). The latter results from the fact that utilities generally prepare billings to customers on the basis of meter readings, and it is not practical for utilities to read all meters simultaneously at year-end and bill all customers as of that time. Utilities that meter their service make extensive use of cycle billing, which, in substance, consists of billing part of their customers each

[5]GASB *Statement No. 20* and GASB *Statement No. 34* provide guidance on business-type accounting and financial reporting for proprietary activities. This guidance clarifies the authoritative status of FASB pronouncements in determining generally accepted accounting principles (GAAP) for proprietary activities given the GAAP hierarchy provided for in *Statement on Auditing Standards No.* 69, "The Meaning of 'Present Fairly in Conformity with Generally Accepted Accounting Principles' in the Independent Auditor's Report" (AICPA, 1992). GASB *Statement No. 20* gives governments an option between two accounting and financial reporting approaches for proprietary funds. The first approach requires consistent use of all GASB pronouncements and applicable pronouncements of FASB and its predecessors (Accounting Principles Board and Committee on Accounting Procedure) issued on or before November 30, 1989, unless those pronouncements conflict with or contradict GASB pronouncements. The second approach requires consistent use of all GASB pronouncements and all applicable pronouncements (both before and after November 30, 1989) of FASB and its predecessors, unless those pronouncements conflict with or contradict GASB pronouncements. Thus, under the first approach, unless GASB directs otherwise, governments are not required to change their accounting procedures if FASB issues a standard that supersedes or amends a standard issued on or before November 30, 1989. This date (November 30, 1989) is significant as the date the Financial Accounting Foundation resolved a conflict over jurisdiction of the FASB and GASB.

Illustration 7–5

TOWN OF BRIGHTON
WATER UTILITY FUND
STATEMENT OF NET ASSETS
AS OF DECEMBER 31, 2001

ASSETS			
Current and Accrued Assets:			
Cash		$ 126,000	
Customer accounts receivable	$69,000		
Less: Accumulated provision for uncollectibles	2,900	66,100	
Accrued utilities revenues		14,800	
Materials and supplies		28,700	
Total Current and Accrued Assets			$ 235,600
Restricted Assets:			
Cash		6,600	
Investments		556,000	562,600
Utility Plant:			
Utility plant in service		3,291,825	
Less: Accumulated depreciation		440,325	
Utility Plant—Net		2,851,500	
Construction work in progress		125,000	
Net Utility Plant			2,976,500
Total Assets			3,774,700
LIABILITIES			
Current Liabilities:			
Accounts payable		33,200	
Customer advances for construction		21,000	
Total Current Liabilities			54,200
Liabilities Payable from Restricted Assets:			
Customer deposits			23,700
Long-Term Liabilities:			
Revenue bonds payable (net of unamortized discount of $5,300)			1,744,700
Total Liabilities			1,822,600
NET ASSETS			
Invested in capital assets, net of related debt			1,231,800
Restricted for payment of debt service			538,900
Unrestricted			181,400
Total Net Assets			$1,952,100

day, instead of billing by calendar months. Under this plan, meter reading is a continuous day-by-day operation, with billings following shortly after the filing of the meter readers' reports. Individual meters are read on approximately the same day each month, or every other month, in order that each bill cover approximately the same number of days of usage. Cycle billing eliminates the heavy peak load of accounting and clerical work that results from uniform billing on a calendar month basis. It does, however, result in a sizable amount of unbilled receivables on any given date, thus requiring accrual of unbilled receivables (Accrued Utilities Revenues, in regulatory terminology) as of the financial statement date in order to state assets and sales properly.[6]

Restricted Assets

The section below Current and Accrued Assets in Illustration 7–5 is captioned Restricted Assets, the caption most commonly used when the use of assets is restricted by contractual agreements or legal requirements. Some governments that use regulatory terminology report restricted assets of utilities under the broader caption, Other Property and Investments. Other Property and Investments may include, in addition to restricted assets, the carrying value of property not being used for utility purposes or being held for future utility use.

Cash and Investments are the only two items reported under the Restricted Assets caption of the balance sheet shown in Illustration 7–5. Those items are restricted for return of customer deposits and for retirement of revenue bonds pursuant to the bond covenants. The amount of assets segregated, $562,600, is offset by liabilities currently payable from restricted assets (in the case of the Town of Brighton, Customer Deposits of $23,700) and restrictions of net assets (in this case, restricted for payment of debt service, $538,900). This *fund within a fund* approach permits segregation of assets, related liabilities, and restricted net assets within a single enterprise fund. Net assets should be restricted in the amount of the net assets of each restricted "fund" within the Enterprise Fund, as shown in Illustration 7–5. Other items commonly reported in Restricted Assets include assets set aside to fund depreciation for capital improvements or grants and contributions restricted for capital acquisition or improvement.

Utility Plant

Utility Plant in Service is a control account, supported in whatever detail is required by regulatory agencies and by management needs. For example, water utilities commonly have six subcategories of plant assets: intangible plant, source of supply plant, pumping plant, water treatment plant, transmission and distribution plant, and general plant. Each of the six subcategories is supported by appropriate subsidiary accounts. For example, intangible plant consists of the costs of organization, franchises and consents, and any other intangible costs "necessary and valuable in the conduct of utility operations." Source of supply plant consists of land and land rights; structures and improvements; collecting and impounding reservoirs; lake, river, and other intakes; wells and springs; infiltration galleries and tun-

---

[6]Some governments use the same or similar chart of accounts for utilities as those of regulated profit-seeking enterprises in the same industry. The principal regulatory bodies are the National Association of Regulatory Utility Commissioners (NARUC), an association of state regulatory utility commissioners, and the Federal Energy Regulatory Commission (FERC), which has jurisdiction over certain utilities in interstate commerce.

nels; supply mains; and other water source plant. Each of the accounts within each subcategory is supported by necessary subsidiary records for each individual asset detailing its description, location, cost, date of acquisition, estimated useful life, salvage value, depreciation charges, and any other information needed for management planning and control, regulatory agency reports, financial statements, or special reports to creditors.

Construction Work in Progress. The other Utility Plant item shown on the Balance Sheet, Illustration 7–5, is Construction Work in Progress. This account represents the accumulated costs of work orders for projects that will result in items reportable as Utility Plant when completed and is, of course, supported by the work orders for projects in progress. Each work order, in turn, is supported by documents supporting payments to contractors and to suppliers, or supporting charges for materials, labor, and overhead allocable to the project.

The Uniform System of Accounts for water, sewer, gas, and electric utilities published by NARUC all contain a section on Utility Plant Instructions that, among other items, specifies the components of construction cost. Generally, the components are in agreement with those listed in any intermediate accounting text. One item long recognized in utility accounting and accepted by the FASB is the Allowance for Funds Used During Construction (AFUDC).[7]

AFUDC includes the net cost for the period of construction of borrowed funds used for construction purposes *and a reasonable rate on other funds so used.* Thus, interest paid, accrued, or imputed during the period of construction of a utility plant asset is included as a cost of the asset. Interest paid or accrued, known as the *debt component* of AFUDC, is deducted from Interest on Long-Term Debt in the Other Income and Deductions section of the utility's operating statement (see Illustration 7–7). This practice accomplishes two things: (1) it discloses to financial statement readers the amount of interest that was capitalized during the year, and (2) it reduces the reported interest expense, thus increasing reported net income for the period (presumably slowing down utilities' requests for rate increases). If construction is financed, in part, by use of resources generated by operations of the utility, regulatory authorities allow interest to be imputed on these "equity" funds and capitalized. Since imputed interest is not viewed by accountants as an expense, it is offset by reporting the *equity component* of AFUDC as nonoperating income.

Current Liabilities

Items commonly found in the Current Liabilities section of a Utility Balance Sheet are shown under that caption in Illustration 7–5. Accounts Payable needs no comment here. The other item, **Customer Advances for Construction**, results from the practice of utilities of requiring customers to advance to the utility a sizable

---

[7]Financial Accounting Standards Board, *Statement of Financial Accounting Standards No. 71*, "Accounting for the Effects of Certain Types of Regulation" (Norwalk, CT, 1982), par. 15, as amended by *Statement of Financial Accounting Standards No. 90* (Norwalk, CT, 1986), par. 8, and *Statement of Financial Accounting Standards No. 92* (Norwalk, CT, 1987), pars. 8 and 9.

portion of the estimated cost of construction projects to be undertaken by the utility at the request of the customer. If the advances are to be refunded, either wholly or in part, or applied against billings for service rendered after completion of the project, they are classified as shown in Illustration 7–5. When a customer is refunded the entire amount to which he or she is entitled according to the agreement or rule under which the advance was made, the balance, if any, is reported as Contributions from Customers in the Statement of Revenues, Expenses, and Changes in Net Assets. Other items commonly reported under Current Liabilities include accrued expenses, amounts due to other funds, and current portions of long-term liabilities. Some governments also report customer deposits under the Current Liabilities caption.[8]

Liabilities Payable from Restricted Assets

Liabilities payable from restricted assets should be displayed separately from current liabilities as shown in Illustration 7–5. In addition to customer deposits, the current portion of revenue bonds payable, if any, would be reported here since restricted assets have been set aside for that purpose. The Town of Brighton follows the common practice of most utilities and requires all new customers to deposit a sum of money with the utility as security for the payment of bills. In many, but not all, jurisdictions utilities are required to pay interest on customer deposits at a nominal rate. Regulatory authorities or local policy may require utilities to refund the deposits, and interest, after a specified period of time if the customer has paid all bills on time. The utility may be required, as was the Town of Brighton Water Fund, to segregate cash or investments in an amount equal to the liability for Customer Deposits. Customer Advances for Construction are contractually different from Customer Deposits and are less likely to be reported separately as restricted assets and liabilities, unless agreements with developers make it necessary to restrict assets for this purpose.

Long-Term Liabilities

Bonds are the customary form of long-term liabilities. Bonds issued by a utility are usually secured by the pledge of certain portions of the utility's revenue, the exact terms of the pledge varying with individual cases; bonds of this nature are called **revenue bonds.** Some utility bonds are secured not only by a pledge of a certain portion of the utility's revenues but also by an agreement on the part of the town's or city's general government to subsidize the utility in any year in which its normal revenue is inadequate for compliance with the terms of the bond indenture. Other utility bonds carry the pledge of the governmental unit's full faith and credit, although the intent is to service them from utility revenues rather than general taxes. The latter are, therefore, technically **general obligation bonds.** GASB standards provide that general obligation bonds intended to be serviced from utility revenues be reported as a liability of the enterprise fund. Similarly, special assessment debt may be assumed by an enterprise fund if the assets constructed by special assessment financing are used in enterprise fund operations.

---

[8]Generally, customer deposits should be reported as Liabilities Payable from Restricted Assets, a special category of current liabilities, as explained in the following section.

Governmentally owned utilities may have received long-term interfund loans from the government's General Fund or other funds. Also, enterprises may acquire assets under a capital lease arrangement. The portion of interfund loans, required lease payments, or bond or other debt issues to be paid within one year from balance sheet date should be reported as a current liability; the remainder is properly reported in the Long-term Liabilities section of the Utility Statement of Net Assets. (Alternatively, a Balance Sheet may be presented.) Long-term bonds payable should be reported net of unamortized discount or premium, as shown in Illustration 7–5, or else unamortized discount or premium can be reported as an offset against bonds payable at par on the Statement of Net Assets.

Net Assets

As discussed in earlier chapters for the government-wide Statement of Net Assets, GASB *Statement No. 34* requires that net assets be reported in three categories: invested in capital assets, net of related debt; restricted; and unrestricted. The same three categories apply to the net assets (total assets minus total liabilities) of an enterprise fund, as shown in Illustration 7–5. Restrictions may be placed by law or regulation, or contractually by agreement with creditors or other outside parties. Illustration 7–5 shows a typical restriction—a sinking fund created pursuant to a bond indenture for repayment of revenue bond principal. Unrestricted net assets represent the residual amount of net assets after segregating investment in capital assets, net of related debt, and restricted net assets.

Illustrative Accounting for a Water Utility Fund

The discussion in preceding pages of the balance sheet accounts of a water utility includes by implication the essential characteristics of accounting necessary for both governmentally owned utilities and investor-owned utilities. In this section, accounting for characteristic transactions of a utility fund is illustrated in general journal entry format for the year following the Statement of Net Assets presented in Illustration 7–5.

It is assumed the Town of Brighton is located in a state that permits enterprise funds to operate without formal legal approval of their budgets. Utility, or other enterprise, management must prepare operating budgets and capital expenditure budgets as management tools. For the illustrative case, it is assumed the budgets are submitted to the Town administrators, to the Town legislative body, and to the public, for information, not for legal action. Accordingly, the budget is not formally recorded in enterprise fund accounts. Similarly, utility management must be informed periodically of the status of outstanding construction contracts and purchase orders, but encumbrances need not be recorded in the accounts in order to accomplish this.

The nature of the Accrued Utilities Revenues account was explained previously in the section on Current and Accrued Assets. In the year following the one for which the statement of net assets is shown, it is not feasible when customers' bills are prepared to determine whether a portion of the bill has been accrued and, if so, how much. The simplest procedure, therefore, is to reverse the accrual entry as of the start of the new fiscal year. Assuming the entire December 31, 2001, Town of Brighton Water Utility Fund revenues accrual has been credited to Sales of Water, the following entry is appropriate as of January 1, 2002:

	Debits	Credits
1. Sales of Water	14,800	
Accrued Utility Revenues		14,800

When utility customers are billed during the year, appropriate revenue accounts are credited. Assuming during 2002 the total bills to nongovernmental customers amounted to $696,000, bills to the Town of Brighton General Fund amounted to $30,000, and all revenue was from sales of water, the following entry summarizes the events:

	Debits	Credits
2. Customer Accounts Receivable	696,000	
Due from General Fund	30,000	
Sales of Water		726,000

If collections from nongovernmental customers totaled $680,000 for water billings, Entry 3 is needed:

	Debits	Credits
3. Cash	680,000	
Customer Accounts Receivable		680,000

Materials and supplies in the amount of $138,000 were purchased during the year by the Water Utility Fund. The liability is recorded as:

	Debits	Credits
4. Materials and Supplies	138,000	
Accounts Payable		138,000

Materials and supplies chargeable to the accounts itemized in the entry below were issued during the year.

	Debits	Credits
5. Source of Supply Expenses	18,000	
Pumping Expenses	21,000	
Water Treatment Expenses	24,000	
Transmission and Distribution Expenses	13,000	
Construction Work in Progress	66,000	
Materials and Supplies		142,000

Payrolls for the year were chargeable to the accounts shown in the entry below. Tax Collections Payable is the account provided in the NARUC and FERC systems to report "the amount of taxes collected by the utility through payroll deductions or otherwise pending transmittal of such taxes to the proper taxing authority." Taxes Accrued is the account provided in the NARUC and FERC systems to report the liability for taxes that are the expense of the utility, such as the employer's share of social security taxes. In the entry below, it is assumed that the employer's share of social security taxes is charged to the same accounts that the employees' gross earnings are; it is also assumed that checks have been issued for employees' net earnings.

	Debits	Credits
6. Source of Supply Expenses	8,200	
Pumping Expenses	15,700	
Water Treatment Expenses	17,500	
Transmission and Distribution Expenses	76,250	
Customer Accounts Expenses	96,550	
Sales Expenses	17,250	
Administrative and General Expenses	83,150	
Construction Work in Progress	30,400	
Taxes Accrued		13,800
Tax Collections Payable		51,750
Cash		279,450

Bond interest in the amount of $105,000 was paid; the bonds were issued to finance the acquisition of utility plant assets. Amortization of debt discount and expense amounted to $530.

	Debits	Credits
7. Interest on Long-Term Debt	105,000	
Amortization of Debt Discount and Expense	530	
Unamortized Debt Discount and Expense		530
Cash		105,000

Bond interest in the amount of $12,900 was properly capitalized as part of construction work in progress during the year. (The Town of Brighton does not impute interest on its own resources during construction.)

	Debits	Credits
8. Construction Work in Progress	12,900	
Allowance for Funds Used During Construction		12,900

Construction projects on which costs totaled $220,000 were completed and the assets placed in service:

	Debits	Credits
9. Utility Plant in Service	220,000	
Construction Work in Progress		220,000

Collection efforts were discontinued on bills totaling $3,410. The customers owing the bills had paid deposits to the water utility totaling $2,140; the deposits were applied to the bills, and the unpaid remainder was charged to Accumulated Provision for Uncollectible Accounts (Entry 10a). Restricted assets (cash) is reduced by $2,140, the amount of the decrease in Customer Deposits (Entry 10b).

	Debits	Credits
10a. Customer Deposits	2,140	
Accumulated Provision for Uncollectible Accounts	1,270	
Customer Accounts Receivable		3,410
10b. Cash	2,140	
Cash—Customer Deposits		2,140

Customers' deposits amounting to $1,320 were refunded by check to customers discontinuing service (see Entry 11a). Deposits totaling $2,525 were received from new customers (see Entry 11b).

	Debits	Credits
11a. Customer Deposits	1,320	
Cash—Customer Deposits		1,320
11b. Cash—Customer Deposits	2,525	
Customer Deposits		2,525

Customers' advances for construction in the amount of $14,000 were applied to their water bills; in accord with the agreement with the customers and NARUC recommendations, the remainder of the advances were transferred to Capital Contributions from Customers.

12. Customers Advances for Construction	21,000	
Customer Accounts Receivable		14,000
Capital Contributions from Customers		7,000

Payments of Accounts Payable for materials and supplies used in operations totaled $67,200, and payment of Accounts Payable for materials used in construction totaled $66,000. Payments of Taxes Accrued amounted to $13,500, and payments of Tax Collections Payable amounted to $50,000.

13. Accounts Payable	133,200	
Taxes Accrued	13,500	
Tax Collections Payable	50,000	
Cash		196,700

The Water Utility Fund agreed to pay $25,000 to the Town General Fund as a contribution in lieu of property taxes. The entry in the General Fund is illustrated in Chapter 4 (see Chapter 4, illustrative Entry 22a). The following entry records the event in the accounts of the Water Utility Fund:

14. Contribution in Lieu of Taxes	25,000	
Due to General Fund		25,000

During the year interest in the amount of $44,500 was received in Cash on restricted investments. The amount of $1,375 is allocable to investments of customer deposit assets and is unrestricted as to use; the remaining $43,125 adds to the amount restricted for revenue bond repayment.

15a. Cash	1,375	
Cash—Bond Repayment	43,125	
Interest and Dividend Income		44,500
15b. Net Assets—Unrestricted	43,125	
Net Assets—Restricted for Bond Repayment		43,125

At year-end, entries to record depreciation expense, the provision for uncollectible accounts, and unbilled customers accounts receivable should be made as illustrated by Entry 16. In accord with regulatory terminology, Customer Accounts Expense, instead of Bad Debts Expense, is debited for the amount added to Accumulated Provision for Uncollectible Accounts. Amounts are assumed.

	Debits	Credits
16. Depreciation Expense	102,750	
Customer Accounts Expenses	3,980	
Accrued Utility Revenues	15,920	
Accumulated Provision for Depreciation of Utility Plant		102,750
Accumulated Provision for Uncollectible Accounts		3,980
Sales of Water		15,920

In accord with the revenue bond indenture, $100,000 unrestricted cash was invested in U.S. Government Securities for eventual retirement of revenue bonds. Net assets are restricted in an amount equal to the increase in restricted assets. In addition, investments from restricted cash for bond repayment amounted to $40,000.

	Debits	Credits
17a. Investments—Bond Repayment	140,000	
Cash		100,000
Cash—Bond Repayment		40,000
17b. Net Assets—Unrestricted	100,000	
Net Assets—Restricted for Bond Repayment		100,000

Nominal accounts for the year were closed:

	Debits	Credits
18. Sales of Water	727,120	
Capital Contributions from Customers	7,000	
Allowance for Funds Used During Construction	12,900	
Interest and Dividend Revenue	44,500	
Source of Supply Expenses		26,200
Pumping Expenses		36,700
Water Treatment Expenses		41,500
Transmission and Distribution Expenses		89,250
Customer Account Expenses		100,530
Sales Expenses		17,250
Administrative and General Expenses		83,150
Interest on Long-Term Debt		105,000
Amortization of Debt Discount and Expense		530
Contribution in Lieu of Taxes		25,000
Depreciation Expense		102,750
Net Assets—Unrestricted		163,660

In addition, Net Assets—Invested in Capital Assets, Net of Related Debt, would be increased for depreciation and amortization of debt discount and increased or decreased, as appropriate, for the net change in utility plant during the year. Decreases are recorded as a debit to Net Assets—Invested in Capital Assets, Net of Related Debt, and as a credit to Net Assets—Unrestricted. The reverse entry would be required for increases in capital asset balances.

Illustrative Statements

Statement of Net Assets. The Statement of Net Assets for a water utility, and definitions of certain balance sheet categories and items peculiar to regulated utilities, are explained at length in the sections of this chapter preceding the illustrative entries. The Statement of Net Assets of the Town of Brighton Water Utility Fund as of December 31, 2002, is shown as Illustration 7–6. Note the amount due

Illustration 7–6

TOWN OF BRIGHTON
WATER UTILITY FUND
STATEMENT OF NET ASSETS
AS OF DECEMBER 31, 2002

ASSETS			
Current and Accrued Assets:			
Cash		$ 128,365	
Customer accounts receivable	$67,590		
Less: Accumulated provision for uncollectibles	5,610	61,980	
Accrued utilities revenues		15,920	
Due from General Fund		5,000	
Materials and supplies		24,700	
Total Current and Accrued Assets			$ 235,965
Restricted Assets:			
Cash		8,790	
Investments		696,000	704,790
Utility Plant:			
Utility plant in service		3,511,825	
Less: Accumulated depreciation		543,075	
Utility Plant—Net		2,968,750	
Construction work in progress		14,300	
Net Utility Plant			2,983,050
Total Assets			3,923,805
LIABILITIES			
Current Liabilities:			
Accounts payable		38,000	
Taxes accrued		300	
Tax collection payable		1,750	
Total Current Liabilities			40,050
Liabilities Payable from Restricted Assets:			
Customer deposits			22,765
Long-Term Liabilities:			
Revenue bonds payable (net of unamortized discount of $4,770)			1,745,230
Total Liabilities			1,808,045
NET ASSETS			
Invested in capital assets, net of related debt			1,237,820
Restricted for payment of debt service			682,025
Unrestricted			195,915
Total Net Assets			$2,115,760

Illustration 7–7

TOWN OF BRIGHTON
WATER UTILITY FUND
STATEMENT OF REVENUES, EXPENSES,
AND CHANGES IN NET ASSETS
FOR THE YEAR ENDED DECEMBER 31, 2002

Utility Operating Revenue:		
Sales of water		$ 727,120
Operating Expenses:		
Source of supply expenses	$ 26,200	
Pumping expenses	36,700	
Water treatment expenses	41,500	
Transmission and distribution expenses	89,250	
Customer account expenses	100,530	
Sales expenses	17,250	
Administrative and general expenses	83,150	
Depreciation expense	102,750	
Contribution in lieu of taxes	25,000	
Total Operating Expenses		522,330
Utility Operating Income		204,790
Other Income and Deductions:		
Interest and dividend revenue	(44,500)	
Interest on long-term debt	105,000	
Amortization of debt discount and expense	530	
Allowance for funds used during construction	(12,900)	
Total Other Income and Deductions		48,130
Income before Contributions		156,660
Capital contributions from customers		7,000
Change in Net Assets		163,660
Total Net Assets, January 1, 2002		1,952,100
Total Net Assets, December 31, 2002		$2,115,760

to the General Fund is offset against the amount due from that fund, and only the net amount of the receivable, $5,000, is shown as an asset.

Operating Statement. The results of the operations of the Town of Brighton's Water Utility Fund for the year ended December 31, 2002, are shown in Illustration 7–7, the Statement of Revenues, Expenses, and Changes in Net Assets. The classifications used in the statement are consistent with NARUC and FERC recommendations.

Statement of Cash Flows. GASB standards require that a Statement of Cash Flows be prepared for all proprietary funds as a part of a full set of annual financial statements. As discussed at length earlier in this chapter, GASB standards for preparation of a cash flow statement differ from FASB standards; the main difference being that GASB standards specify four major categories of cash flows rather than three. The Statement of Cash Flows for the Town of Brighton for the year ended December 31, 2002 (Illustration 7–8), utilizes only three of the four categories of cash flows since the Town had no cash flows from noncapital financing activities. *Cash flows from operating activities* (Illustration 7–8) were provided by receipts from customers (Entry 3) and the net increase in refundable customer deposits (Entries 11a and 11b). Note that the application of customer deposits to pay overdue bills (Entries 10a and 10b) has no effect on total cash and cash equivalents. Cash from operating activities was used to pay employees (Entries 6 and 13). As suggested in the GASB *Implementation Guide* on reporting cash flows,[9] all employee-related items (in this case Taxes Accrued and Tax Collections Payable) have been added to the amount actually paid to employees. Payroll taxes and fringe benefits may be included in a separate line "cash payments for taxes, duties, fines, and other fees or penalties," if significant in amount. "Cash paid to employees for services" in the amount of $312,550 is calculated as the net cash paid directly to employees, $279,450, less $30,400 capitalized as Construction Work in Progress (Entry 6) plus $63,500 paid for Taxes Accrued and Tax Collections Payable (Entry 13). Finally cash from operating activities was used to pay suppliers (Entry 13). Although suppliers were paid $133,200 in total, only $67,200 of this amount applied to operating activities.

Cash flows from capital and related activities in Illustration 7–8 show two uses of cash. The first item, acquisition and construction of capital assets, is calculated as the sum of $30,400 (Entry 6) and $66,000 (Entry 13). The other item, interest paid on long-term bonds, reflects bond interest in the amount of $105,000 paid in cash (Entry 7).

Cash flows from investing activities show cash provided by interest and dividend income (Entry 15a) and cash used by purchase of investments (Entry 17a).

As shown in Illustration 7–8, two reconciliations are required. The first reconciliation is necessary because the Town of Brighton's Statement of Cash Flows reports changes in *total* cash and cash equivalents, whereas the Balance Sheet shows two components of cash and cash equivalents: that included in Current and Accrued Assets and that included in Restricted Assets, respectively.[10] GASB standards also require a reconciliation of operating income to net cash provided by operating activities.

External Financial Reporting of Enterprise Funds

As shown in Illustrations 2–1 and 2–2, the totals for all enterprise funds, with interfund transactions between enterprise funds eliminated, are reported in the business-

[9]Governmental Accounting Standards Board, *Implementation Guide*, "Guide to Implementation of GASB Statement 9 on Reporting Cash Flows of Proprietary and Nonexpendable Trust Funds and Governmental Entities That Use Proprietary Fund Accounting," (Norwalk, CT, 1992), p. 23.

[10]Ibid., p. 28.

Illustration 7–8

TOWN OF BRIGHTON
WATER UTILITY FUND
STATEMENT OF CASH FLOWS
FOR THE YEAR ENDED DECEMBER 31, 2002

Cash flows from operating activities:	
Cash received from customers	$680,000
Cash provided from customer deposits	1,205
Cash paid to employees for services	(312,550)
Cash paid to suppliers	(67,200)
Net cash provided by operating activities	301,455
Cash flows from capital and related financing activities:	
Acquisition and construction of capital assets	(96,400)
Interest paid on long-term bonds	(105,000)
Net cash used for capital and related financing activities	(201,400)
Cash flows from investing activities:	
Interest and dividend income	44,500
Purchases of restricted investments	(140,000)
Net cash used for investing activities	(95,500)
Net increase in cash and cash equivalents	4,555
Cash and cash equivalents, January 1, 2002	132,600
Cash and cash equivalents, December 31, 2002	$137,155

Reconciliation of Cash and Cash Equivalents to the Balance Sheet

	End of Year	*Beginning of Year*
Cash and cash equivalents in current and accrued assets	$128,365	$126,000
Restricted cash and cash equivalents	8,790	6,600
Total cash and cash equivalents	$137,155	$132,600

Reconciliation of Utility Operating Income to Net Cash Provided by Operating Activities

Utility operating income		$204,790
Adjustments:		
Depreciation expense	$102,750	
Increase in accounts payable	4,800	
Increase in accrued liabilities	2,050	
Decrease in customer deposits	(935)	
Decrease in inventories	4,000	
Increase in interfund receivables	(5,000)	
Increase in accrued receivables	(1,120)	
Decrease in customer accounts receivable	4,120	
Customer advances applied to customer receivables	(14,000)	
Total adjustments		96,665
Net cash provided by operating activities		$301,455

type activities columns of the government-wide financial statements. Governments must also prepare three fund financial statements for their major enterprise funds (see the Glossary for a definition of major funds) and the total of their internal service funds. These statements are a Statement of Net Assets (or Balance Sheet), a Statement of Revenues, Expenses, and Changes in Net Assets, and a Statement of Cash Flows. Illustrative proprietary fund statements are presented in Illustrations 2–6, 2–7, and 2–8. As those statements show, a separate column is provided for internal service funds under the column head "Governmental Activities—Internal Service Funds." The amounts shown in this column are the totals for all internal service funds, since major fund reporting does not apply to the internal service funds.

Events in Following Year

Earlier in this chapter, the establishment of a Supplies Fund by the Town of Brighton as of January 1, 2003, is illustrated. The Water Utility Fund advanced $130,000 to the Supplies Fund as a long-term loan. The entry by the Supplies Fund is illustrated in Entry 2 in the "Illustrative Case—Supplies Fund" section earlier in this chapter; the corresponding entry in the Water Utility Fund would be:

	Debits	*Credits*
Interfund Loan to Supplies Fund—Noncurrent	130,000	
Cash		130,000

Toward the end of 2003, the Supplies Fund paid its first installment of $6,500 to the Water Utility Fund as a partial repayment of the long-term advance. Entry 9 of the illustrative entries for the Supply Fund shown earlier in this chapter illustrates the effect on the accounts of the Supplies Fund. The effect on the accounts of the Water Utility Fund is recorded by the following entry:

Cash	6,500	
Interfund Loan to Supplies Fund—Noncurrent		6,500

Regulatory Accounting Principles (RAP)

Investor-owned utilities, and governmentally owned utilities in some states, are required to report in a prescribed manner to state regulatory commissions. Electric and certain other utilities subject to the Federal Power Act must also file reports with the FERC. As mentioned at several points in this chapter, both NARUC and FERC prescribe charts of accounts and uniform financial statement formats for reporting to regulatory agencies. Even though the Town of Brighton follows GAAP rather than **regulatory accounting principles** (RAP) in preparing its financial statements, the Town uses the chart of accounts and some of the financial statement captions provided for in regulatory publications. The illustrative financial statements shown earlier in this chapter are typical of those for water funds included in comprehensive annual financial reports.

For utilities that are required to report to a state rate regulatory commission or the FERC, accounting and reporting procedures under RAP are quite different from GAAP. Because plant assets and long-term debt are customarily a dominant share of the total assets and total debt of utilities, and current assets and current liabilities are relatively insignificant in amount, the regulatory balance sheet format displays plant assets before current assets and long-term debt before current liabilities. In Illustration 7–5, for example, Net Utility Plant amounts to almost 79 percent of total assets, and long-term debt is almost 96 percent of total debt.

Under regulatory reporting Utility Plant in Service is stated at original cost. Original cost is a regulatory concept that differs from historical cost, a concept commonly used in accounting for assets of nonregulated businesses. In essence, **historical cost** is the amount paid for an asset by its present owner. In contrast, **original cost** is *the cost to the owner who first devoted the property to public service*. When a regulated utility purchases plant assets from another utility, it must record in its accounts the amounts shown in the accounts of the seller for the Utility Plant purchased and for the related accumulated depreciation. Any premium paid by the present owner over and above such cost less depreciation is in the general nature of payments for goodwill by nonutility enterprises. But utilities enjoy monopoly privileges and are subject to corresponding restrictions. One of the restrictions is that earnings shall not exceed a fair rate of return. Since goodwill is the capitalized value of excess earnings, utilities can have no goodwill (in the accounting sense). Premium on plant purchased is therefore accounted for as **Utility Plant Acquisition Adjustments**. The amount of acquisition adjustment capitalized is amortized over a period of time determined by the appropriate regulatory body; accumulated amortization is disclosed in the Accumulated Provision for Amortization of Utility Plant Acquisition Adjustments account.

Other asset sections of balance sheets prepared in the regulatory format are Other Property and Investments and Deferred Debits. One item usually reported in the former section is Special Funds, which is similar to the Restricted Assets section of the GAAP-format balance sheets shown in Illustrations 7–5 and 7–6. Thus, as mentioned previously, Other Property and Investments is broader in scope than Restricted Assets and may contain items other than restricted assets. One item typically reported under the Deferred Debits caption is Unamortized Debt Discount and Expense, which under GAAP is reported as an offset to the related long-term debt.

Accounting for Nonutility Enterprises

Early in this chapter it was stressed that each governmentally owned enterprise should follow the accounting and financial reporting standards developed for investor-owned enterprises in the same industry. Generally, the standards developed by the Financial Accounting Standards Board, and its predecessors, have been accepted by the GASB as applying to Internal Service Funds and Enterprise Funds.[11] Consequently, many sections earlier in this chapter, which discuss generally accepted accounting principles applicable to Internal Service Funds (such as "Assets Acquired under Lease Agreements"), apply equally to enterprise funds accounting for activities other than utilities.

Accounting for Municipal Solid Waste Landfills

According to Environmental Protection Agency (EPA) estimates, there are approximately 6,000 municipal solid waste landfills (MSWLFs) in the United States, of which about 80 percent are owned by state or local general purpose or

[11]See Footnote 5.

special purpose governments.[12] An EPA Rule, "Solid Waste Disposal Facility Criteria" (40 *Code of Federal Regulations*, parts 257 and 258), establishes certain closure requirements for MSWLFs and imposes stringent criteria for location, design, and operation of landfills, groundwater monitoring and corrective action, postclosure care, and financial assurance. State governments are assigned primary responsibility for implementing and enforcing the EPA rule, and may increase or reduce its provisions based on site conditions existing within their states.

MSWLF owners and operators may incur a variety of costs, both during the period of operation and after closure. These costs include the cost of equipment and facilities (including final covering of the MSWLF upon closure) and cost of services for such items as postclosure maintenance and monitoring for a period of 30 years after closure. The EPA requires owners and operators to estimate in detail the current dollar cost of hiring a third party to close the largest area of an MSWLF expected to require a final cover and to care for the MSWLF over the 30-year postclosure period. Each year the closure and postclosure cost estimates must be adjusted for inflation and revised as necessary to reflect changes in plans or conditions. Owners and operators of MSWLFs must provide assurances that adequate financial resources will be available to cover the estimated costs of closure, postclosure care, and remediation or containment of environmental hazards when the landfill has been filled to capacity. Several forms of financial assurance are acceptable, including third-party trusts, surety bonds, letters of credit, insurance, or state-sponsored plans.

GASB standards provide guidance both for measuring and reporting estimated total closure and postclosure costs. Although the detailed cost estimation procedures are beyond the scope of this chapter, reporting requirements for MSWLFs that use proprietary fund accounting are described briefly. An expense and a liability should be recognized each period for a portion of the estimated total current cost of MSWLF closure and postclosure care. The portion of total cost to be recognized is based on the units-of-production method so that estimated total current cost is assigned to periods on the basis of landfill usage rather than the passage of time. Recognition begins in the period in which the MSWLF first accepts solid waste and continues each period until closure. Estimated total closure and postclosure costs should be reevaluated each year during operation of the landfill and the cumulative effect of changes in the estimated costs, if any, should be reported in the period of the change. Costs of equipment, facilities, services, or final cover acquired during the period are reported as a reduction of the accrued liability and not as capital assets. Equipment and facilities installed prior to commencement of operation of the landfill should be fully depreciated by the closure date.

Assets held by third-party trustees or in surety standby trusts to meet financial assurance requirements should be reported as "amounts held by trustee" in the restricted assets section of the balance sheet and as net assets restricted for closure and postclosure costs. Earnings on such investments should be reported as revenue.

---

[12]Governmental Accounting Standards Board, *Statement of Governmental Accounting Standards No. 18*, "Accounting for Municipal Solid Waste Landfill Closure and Postclosure Costs" (Norwalk, CT, 1993), par. 24.

GASB standards also provide guidance for reporting of MSWLFs in governmental fund types or by other entities such as colleges and universities. Accounting for MSWLFs in the General Fund, for example, requires that an expenditure and fund liability be reported for the current closure and postclosure costs to the extent that an accrued liability would be settled with available fund resources; any remaining liability would be reported in the governmental activities category at the government-wide level, as discussed in Chapter 6. Regardless of the fund type or entity reporting the MSWLF activities, GASB standards require the following note disclosures.[13]

1. The nature and source of landfill closure and postclosure care requirements (federal, state, or local laws or regulations).
2. That recognition of a liability for closure and postclosure care costs is based on landfill capacity used to date.
3. The reported liability for closure and postclosure care at the Balance Sheet date (if not apparent from the financial statements) and the estimated total current cost of closure and postclosure care remaining to be recognized.
4. The percentage of landfill capacity used to date and approximate remaining landfill life in years.
5. How closure and postclosure care financial assurance requirements, if any, are being met. Also, any assets restricted for payment of closure and postclosure care costs (if not apparent from the financial statements).
6. The nature of the estimates and the potential for changes due to inflation or deflation, technology, or applicable laws or regulations.

While municipal solid waste landfills may seem to be a dull topic, the costs of improving landfills to meet increased EPA standards, providing financial assurance, and complying with accounting and reporting requirements may be significant for many governmental units.

Required Segment Information

GASB *Statement No. 34* identifies a *segment* as:

> an identifiable activity reported as or within an enterprise fund or an other stand-alone entity for which one or more revenue bonds or other revenue-backed debt instruments (such as certificates of participation) are outstanding (par. 122).

If, however, a segment is already reported as a major fund then segment reporting is not required for that activity. Emphasis is placed on identifiable streams of revenues pledged for the support of revenue bonds, along with related expenses, gains, losses, assets, and liabilities of the same activity. Segment disclosure requirements are largely met by condensed financial statements, as follows:[14]

[13]GASB, *Codification*, Sec. L10.116.
[14]GASB *Statement No. 34*, par. 122.

1. Type of goods or services provided by the segment.
2. Condensed statement of net assets:
   a. Total assets—distinguishing between current assets, capital assets, and other assets. Amounts receivable from other funds or component units should be reported separately.
   b. Total liabilities—distinguishing between current and long-term amounts. Amounts payable to other funds or component units should be reported separately.
   c. Total net assets—distinguishing among restricted (separately reporting expendable and nonexpendable components); unrestricted; and amounts invested in capital assets, net of related debt.
3. Condensed statement of revenues, expenses, and changes in net assets:
   a. Operating revenues (by major source)
   b. Operating expenses. Depreciation should be identified separately.
   c. Operating income (loss).
   d. Nonoperating revenues (expenses)—with separate reporting of major revenues and expenses.
   e. Capital contributions and additions to permanent and term endowments.
   f. Special and extraordinary items.
   g. Transfers.
   h. Change in net assets.
   i. Beginning net assets.
   j. Ending net assets.
4. Condensed statement of cash flows:
   a. Net cash provided (used) by:
      (1) Operating activities.
      (2) Noncapital financing activities.
      (3) Capital and related financing activities.
      (4) Investing activities.
   b. Beginning cash and cash equivalent balances.
   c. Ending cash and cash equivalent balances.

Key Terms

Cash equivalents 285
Customer advances for construction 297
General obligation bonds 298
Historical cost 309
Original cost 309
Regulatory accounting principles 308
Revenue bonds 298
Utility plant acquisition adjustment 309

Selected References

American Institute of Certified Public Accountants. Audit and Accounting Guide. *Audits of State and Local Governmental Units*. Revised. New York, 1999.

Financial Accounting Standards Board. *Statement of Financial Accounting Standards No. 71*, "Accounting for the Effects of Certain Types of Regulation." Norwalk, CT, 1982.

Governmental Accounting Standards Board. *Codification of Governmental Accounting and Financial Reporting Standards as of June 30, 1999*. Norwalk, CT, 1999.

Questions

7–1. Explain how internal service funds and enterprise funds are similar and how they are different.

7–2. Explain the generally accepted accounting principles utilized by proprietary funds.

7–3. What are the benefits of establishing internal service funds? What kinds of activities are typically accounted for in internal service funds?

7–4. "Since the reason for the establishment of internal service funds is to facilitate management of resources, and not primarily to demonstrate compliance with law, they may be established at the discretion of governmental administrators." Comment.

7–5. Since internal service funds are expected to cover the cost of their operations by charges to departments or agencies using their services, they should use the accrual basis of accounting for both revenue recognition and expenditure recognition. Discuss.

7–6. What are some of the more important considerations in establishing a pricing policy for an internal service fund?

7–7. In general, how may an administrator or accountant determine the accounting and financial reporting standards applicable to a nonregulated governmental enterprise? A governmental enterprise in a regulated industry?

7–8. What is the purpose of the Restricted Assets section of an Enterprise Fund Statement of Fund Net Assets used to account for a utility? Provide examples of items that might be reported in the Restricted Assets section.

7–9. If a governmental unit issues tax-supported bonds or special assessment bonds that are to be serviced by enterprise fund revenues, what treatment should be given to the bonds in the Enterprise Fund Balance Sheet? In the notes to the government-wide statements?

7–10. What is the meaning of *original cost* as used in public utility accounting? In your answer make clear how *original cost* differs from *historical cost*.

7–11. What are the categories of cash flows required in a proprietary fund statement of cash flows prepared in conformity with GASB standards? What kinds of transactions are reported in each category?

7–12. Explain why utilities customarily need to present an Accrued Utilities Revenues account in their Statement of Fund Net Assets. How should the amount of the accrual be determined?

7–13. What is meant by "segment information for enterprise funds"? To what source should persons concerned with governmental financial report preparation go to determine the required disclosures?

7–14. Explain how the expense and liability of a period for the estimated current cost for closure and postclosure of a municipal solid waste landfill accounted for in a proprietary fund should be determined. Does this appear rational? Explain.

7–15. What disclosures are required in the Notes to the Financial Statements for a municipal solid waste landfill, regardless of the fund type or entity used to account for it?

Cases

7–1. Internal Service Fund Policies. The formal financial objectives and funding policies for the internal service funds of the City of Columbia, Missouri, are presented below and on the next page. Read these policies and respond to the questions that follow.

A Resolution

establishing a formal policy with respect to the financial objectives for internal service funds; and establishing a policy regarding generation of funds required for capital outlay.

BE IT RESOLVED BY THE COUNCIL OF THE CITY OF COLUMBIA, MISSOURI AS FOLLOWS:

SECTION 1. That internal service funds such as Data Processing, Vehicle Maintenance, Utilities Accounts and Billing, Public Buildings, and Printing are funds whose financial objective should be to only recover the complete cost of operations without producing any significant amount of profit in excess of the fund's requirements.

SECTION 2. That Section 1 is consistent with practices of "Governmental Accounting, Auditing, and Financial Reporting."

SECTION 3. That in computing an internal service funds revenue requirement for rate setting purposes, the rate base should include such items as debt expense, interest expense, operating expense, prorated reserve (accumulated over time to allow for purchase option under lease/purchase arrangements), and either depreciation expense or estimated capital outlay, either of which are usually financed 100% internally through rates.

SECTION 4. That since working capital in different funds varies because of many factors it should be reviewed more closely with the budgetary process to assure captive users that the cash account is not a result of billings in excess of revenue requirements.

SECTION 5. That if it appears that cash buildup has occurred in excess of reasonable revenue requirements, rates should be adjusted in the budgetary process; cost recoveries, either over or under, should be rolled forward.

SECTION 6. That generation of funds for capital outlay be allowed either 100% internally through rates or through budgeted depreciation expense when lease/purchase agreements are used, in which case, an amount should be included in the rate base for a prorated reserve which, accumulated over time, will enable purchase of such capital outlay at some future date.

Allowable costs used in determining revenue requirements for the City of Columbia's internal service funds are diagrammed in the next box.

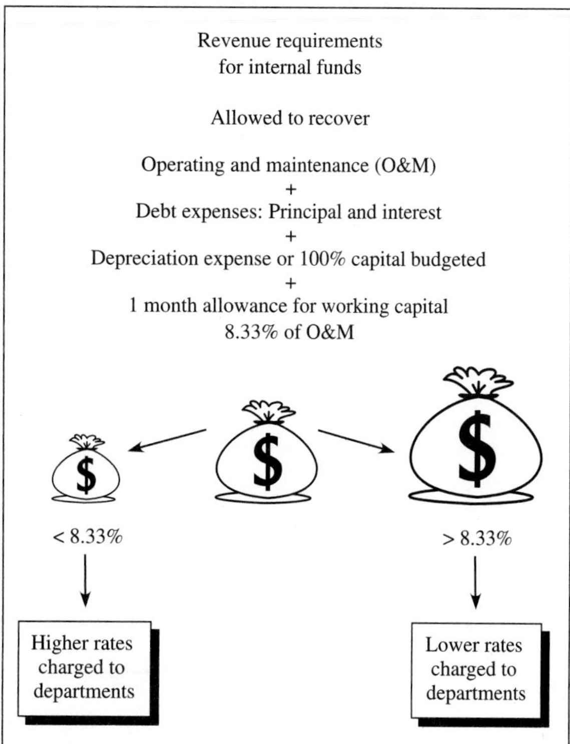

Required

a. Do the City of Columbia's financial objectives and funding policies appear to promote sound resource management?

b. Evaluate the reasonableness of the factors used to determine billing rates/revenue requirements from the viewpoint of

(1) A City Council member.

(2) The Mayor or City Manager.

(3) A department head.

c. Is having a uniform policy for all internal service funds optimal, or would it be better to tailor the revenue requirements to the needs of each individual fund? Explain.

7–2. Building Maintenance Fund. The Balance Sheet and Statement of Revenues, Expenditures, and Changes in Fund Balance for the Building Maintenance Fund, an internal service fund of Coastal City, are reproduced below. No further information about the nature or purposes of this fund is given in the annual report.

COASTAL CITY
BUILDING MAINTENANCE FUND
BALANCE SHEET
AS OF DECEMBER 31, 2001

Assets

Assets:	
Cash and investments	$152,879
Accounts receivable	2,116
Inventory	779,000
Prepaid expenses	19,854
Total Assets	$953,849

Liabilities and Fund Equity

Liabilities:	
Accounts payable	$ 35,675
Other accrued liabilities	109,099
Accrued annual leave	227,369
Total Liabilities	372,143
Fund equity:	
Fund balance	581,706
Total Liabilities and Fund Equity	$953,849

COASTAL CITY
BUILDING MAINTENANCE FUND
STATEMENT OF REVENUES, EXPENDITURES, AND CHANGES IN FUND BALANCE
YEAR ENDED DECEMBER 31, 2001

Revenues:	
Billings to Departments	$10,774,781
Miscellaneous	100,344
Total Billings	10,875,125
Expenditures:	
Salaries and employee benefits	3,353,413
Supplies	3,409,096
Operating services and charges	495,143
Maintenance and repairs	3,536,443
Total expenditures	10,794,095
Excess of Revenues over Expenditures	81,030
Fund Balance, January 1, 2001	500,676
Fund Balance, December 31, 2001	$ 581,706

Required

a. Judging from the information presented, does the Building Maintenance Fund appear to be accounted for and operated, financially, as an internal service fund should be?

b. If you were the manager of a City department that uses the services of the Building Maintenance Fund, what would you want to know in addition to the information disclosed in the financial statements?

7–3. Mass Transit System. The City of Dixon operates a mass transit system (DTS) consisting of a network of bus and trolley routes. The following information is provided about the operations and financing of the mass transit system.*

1. Operating revenues for the most recent fiscal year amounted to $549,420; operating expenses for the same year amounted to $1,011,843. Operating revenues have covered only 45 to 50 percent of operating expenditures since DTS was established five years ago.
2. The operating deficit (from part 1) of $462,423 was financed jointly by $362,423 from the City's General Fund and $100,000 in operating grants from the Urban Mass Transit Administration (UMTA). Capital contributions over the past five years have amounted to $3,334,286 divided about evenly between the City and capital grants from the UMTA.
3. Transit system managers have been pressured at times by City officials to increase bus and trolley fares but are strongly opposed because they believe DTS ridership would drop significantly. Advocates for disadvantaged groups have also lobbied hard to keep the current fares. Thus, for at least the next several years, the City plans to provide an annual operating subsidy to DTS to cover its operating deficit, less any operating grants received from UMTA or other sources.
4. Until now DTS has been accounted for and reported as an enterprise fund of the City. The City Finance Director and the head of the mass transit system would like to continue to use enterprise fund accounting; however, influential members of the Finance Committee of the City Council are insisting that, since DTS is never expected to break even, it should be accounted for and reported as a special revenue fund, Changing to a special revenue fund also means that DTS will require Council-approved appropriations for its expenditures.

Required

Based on the information provided for the City of Dixon mass transit system, should the activities of DTS be accounted for in an enterprise fund or as a special revenue fund? Explain fully.

---

*The authors are indebted to Charles M. Hicks for providing the information from which this case was adapted.

Exercises and Problems

7–1. Examine the CAFR. Utilizing the annual report obtained for Exercise 1–1, follow these instructions:

a. **Internal Service Funds.**

(1) *Use of Funds.* What activities of the governmental unit are reported as being administered by internal service funds (working capital funds, revolving funds, rotary funds, industrial funds, and intragovernmental service funds are other names used for funds of the type discussed in Chapter 7)? If internal service funds are not used by the reporting entity, does the report disclose how activities such as purchasing, motor pools, printing, data processing, and other activities commonly used by more than one fund are financed and accounted for? Does the report state the basis of accounting used for the internal service funds? Are all funds in this category accounted for on the same basis? If so, is the financial statement presentation consistent with the stated basis? If the basis of accounting is not stated, analyze the statements to determine which basis is used—full accrual, modified accrual, or cash basis.

(2) *Fund Disclosure.* In the balance sheet(s) or Statement(s) of Fund Net Assets of the internal service fund(s), are assets classified in accord with practices of profit-seeking businesses, or are current, capital, and other assets not separately displayed? If there are receivables other than from other funds or other governmental units, are allowances for estimated uncollectibles provided? Are allowances for depreciation deducted from related capital-asset accounts?

Are current liabilities and long-term debt properly distinguished in the balance sheet? Are long-term loans from other funds properly distinguished from capital contributions received from other funds?

Are budgetary accounts (Estimated Revenues, Appropriations, Encumbrances) used by the internal service funds? From what sources were revenues actually obtained by each internal service fund? How are costs and expenses of each fund classified: by character, object, function, or activity (see Chapter 3 for definitions of these terms)? Are noncash expenses, such as depreciation, separately disclosed? Do the revenues of each fund exceed the costs and expenses of the period? Compute the net income (or net loss) of each fund in this category as a percentage of its operating revenue for the period. Does the net income (or net loss) for any fund exceed 5 percent of operating revenues? If so, do the statements, or the accompanying text, explain what the excess is being used for, or how the deficiency is being financed?

(3) *Statement of Cash Flows.* Is a Statement of Cash Flows presented for internal service funds? If so, how does the cash provided by operations shown in this statement relate to the revenues and expenses shown in the Statement of Revenues, Expenses, and Changes in Retained Earnings? Are cash flows from financing activities presented separately for noncapital- and capital-related activities? Is there a section for cash flows from investing activities?

(4) *Government-wide Financial Statements*. If the government has adopted GASB *Statement No. 34*, is there a column for business-type activities on the Statement of Net Assets and Statement of Activities? Is there any evidence that the internal service fund account balances were collapsed into the governmental activities column; for example, is there an account called Internal Balances? If enterprise funds are the predominant participants in the internal service fund, do you see evidence that the internal service fund balances are reported in the business-type activities column of the government-wide statements?

b. **Enterprise Funds.**

(1) *Use of Funds*. What activities of the governmental unit are reported as being administered by enterprise funds? Does the governmental unit own and operate its water utility? Electric utility? Gas utility? Transportation system? Are combining statements presented for all enterprise funds, or are separate statements presented for each enterprise fund? Are all enterprise funds accounted for on the full accrual basis? Are all funds in this category earning revenues at least equal to costs and expenses? If not, how is the operating deficit being financed? What sources furnished the original investment in fund assets? Do the notes include segment information on individual enterprise funds where applicable (see "Required Segment Information" section of Chapter 7)?

Are sales to other funds or other governmental units separately disclosed? Are there receivables from other funds? Other governmental units? How are receivables from component units, if any, disclosed? Is there any evidence that enterprise funds contribute amounts to the General Fund in lieu of taxes to help support services received by the enterprise? Is there any evidence that enterprise funds make excessively large contributions to the General Fund or any other funds?

(2) *Utility Funds*. Is it possible to tell from the report whether utilities of this governmental unit are subject to the same regulations as investor-owned utilities in the same state? (If the utility statements follow the format of the NARUC and the FERC, as described in Chapter 7, there is a good chance the governmentally owned utilities are subject to at least some supervision by a regulatory agency.) What rate of return on sales (or operating revenues) is being earned by each utility fund? What rate of return on total assets is being earned by each utility fund?

Is depreciation taken on utility plant? Are accounting policies and accounting changes properly disclosed? If so, what method of depreciation is being used? Is the *original cost* basis used for plant assets—is a plant acquisition adjustment account shown? If so, over what period is the acquisition being amortized?

Does each utility account for its own debt service and construction activities in the manner described in Chapter 7? What Special Funds, or Restricted Assets, are utilized by each utility?

(3) *Nonutility Enterprise Funds*. Are nonutility enterprise funds accounted for in the same manner as investor-owned enterprises in the same industries? (In order to answer this, you may need to refer to publications of trade

associations or to handbooks or encyclopedias of accounting systems found in business libraries.) If you cannot find information about investor-owned counterparts of the governmental nonutility enterprise funds, do the statements of the latter provide evidence that generally accepted accounting principles devised for profit-seeking businesses were used?

(4) *Government-wide Financial Statements*. If the government has adopted GASB *Statement No. 34*, what proportion of the net assets of the business-type activities are reported as invested in capital assets, restricted, and unrestricted? Were the business-type activities profitable; that is, did revenues exceed expenses?

7–2. Multiple Choice. Choose the best answer.

1. Which of the following is *not* an appropriate reason to establish an internal service fund?
   a. To improve the management of resources.
   b. To develop a cash reserve to meet future contingencies.
   c. To determine whether user charges are sufficient to cover operating costs.
   d. To determine whether costs are reasonable in relation to benefits.
2. Which of the following is a correct statement of the role of budgeting in proprietary funds?
   a. Fund managers should have discretion to operate within a flexible budget, consistent with pricing and other policies established by the legislative body.
   b. Expenditures from proprietary fund resources require legislative appropriations.
   c. To ensure appropriations are not overspent, all proprietary funds should use encumbrance procedures.
   d. Proprietary fund managers should ensure that goods and services are not provided to other funds or departments unless a valid appropriation exists for the goods or services ordered.
3. According to GASB *Statement No. 34*, after an interfund transfer from the General Fund to a proprietary fund is recorded as "Contributions and Transfers" on the Statement of Revenues, Expenses, and Changes in Fund Net Assets, how is it reported on the Statement of Net Assets?
   a. Contributed capital in the Fund Equity section.
   b. Retained earnings in the Fund Equity section.
   c. Long-term liability.
   d. Unrestricted Net Assets.
4. Watt County operates a centralized data processing center as an internal service fund to provide services to other funds and departments. In 2001, this fund billed the Parks and Recreation Fund $75,000 for data processing services. What account should Watt's internal service fund credit to record the billing to the Parks and Recreation Fund?
   a. Interfund Exchanges.
   b. Billings to Departments.
   c. Interfund Transfers In.
   d. Data Processing Expenses.

5. If an internal service fund is intended to operate on a cost-reimbursement basis, then user charges should:
   a. Cover the full costs, both direct and indirect, of operating the fund.
   b. Cover at a minimum the direct costs of operating the fund.
   c. Cover the full costs of operating the fund *and* provide for future expansion and replacement of capital assets.
   d. Any of the above could be an appropriate basis for establishing user charges, depending on the policy followed by a particular government.
6. During 2001 Bell City reported the following operating receipts from self-sustaining activities paid for by users of the services rendered:

Operations of water supply plant	$5,000,000
Operations of transit system	900,000

   What amounts should be reported as operating revenues of Bell's enterprise funds?
   a. $0.
   b. $900,000.
   c. $5,000,000.
   d. $5,900,000.
7. Interest capitalized as a part of the cost of assets constructed by a governmentally owned utility properly consists of:
   a. Net interest paid and accrued during the period of construction on money borrowed for construction purposes.
   b. Net interest paid and accrued during the period of construction on money borrowed for construction purposes, and interest imputed on other money used for construction.
   c. Only net interest actually paid during the period of construction.
   d. None of the above.
8. The proceeds of tax-supported bonds issued for the benefit of an enterprise fund and being serviced by a debt service fund:
   a. Should not be reported by the enterprise fund at all.
   b. Should be reported in the notes to enterprise fund statements, but not in the body of any of the statements.
   c. Should be reported in the enterprise fund as Long-Term Debt.
   d. Should be reported in the enterprise fund as a contribution or interfund transfer in the Statement of Changes in Fund Net Assets.
9. Under GASB standards capital assets received by gift or contribution by a proprietary fund, or acquired from grants, entitlements, and shared revenues restricted for acquisition of capital assets, should:
   a. Not be depreciated.
   b. Be depreciated only in the government-wide statements.

c. Be depreciated or not be depreciated at the option of the governmental unit, provided a consistent policy is followed.

d. Be depreciated in the normal manner in both the business-type activities column in the government-wide statements and in the proprietary fund statements.

10. The financial statements required by GASB *Statement No. 34* for a proprietary fund are:

a. Balance Sheet and Statement of Revenues, Expenditures, and Changes in Net Assets.

b. Balance Sheet; Statement of Revenues, Expenditures, and Changes in Fund Balance; Statement of Cash Flows.

c. Statement of Net Assets; Statement of Revenues, Expenses, and Changes in Net Assets; Statement of Cash Flows.

d. Balance Sheet and Statement of Revenues, Expenses, and Changes in Retained Earnings.

7–3. Central Garage Internal Service Fund. Your examination of the accounts of your new client, the City of Delmas, as of June 30, 2001, revealed the following:

1. On December 31, 2000, the City paid $115,000 out of General Fund revenues for a central garage to service its vehicles, with $67,500 being applicable to the building, which has an estimated life of 25 years; $14,500 to land; and $33,000 to machinery and equipment, which has an estimated life of 15 years. A $12,200 cash contribution was received by the garage from the General Fund on the same date.
2. The garage maintains no records, but a review of deposit slips and canceled checks revealed the following:

Collections for services to General Fund departments	$30,000
Office salaries	6,000
Utilities	700
Mechanics' wages	11,000
Inventory of supplies	9,000

3. The garage had uncollected billings of $2,000, accounts payable for supplies of $500, and an inventory of materials and supplies of $1,500 at June 30, 2001.

Required

Prepare journal entries that should be made to establish an Internal Service Fund for the City of Delmas and to record the events for the period given. Also prepare any necessary adjusting and closing entries as of June 30, 2001, the end of the fiscal year.

(AICPA, adapted)

7–4. Central Garage ISF. The City of Ashville operates a central garage through an Internal Service Fund to provide garage space and repairs for all city-owned-and-operated vehicles. The Central Garage Fund was established by a contribution of

$300,000 from the General Fund on July 1, 1999, at which time the land and building were acquired. The after-closing trial balance at June 30, 2001, was as follows:

	Debits	*Credits*
Cash	$110,000	
Due from Other Funds	20,000	
Inventory of Supplies	90,000	
Land	50,000	
Building	250,000	
Allowance for Depreciation—Building		$ 20,000
Machinery and Equipment	65,000	
Allowance for Depreciation—Machinery and Equipment		12,000
Vouchers Payable		42,000
Net Assets—Invested in Capital Assets		333,000
Nets Assets—Unrestricted		178,000
	$585,000	$585,000

The following information applies to the fiscal year ended June 30, 2002:

1. Supplies were purchased on account for $92,000; the perpetual inventory method is used.
2. The cost of supplies used during the year ended June 30, 2002, was $110,000. A physical count taken as of that date showed materials and supplies on hand totaled $72,000 at cost.
3. Salaries and wages paid to employees totaled $235,000, including related costs.
4. A billing was received from the Enterprise Fund for utility charges totaling $30,000, and was paid.
5. Depreciation of the building was recorded in the amount of $10,000; depreciation of the machinery and equipment amounted to $9,000.
6. Billings to other departments for services rendered to them were as follows:

General Fund	$270,000
Water and Sewer Fund	87,000
Special Revenue Fund	40,000

7. Unpaid interfund receivable balances at June 30, 2002, were as follows:

General Fund	$10,000
Special Revenue Fund	17,000

8. Vouchers payable at June 30, 2002, were $16,000.
9. Closing entries for the Central Garage Fund at June 30, 2002, were prepared.

Required

a. Prepare journal entries to record all of the transactions for this period in the Central Garage Fund accounts.

b. Assuming that the City of Ashville has no other internal service funds, name the basic financial statements in which the financial data of the Central Garage Fund should be reported.

7–5. Automotive Service Fund. As of the beginning of a certain year, the Automotive Service Fund of the City of Clarkton had the following post-closing trial balance as of September 30, 2001:

	Debits	*Credits*
Cash	$ 11,000	
Due from Other Funds	20,200	
Service Supplies Inventory	35,300	
Machinery and Equipment	90,000	
Allowance for Depreciation—Machinery and Equipment		$ 18,000
Buildings	210,000	
Allowance for Depreciation—Buildings		70,000
Land	37,000	
Due to Federal Government		1,500
Due to Other Funds		800
Accounts Payable		12,700
Net Assets—Invested in Capital Assets		249,000
Net Assets—Unrestricted		51,500
	$403,500	$403,500

During the fiscal year ended September 30, 2002, the following transactions (summarized) occurred:

1. Employees were paid $290,000 wages in cash; additional wages of $43,500 were withheld for federal income and social security taxes. The employer's share of social security taxes amounted to $23,375.
2. Cash remitted to the federal government during the year for withholding taxes and social security taxes amounted to $65,500.
3. Utility bills received from the City's Utility Fund during the year amounted to $23,500.
4. Office expenses paid in cash during the year amounted to $10,500.
5. Service supplies purchased on account during the year totaled $157,500.
6. Parts and supplies used during the year totaled $152,300 (at cost).
7. Charges to departments during the fiscal year were as follows:

General Fund	$294,000
Street Fund	266,000

8. Unpaid balances at year-end were as follows:

General Fund	$10,000
Street Fund	20,000

9. Payments to the Utility Fund totaled $21,800.
10. Accounts Payable at year-end amounted to $13,250.
11. Annual depreciation is recorded at the following rates:

Machinery and Equipment	10%
Buildings	3

12. Revenue and expense accounts for the year were closed.

Required

a. Prepare a Statement of Revenues, Expenses, and Changes in Net Assets for the year. Classify expenses as to direct and indirect costs. Wages and payroll taxes are considered to be 90 percent direct and 10 percent indirect. Utility services are estimated to be 80 percent direct and 20 percent indirect. Parts and supplies used, and depreciation of machinery and equipment are considered direct costs; all other costs are considered indirect costs.

b. Comment on the evident success of the pricing policy of this fund, assuming that user charges are intended to cover all operating expenses, including depreciation, but are not expected to provide a net income in excess of 3 percent of billings to departments.

c. Prepare a Statement of Net Assets for the Automotive Service Fund as of September 30, 2002.

d. Prepare a Statement of Cash Flows for the Automotive Service Fund for the year ended September 30, 2002.

7–6. Insurance Internal Service Fund. The City of Dalton operates an Internal Service Fund to manage and contract for the various kinds of insurance carried by the City. It pays all premiums to the insurers; then, as premiums expire, they are charged to the specific funds to which they pertain. Operating costs, consisting of personnel, rent, utilities, and miscellaneous other expenses, are charged to the insured funds by adding an "operating charge" to expired premium charges. For the current year, the operating charge is 10 percent of premium expirations billed. Operating surpluses or deficits are usually small in amount and are closed at year-end to Net Assets—Unrestricted. Insurers pay directly to insured funds and all losses are borne by the applicable funds; neither are recorded in the Insurance Fund. At June 30, 2001, the trial balance of the Insurance Fund was as follows:

Cash	$ 5,650	
Due from Other Funds	30,000	
Prepaid Insurance Premiums	236,945	
Vouchers Payable		$105,945
Net Assets—Unrestricted		166,650
	$272,595	$272,595

During the year ended June 30, 2002, the following transactions, in summary form, occurred:

1. The fund was billed by insurance companies for $132,625 in premiums falling due on insurance coverage for the various funds of the city.
2. A total of $216,700 was charged to various funds on account of premiums that expired during the year in the amount of $197,000 and $19,700 of operating charges thereon.
3. Operating Expenses paid in cash during the year were:

Salaries and Wages	$12,400
Rent	5,200
Utilities	860
Miscellaneous	800
Total	$19,260

The rent and the utilities were paid to other funds; Miscellaneous was paid to external suppliers.

4. A total of $4,000 was received from insurance companies as premium adjustments during the year. This amount, plus $300 billed previously for operating charges, was credited to the amount owed by various funds for the current year's expirations.
5. $127,000 was paid on amounts owed to insurance companies, for the benefit of funds and agencies of the City of Dalton.
6. Additional permanent financing for the fund was received in the form of a $75,000 contribution of cash from the General Fund.
7. $170,500 was collected from the various funds. Of this amount, $155,000 was for expirations of premiums and $15,500 was for the related operating charge, both previously billed.
8. Prepare appropriate closing entries as of June 30, 2002.

Required

a. State what you consider to be the justification for operation of a separate fund for accounting for insurance premium payments and expirations.

b. In the fund described above there are no transactions related to settlement of losses. State the reason why.

c. Prepare entries in general journal form to record the transactions of the Insurance Fund, including closing entries, for the fiscal year ended June 30, 2002.

d. Prepare a Statement of Net Assets as of June 30, 2002.

e. Prepare a Statement of Revenues, Expenses, and Changes in Net Assets for the fiscal year ended June 30, 2002.

f. Prepare a Statement of Cash Flows for the fiscal year ended June 30, 2002.

7–7. Utility Plant Fund. Webster City issued bonds for the construction of an addition to its utility plant that totaled $9,000,000 and bore interest at the rate of 6 percent per year. The bonds were sold at par on January 15, 2001, the day the construction contract was signed; proceeds were invested on that date at the rate of 6 percent per year. On March 15, investments in the face amount of $1,500,000 plus accrued interest, were sold, in order to make a progress payment to the contractor. Investments in the face amount of $1,500,000, plus accrued interest, were sold on May 15 in order to make the second progress payment to the contractor. On July 15, semiannual bond interest due was paid. Also on July 15, semiannual interest on investments on hand on that date was collected, then investments in the face amount of $3,000,000 were sold in order to make a progress payment to the contractor. On September 15, investments in the face amount of $3,000,000, plus accrued interest, were sold in order to make a progress payment to the contractor. On November 15, 2001, cash in the amount of $3,000,000 derived from operations of the utility was used for the final payment to the contractor; the utility plant addition was deemed completed on that date.

Required

a. From the information above:

(1) Compute the bond interest paid or accrued during the period of construction, January 15–November 15.

(2) Compute interest earned during the period of construction on the investment of the bond proceeds.

(3) Show in general journal form the entry to capitalize the net interest cost as a part of the cost of the plant addition, as required by GASB standards.

b. Assuming the amount of interest on utility resources generated from operations and used for construction that is to be capitalized as a part of the cost of the addition to the utility plant is $202,250, show in general journal form the entry to capitalize the imputed interest.

c. State, or illustrate, how the debt component of the Allowance for Funds Used During Construction (see your answer to part *a*(3) of this problem) should be reported in the utility's operating statement for the fiscal year ended December 31, 2001.

d. State, or illustrate, how the equity component of the Allowance for Funds Used During Construction (see your answer to part *b* of this problem) should be reported in the utility's operating statement for the fiscal year ended December 31, 2001.

7–8. Water Utility Fund. The Council of the City of Templeton directed that $1,000,000 cash be transferred from the City's General Fund as a permanent contribution to a newly created Water Utility Fund. The Water Utility Fund is *not* regulated by any regulatory agency. The cash is intended to cover the purchase price of the Southland Water Company, plus an additional amount to serve as initial working capital for the new activity. At June 30, 2001, the effective date of purchase, the Southland Company had the following after-closing trial balance:

	Debits	*Credits*
Utility Plant in Service	$2,195,000	
Allowance for Depreciation—Utility Plant		$1,357,000
Cash	29,000	
Accounts Receivable	64,000	
Estimated Uncollectible Receivables		26,000
Materials and Supplies	66,000	
Vouchers Payable		99,000
Miscellaneous Accruals		28,000
Capital Stock		1,000,000
Retained Earnings	156,000	
	$2,510,000	$2,510,000

The acquisition occurred as follows:

1. The General Fund contribution was received on June 27, 2001.
2. As of June 30, 2001, the City of Templeton Water Utility Fund acquired the assets of the Southland Water Company, excluding cash. Receivables were purchased at half of their face value. When the purchased assets were recorded, the allowance for uncollectible receivables was increased to establish the new book value of receivables. The vendor's liabilities were assumed. A cash payment of $900,000 was made for the net assets of the water utility. (Hint: Record Accounts Receivable, Materials and Supplies, Accounts Payable, and Miscellaneous Accruals at the amounts shown in the trial balance. Increase Estimated Uncollectible Receivables to $32,000. Amounts shown for Southland Water Company's Cash, Capital Stock, and Retained Earnings accounts should not be recorded by the Water Utility Fund.)

Required

a. Record in general journal form the entries that should be made in the Water Utility Fund for the events of June 27 and June 30, 2001.

b. Prepare in conformity with GAAP a Statement of Net Assets for the City of Templeton Water Utility Fund as of June 30, 2001.

7–9. This problem continues the preceding problem. During the year ended June 30, 2002, the following transactions and events occurred in the City of Templeton Water Utility Fund:

1. On July 1, 2001, to finance needed plant improvements, the Water Utility Fund borrowed $500,000 from a local bank on notes secured by a pledge of water utility revenues. The notes mature in five years and bear interest at the annual rate of 8 percent.
2. Accrued expenses at June 30, 2001, were paid in cash.
3. Billings to nongovernmental customers for water usage during the year totaled $632,000; billings to the General Fund totaled $40,000.
4. Liabilities for the following were recorded during the year:

Materials and supplies	$ 88,000
Source of supply expenses	32,000
Pumping expenses	40,500
Water treatment expenses	51,500
Transmission and distribution expenses	68,000
Customer accounts expenses	93,000
Administrative and general expenses	76,000
Construction work in progress	357,000
Total	$806,000

5. Materials and supplies were used by the following departments in the following amounts: Source of Supply, $10,800; Pumping, $6,500; Treatment, $34,500; Transmission and Distribution, $32,200; total, $84,000.
6. On July 2, 2002, utility plant assets that had a historical cost of $25,000 were sold for $15,000 cash.
7. $28,000 of old accounts receivable were written off.
8. During fiscal 2002, the utility instituted a program of deposits to reduce meter damage and customer defaults on water bills. Cash amounting to $15,000 was collected during the year (debit Cash—Customer Deposits).
9. Accounts receivable collections totaled $460,000 for the fiscal year from nongovernmental customers and $38,000 from the General Fund.
10. $800,000 of accounts payable were paid in cash.
11. $500 was recorded as interest expense accumulated on customers' deposits (credit Customer Deposits).
12. Depreciation expense for the year of $47,050 was recorded.
13. Bills for materials and supplies, $7,000, were received and approved for payment on June 30, 2002.
14. One year's interest on notes payable was paid.
15. Interest on long-term notes was charged to Construction Work in Progress.
16. The provision for uncollectible accounts was increased by an amount equal to 1 percent of the sales of water to nongovernmental customers for the year.
17. Cash in the amount of $100,000 was transferred to Restricted Assets—Cash for eventual redemption of five-year notes. As required by the loan agreement, net assets in the same amount were recorded as restricted.
18. Operating statement accounts for the year were closed.

Required

a. Record the transactions for the year in general journal form.

b. Prepare a Statement of Net Assets as of June 30, 2002.

c. Prepare a Statement of Revenues, Expenses, and Changes in Net Assets for the year ended June 30, 2002.

d. Prepare a Statement of Cash Flows for the City of Templeton Water Utility Fund for the fiscal year ended June 30, 2002, assuming that cash outflows for operating activities included $310,000 for wages and salaries.

e. On the basis of your analysis of the financial statements, comment on any matters that should be brought to the attention of the management of the City of Templeton Water Utility Fund. What actions do you suggest management should take?

Continuous Problem

7–B. Internal Service Fund. The City of Bingham established a Stores and Services Fund to be operated as an internal service fund to improve purchasing procedures and facilitate inventory management.

Required

a. Open a general journal for the Stores and Services Fund; enter the following transaction:

In June 2002, the Stores and Services Fund recorded the receipt of the long-term loan from the General Fund (see Transaction 15 of part *g* of Problem 4–B).

b. Although no further transactions took place in the year ended June 30, 2002, the Stores and Services Fund was required to prepare (1) a Statement of Net Assets as of that date and (2) a Statement of Cash Flows for the year ended June 30, 2002, for inclusion in the City of Bingham's annual report.

c. In order to put the Stores and Services Fund on a completely self-sustaining basis, it was decided to charge using departments for the cost of stores plus a markup sufficient to recover expected cash expenses plus depreciation of equipment. Stores issues for one year were forecast to be $300,000 at cost. Compute the markup rate based on cost from the following information:

In addition to rent of $500 per month, the estimated expenses were $3,600 a year for utilities; $46,800 for salaries and fringe benefits; and $2,400 a year for operation and maintenance of warehouse equipment. The warehouse equipment was in the basement of City Hall; nobody was quite clear as to when it had been purchased, for what purpose, by whom, or how much it had cost. It was usable, however; and after it was cleaned and minor repairs were made by the Department of Public Works employees, the equipment was turned over to the Stores and Services Fund. The fair value of the equipment is estimated to be $12,000; its remaining useful life is estimated at 10 years.

d. Record in the Stores and Services Fund general journal all of the following transactions, which took place in July 2002. Use account titles and practices illustrated in Chapter. 7.

(1) Warehouse and office space was not available in city-owned buildings; space was rented in a privately owned building for $500 a month. Five percent of the space is assigned to Purchasing, 5 percent to Administration, and 90 percent to Warehousing. Six months' rent was paid in advance. (Charge Prepaid Rent.)

(2) Record the fair value of the equipment contributed to the Stores and Services Fund. Assume the General Fund was given credit for the contribution.

(3) Invoices for stores received were approved for payment in the amount of $30,000.

(4) Vouchers amounting to $20,000 were paid, as was payroll totaling $3,600. (For the payroll, charge Purchasing Expenses, $800; Administrative Expenses, $800; and Warehousing Expenses, $2,000.)

(5) Invoices for utilities for the month were approved for payment in the amount of $300. (Charge to Warehousing Expenses.)

(6) Stores costing $25,000 were issued to the General Fund; an interfund invoice in the proper amount was prepared.

(7) Expenses for operation and maintenance of warehouse equipment totaled $200. This amount was approved for payment.

(8) The Stores and Services Fund used stores of its own that had cost $100. (Charge Administrative Expenses.)

(9) Adjusting and closing entries were recorded as of the end of the first month of operations.

e. Prepare a Statement of Revenues and Expenses and Changes in Net Assets for this fund for July 2002.

Enterprise Fund. The city water utility is owned and operated by the City of Bingham. The water utility was originally constructed and operated by a private corporation, but it was sold to the City 30 years before the year for which transactions are given. The post-closing trial balance of the Water Utility Fund, as of June 30, 2001, follows.

CITY OF BINGHAM
WATER UTILITY FUND
TRIAL BALANCE
AS OF JUNE 30, 2001

	Debits	*Credits*
Cash	$ 144,952	
Customer Accounts Receivable	77,720	
Accumulated Provision for Uncollectible Accounts		$ 2,360
Due from Other Funds	7,000	
Inventory of Supplies	47,073	
Restricted Cash—Customer Deposits	27,638	
Utility Plant in Service	9,500,695	
Accumulated Depreciation—Utility Plant		2,006,139
Property Held for Future Use	100,000	
Construction Work in Progress	594,700	
Accounts Payable		39,210

	Debits	Credits
Matured Interest Payable		217,050
Customer Deposits		27,638
Revenue Bonds Payable, 6%		7,235,000
Unamortized Bond Discount	32,600	
Net Assets, Unrestricted		18,125
Net Assets, Invested in Plant (net)		986,856
Totals	$10,532,378	$10,532,378

You will need the following additional information about accounts shown on the June 30, 2001, trial balance:

Matured Interest represents six months' accrual of interest on the 6 percent Revenue Bonds. Interest is payable annually on January 1 of each year. Unamortized Bond Discount is credited once a year for the amortization applicable to the year. Amortization is computed by the straight-line method. The balance of $32,600 is to be amortized over 20 years commencing July 1, 2001.

Required

f. Open a general journal for the Water Utility Fund and enter the transactions shown, as necessary. All transactions occurred during the year ended June 30, 2002. Use the account titles shown in this chapter.

(1) Billings to nonmunicipal customers for water service for the year totaled $1,468,368. Billings to the City of Bingham for water service totaled $20,000.

(2) Collections from customers totaled $1,445,568; from the City, $7,000.

(3) Construction work authorized amounted to $234,000. As a part of this, a contract for $112,000 was signed with a private firm; the remainder of the work was to be done by water utility employees.

(4) Materials and supplies in the amount of $260,800 were ordered. All of these were received during the period. The invoices agreed with the purchase orders and receiving reports and were approved for payment. A perpetual inventory system is used for all materials and supplies.

(5) Payrolls totaling $289,765 for operations; $83,210 for maintenance; and $36,000 for construction were paid.

(6) Materials and supplies issued during the period amounted to $120,000 for operations; $52,000 for maintenance; and $84,000 for construction.

(7) All bond interest due during the year was paid. Debt discount was amortized on the straight-line basis.

(8) Interest of $14,500 was charged to Construction Work in Progress.

(9) A progress billing for $56,000 was received from the construction contractor and paid.

(10) Certain assets under construction at the start of the year and certain of those started during the year were completed and placed in service. The costs incurred on this construction totaled $456,350.

(11) The water utility paid $178,342 to the general fund as a contribution in lieu of property taxes.

(12) Collection efforts were discontinued on bills amounting to $1,965; the customers owing the bills had paid deposits and interest to the water utility in the amount of $672.

(13) Customer deposits and interest thereon amounting to $1,274 were applied to the final bills of customers discontinuing service. Additional deposits and interest amounting to $1,510 were refunded by check to customers discontinuing service. Deposits totaling $3,427 were received from new customers.

(14) Accounts payable paid during the year amounted to $167,600 for operating supplies and $84,000 for materials used in construction.

(15) Interest on deposits amount to $628 (charge Operation Expense). Depreciation on utility plant was 2 percent of the beginning balance (round charge to the nearest dollar). The Accumulated Provision for Uncollectible Accounts should equal $2,910 at year-end. Make these and all other adjusting and closing entries necessary at year-end, including the entry for accrual of six months' interest on bonds payable.

g. Prepare a Statement of Net Assets for the Water Utility Fund as of the end of the year, June 30, 2002.

h. Prepare a Statement of Revenue, Expenses, and Changes in Net Assets for the Water Utility Fund for the year ended June 30, 2002.

i. Prepare a Statement of Cash Flows for the Water Utility Fund for the year ended June 30, 2002.

Chapter 8 Accounting for Fiduciary Activities—Agency and Trust Funds

Learning Objectives

After reading this chapter, you should be able to:

- Explain the purposes of fiduciary funds and distinguish among agency funds and trust funds (private-purpose, investment, and pension).
- Describe the uses for and characteristics of agency funds.
- Explain the operations of, and accounting and financial reporting for commonly used agency funds.
- Explain the creation, operation, accounting, and financial reporting for:
  - A cash and investment pool (including an investment trust fund),
  - A private-purpose trust fund, and
  - A pension trust fund.

Fiduciary funds, under the GASB *Statement No. 34* reporting model, are used to account for only those activities in which a governmental unit holds assets as an agent or trustee for individuals, organizations, or other governmental units. These private-purpose fiduciary activities are accounted for in agency funds, investment trust funds, private-purpose trust funds, and pension trust funds. Resources that are held in trust for the benefit of the government's own programs or its citizenry should be accounted for in a governmental fund rather than a fiduciary fund. Such public-purpose trusts should be accounted for as special revenue funds if the resources are expendable for the trust purpose. A permanent fund, as illustrated in Chapter 4, should be used to account for trusts in which the trust principal is permanently restricted, but earnings may be used for the specified *public* purpose.

In law, there is a clear distinction between an agency relationship and a trust relationship. In accounting practice, the legalistic distinctions between trust funds and agency funds are not of major significance. The important and perhaps the sole consideration from an accounting standpoint is what can and what cannot be done with the fund's assets in accordance with laws and other pertinent regulations? The name of a particular fund is not a reliable criterion for determining the correct accounting basis for trust and agency funds. Merely calling a fund by one name or another has no influence on the transactions in which it may engage. Trust funds differ from agency funds principally in degree: trust funds often exist over a longer period of time than an agency fund; represent and develop vested interests of a beneficiary to a greater extent; and involve more complex administration and financial accounting and reporting. Agency funds are used only if the governmental unit holds resources in a purely custodial capacity for others. As noted above, specific accounting procedures and limitations depend on the enactment that brought about creation of a particular trust or agency fund, plus all other regulations under which it operates. Regulations include pertinent statutes, ordinances, wills, trust indentures, and other instruments of endowment, resolutions of the governing body, statements of purposes of the fund, kinds and amounts of assets held, and others. This aggregate of factors, or such as are applicable to a given fund, determines the transactions in which it may and should engage.

This chapter illustrates accounting and financial reporting requirements for fiduciary funds. Because fiduciary activities benefit only other individuals, organizations, and governments, rather than the reporting government, GASB *Statement No. 34* excludes the reporting of fiduciary activities in the government-wide financial statements. Thus, fiduciary activities are reported only in the fiduciary fund financial statements.

Agency Funds

GASB standards identify *agency funds* as one of the four types of fiduciary funds. **Agency funds** are used to account for assets held by a governmental unit acting as agent for one or more other governmental units, or for individuals or private organizations. Similarly, if a fund of a governmental unit regularly receives assets that are to be transmitted to other funds of that unit, an agency relationship exists. Assets accounted for in an agency fund belong to the party or parties for which the governmental unit acts as agent. Therefore, *agency fund assets are offset by liabilities equal in amount; no fund equity exists*. GASB *Statement No. 34* requires agency fund assets and liabilities to be recognized on the accrual basis. Revenues, expenditures, and expenses are not recognized in the accounts of agency funds, however.

Unless use of an agency fund is mandated by law, by GASB standards, or by decision of the governing board of a governmental unit, an agency relationship may be accounted for within governmental and/or proprietary funds. For example, local governmental units must act as agent of the federal and state governments in the collection of employees' withholding taxes, retirement contributions, and social security taxes. In the absence of contrary legal requirements or administrative decisions, it is perfectly acceptable to account for the withholdings, and the remittance to federal and state governments, within the funds that account for the gross pay of the employees, as is shown by the illustrative entries in Chapter 4. In general, if an agency relationship is incidental to the primary purposes for which a given fund exists, the relationship is ordinarily discharged on a rather current basis, and the amounts of assets held as agent tend to be small in relation to fund assets, there is no need to create an agency fund unless required by law or administrative decision.

Agency Fund for Special Assessment Debt Service

Readers of Chapters 5 and 6 of this text should recall that GASB standards specify that a governmental unit that has *no* obligation to assume debt service on special assessment debt in the event of property owners' default, but does perform the functions of billing property owners for the assessments, collecting installments of assessments and interest on the assessments, and *from the collections* paying interest and principal on the special assessment debt, should account for those activities by use of an agency fund.

To illustrate *agency fund* accounting for special assessment debt service activities, assume the same information used in Chapter 6 for the City of X except that the governmental unit is not obligated in any manner for the special assessment debt. When the assessments in the amount of $480,000, payable in 10 equal installments, were levied on benefited property owners, the following journal entry was made in the agency fund.

	Debits	*Credits*
1. Assessments Receivable—Current	48,000	
Assessments Receivable—Deferred	432,000	
Due to Special Assessment Bondholders—Principal		480,000

All current assessments receivable were collected (see Entry 2) along with $24,000 interest (5 percent on the previous unpaid receivable balance). As indicated in Chapter 6, any amounts not collected by the due date should be reclassified as Assessments Receivable—Delinquent.

	Debits	*Credits*
2. Cash	72,000	
Assessments Receivable—Current		48,000
Due to Special Assessment Bondholders—Interest		24,000

Special assessment bond principal in the amount of $48,000 and interest in the amount of $24,000 were paid during the current year.

	Debits	Credits
3. Due to Special Assessment Bondholders—Principal	48,000	
Due to Special Assessment Bondholders—Interest	24,000	
Cash		72,000

The second installment of assessments receivable was reclassified at year-end from the Deferred category to the Current category.

	Debits	Credits
4. Assessments Receivable—Current	48,000	
Assessments Receivable—Deferred		48,000

This pattern of journal entries will be repeated during each of the remaining nine years until all special assessment bonds are retired.

Tax Agency Funds

An agency relationship that does, logically, result in the creation of an agency fund is the collection of taxes, or other revenues, by one governmental unit for several of the funds it operates and for other governmental units. State governments commonly collect sales taxes, gasoline taxes, and many other taxes that are apportioned to state agencies and to local governmental units within the state. At the local government level, it is common for an elected county official to serve as collector for all property taxes owed by persons or corporations owning property within the county. Taxes levied by all funds and units within the county are certified to the County Collector for collection. The County Collector is required by law to make periodic distributions of tax collections for each year to each fund or unit in the proportion the levy for that fund or unit bears to the total levy for the year. In many jurisdictions, the law provides that units may request advances or "draws" from the tax agency fund prior to regular distributions; advances are usually limited by law to a specified percentage, often 90 percent, of collections for the period from the last distribution until the date of the advance.

Tax agency fund accounting would be quite simple if all taxes levied for a given year were collected in that year. It is almost always true, however, that collections during any year relate to taxes levied in several prior years as well as taxes levied for the current year, and sometimes include advance collections of taxes for the following year. In many jurisdictions, not only does the total tax rate vary from year to year but the proportion that the rate of each unit (and each fund) bears to the total rate also varies from year to year. Additionally, interest and penalties on delinquent taxes must be collected at statutory rates or amounts at the time delinquent taxes are collected; interest and penalties collected must be distributed to participating funds and units in the same manner that tax collections are distributed.

Illustration of Composition of Total Tax Rates

Assume that the County Collector of Campbell County is responsible for collecting the taxes due in 2002 for the funds and units located within the County. Ordinarily, the taxes levied for each fund and unit within the County are shown in columnar form in a newspaper advertisement as legal notice to taxpayers. In order

Illustration 8–1

COMPOSITION OF TAXES TO BE COLLECTED
BY COUNTY COLLECTOR OF CAMPBELL COUNTY
FOR CERTAIN UNITS WITHIN THE COUNTY
FOR THE YEAR 2002

	Washington Township	*City of Washington*
Total State Rate	$0.01	$ 0.01
County Funds:		
General	1.08	1.08
Capital Projects	0.09	0.09
Debt Service	0.20	0.20
Welfare	0.11	0.11
Total County Rate	1.48	1.48
Library Fund	0.25	0.25
Township Funds:		
General	0.07	0.07
Fire Protection	0.23	—
Total Township	0.30	0.07
School Funds:		
General	4.50	4.50
Capital Projects	0.18	0.18
Debt Service	0.38	0.38
Total School Rate	5.06	5.06
City Funds:		
General		2.53
Street		0.33
Pension		0.25
Debt Service		0.08
Total City Rate		3.19
Total Tax Rates per $100 Assessed Valuation	$7.10	$10.06

to keep the illustrations in this text legible and comprehensible, Illustration 8–1 shows two columns of such a legal advertisement. Real property tax statements are prepared for each parcel of property located within the jurisdiction for which a tax agency fund is operated. Whether each statement discloses the amount of tax that will be distributed to all of the entities that levy taxes on that parcel, or whether the statement shows only the total tax payable to the County Collector, the Collector's Office must be able to compute and distribute all taxes collected to the appropriate units and funds.

For example, Illustration 8–1 shows that a parcel of property located in Washington Township outside the City of Washington would be taxed at the rate of $7.10 per $100 of assessed valuation; whereas if the parcel were inside the city limits, the tax rate would be $10.06. Therefore, if a parcel of property located in Washington Township outside the City had an assessed valuation of $10,000, the total real property tax payable in 2002 would be $710, but a parcel with the same assessed valuation located within the City would be taxed at $1,006. The total of each of these tax statements is comprised of the taxes levied for each unit, as shown in Illustration 8–1. In turn, the taxes levied for each unit are comprised of the taxes levied for funds of that unit, as also shown in Illustration 8–1. The relationship between direct and overlapping debt is discussed in Chapter 6. Note that Illustration 8–1 shows that a person or organization owning property within the City of Washington is required to pay 66 cents of the total rate for debt service (20 cents to Campbell County, 38 cents to the school district, and 8 cents to the City of Washington). Illustration 8–2 summarizes the composition of each tax statement by governmental unit.

In those states in which taxes are levied on personal property, the funds and units that levy the personal property taxes are generally assumed to be the ones that levy taxes on the residence of the owner, unless there is convincing evidence that the situs of the personal property is at another location. Inasmuch as the tax rate levied for each unit and each fund often varies from year to year, it is necessary that all tax collections be identified with the year for which the taxes were levied as well as with the particular parcels for which taxes were collected.

Operation of the Collector's Office often requires the use of substantial administrative, clerical, and computer time and provision of extensive building and computer facilities. Accordingly, it is common for the Collector to be authorized to

Illustration 8–2

2002 TAXES PAYABLE
TO CAMPBELL COUNTY COLLECTOR FOR
PARCEL WITH ASSESSED VALUATION OF $10,000

	Parcel Located	
Amount Levied by	*Outside City*	*In City*
State	$ 1.00	$ 1.00
County	148.00	148.00
Library	25.00	25.00
Township	30.00	7.00
School	506.00	506.00
City	—	319.00
Total	$710.00	$1,006.00

withhold a certain percentage from the collections for each unit, and to remit to the County General Fund (or other fund bearing the expenditures for operating the Tax Agency Fund) the total amount withheld from the collections of other funds.

Accounting for Tax Agency Funds

Taxes levied each year should be recorded in the accounts of each fund of each governmental unit in the manner illustrated in preceding chapters. Although an allowance for estimated uncollectible current taxes would be established in each fund, the *gross* amount of the tax levy for all funds should be recorded in the Tax Agency Fund as a receivable. Note the receivable is designated as belonging to other funds and units, and the receivable is offset in total by a liability. Assuming total real property taxes certified for collection during 2002 amounted to $10,516,400, the Tax Agency Fund entry would be:

	Debits	Credits
1. Taxes Receivable for Other Funds and Units—Current	10,516,400	
Due to Other Funds and Units		10,516,400

It would be necessary, of course, for the County Collector to keep records of the total amount of 2002 taxes to be collected for each of the funds and units that participate in the Tax Agency Fund in order to distribute tax collections properly. Assume that the 2002 taxes were levied for the following units (in order to reduce the detail in this example, a number of the units are combined):

State	$ 10,400
Campbell County	1,480,000
Washington School Corporation	5,060,000
City of Washington	2,400,000
Other units (should be itemized)	1,566,000
	$10,516,400

If collections of 2002 taxes during a certain portion of the year amounted to $5,258,200, the Tax Agency Fund entry would be:

2. Cash	5,258,200	
Taxes Receivable for Other Funds and Units—Current		5,258,200

The tax collections must in an actual case be identified with the parcels of property against which the taxes were levied, because the location of each parcel determines the governmental units and funds that should receive the tax collections. Assuming for the sake of simplicity that the collections for the period represent collections of 50 percent of the taxes levied against each parcel in Campbell County, and that the County General Fund is given 1 percent of all collections for units other than the County as reimbursement for the cost of operating the Tax Agency Fund, the distribution of the $5,258,200 collections would be:

	Taxes Collected (50% of Levy)	Collection Fee (Charged) Received	Cash to Be Distributed
State	$ 5,200	$ (52)	$ 5,148
Campbell County	740,000	45,182	785,182
Washington School Corporation	2,530,000	(25,300)	2,504,700
City of Washington	1,200,000	(12,000)	1,188,000
Other units (should be itemized)	783,000	(7,830)	775,170
	$5,258,200	$ -0-	$5,258,200

If cash is not distributed as soon as the above computation is made, the entry by the Tax Agency Fund to record the liability would be:

	Debits	Credits
3. Due to Other Funds and Units	5,258,200	
Due to State		5,148
Due to Campbell County		785,182
Due to Washington School Corporation		2,504,700
Due to City of Washington		1,188,000
Due to Other Units		775,170

If, as is likely, collections during 2002 include collections of taxes that were levied for 2001, 2000, and preceding years, computations must be made to determine the appropriate distribution of collections for each tax year to each fund and unit that levied taxes against the property for which collections have been received.

When cash is distributed by the Tax Agency Fund, the liability accounts shown in Entry 3 should be debited and Cash credited. If cash is advanced to one or more governmental units or funds prior to a regular periodic distribution, the debits to the liability accounts may precede the credits. By year-end, all advances should be settled, all distributions computed and recorded, and all cash distributed to the units and funds for which the Tax Agency Fund is being operated. Therefore, if all those events have taken place, the year-end Balance Sheet for the Tax Agency Fund would consist of one asset: Taxes Receivable for Other Funds and Units—Delinquent; and one liability: Due to Other Funds and Units.

Entries Made by Funds and Units Participating in Tax Agency Funds

Each unit that receives a distribution must record the appropriate portion of it in each of the funds it maintains. In each fund it must also record the fact that cash received differs from the amount of taxes collected by the fee paid to the County General Fund. The fee paid is, of course, recorded as an Expenditure. For example, the computation for the entries to be made by the various funds of Washington School Corporation would be (using the rates shown in Illustration 8–1):

	2002 Rate	Collections of 2002 Taxes	Collection Fee Paid	Cash Received
School Funds:				
General	$4.50	$2,250,000	$22,500	$2,227,500
Capital Projects	0.18	90,000	900	89,100
Debt Service	0.38	190,000	1,900	188,100
Total	$5.06	$2,530,000	$25,300	$2,504,700

From the computations it can be seen that the entry made in the Washington School Corporation General Fund for the 2002 collections distributed should be:

	Debits	Credits
Cash	2,227,500	
Expenditures	22,500	
Taxes Receivable—Current		2,250,000

Similar entries would be made in the other two funds of the Washington School Corporation and in all the funds of units that paid a tax collection fee to the County General Fund. Collection by the County General Fund of taxes collected for it and the fee collected for it is computed as follows.

	2002 Rate	Collections of 2002 Taxes	Collection Fee	Cash Received
County Funds:				
General	$1.08	$540,000	$45,182	$585,182
Capital Projects	.09	45,000	–0–	45,000
Debt Service	.20	100,000	–0–	100,000
Welfare	.11	55,000	–0–	55,000
Total	$1.48	$740,000	$45,182	$785,182

The entry to be made in the General Fund of Campbell County for the 2002 collections distributed should be:

Cash	585,182	
Taxes Receivable—Current		540,000
Revenues		45,182

"Pass-Through" Agency Funds

Grants, entitlements, or shared revenues from the federal or a state government often pass through a lower level of government (primary recipient) before distribution to a secondary recipient. Accounting for such "pass-through" grants depends on whether the primary recipient government is deemed to have *administrative involvement* or *direct financial involvement* in the grants. According to GASB standards:

> A recipient government has administrative involvement if, for example, it (a) monitors secondary recipients for compliance with program-specific requirements, (b) determines eligibility of secondary recipients or projects, even if using grantor-established criteria, or (c) has the ability to exercise discretion in how the funds are allocated. A recipient government has direct financial involvement if, for example, it finances some direct program costs because of a grantor-imposed matching requirement or is liable for disallowed costs.[1]

More often than not, the criteria for administrative or direct financial involvement are met, in which case the primary recipient government must recognize a revenue for the receipt and an expenditure or expense for the transfer in a governmental fund, private-purpose trust fund, or proprietary fund. If, however, neither administrative nor financial involvement is deemed to exist, then a "Pass-Through" Agency Fund must be used and no revenue or expenditure/expense is recognized.

To illustrate accounting for a "Pass-Through" Agency Fund, assume that $5 million of federal financial assistance is received by a state government from the federal government, the full amount of which must be passed to local governments according to predetermined eligibility requirements and in amounts according to a predetermined formula. Since the state government is serving merely as a "cash conduit" in this case, the use of a Pass-Through Agency Fund is deemed appropriate. The entry to record receipt of the $5 million in the Pass-Through Agency Fund would be:

	Debits	*Credits*
Cash	5,000,000	
Due to Other Units		5,000,000

Assuming all monies were disbursed to the secondary recipients during the current fiscal year, the Pass-Through Agency Fund entry would be:

Due to Other Units	5,000,000	
Cash		5,000,000

The receipt of Cash or other assets from a Pass-Through Agency Fund should be accounted for by the recipient in conformity with GASB standards discussed previously: Governmental fund types are to recognize all grants as revenue when the grant proceeds are available for use for the purposes of the fund and eligibility requirements have been met. If grant proceeds are available immediately, the Revenues account is credited; if some eligibility requirement must be met, the Deferred Revenues account should be credited at the time the grant proceeds are recognized

[1]GASB *Statement No. 24*, par. 5 (GASB, Norwalk, CT), 1994.

as assets, and amounts transferred from Deferred Revenues to Revenues as eligibility requirements are met. Proprietary fund types recognize as nonoperating revenues the proceeds of grants for operating purposes, or that may be expended at the discretion of the recipient government; if the terms of the grant restrict the use of the proceeds to the acquisition or construction of capital assets, the proceeds must be recorded as capital contributions (see Chapter 7).

Financial Reporting of Agency Funds

As mentioned earlier in this chapter, fiduciary activities are reported only in the fiduciary fund financial statements; they have no effect on the governmental or business-type activities of the primary government reported in the government-wide financial statements. As shown in Illustration 2–9, agency fund financial information is reported in a separate column of the Statement of Fiduciary Net Assets. Agency funds are not included in the Statement of Changes in Fiduciary Net Assets (see Illustration 2–10) because they have no net assets (assets minus liabilities equals zero net assets) and therefore have no *changes* in net assets. GASB standards do not require disclosure of the assets and liabilities of individual agency funds, but a government may optionally include in its Comprehensive Annual Financial Report a combining statement of net assets displaying the assets and liabilities of each agency fund in separate columns.

Trust Funds

In addition to agency funds, just discussed, the Fiduciary Fund classification includes Investment Trust Funds, Private-Purpose Trust Funds, and Pension Trust Funds.

Historically, trust funds have been created to account for assets received by the government in a trust agreement in which the assets are to be invested to produce income to be used for specified purposes (generally cultural or educational). The majority of such trusts benefit the government's own programs or its citizenry. As discussed and illustrated in Chapter 4, under GASB *Statement No. 34*, trusts that benefit the government's own program or citizens at large are now accounted for as either special revenue funds or *permanent funds*, depending on whether the principal of the gift is expendable for the specified purpose or permanently restricted for investment, with only the earnings therefrom expendable for the specified purposes. As discussed in Chapter 4, both special revenue funds and permanent funds are governmental fund types. Under the provisions of *Statement No. 34*, only trusts that benefit others, such as individuals, organizations, or other governments, are accounted for in fiduciary funds.

The following section illustrates the accounting for an Investment Pool, in which some participants are other (external) governments and some are funds of the sponsoring government. **External investment pools** are centrally managed investment portfolios (pools) that manage the investments of other governments and perhaps not-for-profit organizations outside the reporting entity of the government that administers the pool (the sponsoring government). An **investment trust fund** is used to account for the assets, liabilities, net assets, and changes in net assets corresponding to the equity of the *external* participants. Typically, as in the following example, the sponsoring government also participates in the pool; however, its equity is considered *internal* and is not reported in the financial statements of the investment trust fund. Instead, the net assets and changes therein relating to the internal portion of the pool are presented in the financial statements of each participating fund, and in the governmental activities and business-type activities of the sponsoring government's government-wide financial statements. As mentioned earlier in this chapter, the financial information for investment trust funds is reported only in the fiduciary fund financial statements (those shown in Illustrations 2–9 and 2–10) and is not reported in the government-wide financial statements.

Investment Pools—Investment Trust Fund Accounting

Effective management of investments (and in some cases idle cash) often is enhanced by placing the investments of the funds in a pool under the control of the Treasurer or a professional investment manager, either within the Treasurer's office or in a financial institution such as a bank or investment firm. If the investment pool is an *internal investment pool* (participating funds are all within the same governmental unit), the investments in the pool may properly be placed under accounting control by use of an agency fund. However, each participating fund is required for financial reporting purposes to report its proportionate share of pooled cash and investments as fund assets and the assets and liabilities of the agency fund are not reported in the governmental unit's external financial statements.[2] For internal management purposes, it may be more useful for participating funds to use the account title Equity in Pooled Cash and Investments, the account title used in the illustrative agency fund journal entries shown later in this section.

If an investment pool has *external* participants, GASB standards require that an *investment trust fund* be established to account for the external investment pool.[3] Investment trust funds are accounted for using an economic resources measurement focus and the full accrual basis of accounting.

Creation of an Investment Pool

Earnings on pooled investments and changes in fair value of investments are allocated to the participants having an equity in the pool in proportion to their relative contributions to the pool. To ensure an equitable division of earnings and changes in fair value, it is necessary to revalue all investments in the pool, and all investments being brought into the pool or removed from the pool, to their **fair value** as of the time that investments of a fund are being brought into or removed from the pool.[4] Each fund of the sponsoring government and external participant that contributes investments to the pool should debit Equity in Pooled Investments, or some similar account, for the fair value of the investments, credit the Investments account for the carrying value (cost or fair value at the time the

[2]GASB, *Codification*, Sec. I50.112.

[3]Ibid., Sec. I50.116.

[4]GASB standards define *fair value* as the amount at which an investment could be exchanged in a current transaction between willing parties, other than in a forced liquidation sale. GASB, *Codification*, Sec. I50.105.

Illustration 8–3 Assets Transferred to Create Drew County Investment Pool

Assets Transferred	*Fair Value at 12-31-01*	*Fair Value at 1-10-02*	*Change in Fair Value*	*Accrued Interest*
Drew County Debt Service Fund:				
Cash	$ 1,000,000	$ 1,000,000	$ –0–	$ –0–
U.S. Agency Obligations	13,373,000	13,425,000	52,000	425,000
Town of Calvin Debt Service Fund:				
U.S. Treasury Bills	9,568,000	9,545,000	(23,000)	192,000
U.S. Agency Obligations	158,700	160,000	1,300	3,000
Calvin Independent School District Capital Projects Fund:				
U.S. Agency Obligations	2,789,000	2,800,000	11,000	76,900
Repurchase Agreements	2,060,000	2,060,000	–0–	13,100
Totals	$28,948,700	$28,990,000	$41,300	$710,000

investments were previously marked to fair value), and credit or debit Revenues—Change in Fair Value of Investments, depending on whether the current fair value is higher or lower than carrying value, respectively. Note that a net debit balance in the Revenues—Change in Fair Value of Investments account would be reported as a contra-revenue item in the operating statement of the appropriate fund, as a component of investment income, and not as an expenditure or expense.

Illustration of the Creation of an Investment Fund. On January 10, 2002, Drew County decided to create a new investment pool, to be accounted for as an *investment trust fund*. Operating expenses of the pool, primarily for personnel time, office supplies, computer, telephone, and postage, are considered nominal and therefore will not be charged to the pool. The initial participants in the pool are the County's own Debt Service Fund and two external participants, the Town of Calvin's Debt Service Fund and the Calvin Independent School District's Capital Projects Fund. As discussed previously, the equity pertaining to the Drew County Debt Service Fund represents an *internal* investment pool, so its proportionate share of the Investment Pool's assets are allocated back to the Debt Service Fund for financial reporting purposes and are not reported as part of the Investment Trust Fund. The proportionate share of assets allocated to *external* participants, however, is properly reported in the financial statements of the Investment Trust Fund.

Illustration 8–3 shows the specific cash and investments that were transferred on January 10, 2002, to create the Drew County Investment Pool.

At the time the Drew County Investment Pool is created, journal entries are required in the accounts of the Drew County Debt Service Fund and Town of Calvin Debt Service Fund, the Calvin Independent School District Capital Projects Fund, and the Investment Trust Fund to record creation of the fund. The journal entries in the Drew County Debt Service Fund and Drew County Investment

Trust Fund (the Investment Pool) to create the investment pool are shown in Entries 1a and 1b below. Entries in the funds of the external participants would be similar to that for the Drew County Debt Service Fund and therefore are omitted here for the sake of brevity.

	Debits	Credits
Drew County Debt Service Fund:		
1a. Equity in Pooled Investments	14,850,000	
Cash		1,000,000
Investments—U.S. Agency Obligations		13,373,000
Revenues—Change in Fair Value of Investments		52,000
Revenues—Investment Earnings		425,000
Drew County Investment Pool:		
1b. Cash	1,000,000	
Investments—U.S. Treasury Bills	9,545,000	
Investments—U.S. Agency Obligations	16,385,000	
Investments—Repurchase Agreements	2,060,000	
Accrued Interest Receivable	710,000	
Due to Debt Service Fund		14,850,000
Additions—Deposits in Pooled Investments—Town of Calvin		9,900,000
Additions—Deposits in Pooled Investments—Calvin Independent School District		4,950,000

A trial balance prepared for the Drew County Investment Pool immediately after Entry 1b has been posted to the Pool's general ledger is presented in Illustration 8–4.

Illustration 8–4

DREW COUNTY
INVESTMENT POOL
TRIAL BALANCE
AS OF JANUARY 10, 2002

Account Title	*Debits*	*Credits*
Cash	$ 1,000,000	
Investments—U.S. Treasury Bills	9,545,000	
Investments—U.S. Agency Obligations	16,385,000	
Investments—Repurchase Agreements	2,060,000	
Accrued Interest Receivable	710,000	
Due to Debt Service Fund		$14,850,000
Additions—Deposits in Pooled Investments—Town of Calvin		9,900,000
Additions—Deposits in Pooled Investments—Calvin Independent School District		4,950,000
Totals	$29,700,000	$29,700,000

On February 1, 2002, Drew County sold tax-supported bonds in the amount of $15,000,000 to finance the construction of roads and bridges. The proceeds of the bonds are added to the pool for investment until such time as they are needed for Capital Projects Fund disbursements. As of February 1, 2002, the U.S. Treasury bills in the pool have a current fair value of $9,535,000 ($10,000 less than the carrying value reported in the trial balance sheet shown in Illustration 8–4), and the U.S. Agency Obligations in the pool have a fair value of $16,695,000 ($310,000 more than the carrying value reported in the trial balance); the fair value of the repurchase agreement is the same as reported in the trial balance. The balance of the Cash account was still $1,000,000 as of February 1, 2002. Therefore, total assets of the pool, revalued to fair value as of February 1, 2002, amount to $30,000,000 (a net increase of $300,000 over the carrying values previously reported).

In the Investment Pool accounts, the $300,000 increase in carrying value of assets should be credited to a liability account for the share of the internal participant (Drew County's Debt Service Fund) and to "Additions" accounts (addition to net assets, similar to revenue) for the shares of the external participants, based on their equitable proportions in the pool just prior to the asset revaluation. The liability to the Debt Service Fund, therefore, is increased by $150,000 (300,000 × 14,850/29,700); Additions—Change in Fair Value—Town of Calvin is credited for $100,000 (300,000 × 9,900/29,700); and Additions—Change in Fair Value—Calvin Independent School District is credited for $50,000 (300,000 × 4,950/29,700). Note that the equity of each participant in the pool remains proportionately the same (i.e., the amount due to the Town of Calvin is $10,000,000 after revaluing the investments to current fair value; total liabilities and net assets (if the Additions accounts were closed) of the pool are $30,000,000; 10,000/30,000 = 9,900/29,700, etc.). The journal entry in the Investment Pool summarizing the revaluation of investments and the Capital Projects entry into the Investment Pool is given as:

	Debits	*Credits*
Drew County Investment Pool:		
2. Cash	15,000,000	
Investments—U.S. Agency Obligations	310,000	
Investments—U.S. Treasury Bills		10,000
Due to Debt Service Fund		150,000
Due to Capital Projects Fund		15,000,000
Additions—Change in Fair Value of Investments—Town of Calvin		100,000
Additions—Change in Fair Value of Investments—Calvin Independent School District		50,000

After revaluation of investments in the pool and receipt of $15,000,000 cash from proceeds of bonds sold to finance road and bridge construction, the Trial Balance of the Investment Pool becomes as shown in Illustration 8–5.

Operation of a Cash and Investment Pool

Although the capital projects fund invested $15,000,000 cash in the pool, upon admission to the pool that Fund no longer has a specific claim on the cash of the

Illustration 8–5

DREW COUNTY
INVESTMENT POOL
TRIAL BALANCE
AS OF FEBRUARY 1, 2002

Account Title	*Debits*	*Credits*
Cash	$16,000,000	
Investments—U. S. Treasury Bills	9,535,000	
Investments—U.S. Agency Obligations	16,695,000	
Investments—Repurchase Agreements	2,060,000	
Accrued Interest Receivable	710,000	
Due to Debt Service Fund		$ 15,000,000
Due to Capital Projects Fund		15,000,000
Additions—Deposits in Pooled Investments—Town of Calvin		9,900,000
Additions—Deposits in Pooled Investments—Calvin Independent School District		4,950,000
Additions—Change in Fair Value of Investments—Town of Calvin		100,000
Additions—Change in Fair Value of Investments—Calvin Independent School District		50,000
Totals	$45,000,000	$45,000,000

pool; rather, it (and each other Fund or unit that is a member of the pool) has a proportionate interest in each of the assets of the pool, and will share in earnings, gains, and losses of the pool in that proportion. Ordinarily, it is inconvenient and unnecessary to apportion to liability and additions to net asset accounts for each receipt of dividends or interest and each revaluation of the portfolio to fair value (some pools revalue to fair value daily). It is simpler to accumulate the earnings in an *Undistributed Earnings on Pooled Investments* account and the unrealized and realized gains and losses in a *Reserve for Change in Fair Value of Pooled Investments* account (both of these accounts are clearing accounts), and to make periodic distributions from these accounts to the specific liability and additions to net asset accounts for pool participants.

The frequency of distributions depends on whether all cash of all funds is pooled along with investments, or whether each fund retains an operating cash account. In the former case, the pool would have frequent receipts attributable to collections of revenues and receivables of the funds, and would have daily disbursements on behalf of the funds; in this case, the interest of each fund in the pool would have to be recomputed each day. If, however, a working cash balance is retained in each active fund, the receipts and disbursements of pool cash would be much less frequent, and the distribution of gains and losses, and earnings, and recomputation of the interest of each fund in the pool could be correspondingly less frequent.

As an example of accounting for earnings on investments of a pool, assume the pool shown in Illustration 8–5 collects interest of $1,610,000, including $710,000 accrued as of March 31, 2002. An appropriate entry would be:

	Debits	*Credits*
3. Cash	1,610,000	
Accrued Interest Receivable		710,000
Undistributed Earnings on Pooled Investments		900,000

By the time the earnings are to be distributed, the fair value of all investments may have changed. Even if this is true, the proportionate interest of each fund will not have changed because each participant continues to bear gains and losses in the same proportion until a participant changes all participants' proportionate interest in the pool by contributing additional assets to the pool or taking assets out of the pool. Therefore, in this example, when earnings are distributed the shares apportioned to the funds are: Drew County Debt Service Fund, 15/45 or 3/9; Drew County Capital Projects Fund, 15/45 or 3/9; Town of Calvin, 10/45 or 2/9; and Calvin Independent School District, 5/45 or 1/9. The entry in the Investment Pools to distribute $900,000 of earnings is:

Drew County Investment Pool:		
4a. Undistributed Earnings on Pooled Investments	900,000	
Due to Debt Service Fund		300,000
Due to Capital Projects Fund		300,000
Additions—Investment Earnings—Town of Calvin		200,000
Additions—Investment Earnings—Calvin Independent School District		100,000

After the distribution, each participant has the same proportionate interest in the assets of the pool as it had before the distribution.

As noted previously, internal management of the pool is enhanced if each participant that is a member of the pool maintains an asset account with a title such as Equity in Pooled Investments. The balance of this account in each member's fund should be the reciprocal of the pool's account that reports the pool's liability or net asset balance to that participant (depending on whether the participant is an internal member or external member). Thus, in the Drew County example, the Drew County Debt Service Fund's Equity in Pooled Investments had a debit balance of $15,000,000 as of March 31, 2002, before the earnings distribution. Upon notification of the earnings distribution on the pooled investments, the Debt Service Fund would make the following entry:

	Debits	Credits
Drew County Debt Service Fund:		
4b. Equity in Pooled Investments	300,000	
Revenues—Investment Earnings		300,000

Interest and dividends earned on pooled investments would, of course, increase the equity of the members of the pool, as would realized gains on the sales of investments (excess of fair value on date of sale over carrying price) and unrealized gains resulting from periodic revaluation of the pooled investment portfolio to fair value in times of rising market values of securities held in the portfolio. Realized losses on securities sold (deficit of fair value at prior revaluation date compared with fair value at the sale date), and unrealized losses resulting from periodic revaluation of the portfolio in times of falling market values, both decrease the equity of funds that are members of the pool. In the Drew County Investment Pool example, each member fund maintains an operating cash account. Consequently, the pool does not need to distribute gains and losses daily, so it accumulates realized and unrealized gains and losses in a *Reserve for Change in Fair Value of Pooled Investments* account. This procedure allows a netting of gains and losses in each account, so that only the net realized and unrealized gain (or loss) need be distributed to pool participants, thus saving some clerical or computer time.

GASB standards require that realized and unrealized gains and losses be reported as a single amount, "Change in Fair Value of Investments," as a component of investment income, rather than being reported as separate amounts in the financial statement. However, realized and unrealized gains and losses can be disclosed in the notes to the financial statements, if desired.[5] If a governmental unit intends to disclose realized and unrealized gains or losses, or needs such information for internal management purposes, it may be useful to maintain a separate *Allowance for Changes in Fair Value of Pooled Investments* (a contra-asset account) to record all changes in fair value rather than increasing and decreasing the balance of the investment accounts. This technique permits the investment accounts to be carried at cost.

Assume that during fiscal 2002 the realized gains on sales of pooled investments of the Drew County Cash and Investments Pool, all credited to the Reserve for Change in Fair Value of Pooled Investments, amounted to $235,000 (measured as excess of fair value at the sale dates over prior fair value). During the year, realized losses, all debited to the Reserve account, totaled $50,000 (measured as the deficit of fair value at the sale dates under prior fair value). Thus, there was a net credit of $185,000 for realized gains and losses for the period. Similarly, assume the net effect

[5] GASB, *Codification*, Sec. 1600.113. If the entity opts, however, to disclose realized gains and losses, they must be measured independently of the basis used for accounting recognition in the pool. That is, the realized gains and losses reported in the notes must be measured as the fair value at the sale date of the investments over (under) cost, rather than over (under) fair value at the prior revaluation date.

of marking the portfolio to fair value is an unrealized gain of $265,000, which is credited to the Reserve account. The net effect of recognizing these gains and losses in the accounts of the Investment Pool, pending distribution, is summarized in Entry 5.

	Debits	Credits
Drew County Investment Pool:		
5. Investments (specific investments should be debited or credited here)	450,000	
Reserve for Change in Fair Value of Investments		450,000

Assuming no participants have joined the pool or withdrawn from the pool, and the four participants that have continued to be members of the pool have not transferred additional assets to the pool, nor withdrawn any, the realized and unrealized net gains of $450,000 should be distributed to the member funds in the proportions used for the distribution of earnings (3/9, 3/9, 2/9, and 1/9). The distribution is shown in the following entry:

	Debits	Credits
Drew County Investment Pool:		
6. Reserve for Change in Fair Value of Investments	450,000	
Due to Debt Service Fund		150,000
Due to Capital Projects Fund		150,000
Additions—Change in Fair Value of Investments—Town of Calvin		100,000
Additions—Change in Fair Value of Investments—Calvin Independent School District		50,000

At December 31, 2002, interest earnings of $720,000 had accrued and were recorded, as shown in Entry 7 below:

	Debits	Credits
Drew County Investment Pool:		
7. Accrued Interest Receivable	720,000	
Undistributed Earnings on Pooled Investments		720,000

Assuming that the accrued interest was immediately distributed to pool participants in the same proportions listed for Entry 6, the following entry would be made to record the distribution:

	Debits	Credits
Drew County Investment Pool:		
8. Undistributed Earnings on Pooled Investments	720,000	
Due to Debt Service Fund		240,000
Due to Capital Projects Fund		240,000
Additions—Investment Earnings—Town of Calvin		160,000
Additions—Investment Earnings—Calvin Independent School District		80,000

Both entries 6 and 8 would, of course, lead to entries to recognize an increase in each participant's Equity in Pooled Investments and Revenues. Those entries would be similar to Entry 4b and thus are not shown here.

After all earnings and changes in fair value have been accounted for by the entries illustrated, the equities and proportionate interests of the participants are:

Debt Service Fund	$15,690,000, or 3/9 of total
Capital Projects Fund	15,690,000, or 3/9 of total
Town of Calvin	10,460,000, or 2/9 of total
Calvin Independent School District	5,230,000, or 1/9 of total
Total	$47,070,000

Withdrawal of Assets from the Pool

If a participant in a pool withdraws part of its equity from a pool, that participant's proportionate interest is decreased and all other participants' proportionate interest is increased. Before a withdrawal is made, there should be an apportionment of earnings, gains, and losses to date. The same is true in the event of complete withdrawal of one or more participants from the pool.

Continuing with the Drew County Investment Pool example, assume the Debt Service Fund needs to withdraw $5,000,000 from the pool to retire matured bonds. Ignoring the fact that in most practical cases it would be necessary to first sell some investments, the entry in the Investment Pool agency fund for the withdrawal is given as:

	Debits	*Credits*
Drew County Investment Pool:		
9a. Due to Debt Service Fund	5,000,000	
Cash		5,000,000

The corresponding entry in the Debt Service Fund is:

9b. Cash	5,000,000	
Equity in Pooled Investments		5,000,000

After withdrawal of $5,000,000 by the Debt Service Fund, the proportionate interests in the pool become:

Debt Service Fund	$10,690,000, or 25.4% of total
Capital Projects Fund	15,690,000, or 37.3% of total
Town of Calvin	10,460,000, or 24.9% of total
Calvin Independent School District	5,230,000, or 12.4% of total
Total	$42,070,000

Closing Entry

To assist in preparing financial statements, the Additions accounts (see Entries 1b, 2, 4a, 6, and 8), which reflect changes in the external participants' proportionate interest due to net new deposits/withdrawals, investment earnings, and changes in fair value, must be closed to the appropriate net asset accounts, as shown in Entry 10 below:

Drew County Investment Pool:		
10. Additions—Deposits in Pooled Investments—Town of Calvin	9,900,000	
Additions—Deposits in Pooled Investments—Calvin Independent School District	4,950,000	
Additions—Investment Earnings—Town of Calvin	360,000	
Additions—Investment Earnings—Calvin Independent School District	180,000	

Additions—Change in Fair Value of Investments— Town of Calvin	200,000	
Additions—Change in Fair Value of Investments— Calvin Independent School District	100,000	
Net Assets Held in Trust for Participants—Town of Calvin		10,460,000
Net Assets Held in Trust for Participants— Calvin Independent School District		5,230,000

Illustrative Financial Statements

Illustrative fiduciary fund statements, prepared for internal management purposes, are presented in Illustrations 8–6 and 8–7. These statements are prepared as of December 31, 2002, Drew County's fiscal year-end. These statements also provide the information to be reported in a column of the Statement of Fiduciary Fund Net Assets (see Illustration 2–9) and Statement of Changes in Fiduciary Fund Net Assets (see Illustration 2–10). It should be noted that only the $15,690,000 of assets representing the 37.3 percent proportionate interest of the *external* participants (the Town of Calvin and the Calvin Independent School District) is reported in the fiduciary fund (Investment Trust Fund) financial statements. The 62.7 percent proportionate interests of Drew County's own funds are reported as Equity in Pooled Investments (or as Cash, Investments, and Interest Receivable, if desired) in the Balance Sheet—Governmental Funds.

Illustration 8–6

DREW COUNTY
INVESTMENT POOL
STATEMENT OF NET ASSETS
AS OF DECEMBER 31, 2002

ASSETS		
Cash (Note A)		$ 4,702,898
Investments (Note A)		10,718,579
Accrued interest receivable (Note A)		268,524
Total Assets		15,690,000
LIABILITIES		
Total Liabilities		-0-
NET ASSETS		
Held in trust for participants—		
Town of Calvin	$10,460,000	
Calvin Independent School District	5,230,000	
Total Net Assets		$15,690,000

Note A: The amounts allocated to Cash, Investments, and Accrued Interest Receivable are the proportionate amounts for the external participants calculated by taking the ratio of 15,690/42,070 times the totals for these three items in the accounts of the Investment Pool.

Illustration 8–7

DREW COUNTY
INVESTMENT POOL
STATEMENT OF CHANGES IN NET ASSETS
FOR THE YEAR ENDED DECEMBER 31, 2002

ADDITIONS	
Deposits of participants	$14,850,000
Investment earnings	540,000
Increase in fair value of investments	300,000
Total Additions	15,690,000
DEDUCTIONS	
Total Deductions	-0-
Change in Net Assets	15,690,000
Net Assets, January 1, 2002	-0-
Net Assets, December 31, 2002	$15,690,000

Private-Purpose Trust Funds

The fair value of assets placed in trust under a trust agreement is referred to as the principal, or corpus, of the trust. Under the reporting model being superseded by GASB *Statement No. 34*, if the principal of the trust must be held intact in order to produce income, the trust is called nonexpendable. Nonexpendable trust funds are often called endowment funds. The income from the assets of a nonexpendable trust may be used only for the purposes specified by the trustor; therefore, the income is expendable. If the principal amount can be expended for the specified purpose, the trust is referred to under the model being superseded as an expendable trust fund.

Not all trust funds require the historic distinction between corpus and income; loan funds operated as trust funds are usually nonexpendable both as to principal and income, whereas public employee retirement systems are funds whose principal and income are both expendable for specified purposes.

In addition to the nonexpendable versus expendable classification, trust funds may also be classified as public or private. Public trust funds are those whose principal or income, or both, must be used for some public purpose; the beneficiaries of private trust funds are private individuals, organizations, or other governments. Funds established for the purpose of holding performance deposits of licensees under a governmental unit's regulatory activities are examples of private trust funds. Funds used to account for escheat property arising from the estate of persons who die intestate without any known heirs is another example of a private trust fund. GASB *Statement No. 34* refers to these trusts as public-purpose and private-purpose.

Statement No. 34 significantly changes accounting and financial reporting practices for trusts referred to in the previous reporting model as nonexpendable and expendable trusts. Because most of these trusts are created for public purposes (for example, to maintain parks and cemeteries or to acquire art for public buildings), they are considered governmental rather than fiduciary activities under the new reporting model. Thus, nonexpendable public-purpose trusts are now accounted for as permanent funds and expendable public-purpose trusts are accounted for as special revenue funds. These governmental fund types were discussed and illustrated in Chapter 4.

Private-purpose trust funds are relatively few compared with public-purpose trust funds. Further, private-purpose trust funds follow accounting and financial reporting practices that are quite similar to those illustrated in the previous section on investment trust funds. A private-purpose trust fund whose principal is permanently restricted for investment, with earnings available for a specified private purpose, is accounted for in a manner similar to the City of Columbia Library Endowment Fund illustrated in Chapter 4 as a Permanent Fund. The principal difference is that financial information for a private-purpose trust is reported in the Statement of Fiduciary Net Assets and Statement of Changes in Fiduciary Net Assets, whereas that for a permanent fund is reported in the Balance Sheet—Governmental Funds and Statement of Revenues, Expenditures, and Changes in Fund Balances—Governmental Funds. Even though a private-purpose trust reports additions and deductions from net assets (see Illustration 8–7 for an example), those items are measured in essentially the same manner as revenues and expenditures of a permanent fund. Because there is little difference in accounting and reporting for private-purpose trusts and permanent funds and investment trust funds, already illustrated, no journal entries or financial statements are provided in this chapter for private-purpose funds.

Pension Accounting

Assets held by public pension plans for fiscal year 1996–97 amounted to nearly $1.5 trillion.[6] Thus, it is not surprising that the GASB has devoted substantial effort to improving accounting and financial reporting for pension plans. This section provides an overview of the accounting and reporting requirements for pension plans, as well as the governmental employers that sponsor such plans.

Pension plans are of two general types, *defined contribution plans* and *defined benefit plans*. A **defined contribution plan** specifies the amount or rate of contribution, often a percentage of covered salary, that the employer and employees must contribute to the members' accounts in the pension plan. The level of benefits payable upon retirement is determined by the total amount of contributions to a member's account, earnings on investments, and allocations of forfeited contributions of

[6] U.S. Bureau of the Census, *Summary of State and Local Government Employee-Retirement System Finances: Fiscal Year 1996–97*, Table 1.

other members credited to the account.[7] Because future benefits are neither formula-based nor guaranteed, the risk associated with defined contribution plans rests primarily with employees; the employer's responsibility essentially ends once the required contribution is made. Such plans ordinarily are *not* administered on an actuarial basis; therefore, accounting and financial reporting requirements for both the plan and the employer are straightforward and present few complications. Essentially, the plan reports the fair value of pension assets and any liability for accrued plan benefits; the employer reports expenditures/expenses for the amount contributed to the plan. Both the plan and the employer are required to provide in the Notes to the Financial Statements a brief description of the plan, classes of employees covered, plan provisions, contribution requirements, significant accounting policies for the plan, and concentrations of investments in any one organization that exceed 5 percent or more of plan net assets.[8]

A **defined benefit plan** provides a specified amount of benefits based on a formula that may include such factors as age, salary, and years of employment.[9] Determining the present value of projected pension benefits involves numerous factors, such as employee mortality, employee turnover, salary progression, and investment earnings. To ensure that plan assets will be adequate to cover future benefits, professional actuaries are engaged to calculate the present value of benefits and the required contributions that must be made by employers and, in some cases, employees. Of course, the basic assumptions underlying actuaries' projections may change over time, giving rise to periodic revisions in the required contributions. Because of the need to rely extensively on actuaries' estimates, it is not surprising that accounting for defined benefit plans is much more complex than for defined contribution plans. The remainder of this section provides a summary overview of the accounting and financial reporting requirements for defined benefit pension plans; a complete discussion of these plans is considerably beyond the scope of this text.

The illustrative transactions for defined benefit pension plan accounting discussed in this section are based on a "single-employer plan," that is, a single plan administered by a single governmental employer. Readers should be aware, however, that many governments sponsor multiple pension plans for different classes of employees (for example, a plan for general employees and one or more separate and usually more generous plans for public safety employees). Further, in some states, some or all local government employees participate in a statewide defined benefit pension plan, rather than one sponsored by the local government itself. Such plans or groups of plans are often referred to as **Public Employee Retirement Systems** (PERS). The GASB standards that apply to a single-employer plan apply as well to multiple-employer plans, although accounting and reporting for multiple-employer plans are more complex.

Under GASB *Statement No. 34*, pension plans are accounted for in the basic fiduciary fund statements of the sponsoring government. Some plans are adminis-

---

[7]GASB, *Codification*, Sec. Pe5.525.

[8]Ibid., Sec. Pe6.104.

[9]Ibid., Sec. Pe5.524.

tered as legally separate entities and therefore publish "stand-alone" financial statements, as well as reporting their pension fund financial information in the fiduciary funds statements of the sponsoring governments.

Until 1996, governments had considerable latitude regarding the choice of accounting method for pension plans. GASB *Statement No. 1*, issued in 1984, permitted governments to follow either the pension accounting and reporting standards set forth in NCGA *Statement 1*, in NCGA *Statement* 6, or in FASB *Statement No. 35*, pending the issuance by the GASB of a statement or statements on pension accounting and financial reporting. GASB *Statement No. 5*, "Disclosure of Pension Information by Public Employee Retirement Systems and State and Local Governmental Employers," issued in late 1986, superseded the disclosure requirements of the three statements just cited. Those disclosures were very extensive, often resulting in more than 10 pages of pension-related disclosures in the Notes to the Financial Statements. After several years of effort, the GASB issued three new standards that collectively provide comprehensive guidance on pension accounting and financial reporting. These standards provide accounting and reporting guidance for defined benefit pension plans (GASB *Statement No. 25)*, postemployment healthcare plans administered by defined benefit pension plans (GASB *Statement No. 26)*, and the sponsor/employer (GASB *Statement No. 27)*. Complete texts of these standards can be found in the GASB's *Codification of Governmental Accounting and Financial Reporting Standards*, Sections Pe5, Po50, and P20, respectively. Most observers agree that the new standards have helped to achieve more uniform reporting of governmental pension plans. Moreover, required note disclosures have been reduced substantially under the new standards.

Required Financial Reporting for Defined Benefit Pension Plans

GASB standards establish a financial reporting framework for defined benefit pension plans that includes both required financial statements and required schedules of historical trend information. The schedules are *required supplementary information* that must follow immediately after the financial statements.[10] Two financial statements and two supplementary schedules of historical trend data are required. These requirements are described as:

a. A *statement of plan net assets* showing plan assets, liabilities, and net assets. Plan assets should be reported at fair value. (See Illustration 8–8 for an example of a PERS that administers three defined benefit pension plans.)
b. A *statement of changes in plan net assets* showing additions to plan net assets, deductions from plan net assets, and net increase (decrease) in plan net assets. (See Illustration 8–9.)
c. A *schedule of funding progress* showing historical trend data about the actuarially determined status of plan funding "from a long-term, ongoing perspective and the progress made in accumulating sufficient assets to pay benefits when due." (See Illustration 8–10.)

[10]Ibid., Sec. Pe5.111.

Illustration 8–8

COLUMBINE RETIREMENT SYSTEM
STATEMENTS OF PLAN NET ASSETS
AS OF JUNE 30, 19X2, AND 19X1
(IN THOUSANDS)

	State Employees	*School Districts*	*Municipal Employees*	*19X2 Total*	*19X1 Total*
Assets					
Cash and short-term investments	$ 66,129	$ 116,988	$ 27,014	$ 210,131	$ 440,146
Receivables:					
Employer	16,451	18,501	2,958	37,910	45,770
Employer—long-term		986		986	1,088
Interest and dividends	33,495	48,299	4,951	86,745	81,183
Total receivables	49,946	67,786	7,909	125,641	128,041
Investments at fair value:					
U.S. Government obligations	541,289	780,541	80,001	1,401,831	1,571,404
Municipal bonds	33,585	48,416	4,969	86,970	86,417
Domestic corporate bonds	892,295	1,217,251	191,801	2,301,347	1,961,288
Domestic stocks	1,276,533	1,784,054	183,893	3,244,480	3,230,446
International stocks	461,350	665,269	68,187	1,194,806	1,187,703
Mortgages	149,100	209,099	24,453	382,652	319,745
Real estate	184,984	266,748	27,350	479,082	420,806
Venture capital	26,795	38,638	3,960	69,393	37,120
Total investments	3,565,931	5,010,016	584,614	9,160,561	8,814,929
Properties, at cost, net of accumulated depreciation of $5,164 and $4,430, respectively	6,351	8,924	1,040	16,315	16,093
Total Assets	3,688,357	5,203,714	620,577	9,512,648	9,399,209
Liabilities					
Refunds payable and other	4,212	1,849	429	6,490	37,211
Net assets held in trust for pension benefits	$3,684,145	$5,201,865	$620,148	$9,506,158	$9,361,998

Source: GASB, *Codification*, Sec. Pe5.901, Illustration I.

d. A *schedule of employer contributions* showing historical trend data about the *annual required contributions of the employer* (ARC) and employer contributions in relation to ARC.[11] (See Illustration 8–11.)

[11]Ibid.

Illustration 8–9

COLUMBINE RETIREMENT SYSTEM
STATEMENTS OF CHANGES IN PLAN NET ASSETS
FOR THE YEARS ENDED JUNE 30, 19X2, AND 19X1
(IN THOUSANDS)

	State Employees	*School Districts*	*Municipal Employees*	*19X2 Total*	*19X1 Total*
Additions:					
Contributions:					
Employer	$ 137,916	$ 157,783	$ 19,199	$ 314,898	$ 284,568
Employer—long-term		102		102	102
Plan member	90,271	117,852	16,828	225,651	216,106
Total contributions	228,887	275,737	36,027	540,651	500,776
Investment income					
Net appreciation (depreciation) in fair value of investments	(241,408)	(344,429)	(35,280)	(621,117)	788,913
Interest	157,371	225,446	23,098	405,915	422,644
Dividends	123,953	177,654	18,191	319,798	560,848
Real estate operating income, net	10,733	15,383	1,575	27,691	25,296
	50,649	74,054	7,584	132,287	1,797,701
Less investment expense	54,081	61,872	7,529	123,482	500,674
Net investment income	(3,432)	12,182	55	8,805	1,297,027
Total additions	225,455	287,919	36,082	549,456	1,797,803
Deductions:					
Benefits	170,434	172,787	18,073	361,294	325,881
Refunds of contributions	15,760	13,200	3,671	32,621	38,406
Administrative expense	4,984	5,703	694	11,381	12,681
Total deductions	191,168	191,690	22,438	405,296	376,968
Net increase	34,287	96,229	13,644	144,160	1,420,835
Net assets held in trust for pension benefits:					
Beginning of year	3,649,858	5,105,636	606,504	9,361,998	7,941,163
End of year	$3,684,145	$5,201,865	$620,148	$9,506,158	$9,361,998

Source: GASB, *Codification*, Sec. Pe5.901, Illustration I.

In addition, the plan is required to provide notes to the financial statements *and* notes to the required schedules. The notes to the financial statements should disclose the following information:

a. Plan description, including:
1. Identification of the type of plan.
2. Classes of employees covered.
3. Brief description of benefit provisions.

Illustration 8–10 Required Supplementary Information

SCHEDULES OF FUNDING PROGRESS
(DOLLAR AMOUNTS IN THOUSANDS)

Actuarial Valuation Date	*Actuarial Value of Assets (a)*	*Actuarial Accrued Liability (AAL) —Entry Age (b)*	*Unfunded AAL (UAAL) (b – a)*	*Funded Ratio (a/b)*	*Covered Payroll (c)*	*UAAL as a Percentage of Covered Payroll ((b – a)/c)*
SEPP						
12/31/W6	$2,005,238	$2,626,296	$621,058	76.4%	$ 901,566	68.9%
12/31/W7	2,411,610	2,902,399	490,789	83.1	956,525	51.3
12/31/W8	2,709,432	3,331,872	622,440	81.3	1,004,949	61.9
12/31/W9*	3,001,314	3,604,297	602,983	83.3	1,049,138	57.5
12/31/X0	3,366,946	3,930,112	563,166	85.7	1,093,780	51.5
12/31/X1	3,658,323	4,284,961	626,638	85.4	1,156,346	54.2
SDEPP						
12/31/W6	$2,888,374	$3,499,572	$611,198	82.5%	$1,205,873	50.7%
12/31/W7	3,473,718	3,867,483	393,765	89.8	1,279,383	30.8
12/31/W8	3,902,705	4,439,761	537,056	87.9	1,344,151	40.0
12/31/W9*	4,323,137	4,802,700	479,563	90.0	1,403,255	34.2
12/31/X0	4,849,798	5,236,922	387,124	92.6	1,462,965	26.5
12/31/X1	5,269,502	5,709,764	440,262	92.3	1,546,650	28.5
MEPP						
12/31/W6	$ 301,305	$ 342,842	$ 41,537	87.9%	$ 163,508	25.4%
12/31/W7	362,366	378,885	16,519	95.6	173,476	9.5
12/31/W8	407,117	434,949	27,832	93.6	182,258	15.3
12/31/W9*	450,975	470,512	19,537	95.8	190,272	10.3
12/31/X0	505,714	513,044	7,330	98.6	198,368	3.7
12/31/X1	549,696	559,367	9,671	98.3	209,715	4.6

*Revised economic and noneconomic assumptions due to experience review.

Source: GASB, *Codification*, Sec. Pe5.901, Illustration I.

b. Summary of significant accounting policies.

c. Description of contributions and reserves, including:
1. The authority under which contributions are made.
2. Funding policies.
3. Required contribution rates of active plan members.
4. Brief description of any long-term contracts for contributions.
5. Balances of the plan's legally required reserves at the reporting date.[12]

The notes to the required schedules should provide:

a. Identification of actuarial methods used and significant actuarial assumptions for the most recent year covered by the required supplementary schedules.

[12]Ibid., Sec. Pe5.124.

Illustration 8–11

SCHEDULES OF EMPLOYER CONTRIBUTIONS
(DOLLAR AMOUNTS IN THOUSANDS)

	Employer Contributions					
	SEPP		SDEPP		MEPP	
Year Ended June 30	*Annual Required Contribution*	*Percentage Contributed*	*Annual Required Contribution*	*Percentage Contributed*	*Annual Required Contribution*	*Percentage Contributed*
19W7	$100,729	100%	$115,935	100%	$15,042	100%
19W8	106,030	100	122,682	100	15,959	100
19W9	112,798	100	129,822	100	16,768	100
19X0	118,735	100	137,378	100	17,505	100
19X1	124,276	100	142,347	100	18,049	100
19X2	137,916	100	157,783	100	18,653	100

Source: GASB, *Codification*, Sec. Pe5.901, Illustration I.

b. Factors such as changes in benefit provisions, employees covered by the plan, or actuarial methods or assumptions used that significantly affect the trends reported in the schedules.[13]

Statement of Plan Net Assets

Illustration 8–8, reproduced from the GASB *Codification*, presents the statements of plan net assets for the hypothetical Columbine Retirement System, a public employee retirement system (PERS). Columbine administers three pension plans: the state employees' plan, the school districts' plan, and the municipal employees' plan. As shown, plan investments should be reported at fair value (last reported sales price) for all investments in securities that trade on active exchanges. Investments in mortgages should be based on the discounted present value of future interest and principal payments to be received. Investments in real estate should be reported at fair value based on independent appraisals. All other investments should be reported at estimated fair value, including institutional price quotes for debt securities for which trade prices are unavailable.

Depreciable assets of a PERS, that is, assets held as property, plant, and equipment for use by the PERS, should be reported at cost less accumulated depreciation. Cash and short-term investments (reported at cost), and receivables typically represent a minor part of the total assets of a PERS. An astute reader will note also the assets of a PERS are not classified as current and noncurrent; the distinction not being important since short-term liabilities typically are immaterial in relation to available plan assets. PERS liabilities, usually short term (e.g., benefits due but

[13]Ibid., Sec. Pe5.132.

unpaid, refunds for terminated employees, vouchers payable, accrued expenses, and payroll taxes payable), are reported as a deduction from PERS assets; the difference is captioned "Net assets held in trust for pension benefits."

Statement of Changes in Plan Net Assets

The *Statements of Changes in Net Plan Assets* for the Columbine Retirement System is presented in Illustration 8–9. This statement reports employer and employee contributions and investment income as additions to net assets rather than as revenues. Similarly, benefits paid, refunds of contributions, and administrative expense are reported under the caption deductions from net assets rather than as expenses. The net increase (decrease) in net assets is added to beginning-of-period net assets to calculate end-of-period net assets. Additions and deductions are recognized on the accrual basis.

Schedule of Funding Progress

An example *Schedules of Funding Progress* is presented in Illustration 8–10. This schedule shows funding progress of the plan in relation to *actuarial* requirements. A key measure of how well the plan is funded is the *funded ratio*. The **funded ratio** is the ratio of *actuarial value of assets* to *actuarial accrued liability* (AAL). **Actuarial value of assets** is the value of plan assets used by the actuary; the methods of determination for the various assets should be disclosed in the notes.[14] **Actuarial accrued liability** is determined by using any of several generally accepted actuarial methods (consistently applied, of course)—in this case, the Entry Age method—and is the present value of projected benefits, other than normal costs (benefits earned from current and future employee service). Thus, AAL arises primarily from past underfunding and ad hoc changes in plan provisions. Both the Schedule of Funding Progress and the other required schedule, the Schedule of Employer Contributions, should present information for the current year and as many prior years for which comparable data can be provided. By the sixth and subsequent years after implementation of GASB *Statement No. 25*, information should be provided for the current and five prior years (six years in total).

Schedule of Employer Contributions

The key information the reader should note in the *Schedules of Employer Contributions* shown in Illustration 8–11 is the *annual required contribution* (ARC) and what percentage of the ARC the employer has contributed. **Annual required contribution** is an actuarially determined amount that the employer should contribute each year to ensure full actuarial funding of the plan. Calculation of the ARC is discussed later in the section headed "Employer's Pension Accounting."

Alternative Reporting and Disclosure

The two financial statements and two schedules discussed previously, and related note disclosures, are those required in the stand-alone statements of a plan or PERS. The financial information and note disclosures required should also be

[14]The definitions paraphrased here and following are based on those provided in GASB, *Codification*, Sec. Pe5.A-1 and A-3.

Illustration 8–12

JOHNSON COUNTY EMPLOYEE RETIREMENT SYSTEM
STATEMENT OF PLAN NET ASSETS
JUNE 30, 2001

Assets	
Cash	$ 28,569
Accrued interest receivable	2,507,612
Investments (at fair value):	
Bonds	71,603,976
Common stocks	31,957,205
Commercial paper and repurchase agreements	12,570,401
Properties, at cost, net of accumulated depreciation of $17,673	22,644
Total assets	118,690,407
Liabilities	
Accounts payable and accrued expenses	401,581
Net assets held in trust for pension benefits	$118,288,826

reported in the employer government's statement of fiduciary net assets and statement of changes in fiduciary net assets and related notes.[15]

Illustrative Transactions for a Defined Benefit Pension Plan

Assume the Johnson County Employee Retirement Plan started the fiscal year beginning July 1, 2001, with the Statement of Plan Net Assets presented in Illustration 8–12. During fiscal year 2002 , the following transactions occurred that require journal entries as shown.

Accrued interest receivable as of June 30, 2001 was collected:

	Debits	*Credits*
1. Cash	2,507,612	
Accrued Interest Receivable		2,507,612

Member contributions in the amount of $8,009,400 and employer contributions in the amount of $14,126,292 were received in cash:

2. Cash	22,135,692	
Additions—Member Contributions		8,009,400
Additions—Employer Contributions		14,126,292

Annuity benefits in the amount of $3,134,448 and disability benefits in the amount of $287,590 were recorded as liabilities:

[15]GASB *Statement No. 34* (Norwalk, CT, 1999), par. 106.

	Debits	Credits
3. Deductions—Annuity Benefits	3,134,448	
Deductions—Disability Benefits	287,590	
Accounts Payable and Accrued Expenses		3,422,038

Accounts payable and accrued expenses paid in cash amounted to $3,571,969:

	Debits	Credits
4. Accounts Payable and Accrued Expenses	3,571,969	
Cash		3,571,969

Terminated employees whose benefits were not vested were refunded $2,057,265 in cash:

	Debits	Credits
5. Deductions—Refunds to Terminated Employees	2,057,265	
Cash		2,057,265

Investment income received in cash amounted to $9,440,769; $4,882,076 interest income was accrued at year-end. In addition, the fair value of investments in bonds decreased during the year by $5,626,382 and the fair value of investments in common stocks increased by $3,427,600.

	Debits	Credits
6a. Cash	9,440,769	
Accrued Interest Receivable	4,822,076	
Additions—Investment Income		14,262,845
6b. Investment in Common Stock	3,427,600	
Deductions—Change in Fair Value of Investments	2,198,782	
Investment in Bonds		5,626,382

Commercial paper and repurchase agreements carried at a cost of $1,354,568 matured, and cash in that amount was received:

	Debits	Credits
7. Cash	1,354,568	
Commercial Paper and Repurchase Agreements		1,354,568

Common stocks carried at fair value of $6,293,867 were sold for that amount; $1,536,364 was reinvested in common stocks and the remainder in bonds. An additional amount of $29,229,967 was also invested in bonds:

	Debits	Credits
8a. Cash	6,293,867	
Investment in Common Stocks		6,293,867
8b. Investment in Bonds	33,987,470	
Investment in Common Stocks	1,536,364	
Cash		35,523,834

Administrative expenses for the year totaled $568,219 all paid in cash:

	Debits	Credits
9. Deductions—Administrative Expenses	568,219	
Cash		568,219

Equipment costing $11,059, on which depreciation in the amount of $5,000 had accumulated, was sold for $6,059 cash:

	Debits	Credits
10. Accumulated Depreciation—Equipment	5,000	
Cash	6,059	
Equipment		11,059

Equipment costing $15,000 was purchased:

	Debits	Credits
11. Equipment	15,000	
Cash		15,000

Depreciation expenses for the year amounted to $12,000 (charge to Administrative Expenses):

	Debits	Credits
12. Deductions—Administrative Expenses	12,000	
Accumulated Depreciation—Equipment		12,000

Nominal accounts for the year were closed:

	Debits	Credits
13. Additions—Member Contributions	8,009,400	
Additions—Employer Contributions	14,126,292	
Additions—Investment Income	14,262,845	
Deductions—Annuity Benefits		3,134,448
Deductions—Disability Benefits		287,590
Deductions—Refunds to Terminated Employees		2,057,265
Deductions—Administrative Expenses		580,219
Deductions—Change in Fair Value of Investments		2,198,782
Net Assets Held in Trust for Pension Benefits		28,140,233

Entries 1 through 13 result in the financial statements shown as Illustrations 8–13 and 8–14, when applied to the accounts existing at the beginning of the period as shown in Illustration 8–12.

Illustration 8–13

JOHNSON COUNTY EMPLOYEE RETIREMENT SYSTEM
STATEMENT OF PLAN NET ASSETS
JUNE 30, 2002

Assets	
Cash	$ 30,849
Accrued interest receivable	4,822,076
Investments (at fair value):	
Bonds	99,965,064
Common stocks	30,627,302
Commercial paper and repurchase agreements	11,215,833
Properties, at cost, net of accumulated depreciation of $24,673	19,585
Total assets	146,680,709
Liabilities	
Accounts payable and accrued expenses	251,650
Net assets held in trust for pension benefits	$146,429,059

Illustration 8–14

JOHNSON COUNTY EMPLOYEE RETIREMENT SYSTEM
STATEMENT OF CHANGES IN PLAN NET ASSETS
FOR THE FISCAL YEAR ENDED JUNE 30, 2002

Additions:	
Contributions:	
Employer	$ 14,126,292
Plan members	8,009,400
Total contributions	22,135,692
Investment income:	
Net decrease in fair value of investments	(2,198,782)
Interest and dividends	14,262,845
Total investment income	12,064,063
Total additions	34,199,755
Deductions:	
Annuity benefits	3,134,448
Disability benefits	287,590
Refunds to terminated employees	2,057,265
Administrative expenses	580,219
Total deductions	6,059,522
Net increase	28,140,233
Net assets, July 1, 2001	118,288,826
Net assets, June 30, 2002	$146,429,059

Employer's Pension Accounting

GASB standards for the employer's accounting for defined benefit pension plans provide guidance for measurement, recognition, and display of the employer's pension information. In addition to general purpose government employers, the standards apply also to governmental public benefit corporations and authorities, utilities, hospitals, and other health care providers, colleges and universities, and, if they are employers, to public employee retirement systems.

Many of the note and statistical disclosures applicable to defined benefit pension plans, discussed in the preceding paragraphs, apply as well to the employer. If the plan (or PERS) is deemed to be part of the government's reporting entity, then many of the employer's required disclosures are redundant of those required of the plan (a pension trust fund). In this case, the employer need not make disclosures that would duplicate those made by the plan. If the plan issues a stand-alone financial report, however, the employer will have to make many of the same disclosures in the CAFR that the plan makes in its stand-alone report. Because of the similarity of the disclosures and supplementary information required of the employer to those enumerated previously for the plan, the reader is referred to GASB *Codification*, Sec. P20.117, for specific disclosure requirements applicable to the employer.

Illustration 8–15

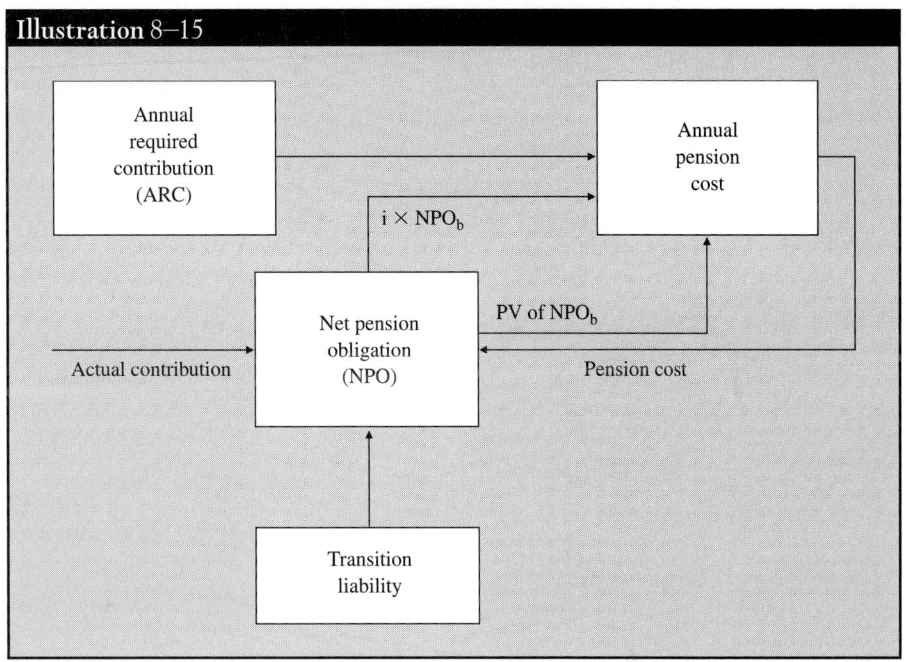

Whether a government employer accounts for payroll in a governmental fund or proprietary fund, or both, there are three primary measures to be calculated and reported: (1) *annual required contribution* (ARC), (2) *annual pension cost,* and (3) *net pension obligation* (NPO).

Calculation of Annual Pension Cost and Net Pension Obligation. *Annual pension cost* must be calculated and disclosed in the notes to the employer's financial statements. As shown in Illustration 8–15, the *annual required contribution* (ARC) is the starting point for understanding the calculation of annual pension cost. A discussion of the detailed procedures for calculating ARC is well beyond the scope of this text; therefore, only identification of the components of ARC is discussed here.

ARC is calculated in accordance with certain parameters provided in GASB standards. The parameters require that for financial reporting purposes an actuarial valuation be performed at least biennially and that ARC be based on an actuarial valuation as of a date not more than 24 months prior to the beginning of the current fiscal year. A component of ARC is the **actuarial present value of total projected benefits,** allowing for projected salary increases and additional statutory or contractual agreements such as ad hoc cost-of-living increases and other types of postemployment benefit increases.

The parameters used to calculate ARC also provide broad guidance regarding actuarial and economic assumptions, even though any of six actuarial methods are permitted, subject to the limitation that in most cases the same actuarial method should be used both for funding and financial reporting purposes. Further, both the plan and the employer should use the same actuarial method.

An employer's ARC should include **normal cost** (i.e., the actuarial present value of benefits allocated to the current year by the actuarial cost method being used) and amortization of any **unfunded actuarial liability** (same as *unfunded actuarial accrued liability* defined previously in the discussion of the required Schedule of Funding Progress). The provision for amortization can be determined using either level dollar amounts each year or a level percentage of the projected payroll. The amortization period must fall between defined maximum and minimum amortization periods. The maximum amortization period for the first 10 years after June 15, 1996, the effective date of GASB *Statement No. 25*, is 40 years. After the first 10 years the maximum period is 30 years. If there is a significant decrease in the total unfunded actuarial liability caused by a change in actuarial cost method or a change in asset valuation method, the decrease must be amortized over a period of not less than 10 years.

Once ARC has been calculated, it becomes an input to the calculation of annual pension cost (see Illustration 8–15). If there were no *net pension obligation* (NPO), the annual pension cost would be the same as ARC, and that would be the amount the employer should contribute during the period to the plan in order to fully fund current-period accrued benefits. If the employer has undercontributed in the past, then ARC will contain an amount for the amortization of the unfunded actuarial liability. Moreover, if actual contributions have been less than annual pension cost, NPO will have a positive balance. Thus, annual pension cost will be affected by the existence of an NPO, in addition to ARC. Before discussing the precise calculation of annual pension cost in the presence of an NPO, it will be useful to first examine the components of NPO.

Net Pension Obligation. **Net pension obligation** (NPO) has two components: (1) the transition pension liability (or asset), if any, existing at the date GASB *Statement No. 27* was implemented and (2) the cumulative difference from the implementation date of *Statement No. 27* to the current balance sheet date between annual pension cost (the amount that should be contributed) and the employer's actual contributions. These inputs to NPO (actual contribution, annual pension cost, and transition liability) are shown clearly in Illustration 8–15.

Annual Pension Cost. When an employer has an NPO, **annual pension cost** is equal to: (1) the ARC, plus (2) one year's interest on the beginning-of-year NPO, and minus or plus (3) an adjustment for any amounts already included in ARC for past amortization of contribution deficiencies or excess contributions. The adjustment is minus if the beginning balance of NPO is positive (contribution deficiencies) and plus if NPO is negative (excess contributions). As shown in Illustration 8–15, the adjustment to ARC is approximated by deducting an amount equal to the present value of the beginning balance of NPO. Illustration 8–16 provides a numerical example of how annual pension cost and NPO are related and how each is calculated.

Illustration 8–16 Calculation of Annual Pension Cost and Net Pension Obligation

Annual required contribution (ARC)	$165,485
Interest on net pension obligation (i × NPO_b)	5,070
Adjustment to annual required contribution (PV of NPO_b)	(3,692)
Annual pension cost	166,863
Contributions made during the year	(157,982)
Increase in net pension obligation	8,881
Net pension obligation, January 1, 2001	67,594
Net pension obligation, December 31, 2001	$ 76,475

Source: Based on example shown in GASB, *Codification,* Sec. P20.902.

Employer Reporting of Pension Expenditure/ Expense

Referring to Illustrations 8–15 and 8–16, a governmental employer that reports pension expenditures in a governmental fund should recognize the expenditures on the modified accrual basis. Thus, the amount recognized will be the actual amount contributed to the plan during the year. If the amount of pension expenditures for the year is less than annual pension cost, the difference should be added to NPO. If the expenditures amount is greater than annual pension cost, the difference should be deducted from NPO. Any cumulative positive balance of NPO, including a transition liability, should be reported in the Statement of Net Assets at the government-wide level. A negative NPO balance should be used to reduce any other liability to the plan to zero, but should not be reported as an asset. Annual pension cost should be disclosed in the Notes to the Financial Statements. Under- or overfunding by a proprietary fund employer should be reported in the same manner except the NPO should be reported in the Balance Sheet of the proprietary fund. The amount of pension expense recognized in the proprietary fund should be the same as the annual pension cost. This amount would also be recognized as program expenses in the government-wide Statement of Activities, both for governmental activities and business-type activities.

Required Disclosures for Other Postemployment Benefits (OPEB)

Since unfunded other postemployment benefits (OPEB), such as health care benefits for retirees, may represent a material liability, GASB standards require certain disclosures by governmental employers that provide OPEB. If the OPEB plan is administered by a defined benefit pension plan, the OPEB follows the standards set forth in GASB *Statement No. 26* and codified in GASB *Codification*, Sec. Po50. Those standards impose financial reporting and disclosure requirements on the OPEB plan that are very similar to those for defined benefit pension plans, and thus do not need to be elaborated on here.

For OPEB plans that are not administered as part of a defined benefit pension plan, GASB standards provide disclosure standards only; financial display issues relating to such OPEB plans are being examined in a separate project by the GASB.[16] The Notes to the Financial Statements should provide, at a minimum, the following disclosures, either separately for each OPEB or in the aggregate for all OPEB provided:

a. Description of the OPEB; employee groups covered; eligibility requirements; and the employer and participant obligations to contribute, quantified in some manner.

b. Description of the statutory, contractual, or other authority under which OPEB provisions and obligations to contribute are established.

c. Description of the accounting and financing or funding policies followed.

d. Expenditure/expense information. If OPEB are financed on a pay-as-you-go basis, the employer should disclose expenditures/expenses recognized during the period by the employer (net of participant contributions) and the number of participants currently eligible to receive benefits. If OPEB are advance funded on an actuarially determined basis, the employer should disclose the number of active plan participants, the employer's actuarially required and actual contributions for the period (net of participant contributions), the amount of net assets available for the OPEB, and the actuarial accrued liability and unfunded actuarial accrued liability.

e. Description (and dollar effect, if measurable) of any significant matters that affect the comparability of the disclosures with those for the previous period.

f. Any additional information that the employer believes will help users assess the nature and magnitude of the cost of the employer's commitment to provide OPEB.

Employers that advance fund an OPEB through a pension plan have the option of following required employer pension disclosures, discussed previously in this chapter, or the OPEB disclosures just listed.

Key Terms

[16]GASB, *Codification,* Sec. P50.105. If the GASB should issue new standards on recognition and measurement for postemployment benefits other than pension benefits, the publisher will provide an update to adopters of this edition of the text.

Selected References

American Institute of Certified Public Accountants. Audit and Accounting Guide, *Audits of State arid Local Governmental Units*, revised. New York, 1999.

Governmental Accounting Standards Board. *Codification of Governmental Accounting and Financial Reporting Standards as of June 30, 1999*. Norwalk, CT, 1999.

Questions

8–1. Explain the distinction(s) between *agency funds* and *trust funds*.

8–2. Why are *fiduciary funds* used by governmental units?

8–3. Must an agency fund be used to account for withholding taxes, retirement contributions, and (if applicable) social security taxes of General Fund employees?

8–4. Why do agency funds have no fund equity?

8–5. Under what circumstances should a governmental unit use an agency fund to account for special assessment debt service? What is the rationale for using an agency fund for these transactions?

8–6. What are the most important factors that cause tax agency fund accounting to be complex?

8–7. Why is it considered reasonable for a governmental unit that operates a tax agency fund to charge other governmental units a fee for collecting their taxes, if state law permits such a charge?

8–8. What is a Pass-Through Agency Fund? How does such a fund differ from a Tax Agency Fund?

8–9. Why would pooled investments be revalued to fair value when a fund is added to the pool, or when a fund withdraws from the pool?

8–10. Explain the essential differences between a *defined benefit pension plan* and a *defined contribution pension plan*. Which involves the more complex accounting and reporting requirements? Why?

8–11. What are the required financial statements and supplementary schedules that must be reported by a defined benefit pension plan in its stand-alone financial report, or in the CAFR of the employer (sponsor government), if applicable?

8–12. Describe the disclosures a defined benefit plan is required to make in the notes to its required financial statements and the notes to the required supplementary schedules.

8–13. How is annual pension cost calculated? How does an employer government's pension expenditure or expense relate to annual pension cost?

8–14. Explain how *net pension obligation* (NPO) is calculated, and how it should be reported/disclosed in the employer's financial report.

8–15. Explain how financial reporting requirements differ between other postemployment benefits (OPEB) plans administered by a defined benefit pension plan and those that are not administered by a pension plan.

Case

8–1. Fiduciary Funds. Boise City, Idaho, described the following funds in which it holds money in a fiduciary capacity in its Comprehensive Annual Financial Statement for the year ended September 30, 1998:

Deferred Compensation Fund: to account for the assets in the deferred compensation plans of the City held in trust for the exclusive benefit of employees.

Dedicated Trust Funds: to account for monies which are dedicated for a specific purpose. The principal must remain intact; only the interest income is used for current operations.

Housing Rehabilitation Fund: to account for several revolving loan funds that provide low interest loans for housing. Various federal grants were used to establish the existing fund balance. The collection of the loans are used to run the program and make new loans to qualified citizens.

Boise City Trust Fund: to account for items which must be held in trust for any reason. The major item accounted for in this fund is the Boise Improvement District payments.

Required

Determine whether each of the funds described above should be accounted for as fiduciary activities (e.g., agency fund, investment trust fund, private-purpose trust fund, or pension trust fund), or governmental activities (e.g., special revenue fund or permanent trust fund) according to GASB *Statement No. 34* standards. Explain your reasoning.

Exercises and Problems

8–1. Examine the CAFR. Utilizing the annual report obtained for Exercise 1–1, follow the instructions below:

a. Agency Funds. Are employees' and employer's FICA tax contributions and contributions to other retirement funds accounted for by the General Fund, by an agency fund, or in some other manner (describe)?

Does the governmental unit operate a tax agency fund? Participate in a tax agency fund operated by another governmental unit?

Does the government act as agent for owners of property within a special assessment district, and for the creditors of those property owners? Do the Notes to the Financial Statements disclose the agency relationship clearly and fully?

Does the governmental unit operate one or more pass-through agency funds? If so, describe. If not, is there any evidence that the governmental unit received grants, entitlements, or shared revenues that might properly have been accounted for by a pass-through agency fund?

b. *Cash and Investment Pools*. Does the governmental unit operate, or participate in, a cash and investments pool? If so, is the pool accounted for as an investment trust fund? If there is a cash and investment pool and it is not accounted for as an agency fund or as an investment trust fund, how is it accounted for? Explain.

c. *Financial Statements*. Are agency funds properly disclosed in the financial statements? Explain the reasons for your answer.

d. *General*. Are all fiduciary funds shown in a Statement of Fiduciary Net Assets and a Statement of Changes in Fiduciary Net Assets?

Does the report state the basis of accounting used for trust and agency funds? Are all funds in this category accounted for on the same basis? If so, is the financial statement presentation consistent with the stated basis? If the basis is not stated, analyze the statements to determine which basis is used—full accrual, modified accrual, or cash basis. Are the bases used consistent with those required by GASB standards discussed in the text? Does the report include an investment trust fund? If so, is the fund accounted for on the accrual basis?

e. *Trust Funds*. Does the report contain a schedule or list of investments of trust funds? Are investments reported at fair value? Is the net increase (decrease) in the fair value of investments reported separate from interest and dividend income?

If trust funds own depreciable assets, is depreciation taken? If so, is depreciation considered a charge against principal or against income? Are any trust funds operated as profit-seeking businesses? If so, does the annual report contain income statements for the businesses?

f. *Pension Trust Funds*, or PERS. Are the government employees covered by a Retirement Fund operated by a local government, by the state, by the federal Social Security Administration, or by two or more of these?

If the government operates one or more Pension Plans, or retirement systems, are the Pension Plan financial statements accompanied by a separate audit report, or are they included in the auditor's opinion accompanying the other funds? Are the Pension Plan statements accompanied by an actuary's report? If not, is reference made to the actuary's report in the Statement of Fiduciary Net Assets, in Notes to the Financial Statements, or in the Auditor's Report? Does the Pension Plan have an "actuarial deficiency" or an "unfunded actuarial liability"? If so, is this condition explained in the notes accompanying the statement? Is a net pension obligation (NPO) reported in the government-wide Statement of Net Assets and/or in a proprietary fund?

Are the financial statements in the format shown in Illustrations 8–8 and 8–9? Is all the pension information specified in GASB standards and discussed in Chapter 8 presented in the Notes to the Financial Statements? Are the required supplementary schedules and related notes to the schedules reported in the comprehensive annual financial report?

8–2. Multiple Choice. Choose the best answer.

1. Which of the following accounts of an agency fund is (are) closed at the end of the fiscal year?

   a. The budgetary accounts.
   b. The operating statement accounts.
   c. Both *a* and *b.*
   d. None of the above.

2. GASB standards require each state and local governmental unit to display in agency fund financial statements:
   a. Investment transactions of internal investment pools.
   b. Investment transactions of external investment pools.
   c. Collections of special assessments and interest thereon, and from those collections payment of interest on and principal of special assessment debt for which the government has no obligation.
   d. All of the above.
3. Taxes collected by the County Collector for distribution to other Funds of the County and/or to governmental units within the County should be accounted for in an:
   a. Enterprise Fund.
   b. Internal Service Fund.
   c. Investment Trust Fund.
   d. Agency Fund.
4. Taxes certified to the County Collector of Leigh County by other County Funds and by other governmental units within the County should be recorded by the Collector by a debit to:
   a. Taxes Receivable—Current and a credit to Revenues.
   b. Taxes Receivable—Current and a credit directly to Fund Balance.
   c. Taxes Receivable for Other Funds and Units—Current and a credit to Due to Other Funds and Units.
   d. Taxes Receivable—Current and a credit to Due to County General Fund.
5. Agency fund financial data should be displayed in the basic financial statements in:
   a. The same basic statements as the governmental funds of the primary government.
   b. The same basic statements as the proprietary funds of the primary government.
   c. The same basic statements as all trust funds of the primary government.
   d. None of the basic financial statements.
6. Agency fund financial information should be displayed in the CAFR in the:
   a. Statement of Fiduciary Net Assets.
   b. Government-wide financial statements.
   c. Individual statements of each agency fund.
   d. Statistical section of the CAFR.

Items 7 through 10 relate to the following information:

The City Council of the City of Haysville decided to pool the investments of its General Fund with that of Haysville School and Haysville Township, each of which carried its investments at fair value as of the prior balance sheet date. All investments are revalued to current fair value at the date of the creation of the pool. At that date, the prior and current fair value of the investments of each of the participants were as follows:

	Investments	
	Prior Fair Value	*Current Fair Value*
General Fund	$ 600,000	$ 590,000
Haysville School	3,600,000	3,640,000
Haysville Township	1,800,000	1,770,000
Total	$6,000,000	$6,000,000

7. At the date of the creation of this external investment pool each of the participants should:
   a. Debit its Fund Balance account and credit its Investments account for the prior fair value of the assets transferred to the pool.
   b. Debit or credit its Investments account as needed to adjust its carrying value to current fair value. The offsetting entry in each fund should be to Fund Balance.
   c. Debit Equity in Pooled Investments for the current fair value of investments pooled, credit Investments for the prior fair value of investments pooled, and credit or debit Revenues—Change in Fair Value of Investments for the difference.
   d. Make a memorandum entry only.
8. At the date of creation of the pool, the City of Haysville should account for all the pooled investments in:
   a. An investment trust fund at fair value at the date the pool is created.
   b. An agency fund at fair value as of the prior balance sheet date.
   c. Its General Fund at fair value at the date the pool is created.
   d. Its General Fund at fair value as of the prior balance sheet date.
9. One day after creation of the pool, the investments that had belonged to Haysville Township were sold by the pool for $1,760,000.
   a. The loss of $40,000 is borne by each participant in proportion to its equity in the pool.
   b. The loss of $10,000 is borne by each participant in proportion to its equity in the pool.
   c. The loss of $40,000 is considered to be a loss borne by Haysville Township.
   d. The loss of $10,000 is considered to be a loss borne by Haysville Township.
10. One month after creation of the pool, earnings on pooled investments totaled $59,900. It was decided to distribute the earnings to the participants, rounding the distribution to the nearest dollar. The Haysville School Fund should receive:

a. $36,000.
b. $35,940.
c. $36,339.
d. $37,000.

8–3. Multiple Choice. Choose the best answer.

1. Which of the following is *not* a fiduciary fund?
   a. Permanent Fund.
   b. Agency Fund.
   c. Investment Trust Fund.
   d. Pension Trust Fund.
2. Which of the following is a fiduciary fund that may be either expendable or nonexpendable (i.e., the principal of the fund is permanently restricted for investment with only the earnings therefrom expendable for specified purposes)?
   a. Investment Trust Funds.
   b. Private-purpose Trust Funds.
   c. Pension Trust Funds.
   d. Permanent Fund.
3. Which of the following fiduciary fund types is most likely to require formal legislative approval (appropriation procedures) for expenditures?
   a. Investment Trust Funds.
   b. Pension Trust Funds.
   c. Agency Funds.
   d. None of the above.
4. A Statement of Cash Flows is required by GASB standards for which of the following fiduciary fund types?
   a. Investment Trust Funds.
   b. Private-purpose Trust Funds.
   c. Pension Trust Funds.
   d. None of the above.
5. An Investment Trust Fund is used to report the net assets available to the:
   a. Sponsoring government only.
   b. External participants only.
   c. Financial institution that acts as custodian for the fund's investments.
   d. All of the above.
6. Arkmo City has a single pension plan for its employees, all of whose salaries and wages are paid from the General Fund. Ordinarily, the City's General Fund should report an expenditure for its annual pension contribution to a defined benefit plan in an amount equal to the:
   a. Annual required contribution.
   b. Annual pension cost.
   c. Net pension obligation.
   d. Actual contribution.

7. GASB's pension standards require defined benefit pension plans to provide which of the following statements and schedules?
   a. Balance Sheet, Statement of Revenues and Expenses, Cash Flow Statement, and a Schedule of Actual and Required Contributions.
   b. Balance Sheet, Statement of Revenues and Expenditures, and a Schedule of Funding Progress.
   c. Statement of Plan Net Assets, Statement of Changes in Plan Net Assets, Schedule of Funding Progress, and a Schedule of Employer Contributions.
   d. Balance Sheet, Statement of Pension Activities, Schedule of Funding Progress, and a Statement of Plan Assets and Projected Pension Benefits—Funded and Unfunded.
8. Regarding financial reporting by governmental employers and defined benefit pension plans, which of the following is a correct statement?
   a. Expenditures and/or expenses incurred by governmental employers need not be reported separately in governmental and proprietary funds if the pension plan is determined to be a part of the governmental reporting entity.
   b. Expenditures and/or expenses incurred by governmental unit employers, and other pension-related financial information pertaining to employers, should be distinguished from financial information required to be reported by the pension plan.
   c. When a pension plan is considered to be part of a governmental reporting entity, its financial information need not be reported in the Fiduciary Funds financial statements.
   d. Disclosure of pension plan financial information is required only when there is a positive net pension obligation.

Items 9 and 10 are based on the following information:

Elm City contributes to and administers a single-employer defined benefit pension plan on behalf of its covered employees. The plan prepares its own stand-alone financial report and is not accounted for in a pension trust fund. The annual pension cost and actual contributions made for the past three years, along with the percentage of annual covered payroll, were as follows:

	Actual Contribution		**Annual Pension Cost**	
	Amount	*Percent*	*Amount*	*Percent*
2002	$25,000	26	$25,000	26
2001	7,500	12	15,000	24
2000	–0–	—	9,000	20

9. What account should be credited by the pension plan to record the year 2002 employer contribution of $25,000?
   a. Revenues—Employer Contributions.
   b. Other Financing Sources—Interfund Transfers In.

c. Due from General Fund.
d. Additions—Employer Contributions.

10. To record the year 2002 pension contribution of $25,000, what account would be debited in the General Fund for the employer pension contributions?
    a. Other Financing Uses—Interfund Transfers Out.
    b. Expenditures.
    c. Pension Expense.
    d. Due to Pension Fund.

8–4. Tax Agency Fund. For the three years indicated, the rates applicable to real property within the Town of Truxton were as shown below (rates are in terms of dollars and cents per $100 assessed valuation):

Fund or Unit	*2000*	*2001*	*2002*
Town General Fund	$3.12	$ 3.18	$ 3.30
Town Debt Service Fund	0.44	0.50	0.60
Total Town Rate	3.56	3.68	3.90
Truxton School Corp.	4.70	4.90	5.00
Canton County Library	0.13	0.20	0.30
Canton County	1.54	1.65	1.80
Total Rate	$9.93	$10.43	$11.00

Taxes on all real property located within Canton County are collected by the County Collector, who then distributes collections to the County Funds and to governmental units located within the County. Collections during the second half of 2002 totaled $6,800,000 from property located within the Town of Truxton, which represented collections of the following levies in the following amounts:

From 2000 levy	$ 72,000
From 2001 levy	360,000
From 2002 levy	6,368,000

Required

a. Assuming state law prohibits the County Collector from charging funds and units for the collection service, how much of the $6,800,000 collected in the second half of 2000 should be remitted by the County Collector to the Truxton Town Treasurer? Show computations in good form.

b. How much of the Town's share of collections of the 2002 levy, as computed in part *a* of this problem, should be remitted to the Town's Debt Service Fund? Show computations in good form.

8–5. The County Collector of Springer County is responsible for collecting all property taxes levied by funds and units within the boundaries of the County. In order to reimburse the County for estimated administrative expenses of operating the Tax Agency Fund, the agency fund deducts 1 percent from the collections for the Town, the School District, and the townships. The total amount deducted is added to the collections for the County and remitted to the County General Fund.

The following events occurred in 2002:

1. Current-year tax levies to be collected by the agency fund were:

County General Fund	$1,420,000
Town of Cronan General Fund	2,287,100
Springer Co. Consolidated School District	3,920,000
Various Townships	960,000
Total	$8,587,100

2. $15,100 was charged back to the Town of Cronan because of errors in the computation of that unit's current taxes.
3. $4,190,000 of current taxes were collected during the first half of 2001.
4. Liabilities to all funds and units as the result of the first half-year collections were recorded. (A schedule of amounts collected for each participant, showing amount withheld for the County General Fund and net amounts due the participants, is recommended for determining amounts to be recorded for this transaction. Round computation of the final amounts to the nearest dollar.)
5. All money in the Tax Agency Fund was distributed.

Required

a. Make journal entries for each of the foregoing transactions that affected the Tax Agency Fund.

b. Make journal entries for each of the foregoing transactions that affected the County General Fund. Begin with the tax levy entry, assuming 3 percent of the gross levy will be uncollectible.

c. Make journal entries for each of the foregoing entries that affected the Town of Cronan General Fund. Begin with the tax levy entry, assuming 3 percent of the gross levy will be uncollectible.

8–6. Special Assessment Agency Fund. The City of Fayette agreed to bill each owner of each parcel of property within Special Assessment District No. 21 for each installment of the owner's share of the total assessment for the construction project being undertaken by that Special Assessment District. The City agreed to collect the installments and interest thereon, and agreed to use the collections to pay interest and principal due on debt incurred for the construction project, although the City is not obligated in any manner for the special assessment debt.

Required

a. Name the fund type that should be used by the City of Fayette to record the activities described above. Explain the reason for your answer.

b. If the total assessment for the project to be undertaken by the Special Assessment District is $3,600,000, to be collected in three equal annual installments, show in general journal form the entry that should be made for the total assessment, assuming all installments are to be used for service of debt incurred for this project.

c. Show in general journal form the entry that should be made for collections from owners of property within Special Assessment District No. 21 of the first installment amounting to $1,276,000 ($1,160,000 for principal and $116,000 for interest).

d. Show in general journal form the entry that should be made to record the payment of interest amounting to $110,000 and principal amounting to $1,150,000 on debt incurred for the Special Assessment District No. 21 project.

e. Assuming all transactions described above occurred in the fiscal year ended June 30, 2001, and the City of Fayette had no other transactions during that year with the property owners or creditors of Special Assessment District No. 21, name the basic financial statement, or statements, of the City of Fayette in which the results of the transactions described above should be reported, and state which information about the transactions should be reported in each statement you name.

8–7. Pass-Through Agency Fund. Marshall County customarily receives from various federal government agencies resources that are designated for the use of the governmental units within the County. These resources are accounted for by the County in a Pass-Through Agency Fund.

Required

Show in general journal form the entries in the Pass-Through Fund for the following events and transactions, which occurred in 2001.

(1) The County received in cash a grant of $40,000,000, which is to be distributed to various units within the County in a manner not yet specified.

(2) Official notice was received that $17,000,000 of the above grant is to be distributed to the City of Pittsfield for public improvements. The distribution was made.

(3) Official notice was received that $16,000,000 was to be distributed to Marshall Schools. The distribution was made. Remaining cash was invested in marketable securities.

(4) The County received in cash a grant of $3,000,000, to be distributed to law enforcement agencies throughout the County in a manner yet to be specified. The cash was invested in marketable securities.

8–8. Investment Trust Fund. The City Council of the City of Liberty decided to pool the investments of its General Fund with Liberty Schools and Liberty Township in an Investment Pool to be managed by the City, each of which had accounted for its investments at fair value as of the end of the last fiscal year. At the date of the creation of the pool, the current fair value of the investments of each of the participants were as follows:

	Investments	
	Prior Fair Value	*Current Fair Value*
City of Liberty General Fund	$ 800,000	$ 790,000
Liberty Schools	4,600,000	4,740,000
Liberty Township	3,000,000	3,060,000
Total	$8,400,000	$8,590,000

Required

a. Show the entry that should be made by (1) the City of Liberty, (2) Liberty Schools, and (3) Liberty Township to do the following: open a new asset account, Equity in Investment Pool, in the amount of the current fair value of the investments transferred to the pool; close the existing Investments account; and debit or credit the Revenues account of each fund as needed to balance the entry.

b. Show in general journal form the entries to be made in the accounts of the Investment Pool Trust Fund to record the following transactions of the first year of its operations:

(1) Record at current fair value the investments transferred to the pool; assume the investments of the City's General Fund were in U.S. Treasury bills, and the investments of both the schools and the township were in certificates of deposit.

(2) Certificates of deposit that had been recorded at a fair value of $1,000,000 matured. The pool received $1,050,000 in cash ($1,000,000 for the face of the CDs and $50,000 interest). The entire amount was reinvested in a new issue of certificates of deposit.

(3) Interest on Treasury bills was collected in the amount of $50,000, and interest on certificates of deposit was collected in the amount of $300,000. These amounts were reinvested in Treasury bills.

(4) Interest on certificates of deposit accrued at year-end amounted to $28,250.

(5) At the end of the year, it was decided to compute and record the pool's liability or net assets held for each of the three participants for its proportionate share of earnings on the pooled investments. Carry your computation of each fund's proportionate share to four decimal places. Round the amount of the distribution to each fund to the nearest dollar.

c. Record in each of the participant's funds the increase in its Equity in Investment Pool.

8–9. Pension Plan calculation. The Village of Vandover administers a defined benefit pension plan for its police and fire personnel. Employees are not required to contribute to the plan. The Village received from the actuary and other sources the following information about the Public Safety Employees' Pension Fund as of December 31, 2001.

Item	Amount
Annual required contribution	$ 49,600
Net pension obligation, 1/1/2001	147,300
Present value of net pension obligation as of 1/1/2001	12,400
Interest rate applicable to beginning net pension obligation	8%
Transition liability	–0–

Required

Assuming the Village of Vandover contributes $45,000 cash to the plan on December 31, 2001, calculate the employer's

a. Annual pension cost.

b. Net pension obligation, as of December 31, 2001.

8–10. Pension Plan Financial Statements. The State of Arkoma operates a Public Employee Retirement System for all employees of the state. The trial balance of the PERS as of June 30, 2001, follows (in thousands of dollars):

	Debits	Credits
Cash	$ 6,254	
Accrued Interest Receivable	32,955	
Investments, at fair value	1,961,986	
Equipment and Fixtures	15,200	
Accumulated Depreciation—Equipment and Fixtures		$ 3,110
Accounts Payable and Accruals		33,396
Net Assets Held in Trust for Pension Benefits, July 1, 2000		1,647,748
Member Contributions		112,126
Employer Contributions		197,768
Interest and Dividend Income		199,679
Change in Fair Value of Investments	92,600	
Annuity Benefits	43,882	
Disability Benefits	4,026	
Refunds to Terminated Employees	28,801	
Administrative Expenses	8,123	
Totals	$2,193,827	$2,193,827

Required

a. Prepare a Statement of Changes in Net Plan Assets for the State of Arkoma Public Employee Retirement System for the year ended June 30, 2001, in as much detail as possible.

b. Prepare a Statement of Net Plan Assets as of June 30, 2001, for the State of Arkoma Public Employee Retirement System.

Continuous Problem

8–B. The City of Bingham utilizes a Pass-Through Agency Fund to account for grants, entitlements, and shared revenues that may be used in more than one fund pending determination by the City Council of the City of Bingham, or which the City of Bingham receives as primary recipient of grants, and that must be transmitted, without discretion of the City of Bingham, to other governmental units.

The Pass-Through Agency Fund had disbursed all cash received during the fiscal year ended June 30, 2001, and had no assets or liabilities on that date.

Required

a. Open a general journal for the City of Bingham Pass-Through Agency Fund and record the following events and transactions that occurred during the fiscal year ended June 30, 2002:

(1) The City of Bingham is designated as the primary recipient of a grant from a federal agency. The City must remit 80 percent of the grant proceeds to the Bingham School Corporation and 20 percent of the grant proceeds to Bingham Township, both of which are governmental units independent of the City of Bingham. In January 2002, the grantor agency informed the City of Bingham that the total amount of the grant is to be $800,000; the entire amount is to be paid to the City within 60 days of notification.

(2) The City receives cash in the full amount of the grant, $800,000.

(3) The City remits the amounts due to the secondary recipients of the grant: Bingham School Corporation and Bingham Township.

b. The City of Bingham (see Problems 2–B through 7–B) has had an Employees' Retirement Fund for many years. The fund is financed by actuarially determined contributions from the City's General Fund; the employees make no contribution. Administration of the Retirement Fund is handled by General Fund employees, and the Retirement Fund does not bear any administrative expenses.

The Statement of Plan Net Assets for the Employees' Retirement Fund (a pension trust fund) as of the end of the fiscal year prior to the one with which this problem is concerned is shown below:

CITY OF BINGHAM
EMPLOYEES' RETIREMENT FUND
STATEMENT OF PLAN NET ASSETS
AS OF JUNE 30, 2001

Assets	
Cash	$ 8,360
Accrued interest receivable	15,000
Investments, at fair value	750,840
Total Assets	$774,200
Liabilities	
Accounts payable and accrued expenses	6,000
Net Assets Held in Trust for Pension Benefits	$768,200

Record in the general journal for the Employees' Retirement Fund the following events and transactions, which occurred during the year ended June 30, 2002:

(1) The interest receivable on investments as of the beginning of the year was collected in cash.

(2) A liability for annuities payable was recorded in the amount of $75,000.

(3) Contributions from the General Fund in the amount of $176,390 were received in cash.

(4) Interest earnings received in cash amounted to $30,000; additional interest earnings were accrued in the amount of $16,000.

(5) Accounts Payable for Annuities in the amount of $78,000 were paid.

(6) Investments held at June 30, 2001, increased in fair value during the year by $32,600.

(7) Additional investments were purchased at a cost of $150,000.

(8) Nominal accounts for the year were closed.

c. Prepare a Statement of Plan Net Assets as of June 30, 2002, for the Employee's Retirement Fund.

d. Prepare a Statement of Changes in Plan Net Assets for the year ended June 30, 2002.

Financial Reporting of State and Local Governments

Learning Objectives

After studying this chapter, you should be able to:

- Describe the financial reporting requirements of the GASB *Statement No. 34* reporting model.
- Explain the key concepts and terms used in describing the governmental reporting entity.
- Apply the GASB criteria used to determine whether a potential component unit should be included in the reporting entity, and the manner of reporting component units.
- Identify and describe the contents of a Comprehensive Annual Financial Report (CAFR).
- Identify and explain contemporary financial reporting issues.
- Describe the required funds and account groups, characteristics of the funds and account groups, and required financial statements under the financial reporting model being superseded by GASB *Statement No. 34* (Appendix).

Chapters 2 through 8 present extended discussions of the principles of accounting for governmental, proprietary, and fiduciary funds, and governmental and business-type activities at the government-wide level. Chapters 1 and 2 provide overviews of GASB *Statement No. 34* financial reporting requirements, and financial reporting requirements for specific fund types are discussed in several chapters. This chapter presents the *Statement No. 34* reporting requirements in more depth and discusses contemporary financial reporting issues that the GASB may focus on in the future. In addition, for those who may wish to contrast and compare the previous reporting model to the new model specified by *Statement No. 34*, a comprehensive summary of the previous model is provided in an appendix to this chapter.

The Governmental Reporting Entity

The objectives of accounting and financial reporting for governmental units set forth in the GASB's *Concepts Statement No. 1* are discussed in Chapter 1. *Concepts Statement No. 1* does not deal with the practical problem of deciding what a "governmental unit" is. The average citizen—including accountants whose only experience has been with business organizations—has only a vague knowledge, and little understanding, of the overlapping layers of general purpose and special purpose governmental organizations that have some jurisdiction over us wherever we may live and work. Illustration 8–1 indicates the layers of general purpose governments that levy taxes on property. The School Funds in that illustration show that taxes are also levied by special purpose governmental units (an independent school district, in that illustration). Omitted from that illustration, for the sake of brevity, are taxes levied by any special districts. Special districts are defined by the Bureau of the Census as "independent special-purpose governmental units (other than school districts) that exist as separate entities with substantial administrative and fiscal independence from general-purpose local governments."[1] About 40 percent of the local governments in the United States are classified as special districts.[2]

Although the Census definition stresses the independence of special districts, in many instances they were created to provide a vehicle for financing services demanded by residents of a general purpose governmental unit that could not be financed by the general purpose unit because of constitutional or statutory limits on the rates or amounts it could raise from taxes, other revenue sources, and debt. Building authorities are an example of special districts created as a financing vehicle.

In addition to special districts, defined by the Bureau of the Census as independent entities whose financial activities are often closely related to those of one or more general governmental units, it is common for certain governmental activities to be carried on by commissions, boards, and other agencies that are not considered as independent of a general governmental unit by the Bureau of the Census

[1]U.S. Department of Commerce, Bureau of the Census, *1997 Census of Governments* 1, no. 1 (Washington, DC: U.S. Government Printing Office, 1998), p. VII.

[2]Ibid.

but that may have some degree of fiscal and administrative independence from the governing board of the general governmental unit. In past years, some governments have included in their annual reports the financial statements of such semi-independent boards and commissions, and even certain of the special districts, whereas other governments have excluded from their reports the financial data of semi-independent and independent entities.

In order to reduce disparity in reporting and to promote the preparation of financial reports consistent with GASB *Concepts Statement No. 1*, GASB *Codification* Section 2100 provides authoritative guidance on defining the reporting entity, and Section 2600 presents guidance on reporting entity and component unit presentations and disclosure.

Entity Definition Criteria

GASB *Codification* Section 2100 notes that all government organizations are ultimately responsible to elected governing officials at the federal, state, or local level. Elected officials of the primary government are accountable to the citizens for those organizations that are financially dependent on the primary government, or for which the primary government can impose its will. Thus, Section 2100 takes the position that governmental financial reporting should report the elected officials' accountability for such organizations. It should be emphasized that Section 2100 deals only with criteria for defining a governmental reporting entity; it does not establish standards for the incorporation of financial data of component units in the financial statements of the reporting entity. Standards for the incorporation of financial data are set forth in Section 2600.

Definitions of key terms and concepts needed to understand and apply reporting entity criteria are given in Section 2100.501, as amended by GASB *Statement No. 34*, from which selected terms and concepts are provided here:

> **Financial Reporting Entity.** A primary government, organizations for which the primary government is financially accountable, and other organizations for which the nature and significance of their relationship with the primary government are such that exclusion would cause the reporting entity's basic financial statements to be misleading or incomplete. The nucleus of a financial reporting entity usually is a primary government. However, a governmental organization other than a primary government (such as a component unit, a joint venture, a jointly governed organization, or other stand-alone government) serves as the nucleus for its own reporting entity when it issues separate financial statements.
>
> **Primary Government.** A state government or general purpose local government. Also, a special purpose government that has a separately elected governing body, is legally separate, and is fiscally independent of other state or local governments.
>
> **Component Units.** Legally separate organizations for which the elected officials of the primary government are financially accountable. In addition, a component unit can be another organization for which the nature and significance of its relationship with a primary government are such that

exclusion would cause the reporting entity's financial statements to be misleading or incomplete.

Blending (Blended). The method of reporting the financial data of a component unit that presents the component unit's balances and transactions in a manner similar to the presentation of the balances and transactions of the primary government.

Discrete Presentation (Discretely Presented). The method of reporting financial data of component units in a column(s) separate from the financial data of the primary government. An integral part of this method of presentation is that major component unit supporting information is required to be provided in the reporting entity's basic financial statements by (*a*) presenting each major component unit in a separate column in the reporting entity's statements of net assets and activities, (*b*) including combining statements of major component units in the reporting entity's basic statements after the fund financial statements, or presenting condensed financial statements in the notes to the reporting entity's basic financial statements.

Financial Accountability (Financially Accountable). The level of accountability that exists if a primary government appoints a voting majority of an organization's governing board and is either able to impose its will on that organization or there is a potential for the organization to provide specific financial benefits to, or impose specific financial burdens on, the primary government. A primary government may also be financially accountable for governmental organizations with a separately elected governing board, a governing board appointed by another government, or a jointly appointed board that is fiscally dependent on the primary government.

Jointly Governed Organizations. A regional government or other multigovernmental arrangement that is governed by representatives from each of the governments that create the organization, but that is not a joint venture because the participants do not retain an ongoing financial interest or responsibility.

Joint Venture. A legal entity or other organization that results from a contractual arrangement and that is owned, operated, or governed by two or more participants as a separate and specific activity subject to joint control, in which the participants retain (*a*) an ongoing financial interest or (*b*) an ongoing financial responsibility.

Legally Separate Organization (Separate Legal Standing). An organization created as a body corporate or a body corporate and politic or otherwise possessing similar corporate powers. An organization that has separate legal standing has an identity of its own as an "artificial person" with a personality and existence distinct from that of its creator and others.

Other Stand-Alone Government. A legally separate governmental organization that (*a*) does not have a separately elected governing body and (*b*) does not meet the definition of a component unit. Other stand-alone governments include some special purpose governments, joint ventures, jointly governed organizations, and pools.

The definition of the reporting entity is based primarily on the notion of financial accountability. A primary government is financially accountable for the organizations that make up its legal entity. It is also financially accountable for legally separate organizations if its officials appoint a voting majority of an organization's governing body and either it is able to impose its will on that organization or there is a potential for the organization to provide specific financial benefits to, or to impose specific financial burdens on, the primary government.

A primary government has the ability to impose its will on an organization if it can significantly influence the programs, projects, or activities of, or the level of services performed or provided by, the organization. A financial benefit or burden relationship exists if the primary government (*a*) is entitled to the organization's resources; (*b*) is legally obligated or has otherwise assumed the obligation to finance the deficits of, or provide financial support to, the organization; or (*c*) is obligated in some manner for the debt of the organization.

Some organizations are included as component units because of their fiscal dependency on the primary government. An organization is fiscally dependent on the primary government if it is unable to adopt its budget, levy taxes, or set rates or charges, or issue bonded debt without approval by the primary government.[3]

The flowchart in Illustration 9–1 shows the decision process for inclusion or exclusion of a potential component unit (PCU) and how the PCU should be presented in the financial statements or the notes thereto. *Codification* Section 2100.902–.920 provides several examples of the application of the reporting entity criteria in specific circumstances.

GASB standards require that most component units be **discretely presented** (as defined previously) since they are legally separate organizations.[4] If, however, a component unit is, in substance, a part of the primary government, **blended reporting** is required. An example of the latter is a building authority established to finance and construct public facilities for the primary government, with debt service provided by lease payments made by the primary government. Blended reporting is accomplished by including component units' financial data for particular funds and activities with that for the same fund types and activities of the primary government. For example, special revenue fund data of the component units, if major funds, should be reported in separate columns of the basic fund financial statements alongside the primary government's major special revenue funds (or in combining statements if nonmajor funds) and in the governmental activities column of the government-wide financial statements. One exception is that the General Fund data of a blended component unit should be reported as a special revenue fund (either as a major or nonmajor fund, as appropriate) in the reporting entity's

[3]GASB, *Codification*, Sec. 2100.

[4]GASB, *Codification*, Sec. 2600, 107–114.

Illustration 9–1 Decision Process for Inclusion or Exclusion of PCU

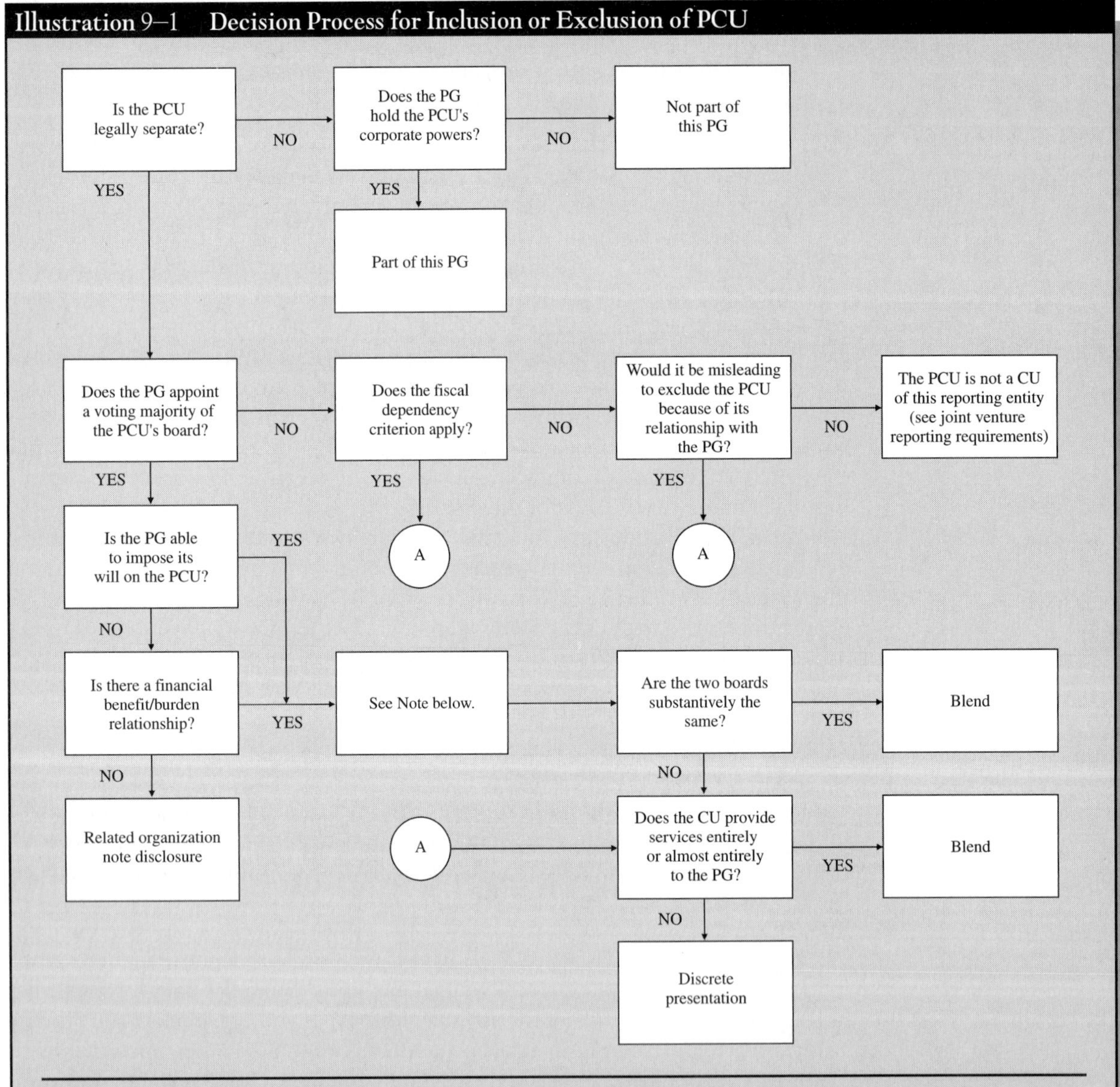

Note: A potential component unit (PCU) for which a primary government (PG) is financially accountable may be fiscally dependent on another government. An organization should be included as a component unit (CU) of only one reporting entity. Professional judgment should be used to determine the most appropriate reporting entity. A primary government that appoints a voting majority of the governing board of a component unit of another government should make the disclosures required for related organizations.

Source: GASB, *Codification*, Sec. 2100.901.

financial statements.[5] Thus, the General Fund column presents only the data for the primary government's General Fund.

Governmental Financial Reports

Once the reporting entity has been determined in accord with the criteria discussed in the preceding section, persons responsible for preparing financial reports for the reporting entity should follow the guidance given in currently effective authoritative literature to determine the content of financial reports to be issued for external users. Chapter 2 contains a summary of the standards GASB *Statement No. 34* sets forth for the content of the comprehensive annual financial report (CAFR) of a state or local governmental reporting entity. Chapters 3 through 8 elaborate on the application of those standards to accounting and financial reporting for each of the funds and government-wide activities. Although much of the discussion in preceding chapters is concerned with general purpose external financial reporting, the needs of administrators, legislators, and other users not properly classifiable as "external" have been given some attention. In the following paragraphs, the discussion in preceding chapters is briefly summarized and placed in perspective.

Need for Periodic Reports

Persons concerned with the day-to-day operations and activities accounted for by governmental funds and groups should be familiar with much of the data processed by the accounting information system because it results from the events and transactions with which they are involved. It is easy for these persons to become overconfident of the intuitive "feel" they develop from their daily involvement. Past events were not always as remembered, and the relative significance of events changes over time. Similarly, administrators at succeedingly higher levels in the organization may feel that participation in decision making and observation of the apparent results of past decisions obviate the necessity for periodic analysis of accounting and statistical reports prepared objectively and with neutrality. However, the memory and perceptions of administrators at higher levels are also subject to failure. Therefore, it is generally agreed that it is useful for financial reports to be prepared and distributed at intervals throughout a fiscal period as well as at period-end.

Interim Financial Reports

Administrators of a governmental unit have the greatest need for interim financial reports, although members of the legislative branch of the governmental unit (particularly those on its finance committee) may also find them of considerable use. Other users of interim reports are news media and residents who are particularly concerned with aspects of the financial management of the unit.

[5] GASB, *Statement No. 34*, par. 114.

Although the particular statements and schedules that should be prepared on an interim basis are a matter of local management preference, the authors believe the following statements and schedules should be useful for budgetary and cash management during the fiscal year.

1. Statement of Actual and Estimated Revenue (for the General and special revenue funds and each other fund type for which budgets have been legally adopted).
2. Statement of Actual and Estimated Expenditures (for the General and special revenue funds and for each other fund type for which budgets have been legally adopted).
3. Comparative Statement of Revenue and Expense (for each enterprise and internal service fund and for similar fiduciary funds).
4. Combined Statement of Cash Receipts, Disbursements, and Balances—All Funds.
5. Forecast of Cash Positions—All Funds.

Other statements and schedules, in addition to those listed above, may be needed, depending on the complexity and scope of a governmental unit's activities. A statement of investments held and their cost and fair values is an example of an additional statement that may be useful. Schedules of past-due receivables from taxes, special assessments, and utility customers may also be needed at intervals.

Complete interim reports should be prepared and distributed at regular intervals throughout a fiscal period, generally monthly, although small governmental units that have little financial activity may find a bimonthly or quarterly period satisfactory. Partial interim reports dealing only with those items of considerable current importance should be prepared and distributed as frequently as their information would be of value. For example, reports of the fair values of investments and of purchases and sales may be needed by a relatively small number of users on a daily basis during certain critical periods.

Annual Financial Reports

Governmental annual financial reports are needed by the same individuals and groups who should receive interim reports. They are also often required to be distributed to agencies of higher governmental jurisdictions and to major creditors. Other users include financial underwriters; debt insurers; debt rating agencies; debt analysts; libraries; other governmental units; associations of governmental administrators, accountants, and finance officers; and college professors and students.

A comprehensive annual financial report (CAFR) should be prepared and published by each state and local governmental unit as a matter of public record. The comprehensive annual financial report is the governmental unit's official annual report prepared and published as a matter of public record. GASB standards make it clear that a primary government is the nucleus of a financial reporting entity for which a CAFR is prepared. However, a governmental organization other than a primary government (e.g., a component unit, joint venture, jointly governed organization, or other stand-alone government) serves as the nucleus of its own reporting entity. The separately issued financial statements of such a reporting entity should follow the same reporting entity standards as those for a primary government and its component units. Specifically, Codification Section 1100.112 requires that the Section 2100 criteria for defining a reporting entity be applied in layers "from the bottom up." For each layer, reporting entity definition and display requirements must be applied before the layer is included in the financial statements for the next higher layer.

In addition to the required management's discussion and analysis (MD&A), basic financial statements (government-wide and fund), and required supplementary information other than the MD&A, the CAFR should contain introductory material, individual fund and combining financial statements, schedules necessary to demonstrate legal compliance, and statistical tables.

Introductory Section. The introductory section of a CAFR should include the table of contents, the letter of transmittal, and other material deemed appropriate by management.

The letter of transmittal may be a letter from the chief finance officer addressed to the chief executive and governing body of the governmental unit, or it may be a narrative over the signature of the chief executive. In either event, the letter or narrative material should cite legal and policy requirements for the report. The introductory section may also include summary discussion of factors relating to the government's service programs and financial matters. Matters discussed in the introductory section should not duplicate those discussed in the MD&A. Because the MD&A is part of the information reviewed (but not audited) by the auditor, it presents only information based on facts known to exist as of the reporting date. Ordinarily, the introductory section is not covered by the auditor's report and therefore may present information of a more subjective nature, including prospective information such as forecasts or expectations.

Financial Section. The financial section of a comprehensive annual financial report should include: (1) an auditor's report, (2) MD&A, (3) basic financial statements (including notes), (4) required supplementary information (RSI) other than the MD&A, and (5) combining and individual fund statements.

Laws relating to the audit of governmental units vary markedly from state to state. In some, all state agencies and all governmental units created pursuant to the state law are required to be audited by an audit agency of the state government. In others, local governmental units are audited by independent Certified Public Accountants. In still others, some governmental units are audited by the state audit agency and some by independent Certified Public Accountants. In any event, the auditor's report should accompany the MD&A, basic financial statements, and RSI other than MD&A presented in the CAFR. Chapter 11 illustrates auditors' reports and explains their significance.

The financial section should contain sufficient information to disclose fully and present fairly the financial position and results of financial operations during the fiscal year. GASB Codification Section 2200, as revised by GASB *Statement*

No. 34, identifies the minimum requirements for general purpose external financial reporting as consisting of the:

1. MD&A
2. Basic Financial Statements
   a. Government-wide financial statements
      (1) Statement of Net Assets (see Illustration 2–1)
      (2) Statement of Activities (see Illustration 2–2)
   b. Fund financial statements
      (1) Governmental Funds
         (a) Balance sheet (see Illustration 2–3)
         (b) Statement of revenues, expenditures, and changes in fund balances (see Illustration 2–4)
      (2) Proprietary funds
         (a) Statement of fund net assets (see Illustration 2–6)
         (b) Statement of revenues, expenses, and changes in fund net assets (see Illustration 2–7)
         (c) Statement of cash flows (see Illustration 2–8)
      (3) Fiduciary funds (including component units that are fiduciary in nature)
         (a) Statement of fiduciary net assets (see Illustration 2–9)
         (b) Statement of changes in fiduciary net assets (see Illustration 2–10)
   c. Notes to the financial statements
3. Required supplementary information other than MD&A
   a. Budgetary comparison schedule (see Illustration 3–2)
   b. Schedules showing assessed infrastructure asset condition, required asset preservation amount, basis for condition measurement, and established asset condition level (only for governments adopting the modified approach for reporting infrastructure).

In addition to the preceding minimum requirements, state and local governments may provide in the financial section of the CAFR combining financial statements for nonmajor funds of each fund type and individual fund statements for the General Fund or for a nonmajor fund that is the only fund of a given type (for example, a debt service fund that is the only fund of that type).

An MD&A was the first item listed above as part of the minimum requirements for general purpose financial reporting. Examples of all required basic financial statements were provided in Chapter 2; however, no example is provided in Chapter 2 for an MD&A. Because the authors have not yet received any government's annual report prepared under the GASB *Statement No. 34* reporting model, we do not yet have a real-world example of an MD&A to provide. The authors will provide an example of an actual city's MD&A in the next edition to the text. Meanwhile, an example included in GASB *Statement No. 34* is presented in Illustration 9–2. As shown in Illustration 9–2, the MD&A should provide an overview of the governmental unit's financial activities and financial highlights for the year.

Illustration 9–2 Management's Discussion and Analysis (MD&A)

Our discussion and analysis of Sample City's financial performance provides an overview of the City's financial activities for the fiscal year ended December 31, 2002. Please read it in conjunction with the transmittal letter on page xxx and the City's financial statements, which begin on page xxx.*

FINANCIAL HIGHLIGHTS

- The City's net assets remained virtually unchanged as a result of this year's operations. While net assets of our business-type activities increased by $3.2 million, or nearly 4 percent, net assets of our governmental activities *decreased* by $3.1 million, or nearly 2.5 percent.
- During the year, the City had expenses that were $6.3 million more than the $99.5 million generated in tax and other revenues for governmental programs (before special items). This compares to last year, however, when expenses exceeded revenues by $8.9 million.
- In the City's business-type activities, revenues increased to $15 million (or 5.6 percent) while expenses decreased by 1.7 percent.
- Total cost of all of the City's programs was virtually unchanged (increasing by $800,000, or less than 1 percent) with no new programs added this year.
- The General Fund reported a deficit this year of $1.3 million despite the one-time proceeds of $3.5 million from the sale of some of our park land.
- The resources available for appropriation were $1.1 million less than budgeted for the General Fund. However, we kept expenditures within spending limits primarily through a mid-year hiring and overtime freeze and our continuing staff restructuring efforts.

USING THIS ANNUAL REPORT

This annual report consists of a series of financial statements. The Statement of Net Assets and the Statement of Activities (on pages xxx and xxx–xxx) provide information about the activities of the City as a whole and present a longer-term view of the City's finances. Fund financial statements start on page xxx. For governmental activities, these statements tell how these services were financed in the short term as well as what remains for future spending. Fund financial statements also report the City's operations in more detail than the government-wide statements by providing information about the City's most significant funds. The remaining statements provide financial information about activities for which the City acts solely as a trustee or agent for the benefit of those outside of the government.

REPORTING THE CITY AS A WHOLE

The Statement of Net Assets and the Statement of Activities

Our analysis of the City as a whole begins on page xxx. One of the most important questions asked about the City's finances is, "Is the City as a whole better off or worse off as a result of the year's activities?" The Statement of Net Assets and the Statement of Activities report information about the City as a whole and about its activities in a way that helps answer this question. These statements include *all* assets and liabilities using the *accrual basis of accounting*, which is similar to the accounting used by most private-sector companies. All of the current year's revenues and expenses are taken into account regardless of when cash is received or paid.

These two statements report the City's *net assets* and changes in them. You can think of the City's net assets—the difference between assets and liabilities—as one way to measure the City's financial

*Note: The preparer would cite the page numbers each place indicated by xxx.

Illustration 9–2 Continued

health, or *financial position*. Over time, *increases or decreases* in the City's net assets are one indicator of whether its *financial health* is improving or deteriorating. You will need to consider other nonfinancial factors, however, such as changes in the City's property tax base and the condition of the City's roads, to assess the *overall health* of the City.

In the Statement of Net Assets and the Statement of Activities, we divide the City into three kinds of activities:

- Governmental activities—Most of the City's basic services are reported here, including the police, fire, public works, and parks departments, and general administration. Property taxes, franchise fees, and state and federal grants finance most of these activities.
- Business-type activities—The City charges a fee to customers to help it cover all or most of the cost of certain services it provides. The City's water and sewer system and parking facilities are reported here.
- Component units—The City includes two separate legal entities in its report—the City School District and the City Landfill Authority. Although legally separate, these "component units" are important because the City is financially accountable for them.

REPORTING THE CITY'S MOST SIGNIFICANT FUNDS

Fund Financial Statements

Our analysis of the City's major funds begins on page xxx. The fund financial statements begin on page xxx and provide detailed information about the most significant funds—not the City as a whole. Some funds are required to be established by State law and by bond covenants. However, the City Council establishes many other funds to help it control and manage money for particular purposes (like the Route 7 reconstruction project) or to show that it is meeting legal responsibilities for using certain taxes, grants, and other money (like grants received from the U.S. Department of Housing and Urban Development). The City's two kinds of funds—*governmental* and *proprietary*—use different accounting approaches.

- Governmental funds—Most of the City's basic services are reported in governmental funds, which focus on how money flows into and out of those funds and the balances left at year-end that are available for spending. These funds are reported using an accounting method called *modified accrual* accounting, which measures cash and all other *financial* assets that can readily be converted to cash. The governmental fund statements provide a detailed *short-term view* of the City's general government operations and the basic services it provides. Governmental fund information helps you determine whether there are more or fewer financial resources that can be spent in the near future to finance the City's programs. We describe the relationship (or differences) between governmental *activities* (reported in the Statement of Net Assets and the Statement of Activities) and governmental *funds* in a reconciliation at the bottom of the fund financial statements.
- Proprietary funds—When the City charges customers for the services it provides—whether to outside customers or to other units of the City—these services are generally reported in proprietary funds. Proprietary funds are reported in the same way that all activities are reported in the Statement of Net Assets and the Statement of Activities. In fact, the City's enterprise funds (a component of proprietary funds) are the same as the business-type activities we report in the government-wide statements but provide more detail and additional information, such as cash flows, for proprietary funds. We use internal service funds (the other component of proprietary funds) to report activities that provide supplies and services for the City's other programs and activities—such as the City's Telecommunications Fund.

Illustration 9–2 Continued

THE CITY AS TRUSTEE

Reporting the City's Fiduciary Responsibilities

The City is the trustee, or *fiduciary*, for its employees' pension plans. It is also responsible for other assets that—because of a trust arrangement—can be used only for the trust beneficiaries. All of the City's fiduciary activities are reported in separate Statements of Fiduciary Net Assets and Changes in Fiduciary Net Assets on pages xxx and xxx. We exclude these activities from the City's other financial statements because the City cannot use these assets to finance its operations. The City is responsible for ensuring that the assets reported in these funds are used for their intended purposes.

THE CITY AS A WHOLE

The City's *combined* net assets were virtually unchanged from a year ago—*increasing* from $209.0 million to $209.1 million. In contrast, last year net assets *decreased* by $6.2 million. Looking at the net assets and net expenses of governmental and business-type activities separately, however, two very different stories emerge. Our analysis below focuses on the net assets (Table 1) and changes in net assets (Table 2) of the City's governmental and business-type activities.

Table 1
Net Assets (in Millions)

	Governmental Activities		Business-type Activities		Total Primary Government	
	2002	*2001*	*2002*	*2001*	*2002*	*2001*
Current and other assets	$ 54.3	$ 49.0	$ 13.8	$ 15.7	$ 68.1	$ 64.7
Capital assets	170.0	162.1	151.4	147.6	321.4	309.7
Total assets	224.3	211.1	165.2	163.3	389.5	374.4
Long-term debt outstanding	(79.3)	(61.8)	(78.3)	(77.3)	(157.6)	(139.1)
Other liabilities	(21.4)	(22.6)	(1.4)	(3.7)	(22.8)	(26.3)
Total liabilities	(100.7)	(84.4)	(79.7)	(81.0)	(180.4)	(165.4)
Net assets:						
Invested in capital assets, net of debt	103.7	100.3	73.1	71.6	176.8	171.9
Restricted	22.8	27.1	1.4	2.8	24.2	29.9
Unrestricted (deficit)	(2.9)	(0.7)	11.0	7.9	8.1	7.2
Total net assets	$123.6	$126.7	$ 85.5	$ 82.3	$209.1	$209.0

Net assets of the City's governmental activities decreased by 2.5 percent ($123.6 million compared to $126.7 million). *Unrestricted* net assets—the part of net assets that can be used to finance day-to-day operations without constraints established by debt covenants, enabling legislation, or other legal requirements—changed from a $700,000 deficit at December 31, 2001, to a $2.9 million deficit at the end of this year.

Illustration 9–2 Continued

This deficit in unrestricted governmental net assets arose primarily because of three factors. First, the City did not include in past annual budgets the amounts needed to fully finance liabilities arising from property and casualty claims. The City does not purchase commercial insurance to cover these claims. The City also did not include in past budgets amounts needed to pay for unused employee vacation and sick days. The City will need to include these amounts in future years' budgets as they come due. Second, during the past two years, tax revenues and State grants have fallen short of amounts originally anticipated. Finally, the City Council decided to draw down accumulated cash balances to delay the need to approve new tax increases. These factors are discussed in greater detail below.

The net assets of our business-type activities increased by 3.9 percent ($85.5 million compared to $82.3 million) in 2002. This increase, however, cannot be used to make up for the *decrease* reported in governmental activities. The City generally can only use these net assets to finance the continuing operations of the water and sewer and parking operations.

Table 2
Changes in Net Assets (in Millions)

	Governmental Activities		Business-type Activities		Total Primary Government	
	2002	*2001*	*2002*	*2001*	*2002*	*2001*
Revenues						
Program revenues:						
Charges for services	$ 15.8	$ 14.6	$12.7	$11.9	$ 28.5	$ 26.5
Federal grants	2.5	2.4	1.6	1.5	4.1	3.9
State grants and entitlements	7.5	8.3	—	—	7.5	8.3
General revenues:						
Property taxes	56.1	53.6	—	—	56.1	53.6
Other taxes	13.3	13.0	—	—	13.3	13.0
Federal entitlements	1.5	1.4	—	—	1.5	1.4
Other general revenues	2.8	2.6	0.7	0.8	3.5	3.4
Total revenues	99.5	95.9	15.0	14.2	114.5	110.1
Program expenses						
General government	9.6	9.3	—	—	9.6	9.3
Public safety	34.9	33.8	—	—	34.9	33.8
Public works	10.1	10.5	—	—	10.1	10.5
Engineering services	1.3	1.4	—	—	1.3	1.4
Health and sanitation	6.7	6.5	—	—	6.7	6.5
Cemetery	0.7	0.5	—	—	0.7	0.5
Culture and recreation	11.5	11.9	—	—	11.5	11.9
Community development	3.0	3.3	—	—	3.0	3.3
Education	21.9	21.3	—	—	21.9	21.3
Interest on long-term debt	6.1	6.3	—	—	6.1	6.3
Water	—	—	3.6	3.7	3.6	3.7

Illustration 9–2 Continued

Table 2 (continued)

	Governmental Activities		Business-type Activities		Total Primary Government	
	2002	2001	2002	2001	2002	2001
Sewer	—	—	4.9	4.8	4.9	4.8
Parking facilities	—	—	2.8	3.0	2.8	3.0
Total expenses	105.8	104.8	11.3	11.5	117.1	116.3
Excess (deficiency) before special items and transfers	(6.3)	(8.9)	3.7	2.7	(2.6)	(6.2)
Special items—park land sale	2.7	—	—	—	2.7	—
Transfers	0.5	(0.4)	(0.5)	0.4	—	—
Increase (decrease) in net assets	$ (3.1)	$ (9.3)	$ 3.2	$ 3.1	$ 0.1	$ (6.2)

The City's total revenues (excluding special items) increased by 4 percent ($4.4 million). The total cost of all programs and services was virtually unchanged (increasing by $800,000, or less than 1 percent) with no new programs added this year. Even with this low growth in expenses and the sale of 1,170 acres of park land on the City's south side for a gain of $2.7 million, the City still did not cover this year's costs. The factors that led to the accumulated deficit also were the primary reasons for this year's shortfall. Our analysis below separately considers the operations of governmental and business-type activities.

GOVERNMENTAL ACTIVITIES

Revenues (excluding the sale of park land) for the City's governmental activities increased by 3.8 percent ($3.6 million), while total expenses increased just under 1 percent ($1 million). With the gain on the sale of the park land, the decrease in net assets for governmental activities was narrowed to $3.1 million in 2002. This compares to a $9.3 million decrease in net assets in 2001.

The City's management took three major actions this year to avoid the level of deficit reported last year. Two of these actions increased revenues and the third reduced expenses:

- The City increased property tax rates by an average of 5 percent. This increase, the first in four years, raised the City's tax revenues by $2.5 million in 2002. Based on increases in the total assessed valuation, property tax revenues are budgeted to increase by an additional $2.8 million next year.
- The City sold three parcels of park land for $3.5 million, giving the City a gain (net of the $823,000 originally paid for the land) of $2.7 million. This was a one-time special item. Although this property has been added back to the tax rolls, the tax revenues it may generate are not expected to increase resources in any single year to the same level we recognized from selling the land.
- The City imposed a hiring and overtime freeze in midyear (excluding the City's police, fire, and sanitation departments) that resulted in approximately a $2.2 million savings in wages and related benefits expenses reported in 2002 compared to 2001. This freeze, plus cost savings of $500,000 from our continuing staff restructuring efforts, held down the increase in expenses.

Illustration 9–2 Continued

Despite the rate increase, property tax revenues lagged by $680,000 compared to the final budget estimates because delays in several major commercial and residential developments precluded adding them to this year's tax rolls. More than half of the City's other revenue sources also fell short of the final budget estimates. These shortfalls include franchise fee revenues, which vary based on sales generated by businesses operated within the City. The fire at the State Street Mall affected many retail businesses in the City, as discussed on page xxx. In addition, grant revenues were lower than expected because of overall state cutbacks.

The cost of all *governmental* activities this year was $105.8 million compared to $104.8 million last year. However, as shown in the Statement of Activities on pages xxx–xxx, the amount that our taxpayers ultimately financed for these activities through City taxes was only $80 million because some of the cost was paid by those who directly benefited from the programs ($15.8 million) or by other governments and organizations that subsidized certain programs with grants and contributions ($10.0 million). Overall, the City's governmental program revenues, including intergovernmental aid and fees for services, increased in 2002 from $25.3 million to $25.8 million, principally based on increases in fees charged for services. The City paid for the remaining "public benefit" portion of governmental activities with $69.4 million in taxes (some of which could only be used for certain programs) and with other revenues, such as interest and general entitlements.

Table 3 presents the cost of each of the City's five largest programs—police, fire, public works, education, and parks and recreation—as well as each program's *net* cost (total cost less revenues generated by the activities). The net cost shows the financial burden that was placed on the City's taxpayers by each of these functions.

Table 3
Governmental Activities (in Millions)

	Total Cost of Services		Net Cost of Services	
	2002	*2001*	*2002*	*2001*
Police department	$ 20.3	$ 19.7	$19.5	$19.1
Fire department	9.4	9.2	8.7	8.4
Public works	10.1	10.5	7.0	7.3
Education	21.9	21.3	21.9	21.3
Parks and recreation	9.9	9.7	4.4	4.6
All others	34.2	34.4	18.5	18.3
Totals	$105.8	$104.8	$80.0	$79.0

BUSINESS-TYPE ACTIVITIES

Revenues of the City's business-type activities (see Table 2) increased by 5.6 percent ($15 million in 2002 compared to $14.2 million in 2001) and expenses *decreased* by 1.7 percent. The factors driving these results include:

- The City water and sewer system, benefiting from growth in hook-ups by residential customers who are converting from septic systems, saw its operating revenues climb 10 percent to $11.3 million, but operating expenses rose only 4 percent, to $6.9 million. High maintenance costs—caused by the harsh winter months in 2001—did not occur this year.

Illustration 9–2 Continued

- The City parking facilities, however, continued to operate at a deficit (by $1.4 million this year versus $1.3 million in 2001). In both years, this decrease is attributable primarily to the largest of the three City-owned garages, located on State Street. This year, the garage had to be closed for two extended periods due to ruptured gas lines beneath nearby streets, which now have been repaired, and the State Street Mall fire. These closings stopped revenues from being generated by the garage for two months, while only slightly reducing expenses.

THE CITY'S FUNDS

As the City completed the year, its governmental funds (as presented in the balance sheet on pages xxx–xxx) reported a *combined* fund balance of $34.9 million, which is slightly below last year's total of $35.0 million. Included in this year's total change in fund balance, however, is a deficit of $1.3 million in the City's General Fund. Furthermore, without the cash from the sale of park land, fund balances would be $3.5 million lower. The primary reasons for the General Fund's deficit mirror the governmental activities analysis highlighted on pages xxx and xxx. In addition, these other changes in fund balances should be noted:

- The City spent $11.3 million this year on the Route 7 reconstruction project, reducing the beginning fund balance in that capital projects fund by the same amount. This reduction was expected because capital fund balances at the beginning of this year included the proceeds of general obligation bonds issued last year to finance that project. Although these and other capital expenditures reduce available fund balances, they create new assets for the City as reported in the Statement of Net Assets and as discussed in Note 1 to the financial statements.
- In the same way, the fund balance of the Community Redevelopment Fund increased by $17.5 million this year when community redevelopment housing bonds were issued. By year-end, only $2.2 million of the debt proceeds had been used for construction of new housing units and $2.3 million was transferred to the Debt Service Fund. Overall, fund balance in the Community Redevelopment Fund increased by $13.1 million.
- Each year, the State provides the City with a portion of the gasoline tax revenues it collects. This money can only be used to replace, maintain, or improve the City's roads. This year, $3 million of these resources, including $1.7 million accumulated in previous years, was used primarily on ten major repaving projects.

GENERAL FUND BUDGETARY HIGHLIGHTS

Over the course of the year, the City Council revised the City budget several times. These budget amendments fall into three categories. The first category includes amendments and supplemental appropriations that were approved shortly after the beginning of the year and reflect the actual beginning balances (versus the amounts we estimated in October 2001). The second category includes changes that the Council made during the third quarter to take into account the mid-year hiring and overtime freeze and some of the City's staff restructuring efforts. The principal amendment in this case was to eliminate the original budget contingency appropriation used in the past to cover employee overtime and charges associated with staff turnover. In addition, the Council revised its estimated resources to reflect its decision to sell an additional parcel of park land. Finally, the Council approved several increases in appropriations to prevent budget overruns.

Even with these adjustments, the actual charges to appropriations (expenditures) were $1.3 million below the final budget amounts. The most significant positive variance ($534,646) occurred in the City's general government account, where the staff restructuring and hiring freeze resulted in a 10 percent reduction of the general administration workforce.

Illustration 9–2 Continued

On the other hand, resources available for appropriation were $1.1 million below the final budgeted amount. As we noted earlier, property and franchise tax collections were less than expected. Reductions in State funding also affected grant resources available for appropriation. These shortfalls were partially offset by an increase in public service taxes. This increase resulted from a 15 percent increase in utility and cable television taxes, which was approved by the City Council in the third quarter.

The City's General Fund balance of $1.7 million reported on pages xxx–xxx differs from the General Fund's *budgetary* fund balance of $1.4 million reported in the budgetary comparison schedule on page xxx. This is principally because *budgetary* fund balance excludes $182,821 of supplies inventories that are reported as expenditures for budgetary purposes when they are purchased and $40,292 of encumbrances reported as expenditures for budgetary purposes.

CAPITAL ASSET AND DEBT ADMINISTRATION

Capital Assets

At the end of 2002, the City had $321 million invested in a broad range of capital assets, including police and fire equipment, buildings, park facilities, roads, bridges, and water and sewer lines. (See Table 4 below.) This amount represents a net increase (including additions and deductions) of just under $12 million, or 3.8 percent, over last year.

Table 4
Capital Assets at Year-end (Net of Depreciation, in Millions)

	Governmental Activities		Business-type Activities		Totals	
	2002	*2001*	*2002*	*2001*	*2002*	*2001*
Land	$ 27.1	$ 29.4	$ 3.8	$ 3.7	$ 30.9	$ 33.1
Buildings and improvements	30.2	30.5	115.5	113.6	145.7	144.1
Equipment	21.2	22.9	1.2	1.0	22.4	23.9
Infrastructure	91.5	79.3	30.9	29.3	122.4	108.6
Totals	$170.0	$162.1	$151.4	$147.6	$321.4	$309.7

This year's major additions included (in millions):

Route 7 reconstruction project, paid for with proceeds of general obligation bonds issued last year	$11.3
Replacement of older segments of the wastewater collection system and treatment facilities, paid for with proceeds from a revenue note issued last year	3.2
Redevelopment housing construction, paid for with revenue bonds issued this year	2.2
Land acquired through the City's power of eminent domain, paid for with General Fund resources	2.0
Water distribution mains, hydrants, and meters, paid for with water and sewer revenue bonds issued this year	1.6
	$20.3

Illustration 9–2 Continued

The City's fiscal-year 2003 capital budget calls for it to spend another $16 million for capital projects, principally for the completion of its Route 7 construction project and to create housing units in the City's new community redevelopment housing program. The City has no plans to issue additional debt to finance these projects. Rather, we will use bond proceeds from the community redevelopment bonds issued this year and resources on hand in the City's Gas Tax Fund. More detailed information about the City's capital assets is presented in Note 1 to the financial statements.

DEBT

At year-end, the City had $158 million in bonds and notes outstanding versus $141 million last year—an increase of 12 percent—as shown in Table 5.

Table 5
Outstanding Debt, at Year-end (in Millions)

	Governmental Activities		Business-type Activities		Totals	
	2002	*2001*	*2002*	*2001*	*2002*	*2001*
General obligation bonds (backed by the City)	$32.6	$32.7	$—	$—	$ 32.6	$ 32.7
Revenue bonds and notes (backed by specific tax and fee revenues)	46.7	30.7	78.3	77.3	125.0	108.0
Totals	$79.3	$63.4	$78.3	$77.3	$157.6	$140.7

New debt resulted mainly from issuing revenue bonds for two new projects—$18 million of community redevelopment housing bonds and $3.6 million of water system improvement bonds. In addition, to improve cash flow and to take advantage of lower interest rates, the City management decided to refinance nearly $43 million of two general obligation debt issues and one revenue bond issue by issuing refunding bonds. By refinancing the debt, the City will save $2.3 million in principal and interest over the next 15 years.

The City's general obligation bond rating continues to carry the fourth highest rating possible, a rating that has been assigned by national rating agencies to the City's debt since 1995. All of the City's other debt—principally, revenue bonds and notes—carries the fifth highest rating. The State limits the amount of general obligation debt that cities can issue to 3 percent of the assessed value of all taxable property within the City's corporate limits. The City's outstanding general obligation debt is significantly below this $134 million state-imposed limit.

As noted earlier, the City did not previously purchase commercial insurance for property and casualty claims and has claims and judgments of $7.9 million outstanding at year-end compared with $8.1 million last year. Other obligations include accrued vacation pay and sick leave. More detailed information about the City's long-term liabilities is presented in Note 2 to the financial statements.

Illustration 9–2 Concluded

ECONOMIC FACTORS AND NEXT YEAR'S BUDGETS AND RATES

The City's elected and appointed officials considered many factors when setting the fiscal-year 2003 budget, tax rates, and fees that will be charged for the business-type activities. One of those factors is the economy. The City's nonagricultural employment growth has mirrored its population growth during 1998–2002, averaging annual gains of 4.2 percent. Unemployment in the City now stands at 3.9 percent versus 4.1 percent a year ago. This compares with the State's unemployment rate of 4.4 percent and the national rate of 4.9 percent.

Inflation in the metropolitan area continues to be somewhat higher than the national Consumer Price Index (CPI) increase. The City's CPI increase was 3.2 percent for fiscal year 2002 compared with the average U.S. city rate of 3 percent and the national rate of 2.8 percent. Inflation has been higher here due in part to residential housing market and energy price increases in 2001–2002.

These indicators were taken into account when adopting the General Fund budget for 2003. Amounts available for appropriation in the General Fund budget are $96.4 million, an increase of 4 percent over the final 2002 budget of $92.7 million. Property taxes (benefiting from the 2002 rate increases and increases in assessed valuations), public service taxes (with rate increases discussed on page xxx), and grant revenue (boosted by increased State funding in several of our current programs) are expected to lead this increase. The City will use these increases in revenues to finance programs we currently offer and the effect that we expect inflation to have on program costs. Budgeted expenditures are expected to rise nearly 4 percent, to $95.9 million from $92.2 million in 2002. Increased wage and cost-of-living adjustments, based on agreements reached with the police, fire, and sanitation department unions in 2002 of roughly $800,000, are the largest increments. The City has added no major new programs or initiatives to the 2003 budget.

If these estimates are realized, the City's budgetary General Fund balance is expected to increase modestly by the close of 2003. More importantly, however, this will have been accomplished without selling capital assets or restructuring long-term debt to alleviate cash flow pressures, both actions needed in the current year. In addition, the City recently purchased commercial insurance for all property and casualty claims incurred after December 31, 2002.

As for the City's business-type activities, we expect that the 2003 results will also improve based on these recent rate decisions:

- The Public Service Commission approved a 2 percent rate increase for all water customers effective January 1. Sewer charges will not change.
- The City Council authorized a 15 percent increase in parking fees, both at the City-owned garages and for on-street meters.

CONTACTING THE CITY'S FINANCIAL MANAGEMENT

This financial report is designed to provide our citizens, taxpayers, customers, and investors and creditors with a general overview of the City's finances and to show the City's accountability for the money it receives. If you have questions about this report or need additional financial information, contact the City Controller's Office, at City, 1501 Coolidge Avenue, City, State.

Source: Governmental Accounting Standards Board, GASB *Statement No. 34* (Norwalk, CT, 1999), Appendix C, pp. 183–197.

It should provide a narrative explanation of the contents of the CAFR, including the nature of the government-wide and fund financial statements, and the distinctions between those statements. The remainder of the MD&A should describe the governmental unit's financial condition, financial trends of the government as a whole and of its major funds, budgetary highlights, and activities affecting capital assets and related debt. Finally, the MD&A should discuss economic factors and budget and tax rates for the next year.

Statistical Tables. In addition to the output of the accounting information system presented in the financial section of the governmental annual report, statistical tables reflecting social and economic data, financial trends, and the fiscal capacity of the government are needed by the reader who is more than casually interested in the activities of the governmental unit. Tabulations required by the GASB for inclusion in a CAFR are:

1. General Governmental Expenditures by Function—Last Ten Fiscal Years.
2. General Revenues by Source—Last Ten Fiscal Years.
3. Property Tax Levies and Collections—Last Ten Fiscal Years.
4. Assessed and Estimated Actual Value of Taxable Property—Last Ten Fiscal Years.
5. Property Tax Rates—All Overlapping Governments—Last Ten Fiscal Years.
6. Special Assessment Billings and Collections—Last Ten Fiscal Years (if the government is obligated in some manner for related special assessment debt).
7. Ratio of Net General Bonded Debt to Assessed Value and Net Bonded Debt per Capita—Last Ten Fiscal Years.
8. Computation of Legal Debt Margin (if not presented in the financial section).
9. Computation of Overlapping Debt (if not presented in the financial section).
10. Ratio of Annual Debt Service for General Bonded Debt to Total General Expenditures—Last Ten Fiscal Years.
11. Revenue Bond Coverage—Last Ten Fiscal Years.
12. Demographic Statistics.
13. Property Value, Construction, and Bank Deposits—Last Ten Fiscal Years.
14. Principal Taxpayers.
15. Miscellaneous Statistics.

Classification of governmental expenditures by function, classification of revenues by source, and other meaningful classifications of revenues and expenditures are discussed at some length in Chapter 3. Assessment of property and the levy and collection of property taxes are discussed in Chapter 4 and in subsequent chapters as appropriate. Reporting of the ratio of net general bonded debt to assessed valuation and the ratio per capita, as well as the computation of legal debt limit, legal debt margin, and direct and overlapping debt and future debt service requirements, are all illustrated and discussed in Chapter 6. Information about investments held for the various funds is often presented in the statistical section of a CAFR, although, as shown in Chapter 6, the information may also be presented in other sections of the report. Additional information listed by the GASB as desirable for presentation in the statistical section of the CAFR is generally self-explanatory. The demographic statistics and miscellaneous statistics often presented are those that are of interest to debt insurers, debt rating agencies, creditors and potential creditors, and organizations considering locating in the area included in the reporting entity, such as population, per capita income, unemployment rate, average education of the workforce, fire protection data, police protection data, information about public schools and colleges and universities, recreation and cultural facilities, and parking facilities. Additionally, it seems to be common for state laws to require local governments to list administrators and their salaries, and to list property, casualty, and fidelity insurance coverage carried by the reporting entity.

Preparation of Basic Financial Statements

The basic financial statements that must be presented to meet minimum general purpose financial reporting requirements were described earlier in this chapter. Although GASB-furnished examples of the basic statements are provided in Chapter 2, it will be instructive to illustrate preparation of those statements for the Town of Brighton, the hypothetical town used for illustrative purposes in several of the preceding chapters. In the prior chapters illustrative journal entries were provided for fund and government-wide activities as follows:

Chapter	*Illustrative Entries for*	*Fiscal Year Ending*
4	General Fund/Governmental Activities	December 31, 2002
5	Capital Projects Fund/Governmental Activities	December 31, 2002
6	Regular Serial Bond Debt Service Fund/ Governmental Activities	December 31, 2002
	Deferred Serial Bond Debt Service Fund/ Governmental Activities	December 31, 2002
	Term Bond Debt Service Fund	December 31, 2002
7	Supplies Fund (an internal service fund)	December 31, 2003
	Water Utility Fund (an enterprise fund)	December 31, 2002

For sake of brevity, entries in the governmental activities general journal were omitted in Chapter 6 for the Term Bond Debt Service Fund. Nevertheless, the effects of those transactions are included in the illustrative government-wide financial statements presented later in this section. Recall from Chapter 7 that the business-type activities column of the government-wide statements simply reports information for the enterprise funds (internal service fund information is reported in the governmental activities column). Further, enterprise funds report using the same measurement focus (flow of economic resources) and basis of accounting (accrual) as the government-wide financial statements. Thus, unlike governmental activities, which use a different measurement focus and basis of accounting than governmental funds, there is no need for a separate set of accounting records to record government-wide business-type transactions. The accounting information reported in enterprise funds can easily be aggregated for reporting at the government-wide level. Since, in the case of the Town of Brighton, the Water Utility Fund is the only enterprise fund, its financial information will simply be reported in the business-type activities column of the government-wide financial statements. A different fiscal year (2003) was used for the Supplies Fund (an internal service fund) to avoid needing to include its interfund transactions in the General Fund in Chapter 4 and to simplify preparation of the government-wide financial statements for the Town of Brighton. Thus, the Supplies Fund is not included in the financial statements illustrated in this section.

The governmental activities column of the government-wide financial statements for the Town of Brighton, presented later in this section, includes all pertinent financial information, other than budget-related, arising from transactions of the General Fund, the capital projects fund (see Chapter 5), and the three debt service funds (see Chapter 6). In addition, the direct expenses of the functions reported in the Statement of Activities include depreciation on the general capital assets assigned to those functions, or allocated to the functions on a rational basis, such as square footage of usage for functions that share public buildings.

All changes in government-wide net assets that occurred due to transactions during fiscal year 2002 in the General Fund, Capital Projects Fund, Regular Serial Bond Debt Service Fund, Deferred Serial Bond Debt Service Fund, and the Term Bond Debt Service Fund are reflected in the pre-closing general ledger trial balance for governmental activities presented in Illustration 9–3. The amounts shown for certain revenue and expense accounts are assumed amounts that reflect many transactions that were not illustrated in Chapter 4, as were certain amounts that were reported in the General Fund Statement of Revenues, Expenditures, and Fund Balances shown in Illustration 4–6.

Before preparing the government-wide financial statements, an adjusting entry should be made to record fiscal year 2002 depreciation expense for the general capital assets, as well as other appropriate adjusting entries. Using assumed amounts for depreciation and assuming depreciation is assigned to functions in the amounts

Illustration 9–3

TOWN OF BRIGHTON
PRE-CLOSING TRIAL BALANCE
GOVERNMENTAL ACTIVITIES GENERAL LEDGER
DECEMBER 31, 2002

	Debits	Credits
Cash	$ 391,451	
Taxes Receivable—Delinquent	680,900	
Estimated Uncollectible Delinquent Taxes		$ 96,000
Interest and Penalties Receivable	3,085	
Estimated Uncollectible Interest and Penalties		1,985
Interest Receivable	20,500	
Inventory of Materials and Supplies	61,500	
Investments	1,393,972	
Land	1,214,600	
Buildings	15,476,248	
Accumulated Depreciation—Buildings		10,968,347
Equipment	6,369,477	
Accumulated Depreciation—Equipment		4,059,444
Improvements Other Than Buildings	16,693,626	
Accumulated Depreciation—Improvements Other Than Buildings		5,148,162
Vouchers Payable		396,800
Interest Payable		85,500
Due to Federal Government		126,520
Due to State Government		39,740
Internal Balances		5,000
Current Portion of Long-Term Debt		320,000
Bonds Payable		4,180,000
Net Assets—Invested in Capital Assets, Net of Related Debt		15,830,018

shown, the journal entry to record the adjusting entry for depreciation in the governmental activities general journal is given as:

	Debits	Credits
Governmental Activities:		
Expenses—General Government	114,746	
Expenses—Public Safety	229,493	
Expenses—Public Works	672,288	
Expenses—Health and Welfare	95,622	
Expenses—Parks and Recreation	133,871	
Accumulated Depreciation—Buildings		527,240
Accumulated Depreciation—Equipment		428,980
Accumulated Depreciation—Improvements Other than Buildings		289,800

Illustration 9–3 (concluded)

	Debits	*Credits*
Net Assets, Restricted for Debt Service		1,659,978
Net Assets, Unrestricted		349,900
Program Revenues—Charges for Services—General Government		213,200
Program Revenues—Charges for Services—Parks and Recreation		82,464
Program Revenues—Operating Grants and Contributions—Public Safety		100,000
Program Revenues—Operating Grants and Contributions—Health and Welfare		184,100
Program Revenues—Capital Grants and Contributions—Public Safety		300,000
General Revenues—Property Taxes		2,599,636
General Revenues—Sales Taxes		485,000
General Revenues—Interest and Penalties on Delinquent Taxes		11,400
General Revenues—Fines and Forfeits		310,800
General Revenues—Miscellaneous		28,400
General Revenues—Taxes—Restricted for Debt Service		337,000
General Revenues—Investment Earnings—Restricted for Debt Service		107,245
Expenses—General Government	788,659	
Expenses—Public Safety	1,646,321	
Expenses—Public Works	1,546,874	
Expenses—Health and Welfare	959,564	
Expenses—Parks and Recreation	562,362	
Expenses—Interest on Tax Anticipation Notes	13,500	
Expenses—Interest on Long-Term Debt	204,000	
Totals	$48,026,639	$48,026,639

The pre-closing trial balance presented in Illustration 9–3 provides all the information needed for the governmental activities column of the government-wide financial statements, including the effects of the preceding adjusting entry for depreciation.

Portions of closing entries for the temporary accounts of the governmental activities were discussed or illustrated in earlier chapters. The complete closing entry to close all temporary accounts of the governmental activities general ledger would be:

	Debits	Credits
Governmental Activities:		
Program Revenues—Charges for Services—General Government	213,200	
Program Revenues—Charges for Services—Parks and Recreation	82,464	
Program Revenues—Operating Grants and Contributions—Public Safety	100,000	
Program Revenues—Operating Grants and Contributions—Health and Welfare	184,100	
Program Revenues—Capital Grants and Contributions—Public Safety	300,000	
General Revenues—Property Taxes	2,599,636	
General Revenues—Sales Taxes	485,000	
General Revenues—Interest and Penalties on Delinquent Taxes	11,400	
General Revenues—Fines and Forfeits	310,800	
General Revenues—Miscellaneous	28,400	
General Revenues—Taxes—Restricted for Debt Service	337,000	
General Revenues—Investment Earnings—Restricted for Debt Service	107,245	
Net Assets—Unrestricted	962,035	
Expenses—General Government		788,659
Expenses—Public Safety		1,646,321
Expenses—Public Works		1,546,874
Expenses—Health and Welfare		959,564
Expenses—Parks and Recreation		562,362
Expenses—Interest on Tax Anticipation Notes		13,500
Expenses—Interest on Long-Term Debt		204,000

In addition to the closing entry shown above, entries are required to reclassify the three net asset accounts to their correct amounts as of December 31, 2002. By comparing the pre-closing trial balance (see Illustration 9–3) to the governmental activities column of the Statement of Net Assets as of December 31, 2001 (see Illustration 4–1), one can easily verify that the balances of the two accounts Net Assets—Invested in Capital Assets, Net of Related Debt and Net Assets—Restricted for Debt Service in the pre-closing trial balance are the same as those reported at the end of the prior year. That is, these accounts have not yet been updated to reflect changes in general capital asset transactions and related debt, and changes in net assets restricted for debt service.

From the information in the trial balance, the total amount of capital assets, net of accumulated depreciation, as of December 31, 2002, is calculated as $19,577,998. Therefore, the correct balance of Net Assets—Invested in Capital Assets, Net of Related Debt is $15,077,998 ($19,577,998, less related debt of $4,500,000), a decrease of $752,020 during the year. Since capital debt increased by $1,000,000 (from $3,500,000 to $4,500,000) during the year and accumulated depreciation totaled $1,246,020, capital asset acquisitions during the year must have exceeded dispositions by $1,494,000 ($1,000,000 + $1,246,020 – $752,020). The Town of Brighton Fire Station (see Entry 16 on page 196 in Chapter 5) was completed during the year at a cost of $1,494,000, which accounts in full for capital asset acquisitions during 2002.

Based on the assets reported in the combined debt service funds balance sheet presented in Illustration 6–8, assets reported in the governmental activities trial balance must include amounts totaling $1,666,723 for cash, investments, and taxes and interest receivable that are restricted for debt service. Thus, the correct balance for Net Assets–Restricted for Debt Service as of December 31, 2002, must also be $1,666,723, an increase of $6,745 from its current balance of $1,659,978.

Based on the foregoing analysis, the journal entry to reclassify the governmental activities net asset accounts to the appropriate amounts is given as:

	Debits	Credits
Governmental Activities:		
Net Assets—Invested in Capital Assets, Net of Related Debt	752,020	
Net Assets—Restricted for Debt Service		6,745
Net Assets—Unrestricted		745,275

The Town of Brighton's government-wide Statement of Net Assets and Statement of Activities are presented in Illustrations 9–4 and 9–5. Compared with the trial balance shown in Illustration 9–3, it is apparent that the financial statements are highly condensed. For example, taxes receivable, interest and penalties receivable, and interest receivable are reported as a single receivables amount, net of related estimated uncollectible amounts. Detail of the receivables and uncollectibles should be disclosed in the notes to the financial statements. Similarly, because the detail of capital assets, including depreciation expense and accumulated depreciation, should be disclosed in the notes to the financial statements, it is acceptable to report the aggregate net amount for capital assets on a single line. The Town has also decided to report all current liabilities, except for the current portion of long-term debt, as a single amount for vouchers payable and accrued liabilities. Such highly condensed reporting is consistent with the GASB's objective to "enhance the understandability and usefulness of the general purpose external financial reports of state and local governments" by providing an overview of the financial condition and results of activities of the government as a whole, in addition to more detailed fund financial statements and detailed disclosures in the notes to the financial statements.[6]

As shown in Illustrations 9–4 and 9–5, the two government-wide financial statements should also report amounts for discretely presented component units. Because the Town of Brighton has no component units, only primary government information is presented. In order to minimize line-item detail in the financial statements, and thus make the financial statements easier to understand, immaterial amounts for specific items may be reported with the amounts for broadly similar items. For example, in the Town of Brighton's Statement of Activities, it would have been acceptable to report the relatively small amount of revenue from interest and penalties on delinquent taxes as part of revenues from property taxes.

[6]GASB, *Statement No. 34*, par. 1.

Illustration 9–4

TOWN OF BRIGHTON
STATEMENT OF NET ASSETS
DECEMBER 31, 2002

	Primary Government			
	Governmental Activities	*Business-Type Activities*	*Total*	*Component Units (None)*
Assets				
Cash	$ 391,451	$ 137,155	$ 528,606	
Investments	1,393,972	696,000	2,089,972	
Receivables (net)	606,500	77,900	684,400	
Internal balances		5,000		
Materials and supplies	61,500	24,700	86,200	
Capital assets (net)	19,577,998	2,983,050	22,561,048	
Total Assets	22,031,421	3,923,805	25,950,226	
Liabilities				
Vouchers payable and accrued liabilities	648,560	62,815	711,375	
Internal balances	5,000			
Current portion of long-term debt	320,000		320,000	
Bonds payable	4,180,000	1,745,230	5,925,230	
Total Liabilities	5,153,560	1,808,045	6,956,605	
Net Assets				
Invested in capital assets net of related debt	15,077,998	1,237,820	16,315,818	
Restricted for debt service	1,666,723	682,025	2,348,748	
Unrestricted	133,140	195,915	329,055	
Total Net Assets	$16,877,861	$2,115,760	$18,993,621	

Fund Financial Statements

In addition to the MD&A and government-wide financial statements, the Town of Brighton would also prepare several required fund financial statements. The latter include a Balance Sheet—Governmental Funds and a Statement of Revenues, Expenditures, and Changes in Fund Balances—Governmental Funds. The Town would also prepare proprietary fund financial statements for its only other fund, the Water Utility Fund. The Statement of Net Assets; Statement of Revenues, Expenses, and Changes in Net Assets; and Statement of Cash Flows for the Water Utility Fund were provided in Chapter 7 as Illustrations 7–6, 7–7 and 7–8, and thus are not shown again in this chapter.

Illustration 9–6 presents the Balance Sheet—Governmental Funds for the Town of Brighton. Both the Fire Station Capital Projects Fund and the Deferred Serial Bond Debt Service Fund meet the criteria of a *major fund* established by

Illustration 9–5

TOWN OF BRIGHTON
STATEMENT OF ACTIVITIES
FOR THE YEAR ENDED DECEMBER 31, 2002

		Program Revenues			Net (Expenses) Revenues and Changes in Net Assets			
					Primary Government			
Functions/Programs	*Expenses*	*Charges for Services*	*Operating Grants and Contributions*	*Capital Grants and Contributions*	*Governmental Activities*	*Business-type Activities*	*Total*	*Component Units*
Primary government:								
Governmental activities:								
General government	$ 788,659	$ 213,200			$ (575,459)		$ (575,459)	
Public safety	1,646,321		$100,000	$300,000	(1,246,321)		(1,246,321)	
Public works	1,546,874				(1,546,874)		(1,546,874)	
Health and welfare	959,564		184,100		(775,464)		(775,464)	
Parks and recreation	562,362	82,464			(479,898)		(479,898)	
Interest on long-term debt	204,000				(204,000)		(204,000)	
Interest on tax-anticipation notes	13,500				(13,500)		(13,500)	
Total governmental activities	5,721,280	295,664	284,100	300,000	(4,841,516)		(4,841,516)	
Business-type activities:								
Water	614,960	727,120		7,000		$119,160	119,160	
Total primary government	$6,336,240	$1,022,784	$284,100	$307,000	$(4,841,516)	$119,160	$(4,722,356)	
General revenues:								
Taxes:								
Property taxes levied for general purposes					2,599,636		2,599,636	
Property taxes levied for debt service					337,000		337,000	
Sales taxes					485,000		485,000	
Fines and forfeits					310,800		310,800	
Investment earnings					107,245	44,500	151,745	
Interest and penalties on delinquent taxes					11,400		11,400	
Miscellaneous					28,400		28,400	
Total general revenues					3,879,481	44,500	3,923,981	
Increase (decrease) in unrestricted net assets					(962,035)	163,660	(798,375)	
Net assets, January 1, 2002					17,839,896	1,952,100	19,791,996	
Net assets, December 31, 2002					$16,877,861	$2,115,760	$18,993,621	

Illustration 9–6

TOWN OF BRIGHTON
BALANCE SHEET
GOVERNMENTAL FUNDS
DECEMBER 31, 2002

	General Fund	*Deferred Serial Bond Debt Service Fund*	*Term Bond Debt Service Fund*	*Total Governmental Funds*
ASSETS				
Cash	$ 145,800	$ 245,038	$ 613	$ 391,451
Investments		1,310,656	83,316	1,393,972
Receivables (net)	579,400	25,500	1,600	606,500
Inventory of supplies	61,500			61,500
Total assets	$ 786,700	$1,581,194	$ 85,529	$2,453,423
LIABILITIES AND FUND BALANCES				
Liabilities:				
Vouchers payable	$ 396,800			$ 396,800
Due to other governments	166,260			166,260
Due to other funds	5,000			5,000
Total liabilities	568,060			568,060
Fund balances:				
Reserved for:				
Encumbrances	70,240			70,240
Inventory of supplies	61,500			61,500
Unreserved, reported in:				
General fund	86,900			86,900
Debt service funds		1,581,194	85,529	1,666,723
Total fund balances	218,640	1,581,194	85,529	1,885,363
Total liabilities and fund balances	$ 786,700	$1,581,194	$ 85,529	$2,453,423

GASB *Statement No. 34* (see the glossary for definition of this term and the criteria for determining if a fund is a major fund.) Neither the Fire Station Capital Projects Fund nor the Regular Serial Bond Debt Service Fund has any assets or liabilities at December 31, 2002. Consequently, the two funds do not appear in the Town of Brighton Balance Sheet—Governmental Funds shown in Illustration 9–6. The Town's Statement of Revenues, Expenditures, and Changes in Fund Balances is shown in Illustration 9–7. Because all governmental funds had activity during the year, they are all included in the operating statement. The two nonmajor funds (the Regular Serial Bond Debt Service Fund and the Term Debt Service Fund) are combined in a single column under the heading *Other Governmental Funds*.

Illustration 9–7

TOWN OF BRIGHTON
STATEMENT OF REVENUES, EXPENDITURES, AND CHANGES IN FUND BALANCES
GOVERNMENTAL FUNDS
FOR YEAR ENDED DECEMBER 31, 2002

	General Fund	*Fire Station Capital Projects Fund*	*Deferred Serial Bond Debt Service Fund*	*Other Governmental Funds*	*Total Governmental Funds*
REVENUES					
Property taxes	$2,599,636		$ 190,000	$117,000	$2,906,636
Interest and penalties	11,400				11,400
Sales taxes	485,000				485,000
Licenses and permits	213,200				213,200
Fines and forfeits	310,800				310,800
Intergovernmental	284,100	$ 300,000			584,100
Charges for services	82,464				82,464
Investment earnings			104,100	3,145	107,245
Miscellaneous	28,400			30,000	58,400
Total revenues	4,015,000	300,000	294,100	150,145	4,759,245
EXPENDITURES					
Current:					
General government	649,400				649,400
Public safety	1,305,435				1,305,435
Public works	778,300				778,300
Health and welfare	850,325				850,325
Parks and recreation	419,500				419,500
Contributions to retirement plans	179,100				179,100
Miscellaneous	14,200				14,200
Debt service:					
Principal			200,000		200,000
Interest			95,000	111,000	206,000
Capital outlay:		1,494,000			1,494,000
Total expenditures	4,196,260	1,494,000	295,000	111,000	6,096,260
Excess (deficiency) of revenues over expenditures	(181,260)	(1,194,000)	(900)	39,145	(1,337,015)
OTHER FINANCING SOURCES (USES)					
Proceeds of long-term capital debt		1,200,000			1,200,000
Interfund transfers in (out)		(6,000)		6,000	
Total other financing sources (uses)		1,194,000		6,000	1,200,000
Net change in fund balances	(181,260)		(900)	45,145	(137,015)
Fund balances, January 1, 2002	399,900		1,582,094	40,384	2,022,378
Fund balances, December 31, 2002	$ 218,640		$1,581,194	$ 85,529	$1,885,363

Required Reconciliations

GASB *Statement No. 34* requires that the financial information reported in the governmental funds balance sheet be reconciled to that reported in the governmental activities column of the government-wide statement of net assets. Similarly, the information reported in the governmental funds statement of revenues, expenditures, and changes in fund balances must be reconciled to that reported as governmental activities in the government-wide statement of activities. The need for reconciliation arises from the use of different measurement focuses and bases of accounting, as discussed at several points in prior chapters. Because enterprise funds are accounted for on the accrual basis, using the economic resources measurement focus, usually there will be no need for a reconciliation between the enterprise fund financial information and that of business-type activities at the government-wide level.

Items that typically differ between governmental fund statements and governmental activities at the government-wide level, and thus should be included in the reconciliation, include:

1. Capital outlays that are reported as expenditures in governmental funds but as capital assets at the government-wide level.
2. Disposition of capital assets that are reported as other financing sources in governmental funds but as reduction of capital assets and gains/losses at the government-wide level.
3. Depreciation on capital assets that is not reported in governmental funds but is reported as expenses and contra-assets at the government-wide level.
4. Issuance of long-term debt that is reported as other financing sources in governmental funds but as an increase in general long-term liabilities at the government-wide level.
5. Retirement of long-term debt that is reported as an expenditure in governmental funds but as a reduction of general long-term liabilities at the government-wide level.
6. Some revenues that do not provide current financial resources are not recognized in governmental funds but are recognized at the government-wide level.

Illustration 2–5 presents an example of a separate schedule prepared to reconcile changes in governmental fund balances to change in governmental activity net assets. GASB *Statement No. 34* permits reconciliations to be provided on the face of the governmental fund basic financial statements or in accompanying schedules.

Current Financial Reporting Issues

GASB reporting objectives emphasize the role of accountability in external financial reporting. Indeed, accountability is considered to be "the paramount objective from which all other objectives must flow."[7] GASB *Concepts Statement No. 1*

[7]GASB, *Codification*, Appendix B, *Concepts Statement No. 1*, par. 76.

expands the definition of accountability beyond the traditional notion of accountability for expenditures of financial resources in conformity with the legally adopted budget. GASB's concept of accountability also includes accountability for the efficient and effective use of resources in providing government services and for interperiod equity, or the extent to which current-year revenues are sufficient to pay for current-year services. The new GASB *Statement No. 34* reporting model, upon which the first nine chapters of this Twelfth Edition of the text are based, represents a step toward meeting broader accountability objectives. The GASB continues to encourage experimentation with service efforts and accomplishments reporting, as discussed next. In addition, it has on its technical agenda projects that deal with unfinished reporting issues such as note disclosures, affiliated organizations, other post-employment benefits, and conceptual framework topics such as the efficacy of alternative communication media and definition of the elements of basic financial statements.

Service Efforts and Accomplishments (SEA)

GASB, as mentioned previously, has expanded the accountability reporting objective to include reporting on the efficient and effective use of resources. GASB *Codification* Section 100.177c states:

> Financial reporting should provide information to assist users in assessing the service efforts, costs, and accomplishments of the governmental entity.

The lack of a bottom-line measure of performance for a governmental entity, such as "profit" for a for-profit entity, means that *nonfinancial* measures of **service efforts and accomplishments** (SEA), and related costs, are necessary for informed decision making by citizens, elected officials, appointed officials, investors and creditors, and others having an interest in the government's performance. Advances in information technology, the growing number of highly qualified public managers, and increasing public demand for accountability now make feasible more sophisticated performance measurement and reporting systems than in the past. Thus, the GASB has sponsored and conducted extensive research on SEA measures for several service areas, including, among others, elementary and secondary education, higher education, fire departments, police departments, hospitals, public health, mass transit, road maintenance, and sanitation collection and disposal.

Based on the research to date, GASB issued in 1994 *Concepts Statement No. 2*, which identified three broad categories of SEA measures: (1) measures of service efforts, (2) measures of service accomplishments, and (3) measures that relate efforts to accomplishments.[8] Measures of service efforts, or **input measures,** relate to the amount of financial and nonfinancial resources (such as money and materials) used in a program or process.[9] Measures of service accomplishments are of two

---

[8]Governmental Accounting Standards Board, *Concepts Statement No. 2*, "Service Efforts and Accomplishments Reporting" (Norwalk, CT, April 1994).

[9]The discussion of SEA measures in this paragraph is paraphrased from the discussion in *Concepts Statement No. 2*, pars. 50–53.

types: outputs and outcomes. **Output measures** are quantity measures that reflect either the quantity of a service provided, such as the number of lane-miles of road repaired, or the quantity of service provided that meets a specified quality requirement, such as the number of lane-miles of road repaired to a specified minimum condition. **Outcome measures** gauge accomplishments, or the results of services provided, such as the percentage of lane-miles of road in excellent, good, or fair condition. Such measures are particularly useful when compared with established objectives or norms, or with results from previous years. Finally, measures that relate efforts to accomplishments are essential to assessing efficiency and effectiveness. **Efficiency measures** relate the quantity or cost of resources used to unit of output (e.g., cost per lane-mile of road repaired). Measures that relate resource costs to outcomes are useful in evaluating how effectively service objectives are being met and at what cost (e.g., the cost per lane-mile of road maintained in excellent, good, or fair condition). Additional quantitative and narrative explanation may be necessary to help users fully assess the entity's performance.

The authors believe that some form of SEA reporting, possibly as a required supplemental disclosure in the CAFR, or perhaps in a separately issued "performance" report, may eventually be required by GASB. However, there is currently little consensus as to what kinds of measures should be reported, and even whether setting standards for SEA reporting is within the scope of GASB's mandate. Thus, considerable experimentation and deliberation will be required before GASB can issue a standard on SEA reporting. SEA is discussed in greater depth in Chapter 13.

Other Reporting Issues

GASB has established a number of other projects on reporting issues. These include accounting for postemployment benefits other than pensions, note disclosures, and accounting for government-owned or affiliated organizations of colleges and universities.[10] It should be obvious from the preceding discussion that governmental accounting has changed rapidly in recent years. Developments in this area are expected to continue at a rapid pace for the forseeable future.

Popular Reporting

Although the CAFR has evolved to meet the diverse information needs of financial report users (i.e., citizens, legislative and oversight bodies, and investors and creditors), it is widely recognized that most citizens are unable to read and comprehend the CAFR. Indeed, only a relatively few sophisticated analysts with taxpayer associations, citizen watchdog groups, and the media find the CAFR to be useful. To better communicate financial results to citizens, a growing number of governments prepare and distribute **popular reports** that provide highly condensed financial information, budget summaries, and narrative descriptions. They are usually short in length and employ a variety of graphical techniques to enhance under-

[10]As standards are issued in these areas, the publisher will provide updates to adopters of this edition of the text.

standability. Popular reports are intended to supplement the CAFR, not replace it. Since they do not present minimum data required for complete and fair presentation, popular reports are considered "summary data" and are unaudited.[11] Both GASB and the Government Finance Officers Association (GFOA), however, recognize the value of popular reports. GASB has published a commissioned research report on popular reporting,[12] and the GFOA has established an award program for excellence in popular reporting. As citizens continue to demand greater accountability from their elected and appointed officials, popular reporting is likely to become more common.

Persons concerned with decision making for governmental bodies, auditors, bond analysts and investors, and others have a need to understand and evaluate both financial and nonfinancial information not incorporated in the comprehensive annual financial report. Chapter 10 explains how to use financial statements in evaluating the financial condition of governments. Chapter 13 introduces the subject of budgeting as a means of aiding administrators and legislators in evaluating alternative plans and, after plans are decided on, in evaluating whether activities are conducted according to plan.

---

[11]Audit standards issued by the American Institute of Certified Public Accountants permit auditors to express their opinion that a popular report (and other forms of summary data) is fairly stated in relation to the general purpose financial statements from which it is derived. Current AICPA guidance does not permit auditors to express an opinion on popular reports that they are fairly presented in conformity with GAAP.

[12]Frances H. Carpenter and Florence C. Sharp, *Research Report*, "Popular Reporting: Local Government Financial Reports to the Citizenry" (Norwalk, CT: GASB, 1992).

APPENDIX
SUMMARY OF THE NATURE AND ACCOUNTING CHARACTERISTICS OF FUNDS AND ACCOUNT GROUPS—GASB REPORTING MODEL BEING SUPERSEDED BY *STATEMENT NO. 34*

This appendix presents a brief overview of the current financial reporting model that is being superseded by GASB *Statement No. 34*. Such an overview may be useful to readers who wish to better understand the historical perspective for the *Statement No. 34* reporting model, or who wish to know more about the former model because they anticipate being involved with one or more governmental units that have not yet adopted *Statement No. 34*. Familiarity with the former model may be useful knowledge given that many governments are expected to continue indefinitely to use their existing fund accounting systems and prepare the reclassification entries needed for the government-wide financial statements. The nature of such reclassifications is discussed later in this appendix.

As discussed in Chapters 2 and 3, a fund is an independent fiscal and accounting entity with a self-balancing set of accounts recording assets and resources, and related liabilities, reserves, and equities, segregated for the purpose of carrying on specific activities or attaining certain objectives in compliance with legal restrictions or agreements. As in the GASB *Statement No. 34* reporting model, fund types in the former model are classified in three major categories—governmental funds, proprietary funds, and fiduciary funds. In addition, in the former reporting model, there are two account groups used to account for general fixed assets and general long-term liabilities.

Account groups are not fiscal entities and thus are not funds. Under the former model, four types of funds are classified as governmental funds: general funds, special revenue funds, capital projects funds, and debt service funds. Internal service funds and enterprise funds are classified as proprietary funds. Fiduciary funds is the generic name for all trust and agency funds. The two account groups are the General Fixed Assets Account Group and the General Long-Term Debt Account Group.

Classification of funds by major category is helpful because the principal accounting recommendations differ by category: *Governmental* fund revenues and expenditures should be recognized on the **modified accrual basis** of accounting. Governmental fund operating statements have a flow of financial resources measurement focus. Governmental funds do not account for fixed assets (referred to as capital assets in the new reporting model) used in their operations, nor for long-term debt. *Proprietary* fund revenues and expenses should be recognized on the **full accrual basis.** Proprietary fund operating statements have an income determination focus. Proprietary funds account for fixed assets used in their operations and for long-term debt serviced by revenues from their operations. In the former model *fiduciary* funds consist of investment trust funds, nonexpendable trust funds, and pension trust funds, all of which are accounted for in a manner similar to proprietary funds; and Expendable Trust Funds and Agency Funds, both of which are accounted for in a manner similar to governmental funds. The two account groups exist to account for fixed assets and long-term debt not accounted for by the governmental funds. Illustration 9–8 presents a comparison of the principal accounting characteristics of funds and account groups provided for use by state and local governmental units by GASB standards. The following sections of this chapter summarize the nature, purposes, and accounting characteristics of each fund and group.

Governmental Funds

General Funds and Special Revenue Funds. The *General Fund* is the name given to the entity that accounts for all of the assets and resources used for financing the general administration of the governmental unit and the traditional services provided to its residents.

Operating funds and current funds are names sometimes given to funds that function as a General Fund.

The typical governmental unit now engages in many activities financed by revenues designated by law for a particular operating purpose. In order to demonstrate compliance with such laws, it is recommended that a *special revenue fund* be used to account for the receipt and use of each such restricted category of revenue.

Both general funds and special revenue funds are sometimes known as *revenue funds*. In terms of accounting characteristics, both types are alike. The effect of the budget when it becomes a legal document is recorded in the accounts of each type. Estimated Revenues, a control account for all sources of revenues available to the fund and to be utilized during the budget period, is debited for the total amount of revenues expected to be recognized during the budget period; Estimated Other Financing Sources, a control account for all sources of financial resource inflows not classified by the GASB as revenues, is debited for the total other financing sources expected to be recognized during the budget period. Appropriations, a control account for all categories of expenditures authorized in the legally approved budget, is credited; Estimated Other Financing Uses, a control account for all categories of financial resource outflows not classified by the GASB as expenditures, is credited for the total other financing uses authorized for the budget period. Fund Balance, the account that is similar to a capital account of a profit-seeking entity, is debited or credited for the difference between Estimated Revenues plus Estimated Other Financing Sources less Appropriations and Estimated Other Financing Uses.

Accounting for general and special revenue funds differs from accounting for profit-seeking entities in more respects than just the obvious one of formally recording the budget in the accounts. Two principal differences are:

1. Expenditures are made for the purposes specified in the Appropriations Budget and are not made in the hope of generating revenue (as is true of profit-seeking entities); therefore, income determination, which is the principal focus of accounting for profit-seeking entities, is of no concern in accounting for general and special revenue funds.
2. The sources and amounts of revenues and other financing sources relate to a budget for a particular time period, generally one year, so general and special revenue funds can be said to have a year-to-year life rather than an indefinite life, as is true of a profit-seeking entity. Thus, the going-concern assumption that is basic to accounting for profit-seeking entities is not applicable to accounting for revenue funds; flow of financial resources is the focus of general and special revenue funds.

Legally approved appropriations are authorizations to incur liabilities for specified purposes in specified amounts during a specified time period. Penalties provided by law may be imposed on governmental administrators who expend governmental resources in a manner in any way contrary to that authorized in appropriation ordinances or statutes. For that reason, it is recommended that Encumbrances, a control account supported by the appropriations expenditures subsidiary ledger, be debited, and Reserve for Encumbrances, a Fund Equity account, be credited when purchase orders, contracts, or other commitment documents are issued. When goods or services have been received, a liability is incurred and an appropriation is deemed to have been expended (under accrual accounting theory); thus, if the appropriation has previously been encumbered, it is necessary to reverse the encumbrance entry at the time the Expenditure account is debited and the liability account is credited.

Revenues of a general or special revenue fund are to be recognized on the modified accrual basis. That is, those items of revenue that are "susceptible to accrual" (measurable and available), such as property taxes, are recorded on the accrual basis; other items of revenue are generally recorded on the cash basis. Revenues and Expenditures are operating statement accounts and are closed to Fund Balance at the end of a fiscal period. Estimated

Illustration 9–8 Comparison of Characteristics of Funds and Account Groups of State and Local Governmental Units under Reporting Model Standards Being Superseded

	Governmental Funds			
Characteristic	*General*	*Special Revenue*	*Capital Projects*	*Debt Service*
Focus	Liquidity	Liquidity	Liquidity	Liquidity
Length of Life	Year to year	Year to year	From approval of project until completion	From issue of general debt until final liquidation
Balance Sheet Accounts:				
Current Assets	Yes	Yes	Yes	Yes
Fixed Assets	No	No	No	No
Assets Available and to Be Provided	—	—	—	—
Current Liabilities	Yes	Yes	Yes	Yes
Fixed Liabilities	No	No	No	No
Fund Equity:				
Fund Balance—Reserved	Yes	Yes	Yes	No
Fund Balance—Available	Yes	Yes	Yes	Yes
Contributed Capital	—	—	—	—
Retained Earnings	—	—	—	—
Invested in G.F.A.	—	—	—	—
Operating Statement Accounts—Basis of Recognition:				
Revenues	Modified Accrual	Modified Accrual	Modified Accrual	Modified Accrual
Expenditures	Full Accrual	Full Accrual	Full Accrual	Modified Accrual
Expenses	—	—	—	—
Budgetary Accounts:				
Estimated Revenues	Yes	Yes	No	Yes
Appropriations	Yes	Yes	No	Yes
Encumbrances	Yes	Yes	Yes	No

Notes: 1. An Agency Fund recognizes, on the modified accrual basis, assets to be collected on behalf of the funds and units that are parties to the agency relationship. Since all assets belong to other funds and units, the assets are offset by liabilities to other funds and units.

2. Long-term debt of an Internal Service Fund is usually owed to another fund rather than to external creditors.

3. Accumulated depreciation may be recorded in this group; related expense should not be recorded in any governmental fund.

Source: Adapted from a comparative chart prepared by Professor W. David Brooks, CPA, of Chemeketa Community College, Salem, Oregon.

Revenues, Estimated Other Financing Sources, Appropriations, Estimated Other Financing Uses, and Encumbrances, all referred to as *budgetary* accounts, are also closed to Fund Balance at the end of a fiscal period. Therefore, when budgetary and operating statement accounts have been closed, the balance sheet accounts remain open and their balances are reported in a balance sheet for the General Fund and in a combining balance sheet for the special revenue fund type. The balance sheet accounts of a general or special revenue fund consist of accounts for financial resources available for fund operations, current liabilities to be paid from fund assets, and Fund Equity. If prepaid items and/or inventories of materials

Fiduciary Funds			Proprietary Funds		Account Groups	
Agency	*Expendable Trust*	*Nonexpendable, Investment, and Pension Trust*	*Internal Service*	*Enterprise*	*General Fixed Assets*	*General Long-Term Debt*
Liquidity	Liquidity	Going concern	Going concern	Going concern	—	—
Duration of agency	Duration of trust	Duration of trust	Decision of governing board	Decision of governing board	As long as general fixed assets exist	As long as unmatured long-term general debt exists
(Note 1)	Yes	Yes	Yes	Yes	No	No
No	No	Yes	Yes	Yes	Yes	No
—	—	—	—	—	—	Yes
(Note 1)	Yes	Yes	Yes	Yes	No	No
No	No	Yes	(Note 2)	Yes	No	Yes
—	Yes	No	—	—	—	—
—	Yes	Yes	—	—	—	—
—	—	—	Yes	Yes	—	—
—	—	—	Yes	Yes	—	—
—	—	—	—	—	Yes	—
—	Modified Accrual	Full Accrual	Full Accrual	Full Accrual	—	—
—	Full Accrual	—	—	—	—	—
—	—	Full Accrual	Full Accrual	Full Accrual	(Note 3)	—
—	Yes	—	—	—	—	—
—	Yes	—	—	—	—	—
—	Yes	—	—	—	—	—

and supplies are owned by a revenue fund, they should be included as an asset, but Fund Equity should be *reserved* in an equivalent amount. Unreserved Fund Balance, therefore, represents the net amount of financial resources available for appropriation and expenditure for legally approved purposes or for authorized other financing uses.

Capital Projects Funds. The receipt and disbursement of all monies from the sale of tax-supported or special assessment bonds issued for the construction or acquisition of capital facilities, along with the receipt and disbursement of all monies from other sources (such as grants from governmental units, special assessments, transfers from other funds, or gifts from citizens for the construction or acquisition of capital facilities), are accounted for by capital projects funds. The acquisition of general fixed assets under a capital lease is also recorded in a governmental fund, usually a capital projects fund.

A capital projects fund exists because certain resources are dedicated to a given capital purpose; all activities of the fund have the objective of accomplishing that purpose. Therefore, it is not considered necessary for budgetary accounts other than Encumbrances to be used. Encumbrances and Reserve for Encumbrances are considered desirable because of the large number of commitment documents that are issued for a typical governmental capital project. The encumbrance entry is reversed and Construction Expenditures of a capital projects fund are recognized when goods and services are received and the corresponding liability is recorded. Revenues of a capital projects fund are recognized on the same accrual basis as general and special revenue funds. The life of a capital projects fund is the length of time from legal approval of the project until completion of the project and formal acceptance of the capital assets by the governmental unit. The life of a capital projects fund generally does not coincide with a fiscal period; therefore, operating statement accounts and encumbrances are ordinarily closed at year-end to facilitate preparation of annual statements. Neither the fixed assets nor any long-term liabilities resulting from the project are accounted for by a capital projects fund. Only assets that will be converted into cash and disbursed for the project are to be accounted for by a fund of this type. Similarly, only liabilities that are to be paid out of fund assets are accounted for by capital projects funds. Fund Balance of a capital projects fund represents the excess of current assets over the sum of current liabilities and expected liabilities (Reserve for Encumbrances) or, therefore, the amount available for expenditure for the approved purposes of the fund.

Debt Service Funds. Tax-supported long-term debt issued and the interest thereon must be serviced primarily from revenue raised in years subsequent to the issue. Special assessment long-term debt for which a general government is obligated in some manner is expected to be serviced from collections of assessments and interest thereon. Laws of superior jurisdictions and bond indentures commonly require local governmental units to establish funds to account for debt service revenue.

It is recommended that debt service funds record Estimated Revenues and Appropriations (and Estimated Other Financing Sources and Estimated Other Financing Uses, if needed). Encumbrance accounting is ordinarily not needed for debt service funds because the only appropriations for these funds are for the payment of interest and the payment of principal of matured debt.

Although a major portion of the revenues of a debt service fund for tax-supported bonds arises from taxes, a portion of the revenues arises from interest on investments. Special assessments against property benefited by a special assessment project, and interest on the assessments, furnish revenues for debt service of special assessment bonds. Since the fund must stay in existence until all general long-term debt is repaid, in most cases the fund may be said to have an unlimited life.

The accrual basis of accounting specified for debt service funds has the same meaning for the revenues of debt service funds as it has for general and special revenue funds, but whereas the expenditures of a general or special revenue fund are to be accounted for on the full accrual basis, the expenditures of a debt service fund for interest and matured bonds are to be accounted for in the fiscal year in which appropriations for the payment of interest and principal are made—generally, the year in which the items become due.

As is true of general and special revenue funds and capital projects funds, a regular serial bond debt service fund accounts for only current assets and current liabilities (matured interest and matured principal payments), and the Fund Balance represents the excess of current assets available for fund purposes. A term bond debt service fund or a deferred serial bond debt service fund ordinarily is expected to accumulate assets over the life of the bonds; it is prudent for the assets to be held in the form of high-quality investments that are readily marketable or that will mature by the time cash is needed. The debt to be retired by the debt service fund is recorded by the general long-term debt group, not the debt service fund (until maturity).

Proprietary Funds

Internal Service Funds. If governmental resources are segregated for the purpose of providing services to several departments or funds of the same governmental unit or to other governmental units, the resources are accounted for by an internal service fund. The internal service fund type may be operated under many different levels of legislative supervision; in this summary it is assumed the financial objective of the fund is to recover through user charges the full cost of operations and to earn enough net income to allow for replacement of inventories and facilities in periods of rising prices. Accordingly, although budgets should be prepared for managerial use, it is not necessary to record the budget in the accounting system. Full accrual accounting should be used for revenues and for *costs* and *expenses* (these terms are used rather than *expenditures* because the latter refers to appropriation accounting). The life of an internal service fund is indefinite, so the going-concern assumption should be applied to accounting decisions. Current assets and fixed assets used in internal service fund operations should be accounted for by the internal service fund. Long-term debt to be repaid from earnings of the fund should also be accounted for by the internal service fund, as should all other liabilities to be paid from fund assets. Since net income is retained in the fund, a Retained Earnings account is needed as well as accounts that disclose the amount and source of the permanent equity of the fund.

Enterprise Funds. In contrast to internal service funds, resources utilized by a governmental unit to provide services on a user-charge basis to the general public are accounted for by an Enterprise Fund. Governmentally owned utilities are common examples of activities accounted for by enterprise funds. Almost any form of business engaged in by individuals, partnerships, and corporations may also be owned and operated by a governmental unit, however, and would be accounted for by an enterprise fund. Utilities or other enterprises that would be regulated if they were investor-owned should use the charts of accounts and accounting and statistical definitions required of investor-owned enterprises in the same industry. Other governmentally owned enterprises should use charts of accounts and definitions established by trade associations for the appropriate industry. In general, principles of accounting established for profit-seeking entities apply. Differences between regulatory accounting and accounting for nonregulated industries are discussed in Chapter 7.

In addition to operations financed primarily through user charges, the enterprise fund structure may be used to account for any other operations for which the governing body of the governmental unit desires a periodic determination of revenues earned, expenses incurred, and/or net income.

The life of an enterprise is assumed to be indefinite. Full accrual accounting is used. All assets used in fund operations and all debt to be serviced from fund earnings are included in enterprise fund accounts. A Retained Earnings account as well as accounts that disclose the amount and source of the contributed equity of the fund are utilized.

Fiduciary Funds

Trust and agency funds are used to account for assets held by a state or local government in a fiduciary capacity. A governmental unit that collects taxes for other units would have need for an agency fund, for example. Employees' retirement plans, also referred to as *Public Employee Retirement Systems* (PERS), are often accounted for in pension trust funds.

However, some PERS are organized as separate legal entities and therefore publish their own stand-alone financial statements, rather than report as a pension trust fund.

Agency Funds. An agency relationship may be accounted for satisfactorily within the accounting structure of the General Fund, or other fund, if the amounts collected pursuant to the agency are small in relation to total fund assets, and if the amounts are remitted to the owner without an appreciable lapse of time. If the amounts collected are relatively large, however, or if they are held for an appreciable time, or if the law or GASB standards (discussed in Chapter 8) require it, agency funds should be established. A very simple set of proprietary accounts ordinarily suffices for an agency fund because all fund assets are held as agent and are entirely offset by a liability to the owner. At year-end, if all assets have been collected and have been remitted to the owner, the agency fund would have no balances to report in the annual statements. The former GASB standards provide that agency fund assets and liabilities are to be accounted for on the basis used by governmental fund types.

Trust Funds. Trust funds differ from agency funds in that a trust fund generally holds assets and manages them for the beneficiaries over a substantial period of time. As discussed in Chapter 8, trust fund accounting problems often relate to the distinction between trust principal and trust income, and to the distinction between expendability and nonexpendability. *Expendable trust funds*, in general, are those that are created to account for trust income expendable for purposes specified by the trustor. Thus, expendable trust funds are similar in nature to special revenue funds, and GASB standards provide that the measurement focus and basis of accounting for expendable trust funds be the same as for governmental funds.

Nonexpendable trust funds are created to account for trust principal, or corpus, held for purposes specified by the trustor—often, the generation of net income to be transferred to an expendable trust. If the generation of net income is the objective of a trust fund, it seems obvious that accounting principles derived for profit-seeking entities and proprietary funds are applicable. Thus, fixed assets given by the donor as a part of the trust principal, or acquired in pursuit of the trust objectives, and long-term debt related to trust assets are accounted for by the trust fund, as well as current assets and current liabilities of the trust.

Investment Trust Funds are used to account for external investment pools, those which invest the monies of governmental and not-for-profit organizations *external* to the government that administers the pool. The assets of such pools must be reported at fair value as of the balance sheet date. Investment trust funds are accounted for on the full accrual basis, similar to the accounting for proprietary funds and nonexpendable trust funds.

Pension Trust Funds are accounted for as explained in Chapter 8. Since this type of trust fund generally has an objective of maximizing earnings from its investments (although the nature of investments that may be held is usually subject to legal restriction), GASB standards require that pension trusts be accounted for in a manner similar to proprietary funds.

Account Groups

General Fixed Assets. Only proprietary funds and fiduciary funds similar to proprietary funds routinely account for property, plant, and equipment used in their operations. All other funds account only for assets that will be turned into cash during the regular operations of the fund. Thus, property, plant, and equipment acquired by governmental funds and fiduciary funds similar to governmental funds are brought under accounting control by the creation of a General Fixed Assets Account Group. No other assets are recorded in the General Fixed Assets Account Group. No liabilities at all are recorded in the accounts of this group. The credit-balance accounts that offset the fixed assets accounts to create a self-balancing group show the source of the investment in general fixed assets.

Depreciation of general fixed assets is not recorded by any fund. It is permissible, but not required, for depreciation to be recorded in the General Fixed Assets Account Group as a deduction from the Investment in General Fixed Assets accounts. Accumulated depreciation accounts would then be deducted from related assets in the Statement of General Fixed Assets.

General Long-Term Debt. Debt instruments backed by the taxing power of a governmental unit are obligations of the governmental unit as a whole and not of the individual funds. The General Long-Term Debt Account Group (GLTDAG) was created to account for such debt. The GLTDAG is also used to account for special assessment long-term debt for which the government is obligated in some manner; the present value of capital lease payments; the noncurrent portions of claims, judgments, and compensated absences to be paid when due by use of the resources of governmental funds; and any unfunded liability for pensions of employees of activities accounted for by governmental funds. No assets are recorded in the group. The amount of long-term (and intermediate-term) debt is offset by accounts entitled Amounts Available in Debt Service Funds for Payment of _____ and Amounts to Be Provided for Payment of _____.

Summary of Interfund Transactions—Model Being Superseded by Statement No. 34

Transactions, or events, that affect the accounts of more than one fund or account group of a single governmental unit have been noted in the preceding discussions. A brief review of interfund transactions and events at this point should aid the reader in reinforcing his or her understanding of the relationships that exist among the funds and groups under the former reporting model.

Each fund is (1) a fiscal entity, (2) an accounting entity, and, in a sense, (3) a legal entity. Each account group is only an accounting entity, not a fiscal entity nor, in any sense, a legal entity. Events and transactions that must be recognized in more than one accounting entity of a single governmental unit may be classified in the following manner:

I. Transactions and Transfers between Funds
   - A. Interfund loans and advances
   - B. Transactions that would be treated as revenues, expenditures, or expenses if they involved organizations external to the governmental unit (quasi-external transactions)
   - C. Transactions that reimburse a fund for expenditures made by it on behalf of another fund
   - D. Recurring periodic transfers made primarily for the purpose of shifting resources from one fund to another (operating transfers)
   - E. Nonrecurring transfers made in compliance with special statutes or ordinances that do not qualify as revenues or expenditures to the receiving or disbursing funds (equity transfers)

II. Events Requiring Recognition in More than One Accounting Entity
   - A. Acquisition of general fixed assets
   - B. Creation of tax-supported and special assessment long-term debt, or repayment of principal of such long-term debt

Examples of each of the seven classes of interfund events or transactions, and entries that record them in each affected fund or group, are illustrated in the following paragraphs.

Transactions and Transfers between Funds

Interfund Loans and Advances. Under the former reporting model, the terms *loans* and *advances* were used to indicate amounts temporarily transferred from one fund to another but that will have to be repaid in due time.

Since each fund is a fiscal entity, the interfund receivables and payables resulting from loans and advances must be disclosed in a Combined Balance Sheet. They may not be eliminated, as would be proper in the preparation of consolidated statements for parent and subsidiary profit-seeking corporations.

Interfund loans and advances are discussed and illustrated in earlier chapters. The Supplies Fund of the Town of Brighton received a $130,000 long-term advance from the Water

Utility Fund of the Town. (The Supplies Fund also received a contribution from the General Fund, which is reviewed below under the Nonrecurring Transfers heading.) The effect of the advance on each fund under the former model is:

	Debits	Credits
Supplies Fund		
Cash	130,000	
Advance from Water Utility Fund		130,000
Water Utility Fund		
Long-Term Advance to Supplies Fund	130,000	
Cash		130,000

Partial repayment of the advance was made at year-end:

	Debits	Credits
Supplies Fund		
Advance from Water Utility Fund	6,500	
Cash		6,500
Water Utility Fund		
Cash	6,500	
Long-Term Advance to Supplies Fund		6,500

Transactions to Be Reported as Revenues and Expenditures. In the former model, interfund transactions that would result in the recognition of revenues, expenditures, or expenses if one of the parties were external to the governmental unit were called **quasi-external transactions**. One of the most common examples of this type of interfund transaction, which properly results in the recognition of revenue by one fund and the recording of an expenditure by another fund, is the provision to the General Fund of fire hydrants and water for fire protection by a municipally owned water utility; illustrative entries are given in Chapters 4 and 7 for this type of interfund transaction. The effect on the general ledger accounts of the Town of Brighton's General Fund and Water Utility Fund for fire protection service provided by the utility is:

	Debits	Credits
General Fund		
Expenditures	30,000	
Due to Other Funds		30,000
Water Utility Fund		
Due from Other Funds	30,000	
Sales of Water		30,000

The Water Utility Fund of the Town of Brighton received services from General Fund departments, as is also common. The entries to record the resulting expense and revenues, as given in Chapters 4 and 7, are:

	Debits	Credits
General Fund		
Due from Other Funds	25,000	
Revenues		25,000
Water Utility Fund		
Contribution in Lieu of Taxes	25,000	
Due to Other Funds		25,000

The net effect of the transactions between the two funds of the Town of Brighton is that the General Fund owes the Water Utility Fund $5,000. It is considered proper for the Balance Sheet of each fund, and the Combined Balance Sheet for all funds, to display this net amount as a receivable or payable. It should be stressed, however, that it is *not* acceptable to offset a receivable from one fund against a payable to a different fund.

Transactions in the Nature of Reimbursements of Expenditures. If one fund performs services for another fund on an incidental rather than recurring basis, administrators and accountants may consider it more reasonable for the fund receiving the services to reimburse the fund rendering the services for their cost (or estimated cost) rather than to treat the transaction as a quasi-external transaction in the manner described above. For example, if the city engineers' office, a General Fund department, performed services of an incidental nature for the Street Fund (assumed to be a special revenue fund in this example), the following entries would reflect the reimbursement given to the General Fund by the Street Fund (assuming $2,600 is thought to reflect fairly the expenditure the city engineers' office incurred for the benefit of the Street Fund):

	Debits	*Credits*
General Fund		
Cash	2,600	
Expenditures		2,600
Street Fund		
Expenditures	2,600	
Cash		2,600

Similarly, it is not uncommon for an amount to be recorded as an expenditure, or expense, of one fund which, in fact, should have been recorded as an expenditure, or expense, of another fund. This may occur because of incorrect account coding, data entry error, or lack of adequate information at the time the transaction was recorded. Since the general rule is that revenues, expenditures, and expenses should be reported as such only once, it is considered proper for the fund that should have borne the expenditure, or expense, to debit the appropriate expenditure, or expense, account when it recognizes its liability to the fund that first recorded the expenditure. Similarly, the fund that erroneously recorded the expenditure should debit a receivable from the fund that should have recognized the expenditure, or expense, and should credit the expenditure, or expense, account originally debited.

Recurring Periodic Shifts of Resources (Operating Transfers). A common example of a transfer of resources that would occur at regular periodic intervals, but that would not result in a true expenditure to the fund raising the revenue, or true revenue to the fund receiving the transfer, is the situation in which revenue to be used for debt service is raised by the General Fund and transferred to a debt service fund. Under the former reporting model, the entry in the General Fund for the shift of resources from the General Fund to the debt service fund would be (amount assumed):

General Fund		
Operating Transfers Out	128,000	
Cash		128,000

The corresponding entry in the Debt Service Fund would be:

	Debits	Credits
Debt Service Fund		
Cash	128,000	
Operating Transfers In		128,000

The transfer illustrated above also has an effect on the General Long-Term Debt Account Group if a portion of the transfer is to be used for payment of debt principal. Assuming $50,000 of the $128,000 is to be used for debt principal payment, the entry in the GLTDAG would be:

	Debits	Credits
General Long-Term Debt Account Group		
Amount Available in Debt Service Fund for Payment of Regular Serial Bonds	50,000	
Amount to Be Provided for Payment of Regular Serial Bonds		50,000

Nonrecurring Transfers Made in Compliance with Special Statutes (Residual Equity Transfers). In Chapter 7, the first entry in the illustrative case of the Town of Brighton Supplies Fund reflects the transfer of inventory and cash from the General Fund of that town as a contribution of working capital that is not expected to be repaid. This transfer would have to have been authorized by appropriate legal action and therefore is an example of a nonrecurring transfer made in compliance with special statutes or ordinances that does not result in revenues or expenditures to the receiving or disbursing fund. The transfer is stated to have taken place in the year following the year for which illustrative entries are shown for the Town of Brighton General Fund, so the entries in that fund are not shown in Chapter 4. The entries to be made by both funds under the former model at the time of the transfer are:

	Debits	Credits
General Fund		
Equity Transfers Out*	91,500	
Cash		30,000
Inventory of Supplies		61,500
Supplies Fund		
Cash	30,000	
Inventory of Supplies	61,500	
Equity Transfers In†		91,500

*In the General Fund the Equity Transfers Out account would be closed to Fund Balance; the Reserve for Inventory of Supplies account would also be closed to Fund Balance since the General Fund no longer accounts for the inventory.

†In the Supplies Fund the Equity Transfers In account would be closed to the Contribution from General Fund account.

An example similar to the one discussed above is the contribution of equity by a General Fund to a utility fund. The return of part or all of such contributions would also be a transfer of the nature comprehended in this category. A further example would be the transfer of residual equity balances of discontinued funds to general or debt service funds, normally required by statute.

Events Requiring Recognition in More Than One Accounting Entity

Acquisition of General Fixed Assets. Preceding discussions of the General Fixed Assets Account Group emphasized that the group was created to place under accounting control assets acquired through expenditures of General Funds, special revenue funds, and capital projects funds, none of which accounts for fixed assets. Chapter 5 illustrates several sets of entries in funds financing the acquisition of general fixed assets and corresponding entries in the governmental activities general journal at the government-wide level. By contrast, the corresponding entries under the former model to record the purchase of office equipment by the General Fund of a state or local governmental unit are shown below:

	Debits	Credits
General Fund		
Expenditures	1,450	
Vouchers Payable		1,450
General Fixed Assets Account Group		
Equipment	1,450	
Investment in General Fixed Assets—General Fund Revenues		1,450

The acquisition of general fixed assets by use of a capital lease agreement results in three sets of entries at the inception of the lease: the assets must be recorded in the General Fixed Assets Account Group, the related liability must be recorded in the General Long-Term Debt Account Group, and an Expenditure and an Other Financing Source must be recorded in a governmental fund (including, if appropriate, a capital projects fund). Entries at the inception of one hypothetical capital lease are illustrated in Chapters 5 and 6.

Creation or Repayment of General Long-Term Debt. Under the former model, the issuance of tax-supported bonds to finance the acquisition of capital facilities were recorded in the appropriate fund and the General Long-Term Debt Account Group. In the Town of Brighton case presented in Chapter 6, the town has outstanding a deferred serial bond issue in the amount of $2,000,000. At the time the bonds were sold, assuming they were sold at par for the acquisition of capital facilities, the following entries were necessary:

Capital Projects Fund		
Cash	2,000,000	
Proceeds of Bonds		2,000,000
General Long-Term Debt Account Group		
Amount to Be Provided for Payment of Deferred Serial Bonds	2,000,000	
Deferred Serial Bonds Payable		2,000,000

Later, after cash for bond repayment has been received by the debt service fund and the GLTDAG has recorded that amount in the Amount Available account, and removed it from the Amount to Be Provided account, assume the first $200,000 of bonds matures and the liability is transferred from the General Long-Term Debt Account Group to the debt service fund for payment, as shown in the following entries:

Debt Service Fund		
Expenditures—Bond Principal	200,000	
Bonds Payable		200,000
General Long-Term Debt Account Group		
Deferred Serial Bonds Payable	200,000	
Amount Available in Debt Service Fund for Payment of Deferred Serial Bonds		200,000

General long-term debt arising from a capital lease agreement is recorded at the inception of the lease, as noted in the section above. Under the former model, the payment of rentals during the term of the lease required entries in a governmental fund (ordinarily a debt service fund) and in the General Long-Term Debt Account Group.

Illustrations 9–9 through 9–13 provide examples of the general purpose financial statements specified in the financial reporting model being superseded by GASB *Statement No. 34*.

Illustration 9–9

NAME OF GOVERNMENTAL UNIT
COMBINED BALANCE SHEET—ALL FUND TYPES, ACCOUNT GROUPS,
AND DISCRETELY PRESENTED COMPONENT UNITS
DECEMBER 31, 2002

	Primary Government's Fund Types and Account Groups					
	Governmental Fund Types				Proprietary Fund Types	
	General	*Special Revenue*	*Debt Service*	*Capital Projects*	*Enterprise*	*Internal Service*
Assets:						
Cash	$258,500	$101,385	$ 598,366	$461,917	$ 257,036	$ 29,700
Investments	130,000	37,200	160,990	—	111,800	—
Receivables, net	155,300	77,760	264,666	213,540	161,985	12,000
Investment in joint venture	—	—	—	—	2,300,000	—
Due from component units	65,000	—	—	—	—	—
Lease receivable from primary government	—	—	—	—	—	—
Fixed assets, net	—	—	—	—	4,281,759	103,100
Amount available	—	—	—	—	—	—
Amounts to be provided	—	—	—	—	—	—
Total assets	$608,800	$216,345	$1,024,022	$675,457	$7,112,580	$144,800
Liabilities:						
Accounts payable	$ 50,512	$ 15,380	—	$ 29,600	$ 57,000	$ 15,000
Due to primary government	—	—	—	—	—	—
Lease payable to component unit	—	—	—	—	810,000	—
Revenue bonds payable	—	—	—	—	—	—
Tax-supported bonds payable	—	—	—	—	—	—
Total liabilities	50,512	15,380	—	29,600	867,000	15,000
Equity:						
Investment in general fixed assets	—	—	—	—	—	—
Contributed capital	—	—	—	—	4,103,224	95,000
Retained earnings	—	—	—	—	2,142,356	34,800
Fund balances:						
Reserved	76,000	93,000	—	500,000	—	—
Unreserved	482,288	107,965	$1,024,022	145,857	—	—
Total equity	558,288	200,965	1,024,022	645,857	6,245,580	129,800
Total liabilities and equity	$608,800	$216,345	$1,024,022	$675,457	$7,112,580	$144,800

Source: Based on Example I, GASB, *Codification*, Sec. 2600.905.

Fiduciary Fund Types	Account Groups		Totals—Memorandum Only Primary Government	Component Units	Totals—Memorandum Only Reporting Entity
Trust and Agency	*General Fixed Assets*	*General Long-Term Debt*	*December 31, 2002*	*December 31, 2002*	*December 31, 2002*
$ 216,701	—	—	$ 1,923,605	$ 1,656,960	$ 3,580,565
1,239,260	—	—	1,679,250	893,227	2,572,477
328,855	—	—	1,214,106	87,329	1,301,435
—	—	—	2,300,000	—	2,300,000
—	—	—	65,000	—	65,000
—	—	—	—	810,000	810,000
—	$7,326,500	—	11,711,359	19,191,577	30,902,936
—	—	$1,024,022	1,024,022	—	1,024,022
—	—	5,381,978	5,381,978	193,000	5,574,978
$1,784,816	$7,326,500	$6,406,000	$25,299,320	$22,832,093	$48,131,413
—	—	—	$ 167,492	$733,710	$ 901,202
—	—	—	—	65,000	65,000
—	—	—	810,000	—	810,000
—	—	—	—	2,776,000	2,776,000
—	—	$6,406,000	6,406,000	193,000	6,599,000
—	—	6,406,000	7,383,492	3,767,710	11,151,202
—	$7,326,500	—	7,326,500	7,836,545	15,163,045
—	—	—	4,198,224	8,841,640	13,039,864
—	—	—	2,177,156	1,359,581	3,536,737
$1,784,816	—	—	2,453,816	226,617	2,680,433
—	—	—	1,760,132	800,000	2,560,132
1,784,816	7,326,500	—	17,915,828	19,064,383	36,980,211
$1,784,816	$7,326,500	$6,406,000	$25,299,320	$22,832,093	$48,131,413

Illustration 9–10

NAME OF GOVERNMENTAL UNIT
COMBINED STATEMENT OF REVENUES, EXPENDITURES, AND CHANGES IN FUND BALANCES— ALL GOVERNMENTAL FUND TYPES AND DISCRETELY PRESENTED COMPONENT UNITS
FOR THE FISCAL YEAR ENDED DECEMBER 31, 2002

	Primary Government's Fund Types							
	Governmental Fund Types				Fiduciary Fund Type			
	General	*Special Revenue*	*Debt Service*	*Capital Projects*	*Expendable Trust*	*Totals— Memorandum Only Primary Government December 31, 2002*	*Component Units*	*Totals— Memorandum Only Reporting Entity December 31, 2002*
Revenues:								
Taxes	$ 881,300	$ 189,300	$ 380,587	—	—	$1,451,187	$ 675,327	$2,126,514
Intergovernmental	186,500	831,100	41,500	$1,250,000	—	2,309,100	233,474	2,542,574
Licenses and permits	191,700	—	—	—	—	191,700	13,942	205,642
Miscellaneous	—	—	—	—	$ 2,000	2,000	—	2,000
Total revenues	1,259,500	1,020,400	422,087	1,250,000	2,000	3,953,987	922,743	4,876,730
Expenditures:								
Current:								
General government	1,078,375	—	—	—	—	1,078,375	233,587	1,311,962
Public safety	204,095	534,200	—	—	—	738,295	—	738,295
Highways and streets	—	502,400	—	—	—	502,400	—	502,400
Education	—	—	—	—	—	—	658,923	658,923
Capital outlay	—	—	—	1,437,100	2,000	1,439,100	102,500	1,541,600
Debt service:								
Principal	—	—	315,500	—	—	315,500	33,400	348,900
Interest	—	—	368,420	—	—	368,420	14,800	383,220
Total expenditures	1,282,470	1,036,600	683,920	1,437,100	2,000	4,442,090	1,043,210	5,485,300

Other financing sources (uses):								
Proceeds of general obligation bonds	—	—	—	1,365,500	—	1,365,500	—	1,365,500
Operating transfers in	—	—	77,030	—	—	77,030	—	77,030
Operating transfers from primary government	—	—	—	—	—	—	100,000	100,000
Operating transfers out	(74,500)	—	—	—	—	(74,500)	—	(74,500)
Operating transfers to component units	(200,000)	(75,000)	—	—	—	(275,000)	—	(275,000)
Total other financing sources (uses)	(274,500)	(75,000)	77,030	1,365,500	—	1,093,030	100,000	1,193,030
Excess of revenues and other sources over (under) expenditures and other uses	(297,470)	(91,200)	(184,803)	1,178,400	—	604,927	(20,467)	584,460
Net income from golf course operations	—	—	—	—	—	—	2,350	2,350
Fund balance—beginning	855,758	292,165	1,208,825	(532,543)	33,163	1,857,368	1,352,056	3,209,424
(Increase) in reserves	(76,000)	(93,000)	—	(500,000)	—	(669,000)	(226,617)	(895,617)
Fund balance—ending	$ 482,288	$ 107,965	$1,024,022	$ 145,857	$33,163	$1,793,295	$1,107,322	$2,900,617

Source: Based on Example I, GASB, *Codification*, Sec. 2600.905.

Illustration 9–11

NAME OF GOVERNMENTAL UNIT
COMBINED STATEMENT OF REVENUES, EXPENDITURES, AND CHANGES IN FUND BALANCES—
BUDGET AND ACTUAL—GENERAL AND SPECIAL REVENUE FUND TYPES OF THE PRIMARY GOVERNMENT
NON-GAAP PRESENTATION
FOR THE FISCAL YEAR ENDED DECEMBER 31, 2002

	General Fund			Special Revenue Funds			Totals (memorandum only)		
	Budget	*Actual*	*Actual Over (Under) Budget*	*Budget*	*Actual*	*Actual Over (Under) Budget*	*Budget*	*Actual*	*Actual Over (Under) Budget*
Revenues:									
Taxes	$ 882,500	$ 881,300	$ (1,200)	$ 189,500	$ 189,300	$ (200)	$1,072,000	$1,070,600	$ (1,400)
Intergovernmental	200,000	186,500	(13,500)	837,600	831,100	(6,500)	1,037,600	1,017,600	(20,000)
Licenses and permits	195,000	191,700	(3,300)	—	—	—	195,000	191,700	(3,300)
Miscellaneous	—	—	—	—	—	—	—	—	—
Total revenues	1,277,500	1,259,500	(18,000)	1,027,100	1,020,400	(6,700)	2,304,600	2,279,900	(24,700)
Expenditures and encumbrances:									
Current:									
General government	1,150,000	1,148,375	(1,625)	—	—	—	1,150,000	1,148,375	(1,625)
Public safety	212,000	210,095	(1,905)	580,000	577,200	(2,800)	792,000	787,295	(4,705)
Highways and streets	—	—	—	555,000	552,400	(2,600)	555,000	552,400	(2,600)
Total expenditures and encumbrances	1,362,000	1,358,470	(3,530)	1,135,000	1,129,600	(5,400)	2,497,000	2,488,070	(8,930)
Other financing sources (uses):									
Operating transfers out	(74,500)	(74,500)	—	—	—	—	(74,500)	(74,500)	—
Operating transfers to component units	(200,000)	(200,000)	—	(75,000)	(75,000)	—	(275,000)	(275,000)	—
Total other financing sources (uses)	(274,500)	(274,500)	—	(75,000)	(75,000)	—	(349,500)	(349,500)	—
Excess of revenues over (under) expenditures, encumbrances, and other uses	(359,000)	(373,470)	(14,470)	(182,900)	(184,200)	(1,300)	(541,900)	(557,670)	(15,770)
Fund balance—beginning	855,758	855,758	—	292,165	292,165	—	1,147,923	1,147,923	—
Fund balance—ending	$ 496,758	$ 482,288	$(14,470)	$ 109,265	$ 107,965	$(1,300)	$ 606,023	$ 590,253	$(15,770)

Source: Prepared by authors in conformity with GASB, *Codification*, Sec. 2600.905.

Illustration 9–12

NAME OF GOVERNMENTAL UNIT
COMBINED STATEMENT OF REVENUES, EXPENSES, AND CHANGES IN FUND EQUITY—
ALL PROPRIETARY FUND TYPES, SIMILAR TRUST FUNDS, AND DISCRETELY PRESENTED
COMPONENT UNITS
YEAR ENDED DECEMBER 31, 2002

	Primary Government						
	Proprietary Fund Types		Fiduciary Fund Types		Totals—Memorandum Only		Totals—Memorandum Only
	Enterprise	*Internal Service*	*Non-expendable Trust*	*Pension Trust*	*Primary Government*	*Component Units*	*Reporting Entity*
Operating revenues:							
Charges for services	$ 650,333	$109,817	—	—	$ 760,150	$1,189,631	$ 1,949,781
Interest	—	—	—	$ 20,150	20,150	—	20,150
Contributions	—	—	—	60,686	60,686	—	60,686
Total operating revenues	650,333	109,817	—	80,836	840,986	1,189,631	2,030,617
Operating expenses:							
Cost of services	357,305	72,999	—	—	430,304	1,018,008	1,448,312
General and administrative	91,226	6,350	—	2,500	100,076	181,856	281,932
Depreciation	123,500	25,050	—	—	148,550	460,102	608,652
Benefit payments	—	—	—	21,000	21,000	—	21,000
Refunds	15,225	—	—	10,520	25,745	—	25,745
Total operating expenses	587,256	104,399	—	34,020	725,675	1,659,966	2,385,641
Operating income (loss)	63,077	5,418	—	46,816	115,311	(470,335)	(355,024)
Nonoperating revenues (expenses):							
Operating grants	55,000	—	—	—	55,000	410,000	465,000
Net income from joint venture	145,000	—	—	—	145,000	—	145,000
Interest revenue	8,830	—	$10,790	—	19,620	82,522	102,142
Interest expense and fiscal charges	(62,988)	—	—	—	(62,988)	(248,320)	(311,308)
Tax revenues	—	—	—	—	—	100,000	100,000
Total nonoperating revenue (expenses)	145,842	—	10,790	—	156,632	344,202	500,834
Income (loss) before operating transfers	208,919	5,418	10,790	46,816	271,943	(126,133)	145,810
Operating transfers in	—	65,000	—	—	65,000	—	65,000
Operating transfers from primary government	—	—	—	—	—	175,000	175,000
Operating transfers out	(56,740)	—	(10,790)	—	(67,530)	—	(67,530)
Net income	152,179	70,418	—	46,816	269,413	48,867	318,280
Fund equity—beginning	5,420,735	59,382	296,198	1,408,639	7,184,954	9,445,032	16,629,986
Contributions—capital grants	672,666	—	—	—	672,666	400,000	1,072,666
Fund equity—ending	$6,245,580	$129,800	$296,198	$1,455,455	$8,127,033	$9,893,899	$18,020,932

Source: Based on Example 4, GASB, *Codification*, Sec. 2200.906.

Illustration 9–13

NAME OF GOVERNMENTAL UNIT
COMBINED STATEMENT OF CASH FLOWS—ALL PROPRIETARY FUND TYPES, AND DISCRETELY PRESENTED COMPONENT UNITS
YEAR ENDED DECEMBER 31, 2002

	Primary Government					
	Proprietary Fund Types		Fiduciary Fund Types	Totals—Memorandum Only		Totals—Memorandum Only
	Enterprise	*Internal Service*	*Nonexpendable Trust*	*Primary Government*	*Component Units*	*Reporting Entity*
Cash flows from operating activities:						
Cash received from customers	$605,000	$110,410	—	$715,410	$1,220,000	$1,935,410
Cash paid to suppliers and employees	(450,000)	(95,000)	—	(545,000)	(1,150,000)	(1,695,000)
Net cash provided by operating activities	155,000	15,410	—	170,410	70,000	240,410
Cash flows from noncapital financing activities:						
Operating grants	55,000	—	—	55,000	410,000	465,000
Operating transfers in from other funds	—	65,000	—	65,000	—	65,000
Operating transfers out to other funds	(56,740)	—	$(10,790)	(67,530)	—	(67,530)
Operating transfer from primary government	—	—	—	—	175,000	175,000
Net cash provided (used) by (for) noncapital financing activities	(1,740)	65,000	(10,790)	52,470	585,000	637,470
Cash flows from capital and related financing activities:						
Purchase of capital assets	(700,000)	(70,000)	—	(770,000)	(200,000)	(970,000)
Principal payments—capital leases	(81,000)	—	—	(81,000)	—	(81,000)
Interest payments—capital leases	(62,988)	—	—	(62,988)	—	(62,988)
Interest payments—revenue bonds	—	—	—	—	(248,320)	(248,320)
Contributions from state government	672,666	—	—	672,666	400,000	1,072,666
Net cash provided (used) by (for) capital and related financing activities	(171,322)	(70,000)	—	(241,322)	(48,320)	(289,642)

Cash flows from investing activities:						
Receipt of interest	8,830	—	10,790	19,620	82,522	102,142
Net income from joint venture	145,000	—	—	145,000	—	145,000
Net cash provided by investing activities	153,830	—	10,790	164,620	82,522	247,142
Net increase (decrease) in cash and cash equivalents	135,768	10,410	—	146,178	689,202	835,380
Cash and cash equivalents at beginning of year	121,268	19,290	15,300	155,858	440,798	596,656
Cash and cash equivalents at end of year	$257,036	$ 29,700	$ 15,300	$302,036	$1,130,000	$1,432,036
Reconciliation of operating income to net cash provided by operating activities:						
Operating income (loss)	$ 63,077	$ 5,418	$ -0-	$ 68,495	$ (470,335)	$ (401,840)
Adjustments to reconcile operating income to net cash provided by operating activities:						
Depreciation	123,500	25,050	—	148,550	460,102	608,652
Decrease (increase) in investments	(9,812)	—	—	(9,812)	62,115	52,303
Decrease (increase) in accounts receivable	(15,315)	(7,795)	—	(23,110)	29,116	6,006
Increase (decrease) in accounts payable	(6,450)	(7,263)	—	(13,713)	(10,998)	(24,711)
Total adjustments	91,923	9,992	-0-	101,915	540,335	642,250
Net cash provided by operating activities	$155,000	$ 15,410	$ -0-	$170,410	$ 70,000	$ 240,410

Source: Format based on GASB, *Codification*, Sec. 2450.901.

Illustration 9–14 Comparison of Former Reporting Model and GASB *Statement No. 34* Reporting Model

	Former Model	Statement No. 34 *Model*
1. Fund Structure:		
a. Governmental Funds	General, special revenue, debt service, capital projects	General, special revenue, debt service, capital projects, permanent
b. Proprietary Funds	Enterprise, internal service	Enterprise, internal service (internal service reported as governmental activities at government-wide level)
c. Fiduciary Funds	Agency, expendable trust, nonexpendable trust, investment trust, pension trust	Agency, investment, private-purpose trust, pension trust
d. Account Groups	General Fixed Assets Account Group, General Long-Term Debt Account Group	None. General capital assets and general long-term liabilities are accounted for in the governmental activities category at the government-wide level
2. Required financial statements	Combined financial statements (see Illustrations 9–9 through 9–13)	MD&A, basic financial statements (government-wide and fund), and required supplementary information (RSI) other than MD&A
3. Basis of Accounting and Measurement focus	Governmental, agency, and expendable trust use modified accrual and flow of current financial resources measurement focus. Proprietary, investment trust, nonexpendable trust, and pension trust use accrual basis and flow of economic resources measurement focus	Governmental funds use modified accrual and flow of current financial resources measurement focus. All other funds and all activities at the government-wide level use the accrual basis and flow of economic resources measurement focus.

Note that these statements are referred to as *combined* financial statements. In these statements, each type of fund is reported in a separate column, whereas in the *Statement No. 34* model only major funds are reported in separate columns.

Comparison of Model Being Superseded and the GASB Statement No. 34 *Reporting Model*

Illustration 9–14 presents comparisons of the former financial reporting model and the GASB *Statement No. 34* model that is being implemented on a phased basis as discussed in Chapter 1 and other chapters of the text.

Preparation of Government-wide Financial Statements by Governments Using the Former Fund Accounting Model

As indicated in Chapter 3, some governments have substantial investments in their fund accounting computer systems. Many of these governments will continue to use these systems, even after implementation of the GASB *Statement No. 34* reporting model. This presents no major problems provided entries are made at year-end to reclassify the fund-based data for governmental funds and the internal service fund as appropriate for the government-wide financial statements. These reclassification entries involve the items that differ between governmental funds and governmental activities at the government-wide level because they use different accounting bases and measurement focuses. Generally, these items are the same as those disclosed in the reconciliation schedules discussed earlier in this chapter.

Key Terms

Blended presentation, 390
Component unit, 389
Discrete presentation, 390
Efficiency measures, 420
Financial accountability, 390
Financial reporting entity, 389
Full accrual basis, 422
Input measures, 419
Joint venture, 390
Jointly governed organizations, 390
Legally separate organizations, 390
Modified accrual basis, 422
Other stand-alone government, 390
Outcome measures, 420
Output measures, 420
Popular reports (or reporting), 420
Primary government, 389
Quasi-external transaction, 430
Service efforts and accomplishments, 419

Selected References

American Institute of Certified Public Accountants, Audit and Accounting Guide. *Audits of State and Local Governmental Units*. Revised, New York, 1999.

Governmental Accounting Standards Board. *Codification of Governmental Accounting and Financial Reporting Standards as of June 30, 1999*. Norwalk, CT, 1999.

Questions

9–1. *a.* State the principal reasons for the use of funds in accounting for governmental units.

b. List five kinds of funds frequently found in the accounting system of a municipality, and briefly discuss the content of each.

9–2. What is the minimum number of funds a government could keep if it were attempting to adhere to GASB standards? Explain.

9–3. Describe some of the reasons why a government should prepare periodic or interim reports.

9–4. The Mayor of a city contends that since he is the elected head of all city activities, he has authority to transfer assets from one fund to another on a temporary basis because "it is all in the family." What is the merit, if any, of the Mayor's contention?

9–5. William Bates is executive vice president of Mavis Industries, Inc., a publicly held industrial corporation. Bates has just been elected to the City Council of Gotham City. Prior to assuming office as a member of the City Council, he asks you as his CPA to explain the major differences that exist in accounting and financial reporting for a large city when compared to a large industrial corporation.

Required

a. Describe the major differences that exist in the purpose of accounting and financial reporting and in the types of financial reports of a large city when compared to a large industrial corporation.

b. Why are inventories often ignored in accounting for local governmental units? Explain.

c. Under what circumstances should depreciation be recognized in accounting for local governmental units? Explain.

(AICPA)

9–6. What are the three major sections of a CAFR and what are the contents of each?

9–7. What additional steps must be taken to convert fund financial statements to government-wide statements at the end of the year?

9–8. Listed below are four independent transactions or events that relate to a local government.

1. $25,000 was disbursed from the General Fund (or its equivalent) for the cash purchase of new equipment.
2. An unrestricted cash gift of $100,000 was received from a donor.
3. Listed common stocks with a total carrying value of $100,000 were sold by the permanent fund for $105,000, before any dividends were declared on these stocks. There are no restrictions on the gain.
4. General obligation bonds with a face amount of $1,000,000 were sold at par, with the proceeds required to be used solely for construction of a new building. This building was completed at a total cost of $1,000,000, and the total amount of bond issue proceeds was disbursed in connection therewith. Disregard interest capitalization.

Required

For each of the above-listed transactions or events, prepare journal entries, without explanations, specifying the affected funds and governmental activity category and showing how these transactions or events should be recorded by a local government whose debt is serviced by general tax revenues.

9–9. Explain the criteria currently prescribed by GASB standards for determining whether an organization is a primary government and whether it is financially accountable for another organization. Assuming a decision has been made to include a component unit in the reporting entity, how does one determine whether to report the component unit by discrete presentation or by blending?

9–10. What are some of the current issues that the GASB has on its agenda now that they have completed the "financial reporting model" prescribed by GASB *Statement No. 34*?

Cases

9–1. Reporting Entity. The following example of application of reporting entity criteria is based on an example contained in GASB *Codification* Section 2100.

The Greater Metropolis Urban Development Authority (GMUDA) was authorized as a nonprofit corporation by the state legislature and created by the City of Metropolis Council to attract new industry and participate in long-range planning of the City. Although the City Council appoints GMUDA's governing board, the Board has complete authority to hire management and all other employees. The City has no role in monitoring or participating in the day-to-day operating activities of GMUDA.

Per its state charter, GMUDA has separate taxing powers and levies taxes on all commercial and industrial properties located within the designated development district. GMUDA's tax levies are completely independent of the City's, other than they are levied on some of the same taxpayers. GMUDA performs some services for the Chamber of Commerce and other local business organizations for a fee. However, its primary source of revenues is property taxes. GMUDA receives no financial subsidies of any kind from the City and the City is not obligated in any manner for the authority's debt. Even though GMUDA does not require the City's approval of its operating budget, it routinely sends the budget to the City Council for review. The City Attorney has ruled that the City Council has no option but to approve the budget as submitted.

Required

a. Using the reporting entity flow chart presented in Illustration 9–2, and the reporting entity definitions and criteria discussed in Chapter 9, determine whether or not the Greater Metropolis Urban Development Authority should be included in the reporting entity of which the City of Metropolis is the primary government? If so, should GMUDA be reported by blending or by discrete presentation? Explain your rationale for the inclusion/exclusion decision and, if applicable, method of display.

b. Assume the same facts as in Part *a* above except that the City Council has the power to remove members of GMUDA's board for cause. Also, the City must approve all debt issuances and all expenditures in excess of $100,000. Do your conclusions made in Part *a* above change in light of the different facts in Part *b*? Explain fully.

9–2. Letter of Transmittal. The letter of transmittal to the Mayor and Council accompanying the annual financial statements of the Town of Stevens is presented below. (Note: This case is based on an actual letter of transmittal and financial statements received by one of the authors quite some time ago; however, the name of the Town and certain other facts have been changed.)

LETTER OF TRANSMITTAL

To the Honorable Mayor and Town Council
Town of Stevens

Gentlemen:

We are attaching the financial report for the Town of Stevens for the year 2002. The statements and organization of this report are designed to conform to generally accepted principals [sic] and standards of government accounting and reporting. A review of this report will reveal much information about the financial position and movements of the Town, some of which it is hoped will be valuable and some of which we fear will be tiresome and redundant.

Plans and performance for 2002 did not exactly match. Hopes for major street repair and water line replacement on Castle Avenue were frustrated by the need to follow the county engineering and road department on its Jones Street relocation project. This meant relocating 300 feet of 6-inch main line, the rebuilding of two laterals, 12 services and the digging out and adjusting of 10 valve covers a number of times. This work, which was not anticipated, occupied most of the summer and partly explained why the water line maintenance cost was $97,418 for 2002 as compared with $46,554 for last year. It is hoped that this deferred work can be accomplished next year.

For the first time in a number of years the streets were hand-cleaned of old dirt and the remains of the winter debris. Although a new and richer layer of gum wrappers, beer cans, and cigarette packs corrected this condition, the Town's purchase of a Wayne sweeper in August puts the Town temporarily one up in its long struggle for clean streets. An additional help is that a tough antilitter ordinance was passed.

The new Town Hall was purchased on a contract for $90,900 payable at $30,000 per year, the first installment of which was met in 2002. We thus own outright the Town Hall from the front door to the west end of the fireplace. A new roof was installed and arrangements made to have part of the interior repaired next year.

At the moment the Town's financial position is not too grim. This may be changed in attempting to solve the remaining problems of sewage disposal and providing additional water to the areas the Town is required to serve.

/s/ Treasurer-Clerk

THE TOWN OF STEVENS
GENERAL FUND

Balance Sheet—December 31, 2002 Form A–1

Assets:	
Petty cash	500
Cash on deposit with treasurer	(16,405)
Temporary investments (S–9)	100,000
Inventory of supplies	3,800
Total Assets	87,895

Liabilities, reserves, and surplus:	
Warrants payable	8,587
Contract payable—new town hall	60,900
Cumulative reserve fund	53,298
Deficit (A–2)	(34,890)
	87,895

Analysis of Changes in Fund Balance Form A–2

	Estimated	*Actual*	*Excess or Deficiency*
Surplus—Jan. 1, 2002	43,030	43,030	
Add: Revenues (A–3)	288,200	303,880	15,680
Total	331,230	346,910	15,680
Less: Town hall contract		90,900	(90,900)
Expenditures (A–4)	310,200	290,900	19,300
Deficit—Dec. 31, 2002	21,030	(34,890)	55,920

Statement of Revenues—Estimated and Actual Form A–3

	Estimated	*Actual*	*Difference*
General property tax	140,000	94,636	45,364
Special tax—utilities	33,000	31,400	1,600
Licenses and permits	10,000	8,146	1,854
Fines and penalties	9,000	21,275	(12,275)
Rental income	7,200	6,700	500
Revenue from other agencies:			
Aid to Cities	7,000	23,457	(16,457)
State liquor tax	39,000	38,795	205
Motor vehicle excise tax	35,000	38,374	(3,374)
Expense sharing—Fire district 2	8,000	4,853	3,147
Interest income		4,750	(4,750)
Other income		31,494	(31,494)
	288,200	303,880	15,680

THE TOWN OF STEVENS
GENERAL FUND

Statement of Expenditures Compared with Authorizations Form A–4

	Appropriated	*Expended*	*Actual Under (Over) Estimate*
Police:			
Salaries	123,000	123,482	(482)
FICA tax	5,500	5,495	4
Retirement	7,400	7,228	171
Industrial insurance	3,000	1,666	1,333
Hospital insurance	3,000	2,644	355
Vehicle care	1,500	4,763	(3,263)
Police bond	700	550	150
Motor fuel	8,000	11,641	(3,641)
Supplies	2,000	2,892	(892)
Total	154,100	160,364	(6,264)
Clerk:			
Salaries	21,000	21,335	(335)
FICA tax	1,000	1,067	(67)
Retirement	2,300	2,345	(45)
Hospital	1,200	527	672
Bond	150	140	10
Office supplies	2,500	2,997	(497)
Total	28,150	28,413	(263)
Fire Department:			
Salaries	12,000	8,120	3,880
Pensions	6,000	2,655	3,345
Hydrant rental	12,000	12,000	–0–
Vehicle care	2,000	240	1,759
Equipment repair		511	(511)
Heat and lights		5,102	(5,102)
Motor fuel	1,500	272	1,227
Supplies	1,000	1,252	(252)
Total	34,500	30,156	4,344
General Government:			
Census	1,000	897	103
Elections	800		800
Attorney fees	10,000	1,500	8,500
Police judge	9,000	6,000	3,000
Councilmen:			
Salaries (Ord. #581)		3,666	(3,666)
Retirement		374	(374)
FICA tax		171	(171)
Heat and lights	8,000	4,762	3,238
Telephone	1,500	1,687	(187)
Building repair	5,000	6,356	(1,356)
Audit fee	4,000		4,000
Printing	2,000	302	1,698

	Appropriated	*Expended*	*Actual Under (Over) Estimate*
Advertising	2,850	2,256	594
Postage	500	469	31
Surety bonds and insurance	15,000	12,850	2,150
Janitor service	1,800	1,440	359
Library	19,000	15,110	3,890
Travel and subsistence	2,000	1,975	24
Association dues	2,000	1,875	124
Planning commission	3,000		3,000
Miscellaneous	3,500	3,948	(448)
Supplies	1,000	1,030	(30)
Household supplies	1,500	525	974
Driver education		4,770	(4,770)
Total	93,450	71,967	21,483
Combined totals—General Fund	310,200	290,900	19,300

Required

The remainder of the report deals with other funds and account groups of the Town of Stevens; those statements are not reproduced because they are similar to the General Fund statements above. On the basis of the material given you, prepare a written evaluation of the information produced by the Town's accounting system from the standpoint of its usefulness to:

a. Town administrators.

b. The Town Council (the legislative body).

c. Taxpayers and citizens of the town.

d. Creditors of the town.

9–3. Internet Case—Popular Reports. You have just been hired as an accountant for a large metropolitan city in the eastern part of the country. Your first assignment is to assist the Finance Director in the preparation of a "popular report." The city has long been concerned with the difficulty that most citizens have in understanding the Comprehensive Annual Financial Report. The Finance Director tells you that she saw the State of New York's popular report at a conference and was quite impressed.

Required

a. Try to obtain a copy of the State of New York's popular report as well as those of other local governments by going to their Internet websites. The website of most states can be accessed by going to http://www.state.______.us and inserting the two-letter abbreviation for the state in the blank. Most cities are accessible by going to http://www.city.______.______.us where the first blank is the name of the city and the second blank is the two-letter abbreviation for the state.

b. Evaluate the usefulness of the popular reports you are able to obtain from the perspective of a citizen. In particular, focus on financial accounting information. Do you have adequate information to determine if the government has a strong financial position and condition? Does the city report any service efforts and accomplishments (SEA) information?

Exercises and Problems

9–1. Examine the CAFR. Utilizing the CAFR obtained for Exercise 1–1 and your answers to the question asked in Exercise 1–1, and the corresponding exercises in Chapters 2 through 8, comment on the following:

a. Analysis of Introductory Section. Does the report contain all introductory material specified by the GASB? Is the introductory material presented in such a manner that it communicates significant information effectively—do you understand what they are telling you and why they are telling it to you? On the basis of your study of the entire report, list any additional information you feel should have been included in the introductory section and explain why you feel it should have been included. On the basis of your study of the entire report, do you think the introductory material presents the information fairly? Comment on any information in the introductory section you feel is superfluous, and explain why.

b. Analysis of Financial Statements.

1. Do the statements, notes, and schedules in the financial section present the information required by the GASB? Are Total columns provided in the basic financial statements and schedules for the primary government and the reporting entity? If so, are the Total columns for the current year compared with Total columns for the prior year? Are the basic financial statements and notes cross-referenced to each other? Are they cross-referenced to the statements and schedules of individual funds?
2. Review your answers to the questions asked in Exercises 3–1 and 4–1 in light of your study of subsequent chapters of the text and your analysis of all portions of the annual report. If you feel your earlier answers were not entirely correct, change them in accord with your present understanding of generally accepted accounting principles and proper disclosure of the financial position and financial operations of a governmental reporting entity.
3. Review your answers to Exercise 5–1 and all subsequent exercises in this series in light of knowledge you have gained since you prepared the answers. If any of your earlier answers should be changed, change them.

c. Analysis of Statistical Section. Are statistical tables presented in the annual report in conformity with GASB standards? Make note of any data omitted. Make note of any additional data presented. If data have been omitted, to what extent does each omission impair your ability to understand the report? To what extent does each additional table, chart, graph, or other statistical presentation add to your understanding of the governmental reporting entity, its problems, its financial position, past and probable future changes in its financial position, financial operations, or past and probable future changes in financial operations?

d. *GFOA Certificate of Achievement.* Does the report include a copy of a GFOA Certificate of Achievement for Excellence in Financial Reporting or refer to the fact that the governmental unit has received one? If the report has been awarded a certificate, does your review indicate it was merited? If the report has not been awarded a certificate, does your review indicate that the report should be eligible for one?

e. *Service Potential of the* CAFR. Specify the most important information needs that a governmental annual report should fulfill for each of the following:

(1) Administrators.

(2) Members of the legislative branch.

(3) Interested residents.

(4) Creditors or potential creditors.

In what ways does the CAFR you have analyzed meet the information needs you have specified for each of the four groups, assuming members of each group make an effort to understand reports equivalent to the effort you have made? In what way does the report fail to meet the information needs of each of the four groups?

f. Does your CAFR present any service efforts and accomplishments (SEA) data in the introductory section, statistical section, or elsewhere in the CAFR? If so, are measures provided for both service efforts and service accomplishments? From the data and/or narrative provided can you infer whether major service functions of the governmental unit were carried out efficiently and economically, and that program activities are having the desired effects?

9–2. Multiple Choice. Choose the best answer.

1. One of the differences between accounting for a governmental unit and accounting for a business is that a government should:

   a. Use only the cash basis of accounting.

   b. Not record depreciation expense in any of its funds.

   c. Use only the modified accrual basis of accounting.

   d. Always establish and maintain complete self-balancing accounts for each fund.

2. Which of the following funds of a governmental unit integrates budgetary accounts into the accounting system?

   a. Special Revenue.

   b. Enterprise.

   c. Internal Service.

   d. Investment Trust Fund.

3. Which of the following items would generally be recognized as revenue in the General Fund of a governmental unit?

   a. Receipts from a city-owned parking structure that is operated on a business basis.

   b. Property taxes.

   c. Interest earned on investments held to finance pension payments to retired employees.

   d. Revenues from internal service funds.

4. Cook County received goods that had been approved for purchase but for which payment had not yet been made. Should the accounts listed below be increased?

	Encumbrances	*Expenditures*
a.	No	No
b.	No	Yes
c.	Yes	No
d.	Yes	Yes

5. Proceeds of General Obligation Bonds is an account of a governmental unit that would be included in the:
   a. Enterprise Fund.
   b. Pension Trust Fund.
   c. Capital Projects Fund.
   d. Investment Trust Fund.
6. What journal entry should be made at the end of the fiscal year to close Encumbrances?
   a. Debit Fund Balance and credit Encumbrances.
   b. Debit Encumbrances and credit Reserve for Encumbrances.
   c. Debit Reserve for Encumbrances and credit Encumbrances.
   d. None. The account is only closed when no encumbrance documents are outstanding.
7. Which of the following funds ordinarily should account for the payment of interest and principal on revenue bond debt?
   a. Debt Service.
   b. Capital Projects.
   c. Permanent Fund.
   d. Enterprise.
8. The Appropriations Control account of a governmental unit is debited when:
   a. Supplies are purchased.
   b. Expenditures are recorded.
   c. The budgetary accounts are closed.
   d. The budget is recorded.
9. Equipment in general governmental service that had been constructed 10 years before by the Capital Projects Fund was sold. The receipts were accounted for as unrestricted revenue. Under the reporting model being superseded by GASB *Statement No. 34*, entries are necessary in the:
   a. General Fund and Capital Projects Fund.
   b. General Fund and General Fixed Assets Account Group.
   c. General Fund, Capital Projects Fund, and Enterprise Fund.
   d. General Fund, Capital Projects Fund, and General Fixed Assets Account Group.
10. The members of the Library Board of the City of Fayetteville are appointed by the City Council of the City of Fayetteville, and the City Council has agreed to finance any operating deficits of the Library. Under these conditions:

a. The Library is a primary government.

b. The City is a primary government.

c. Financial data of the Library should be included in the financial statements of the reporting entity, in the manner specified in GASB standards.

d. Both *b* and *c*.

(AICPA, adapted)

9–3. Multiple Choice. Choose the best answer.

1. Self-supporting activities provided to the public on a user-charge basis are accounted for in what fund type?

   a. Agency.

   b. Enterprise.

   c. Internal Service.

   d. Special Revenue.

Items 2 through 5 are based on the following information:

The following related entries were recorded in sequence in the General Fund of a city:

Encumbrances	12,000	
Reserve for Encumbrances		12,000
Reserve for Encumbrances	12,000	
Encumbrances		12,000
Expenditures	12,350	
Vouchers Payable		12,350

2. The sequence of entries indicates that:

   a. An adverse event was foreseen, and a reserve of $12,000 was created; later the reserve was canceled, and a liability for the item was acknowledged.

   b. An order was placed for goods or services estimated to cost $12,000; the actual cost was $12,350, for which a liability was acknowledged on receipt.

   c. Encumbrances were anticipated but later failed to materialize and were reversed. A liability of $12,350 was incurred.

   d. The first entry was erroneous and was reversed; a liability of $12,350 was acknowledged.

3. Entries similar to those for the General Fund may also appear on the books of the City's:

   a. Internal Service Fund.

   b. Agency Fund.

   c. Pension Trust Fund.

   d. Special Revenue Fund.

4. Assuming GASB standards were followed, the entries:

   a. Occurred in the same fiscal period.

   b. Did not occur in the same fiscal period.

   c. Could have occurred in the same fiscal period.

   d. Reflect the equivalent of a "prior period adjustment" had the entity concerned been operated for profit.

5. Immediately after the first entry was recorded, the city had a balanced General Fund budget for all transactions. What would be the effect of recording the second and third entries?
   a. Not change the balanced condition of the budget.
   b. Cause the city to show a surplus.
   c. Cause the city to show a deficit.
   d. Not affect the current budget but would affect the budget of the following fiscal period.
6. What would be the incremental effect on the General Fund Fund Balance in the current fiscal year of recording a $15,000 purchase for a new automobile out of General Fund resources, for which a $14,600 encumbrance had been recorded in the General Fund in the previous year?
   a. Reduce the Fund Balance $15,000.
   b. Reduce the Fund Balance $14,600.
   c. Reduce the Fund Balance $400.
   d. Have no effect on the Fund Balance.
7. The activities of a central data processing department that offers data processing services at a discount to other departments of a certain city should be accounted for in:
   a. An Enterprise Fund.
   b. An Internal Service Fund.
   c. A Special Revenue Fund.
   d. The General Fund.
8. The initial contribution of cash from the General Fund in order to establish an Internal Service Fund would require the General Fund to credit Cash and debit:
   a. Accounts Receivable—Internal Service Fund.
   b. Interfund Transfers Out.
   c. Equity Contributions.
   d. Interfund Loans Receivable—Noncurrent.
9. The premium received at the time an issue of general obligation bonds is sold is usually considered an other financing source of what fund?
   a. Debt Service.
   b. Enterprise Fund.
   c. General.
   d. Special Revenue.
10. Brockton City's Debt Service Fund (for term bonds) recorded estimated other financing sources and estimated revenues for the current fiscal year of $15,000 and $7,000, respectively. The actual transfers in and interest earnings for future repayment of principal were $16,000 and $6,500, respectively. What are the necessary amounts to record the year's actual transfers and earnings in the Debt Service Fund and in the governmental activities general journal at the government-wide level, respectively?
    a. $22,500 and $22,000.
    b. $22,000 and $22,000.

c. $22,500 and $22,500.

d. $22,500 and no entry.

(AICPA, adapted)

9–4. Multiple Choice. Choose the best answer.

1. Which of the following is an appropriate basis of accounting for a proprietary fund of a governmental unit?

	Cash Basis	*Accrual Basis*
a.	Yes	Yes
b.	Yes	No
c.	No	No
d.	No	Yes

2. The budget of a governmental unit, for which the appropriations exceed the estimated revenues, was adopted and recorded in the general ledger at the beginning of the year. During the year, expenditures and encumbrances were less than appropriations; whereas revenues equaled estimated revenues. The Budgetary Fund Balance account is:
   a. Credited at the beginning of the year and debited at the end of the year.
   b. Credited at the beginning of the year and *not* changed at the end of the year.
   c. Debited at the beginning of the year and credited at the end of the year.
   d. Debited at the beginning of the year and *not* changed at the end of the year.
3. Which of the following amounts are included in a General Fund's Encumbrance account?
   I. Outstanding vouchers payable amounts.
   II. Outstanding purchase order amounts.
   III. Excess of the amount of a purchase order over the actual expenditure for that order.
   a. I only.
   b. I and III.
   c. II only.
   d. II and III.
4. Property taxes levied in fiscal year 2001 to finance the General Fund budget of fiscal year 2002 should be reported as General Fund revenues in fiscal year 2002:
   a. Regardless of the fiscal year in which collected.
   b. For the amount collected in fiscal year 2002 only.
   c. For the amount collected before the end of fiscal year 2002 only.
   d. For the amount collected before the end of fiscal year 2002 or shortly thereafter.
5. Repairs that have been made for a governmental unit, and for which a bill has been received, should be recorded in the General Fund as a debit to an:
   a. Expenditure.
   b. Encumbrance.
   c. Expense.
   d. Appropriation.

6. Brockton City serves as collecting agency for the local independent school district and for a local water district. For this purpose, Brockton has created a single Agency Fund and charges the other entities a fee of 1 percent of the gross amounts collected. (The service fee is treated as General Fund revenue.) During the latest fiscal year, a gross amount of $268,000 was collected for the independent school district and $80,000 for the water district. As a consequence of the foregoing, Brockton's General Fund should:
   a. Recognize receipts of $384,000.
   b. Recognize receipts of $344,520.
   c. Record revenue of $3,480.
   d. Record encumbrances of $344,520.

Items 7 and 8 are based on the following information:

During the year ended December 31, 2001, Leyland City received a state grant of $500,000 to finance the purchase of buses and an additional grant of $100,000 to aid in the financing of bus operations in 2001. Only $300,000 of the capital grant was used in 2001 for the purchase of buses, but the entire operating grant of $100,000 was spent in 2001.

7. If Leyland's bus transportation is accounted for as part of the City's General Fund, how much should Leyland report as grant revenues for the year ended December 31, 2001, assuming the City follows the GASB *Statement No. 34* reporting model?
   a. $100,000.
   b. $300,000.
   c. $400,000.
   d. $600,000.
8. If Leyland's bus transportation system is accounted for as an Enterprise Fund, how much should Leyland report as grant revenues for the year ended December 31, 2001?
   a. $100,000.
   b. $300,000.
   c. $400,000.
   d. $600,000.
9. The comprehensive annual financial report (CAFR) of a governmental reporting entity should contain a Statement of Revenues, Expenses, and Changes in Fund Net Assets for:

	Governmental Funds	*Proprietary Funds*
a.	No	Yes
b.	No	No
c.	Yes	No
d.	Yes	Yes

10. The comprehensive annual financial report (CAFR) of a governmental reporting entity should contain a Statement of Cash Flows for:

	Governmental Funds	*Proprietary Funds*
a.	Yes	No
b.	Yes	Yes
c.	No	Yes
d.	No	No

(AICPA, adapted)

9–5. Independent Transactions. The following transactions represent practical situations frequently encountered in accounting for state and local governments for a calendar year. Each transaction is independent of the others.

1. The City Council of Bernardville adopted a budget for the general operations of the government during the new fiscal year. Revenues were estimated at $695,000. Legal authorizations for budgeted expenditures were $650,000.
2. Taxes of $160,000 were levied for the Special Revenue Fund of Millstown. One percent was estimated to be uncollectible.
3. *a.* On July 25, office supplies estimated to cost $2,390 were ordered for the City Manager's office of Bullersville. Bullersville, which operates on the calendar year, does not maintain an inventory of such supplies.
   b. The supplies ordered July 25 were received on August 9, accompanied by an invoice for $2,500.
4. On October 10, the General Fund of Washingtonville repaid to the Utility Fund a loan of $1,000 plus $40 interest. The loan had been made earlier in the fiscal year.
5. A prominent citizen died and left 10 acres of undeveloped land to Harper City for a future park site. The donor's cost of the land was $55,000. The fair value of the land was $85,000 at the time its ownership was transferred to the City.
6. *a.* On March 6, Dahlstrom City issued 9 percent special assessment bonds payable in five years, at face value of $90,000. Interest is payable annually. Dahlstrom City, which operates on the calendar year, will use the proceeds to finance a curbing project. In case of default by property owners, the City agreed to assume debt service.
   b. On October 29, the full $84,000 cost of the completed curbing project was recorded as a liability. Also, appropriate closing entries were made with regard to the project. Cash in the amount of the residual equity was transferred to the Debt Service Fund to be used for interest payments.
7. *a.* Conrad Thamm, a citizen of Basking Knoll, donated common stock valued at $22,000 to the City under a private-purpose trust agreement. Under the terms of the agreement, the principal amount is to be kept intact; use of revenue from the stock is restricted to financing academic college scholarships for needy students.
   b. On December 14, dividends of $1,100 were received on the stock donated by Mr. Thamm.

8. *a.* On February 23, the Town of Lincoln, which operates on the calendar year, issued 9 percent general obligation bonds with a face value of $3,000,000 payable February 23, to finance the construction of an addition to the city hall. The bonds were sold for $3,080,000. The premium was recorded directly in the Debt Service Fund and is to be held for bond repayment at maturity.
   b. On December 31, the addition to the city hall was officially approved, the full cost of $2,970,000 was paid to the contractor, and appropriate closing entries were made with regard to the project. (Assume no entries have been made with regard to the project since February 23.) The residual equity of the Construction Fund was transferred to the Debt Service Fund to be held for bond repayment at maturity.

Required

For each transaction, prepare the necessary journal entries for *all* of the funds involved and in the government-wide general journal. No explanation of the journal entries is required. Use the following headings for your workpaper:

Trans-action Number	*Journal Entries*	*Dr.*	*Cr.*	*Fund or Activity*

In the far right column, indicate in which fund or activity each entry is to be made, using the coding below:

Funds:	
General	GF
Special Revenue	SRF
Capital Projects	CPF
Debt Service	DSF
Enterprise	EF
Internal Service	ISF
Private-Purpose Trust	PPT
Government-wide level:	
Government-type activity	GTA
Business-type activity	BTA

(AICPA, adapted)

9–6. Comprehensive Set of Transactions. The Village of Dexter was recently incorporated and began financial operations on July 1, 2001, the beginning of its fiscal year.

The following transactions occurred during this first fiscal year, July 1, 2001, to June 30, 2002.

1. The Village Council adopted a budget for general operations during the fiscal year ending June 30, 2002. Revenues were estimated at $2,000,000. Legal authorizations for budgeted expenditures were $1,970,000.
2. Property taxes were levied in the amount of $1,950,000; it was estimated that 2 percent of this amount would prove uncollectible. These taxes are available as of the date of levy to finance current expenditures.
3. During the year, a resident of the Village donated marketable securities valued at $250,000 to the Village under the terms of a trust agreement. The terms of the trust agreement stipulated that the principal amount is to be kept intact; use of revenue generated by the securities is restricted to financing college

scholarships for needy students. A permanent fund will be used to account for the endowment. Earnings are transferred to the Scholarship Fund, a special revenue fund. Revenue earned and received on these marketable securities amounted to $27,500 through June 30, 2002.

4. A General Fund transfer of $100,000 was made to establish an Internal Service Fund to provide for a permanent investment in inventory.
5. The Village decided to install lighting in a subdivision of the Village; a special assessment project was authorized to install the lighting at a cost of $375,000. Assessments were levied for $360,000; the Village's share of cost was $15,000. All assessments were collected during the year, as was the transfer from the Village's General Fund.
6. A contract for $375,000 was let for the installation of the lighting. At June 30, 2002, the contract was completed. The contractor was paid all but 5 percent, which was retained to ensure compliance with the terms of the contract. Encumbrance accounting is used.
7. During the year, the Internal Service Fund purchased various supplies at a cost of $95,000.
8. Cash collections recorded by the General Fund during the year were as follows:

Property taxes	$1,930,000
Licenses and permits	35,000

9. The Village Council decided to build a village hall at an estimated cost of $2,500,000 to replace space occupied in rented facilities. In order to finance the project, 6 percent bonds were sold at their face value of $2,500,000. No contracts have been signed for this project, and no expenditures have been made.
10. A purchase order in the amount of $100,000 was issued for a truck for use by the street department, a General Fund department. The truck was received, and a voucher in the amount of $102,500 was approved and paid.

Required

Prepare journal entries to properly record each of the above transactions in the appropriate fund(s) or activity of Dexter Village for the fiscal year ended June 30, 2002. Use the following funds and government-wide activities, as necessary:

General Fund	GF
Capital Projects Fund	CPF
Internal Service Fund	ISF
Permanent Fund	PF
Scholarship Fund (a special revenue fund)	ISF
Governmental-Type Activity	GTA

Each journal entry should be numbered to correspond with the transactions described above. Do *not* prepare closing entries for any fund.

Your answer sheet should be organized as follows:

Transaction Number	*Fund or Activity*	*Account Title and Explanation*	*Amounts*	
			Debits	*Credits*

(AICPA, adapted)

9–7. General Fund Adjusting and Closing Entries. You have been engaged by the Town of Rego to examine its June 30, 2001, balance sheet. You are the first CPA to be engaged by the Town and find that employees of the Town are unaware of governmental accounting and financial reporting standards. The Town clerk stated that the books had not been closed and presented the following preclosing trial balance of the General Fund as of June 30, 2001:

	Debits	*Credits*
Cash	$ 550,000	
Taxes Receivable—Current Year	159,200	
Estimated Losses—Current-Year Taxes Receivable		$ 18,000
Taxes Receivable—Prior Year	28,000	
Estimated Losses—Prior-Year Taxes Receivable		30,200
Estimated Revenues	1,310,000	
Appropriations		1,348,000
Donated Land	127,000	
Expenditures—Building Addition Constructed	250,000	
Expenditures—Serial Bonds Paid	56,000	
Other Expenditures	1,005,000	
Special Assessment Bonds Payable		500,000
Revenues		1,354,000
Accounts Payable		126,000
Fund Balance		109,000
	$3,485,200	$3,485,200

Additional Information

1. The estimated losses of $18,000 for current-year taxes receivable were determined to be a reasonable estimate.
2. Included in the Revenues account is a credit of $127,000 representing the value of land donated by the state to be used for a town park.
3. The Expenditures—Building Addition Constructed account balance is the cost of an addition to the Town Hall building. This addition was constructed and completed in June 2001. The General Fund recorded the payment as authorized.
4. The Expenditures—Serial Bonds Paid account reflects the annual retirement of general obligation bonds issued to finance the construction of the Town Hall. Interest payments of $24,000 for this bond issue are included in the Other Expenditures account.
5. Operating supplies ordered in the prior fiscal year and chargeable to that year were received, recorded, and consumed in July 2000. The outstanding purchase orders for these supplies, which were not recorded in the accounts at June 30, 2000, amounted to $28,800. The vendors' invoices for these supplies totaled $30,400. Appropriations lapse one year after the end of the fiscal year for which they are made.
6. Outstanding purchase orders at June 30, 2001, for operating supplies totaled $10,100. These purchase orders were not recorded on the books.

7. The special assessment bonds were sold in June 2001 to finance a street paving project. No contracts have been signed for this project, and no expenditures have been made.
8. The balance in the Revenues account includes credits for $100,000 for a note issued to a bank to obtain cash in anticipation of tax collections and for $5,000 for the sale of scrap iron from the Town's water plant. The note was still outstanding at June 30, 2001. The operations of the water plant are accounted for in the Water Fund.

Required

a. Prepare the formal adjusting and closing journal entries for the General Fund for the fiscal year ended June 30, 2001. Assume capital projects and debt service legally may be accounted for in the General Fund.

b. The foregoing information disclosed by your examination was recorded only in the General Fund even though other funds were involved. Prepare the formal adjusting journal entries for any other funds involved, assuming that financial statements are to be prepared in conformity with GAAP.

(AICPA, adapted)

Continuous Problem

9–B. *a.* Assemble all statements and schedules prepared for your solutions to Problems 2–B through 8–B. Assume that the balances in the Governmental Activities general ledger at the beginning of the fiscal year were as follows:

CITY OF BIRMINGHAM
POST-CLOSING TRIAL BALANCE
GOVERNMENTAL ACTIVITIES GENERAL LEDGER
AS OF JUNE 30, 2001

Account Title	*Debits*	*Credits*
Cash	$ 550,000	
Taxes Receivable—Delinquent	286,000	
Estimated Uncollectible Delinquent Taxes		$ 62,400
Interest and Penalties Receivable on Taxes	13,376	
Estimated Uncollectible Interest and Penalties		662
Special Assessments Receivable—Current	66,000	
Special Assessments Receivable—Deferred	594,000	
Investments for Special Assessment Bond Payment	260,000	
Land	600,000	
Buildings	5,200,000	
Accumulated Depreciation—Buildings		1,400,000
Equipment and Miscellaneous	3,930,000	
Accumulated Depreciation—Equipment and Miscellaneous		1,943,000
Improvements Other Than Buildings	16,560,000	
Accumulated Depreciation—Improvements Other Than Buildings		7,320,000
Infrastructure	5,000,000	
Accumulated Depreciation—Infrastructure		1,200,000
Vouchers Payable		187,000
Internal Balances		7,000

Account Title	Debits	Credits
Deferred Revenues		594,000
Tax-Supported Serial Bonds Payable—6%		6,000,000
Special Assessment Term Bonds Payable—8%		600,000
Capital Lease Obligations Payable		1,020,000
Net Assets—Invested in Capital Assets, Net of Related Debt		11,807,000
Net Assets—Restricted for Debt Service		835,000
Net Assets—Unrestricted		83,314
Totals	$33,059,376	$33,059,376

b. Create a general ledger for Governmental Activities. Enter the beginning balances from the June 30, 2001, post-closing trial balance presented above. Post the journal entries made in the Governmental Activities general journal in Problems 4-B through 6-B in the general ledger. Assume all charges for services revenue are for the General Government function.

c. Prepare an adjusting journal entry to record depreciation expense on general capital assets using these assumed amounts: General Government $160,000; Public Safety $320,000; Public Works $120,000; Health $40,000; Public Welfare $40,000; Recreation $80,000. Total depreciation expense applies to Buildings $60,000; Equipment and Miscellaneous $120,000; Improvements Other Than Buildings $520,000; and Infrastructure $60,000. Post these changes to the Governmental Activities general ledger and prepare a preclosing trial balance for Governmental Activities as of June 30, 2002, that includes the effects of the preceding entry for depreciation. Note: For the sake of simplicity, we assume no change in fair value of investments.

d. From your solutions to Problems 2-B through 8-B, prepare the following statements for the year ended June 30, 2002. (Note: The City of Bingham is a primary government and has no other organizations for which it is accountable as component units.):

1. Government-wide Statement of Net Assets
2. Government-wide Statement of Activities
3. Balance Sheet—Governmental Funds
4. Statement of Revenues, Expenditures, and Changes in Fund Balances—Governmental Funds (with reconciliation of this statement to the government-wide Statement of Activities)
5. Statement of Net Assets—Proprietary Funds
6. Statement of Revenues, Expenses, and Changes in Fund Net Assets—Proprietary Funds
7. Statement of Cash Flows—Proprietary Funds
8. Statement of Fiduciary Net Assets
9. Statement of Changes in Fiduciary Net Assets

e. Prepare closing entries for the temporary accounts of the Governmental Activities general ledger, as well as the entry to reclassify the three net asset accounts to their correct amounts as of June 30, 2002.

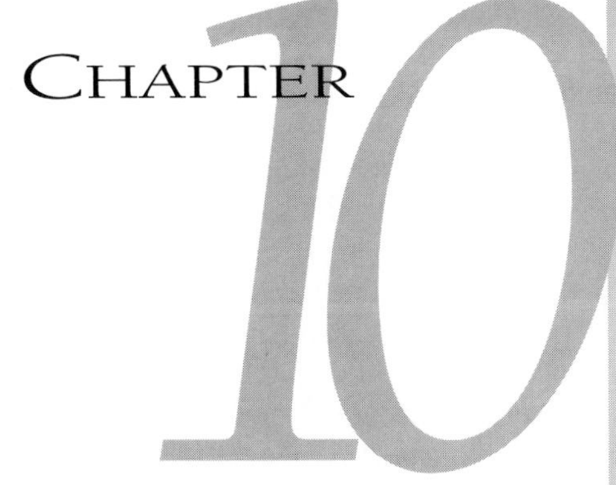

CHAPTER 10 Analysis of Governmental Financial Performance

Learning Objectives

After studying this chapter, you should be able to:

- Explain the importance of evaluating governmental financial performance.
- Distinguish and describe key financial performance concepts, such as:
  - Financial position.
  - Financial condition.
  - Interperiod equity.
- Explain the relationships among environmental factors, organizational factors, and financial factors in determining governmental financial condition.
- Identify, calculate, and interpret key economic and financial ratios that measure financial condition.
- Describe how financial performance is related to the operating performance of a governmental entity.

The Need to Evaluate Financial Condition

Over the past three decades, numerous financial crises have underscored the need for an effective system to provide taxpayers, creditors, managers, legislative and oversight bodies, and others with an *early warning* of impending financial difficulty. Municipalities that have experienced financial crises during this period include such highly publicized cases as Boston; Bridgeport, Connecticut; Cleveland; Miami; New York City; Orange County, California; and Washington, DC. Recent cases include Orange County, which filed for bankruptcy in 1994 after suffering investment losses estimated variously from $1.5 to $2.1 billion,[1] and the cities of Miami, Florida, and Washington, DC. Because of their current financial crises, both Miami and Washington, DC, are (as of May 2000) in a state of public *receivership*—the financial management of both cities has been handed over to public boards until fiscal integrity has been restored.[2]

By far, the fiscal crisis with the greatest impact was that of New York City. In the aftermath of the City's default on several billion of short-term debt in 1975, deficient financial reporting was singled out as one of the contributing factors.[3] Indeed, several published studies following the New York City crisis found widespread deficiencies in municipal financial reporting. For example, a joint Coopers & Lybrand/University of Michigan study of 46 municipalities conducted in 1976 found the following percentages of noncompliance with required disclosures: accounting policies for pensions, 63 percent; accrued vacation and sick leave pay, 84 percent; overlapping debt, 50 percent; lease obligations, 93 percent; description of significant accounting policies, 46 percent; annual report issued within 90 days of fiscal year-end, 61 percent; and preparation of interim financial reports for the general and special revenue funds, 39 percent and 63 percent, respectively.[4] Another study conducted for the National Council on Governmental Accounting (NCGA), the standards-setting body that preceded the GASB, noted that:

> In many instances, the financial reports of those [financially distressed] jurisdictions did not permit the general public to appreciate their precarious situation until it was too late. In response to pressures brought by lenders, these jurisdictions have had to alter materially and improve their reporting practices.[5]

---

[1]"Bitter Fruit: Orange County, Mired in Investment Mess, Files for Bankruptcy," *The Wall Street Journal*, December 7, 1994, pp. A1, A4.

[2]James Seemuth, "Gloom Over Miami: City Government Projects $68 Million Deficit in Its Budget for 1997," *Florida Trend* 39, no. 9 (January 1997), p. 26; and Katherine Barrett and Richard Greene, "Capital of Bad Management (Washington, DC, A Special Report Ranking the Cities)" *Financial World*, no. 164 (March 14, 1995), pp. 50–55.

[3]Soybel (1992) summarizes the City's serious accounting deficiencies, including those identified in the SEC's study of the default. See Virginia E. Soybel, "Municipal Financial Reporting and the General Obligation Bond Market: New York City, 1961–1975," *Journal of Accounting and Public Policy* 2, no. 3 (Fall 1992), pp. 207–32.

[4]Coopers & Lybrand and the University of Michigan, *Financial Reporting Practices of the American Cities, A Public Report* (New York: Coopers & Lybrand, 1976.)

[5]W. D. Haseman and R. P. Strauss, "The Quality of Financial Reporting by General Purpose Local Governments," in *Objectives of Accounting and Financial Reporting for Governmental Units: A Research Study*, vol. II (Chicago: NCGA, 1981), p. 2–1.

As the foregoing quotation suggests, the widespread financial distress of many cities in the 1970s, particularly the default of New York City, was a double-edged sword. Although it created consternation and hardship for the cities involved (as well as for the municipal credit markets), it unleashed forces that transformed the quality of governmental financial management and financial reporting nationwide. Strong pressure from the credit markets and the effective leadership of national professional organizations such as the Government Finance Officers Association (GFOA) (then known as the Municipal Finance Officers Association) and the National Association of State Auditors, Comptrollers, and Treasurers (NASACT) were major factors in the rapid improvement of both financial reporting standards and compliance with those standards. Because of these improvements, deteriorating financial performance is much more likely to be detected now than in the past.

New York City's default led also to considerable research on measuring financial condition. In 1980, the International City Management Association (ICMA) (since renamed the International City and County Management Association) published a series of five handbooks that dealt with evaluating financial condition, implementing a financial trend monitoring system, identifying unsound financial practices, setting long-range financial goals, and identifying tools for improving financial decisions.[6] These handbooks resulted from a three-year research project funded by a National Science Foundation grant. Some local governments that participated in field testing, as well as other governments, continue to use the financial trend monitoring system developed in the handbooks to monitor their financial condition. The third-edition ICMA handbook (see footnote 6), together with various publications of the municipal credit market, remain the main sources of guidance for monitoring and evaluating governmental financial condition, including how to use financial and other information for these purposes.

Despite the widespread improvements in financial management over the past 20 years, instances of poor financial management continue to crop up. As mentioned earlier, three recent examples are Orange County, California, and the cities of Miami, Florida, and Washington, DC. Orange County officials issued billions of dollars in short-term, reverse-repurchase debt instruments to leverage the acquisition of interest rate–sensitive derivative investments known as *inverse floaters*. When interest rates were low, the County's investment pool earned well above normal returns; however, when interest rates increased in 1994, the derivative investments lost significant value, triggering a default on the short-term debt and forcing the County, traditionally one of the wealthiest and most conservative in the nation, to declare bankruptcy.[7]

---

[6]In 1986, the ICMA published a revised, single handbook, *Evaluating Financial Condition: A Handbook for Local Government*, which integrates and updates information from all the handbooks. The third edition of this handbook was published in 1994. Sanford M. Groves and Maureen G. Valente, *Evaluating Financial Condition: A Handbook for Local Government*, 3rd ed. (Washington, DC: ICMA, 1994).

[7]Laura Jaweski, "Orange County Borrowed $1 Billion Even as Its Investment Losses Piled Up," *The Wall Street Journal*, December 5, 1994, pp. A3–A4.

In 1996, an FBI investigation known as Operation Green Palm uncovered massive payoffs, kickbacks, and other financial wrongdoing in Miami, involving, among other officials, a City Commission member, the City Manager, and the City's Finance Director. City officials were also accused of using funds designated for pensions, capital projects, and other purposes to hide a $68 million operating budget deficit that threatened to force the City into bankruptcy.[8] To avoid bankruptcy and restore fiscal integrity, the Governor of Florida appointed a *Financial Emergency Oversight Board.* As a result, the City has made substantial progress toward recovery. Miami voters narrowly defeated a measure on September 4, 1997, that would have abolished the City of Miami as a separate entity and turned its governance over to Dade County.

A 1995 survey of major U.S. cities by Barrett and Greene for *Financial World* ranked Washington, DC, worst among 30 cities surveyed in terms of financial management. Unlike Miami, the reason for Washington, DC's poor showing relates primarily to economic factors and serious mismanagement, rather than corruption. In commenting on the City's mismanagement, which had created a projected $722 million budget deficit for fiscal 1995, Barrett and Greene note:

> It's midyear 1993, Sharon Pratt Kelly, then the mayor of Washington, D.C., is short of revenues to balance her books. Money isn't coming in as quickly as expected. Expenses are up. The mayor's plans to cut staff dramatically have been torn to shreds by the unions and city agencies. So the mayor simply adds a fifth quarter to 1993. This moves the income scheduled to come in from property tax in the first quarter of 1994 to 1993. No more cash actually pours into her coffers. But on paper it does give her about $180 million. The Monopoly money gets spent just as if it were real cash.[9]

A Memorandum of Agreement between the District of Columbia Financial Responsibility and Management Assistance Authority signed January 2, 1999, conveys back to the Mayor of Washington, DC, control over operations, but retains statutory oversight responsibilities.

These current financial crises illustrate an ongoing need to monitor the financial well-being of governments. Moreover, increasing demands for services in the face of a growing unwillingness of taxpayers to pay higher taxes have created a nationwide movement, at all levels of government, to develop performance measurement systems to enhance the efficient and effective delivery of services. Whereas such systems may not have been feasible 10 or 20 years ago because of limited data collection and processing capabilities, recent technological developments, such as computer networking, the Internet, shared databases, and data warehousing, now make such systems not only feasible but necessary, especially for larger governments.

---

[8]Linda Robinson, "The Drive to Abolish the City of Miami: Charges of Corruption Would Be Thigh-Slapping Entertainment if the Place Weren't Going Broke," *U.S. News and World Report* 121, no. 22 (December 2, 1996), pp. 39–40.

[9]Barrett and Greene, "Capital of Bad Management," p. 50.

Evaluating Financial Condition

Preventing financial crises such as those discussed earlier in this chapter requires an early warning system to identify trends or practices that may adversely impact financial condition. Ensuring that the government has the financial capacity to sustain desired services is the primary reason for internal managers to monitor financial condition. Bond investors and creditors have a similar interest in evaluating financial condition, namely, to assess the government's ability to make future interest and principal payments, even in the face of adverse economic trends or other events (for example, natural disasters). Knowledge that internal managers are employing a system to track financial trends provides investors and creditors with added confidence in the quality of the government's financial management, particularly if such trend data are shared with credit analysts. Credit analysts also have more than a passing interest in the government's ability to provide services in the long run since experience has shown that, in times of fiscal crisis, expenditures for vital services often take priority over debt service payments.

Legislative bodies have responsibility for helping formulate sound fiscal policies for the government they serve, whereas oversight bodies have responsibility for monitoring, and in some cases establishing, the fiscal policies of governmental units for which they have oversight responsibility. Some states, for example, impose uniform financial accounting and reporting systems that all municipalities within the state must follow. Municipalities may also be required to submit annual financial reports to a state oversight body. Finally, legislative and oversight bodies typically have responsibilities to monitor executives' compliance with laws and regulations.

Although citizens should have an interest in the government's overall financial condition, often their interests lie more narrowly with a particular program or with rising tax rates or service fees. Moreover, citizens' interests usually are represented through intermediaries such as the media, taxpayer *watchdog* groups, special interest groups, and groups that serve the public interest, such as the League of Women Voters. Thus, citizen groups typically have little interest or involvement in evaluating the overall financial condition of government, even though they may suffer severe cutbacks in governmental services in the event of a financial crisis.

The remainder of this chapter focuses on the ICMA financial trend monitoring system that *internal managers* may use to monitor and evaluate the financial condition of their government and similar methods used by *investors and creditors* to assess financial condition, or, more specifically, general obligation creditworthiness. Presumably, these methods can be useful as well for legislative and oversight bodies and citizen groups.

As mentioned earlier in this chapter, the *financial trend monitoring system* was developed by the ICMA in the wake of the New York City default for financial managers to use in tracking the financial performance of their own governments. Credit market analysts, particularly analysts with the major rating agencies, have developed proprietary (in-house) approaches for evaluating the general obligation creditworthiness of governmental units that issue bonds. Although evaluation objectives differ slightly between internal and external evaluation systems, and among the approaches used by external users, both types focus on many of the same kinds of factors. Prior to examining systems for evaluating financial condition, it is important to distinguish between the key terms *financial position* and *financial condition*.

Financial Position versus Financial Condition

Various definitions have been developed for the terms *financial position* and *financial condition*. A GASB research study notes that **financial position** "tends to be a shorter-run concept compared with financial condition."[10] The GASB study further notes that "*financial position* for governmental funds focuses on assets and liabilities that require cash or are normally converted to cash in the near future and can generally be determined from the financial statements alone."[11] Thus, *financial position* is closely related to the concept of liquidity. By contrast, the GASB study defines **financial condition** as:

> The probability that a government will meet both its financial obligations to creditors, consumers, employees, taxpayers, suppliers, constituents, and others as they become due and its service obligations to constituents, both currently and in the future.[12]

Similarly, the ICMA handbook summarizes *financial condition* as "a local government's ability to finance its services on a continuing basis."[13] The handbook notes more specifically that *financial condition* "refers to a government's ability to (1) maintain existing service levels, (2) withstand local and regional economic disruptions, and (3) meet the demands of natural growth, decline, and change."[14] Definitions of both the GASB study and the ICMA handbook make it clear that *financial condition* is similar to the common accounting term *solvency*. The ability to maintain existing or provide increasing service levels is related also to the accountability concept of *interperiod equity*, a term the GASB defines as determining "whether current-year revenues are sufficient to pay for the services provided that year and whether future taxpayers will be required to assume burdens for services previously provided."[15] Excessive shifting of the burden to pay for current services to future taxpayers may threaten the government's ability to sustain the current level of services or to expand services to meet future population growth.

Internal Financial Trend Monitoring

Both the GASB study and the revised ICMA Handbook point out that financial condition is a complex, multidimensional concept whose measurement requires analysis of a multitude of factors. The GASB study identifies the major categories of factors as economy and demographics; revenue base; current and capital expen-

---

[10]Robert Berne, *Research Report*, "The Relationship Between Financial Reporting and the Measurement of Financial Condition" (Norwalk, CT: GASB, 1992), pp. 16–17.

[11]Ibid., p. 17.

[12]Ibid.

[13]Groves and Valente, *Evaluating Financial Condition*, p. 2.

[14]Ibid.

[15]Governmental Accounting Standards Board, *Concepts Statement No. 1*, "Objectives of Financial Reporting" (Norwalk, CT: GASB, 1987), par. 61.

ditures; debt, pensions and other postemployment benefits; internal resources; management capabilities; infrastructure; and willingness to raise revenues and to provide needed public services.[16] Perusal of this list suggests that evaluation of some categories such as management capabilities, infrastructure, and willingness to raise revenues and provide services are largely qualitative judgments. Thus, unlike the rather straightforward evaluation of the financial condition of a business entity based on analysis of profitability and well-understood financial ratios, evaluation of governmental financial condition involves subjective judgments about the interplay of complex environmental, organizational, and financial factors.

Illustration 10–1 shows the framework developed by the ICMA for internal managers to use in evaluating financial condition. Environmental factors such as community needs and resources, economic conditions, political culture, intergovernmental constraints, and natural disasters and emergencies largely determine revenue capacity and demand for services. How fiscal policy within the governmental unit responds to environmental demand and changes in the environment is a major factor determining how environmental factors are translated into financial factors. Financial factors (identified in Illustration 10–1 as revenues, expenditures, operating position, debt structure, unfunded liabilities, and condition of capital plant) are the result of management and legislative policies in response to environmental demands and resources. Measures of financial condition include ratios consisting of one financial amount divided by another financial amount (such as fund balance divided by revenues) and ratios consisting of financial amounts divided by demographic or economic measures (such as debt divided by population).

Although identifying financial indicators and interpreting them is more of an art than a science, the ICMA provides a large number of potentially useful indicators grouped into 12 categories or factors corresponding to the environmental, organizational, and financial dimensions shown in Illustration 10–1. Examining changes in indicators over time and relationships among indicators can yield useful information on financial issues, such as whether revenue trends are adequate to meet expenditure trends, the adequacy of financial reserves to withstand revenue shortfalls or unforeseen expenditure requirements, current debt burden and future debt capacity, future service demands and ability of the governmental unit to meet those demands, adequacy of enterprise fund revenues to meet debt covenant requirements, and what portions of operating costs could be met by user charges rather than by taxes. However, making a reasonable judgment about the financial condition of a particular entity requires a sound understanding of how environmental factors influence the demand for and capacity to supply services, how organizational factors influence fiscal policy given a particular level or trend in the demand for and capacity to supply services, and how to measure the financial outcomes of the entity's fiscal policy. Each of these sets of factors is discussed at some length prior to moving to the identification, calculation, and interpretation of financial ratios.

---

[16]Berne, *Research Report*, p. 25.

Illustration 10–1 Factors Affecting Financial Condition

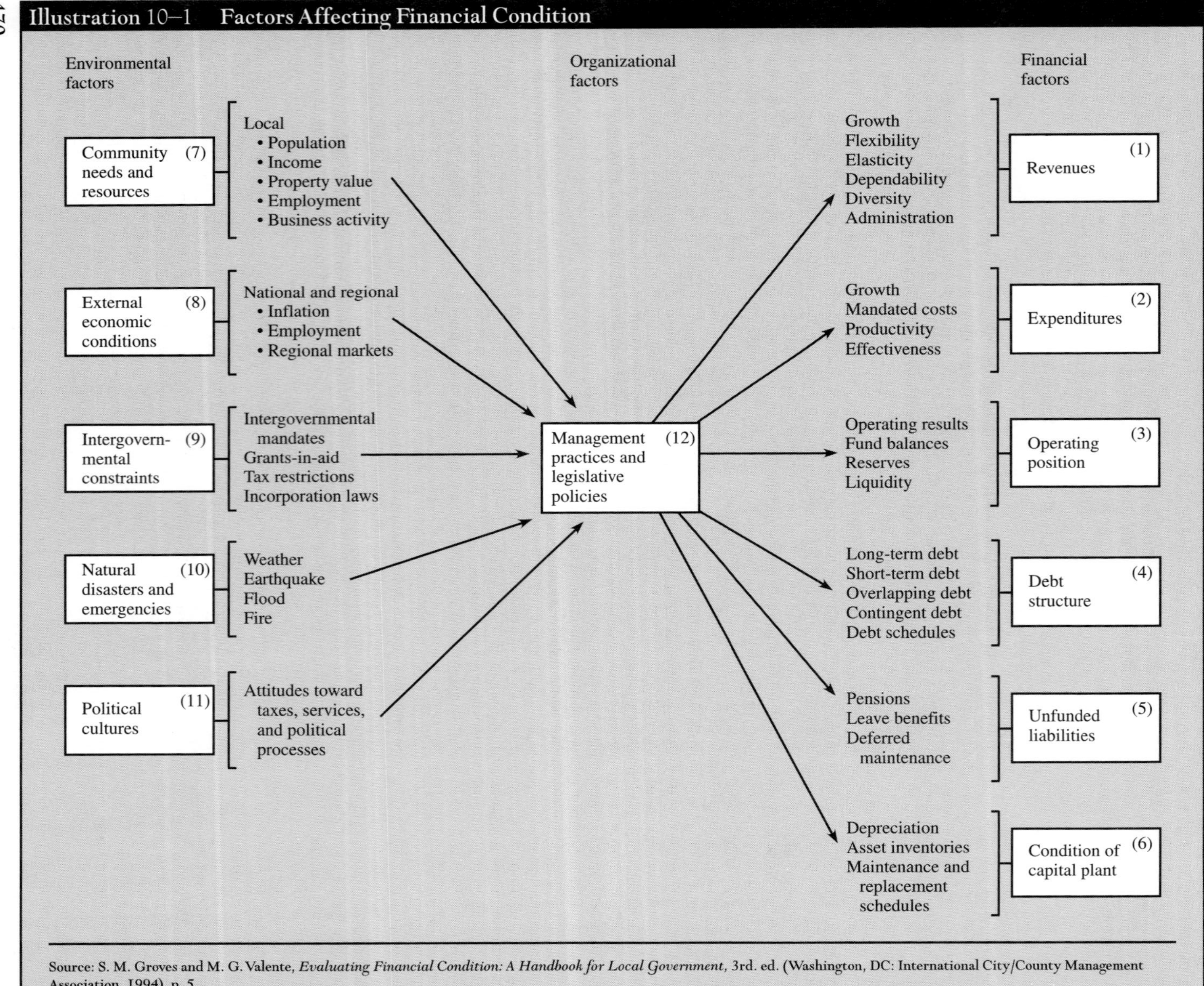

Source: S. M. Groves and M. G. Valente, *Evaluating Financial Condition: A Handbook for Local Government*, 3rd. ed. (Washington, DC: International City/County Management Association, 1994), p. 5.

Environmental Factors

Community needs and resources (see Illustration 10–1) determine in part the kinds and levels of services that are needed and the capacity to provide those services. Other environmental factors such as the legal and fiscal constraints under which the government operates, the kinds of major disruptions to which the government is susceptible, and the political culture of the government also affect the demand for services and the government's capacity to provide services.

Community Needs and Resources. This category consists of factors (see Illustration 10–1) that determine the demand for services such as population demographics (growth, density, and composition), median age, and percentage of households below the poverty level, as well as the capacity to provide services, such as personal income per capita, property values, employment (level, diversity, and types), and level of business activity. Some indicators affect both the demand for and capacity to provide services, for example a low personal income per capita generally is correlated with both high demand and low capacity, whereas high personal income is correlated with low demand and high capacity. The reason for this two-sided effect may be that personal income itself is the result of other factors such as the employment base, educational level, and median age. Thus, even when evaluating factors within a single category, the factors are often interrelated, making it difficult to assess any single factor in isolation. These difficulties notwithstanding, the more diversified and stable the employment base is, the higher are property values and personal income, and the more robust is business activity (for example, building permits, bank deposits, and retail sales), the lower will be demand for services and the higher the capacity to provide services. Population and related demographics such as growth, composition by age and race, housing patterns, and location (urban, rural, or suburban) also may strongly affect the demand for and capacity to provide services. A constant enigma in public finance is that the greater the need for services, the lower is the capacity to provide them, and vice versa.

Illustration 10–2 presents the trend, description, and analysis of one of the City of Columbia, Missouri's business activity indicators: Indicator 36-B, Retail Sales. This information is taken from its Financial Trend Manual for the years 1989 through 1998. The City of Columbia was a test city for the ICMA financial condition research project in the late 1970s and has since continued to use the trend monitoring system to monitor its financial condition. Based on the City's own analysis, it appears that retail sales have been growing at a satisfactory rate.

External Economic Conditions. Obviously, no local or state government operates independently of the regional and national economy. Regional economic activity affects local business activity, employment, and income, by influencing the demand for manufactured, agricultural, and service products, and the levels of wholesale and retail sales. Similarly, inflation at the national level influences regional and local prices, including wages and the cost of debt financing. Although consideration of external economic conditions is essential to assessing the local economy, the linkages are generally difficult to pinpoint and quantify.

Illustration 10–2 Indicator 36–B—Business Activity: Retail Sales

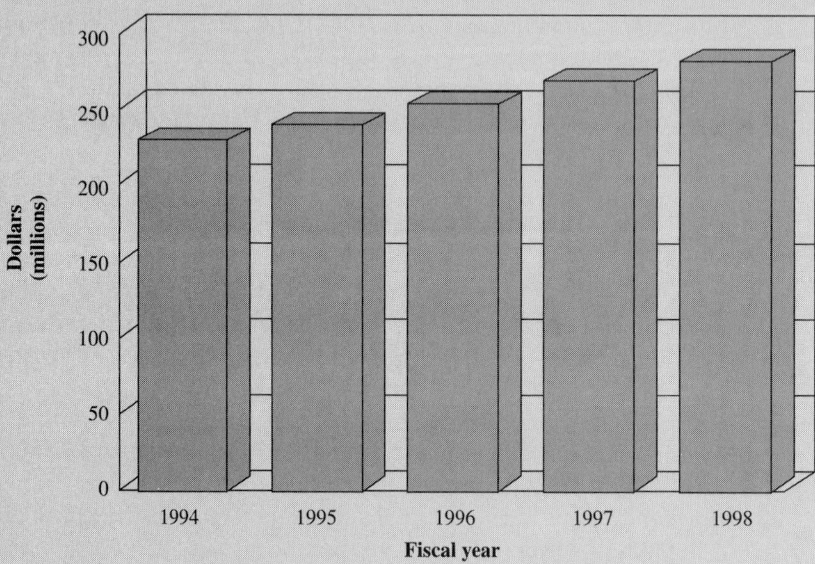

Warning Trend:
Decline in Business Activity as Measured by Retail Sales (constant dollars)
Formulation:
Retail Sales (constant dollars)

	Fiscal Year				
	1994	*1995*	*1996*	*1997*	*1998*
Estimated retail sales	1,056,384,400	1,133,710,600	1,207,907,000	1,269,536,600	1,339,671,700
Consumer price index	447.5	459.0	470.4	483.0	491.3
Retail sales in constant dollars	236,063,553	246,995,773	256,782,951	262,844,017	272,678,954

Description:
The level of retail sales can affect the City's financial condition in two ways. First, it directly affects revenue yields to the extent that they are reliant on sales tax receipts. And second, the affect is indirect to the extent that changes in retail sales affect other demographic and economic areas such as employment base, personal income, etc. This in turn can create further declines in such business activity.

Analysis:
Constant dollar retail sales increased 35.31 percent from FY 89 to FY 98. This reflects on the ability of the business sector to maintain and increase future retail sales growth. The growth in sales tax has ranged from approximately 5 percent to 9 percent for the past ten years. Any constant dollar decline in retail sales may need to be monitored closely in the future. However, there has been a positive trend for the period studied.

Source: City of Columbia, Missouri, *Ten Year Revenue, Expenditures, and Financial Trend Manual*, FY 1989–1998, pp. 362–63.

Intergovernmental Constraints. Most local governments operate under various legal constraints imposed by the state government. Moreover, the federal government imposes constraints as a condition for receiving federal financial assistance. Among the state-imposed constraints may be legal limitations on the ability of local governments to raise revenues and issue debt. If such limitations exist, the current levels of revenues and debt subject to such limits should be compared to the authorized limits. Of particular importance is considering the extent to which legal limits may impede needed acquisition of capital assets and future growth in services.

Natural Disasters and Emergencies. The need to consider and plan for natural disasters is incumbent on all top governmental officials. Certainly, no place is immune from such events, although some locations are more vulnerable than others. The question that should be asked is: What would happen if a major earthquake or hurricane were to strike? Related questions that need to be asked are: (1) Does the City have sufficient insurance and reserves to cover possible losses? (2) Does the government have sufficient resources (and a plan) for evacuation, protection against looting, and cleanup?

Political Culture. This perhaps is the most difficult of all factors to measure, but certainly critically important to determining how the administration will react to the other environmental factors in shaping the government's fiscal policy. Political culture includes such factors as form of government (e.g., mayor-council—weak or strong, council-manager, commission) and the entity's economic, political, and social history. The entity's history may reveal underlying community philosophies regarding willingness to support higher taxes, issuances of long-term debt, and increased social services.

Organizational Factors

Management Practices and Legislative Policies. As indicated by their pivotal location in Illustration 10–1, *management practices and legislative policies* play a crucial role in determining fiscal policy in response to the environmental factors just discussed. Sound financial management and the political will to resist easy solutions can minimize financial problems that might otherwise result from such factors as economic downturns, plant closings, or natural disasters. Financial crises often build over a number of years during economic recessions. Politicians may be either unwilling or unable to curtail expenditures for services in response to revenue shortfalls. Results of past policies, such as heavy reliance on debt or an excessive labor force, may make it difficult or infeasible to reduce expenditures sufficiently in the short run. Short-run solutions, such as deferring needed maintenance, curtailing capital expenditures, or underfunding pensions, may lead to even greater problems in the future. Thus, sound financial management means planning for adverse environmental conditions or events and devising long-run solutions when problems do occur. Although management practices and legislative policies are critical determinants of financial condition, they are among the most difficult factors to measure. Among indicators that credit analysts use to assess management quality are the legal and political relationship between a local government and the state government, growth of services relative to capacity, background and experience of key government managers, accounting and budgeting practices, debt management, and tax policies.[17] Evidence of mismanagement or deficient fiscal policies may include deferral of maintenance; underfunding of pensions; decline in tax collection rates; use of one-time revenues, long-term reserves, debt proceeds, or the proceeds from the sale of assets to balance the operating budget; and accounting gimmickry.[18]

Financial Factors

Examples of governmental fund financial ratios typically used in assessing financial condition in the ICMA trend monitoring system are shown in Illustration 10–3. Although the ratios contained in Illustration 10–3 represent what the authors consider key ratios, they are not intended to represent all the ratios that might be useful in evaluating financial condition. In fact, the ICMA handbook provides for a total of 27 financial indicators. The 13 ratios given in Illustration 10–3 cover each of the financial factors shown on the right-hand side of Illustration 10–1, except for condition of capital plant. Most governmental entities do not include information on the condition of capital plant in their CAFR. Descriptive information on miles of street, miles of sewer, number of fire and police stations, number of employees, and so on, are often provided, but seldom is any information provided about the *condition* of capital plant. Although the lack of such disclosures creates problems for *external* analysts, internal users can obtain information on maintenance effort and condition of equipment from the Public Works Department. Such information when combined with information on maintenance expenditures and capital outlay can provide useful indicators of the condition of capital plant.

The data to calculate the 13 financial ratios shown in Illustration 10–3 are readily obtainable from most CAFRs. Except for population, which is usually disclosed in the statistical section, data for the first 8 ratios and ratio 11 can be obtained from the Statement of Revenues, Expenditures, and Changes in Fund Balances—Governmental Funds (see Illustration 2–4) and the Balance Sheet—Government Funds (see Illustration 2–3). Data for the remaining ratios usually can be found in the Notes to the Financial Statements.

In calculating ratios 1 through 8, some analysts prefer to utilize General Fund data only, whereas others will utilize combined data for all governmental fund types. This decision will depend, in part, on how large the General Fund is relative to all governmental fund types. In calculating operating revenues, capital project fund revenues should be excluded since the capital project fund is not an operating fund. For purposes of calculating revenues and expenditures in these ratios, other financing sources are often added to revenues and other financing uses are often added to expenditures. The government-wide financial statements prescribed by GASB *Statement No. 34* offer additional opportunities for analysis of financial factors relating to the governmental entity as a whole.

---

[17]Standard & Poor's, *Municipal Finance Criteria* (New York: Standard & Poor's, 1995), pp. 23–24.
[18]Groves and Valente, *Evaluating Financial Condition*, pp. 146–51.

Illustration 10–3 Financial Ratios Based on CAFR Governmental Funds Information

Financial Ratios	Explanation for Ratio
Revenue measures:	
1. Total revenues / Population	Indicates demand for resources and the entity's ability and willingness to provide resources. Over time shows how revenues are changing relative to population changes. A high ratio, and increasing trend, in relation to ratio 3 below, is desirable. However, a high ratio may also suggest less flexibility for obtaining additional revenues.
2. Own source revenues / Total revenues	Indicates extent of fiscal self-reliance; a high ratio is viewed as a positive characteristic.
Expenditure measures:	
3. Total expenditures / Population	Indicates cost of providing services per capita. Over time it reflects changes in expenditures relative to changes in population. A high ratio may indicate inefficiency or that cost of services may eventually exceed residents' ability to pay for services.
4. Operating expenditures / Total expenditures	Operating expenditures = Total expenditures − Capital expenditures. A high ratio may indicate inadequate financial capacity to maintain infrastructure. Capital expenditures are often one of the first discretionary expenditures cut when fiscal stress occurs. Deferred capital expenditures create a need for increased capital expenditures in the future.
Operating position liquidity measures:	
5. Total revenues / Total expenditures	Indicates relationship of inflow from revenues to outflow for expenditures; a high ratio is viewed as a positive characteristic.
6. Unreserved fund balance(s) / Operating revenues	Indicates availability of "financial reserves" to meet unforeseen contingencies and for appropriation for future operations. A ratio below 5 percent is often regarded by the debt rating agencies as a red flag indicating probable fiscal stress.
7. (Cash + Short-term investments) / Current liabilities	Indicates liquidity or "cash position"; a ratio of less than one is considered as a negative factor, particularly if it occurs in consecutive years.
8. Current liabilities / Operating revenues	Indicates the ability of the government to meet its current liabilities.
Debt structure measures:	
9. Net tax-supported long-term debt / Net assessed valuation	Net tax-supported debt is direct tax-supported debt less amount available in debt service funds. Indicates the government's ability to repay its net general long-term debt; a ratio of 10 percent or more is viewed as a negative factor. This may not be a valid benchmark in states that have extremely low assessment ratios, such as Missouri, which averages 24 percent.
10. Net tax-supported long-term debt / Population	An alternative indicator measure of general long-term debt burden is debt per capita. A debt burden greater than $1,200 per capita or level of debt exceeding 90 percent of amount authorized by law may be considered a warning signal.
11. Debt service / Operating revenues	Indicates extent of the government's fixed costs for paying principal and interest on its direct tax-supported debt. A ratio of 20 percent or more is considered a warning signal; 10 percent or below is considered good.
Unfunded liabilities:	
12. Unfunded pension liability / Net assessed valuation	When compared with ratio 9 above, this ratio indicates the level of unfunded liabilities relative to net tax-supported bonded debt. Other useful ratios would be unfunded "other postemployment benefits" or unfunded accrued vacation and sick leave divided by net assessed valuation.
13. Pension plan assets / Benefits paid	Indicates the amount of accumulated cash and investments relative to annual benefits paid. Over time, a decline in this ratio may indicate serious problems in the management or design of the pension plan.

Source: These ratios are adapted from S. M. Groves and M. G. Valente, *Evaluating Financial Condition: A Handbook for Local Government*, 3rd ed. (Washington, DC: International City/County Management Association, 1994).

Using Financial Reports in Evaluating Financial Condition

Given the complex analytical framework just discussed, one might question the usefulness of the Comprehensive Annual Financial Report in evaluating financial condition. A common complaint is that the fund financial statements in the typical CAFR do not portray a clear picture of the governmental entity's financial condition. In fact, many trained analysts find the introductory and statistical sections of the CAFR, and the Notes to the Financial Statements, to be more useful than the financial statements for assessing financial condition. This is not surprising since the introductory and statistical sections of the CAFR and the Notes to the Financial Statements provide important information on environmental and organizational factors (such as those shown in Illustration 10–1), and how they relate to financial factors. Moreover, as discussed in Chapters 1 and 9, the fund financial statements prepared by state and local governments focus on short-term *financial position*, rather than long-term *financial condition*. Many governments further enhance the understandability of their CAFR by providing excellent narrative and graphical explanation of economic and financial factors, including trend data, comparisons with other governments, and forecasts in the introductory section.

In the authors' view, the fact that many find the introductory and statistical sections to be as useful as financial statements for evaluating financial condition is a reflection of the complex nature of financial condition rather than an indictment of financial statements. These complexities and the lack of a "bottom-line" performance measure (profit) may also explain why the CAFR has evolved to its present form, and provides justification for publishing a complete CAFR rather than just basic financial statements. From this perspective, the basic financial statements (illustrated in Chapter 2) are not useless; they provide useful information for calculating financial ratios essential to understanding the entity's financial position, an important component of financial condition.

Use of Benchmarks to Aid Interpretation

Regardless of how the ratios are calculated, the more difficult task is how to interpret the ratios to make an informed judgment about financial condition. Checking each ratio against the applicable "red-flag" level shown in Illustration 10–3 may provide early warning signals about low liquidity, over-reliance on intergovernmental revenues, an imbalance between revenues and expenditures, excessive debt burden, and poor management of retirement plans. Five- or 10-year trends in these ratios are essential in pinpointing emerging or existing problem areas.

In addition to comparing ratios to established red-flag levels, **benchmarking** can be a very useful tool. For internal trend monitoring purposes, comparing current-period ratios to those of prior years provides useful information, particularly when the data are displayed in graphs. Illustration 10–4 shows the use of time-series trend monitoring by the City of Columbia, Missouri, along with credit industry benchmarking, to display data for the years 1993 through 1998 for Indicator 16, Excess of Revenues over Expenditures (of the General Fund). (See Illustration 10–6.) Besides showing the time-series data in both graphical and tabular form, the City explains the manner of formulating the indicator and provides a narrative

Illustration 10–4 Indicator 16—Excess of Revenues over Expenditures: General Fund

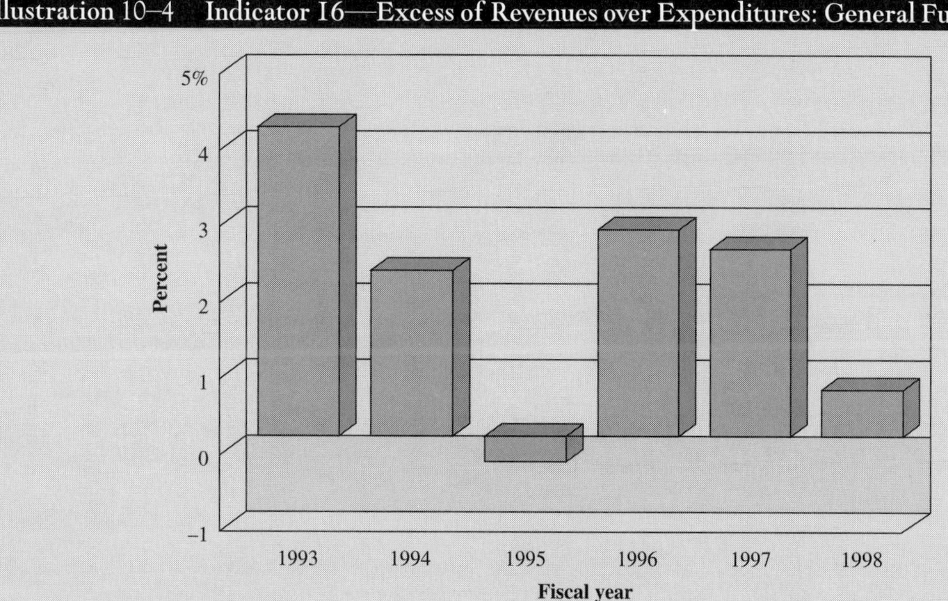

Warning Trend:
Increasing Amount of General Fund Operating Deficits as a Percent of Operating Revenues and Transfers

Formulation:

$$\frac{\text{General Fund operating (deficits) surpluses}}{\text{Operating revenues and transfers}}$$

	Fiscal Year					
Fiscal Year	*1993*	*1994*	*1995*	*1996*	*1997*	*1998*
General Fund operating surplus (deficit)*	1,296,056	742,880	(122,256)	1,122,324	1,005,174	323,804
Operating revenues and transfers†	32,156,759	34,412,828	36,945,336	38,794,027	41,207,631	43,532,800
General Fund operating surpluses (deficits) as a percentage of operating revenues and transfers	4.03%	2.16%	−0.33%	2.89%	2.44%	0.74%

*Not including encumbrances.

†Operating revenues and transfers: General Fund revenues plus operating transfers from other funds and increase in obligations under capital leases and appropriated Fund Balance where applicable.

(continued)

description and interpretation of the indicator. In addition, the City provides both time-series warning trend and credit industry benchmark information and a complete analysis of the trend information that is provided.

Illustration 10–4 (concluded)

Description:
An operating deficit will occur as operating expenditures exceed operating revenues. However, this does not necessarily mean the budget will be out of balance. Reserves (fund balances) and transfers are sometimes used to cover the difference. Continuing use of reserves and the unjustifiable transfer of funds to balance the deficit may indicate a revenue/expenditure problem.

The existence of an operating deficit in one year is not cause for concern, but frequent and increasing deficits can indicate that current revenues are not supporting current expenditures, and that serious problems may lie ahead.

Credit Industry Benchmarks:
A current year operating deficit would be considered a minor warning signal, and the reasons and manner of funding would be carefully examined before it was even considered a negative factor. However, the following situations would be looked at with considerably more attention and would probably be considered negative factors:

1. Two consecutive years of operating fund deficits.
2. A current year deficit greater than the previous year's deficit.
3. A current operating fund deficit in two or more of the last five years.
4. An abnormally large deficit (5% to 10% of operating revenues) in any one year.

Analysis:
FY 95 shows a deficit percentage of −0.33%, the first deficit in 10 years. This is not cause for alarm as we have not experienced any other deficits in the period shown and FY 98 reflects a 0.74% surplus percentage of Operating Revenues and Transfers. The adopted budget for FY 99 reflects a balanced budget with $100,000 Contingency and $29,837 for the City Council to allocate to programs or projects during the fiscal year. The FY 99 budget provides for increases in personnel and capital costs. Management and City Council are addressing avenues for increasing the City's revenue base.

Operating Revenues and Transfers increase primarily due to increases in sales tax, intragovernmental revenues, fees and service charges, operating transfers, public safety, health and environment, and appropriation of prior year fund balance. For ten years the General Fund has appropriated amounts from the prior year's fund balance ranging from $0 to $2,338,381. The appropriated fund balance for FY 98 is $2,338,381.

Source: City of Columbia, Missouri, *Ten Year Revenue, Expenditure, and Financial Trend Manual*, FY 1989–FY 1998, pp. 292–93.

Internal managers and external analysts can also compare specific ratios to national and state medians published by Moody's Investors Service,[19] or to comparative ratios published by Dr. Kenneth Brown of Southwest Missouri State University for both cities and counties.[20] Dr. Brown's benchmark data are grouped by state, Census Bureau region, and population range and are based on annual financial data collected by the GFOA. His publication provides comparative ratio data for the 25th, 50th, and 75th percentiles, by group, for ratios 1 and 2, 4 through 8, and 10 and 11 of the 13 ratios shown in Illustration 10–3. Dr. Brown's ratios are based mainly on General Fund financial data. For readers who may have forgotten their statistics, the 50th percentile corresponds to the median.

[19]Moody's Investor's Service, Inc., [year] *Medians: Selected Indicators of Municipal Performance* (New York: Moody's, annual).

[20]*Dr. Kenneth W. Brown's Comparative Ratios for Cities: Developed for Analyses of FY 1999 Financial Statements* website http://courses.smsu.edu/kwb237f/ratios/.

Illustration 10–5 presents Dr. Brown's comparative ratios for 513 cities located in the U.S. Census Bureau's Midwest Region and other three regions. The column headed *Best* indicates whether a high or low measure is preferred. Comparing the 25th and 75th percentile values shows the values for some ratios are highly variable across cities. This fact should also be kept in mind when comparing a city's ratios to ratios from a comparison group.

How should financial condition be evaluated and interpreted? After each indicator (ratio) is calculated, it should be compared with the same indicator from prior years, as well as against any credit market or other *red flags*. If available, each indicator can be compared with a comparative benchmark value, such as those from Moody's Medians (see footnote 19) or those published by Dr. Brown. A table can then be prepared listing each indicator and showing whether the indicator is positive (+) or negative (−). Such a table for the City of Columbia, Missouri, showing 36 indicators (for all financial factors plus community needs and resources) is shown in Illustration 10–6. Alternative measures are calculated for some indicators. Further, the City of Columbia could calculate the 10 ratios contained in Dr. Brown's database and compare them to the comparison ratios. The 10-point test is based on instructions in Dr. Brown's publication. Scores should be interpreted as follows: For each ratio, if the City of Columbia's ratio is in the first quartile (below the 25th percentile comparison ratio), score −1; if in the second quartile (at or above the 25th percentile but below the 50th percentile), score 0; if in the third quartile (at or above the 50th percentile, but below the 75th percentile), score +1; and if in the fourth quartile (at or above the 75th percentile), score +2. The total score for each column is interpreted as follows:

Score	*Percentile*	*Relation to Score of Other Cities*
14	99th	Only 1% scored higher
12	95th	Only 5% scored higher
10	90th	Only 10% scored higher
8	75th	Only 25% scored higher
5	50th	50% scored higher
2	25th	75% scored higher
0	10th	90% scored higher
−2	5th	95% scored higher
−4	1st	99% scored higher

Since the City of Columbia's total scores ranged from 6 to 10, depending on which comparison group was used, it scored quite well on these benchmarks. Further, the large number of + signs included in Illustration 10–6 suggests that the City is in sound financial condition.

A caveat to keep in mind in using benchmarks from other states is that local government organizational structures differ significantly from state to state, and these differences may have a large effect on some ratios. A good example is that in

Illustration 10–5 FY 1999 Comparative Ratios for Cities: Comparison Group–Cities by U.S. Census Region

		MIDWEST					NORTHEAST				
	Ratio	*No.*	*Best*	*25%*	*50%*	*75%*	*No.*	*Best*	*25%*	*50%*	*75%*
1	Total Revenues to Population	513	HIGH	553.972	685.864	838.392	118	HIGH	703.460	1758.486	2250.686
2	Local GF Revenues to Total GF Revenues	513	HIGH	0.702	0.849	0.954	118	HIGH	0.769	0.896	0.950
3	Operating Transfers In to Total GF Revenues and Operating Transfers In	513	LOW	0.041	0.009	0.000	118	LOW	0.016	0.003	0.000
4	Operating Expenditures to Total Expenditures	513	LOW	0.919	0.851	0.757	118	LOW	0.959	0.923	0.883
5	Total Revenues to Total Expenditures	513	HIGH	0.861	0.954	1.035	118	HIGH	0.927	0.969	1.021
6	Unreserved GF Balance to GF Revenues	513	HIGH	0.191	0.330	0.487	118	HIGH	0.069	0.121	0.185
7	Total GF Cash to GF Liabilities	513	HIGH	0.931	1.825	3.920	118	HIGH	0.851	1.340	2.121
8	Total GF Liabilities to GF Revenues	513	LOW	0.291	0.170	0.090	118	LOW	0.179	0.117	0.080
9	Direct General Long-Term Debt to Population	513	LOW	508.175	260.752	66.709	118	LOW	1013.559	546.666	283.884
10	Debt Service to Total Revenues	513	LOW	0.136	0.080	0.043	118	LOW	0.070	0.001	0.000

		SOUTHERN					WESTERN				
1	Total Revenues to Population	552	HIGH	494.760	632.571	824.777	387	HIGH	553.835	727.349	978.516
2	Local GF Revenues to Total GF Revenues	552	HIGH	0.816	0.905	0.983	387	HIGH	0.828	0.887	0.930
3	Operating Transfers In to Total GF Revenues and Operating Transfers In	552	LOW	0.082	0.024	0.000	387	LOW	0.080	0.024	0.001
4	Operating Expenditures to Total Expenditures	552	LOW	0.991	0.923	0.844	387	LOW	0.947	0.880	0.779
5	Total Revenues to Total Expenditures	552	HIGH	0.878	0.964	1.039	387	HIGH	0.902	0.982	1.064
6	Unreserved GF Balance to GF Revenues	552	HIGH	0.181	0.271	0.417	387	HIGH	0.154	0.266	0.445
7	Total GF Cash to GF Liabilities	552	HIGH	1.778	3.316	6.028	387	HIGH	1.397	2.585	4.722
8	Total GF Liabilities to GF Revenues	552	LOW	0.131	0.085	0.060	387	LOW	0.162	0.104	0.064
9	Direct General Long-Term Debt to Population	552	LOW	564.115	160.050	0.000	387	LOW	287.576	36.096	0.000
10	Debt Service to Total Revenues	552	LOW	0.108	0.042	0.000	387	LOW	0.121	0.066	0.024

Source: Dr. Kenneth W. Brown's website http://courses.smsu.edu/kwb237f/ratios/.

Illustration 10–6 Columbia Financial Trend Monitoring System: Summary 1989–1998

		State of Indicator*		
Indicator	*Description of Indicator*	*General Fund/ Government Funds*	*Enterprise/Internal Service Funds*	*Community Needs and Resources*
Chart A	Columbia Financial Trend Monitoring System: Warning Trends/Factors			
Revenues:				
Chart B	Impact of Inflation on City Revenues	+		
1	Revenues per Capita: General Fund	+		
2-A	Restricted Revenues: Governmental Funds	+		
2-B	Restricted Revenues: Enterprise Funds		+	
3	Intergovernmental Revenues: General Fund	+		
4	Elastic Tax Revenues: General Fund	+		
5	Operating Transfers from Other Funds: General Fund	+		
6	Temporary Revenues: Governmental Funds	+		
7	Property Tax Revenues: General Fund	+		
8	Uncollected Property Taxes: General Fund	+		
9	Service Charges Coverage: General Fund	+		
10	Revenues—Budgeted vs. Actual: General Fund	+		
Expenditures:				
Chart C	Impact of Inflation on City Expenditures	+	+	
11-A	Expenditures per Capita: General Fund	+		
11-B	Expenses per Capita: Enterprise Funds		+	
12-A	Employees per Capita: General Fund	+		
12-B	Employees per Capita: Enterprise Funds and Internal Service Funds		+	
13	Fixed Costs: All Funds	Monitor	Monitor	
14	Fringe Benefits	+	+	
15	Expenditures: General Fund over/under Budget	+		
Operating Position:				
16	Excess of Revenues over Expenditures: General Fund	+		
17	Enterprise Retained Earnings/Loss		+	
18	General Fund Balances	+		
19-A	Liquidity: General Fund	+		
19-B	Liquidity: Enterprise Funds		+	
20-A	Revenues to Expenditures: Governmental Funds & Expendable Trust Funds	+		
20-B	Revenues to Expenses: Proprietary Funds & Nonexpendable Trust Funds		+	
21-A	Current Liabilities: General Fund	+		
21-B	Current Liabilities: Enterprise Fund		+	
22-A	General Obligation Long-Term Debt: per Assessed Valuation	+		
22-B	General Obligation Long-Term Debt: per Capita	+		
23-A	Debt Service: General Obligation Bonds	+		
23-B	Debt Service: Revenue Bonds		+	

(continued)

Illustration 10–6 *(concluded)*

		State of Indicator*		
Indicator	*Description of Indicator*	*General Fund/ Government Funds*	*Enterprise/Internal Service Funds*	*Community Needs and Resources*
Unfunded Liabilities:				
24	Pension Assets	+	+	
25	Accumulated Employee Leave	+	+	
26-A	Maintenance Effort: Streets & Sidewalks	+		
26-B	Maintenance Effort: Water & Electric Utilities		+	
27	Capital Outlay: General, Internal Service, & Enterprise Funds	Monitor	Monitor	
28	Depreciation: Enterprise & Internal Service Funds		+	
Community Needs & Resources:				
29	Population			+
30	Median Age			+
31	Household Effective Buying Income			+
32	Public Assistance Recipients			Monitor
33	Property Value			+
34	Residential Development			+
35	Employment Base			+
36-A	Business Activity: Business License Accounts			+
36-B	Business Activity: Retail Sales			+

*State of Indicator: + = Positive Trend; − = Negative Trend; Monitor = Needs to be closely monitored.

Source: City of Columbia, Missouri, *Ten Year Revenue, Expenditure, and Financial Trend Manual,* FY1989–FY1998, pp. 239–40.

a few states local school districts are legally part of the government of the city in which they are located, whereas in most states the school districts are independent governmental units. In those states in which schools are part of the city government, per capita measures such as ratios 1, 3, and 10 may be much larger than in the other states.

In addition to analyzing ratios, one should evaluate the stability, flexibility, and diversity of revenue sources; budgetary control over revenues and expenditures; adequacy of insurance protection; level of overlapping debt; and growth of unfunded employee-related benefits. Socioeconomic and demographic trends should also be analyzed, including trends in employment, real estate values, retail sales, building permits, population, personal income, and welfare. Much of this information is contained in the statistical section of the CAFR; the remainder can be obtained from the U.S. Bureau of the Census publications available in most university libraries.

Despite the complexity of evaluating governmental financial condition, there are recognizable signals of fiscal stress.[21] These include: (1) a decline or inadequate growth in revenues relative to expenditures, (2) declining property values, (3) declining economic activity (such as increasing unemployment, declining retail sales, and declining building activity), (4) erosion of capital plant, particularly infrastructure, (5) increasing levels of unfunded pension and other postemployment obligations, and (6) inadequate capital expenditures. Warning signals such as these, particularly if several exist simultaneously, may indicate a potential fiscal crisis unless the government takes action to increase revenues or decrease spending.

Credit Analyst Models

As discussed earlier in this chapter, credit analysts are concerned with assessing a government's ability to pay interest and principal when due. Credit analysts typically examine the same kinds of information that internal managers use in evaluating financial condition. Of course, internal managers have access to *all* information generated by the government, for as far back as data are retained, whereas credit analysts have access only to what management provides or what they require from management. Thus, internal managers have an informational advantage with respect to their own government. Credit analysts with the major bond rating agencies (Moody's Investors Service and Standard & Poor's), or with companies that insure bonds against default, may have an informational advantage with respect to *benchmark* information, in that they have data from thousands of entities whose bonds are rated or insured. Moreover, these analysts develop extensive multiple-year libraries, including budgets and CAFRs, for the entities whose bonds are rated or insured, and they often visit the entity for discussions with management. Analysts with investment firms (underwriters and brokers) tend to collect and process much less information than do bond rating and insurer organizations. Rather, these analysts rely in part on agency ratings to help them properly determine the credit risk of municipal bonds.

Both Moody's and Standard & Poor's examine factors in the following four groups: (1) economic, (2) financial, (3) debt, and (4) administrative/political.[22] Moody's is known to emphasize debt factors in its analyses, whereas Standard & Poor's emphasizes the issuer's economic base.[23] Nevertheless, both agencies thoroughly examine factors in each of the four groups. Although little is known about which specific factors are examined in each group, or how factors are weighted in assigning ratings, the bond market literature suggests the agencies examine many, if not most, of the same factors that are considered for internal financial trend monitoring. Thus, there is little need to describe the credit analysis models, beyond this basic discussion. One should note, however, that the ratings themselves are often viewed, particularly by investors, as crude indicators of long-term financial condi-

[21]See, for example, Groves and Valente, *Evaluating Financial Condition*, Part 2.

[22]Robert Lamb and Stephen P. Rappaport, *Municipal Bonds*, 2nd ed. (New York: McGraw-Hill, 1987), pp. 40–44.

[23]Ibid.

tion. For example, a Moody's Aaa rating indicates a city is likely in better financial condition than a city with a Baa rating (the lowest *investment grade* rating). Further, ratings assigned to general obligation (GO) bonds often apply to all GO bonds of the same issuer. This is not necessarily the case, however. For example, GO bonds issued with state credit backing or other credit enhancement may carry a higher rating than the ordinary GO bonds of the same issuer. Insured bonds and certain defeased[24] bonds are automatically assigned the top rating category by both Moody's and Standard & Poor's.

Relation of Financial Performance to Operating Performance

This chapter describes the evaluation of financial condition. Continued sound financial condition is an indication of quality financial management and good financial performance. Achieving strong financial performance, however, does not ensure efficient and effective operating performance. Although it is difficult to provide an adequate level of services without sufficient financial resources, achieving efficient and effective use of *productive* resources requires innovative budgeting and management techniques. We defer discussion of these techniques until Chapter 13. In reading Chapter 13, one should keep in mind the importance of maintaining sound financial condition if service levels are to be sustained.

Key Terms

Benchmarking, 476
Financial condition, 468
Financial position, 468

Selected References

Berne, Robert. *Research Report*, "The Relationship Between Financial Reporting and the Measurement of Financial Condition." Norwalk, CT: GASB, 1992.

Brown, Kenneth W. *Comparative Ratios for Cities*. Springfield, MO: Solstice Publications, 1997.

———. "The 10-Point Test of Financial Condition: Toward an Easy-to-Use Assessment Tool for Smaller Cities." *Government Finance Review*, December 1993, pp. 21–26.

Governmental Accounting Standards Board. *Concepts Statement No. 1*, "Objectives of Financial Reporting." Norwalk, CT: GASB, 1987.

Groves, Sanford M., and Maureen G. Valente. *Evaluating Financial Condition: A Handbook for Local Government*, 3rd ed. Washington, DC: ICMA, 1994.

Lamb, Robert, and Stephen P. Rappaport. *Municipal Bonds*, 2nd ed. New York: McGraw-Hill, 1987.

The Bond Market Association. *Fundamentals of Municipal Bonds*, 5th ed. New York: PSA, 2000.

[24]See Chapter 6 for a discussion of defeased bonds.

Questions

10–1. Explain why a city government needs an effective system to monitor and evaluate financial condition.

10–2. Discuss and compare the quality of governmental financial reporting now and that at the time of the New York City default (mid-1970s). How does the quality of financial reporting affect the ability to evaluate financial condition?

10–3. Explain some typical causes of municipal financial crises.

10–4. How do the objectives of evaluating financial condition differ between internal managers and credit analysts? How are their objectives similar?

10–5. "Citizens have a strong interest in evaluating their city's financial condition." Do you agree with this statement? Why or why not?

10–6. Distinguish *financial position* from *financial condition*.

10–7. How is *interperiod equity* related to *financial condition*?

10–8. Why are management practices and legislative policies considered to be critically important in evaluating financial condition?

10–9. Explain how environmental factors influence a city's fiscal policy.

10–10. "Financial statements are virtually useless in evaluating a city's financial condition." Do you agree with this statement? Why or why not?

Cases

10–1. Comparative Ratios. The Combined Balance Sheet—All Fund Types and Account Groups; Combined Statement of Revenues, Expenditures, and Changes in Fund Balances—All Governmental Fund Types and Expendable Trust Funds; selected demographic statistics; and information on general bonded debt and assessed valuations of taxable property for the City of Marshall are provided on pages 488–497. The City has not yet implemented GASB *Statement No. 34*.

Required

a. Using the financial statements and other information provided, calculate the 10 ratios for which Dr. Kenneth Brown's comparative ratios for Midwest states are provided in Illustration 10–5 of this chapter.

Calculate ratios as follows: (Note: Use all revenues and expenditures as reported; do not include operating transfers in and out.) (GF = General Fund, SRF = special revenue funds, DSF = debt service funds, CPF = capital projects funds)

Ratio No.	*Numerator*	*Denominator*
1.	Total governmental fund revenues (GF + SRF + DSF + CPF)	Population
2.	GF Revenues minus GF Intergovernmental Revenues	GF Revenues

Ratio No.	Numerator	Denominator
3.	GF Operating Transfers In	GF Revenues plus GF Operating Transfers In
4.	GF Expenditures + SRF Expenditures + DSF Expenditures	GF Expenditures + SRF Expenditures + DSF Expenditures + CPF Expenditures
5.	Same as ratio 1	Same as ratio 4
6.	Unreserved Fund Balance of the GF (both designated and undesignated)	GF Revenues
7.	GF Cash + GF Investments	GF Total Liabilities
8.	GF Total Liabilities	GF Revenues
9.	Direct Debt (Use Total Debt)	Population
10.	Total Debt Service Expenditures	Same as numerator of ratio 1

b. Compare each ratio calculated in part *a* above to the comparative ratios provided in Illustration 10–5. Prepare a 10-point test of financial condition for FY 2002 (even though the comparative data are intended for FY 1999) and interpret the City's financial condition. (See explanation in text about scoring method.) Assume the City of Marshall is in the Midwest Region.

c. Provide an overall assessment of the City's financial condition using all information, both financial and nonfinancial, provided.

10–2. Comprehensive Case. (Different city for each student. Works well as a term or semester project.)

Objective and General Requirements: The objective of this case is to help you obtain a better understanding of how to use financial and nonfinancial information to assess the current and long-term financial condition of a city of your choice, or one assigned by your instructor. You should write or call the city to obtain their CAFR, or, alternatively, your instructor may provide you with a CAFR. It is recommended that you use a city with a population of at least 25,000 to increase the chances of obtaining a complete usable CAFR. Be sure to specify that you need the full CAFR. Be prepared to contact two or three cities if necessary to ensure you receive at least one.

You will use the information provided in the city's CAFR, as well as data from the U.S. Census Bureau and other data sources you may locate, to assess the current financial position and long-term financial condition or solvency of the city. Your conclusions must, of course, be based on an in-depth analysis of all information provided in the CAFR, as well as your other sources. Because evaluation of municipal financial condition is more of an art than a science, you may have to be creative and resourceful to do a good job.

Overview: For purposes of this project, financial condition is broadly defined as the ability of a city to provide an adequate range of services on a continuing basis. Specifically, it refers to a city's ability to (1) maintain existing service levels, (2) withstand major economic disruptions, and (3) meet the demands of a changing society in a changing economy. *Current* financial position can (*continued* on p. 498)

CITY OF MARSHALL
COMBINED BALANCE SHEET—ALL FUND TYPES AND ACCOUNT GROUPS
JUNE 30, 2002

	Governmental Fund Types			
	General	*Special Revenue*	*Debt Service*	*Capital Projects*
Assets and Other Debits				
Assets:				
Cash and pooled cash investments	$ 592,976	$ 282,360	$ 36,177	$ 619,283
Cash and pooled cash investments—nonexpendable trust	—	—	—	—
Investments	103,526	3,800,299	150,000	6,453,100
Investments held by deferred compensation plan administrators—Note 9	—	—	—	—
Receivables:				
Property tax	44,583	12,608	24,350	—
Accounts and unbilled usage (net of allowance for uncollectibles)	23,709	7,153	—	634
Special assessments	—	2,657	—	6,810
Interest	8,992	25,215	420	7,189
Due from other funds—Note 3	34,787	1,921	—	—
Due from component unit—Note 3	—	—	—	—
Advance to other funds—Note 3	—	65,603	—	108,272
Due from other governments	93,949	233,712	—	265,328
Inventories, at cost	41,837	—	—	—
Prepaid items	205,046	7,135	—	—
Deferred charges	—	83,855	—	—
Restricted assets:				
Cash	—	—	—	—
Investments	—	—	—	—
Land and improvements—Note 4	—	—	—	—
Buildings and structures—Note 4	—	—	—	—
Equipment and vehicles—Note 4	—	—	—	—
Sanitary sewers and lift stations	—	—	—	—
Construction in progress—Note 4	—	—	—	—
Accumulated depreciation	—	—	—	—
Other Debits:				
Amount available in debt service fund	—	—	—	—
Amount to be provided for retirement of general long-term debt	—	—	—	—
Total Assets and Other Debits	$1,149,405	$4,522,518	$210,947	$7,460,616

Proprietary Fund Types		Fiduciary Fund Type	Account Groups		
Enterprise	*Internal Service*	*Trust and Agency*	*General Fixed Assets*	*General Long-Term Debt*	*Totals Primary Government (Memorandum Only)*
$ 320,031	$ 78,798	$ 106,590	—	—	$ 2,036,215
—	—	2,517	—	—	2,517
3,506,055	777,808	147,445	—	—	14,938,233
—	—	2,352,314	—	—	2,352,314
—	—	—	—	—	81,541
748,789	—	—	—	—	780,285
—	—	—	—	—	9,467
70,577	9,926	940	—	—	123,259
1,807	—	—	—	—	38,515
148,663	—	—	—	—	148,663
19,667	—	—	—	—	193,542
1,238	175	—	—	—	594,402
41,973	—	—	—	—	83,810
59,999	6,150	607	—	—	278,937
—	—	—	—	—	83,855
—	—	—	—	—	—
911,445	—	—	—	—	911,445
3,081,964	—	—	$ 1,007,674	—	4,089,638
5,936,704	—	—	4,215,180	—	10,151,884
10,910,421	2,795	—	7,048,018	—	17,961,234
5,480,786	—	—	—	—	5,480,786
1,005,484	—	—	—	—	1,005,484
(9,492,366)	(2,795)	—	—	—	(9,495,161)
—	—	—	—	$ 196,004	196,004
—	—	—	—	17,852,743	17,852,743
$22,753,237	$872,857	$2,610,413	$12,270,872	$18,048,747	$69,899,612

(continued)

CITY OF MARSHALL
COMBINED BALANCE SHEET—ALL FUND TYPES AND ACCOUNT GROUPS
JUNE 30, 2002
(CONTINUED)

	Governmental Fund Types			
	General	*Special Revenue*	*Debt Service*	*Capital Projects*
Liabilities, Equity, and Other Credits				
Liabilities:				
Accounts payable	$120,564	$138,873	—	$399,605
Accrued payroll and payroll benefits	153,000	3,668	—	—
Compensated absences payable—Note 5	111,680	7,389	—	—
Retainage payable	—	17,651	—	83,083
Advantage from other funds—Note 3	—	19,667	—	—
Deferred revenues	10,236	58,362	$ 235	7,228
Due to other governments	—	192,030	—	—
Due to other funds—Note 3	—	28,186	—	3,608
Due to primary government—Note 3	—	—	—	—
Due to employees	—	—	—	—
Due to general public	—	—	—	—
Matured interest payable	—	—	14,708	—
Liabilities payable from restricted assets:				
Customers' deposits	—	—	—	—
Accrued interest payable	—	—	—	—
Current portion of revenue bonds (net of $1,313 unamortized discounts)	—	—	—	—
General obligation bonds and notes payable—Note 5	—	—	—	—
Urban renewal tax increment revenue bonds—Note 5	—	—	—	—
Revenue bonds payable (net of $68,572 unamortized discounts)—Note 5	—	—	—	—
Total Liabilities	395,480	465,826	14,943	493,524

Proprietary Fund Types		Fiduciary Fund Type	Account Groups		
Enterprise	*Internal Service*	*Trust and Agency*	*General Fixed Assets*	*General Long-Term Debt*	*Totals Primary Government (Memorandum Only)*
$ 241,110	$181,952	$ 5,465	—	—	$ 1,087,569
23,359	—	75,404	—	—	255,431
97,219	—	—	—	$ 608,747	825,035
19,043	—	—	—	—	119,777
173,875	—	—	—	—	193,542
232	—	—	—	—	76,293
10,506	—	1,045	—	—	203,581
684	—	6,037	—	—	38,515
—	—	—	—	—	—
—	—	2,352,576	—	—	2,352,576
—	—	36,048	—	—	36,048
—	—	—	—	—	14,708
—	—	—	—	—	—
27,917	—	—	—	—	27,917
48,687	—	—	—	—	48,687
—	—	—	—	16,945,000	16,945,000
—	—	—	—	495,000	495,000
5,851,428	—	—	—	—	5,851,428
6,494,060	181,952	2,476,575	—	18,048,747	28,571,107

(continued)

CITY OF MARSHALL
COMBINED BALANCE SHEET—ALL FUND TYPES AND ACCOUNT GROUPS
JUNE 30, 2002
(CONCLUDED)

	Governmental Fund Types			
	General	*Special Revenue*	*Debt Service*	*Capital Projects*
Liabilities, Equity, and Other Credits				
Fund Equity and Other Credits:				
Contributed capital—Note 6	—	—	—	—
Investment in general fixed assets	—	—	—	—
Reserved retained earnings:				
Reserved for bond and interest payments	—	—	—	—
Reserved for improvements	—	—	—	—
Reserved for advance to other funds	—	—	—	—
Unreserved retained earnings	—	—	—	—
Reserved fund balances:				
Reserved for endowments	—	—	—	—
Reserved for inventories	$ 41,837	—	—	—
Reserved for prepaid items	205,046	$ 7,135	—	—
Reserved for employees retirement systems	—	2,115,078	—	—
Reserved for advance to other funds	—	65,603	—	$ 108,272
Reserved for debt service	—	—	$196,004	—
Unreserved fund balances:				
Designated for future equipment and capital maintenance	35,732	—	—	—
Designated for future cash flow	59,475	—	—	—
Undesignated	411,835	1,868,876	—	6,858,820
Total Fund Equity and Other Credits	753,925	4,056,692	196,004	6,967,092
Total Liabilities, Equity, and Other Credits	$1,149,405	$4,522,518	$210,947	$7,460,616

See Notes to Financial Statements (not provided here).

	Proprietary Fund Types		**Fiduciary Fund Type**	**Account Groups**		
	Enterprise	*Internal Service*	*Trust and Agency*	*General Fixed Assets*	*General Long-Term Debt*	*Totals Primary Government (Memorandum Only)*
	$ 7,433,430	—	—	—	—	$ 7,433,430
	—	—	—	$12,270,872	—	12,270,872
	661,445	—	—	—	—	661,445
	250,000	—	—	—	—	250,000
	19,667	—	—	—	—	19,667
	7,894,635	$690,905	—	—	—	8,585,540
	—	—	$ 2,521	—	—	2,521
	—	—	—	—	—	41,837
	—	—	—	—	—	212,181
	—	—	8,359	—	—	2,123,437
	—	—	—	—	—	173,875
	—	—	—	—	—	196,004
	—	—	—	—	—	35,732
	—	—	—	—	—	59,475
	—	—	122,958	—	—	9,262,489
	16,259,177	690,905	133,838	12,270,872	—	41,328,505
	$22,753,237	$872,857	$2,610,413	$12,270,872	$18,048,747	$69,899,612

CITY OF MARSHALL
COMBINED STATEMENT OF REVENUES, EXPENDITURES, AND CHANGES IN FUND BALANCES—ALL GOVERNMENTAL FUND TYPES AND EXPENDABLE TRUST FUNDS
FOR THE FISCAL YEAR ENDED JUNE 30, 2002

	Governmental Fund Types				Fiduciary Fund Types	Totals Primary Government (Memorandum Only)
	General	*Special Revenue*	*Debt Service*	*Capital Projects*	*Expendable Trust*	
Revenues:						
Property tax	$4,778,343	$1,349,285	$2,651,407	—	—	$ 8,779,035
Tax increment financing revenues	—	92,028	—	—	—	92,028
Other city taxes	236,954	3,461	6,668	—	—	247,083
Use of money and property	156,570	158,039	49,392	$ 251,374	$ 5,363	620,738
Licenses and permits	196,185	—	—	—	—	196,185
Intergovernmental	971,061	2,637,743	—	818,715	—	4,427,519
Charges for services	302,446	—	—	1,079	40,372	343,897
Special assessments	—	2,658	—	1,530	—	4,188
Miscellaneous	281,714	73,270	—	22,374	60,713	438,071
Total Revenues	6,923,273	4,316,484	2,707,467	1,095,072	106,448	15,148,744
Expenditures:						
Current:						
Community Protection Program	5,048,950	369,780	—	—	10,062	5,428,792
Human Development Program	1,532,342	59,748	—	—	72,338	1,664,428
Home and Community Environment Program	1,245,616	2,053,088	—	—	—	3,298,704
Policy and Administration Program	882,488	2,127	—	—	—	884,615
Total Current Expenditures	8,709,396	2,484,743	—	—	82,400	11,276,539
Capital outlay	—	—	—	4,752,596	—	4,752,596
Debt Service:						
Principal	13,839	73,333	2,055,000	—	—	2,142,172
Interest and other fiscal charges	—	—	725,779	—	—	725,779
Other debt service costs	—	—	2,407	—	—	2,407
Total Debt Service	13,839	73,333	2,783,186	—	—	2,870,358
Total Expenditures	8,723,235	2,558,076	2,783,186	4,752,596	82,400	18,899,493
Excess (Deficiency) of Revenues Over (Under) Expenditures	(1,799,962)	1,758,408	(75,719)	(3,657,524)	24,048	(3,750,749)
Other Financing Sources (Uses):						
Sale of general fixed assets	2,687	—	—	—	—	2,687
Proceeds of general obligation bonds	—	—	—	8,736,155	—	8,736,155
Proceeds of general obligation capital loan notes	250,000	—	—	—	—	250,000
Operating transfers in	2,063,770	2,375	56,000	608,320	—	2,730,465
Operating transfers out	(189,057)	(2,300,935)	—	(435,394)	—	(2,925,386)
Total Other Financing Sources (Uses)	2,127,400	(2,298,560)	56,000	8,909,081	—	8,793,921
Excess (Deficiency) of Revenues and Other Financing Sources Over (Under) Expenditures and Other Financing Uses	327,438	(540,152)	(19,719)	5,251,557	24,048	5,043,172
Fund balances at beginning of year	427,894	4,596,844	215,723	1,715,535	98,910	7,054,906
Decrease in reserve for inventory	(1,407)	—	—	—	—	(1,407)
Fund balances at end of year	$ 753,925	$4,056,692	$ 196,004	$6,967,092	$122,958	$12,096,671

CITY OF MARSHALL
DEMOGRAPHIC STATISTICS
(UNAUDITED)

					School Enrollment		
Year	*Population*	*Median Age (Zip 50158)*	*Retail Sales*	*Number of Businesses*	*Public*	*Private*	*Unemployment Rate*
1992	26,938	N/A	$183,882,515	3,287	4,999	287	6.20
1993	26,938	28.8	199,298,854	3,327	5,007	300	4.10
1994	26,938	N/A	214,882,189	3,312	4,990	305	3.90
1995	25,178	36.7	225,091,244	3,314	4,869	307	3.70
1996	25,178	N/A	238,200,615	3,326	4,883	301	4.00
1997	25,178	N/A	242,596,231	3,362	4,891	304	4.50
1998	25,178	37.1	257,104,537	3,489	4,782	285	4.30
1999	25,178	37.2	288,619,825	3,519	4,872	304	3.30
2000	25,178	37.2	289,608,208	3,513	4,958	285	3.60
2001	25,178	37.8	298,889,577	3,480	4,995	285	3.80

Marshall County

Year	*Per Capita Income*	*Median Household Income*	*Median Age*	*Retail Sales*	*Number of Businesses*	*Unemployment Rate*
1992	$14,305	N/A	N/A	$204,248,849	4,764	6.10
1993	14,706	$25,263	33.3	218,790,354	4,779	4.10
1994	15,915	26,634	33.6	233,427,717	4,726	3.80
1995	17,280	27,114	36.7	244,137,122	4,668	3.70
1996	17,894	N/A	N/A	258,648,375	4,631	4.00
1997	18,814	N/A	N/A	262,118,716	4,608	4.30
1998	18,844	31,456	37.1	272,526,510	4,669	4.10
1999	20,748	33,091	37.2	304,752,174	4,683	3.20
2000	N/A	29,479	37.4	306,775,790	4,607	3.40
2001	N/A	35,810	37.9	315,917,997	4,531	3.60

CITY OF MARSHALL
RATIO OF GENERAL BONDED DEBT TO ASSESSED VALUES AND GENERAL BONDED DEBT PER CAPITA
LAST TEN FISCAL YEARS
(UNAUDITED)

Fiscal Year	General Obligation Bonded Debt	TIF Debt	Total Bonded/ TIF Debt	Assessed Value of Property*[1]
1992–93	$13,550,000	—	$13,550,000	$543,435,685
1993–94	13,615,000	—	13,615,000	545,498,178
1994–95	12,655,000	—	12,655,000	545,372,168
1995–96	11,710,000	—	11,710,000	551,921,255
1996–97	11,050,000	—	11,050,000	576,216,321
1997–98	9,805,000	—	9,805,000	585,744,670
1998–99	13,375,000	$ 515,000	13,890,000	614,238,646
1999–00	11,710,000	515,000	12,225,000	638,734,005
2000–01	9,955,000	515,000	10,470,000	729,253,341
2001–02	13,045,000	4,395,000	17,440,000	738,087,652

Fiscal Year	Population[2]	Ratio of Bonded/TIF Debt to Assessed Value	Bonded/TIF Debt per Capita
1992–93	26,938	2.49%	$503.01
1993–94	26,938	2.50	505.42
1994–95	26,938	2.32	469.78
1995–96	25,178	2.12	465.09
1996–97	25,178	1.92	438.88
1997–98	25,178	1.67	389.43
1998–99	25,178	2.26	551.67
1999–00	25,178	1.91	485.54
2000–01	25,178	1.44	415.84
2001–02	25,178	2.36	692.67

*Sources: Assessed value includes the addition of regular realty and tax increment financing (TIF).

[1]County Auditor's Office and City Assessor.

[2]United States Census Bureau.

CITY OF MARSHALL
COMPUTATION OF DIRECT AND OVERLAPPING DEBT
AS OF JUNE 30, 2002
(UNAUDITED)

Name of Governmental Unit	*Debt Outstanding*[1]	*Percentage Applicable to City of Marshall*[2]	*City of Marshall Share of Debt*
City of Marshall	$17,440,000	100.00%	$17,440,000
Green Valley Schools	12,705,000	54.90	6,975,045
Marshall Schools	195,000	0.08	156
Marshall Community School District	2,010,000	83.62	1,680,762
Marshall County	—	54.30	—
Total direct and overlapping debt	$32,350,000		$26,095,963

Sources:

[1]**Individual units.**

[2]**Marshall County Auditor's Office.**

CITY OF MARSHALL
RATIO OF ANNUAL DEBT SERVICE EXPENDITURES FOR GENERAL DEBT TO TOTAL GENERAL EXPENDITURES: GENERAL, SPECIAL REVENUE, AND DEBT SERVICE FUNDS
LAST TEN FISCAL YEARS
(UNAUDITED)

Fiscal Year	*Principal*	*Interest and Other Fiscal Charges*	*Total Debt Service**	*Total General Expenditures†*	*Ratio of Debt Service to Total Expenditures*
1992–93	$ 775,000	$1,038,661	$1,813,661	$ 9,500,890	19.09%
1993–94	811,250	990,201	1,801,451	9,506,113	18.95
1994–95	892,500	1,015,896	1,908,396	10,177,688	18.75
1995–96	1,006,396	1,012,734	2,019,130	11,661,441	17.31
1996–97	1,146,204	906,275	2,052,479	11,809,777	17.38
1997–98	2,775,819	898,607	3,674,426	12,994,768	28.28
1998–99	1,500,362	856,064	2,356,426	12,547,004	18.78
1999–00	1,759,609	799,144	2,558,753	12,499,729	20.47
2000–01	1,848,173	709,173	2,557,346	13,020,476	19.64
2001–02	2,142,172	728,186	2,870,358	14,046,846	20.43

***General obligation debt paid from property taxes.**

†Expenditures do not include transfers out.

(*continued* from page 487) be assessed to some extent by examining the relationship between financial inflows and outflows, the adequacy of fund balances, level of short-term debt (relative to cash, investments, and receivables), and management's comments in the introductory section of the CAFR. As discussed in the text, assessment of *financial condition* is more complicated, however. An assessment of financial condition requires estimates of the dynamic balance between the probable levels of service demand and the capacity of the city to continue to provide those services. To make such an assessment one must therefore consider critical social and economic factors that may impact on the demand for services or the capacity to provide services, or both. Additional guidance, largely gleaned from the discussion in this chapter, follows. (Note: Not all these items will apply in every case.)

Assessing Financial Condition:

1. Analysis of revenues and revenue sources.
   a. How stable and flexible are the city's revenue sources in the event of adverse economic conditions?
   b. Is the revenue base well diversified or is the city heavily reliant on one or two major sources?
   c. Has the city been relying on intergovernmental revenues for an excessive portion of its operating expenditures?
2. Analysis of reserves.
   a. Are the levels of financial reserves (i.e., fund balances and contingency funds) adequate to meet unforeseen operational requirements or catastrophic events?
   b. Is insurance protection adequate to cover losses due to lawsuits or damage to property?
   c. Is an adequate amount of cash and securities on hand, or could the city borrow quickly to cover short-term obligations?
3. Analysis of expenditures.
   a. Are there any components of expenditures that exhibit sharp growth?
   b. Is adequate budgetary control being exercised over expenditures?
   c. How does the growth pattern of operating expenditures over the past 10 years compare with that of revenues?
4. Analysis of debt burden.
   a. What has been the 10-year trend in general obligation long-term debt relative to population trend and trends in revenue capacity?
   b. Are there significant debts of other governmental units being supported by the same taxable properties (e.g., a school district, a county)? What has been the trend for this "overlapping" debt?
   c. Are there significant levels of short-term operating debt? If so, has it shown indications of growth?
   d. Are there any significant quasi-debts (e.g., lease obligations, unfunded pension liabilities, accrued employee benefits) or contingent liabilities?
   e. Are there any risky investments such as derivatives disclosed in the notes to the financial statements? Are the types of investments adequately explained and are their risks adequately disclosed?

5. Socioeconomic factors.

   What have been the trends in demographic and economic indicators such as real estate values, building permits, retail sales, population, income per capita, percent of population below the poverty level, average age, average educational level, employment and unemployment, and business licenses? (Note: Many of these items and other potentially useful information can be obtained from the *City and County Data Book* published by the U.S. Bureau of the Census. This book is available in the reference area of most university libraries. Selected data can be obtained from the Census Bureau's Internet site also at http://www.census.gov.)

6. Potential "red flags" or warning signs.
   - *a.* Decline in revenues.
   - *b.* Decline in property tax collection rate.
     - (1) Less than 92 percent of current levy collected?
     - (2) Property taxes greater than 90 percent of legal tax limit?
     - (3) Decreasing tax collections in two of the last three years?
   - c. Expenditures increasing more rapidly than revenues.
   - *d.* Declining balances of liquid resources and fund balances.
     - (1) General fund deficit in two or more of the last five years?
     - (2) General fund balance less than 5 percent of general fund revenues and operating transfers in?
   - *e.* Growing debt burden.
     - (1) Short-term debt greater than 5 percent of operating revenues?
     - (2) Two-year trend of increasing short-term debt?
     - (3) Short-term interest and current-year debt service on general obligation debt greater than 20 percent of operating revenue?
     - (4) Debt per capita ratio 50 percent higher than four years ago?
   - *f.* Growth of unfunded pension and other employee-related benefits such as compensated absences and postemployment health care benefits.
   - *g.* Deferral of needed maintenance on capital plant.
   - *h.* A decrease in the value of taxable properties, retail sales levels, or disposable personal income.
   - i. Decreasing revenue support from federal or state government.
   - j. Increasing unemployment.
   - k. Unusual climatic conditions or the occurrence of natural disasters.
   - l. Ineffective management and/or dysfunctional political circumstances.

As part of evaluating the foregoing factors, it is recommended that you compute as many of the ratios shown in Illustration 10–3 of the text as you can, consistent with data availability in your CAFR. For ratios 1 through 5 you may wish to use total governmental funds operating revenues and expenditures, as usually reported among the first tables in the statistical section of the CAFR. You may wish to show these computations in an appendix to your paper.

Required

Using the information in your CAFR and other sources as discussed above, prepare a report providing the results of your analysis. Your instructor will provide specific guidance, but it is recommended that the report be about eight (8) pages of text, double-spaced, typed with 12-point font size. The report should have an appendix providing a few graphs and/or tables to provide support for your analysis. In particular, graphs showing general revenues and expenditures in the same graph for the past 10 years, key debt ratios for the past 10 years, and selected demographic and socioeconomic trends are particularly helpful. You should carefully decide what data are most relevant to your study and include only those data in your graphs and/or tables. Using headings in the report corresponding to each major area in the preceding outline may help focus your report.

10–3. Internet Case. Use any of the several Internet search engines to locate the websites for Moody's Investors Service and Standard & Poor's (Spell precisely as shown. You may wish also to visit the website of a third rating service: Fitch Investors Service.) Locate and print their bond-rating categories. Do they provide any information on how they perform municipal (tax-backed) bond-rating evaluations? If so, summarize those procedures and compare them to the procedures described in this chapter.

Exercises and Problems

10–1. Examine the CAFR. Utilizing the CAFR obtained for Exercise 1–1, and used in Chapters 2 through 9, calculate insofar as possible the 13 financial ratios shown in Illustration 10–3. Evaluate the ratios in terms of the red flags and benchmarks provided in Illustration 10–3 and long-term trend data for each ratio, if available. In your opinion, is the governmental entity whose CAFR you have analyzed in sound financial condition? Explain your conclusions.

10–2. Multiple Choice. Choose the best answer.

1. Which of the following groups or parties generally has taken the *least* initiative to evaluate the financial condition of a city?
   a. Credit market analysts.
   b. Citizens.
   c. Internal managers.
   d. Legislative and oversight bodies.
2. Which of the following improvements was *not* influenced by the default of New York City in 1975?
   a. Improvements in financial reporting standards.
   b. Improvements in the quality of financial reporting in terms of reporting in conformity with GAAP.
   c. Improvements in the quality of municipal elections.
   d. Improvements in the quality of financial management.
3. Which of the following terms or concepts focuses primarily on assets and liabilities that require cash, or are normally converted to cash or require the use of cash in the near future, and can generally be determined from fund-based financial statements alone?

a. Interperiod equity.
b. Financial condition.
c. Solvency.
d. Financial position.

4. The concept of *financial condition* refers to a governmental unit's ability to:
   a. Maintain existing service levels.
   b. Withstand local and regional economic disruptions.
   c. Meet the demands of natural growth, decline, and change.
   d. All of the above.
5. Which of the following environmental factors primarily determines a city's demand for services and its capacity to provide those services?
   a. Intergovernmental constraints.
   b. Community needs and resources.
   c. Political culture.
   d. Management policies and legislative policies.
6. The group of factors that largely determines how fiscal policy is influenced by environmental factors is:
   a. Natural disasters and emergencies.
   b. Unfunded liabilities.
   c. External economic conditions.
   d. Management practices and legislative policies.
7. Which of the following would *not* be an effective means of *benchmarking*?
   a. Comparing key ratios of the city to those of special purpose governments in the area.
   b. Comparing current-period ratios to those of prior periods.
   c. Comparing current-period ratios to *early warning* or *red flag* levels.
   d. Comparing current-period ratios to published medians of the same ratios for similar size cities or cities in the same geographic region.
8. Which of the following conditions may signal impending fiscal stress?
   a. Increasing unemployment.
   b. Increasing property values.
   c. Increasing retail sales.
   d. All of the above.
9. Credit rating agencies such as Moody's and Standard & Poor's examine factors in which of the following four major groups in assessing creditworthiness for purposes of rating tax-supported bonds?
   a. Economic, scope of services, financial, and debt.
   b. Economic, financial, debt, and administrative/political.
   c. Economic, financial, administrative/political, and education.
   d. Economic, financial, debt, and education.

10. Which of the following statements is correct regarding the relationship between *financial condition* and *operating performance*?
    a. Sound financial condition ensures efficient and effective operating performance.
    b. Sound financial condition may be a necessary but not sufficient condition for achieving efficient and effective operating performance.
    c. Efficient and effective operating performance ensures sound financial condition.
    d. Both *a* and *c*.

10–3. Financial Condition. Write the numbers 1 through 10 on a sheet of paper. Beside each number write a "+" if a high or increasing value of the item is generally associated with *stronger* financial condition, a "−" if a high or increasing value of the item is generally associated with a *weaker* financial condition, and "NE" if the item generally has *no effect* on financial condition or the direction of the effect cannot be predicted.

1. Personal income per capita.
2. Inflation rate.
3. Percentage of households below the poverty level.
4. Bank deposits.
5. Property values.
6. Population growth.
7. Political party of the mayor.
8. Unfunded pension liability.
9. Level of overlapping debt.
10. Reserves for self-insurance.

10–4. Test of Financial Condition. The City of Calloway is a small city located in the Western Region, as defined by the U.S. Census Bureau. The City Finance Director desires to compare ratios for the City to the 10 benchmark ratios produced by Dr. Kenneth Brown, as discussed in this chapter. The results of her calculations are shown below:

Ratio No.	*City of Calloway*
1	$435.78
2	0.860
3	0.091
4	0.680
5	0.823
6	0.184
7	1.432
8	0.051
9	$35.82
10	0.102

Required

Prepare the 10-point test of financial condition discussed on page 479 and using the 50th percentile of the comparative ratios in Illustration 10–5. Prepare a brief analysis of how the City's financial condition compares with other cities in the Western Region.

Continuous Problem

10–B. After calculating the financial ratios presented in Illustration 10–3 and examining the financial statements and schedules prepared for 9–B, prepare a letter of transmittal to accompany the basic financial statements and the individual fund and account group statements. Your letter of transmittal should be addressed to the Honorable Mayor, City Council, and City Manager of the City of Bingham and should inform them of the accounting and budgeting policies employed by the City and explain in some detail which financial statements and schedules are enclosed. Your letter should also summarize the financial condition of the City and its funds, and, in general, note significant changes since the end of the prior year. (Trial balances and balance sheets as of June 30, 2001, given at the beginning of each "B" problem, as needed, give you information about the financial condition of funds at the end of the prior year.)

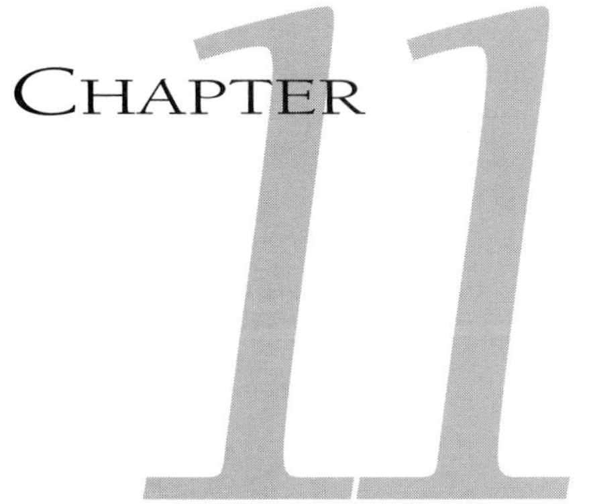

CHAPTER 11

Auditing of Governmental and Not-for-Profit Organizations

Learning Objectives

After studying this chapter, you should be able to:

- Explain the essential characteristics of financial audits by independent CPAs, including:
  - The objective(s) of financial audits.
  - The source and content of generally accepted auditing standards (GAAS).
  - The types of audit reports that can be rendered.
  - The contents of an unqualified and a qualified audit report.
- Explain what is meant by generally accepted government auditing standards (GAGAS), the source of GAGAS, and why GAGAS are much broader than GAAS.
  - Financial audits.
  - Performance audits
- Explain the characteristics of a single audit, including
  - The purpose.
  - Which entities must have a single audit.
  - What auditing work is required.
  - How major programs are selected for audit.
  - What reports must be rendered, when and to whom.
- Describe the role of audit committees.

Financial statements of governmental entities, colleges and universities, hospitals and other health care organizations, voluntary health and welfare organizations, and other not-for-profit organizations are the representations of the officials responsible for the financial management of the entity. In order for users of the financial statements to have the assurance that the statements are prepared in conformity with accounting and financial reporting standards established by authoritative bodies, and that all material facts are disclosed, the statements should be accompanied by the report of an independent auditor. Audits for this purpose are called *financial audits*, or attest audits. Other audits discussed in this chapter focus on determining whether managers of an organization are using resources entrusted to them efficiently and effectively in accomplishing organizational objectives, or whether program goals are being attained. These audits are called *performance audits*.

Financial Audits by Independent CPAs

The auditor's objective in performing a financial audit is to render a report expressing his or her opinion that the financial statements present fairly the financial position, results of operations, and, where appropriate, cash flows of the organization. "Present fairly" means in conformity with generally accepted accounting principles. Auditing standards prescribe standard wording of audit reports to ensure that report users clearly understand the responsibilities of management and those of the auditor, what was audited, the scope of audit, and the nature of the audit opinion.

Audits of State and Local Governments

In the case of state and local government units, audits may be performed by independent certified public accountants (CPAs) or by state or federal audit agencies. In performing audits, auditors are professionally and ethically obligated by Rule 202 of the American Institute of Certified Public Accountants' (AICPA) *Code of Professional Conduct* to follow **generally accepted auditing standards (GAAS)**—standards set by the AICPA and promulgated in *Statements on Auditing Standards*. GAAS have been summarized by the AICPA in the three general standards, three standards of field work, and four standards of reporting shown in Illustration 11–1. These 10 standards are amplified by numerous *Statements on Auditing Standards* published in codified form in the AICPA's *Professional Standards*. Failure to follow GAAS can result in severe sanctions, including, in some instances, loss of the auditor's license to practice as a CPA and expulsion from the AICPA. It is the auditor's duty to adhere to auditing standards, and it is his or her technical qualifications and independence from the entity being audited that add credibility to reported financial information and increase financial statement users' confidence in the information.

In addition to the obligation to follow GAAS, auditors may be engaged to perform an audit that requires they follow generally accepted government auditing standards (GAGAS). Audits conducted under GAGAS are discussed later in this chapter.

Illustration 11–1 Generally Accepted Auditing Standards—AICPA

General Standards

1. The audit is to be performed by a person or persons having adequate technical training and proficiency as an auditor.
2. In all matters relating to the assignment, an independence in mental attitude is to be maintained by the auditor or auditors.
3. Due professional care is to be exercised in the performance of the audit and the preparation of the report.

Standards of Field Work

1. The work is to be adequately planned and assistants, if any, are to be properly supervised.
2. A sufficient understanding of the internal control structure is to be obtained to plan the audit and to determine the nature, timing, and extent of tests to be performed.
3. Sufficient competent evidential matter is to be obtained through inspection, observation, inquiries, and confirmations to afford a reasonable basis for an opinion regarding the financial statements under audit.

Standards of Reporting

1. The report shall state whether the financial statements are presented in accordance with generally accepted accounting principles.
2. The report shall identify those circumstances in which such principles have not been consistently observed in the current period in relation to the preceding period.
3. Informative disclosures in the financial statements are to be regarded as reasonably adequate unless otherwise stated in the report.
4. The report shall either contain an expression of opinion regarding the financial statements, taken as a whole, or an assertion to the effect that an opinion cannot be expressed. When an overall opinion cannot be expressed, the reasons therefore should be stated. In all cases where an auditor's name is associated with financial statements, the report should contain a clear-cut indication of the character of the auditor's work, if any, and the degree of responsibility the auditor is taking.

Source: AICPA *Professional Standards,* 1999 AU 150.02.

Types of Audit Reports

Illustration 11–2 shows the standard audit report wording for an unqualified audit opinion on the general purpose financial statements (GPFS) of a state or local government for a government that reports under the reporting model being superseded by GASB *Statement No. 34*. See the appendix to Chapter 9 for a description of these financial statements. The first paragraph of the auditor's report is called the *opening* or *introductory paragraph*. In the first sentence of that paragraph, the auditor specifies the financial statements on which the opinion is being expressed. Since 1986, GASB standards (Codification Section 2200.134) have stated that the general purpose financial statements are the statements that must be presented for conformity with generally accepted accounting principles (GAAP). The comprehensive annual financial report (CAFR) should include combining and individual fund financial statements, as well as the general purpose financial statements; but in the auditor's report shown in Illustration 11–2, the auditor accepts responsibility only for the combined statements, not for the combining statements or for the individual fund and account group financial statements. This

Illustration 11–2 Unqualified Opinion on General-Purpose Financial Statements Submitted Together with Combining, Individual Fund, and Account Group Financial Statements and Supporting Schedules as Supplementary Data

Independent Auditor's Report

We have audited the accompanying general-purpose financial statements of the City of Example, Any State, as of and for the year ended June 30, 19X1, as listed in the table of contents. These general-purpose financial statements are the responsibility of the City of Example's management. Our responsibility is to express an opinion on these general-purpose financial statements based on our audit.

We conducted our audit in accordance with generally accepted auditing standards. Those standards require that we plan and perform the audit to obtain reasonable assurance about whether the financial statements are free of material misstatement. An audit includes examining, on a test basis, evidence supporting the amounts and disclosures in the financial statements. An audit also includes assessing the accounting principles used and significant estimates made by management, as well as evaluating the overall financial statement presentation. We believe that our audit provides a reasonable basis for our opinion.

In our opinion, the general-purpose financial statements referred to above present fairly, in all material respects, the financial position of City of Example, Any State, as of June 30, 19X1, and the results of its operations and the cash flows of its proprietary fund types and nonexpendable trust funds for the year then ended in conformity with generally accepted accounting principles.

The combining and individual fund and account group financial statements and schedules listed in the table of contents are presented for purposes of additional analysis and are not a required part of the general-purpose financial statements of City of Example, Any State. Such information has been subjected to the auditing procedures applied in the audit of the general-purpose financial statements and, in our opinion, is fairly stated, in all material respects, in relation to the general-purpose financial statements taken as a whole.

[Signature]

[Date]

Source: American Institute of Certified Public Accountants, Audit and Accounting Guide: *Audits of State and Local Governmental Units* (New York: AICPA, 1999), App. A, Example A.2.

is also clear from the first sentence of the fourth paragraph of the auditor's report. Inasmuch as combined statements are prepared from combining and individual fund and account group statements, the auditor would apply auditing procedures to financial data reported in combining and individual fund and account group statements from which the combined statements were derived. If the auditor is expressing an opinion on the GPFS, and they are issued separately from a CAFR, then the fourth paragraph is not required. If the government officials desire an audit report on combining statements, or individual fund statements, that fact should be made explicit in the written *engagement letter* before the start of the audit so the auditor can modify the scope of the examination appropriately. The opening paragraph also states that the financial statements are the responsibility of the entity's management.

The first sentence of the second or *scope paragraph* of the auditor's report (Illustration 11–2) states that the examination was made "in accordance with generally accepted auditing standards." That phrase has a definite meaning to professional auditors—a meaning they have been trying for many years to communicate to clients, bankers, judges, legislators, and every other group with a need to understand what an auditor's report means.

The scope paragraph also includes a statement that GAAS require that the auditor plan and perform the audit to obtain reasonable assurance as to whether the financial statements are free of material misstatements. In addition, the scope paragraph includes a statement that an audit includes: (1) examining, on a test basis, evidence supporting the amounts and disclosures in the financial statements, (2) assessing the accounting principles used and significant estimates made by management, and (3) evaluating the overall financial statement presentation. Finally, the scope paragraph includes a statement that the auditor believes that the audit provides a reasonable basis for the opinion rendered.[1]

The third paragraph of the auditor's report (Illustration 11–2) is referred to as the *opinion paragraph.* In that paragraph, the financial statements on which the auditor is expressing an opinion are identified as presenting fairly in conformity with generally accepted accounting principles the financial position of the reporting entity as of a certain date; the results of its operations for the fiscal year ended on that date; and, where applicable, cash flows during the fiscal year. The auditor states a professional opinion that the financial statements described in the report are fairly presented in conformity with GAAP.

The introductory, scope, and opinion paragraphs would be sufficient if the independent auditor's report accompanied separately issued GPFS. If the auditor's report is associated with the GPFS in the financial section of a CAFR, or is associated with the basic financial statements in the GASB *Statement No. 34* reporting model, a fourth paragraph known as the *explanatory paragraph* is added. The purpose of the explanatory paragraph is to explain that the combining and individual fund financial statements and schedules are not a required part of the GPFS or basic statements, but that such information has been subjected to auditing procedures applied in the audit of the GPFS, and, in the auditor's opinion, is fairly presented in all material respects in relation to the GPFS taken as a whole.[2]

If the auditor determines the financial statements contain a departure from GAAP, the effect of which is material, or there has been a material change between periods in accounting principles, or in the method of their application, the auditor may not express an unqualified opinion.

---

[1]American Institute of Certified Public Accountants, Inc., *Professional Standards* AU 508.08 (New York: AICPA, 1999).

[2]The authors will present in an Update Bulletin any changes the AICPA may make to the Independent Auditor's Report to conform with GASB *Statement No. 34*.

One example that precludes an unqualified opinion is a stand-alone consolidated report that some governments have issued on an experimental basis. If an audit opinion is to be rendered on such a report it must be an *adverse opinion* stating the report does not present fairly in conformity with GAAP.[3] It is also possible that the auditor cannot express an unqualified opinion because the scope of the examination was affected by conditions that precluded the application of one or more auditing procedures the auditor considered necessary in the circumstances. If it is not appropriate for the auditor to express an unqualified opinion, the auditor should consult relevant authoritative pronouncements to determine if a *qualified opinion* (see Illustration 11–3) should be issued, or if an opinion should be *disclaimed*. Expanded discussion of the nature of each of these types of opinions, and the conditions that would warrant the use of each, is beyond the scope of this text. Interested readers are referred to current collegiate auditing texts and to the pronouncements of the AICPA.[4]

Before any audit work is done, there should be a clear understanding of the scope of each engagement by all interested parties. A written memorandum of the engagement, or **engagement letter**, specifying the scope of the work to be done should be prepared in advance and copies retained by both the auditor and auditee. A written record of the agreement is essential for the protection of both parties. Independent public accountants have had the need for specific, written memorandums of the scope of engagements forcefully pointed out to them by a number of well-known liability cases.

Governmental units often engage more than one audit firm to conduct annual audits. Some component units such as airports, hospitals, and utilities may have their own governing boards and select their own auditor, yet meet the criteria discussed in Chapters 2 and 9 for inclusion in the governmental reporting entity. The principal auditor for the governmental unit (the auditor of the General Fund of the primary government) must in this case decide whether to make reference to the other auditor in his or her audit report or to assume responsibility for the work performed by the other auditor without reference in the audit report. If reference is made to the other auditor, the principal auditor's report should disclose the magnitude of the portion of the financial statements audited by the other auditor. An audit report making reference to another auditor is not a qualified report, unless some other reason exists for qualification.

Auditing procedures deemed particularly applicable to audits of state and local governments by independent CPAs are published in the AICPA Audit and

---

[3]Because consolidated reports are based on different accounting principles than are used for certain fund types of the GPFS, the auditor must render an adverse opinion. Auditors may, however, issue a restrictively worded report that certain summary information of the type published by some governments in "popular reports" is fairly presented in relation to the GPFS from which it has been derived. The auditor must have audited the GPFS and must refer to that audit in the "in relation to" report on the summary information. Source: American Institute of Certified Public Accountants, Audit and Accounting Guide, *Audits of State and Local Governmental Units* (New York: AICPA, 1999, pars. 18.23–18.32.

[4]A convenient source of information on currently effective pronouncements is a publication of the American Institute of Certified Public Accountants: AICPA *Professional Standards*.

Illustration 11–3 Qualified Opinion on General-Purpose Financial Statements That Omit One or More, but Not All, Component Units of the Financial Reporting Entity*

Independent Auditor's Report

We have audited the accompanying general-purpose financial statements of the City of Example, Any State, as of and for the year ended June 30, 19X1, as listed in the table of contents. These general-purpose financial statements are the responsibility of City of Example's management. Our responsibility is to express an opinion on these general-purpose financial statements based on our audit.

We conducted our audit in accordance with generally accepted auditing standards. Those standards require that we plan and perform the audit to obtain reasonable assurance about whether the financial statements are free of material misstatement. An audit includes examining, on a test basis, evidence supporting the amounts and disclosures in the financial statements. An audit also includes assessing the accounting principles used and significant estimates made by management, as well as evaluating the overall financial statement presentation. We believe that our audit provides a reasonable basis for our opinion.

The general-purpose financial statements referred to above do not include financial data of the (*identify the component unit [s] omitted*), which should be included in order to conform with generally accepted accounting principles. If the omitted component unit(s) had been included,† the assets and revenues of the [*identify fund types(s)*—for example, *special revenue fund type—or component unit column(s)]* would have been increased by $XXX,XXX and $XXX,XXX, respectively, there would have been an excess of expenditures over revenues in that fund type *[or component unit(s)]* of $XXX,XXX for the year, and the *[identify fund type(s) or discretely presented component unit column(s)]* fund balance would have been a deficit of $XXX,XXX.

In our opinion, except for the effects on the financial statements of the omission described in the preceding paragraph, the general-purpose financial statements referred to above present fairly, in all material respects, the financial position of City of Example, Any State, as of June 30, 19X1, and the results of its operations and the cash flows of its proprietary fund types and nonexpendable trust funds for the year then ended in conformity with generally accepted accounting principles.

[Signature]

[Date]

---

*There may be circumstances when, based on professional judgment, the auditor may determine that an adverse opinion on the general-purpose financial statements is appropriate. In such a case, a separate explanatory paragraph should state all the substantive reasons for the adverse opinion and the principal effects of those matters. If an adverse opinion is to be rendered, the last two paragraphs of this report should be replaced with the following paragraphs:

The general-purpose financial statements referred to above do not include financial data of the *[identify the component unit(s) omitted]*, which should be included in order to conform with generally accepted accounting principles.

Because of the departure from generally accepted accounting principles identified above, as of June 30, 19X1, the assets and revenues of the *[identify fund type(s)*—for example, *special revenue fund type—or component column(s)]* would have increased by $XXX,XXX and $XXX,XXX, respectively, there would have been an excess of expenditures over revenues in the fund type *[or component unit(s)]* for the year of $XXX,XXX and the *[identify fund type(s) or component unit(s)]* fund balance would have been a deficit of $XXX,XXX.

In our opinion, because of the effects of the matters discussed in the preceding paragraphs, the general-purpose financial statements referred to above do not present fairly, in conformity with generally accepted accounting principles, the financial position of City of Example, Any State, as of June 30, 19X1, or the results of its operations or the cash flows of its proprietary fund types or nonexpendable trust funds for the year then ended.

†If the amounts applicable to the omitted component unit have not been audited, insert the phrase *based on unaudited information.*

Source: American Institute of Certified Public Accountants, Audit and Accounting Guide, *Audits of State and Local Governmental Units* (New York: AICPA, 1999), Appendix A, Example A.5.

Accounting Guide, *Audits of State and Local Governmental Units*. The Audit Guide and other authoritative auditing literature provide guidance to all auditors, not just independent CPAs, whose function it is to examine financial statements, and the underlying records, for the purpose of determining whether the statements present fairly the financial position as of a certain date, and the results of operations and cash flows for a fiscal period, in conformity with generally accepted accounting principles.

The audit guide emphasizes the importance of testing for compliance with laws and regulations that may have a material effect on the determination of financial statement amounts. The guide notes that:

> The auditor is required to design the audit to provide reasonable assurance that the financial statements are free of material misstatement resulting from violations of laws and regulations, error, or fraud.[5]

Audits conducted under the government auditing standards issued by the U.S. General Accounting Office place even greater emphasis on testing and reporting on compliance with laws and regulations. These standards are discussed next.

Government Auditing Standards

Audit standards that are to be followed by auditors of federal organizations, programs, activities, functions, and federal funds received by contractors, state and local governmental organizations, and nonprofit organizations are much broader in scope than the audit standards discussed in the first section of this chapter. The General Accounting Office under the direction of the Comptroller General of the United States has developed government auditing standards. **Generally accepted government auditing standards (GAGAS)** are set forth and explained in the publication *Government Auditing Standards*—because of the color of its cover, the document is generally referred to as the yellow book. Generally accepted auditing standards (GAAS), shown in Illustration 11–1, were used as a basis for federal auditing standards. Reasons why the standards established by the AICPA were deemed to be too narrow in scope for audits of governmental entities are expressed in the Introduction of the yellow book:

> Our system of managing public programs today rests on an elaborate structure of relationships among all levels of government. Officials and employees who manage these programs must render an account of their activities to the public. While not always specified by law, this accountability concept is inherent in the governing processes of this Nation.
>
> The need for accountability has caused a demand for more information about government programs and services. Public officials, legislators, and citizens want and need to know whether *government funds are handled properly and in compliance with laws and*

[5]American Institute of Certified Public Accountants, Audit and Accounting Guide, *Audits of State and Local Governmental Units*, Revised (New York: AICPA, 1999), par. 5.09.

> *regulations*. They also want and need to know whether government *organizations, programs, and services are achieving their purposes and whether these organizations, programs, and services are operating economically and efficiently*. [Emphasis added.][6]

Types of Audits

As the italicized phrases in the preceding quote suggest, the scope of audits conducted under *Government Auditing Standards* is much broader than that of audits of business entities. In fact, the term *audit* in the yellow book refers to both financial and performance audits. **Financial audits** are intended to provide an auditor's opinion that financial statements present fairly, in all material respects, an entity's financial position, results of operations, and, where appropriate, cash flows, in conformity with GAAP, or that financial reports comply with other finance-related criteria. **Performance audits** are intended to provide an auditor's independent determination (but not an opinion) of the extent to which government officials are efficiently, economically, and effectively carrying out their responsibilities, or of whether governmental programs are producing the desired results. The yellow book provides that, in any given audit, auditors may perform a combination of financial statement, finance-related, and economy, efficiency, and program results audits. Accordingly, *Government Auditing Standards* place on those who authorize or plan governmental audits the responsibility to provide audit coverage that is sufficiently broad to fulfill the reasonable needs of potential users of audit reports.[7] Illustration 11–4 contrasts and compares the objectives and characteristics of financial and performance audits. Performance audits are often done by internal auditors or state audit agencies. An engagement letter between the auditor and the organization should clearly specify what type of audit is to be performed and which auditing standards will be followed.

Generally Accepted Government Auditing Standards

The first edition (1972) of the yellow book presented a single set of auditing standards that were similar to the AICPA statement of generally accepted auditing standards (GAAS) shown in Illustration 11–1. Subsequent revisions of the yellow book in 1981, 1994, and 1999, however, have developed a progressively broader set of standards, reflecting the need to provide standards for performance audits in addition to financial audits. The broader standards also reflect the unique auditing and operating environments of government and not-for-profit organizations. Government auditing standards now differ so much from GAAS that the term *generally accepted government auditing standards* (GAGAS) is typically used to distinguish the yellow book standards from GAAS.[8] GAGAS, as presented in the yellow book, consist of four general standards, plus nine field work standards for financial audits, five field work standards for performance audits, nine reporting standards for

---

[6]Comptroller General of the United States, *Government Auditing Standards, 1999 Revision* (Washington, DC: U.S. General Accounting Office, 1999), pars. 1.10–1.11.

[7]Ibid, par. 1.13(f).

[8]Another acronym often used to denote government auditing standards is GAS, which is the abbreviation for the publication *Government Auditing Standards*. These terms are used interchangeably; however, the term GAGAS is used in this text.

Illustration 11–4 Types of Government Audits

Financial Audits

1. Financial statement audits provide reasonable assurance about whether the financial statements of an audited entity present fairly the financial position, results of operations, and cash flows in conformity with generally accepted accounting principles, or in conformity with any of several other bases of accounting discussed in auditing standards issued by the AICPA.
2. Financial-related audits include determining whether (*a*) financial information is presented in accordance with established or stated criteria, (*b*) the entity has adhered to specific financial compliance requirements, or (*c*) the entity's internal control structure over financial reporting and/or safeguarding assets is suitably designed and implemented to achieve the control objectives.

Performance Audits

1. Economy and efficiency audits include determining (*a*) whether the entity is acquiring, protecting, and using its resources (such as personnel, property, and space) economically and efficiently; (*b*) the causes of inefficiencies or uneconomical practices; and (*c*) whether the entity has complied with laws and regulations on matters of economy and efficiency.
2. Program audits include determining (*a*) the extent to which the desired results or benefits established by the legislature or other authorizing body are being achieved; (*b*) the effectiveness of organizations, programs, activities, or functions; and (*c*) whether the entity has complied with significant laws and regulations applicable to the program.

Source: *Government Auditing Standards* (Washington, DC: U.S. General Accounting Office, 1999), pars. 2.4–2.7.

financial audits, and five reporting standards for performance audits. Thus, GAGAS consist of 32 standards, compared with 10 for GAAS.

The four general standards presented in *Government Auditing Standards* consist of, in paraphrased and expanded form, the three GAAS general standards shown in Illustration 11–1 and one additional general standard on quality control. In explaining the first general standard relating to adequacy of professional proficiency, the yellow book states:

> This standard places responsibility on the audit organization to ensure that each audit is conducted by staff who collectively have the knowledge and skills necessary for that audit. They should also have a thorough knowledge of government auditing and of the specific or unique environment in which the audited entity operates, relative to the nature of the audit being conducted.[9]

To ensure that auditors conducting audits under GAGAS maintain adequate technical proficiency, the yellow book requires that each auditor responsible for planning, directing, conducting, or reporting on audits under GAGAS complete at least 80 hours of continuing education (CE) and training every two years.[10] At least 20 hours of the 80 hours of CE must be completed in each year of the two-year period, and at least 24 of the 80 hours must be on subjects directly related to the

[9] *Government Auditing Standards*, par. 3.4.

[10] Ibid., par. 3.6.

government or not-for-profit environment and to government or not-for-profit auditing. To further ensure the quality of such audits, the fourth general standard requires each audit organization to have an "appropriate internal quality control system" and undergo an external quality control review at least once every three years by an audit organization not affiliated with the audit organization being reviewed.[11]

The nine field work standards for financial audits contained in GAGAS emphasize the importance of audit follow-up on prior audit findings; detection and reporting of irregularities, illegal acts, and other instances of noncompliance with laws and regulations; and understanding and testing of internal controls. Of the nine GAGAS field work standards, six are also required by GAAS, either by the three field work standards listed in Illustration 11–1 or by various *Statements on Auditing Standards*.

Similarly, the nine GAGAS reporting standards for financial audits incorporate the four GAAS reporting standards shown in Illustration 11–1. Additional reporting standards cover reporting on compliance, required communications, internal controls, report distribution, and irregularities and illegal acts.

The GAGAS field work and reporting standards for performance audits overlap to a small degree those of GAAS, but largely are unique in recognition that the objective of performance audits is to provide evidence to assess performance of a governmental organization, program, activity, or function, rather than to render a professional opinion. Thus, testing for compliance with laws and regulations, though of critical importance in a financial audit, may be relatively less so if the audit objective in a performance audit is to assess the efficiency and effectiveness of a program, and there are no laws and regulations that would have a material effect on the program.

Single Audit

Federal grants-in-aid to state and local governments grew from $2.2 billion in 1950 to $253.3 billion in 1998. Although grants-in-aid originate from more than 1,000 different programs administered by more than 50 federal departments and agencies, about 92% of the grants-in-aid in 1998 were made by five departments: the Department of Health and Human Services (54.4%), Department of Transportation (10.7%), Department of Housing and Urban Development (10.7%), Department of Agriculture (7.5%), and the Department of Education (8.5%).[12]

History of the Single Audit

Until the mid-1980s each federal agency established accounting, reporting, and auditing requirements for each program it administered, and these requirements differed from agency to agency. The requirements for programs administered by a

[11]Ibid., pars. 3.31–3.33.

[12]U.S. Census Bureau, U. S. Dept. of Commerce, "Federal Aid to States for Fiscal Year 1998," April 1999. See also http://www.census.gov/govs/www/cffr98.html.

given agency also often differed from program to program and from year to year. Furthermore, each agency had the right to make on-site audits of grant funds, and often did. Since even a relatively small local governmental unit might have during any given fiscal year several dozen active federal grants (each with different accounting, reporting, and auditing requirements), the amount of time spent keeping track of conflicting requirements, and providing facilities for a succession of different groups of auditors, became extremely burdensome. Efforts were made in the 1960s to standardize grant accounting, reporting, and auditing requirements, but with only modest success. In 1979, the Office of Management and Budget (OMB) issued Attachment P, *Audit Requirements*, OMB Circular A–102, *Uniform Administrative Requirements for Grants-in-Aid to State and Local Governments*. Attachment P was intended to ensure that audits were made on an organizationwide basis, rather than on a grant-by-grant basis. This concept is called the **single audit.**

Experience with Attachment P led to the enactment of the Single Audit Act of 1984. The purposes of the act were to:

(1) Improve the financial management of state and local governments with respect to federal financial assistance programs,
(2) Establish uniform requirements for audits of federal financial assistance provided to state and local governments,
(3) Promote the efficient and effective use of audit resources, and
(4) Ensure that federal departments and agencies, to the maximum extent practicable, rely upon and use audit work done pursuant to chapter 75 of title 31, United States Code (as added by this Act).

In 1985, OMB issued Circular A–128, *Audits of State and Local Governments*, to provide administrative guidance to federal program managers, state and local government recipients of federal financial assistance, and auditors in implementing and complying with the Single Audit Act. Each state and local government that received federal financial assistance equal to or in excess of $100,000 in any of its fiscal years was required to have an audit made for such fiscal year in accordance with the provisions of the Single Audit Act and OMB Circular A–128. The 1984 Act applied only to state and local governments, even though a large amount of federal assistance was also being provided to not-for-profit organizations, particularly institutions of higher education. In order to extend the benefits of the single audit to not-for-profit organizations, the OMB issued in 1990 Circular A–133, *Audits of Institutions of Higher Education and Other Nonprofit Institutions*, which administratively required single audits for institutions of higher education and other not-for-profit organizations.

Subsequent studies by the U.S. General Accounting Office found that the Single Audit Act of 1984 had improved accountability over federal assistance, strengthened the financial management of state and local governments and not-for-profit organizations, and reduced the overall audit burden. In evaluating benefits relative to costs, however, it was apparent that thousands of single audits were being imposed on small entities that in aggregate accounted for only a small percentage of total federal assistance.

Single Audit Act Amendments of 1996

Recognizing the need to further improve the Single Audit Act, Congress passed the Single Audit Act Amendments of 1996 (P.L. 104–156). The purposes of the amendments are essentially the same as the four purposes of the Single Audit Act of 1984, listed above, plus one additional purpose: to reduce [audit] burdens on state and local governments, Indian tribes, and not-for-profit organizations.

The 1996 Act:

1. Raises the threshold for a single audit from $100,000 to $300,000, thus exempting thousands of smaller entities from the single audit requirement.
2. Extends the statutory requirement for single audit coverage to not-for-profit organizations as well as state and local governments.
3. Establishes a risk-based approach for selecting programs for audit testing, ensuring greater audit coverage for high-risk programs.
4. Improves the contents and timeliness of single audit reporting.
5. Increases administrative flexibility by giving OMB the authority to revise certain audit requirements periodically without seeking further amendments to the Single Audit Act.

In June 1997, OMB issued a revised Circular A–133, *Audits of States, Local Governments, and Non-Profit Organizations*, which provides administrative guidance in implementing the Single Audit Act Amendments of 1996 (the 1996 amendments essentially replace the 1984 act). The revised Circular A–133 provides uniform guidance for administering and conducting *all* single audits and thus replaces Circular A–128, which previously covered only single audits of state and local governments. Moreover, Circular A–133 amends the previous A–133, which covered only not-for-profit organizations.[13]

Who Must Have a Single Audit?

Illustration 11–5 provides a flowchart to determine if an entity must have a single audit or other type of audit. As Illustration 11–5 shows, nonfederal entities that *expend* $300,000 or more in a year in federal awards must have a single audit or a **program-specific audit** for that year. The election of a program-specific audit applies when an auditee expends federal awards under only one program, or a cluster of related programs, and the program's (cluster's) laws, regulations, or grant agreements do not require an entitywide financial statement audit. A program-specific audit is usually performed on the financial statements of the particular program and examines matters related to the program such as internal controls and compliance with pertinent laws, regulations, and agreements. In many cases a program-specific audit guide will be available to provide detailed audit guidance for conducting the program-specific audit.

Illustration 11–5 shows that nonfederal entities that expend less than $300,000 of federal awards during the fiscal year generally are exempt from federal audit

[13]The OMB revises its *Compliance Supplement* regularly. Other guidance for the auditor comes from the AICPA, SOP 98–3, *Audits of States, Local Governments, and Not-for-Profit Organizations Receiving Federal Awards* (New York: AICPA, 1998).

Illustration 11–5 Determining Applicability of the Single Audit

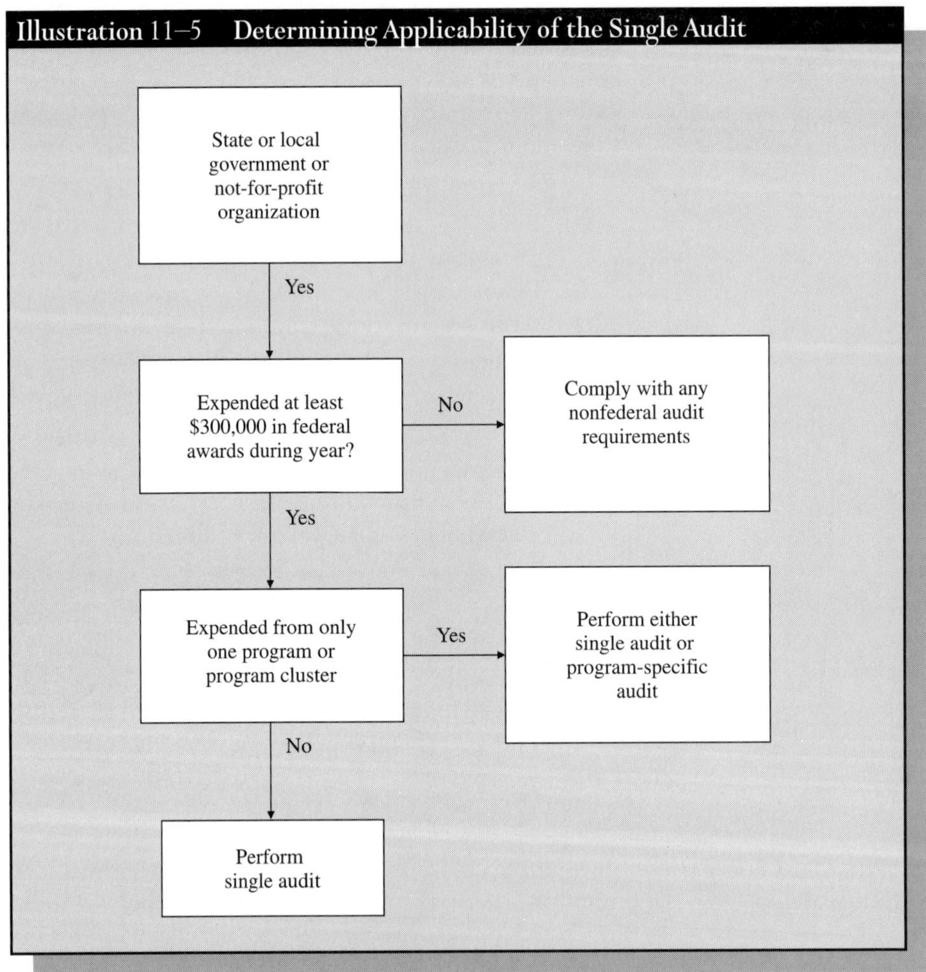

requirements for that year. Nonetheless, any federal awarding agency may conduct or arrange for additional audits it deems necessary. Such additional audits should be rare, should build upon work performed for other audits, and should be paid for by the federal agency conducting or requesting the audit. Some states have voluntarily adopted federal GAGAS and single audit requirements that may apply under state audit mandates, even if federal awards expended are less than $300,000 and no other federal audit requirement exists. In other states that do not mandate their own requirements for GAGAS audits or single audits, annual audits of local governments and not-for-profit organizations, when required, will be performed in conformity with AICPA GAAS, discussed earlier in this chapter.

The foregoing discussion raises two terminology questions. First, what kinds of entities are included in the term *nonfederal entities?* Circular A–133 defines a nonfederal entity as a state or local government, or nonprofit organization. Second, what is meant by the term *federal awards?* A–133 defines federal awards as:

> Federal financial assistance [defined by OMB as grants, loans, loan guarantees, property, cooperative agreements, interest subsidies, insurance, food commodities, direct appropriations, and other assistance] and federal cost-reimbursement contracts that nonfederal entities receive directly from federal awarding agencies or indirectly from pass-through entities. It does not include procurement contracts, under grants or contracts, used to buy goods or services from vendors. Any audits of such vendors shall be covered by the terms and conditions of the contract. Contracts to operate federal government owned, contractor operated facilities are excluded from the requirements of this part, as are payments for Medicare services provided.[14]

An important change made by the 1996 amendments is that the required audit threshold is now based on federal awards *expended* rather than *received*, as was previously the case. Unfortunately, calculating federal awards expended is not as straightforward as it might seem. The basic rule is that a federal award has been expended at the point in time when the awarding agency has become at risk and the nonfederal recipient has become accountable for how the award is being used. Risk exposure and a duty of accountability normally arise when activity occurs that requires the nonfederal entity to begin complying with laws, regulations, or contractual provisions relating to the award. Typical examples are expenditure/expense transactions (such as incurring labor costs, purchasing or using supplies, and paying utility bills) associated with grants, cost-reimbursement contracts, cooperative agreements, and direct appropriations; disbursement of funds by a pass-through entity to a subrecipient; the receipt of property; the receipt or use of program income (such as charges to program beneficiaries for services rendered and rental from program facilities); and the distribution or consumption of food commodities. Amounts expended would normally be determined using the entity's basis of accounting. Thus, either an expenditure or expense may enter into the calculation of federal awards expended. Federal noncash assistance received such as free rent (if received by a nonfederal entity to carry out a federal program), food stamps, commodities, and donated property should be valued at fair value at the time of receipt or the assessed value provided by the awarding federal agency.

If federal awards involve loan, loan guarantee, and insurance programs, the federal award expended is the amount to which the federal government is at risk for the loans. Generally this will be the amount of loans made (or received) during the year, plus any loan balances from previous years for which the federal government imposes continuing compliance requirements, plus any interest subsidy, cash, or administrative cost allowance received.[15] To the extent new and previously issued loans may have been repaid during the year, adjustments would need to be made. This is because the federal awards expended under a loan or insurance program are

---

[14]Office of Management and Budget, OMB Circular No. A–133, *Audits of States, Local Governments, and Non-Profit Organizations* (Washington, DC. OMB, 1997), par. ___ .105.

[15]Ibid., par ___ .205(b).

Illustration 11–6 Determining Federal Awards Expended for a Hypothetical Direct Loan Program

Loan Activity	*Amounts*	*Highest Balance*
Balance, beginning of year	$200,000	
New loans during year	150,000	
		$320,000*
Loans repaid during year	(100,000)	
Balance, end of year	$250,000	

*$320,000 is assumed to have been the highest loan balance outstanding at any point during the year. Because the federal government was at risk at one point during the year for $320,000, that is the amount of federal awards deemed to have been expended.

the highest amount of risk exposure of the federal government during the year. Thus, if the total loan balance varies during the year, the highest loan balance outstanding at any point during the year is the amount of federal awards expended.

Illustration 11–6 provides an example of how federal awards expended would be calculated for a hypothetical direct loan program administered by a local government or not-for-profit organization. Although neither the beginning nor ending loan balances exceed the $300,000 single audit threshold, it is assumed that at one point during the year the loan balance reached $320,000. Because at that point in time the federal government was at risk for $320,000, and the nonfederal entity had compliance duties for the $320,000 in loans outstanding, federal awards are deemed to have been expended in the same amount. If this was the only federal program for which awards were received during the year, the entity would have the option of having a single audit or a program-specific audit.

What Does the Single Audit Require?

The 1996 Amendments to the Single Audit Act of 1984 mandate the following audit requirements for the single audit:

1. An annual audit must be performed encompassing the nonfederal entity's financial statements and schedule of expenditures of federal awards. (Note: A biennial audit is permissible under certain restrictive conditions provided for in the 1996 amendments.)
2. The audit must be conducted by an independent auditor in accordance with generally accepted government auditing standards (GAGAS) and cover the operations of the entire nonfederal entity. Alternatively, a series of audits that cover departments, agencies, and other organizational units is permitted if the series of audits encompasses the financial statements and schedule of expenditures of federal awards for each such department, agency, or other organizational unit, which in aggregate are considered to

be a nonfederal entity. *Independent auditor* means an external federal, state, or local auditor who meets the GAGAS independence standards or an independent public accountant.

3. The auditor must determine whether the financial statements are presented fairly in all material respects with GAAP and whether the schedule of federal financial awards is presented fairly in relation to the financial statements taken as a whole.
4. For each major program, the auditor must obtain an understanding of the internal controls pertaining to the compliance requirements for the program, assess control risk and perform tests of controls, unless the controls are deemed to be ineffective. (Note: OMB Circular A–133 requires the auditor to obtain an understanding of and conduct testing of internal controls to support a low assessed level of control risk; that is, as if high reliance will be placed on the internal controls). In addition, for each major program the auditor shall determine whether the nonfederal entity has complied with laws, regulations, and contract or grant provisions pertaining to federal awards of the program. In auditing compliance auditors test compliance with the requirements listed for each program in the A–133 *Compliance Supplement* published by the OMB. The *Compliance Supplement* details compliance auditing requirements for many federal programs, listed by *Catalog of Federal Domestic Assistance* (CFDA) title and number.
5. The audit assigns certain responsibilities to federal awarding agencies and nonfederal entities that act as "pass-through" agents in passing federal awards to subrecipient nonfederal entities.

Compliance Audits. As noted in item (4) above, Circular A–-133 requires the auditor to express an opinion that the auditee complied with laws, regulations, and grant or contract provisions that could have a direct and material effect on each major program. To gather sufficient evidence to support his or her opinion in such **compliance audits,** the auditor tests whether each major program was administered in conformity with administrative requirements contained in OMB Circular A–102, *Uniform Administrative Requirements for Grants and Cooperative Agreements to State and Local Governments*, or OMB Circular A–110, *Uniform Administrative Requirements for Grants and Cooperative Agreements with Institutions of Higher Education, Hospitals, and Other Nonprofit Organizations*, as appropriate. The auditor also tests for compliance with the detailed compliance requirements for major programs provided in the A–133 *Compliance Supplement* or other guidance provided by federal awarding agencies. Many compliance requirements are generic and thus apply to compliance audits of most federal programs. The *Compliance Supplement* identifies 14 generic compliance requirements, although not all the requirements apply to every major program. Moreover, there are additional compliance requirements specified for some programs. Detailed discussion of the 14 compliance requirements is beyond the scope of this text. In general, however, they relate to such matters as allowed and unallowed activities; allowed and unallowed costs; eligibility of program beneficiaries; responsibilities of the nonfederal entity regarding matching, level of effort, and earmarking; management of equipment and real property acquired from federal awards; and required reporting.

Auditee Responsibilities. OMB Circular A–133 also details the responsibilities of auditees (nonfederal entities). Auditees are responsible to identify in the accounts all federal awards received and expended, and the federal programs under which they were received. Identification of the federal program includes the CFDA title and number, award number and year, and name of the federal agency. In addition, auditees are responsible for maintaining appropriate internal controls and systems to ensure compliance with all laws, regulations, and contract or grant provisions applicable to federal awards. Finally, auditees must prepare appropriate financial statements and the schedule of expenditures of federal awards, ensure that audits are properly performed and submitted when due, and follow up and take appropriate corrective action on audit findings. The latter requirement includes preparation of a summary schedule of prior audit findings and a corrective action plan for current year audit findings.

How Are Programs Selected for Audit?

Illustration 11–7 shows the procedures and criteria for selecting major programs for audit. A **major program** is a federal award program selected for audit using the procedures described below and shown in Illustration 11–7, or by request of a federal awarding agency. Use of a **risk-based approach** for selecting major programs for audit ensures that audit effort is concentrated on the highest risk programs. The risk-based approach is applied as follows:

1. Identify the "larger" federal programs and analyze them according to the Type A criteria. Programs not meeting Type A criteria are identified as Type B programs. Type A programs are determined using the following sliding scale:

Federal Awards Expended	*Threshold for Type A Program*
$300,000 to $100 million	Larger of $300,000 or 3% (.03) of total federal awards expended
More than $100 million to $10 billion	Larger of $3 million or .3% (.003) of total federal awards expended
More than $10 billion	Larger of $30 million or .15% (.0015) of total federal awards expended

2. Identify low-risk Type A programs: programs previously audited in at least one of the two most recent audit periods as a major program, with no audit findings in the most recent audit period; programs with no significant changes in personnel or systems that would have significantly increased risk; and programs that, in the auditor's professional judgment, are low

Illustration 11–7 Risk-Based Approach for Selecting Major Programs for Audit

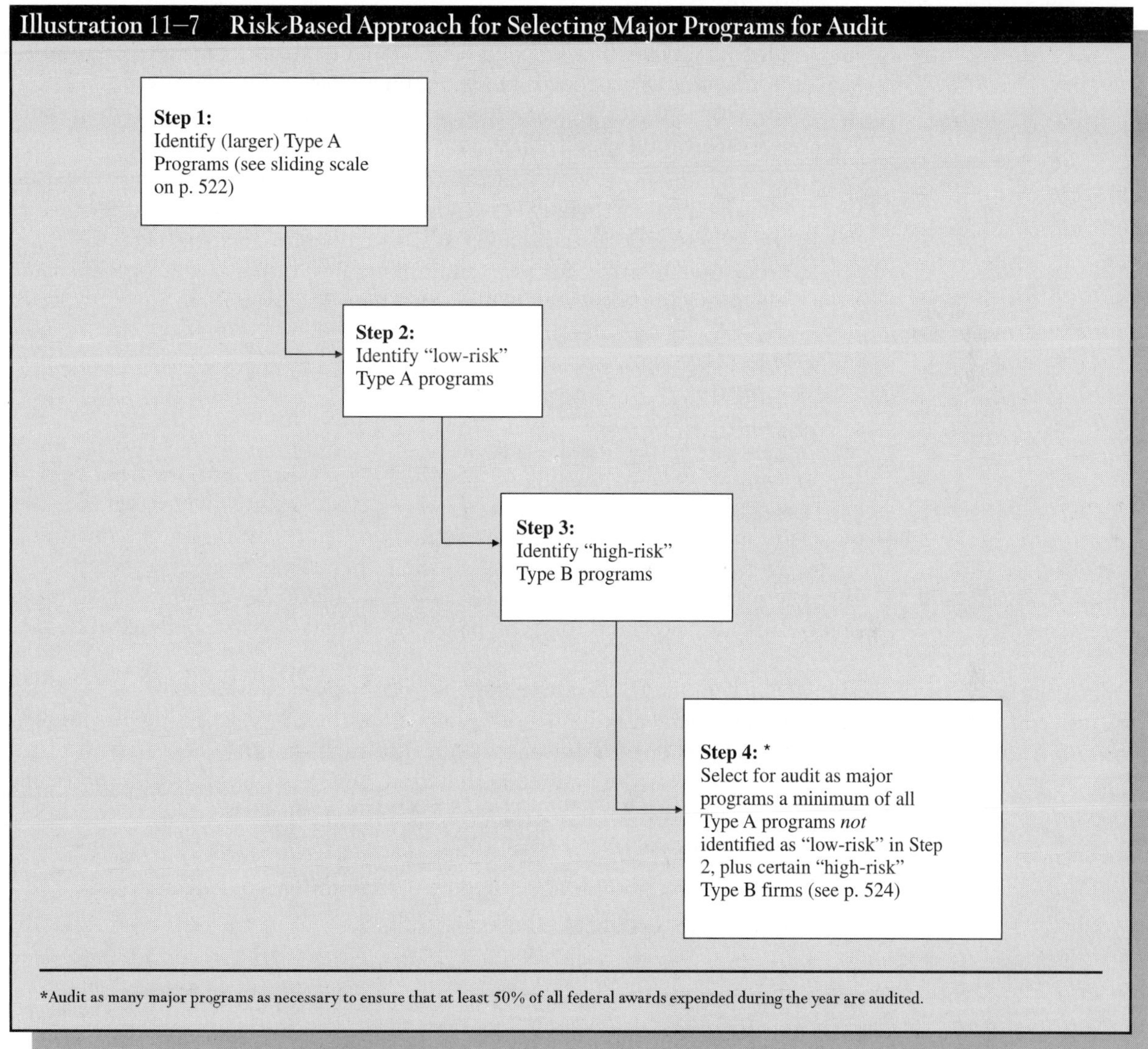

Step 1:
Identify (larger) Type A Programs (see sliding scale on p. 522)
Step 2:
Identify "low-risk" Type A programs
Step 3:
Identify "high-risk" Type B programs
Step 4: *
Select for audit as major programs a minimum of all Type A programs *not* identified as "low-risk" in Step 2, plus certain "high-risk" Type B firms (see p. 524)

*Audit as many major programs as necessary to ensure that at least 50% of all federal awards expended during the year are audited.

risk, after considering such factors as the inherent risk of the program, the level of oversight exercised by federal awarding agencies and pass-through agencies, and the phase of a program in its life cycle. New programs, for example, tend to be more risky than more mature programs.

3. Identify Type B programs that, based on the auditor's professional judgment and criteria discussed above, are high risk. The auditor is not expected to perform risk assessments on relatively small federal programs.

Risk assessments are performed only for those Type B programs that are (*a*) \$100,000 or .3% (.003) of total federal awards expended when total federal awards expended are less than or equal to \$100 million or (*b*) \$300,000 or .03% (.0003) of total federal awards expended when total federal awards expended are more than \$100 million.

4. At a minimum, audit as major programs all Type A programs *not* identified as low risk and certain high-risk Type B programs, using one of the following options: (*a*) audit at least half of the high-risk Type B programs; but not required to audit more Type B than Type A programs identified as low risk; or (*b*) audit one high-risk Type B program for each Type A program identified as low risk.
5. *Percentage of coverage rule:* As many major programs as necessary must be audited to ensure that at least 50% of total federal awards expended are audited.

In addition to the possibility of reduced audit coverage resulting from individual Type A programs being classified as low risk, A–133 also provides that the auditee itself can be classified as low risk and thereby receive even greater reduction in audit coverage.[16] An auditee that meets the rather stringent criteria prescribed in Circular A–133 to be a low-risk auditee needs only to have audited a sufficient number of major programs to encompass 25% of total federal awards expended.

What Reports Are Required for the Single Audit?

The 1996 amendments require that all auditors' reports for the single audit be submitted to the federal clearinghouse designated by the OMB within the earlier of 30 days after receipt of the auditor's report(s) or nine months after the end of the audit period.[17] Both the auditee and auditor have responsibilities for particular reports that comprise the reporting package.

The reporting package consists of:

1. Financial statements and schedule of expenditures of federal awards.
2. Summary schedule of prior audit findings.
3. Auditors' reports.
4. Corrective action plan.

The auditee is responsible for preparing all the documents described in items (1), (2), and (4) above. The auditor is responsible for preparing the various auditors' reports in item (3) and for following up on prior year audit findings, including testing the accuracy and reasonableness of the summary schedule of prior audit findings. In addition, both the auditee and auditor have responsibilities for completing and

[16]An auditee is considered "low risk" if unqualified opinions have been received on annual single audits with no deficiencies in internal control and no audit findings.

[17]A three-page data collection form (SF-SAC) is sent to the Federal Audit Clearinghouse, Bureau of the Census, Department of Commerce, currently in Jeffersonville, Indiana, along with the single audit reporting package. Electronic submission of Form SF-SAC began in 1999. A copy is reproduced in the Instructor's Guide that accompanies this text.

submitting the comprehensive data collection form that accompanies the reporting package to the clearinghouse. A complete description of the numerous data elements that must be provided on the data collection form is beyond the scope of this text. In general, however, the form provides for extensive descriptive data about the auditee, the auditor, identification of types and amounts of federal awards and major programs, types of reports issued by the auditor, and whether the auditor identified internal control deficiencies or significant noncompliance with laws, regulations, and grant provisions. Both a senior-level representative of the auditee and auditor must sign the data collection form, certifying its accuracy and completeness.

Auditor's Reports. OMB Circular A–133 specifies several reports that the auditor must submit for each single audit engagement. These reports can be in the form of separate reports for each requirement or a few combined reports. The auditor's report on the financial statements should indicate that the audit was conducted in accordance with GAAS and GAGAS. Other auditor's reports required by the single audit should indicate the audits were conducted in accordance with GAAS, GAGAS, and provisions of Circular A–133. The required single audit reports, whether made as separate reports or combined, must include:

1. An opinion (or disclaimer of opinion) as to whether the financial statements are presented fairly in conformity with GAAP and whether the schedule of expenditures of federal awards is presented fairly in relation to the financial statements taken as a whole.
2. A report on internal controls related to the financial statements and major programs.
3. A report on compliance with laws, regulations, and provisions of grant or contract agreements that could have a material effect on the financial statements. The report must also include an opinion on compliance matters related to major programs audited that could have a direct and material effect on each major program. Where applicable, include findings of noncompliance in the separate schedule of findings and questioned costs, described in item (4) below.
4. A schedule of findings and questioned costs, containing the following:
   (*a*) A summary of the auditor's results, including such information as type of opinion rendered on the financial statements, reportable conditions relating to internal control weaknesses, material noncompliance affecting the financial statements, major programs audited, type of opinion on compliance for major programs and reportable conditions in internal control affecting major programs, and a statement as to whether the auditee qualified as low risk.
   (*b*) Findings related to the audit of the financial statements required to be reported by the yellow book (GAGAS). These relate primarily to the auditor's responsibility to ensure adequate communication of material irregularities and illegal acts.
   (*c*) Audit findings and questioned costs. Audit findings are discussed next.

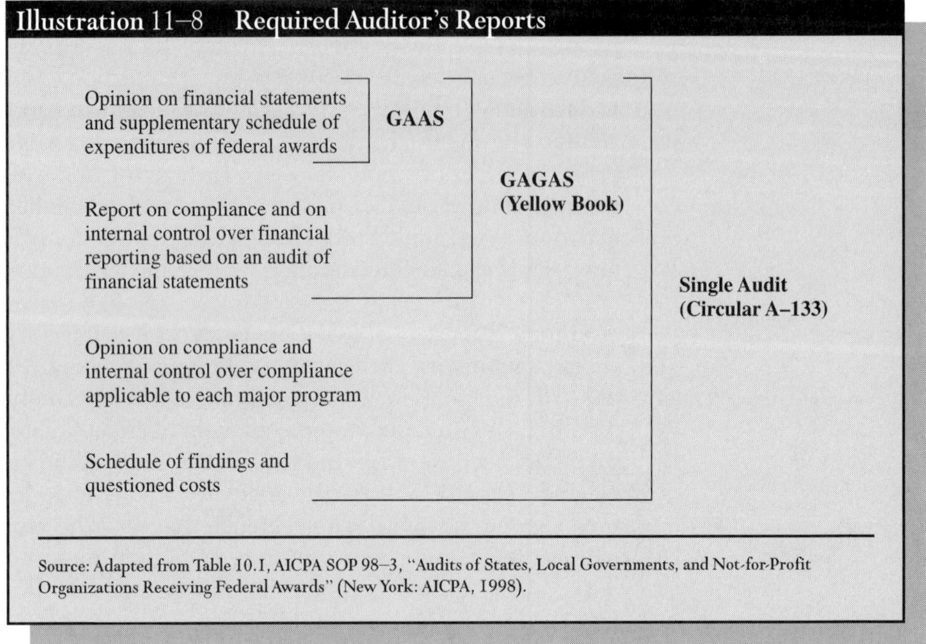
Illustration 11–8 Required Auditor's Reports

Source: Adapted from Table 10.1, AICPA SOP 98–3, "Audits of States, Local Governments, and Not-for-Profit Organizations Receiving Federal Awards" (New York: AICPA, 1998).

Illustration 11–8 shows the relationship of the required auditor's reports under GAAS, GAGAS, and the Single Audit (OMB Circular A–133).

Reporting Audit Findings. As listed in item (4) above auditors must prepare a schedule of findings and questioned costs. **Audit findings** reported in the schedule provide detail on such matters as internal control weaknesses, instances of noncompliance, questioned costs, fraud, and material misrepresentations (by the auditee) in the schedule of prior audit findings.

Regarding reporting on internal controls, item (4a) above uses the term **reportable condition.** This term is used in AICPA authoritative audit publications and adopted in the yellow book and Circular A–133. In the context of GAGAS audits, a reportable condition is a significant deficiency in the design or operation of the internal control structure that could adversely affect the entity's ability to administer a federal award program in accordance with laws and regulations. A **material weakness** is a reportable condition of such magnitude that the internal control structure elements do not reduce the risk of material noncompliance to an acceptably low level.

A **questioned cost** arises from an audit finding, generally relating to noncompliance with a law, regulation, or agreement, where the costs are either not supported by adequate documentation or appear unreasonable. Cost principles to be followed by nonfederal entities in the administration of federal awards are prescribed by (1) OMB Circular A–21, *Cost Principles for Educational Institutions*,

(2) OMB Circular A–87, *Cost Principles for State, Local, and Indian Tribal Governments*, and (3) OMB Circular A–122, *Cost Principles for Non-Profit Organizations*. The circulars define concepts such as direct and indirect costs, allowable and unallowable costs, and methods for calculating indirect cost rates.

The cost principles in these circulars are similar, but differ to meet the unique environment of each type of organization. Recovery of indirect costs (such as depreciation, general administrative costs, library costs, and interest expense) is based on rates approved by the federal government in cost allocation plans (state, local, and Indian tribal governments only) or indirect cost rate proposals (all other nonfederal agencies). Unallowable costs are generally consistent across the three circulars. Bad debt expenses and political/lobbying costs are generally unallowable. Some costs, such as advertising and public relations costs, are allowable, subject to certain restrictions. The auditing of program costs is inherently complex and professional judgment is often required to determine the appropriate classification of costs. This is particularly true in auditing institutions of higher education. Individuals who audit federal awards must be familiar with the applicable cost circular and ascertain that the methods of charging costs to cost pools and federal programs conform to approved cost allocation plans or indirect cost rate proposals.

Circular A–133 requires that *known questioned costs* greater than $10,000, identified in auditing a major program, be reported in the schedule of findings and questioned costs. A known questioned cost is one that the auditor has specifically identified in performing audit procedures. In evaluating the impact of a known questioned cost, the dollar impact also includes a best estimate of "likely questioned costs." Thus the auditor must also report known questioned costs if the likely questioned costs exceed $10,000, even if the known dollar amount is zero. Nonmajor programs are not normally audited for compliance (except for audit follow-up of a program that was previously audited as a major program); however, if the auditor becomes aware of a known questioned cost in a nonmajor program, he or she must also report it in the schedule of findings and questioned costs.

Other Single Audit Requirements

Audit Working Papers. The 1999 revision to the yellow book (GAGAS) requires that auditors make their audit working papers available to other auditors and to oversight officials from federal awarding agencies and cognizant agents for quality review purposes. The 1996 amendments to the Single Audit Act are even more explicit in requiring independent auditors to provide access to federal oversight officials. Federal agency access also includes the right to obtain copies of the working papers. Circular A–133 reemphasizes this requirement and the GAGAS requirement that auditors retain all working papers and reports for a minimum of three years.

Cognizant Agents. OMB Circular A–133 provides that a **cognizant agency for audit responsibilities** will be designated for each nonfederal entity expending more than $25 million a year in federal awards. The cognizant agency will be the federal awarding agency that provides the predominant amount of direct funding unless the OMB specifically designates a different cognizant agency. Among the cognizant agency's responsibilities are providing technical audit advice and liaison to auditees and auditors, obtaining or conducting quality control reviews of selected audits made by nonfederal auditors, communicating to affected parties deficiencies identified by quality control reviews (including, when necessary, referral of deficiencies to state licensing agencies and professional bodies for possible disciplinary action), and promptly communicating findings of irregularities and illegal acts to affected federal agencies and appropriate federal law enforcement agencies. Nonfederal entities expending less than $25 million in federal awards are assigned an **oversight agency.** The oversight agency is the agency that makes the predominant amount of direct funding to the nonfederal entity. An oversight agency has responsibilities similar to a designated cognizant agency, but less extensive.

Audit Committees

An **audit committee** is typically a committee of the governing board whose function it is to help select the auditor, monitor the audit process, review results of the audit, assist the governing board in understanding the results of the audit, and participate with both management and the independent auditor in resolving internal control or other deficiencies identified during the audit. Audit committees usually consist of selected members of the governing board (e.g., the city council or school board) and sometimes outside members in order to increase the independence of the committee.

Audit committees, when properly organized and utilized, can provide substantial benefit to all concerned parties. The audit committee can strengthen the stewardship reporting function of the governing board; it can also improve communications between the independent auditor and management and enhance the auditor's independence by serving as an objective buffer between the auditor and management. For taxpayers and creditors, audit committees help ensure maximum value and benefit from the audit.

Although most major corporations now consider an audit committee to be an important aspect of corporate governance, governmental units have been slow to establish audit committees. Perhaps, as the benefits of having an audit committee become apparent, we can anticipate greater use of these committees in the future.

Key Terms

Audit committee, 528
Audit findings, 526
Cognizant agency for audit responsibilities, 527
Compliance audit, 521
Engagement letter, 510
Financial audits, 513
Generally accepted auditing standards (GAAS), 506
Generally accepted government auditing standards (GAGAS), 512
Major programs, 522

Material weakness, 526
Oversight agency, 528
Performance audits, 513
Program-specific audit, 517
Questioned cost, 527
Reportable condition, 526
Risk-based approach, 522
Single audit, 516

Selected References

American Institute of Certified Public Accountants. Audit and Accounting Guide. *Audits of State and Local Governmental Units*. Revised. New York: AICPA, 1999.

______ . *Statement of Position* 98–3, "Audits of States, Local Governments, and Not-for-Profit Organizations Receiving Federal Awards." New York: AICPA, 1998.

______ . *Statement on Auditing Standards, No. 1*, et seq. New York, 1973 to date.

Comptroller General of the United States. *Government Auditing Standards*. Washington, DC: Superintendent of Documents, U.S. Government Printing Office, 1999 revision.

Office of Management and Budget. *Circular A–133*, "Audits of Institutions of Higher Education and Other Nonprofit Organizations." Washington, DC: Superintendent of Documents, U.S. Government Printing Office, 1997.

______ . *Compliance Supplement for Single Audits of State and Local Governments*. Washington, DC. Superintendent of Documents, U.S. Government Printing Office, 2000.

[Note: AICPA documents must be ordered from the AICPA; all others can be downloaded at no charge by following website links at http://www.financenet.gov.]

Questions

11–1. What assurance does the independent auditor provide users of financial statements of governmental and not-for-profit entities?

11–2. What information is contained in the *opening paragraph* of an auditor's report prepared in conformity with the AICPA's standard wording?

11–3. What is the meaning of the term *scope paragraph* (of an auditor's report prepared in conformity with the AICPA's standard wording)? The term *opinion paragraph?*

11–4. The standard report used by certified public accountants sets forth that the financial statements are presented in conformity with "generally accepted accounting principles." How may an auditor determine the meaning of this phrase in the case of a state or local government?

11–5. What is the meaning of the term *unqualified opinion* as used in auditing literature?

11–6. Define GAGAS. How do GAGAS differ from GAAS?

11–7. What are the two major types of audits described in the General Accounting Office's *Government Auditing Standards* (the yellow book), and how do they differ?

11–8. GAGAS consists of 32 standards compared to only 10 for GAAS. Why is this the case?

11–9. Describe briefly the single audit concept set forth in the Single Audit Act of 1984, the 1996 amendments, and OMB Circular A–133.

11–10. Explain the key provisions of the 1996 amendments to the Single Audit Act of 1984.

11–11. Which nonfederal entities are required to have a single audit? Explain.

11–12. What audit work is required for a single audit?

11–13. Explain how federal award programs are selected for audit under the risk-based approach.

11–14. Discuss some of the *auditee's* responsibilities under the Single Audit Act.

11–15. Distinguish between the terms *reportable condition* and *material weakness* in reporting internal control findings.

11–16. Define the term *questioned cost*. What criteria does an auditor use to determine whether a questioned cost must be reported?

11–17. What documents comprise the single audit reporting package that must be sent to the federal clearinghouse?

11–18. Describe the audit reports the auditor must submit upon completion of a single audit.

11–19. Which nonfederal entities are assigned a cognizant agency for audit responsibilities? What are the cognizant agency's responsibilities?

11–20. What are the benefits of having an audit committee?

Cases

11–1. Single Audit. Background. Mountain Lake Mental Health Affiliates, a nongovernmental not-for-profit organization, has contacted Bill Wise, CPA, about conducting an annual audit for their first year of operations. The governing board wishes to obtain an audit of the financial statements and, having received favorable information about Mr. Wise's ability to conduct such audits, has decided not to issue a request for proposals from other audit firms. Cybil Civic, president of the board, heard from a friend associated with a similar organization that $5,000 is an appropriate price for such an audit and has offered Mr. Wise the audit for that price. Although Mr. Wise agrees that $5,000 would be reasonable for a typical financial statement audit of an organization of Mountain Lake's type and size, he refuses to contract for the audit at that price until he is able to estimate the extent of audit work that would be involved.

Facts. In discussions with Mountain Lake's controller, Mr. Wise obtains the following information about the organization for the year just ended:

1. Mountain Lake received a $200,000 grant from the City of Mountain Lake, of which 50 percent was stated as being from federal sources. $150,000 was expended during the year, ratably from federal and nonfederal sources.
2. Unrestricted gifts of $50,000 were received from private donors; $40,000 was spent during the year.
3. The organization received $300,000 from Medicare for mental health services rendered during the year.
4. A building owned by the U.S. Department of Health and Human Services is occupied by Mountain Lake for rent of $1 per year. The fair value of the rental has been appraised at $30,001.

5. Mountain Lake carried out a program with the Federal Bureau of Prisons to provide alcohol and drug abuse counseling services for prisoners at a nearby federal prison. Services are provided on a "units of service" reimbursement basis. Each unit of service is reimbursed at the rate of $100 and the contract provides for maximum reimbursement of $200,000. Actual units of service for the year were 2,200. Direct costs incurred for these services amounted to $150,000 in total.

Required

a. Based on the foregoing facts, is Mountain Lake Mental Health Affiliates required to have a single audit? Explain your answer.

b. Should Mr. Wise accept the audit engagement for a $5,000 fee? Why or why not?

(Note: The authors are indebted to James Brown, a partner with Baird, Kurtz & Dobson in Springfield, Missouri, for providing the example on which Case 11–1 is based.)

11–2. Single Audit and Major Programs. The City of Salem expended federal awards from the following programs during its most recent fiscal year.

Program	*Amount Expended*
1. Community Service Block Grants	$ 400,000
2. Solid Waste Management Assistance	300,000
3. Emergency Federal Law Enforcement Assistance	250,000
4. Low Income Home Energy Assistance	200,000
5. Community Economic Adjustment Planning Assistance	150,000
6. Air Pollution Control Program	50,000
Total	$1,350,000

Other Information

The auditor has rendered an unqualified report on the financial statements and found no reportable conditions or material weaknesses in internal control at the financial statement level. In addition, the auditor has given an unqualified opinion on the Schedule of Expenditures of Federal Awards, from which the preceding information was obtained. Next the auditor must determine which major federal award programs require internal control evaluation and compliance testing.

Following the risk-based approach, the auditor, with the concurrence of the oversight agency, has classified programs 2 and 4 as low risk. Program 6 was not assessed as to risk due to its small size.

Required

a. Which programs should the auditor audit as major programs for the year just ended? Explain your rationale.

b. How would your answer to requirement *a* differ if program 2 had not been classified as low risk?

11–3. Internet Case. The Town of Grandview Health Department receives pass-through funds from the State Department of Social Services to assist in administering the federally funded Special Supplemental Nutrition Program for Women, Infants, and Children (WIC). At the request of the State Department of Social Services, the town of Grandview has engaged you to perform a program-specific audit of its expenditures of federal awards for the WIC program. Although you are unfamiliar with this particular program, you have extensive experience in governmental auditing and have audited many other federal programs.

Required

Utilize the Internet to answer the following question about this program.

a. What is the Catalog of Federal Domestic Assistance (CFDA) number for this program? (Relevant website is: http://www.gsa.gov/fdac. Use the index at that site to search for the catalog.)

b. Describe the purpose of this program.

c. Who are the eligible beneficiaries of the program?

d. Which of the 14 compliance items listed in the A–133 *Compliance Supplement* are applicable to auditing compliance for this program? (Hint: Access Parts 2, 3, and 4 of the *Compliance Supplement* at website http://www.whitehouse.gov/OMB/circulars/.

e. Depending on your instructor's preference, either print the compliance audit requirements for this program from Part 4 of the compliance supplement (about nine pages) or summarize them in a brief report.

11–4. Auditor Selection. For its most recent fiscal year Jeffcoat County expended $900,000 in federal awards from various federal programs. In each of the last three years, Jeffcoat County received a single audit from a large, national accounting firm. Until last year the County had always received unqualified audit opinions and had received no reportable conditions or significant findings of noncompliance. Last year, however, the accounting firm rendered a qualified opinion for its audit of financial statements. In addition, it identified many reportable conditions in its evaluation of internal controls related to the financial statements and major programs, three of which were reported as material weaknesses. Several findings of noncompliance with laws, regulations, and grant agreements were also identified, resulting in a qualified opinion on the compliance report for major programs.

Jeffcoat County's Director of Finance, who had been hired early last year, expressed strong disagreement with the qualified opinions and reported findings and vowed to switch auditors for the current year's single audit. Accordingly, the County solicited bids for the current year audit and received bids ranging from $6,000 to $59,000 to conduct the audit. By mutual agreement, the incumbent audit firm did not tender a bid. The $6,000 bid was received from Mary Benson, CPA, a local accountant, who 20 years earlier had conducted grant audits for local governmental and not-for-profit organizations. Ms. Benson had not done an audit of federal awards during the past 20 years, nor had she received any continuing professional education or peer evaluation for such audits. She had bid on the County audit in the hope of using it as a springboard for building a practice in federal program auditing to replace declining revenues from tax services. Given current budget constraints, Ms. Benson received strong support from a majority of the County Commissioners. Commissioners noted the fact that she held a valid CPA license from the state and had relevant experience. Furthermore, the Director of Finance felt that a local auditor would be less critical of the County's financial management and reporting practices. Based on these considerations, Ms. Benson was selected to perform the single audit for the current year.

Required

(Note: For guidance in answering the following questions you may wish to access OMB Circular A–133. Conduct your search at http://www.whitehouse.gov/omb/circulars.)

a. Is Ms. Benson qualified to conduct the single audit for Jeffcoat County? Why or why not?

b. What are some of the potential ramifications of selecting Ms. Benson to conduct this year's audit?

Exercises and Problems

11–1. Examine the CAFR. Using the CAFR you obtained for Exercise 1–1, answer the following questions:

a. Auditors. Was this CAFR audited by external certified public accountants (CPAs) or by state or local governmental auditors?

b. Audit Opinion. What type of opinion did this entity receive? If it was qualified, what reason was given? Was an opinion expressed on the combining statements as well as the basic (or general purpose) financial statements?

c. Auditing Standards. Did the auditor use generally accepted auditing standards (GAAS), generally accepted governmental auditing standards (GAS or GAGAS), or both?

d. Paragraphs. How many paragraphs are there in the auditor's report? Can you identify the introductory, scope, opinion, and any explanatory paragraphs?

e. Single Audit. Can you tell if this entity was required to have a Single Audit? If so, are the required Single Audit reports contained within the cover of the CAFR that you are examining? If the entity does receive federal financial assistance, but you see no mention of the Single Audit in the Auditor's Report, where do you expect that Single Audit report to be?

11–2. Multiple Choice. Choose the best answer.

1. The scope paragraph of an independent auditor's report on a financial audit of a local governmental unit:

a. States that generally accepted auditing standards require that the auditor plan and perform the audit to obtain reasonable assurance as to whether the financial statements are free of material misstatement.

b. Identifies the financial statements on which the auditor is expressing an opinion.

c. States whether, in the auditor's opinion, the financial statements present fairly in conformity with generally accepted accounting principles the financial position of the reporting entity.

d. All of the above.

2. An unqualified opinion paragraph of an independent auditor's report on a financial audit of a local government unit:
   a. States that, in the auditor's opinion, the combined financial statements present fairly the financial position, results of operations, and cash flows in conformity with generally accepted accounting principles.
   b. States that, in the auditor's opinion, the financial statements of the individual funds and account groups accurately present the financial condition as of a certain date, and the results of operations for the year then ended.
   c. States that the combining financial statements fairly present the financial condition as of a certain date, and the results of operations for the year then ended.
   d. None of the above.
3. Which of the following is *not* one of the types of opinions an auditor may render in accordance with GAAS?
   a. Unqualified.
   b. Qualified.
   c. Satisfactory.
   d. Adverse.
4. Which of the following *best* describes the relationship between GAAS and GAGAS?
   a. GAAS do not apply to audits conducted in accordance with the yellow book.
   b. GAAS apply to independent CPA auditors; GAGAS apply to governmental auditors.
   c. Audits done in accordance with GAGAS must also be done in accordance with GAAS.
   d. Audits of state and local governmental units always require that the audit be conducted in accordance with both GAAS and GAGAS.
5. Financial audits, as defined in the GAO's *Government Auditing Standards*, may include determining
   a. Whether the financial statements present fairly the entity's financial position, results of operations, and cash flows in conformity with GAAP.
   b. Whether financial information is presented in accordance with established or stated criteria.
   c. Whether the entity has adhered to specific financial compliance requirements.
   d. All of the above.
6. Performance audits, as defined in the GAO's *Governmental Auditing Standards*:
   a. Provide a basis for an auditor's opinion as to whether the entity is acquiring, protecting, and using its resources economically and efficiently.
   b. Include determining whether or the extent to which government officials are efficiently, economically, and effectively carrying out their responsibilities.
   c. Provide assurance that operations are in compliance with *all* applicable laws and regulations that may have a material effect on the financial statements.
   d. Are performed by the internal audit staff to assist the entity's independent auditor.

7. When performing an audit of a city that is subject to the requirements of the Single Audit Act of 1984 and the 1996 amendments, an auditor should adhere to:
   a. Governmental Accounting Standards Board's *General Standards*.
   b. Governmental Finance Officers Association's *Governmental Accounting, Auditing, and Financial Reporting Principles*.
   c. General Accounting Office's *Government Auditing Standards*.
   d. Securities and Exchange Commission's *Regulation S–X*.
8. When engaged to audit a governmental entity in accordance with *Government Auditing Standards*, an auditor prepares a written report on the internal control structure:
   a. In all audits, regardless of circumstances.
   b. Only when the auditor has noted reportable conditions.
   c. Only when requested by the governmental entity being audited.
   d. Only when requested by the federal government funding agency.
9. Kent is auditing an entity's compliance with requirements governing a major federal financial assistance program in accordance with the Single Audit Act. Kent detected noncompliance with requirements that have a material effect on that program. Kent's report on compliance should express a (an):
   a. Unqualified opinion with a separate explanatory paragraph.
   b. Qualified opinion or an adverse opinion.
   c. Adverse opinion or a disclaimer of opinion.
   d. Limited assurance on the items tested.
10. What is an auditor's responsibility for supplementary information required by GASB that is placed outside the basic financial statements?
   a. Label the information as unaudited and expand the auditor's report to include a disclaimer on the information.
   b. Add an explanatory paragraph to the auditor's report and refer to the information as "required supplementary information."
   c. Apply limited procedures to the information and report deficiencies in, or the omission of, the information.
   d. Audit the required supplementary information in accordance with generally accepted government auditing standards.

(Items 7–10, A-ICPA, adapted)

11–3. Qualified Audit Opinion. On September 23, 2002, the CPA firm of Green and Jones completed its audit of the City of Deerfield's general purpose financial statements (GPFS) for the year ended June 30, 2002. The City presents its financial position, results of operations, and cash flows using the financial statements prescribed by generally accepted accounting principles. However, Green and Jones believe that the Deerfield Cultural Center, a theater for the performing arts and financially subsidized by the City, meets the criteria specified by GASB for inclusion as a component unit in Deerfield's GPFS. Deerfield's finance director has steadfastly refused to include the cultural center in Deerfield's GPFS on the basis that it would cause the financial statements to be misleading. Green and Jones feel compelled to issue an "except for" qualified audit opinion to bring attention to this departure from GAAP, although they believe the financial statements present fairly in all other respects. Green and Jones have determined that the effect of including the cultural center in Deerfield's GPFS would have been to increase the reported assets and revenues of the enterprise funds by $450,000 and $127,000, respectively, and increase the excess of revenues over expenses in that fund type by $5,200 for the year ended June 30, 2002.

Required

Prepare the qualified audit report that Green and Jones, CPAs, should render on the City of Deerfield's GPFS for the year ended June 30, 2002.

11–4. Audit Field Work. Jones and Todd, a local CPA firm, received an invitation to bid for the audit of a local, federally assisted program. The audit is to be conducted in accordance with generally accepted government auditing standards (GAGAS) published by the General Accounting Office (GAO). Jones and Todd has become familiar with GAGAS and recognizes that GAGAS are not inconsistent with generally accepted auditing standards (GAAS) issued by the AICPA. GAGAS, unlike GAAS, are concerned with more than the financial aspects of an entity's operations. GAGAS are broader because they provide standards for two types of audits, financial audits and performance audits. Jones and Todd has been engaged to perform the following specific audits, encompassing both a financial and a performance audit for the program:

1. An examination of whether (*a*) financial transactions, accounts, and reports are presented in accordance with the criteria stated in the program; (*b*) the entity has complied with applicable financial compliance requirements specified by the program; and (*c*) the entity's internal control structure achieves control objectives.
2. A review of efficiency and economy in the use of resources, such as personnel and equipment, including compliance with applicable laws and regulations concerning economy and efficiency.
3. A review to determine whether desired results are effectively achieved (program results), including compliance with laws and regulations applicable to the program.

Required

a. Jones and Todd should perform sufficient audit work to satisfy the financial and compliance element of the GAO standards. What should such audit work determine?

b. After making appropriate review and inquiries, what uneconomical practices or inefficiencies should Jones and Todd be alert to in satisfying the efficiency and economy element encompassed by the GAO standards?

c. After making appropriate review and inquiries, what should Jones and Todd consider to satisfy the program results element encompassed by the GAO standards?

(AICPA, adapted)

11–5. Compliance with Laws and Regulations. The City of Granville receives grants from various state agencies as well as grants from several federal government agencies.

The City engaged Hall & Hall, CPAs, to audit its financial statements for the year ended July 31, 2002, in accordance with *Government Auditing Standards*. Accordingly, the auditor's reports are to be submitted by the City of Granville to granting government agencies, which make the reports available for public inspection.

The auditor's separate report on compliance with laws and regulations that was drafted by a staff accountant of Hall & Hall at the completion of the engagement contained the statements below. It was submitted to the engagement partner who reviewed matters thoroughly and properly concluded that no material instances of noncompliance were identified.

1. A statement that the audit was conducted in accordance with generally accepted auditing standards and with *Government Auditing Standards* issued by the Comptroller General of the United States.
2. A statement that the auditor's procedures included tests of compliance.
3. A statement that the standards require the auditors to plan and to perform the audit to detect all instances of noncompliance with applicable laws and regulations.
4. A statement that management is responsible for compliance with laws, regulations, contracts, and grants.
5. A statement that the auditor's objective was to provide an opinion on compliance with the provisions of laws and regulations equivalent to that to be expressed on the financial statements.
6. A statement of negative assurance that, with respect to items tested, nothing came to the auditor's attention that caused the auditors to believe that the entity had not complied, in all material respects, with the provisions of laws, regulations, contracts, and grants.
7. A statement that the report is intended only for the information of the specific legislative or regulatory bodies, and that this restriction is intended to limit the distribution of the report.

Required

For each of above statements indicate whether each is an appropriate or inappropriate element within the report on compliance with laws and regulations. If a statement is not appropriate, explain why.

(AICPA, adapted)

11–6. Auditor's Report. The report of the independent auditors that appeared in an annual financial report for Plains City is reproduced below.

Required

Compare this report with the ones shown in Illustrations 11–2 and 11–3 and discuss the likely reasons for the different wording. What type of opinion is rendered in this report? (The exhibits and tables referred to in the report are not included here.)

Independent Auditors' Report

The Honorable Mayor and Members of the City Council, Plains City

We have audited the general purpose financial statements of Plains City as of and for the year ended December 31, 2001. These general purpose financial statements are the responsibility of Plains City management. Our responsibility is to express an opinion on these general purpose financial statements based on our audit.

We conducted our audit in accordance with generally accepted auditing standards. Those standards require that we plan and perform the audit to obtain reasonable assurance about whether the general purpose financial statements are free of material misstatement. An audit includes examining, on a test basis, evidence supporting the amounts and disclosures in the general purpose financial statements. An audit also includes assessing the accounting principles used and significant estimates made by management, as well as evaluating the overall general purpose financial statement presentation. We believe that our audit provides a reasonable basis for our opinion.

The general purpose financial statements referred to above do not include the general fixed assets account group, which should be included in order to conform with generally accepted accounting principles. The amount that should be recorded in the general fixed assets account group is not known as Plains City does not maintain records of general fixed assets.

In our opinion, except for the effect on the financial statements of the omission described in the preceding paragraph, the general purpose financial statements referred to above present fairly, in all material respects, the financial position of Plains City at December 31, 2001, and the results of its operations and cash flows of its proprietary fund types and nonexpendable trust funds for the year then ended, in conformity with generally accepted accounting principles.

Our audit was made for the purpose of forming an opinion on the general purpose financial statements of Plains City taken as a whole. The combining and individual fund and account group financial statements and schedules listed in the table of contents and the schedule of expenditures of federal awards are presented for purposes of additional analysis and are not a required part of the general purpose financial statements of Plains City. Such information has been subjected to the auditing procedures applied in the audit of the general purpose financial statements and, in our opinion, is fairly presented in all material respects in relation to the general purpose financial statements taken as a whole.

[*Signature*]
[*Date*]

11–7. Single Audit. Tri-States Community Service Agency expended federal awards during their most recent fiscal year in the following amounts for the programs shown:

Program 1	$ 450,000
Program 2	350,000
Program 3	140,000
Program 4	60,000
Total	$1,000,000

Additional information: Programs 1 and 2 were audited as major programs in each of the two preceding fiscal years, with no audit findings reported. Although neither Program 1 nor 2 is considered inherently risky, a new manager, recently graduated from the state university, was appointed during the current year to manage activities related to Program 2.

Required

a. Assuming the auditor classifies Programs 2 and 3 as high risk and Program 1 as low risk, which programs would be audited as major programs? Explain.

b. Explain what audit work would be required to audit the major programs.

11–8. Conformity with GAAP. You are auditing the accounts of the clerk-treasurer of the Town of Belton. You find, in the ledger, accounts for a General Fund, a Street Fund, and a Capital Projects Fund. The legally approved budget for the Street Fund for the year you are examining consisted of the following three appropriations only:

Labor	$60,000
Materials	66,000
Equipment	24,000

In the appropriation and disbursement ledger accounts, you find the record of transactions for the Street Fund shown as follows:

LABOR ACCOUNT

Date	Description	Warrant	Appropriation	Disbursements	Appropriation Balance
Jan. 1	From advertised budget		$60,000		$60,000
31	Street labor	115-142		$ 6,000	54,000
Feb. 28	Street labor	219-241		7,000	47,000
Mar. 31	Street labor	252-263		6,000	41,000
Apr. 30	Street labor	274-294		5,000	36,000
June 30	Labor on municipal parking lots	371-388		8,000	28,000
Aug. 31	Street labor	400-424		10,000	18,000
Oct. 31	Street labor	510-523		10,000	8,000
Dec. 31	Street labor	600-621		8,000	–0–

MATERIALS ACCOUNT

Date	Description	Warrant	Appropriation	Disbursements	Appropriation Balance
Jan. 1	From advertised budget		$66,000		$66,000
20	Asphalt mix for street repair	109		$ 6,000	60,000
Feb. 21	Repair of truck used on streets	217		2,000	58,000
Mar. 12	Purchased used truck for street department	268		12,000	46,000
Apr. 15	Auditor of State, gasoline tax distribution		4,920		50,920
May 31	Gas and oil for street trucks	301		3,000	47,920

MATERIALS ACCOUNT (CONCLUDED)

Date	Description	Warrant	Appropriation	Disbursements	Appropriation Balance
June 6	Tile	367		4,000	43,920
July 14	Concrete for building fireplaces in park	425		6,900	37,020
Aug. 7	Street lights (utility bill)	451		7,220	29,800
Sep. 29	Refund received on tile purchased by warrant No. 367		100		29,900
Oct. 18	Labor on streets	524–532		12,000	17,900
Nov. 2	Reimbursement for cutting weeds on private property		640		18,540
Dec. 11	To contractor for paving street	622		20,000	(1,460)
31	Additional appropriations as advertised on this date		1,460		–0–

EQUIPMENT ACCOUNT

Date	Description	Warrant	Appropriation	Disbursements	Appropriation Balance
Jan. 1	From advertised budget		$24,000		$24,000
9	Grading equipment			$16,000	8,000
Feb. 10	Fire hydrants	189		6,000	2,000
19	Shovels, picks, and hand tools	208		1,420	580

Required

a. Comment on whether accounting for the Street Fund appears in conformity with generally accepted accounting principles. Explain fully.

b. As the auditor, would you be able to render an unqualified opinion on the financial statements of the Town of Belton? Would your answer depend on whether you are engaged to report on the financial statements at the individual fund level rather than at the combined level (general purpose financial statements)?

11–9. Auditor's Opinion. The City of Clayton's Balance Sheet as of December 31, 2002, is shown below. The *Annual Report for 2002* also includes a Statement of Changes in Cash for that year and an operating statement for that year. No Auditor's Report is associated with these three financial statements. Assuming you made an audit for 2002 and found no material errors in the amounts presented in the statements, could you express the opinion that the statements present fairly the financial position of the City at December 31, 2002, and the results of its operations for the year then ended in conformity with generally accepted accounting principles? Why or why not? Be explicit.

CITY OF CLAYTON
Balance Sheet
As of December 31, 2002
Assets

Cash	$ 155,155
Accounts receivable	
Current-year property taxes	58,792

Prior-year property taxes	2,921	
Other taxes	514	
Municipal services—usage	71,861	
Municipal services—tap fees	9,077	
Toll bridges	30,598	
School district	5,242	
Other	173	
Total current assets		$ 334,333
Property, plant, and equipment:		
Library—building and equipment	$ 16,550	
Storage shed	14,742	
Public Safety Dept.—building and equipment	266,317	
Municipal Services Dept.—land, building, and equipment	2,325,893	
Highway Department	28,755	
Cemetery	21,595	
Town office—equipment	4,369	
Land	12,000	
Toll bridges	22,500	
Total property, plant, and equipment	2,712,721	
Less: Accumulated depreciation	(283,357)	2,429,364
Total assets		$2,763,697

Liabilities and Equity

Accounts payable	$ 1,725	
Tax anticipation notes	250,000	
Current portion—long-term debt:		
Bonds	85,000	
Notes	84,304	
Due school district	46,089	
Total current liabilities	467,118	
Long-term debt:		
Bonds	1,395,000	
Notes	373,416	
Total liabilities		$2,235,534
Equity	850,421	
Less: Wind recovery costs	(322,258)	528,163
Total liabilities and equity		$2,763,697

Continuous Problem

11–B. Prepare the audit report you believe would be appropriate for a certified public accountant to provide on the basic financial statements of the City of Bingham (see 9–B). Explain the rationale for the nature of the audit report (qualified or unqualified) rendered.

CHAPTER 12

Accounting and Reporting for the Federal Government

Learning Objectives

After studying this chapter, you should be able to:

- Describe the financial management structure of the federal government.
- Describe the process for establishing generally accepted accounting principles for federal agencies.
- Explain the concepts underlying federal agency accounting and financial reporting.
- Identify the financial statements required of federal agencies.
- Contrast and compare budgetary accounting with proprietary accounting.
- Make budgetary and proprietary journal entries and prepare financial statements for federal agencies.
- Contrast and compare accounting for state and local governments with federal agencies.
- Describe government-wide financial statements for the federal government.

An accounting structure has been provided for the federal government of the United States of America by statutes since 1789. The professional accounting consultants to the first and second Hoover Commissions generally are given credit for being among the first to provide direction to the effort to improve federal government accounting. Recent years have seen major institutional change that is providing the impetus for even greater change in federal accounting. Among these changes are the Chief Financial Officers Act of 1990, the creation of the Federal Accounting Standards Advisory Board (FASAB) in 1990, the Government Performance and Results Act of 1993 (GPRA), the Government Management Reform Act of 1994 (GMRA), and the Federal Financial Management Improvement Act of 1996. Federal accounting standards are similar in some respects to those used by private sector entities, and in other respects are like those developed for state and local governments, as discussed in Chapters 1–9 of this text. Important differences do exist, however. This chapter focuses on the unique aspects of accounting for federal agencies.

Federal Government Financial Management Structure

The United States Code (31 U.S.C. §3512) requires the head of each executive agency to establish, evaluate, and maintain adequate systems of accounting and internal control. Despite this requirement, many federal agencies have been slow to establish effective financial management systems. To help ensure that federal agencies correct their deficient accounting and reporting systems, Congress enacted the **Federal Financial Management Improvement Act of 1996 (FFMIA).** The Act states:

> To rebuild the accountability and credibility of the Federal Government, and restore public confidence in the Federal Government, agencies must incorporate accounting standards and reporting objectives established for the Federal Government into their financial management systems so that all the assets and liabilities, revenues, and expenditures or expenses, and the full costs of programs and activities of the Federal Government can be consistently and accurately recorded, monitored, and uniformly reported throughout the Federal Government.[1]

The FFMIA further requires that each agency "shall implement and maintain financial management systems that comply substantially with federal financial management systems requirements, applicable federal accounting standards, and the United States Government Standard General Ledger at the transaction level."[2] The Act also requires that each audit of a federal agency's financial statements shall report whether the agency is in compliance with the preceding requirement. If not

[1]Public Law 104-208, 104th Congress, Federal Financial Management Improvement Act of 1996, Sec. 802(a)(5).

[2]Ibid., Sec. 803(a).

in compliance, the agency must establish a remediation plan that will ensure compliance no later than three years after the date of determination of noncompliance.

Federal statutes assign responsibility for establishing and maintaining a sound financial management structure for the federal government as a whole to three principal officials: the Comptroller General, the Secretary of the Treasury, and the Director of the Office of Management and Budget (OMB). Responsibilities assigned to each of these officials and the Director of the Congressional Budget Office are discussed briefly, after which recent cooperative efforts of these officials to enhance the quality of federal financial management under the auspices of the Joint Financial Management and Improvement Program (JFMIP) will be examined.

Comptroller General

The Comptroller General of the United States is the head of the General Accounting Office (GAO), an agency of the legislative branch of the government. The Comptroller General is appointed by the President with the advice and consent of the Senate for a term of office of 15 years. Since 1950, the United States Code (31 U.S.C. §3511) has assigned to the Comptroller General responsibility for prescribing the accounting principles, standards, and related requirements to be observed by each executive agency in the development of its accounting system. The executive branch has never acknowledged the constitutional authority of the Comptroller General to set accounting standards for the executive branch. Moreover, the Chief Financial Officers Act of 1990 assigns significant responsibility for establishing policies and procedures for approving and publishing accounting principles and standards (particularly as regards agency financial reporting) to the Director of the Office of Management and Budget. Thus, both under the law and in fact, the responsibility for prescribing accounting principles and standards is now a joint responsibility.

Just as the appropriational authority of state and local governments rests in their legislative bodies, the appropriational authority of the federal government rests in the Congress. The Congress is, therefore, interested in determining that financial and budgetary reports from executive, judicial, and legislative agencies are reliable; that agency financial management is intelligent, efficient, and economical; and that legal requirements have been met by the agencies. Under the assumption that the reports of an independent audit agency would aid in satisfying these interests of the Congress, the General Accounting Office was created as the audit agency of the Congress itself. The standards of auditing followed by the GAO are discussed in some detail in Chapter 11. Briefly, the standards are set forth in the publication *Government Auditing Standards*, often referred to as the "yellow book," and are usually followed by independent CPAs when auditing federal grants and contracts, as well as by some state audit agencies, and federal Inspectors General.

Secretary of the Treasury

The Secretary of the Treasury is the head of the Department of the Treasury, a part of the executive branch of the federal government. The Secretary of the Treasury is a member of the Cabinet of the President, appointed by the President with the advice and consent of the Senate to serve an indefinite term of office. The Department of the Treasury was created in 1789 to receive, keep, and disburse monies of the United States, and to account for them. From the beginning, the word *receive* was construed as *collect*, and the Internal Revenue Service, Bureau of Customs, and other agencies active in the enforcement of the collections of revenues due the federal government are parts of the Department of the Treasury, as are the Bureau of the Mint, the Bureau of Engraving and Printing, the Bureau of Public Debt, the Office of Treasurer of the United States, and the Bureau of Government Financial Operations. Although there is no complete centralized accounting system for the federal government at this time, the Secretary of the Treasury, in coordination with the Director of OMB and the Comptroller General, has for more than two decades published prototype consolidated financial statements for the United States Government as a whole. Beginning with Fiscal Year 1997, the consolidated financial statements are no longer prepared on a prototype basis; they are now an official report of the federal government as described later in this chapter.

The Secretary of the Treasury is responsible for the preparation of reports that will inform the President, the Congress, and the public on the financial condition and operations of the government (31 U.S.C. §3513). An additional responsibility of the Secretary of the Treasury is the maintenance of a system of central accounts of the public debt and cash to provide a basis for consolidation of the accounts of the various executive agencies with those of the Department of the Treasury.

Statutes provide that the reports of the Secretary of the Treasury shall include financial data needed by the Office of Management and Budget, and that the Department of the Treasury system of central accounting and reporting shall be consistent with the principles, standards, and related requirements prescribed for federal agency accounting systems. Instructions and requirements relating to central accounting, central financial reporting, and various other fiscal matters have been codified by the Department of the Treasury in the *Treasury Financial Manual* for guidance of departments and agencies.

The Department of the Treasury through its Financial Management Service (FMS) also provides support for the interagency Standard General Ledger Board, which maintains the *U.S. Government Standard General Ledger*, subject to the approval of the OMB. The *Standard General Ledger* was developed by an interagency task force under the direction of the OMB and was originally published by the OMB in 1986. The *Standard General Ledger* is intended to (1) provide an accounting structure that will standardize financial information accumulation and processing, (2) enhance financial control, and (3) support budget reporting and external financial reporting. Implementation of the *Standard General Ledger* has enhanced the ability of central agencies to more accurately consolidate accounting data derived from individual agency accounting records. The chart of accounts presented in the *Standard General Ledger* is based on a standardized coding system for asset, liability, equity, budgetary, revenue, expense, and "gains/losses/extraordinary items, etc." accounts and provides flexibility so that agency-specific accounts may be incorporated. In addition to the chart of accounts, the *Standard General Ledger* publication provides account descriptions; illustrates the manner in which accounting transactions should be recorded; discusses data elements, subaccounts, and definitions; and illustrates crosswalks to external reports. Accounting for typical transactions of a federal agency illustrated in a later section of this chapter is based on the *Standard General Ledger* structure.

Director of the Office of Management and Budget

The Director of the Office of Management and Budget is appointed by the President and is a part of the Executive Office of the President. As the direct representative of the President with the authority to control the size and nature of appropriations requested of each Congress, it is obvious that the Director of the OMB is an extremely powerful figure in the federal government.

Congressional requirements for the budget have a number of accounting implications in addition to the explicit historical comparisons that necessitate cooperation among the OMB, the Department of the Treasury, and the GAO. Implicit in the requirements for projections of revenues and receipts is the mandate that the OMB coordinate closely with the Council of Economic Advisers in the use of macroeconomic (the study of the economic system in its aggregate) and **macroaccounting** (accounting for the economy in the aggregate) forecasts. Macroaccounting is beyond the scope of this text, yet the subject is of great, and increasing, importance in the financial management of the federal government.

The OMB is assigned major responsibilities under the Chief Financial Officers Act of 1990 for establishing policies and procedures for approving and publishing financial accounting principles and standards to be followed by executive branch agencies. Pursuant to the Act, an Office of Federal Financial Management has been established within the OMB, headed by a controller appointed by the President. The Act also authorizes each major department or agency of the federal government to have a Chief Financial Officer (CFO) and a deputy CFO. Under the Act, the Director of the OMB is required to prepare and update each year a five-year financial plan for the federal government. The OMB issues Circulars and Bulletins relating to financial reporting and management of federal agencies.

Director of the Congressional Budget Office

The Congressional Budget and Impoundment Control Act of 1974 established House and Senate budget committees, created the Congressional Budget Office (CBO), structured the congressional budget process, and enacted a number of other provisions to improve federal fiscal procedures. The Director of the CBO is appointed for a four-year term by the Speaker of the House of Representatives and the President *pro tempore* of the Senate. The CBO gathers information for the House and Senate budget committees with respect to the budget (submitted by the executive branch), appropriation bills, and other bills providing budget authority or tax expenditures.[3] The CBO also provides the Congress with information concerning revenues, receipts, estimated future revenues and receipts, changing revenue conditions, and any related information-gathering and analytic functions assigned to the CBO; its Director is responsible for working with the Comptroller General, the Secretary of the Treasury, and the Director of the Office of

[3]A *tax expenditure* is a revenue loss attributable to provisions of federal tax laws that allow special exclusion, exemption, or deduction from gross income, or that provide a special credit, a preferential rate of tax, or a deferral of tax liability.

Illustration 12–1 Federal Government Financial Management Structure

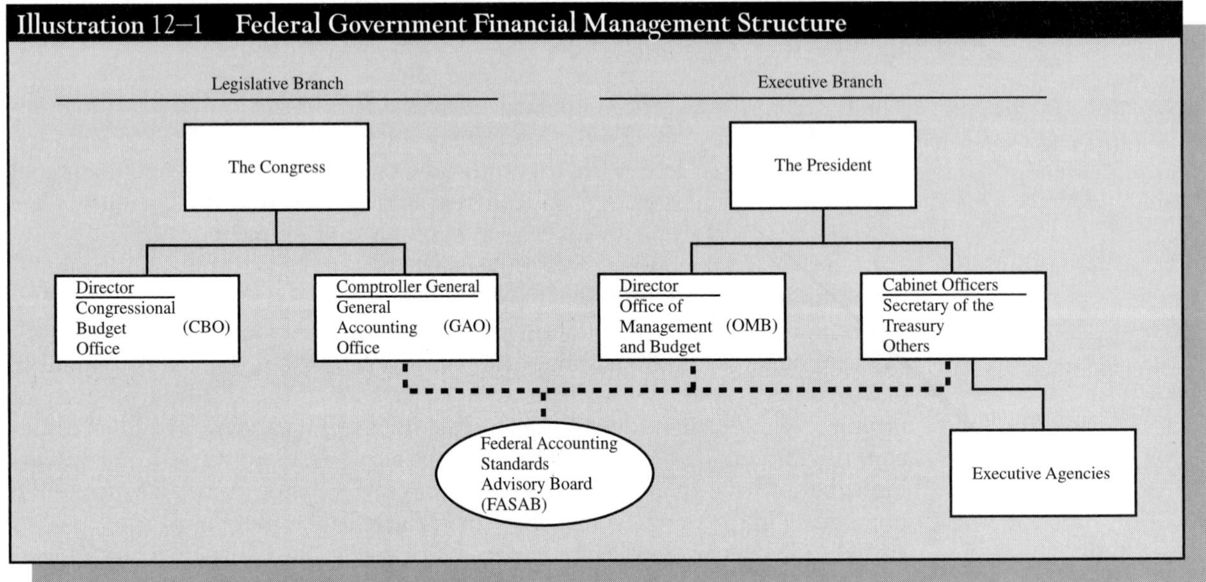

Management and Budget in developing central files of data and information to meet the recurring requirements of the Congress.

Illustration 12–1 shows in chart form the interrelationships among the officials and organizations whose accounting and financial management responsibilities are discussed above.

Process for Establishing Generally Accepted Accounting Principles for Federal Agencies

The three officials or "principals" of the Joint Financial Management Improvement Program (JFMIP)—the Comptroller General, the Director of OMB, and the Secretary of the Treasury—have joint statutory responsibilities for improving financial management in the federal government. Although accounting principles and standards were prescribed for many years by *Title 2* of the *General Accounting Office Policy and Procedures Manual for Guidance of Federal Agencies*, not all federal agencies complied with that guidance. The diverse financial systems used among and within federal departments and agencies made it difficult to achieve uniform financial reporting and to educate and train federal financial managers.

To establish an improved and more generally accepted structure for setting accounting principles and standards, the three principal sponsors of the JFMIP signed a memorandum of understanding in October 1990 creating the **Federal Accounting Standards Advisory Board (FASAB).** The nine-member board utilizes a due process similar to that of FASB and GASB. The board is comprised of one member from each of the three principal sponsors; one member from each of the following federal constituencies: the Congressional Budget Office, defense and international agencies, and civilian agencies; and three members from the nonfederal "general financial community" (defined as the accounting and auditing community and academia). According to OMB *Circular A-134*, "Financial Accounting Principles and Standards" (par. 2):

> The role of the FASAB is to deliberate upon and make recommendations to the Principals on accounting principles and standards for the Federal Government and its agencies. The MOU [memorandum of understanding] states that if the Principals agree with the recommendations, the Comptroller General and the Director of OMB will publish the accounting principles and standards.

During its first decade, the FASAB has issued three Statements of Federal Financial Accounting Concepts (SFFAC), 14 Statements of Federal Financial Accounting Standards (SFFAS), and three Statements of Recommended Accounting Standards (SRAS). These statements collectively provide general and specific accounting and financial reporting standards on a variety of topics, including assets; liabilities; inventory and related property; property, plant, and equipment; revenues and other financial sources; direct loans and loan guarantees; managerial cost accounting concepts; and supplementary stewardship reporting. This chapter provides only an overview of these initial basic standards; detailed discussion of the many complex issues covered by these standards is beyond the scope of this text.[4] The authoritative status of SFFASs is made clear by OMB *Circular A-134:*

> SFFASs shall be considered generally accepted accounting principles (GAAP) for Federal agencies.[5] Agencies shall apply the SFFASs in preparing financial statements in accordance with the requirements of the Chief Financial Officers Act of 1990. Auditors shall consider SFFASs as authoritative references when auditing financial statements. (par. 5.b)

Hierarchy of Accounting Principles and Standards

OMB *Bulletin 97-01* acknowledges that federal agencies may engage in transactions that are not addressed by the SFFASs issued to date. Thus, the Bulletin establishes the following hierarchy of generally accepted accounting principles for the federal government:

1. Individual standards (SFFASs) agreed to by the Director of OMB, the Controller General, and the Secretary of the Treasury and published by OMB and the General Accounting Office.
2. Interpretations related to the SFFASs issued by OMB in accordance with the procedures outlined in OMB *Circular A-134*, "Financial Accounting Principles and Standards."

[4]The FASAB continues to deliberate on additional standards that may extend or modify statements that have been issued to date. Students who desire information about current FASAB projects, including exposure drafts of possible new standards, should consult FASAB's Internet site at http://www.financenet.gov/fasab.

[5]The American Institute of CPAs accorded Rule 203 (Code of Professional Conduct) recognition to federal government standards as generally accepted accounting principles on October 19, 1999.

3. Requirements contained in OMB's Form and Content Bulletin in effect for the period covered by the financial statements [currently OMB *Bulletin 97-01*].
4. Accounting principles published by other authoritative standard-setting bodies and other authoritative sources (*a*) in the absence of other guidance in the first three parts of this hierarchy, and (*b*) if the use of such accounting principles improves the meaningfulness of the financial statements.[6]

Conceptual Framework

Accounting standards recommended by the FASAB, and issued by the Comptroller General and the OMB for federal agencies, are intended to be consistent with a conceptual framework the FASAB is developing. In this respect, the FASAB is following the general pattern established by the FASB, which attempts to issue standards consistent with its several Statements of Financial Accounting Concepts; and the GASB, which looks to its *Concepts Statement No. 1*, "Objectives of Financial Reporting" (see Chapter 1 of this text). To date, the FASAB has issued three concepts statements: *Statement of Federal Financial Accounting Concepts (SFFAC) No. 1*, "Objectives of Federal Financial Reporting 58," 1; *SFFAC No. 2*, "Entity and Display 58," 1; and *SFFAC No. 3*, "Management's Discussion and Analysis." *SFFAC No. 1* is considerably broader in scope than either the FASB's or GASB's concepts statements on objectives. The FASAB, for example, intends to set standards for internal management accounting and performance measurement, as well as for external financial reporting. The FASAB objectives are described briefly in the next section.

Objectives

SFFAC No. 1 identifies four objectives of federal financial reporting, all of which rest on the foundation of accountability. The objectives in brief are to assist report users in evaluating *budgetary integrity*, *operating performance*, *stewardship*, and adequacy of *systems and controls*. *Budgetary integrity* pertains to accountability for raising monies through taxes and other means in accordance with appropriate laws, and expenditures of these monies in accordance with budgetary authorization. Accountability for *operating performance* is accomplished by providing report users information on service efforts and accomplishments—how well resources have been managed in providing services efficiently and economically, and effectively, in attaining planned goals. *Stewardship* relates to the federal government's accountability for the general welfare of the nation. To assess stewardship, report users need information about the "impact on the country of the government's operations and investments for the period and how, as a result, the government's and the nation's financial conditions have changed and may change in the future" (par. 134).

[6]OMB, *Bulletin 97-01*, "Formats and Instructions for the Form and Content of Agency Financial Statements" (Washington, DC: October 1996), par. VIII.

Finally, financial reporting should help users assess whether financial management *systems and controls* (internal accounting and administrative controls) "are adequate to ensure that (1) transactions are executed in accordance with budgetary and financial laws and other requirements, are consistent with the purposes authorized, and are recorded in accordance with federal accounting standards, (2) assets are properly safeguarded to deter fraud, waste, and abuse, and (3) performance measurement information is adequately supported" (par. 146).

Unlike the FASB and the GASB, which focus their standards on external financial reporting, the FASAB and its sponsors are concerned with both internal and external financial reporting. Accordingly, the FASAB has identified four major groups of users of federal financial reports: citizens, Congress, executives, and program managers. Given the broad role the FASAB has been assigned, future standards recommended by the Board may focus on cost accounting systems and controls, and the use of financial information in service efforts and accomplishments measures, as well as on financial accounting and reporting. The Memorandum of Understanding among the sponsors provides, however, that FASAB jurisdiction does not extend to agency budgetary accounting and the manner of controlling expenditures of budgetary resources.

Reporting Entity

SFFAC No. 2, "Entity and Display," provides additional conceptual guidance for federal agency financial reporting. *SFFAC No. 2:*

a. Specifies the types of entities that should provide financial reports.
b. Establishes guidelines for defining each type of reporting entity.
c. Identifies the types of financial statements each type of reporting entity should provide.
d. Suggests the types of information each type of statement should convey.[7]

As discussed in Chapter 9 for state and local governments, accountability reporting is facilitated by including as part of the reporting entity all separate entities for which there is financial accountability or financial interdependence. *SFFAC No. 2* discusses three perspectives from which the federal government can be viewed for accounting and reporting purposes: organizational, budget, and program. From the *organizational perspective*, the government is viewed as a collection of departments and agencies that provide governmental services. From the *budget perspective*, the government is viewed as a collection of expenditure (appropriations or funds) or receipt budget accounts. **Budget accounts** are generally quite broad in scope and are not the same as the Standard General Ledger accounts used for accounting purposes. A budget account may cover an entire organization or a group of budget accounts may aggregate to cover an organization. A budget account may also aggregate to form federal or trust funds as discussed later in this chapter. From

[7]Paraphrased from FASAB, *Report Number 1*, *Reporting Relevant Financial Information*, "Overview of Federal Accounting Concepts and Standards" (as of September 30, 1996) (Washington, DC: 1996), p. 11.

the *program perspective* the government is viewed as an aggregation of programs (or functions) and activities.

Most programs are financed by more than one budget account and some programs are administered by more than one organization. Similarly, some organizations administer multiple programs. Thus, in defining the reporting entity, it is necessary to consider the interacting nature of the perspectives. An entity must meet the following three criteria to be considered a reporting entity:

1. There is a management responsible for controlling and deploying resources, producing outputs and outcomes, executing the budget or a portion thereof (assuming that the entity is included in the budget), and held accountable for the entity's performance.
2. The entity's scope is such that its financial statements would provide a meaningful representation of operations and financial condition.
3. There are likely to be users of the financial statements who are interested in and could use the information in the statements to help them make resource allocation and other decisions and hold the entity accountable for its deployment and use of resources (par. 29).

To reduce uncertainty in identifying the lower level reporting entities, *SFFAC No. 2* presents two additional kinds of criteria to use in deciding what to include in the reporting entity. First is a *conclusive criterion*, which is an inherent conclusion that an organization should be included in the reporting entity. As noted in *SFFAC No. 2*, "Appearance in the Federal budget section currently entitled 'Federal Program by Agency and Account' is a conclusive criterion. Any organization, program, or budget account . . . should be considered part of the U.S. Federal Government, as well as part of the organization with which it appears" (par. 42). Second are *indicative criteria*, which either individually or collectively may indicate that an organization should be included in the reporting entity. These criteria, listed below, are similar to those established by the GASB and discussed in Chapter 9.

1. It exercises any sovereign power of the government to carry out Federal functions.
2. It is owned by the Federal Government, particularly if the ownership is of the organization and not just the property.
3. It is subject to the direct or continuing administrative control of the reporting entity, as revealed by such features as (1) the ability to select or remove the governing authority or the ability to designate management, particularly if there is to be a significant continuing relationship with the governing authority or management with respect to carrying out important public functions (in contrast to selections and designations in which there is little continuing communication with, or accountability to, the appointing official); (2) authority to review and modify or approve budget requests, budgetary adjustments, or amendments or rate or fee changes; (3) ability to veto, overrule, or modify governing body decisions

> or otherwise significantly influence normal operations; (4) authority to sign contracts as the contracting authority; (5) approval of hiring, reassignment, and removal of key personnel; (6) title to, ability to transfer title to, and/or exercise control over facilities and property; and (7) right to require audits that do more than just support the granting of contracts. (*SFFAC No. 2*, par. 44)

SFFAC No. 2 addresses also the nature of the financial statements that should be included in the financial report of a reporting entity and the recommended format and content of the financial statements. Thus, it provides clear and strong direction to the FASAB and its three sponsoring agencies in setting accounting and reporting standards for the federal government, and leaves little discretion to go down a different path.

Management's Discussion and Analysis

SFFAC No. 3, "Management's Discussion and Analysis," provides guidance for the MD&A included in the general purpose federal financial report (GPFFR). The MD&A is described as an "important vehicle for (1) communicating managers' insights about the reporting entity, (2) increasing the understandability and usefulness of the GPFFR, and (3) providing accessible information about the entity and its operations, service levels, successes, challenges, and future."[8] One difference between the FASAB's concept statement on the MD&A and the GASB's MD&A requirement in *Statement No. 34* is that federal agencies should address the reporting entity's performance goals and results in addition to financial activities.

Funds Used in Federal Accounting

FASAB's standards do not focus on fund accounting, but Congress regularly passes laws that create, define, and modify funds for various purposes. Fund accounting is needed for federal agencies to demonstrate compliance with requirements of legislation for which federal funds have been appropriated or otherwise authorized to carry out specific activities, and also for financial reporting.

Two general types of funds are found in federal government accounting: (1) those used to account for resources derived from the general taxation and revenue powers or from business operations of the government and (2) those used to account for resources held and managed by the government in the capacity of custodian or trustee. Six kinds of funds are specified within the two general types:

1. Funds derived from general taxing and revenue powers and from business operations.
   a. General Fund accounts.
   b. Special fund accounts.
   c. Revolving fund accounts.
   d. Management fund accounts.

---

[8]*Statement of Federal Financial Accounting Concepts No. 3*, "Management's Discussion and Analysis," Federal Accounting Standards Advisory Board, April 1999, p. i.

2. Funds held by the government in the capacity of custodian or trustee.
   a. Trust fund accounts.
   b. Deposit fund accounts.

General Fund. The General Fund is credited with all receipts that are not dedicated by law and is charged with payments out of appropriations of "any money in the Treasury not otherwise appropriated" and out of general borrowings.

Strictly speaking, there is only one General Fund in the entire federal government. The Bureau of Government Financial Operations of the Department of the Treasury accounts for the centralized cash balances (the cash is under the control of the Treasurer of the United States; cash accounts subsidiary to those of the Bureau of Government Financial Operations are maintained by the Treasurer), the appropriations control accounts, and unappropriated balances. On the books of an agency, each appropriation is treated as a fund with its own self-balancing group of accounts; these agency "appropriation funds" are subdivisions of *the* General Fund.

Special Funds. Receipt and expenditure accounts established to account for receipts of the government that are earmarked by law for a specific purpose, but that are not generated from a cycle of operations for which there is continuing authority to reuse such receipts (as is true for revolving funds), are classified as *special fund accounts* in federal usage. The term and its definition are very close to that of the classification "special revenue funds" used in accounting for state and local governments.

Revolving Funds. A revolving fund is credited with collections, primarily from other agencies and accounts, that are earmarked by law to carry out a cycle of business-type operations, in which the government is the owner of the activity. This type of fund is quite similar to internal service funds.

Management (Including Working Funds). These are funds in which there are merged monies derived from two or more appropriations, in order to carry out a common purpose or project, but not involving a cycle of operations. Management funds include consolidated working funds that are set up to receive (and subsequently disburse) advance payments, pursuant to law, from other agencies or bureaus.

Trust Funds. Trust funds are established to account for receipts that are held in trust for use in carrying out specific purposes and programs in accordance with agreement or statute. In distinction to revolving funds and special funds, the assets of trust funds are frequently held over a period of time and may be invested in order to produce revenue. For example, the assets of the Federal Old Age and Survivors Insurance Trust Fund are invested in U.S. securities.

The corpus of some trust funds is used in business-type operations. In such a case, the fund is called a *trust revolving fund*. The term "trust fund" is used by Congress to describe some funds that in state and local governmental accounting would be called special revenue funds. An example is the Highway Trust Fund. Other federal trust funds, such as those used to account for assets that belong to Native Americans, are true trust funds.

Deposit Funds. Combined receipt and expenditure accounts established to account for receipts held in suspense temporarily and later refunded or paid to some other fund, or receipts held by the government as a banker or agent for others and paid out at the discretion of the owner, are classified within the federal government as deposit fund accounts. They are similar in nature to the agency funds established for state and local governmental units.

Required Financial Reporting

OMB *Bulletin 97-01* specifies the form and content of financial statements for 24 major executive departments and agencies that have been designated as reporting entities. OMB *Bulletin 97-01* specifies that the *annual financial statement* of a reporting entity is comprised of "(1) an overview of the reporting entity, (2) principal statements and related notes, (3) required supplemental stewardship information, and (4) required supplemental information" (par. VI). These requirements are discussed briefly in the following paragraphs.

Overview of Reporting Entity

OMB *Bulletin 97-01* requires a brief narrative overview of the reporting entity, which should provide a "clear and concise description of the reporting entity and its mission, activities, program and financial results, and financial condition" (p. 11). The overview is also referred to as the Management Discussion and Analysis (MD&A). This requirement is intended to assist in the government-wide implementation of the Government Performance and Review Act (GPRA), which became effective in fiscal year 1999.

SFFAS No. 15 (April 1999) requires that an 58/58 MD&A be included in a federal agency's general purpose federal financial report as required supplementary information. The conceptual basis for the role and importance of this statement were described earlier in the chapter with the discussion of the three FASAB concepts statements. This standard requires MD&A to address the entity's mission and organizational structure; performance goals and results; financial statements; systems, controls, and legal compliance; and forward-looking information regarding the possible effects of currently known demands, risks, uncertainties, and trends.

Financial Statements

OMB *Bulletin 97-01* specifies essentially the same financial statements recommended by *SFFAC No. 2*. It also provides detailed descriptions and instructions for completing each part of each statement. These statements include a (1) Balance Sheet, (2) Statement of Net Cost, (3) Statement of Changes in Net Position,

Illustration 12–2

DEPARTMENT/AGENCY
REPORTING ENTITY
CONSOLIDATED BALANCE SHEET
AS OF SEPTEMBER 30, 19XX
(IN DOLLARS/THOUSANDS/MILLIONS)

	19xx	19xx
Assets		
Entity Assets:		
Intragovernmental:		
Fund Balance with Treasury (Note 2)	$ xxx	$ xxx
Investments (Note 4)	xxx	xxx
Accounts receivable, net (Note 5)	xxx	xxx
Interest receivable (net)	xxx	xxx
Other assets (Note 6)	xxx	xxx
Governmental:		
Investments (Note 4)	xxx	xxx
Accounts receivable, net (Note 5)	xxx	xxx
Interest receivable (net)	xxx	xxx
Credit program receivables and related foreclosed property, net (Note 7)	xxx	xxx
Cash and other monetary assets (Note 3)	xxx	xxx
Inventory and related property, net (Note 8)	xxx	xxx
General property, plant, and equipment, net (Note 9)	xxx	xxx
Other assets (Note 6)	xxx	xxx
Total Entity Assets	xxx	xxx
Nonentity Assets:		
Intragovernmental:		
Fund Balance with Treasury (Note 2)	xxx	xxx
Accounts receivable, net (Note 5)	xxx	xxx
Interest receivable (net)	xxx	xxx
Other assets (Note 6)	xxx	xxx
Governmental:		
Accounts receivable, net (Note 5)	xxx	xxx
Interest receivable (net)	xxx	xxx
Cash and other monetary assets (Note 3)	xxx	xxx
Other assets (Note 6)	xxx	xxx
Total Nonentity Assets	x,xxx	x,xxx
Total Assets	$x,xxx	$x,xxx

(4) Statement of Budgetary Resources, (5) Statement of Financing, and (6) Statement of Custodial Activity. Each of these statements is discussed briefly in the following paragraphs.

Illustration 12–2 (concluded)

	19xx	19xx
Liabilities		
Liabilities Covered by Budgetary Resources:		
Intragovernmental liabilities:		
Accounts payable	$ xxx	$ xxx
Interest payable	xxx	xxx
Other intragovernmental liabilities (Note 11)	xxx	xxx
Governmental liabilities:		
Accounts payable	xxx	xxx
Interest payable	xxx	xxx
Liabilities for loan guarantees (Note 7)	xxx	xxx
Lease liabilities (Note 12)	xxx	xxx
Pensions, other retirement benefits and other postemployment benefits (Note 13)	xxx	xxx
Insurance liabilities (Note 14)	xxx	xxx
Other governmental liabilities (Note 11)	xxx	xxx
Total Liabilities Covered by Budgetary Resources	x,xxx	x,xxx
Liabilities Not Covered by Budgetary Resources:		
Intragovernmental liabilities:		
Accounts payable	xxx	xxx
Debt (Note 10)	xxx	xxx
Other intragovernmental liabilities (Note 11)	xxx	xxx
Governmental liabilities:		
Accounts payable	xxx	xxx
Debt (Note 10)	xxx	xxx
Lease liabilities (Note 3)	xxx	xxx
Pensions, other retirement benefits and other postemployment benefits (Note 13)	xxx	xxx
Insurance liabilities (Note 14)	xxx	xxx
Other governmental liabilities (Note 11)	xxx	xxx
Total Liabilities Not Covered by Budgetary Resources	x,xxx	x,xxx
Total Liabilities	$x,xxx	$x,xxx
Net Position		
Unexpended Appropriations (Note 15)	$ xxx	$ xxx
Cumulative Results of Operations	xxx	xxx
Total Net Position	xxx	xxx
Total Liabilities and Net Position	$x,xxx	$x,xxx

Note: This statement is shown as presented in OMB *Bulletin 97-01*. Notes to Financial Statements are not provided.
Source: OMB, *Bulletin 97-01*, pp. 15–17.

Balance Sheet. An example Balance Sheet from OMB *Bulletin 97-01* is presented in Illustration 12–2. *Bulletin 97-01* permits agencies considerable latitude regarding the level of aggregation to be used in preparing the financial statements. Agencies can use either a single-column (consolidated) format or a multicolumn format displaying financial information for component units or lines of business. If consolidated reporting is used, *Bulletin 97-01* (p. 9) requires a separate column presenting the intraentity transactions (for example, eliminations of intercomponent unit receivables and payables) in the *consolidating* statements underlying the consolidated statements. If consolidated financial information is provided, comparative totals for the prior year must be presented for the Balance Sheet, the Statement of Budgetary Resources, and the Statement of Custodial Activity.

Assets. As shown in Illustration 12–2, *entity assets* are reported separately from *nonentity assets* and *intragovernmental assets* are reported separately from *governmental assets*. These are the asset classifications specified in *Statement of Federal Financial Accounting Standards (SFFAS) No. 1*. **Entity assets** are those the reporting entity has authority to use in its operations, whereas **nonentity assets** are held by the entity but are not available for the entity to spend. An example of a nonentity asset is federal income taxes collected by the Internal Revenue Service for the U.S. government. **Intragovernmental assets (liabilities)** are claims by (against) a reporting entity that arise from transactions between that entity and other reporting entities. **Governmental assets (liabilities)** arise from transactions of the federal government or an entity of the federal government with nonfederal entities.

SFFAS No. 1 provides specific standards relating to Cash, Fund Balance with Treasury, Accounts Receivable, Interest Receivable, and various other asset categories. In most federal agencies *Fund Balance with Treasury* is used rather than *Cash* to indicate that the agency has a claim against the U.S. Treasury on which it may draw to pay liabilities. Only a few large federal departments and agencies, such as the Department of Defense, are authorized to write and issue checks directly against their balances with the Treasury. Most departments and agencies must request that the Treasury issue checks to pay their liabilities. If a federal agency does have the right to maintain one or more bank accounts, bank balances would be reported as *Cash*.

Consistent with the manner in which business entities report inventories, *SFFAS No. 3*, "Accounting for Inventory and Related Property," distinguishes inventory from consumable supplies. Inventory is defined as "tangible personal property that is (1) held for sale, (2) in the process of production for sale, or (3) to be consumed in the production of goods for sale or in the provision of services for a fee" (p. 4). Inventory may be valued at either historical cost or latest acquisition cost. Supplies to be consumed in normal operations are reported as *operating materials and supplies*. *SSFAS No. 3* also defines several additional types of inventory or related property: (1) stockpile materials, (2) seized and forfeited property, (3) foreclosed property, and (4) goods held under price support and stabilization programs. Discussion of these other types is beyond the scope of this text.

SSFAS No. 6, "Accounting for Property, Plant, and Equipment" establishes standards for several categories of property, plant, and equipment (PP&E).

1. **General PP&E.** PP&E used to provide general government goods and services.

2. **Federal mission PP&E.** PP&E such as military weapon systems and space exploration equipment or PP&E that exhibits other characteristics set by the FASAB.[9]
3. **Heritage assets.** PP&E such as the Washington Monument that possess educational, cultural, or natural characteristics.
4. **Stewardship land.** Land other than that included in general PP&E (for example, national parks).

Categories (2), (3), and (4) are collectively referred to as **stewardship PP&E.** *SSFAS No. 6* provides that for these assets, acquisition, replacement, construction, reconstruction, and improvements will be reported as a cost (i.e., expense) in the period incurred. They are not reported on the Balance Sheet and are not depreciated. Category (1) PP&E are capitalized at acquisition cost and, except for land, are depreciated over their useful lives.

Liabilities. *SSFAS No. 1* provides specific accounting standards for Accounts Payable, Interest Payable, and Other Current Liabilities. OMB *Bulletin 97-01* provides additional guidance on reporting liabilities. For example, it requires separate Balance Sheet reporting of liabilities covered by budgetary resources (funded) and liabilities not covered by budgetary resources (unfunded). *Liabilities covered by budgetary resources* are those for which monies have been made available either through congressional appropriations or current earnings of the entity. *Liabilities not covered by budgetary resources* result from the receipt of goods or services in the current or prior periods but for which monies have not yet been made available through congressional appropriations or current earnings of the entity. Examples of the latter are liabilities for accrued leave, capital leases, and pensions.

SFFAS No. 5, "Accounting for Liabilities of the Federal Government," establishes standards for liabilities not covered in *SFFAS No. 1* and *No. 2*. The Statement defines a *liability* as "a probable future outflow or other sacrifice of resources as a result of past transactions or events" (par. 19). *SFFAS No. 5* provides the following recognition criteria for liabilities arising from the transactions or events indicated:

1. *Exchange transactions.* Recognize the liability when one party receives goods or services in exchange for a promise to provide money or other resources in the future.
2. *Nonexchange transactions* (for example, grants and entitlements). Recognize a liability for any unpaid amounts due at the end of the fiscal period.
3. *Government-related events* (nontransactions-based events that involve interaction between federal entities and their environment; for example,

[9]The FASAB has issued an exposure draft of a standard that would amend *SFFAS No. 6*. The proposed standard would restrict use of the federal mission category to certain national defense assets. FASAB, *Exposure Draft*, "Amendments to Accounting for Property, Plant, and Equipment" (FASAB, Washington, DC, February 1998).

damage to private property). Recognize a liability when the event occurs if the future outflow of resources is probable and measurable.

4. *Government-acknowledged events* (events for which the government *chooses* to acknowledge responsibility. For example, damage from a natural disaster). Recognize liability when the government formally acknowledges responsibility for an event and a nonexchange or exchange transaction has occurred.
5. *Contingencies*. Generally disclosed in the notes or, in some cases such as contingencies related to government-acknowledged events, not disclosed at all.
6. *Capital leases*. Criteria for a capital lease are essentially the same as those specified by the FASB for commercial entities and the GASB for state and local governmental entities (see Chapter 5 of this text). A liability should be recognized in the amount of the present value of the rental and other minimum lease payments.
7. *Federal debt* (for example, U.S. Treasury bonds). Recognize a liability when an exchange transaction occurs between involved parties. Original issue premiums and discounts are amortized using the effective interest method.
8. *Pensions, other retirement benefits, and other postemployment benefits*. Recognize an expense at time employees' services are rendered. Any unfunded portion of cost calculated using the "Aggregate Entry Age Normal Cost" method should be reported as a liability.
9. *Insurance and guarantee programs* (other than social insurance and loan guarantee programs). Recognize a liability for unpaid claims incurred as a result of insured events that have already occurred. (Note: Loan guarantee program liabilities are covered by *SFFAS No. 2*. Reporting of social insurance programs, such as social security, is covered in *SFFAS No. 8*, "Supplementary Stewardship Reporting.")

SFFAS No. 5 also requires disclosure in the Notes to the Financial Statements of the condition and estimated cost to remedy deferred maintenance on PP&E. In addition, it provides standards for measurement and recognition of expenses and liabilities related to environmental cleanup and closure costs from removing general PP&E from service.

Net Position. OMB *Bulletin 97-01* requires that the fund balances of the entity's funds be reported in the Balance Sheet as **Net Position.** The components of net position are (1) **Unexpended Appropriations,** the amount of unexpended budget authority appropriated by Congress, both available and unavailable, and (2) **Cumulative Results of Operations,** the net difference between expenses/losses and financing sources, including appropriations, revenues, and gains, since the inception of the activity. Effective with fiscal year 1998, Cumulative Results of Operations also includes the net investment of the government in the reporting entity. The net investment of the government in the reporting entity includes the acquisition cost of capitalized fixed assets financed by appropriations; the additional investment in a revolving fund to commence operations or begin a new activity; less the reduction in investment due to depreciation, amortization, sales or exchanges, donations, other disposals, the return of initial investment to an investor, or transfer to another entity or revolving fund. Cumulative Results of Operations would also include any other items that would affect the net position, including, for example, the fair market value of donated assets, plus any costs incurred to place the donated assets in use, and assets (net of liabilities) transferred to or from other federal entities without reimbursement.

Statement of Net Cost. Illustration 12–3 presents an example Consolidating Statement of Net Cost. This statement is intended to show the components of the net cost of the reporting entity's operations, both for the entity as a whole and for

Illustration 12–3

REPORTING ENTITY
DEPARTMENT/AGENCY
CONSOLIDATING STATEMENT OF NET COST
FOR THE YEAR ENDING SEPTEMBER 30, 19XX
(IN DOLLARS/THOUSANDS/MILLIONS)

	Suborganization A	*Suborganization B*	*Suborganization C*	*Intraagency Eliminations*	*Consolidated Totals*
Costs:					
Crosscutting Programs:					
Program A:					
Intragovernmental	$xxx	—	$xxx	$(xx)	$xxx
With the public	xxx	—	—	—	xxx
Total	xxx	—	xx	(xx)	xxx
Less earned revenues	(xx)	—	(xx)	xx	(xx)
Net program costs	xxx	—	xx	(xx)	xxx
Other programs (Note XX):					
Program B:	—	xx	—	—	xx
Program C:	—	xx	—	—	xx
Program D:	—	xx	—	—	xx
Program E:	—	—	xx	—	xx
Program F:	—	—	xx	—	xx
Program G:	xx	—	—	—	xx
Program H:	xx	—	—	—	xx
Other programs:	—	—	xx	—	xx
Cost not assigned to programs	xx	xx	xx	—	xx
Less earned revenues not attributed to programs	—	—	(xx)	—	xx
Deferred maintenance (Note X)					
Net Cost of Operations	$xxx	$xxx	$xxx	$(xx)	$xxx

Source: OMB, *Bulletin 97-01*, p. 25.

Illustration 12–4

DEPARTMENT/AGENCY
REPORTING ENTITY
CONSOLIDATING STATEMENT OF CHANGES IN NET POSITION
FOR THE YEARS ENDED SEPTEMBER 30, 19XX
(IN DOLLARS/THOUSANDS/MILLIONS)

	Suborganization A	*Suborganization B*	*Suborganization C*	*Intraagency Eliminations*	*Consolidated Totals*
Net Cost of Operations	$xxx	$xxx	$xxx	$xxx	$xxx
Financing Sources (other than exchange revenues):					
Appropriations Used	xxx	xxx	xxx	xxx	xxx
Taxes (and other nonexchange revenues)	xxx	xxx	xxx	xxx	xxx
Donations (nonexchange revenue)	xxx	xxx	xxx	xxx	xxx
Imputed financing	xxx	xxx	xxx	xxx	xxx
Transfers-in	xxx	xxx	xxx	xxx	xxx
Transfers-out	(xxx)	(xxx)	(xxx)	(xxx)	(xxx)
Net Results of Operations	xxx	xxx	xxx	xxx	xxx
Prior-Period Adjustments	xxx	xxx	xxx	xxx	xxx
Net Change in Cumulative Results of Operations	xxx	xxx	xxx	xxx	xxx
Increase (Decrease) in Unexpended Appropriations	xxx	xxx	xxx	xxx	xxx
Change in Net Position	xxx	xxx	xxx	xxx	xxx
Net Position—Beginning of Period	xxx	xxx	xxx	xxx	xxx
Net Position—End of Period	$xxx	$xxx	$xxx	$xxx	$xxx

Source: OMB, *Bulletin 97-01*, p. 30.

each of its responsibility centers or segments. If the reporting entity has a complex organizational structure, it may need to provide supporting schedules in the Notes to the Financial Statements to provide net cost information for its major programs and activities.

Statement of Changes in Net Position. An example Consolidating Statement of Changes in Net Position is shown in Illustration 12–4. The purpose of this statement is to communicate all changes in the reporting entity's net position, as well as that for major responsibility segments (organizational subunits or major programs and activities). Net cost of operations is obtained from the bottom line of the Statement of Net Cost (see Illustration 12–3) and includes gross costs less exchange (earned) revenues. The net cost of operations less nonexchange (nonearned) financing sources provides the *net results from operations*—the equivalent of net income. Further additions or deductions, as appropriate, of prior-period

Illustration 12–5

DEPARTMENT/AGENCY
REPORTING ENTITY
STATEMENT OF BUDGETARY RESOURCES
FOR THE YEARS ENDED SEPTEMBER 30, 19XX
(IN DOLLARS/THOUSANDS/MILLIONS)

	19xx	*19xx*
Budgetary Resources:		
Budget authority (line 1)	$xxx	$xxx
Unobligated balances—beginning of period (line 2A)	xxx	xxx
Spending authority from offsetting collections (line 3)	xxx	xxx
Adjustments (lines 4–6)	xxx	xxx
Total budgetary resources (line 7)	$xxx	$xxx
Status of Budgetary Resources:		
Obligations incurred (line 8)	$xxx	$xxx
Unobligated balances—available (line 9)	xxx	xxx
Unobligated balances—not available (line 10)	xxx	xxx
Total, status of budgetary resources (line 11)	$xxx	$xxx
Outlays:		
Obligations incurred (line 8)	$xxx	$xxx
Less: Spending authority from offsetting collections and adjustments (lines 3A, B, D, & 4A)	(xxx)	(xxx)
Obligated balance, net—beginning of period (line 12)	xxx	xxx
Obligated balance transferred, net (line 13)	xxx	xxx
Less: Obligated balance, net—end of period (line 14)	(xxx)	(xxx)
Total outlays (line 15)	$xxx	$xxx

Source: OMB, *Bulletin 97-01*, p. 33.

adjustments (due to material errors or accounting changes), change in cumulative results of operations, and unexpended appropriations comprise the total change in net position.

Statement of Budgetary Resources. The Statement of Budgetary Resources (see Illustration 12–5) presents the availability of budgetary resources and the status of those resources at year-end. OMB *Circular A-34*, "Instructions on Budget Execution," provides the definitions and guidance for budgetary accounting and reporting. As shown in Illustration 12–5, the equation for this statement is Budgetary resources = Status of budgetary resources. Available **Budgetary Resources** includes new budgetary authority for the period plus unobligated budgetary authority carried over from the prior period and offsetting collections, if any, and plus/minus any budgetary adjustments. The *Status of Budgetary Resources* section consists of obligations

Illustration 12–6

DEPARTMENT/AGENCY
REPORTING ENTITY
STATEMENT OF FINANCING
FOR THE YEAR ENDED SEPTEMBER 30, 19XX
(IN DOLLARS/THOUSANDS/MILLIONS)

Obligations and Nonbudgetary Resources:		
Obligations incurred	$xxx	
Less: Spending authority for offsetting collections and adjustments	xxx	
Donations not in the budget	xxx	
Financing imputed for cost subsidies	xxx	
Transfers-in (out)	xxx	
Exchange revenue not in the budget	xxx	
Other	xxx	
Total Obligations, as Adjusted, and Nonbudgetary Resources		$xxx
Resources That Do Not Fund Net Cost of Operations:		
Change in amount of goods, services, and benefits ordered but not yet received or provided	(xxx)	
Costs capitalized on the Balance Sheet	(xxx)	
Financing sources that fund costs of prior periods	(xxx)	
Other	(xxx)	
Total Resources That Do Not Fund Net Cost of Operations		(xxx)
Costs That Do Not Require Resources:		
Depreciation and amortization	xxx	
Revaluation of assets and liabilities	xxx	
Other	xxx	
Total Costs That Do Not Require Resources		xxx
Financing Sources Yet to Be Provided		xxx
Net Cost of Operations		$xxx

Source: OMB, *Bulletin 97-01*, p. 35.

incurred (that is, budget authority expended and amounts reserved for undelivered orders) plus any current budgetary authority that is still available to finance operations of the current period (Unobligated balances—available, line 9 in Illustration 12–5) or those of prior periods (Unobligated balances—not available, line 10). The lower portion of the Statement of Budgetary Resources reconciles obligations incurred during the period to total budgetary outlays for the period, after adjusting for offsetting collections and budgetary adjustments, and the change during the year in obligations carried forward.

Statement of Financing. Another required statement is the Statement of Financing (see Illustration 12–6). This statement reconciles the budget-based information in the Statement of Budgetary Resources to the accrual-based *net cost of operations*

Illustration 12–7

DEPARTMENT/AGENCY
REPORTING ENTITY
STATEMENT OF CUSTODIAL ACTIVITY
FOR THE YEARS ENDED SEPTEMBER 30, 19XX
(IN DOLLARS/THOUSANDS/MILLIONS)

	19xx	*19xx*
Sources of Collections:		
Cash collections (by type of tax or duty)	$xxx	$xxx
Less refunds and other payments	(xxx)	(xxx)
Net collections	xxx	xxx
Accrual adjustment	xxx	xxx
Total revenue	xxx	xxx
Disposition of Collections:		
Transferred to others net of refunds (by recipient)	xxx	xxx
Increase (decrease) in amounts to be transferred	xxx	xxx
Retained by the entity	xxx	xxx
Total disposition of revenue	xxx	xxx
Net Custodial Activity	$ 0	$ 0

Source: OMB, *Bulletin 97-01,* p. 38.

information in the Statement of Net Costs. Total budgetary and nonbudgetary resources available to fund current-period operations are reported in the upper section captioned *Obligations and Nonbudgetary Resources*. The *Resources That Do Not Fund Net Cost of Operations* section essentially deducts items that were included in sources or uses of budgetary resources, but were not included as part of the *net cost of operations* on the accrual basis. The third section, *Costs That Do Not Require Resources*, are items that would have been included in the measurement of the net cost of operations but that did not require financing. The final section, *Financing Sources Yet to Be Provided*, would typically be required for an increase in unfunded liabilities, such as unfunded annual leave. An accrual for annual leave would have been included in the net cost of operations, but not as an obligation incurred for budgetary purposes. Of course, this item would be deducted in a future period when the leave is funded as *financing sources that fund costs of prior periods* in the third section.

Statement of Custodial Activity. OMB *Bulletin 97-01* requires entities that "collect nonexchange revenue for the General Fund of the Treasury, a trust fund, or other recipient entities" (p. 39) to prepare a Statement of Custodial Activity (see Illustration 12–7). This statement usually would be required of agencies that collect taxes or duties, such as the Internal Revenue Service or the U.S. Customs Service (OMB *Bulletin 97-01*, p. 39). As shown in Illustration 12–7, the Statement of

Custodial Activity essentially reports on the agency's fiduciary responsibility to account for how much has been collected and accrued, and how the monies were distributed.

Required Supplemental Information

SFFAS No. 8, "Supplementary Stewardship Reporting," requires that information on *Stewardship Property, Plant, and Equipment* (heritage assets, federal mission PP&E, and stewardship land, described earlier in this chapter) be disclosed to "highlight their long-term-benefit nature and to demonstrate accountability over them" (*SFFAS No. 8*, Summary). OMB *Bulletin 97-01* requires that the costs related to stewardship PP&E be recognized on the face of the Statement of Net Costs or be disclosed in the Notes to the Financial Statements. Disclosures are also required about deferred maintenance for both general and stewardship PP&E.

Information about *stewardship investments*, such as the amount of annual investments and description of major programs related to these investments, must also be disclosed. **Stewardship investments** are beneficial investments of the government in such items as nonfederal physical property (property financed by the federal government but owned by state or local governments), human capital, and research and development. In addition, pursuant to applicable federal accounting standards, *Bulletin 97-01* discusses the required disclosures about environmental cleanup costs, detail of budgetary resources and obligations, and incidental amounts of custodial collections and distributions that may not warrant separate reporting in a Statement of Custodial Activity.

Accounting for Social Insurance

SRAS No. 17 (August 1999) presents accounting standards for several federal social insurance programs: Social Security, Medicare and Supplementary Medical Insurance (Part B), Railroad Retirement benefits, Black Lung benefits, and Unemployment Insurance. In general, a liability is recognized when payments are due and payable to beneficiaries or service providers, and supplementary stewardship information is required to facilitate assessing long-term sustainability of programs and the nation's ability to raise resources from future program participants to pay for benefits proposed to present participants.

The FASAB acknowledges that although this standard is a major step forward in federal financial reporting, there is much more work to do in properly accounting for social insurance. Social insurance is a complex and unique blend of nonexchange transactions, such as annual governmental assistance programs, and exchange transactions, such as long-term pension programs. The FASAB decided in earlier studies on liabilities (*SFFAS No. 5*) and Supplementary Stewardship Reporting (*SFFAS No. 8*) that social insurance programs were unique enough to require a separate project. Required supplementary information includes long-range cash-flow projections, projections of the ratio of amounts paid into and out of the programs, and actuarial values of benefits and contributions/income from or on behalf of participants (both current and future). Note that this is a *recommended* standard and has no authoritative standing until approved by the three principals, at which time it will be called an SFFAS, rather than an SRAS.

Dual-Track Accounting System

Financial reports of federal agencies must be based on historical costs to indicate whether an entity has complied with laws and regulations (e.g., 31 U.S.C. §1341). Congressional policy, as expressed in 31 U.S.C. §3512 and the Federal Financial Management Improvement Act of 1996, calls for using cost information in budgeting and in managing operations. This law also provides for using cost-based budgets, at such time as may be determined by the President, in developing requests for appropriations. This law has not been implemented because of deficient cost accounting systems. Federal agencies are struggling to implement *SFFAS No. 4* and the Government Performance Review Act, both of which require more cost information than some agencies currently produce. All departments and agencies, therefore, should have budget and accounting systems that have the capability to produce cost-based budgets. In this context, cost is the value of goods and services used or consumed by a government agency within a given period, regardless of when they were ordered, received, or paid for. In any given year, the obligations incurred may be less than, equal to, or greater than the costs recognized for that period, due to changes in inventories, obligations, and so on. At the completion of a program, however, obligations and costs are identical.

The accounting system of a federal agency must provide information needed for financial management as well as information needed to demonstrate that agency managers have complied with budgetary and other legal requirements. Accordingly, federal agency accounting is based on a *dual-track system;* one track being a self-balancing set of *proprietary* accounts intended to provide information for agency management, and the other track being the self-balancing set of *budgetary* accounts needed (1) to assure that available budgetary resources and authority are not overexpended or overobligated and (2) to facilitate standardized budgetary reporting requirements. The dual-track system is not likely to change in the near future since the FASAB's role specifically excludes budgetary accounting. Illustration 12–8 summarizes key differences between budgetary and proprietary track accounting in terms of the timing of the recognition of events and transactions. The use of the dual-track system is illustrated in the next section.

Illustrative Transactions and Entries[10]

The basic budgetary authority for a federal agency can come from many different sources. Only one of those sources is illustrated here—basic operating appropriations. The flow of budgetary authority generally follows a sequence of events described as follows:

1. The Congressional **appropriation** is enacted into law and provides budget authority to fund an agency's operations for the year.

[10]The illustrative journal entries shown in this section are modeled on the account titles prescribed by the U.S. Government Standard General Ledger, except that we have added fiscal year designations after certain accounts for instructional purposes. The financial statements that follow are based on those specified by OMB *Bulletin No. 97-01*.

Illustration 12–8 Summary of Key Differences between Budgetary and Proprietary Accounting in Recognition of Events That Constitute Transactions

Budgetary Accounting	*Proprietary Accounting*
Entries are made for commitment of funds in advance of preparing orders to procure goods and services.	Entries are not made for commitments.
Entries are made for obligation of funds at the time goods and services are ordered.	Entries are not made for obligations.
Entries are made to expend appropriations when goods and services chargeable to the appropriation are received, regardless of when they are used and regardless of when they are paid for.	Goods and services that will last more than a year and otherwise meet the criteria to qualify as assets are capitalized and expensed when consumed, regardless of what appropriation funded them and when they are paid for.
Entries are only made against an appropriation for transactions funded by the appropriation.	Goods and services consumed in the current period for which payment is to be made from one or more subsequent appropriations is recognized as an expense in the current period.
Entries are not made against an appropriation for transactions not funded by the appropriation.	Goods and services consumed in the current period but paid for in prior periods are expensed in the current period.

Source: U.S. General Accounting Office, *GAO Accounting Guide: Basic Topics Relating to Appropriations and Reimbursables* (Washington, DC: GAO, 1990), p. 3–2.

2. An **apportionment,** usually quarterly, is approved by the Office of Management and Budget and may be used by the agency to procure goods and services for the quarter.
3. The head of the agency or his designee authorizes an **allotment** of the apportionment for procurement of goods and services.
4. Authorized agency employees reserve allotted budget authority in the estimated amount of an order as a **commitment** prior to the actual ordering of goods and services.
5. **Obligation** of the allotment occurs when a formal order is placed for acquisition of goods and services, charging the allotment with the latest estimate of the cost of goods or services ordered.
6. An **expended appropriation** occurs when goods or services have been received.

It should be noted that the term *expended appropriation* means the budget authority has been used and is no longer available to provide for goods and services. It does

Illustration 12–9 Relationship among Budgetary Accounts

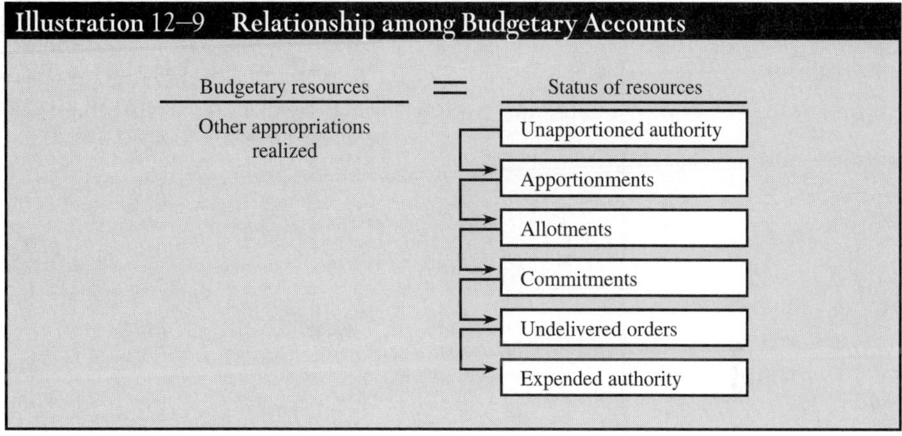

not necessarily mean that cash has been disbursed; it may be that only a liability has been incurred. A *commitment* (item 4 above) does not legally encumber an appropriation, but its use is recommended for effective planning and fund control. Some agencies, however, use commitments only for certain spending categories.[11]

As shown in Illustration 12–9, the full amount of an agency's appropriation for the year is reported as a budgetary resource that, at a given point during the period, is distributed among the budgetary accounts shown under "Status of Resources." As discussed above, and in the following illustrative transactions, budgetary authority normally flows down the accounts, culminating ultimately in the expending of authority. If the agency whose September 30, 2001, Post-Closing Trial Balance is shown in Illustration 12–10 receives from Congress a one-year appropriation for fiscal year 2002 (FY 2002) in the amount of $2,500,000, the Treasury's Bureau of Government Financial Operations would prepare a formal notice to the agency after the appropriation act has been signed by the President. The following entries would be made in the agency accounts:

	Debits	*Credits*
1a. *Budgetary:*		
Other Appropriations Realized—2002	2,500,000	
Unapportioned Authority—2002		2,500,000
1b. *Proprietary:*		
Fund Balance with Treasury—2002	2,500,000	
Unexpended Appropriations—2002		2,500,000

The *Other Appropriations Realized* account is used in the U.S. Standard General Ledger to distinguish basic operating appropriations from specific appropriation authority that earmarks appropriations for specific purposes.

[11]For a discussion of these commitments, see U.S. General Accounting Office, GAO *Accounting Guide: Basic Topics Relating to Appropriations and Reimbursables* (Washington, DC: GAO, 1990),p. 2–3.

Illustration 12–10

FEDERAL AGENCY
POST-CLOSING TRIAL BALANCE
AS OF SEPTEMBER 30, 2001

	Debits	Credits
Proprietary Accounts:		
Fund Balance with Treasury—2001	$ 675,000	
Operating Materials and Supplies	610,000	
Equipment	3,000,000	
Accumulated Depreciation on Equipment		$ 600,000
Accounts Payable		275,000
Unexpended Appropriations—2001		400,000
Cumulative Results of Operations		3,010,000
	$4,285,000	$4,285,000
Budgetary Accounts:		
Other Appropriations Realized—2001	$ 400,000	
Undelivered Orders—2001		$ 400,000
	$ 400,000	$ 400,000

When the Office of Management and Budget approves the quarterly apportionment, the agency would be notified. Assuming the OMB approved apportionments of $2,500,000 during FY 2002, the agency would record the apportionments as follows:[12]

	Debits	Credits
2. *Budgetary:*		
Unapportioned Authority—2002	2,500,000	
Apportionments—2002		2,500,000

If, during FY 2002, the agency head allotted to subunits within the agency the entire apportionment, the event would be recorded in the agency accounts in the following manner:

	Debits	Credits
3. *Budgetary:*		
Apportionments—2002	2,500,000	
Allotments—2002		2,500,000

All three entries—for the annual appropriation, for the apportionment by the OMB, and for the agency allotments—would be made as of October 1, the first day of fiscal year 2002, although in some years the appropriation bill might not have been actually enacted by that date. Fiscal year 2002 runs through September 30,

[12]OMB ordinarily does not have authority to withhold apportionments. If OMB does withhold a portion of an apportionment, special accounts would be used. This requirement is beyond the overview scope of our coverage here.

2002. The substance of the three entries is that agency managers had obligational spending authority for the year totaling $2,500,000 to finance agency operations. As discussed in Chapters 3 and 4 for state and local government accounting, federal agencies are legally constrained to manage the activities of the agency so they do not exceed their obligational authority. It should also be noted that if the OMB should withhold any portion of the annual appropriations, that amount would not be available to the agency. Further, for single-year appropriations, any apportionments and allotments not expended or obligated ordinarily must be returned to the U.S. Treasury at the end of the fiscal year.

Operations of the example agency for FY 2002 are summarized in the following journal entries:

Commitments were recorded during FY 2002 in the amount of $1,150,000.

	Debits	*Credits*
4. *Budgetary:*		
Allotments—2002	1,150,000	
Commitments—2002		1,150,000

Purchase orders and contracts for goods and services were issued in the amount of $1,144,000 during the year.

5. *Budgetary:*		
Commitments—2002	1,144,000	
Undelivered Orders—2002		1,144,000

Checks for Accounts Payable as of October 1 were requested from the Treasury. The Accounts Payable were for materials received in fiscal year 2001 in the amount of $90,000 and equipment received in the amount of $185,000. This event does not reduce the agency's Fund Balance with Treasury until the checks are actually issued by the Treasury. Instead, most agencies would credit the account *Disbursements in Transit* until notified by the Treasury that the requested checks have been issued. Disbursements in Transit is a current liability account since liabilities to vendors and creditors cannot be considered settled until the checks have actually been issued. If this agency had been one of the few with authority to issue checks directly, then Fund Balance with Treasury would have been credited immediately. Since this agency is not assumed to have check-writing authority, the following entry would be made:

6. *Proprietary:*		
Accounts Payable	275,000	
Disbursements in Transit—2001		275,000

The agency received notification from the Treasury that the checks requested in Transaction 6 had been issued. This notification would be recorded as:

7. *Proprietary:*		
Disbursements in Transit—2001	275,000	
Fund Balance with Treasury—2001		275,000

Goods and equipment ordered in FY 2001 (prior fiscal year) are reported in Illustration 12–10 in the Net Position account, Unexpended Appropriations—

2001, a proprietary account, as amounting to $400,000. A budgetary account Undelivered Orders—2001 also exists in the same amount, as does its offsetting account Other Appropriations Realized—2001. (All other budgetary accounts for 2001 were closed at the end of that fiscal year because all unobligated appropriation authority expired at year-end.) Assuming all the goods and equipment ordered in 2001 were received during the first quarter of FY 2002, one entry is necessary in the budgetary accounts to show that fiscal 2001 obligations are now liquidated and that the prior-year appropriation is expended in the same amount. Entries in proprietary accounts are required to record the debit to Unexpended Appropriations—2001 and the offsetting credit to the Appropriations Used account,[13] and debits to asset accounts and a credit to Accounts Payable. These entries are:

	Debits	Credits
8a. *Budgetary:*		
Undelivered Orders—2001	400,000	
Expended Authority—2001		400,000
8b. *Proprietary:*		
Operating Materials and Supplies	150,000	
Equipment	250,000	
Accounts Payable		400,000
Unexpended Appropriations—2001	400,000	
Appropriations Used		400,000

Operating materials and supplies were received from suppliers during FY 2002 at an actual cost of $1,010,000, for which Undelivered Orders—2002 had been recorded in the estimated amount of $1,005,000. Budgetary track and proprietary track entries for these transactions are shown in Entries 9a and 9b. Because the actual cost of materials and supplies exceeded the estimated amount recorded previously as Undelivered Orders—2002, the $5,000 excess must be debited to Allotments—2002 to record the additional expenditure of obligational authority.

	Debits	Credits
9a. *Budgetary:*		
Undelivered Orders—2002	1,005,000	
Allotments—2002	5,000	
Expended Authority—2002		1,010,000
9b. *Proprietary:*		
Operating Materials and Supplies	1,010,000	
Accounts Payable		1,010,000
Unexpended Appropriations—2002	1,010,000	
Appropriations Used		1,010,000

Payrolls for FY 2002 amounted to $1,188,000. Utilities in the amount of $120,000 were also approved for payment during the year. (The agency does not record commitments for payrolls and other recurring operating expenses.) Checks

[13]Until FY 1998, such capitalized amounts would have been reported in Invested Capital. These amounts, as well as the net effects of operations, are now reported in the net position account, Cumulative Results of Operations, the account to which Appropriations Used is closed at fiscal year-end. Use of the Invested Capital account has been discontinued.

totaling $1,308,000 were requested from the Treasury for these expenses. The debit in the first proprietary track entry is to the control account Operating/Program Expenses. Obviously, each agency would have a subsidiary expense ledger or more detailed expense accounts in their general ledger tailored to its specific needs. The required entries are:

	Debits	Credits
10a. *Budgetary:*		
Allotments—2002	1,308,000	
Expended Authority—2002		1,308,000
10b. *Proprietary:*		
Operating/Program Expenses	1,308,000	
Disbursements in Transit—2002		1,308,000
Unexpended Appropriations—2002	1,308,000	
Appropriations Used		1,308,000

Materials and supplies used in the operating activities during FY 2002 amounted to $1,620,000. The entries would be:

	Debits	Credits
11. *Proprietary:*		
Operating/Program Expenses	1,620,000	
Operating Materials and Supplies		1,620,000

Accounts Payable in the amount of $1,410,000 (see Entries 8b and 9b) were approved for payment and checks were requested from the Treasury. Of this amount, $400,000 will be charged against the FY 2001 Fund Balance with Treasury and $1,010,000 against the FY 2002 Fund Balance with Treasury. The required entry is:

	Debits	Credits
12. *Proprietary:*		
Accounts Payable	1,410,000	
Disbursements in Transit—2001		400,000
Disbursements in Transit—2002		1,010,000

The agency was notified by the Treasury that checks in the amount of $2,718,000 (including $400,000 for Accounts Payable arising from fiscal year 2001—see Entry 12) had been issued during FY 2002. Of the $2,318,000 charged against the FY 2002 Fund Balance with Treasury, $1,010,000 was for operating materials and supplies (see Entry 9b), $1,188,000 was for payrolls, and $120,000 was for utilities expense.

	Debits	Credits
13. *Proprietary:*		
Disbursements in Transit—2001	400,000	
Disbursements in Transit—2002	2,318,000	
Fund Balance with Treasury—2001		400,000
Fund Balance with Treasury—2002		2,318,000

Adjusting Entries

In order to prepare accrual-based financial statements, the following items were taken into account: (1) payroll accrued for the last week of the fiscal year is computed to be $27,000 and (2) invoices or receiving reports for goods received, but for which payment has not yet been approved, totaled $105,000, of which $36,000 worth has been used in operations and $69,000 is in ending inventory. Because the obligations for the items in (1) and (2) have become certain in amount and relevant expense accounts or inventory accounts can be charged, as illustrated below, the amounts should be shown in the financial statements as current liabilities. It is assumed that the goods received had been previously obligated in the amount of $105,000, but no commitment or obligation had been recorded for the accrued payroll. The required entries are:

	Debits	Credits
14a. *Budgetary:*		
Allotments—2002	27,000	
Undelivered Orders—2002	105,000	
Expended Authority—2002		132,000
14b. *Proprietary:*		
Operating/Program Expenses	63,000	
Operating Materials and Supplies	69,000	
Accounts Payable		105,000
Accrued Funded Payroll and Benefits		27,000
Unexpended Appropriations—2002	132,000	
Appropriations Used		132,000

Depreciation of equipment was computed as $300,000 for FY 2002. Inasmuch as depreciation is not an expense chargeable against the appropriation, the accrual of depreciation expense does not affect any of the appropriation, allotment, or obligation accounts. However, it is recorded as in business accounting to measure the cost of activities on an accrual basis. The debit to Accumulated Depreciation reduces the book value of the equipment.

	Debits	Credits
15. *Proprietary:*		
Depreciation and Amortization	300,000	
Accumulated Depreciation on Equipment		300,000

Although not illustrated here, federal agencies also accrue some expenses such as accrued annual leave that will be funded by future-period appropriations. These unfunded accrued expenses require entries in the proprietary track, but require no entries in the budgetary track. The effect of these unfunded expenses is to reduce the balance of Cumulative Results of Operations since the expenses are not offset by a financing source.

Illustrative Financial Statements

After entries illustrated above have been made, the federal agency Balance Sheet at the end of FY 2002 and the other required statements can be prepared. As discussed earlier in this chapter, OMB *Bulletin 97-01* prescribes the form and content of financial statements required to be prepared under the Chief Financial Officers (CFO) Act of 1990 and the Federal Financial Management Improvement Act of 1996 by most executive agencies and departments. The content of each agency's *annual financial statement* and examples of the basic financial statements were provided as Illustrations 12–2 through 12–7, earlier in this chapter.

Basic financial statements are shown in Illustrations 12–12 through 12–15 for the simple federal agency whose transactions were just discussed. These statements are a Balance Sheet, Statement of Changes in Net Position, Statement of Budgetary Resources, and a Statement of Financing. Since the example federal agency used in this chapter had no material custodial activities, no Statement of Custodial Activities is needed. Also, no supplemental financial and management information is provided. In the case of an actual federal entity, such as the Department of Defense, for example, there would be numerous funds, programs, and organizational units, and thus a need for consolidating and consolidated financial statements, as well as required supplemental information.

Prior to preparing the illustrative financial statements, as of and for the fiscal year ended September 30, 2002, lapsed budgetary authority should be closed and a pre-closing general ledger trial balance should be prepared such as that presented in Illustration 12–11. Note that it is standard practice to prepare the U.S. Standard General

Illustration 12–11

FEDERAL AGENCY
PRE-CLOSING TRIAL BALANCE
AS OF SEPTEMBER 30, 2002

	Debits	*Credits*
Proprietary Accounts:		
Fund Balance with Treasury—2002	$ 166,000	
Operating Materials and Supplies	219,000	
Equipment	3,250,000	
Accumulated Depreciation on Equipment		$ 900,000
Disbursements in Transit—2002		0
Accounts Payable		105,000
Accrued Funded Payroll and Benefits		27,000
Unexpended Appropriations—2002		34,000
Cumulative Results of Operations		3,010,000
Appropriations Used—2001		400,000
Appropriations Used—2002		2,450,000
Operating/Program Expenses	2,991,000	
Depreciation and Amortization	300,000	
	$6,926,000	$6,926,000
Budgetary Accounts:		
Appropriations Realized but Withdrawn—2002	$ 16,000	
Other Appropriations Realized—2002	34,000	
Unapportioned Authority—2002	0	
Apportionments—2002	0	
Allotments—2002		$ 0
Commitments—2002		0
Undelivered Orders—2002		34,000
Restorations, Writeoffs, and Withdrawals—2002		16,000
	$ 50,000	$ 50,000

Ledger *pre-closing* trial balance after the expended and withdrawn budgetary authority accounts have been closed, but before the other temporary proprietary accounts are closed. Closing of expended and withdrawn budgetary authority is discussed below.

Total credits to the Expended Authority—2002 account (Entries 9a, 10a, and 14a) amounted to $2,450,000. Thus, the total *unexpended* budgetary authority at the end of FY 2002 is $50,000 ($2,500,000 − $2,450,000). Of the $50,000 unexpended amount, $34,000 is *reserved* in the Undelivered Orders—2002 for goods or services still on order at year-end. However, the $6,000 balance in Commitments—2002 and $10,000 in Allotments—2002 have not been reserved and must be returned to Treasury. The following journal entries are needed to record the lapse of obligational authority for the $16,000 not obligated or reserved by fiscal year-end. As the first entry in Entry 16a shows, unused commitments and allotments (as well as apportionments if there had been a year-end balance) are closed to Other Appropriations Realized—2002, as is the amount of appropriations that was expended. In addition, the $400,000 balance in Expended Authority—2001 is closed to Other Appropriations Realized—2001, which also has a $400,000 balance prior to closing. In order to establish a record of withdrawn appropriations, the second budgetary entry shown below should also be made. In addition, temporary proprietary accounts would be closed as shown in 16b.

	Debits	*Credits*
16a. *Budgetary:*		
Commitments—2002	6,000	
Allotments—2002	10,000	
Expended Authority—2001	400,000	
Expended Authority—2002	2,450,000	
Other Appropriations Realized—2001		400,000
Other Appropriations Realized—2002		2,466,000
Appropriations Realized but Withdrawn—2002	16,000	
Restorations, Write-Offs, and Withdrawals—2002		16,000
16b. *Proprietary:*		
Unexpended Appropriations—2002	16,000	
Fund Balance with Treasury—2002		16,000

Accounting procedures also exist to reverse the second entry under Entry 16a to the extent the actual cost of goods or services received early in FY 2003 exceeds the $34,000 estimated in Undelivered Orders. Essentially, a portion of the budgetary authority that was withdrawn in Entry 16a would be *restored* in this case. These accounting procedures are well beyond the scope of the limited coverage presented in this chapter.

Temporary proprietary accounts should be closed to update the Net Position accounts so the end-of-period balance sheet can be prepared. The necessary closing entry would be:

	Debits	Credits
17. *Proprietary:*		
Appropriations Used	2,850,000	
Cumulative Results of Operations	441,000	
Operating/Program Expenses		2,991,000
Depreciation and Amortization		300,000

The balance sheet for the example federal agency whose pre-closing trial balance is shown in Illustration 12–11 is presented in Illustration 12–12. In more complex agencies, a consolidated balance sheet like the one shown in Illustration 12–2 is usually prepared. The example federal agency is assumed to have only entity assets (those that can be used for the agency's operations) and, except for Fund Balance with Treasury, the remaining assets are governmental. All liabilities (Accounts Payable and Accrued Funded Payroll and Benefits) are assumed to be governmental. Further, all liabilities are covered by budgetary resources. As discussed earlier in this chapter, the *net position* consists of only two items, unexpended appropriations ($34,000 reserved for goods and services on order at year-end) and Cumulative Results of Operations.

A Consolidating Statement of Net Cost for a major federal agency was presented in Illustration 12–3. Because the federal agency used in our example is assumed to have a simple organizational structure and no earned revenues, its Statement of Net Cost would be very simple; net cost would be the same as gross cost. Moreover, since the agency's net suborganization or program costs are reported on the first line of the Statement of Changes in Net Position presented in Illustration 12–13, a Statement of Net Cost would convey little additional information. Therefore, we do not include one here.

Illustration 12–12

FEDERAL AGENCY
BALANCE SHEET
AS OF SEPTEMBER 30, 2002

Assets	
Entity Assets:	
Intragovernmental:	
Fund Balance with Treasury	$ 166,000
Governmental:	
Operating materials and supplies	219,000
Equipment (net of accumulated depreciation of $900,000)	2,350,000
Total Entity Assets	$2,735,000
Liabilities	
Liabilities Covered by Budgetary Resources:	
Governmental liabilities:	
Accounts payable	$ 105,000
Accrued funded payroll and benefits	27,000
Total Liabilities Covered by Budgetary Resources	132,000
Net Position	
Unexpended Appropriations	34,000
Cumulative Results of Operations	2,569,000
Total Net Position	2,603,000
Total Liabilities and Net Position	$2,735,000

Illustration 12–13

FEDERAL AGENCY
STATEMENT OF CHANGES IN NET POSITION
FOR THE YEAR ENDED SEPTEMBER 30, 2002

	Suborganization A	*Suborganization B*	*Consolidated Totals*
Net Cost of Operations (Note A)	$1,316,400	$1,974,600	$3,291,000
Financing Sources:			
Appropriations Used	1,140,000	1,710,000	2,850,000
Net Results from Operations	(176,400)	(264,600)	(441,000)
Prior-Period Adjustments	0	0	0
Net Change in Cumulative Results of Operations	(176,400)	(264,600)	(441,000)
Decrease in Unexpended Appropriations	(146,400)	(219,600)	(366,000)
Change in Net Position	(322,800)	(484,200)	(807,000)
Net Position—Beginning of Year	1,364,000	2,046,000	3,410,000
Net Position—End of Year	$1,041,200	$1,561,800	$2,603,000

Note A: These amounts are taken from the bottom line of the Statement of Net Costs, which is not included here for sake of brevity.

For illustrative purposes, the agency whose Statement of Changes in Net Position is shown in Illustration 12–13, is assumed to have two suborganizations, A and B, and there are no interorganization transactions that require eliminations. Further, 40 percent of total net cost is assigned to suborganization A and 60 percent to B. Since the only financing source for this agency is annual appropriations, the Statement of Changes in Net Position is quite simple, but informative nonetheless.

The example federal agency would also have to prepare a Statement of Budgetary Resources (see Illustration 12–14). The astute reader will note that the equation applicable to this statement is Budgetary resources = Status of budgetary resources. Budgetary resources in this case is $2,884,000, consisting of current-year appropriations of $2,500,000 less expired appropriations of $16,000, plus $400,000 carried forward from prior-year appropriations to cover undelivered orders at the end of the prior year. Since there are no unobligated appropriations that can be carried forward at year-end, the *status of budgetary resources* in this case is simply the amount of budgetary resources expended ($2,850,000) plus $34,000 obligated for goods on order at the end of FY 2002 that had not yet been expended. Outlays are reported in the bottom section of the Statement of Budgetary Resources and are the same as the total amount expended during the year, or $2,850,000 ($2,450,000 chargeable to the current-year appropriation and $400,000 chargeable to the prior-year appropriation).

The final statement presented for the simple federal agency illustrated in this chapter is the Statement of Financing (see Illustration 12–15). This statement is intended to reconcile the budgetary basis expenditure or obligation of budgetary resources (obligations incurred) with the accrual basis net cost of operations. As

Illustration 12–14

FEDERAL AGENCY
STATEMENT OF BUDGETARY RESOURCES
FOR THE YEAR ENDED SEPTEMBER 30, 2002 (NOTE A)

Budgetary resources:	
Budgetary authority (Note B)	$2,484,000
Status of Budgetary Resources:	
Obligations incurred (Note C)	$2,484,000
Total status of budgetary resources	$2,484,000
Outlays:	
Obligations incurred (Note C)	$2,484,000
Obligated balance, net—beginning of period	400,000
Less obligated balance, net—end of year	(34,000)
Total outlays	$2,850,000

Note A: Comparative totals should also be presented for the prior year. Those totals are omitted in this example.

Note B: Total budgetary resources were $2,500,000 appropriation, less $16,000 of expired appropriation at year-end.

Note C: Expended authority of current year of $2,450,000, plus $34,000 obligated budgetary authority for undelivered goods at year-end.

Illustration 12–15

FEDERAL AGENCY
STATEMENT OF FINANCING
FOR THE YEAR ENDED SEPTEMBER 30, 2002

Obligations and Nonbudgetary Resources:	
Obligations incurred (Note A)	$2,484,000
Resources That Fund Net Cost of Operations:	
Change in amount of goods, services, and benefits ordered but not yet received or provided (Note B)	366,000
Costs capitalized on the balance sheet (Note C)	141,000
Total Resources That Fund Net Cost of Operations	507,000
Costs That Do Not Require Resources:	
Depreciation and amortization	300,000
Net Cost of Operations	$3,291,000

Note A: Obligations incurred consist of $2,450,000 expended from the FY 2002 appropriation plus $34,000 obligated for goods on order at the end of FY 2002.

Note B: The change in goods and services on order is a decrease of $366,000 ($400,000 − $34,000).

Note C: Equipment acquisition capitalized at $250,000 minus a net decrease in operating materials and supplies of $391,000. Thus, there was a net *decrease* in capitalization of $141,000, so this amount should be added in reconciling the use of budgetary resources to the net cost of operations.

shown in Illustration 12–15, there are certain resources that affect budgetary resources but do not affect the net cost of operations. These include the net change in the amount of goods, services, or benefits ordered (in this case, the change in Undelivered Orders from the beginning to the end of the year) and the net change in assets capitalized on the balance sheet. As explained in Note C to the statement, $250,000 of equipment purchases were capitalized during the year, but the balance of Operating Materials and Supplies decreased by $391,000, resulting in a net decrease in capitalized assets of $141,000. The lower section of the statement shows an addition for depreciation expense, since it had not been included in obligations incurred but is a part of the net cost of operations.

Summary of Accounting and Reporting for Federal Government Agencies

Illustration 12–16 provides a summary comparison of budgetary and proprietary accounting procedures for state and local governments as compared with federal agencies. Although some similarities exist, there are areas specific to each level of government. As shown in Illustration 12–16, state and local governments do not account for apportionments and most do not account for allotments. Federal agency accounting takes into consideration certain accruals (supplies used and depreciation) generally ignored in state and local government accounting, although as mentioned in several earlier chapters, the new reporting model created by GASB *Statement No. 34* now requires the use of accrual accounting by state and local governments at the government-wide level.

The head of each agency in the executive branch of the federal government has the statutory responsibility for the establishment and maintenance of systems of accounting and internal control in conformity with principles, standards, and requirements established by the Comptroller General, the Secretary of the Treasury, and the Director of the OMB. Federal agency accounting is directed at providing information for intelligent financial management of agency activities and programs to the end they may be operated with efficiency and economy, as well as providing evidence of adherence to legal requirements. As emphasized by the headings of Illustration 12–16, and by the discussions in earlier chapters, accounting for governmental funds is presently focused on legal compliance. The focus of federal agency accounting, in contrast, is broadened to include information needed for the management of agency resources (the *proprietary* track) as well as for compliance with fund control requirements (the *budgetary* track). However, as discussed in Chapters 1–9 of this text, the authors have introduced dual-track accounting for state and local government accounting to meet the full accrual accounting needs at the government-wide level while continuing to focus on legal compliance within the governmental funds.

U.S. Government-wide Financial Report

For the second time in history, the Department of the Treasury issued an annual *Financial Report of the United States Government* that follows FASAB standards and

Illustration 12–16 Comparison of Accounting for State and Local Governmental Fund Types and Accounting for Federal Agencies (journal entries)

Item	State and Local Government Funds Compliance Track Only	Federal Agency: Budgetary Track	Federal Agency: Proprietary Track
1. Passage of appropriations (and for state and local governments, revenue) bills	Estimated Revenues Appropriations Fund Balance	Other Appropriations Realized Unapportioned Authority	Fund Balance with Treasury Unexpended Appropriations
2. Revenues accrued (at expected collectible amount)	Taxes Receivable Estimated Uncollectible Taxes Revenues	No equivalent for taxes; user charges, if any, recognized as billed	No entry*
3. Apportionment by OMB	No equivalent	Unapportioned Authority Apportionments	No entry
4. Allotment by agency head	No equivalent†	Apportionments Allotments	No entry
5. Budget authority reserved prior to ordering goods or services	No equivalent	Allotments Commitments	No entry
6. Goods or services ordered	Encumbrances Reserve for Encumbrances	Commitments Undelivered Orders‡	No entry
7. Goods or services received	Reserve for Encumbrances Encumbrances Expenditures Accounts Payable	Undelivered Orders Expended Authority	Expense or asset account Accounts Payable Unexpended Appropriations Appropriations Used
8. Liability paid (expenditure recorded in 7 above)	Accounts Payable Cash	No entry	Accounts Payable Fund Balance with Treasury§
9. Supplies used	No entry	No entry	Operating/Program Expenses Inventory for Agency Operations
10. Physical inventory (consumption method assumed for state and local governments)	Inventory Expenditures Fund Balance Reserve for Inventory	No entry	Entry for (7) assumes perpetual inventory; would need entry for (10) if physical inventory and book inventory differed
11. Depreciation computed	No entry (computation used for cost reimbursements and management information)	No entry (Not an expenditure of appropriations; will never require a check to be drawn on U.S. Treasury)	Depreciation and Amortization Accumulated Depreciation (on general property, plant, and equipment, but not certain military assets and stewardship assets)
12. Closing entries	Appropriations Revenues Estimated Revenues Encumbrances Expenditures Fund Balance	Expended Authority Other Appropriations Realized; (Also must close any budgetary accounts associated with expired budget authority)	Cumulative Results of Operations Operating/Program Expenses Appropriations Used Cumulative Results of Operations

*Prototype consolidated financial statements of federal government do include an accrual for taxes, fines, and other revenue categories.

†As discussed in Chapter 3, some local governmental units utilize allotment accounting. In such cases, the credit in Entry 1 would be to Unallotted Appropriations, and an Entry 4 would be necessary to record the debit to that account and the credit to Allotments.

‡As illustrated by Entry 4 earlier in this chapter, and by entry 5, some agencies opt to use the interim account Commitments to improve planning for procurement of goods and services. If commitments are not recorded in advance of placing orders the debit for the budgetary track would be "Allotments."

§As indicated in this chapter, the account credited here might be Disbursements in Transit rather than Fund Balance with Treasury.

are audited by the General Accounting Office. Prototype "Consolidated Financial Statements" had been issued since the early 1980s; however, the Government Performance and Results Act of 1993 expanded the requirements of the Chief Financial Officers Act of 1990 and required that 24 federal agencies be audited and comprehensive government-wide financial statements be prepared within three years. These statements are available at http://www.gao.gov/reports.htm.

Not surprisingly, audits for FY 1997 and FY 1998 resulted in a disclaimer of opinion by the Comptroller General of the GAO. That disclaimer stated: "Serious deficiencies in the government's systems, recordkeeping, documentation, financial reporting, and controls, amounts reported in the financial statements and related notes do not provide a reliable source of information for decision-making by the government or public (p. 22)." Major challenges facing the Department of the Treasury include converting cash basis budgets to the accrual basis of accounting, confirming accounts receivable (e.g., of the Internal Revenue Service), taking inventory of the capital assets of the federal government (such as Defense Department equipment), and determining the cost of heritage assets. Twenty of the 24 federal agencies did not comply with the Federal Financial Management Improvement Act (FFMIA) of 1996's requirement that "financial management systems comply substantially with federal accounting standards, financial systems requirements, and the government's standard general ledger at the transaction level (p. 33)."

Given the difficulties agencies have experienced in complying with newly developed federal GAAP, it may be surprising that seven agencies *did* receive unqualified opinions (i.e., Social Security Administration, Department of Labor, General Service Administration, National Science Foundation, National Aeronautics and Space Administration, Nuclear Regulatory Commission, and Federal Emergency Management Agency). The Comptroller General states that "while obtaining unqualified 'clean' audit opinions on federal financial statements is an important objective, it is not an end in and of itself. The key is to take steps to continuously improve internal controls and underlying financial and management information systems as a means to assure accountability, increase the economy, improve the efficiency, and enhance the effectiveness of government (p. 2)." Most indications are that federal accounting is improving at a rapid rate, attributed in part to congressional mandate, but also to increasingly high professional skills and dedication of governmental accountants, auditors, and agency managers.

Key Terms

Allotment, 568
Apportionment, 568
Appropriation, 567
Budget accounts, 551
Budgetary resources, 563
Commitment, 568
Cumulative results of operations, 560
Entity assets, 558

Expended appropriation (authority), 568
Federal Accounting Standards Advisory Board (FASAB), 548
Federal Financial Management Improvement Act, 544
Federal mission property, plant, and equipment, 559
General property, plant, and equipment, 558
Governmental assets (liabilities), 558
Heritage assets, 559
Intragovernmental assets (liabilities), 558
Macroaccounting, 547
Net position, 560
Nonentity assets, 558
Obligation, 568
Stewardship investments, 566
Stewardship land, 559
Stewardship property, plant, and equipment, 559
Unexpended appropriations, 560

Selected References

General Accounting Office. *Accounting Guide: Basic Topics Relating to Appropriations and Reimbursables*. 1990.

Office of Management and Budget. *U.S. Government Standard General Ledger,* 1997.

———. *Bulletin 97-01*, "Form and Content of Agency Financial Statements." 1996.

———. *Circular A-134*, "Financial Accounting Principles and Standards." 1993.

Questions

12–1. Identify which of the following are part of the legislative branch of the federal government and which are part of the executive branch:

a. Secretary of the Treasury.

b. Director of the Office of Management and Budget.

c. Director of the Congressional Budget Office.

d. Comptroller General.

12–2. Describe the institutional process for establishing generally accepted accounting principles for the federal government.

12–3. Discuss the conceptual framework of accounting for federal agencies and compare it to the conceptual framework established by the GASB for state and local governments.

12–4. What are the objectives of financial reporting identified in *Statement of Federal Financial Accounting Concepts No. 1*?

12–5. Describe the criteria developed in *Statement of Federal Financial Accounting Concepts No. 2* for defining the federal reporting entity.

12–6. What is the importance of the Management Discussion & Analysis described in *Statement of Federal Financial Accounting Concepts No. 3* to financial statement users?

12–7. Describe the dual-track system used in federal agency accounting.

12–8. Identify the budgetary accounts used in federal agency accounting and explain the sequential flow of budgetary authority through the accounts.

12–9. Distinguish between a commitment and an obligation in budgetary track accounting for a federal agency.

12–10. What accounts are used to describe the net position of a federal agency?

12–11. Name the financial statements that should be prepared for each federal agency in conformity with OMB *Bulletin 97-1*.

Cases

12–1. Department of Transportation. The Consolidated Balance Sheet and Consolidated Statement of Net Cost for the U.S. Department of Transportation are provided on the following pages. After reading and evaluating these financial statements, use the Internet to answer the following questions or provide the requested information. [You may wish to access the Department of Transportation's Internet homepage at http://www.dot.gov/, then at that site locate a link to "Budget and Financial." The specific website for the Department's 1998 Consolidated Financial Statements was http://www.oig.dot.gov/audits/fe1999081.pdf. Because this information may change over time, you may need to navigate the Department's website as necessary to find the required information.]

a. What organizations comprise the Department of Transportation reporting entity?

b. Were these consolidated financial statements prepared in conformity with FASAB and OMB guidance applicable in FY 1998?

c. What amount of operations was funded by appropriations during FY 1998?

d. Referring to the Statement of Net Cost, does the fact that total expenses exceeded revenues and financing sources by over $20.3 billion indicate unlawful activity or lack of budget compliance for the year?

12–2. Internet Case. At the cutoff date for publication of this edition of the text, 14 Statements of Federal Financial Accounting Standards (SFFASs) had been issued. In addition, as of the cutoff date, OMB *Bulletin 97-01* provided authoritative guidance for the form and content of federal agency financial statements.

Required

Using the Internet [we recommend you search FASAB and OMB links from http://www. financenet.gov], determine if:

a. There have been any additional SFFASs or SRASs issued. If so, list them by name and provide their effective date.

b. Has the OMB replaced *Bulletin 97-01* with a later Bulletin? If so, how do the financial statements required by the later Bulletin compare to those required by *Bulletin 97-01*, as described and illustrated in Chapter 12? [Note: The preceding OMB *Bulletin* on form and content of agency financial statements was OMB *Bulletin 94-01*. Thus, the OMB may not intend to make frequent changes in its reporting guidance.]

U.S. DEPARTMENT OF TRANSPORTATION
CONSOLIDATED BALANCE SHEET
FOR THE PERIOD ENDED SEPTEMBER 30, 1998
(DOLLARS IN THOUSANDS)

	1998 DOT Total
Assets	
Entity:	
Intragovernmental:	
Fund Balance with Treasury	$19,369,862
Investments	27,767,859
Accounts Receivable, Net	388,075
Interest Receivable, Net	135,687
Other Assets	337,203
Total Intragovernmental Assets	$47,998,686
Investments	27
Accounts Receivable, Net	102,329
Interest Receivable, Net	148
Loans Receivable and Related Foreclosed Property, Net	343,628
Cash and Other Monetary Assets	63,115
Inventory and Related Property, Net	2,190,619
General Property, Plant and Equipment, Net	13,821,827
Other Assets	204,197
Total Entity	$64,724,576
Non-Entity:	
Intragovernmental:	
Fund Balance with Treasury	$ 47
Investments	934,240
Interest Receivable, Net	11,428
Total Intragovernmental Assets	$ 945,715
Accounts Receivable, Net	10,055
Total Non-Entity	$ 955,770
Total Assets	$65,680,346
Liabilities	
Liabilities Covered by Budgetary Resources:	
Intragovernmental:	
Accounts Payable	$ 8,524,068
Interest Payable	11,586
Debt	317,159
Other Intragovernmental Liabilities	314,525
Total Intragovernmental Liabilities	9,167,338
Accounts Payable	1,576,054
Liabilities for Loan Guarantees	135,619
Lease Liabilities	687
Other Liabilities	370,697
Total Liabilities Covered by Budgetary Resources	$11,250,395

	1998 DOT Total
Liabilities Not Covered by Budgetary Resources:	
Intragovemmental:	
Debt	$ 24
Environmental Cleanup Costs	59,762
Other Intragovernmental Liabilities	221,144
Total Intragovernmental Liabilities	$ 280,930
Lease Liabilities	103,532
Federal Employee and Veterans' Benefits	21,056,390
Environmental Cleanup Costs	3,277,178
Other Liabilities	1,233,171
Total Liabilities Not Covered by Budgetary Resources	$25,951,201
Total Liabilities	$37,201,596
Net Position	
Unexpended Appropriations	$ 9,353,380
Cumulative Results of Operations	19,125,370
Total Net Position	28,478,750
Total Liabilities and Net Position	$65,680,346

U.S. DEPARTMENT OF TRANSPORTATION CONSOLIDATED STATEMENT OF NET COST FOR THE PERIOD ENDED SEPTEMBER 30, 1998 (DOLLARS IN THOUSANDS)

	1998 DOT Total
Program Costs	
Surface Transportation:	
Intragovernmental	$ 57,944
Public	26,496,518
Total	26,554,462
Less Earned Revenues	(150,882)
Net Program Costs	$ 26,403,580
Air Transportation:	
Intragovernmental	$ 504,332
Public	8,677,118
Total	9,181,440
Less Earned Revenues	(99,149)
Net Program Costs	$ 9,082,291
Maritime Transportation:	
Intragovemmental	$ 957,451
Public	5,032,601
Total	5,990,052
Less Earned Revenues	(587,807)
Net Program Costs	$ 5,402,245

	1998 DOT Total
Cross-Cutting Programs	
Intragovernmental	$ 54,483
Public	1,212
Total	55,695
Less Earned Revenues	(55,695)
Net Program Costs	$ —
Cost Not Assigned to Programs	$ 191,587
Less Earned Revenues Not Attributed to Programs	(33,661)
Deferred Maintenance	
Net Cost of Operations	$ 41,046,042
Financing Sources:	
Appropriations Used	$ 10,076,703
Taxes and Other Non-Exchange Revenue	39,799,313
Donations	96,575
Imputed Financing	407,551
Transfers-In	157,006
Transfers-Out	(10,879,734)
Other	25,069
Net Results of Operations	$ (1,363,559)
Prior Period Adjustments	(19,011,428)
Net Change in Cumulative Results of Operations	$(20,374,987)
Increase (Decrease) in Unexpended Appropriations	(1,909,063)
Change in Net Position	$(22,284,050)
Net Position, Beginning of Period	50,762,800
Net Position, End of Period	$ 28,478,750

12–3. U.S. Government-wide Annual Report. Obtain the most recent audited annual financial statement of the United States Government. It is available from the General Accounting Office (GAO) either in print (e.g., FY98 was issued March 1999 as report GAO/AIMD-99-130) or on the Internet (e.g., http://www.gao.gov/reports.htm).

Required

a. What are the total assets of the U.S. government as a whole? Total liabilities?

b. Was there an increase or decrease in the Net Position of the U.S. Government for this fiscal year (i.e., do revenues exceed the net cost of government operations)?

c. Did the GAO give the Federal Government an unqualified, qualified, adverse, or disclaimer of opinion?

d. What weaknesses or deficiencies did the Comptroller General of the GAO note in his report?

e. What federal agencies received an unqualified opinion for this fiscal year?

Exercises and Problems

12–1. Multiple Choice. Choose the best answer.

1. Federal statutes assign responsibility for establishing and maintaining a sound financial structure for the federal government to the:
   a. Comptroller General.
   b. Director of the OMB.
   c. Secretary of the Treasury.
   d. All of the above.
2. Which of the following is a true statement about the process of setting accounting standards for the federal government?
   a. The FASAB authorizes the issuance of accounting standards.
   b. The FASAB recommends accounting standards, but they have no authoritative standing unless approved by all three principals.
   c. The GASB has primary responsibility for issuing federal government accounting standards; the FASAB has secondary responsibility for federal standards.
   d. Each federal agency is responsible for setting its own accounting standards; those standards take precedence over standards developed by the FASAB.
3. In the GAAP hierarchy for federal agency accounting and financial reporting, the highest level GAAP is (are):
   a. The *Treasury Financial Manual*.
   b. Interpretations of the U.S. General Accounting Office.
   c. Statements of Federal Financial Accounting Standards (SFFASs).
   d. OMB *Bulletin 97-01*, "Form and Content of Agency Financial Statements."
4. Which of the following is *not* one of the principals of the Joint Financial Management Improvement Project?
   a. Executive Director of the FASAB.
   b. Comptroller General.
   c. Director of the OMB.
   d. Secretary of the Treasury.
5. Which of the following is *not* an objective of federal financial reporting?
   a. Assist report users in evaluating budgetary integrity.
   b. Assist report users in evaluating operating performance.
   c. Assist report users in evaluating the reliability of financial information.
   d. Assist report users in evaluating stewardship.
6. When closing entries are made, the Cumulative Results of Operations account will be affected by which of the following transactions or events that occurred during the year?

a. Expiration of budget authority.
b. Purchase of property, plant, and equipment.
c. Depreciation of property, plant, and equipment.
d. Both *b* and *c*.

7. Assuming that an agency's unused appropriations expire at year-end, but appropriations continue in effect for obligated amounts (purchase orders, etc.), which of the following budgetary accounts would likely be found in the agency's post-closing trial balance at year-end?
   a. Commitments and Other Appropriations Realized.
   b. Expended Authority and Undelivered Orders.
   c. Commitments and Undelivered Orders.
   d. Undelivered Orders and Other Appropriations Realized.
8. Which of the following is a correct mathematical relationship among proprietary account balances?
   a. Fund Balance with Treasury equals Unexpended Appropriations.
   b. Net Position equals Total Assets minus Total Liabilities.
   c. Cumulative Results of Operations equals Revenues and Financing Sources minus Operating/Program Expenses.
   d. Disbursements in Transit equals Fund Balance with Treasury minus Accounts Payable and Other Current Liabilities.
9. Which of the following is *not* a component of the changes in net position reported in a federal agency's annual Statement of Changes in Net Position?
   a. Appropriations used during the period.
   b. Change in Cumulative Results of Operations.
   c. Prior-period adjustments.
   d. Commitments.
10. In a Statement of Budgetary Resources prepared in conformity with OMB *Bulletin 97-01*, the amount shown for Total Outlays in the lower section of the statement represents the amount of:
   a. Expended budgetary authority for the current period.
   b. Expenditures accrued but unpaid at the end of the period.
   c. Amount of cash paid for all purposes during the period.
   d. Total reduction in Fund Balance with Treasury during the period.

12–2. Fund Balance with U.S. Treasury. One amount is missing in the following trial balance of proprietary accounts and one amount is missing from the trial balance of budgetary accounts of a certain agency of the federal government. The debits are not distinguished from the credits.

Required

a. Compute each missing amount in the pre-closing trial balance below.

FEDERAL AGENCY
PRE-CLOSING TRIAL BALANCE
SEPTEMBER 30, 2001

Proprietary Accounts:	
Accounts Payable	$ 300,000
Accumulated Depreciation—Plant and Equipment	2,600,000
Appropriations Used	4,000,000
Fund Balance with Treasury—2001	?
Operating Materials and Supplies	1,000,000
Cumulative Results of Operations—10/1/00	6,600,000
Operating/Program Expenses	3,150,000
Depreciation and Amortization	150,000
Plant and Equipment	8,900,000
Unexpended Appropriations—2001	1,500,000
Budgetary Accounts:	
Other Appropriations Realized—2001	?
Expended Authority—2001	4,000,000
Undelivered Orders—2001	1,500,000

b. Compute the net additions to assets other than Fund Balance with Treasury during fiscal year 2001. Clearly label your computations and show all work in good form.

12–3. Federal Agency Financial Statements. Using the data from Problem 12–2:

a. Prepare in general journal form entries to close the budgetary accounts as needed, and to close the operating statement proprietary accounts.

b. Prepare in good form a Balance Sheet for the Federal Agency as of September 30, 2001. [Note: Assume that all assets are *entity assets*, Fund Balance with Treasury is an *intragovernmental asset*, and all other assets are *governmental*. Assume also that all liabilities are covered by budgetary resources.]

c. Prepare in good form a Statement of Changes in Net Position of the Federal Agency for the year ended September 30, 2001, assuming Unexpended Appropriations, as of October 1, 2000, amounted to $1,300,000, and that there are no material suborganizations or programs to be separately reported.

12–4. Federal Agency Transactions. The Balance Sheet for the Rural Assistance Agency of the federal government for the year ended September 30, 2001 is provided as follows:

RURAL ASSISTANCE AGENCY
BALANCE SHEET
AS OF SEPTEMBER 30, 2001
(THOUSANDS)

Assets	
Entity Assets:	
Intragovernmental:	
Fund Balance with Treasury	$2,164
Governmental:	
Property, plant, and equipment, net of accumulated depreciation of $1,790	6,835

Operating materials and supplies	325
Total Assets	$9,324
Liabilities	
Liabilities Covered by Budgetary Resources:	
Accounts payable	$ 240
Accrued funded payroll and benefits	55
Total Liabilities Covered by Budgetary Resources	295
Liabilities Not Covered by Budgetary Resources:	
Accrued unfunded liabilities	340
Total Liabilities	635
Net Position	
Unexpended Appropriations	1,869
Cumulative results of operations	6,820
Total Net Position	8,689
Total Liabilities and Net Position	$9,324

Additional Information:

1. Total Appropriations for the fiscal year ending September 30, 2002, totaled $15,513,000.
2. Accounts Payable reported on the Balance Sheet as of September 30, 2001, in the amount of $240,000 were paid early in fiscal year 2002.
3. Materials and supplies ordered in fiscal 2001 were received in early fiscal year 2002 in the amount of $1,869,000, the same amount as reported for Unexpended Appropriations on the Balance Sheet as of September 30, 2001. All materials and supplies are credited to Accounts Payable upon receipt.
4. Additional materials and supplies were ordered and received during fiscal year 2002 in the amount of $2,050,000. Property, Plant, and Equipment in the amount of $400,000 was also purchased during fiscal year 2002. Upon the agency's request the Treasury paid $400,000 for the Property, Plant, and Equipment. (Note: The $2,050,000 for purchases of materials and supplies was credited to Accounts Payable.)
5. Operating/program expenses for fiscal year 2002 totaled $15,076,000. This amount excluded depreciation expense of $450,000 on Property, Plant, and Equipment, but included accruals at fiscal year-end in the amounts of $60,000 for accrued payroll and benefits and $10,000 for accrued annual leave. [Credit Accrued Unfunded Liabilities for the accrued leave. Note that accrued annual leave is unfunded and therefore does not reduce the balance of Unexpended Appropriations nor does it increase Appropriations Used. The total FY 2002 appropriations used amounted to $11,162,000: $15,076,000 for FY 2002 expenses minus $3,904,000 of materials and supplies consumed minus $10,000 for expenses that will be funded in future years.] Except for materials and supplies in the amount of $3,904,000 consumed in operations and the two accrued items, all other operating/program expenses were paid by checks drawn on the Treasury during the fiscal year.
6. Accounts payable in the amount of $3,654,000 were paid during the year. Of this amount, checks in the amount of $1,869,000 were drawn against Fund

Balance with Treasury—2001; the remainder against Fund Balance with Treasury—2002. In addition, early in FY 2002, the $55,000 reported as accrued funded payroll and benefits on the September 30, 2001, Balance Sheet was paid by charging against Fund Balance with Treasury—2001.

7. There was no property, plant, and equipment sold or otherwise disposed of during fiscal year 2002.

Required

a. Prepare all necessary *proprietary* journal entries only for the Rural Assistance Agency (ignore *budgetary* entries) for fiscal year 2002.

b. Prepare a Comparative Balance Sheet for the Rural Assistance Agency as of September 30, 2001, and 2002.

c. Prepare a Statement of Changes in Net Position for the Rural Assistance Agency for the year ended September 30, 2002.

12–5. Federal Agency Financial Statements. The trial balance of the Federal Science Administration, as of August 31, 2001, is shown below:

	Debits	*Credits*
Proprietary Accounts		
Fund Balance with Treasury—2001	$ 1,635,772	
Operating Materials and Supplies	1,184,186	
Plant and Equipment	7,651,633	
Accumulated Depreciation—Plant and Equipment		$ 2,332,628
Construction Work in Progress	581,818	
Accounts Payable		328,123
Advances from Other Federal Agencies		43,518
Appropriations Used		2,630,724
Unexpended Appropriations		1,264,131
Cumulative Results of Operations—10/1/00		6,842,823
Operating/Program Expenses	2,388,538	
Total Proprietary Accounts	$13,441,947	$13,441,947
Budgetary Accounts:		
Other Appropriations Realized—2001	$ 3,894,855	
Unapportioned Authority—2001		$ 100,000
Apportionments—2001		150,000
Allotments—2001		600,000
Commitments—2001		50,000
Undelivered Orders—2001		364,131
Expended Authority—2001		2,630,724
Total Budgetary Accounts	$ 3,894,855	$ 3,894,855

Required

a. Prepare a Balance Sheet for the Federal Science Administration, as of August 31, 2001.

b. Prepare a Statement of Changes in Net Position for the 11 months ended August 31, 2001, assuming the balance, as of September 30, 2000, for the Unexpended Appropriations—2000 account was $1,210,210.

c. Prepare a Statement of Budgetary Resources for the 11 months ended August 31, 2001, assuming goods on order at the end of the prior year amounted to $1,210,210.

12–6. Transactions and Closing Entries. The Statement of Financial Position of the Throttlebottom Commemorative Commission, of the United States Department of Culture, is given as follows:

THROTTLEBOTTOM COMMEMORATIVE COMMISSION
BALANCE SHEET
SEPTEMBER 30, 2001

Assets		
Entity Assets:		
Intragovernmental:		
Fund Balance with Treasury—2001		$1,650,000
Operating Materials and Supplies		365,000
Equipment	$600,000	
Less: Accumulated Depreciation	60,000	540,000
Total Assets		$2,555,000
Liabilities		
Liabilities Covered by Budgetary Resources:		
Accounts Payable		$ 850,000
Total Liabilities Covered by Budgetary Resources		850,000
Net Position		
Unexpended Appropriations		800,000
Cumulative Results of Operations		905,000
Total Net Position		1,705,000
Total Liabilities and Net Position		$2,555,000

Required

a. Prepare entries in general journal form for the following transactions, which summarize all financial transactions for fiscal year October 1, 2001–September 30, 2002. Use the account titled *Operating/Program Expenses* for all expense items, realizing, of course, that in an actual accounting system, either additional general ledger detail or an expense subsidiary ledger would be used.

(1) An appropriation for FY 2002 in the amount of $12,000,000 is authorized by Congress, and the bill is signed by the President.

(2) The Office of Management and Budget apportioned $11,000,000 to the agency and withheld $1,000,000.

(3) The agency head allotted $11,000,000 to subordinates.

(4) Commitments are recorded in the amount of $10,300,000.

(5) Obligation documents totaling $10,000,000 are recorded for those commitments that had been previously recorded.

(6) Goods and services were received and liabilities recorded for: Payroll, $6,500,000; equipment, $600,000; and materials and supplies, $2,000,000. The equipment and $200,000 worth of the materials and supplies had been ordered in the prior year; the remainder of the materials and the payroll relate to obligations of the current year.

(7) Materials and supplies issued during the period and used in operations, $1,200,000.
(8) Liabilities paid totaled $8,950,000, of which $1,650,000 was paid from Fund Balance with Treasury—2001.
(9) Depreciation is recorded at the rates of 10 percent on the beginning balance and 5 percent on the additions during the year.
(10) Accruals as of September 30, 2002, are recorded for payroll, $350,000; and materials and supplies, $68,000. Obligations had been previously recorded for these amounts.
(11) The withheld and unobligated portions of the appropriation lapsed at year-end.

b. Prepare a trial balance as of September 30, 2002.
c. Prepare closing entries as of September 30, 2002.
d. Prepare a Balance Sheet as of September 30, 2002, in the format used for the September 30, 2001, Balance Sheet.
e. Prepare a Statement of Changes in Net Position for 2002.

12–7. Transactions and Statements. The Flood Control Commission was authorized by Congress to start operations on October 1, 2001.

Required

a. Record the following transactions in general journal form as they should appear in the accounts of the Flood Control Commission. Record all expenses in the "Operating/Program Expenses" account.
(1) The Flood Control Commission received official notice that the one-year appropriation passed by Congress and signed by the President amounted to $7,000,000 for operating expenses.
(2) The Office of Management and Budget notified the Commission of the following schedule of apportionments: first quarter, $2,000,000; second quarter, $2,000,000; third quarter, $1,500,000; and fourth quarter, $1,500,000.
(3) The Flood Control Commissioner allotted $1,000,000 for the first month's operations.
(4) Obligations were recorded for salaries and fringe benefits, $400,000; furniture and equipment, $270,000; materials and supplies, $250,000; rent and utilities, $50,000. The Flood Control Commission does not record commitments prior to recording obligations.
(5) Payroll for the first two weeks in the amount of $170,000 was paid.
(6) Invoices approved for payment totaled $395,000; of the total, $180,000 was for furniture and equipment, $175,000 for materials and supplies, and $40,000 for rent.
(7) Liability was recorded for the payroll for the second two weeks, $160,000; and for the employer's share of FICA taxes for the four weeks, $23,000. [Credit Accrued Funded Payroll and Benefits.]
(8) Accounts payable totaling $189,000 were paid, which included liabilities for materials and supplies, $149,000, and Rent, $40,000. Accrued Funded Payroll and Benefits were paid in the amount of $183,000.

(9) Accruals recorded at month-end were salaries, $30,000, and utilities, $10,000. Materials and supplies costing $60,000 were used during the month. Depreciation of $2,500 was recorded on furniture and equipment for the month. [Note: In practice, this would likely be done in worksheet form for monthly reporting purposes.]

(10) Necessary closing entries were prepared as of October 31, 2001. [Again, for monthly statements, this would be a worksheet entry only.]

b. Prepare a Balance Sheet for the Flood Control Commission as of October 31, 2001, assuming that all of the Commission's assets are entity assets, that Fund Balance with Treasury is intragovernmental, and that all other assets are governmental. Further, all liabilities are covered by budgetary resources.

c. Prepare a Statement of Changes in Net Position for the Flood Control Commission for the month ended October 31, 2001.

d. Prepare a Statement of Budgetary Resources for the Flood Control Commission for the month ended October 31, 2001.

e. Prepare a Statement of Financing for the Flood Control Commission for the month ended October 31, 2001.

12–8. Correction of Errors. The following trial balances were prepared for a federal agency at the end of its first month of existence by a new accountant, whose only prior experience had been as a bookkeeper in the accounting department of a large city.

INTERSTATE PARKS COMMISSION
TRIAL BALANCE
OCTOBER 31, 2001

	Debits	*Credits*
General Fund:		
Accounts Payable		$1,200,000
Allotments		1,600,000
Due from U.S. Treasury	$3,140,000	
Encumbrances	50,000	
Estimated Revenues	3,500,000	
Expenditures	1,410,000	
Fund Balance	50,000	
Inventory of Supplies	50,000	
Reserve for Encumbrances		50,000
Reserve for Inventory		50,000
Revenues		3,400,000
Unallotted Appropriations		1,900,000
	$8,200,000	$8,200,000
General Fixed Assets Account Group:		
Buildings	$ 720,000	
Equipment	180,000	
Improvements Other than Buildings	45,000	
Investment in General Fixed Assets—General Fund Revenues		$1,000,000
Land	55,000	
	$1,000,000	$1,000,000

Early in the second month of the agency's existence (before any transactions of the second month have been posted), you are sent to the agency to see how the new accountant is getting along. After looking over the trial balances, you ask to see the underlying accounts. (These are reproduced below. Related debits and credits are indicated by the same number. Explanations appear with the debit member of each entry.)

General Fund Accounts

Accounts Payable

Checks requested from U.S. Treasury	(7)	260,000	(5)	1,150,000
			(6)	310,000

Allotments

			(3)	1,600,000

Due from U.S. Treasury

OMB Apportionment	(2)	3,400,000	(7)	260,000

Encumbrances

Option to purchase land, building, and equipment, 1,000,000; supplies ordered, 200,000	(4)	1,200,000	(5)	1,150,000

Estimated Revenues

Congressional appropriation	(1)	3,500,000		

Expenditures

Title taken to land, etc., 1,000,000; supplies received, 150,000	(5)	1,150,000	(8)	50,000
Salaries and wages	(6)	310,000		

Fund Balance

To set up Reserve for inventory	(8)	50,000		

Inventory of Supplies

Month-end physical inventory	(8)	50,000		

Reserve for Encumbrances

See explanation in Expenditures account	(5)	1,150,000	(4)	1,200,000

Reserve for Inventory

			(8)	50,000

Revenues

			(2)	3,400,000

Unallotted Appropriations

Allotment for July	(3)	1,600,000	(1)	3,500,000

General Fixed Assets Account Group

Buildings

See GF entry (5); expected life, 30 years	(5)	720,000		

Equipment

See GF entry (5); expected life, 10 years	(5)	180,000		

Improvements Other than Buildings

See GF entry (5); expected life, 15 years	(5)	45,000		

Investment in General Fixed Assets—General Fund Revenues

			(5)	1,000,000

Land

See GF entry (5)	(5)	55,000		

Required

a. Prepare entries in general journal form to state the accounts of the Interstate Parks Commission correctly as of October 31, 2001.

b. Prepare a Balance Sheet for the Interstate Parks Commission as of October 31, 2001, assuming that all of the Commission's assets are entity assets, that Fund Balance with Treasury is intragovernmental, and that all other assets are governmental. Further, all liabilities are covered by budgetary resources.

c. Prepare a Statement of Changes in Net Position for the Interstate Parks Commission for the month ended October 31, 2001.

CHAPTER 13

Budgeting and Costing of Government Services

Learning Objectives

After studying this chapter, you should be able to:

- Explain the objectives of budgeting and cost determination in relation to measuring performance.
- Explain the differences among various budgeting approaches.
- Identify the procedures involved in specific types of budgets including appropriation budgets, revenue budgets, cash budgets, and capital budgets.
- Describe budgeting for performance:
  - Total quality management (TQM).
  - Service efforts and accomplishments (SEA).
- Explain unique aspects of costing government services:
  - Federal contracts and grants.
  - Activity-based costing (ABC).
  - Cost accounting and expenditure accounting.
- Describe the unique budget and cost issues in a nongovernmental, not-for-profit organization.

The 1990s brought a renewed interest in measuring the performance of organizations in the public and not-for-profit sectors, as well as in the private sector. The budget has always played a unique role in governmental entities because it is a legal document. Cost determination has long been a critical task in complying with requirements accompanying federal funds. What appears to be new is the pervasive acceptance across entities that assessing outcomes and accomplishments is key to being accountable to resource providers and remaining viable and competitive as an organization. A challenge is to integrate the functions of management, budgeting, and costing into the accounting information system so that performance can be continuously monitored and improved.

The analysis of government financial performance is discussed in Chapter 10. In this chapter, the roles of budgets, cost determination, and accounting information systems in that process are examined. The concepts and tools are discussed primarily from the perspective of a state or local government or public entity, such as a public university or public hospital; however, many of the issues apply equally well to nongovernmental, not-for-profit organizations.

Objectives of Budgeting

The GASB *Budgeting, Budgetary Control, and Budgetary Reporting* Principle provides that:

> *a.* An annual budget(s) should be adopted by every governmental unit.
> *b.* The accounting system should provide the basis for appropriate budgetary control.
> *c.* Budgetary comparisons should be included in the appropriate financial statements and schedules for governmental funds for which an annual budget has been adopted.

The *Budgeting* Principle is directly related to the *Accounting and Reporting Capabilities* Principle, which specifies that a governmental accounting system must make it possible for a governmental unit (1) to prepare financial reports in conformity with generally accepted accounting principles (GAAP) and (2) to determine compliance with finance-related legal provisions. Chapter 3 is concerned with budgets as legal documents binding on the actions of administrators and with budgetary accounting needed to make it possible to prepare budgetary reports to demonstrate legal compliance. It is also concerned with budgetary comparisons required for the General Fund and major special revenue funds in conformity with GASB's new reporting model.

Budgeting is also an important tool for achieving efficient and effective management of resources. Because of growing public demand for improved government performance, innovative performance measurement systems are being developed at all levels of government. In 1993, for example, the U.S. Congress passed the Government Performance and Results Act, which mandates the development of strategic plans, performance measures, annual performance plans, and performance reporting for all federal agencies.[1]

In 1998, the National Advisory Council on State and Local Budgeting, a cooperative of organizations, issued a document that describes nearly 60 *best* budget practices covering the planning, development, adoption, and execution phases of the budget process.[2] This document recognizes that budgeting is one of the most important activities undertaken by state and local governments in allocating scarce resources to programs and services. Over the years, governments have experimented with various approaches to budgeting. These approaches are described in the next section.

Rational Budgeting Approaches

The legalistic view is that a budget is a plan of financial operation embodying an estimate of proposed expenditures for a given period of time and the proposed means of financing them. In a much more general sense, budgets may be regarded as devices to aid management to operate an organization more effectively. In the general sense, budgets are the financial expression of plans prepared by managers for operating an organization during a time period and for changing its physical facilities and its capital structure.

Types of Budgeting

Incremental Budgeting. A simplistic, and often used, approach to budgeting is called **incremental budgeting**. In essence, an incremental budget is derived from the current year's budget by adding amounts expected to be required by salary and wage increases and increases in the cost of supplies and equipment to be purchased; decreases would result from shrinkage in the scale of operations forced by pressures such as spending limitations mandated by the electorate (for example, California's Proposition 13 in 1978) or cuts in capital equipment purchases. Incremental budgeting focuses largely on resource inputs and typically uses the *line-item* budget format in which the focus is on departmental expenditures for specified purposes, or objects, such as personnel, supplies, equipment, and travel.

Incremental budgeting is often contrasted with *rational* budgeting approaches, which stress the relation of inputs to outputs (quantities of work accomplished) and outcomes (impacts on goals and objectives). Rational budgeting approaches, as

---

[1]Progress on implementation of "The Results Act" is reported on web page http://www.npr.gov/. The Act required agencies to submit their strategic plans to Congress by September 30, 1997. Annual performance plans were developed parallel to budget requests beginning with FY99, and agencies will report on the results achieved in those performance plans beginning in March 2000.

[2]See John Gross, "NACSLB Recommended Budget Practices: What They Are and How to Use Them," *Government Finance Review,* June 1998, pp. 9–14. The report can be obtained at http://www.gfoa.org.

they have evolved, attempt to identify fundamental objectives of the governmental unit, estimate future-year costs and benefits, and systematically analyze alternative ways of meeting the governmental unit's objectives. Three approaches commonly described as rational are performance/program budgeting, planning-programming-budgeting system, and zero-based budgeting. These approaches are discussed next.[3]

Performance Budgeting. The evolution of the concept of a budget from "an estimate of proposed expenditures and the proposed means of financing them" to an "operating plan" was a natural accompaniment to the development of the concept of professional management. In public administration, as in business administration, the concept of professionalism demanded that administrators, or managers, attempt to put the scarce resources of qualified personnel and money to the best possible uses. The legal requirement that administrators of governmental units and agencies submit appropriate requests to the legislative bodies in budget format provided a basis for adapting required budgetary estimates of proposed expenditures to broader management use. The legislative appropriation process has traditionally required administrators to justify budget requests. A logical justification of proposed expenditures is to relate the proposed expenditures of each governmental subdivision to the programs and activities to be accomplished by that subdivision during the budget period. The type of budgeting in which input of resources is related to output of services is sometimes known as **performance budgeting**. Performance budgeting is linked conceptually with *performance auditing* as defined in Chapter 11 of this text. Performance budgeting is a plan for relating resources inputs to the efficient production of outputs; performance auditing is the subsequent evaluation to determine that resources were in fact used efficiently and effectively in accordance with the plan.

Program budgeting is another term sometimes used synonymously with performance budgeting. However, the term is more generally used to refer to a budget format that discloses the full costs of programs or functions without regard to the number of organizational units that might be involved in performing the various aspects of the program or functions. Performance budgeting, at least in its earlier forms, focuses on the relation between inputs and outputs of each organizational unit rather than programs.

The use of performance budgeting in governmental units received significant impetus from the work of the first Hoover Commission for the federal government. The report of this Commission, presented to the Congress in 1949, led to the adoption in the federal government of budgets then known as *cost-based budgets* or *cost budgets*. The use of these designations suggests that a governmental unit desiring to use performance budgeting must have an accrual accounting system, rather than a cash accounting system, in order to routinely ascertain the costs of programs and

[3]More details about these specific budgeting techniques and their application to industries, such as service, not-for-profit, higher education, and health care can be found in Robert Rachlin, *Handbook of Budgeting*, 4th ed. (New York: John Wiley & Sons, 2000).

activities. The recommendations of the second Hoover Commission led to the statutory requirement of both accrual accounting and cost-based budgeting for agencies of the executive branch of the federal government. Federal statutes also require the synchronization of budgetary and accounting classifications and the coordination of these with the organizational structure of the agencies. Subsequently it was realized that the planning and programming functions of federal agencies were not performed by the same organizational segments that performed the budgeting and accounting functions and that plans and programs were thus often not properly related to appropriation requests.

Planning-Programming-Budgeting System. The integration of planning, programming, budgeting, and accounting has considerable appeal to persons concerned with public administration because an integrated system should, logically, provide legislators and administrators with much better information for the management of governmental resources than has been provided by separate systems. In the late 1960s, there was a concentrated effort to introduce a **planning-programming-budgeting system**, called PPBS, throughout the executive branch of the federal government, and to adapt the concept to state and local governmental units and to other complex organizations.

Zero-Based Budgeting. In the 1970s, the wave of interest in PPBS receded and was replaced by widespread discussion of another approach to wedding the legally required budget process to a rational process of allocating scarce resources among alternative uses: The approach was called **zero-based budgeting** or ZBB. As the name indicates, the basic concept of ZBB is that the very existence of each activity be justified each year, as well as the amounts of resources requested to be allocated to each activity.

Many governmental units of various sizes have experimented with performance budgeting, program budgeting, PPBS, ZBB, and mixed approaches to rational budgeting.[4] Successful implementation of these approaches, particularly PPBS, requires formulation of the governmental unit's fundamental objectives and identification and evaluation of alternative ways of achieving the objectives. Techniques used to evaluate alternatives are sometimes referred to as *systems analysis*, *cost/benefit analysis*, and *cost-effectiveness analysis*. Techniques for "productivity measurement" or "productivity evaluation" are also often utilized by administrators who use the budgeting process as an aid in the allocation of scarce resources among competing demands for services. Quantitative techniques such as model building and simulation studies are utilized as aids in evaluating alternative allocations of governmental resources just as they are for evaluating business alternatives.

However simple or however sophisticated the methods used to develop information to aid in the resource allocation process, any method can produce useful

[4]See Daniel E. O'Toole, James Marshall, and Timothy Grewe, "Current Local Government Budgeting Practices," *Government Finance Review*, December 1996, pp. 25–29, for the results of a survey of budgeting practices of members of the Government Finance Officers Association.

output only if the data input are sufficiently reliable. Chapters 2 through 9 are intended to provide the reader with the background needed to understand data produced in conformity with GASB standards. Modifications that would facilitate rational budgeting are discussed later in this chapter.

Interrelation of Policy Setting, Service Delivery, and Evaluation Activities

Illustration 13–1 is a graphic representation of the interrelations among the processes of policy setting, service delivery, and evaluation in one city. Illustration 13–1 shows that budget preparation is constrained by evaluation of prior years' action plans and accomplishments, generation of data about the city, and adjustment of goals and policies. Not specifically presented in the chart is the necessity of recognizing the impact on the city's action plans of changes in federal and state policies, programs, and revenues and expenditures structures. Note that this city uses the term *corporate* as governments are public corporations.

Budgeting Procedures

Budgeting Governmental Appropriations

Appropriations budgets are an administration's requests for authorization to incur liabilities for goods, services, and facilities for specified purposes. In practice, the preparation of appropriations budgets for any one year is related to the administration's budget of revenues since the revenues budget is the plan for financing the proposed appropriations. If the program, or performance, budget concept is followed, appropriations budgets are prepared for each existing and continuing work program or activity of each governmental subdivision; for each program authorized or required by action of past legislative bodies but not yet made operative; and for each new program the administration intends to submit to the legislative body for approval.

In business budgeting, each ongoing program should be subjected to rigorous management scrutiny at budget preparation time to make sure there is a valid reason for continuing the program at all: This is the fundamental idea of zero-based budgeting. If the program should be continued, then management must decide whether the prior allocation of resources to the program is optimal, or whether changes should be made in the assignment of personnel, equipment, space, and money. In a well-managed governmental unit, the same sort of review is given to each continuing program. The mere fact that the program was authorized by a past legislative body does not mean the administration may shirk its duty to recommend discontinuance of a program that has ceased to serve a real need. If the program should be continued, in the judgment of the administration, the appropriate level of activity and the appropriate allocation of resources must be determined; this determination takes far more political courage and management skill than the common practice of simply extrapolating the trend of historical activity and historical cost.

If the administration is convinced that a program should be continued and the prior allocation of resources is relatively appropriate, the preparation of the appropriations budget is delegated to the persons in charge of the program. In the case of

Illustration 13–1 Integrated Budgeting Planning System

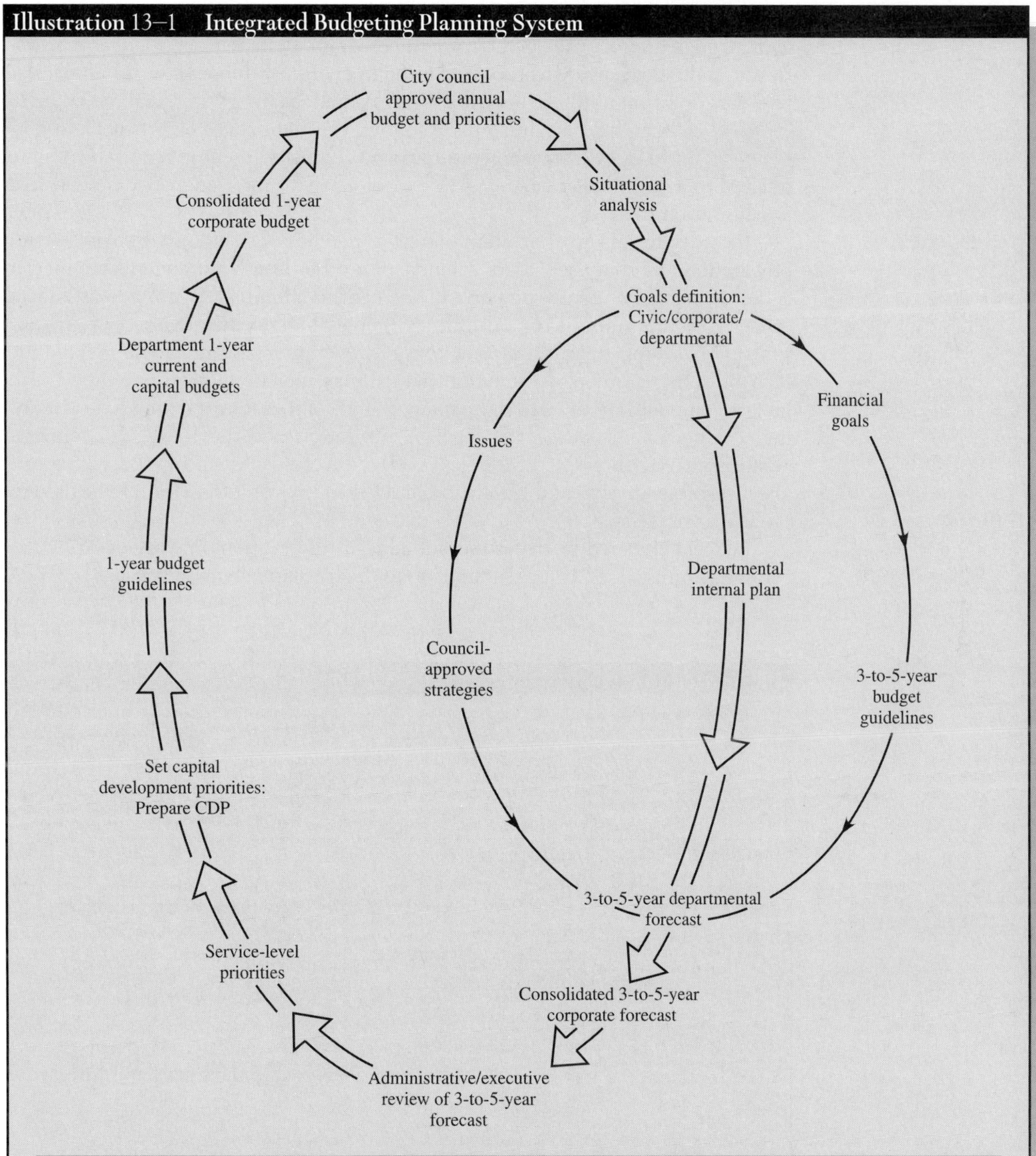

Source: Adapted from Peter P. Fernandes and Myriam P. Laberge, "Setting Local Government Priorities through the Budget Process," *Government Finance Review*, April 1986, p. 23. Reprinted with permission of the Government Finance Officers Association.

a new program, the administration states the objectives of the program and sets general guidelines for the operation of the program, then delegates budget preparation to individuals who are expected to be in charge of the program when legislative authorization and appropriations are secured. State laws or local ordinances typically require that certain steps be followed in the budgeting process and may prescribe dates by which each step must be completed. These requirements are referred to as the **budget calendar**. A budget calendar for a small city is presented in Illustration 13–2.

In order to ensure that administrative policies are actually used in budget preparation and that the budget calendar and other legal requirements are met, it is customary to designate someone in the central administrative office as budget officer. In addition to the responsibilities enumerated, the **budget officer** is responsible for providing technical assistance to the operating personnel who prepare the budgets. The technical assistance provided may include clerical assistance with budget computations as well as the maintenance of files for each program containing: (1) documents citing the legal authorization and directives, (2) relevant administrative policies, (3) historical cost and workload data, (4) specific factors affecting program costs and workloads, and (5) sources of information to be used in projecting trends.

Budgets prepared by departmental administrators should be reviewed by the central administration before submission to the legislative branch because the total

Illustration 13–2

SAMPLE CITY
BUDGET CALENDAR
YEAR ENDING SEPTEMBER 30

Date	*Event*	*Requirement or Action*
July 20	1st Budget Workshop	Draft budget and documentation.
August 4	2nd Budget Workshop	Draft budget and documentation.
August 11	Regular Council Meeting/ 3rd Budget Workshop	Long-term GF projections, capital outlay and analysis of budget increases.
August 25	Regular Council Meeting/ 4th Budget Workshop	Budget presentations by County Health District, Chamber of Commerce, and other organizations.
September 1	Special Council Meeting/ 5th Budget Workshop	Water/Sewer budget presentation. Call for public hearing to be held September 8.
September 3	Newspaper Publication	Publish notice of public hearing on budget to be held on September 8.
September 8	Regular Council Meeting	Public hearing on proposed budget.
September 15	Special Council Meeting	First reading of budget ordinance.
September 22	Regular Council Meeting	Second reading and vote on adoption of budget ordinance.

of departmental requests frequently exceeds the total of estimated revenues, and it is necessary to trim the requests in some manner. Central review may also be necessary to make sure enough is being spent on certain programs. Good financial management of the taxpayers' dollars is a process of trying to determine the optimum dollar input to achieve the desired service output, not a process of minimizing input. Even though the appropriations budget is a legally prescribed document, the administration should not lose sight of its managerial usefulness.

It should be emphasized that governmental budgets submitted to the legislative branch for action must be made available for a certain length of time for study by interested citizens, and one or more public hearings must be held before the legislative branch takes final action. Ordinarily, few citizens take the trouble to study the proposed budgets in detail; however, newspaper and television reporters often publicize proposed appropriations, especially those for programs, activities, and functions deemed particularly newsworthy. News reporters also publicize increases in taxes and fees proposed to finance budgeted appropriations. Representatives of such organizations as the state or local Chamber of Commerce and League of Women Voters analyze the budgets in detail and furnish analyses to their members, the public, and news media. Generally, such broadly based organizations attempt to be even-handed in their budget analyses. In many instances, however, members of special interest groups also sift through the proposed budget to determine the proposed allocation of resources to the programs, activities, and functions of interest to the groups they represent; budget analyses of special interest groups are not intended to be even-handed. If the proposed budget does not meet the interests of the group as well as they think they can expect realistically, the groups may be counted on to attempt to influence the votes of the members of the legislative branch to change the budget before it is enacted into law. Thus it is evident that the governmental process involves political and social considerations and, at higher levels of government, aggregate economic considerations, all of which may be more important to many voters, administrators (bureaucrats), and legislators (politicians) than financial considerations. The relationship among these stakeholders is presented graphically in Illustration 13–3. Governmental budgeting considerations are consistent with the overall goal of governmental accounting and financial reporting, discussed in Chapter 1.

Comparable considerations exist for business enterprises. A profit-seeking business will succeed in the long run only if it serves the needs of its customers and of society in general: The financial managers of a business must budget within this framework. In business budgeting, revenues and expenses of any year are interrelated; expenses are incurred in the effort to produce revenue, and the production of revenue enables the further incurring of expenses and the further production of revenue. Revenues and expenses are interdependent variables in business budgeting.

Business budgeting concepts are appropriate for governmental activities run on a business basis. A similar interrelationship may be said to exist at the federal government level in the cases of certain General Fund expenditures made in order to stimulate segments of the economy; the costs of increasing economic activity tend to be recouped by increased tax revenue. For general governmental activities,

Illustration 13–3 The Governmental Budget Decision Process

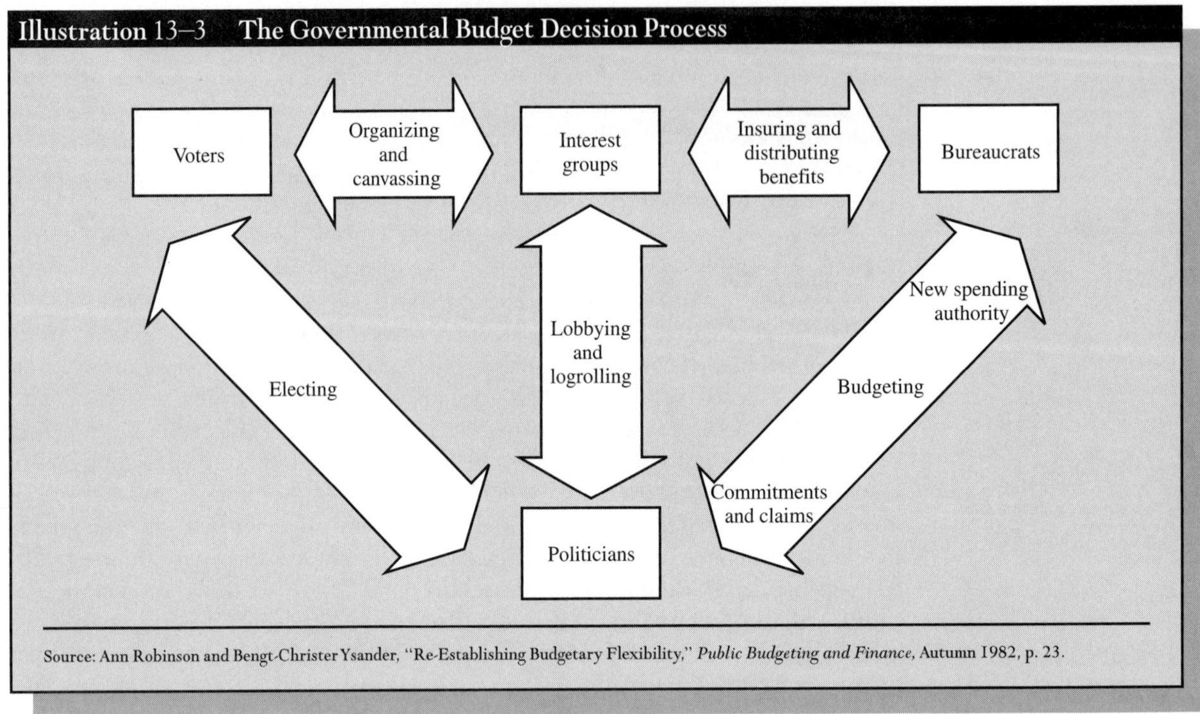

Source: Ann Robinson and Bengt-Christer Ysander, "Re-Establishing Budgetary Flexibility," *Public Budgeting and Finance,* Autumn 1982, p. 23.

however, revenues and expenditures are not interdependent variables. Expenditures are made in order to render a service to the citizens, and not in order to generate revenue. Similarly, although revenues may vary from month to month, the variation of revenues has little direct effect on the incurring of expenditures.

Budgeting Governmental Revenues

Although governmental revenues and expenditures are not interdependent variables as business revenues and expenses are, the availability of revenues is a necessary prerequisite to the incurring of expenditures. Some states and local governments may operate at a deficit temporarily, but it is generally conceded that they may not do so indefinitely. Thus, wise financial management calls for the preparation of revenues budgets, at least in rough form, prior to the preparation of detailed operating plans and finalizing appropriations budgets.

Revenues is a term that has a precise meaning in governmental accounting. The GASB states that the term *revenues* "means increases in (sources of) fund financial resources other than from interfund transfers and debt issue proceeds."[5] For purposes of budgeting inflows of financial resources of a fund, it does not seem particularly valuable to distinguish among revenues, as defined by the GASB,

[5]GASB, *Codification*, Sec. 1800, 114.

interfund transfers, and debt issue proceeds, other than to keep budgeting terminology consistent with accounting and financial reporting terminology.

Sources of revenue and other financial inflows available to a given local governmental unit are generally closely controlled by state law; state laws also establish procedures for the utilization of available sources and may impose ceilings on the amount of revenue a local government may collect from certain sources. Sources generally available for financing routine operations include property taxes, sales taxes, income taxes, license fees, fines, charges for services, grants or allocations from other governmental units, and revenue from the use of money or property. Chapter 3 of this text describes revenue sources and discusses revenue accounting in some detail. The present discussion is, therefore, limited to the broad aspects of governmental revenue budgeting.

Within the framework set by legal requirements and subject to the approval of the legislative body (which, in turn, reacts to the electorate), the determination of revenue policy is a prerogative of the administration. Major considerations underlying the policy formulation are set forth in the preceding section of this chapter. After policies are established, the technical preparation of the revenues budget is ordinarily delegated to the budget officer. In order to facilitate budget preparation, experienced budget officers generally keep for each revenue source a file containing (1) a copy of legislation authorizing the source and any subsequent legislation pertaining to the source; (2) historical experience relative to collections from the source, including collections as a percentage of billings, where applicable; (3) relevant administrative policies; and (4) specific factors that affect the yield from the source, including for each factor the historical relationship of the factor to revenue procedures to be used in projecting the trend of factors affecting yield, and factors affecting collections. Graphic presentations of these factors are also frequently included in the file. Finance officers of large governmental units use more sophisticated statistical and econometric methods of revenue forecasting, particularly to evaluate alternative assumptions, but the method described here is generally used for preparation of a legal revenues budget.

Budgeting Capital Expenditures

Accounting principles for business enterprises and for proprietary funds of governmental units require the cost of assets expected to benefit more than one period to be treated as a balance sheet item, rather than as a charge against revenues of the period. No such distinction exists for governmental fund types. Expenditures for long-lived assets to be used in the general operations of a governmental unit are treated in the appropriations process in the same manner as are expenditures for salaries, wages, benefits, materials, supplies, and services to be consumed during the accounting period. Accounting control over long-lived assets used in general operations is established, however, as described in Chapter 5 of this text.

Effective financial management requires the plans for any one year to be consistent with intermediate- and long-range plans. Governmental projects such as the construction or improvement of streets; construction of bridges and buildings; acquisition of land for recreational use, parking lots, and future building sites; and urban renewal all may require a consistent application of effort over a span of years. Consequently, administrators need to present to the legislative branch and to the public a multiyear capital improvements program, as well as the budget for revenues, operating expenditures, and capital outlays requested for the forthcoming year.

Effective financial management also requires nonfinancial information such as physical measures of capital assets, their service condition, and their estimated replacement cost. Nonfinancial information of these types is useful for purposes of forecasting future asset repair and replacement schedules, repair and replacement costs, and financing requirements.

Revenues and Expenditures budgets would best be prepared on the same basis as the accounts and financial reports: modified accrual, in the case of governmental funds—particularly general funds and special revenue funds. Although it is highly desirable for persons concerned with the financial management of governmental units (or any other organization) to foresee the effects of operating plans and capital improvement plans on receivables, payables, inventories, and facilities, it is absolutely necessary to foresee the effects on cash. An organization must have sufficient cash to pay employees, suppliers, and creditors amounts due at the times due, or it risks labor troubles, an unsatisfactory credit rating, and consequent difficulties in maintaining its capacity to render services at acceptable levels to its residents. An organization that maintains cash balances in excess of needs fails to earn interest on temporary investments; therefore, it is raising more revenues than would otherwise be needed, or failing to offer services.

Cash Receipts Budgeting

In Chapter 4 it was noted, that in a typical governmental unit, cash receipts from major sources of revenues of general funds and special revenue funds are concentrated in a few months of each fiscal year, whereas cash disbursements tend to be approximately level month by month. Under the heading "Tax Anticipation Notes Payable" in Chapter 4, reference is made to cash forecasting done by the Treasurer of the Town of Brighton in order to determine the amount of **tax anticipation notes** to be issued. The cash forecasting method illustrated in that chapter is quite crude but often reasonably effective if done by experienced persons. Sophisticated cash budgeting methods used in well-managed governmental units require additional data, such as historical records of monthly collections from each revenue source including percentage of billings, where applicable. In addition to the historical record of collections, the budget files should contain analyses of the factors affecting the collections from each source, so that adjustments to historical patterns may be made, if needed, for the budget year.

Property taxes are often the largest recurring cash receipt in a government; however, all other expected cash receipts must be included in the cash budget. More difficult to project are self-assessed taxes, such as income taxes; nonrecurring receipts, such as those from the sale of assets; and income earned on **sweep accounts**, arrangements where a bank automatically "sweeps" cash that exceeds the target balance into short-term cash investments.

Cash Disbursements Budgeting

Except for special provisions regarding expenditures of debt service funds, the expenditures of all other governmental funds (and of all proprietary funds) are to be recognized and budgeted on the full accrual basis. Therefore, the conversion of the approved appropriations budget into a cash disbursements budget involves a knowledge of personnel policies, purchasing policies, and operating policies and plans, which should govern the timing of expenditures of appropriations, and the consequent payment of liabilities. Information as to current and previous typical time intervals between the ordering of goods and contractual services, their receipt, and the related disbursements should be available from the appropriation expenditures ledgers and cash disbursement records. In the case of salaries and wages of governmental employees, the cash disbursements budget for each month is affected by the number of paydays that fall in the month, rather than that number of working days in the month.

After monthly cash receipts budgets are prepared for all sources of revenues of each fund and cash disbursements budgets are prepared for all organization units, and so forth, it is possible, and desirable, to match the two in order to determine when and for how long cash balances will rise to unnecessarily high levels, or fall to levels below those prudent management would require (or even to overdraft positions). Note the preceding sentence is concerned with cash receipts and disbursements of all funds of a governmental unit, not a single fund. There is no reason for bank accounts and fund cash accounts to agree, except in total. Effective cash planning and control suggests that *all* cash be put under control of the Treasurer of the governmental unit.

As shown in Illustration 13–4, cash receipts for the Town of Brighton are highest in April, May, and November, presumably when taxes are collected. Disbursements are fairly constant across the year, except for January, which may be when capital assets are acquired. The pattern of short-term borrowing, repayment, and investment seems to indicate that the City's cash and investment policies include: (1) a target monthly cash balance of at least $425,000, (2) new borrowing made in increments of $5,000, and (3) cash exceeding the target used to repay short-term borrowing; any remaining excess is invested. A very small governmental unit that has few receipts and infrequent disbursements may be able to plan temporary investments and short-term borrowings on the basis of cash budgets for periods longer than one month, perhaps quarterly or semiannually. Conversely, a governmental unit with considerable cash activity involving large sums might need to budget cash receipts and cash disbursements on a daily basis to maintain adequate, but not excessive, cash balances.

Budgeting, by definition, involves planning on the basis of assumptions about economic conditions, salary levels, numbers of employees at each salary level, prices of supplies and capital acquisitions, and other factors that cannot be foreseen with great accuracy. Accordingly, it is necessary at intervals throughout the year to compare actual receipts with budgeted receipts, source by source; and actual disbursements with budgeted disbursements for each organizational unit, function and object; not only for the sake of control (cash control is discussed in the next section of this chapter) but for the sake of evaluating the budget and, if necessary, revising the budget in light of new knowledge about economic conditions, salary, and price levels, and other factors affecting collections and disbursements.

Illustration 13–4

TOWN OF BRIGHTON
BUDGETED CASH RECEIPTS AND DISBURSEMENTS FOR FY2002
(000 OMITTED)

	January	*February*	*March*	*April*	*May*	*June*	*July*	*August*	*September*	*October*	*November*	*December*
Balance first of month	$ 610	$425	$425	$425	$ 425	$425	$425	$427	$427	$427	$ 427	$425
Expected receipts during month	165	250	295	570	1,096	134	280	370	285	270	892	116
Cash available	775	675	720	995	1,521	559	705	797	712	697	1,319	541
Expected disbursements during month	1,050	240	280	325	320	320	508	325	315	335	320	455
Provisional balance at end of month	(275)	435	440	670	1,201	239	197	472	397	362	999	86
Less: Temporary investments purchased	—	—	—	—	346	—	—	—	—	—	454	—
Less: Repayment of short-term borrowings	—	10	15	245	430	—	—	45	—	—	120	—
Add: Temporary investments sold	—	—	—	—	—	186	160	—	—	—	—	340
Add: Short-term borrowings	700	—	—	—	—	—	70	—	30	65	—	—
Balance at end of month	$ 425	$425	$425	$425	$ 425	$425	$427	$427	$427	$427	$ 425	$426

Budgeting for Performance

During the last twenty years, growth in service demands and cutbacks in unrestricted federal funding forced numerous state and local governments to increase taxes and user fees. Meanwhile, taxpayers have become increasingly more frustrated with paying higher taxes for what they perceive as bloated, inefficient government bureaucracies. Fiscal reform has thus become a popular platform for politicians aspiring to key elective offices. Even though, as discussed previously in this chapter, many governments have experimented with so-called rational budgeting approaches, most of these experiments seem to have had little real impact on improving the efficiency and effectiveness of service delivery. Given their limited success with prior budgeting approaches, political leaders have had little choice but to experiment with recent management innovations in the private sector that might improve the efficiency of government operations and reduce the need for higher taxes.

Many state and local governments are well along in their efforts to link performance measurement systems with budgeting and strategic planning. For example, the Government Finance Officers Association (GFOA) has recognized the cities of Sunnyvale, California; Indianapolis, Indiana; and Glendale, Arizona (among others), with the GFOA's Distinguished Budget Presentation Award for excellence in budgeting for legal compliance and performance.[6] Some states have passed legislation that requires performance measures, both financial and nonfinancial, to be reported by local governments and public institutions, such as colleges and universities. Two innovations being employed by many governments to measure the results or performance of the organization are total quality management and service efforts and accomplishments.

Fortunately, many governments have improved their budgeting practices over the past decade. A major impetus for this improvement has been the Government Finance Officers Association's Distinguished Budget Presentation Awards Program. Voluntary applications for this award increased from 113 in 1984, the year the program was initiated, to 900 in 1998. About 80 percent of the applicants have received the award and many of the unsuccessful applicants received confidential reviewer suggestions that permitted them to subsequently qualify for the award.

Total Quality Management

Total quality management (TQM) is attractive to many government officials because it links customer (taxpayer and other resource provider) satisfaction to improvements in the operating systems and processes used to provide goods and services. TQM seeks to continuously improve the government's ability to meet or exceed customer demands, where the customer might be external, such as taxpayers and service recipients, or internal, such as the customers of an internal service

[6]See Theodore H. Poister and Gregory Streib, "Performance Measurement in Municipal Government: Assessing the State of the Practice," *Public Administration Review*, July/August 1999, pp. 325–35. See also, "Annual Report—Distinguished Budget Presentation Awards Program" of the GFOA, available at www.gfoa.org/awards/budget.htm.

fund. Central to TQM is using customer data to identify and correct problems. Individual governments have tailored their TQM structures to meet their unique requirements, but most incorporate a majority of the following elements:

1. Support and commitment of top-level officials.
2. Customer orientation.
3. Employee involvement in productivity and quality improvement efforts.
4. Employees rewarded for quality and productivity achievement.
5. Training provided to employees in methods for improving productivity and quality.
6. Reduction of barriers to productivity and quality improvement.
7. Productivity and quality measures and standards that are meaningful to the governmental unit.
8. Written vision or mission statements that are linked directly to team-established targets or goals.[7]

The elements of TQM are obviously consistent with those of the rational budgeting approaches (particularly PPBS) previously discussed. Thus governments that have implemented one of the rational budgeting approaches, or a mixed approach, may find it less costly to implement a TQM structure. On the other hand, few governments possess adequate data on customer satisfaction. Moreover, the traditional emphases of government on line-item budgeting, rigid personnel classifications, restrictive procurement regulations, and so on, tend to reduce management autonomy, and thus may be inconsistent with the need under TQM to empower employees to be "entrepreneurial" in improving processes and meeting customer demand. It should also be noted that the objective of TQM is not necessarily to reduce cost but rather to increase "value for the dollar." Insofar as a TQM program successfully adds value, it has the potential to improve the public perception of government, in addition, of course, to improving service delivery.

Element 7 from the preceding list of TQM elements requires that the governmental unit develop meaningful standards for and measures of performance in terms of productivity and quality. In the government and not-for-profit context, the analogous performance terms more typically used are *efficiency* and *effectiveness*, the former relating efforts (resource inputs) to outputs of a service process and the latter relating efforts to outcomes or the results produced by service.

Service Efforts and Accomplishments

Because of growing public demand for greater accountability, a number of governments currently report some **service efforts and accomplishments** (SEA) measures for selected service functions, although there are no generally accepted standards to guide selection of the measures to report. The GASB has conducted and commissioned research into appropriate SEA measures for a variety of service functions,

[7]Adapted from James J. Kline, "Total Quality Management in Local Government," *Government Finance Review*, August 1992, p. 7. See also Andrea Jackson, "Applying TQM Principles to the Finance Department: The City of Auburn Experience," *Government Finance Review*, February 1999.

including, among others, police departments, fire departments, mass transit, public assistance programs, road maintenance, and colleges and universities.[8]

As discussed in Chapter 9, SEA measures fall into three broad categories: (1) service efforts (resources used), (2) service accomplishments (outputs and outcomes), and (3) those that relate service efforts to service accomplishments (efficiency measures and cost-outcome measures). Illustration 13–5 shows recommended SEA indicators for police departments. As shown in Illustration 13–5 the input measures indicate quantities and dollar amounts of resources used in providing police services. The output and outcome indicators collectively indicate service accomplishments, where outputs indicate quantities of work done on particular activities (such as patrol, responding to calls, and investigations) and outcomes indicate the results of activities in achieving desired objectives (such as reduction of deaths, bodily injury, and property loss). SEA measures for key programs or service functions are essential for measuring entity performance and can provide much of the data needed for implementation of a TQM system.

Development of sophisticated rational budgeting approaches and TQM systems requires sophisticated cost accounting systems to determine the full cost of programs or functions. Better managed state and local governmental units are therefore actively developing improved cost accounting systems. One innovative costing approach being implemented by some governments, which can be implemented in tandem with TQM or other performance measurement systems, is activity-based costing (ABC), discussed later in this chapter.

Costing of Government Services

The explosive increase in demand for government services, relative to the increase in resources, has forced the adoption of the techniques of good financial management, including better cost accounting. The use of cost as a measure of the input of resources into a program, as an element of the budget, and as a basis to assess performance has been discussed earlier in this chapter. This section discusses the role of costs in a system that integrates management, budgeting, and costing for a governmental or not-for-profit organization.

Cost accounting, as discussed in standard college texts, is obviously applicable to business operations of governments and health care entities; but its application to nonbusiness activities of a government, not-for-profit organizations, or colleges and universities is not as immediately obvious. However, the same tasks of segregating direct from indirect costs, variable from fixed costs, standard from actual costs, and incremental from sunk costs are as important in capturing the total cost of delivering governmental or not-for-profit program services as they are in private-sector companies. Another similarity with traditional cost accounting in the

[8]Governmental Accounting Standards Board, Research Report, *Service Efforts and Accomplishments Reporting: Its Time Has Come* (Norwalk, CT: GASB, 1990). See the GASB's "Performance Measurement for Government" site at http://www.rutgers.edu/Accounting/raw/seagov/pmg.

Illustration 13–5 Recommended SEA Indicators for Police Departments*

Indicator	*Rationale for Selecting Indicator*
Inputs:	
Budget expenditures	To provide a measure of financial resources used to provide services.
Equipment, facilities, vehicles	To provide a measure of nonpersonnel resources used to provide services.
Number of personnel or hours expended	To provide a measure of the size of the organization and the human resources used to provide services.
Outputs:	
Hours of patrol	To provide a measure of the quantity of patrol service provided; patrol is generally regarded as a primary product of police efforts.
Responses to calls for service	To provide a measure of the quantity of response service provided.
Crimes investigated	To provide a measure of the quantity of services provided by investigation units.
Number of arrests	To provide a measure of the success of police efforts in apprehending criminal offenders.
Persons participating in crime-prevention activities	To provide a measure of the quantity of service provided by crime-prevention units.
Outcomes:	
Deaths and bodily injury resulting from crime	To provide a measure of the effectiveness of police efforts in reducing the incidence of personal harm attributed to criminal activity.
Value of property lost due to crime	To provide a measure of the effectiveness of police efforts in reducing the incidence of property loss due to criminal activity.
Crimes committed per 100,000 population	To provide a measure of the effectiveness of police efforts in reducing criminal activity.
Percentage of crimes cleared	To provide a measure of the effectiveness of police efforts in detection of criminal activity and apprehension of criminal offenders.
Response time	To provide a measure of the quality of police response to calls.
Citizen satisfaction	To provide a measure of the overall effectiveness of police efforts in meeting citizen needs.

context of for-profit organizations is that **job order cost** accounting may be appropriate for some tasks (i.e., recording costs chargeable to specific grants, programs, projects, activities, or departments), and for others **process cost** accounting is more appropriate (i.e., recording continuous activities of governmental units, health care entities, and universities for a time period). In any organization, predetermination of overhead rates involves budgeting the overhead costs that should be incurred at the level of activity chosen as a basis for determination of the rate. Governments and not-for-profit organizations can use **flexible budgeting** to budget costs at different levels of activity and then compare costs that were actually incurred in a period with costs that should have been incurred to achieve that level of output.

Illustration 13–5 *(concluded)*

Indicator	*Rationale for Selecting Indicator*
Efficiency:	
Cost per case assigned; cost per crime cleared	To provide an indication of the cost efficiency of police efforts.
Personnel-hours per crime cleared	To provide an indication of the productivity of personnel in providing police services.
Explanatory variables:	To provide information on factors that are likely to affect the incidence and effects of criminal activity so that measures of output, outcome, and efficiency may be viewed in proper context.
Population by age group	
Unemployment rate	
Number of households; number of business firms	
Percentage of population below poverty level	
Land area	
Dollar value of property within jurisdiction	
Demand:	
Calls for service	
Cases assigned	

*The recommended indicators presented in this exhibit are illustrative. They are intended to serve as a starting point for use in the development of a comprehensive set of SEA indicators for external reporting of an entity's results of operation.

This exhibit does not provide illustrations of indicator disaggregation or of comparison data such as trends, targets, or other comparable entities. Both disaggregation and comparison data are important aspects of SEA reporting.

Source: Government Accounting Standards Board, Research Report, *Service Efforts and Accomplishments Reporting: Its Time Has Come* (Norwalk, CT: GASB, 1990), Exhibit 8–1.

Cost determination, the recasting of data derived from fund accounting to obtain desired cost information, is often a necessary task for governmental and not-for-profit organizations given the poor state of many such organizations' cost accounting systems. Cost determination procedures may be considered statistical if they are done apart from the accounting information system, and may be done at regular intervals or only on a special study basis. The role of cost accounting systems will change dramatically as organizations implement integrated financial management systems, including enterprise resource planning (ERP).[9]

This section presents two other cost accounting issues with special significance to governmental and not-for-profit organizations. The first, acceptance of federal grants and sponsored agreements, brings with it the duty to comply with particular

[9]K. Nicole Fontayne-Mack, "Managing Enterprise Financial Systems Projects: The City of Detroit's Experience," *Government Finance Review*, February 1999.

regulations on allowable costs and methods of spending. The second, activity-based costing, has been adopted by some governments as a key element of performance evaluation systems. Such systems are enhanced by designing accounting systems to provide as much activity-based cost data as possible, even though the need for some statistical cost data outside of the accounting system is inevitable.

Federal Grants and Sponsored Agreements

State and local governmental units and not-for-profit entities, particularly colleges and universities, have found grants from and sponsored agreements with the federal government important, although diminishing, sources of financing. The United States Office of Management and Budget has issued a series of Circulars to set forth *cost principles* to govern payments by the federal government under grant programs, contracts, and other agreements, to state and local governments (OMB *Circular A-87*), educational institutions (OMB *Circular A-21*), and other not-for-profit organizations (OMB *Circular A-122*).[10] The wording of all three Circulars is similar in many respects. They provide that the total cost of a program or contract is the sum of the allowable direct costs incident to its performance, plus its allocable portion of allowable indirect costs, less applicable credits. The terms *allowable costs*, *direct costs*, and *indirect costs*, among others, are defined in the Circulars.

Administrative requirements describing *how* federal expenditures are made are also detailed in OMB Circulars (for example, maintaining a financial management system and competitive bidding for procuring supplies and property). Illustration 13–6 shows the relationship of these Circulars to the organizations they cover. Just as the OMB combined *Circulars A-128* and *A-133* (as discussed in Chapter 11), there is a movement towards a combined circular for cost principles and another for administration requirements covering all types of organizations receiving federal funds. Of course, even with one Circular for educational institutions and not-for-profit agencies (OMB *Circular A-110*), only 12 federal agencies have adopted *A-110* without major changes. Seven agencies, including the Departments of Education, Health and Human Services, and Housing and Urban Development, have made major changes to the version of *A-110* that applies to grants they make. An organization accepting federal funds must follow *all* relevant OMB Circulars.

Allowable Costs. To be an **allowable cost**, the cost must meet the following general criteria:

a. Be necessary and reasonable for proper and efficient performance and administration of federal awards. (A cost is reasonable if it does not exceed that which would be incurred by a prudent person under the circumstances prevailing at the time the decision was made to incur the cost.)

b. Be allocable to federal awards under provisions of *Circular A-87*.

c. Be authorized or not prohibited under state or local laws or regulations.

---

[10]In addition, the Cost Accounting Standards Board (CASB), an independent board within the Office of Management and Budget's Office of Federal Procurement Policy, has instituted 19 standards since its inception in 1970 that apply to federal government contractors.

Illustration 13–6 OMB Grants Management Circulars

	Cost Principles	*Administrative Requirements*
State and local governments	*Circular A-87* "Cost Principles for State, Local and Indian Tribal Governments" (revised 1995, amended 8/29/97)	*Circular A-102* "Grants and Cooperative Agreements with State and Local Governments" known as **"The Common Rule"** (revised 1994, amended 8/29/97)
Educational institutions	*Circular A-21* "Cost Principles for Educational Institutions" (10/27/98)	*Circular A-110* "Uniform Administrative Requirements for Grants and Other Agreements with Institutions of Higher Education, Hospitals, and Other Non-Profit Organizations" (revised 1993, amended 9/30/99)
Nonprofit organizations	*Circular A-122* "Cost Principles for Non-Profit Organizations" (5/19/98)	*Circular A-110* (same as above)

Source: All Circulars are available from the Office of Management and Budget (Washington, DC: Superintendent of Documents, U.S. Government Printing Office) or http:/www.whitehouse.gov/OMB.

d. Conform to any limitations or exclusions, federal laws, terms and conditions of the federal award, or other governing regulations as to types or amounts of cost items.

e. Be consistent with policies, regulations, and procedures that apply uniformly to both federally assisted and other activities of the governmental unit.

f. Be accorded consistent treatment. Consequently, a cost may not be assigned to a federal award as a direct cost if any other cost incurred for the same purpose has been allocated to the federal award as an indirect cost.

g. Except as otherwise provided for, be determined in accordance with generally accepted accounting principles.

h. Not be included as a cost or used to meet cost sharing or matching requirements of any other federal award in either the current or a prior period, except as specifically provided by federal law.

i. Be determined net of all applicable credits (e.g., purchase discounts; rebates or allowances; recoveries or indemnities on losses; sale of publications and scrap; income from personal or incidental services;

insurance refunds or rebates; earnings or imputed earnings on reserves; and adjustments of overpayments or erroneous charges).

j. Be adequately documented.[11]

Each Circular provides standards for determining the allowability of selected items of cost. Certain items of cost are generally allowable whether or not mentioned specifically in a grant, contract, or other agreement document. Certain other cost items are allowable only if specifically approved by the grantor agency, and certain other cost items are unallowable. *Circular A-87* lists 42 cost items ranging alphabetically from Accounting to Underrecovery of Costs under Federal Agreements. Of the 42 cost items, 31 are allowable whether direct or indirect to the extent they pertain to specific grants or to the overall management of all grant programs. Depreciation and use allowances are included in the 31 allowable cost items. As explained in Chapter 5, even though governmental funds do not record depreciation expense, it is now reported for general capital assets at the government-wide level in the GASB *Statement No. 34* reporting model. Moreover, although public colleges and universities formerly did not report depreciation expense, they will report it now that most such institutions will be reporting as a business-type activity under GASB *Statement No. 35*. Consequently, both governmental units and public colleges and universities will find it relatively easy to charge depreciation to federal grants and contracts.

Several of the 31 allowable items are allowable under highly restrictive conditions, and generally require the explicit approval of the grantor agency. An example is advertising costs that are allowable only for such items as recruitment of personnel, procurement of goods and services, and disposal of scrap or surplus materials related to the performance of federal assistance programs. Eleven of the 42 cost items are *unallowable*, including such items as alcoholic beverages, bad debt expenses, contributions and donations, fund-raising and investment management costs, entertainment, general expenses of the state or local government (e.g., salaries of the chief executive, legislatures, judicial department officials), and lobbying. Similar prohibitions apply to colleges and universities under the provisions of *Circular A-21*.

Direct Costs. **Direct costs** are those that can be identified specifically with a particular cost objective. A **cost objective,** in federal terminology, is an organizational unit, function, activity, project, cost center, or pool established for the accumulation of costs. A final, or ultimate, cost objective is a specific grant, project, contract, or other activity (presumably one of interest to the federal agency that provides resources for the activity under a grant, contract, or other agreement). A cost may be direct with respect to a given function or activity but indirect with respect to the grant or other final cost objective of interest to the grantor or contractor. Typical direct costs chargeable to grant programs include compensation of

[11]OMB, *Circular A-87*, Attachment A, C-1.

employees for the time and efforts devoted specifically to the execution of grant programs; cost of materials acquired, consumed, or expended specifically for the purpose of the grant; and other items of expense incurred specifically to carry out the grant agreement. If approved by the grantor agency, equipment purchased and other capital expenditures incurred for a certain grant or other final cost objective would be considered direct costs.

Indirect Costs. **Indirect costs**, according to *Circular A-87*, are those (*a*) incurred for a common or joint purpose benefiting more than one cost objective and (*b*) not readily assignable to the cost objectives specifically benefited, without effort disproportionate to the results achieved. The term *indirect costs* applies to costs originating in the grantee department, as well as to those incurred by other departments in supplying goods, services, and facilities to the grantee department. To facilitate equitable distribution of indirect expenses to the cost objectives served, it may be necessary to establish a number of "pools" of indirect cost within the grantee department. Indirect cost pools should be distributed to benefited cost objectives on bases that produce an equitable result in consideration of relative benefits derived. In certain instances, grantees may negotiate annually with the grantor a predetermined fixed rate for computing indirect costs applicable to a grant, or a lump-sum allowance for indirect costs, but generally grantees must prepare a cost allocation plan that conforms with instructions issued by the U.S. Department of Health and Human Services. Cost allocation plans of local governments will be retained for audit by a designated federal agency. (Audit of federal grants is discussed in some detail in Chapter 11 of this text.)

Activity-Based Costing

Activity-based costing (ABC) was developed for use by manufacturing companies when it became apparent that traditional cost accounting systems were producing distorted product costs. Thus, some products that were thought to be profitable were, on closer inspection, found to be unprofitable, and vice versa. Two Harvard University professors, Robin Cooper and Robert S. Kaplan, made convincing arguments that typical cost accounting systems often understate profits on high-volume products and overstate profits on low-volume specialty items.[12] This problem is attributable, in part, to greater product diversity, shorter product life cycles, shift in production technology from labor to automation, more diverse distribution channels, and greater quality demands, all of which are driven by need to more effectively compete in the global marketplace. The net effect of these trends (which are also applicable to government, at least to some extent) is to create a larger infrastructure of "production support" activities, and thus to shift costs from direct cost categories to indirect cost, or overhead, categories. As a larger proportion of these costs is allocated to products, product cost distortions become a larger problem and may result in poor product decisions.

---

[12]Robin Cooper and Robert S. Kaplan, "Measure Costs Right: Make the Right Decisions," *Harvard Business Review*, September–October 1988, pp. 96–103.

ABC essentially attempts to determine the cost of specific process-related activities, the "drivers" of those costs (e.g., labor-hours, machine-hours, or units of material), and the consumption of cost drivers in producing outputs of goods or services. Emphasis is placed on tracing the specific activities performed to specific outputs of goods or services, rather than on allocating average costs to units of output as done in conventional cost accounting systems. A publication of the Institute of Management Accountants explains the advantage of the ABC approach relative to traditional cost accounting allocations:[13]

> In traditional systems, financial controllers usually create elaborate, step-down, sequential allocations that distribute service department cost to production work centers based on percentage estimates. These allocations are often flawed because they assume arbitrary relationships; for example, using square feet or head count. These measures do not reflect disproportionate resource consumption. Such burden-averaging techniques are convenient for accountants but are not of service to users of information.
>
> With ABC, resource cost drivers replace the step-down allocations with cause-and-effect relationships at the activity level. (p. 13)

Determining the amount of each activity that is consumed in each product or service utilizes materials usage records, observation, and timekeeping systems, but is often augmented with estimates obtained through employee interviews and other means. The cost of designing a system that totally eliminates the need for overhead allocation is likely to be prohibitive. If allocation of "residual" unassigned costs is not potentially distortive, it may be more cost effective to focus ABC design on major activities and cost drivers, and then allocate remaining costs on an appropriate basis.

State-of-the-art approaches, such as total quality management (TQM) and service efforts and accomplishments (SEA) measures, implemented by some governments to improve performance require timely information on the full cost of resources consumed in providing service outputs. To calculate the full cost of services, however, requires careful allocation of indirect costs such as the clerical and administrative costs of general government functions (e.g., chief executive's office, finance department, legal department). The use of inappropriate allocation bases may produce distorted cost estimates for some service outputs in much the same manner that conventional cost systems produce distorted product costs. It is not surprising then that some governments have adopted ABC for key service functions. An article by Bridget Anderson explains the objectives of ABC in a governmental environment as follows:[14]

> The objectives of ABC are to preserve, at a minimum, the present quality and availability of core services but to acknowledge that some of the forces for greater expenditures have not been controlled. It seeks to reduce the costs of service outcomes by:
>
> - reducing the number of service units through program redesign,

---

[13]Gary Cokins, Alan Stratton, and Jack Helbling, *An ABC Manager's Primer: Straight Talk on Activity-Based Costing* (Montvale, NJ: Institute of Management Accountants, 1993).

[14]Bridget M. Anderson, "Using Activity-Based Costing for Efficiency and Quality," *Government Finance Review*, June 1993, pp. 7–9.

- finding lower cost alternatives,
- making volume increases dependent on cost reductions, and
- understanding and controlling the delivery/program design interaction.

A simplified diagram of an ABC cost model used by the City of Indianapolis to identify activity-based costs for snow control and patching chuckholes is shown in Illustration 13–7. Total activities cost for one particular district of the City for the two functions (snow control and chuckhole patching) is $2,600 as displayed in the leftmost table of Illustration 13–7. The five activities are C labor, D labor, salt, SAD (a type of truck), and central service overhead. The drivers identified in Illustration 13–7 are direct labor-hours of C and D labor, tons of salt, SAD (vehicle usage) hours, and total labor-hours for C and D combined to allocate overhead to units of output. The Consumption table shows the driver units of each activity that were consumed for each of the two service functions. Finally, as shown in the Cost per Output table, driver units consumed are multiplied by cost per driver unit and aggregated to determine the total cost of providing snow control and patching chuckholes. The cost for the current period for clearing snow from 12 miles of road

Illustration 13–7 Identification of Activity-Based Costs

Activities

Activity Name	*Total Dollars*
C labor	$1,000
D labor	600
Salt	400
SAD truck	400
Central service O/H	200
Total	$2,600

Activities and Related Drivers

Activity Name	*Driver*
C labor	C hours
D labor	D hours
Salt	Tons of salt
SAD truck	SAD hours
Central serv O/H	Total labor-hours

Consumption

Drivers	*Snow Control*	*Patch Chuckhole*	*Total*
C hours	50	50	100
D hours	10	20	30
Tons of salt	500	0	500
SAD hours	80	70	150
Total labor-hours	60	70	130

Cost per Output

Activities	*Snow Control*	*Patch Chuckhole*	*Total*
C labor	$ 500	$ 500	$1,000
D labor	200	400	600
Salt	400	0	400
SAD truck	213	187	400
Central serv O/H	92	108	200
Total	$1,405	$1,195	$2,600
12 miles of road	$117.08		
14 tons of mix		$85.36	

Source: Bridget M. Anderson, "Using Activity-Based Costing for Efficiency and Quality," *Government Finance Review*, June 1993, p. 8. Reprinted with permission of the Government Finance Officers Association.

was $1,405 or $117.08 per mile. Similarly, the cost of 14 tons of mix for patching chuckholes was $1,195 or $85.36 per ton.

Actual snow removal costs per mile for five geographic cost centers of the City of Indianapolis are presented in Illustration 13–8. As shown in this illustration, the cost per mile for snow removal ranged from $39.96 for 1,846 miles of road in the Southeast cost center to $117.59 for 1,000 miles of road in the Southwest cost center. Subsequent cost analysis by the City's Department of Transportation revealed

Illustration 13–8 Cost Analysis of Snow Removal

	Geographic Cost Center				
	Northwest	*Northeast*	*Center*	*Southwest*	*Southeast*
Activity					
C labor	0.89	1.19	3.08	0.14	0.42
D labor	7.27	11.76	25.29	13.21	7.73
E labor	5.09	5.84	5.59	2.77	1.17
Supervisors	2.27	2.69	3.81	6.10	1.81
T supervisors	2.60	5.10	2.13	2.06	2.08
Personnel Costs	18.12	26.58	39.90	24.28	13.21
Calcium	0.86			4.86	
Salt	36.18	9.25	20.78	43.96	5.24
Sand				0.14	
Direct Materials Costs	37.04	9.25	20.78	48.96	5.24
Central Services	9.35	13.29	19.74	18.63	7.47
Facilities	1.84	3.81	0.94	0.59	0.66
Fixed assets	0.14	0.08	0.05	0.07	0.05
Administration	3.18	4.30	4.98	3.77	2.34
Overhead Costs	14.51	21.48	25.71	23.06	10.52
Crewcab pickup	0.01				
Loader	8.24	3.83	1.43	4.25	0.77
Mini pickup	6.11				
SAD 90	6.24	6.12	0.50	6.51	2.73
SADA 85	1.17	1.93	0.88	4.02	1.67
Sedan	3.31				
TAD 90	2.87	0.79	3.72	2.98	1.89
TADA	10.41	4.25	1.73	2.98	2.85
Dump truck	0.01	0.02			
Unused equipment	0.48	0.55	0.13	0.55	1.08
Rolling Stock Costs	38.85	17.49	8.39	21.29	10.99
TOTAL	$108.52	$74.80	$94.78	$117.59	$39.96
Miles plowed	1,100	1,000	900	1,000	1,846

Source: Bridget M. Anderson, "Using Activity-Based Costing for Efficiency and Quality," *Government Finance Review*, June 1993, p. 9. Reprinted with permission of the Government Finance Officers Association.

that the Southwest cost center was using excessive amounts of salt per mile and was not using an optimal mix of equipment. The Center geographic cost center was using excessive labor. This analysis led to reallocation of both personnel and equipment between cost centers, thus resulting in improved efficiency without loss of quality.[15]

Clerical and Administrative Costs. A very large part of governmental expenditures are incurred for services of a general nature (such as the costs of the chief executive's office, costs of accounting and auditing, or costs of boards and commissions), which are somewhat remote from the results any given subdivision is expected to accomplish. Furthermore, in smaller units of government, many offices or departments perform such a variety of services that separating their costs is practically impossible under their present schemes of organization.

Given the importance and magnitude of key administrative offices, government officials should attempt to measure the efficiency and effectiveness of the activities of these offices just as it would other service activities. The primary difference is that many of these activities, such as those of the finance and legal departments for example, mainly serve customers within the government rather than the general public. Activity-based costing would seem to be a useful tool for measuring the cost of such activities. Possible activities and cost drivers for selected offices are provided below.

Office	*Activities*	*Cost Drivers*
Tax Collector	Preparing tax bills.	Number of bills prepared.
	Collecting tax bills.	Number of bills collected.
	Preparing receipts.	Number of receipts prepared.
	Mailing receipts.	Number of receipts mailed.
	Preparing deposits.	Number of deposits prepared.
Accounting	Recording revenues.	Number of revenue transactions.
	Recording expenditures.	Number of expenditure transactions.
	Processing payroll.	Number of employees.
	Recording purchase orders.	Number of orders.
Public Recorder	Recording documents	Number of documents or number of lines.

This table is intended to be illustrative of the kinds of activities and cost drivers that might apply to certain administrative offices. Obviously, the list is incomplete, but, insofar as the activities and drivers are appropriate for a particular office, costs accumulated by activity could be useful both for internal performance review and pricing services to other offices. As an example of pricing services rendered, the

[15]For an update on this city's experience with ABC, see Mayor Stephen Goldsmith, "The ABCs of Competitive Government: The Indianapolis Experience," *Government Finance Review*, October 1999.

costs of accounting services could be priced to other departments on the basis of the amount of accounting activities they consume. For example, assume that the Public Works Department generates 30 percent of all purchase requisitions processed by the Accounting Department. Arguably, it should then be charged for 30 percent of the total cost of recording purchase orders in the accounting function. Similarly, the costs of recording expenditures could be charged to departments proportionate to the expenditures they make. Although an activity-based costing approach to costing central services seems technologically feasible, much additional research is needed to determine whether the benefits would warrant the considerable costs involved.

In spite of all the difficulties, rational allocation of resources requires the best available information as to benefits expected to result from a proposed program to be matched with the best available information as to costs of the same program. Before a purported benefit can be identified as a true benefit, the objectives of the government and the objectives of the proposed program must be identified. Relative to this, Hinrichs points out:

> The student of government decision making must not always assume that obscure and obfuscated objectives are totally lacking in function. Many times objectives are uncertain, changing, conflicting; this may not be the time for total inaction but instead a time of discovering and discussing objectives in the very process of moving in a general direction. Objectives often are a result of a feed-back process in getting the job underway and in working toward broader goals.[16]

Equally pragmatic, and equally relevant to the present discussion, is a comment by Hatry on the problem of expressing benefits in monetary items:

> Realistically most governmental problems involve major objectives of a nondollar nature. Not only is it very difficult for analysts to assign dollar "values" to such nondollar objectives, but it is also questionable whether it would be desirable even if it could be done. Thus, questions of the value of such effects as reducing death rates, reducing illness incidences and severities, improving housing conditions, and increasing recreational opportunities should not become simply a problem of estimating the dollar values of these things.
>
> The analysts should rather concentrate upon the estimation and presentation, for each alternative, of full information as the actual dollar effects and the effects upon the nonmonetary criteria. *This is the primary function of program analysis*.[17] [Emphasis added]

If the anticipated benefits from a program cannot be stated in quantitative terms, they must be stated verbally. In order to be of value in the management process, the statement must be explicit and in operational terms, not "God and Motherhood" generalities.

---

[16]Harley M. Hinrichs and Graeme M. Taylor, *Program Budgeting and Benefit-Cost Analysis* (Santa Monica, CA: Goodyear Publishing, 1969), p. 13.

[17]Ibid., p. 101.

Budgeting in Nongovernmental Not-for-Profit Organizations

The budgeting and costing issues of not-for-profit organizations, such as voluntary health and welfare organizations (VHWOs) differ from those in governmental entities, in part, because VHWOs rely on grants and contributions in the operation of distinct programs, rather than on taxes or user charges. Grants may be received from governmental entities, other not-for-profit organizations, or foundations; and contributions come from individual donors. Either type of funding may be given to support specified programs or the organization as a whole. Grants are characterized by proposed budgets, authorized direct and indirect costs, grant periods, and periodic reports to the grantor by the recipient agency. The accounting challenge is to capture total costs of each program and to match actual to budgeted costs for each grant. Difficulties arise because shared costs must be allocated across programs, grantors have different fiscal years, and terminology often differs across granting sources. For example, federal government grants may approve *telephone and printing* costs, while a local government grant covers *communication* costs. Further complications come when there are multiple grantors for one program, and multiple programs supported by one grantor as seen in Illustration 13–9.

Accounting Information Systems

Even small organizations have computerized accounting systems. At issue is whether the entity will use a relatively inexpensive commercial package designed for business entities, or higher priced software designed for not-for-profit entities. Whatever the decision, the creation of a chart of accounts is a critical step that must be done at the beginning stages of the organization, and revised each time the agency changes software or has other structural changes in its operation. The chart of accounts provides the framework used to classify transactions that affect programs as well as granting

Illustration 13–9 Relationship of Programs and Grantors in Nonprofit Organizations.

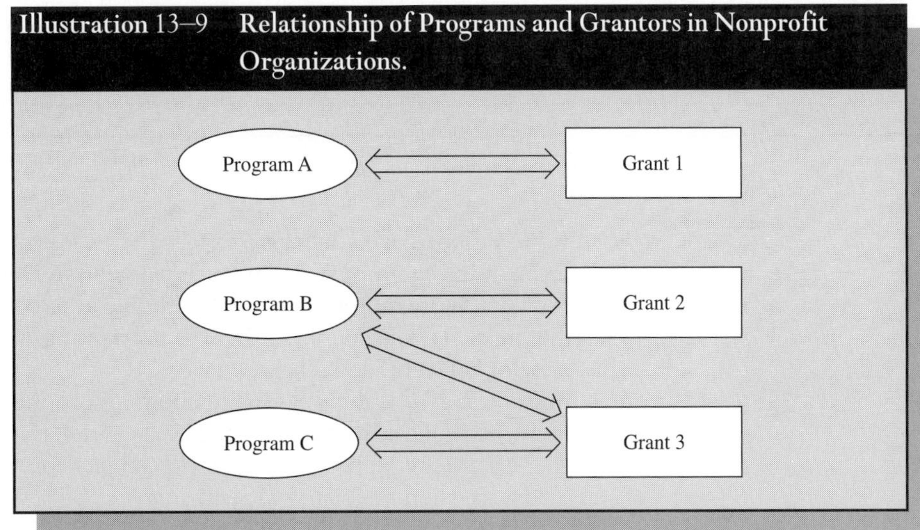

Illustration 13–10 Chart of Accounts for a Nongovernmental, Not-for-Profit Organization

Type of Account X	*Object XX*	*Program X*	*Funding Source XX*
1 = Assets	10 = Cash		
	20 = Accounts receivable		
	30 = Inventory		
	40 = Prepaid expenses		
	50 = Investments		
	60 = Property, plant, and equipment		
	70 = Accumulated depreciation		
2 = Liabilities	10 = Accounts payable		
	20 = Accrued payroll		
	30 = Other accrued liabilities		
3 = Net assets	10 = Unrestricted net assets		
	20 = Unrestricted, designated net assets		
	30 = Temporarily restricted net assets		
	40 = Permanently restricted net assets		
4 = Revenues	10 = Contributions	A = Community Impact	01 = Federal grant
	20 = Grants	B = Youth Commission	02 = Community development block grant
	30 = Charges for services	C = Juvenile Court Advocacy	21 = State grant
	40 = Dues	D = Student Outreach	22 = County grant
	50 = Investment income	E = Safe Schools	23 = City grant
	60 = Special events	F = Parent Effectiveness Training	24 = City Housing Commission grant
	70 = Miscellaneous	G = Advocacy	30 = Ford Foundation grant
5 = Cost of programs	11 = Salaries and wages		31 = Kellogg Foundation grant
6 = Expenses (General and administrative; fund-raising)	12 = Fringe benefits and payroll taxes		32 = Smith Foundation grant
	20 = Travel		33 = Brown Foundation grant
	30 = Supplies, phone, postage, printing		43 = Universal Church
	40 = Occupancy costs		50 = United Way
	60 = Equipment maintenance		
	61 = Depreciation		
	70 = Legal and professional services		
	80 = Miscellaneous		

sources. Decision makers who are expected to use the reports generated by the accounting information system (for example, management, program directors, the Board of Directors, grantors, and donors) should all be considered in the process of creating the chart of accounts so that the accounting system captures information that is useful, relevant, and reliable.

Illustration 13–10 shows a simple chart of accounts for a VHWO that advocates for school-age students at-risk. The agency has seven programs funded, in part, by 12 grantors. Natural expenses (i.e., objects of expenditures or line items) are called *costs* when associated with programs and *expenses* when related to general and administrative or fund-raising activities.

In order to report on activities effectively for various decision makers, the chart of accounts must allow for costs to be characterized by program and grant, as well as natural line item. Some accounting software facilitates this reporting by allowing reports to be prepared based on a range of account numbers in which fields of the account number are *masked* to focus on the distinguishing field in the account number. For the example agency in Illustration 13–10, which has a six-digit account number, a report for the Community Impact program could be generated by printing all revenues and costs for the A program; that is, the range of accounts used in the report would be 4**A** and 5**A** where the * is used as a *wild card* to indicate all numbers. Similarly, if the agency wants a report on the Federal grant, they select 4***01 and 5***01 accounts. Other software may produce the same result by allowing each revenue or cost to be characterized, and consequently sorted, by another item; for example, programs may be considered *classes or jobs* and funding sources may be treated as *customers*. Not surprisingly, more expensive software programs written specifically with not-for-profit agencies and their needs in mind may be more efficient in producing specialized reports.

Conclusion

An entity that integrates its strategic planning, budgeting, and cost/benefit analysis with the management of the resources with which it is entrusted can more effectively document performance than if these financial management functions stand alone. The statement of anticipated benefits from a proposed program, activity, or grant should follow from a statement of objectives for it. The statement of objectives should be expanded into a plan of action to achieve the objectives, which in turn serves as a basis for planning costs to be incurred. Unless this course is followed, administrators and legislators will not be able to allocate resources of the governmental unit wisely, nor will administrators be able to manage resources committed to approved programs. Legislators and the public have a right to expect this integration of long-range analysis and fiscal period planning, so that they may evaluate the actions of the administrators in following the plan as well as the success of the programs in achieving the stated objectives. Cost accounting takes on an even more important role in long-range fiscal planning as organizations evaluate the benefits of privatizing and out-sourcing traditional functions.

Key Terms

Activity-based costing (ABC), 621
Allowable costs, 618
Budget calendar, 606
Budget officer, 606
Common Rule, 619
Cost determination, 617
Cost objective, 620
Direct costs, 620
Flexible budgeting, 616
Incremental budgeting, 601

Questions

13–1. Explain the interrelation among the processes of policy setting, service delivery, evaluation, and budgeting that should exist in a governmental unit.

13–2. If governmental budgets should be prepared to facilitate management of resources, why should the budget documents be subjected to study by individual taxpayers, reporters, and public interest groups, as well as by legislative bodies?

13–3. Explain the costs and benefits of performance budgeting compared with incremental budgeting.

13–4. "Every rational budgeting approach that has been experimented with by governments has been a failure." Do you agree or disagree with this statement? Explain fully.

13–5. What advantages does total quality management (TQM) offer compared with rational budgeting approaches? Is it fundamentally a budgeting approach?

13–6. What are some of the factors to be taken into account in preparing revenue estimates for inclusion in a budget?

13–7. Assuming the typical governmental budget is a collection of departmental budgets, each of which shows only the department's requested appropriation for personal services, materials and supplies, and capital outlays, specify the advantages and disadvantages each of the following groups should find if a city were to convert to a program budget:

a. The city's central administration.

b. The city's departmental administrators.

c. The city's legislative body.

d. The city's taxpayers.

13–8. Why is a good cost accounting system an important component of rational budgeting?

13–9. If governmental units, educational institutions, and not-for-profit health care entities exist in order to provide services needed by the public, or a segment of the public, and are not concerned with the generation of net income, why should they be interested in the determination of costs? Explain your answer.

13–10. The Finance Officer of a small city has heard that certain items of cost may be allowable under federal grants and contracts, even though they were not incurred specifically for the grant or contract. To what source could the Finance Officer go to determine what costs are allowable under federal grants and contracts?

13–11. Explain in your own words what indirect costs are. For what reason would the administrator of a governmental unit or not-for-profit organization want indirect costs allocated to cost objectives?

13–12. What criteria should be applied to the selection of a basis for the allocation of indirect expenses? Explain.

13–13. Below are listed a number of activities and work units often used in measuring output of the activities for purposes of relating cost to output or determining unit costs. For each one, state one or more factors that might make it difficult to evaluate performance of the activity.

Street cleaning—linear mile
Sweeping and collection of leaves—square yard
Earth excavation—cubic yard
Snow and ice removal—cubic yard
Laying of mains—linear foot
Servicing of parking meters—each
School bus operation—student-day
Billing of taxes—bill
Solid waste collection—ton
Recording documents—document

13–14. Explain why conventional cost accounting systems have become less useful in both the business and government setting. How does activity-based costing (ABC) reduce the problems created by conventional cost accounting systems?

Cases

13–1. Activity-Based Costing. The Frumerville Hospital has always determined the full cost of serving patients by accounting for the direct and indirect costs of all hospital operations. The hospital uses the step-down method of allocating indirect costs: The costs of nonrevenue, producing departments are allocated in sequence to departments they serve, whether or not these produce revenue; once the costs of a department have been allocated, the costing process for that department is closed, and it receives no further charges. A new CFO has recently joined the Hospital after a distinguished career in the manufacturing industry. In that capacity, he initiated activity-based costing (ABC), which resulted in a documented savings to the business. As an accounting assistant, you have been asked to meet with the CFO to discuss the issues involved in implementing ABC in this Hospital. A copy of the Hospital's most recent Step-Down Expense Distribution is presented here.

FRUMERVILLE HOSPITAL
STEP-DOWN METHOD—EXPENSE DISTRIBUTION
YEAR ENDED APRIL 30, 19—

	Direct Costs	*Maintenance of Plant*	*Operation of Plant*	*Housekeeping*	*Laundry and Linen*	*Cafeteria*	*Administration*	*Medical Supplies*	*Medical Records*	*Nursing Service*	*Dietary*	*Total Costs*
General Services:												
Maintenance of plant	$ 252,000	$(252,000)	—	—	—	—	—	—	—	—	—	—
Operation of plant	354,600	113,400	$(468,000)	—	—	—	—	—	—	—	—	—
Housekeeping	357,000	2,520	2,340	$(361,860)	—	—	—	—	—	—	—	—
Laundry and linen service	216,000	10,080	16,848	7,236	$(250,164)	—	—	—	—	—	—	—

FRUMERVILLE HOSPITAL
STEP-DOWN METHOD—EXPENSE DISTRIBUTION
YEAR ENDED APRIL 30, 19—

	Direct Costs	Maintenance of Plant	Operation of Plant	Housekeeping	Laundry and Linen	Cafeteria	Administration	Medical Supplies	Medical Records	Nursing Service	Dietary	Total Costs
Cafeteria	23,640	756	14,508	7,236	1,251	$ (47,391)	—	—	—	—	—	—
Administration	844,800	7,560	28,548	25,332	249	6,918	$(913,407)	—	—	—	—	—
Medical supplies	480,000	2,520	6,084	1,809	501	1,707	39,276	$(531,897)	—	—	—	—
Medical records	132,000	2,520	4,680	10,857	—	1,137	25,575	—	$(176,769)	—	—	—
Nursing service	1,800,000	1,764	7,020	2,532	6,504	20,709	466,752	—	—	$(2,305,281)	—	—
Dietary	657,000	10,080	19,188	10,857	3,003	4,596	103,215	—	—	—	$(807,939)	—
Special Services:												
Operating rooms	482,460	25,200	28,548	3,618	41,778	3,459	77,640	79,785	—	—	—	$ 742,488
Delivery rooms	141,000	15,120	14,508	10,857	21,015	1,422	31,968	53,190	—	—	—	289,080
Radiology	300,000	10,080	14,508	14,475	3,003	1,707	29,276	—	—	—	—	383,049
Laboratory	381,000	7,560	16,848	14,475	3,003	3,459	77,640	—	—	—	—	503,985
Blood bank	219,000	2,016	3,744	5,427	249	570	12,789	—	—	—	—	243,795
Cost of medical supplies sold	—	—	—	—	—	—	—	265,947	—	—	—	265,947
Routine Services:												
Medical and surgical	144,000	25,200	219,024	218,202	138,339	—	—	79,785	137,880	1,959,489	807,939	3,729,858
Nursery	13,500	3,024	23,868	7,236	18,762	—	—	26,595	8,838	345,792	—	447,615
Outpatient clinic	192,000	12,600	47,736	21,711	12,507	1,707	39,276	26,595	30,051	—	—	384,183
Totals	$6,990,000	$ 0	$ 0	$ 0	$ 0	$ 0	$ 0	$ 0	$ 0	$ 0	$ 0	$6,990,000

Required

In preparation for the meeting, answer the following questions by examining the Expense Distribution:

a. What "activities" do you consider most appropriate in describing the operations of the Hospital?

b. What are the cost drivers of these programs?

c. What particular problems do you expect to face in implementing ABC in this Hospital?

13–2. Indirect Costs. As a cost reimbursement accountant in a large public research university, you are aware that federal agencies have increased auditing efforts in the area of federal research grants to higher education institutions. In particular, OMB *Circular A-21* detailing allowable costs for colleges and universities receiving federal funds has been revised. The administration has asked you whether it is appropriate to include certain overhead costs in the pool of indirect costs (facilities and administrative costs) that are recovered in most federal research awards. Items include: (1) holiday lights put on the President's university-owned home, (2) library books in the research section of the undergraduate library, (3) cost of a large boat used by the higher administration in meeting with faculty and outside researchers for social events, (4) advertising new graduate programs in the large urban newspaper, (5) clerical salaries in the academic departments where a large amount of research is conducted, and (6) utility bills in the research wing of one of the buildings.

Required

Write a short businesslike memo to the administration giving your opinion about whether these costs would be allowable "indirect costs" to be recovered in part by federal research grants. Defend your position.

13–3. Internet Case. Use the Internet to list as many governments as you can (in the state in which the college or university you are attending is located) that have received the Government Finance Officers Association Distinguished Budget Award since its inception in 1984 until today. Information may be available on the GFOA's own website (http://www.gfoa.org) or the individual city's websites, or by searching the Internet using key words such as *governmental budgeting*. Identify the particular strengths of their budgets for which they were recognized.

Exercises and Problems

13–1. Examine the Budget. Obtain a copy of a recent operating budget document of a governmental unit.* Familiarize yourself with the organization of the operating budget document; read the letter of transmittal or any narrative that accompanies the budgets.

Budgetary practices may differ from the GAAP reporting model as to *basis*, *timing*, *perspective*, and *entity*. GASB standards (*Codification*, Section 2400.113–.122) define these differences as:

1. *Basis* differences arising through the employment of a basis of accounting for budgetary purposes that differs from the basis of accounting applicable to the fund type when reporting on the operations in accordance with GAAP.
2. *Timing* differences that can result in significant variances between budgetary practices and GAAP may include continuing appropriations, project appropriations, automatic reappropriations, and biennial budgeting.
3. *Perspective* differences resulting from the structure of financial information for budgetary purposes. The perspectives used for budgetary purposes include fund structure, and organizational structure, or program structure. In addition, some subsidiary perspective, such as nature of revenue source, special projects, or capital and operating budgets, may also be used. The fund structure and individual fund definitions establish which assets, liabilities, equities, and revenue and expenditure/expense flows are accounted for in a fund. In the traditional view, budgeting, accounting, financial reporting, and auditing would follow the fund perspective.
4. *Entity* differences are the fourth possible type of difference. Frequently, an "appropriated budget" may either include or exclude organizations, programs, activities, and functions that may or may not be compatible with the criteria defining the governmental reporting entity.

* The footnote of Exercise 1–1 suggested that you attempt to obtain an operating budget document from the entity whose CAFR you analyzed for Exercises 1–1 through 10–1. If this was not possible, write the Budget Officer of the city, town, or county of your choice and request a copy of the most recent available operating budget document.

Answer the following questions, which aid in assessing the quality of the budget document you are reviewing.†

Policy Document: Does the operating budget you are reviewing include a coherent statement of organizationwide financial and programmatic policies and goals that address long-term concerns and issues? Does the operating budget document describe the organization's short-term financial and operational policies that guide budget development for the upcoming year? Does the budget document include a coherent statement of goals and objectives of organizational units (e.g., departments, divisions, offices, or programs)? Does the document include a budget message that articulates priorities and issues for the budget for the new year and describes significant changes in priorities from the current year, and the factors producing those changes?

Financial Plan: Does the operating budget document include and describe all funds that are subject to appropriation? Does the document present a summary of major revenues and expenditures, as well as other financing sources and uses? Does the document include summaries of revenues, and other resources, and of expenditures for prior-year actual, current-year budget and/or estimated current-year actual, and proposed budget year? Are major revenue sources described? Are the underlying assumptions for revenue estimates and significant revenue trends explained? Does the document include projected changes in fund balances for governmental funds included in the budget presentation, including all balances potentially available for appropriation?

Does the budget document include budgeted capital expenditures and a list of major capital projects (even if these are authorized in a separate capital budget)? Does the document describe if, and to what extent, capital improvements or other major capital spending will impact the entity's current and future operating budget? Are financial data on current debt obligations provided, describing the relationship between current debt levels and legal debt limits, and explaining the effects of existing debt levels on current and future operations? Is the basis of budgeting explained for all funds, whether GAAP, cash, modified accrual, or some other basis?

Operations Guide: Does the operating budget document describe activities, services, or functions carried out by organizational units? Are objective methods (quantitative and/or qualitative) of measurement of results provided by unit or program? (Information on results should be provided for prior-year actual, current-year budget, and/or estimate, and budget year.) Does the budget document include an organizational chart for the entire organization? Is a schedule(s) or summary table(s) provided giving personnel or position counts for prior, current, and budget years, including descriptions of significant changes in levels of staffing or reorganizations planned for the budget year?

Communication Device: Does the operating budget document provide summary information, including an overview of significant budgetary issues, trends, and resource choices? Does the budget document explain the effect, if any, of other planning processes (e.g., strategic plans, long-range plans, capital improvement plans) upon the budget and budget process? Is the process used to prepare, review, adopt, and amend the budget explained? If a separate capital budget is prepared, is a description provided of the process by which it is prepared and how it relates to the operating budget? Are charts and graphs used, where appropriate, to highlight financial and statistical information? Is narrative information pro-

---

†These questions are paraphrased from the awards criteria established by the Government Finance Officers Association for its Distinguished Budget Presentation Awards Program. Questions are arranged under the four key categories included in the award criteria: **Policy Document, Financial Plan, Operations Guide,** and **Communication Device.**

vided when the messages conveyed by the charts and graphs are not self-evident? Does the document provide narrative, tables, schedules, crosswalks, or matrices to show the relationship between different revenue and expenditure classifications (e.g., funds, programs, organization units)? Is a table of contents provided to make it easy to locate information in the document? Is there a glossary to define terms (including abbreviations and acronyms) that are not readily understood by a reasonably informed lay reader? Does the document include statistical and supplemental data that describe the organization and the community of population it serves, and provide other pertinent background information related to services provided? Finally, is the document printed and formatted in such a way as to enhance understanding and utility of the document to a lay reader? Is it attractive, consistent, and oriented to the reader's needs?

13–2. Multiple Choice. Choose the best answer.

1. The GASB *Budgeting, Budgetary Control, and Budgetary Reporting* Principle provides that:
   a. An annual budget should be adopted for every governmental fund type of a governmental unit.
   b. An annual budget should be adopted by every governmental unit.
   c. Budgetary comparisons should be included in the appropriate financial statements and schedules for governmental funds for which an annual budget has been adopted.
   d. Both *b* and *c* are correct.
2. Which of the following is *not* considered a "rational" budgeting approach?
   a. Incremental budgeting.
   b. Performance budgeting.
   c. Program budgeting.
   d. PPBS.
3. Which of the following budgeting approaches focuses mainly on relating work activity outputs to resource inputs?
   a. Incremental (line-item) budgeting.
   b. Performance budgeting.
   c. Program budgeting.
   d. PPBS.
4. Which of the following budgeting approaches requires formulation of the governmental unit's fundamental objectives and identification and evaluation of alternative ways of achieving objectives?
   a. Incremental (line-item) budgeting.
   b. Performance budgeting.
   c. Program budgeting.
   d. PPBS.
5. Which of the following steps would *not* usually be part of the budgeting process?
   a. Heads of operating departments prepare budget requests.
   b. Budget officer and other central administrators review and make adjustments to departmental requests.
   c. One or more public budget hearings are held.

   d. The Chief Executive (Mayor or City Manager, as appropriate) formally adopts the budget, thus giving it the force of law.

6. Which of the following kinds of information is useful for effective capital budgeting?
   a. A multiple-year forecast of needed capital improvements and proposed means of financing them.
   b. Physical measures of the service condition of plant assets.
   c. Estimated replacement costs to replace plant assets.
   d. All of the above are useful for capital budgeting.
7. Which of the following budgeting approaches is most consistent with total quality management (TQM)?
   a. Incremental (line-item) budgeting.
   b. Performance budgeting.
   c. Program budgeting.
   d. PPBS.
8. Measurement of *efficiency* requires that:
   a. Inputs be related to outputs.
   b. Inputs be related to outcomes.
   c. Outputs be related to outcomes.
   d. Dollar cost of inputs be related to quantities of inputs.
9. Which of the following is the central focus of a TQM system?
   a. Measuring productivity and quality improvement.
   b. Rewarding employees for productivity and quality achievement.
   c. Obtaining the support and commitment of top-level officials.
   d. Continuously meeting or exceeding customer expectations.
10. Measures of service accomplishments include:
   a. Input measures.
   b. Output measures.
   c. Outcome measures.
   d. Both *b* and *c*.

13–3. Multiple Choice. Choose the best answer.

1. Cost principles established by the federal Office of Management and Budget (OMB) apply to which of the following types of entities?
   a. State and local governments.
   b. Colleges and universities.
   c. Not-for-profit organizations such as museums.
   d. All of the above.
2. Which of the following is *not* a general criterion for a cost item to be an "allowable" cost?
   a. Be necessary and reasonable for proper and efficient performance and administration of the federal financial assistance program.
   b. Be approved by the Cost Accounting Standards Board.

c. Be determined in accordance with generally acceptable accounting principles.
d. Be authorized or not prohibited under state or local regulations.

3. Which of the following is an example of an applicable credit?
   a. Purchase discount.
   b. Advertising expense.
   c. A fund equity item that is reserved for capital construction with the permission of the grantor agency.
   d. All of the above.
4. Which of the following cost items would be unallowable by a federal grantor agency?
   a. Depreciation on buildings and equipment.
   b. Advertising expense.
   c. Alcoholic beverages for a Christmas party.
   d. All of the above.
5. Which of the following ordinarily would *not* be classified as a direct cost of a particular grant?
   a. Depreciation on buildings and equipment.
   b. Compensation of employees for time spent working on the specific federal assistance programs.
   c. Materials consumed in performance of the specific federal assistance programs.
   d. None of the above.
6. Costs that are incurred for a common or joint purpose benefiting more than one cost objective and that are not readily assignable to the cost objectives specifically benefited, without effort disproportionate to the results achieved, are referred to as:
   a. Pseudo costs.
   b. Indirect costs.
   c. Direct costs.
   d. Activity-based costs.
7. Which of the following statements about activity-based costing is true?
   a. It is intended to reduce the probability of distorted unit costs that may adversely affect management decisions.
   b. It eliminates the need for allocation of indirect costs.
   c. It permits measuring the true cost of every unit of output (i.e., cost measures that are free from subjective estimates).
   d. All of the above.
8. In activity-based costing, the amount of activity-related cost that is consumed in producing goods or service is measured by the consumption of units of particular allocation bases referred to as:
   a. Activities.
   b. Cost objects.

c. Activity cost drivers.
d. Unit costs.

9. A good cost accounting system facilitates a kind of budgeting in which the costs associated with different levels of activity are planned for. Such a form of budget is referred to as:
   a. Incremental budgeting.
   b. Fixed budgeting.
   c. Rational budgeting.
   d. Flexible budgeting.
10. Determining the cost of depreciation related to the general capital assets of a governmental unit for purposes of charging the cost to a federal grant, or for internal costing of services, is complicated by which of the following factors?
   a. The method of depreciation used does not correspond with actual patterns of asset consumption.
   b. Some capital assets are used for many activities and records of such use may not be adequate.
   c. Depreciation is not recorded in any governmental fund type for such assets, nor is depreciation recorded in the Governmental Activities accounts.
   d. Both *b* and *c* are correct.

13–4. General Fund Budget. A portion of the General Fund operating budget for Southwest City's Street Department is shown below and on the following three pages.

Required

After reading and evaluating the budget information for the Street Department of Southwest City, answer the following questions:

a. Does the City appear to be using program budgeting? If not, what form of budgeting is the City using?
b. Does the budget provide information useful for evaluating the performance of the Street Department's management?
c. Do the goals established for the Street Department appear appropriate? How could they be improved?

SOUTHWEST CITY	GENERAL FUND
ANNUAL BUDGET	DESCRIPTION
FY 2001–2002	STREETS

DEPARTMENT DESCRIPTION

The Street Department is responsible for maintaining all City-owned streets, alleys, and parking lots, keeping them in serviceable condition to ensure the safety and welfare of the public. Activities include repairing damage caused by waterline breaks; repairing potholes and patching utility cuts; repairing base failures; preparing street driving surfaces for annual seal coating program; reconstructing streets to upgrade driving surface and drainage to meet increased traffic volumes; cleaning and repairing drainage ditches and structures; inspecting

SOUTHWEST CITY
ANNUAL BUDGET
FY 2001–2002 *(continued)*

GENERAL FUND
DESCRIPTION
STREETS

and making repairs to City bridges and sidewalks; performing annual crack sealing to prevent water damage to driving surface of streets; performing traffic counts on an as-needed basis; installing and maintaining traffic control signs and paving markings; responding to emergency conditions by barricading, sandbagging, clearing of fallen trees and debris from streets and drainage structures, and sanding of streets during icing conditions; mowing rights-of-way and maintaining street and alley shoulders; installing and maintaining street name signs; and assisting other departments as needed.

Expenditure Summary

Classification	*1999–2000 Actual*	*2000–2001 Budget*	*2000–2001 Estimated*	*2001–2002 Budget*
Personnel	$206,135	$226,748	$227,273	$250,000
Supplies	10,649	11,714	11,818	13,000
Maintenance	70,624	77,686	66,367	73,000
Services	73,768	81,145	60,909	67,000
Capital Outlay	31,927	2,500	34,000	3,000
Total	$393,103	$399,793	$400,367	$406,000

Staffing

Position	*Number*
Superintendent	1
Assistant superintendent	1
Crew leader	2
Equipment operator	6
Total	10

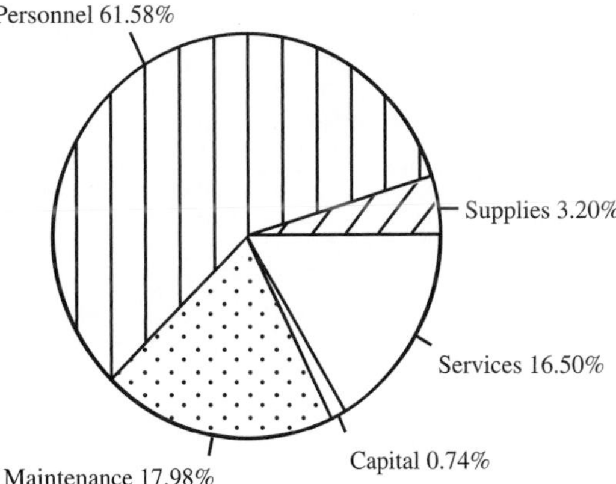

Department Goals

Increase the number of repairs for old utility cuts, upgrade the street driving surface, and prevent future water damage.

Pursue an aggressive weed and grass control program within street gutters, rights-of-way, and behind curbs.

Increase miles of street shoulder repairs to prevent pavement breaking and erosion.

Replace existing noncompliance yield signs with stop signs.

Increase work-hours spent on trimming overhanging limbs and brush in and over streets.

SOUTHWEST CITY
ANNUAL BUDGET
FY 2001–2002 *(continued)*

GENERAL FUND
DEPARTMENTAL GOALS
STREETS

Indicators

Measurement	*1999–00 Actual*	*2000–01 Estimated*	*2001–02 Proposed*
Traffic and street signs	84	159	175
Miles of streets maintained	66	70	70
Square yards of seal coating	42,500	44,800	42,500
Number of utility cuts	136	155	250
Miles of right-of-way mowing	34	172	172
Tons of asphalt for potholes	84	102	175
Tons of asphalt for street leveling	66	40	100
Feet of drainage ditches cleared	3,350	3,750	4,250
Feet of street shoulder bladed	4,150	5,275	6,000
Square yards of sidewalks repaired	40	65	150
Feet of weed control on streets	12,500	16,750	18,000
Miles of streets cleaned	10	19	76

Streets

Account Number	*Account Description*	*FY2000 Actual*	*FY2001 Budget*	*FY2001 Estimated*	*FY2002 Budget*
02-13-00-0101	Salaries—Administrative	$ 4,827.90	$ 4,910.00	$ 4,910.00	$ 4,910.00
02-13-00-0102	Salaries—Operations	27,445.47	29,834.00	29,834.00	36,617.00
02-13-00-0103	Salaries—Supervisory	67,951.32	70,081.00	59,231.00	58,577.00
02-13-00-0104	Salaries—Skilled	42,957.99	42,944.00	55,175.00	69,443.00
02-13-00-0107	Salaries—Overtime	6,584.77	6,854.00	7,604.00	6,500.00
02-13-00-0108	Part-time and hourly	0	1,800.00	0	0
02-13-00-0116	TMRS retirement	12,159.21	11,847.00	12,169.00	11,665.00
02-13-00-0117	Employer's FICA	11,249.99	1,581.00	11,208.00	11,707.00
02-13-00-0118	Hospitalization insurance	12,203.21	13,532.00	13,090.00	15,544.00
02-13-00-0119	Workers' compensation	20,351.76	32,987.00	33,941.00	33,941.00
02-13-00-0120	Unemployment compensation	403.38	378.00	111.00	1,096.00
	Total Personnel	$206,135.00	$226,748.00	$227,273.00	$250,000.00
02-13-00-0210	Chemical supplies	$ 760.95	$ 250.00	$ 0	$ 1,500.00
02-13-00-0220	Clothing supplies	1,638.28	2,164.00	1,520.00	1,600.00
02-13-00-0260	General office supplies	14.79	50.00	6.00	25.00
02-13-00-0270	Janitorial supplies	143.43	50.00	72.00	75.00
02-13-00-0280	Minor tools	609.32	300.00	496.00	400.00
02-13-00-0285	Fuel and vehicle supplies	6,938.49	8,500.00	8,861.00	8,900.00
02-13-00-0290	Other supplies	543.74	400.00	863.00	500.00
	Total Supplies	$ 10,649.00	$ 11,714.00	$ 11,818.00	$ 13,000.00
02-13-00-0302	Building maintenance	$ 0	$ 50.00	$ 93.00	$ 50.00
02-13-00-0304	Street maintenance	17,520.75	20,950.00	20,950.00	18,950.00
02-13-00-0305	Seal coating and overlays	37,457.21	35,488.00	24,481.00	35,275.00
02-13-00-0306	Sidewalks	5,085.75	1,048.00	1,048.00	1,000.00

SOUTHWEST CITY
ANNUAL BUDGET
FY 2001–2002 *(concluded)*

GENERAL FUND
EXPENDITURES
STREETS

Account Number	Account Description	FY2000 Actual	FY2001 Budget	FY2001 Estimated	FY2002 Budget
02-13-00-0307	Street sweeping	0	10,500.00	10,500.00	9,575.00
02-13-00-0401	Heating and air conditioning maintenance	60.00	50.00	225.00	50.00
02-13-00-0420	Machine tools maintenance	1,928.05	1,500.00	1,978.00	1,500.00
02-13-00-0430	Motor vehicle maintenance	5,000.00	5,000.00	5,000.00	3,500.00
02-13-00-0460	Radio maintenance	0	100.00	0	100.00
02-13-00-0480	Signs	3,572.24	3,000.00	2,092.00	3,000.00
	Total Maintenance	$ 70,624.00	$ 77,686.00	$ 66,367.00	$ 73,000.00

13–5. Police Department Budget. The police chief of the Town of Meridian submitted the following budget request for the Police Department for the forthcoming budget year 2002–03.

Item	Actual FY2001	Budget FY2002	Forecast FY2002	Budget FY2003
Personnel	$1,051,938	$1,098,245	$1,112,601	$1,182,175
Supplies	44,442	61,971	60,643	64,450
Maintenance	47,163	45,310	46,139	47,422
Miscellaneous	34,213	36,272	32,198	37,723
Capital outlay	65,788	69,433	67,371	102,210
Totals	$1,243,544	$1,311,231	$1,318,952	$1,433,980

Upon questioning by the newly appointed Town Manager, a recent Masters of Public Administration graduate from a nearby university, the Police Chief explained that he had determined the amounts in the budget request by multiplying the prior year's budget amount by 1.04 (to allow for the expected inflation rate of 4 percent). In addition, the personnel category includes a request for a new uniformed officer at an estimated $40,000 for salary, payroll expenses, and fringe benefits. Capital outlay includes a request for a new patrol vehicle at an estimated cost of $30,000. The amount of $300 was added to the Maintenance category for estimated maintenance on the new vehicle. The Police Chief is strongly resisting instructions from the Town Manager that he justify not only the need for the new uniformed position and additional vehicle but also the need for the *existing* level of resources in each category. The Town Manager has stated she will not request any increase in the Police Department's budget unless adequate justification is provided.

Required

a. Evaluate the strengths and weaknesses of the Police Chief's argument that his budget request is reasonable.

b. Are the Town Manager's instructions reasonable? Explain.

c. Would the Town Council likely support the Town Manager or the Police Chief in this dispute, assuming the Police Chief might take his case directly to the Town Council?

d. What other improvements could be made to the Town's budgeting procedures?

13–6. Allowable Costs. Compensation for personal services rendered during the period of performance under the grant agreement is an allowable cost under OMB *Circular A-87*, as are employee benefits such as vacation leave, sick leave, or employer's contributions to retirement and health plans, and so on, if "the cost thereof is equitably allocated to all related activities, including grant programs."

During 2001, Jane Anderson, an employee of Oak City, was paid an annual salary of $56,000. She took three weeks' paid vacation plus one-week paid sick leave. The employer's contributions to retirement and health plans amounted to 25 percent of Anderson's annual salary. During 2001, Anderson worked 12 weeks on HHS Grant No. 9227. Compute the appropriate charge to that grant for Anderson's salary and fringe benefits (round to the nearest dollar).

13–7. Total Program Costs. On the basis of the following data, prepare a statement for the Town of Chippewa for the year ended June 30, 2002, showing the total cost of solid waste removal and the cost per ton of residential solid waste removed, or cubic yard of commercial solid waste removed (carry unit costs to three decimal places).

	Residential	*Commercial*
By town employees:		
Salaries and wages	$702,000	$481,000
Materials and supplies	$ 39,000	$ 36,090
Equipment use	$300,840	$201,470
Tons collected	165,000	—
Cubic yards collected	—	248,000
Labor-hours	90,000	68,000
By contractors:		
Cost	$ 78,900	$ 48,000
Tons collected	23,000	—
Cubic yards collected	—	30,000

Overhead for town force collection of residential solid waste is $0.948 per labor-hour; for commercial solid waste collection, $0.924 per labor-hour. Overhead for contract residential solid waste collection, 20 percent of cost (exclusive of overhead); for commercial solid waste collection, 15 percent of cost (exclusive of overhead).

13–8. Job Order Costing. The City of Lakeville operates a Shop and Maintenance Department and accounts for its activities by means of an internal service fund. In order to charge the using departments on an equitable basis for work orders filled, the Shop and Maintenance Department uses job order costing. Direct labor, materials used, and any other costs readily identifiable with a specific work order are charged to that work order, and overhead is allocated to each work order at the predetermined rate of 50 percent of direct labor dollars charged to the work order.

As of the end of fiscal year 2001, four work orders were being worked on; costs charged to each during 2001 were:

Work Order No.	*Direct Labor*	*Direct Materials*	*Overhead*	*Total*
871	$1,720	$ 770	$ 860	$3,350
875	240	660	120	1,020
876	860	750	430	2,040
877	380	630	190	1,200
Totals	$3,200	$2,810	$1,600	$7,610

During January 2002, direct labor cost was incurred for the following orders in the amount shown:

Work Order No.	*Amount*
871	$1,200
875	3,600
876	4,400
877	700
878	800
879	1,280
880	360
881	540

During January 2002, materials were used for the following orders in the dollar amounts shown:

Work Order No.	*Amount*
875	$2,600
876	570
877	120
878	440
879	680
880	600
881	1,210
882	80
883	120

The following orders were completed during January for departments accounted for by the funds shown:

Work Order No.	*Fund*
871	Capital Projects Fund (CPF)
875	General Fund (GF)
876	Enterprise Fund (EF)
878	Special Revenue Fund (SRF)

Required:

a. Show in good form your computation of the total costs charged to each work order completed in January 2002.

b. Assuming the department requesting work order 875 had estimated the cost to be $8,500, and the department requesting work order 876 had estimated the cost to be $9,000, show the entries each of these funds should make to record the approval of the invoice received from the Shop and Maintenance Department for the completed work order.

13–9. Allocating Administrative Costs. When the County Commission of Copper County questioned the County Treasurer about his request for additional appropriations, he claimed the large number of tax bills prepared and collected was responsible for the heavy expenses of his office. Since the duties of the Treasurer's office are rather uniform and of limited range, it was decided to attempt a cost study in an effort to determine the reasonableness of the Treasurer's request. As tax bills are numbered serially, it is possible to determine accurately the number prepared and collected. It was decided to divide the activities of the office into general administration, billing, and collecting. General administration consists of supervising the office and providing information to taxpayers, attorneys, and others. It would be measured on the basis of thousands of dollars of collections. Preparing bills and collecting would be measured on the basis of number of bills prepared and collected, respectively. The following information is available about the costs of the office:

1. The salary of the Treasurer is $4,000 per month. His time is devoted to general administration, except that during approximately three months of each year he spends practically all his time on collections.
2. Two regular deputies each receives $1,800 per month. Their time is divided approximately four months to billing, four months to collections, and the remainder to general administration.
3. During the year, the office spent $12,000 for extra help, of which two-thirds was chargeable to billing and one-third to collecting.
4. The office collected $240,000 of delinquent taxes, interest, and penalties during the year, of which the Treasurer retained 4 percent, to be credited equally to administration and collection.
5. Utility bills, stationery and stamps, repairs to office equipment, and retirement contributions, and so on, totaled $81,480 for the year. This was distributed to administration, billing, and collection on the basis of total salaries chargeable to those operations, except $20,600 spent for stamped envelopes was chargeable in total to collections.
6. The number of tax bills prepared during the year was 51,280, of which 740 were unpaid at the end of the year. The $240,000 of delinquent taxes collected during the year was on 625 bills.

7. Collection of current taxes during the year amounted to $3,000,000.

Required

a. Prepare a schedule to show the allocation of the Treasurer's office costs to general administration, billing, and collecting.

b. Prepare a schedule to show the computation of the unit costs for each activity. (The basis for measuring each activity is given above. Carry unit costs to the third decimal place.)

13–10. Activity-Based Costing. Activity-based costing data for various activities relating to signs, one of many responsibilities of the Department of Transportation for the City of Indianapolis, is provided below and on the following pages. Cost data relating to manufacturing, installation, removal, and other activities pertaining to highway signs and showing the level of accomplishment in terms of labor-hours expended for each activity and the total number of signs for each type of activity are provided below.

Required

a. How does this method of accumulating costs compare with a typical cost accounting system that allocates many indirect costs on a predetermined overhead rate basis? Have you learned anything from these data that would not have been provided by a conventional costing system? Explain fully.

b. Can you envision any problems with the ABC approach used here in terms of cost versus benefit analysis?

c. Name some additional service programs that might benefit from a similar costing approach.

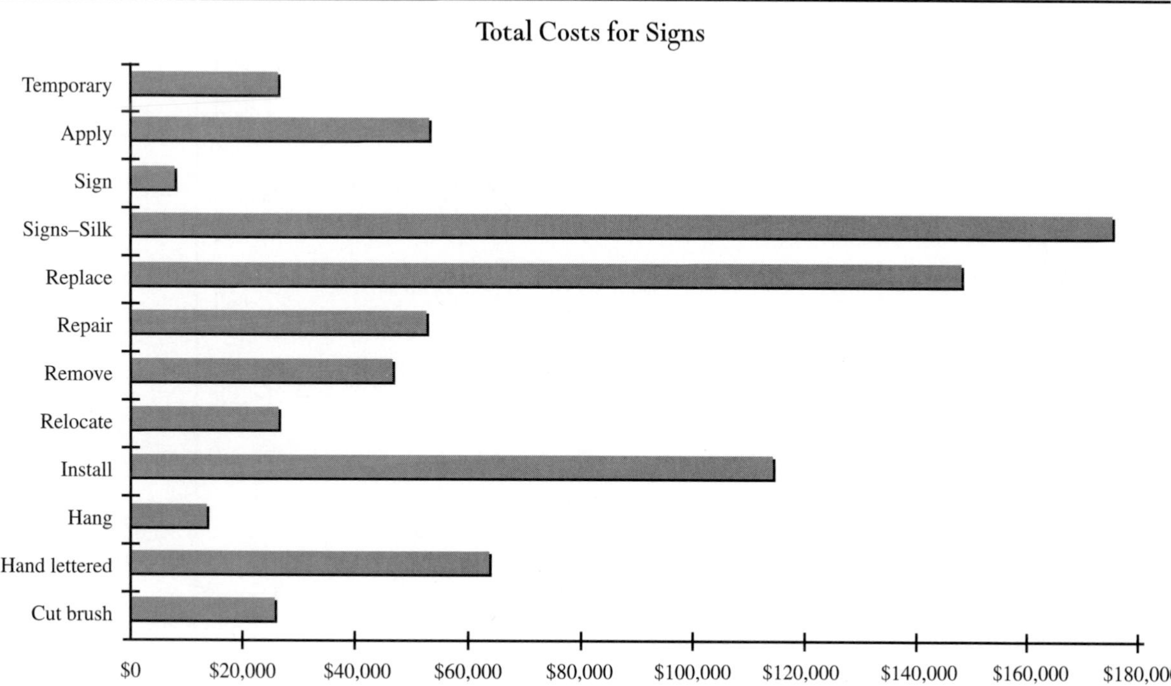

Total Costs for Signs (*concluded*)

Activity	*Cut Brush*	*Hand-Lettered Signs*	*Hang Banners*	*Install Signs*	*Relocate Signs*	*Remove Signs*	*Repair Signs*	*Replace Signs*	*Signs—Silk Screen*	*Sign Cover*	*Apply Sign Face*	*Temporary Installation*	*Total*
Personnel Costs:													
Operations administration	$ 735	$ 3,923	$ 538	$ 2,882	$ 339	$ 1,473	$ 1,787	$ 4,002	$ 5,560	$ 478	$ 2,295	$ 1,077	$ 25,089
Section administration	627	3,348	459	2,460	290	1,257	1,525	3,416	4,746	408	1,959	919	21,416
Section administration OT	3	16	2	12	1	6	7	16	23	2	9	4	103
Sign installation TECH I	2,871	0	838	9,310	0	3,684	5,817	13,286	0	0	0	2,363	38,169
Sign installation TECH II	7,364	0	1,866	26,707	0	12,836	14,173	38,711	0	0	0	8,423	110,080
Sign manufacturer	0	20,965	0	0	0	0	0	0	30,547	814	11,442	0	63,768
Warehouse	0	2,304	2,304	2,304	2,304	2,304	2,304	2,304	2,304	2,304	2,304	2,304	25,344
Total Personnel Costs	11,600	30,556	6,008	43,676	2,934	21,560	25,614	61,735	43,181	4,006	18,009	15,091	283,969
Direct Material Costs:													
Aluminum blank signs	0	0	0	0	0	0	0	0	0	0	7,072	0	7,072
Aluminum	0	4,290	0	0	0	0	0	0	35,450	0	0	0	39,739
Black ink	0	4	0	0	0	0	0	0	85	0	0	0	88
Face cover	0	0	0	0	0	0	0	0	0	0	13,559	0	13,559
Lettering	0	141	0	0	0	0	0	0	218	0	0	0	360
Red ink	0	15	0	0	0	0	0	0	44	0	0	0	59
Sheeting—ENG	0	2,193	0	0	0	0	0	0	10,132	0	0	0	12,324
Sheeting—HI	0	1,625	0	0	0	0	0	0	51,699	0	0	0	53,324
U iron	0	0	0	16,105	0	0	0	16,937	0	0	0	0	33,042
Total Direct Material Costs	0	8,267	0	16,105	0	0	0	16,937	97,628	0	20,630	0	159,567
Overhead Costs:													
Facility	2,138	0	543	7,769	0	3,734	4,123	11,264	0	0	0	2,450	32,021
Fixed assets	403	0	102	1,463	0	703	777	2,122	0	0	0	462	6,032
Central services	1,348	7,191	986	5,284	622	2,701	3,276	7,337	10,194	877	4,207	1,975	45,996
Supplies	3,184	16,989	2,330	12,484	1,469	6,380	7,738	17,333	24,082	2,071	9,939	4,665	108,664
Total Overhead Costs	7,073	24,180	3,961	27,000	2,091	13,518	15,913	38,056	34,276	2,948	14,146	9,552	192,713
Rolling Stock Costs:													
Unused equipment	477	0	121	1,733	0	833	920	2,513	0	0	0	547	7,145
Aerial van 28	883	0	1,980	6,931	0	2,060	1,124	6,850	0	0	0	642	20,471
Crewcab	0	0	0	1,555	0	11	0	0	0	0	0	0	1,566
Double bucket	0	0	0	0	0	0	0	0	0	0	0	797	797
Sign truck	4,171	0	0	10,948	0	6,801	8,334	20,549	0	0	0	3,905	54,709
VL aerial truck	0	0	0	5,664	0	1,122	393	673	0	0	0	1,346	9,197
Total Rolling Stock Costs	5,531	0	2,101	26,831	0	10,827	10,771	30,586	0	0	0	7,236	93,884
Total	$24,204	$63,003	$12,070	$113,611	$5,025	$45,906	$52,298	$147,315	$175,084	$6,954	$52,785	$31,879	$730,133

Signs—Unit Costs and Accomplishments

Activity	*Cut Brush*	*Hand-Lettered Signs*	*Hang Banners*	*Install Signs*	*Relocate Signs*	*Remove Signs*	*Repair Signs*	*Replace Signs*	*Signs—Silk Screen*	*Sign Cover*	*Apply Sign Face*	*Temporary Installation*	*Total*
Personnel Costs:													
Operations administration	1.42	1.60	1.42	0.75	1.42	1.42	1.42	0.89	0.99	1.42	1.86	1.42	16.03
Section administration	1.21	1.37	1.21	0.64	1.21	1.21	1.21	0.76	0.84	1.21	1.59	1.21	13.68
Section administration OT	0.01	0.01	0.01	0.01	0.01	0.01	0.01	0.00	0.00	0.01	0.01	0.01	0.07
Sign installation TECH I	5.54	0.00	2.21	2.43	0.00	3.55	4.62	2.94	0.00	0.00	0.00	3.11	24.41
Sign installation TECH II	14.22	0.00	4.92	6.97	0.00	12.37	11.26	8.57	0.00	0.00	0.00	11.10	69.40
Sign manufacturer	0.00	8.57	0.00	0.00	0.00	0.00	0.00	0.00	5.43	2.41	9.29	0.00	25.70
Warehouse	0.00	0.94	6.08	0.60	9.64	2.22	1.83	0.51	0.41	6.84	1.87	3.04	33.97
Total Personnel Costs	22.40	12.49	15.85	11.40	12.28	20.76	20.35	13.67	7.67	11.89	14.62	19.89	183.26
Direct Material Costs:													
Aluminum blank signs	0.00	0.00	0.00	0.00	0.00	0.00	0.00	0.00	0.00	0.00	5.74	0.00	5.74
Aluminum	0.00	1.75	0.00	0.00	0.00	0.00	0.00	0.00	6.30	0.00	0.00	0.00	8.05
Black ink	0.00	0.01	0.00	0.00	0.00	0.00	0.00	0.00	0.02	0.00	0.00	0.00	0.03
Face cover	0.00	0.00	0.00	0.00	0.00	0.00	0.00	0.00	0.00	0.00	11.01	0.00	11.01
Lettering	0.00	0.06	0.00	0.00	0.00	0.00	0.00	0.00	0.04	0.00	0.00	0.00	0.10
Red ink	0.00	0.01	0.00	0.00	0.00	0.00	0.00	0.00	0.01	0.00	0.00	0.00	0.01
Sheeting—ENG	0.00	0.90	0.00	0.00	0.00	0.00	0.00	0.00	1.80	0.00	0.00	0.00	2.70
Sheeting—HI	0.00	0.66	0.00	0.00	0.00	0.00	0.00	0.00	9.19	0.00	0.00	0.00	9.85
U iron	0.00	0.00	0.00	4.20	0.00	0.00	0.00	3.75	0.00	0.00	0.00	0.00	7.95
Total Direct Material Costs	0.00	3.39	0.00	4.20	0.00	0.00	0.00	3.75	17.36	0.00	16.75	0.00	45.44
Overhead Costs:													
Facility	1.81	2.05	1.81	0.96	1.81	1.81	1.81	1.13	1.26	1.81	2.38	1.81	20.45
Fixed assets	0.34	0.39	0.34	0.18	0.34	0.34	0.34	0.21	0.24	0.34	0.45	0.34	3.86
Central services	2.60	2.94	2.60	1.38	2.60	2.60	2.60	1.62	1.81	2.60	3.41	2.60	29.38
Supplies	6.15	6.95	6.15	3.26	6.15	6.15	6.15	3.84	4.28	6.15	8.07	6.15	69.41
Total Overhead Costs	10.90	12.33	10.90	5.78	10.90	10.90	10.90	6.80	7.59	10.90	14.31	10.90	123.10
Rolling Stock Costs:													
Unused equipment	0.92	0.00	0.32	0.45	0.00	0.80	0.73	0.56	0.00	0.00	0.00	0.72	4.50
Aerial van 28	1.70	0.00	5.22	1.81	0.00	1.99	0.89	1.52	0.00	0.00	0.00	0.85	13.98
Crewcab	0.00	0.00	0.00	0.41	0.00	0.01	0.00	0.00	0.00	0.00	0.00	0.00	0.42
Double bucket	0.00	0.00	0.00	0.00	0.00	0.00	0.00	0.00	0.00	0.00	0.00	1.05	1.05
Sign truck	8.05	0.00	0.00	2.86	0.00	6.55	6.62	4.55	0.00	0.00	0.00	5.14	33.78
VL aerial truck	0.00	0.00	0.00	1.48	0.00	1.08	0.31	0.15	0.00	0.00	0.00	1.77	4.79
Total Rolling Stock Costs	10.67	0.00	5.54	7.01	0.00	10.43	8.55	6.78	0.00	0.00	0.00	9.53	58.52
Total	43.97	28.21	32.29	28.39	23.18	42.09	39.81	31.00	32.62	22.79	45.67	40.33	
Accomplishment	518 hours	2,446 signs	379 hours	3,832 signs	239 hours	1,038 hours	1,259 hours	4,517 signs	5,628 signs	337 hours	1,232 signs	759 hours	

CHAPTER 14

Accounting for Not-for-Profit Organizations

Learning Objectives

After studying this chapter, you should be able to:

- Distinguish not-for-profit organizations (NPOs) from entities in the governmental and commercial sectors of the U.S. economy.
- Identify the authoritative standards-setting body for establishing GAAP for nongovernmental NPOs.
- Explain financial reporting and accounting for NPOs.
  - Accounting for revenue, gains, and support.
  - Accounting for expenses.
  - Accounting for assets.
- Describe optional fund accounting.
- Identify the unique accounting issues of financially interrelated organizations.
- Prepare financial statements using *SFAS No. 117*.

Defining the Not-for-Profit Sector

In the United States more than 1 million entities in the not-for-profit sector receive several hundred billion dollars in revenues and support each year.[1] This diverse sector includes organizations that may be tax-exempt or taxable; charitable or mutually beneficial; a public charity or a private foundation. Not-for-profit organizations (NPOs)[2] are characterized by the absence of owners and dependence on contributions, dues, and charges for services rather than taxes as their source of revenues. The definition of a **not-for-profit organization** recently articulated by the AICPA and FASB is an entity that possesses the following characteristics that distinguish it from a business enterprise.[3, 4]

1. Contributions of significant amounts of resources from resource providers who do not expect commensurate or proportionate pecuniary return.
2. Operating purposes other than to provide goods or services at a profit.
3. Absence of ownership interests like those of business enterprises.

Not-for-profit organizations have the preceding characteristics in varying degrees. NPOs include **voluntary health and welfare organizations (VHWO)** or **human service organizations** (those that receive contributions from the public at large and provide health and welfare services for a nominal or no fee), such as the American Cancer Society, Girl Scouts, and Boy Scouts. There are a variety of other not-for-profit organizations, such as cemetery organizations, civic organizations, fraternal organizations, labor unions, libraries, museums, cultural institutions, performing arts organizations, political parties, private schools, professional and trade associations, social and country clubs, research and scientific organizations, and religious organizations. These organizations are classified more or less by Internal Revenue Code Sections (discussed further in Chapter 15). Illustration 14–1 shows various organizational forms that comprise the not-for-profit sector of the U.S. economy.

Organizations that provide dividends, lower costs, or other economic benefits directly and proportionately to their owners, members, or participants (e.g. mutual insurance companies, credit unions, farm and rural electric cooperatives, and

---

[1]The Independent Sector reports that there are 1.14 million organizations in the independent voluntary, not-for-profit sector [http://www.indepsec.org]. The Internal Revenue Service's Pub. 78 lists almost 500,000 tax-exempt entities to which charitable contributions were deductible by individuals.

[2]The AICPA prefers the term *not-for-profit organizations*. A Texas statute states that "nonprofit corporation" is equivalent to "not-for-profit corporation." Howard L. Oleck and Martha E. Stewart, *Nonprofit Corporations, Organizations & Associations* (Englewood Cliffs, NJ: Prentice Hall, 1994), p. 12. Abbreviations for nongovernmental, not-for-profit entities include NPO, NFP entity, ONPO (other nonprofit organizations), and NGO (nongovermental organizations, a term used in an international context). The abbreviation NPO is used in this chapter, and the terms nonprofit and not-for-profit are used interchangeably.

[3]American Institute of Certified Public Accountants, Audit and Accounting Guide, *Not-for-Profit Organizations* (New York, 1999), par. 1.01.

[4]Financial Accounting Standards Board, *Statement of Financial Accounting Standards No. 116*, "Accounting for Contributions Received and Contributions Made" (Norwalk, CT, 1993), App. D.

Illustration 14–1 Organizational Forms

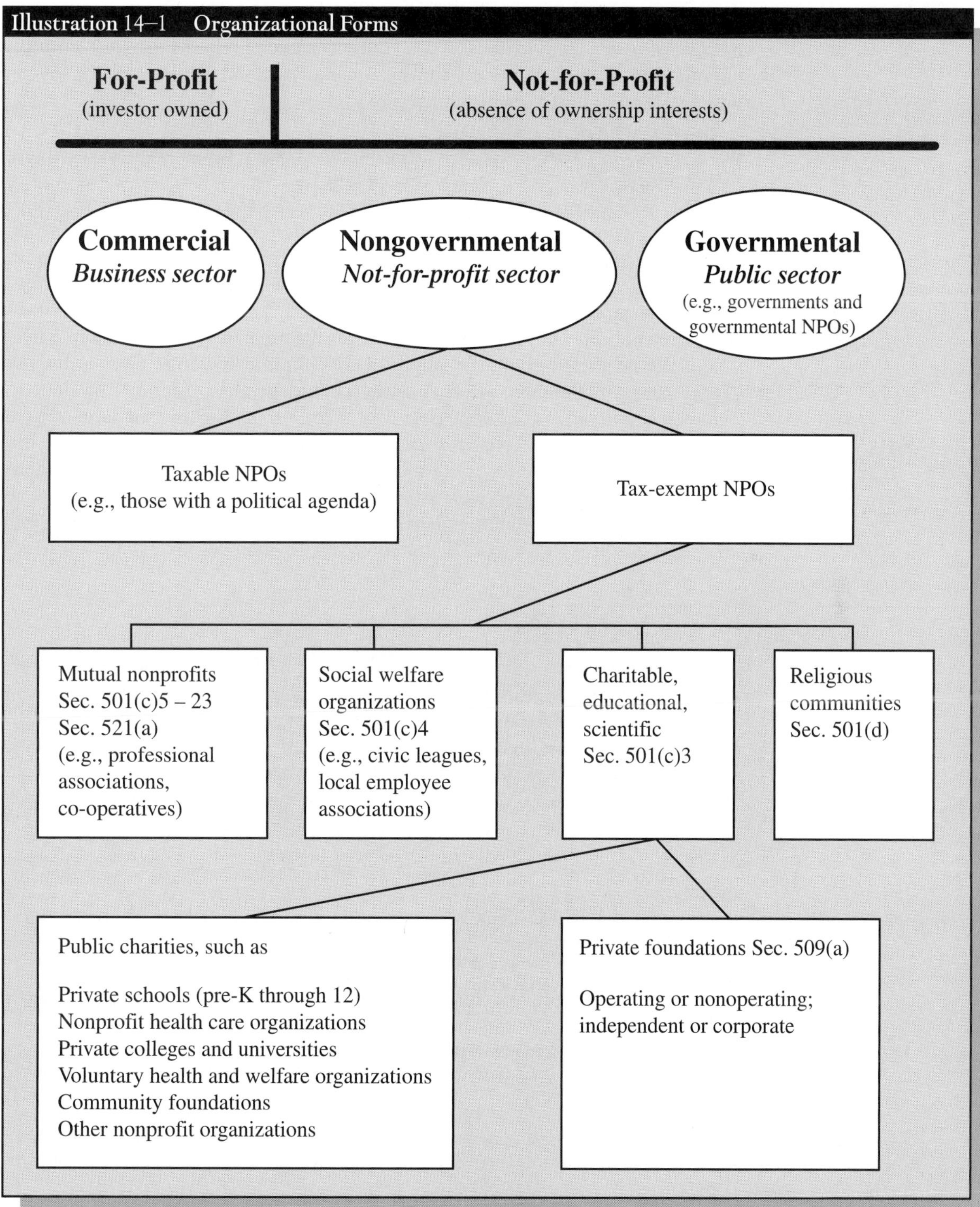

employee benefit plans) are nonprofit because they do not have residual interest owners; however, they do not meet the criteria stated previously for a not-for-profit organization.[5] They operate essentially as commercial businesses and are covered under separate Industry Audit Guides.

There are also "governmental" not-for-profit organizations that may receive tax revenue or be controlled by a government,[6] but are not governments.[7] Examples of entities that receive special tax revenue include libraries and transportation authorities. Governments often control museums, cemeteries, development authorities, housing authorities, public hospitals, public colleges and universities, and other public benefit corporations. Some such organizations are reported as a department or unit of a general purpose government.

Not-for-profit entities are first organized as nonprofit corporations or charitable trusts under a state statute so that they are legally separate from the incorporators. The NPO may then choose to apply to the Internal Revenue Service for tax-exempt status. The IRS, together with the Independent Sector,[8] developed a National Taxonomy of Exempt Entities (NTEE) that divides that largest set of tax-exempt entities, Internal Revenue Code Sec. 501(c)(3) organizations, into 10 functional categories (arts, culture, and humanities; education; environment/animals; health; human services; international/foreign affairs; public/society benefit; religion related; mutual/membership benefit; and others) and 26 major group areas. See Chapter 15 for more discussion of regulation over tax-exempt entities.

GAAP for Nongovernmental NPOs

The FASB assumed primary responsibility for providing guidance on generally accepted accounting principles for nongovernmental not-for-profit entities in 1979.[9] The GASB is responsible for governmental organizations including governmental not-for-profit organizations (see Illustration 1–1, p. 4). These lines of responsibility were most clearly established with the AICPA's *SAS No.* 69, commonly known as "the GAAP hierarchy."[10] Governmental not-for-profit organiza-

[5]Ibid.

[6]The terms *public* and *private* are problematic; for example, *public* charities are in the not-for-profit sector, *public* schools are in the governmental sector, and *publicly* traded companies are in the for-profit sector of our economy. Distinguishing between for-profit, not-for-profit, and governmental/nongovernmental is more useful.

[7]See p. 6 for the definition of a governmental entity.

[8]The Independent Sector is a nonprofit coalition of corporate, foundation, and voluntary organization members with national interest and impact in philanthropy and voluntary action based in Washington, DC.

[9]Financial Accounting Standards Board, *Statement of Financial Accounting Standards No. 32*, "Specialized Accounting and Reporting Principles in AICPA Statements of Position and Guides on Accounting and Auditing Matters" (New York, 1979).

[10]American Institute of Certified Public Accountants, *Statement of Auditing Standards (SAS) No.* 69, "The Meaning of 'Present Fairly in Conformity with Generally Accepted Accounting Principles' in the Independent Auditor's Report" (New York, 1992). The FASB rescinded *SFAS No. 32* upon the issuance of this guidance. An Exposure Draft to amend this statement was issued in November 1999.

tions should apply the principles outlined by the GASB in its financial reporting project (discussed in Chapter 1). They are not permitted to adopt FASB's standards applicable to nongovernmental NPOs. This chapter focuses on nongovernmental not-for-profit entities.[11]

There has been a concerted effort recently among the AICPA, the FASB, and the federal Office of Management and Budget (OMB) to standardize the accounting, financial reporting, and auditing rules for the diverse set of entities in the not-for-profit sector and reduce the inconsistencies across segments of this sector. The AICPA's 1996 Audit and Accounting Guide, *Not-for-Profit Organizations*, superseded three audit guides (Voluntary Health and Welfare Organizations, Colleges and Universities, and Certain Not-for-Profit Organizations) and four statements of Position (*SOPs 74-8, 78-10, 87-2,* and *94-2*). The FASB has completed four of its five not-for-profit agenda items designed to reduce inconsistencies across NPOs: depreciation (*SFAS No. 93*), contributions (*SFAS No. 116*), financial reporting display (*SFAS No. 117*), and investments (*SFAS No. 124*). The remaining item is on financially interrelated entities, and is integrally tied to the for-profit project on consolidations and related matters. Each of these statements is discussed in this chapter. Congress revised the Single Audit Act in 1996 to cover both governmental and not-for-profit entities, and the OMB issued a revision of *Circular A-133* (see Chapter 11)[12] that includes governments, not-for-profit organizations, and health care entities.

Financial Reporting and Accounting

As stated in Chapter 1, the FASB's objectives of financial reporting for not-for-profit agencies are to provide information useful in (1) making resource allocation decisions, (2) assessing services and ability to provide services, (3) assessing management stewardship and performance, and (4) assessing economic resources, obligations, net resources, and changes in them.[13] Users of not-for-profit financial statements include donors, grantors, members, creditors, and others who provide resources to NPOs.

Financial Reporting

FASB *Statement No. 117* requires NPOs to present financial statements showing an aggregate view of the entity.[14] This revolutionary approach effectively moved not-for-profit financial reporting away from the disaggregated, traditional method of fund-based reporting and more toward the commercial for-profit model of financial

---

[11]Governmental Accounting Standards Board, *Statement No. 29*, "The Use of Not-for-Profit Accounting and Financial Reporting Principles by Governmental Entities" (Norwalk, CT, 1996).

[12]Office of Management and Budget, *Circular A-133*, "Audits of Not-for-Profit Organizations Receiving Federal Awards" (Washington, DC, 1997, with 1999 update).

[13]FASB, *Concepts Statement No. 4*, pp. 19–23.

[14]Financial Accounting Standards Board, *Statement of Financial Accounting Standards No. 117*, "Financial Statements for Not-for-Profit Organizations" (Norwalk, CT, 1993).

reporting. Not all users welcomed this change and the impacts of this controversial change will take several years to be assessed.[15]

FASB *Statement No. 117* established minimum standards for general purpose external financial statements for NPOs by requiring a Statement of Financial Position, Statement of Activities, and Statement of Cash Flows, along with Notes to the Financial Statements. Voluntary health and welfare organizations must also present a Statement of Functional Expenses. Although the information specified by *SFAS No. 117* is to be presented for the entity as a whole, the statement permits additional display of disaggregated information, such as fund-based information that may be useful for management of the entity and accountability to donors and others. Comparative statements are encouraged, but not required. Illustrative financial statements for the Community Family Service Agency, Inc., a VHWO, are presented in Illustrations 14–2 through 14–5, although alternative financial statement formats are allowed by *SFAS No. 117*. The amounts shown in the financial statements reflect the illustrative transactions and journal entries presented later in this chapter.

Statement of Financial Position. This statement shows total assets, total liabilities, and the difference, **net assets,** for the organization as a whole. As seen in Illustration 14–2, net assets for this VHWO are categorized into the three classes required by *SFAS No. 117:* unrestricted net assets, temporarily restricted net assets, and permanently restricted net assets. **Unrestricted net assets** arise from contributions either that have no donor restrictions or for which the restrictions have expired, revenues for services provided, and most investment income. Unrestricted net assets can be further segregated into Board-designated and residual available for operations. **Board-designated net assets** are those unrestricted net assets appropriated or set aside by the governing board rather than an external donor and are sometimes subtitled "investments" and "net equity in fixed assets."

Temporarily restricted net assets result from contributions in which the donor imposes restrictions as to purpose (how the asset is used) or time (when the asset is used). When the restrictions are met, these net assets are "released" and reported as increases in unrestricted net assets. **Permanently restricted net assets** are assets for which the donor stipulates that the assets be held in perpetuity, but allows the organization to spend the income. These gifts are also called **endowments** and are nonexpendable. Endowments may take the form of *pure* endowments, *term* endowments, or *quasi*-endowments. Term endowments are classified as temporarily restricted net assets because as the term expires, the assets can be used at the discretion of the NPO. Quasi-endowments are those in which the Board designates that funds be set aside; however, since the Board can reverse that decision, this form of endowment is classified as an unrestricted net asset. Permanently restricted net assets may also be in the form of artwork, land, or other assets that must be used for a certain purpose

[15]See Robert N. Anthony, "The Not-for-Profit Accounting Mess," and Robert H. Northcutt, "Observations on Professor Anthony's Commentary," *Accounting Horizons*, June 1995, pp. 44–55.

Illustration 14–2

COMMUNITY FAMILY SERVICE AGENCY, INC.
STATEMENT OF FINANCIAL POSITION
DECEMBER 31, 2002, AND 2001

	2002	2001
Assets:		
Cash	$ 28,953	$ 58,711
Short-term investments, at fair value	22,000	22,000
Accounts receivable (net)	1,150	2,350
Contributions receivable (net)	6,061	5,165
Supplies, at lower of cost or market	19,100	23,095
Prepaid expense	3,600	3,917
Assets restricted to investment:		
For land, buildings, and equipment:		
Investments, at fair value	15,000	20,000
Contributions receivable (net)	982	10,182
For endowment:		
Investments, at fair value	230,000	230,000
Land, buildings, and equipment, less allowance for accumulated depreciation of $17,961 and $13,776	104,763	103,948
Long-term investments	17,000	17,000
Total assets	$448,609	$496,368
Liabilities and net assets:		
Accounts payable and accrued expenses	$ 44,147	$ 25,911
8¼% mortgage payable, due 2015	48,500	55,000
Total liabilities	92,647	80,911
Net assets:		
Unrestricted	29,627	97,302
Temporarily restricted	96,335	88,155
Permanently restricted	230,000	230,000
Total net assets	355,962	415,457
Total liabilities and net assets	$448,609	$496,368

and may not be sold. Information on temporarily and permanently restricted net assets can be reported on the face of the Statement of Financial Position or in the Notes to the Financial Statements.

SFAS No. 117 recommends that assets and liabilities be listed in their order of liquidation similar to the manner in which they are listed by business enterprises. The nature of assets and any restrictions should be disclosed. In general, restrictions apply to net assets, not to specific assets. However, if cash or other assets received are designated for long-term purposes or have donor-imposed restrictions that limit their use, they should be segregated on the financial statement, as seen in Illustration 14–2.

Statement of Activities. The Statement of Activities presents, in aggregated fashion, all changes in unrestricted net assets, temporarily restricted net assets, permanently restricted net assets, and total net assets for the reporting period. These changes take the form of revenues, gains, expenses, and losses. As seen in Illustration 14–3, there is also a section titled "Net assets released from restrictions" that indicates the reclassification of temporarily restricted support to unrestricted support in the year in which the donor stipulations were met. Reclassifications are made for (1) satisfaction of program or purpose restrictions, (2) satisfaction of equipment acquisition restrictions, sometimes measured by depreciation expense, and (3) satisfaction of time restrictions, either actual donor or implied restrictions.

NPOs have considerable flexibility in presenting financial information as long as it is useful and understandable to the reader. *SFAS No. 117* does not preclude the NPO from using additional classifications, such as operating and nonoperating, expendable and nonexpendable, earned and unearned, and recurring and nonrecurring. An alternative format is presented later in Illustration 14–7.

In the absence of any donor restrictions, contributions including unconditional promises to give are shown as revenue or support increasing unrestricted net assets. Unconditional promises to give that will not be received until future periods must be reported among the temporarily restricted net assets unless explicit donor stipulations or the circumstances surrounding the promise make it clear that the donor intended the contribution to support activities of the current period. If the provisions of a temporarily restricted contribution are met in the period of the gift, then the revenue and expenses *may* be reported in the unrestricted category. If events simultaneously increase one asset class and decrease another, they should be reported as separate items.

Although some NPOs may use the cash basis as a simple method of accounting internally, external financial statements must be prepared on the accrual accounting basis in order to be in conformity with GAAP. In general, all revenues and expenses should be reported at their gross amounts. Exceptions include activities peripheral to the entity's central operations and investment revenue, which may be reported net of related expenses, if properly disclosed. Although revenues are categorized into three classes, all expenses are reported as reductions of unrestricted net assets. In addition, expenses must be reported by their functional classification (e.g., program or supporting) either in this statement or in the Notes to the Financial Statements. Gains and losses on investments and other assets are reported as changes in unrestricted net assets unless their use is temporarily or permanently restricted.

Statement of Cash Flows. *SFAS No. 117* requires a Statement of Cash Flows by amending *SFAS No. 95* to extend its coverage to not-for-profit organizations as

Illustration 14–3

COMMUNITY FAMILY SERVICE AGENCY, INC.
STATEMENT OF ACTIVITIES
YEAR ENDED DECEMBER 31, 2002

Changes in unrestricted net assets:	
Revenues and gains:	
Contributions	$388,196
Program service fees	55,250
Membership dues	1,000
Sales to public (net)	100
Investment income	15,680
Miscellaneous	1,500
Total unrestricted revenues and gains	461,726
Net assets released from restrictions:	
Satisfaction of program requirements	27,400
Satisfaction of equipment acquisition restrictions	4,185
Expiration of time restrictions	5,125
Total net assets released from restrictions	36,710
Total unrestricted revenues, gains, and other support	498,436
Expenses and losses:	
Program services:	
Counseling	185,513
Adoption	69,560
Foster home care	172,531
Special outreach project	62,870
Total program services	490,474
Supporting services:	
Management and general	53,085
Fund-raising	13,978
Total supporting services	67,063
Payments to affiliated organizations	8,574
Total expenses and losses	566,111
Decrease in unrestricted net assets	(67,675)
Changes in temporarily restricted net assets:	
Contributions	43,500
Investment income	1,390
Net assets released from restrictions	(36,710)
Increase in temporarily restricted net assets	8,180
Change in permanently restricted net assets	0
Decrease in net assets	(59,495)
Net assets, December 31, 2001	415,457
Net assets, December 31, 2002	$355,962

well as for-profit entities.[16] As Illustration 14–4 shows, cash flows are reported in three categories: operating, investing, and financing. The direct or indirect method may be used. If the direct method is used, a reconciliation showing the change in total net assets from the Statement of Activities to net cash used for operating activities must be prepared.

Donor-imposed restrictions are not separately reported in the cash flows statement; however, the statement does have some unique aspects. Unrestricted gifts are included with the operating activities; purchases or sales of long-term assets, including investments, are reported in the investing activities section; and the receipt of temporarily and permanently restricted net assets given for long-term purposes are included in the financing activities section, with the related income. The financing activities section also includes the issuance and repayment of long-term debt. Noncash gifts or in-kind contributions (discussed later) are disclosed as noncash investing and financing activities in a separate section.

Notes to the Financial Statements. As with all entities, the notes are an integral part of the financial statements of NPOs. Disclosures include principles applicable to for-profit entities, unless there is a specific exemption for not-for-profit organizations. Examples of required disclosures are those relating to financial instruments; commitments; contingencies; extraordinary items; prior-period adjustments; changes in accounting principles; employee benefits; and credit risks. In addition, the nature and amounts of unrestricted, temporarily restricted, and permanently restricted net assets must be disclosed if not displayed on the face of the financial statements. Notes are encouraged to report the detail of reclassifications, investments, and promises to give. Policy statements regarding whether restricted gifts received and expended in the same period are reported first as temporarily restricted must also be disclosed.

Statement of Functional Expenses. VHWOs must prepare a Statement of Functional Expenses along with their other financial statements. Illustration 14–5 shows a format with functional expenses reported in the columns and the natural classification of expenses shown as rows. The functional expenses are those that relate to the program or mission of the organization as opposed to the management and general and fund-raising expenses required to operate the programs. The natural classification of expenses, or object of expense, includes salaries, supplies, occupancy costs, interest, and depreciation, among other categories the organization considers useful to the readers. The ratio of program expenses to total expenses is often used by watchdog agencies, donors, and others as a measure of an NPO's performance. According to the National Charities Information Bureau, the ratio of program

---

[16]Financial Accounting Standards Board, *Statement of Financial Accounting Standards No. 95*, "Statement of Cash Flows" (Norwalk, CT, 1987).

Illustration 14–4

COMMUNITY FAMILY SERVICE AGENCY, INC.
STATEMENT OF CASH FLOWS
YEAR ENDED DECEMBER 31, 2002

Cash flows from operating activities:	
Cash received from contributors	$349,440
Cash collected on contributions receivable	68,500
Cash received from service recipients	57,200
Cash collected from members	1,000
Investment income	15,680
Miscellaneous receipts	1,750
Cash paid to employees and suppliers	(530,164)
Cash paid to affiliated organizations	(8,574)
Interest paid	(4,540)
Net cash used for operating activities	(49,708)
Cash flows from investing activities:	
Purchase of property and equipment	(5,000)
Proceeds from sale of securities	5,000
Net cash used by investing activities	0
Cash flows from financing activities:	
Proceeds from contributions restricted for:	
Investment in plant	8,660
Future operations	16,400
Other financing activities:	
Interest and dividends restricted for plant acquisition	1,390
Repayment of long-term debt	(6,500)
Net cash provided by financing activities	19,950
Net increase (decrease) in cash	(29,758)
Cash, December 31, 2001	58,711
Cash, December 31, 2002	$ 28,953
Reconciliation of Changes in Net Assets to Net Cash Used for Operating Activities:	
Change in net assets	$ (59,495)
Adjustments to reconcile changes in net assets to net cash provided by operating activities:	
Depreciation	4,185
Decrease in accounts receivable, net	1,200
Decrease in contributions receivable, net	8,304
Decrease in supplies	3,995
Decrease in prepaid expenses	317
Increase in accounts payable and accrued expenses	18,236
Gifts, grants, and bequests restricted for long-term investment	(25,060)
Interest restricted for long-term investment	(1,390)
Cash used for operating activities	$ (49,708)

Illustration 14–5

COMMUNITY FAMILY SERVICE AGENCY, INC.
STATEMENT OF FUNCTIONAL EXPENSES
YEAR ENDED DECEMBER 31, 2002
(WITH COMPARATIVE TOTALS FOR 2001)

	Program Services					Supporting Services			Total Program and Supporting Services Expenses	
	Counseling	*Adoption*	*Foster Home Care*	*Special Outreach Project*	*Total*	*Management and General*	*Fund-Raising*	*Total*	*2002*	*2001*
Salaries	$ 87,720	$36,559	$ 83,610	$13,738	$221,627	$35,153	$ 8,220	$43,373	$265,000	$232,170
Employee benefits	16,882	7,036	16,091	2,644	42,653	6,765	1,582	8,347	51,000	47,035
Payroll taxes	6,720	2,801	6,405	1,051	16,977	2,693	630	3,323	20,300	11,400
Total salaries and related expenses	111,322	46,396	106,106	17,433	281,257	44,611	10,432	55,043	336,300	290,605
Professional fees	25,107	3,929	11,643	18,143	58,822	1,178	—	1,178	60,000	54,600
Supplies	4,049	2,167	4,747	3,950	14,913	790	592	1,382	16,295	8,500
Telephone	3,897	1,430	3,350	190	8,867	600	333	933	9,800	9,610
Postage and shipping	2,840	1,073	2,402	908	7,223	684	210	894	8,117	6,750
Occupancy	8,772	1,415	8,078	2,586	20,851	2,468	581	3,049	23,900	24,600
Rental and maintenance of equipment	3,669	1,520	3,511	—	8,700	—	—	—	8,700	8,750
Printing and publications	2,761	1,420	1,352	1,462	6,995	940	1,565	2,505	9,500	7,200
Travel	7,700	1,500	7,500	5,000	21,700	300	—	300	22,000	24,000
Conferences, conventions, meetings	3,450	887	4,436	4,436	13,209	591	—	591	13,800	13,700
Specific assistance to individuals	9,000	1,000	16,100	3,900	30,000	—	—	—	30,000	28,500
Membership dues	234	187	93	93	607	93	—	93	700	677
Awards and grants to National Headquarters	—	5,500	—	—	5,500	—	—	—	5,500	5,000
Miscellaneous	1,744	843	1,891	4,144	8,622	118	—	118	8,740	5,200
Total before depreciation	184,545	69,267	171,209	62,245	487,266	52,373	13,713	66,086	553,352	487,692
Depreciation of buildings and equipment	968	293	1,322	625	3,208	712	265	977	4,185	4,200
Total expenses	$185,513	$69,560	$172,531	$62,870	$490,474	$53,085	$13,978	$67,063	$557,537	$491,892

expenses to total expenses should be greater than 60 percent.[17] Natural expenses that apply to more than one function must be allocated across program, general and administrative, and fund-raising using a systematic method. Allocation of fund-raising costs is discussed later in this chapter.

Accounting for Revenues, Gains, and Support

Not-for-profit organizations have traditionally distinguished revenues, gains, and support. **Revenues** represent increases in unrestricted net assets arising from bilateral **"exchange transactions"** in which the other party to the transaction is presumed to receive direct tangible benefit commensurate with the resources provided. Examples are membership dues, program service fees, sales of supplies and services, and investment income. **Gains,** such as realized gains on investment transactions and gains on sale or disposal of equipment, are increases in net assets that relate to peripheral or incidental transactions of the entity and often are beyond the control of management. **Support** is an increase in net assets arising from contributions of resources or **"nonexchange transactions"** and include only amounts for which the donor derives no tangible benefits from the recipient agency. Membership dues may be part revenue and part contribution if the value received by the member is less than the dues payment. A government grant is usually considered unrestricted support, unless it is essentially a purchase of services, in which case the recipient is considered a vendor and the grant is classified as revenue. Often organizations present one section in the Statement of Activities for revenues, gains, and support, in which case these distinctions are less important. All revenues, gains, and support should be recognized on the accrual basis and reported at gross amounts to be in conformity with GAAP. Revenue that is restricted by an agreement, such as fees or dues dedicated for a specific purpose, is reported in unrestricted net assets because it does not arise from a restricted gift by a donor.

Contributions. Not-for-profit organizations, in particular voluntary health and welfare organizations, depend on contributions for their operations. A **contribution** is an unconditional transfer of cash or other asset to the entity (or a settlement or cancellation of its liabilities) in a voluntary, nonreciprocal transfer by another entity acting other than as an owner. *SFAS No. 116* provides guidance on contributions where the reporting entity is a donor or donee; however, it does not apply to exchange transactions—those in which the entity is acting as an agent, trustee, or intermediary or to tax exemptions, incentives, or abatements.[18] Donors may restrict the period in which the gift can be used or its purpose, or make the contribution without restrictions. In general, *SFAS No. 116* requires recognition of both unrestricted and restricted gifts as support at fair value at the time of the gift. Restricted support increases either temporarily or permanently restricted net assets, depending on whether the restriction is temporary or permanent. In the absence of donor-imposed restrictions, unrestricted net assets are increased.

---

[17]See the NCIB's "Standards in Philanthropy" at http://www.give.org/standard.cfm.
[18]FASB, *SFAS No. 116*, par. 4.

Promises to give assets to an organization (commonly called *pledges*) can be conditional or unconditional. A **conditional promise to give** depends on the occurrence of a specified future and uncertain event to bind the promissor, such as obtaining matching gifts by the recipient. A conditional promise to give is *not* recognized as support until the conditions on which it depends are substantially met.

An **unconditional promise to give** depends only on the passage of time or demand by the promisee for performance. These promises are recorded as support in the year made. Unconditional pledges payable in the future, or multiyear promises, are treated as temporarily restricted support, then reclassified to the unrestricted net asset class when the period arrives or the donor stipulation is met. The contribution is measured at the present value of future cash flows. Any difference in previously recorded temporarily restricted support and the current value when the period arrives is recorded as contribution revenue, not interest income.

Promises may require the establishment of an allowance for estimated uncollectible pledges, inasmuch as pledges may not be enforceable under law. A description of promises and their terms must be disclosed in the Notes to the Financial Statements. Pledges or intentions to give are not recorded until they have the characteristics of an unconditional promise to give, for example, a written document, partial payment, or a public announcement by the donor.

These *nonexchange* transactions can take the form of cash, securities, capital assets, materials, or services. Cash contributions require that a strong system of internal controls over the safeguarding of this asset be in place; however, they pose no unusual accounting or reporting problems. Donated securities may be received for any purpose, although generally they are received as a part of the principal of an endowment. They are recorded at their fair value at the date of the gift, and the same valuation rule is applied to capital assets received either as a part of an endowment or for use in the operations of the organization. Donations of capital assets, such as land, buildings, or works of art, may be temporarily or permanently restricted. If the donor does not stipulate how the asset should be used, then the gift is classified as unrestricted. If the donor does impose restrictions, such as how long the asset must be used as a building, or if the NPO has a policy implying a time restriction over the useful life of the asset, then the contribution is classified as temporarily restricted. For buildings and equipment, an amount equal to annual depreciation expense is reclassified from temporarily restricted to unrestricted each year.

Donated Materials and Services. One of the basic characteristics that distinguishes not-for-profit organizations from commercial organizations is their reliance on noncash contributions or **gifts in kind.** Sheltered workshops for persons with disabilities often depend heavily on donations of clothing and furniture, thrift shops receive their inventory from donations, and health agencies may obtain contributions of drugs from pharmaceutical houses. Office space may be furnished rent free; and television, radio, and periodicals may publicize fund drives, special events, or the general work of NPOs at no charge. *SFAS No. 116* requires that all unconditional gifts, including material amounts of donated materials, be reported as both a contribution, measured at fair value on the date of the gift, and an expense. An objective, clearly measurable basis for fair value can be established by proceeds from resale by the organization, price lists, market quotations, or appraisals.[19] Donated materials used or consumed in rendering services should be reported as part of the cost of the services rendered.

The services of unpaid workers may well make the difference between an effective organization and one that fails to achieve its objectives. Voluntary health and welfare organizations typically rely on the efforts of volunteer workers to supplement the efforts of paid employees. *SFAS No. 116* requires recognition of contributed services at their fair value if the services received (1) create or enhance nonfinancial assets; or (2) require specialized skills, are provided by individuals possessing those skills, and typically would need to be purchased if not provided by donation (e.g., accountants or secretaries). Although *SFAS No. 116* does not provide an example of the first criterion, a logical example would be recognition of support for donated architectural, legal, or carpentry services related to construction of a building addition. In this example, a capital asset account, rather than a program or support expense, would be debited. In general, nonfinancial assets are assets other than cash and assets readily convertible into cash, such as consumable supplies and capital assets. The second criterion is quite restrictive and results in many donated services not being recognized.

Donated Land, Building, and Equipment. If a donor makes a contribution of real estate or equipment to an NPO without any restrictions on its use, the contribution may be reported as unrestricted or temporarily restricted, depending on the policy of the organization. This policy should be clearly stated in the notes to the financial statements. The donor may stipulate that the gift is temporarily or permanently restricted. In any case, the donation should be recorded at the fair value at the date of the gift. If an NPO receives use of a building for a reduced rate, the difference between the rent paid and the fair market rental value should be reported as a contribution. If the organization receives donations that they intend to sell rather than use, then these contributions should be reported as increases in unrestricted net assets.

Split-Interest Gifts. Donors may arrange to split the interest in a gift among several beneficiaries, including an NPO. These complex legal agreements, often involving charitable lead and remainder trusts, as well as deferred giving programs and gifts of life insurance, are beyond the scope of this book.

Special Events. Special events are fund-raising activities in which something of tangible value is offered to donor participants or designees for a payment that includes a contribution adequate to yield revenue for the sponsoring agency over and above direct expenses. Dinners, dances, golf outings, bazaars, card parties, fashion shows, and sales of candy, cookies, cakes, or greeting cards are typical "special

[19]*SFAS No. 116*, par. 19.

events." The special events category of support is reserved for those events sponsored by the voluntary organization or by an organization over which it has control. If a completely independent organization sponsors an event for the voluntary agency's benefit, the amount given to the agency should be reported as contributions.

Special events may give rise to incidental revenue, such as advertising of programs; incidental revenue is properly reported in the special events category of support. NPOs have traditionally netted direct costs of special events (such as the cost of dinner, rental of ballroom, or cost of prizes) against the gross proceeds of the special event. FASB *Statement No. 117*, par. 138, requires that all special event revenue and direct costs, except those of a peripheral or incidental nature, be reported at their gross amounts. In the Statement of Activities presented in Illustration 14–3 in this chapter, special events support is included as part of the "Contributions" rather than as a separate amount. If desired, NPOs can provide more detailed reporting of support categories, either on the face of the Statement of Activities or in the Notes to the Financial Statements.

Expenses of promoting and conducting special events, such as expenses of printing tickets and posters, mailings, fees and expenses of public relations and fund-raising consultants, and salaries of employees of the voluntary agency attributable to planning, promoting, and conducting special events, are treated as fund-raising expenses and are not charged against special events support.

Accounting for Expenses

Generally accepted accounting principles require that all expenses of NPOs be measured on the accrual basis and be reported as decreases in unrestricted net assets on the Statement of Activities. Depreciation of capital assets, including contributed capital assets, used in the operation of the organization is required by *SFAS No. 93*.[20] Depreciation of art and historical collections is discussed later in this chapter.

Functional Expenses. NPOs have long been required to report some degree of functional expenses; that is, segregation of expenses incurred for operating the *programs* from expenses incurred for *supporting* the programs (e.g., fund-raising or management and general expenses). Depreciation expense should be allocated to programs as well as to support function expenses. Illustration 14–6 presents a chart from the United Way of America's book, *Accounting and Financial Reporting: A Guide for United Ways and Not-for-Profit Human Service Organizations* that shows the relationship between functional and natural or object classifications of expenses. The human service organization used in the illustration is a United Way of America agency operating three programs: adoption, foster home care, and counseling. A local fund-raising organization, such as the United Way, that is intended to allocate most of its inflows to participating agencies rather than to engage directly in offering program services to the public may find it desirable to present

[20]Financial Accounting Standards Board, *Statement of Financial Accounting Standards No. 93* "Recognition of Depreciation by Not-for-Profit Organizations" (Norwalk, CT, 1987).

Illustration 14–6 Functional Basis Financial Package of a Not-for-Profit Human Service Organization

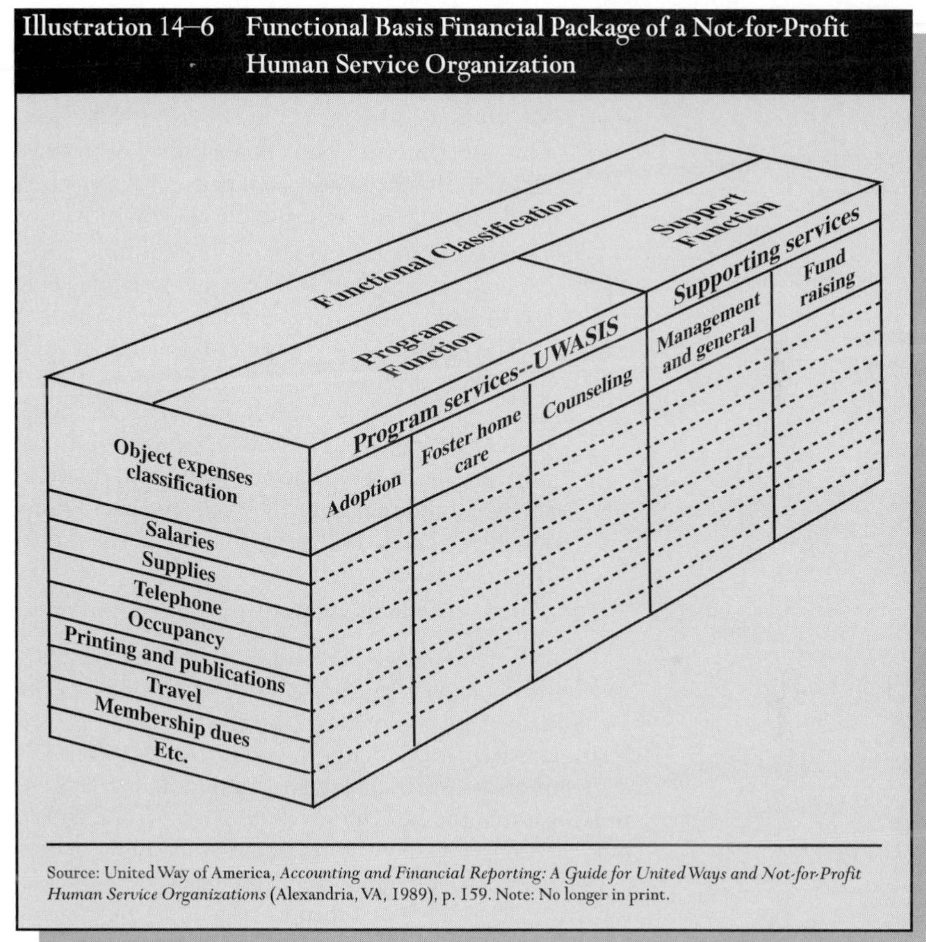

Source: United Way of America, *Accounting and Financial Reporting: A Guide for United Ways and Not-for-Profit Human Service Organizations* (Alexandria, VA, 1989), p. 159. Note: No longer in print.

"allocating and agency relations" or "planning and evaluation" as well as management and general and fund-raising.

Allocation of Costs with a Fund-Raising Appeal. Nonprofit organizations often conduct an activity that combines a program purpose and a fund-raising purpose. For example, a door-to-door campaign to educate the public on its mission *and* solicit contributions. In the past, the cost of this joint activity often was reported entirely as functional program expenses with no allocation to the functional support expense of "fund-raising." AICPA *Statement of Position 98-2* revises *SOP 87-2* on joint costs and makes it more difficult to allocate "educating the public" or "advocacy" costs to program expenses. *SOP 98-2* provides:

1. The total cost of activities that include a fund-raising appeal should be reported as fund-raising costs unless a *bona fide* program or management and general function has been conducted in conjunction with the appeal for funds.
2. The joint costs of a bona fide program or management and general function should be allocated between those cost objectives and fund-raising using an equitable allocation base.
3. Criteria of purpose, audience, and content must be met in order to conclude that a bona fide program or management and general function has been conducted in conjunction with the appeal for funds.

   The *purpose* criterion is met if the activity accomplishes a program or management purpose of the organization other than "educating the public." The *audience* criterion is met if the audience was selected primarily for its need for the program or ability to advance the goals of the organization, rather than the likelihood that they will contribute financially to the cause. The *content* criterion is met if the activity includes a call to action on the part of the targeted audience to advance the mission of the organization.
4. Certain information must be disclosed if joint costs are allocated.[21]

This statement goes beyond *SOP 87-2* by covering total costs, not just joint costs, and applying to state and local governmental entities, as well as to NPOs.

Management and general expenses include the cost of publicity and public relations activities designed to keep the organization's name before prospective contributors. Costs of informational materials that contain only general information regarding the health or welfare program and the costs of informational materials distributed to potential contributors, but not as a part of a fund drive, are considered management and general expenses. The costs of budgeting, accounting, reporting, legal services, office management, purchasing, and similar activities are examples of expenses properly classifiable as management and general expenses.

Fund-raising expenses include the costs of television and radio announcements that request contributions, including the costs of preparing the announcements and purchasing or arranging for the time; the costs of postage, addressing, and maintenance of mailing lists and other fund drive records; the costs of preparing or purchasing fund-raising materials; the costs of public meetings to "kick off" a fund drive; and an appropriate portion of the salaries of personnel who supervise fund-raising activities or keep records of them.

Accounting for Assets

Assets that have different treatment in NPOs than in for-profit entities include investments and collection items.

[21] AICPA, *SOP 98-2*, "Accounting for Costs of Activities of Not-for-Profit Organizations and State and Local Governmental Entities that Include Fund-Raising" (New York, 1998).

Investments. *SFAS No. 124* provides guidance to NPOs on accounting for investments in a manner similar to *SFAS No. 115* for businesses, and removes the inconsistencies in investment accounting across the various audit guides for nongovermental not-for-profit entities.[22] *SFAS No. 124* requires that not-for-profit organizations mark all investments in equity securities that have readily determinable values and all debt securities to market or *fair value*, rather than reporting them at original cost, amortized cost, or lower of cost or market. This statement is simpler than *SFAS No. 115* in that there is no requirement that NPOs classify their investments into trading, available-for-sale, and held-to-maturity categories. It does not apply to investments in securities accounted for under the equity method; consolidated subsidiaries; or investments with no readily determinable market value, such as real estate mortgages, oil and gas interests, and limited partnerships without a publicly traded market value.

Gains and losses are measured as the changes in fair value of the investments. Fair values are determined by quoted market prices, if available; selling price of similar securities; or valuation techniques, such as discounted cash flows. All realized and unrealized gains and losses on investments, as well as investment income (i.e., interest and dividends), are reported in the current period's Statement of Activities. Income and gains (losses) are reported as increases (decreases) in unrestricted net assets, unless their use is restricted by the donor or legally restricted by state law.[23] If restrictions on income exist, then income is reported as an increase in either temporarily or permanently restricted net assets, depending on the nature of the restriction; and gains and losses are reported in the same way as the income. When the restriction is satisfied in the same period the income or gain is earned, then the investment income and gains may be reported as increases in unrestricted net assets as long as the organization has a similar policy for reporting contributions received, reports consistently from period to period, and discloses its accounting policy.

Endowments, gifts that the donor requires be held permanently, pose some additional accounting problems. If the donor requires that a specific investment security be held in perpetuity, then gains and losses on that security are also permanently restricted. However, if the NPO can choose suitable investments, then gains on those investments are reported as increases in unrestricted net assets, unless the income was restricted. The donor may stipulate that part of the net appreciation value (unrealized gain) is restricted, most often done to protect the endowment from the effects of inflation. In this case, gains are reported as permanently restricted net assets until the required net appreciation value is reached, then the remainder is reported as unrestricted. Losses on endowments are more

[22]Financial Accounting Standards Board, *Statement of Financial Accounting Standards No. 124*, "Accounting for Certain Investments Held by Not-for-Profit Organizations" (Norwalk, CT, 1995), and *Statement of Financial Accounting Standards No. 115*, "Accounting for Certain Investments in Debt and Equity Securities" (Norwalk, CT, 1994).

[23]Most states have adopted some version of the Uniform Management of Institutional Funds Act (UMIFA) (1970s) and some have adopted the Uniform Prudent Investors Act (1994), which describes standards of care, portfolio theory, and delegation of investment authority.

complicated, in part, because the donor is often silent regarding any loss. *SFAS No. 124* requires that endowment losses reduce unrestricted net assets if the net appreciation requirement has been reached; otherwise, endowment losses decrease temporarily restricted net assets. In subsequent years, gains that restore the fair value of the endowment assets to the required level are reported as increases in unrestricted net assets.

SFAS No. 124 also requires extensive disclosures such as:

1. Composition of investment return, including investment income, net realized gains and losses on investments reported at other than fair value, and net gains and losses on investments reported at fair value.
2. A reconciliation of investment return to amounts reported in the Statements of Activities, if investment return is separated into operating and nonoperating amounts, together with a description of the policy used to determine the amount that is included in the measure of operations, and a discussion of circumstances leading to any change in that policy.
3. The aggregate carrying amount of investments by major types (e.g., equity securities, U.S. Treasury securities, mutual funds, corporate, debt securities, real estate).
4. The basis for determining the carrying amount for investments not covered by this standard.
5. The method(s) and significant assumptions used to estimate the fair values of investments other than financial instruments, if those other investments are reported at fair value.
6. The aggregate amount of deficiencies for all donor-restricted endowment funds for which the fair value of the investment at the reporting date is less than the level required by donor stipulation or law.
7. The nature of and carrying amount for each individual investment or group of investments that represents a significant concentration of market risk.

NPOs must follow the disclosure guidance in *SFAS Nos. 105, 107,* and *109*.[24]

Collection Items. Certain not-for-profit organizations, particularly museums and libraries, have significant collections. *SFAS No. 116* defines **collections** as works of art, historical treasures, or similar assets that are:

1. Held for public exhibition, education, or research in furtherance of public service rather than financial gain.
2. Protected, kept unencumbered, cared for, and preserved.

[24]Financial Accounting Standards Board, *Statement of Financial Accounting Standards No. 105*, "Disclosure of Information about Financial Instruments with Off-Balance Sheet Risk and Financial Instruments with Concentrations of Credit Risk" (Norwalk, CT, 1990); *SFAS No. 107*, "Disclosures about Fair Value of Financial Instruments" (1991); and *SFAS No. 119*, "Disclosures about Derivative Financial Instruments and Fair Value of Financial Instruments" (1994).

3. Subject to an organizational policy that requires the proceeds of items that are sold to be used to acquire other items for collection.[25]

An NPO may adopt a policy of recognizing collections as assets, or not recognizing them; however, selective capitalization is not allowed. Implementation of *SFAS No. 116* required organizations to either retroactively capitalize their collections, prospectively capitalize the collection, or not capitalize at all.

If an NPO capitalizes its collections, then it should recognize them as assets in the period in which they are acquired, either at cost or fair market value, if contributed. If contributed, collections should be recorded in the appropriate net asset category depending on any restrictions placed on the contribution by the donor. If the organization chooses not to capitalize, then it should provide note disclosure of its collections.

SFAS No. 93 states that works of art or historical treasures do not need to be depreciated so long as their economic benefit is used up so slowly that their estimated useful lives are extraordinarily long. This characteristic exists if (1) the assets individually have cultural, aesthetic, or historic value that is worth preserving perpetually, and (2) the holder has the technological and financial ability to protect and preserve essentially undiminished the service potential of the asset and is doing that.[26]

Optional Fund Accounting

Fund accounting was defined and illustrated in Chapters 1 through 9 for governments as a method of segregating assets, liabilities, and fund balances into separate accounting entities associated with specific activities, donor-imposed restrictions, or obligations. This system makes it possible to determine compliance with laws, regulations, and agreements; and demonstrate that the NPO is meeting its stewardship responsibility to resource providers. Many NPOs still use this accounting method for internal management and grant reporting purposes. As mentioned previously, *SFAS No. 117* permits not-for-profit organizations to also present disaggregated data classified by fund groups, as long as the aggregated net asset statements are also presented. Fund categories described in the AICPA Audit and Accounting Guide, *Not-for-Profit Organizations*, are:

- Unrestricted current funds (or unrestricted operating or general funds).
- Restricted current funds (or restricted operating or specific purpose funds).
- Plant funds (or land, building, and equipment funds).
- Loan funds.
- Endowment funds.

[25]AICPA, Audit and Accounting Guide, *Not-for-Profit Organizations*, par. 7.05; and FASB, *SFAS No. 116*, Appendix D.

[26]FASB, *SFAS No. 93*, par. 6.

- Annuity and life income funds (or split-interest funds).
- Agency funds (or custodian funds).[27]

All NPO funds are self-balancing sets of accounts that are both accounting entities and fiscal entities accounted for on the full accrual basis, except the Agency Fund, which is comprised only of assets and liabilities. The residual difference between total assets and total liabilities in a fund is labeled Fund Balance. Net assets also represent residual interests, but net assets are not the same as fund balances.

Unrestricted current funds are used to account for all resources that may be used at the discretion of the governing Board for carrying on the operations of the organization, including assets designated by the Board for specific purposes. Restricted current funds account for resources that may be used for operations, but have been *restricted* by the stipulations of donors or grantors. Current liabilities are recorded in the appropriate fund depending on which funds will be used to pay them.

Plant funds are used to account for land, buildings, and equipment used by not-for-profit organizations in the conduct of their operations; liabilities relating to the acquisition or improvement of plant assets; and cash, investments, or receivables contributed specifically for acquiring, replacing, or improving plant. Loan funds account for loans made to students, employees, and other constituents; consequently, they appear most often in accounting for colleges and universities (see Chapter 16).

The principal amounts of gifts and bequests that must, under the terms of agreements with donors, be maintained intact in perpetuity, or until the occurrence of a specified event or for a specified time period, are accounted for as endowment funds. Other gifts may take the form of split interests in which donors retain some of the gift (either the income or principal) for a period of time, sometimes until their death. Annuity funds are used when the donor specifies an amount of income to be paid to the donor or to a designated third party for a specified period. A life income fund is used when the donor stipulates that all income will be paid to the donor or a designated third party, with the principal reverting to the NPO upon the donor's death, or some other specified time.

Agency or custodian funds are established to account for assets received by an organization to be held or disbursed only on instructions of the person or organization from whom they were received. Assets accounted for by a custodian fund are assets of the donors, not assets of the organization; income generated from the assets is added to the appropriate liability account. For these reasons, neither the receipt of assets to be held in custody nor the receipt of income from those assets should be reported by the not-for-profit organization as revenue or support. Assets of custodian funds and the offsetting liabilities should not be combined with assets and liabilities of other funds.

NPOs that use fund accounting recognize revenues and expenses for all categories of funds except custodian funds. This practice makes it relatively easy for

[27]AICPA, Audit and Accounting Guide, *Not-for-Profit Organizations*, par. 16.01–16.20.

NPOs to prepare the aggregated entitywide financial statements required by FASB *Statement No. 117*. Unrestricted current fund balance is reported as unrestricted net assets, restricted current fund balances as temporarily restricted net assets, and *pure* endowment fund balance as permanently restricted net assets. The remaining fund balances can contain elements of each category, and the terms of their existence must be examined for donor restrictions. All interfund receivables and payables must be eliminated in preparing entitywide statements. Fund accounting for not-for-profit entities is not illustrated in this chapter.

Financially Interrelated Entities

Not-for-profit organizations may *have control over* or be *financially interrelated with* another entity, such as a for-profit entity or another NPO. At issue is whether the financial statements of the two entities should be combined and what disclosures will provide the decision maker with the fairest picture of the overall organization. AICPA *SOP 94-3* provides guidance to NPOs on reporting affiliated entities and makes uniform the previous guidance in the three former industry audit guides (Colleges and Universities, VHWO, and Certain Not-for-Profit Organizations).[28] In general, the nature of the relationship between the entities should drive the decision to consolidate financial information of two entities and the extent of disclosures if statements are not consolidated.

Investments in For-Profit Entities

If an NPO has a controlling financial interest through direct or indirect ownership of a majority voting interest in a for-profit entity, it should consolidate that entity's financial information with its own, if conditions of *ARB No. 51* and *SFAS No. 94* are met, and the control is not expected to be temporary.[29] If an entity owns less than a controlling interest, but has significant influence over a for-profit entity, it should use the equity method to report investments in that entity if the guidelines in *APB Opinion No. 18* are met.[30] If the entity does not exert influence, then the investment should be reported at fair value according to *SFAS No. 124*. The FASB agenda item on "Consolidations and Other Related Matters" separated nonprofit organizations from its guidance on *control* for the for-profit sector. The FASB is expected to issue final statements on both issues in 2000.[31]

---

[28]American Institute of Certified Public Accountants, Statement of Position 94-3, *Reporting of Related Entities by Not-for-Profit Organizations* (New York, 1994), effective for fiscal years beginning after December 15, 1994, and one year later for smaller organizations.

[29]*Accounting Research Bulletin (ARB) No. 51*, "Consolidated Financial Statements" (New York: AICPA, 1959), and FASB, *SFAS No. 94*, "Consolidation of All Majority-Owned Subsidiaries" (Stamford, CT, 1987).

[30]*Accounting Principles Board (APB) Opinion No. 18*, "The Equity Method of Accounting for Investments" (New York, 1971).

[31]When a statement is issued, the publisher will distribute to faculty members who have adopted this text an Update Bulletin describing this issue and its effect on NPOs.

Financially Interrelated NPOs

In the case of financially interrelated not-for-profit organizations, an NPO should consolidate another NPO in which it has a controlling financial interest and an economic interest. Control exists if one organization can determine the direction of management policies through ownership, contract, or otherwise. Evidence of control might be majority membership on the Board, a charter granting the ability to dissolve the other organization, or contracts assigning oversight responsibility. An **economic interest** exists if the other entity holds or utilizes significant resources that must be used for the purposes of the NPO; or the reporting organization is responsible for the liabilities of the other entity. Examples of economic interests include:

1. Other entities solicit funds in the name of the reporting organization, and the solicited funds are intended by the contributor to be transferred to the reporting organization or used at its discretion.
2. A reporting organization transfers significant resources to another entity whose resources are held for the benefit of the reporting organization.
3. A reporting organization assigns certain significant functions to another entity.
4. A reporting organization provides funds for another entity or guarantees its debt.

If either control *or* an economic interest exists, but not both, related party disclosures required in *SFAS No. 57* should be made, as well as disclosures that identify the other organization and the nature of the relationship. Contributions made to an organization by its governing board members, officers, or employees need not be disclosed if the contributors do not receive a reciprocal economic benefit in consideration for the contribution. Reasonable amounts of salaries, wages, employee benefits, and reimbursement of expenses incurred in connection with a contributor's duties are not considered reciprocal benefits. If a national or international not-for-profit organization has local organizations that determine their own program activities, are financially independent, and control their own assets, consolidated financial statements are not required.

Funds Received as an Intermediary. Community, federated fund-raising, and institutionally related foundations (IRFs)[32] asked the FASB to clarify paragraph 4 of *SFAS No. 116*, which declared that the Statement did not apply to transfers of assets in which the reporting entity was acting as an agent, trustee, or intermediary, rather than as a donor or donee. Therefore, in June 1999, the FASB issued *SFAS*

[32]According to the Council for the Advancement of Secondary Education, there are almost 800 nongovernmental not-for-profit IRC Sec. 501(c)(3) foundations that are related to public institutions such as universities and handle their fund-raising, manage their endowment, and sometimes manage entrepreneurial activities.

No. 136 to clarify that an organization that receives financial assets from a donor, and agrees to transfer them (and/or the return on investment of those assets) to a specified "unaffiliated" beneficiary, should recognize the fair value of the gift as an asset and a liability. Under this rule, most federated fund-raising foundations, such as United Way organizations, are treated as agents when they receive such gifts.

However, if the donor grants the recipient organization **variance power** to redirect the assets to another beneficiary, or if the recipient organization and the specified beneficiary are "financially interrelated" organizations, then the gift is recognized as an asset and as contribution revenue. Captive fund-raisers, such as institutionally related foundations, then, are not considered agents. This statement also provides guidance on the definition of financially interrelated, revocable or reciprocal transfers, required disclosures, and when a beneficiary NPO should recognize its rights to the assets held by another NPO.[33]

Funds Held in Trust by Others. Beneficial interests in perpetual trusts held in trust by third parties under a legal trust instrument created by a donor to generate income for an NPO should not be included in the Balance Sheet of the not-for-profit organization if it has no control over the actions of the trustee, and if the organization is not the remainderman under the trust. The existence of the trust may be disclosed either parenthetically in the Balance Sheet or in Notes to the Financial Statements. Income from such trusts, if significant, should be reported separately in the Statement of Activity.

Illustrative Transactions—Voluntary Health and Welfare Organizations

Preceding sections of this chapter point out the fact that there are many differences among NPOs regarding the kinds of program services provided and in the sources of support and revenue utilized. Accordingly, the transactions and accounting entries presented in this section should be taken as illustrative of those considered appropriate for an organization that offers counseling, adoption, and foster home care, but not necessarily typical of other NPOs. The transactions illustrated in this section are assumed to pertain to the year 2002 of a hypothetical organization called the Community Family Service Agency, Inc. The trial balance of the Community Family Service Agency, Inc., as of December 31, 2001, is shown next.

---

[33]Financial Accounting Standards Board, *Statement of Financial Accounting Standards No. 136*, "Transfers of Assets to a Not-for-Profit Organization or Charitable Trust That Raises or Holds Contributions for Others" (Norwalk, CT, 1999). This statement incorporates and supersedes the 1996 FASB *Interpretation No. 42* with a similar title.

COMMUNITY FAMILY SERVICE AGENCY, INC.
TRIAL BALANCE
AS OF DECEMBER 31, 2001

	Debits	*Credits*
Cash	$ 58,711	
Short-term Investments—Unrestricted	22,000	
Short-term Investments—Temporarily Restricted—Plant	20,000	
Accounts Receivable	2,485	
Allowance for Uncollectible Accounts Receivable		$ 135
Contributions Receivable—Unrestricted	5,424	
Allowance for Uncollectible Contributions—Unrestricted		259
Contributions Receivable—Temporarily Restricted	10,470	
Allowance for Uncollectible Contributions—Temporarily Restricted for Plant		288
Supplies	23,095	
Prepaid Expense	3,917	
Land—Temporarily Restricted	16,900	
Building—Temporarily Restricted	58,000	
Allowance for Depreciation—Building		4,640
Equipment—Temporarily Restricted	42,824	
Allowance for Depreciation—Equipment		9,136
Long-term Investments—Unrestricted	17,000	
Long-term Investments—Permanently Restricted	230,000	
Accounts Payable and Accrued Expenses		25,911
Mortgage Payable		55,000
Unrestricted Net Assets—Undesignated—Available for Operations		67,302
Unrestricted Net Assets—Designated for Special Outreach Project		30,000
Temporarily Restricted Net Assets—Programs		3,900
Temporarily Restricted Net Assets—Plant		79,130
Temporarily Restricted Net Assets—Time		5,125
Permanently Restricted Net Assets		230,000
Totals	$510,826	$510,826

The trial balance as of December 31, 2001, indicates that the plant assets (land, building, and equipment) are temporarily restricted, either explicitly by the donor or by an organization policy implying that donated capital assets will be restricted for the term of their useful life. An amount equal to depreciation expense is reclassified from temporarily restricted to unrestricted net assets each year.

It is also apparent from the trial balance that the donors of temporarily restricted gifts for the programs, the plant, or future periods have also restricted the specific asset or investments. Donors are more likely to restrict these assets than cash. For simplicity, it is assumed that the investments have not changed in fair value from the prior year. Of course, when there is a change, *SFAS No. 124* requires an adjustment to the asset with the unrealized gain or loss reported in the Statement of Activities.

Contributions received in 2001, but specified by donors for unrestricted use in 2002, were transferred from the temporarily restricted to the unrestricted net asset class, as shown by Entry 1.

	Debits	Credits
1. Net Assets Released—Expiration of Time Restrictions—Temporarily Restricted	5,125	
Net Assets Released—Expiration of Time Restrictions—Unrestricted		5,125

Pledges receivable resulting from the 2002 fund drive were recorded. Pledges of $69,500 were unrestricted; in addition, pledges of $16,500 were donor-restricted for a special outreach project to be undertaken in 2002.

2a. Contributions Receivable—Unrestricted	69,500	
Contributions—Unrestricted		69,500
2b. Contributions Receivable—Temporarily Restricted	16,500	
Contributions—Temporarily Restricted—Program		16,500

Cash collected for unrestricted pledges totaled $68,500; collection of accounts receivable amounted to $2,200. Cash collected for restricted pledges made this year totaled $16,500. Cash in the amount of $9,200 was collected for pledges given during a building fund drive in the preceding year.

3a. Cash	70,700	
Contributions Receivable—Unrestricted		68,500
Accounts Receivable		2,200
3b. Cash	16,500	
Contributions Receivable—Temporarily Restricted		16,500
3c. Cash	9,200	
Contributions Receivable—Temporarily Restricted		9,200

The organization sponsored a bazaar to raise funds for the Special Outreach Project. Direct costs of $3,000, considered peripheral or incidental in nature, incurred for this event were paid in cash; the event yielded cash contributions of $10,000.

4a. Cash	10,000	
Contributions—Temporarily Restricted—Program		10,000
4b. Contributions—Temporarily Restricted—Program	3,000	
Cash		3,000

The FY2002 allocation from the United Way of Fairshare Bay amounted, in gross, to $317,000. Related fund-raising expenses to be borne by the Community Family Service Agency totaled $13,200; the net allocation was received in cash.

5. Cash	303,800	
Fund-raising Support Expenses	13,200	
Contributions—Unrestricted		317,000

Salaries expense for the year totaled $265,000; employee benefits expense totaled $51,000; and payroll taxes expense was $20,300. As of year-end, $15,100 of these expenses were unpaid; the balance had been paid in cash.

	Debits	*Credits*
6. Salaries Expense	265,000	
Employee Benefits Expense	51,000	
Payroll Taxes Expense	20,300	
Cash		321,200
Accounts Payable and Accrued Expenses		15,100

Expenses incurred for the Special Outreach Project were professional fees, $17,000; supplies, $4,500; and printing and publications, $1,600. All amounts were paid in cash.

	Debits	*Credits*
7. Professional Fees Expense	17,000	
Supplies Expense	4,500	
Printing and Publications Expense	1,600	
Cash		23,100

Expenses for program services and supporting services were professional fees, $43,000; supplies, $7,800; telephone, $9,800; postage and shipping, $7,800; occupancy, $23,900; rental and maintenance of equipment, $8,700; printing and publications, $7,900; travel, $22,000; conferences, conventions, and meetings, $13,800; specific assistance to individuals, $30,000; membership dues, $700; awards and grants to national headquarters, $5,500; costs of sales to the public, $900; and miscellaneous, $4,200. All expenses were credited to Accounts Payable and Accrued Expenses.

	Debits	*Credits*
8. Professional Fees Expense	43,000	
Supplies Expense	7,800	
Telephone Expense	9,800	
Postage and Shipping Expense	7,800	
Occupancy Expense	23,900	
Rental and Maintenance of Equipment Expense	8,700	
Printing and Publications Expense	7,900	
Travel Expense	22,000	
Conferences, Conventions, and Meetings	13,800	
Specific Assistance to Individuals	30,000	
Membership Dues	700	
Awards and Grants to National Headquarters	5,500	
Cost of Sales to the Public	900	
Miscellaneous Expense	4,200	
Accounts Payable and Accrued Expenses		186,000

Unrestricted support and revenue were received in cash during 2002 from the following sources: legacies and bequests, $15,000; membership dues from individuals, $1,000; program service fees, $55,000; net incidental revenue, $250; investment income, $2,900; and miscellaneous, $1,500.

	Debits	*Credits*
9. Cash	75,650	
Contributions—Unrestricted		15,000
Membership Dues		1,000

	Debits	Credits
Program Service Fees		55,000
Net Incidental Revenue		250
Investment Income—Unrestricted		2,900
Miscellaneous Revenue		1,500

Sales to the public amounted to $1,000 gross for the year. None of this amount was collected by year-end.

	Debits	Credits
10. Accounts Receivable	1,000	
Sales to the Public		1,000

Accounts payable and accrued expenses paid in cash during 2002 totaled $182,864.

	Debits	Credits
11. Accounts Payable and Accrued Expenses	182,864	
Cash		182,864

Contributions received in cash in 2002 but specified by donors for use in 2003 amounted to $20,000. Of this total, $10,000 was unrestricted as to purpose; $6,000 was for restricted program purposes; and $4,000 was for the purchase of equipment. The Agency chooses to report one Contributions Revenue account for temporarily restricted support and keep a subsidiary ledger for time, program, and plant restrictions.

	Debits	Credits
12. Cash	20,000	
Contributions—Temporarily Restricted—Time		10,000
Contributions—Temporarily Restricted—Program		6,000
Contributions—Temporarily Restricted—Plant		4,000

Interest of $4,540 and $6,500 on the principal of the mortgage were paid in cash. Short-term investments that were restricted for the plant were sold at par, $5,000; the proceeds were used to purchase equipment. The Agency has a policy that there is an implied restriction on plant assets and that this restriction is satisfied as the assets are used (measured by depreciation expense).

	Debits	Credits
13a. Miscellaneous Expense	4,540	
Mortgage Payable	6,500	
Cash		11,040
13b. Cash	5,000	
Short-Term Investments—Temporarily Restricted—Plant		5,000
13c. Equipment	5,000	
Cash		5,000

Interest received in cash on short-term investments restricted for the plant amounted to $1,390. Interest received in cash on investments of endowment funds amounted to $12,780. This income was not restricted by the donor.

	Debits	Credits
14a. Cash	1,390	
Investment Income—Temporarily Restricted—Plant		1,390
14b. Cash	12,780	
Investment Income—Unrestricted		12,780

The Community Family Service Agency paid its national affiliates in accord with the affiliation agreements; the amount of the payment in 2002 was $8,574.

	Debits	Credits
15. Payments to Affiliated Organizations	8,574	
Cash		8,574

End-of-the-Year Adjusting Journal Entries. A physical count of supplies, valued at the lower of cost or market, indicated the proper balance sheet value should be $19,100. Prepaid expenses at year-end were $3,600; the decrease is chargeable to postage and shipping expense.

	Debits	Credits
16a. Supplies Expense	3,995	
Supplies		3,995
16b. Postage and Shipping	317	
Prepaid Expense		317

An analysis of the investment accounts indicated that the fair value of the long-term investments was equal to the cost. The allowance for uncollectible accounts receivable appeared adequate and not excessive, but the allowance for uncollectible unrestricted pledges should be increased by $104.

	Debits	Credits
17. Uncollectible Contributions Expense	104	
Allowance for Uncollectible Contributions—Unrestricted		104

Depreciation on buildings and equipment belonging to the Community Family Service Agency is recorded in the amounts shown in entry 18. Since the depreciation reduced the carrying value of the capital assets, a reclassification is made for the net assets temporarily restricted for plant released from restriction.

	Debits	Credits
18a. Depreciation of Buildings and Equipment	4,185	
Allowance for Depreciation—Building		1,145
Allowance for Depreciation—Equipment		3,040
18b. Net Assets Released—Satisfaction of Plant Restrictions—Temporarily Restricted	4,185	
Net Assets Released—Satisfaction of Plant Restrictions—Unrestricted		4,185

End-of-the-Year Reclassification Journal Entries. Miscellaneous expenses for mortgage interest (in entry 13a) and depreciation expense (in entry 18a) were allocated to program services and supporting services. The allocation is assumed to be as shown in entry 19.

	Debits	Credits
19. Counseling Program Expenses	2,480	
Adoption Program Expenses	990	
Foster Home Care Program Expenses	2,510	
Special Outreach Project Program Expenses	2,050	
Management and General Support Expenses	530	
Fund-raising Support Expenses	165	
Miscellaneous Expense		4,540
Depreciation of Buildings and Equipment		4,185

The natural classification of expenses in entry 7 were allocated to the Special Outreach Project.

	Debits	Credits
20. Special Outreach Project Program Expenses	23,100	
Professional Fees Expense		17,000
Supplies Expense		4,500
Printing and Publications Expense		1,600

The remaining natural classification of expenses (in entries 6, 8, and 16b) were allocated to the various program and support categories as shown in entry 21, except Costs of Sales to the Public (entry 8), which will be netted with Sales to the Public.

	Debits	Credits
21. Counseling Program Expenses	183,033	
Adoption Program Expenses	68,570	
Foster Home Care Program Expenses	170,021	
Special Outreach Project Program Expenses	37,720	
Management and General Support Expenses	52,555	
Fund-raising Support Expenses	13,813	
Salaries Expense		265,000
Employee Benefits Expense		51,000
Payroll Taxes Expense		20,300
Professional Fees Expense		43,000
Supplies Expense		11,795
Telephone Expense		9,800
Postage and Shipping Expense		8,117
Occupancy Expense		23,900
Rental and Maintenance of Equipment		8,700
Printing and Publications Expense		7,900
Travel Expense		22,000
Conferences, Conventions, and Meetings		13,800
Specific Assistance to Individuals		30,000
Membership Dues		700
Awards and Grants to National Headquarters		5,500
Miscellaneous Expense		4,200

Unrestricted net assets that were designated by the Board for the Special Outreach Project were deemed no longer necessary; the Board authorized the return of the amount, $30,000, to Unrestricted Net Assets—Undesignated. $27,400 ($3,900 + $23,500) of temporarily restricted funds were spent on the programs this year.

	Debits	Credits
22. Unrestricted Net Assets—Designated for Special Outreach Project	30,000	
Unrestricted Net Assets—Undesignated—Available for Operations		30,000
Net Assets Released—Satisfaction of Program Restrictions—Temporarily Restricted	27,400	
Net Assets Released—Satisfaction of Program Restrictions—Unrestricted		27,400

End-of-the-Year Closing Journal Entries. The following closing journal entries are made: (*a*) reclassifications for net assets released are closed into the appropriate categories of net assets, (*b*) unrestricted support and revenue are closed to unrestricted net assets, (*c*) program and support expenses as well as payments to affiliated organizations are closed to unrestricted net assets, (*d*) temporarily restricted support for programs, plant, and time are closed to temporarily restricted net assets, and (*e*) permanently restricted support is closed to permanently restricted net assets, if any.

		Debits	*Credits*
23a.	Temporarily Restricted Net Assets—Time	5,125	
	Net Assets Released—Expiration of Time Restrictions—Unrestricted	5,125	
	Net Assets Released—Expiration of Time Restriction—Temporarily Restricted		5,125
	Unrestricted Net Assets—Undesignated—Available for Operations		5,125
	Temporarily Restricted Net Assets—Plant	4,185	
	Net Assets Released—Satisfaction of Plant Restrictions—Unrestricted	4,185	
	Net Assets Released—Satisfaction of Plant Restrictions—Temporarily Restricted		4,185
	Unrestricted Net Assets—Undesignated—Available for Operations		4,185
	Temporarily Restricted Net Assets—Program	27,400	
	Net Assets Released—Satisfaction of Program Restrictions—Unrestricted	27,400	
	Net Assets Released—Satisfaction of Program Restrictions—Temporarily Restricted		27,400
	Unrestricted Net Assets—Undesignated—Available for Operations		27,400
23b.	Contributions—Unrestricted	401,500	
	Sales to the Public	1,000	
	Membership Dues—Individuals	1,000	
	Program Service Fees	55,000	
	Net Incidental Revenue	250	
	Investment Income—Unrestricted	15,680	
	Miscellaneous Revenue	1,500	
	Unrestricted Net Assets—Undesignated—Available for Operations		475,930
23c.	Unrestricted Net Assets—Undesignated—Available for Operations	580,315	
	Counseling Program Expenses		185,513
	Adoption Program Expenses		69,560
	Foster Home Care Program Expenses		172,531
	Special Outreach Project Program Expenses		62,870
	Cost of Sales to Public		900
	Uncollectible Contributions Expense		104
	Management and General Support Expenses		53,085
	Fund-raising Support Expenses		27,178
	Payments to Affiliated Organizations		8,574
23d.	Contributions—Temporarily Restricted—Program	29,500	
	Contributions—Temporarily Restricted—Time	10,000	
	Contributions—Temporarily Restricted—Plant	4,000	
	Investment Income—Temporarily Restricted—Plant	1,390	

	Debits	*Credits*
Temporarily Restricted Net Assets—Program		23,500
Temporarily Restricted Net Assets—Plant		1,390
Temporarily Restricted Net Assets—Time		20,000

Note: There were no changes to Permanently Restricted Net Assets.

The effects of the preceding journal entries are reflected in Illustrations 14–2 through 14–5. Illustration 14–7 presents a Statement of Activities prepared according to Format B in *SFAS No. 117*. That is, there are columns displaying the

Illustration 14–7

COMMUNITY FAMILY SERVICE AGENCY, INC.
STATEMENT OF ACTIVITIES
FOR THE YEAR ENDED DECEMBER 31, 2002

	Unrestricted	*Temporarily Restricted*	*Permanently Restricted*	*Total 2002*
Revenues, gains, and other support:				
Contributions (Note A)	$388,196	$43,500		$431,696
Program service fees (Note B)	55,250			55,250
Membership dues	1,000			1,000
Sales to the public (net)	100			100
Investment income	15,680	1,390		17,070
Miscellaneous	1,500			1,500
Net assets released from restrictions:				
Satisfaction of program requirements	27,400	(27,400)		
Satisfaction of equipment acquisition restrictions	4,185	(4,185)		
Expiration of time restrictions	5,125	(5,125)		
Total revenues, gains, and other support	498,436	8,180		506,616
Expenses and losses:				
Program services:				
Counseling	185,513			185,513
Adoption	69,560			69,560
Foster home care	172,531			172,531
Special outreach project	62,870			62,870
Total program expenses	490,474			490,474
Support expenses:				
Management and general	53,085			53,085
Fund-raising	13,978			13,978
Total support expenses	67,063			67,063
Payments to affiliated organizations	8,574			8,574
Total expenses and losses	566,111			566,111
Change in net assets	(67,675)	8,180		(59,495)
Net assets, December 31, 2001	97,302	88,155	$230,000	415,457
Net assets, December 31, 2002	$ 29,627	$96,335	$230,000	$355,962

Note A: Reduced by Special Event fund-raising expense of $13,200 and uncollectible accounts expense of $104.

Note B: Includes $250 net incidental revenue.

changes in the three categories of net assets, which makes it clear that as donor restrictions expire, net assets are reclassified from the temporarily restricted column to the unrestricted net asset column. Illustration 14–3 follows Format A in *SFAS No. 117*, which is a single column and is most useful for multiyear comparisons. *SFAS No. 117* also displays Format C, which reports information in two statements: The first summarizes detailed changes in unrestricted net assets to focus attention on operating activities; and the second reconciles changes in all three categories of net assets. That format is not illustrated in this chapter.

NPOs other than VHWOs may have transactions not illustrated here. For example, deferred revenue arises from exchange transactions, such as subscriptions in a performing arts organization, and long-term debt from a construction project may exist in larger not-for-profit organizations.

Key Terms

Selected References

American Institute of Certified Public Accountants. Audit and Accounting Guide, *Not-for-Profit Organizations*. New York: AICPA, 1999.

———. 1999 Audit Risk Alert. *Not-for-Profit Organizations Industry Developments*. New York: AICPA, 1999.

———. *Statement of Position 98–2*. "Accounting for Costs of Activities of Not-for-Profit Organizations and State and Local Governmental Entities That Include Fund Raising." New York: AICPA, 1998.

Financial Accounting Standards Board. *Statement of Financial Accounting Standards No. 116*, "Accounting for Contributions Received and Made." Norwalk, CT: FASB, 1993.

———. *Statement of Financial Accounting Standards No. 117*, "Financial Statements of Not-for-Profit Organizations." Norwalk, CT: FASB, 1993.

———. *Statement of Financial Accounting Standards No. 136*, "Transfers of Assets to a Not-for-Profit Organization or Charitable Trust That Raises or Holds Contributions for Others." Norwalk, CT: FASB, 1999.

National Assembly of National Voluntary Health and Social Welfare Organizations, Inc., and National Health Council. *Standards of Accounting and Financial Reporting for Voluntary Health and Welfare Organizations ("The Black Book")*, 4th ed. Dubuque, Iowa: Kendall/Hunt Publishing Company, 1998.

Questions

14–1. Identify the key characteristics that distinguish an entity in the not-for-profit sector from one in the public sector or private sector.

14–2. A university has a collection of rare books that it has never recorded as assets. As an independent CPA, under what conditions would you require that the university capitalize these books? Would they then be depreciated?

14–3. Distinguish between *public support* and *revenue*.

14–4. Health and welfare organizations typically rely heavily on the efforts of volunteer workers. Under what conditions should donated services be recognized in the financial statements as contributions and as expenses, assuming the organization is subject to FASB jurisdiction?

14–5. Distinguish between *program services* and *supporting services* as the terms are used in financial reports recommended for use by not-for-profit organizations.

14–6. Why is a Statement of Functional Expenses considered an important financial statement for a voluntary health or welfare organization? How does a Statement of Functional Expenses relate to a Statement of Activities?

14–7. "The financial statements required for voluntary health and welfare organizations are (1) a Balance Sheet, (2) a Statement of Revenue and Expenses and Changes in Fund Balance, (3) a Statement of Functional Expenses, and (4) a Statement of Cash Flows." Do you agree or disagree? Explain.

14–8. "Responsibility for setting financial reporting standards for nongovernmental not-for-profit organizations is vested in the FASB." Do you agree or disagree? Explain.

14–9. "All not-for-profit organizations must use fund accounting to account for their activities." Do you agree or disagree? Why?

14–10. A privately endowed museum reports all investments at market, even if market is in excess of cost. As an independent CPA, would you be required to take exception to this practice?

14–11. How do you determine if one NPO "controls" another for purposes of combining the financial statements of the two organizations?

Cases

14–1. Institutionally Related Foundation. Compass State University Foundation (CSUF), a not-for-profit organization, was created in 1992 to support a public university in its fund-raising efforts and management of its endowment. The Foundation has a self-perpetuating Board of which one-third of its members are selected by the University's President. Under a joint operating agreement, the

University agrees to provide the Foundation with staff, computer and mail services, and office space until such time as the Foundation can be self-sufficient; and to pay the Foundation management fees of 2 percent of the endowment balance, 5 percent of cash gifts received, $.22 per dollar raised, and $1.84 per donor record per year.

From 1986 through 1992, the average donations to the University (both unrestricted and restricted) were $2.2 million and the University Endowment Fund grew very slowly from $5.2 million to $8.3 million. In 1992, the University transferred its entire $8.3 million endowment fund to the Foundation to manage. By 1999, average donations to the Foundation were $8 million and permanently restricted net assets, or endowments, had grown to $24 million. The Foundation's fund-raising and management and general expenses in 1999 totaled $1.5 million and $3 million was returned to the University in the form of scholarships to students and support to faculty.

Required

a. Identify the costs of creating and operating a separate organization, such as the CSUF (e.g., attorney fees to incorporate).

b. Who are the stakeholders in the Foundation and what are their accountability concerns?

c. Assume the role of the President of the University and discuss the advantages and disadvantages of transferring $8.3 million of the University's endowment funds to the Foundation.

d. Referring to item *c* above, assume the role of a donor who established a scholarship endowment with the University 15 years ago. What would you ask about the transfer?

e. Calculate the percentage of total expenses spent on the program and that spent on supporting the programs. Do these ratios seem reasonable?

f. Evaluate the performance of the Foundation based on the information provided. Is the University better off because of the Foundation? Why or why not?

g. From an accounting (not legal) point of view, is the Foundation a separate entity or a component unit of the related public institution?

This case is based on "Compass State University: Managerial Accounting Issues in a Nonprofit Entity," by S. Ravenscroft and S. Kattelus, *Issues in Accounting Education* 13, no. 3, 1998.

14–2. Terms of Gift. The Shelter Association of Gogebic County receives the majority of its funding from the local chapter of the United Way. That federated fund-raising organization has a policy that if a member agency reports unrestricted net assets in excess of one year's budgeted revenues and support, then the excess will be deducted from the next year's allocation. The Association's reporting year ends December 31, and unrestricted net assets are just about equal to last year's revenues and support.

On December 30, Bill Olson contacts the Shelter Association about making a large contribution. It is important to Bill that the gift be made in the current calendar year so that he can deduct the charitable contribution on his personal federal income tax return. However, Bill has heard that the Treasurer of the

Association and several Board members recently left due to allegations of financial mismanagement. He is considering restricting his gift for the direct purposes of acquiring food, clothing, and supplies for the homeless over the next several years so that none of the money could be used by the management for overhead expenses.

Required

Take the position of the certified public accountant for the Association.

a. Do you recommend that the Association persuade Mr. Olson to make the gift unrestricted or restricted? Give your reasons.

b. Mr. Olson asks you how he can be assured that the Association spends his contribution as he intends, assuming that he restricts the purpose of his gift. Explain to Mr. Olson what kind of public information is available to him. Do you consider that information adequate to assess whether the not-for-profit agency was efficient and effective in its use of public donations?

14–3. Internet Case. Look for the website of a nongovernmental not-for-profit entity on the Internet. For example, United Way's address is http://www.unitedway.org. ".Org" indicates that this organization is nonprofit rather than commercial (.com), governmental (.gov), or a university (.edu). Answer the following questions: Are audited financial statements provided on their website? What other kind of financial information do they make available? Take the position of a potential donor to this organization. Find some "benchmarks" (or industry averages) for this type of NPO and evaluate their performance compared to similar organizations. Performance measures may include financial ones, such as percentage of program or support expenses to total expenses, rate of return on investment, and payout rates. Output measures or service efforts and accomplishment (SEA) measures may include number of people served, improvement in test scores, or reduction in crimes. [Hint: Try the National Charities Information Bureau (http://www.give.org) or the Council of Better Business Bureau (CBBB) Philanthropic Advisory Service (PAS) (http://www.bbb.org) for comparisons of not-for-profit agencies.]

Exercises and Problems

14–1. Multiple Choice. Choose the best answer.

1. In a Statement of Activities of a voluntary health and welfare organization, depreciation expense should:
   a. Not be included.
   b. Be included as an element of support.
   c. Be included as an element of changes in fund balances.
   d. Be included as an element of expense.
2. Which of the following funds of a voluntary health and welfare organization does *not* have a counterpart *fund* in governmental accounting?
   a. Land, Building, and Equipment.
   b. Current Unrestricted.

c. Custodian.

d. Endowment.

3. Securities donated to voluntary health and welfare organizations should be recorded:
   a. At the donor's recorded amount.
   b. At fair market value at the date of the gift.
   c. At fair market value at the date of the gift, or the donor's recorded amount, whichever is lower.
   d. At fair market value at the date of the gift, or the donor's recorded amount, whichever is higher.
4. Which of the following is *not* a criterion that must be met under *SFAS No. 116* for contributed services to be recorded?
   a. They create or enhance nonfinancial assets.
   b. They are provided by individuals possessing required skills.
   c. They are provided by licensed professionals.
   d. They would typically need to be bought if not provided by donation.
5. Which of the following factors, if present, would indicate that a transaction is *not* a contribution under *SFAS No. 116*?
   a. The resource provider entered into the transaction voluntarily.
   b. The resource provider received value in exchange.
   c. The transfer of assets was unconditional.
   d. The organization has discretion in the use of the assets received.
6. Which of the following criteria would suggest that an NPO capitalize its works of art, historical treasures, or similar assets?
   a. They are held for public inspection, education, or research in furtherance of public service rather than financial gain.
   b. They are protected, kept unencumbered, cared for, and preserved.
   c. They are subject to be used to acquire other items for the collection.
   d. They are held primarily to be resold for financial gain.

Items 7 and 8 are based on the following information:

Expenditures incurred by a not-for-profit botanical society for the current year were as follows:

Printing of annual report	$10,000
Unsolicited merchandise sent to encourage contributions	$20,000

7. What amount should be classified as Fund-Raising Costs in the Society's Statement of Activity?
   a. $0.
   b. $10,000.
   c. $20,000.
   d. $30,000.
8. What amount should be classified as Supporting Services in the Society's Statement of Activity?

a. $0.
b. $10,000.
c. $20,000.
d. $30,000.

9. Under *SFAS No. 117*, which of the following statements is true?
   a. All nonprofit organizations must include a Statement of Functional Expenses.
   b. Donor-restricted contributions whose restrictions have been met in the reporting period may be reported as unrestricted support.
   c. Statements should focus on the individual unrestricted and restricted funds of the organization.
   d. *SFAS No. 117* contains requirements that are generally more stringent than those for for-profit organizations.
10. Funds held in trust by others under a legal trust instrument created by a donor to generate income for a not-for-profit organization, and over which the not-for-profit organization has no control, should be:
   a. Included with the amounts reported in the Balance Sheet of the not-for-profit organization.
   b. Excluded from the amounts reported in the Balance Sheet of the not-for-profit organization.
   c. Disclosed either parenthetically in the permanently restricted net assets section of the Balance Sheet or in the Notes to the Financial Statements.
   d. Both *b* and *c* are correct.

(Items 1–3, 7–8, and 10, AICPA, adapted)

14–2. Accrual Accounting and Capital Assets. The characteristics of voluntary health and welfare organizations differ in certain respects from the characteristics of state or local governmental units. As an example, voluntary health and welfare organizations derive their revenues primarily from voluntary contributions from the general public or governmental grants, while governmental units derive their revenues from taxes and services provided to their jurisdictions.

Required

a. Distinguish between accrual accounting as it should be applied to the recognition of revenues of a voluntary health and welfare organization and accrual accounting as it is applied to the recognition of governmental fund revenues.
b. Discuss how methods used to account for capital assets differ between voluntary health and welfare organizations and governmental units.

(AICPA, adapted)

14–3. Joint Activities with a Fund-Raising Appeal. Consider the following scenarios relating to activities that include a fund-raising appeal:

1. The Green Group's mission is to protect the environment by increasing the portion of waste recycled by the public. The group conducts a door-to-door canvass of communities chosen because they recycle a low portion of their waste. The canvassers share their knowledge about the environmental problems

caused by not recycling with households, asking them to change their recycling habits. The canvassers also ask for charitable contributions to continue this work, although these canvassers have not participated in fund-raising activities before.

2. Central University's mission is to educate students in various academic pursuits. The political science department holds a special lecture series in which prominent world leaders speak about current events. Admission is priced at $250, which is above the $50 fair value of other lectures on campus, resulting in a $200 contribution. Invitations are sent to prior attendees and to donors who have contributed significant amounts in the past.
3. The mission of Kid's Camp is to provide summer camps for economically disadvantaged youths. It conducts a door-to-door solicitation campaign for its camp programs by sending volunteers to homes in middle-class neighborhoods. The volunteers explain the camp's programs and distribute leaflets explaining the mission of the organization. Solicitors say, "Although your own children most likely are not eligible to attend this camp, we ask for your financial support so that children less fortunate can have this summer camp experience."

Required

Determine for each scenario if the criteria of purpose, audience, and content described in AICPA *SOP 98-2* are met so that the joint costs can be allocated between programs and support expenses. Explain.

14–4. Statement of Functional Expenses. The Rural Human Services Association had the following expenses for the year ended September 30, 2002.

Salaries and fringe benefits	$ 850,000
Professional fees	50,000
Supplies	38,000
Telephone	40,000
Postage and shipping	75,000
Occupancy costs	100,000
Travel and meetings	80,000
Printing and publications	100,000
Depreciation of buildings and equipment	17,000
Total expenses	$1,350,000

Required

a. The programs offered by this Association during that year were Counseling, Outreach, Meals, and Public Education. Supporting services were Management and General, and Fund-Raising. The governing board wants to know the cost of each program service and each supporting service for the year. After discussion with persons engaged in offering each service, and perusal of records of the Association, you determine that the following distribution would be reasonably realistic. Prepare a statement of functional expenses for the year.

	Program Services				Supporting Services	
	Coun-seling	*Out reach*	*Meals*	*Public Education*	*Management and General*	*Fund-Raising*
Salaries and fringes	20%	16%	3%	19%	22%	20%
Professional fees	10	10	20	20	10	30
Supplies	10	15	5	25	25	20
Telephone	10	20	5	20	15	30
Postage and shipping	5	23	15	15	7	35
Occupancy costs	20	10	10	20	20	20
Travel and meetings	25	10	15	15	25	10
Printing and publications	15	5	2	33	20	25
Depreciation	33	15	5	15	20	12

b. If the Rural Human Services Association approached you as a potential contributor, and presented the statement prepared as the solution to part *a* of this problem as evidence of its merit for your contribution, what would be your reaction and why?

14–5. Prepare Financial Statements. Helping Hand Agency of America, Inc., was incorporated as a nongovernmental not-for-profit voluntary health and welfare organization on July 1, 2001. The adjusted trial balance as of June 30, 2002, is provided below:

	Debits	*Credits*
Cash	$ 24,000	
Pledges Receivable—Unrestricted	54,000	
Estimated Uncollectible Pledges		$ 9,000
Inventory	1,000	
Pledges Receivable—Temporarily Restricted	51,000	
Investments—Temporarily Restricted	61,100	
Furniture and Equipment—Temporarily Restricted	3,000	
Accumulated Depreciation		300
Accounts Payable		1,200
Unrestricted Net Assets		–0–
Temporarily Restricted Net Assets		–0–
Permanently Restricted Net Assets		–0–
Contributions—Unrestricted		188,100
Contributions—Temporarily Restricted		121,700
Uncollectible Contributions Expense—Temporarily Restricted	9,000	
Investment Income—Temporarily Restricted		2,100
Salaries Expense	80,000	
Fringe Benefits Expense	5,000	
Occupancy Expense	4,800	
Supplies Expense	8,000	
Printing and Publishing Expense	15,000	
Telephone and Utility Expense	5,200	
Postage and Shipping Expense	1,000	
Depreciation Expense	300	
Totals	$322,400	$322,400

1. Salaries and fringe benefits were allocated to program services and supporting services in the following percentages: public health education, 20 percent; professional education and training, 30 percent; community services, 10 percent; management and general, 15 percent; and fund-raising, 25 percent. All other expenses were allocated in the following percentages: public health education, 15 percent; professional education and training, 20 percent; community services, 10 percent; management and general, 35 percent; and fund-raising, 20 percent.
2. Helping Hand Agency received cash during the year from contributors: $126,000 that was unrestricted and $59,000 that was restricted for investment in the plant. $2,100 of income was earned and received on long-term investments. The Agency spent cash on salaries, $70,000; purchase of goods, $29,000; purchase of furniture and equipment, $3,000; and purchase of investments, $59,000.

Required

Prepare a Statement of Financial Position, Statement of Activities, Statement of Cash Flows, and a Statement of Functional Expenses for Helping Hand Agency of America, Inc., as of and for the year ended June 30, 2002. Follow the format in Illustrations 14–2 through 14–5.

14–6. Membership Dues Revenue. The Professional Persons Association of Middleton is a not-for-profit organization subject to the provisions of the AICPA Audit and Accounting Guide, *Not-for-Profit Organizations*. The dues for members are $50 per year; the fiscal year ends on August 31. Prior to September 1, 2001, 410 members had paid their dues for the year ended August 31, 2002. Prior to September 1, 2002, 457 members had paid their dues for the year ended August 31, 2003; one of these died suddenly on August 30, 2002, and the governing Board decided to return his check to his widow. During the fiscal year ended on August 31, 2002, 36 other members died; 15 members were dropped for nonpayment of dues; and one member was expelled—no dues refunds were made to the estates of the 36 decedents; a $25 refund was made to the person expelled. Offsetting these membership decreases, 123 new members joined in fiscal 2002; membership as of September 1, 2001, had been 2,980 persons. Members admitted during a year are charged dues for the full year.

The Association has reported membership dues revenue on the cash basis in prior years. You bring to the attention of the governing Board the requirement that financial statements should be on the accrual basis, unless cash basis statements are not materially different. Since you are so knowledgeable, the Board asks you to compute membership dues revenue for fiscal 2002 on both the cash basis and the accrual basis and to report to them the amount on each basis *and* your conclusion as to whether the difference between the two is material.

(AICPA, adapted)

14–7. Statement of Activity. A group of civic-minded merchants in Albury City organized the "Committee of 100" for the purpose of establishing the Community Sports Club, a not-for-profit sports organization for local youth. Each of the Committee's 100 members contributed $1,000 toward the Club's capital and in turn received a participation certificate. In addition, each participant agreed to pay dues of $200 a year for the Club's operations. All dues have been collected in full by the end of each fiscal year ending March 31. Members who have discontinued their participation have been replaced by an equal number of new members through transfer of the participation certificates from the former members to the new ones. Following is the Club's trial balance at April 1, 2001:

	Debits	*Credits*
Cash	$ 9,000	
Investments (at market equal to cost)	58,000	
Inventories	5,000	
Land	10,000	
Building	164,000	
Accumulated Depreciation—Building		$130,000
Furniture and Equipment	54,000	
Accumulated Depreciation—Furniture and Equipment		46,000
Accounts Payable		12,000
Participation Certificates (100 at $1,000 each)		100,000
Cumulative Excess of Revenue over Expenses		12,000
	$300,000	$300,000

Transactions for the year ended March 31, 2002, were as follows:

1. Collections from participants for dues	$20,000
2. Snack bar and soda fountain sales	28,000
3. Interest and dividends received	6,000
4. Additions to voucher register:	
House expenses	17,000
Snack bar and soda fountain	26,000
General and administrative	11,000
5. Vouchers paid	55,000
6. Assessments for capital improvements not yet incurred (assessed on March 20, 2002, none collected by March 31, 2002; deemed 100% collectible during year ending March 31, 2003)	10,000
7. Unrestricted bequest received	5,000

Adjustment data:

1. Investments are valued at market, which amounted to $65,000 at March 31, 2002. There were no investment transactions during the year.
2. Depreciation for the year:

Building	$ 4,000
Furniture and equipment	8,000

3. Allocation of depreciation:

House expenses	9,000
Snack bar and soda fountain	2,000
General and administrative	1,000

4. Actual physical inventory at March 31, 2002, was $1,000, and pertains to the snack bar and soda fountain.

Required

On a functional basis:

a. Record the transactions and adjustments in journal entry form for the year ended March 31, 2002. Omit explanations.

b. Prepare the activity statement illustrated in *SFAS No. 117* for the year ended March 31, 2002.

(AICPA, adapted)

14–8. **Prepare Financial Statements.** The University City Art League, Inc., is a nongovernmental not-for-profit organization dedicated to promotion of the arts within the community. The Art League conducts two programs: (1) exhibition and sales of members' art (referred to as "Exhibition") and (2) community art education. Activities of the Art League are administered by a full-time administrator, assisted by a secretary-bookkeeper and several part-time volunteer receptionists. The volunteer receptionists greet visitors, monitor the security of the exhibit hall, and conduct sales of art to the public. Art on exhibit is considered the property of the member artists, not the Art League.

The post-closing trial balance for the University City Art League as of June 30, 2001, the end of its fiscal year, is shown below.

UNIVERSITY CITY ART LEAGUE, INC.
POST-CLOSING TRIAL BALANCE
AS OF JUNE 30, 2001

Account Title	*Debits*	*Credits*
Cash	$ 4,015	
Investments—unrestricted	9,462	
Grants receivable	4,600	
Prepaid expenses	1,060	
Equipment	9,345	
Accumulated depreciation—equipment		$ 2,426
Investments—temporarily restricted for plant	12,649	
Investments—permanently restricted for endowment	4,767	
Accounts payable		1,893
Accrued expenses		756
Long-term notes payable		2,000
Net assets—unrestricted		13,524
Net assets—temporarily restricted		20,532
Net assets—permanently restricted		4,767
Totals	$45,898	$45,898

Following is information summarizing the transactions of the University City Art League, Inc., for the year ended June 30, 2002.

1. During the year unrestricted support was received in cash from the following sources: grants, $11,600, of which $4,600 had been reported as receivable on June 30, 2001; annual giving from fund drives and other unrestricted gifts, $13,861; membership dues, $16,285; sales of members' art, $12,010, of which 20 percent, or $2,402, represents commissions earned by the Art League; tuition and fees for educational courses and workshops, $6,974; and interest on unrestricted investments, $686. Grants receivable as of June 30, 2002, totaled $5,020, of which $3,120 was recognized as current-year revenue and $1,900 was reported as temporarily restricted.
2. Investment earnings were received in cash in the amounts of $925 on plant investments and $344 on endowment investments. (These investment earnings are temporarily restricted as to use.)
3. Expenses incurred for unrestricted activities during the year were as follows: salaries and fringe benefits, $36,300; occupancy, $9,600; utilities, $2,680; postage and supplies, $2,313; and miscellaneous, $1,037. Included in miscellaneous was interest expense of $160, which was paid in cash during the year. As of June 30, 2002, the balances of the following balance sheet accounts were: Prepaid Expenses, $970; Accounts Payable, $2,019; and Accrued Expenses, $727.
4. During the year $2,900 of matured CDs were sold from plant investments to purchase a new computer. The computer was purchased at a cost of $2,835.
5. In accordance with the terms of the Art League endowment, endowment earnings in the amount of $825 were used to provide free art instruction for children with disabilities. This amount was allocated $500 to Community Art Education and $325 to General and Administrative Expenses.
6. Expenses for the year were allocated 20 percent to the Exhibition Program, 25 percent to the Community Art Education Program, 30 percent to General and Administrative Expenses, and 25 percent to Fund-Raising. (Round all amounts to the nearest whole dollar.)
7. Depreciation on equipment in the amount of $1,642 was recorded on the plant assets. This amount was allocated to programs, General and Administrative Expenses, and Fund-Raising in the same proportions as in item 6 above. (Round all amounts to the nearest whole dollar.)
8. $9,608, representing the proceeds of art sales, net of commissions, charged by the Art League, was paid to member artists during the year.
9. In order to prepare financial statements as of year-end, all temporary accounts were closed.

Required

a. Prepare in general journal form all required journal entries to record the transactions summarized above for the year ending June 30, 2002.

b. On the advice of their independent auditor, the Art League does not include support and expenses related to the value of services donated by their volunteer receptionists. Discuss the criteria for recognition of donated services and comment on the auditor's likely rationale for not recognizing them in this specific case.

c. Prepare a Statement of Financial Position in the FASB *Statement No. 117* format shown in Illustration 14–2.

d. Prepare a Statement of Activities in the FASB *Statement No. 117* format shown in Illustration 14–3.

e. Prepare a Statement of Cash Flows in the FASB *Statement No. 117* format shown in Illustration 14–4.

CHAPTER 15

Not-for-Profit Organizations—Regulatory and Taxation Issues

Learning Objectives

After studying this chapter, you should be able to:

- Identify oversight bodies and the source of their authority over not-for-profit organizations (NPOs).
- Describe how and why states regulate NPOs and describe the following:
  - Nonprofit incorporation laws.
  - Registration, licenses, and tax exemption.
  - Lobbying and political influence.
- Identify how the federal government regulates NPOs and describe the following:
  - Tax-exempt status—public charities and private foundations.
  - Unrelated business income tax.
  - Restricting political activity.
  - Intermediate sanctions.
  - Reorganization and dissolution.
- Describe governance issues of NPO Boards including incorporating documents and Board membership.
- Identify how benchmarks and performance measures can be used to evaluate NPOs.

Oversight Authority

The 1990s brought a dramatic increase in the number of nongovernmental not-for-profit organizations (NPOs) in the United States. Along with this growth came very public revelations of financial impropriety and fraud in some of those entities. Some managers were fined and sent to jail for personally profiting from the charities they operated; politicians faced allegations that they used charitable foundations to skirt political contribution laws; and NPOs were converted to for-profit entities before distributing the assets to other charities.[1] Because of well-publicized instances of impropriety and fraud, there has been a growing demand for better accountability by NPOs. Demands for accountability by NPOs may increase further as the not-for-profit sector grows in number and dollars to meet the demand brought about by *devolution*—the shifting of responsibility for social programs from the federal government to local levels.[2]

NPOs are accountable to the state government that grants them their legal existence, the federal government for granting them tax-exempt status, their own governing board, individual donors and grantors, and the public at large. Accountants and auditors play a critical role in assuring these stakeholders that NPOs have complied with applicable laws and regulations, and, in the process, have efficiently and effectively used the assets with which they were entrusted. The purpose of this chapter is to provide an overview of regulations over NPOs by oversight bodies, such as state governments, the federal government, and governing boards. Many of these topics have complex legal aspects that are beyond the scope of this book. For the interested reader, additional references are provided at the end of the chapter.

State Regulation

Oversight responsibility derives from a state's power to give legal life to a nonprofit organization. In the absence of stockholders, the state monitors nonprofit managers whom the public entrusts with funds and grants economic privileges, such as exemption from taxes. The state has responsibility to represent public beneficiaries of charities and to detect cases when managers or directors have mismanaged, diverted, or defrauded the charity and the public.

Legislation regulating NPOs, of course, varies greatly across states; and few states are alike. However, there are some common methods used by states, and sometimes adopted by local governments, to ensure that the public good is protected as NPOs solicit charitable contributions and conduct business. The audited

[1]Steve Stecklow, "New Era Foundation Founder Bennett Is Scheduled for Sentencing This Week," *The Wall Street Journal*, September 15, 1997, p. B2; Leslie Lenkowsky, "Newt Violation Hard to Find," *The Wall Street Journal*, January 3, 1997; "California Blue Cross to Make Payback for Conversion," *National Underwriter* 97, September 6, 1993, pp. 37–41.

[2]Carol J. DeVita, "Viewing Nonprofits across the States," in *Charting Civil Society* (Washington, DC: The Urban Institute, August 1997).

annual financial statements are not always sufficient to satisfy the oversight body that the NPO complied with laws. The accountant often serves the NPO client in preparing specialized reports required by the oversight body.

Nonprofit Incorporation Laws

A group of individuals who share a philanthropic or other vision may operate as an unincorporated association if they are small or expect their endeavor to have a limited life; however, organizers are treated as partners and share liability for any debts incurred by the association. If the organization plans to grow into a long-lived operation, organizers may choose to file articles of incorporation with a state under the nonprofit corporation statutes or charitable trust laws to create a legal entity and limit the liability of the incorporators and directors. These laws differ across the 50 states, but states generally have built into the nonprofit corporation laws the requirement that organizers: (1) choose a name that is not misleading or in use by another corporation, (2) designate a resident agent and address, (3) state a clear purpose for the entity, (4) appoint a Board of Directors, (5) write by-laws that delineate Board responsibilities and operating structure, (6) call at least one Board meeting a year, and (7) require management to report on financial condition and operations at least once a year. Nonprofit incorporation statutes also state the extent to which directors are individually liable for the misapplication of assets through neglect or failure to exercise reasonable care and prudence in administration of the affairs of the corporation. Upon conferring the NPO legal status separate from the incorporators, the state bears oversight responsibility over the NPO.

Registration, Licenses, and Tax Exemption

State regulation of nonprofit corporations has increased since the State of New York established an Office of Charitable Registration in 1955 to administer fund-raising regulations for not-for-profit organizations.[3] Some states require NPOs to register with a specified department of the state (e.g., Attorney General, Secretary of State, Consumer, Regulatory Affairs, or Commerce) or apply for a license in order to solicit funds, hold property, do business in the state, or lobby. For the most part, state and local governments require fees to accompany registration and licenses in order to defray the cost of regulation and monitoring. Failure to file required reports may result in automatic dissolution of the NPO.

License to Solicit Contributions. Some states protect citizens from competitive fund-raising requests by requiring the NPO to obtain a license to solicit charitable contributions. **Charitable solicitation** is the direct or indirect request for money, credit, property, financial assistance, or other things of value on the representation that these assets will be used for a charitable purpose. The Model Act Concerning the Solicitation of Funds for Charitable Purposes was promulgated in 1986 by the National Association of Attorneys General, the National Association of State Charity Officials, and a private-sector advisory group to guide states in designing

[3]Seth Perlman and Betsy Hills Bush, *Fund-Raising Regulation: A State-by-State Handbook of Registration Forms, Requirements, and Procedures, 2000 Supplement* (New York: John Wiley & Sons, 1999).

this type of legislation. Although regulation has been challenged by some charities that argue soliciting is protected free speech, most legislation stands as an efficient way to protect the public from fraud.

States granting licenses usually impose annual compliance reporting on NPOs. A few states require audited annual financial reports to be filed when the level of public support exceeds a certain threshold, such as $250,000 (i.e., Michigan). Some states require a license when an NPO compensates someone for fund-raising, such as a professional fund-raiser or solicitor, and a fee may be required of the organization for the right for each fund-raiser to solicit. Many states also require specific disclosures be put on all written materials mailed to potential donors to indicate that financial information about the organization may be on file with the state. In addition to the state, local governments may regulate charitable solicitation, although sometimes more for its fee revenue potential than for regulatory purposes.

Other Licenses. States or local governments may require a not-for-profit organization to get a license or permit for bingo, raffles, and charity games with maximum prizes. Often licenses or permits are granted for one-day beer, wine, and liquor sales for events.

Taxes. NPOs are often exempted from the taxes levied by state and local governments, such as sales, real or personal property, transfer, employment, or excise taxes. Of course, this privilege varies across the country and, in the case of property taxes, is being challenged by interest groups suspicious of some NPOs' charitable mission and defended by nonprofit coalitions.[4] To be relieved from the tax, the NPO may have to file for specific tax exemption and document that the property is *in use* for charitable purposes. Fund-raising events often give rise to sales tax reporting, both collection of tax from customers and exemption from sales tax paid on the purchase of goods. Often overlooked by the NPO are the excise taxes on telephone and utility bills for which they may not be liable and could recover by filing for a refund.

Lobbying and Political Influence

For the most part, a nonprofit organization cannot be organized primarily to attempt to influence legislation or participate in any political campaigns. Two primary ways that states regulate lobbying and political activity for all organizations are through lobbying acts and campaign finance acts. These laws require organizations to register with the state and then account for lobbying or campaign financing activities. The NPO must determine if it, or someone it hires, is a lobbyist or lobbyist agent and, consequently, subject to these regulations. **Lobbying** is communicating directly with a public official in either the executive or legislative branch of the state government for the purpose of influencing legislation. **Influencing** means to promote, support, affect, modify, oppose, or delay by any means. In one state, the amount of money spent on lobbying each year determines whether the

[4]Citizen Action for Colorado Nonprofits, *Position Paper on Proposed Taxation of Nonprofits* (Denver, CO: May 2, 1996).

NPO must register with a specified state agency. For example, if more than $1,725 is spent on lobbying or more than $425 contributed to any single public official in any 12-month period, the NPO must register, file annual reports detailing its lobbying activity, and specify the amounts contributed to public officials. In addition to registering and reporting, certain prohibitions may exist. For example, compensation of lobbyists cannot be contingent upon certain legal outcomes; no gifts or honorariums can be paid to public officials; and no contributions can be made to campaigns to support (or defeat) ballot questions.

The impact of excessive political activity on NPOs can be significant due to the harsh sanctions for violating these laws, as well as negative publicity that may harm future fund-raising efforts. The ultimate penalty is revocation of exemption from taxes, but more often fines are imposed for engaging in prohibited behavior.

Illustration 15–1 presents a chart that summarizes typical regulation of nongovernmental not-for-profit organizations at the state as well as the federal level.

Federal Regulation

The federal government has encouraged nonprofit associations and charitable contributions since the first revenue act in 1894 and income tax law in 1913 because they serve the common good. The public, then, expects the federal government to monitor those organizations receiving tax benefits to ensure that these privileges are not abused. Of course, NPOs must follow general laws that govern businesses (such as fair labor standards, older workers' benefits protection, equal employment opportunities acts, disabilities acts, civil rights laws, drug-free workplace laws, immigration laws, antidiscrimination and harassment laws, and veterans and whistleblowers' protection), unless they are specifically exempted. This section describes federal laws that are unique to NPOs.

Tax-Exempt Status

Even though a state may have conferred nonprofit corporation status on an organization, that NPO must still apply to the Internal Revenue Service (IRS) for exemption from federal income tax.[5] As shown in Illustration 14–1, not all not-for-profit organizations are tax-exempt. A common reason why an NPO is not exempt from income taxes is that its mission is primarily to influence legislation. The stated purpose of the NPO and the services it will perform determine under which section of the Internal Revenue Code (IRC) of 1986 the NPO requests exemption. The most common classification under IRC Section 501 is Sec. 501(c)(3), which is an organization operated for philanthropic, or charitable, purposes. The **organizational test** for tax-exempt status is that the articles of incorporation must limit the organization's purposes to those described in the categories in IRC Sec. 501 and must not empower it to engage in activities that are not in furtherance of those

[5]Application for income tax exemption is made on Form 1023 for public charities and Form 1024 for all other organizations. NPOs may also qualify for exemption from certain federal excise taxes (e.g., communications, manufacturers, diesel and motor fuels taxes).

Illustration 15–1 Regulations over Not-for-Profit Organizations (varies by state)

State and/or Local Government Regulations

Application to operate under an assumed name
Application to incorporate as a nonprofit corporation or a charitable trust
Annual compliance reporting
Special licenses with particular state departments to operate a health care facility (public health), housing corporation (housing authority), residential care facility (social service), or school (education), or to handle food
Application for exemption from income, franchise, sales, use, real and personal property taxes
Employer registration including payroll tax returns, withholding of state taxes, and unemployment
License to solicit charitable contributions
Registration of political lobbyists, lobbying agents, or lobbying activities
License for one-day beer, wine, and liquor sales
License to conduct charitable games (e.g., bingo, raffles, millionaires parties)
Policies on conflict of interest and self-dealing with directors
License to collect sales and use taxes as a vendor
Freedom of Information Act (FOIA) (if a substantial amount of funds are public)
Open Meetings Act (if governmental in nature)
Notice of plans to merge with another agency
Notice of plans to dissolve, including tax clearance

Federal Government Regulations	*Federal Forms*
Application for a taxpayer/employer identification number	SS-4
Application for tax-exempt status	1023 or 1024
Application for exemption from certain excise taxes	637
Annual reporting	990 or 990-PF
Excise taxes on private foundations	4720
Reporting on unrelated business income tax	990-T
Reporting on lobbying and political contributions	990, 4720, 1120-POL
Election to make expenditures to influence legislation	5786
Payroll employment taxes	W-2, W-4, W-9, 940, 941
Statements to independent contractors earning more than $600 per year	1099
Appraisals for noncash contributions over $5,000 (the donor has primary responsibility for this regulation)	8283, 8282
Substantiation of gifts of cash over $250	
Application for bulk postal permit	Local post office
Financial reporting, audit, cost, and administrative requirements under OMB Circulars	

purposes. Nonprofit hospitals have been criticized for not providing an adequate amount of free services as a benefit to society, as stated in their application for tax-exempt status and required by tax law. Illustration 15–2 shows some of the more than twenty classifications of statutory exemptions under which tax-exempt organizations fall.

An individual can receive a charitable contribution deduction by making a donation to a Sec. 501(c)(3) organization and other exempt organizations but only if the gift is used for charitable purposes. Many categories of tax-exempt organizations, such as business leagues, social clubs, and cooperatives, cannot offer donors the advantage of a charitable deduction from income taxes because they operate

Illustration 15–2 Tax-Exempt Status According to the Internal Revenue Code (selected)

Section of 1986 Internal Revenue Code	*Description of Organization and Its Activities*
501(c)(1)	Federal and related agencies, such as Federal Deposit Insurance Corporation
501(c)(3)	Religious, charitable, scientific, literary, educational, testing for public safety, to foster national or international amateur sports competition, or prevention of cruelty to children or animals organizations
501(c)(4)	Civic leagues, social welfare organizations, and employee unions: to promote community welfare
501(c)(5)	Labor unions, agricultural, and horticultural organizations: to educate to improve conditions of work
501(c)(6)	Business leagues, chambers of commerce, real estate boards: to improve business conditions
501(c)(7)	Social and recreational clubs: for pleasure and social activities
501(c)(8)	Fraternal beneficiary society and associations: lodges providing for payment of insurance benefits to members
501(c)(9)	Voluntary employees' beneficiary associations: to provide insurance benefits to members
501(c)(13)	Cemetery companies: burial activities
501(c)(14)	State-chartered credit unions, mutual reserve funds: loans to members
501(c)(20)	Group legal service plans: provided by a corporation for its members
501(d)	Religious and apostolic associations: religious communities
501(e)	Cooperative hospital service organizations: to perform cooperative services for hospitals
501(f)	Cooperative service organizations: operating educational organizations
501(k)	Child care organizations
521(a)	Farmers' cooperative associations: marketing and purchasing for agricultural producers
529	Qualified state tuition programs

primarily for the benefit of members and not the public at large. Another advantage of tax exemption under Sec. 501(c)(3) is the opportunity to apply for grants from foundations and government agencies, which often limit funding to public charities. An organization that is not a Sec. 501(c)(3) organization must disclose to donors that contributions are *not* tax-deductible. Independent charitable organizations may voluntarily join together as a **federated fund-raising organization** to raise and distribute money among themselves. Examples of such federations are the United Way and community chests.

Annual Compliance Reporting. Form 990 is the primary tool the federal government uses to collect information about the NPO and its activities. The IRS expands the form as Congress requires more information to be furnished by tax-exempt organizations. The form must be made available to the public for three years.[6] Failure to file this form brings significant penalties, unless an extension is granted. Annual reporting requirements do not apply to federal agencies, churches and their affiliates, and NPOs with gross receipts less than $25,000.

Form 990 provides useful information for donors, grantors, regulators, and researchers. Among the information included on Form 990 is identification of the four largest program services; a list of directors and officers and their compensation; a report of expenses segregated into the functional categories of unrelated business income, program, and support; and a list of major contributors, although the latter item need not necessarily be public information. Illustration 15–3 delineates the kinds of information that are required on the annual reporting Form 990.

Public Charities versus Private Foundations. Tax-exempt status brings with it potential liability for penalties in the form of excise taxes, such as those for certain activities of private foundations, unrelated business income, some activity of feeder organizations, and excess lobbying. IRC Sec. 501(c)(3) encompasses private foundations and public charities. A **private foundation** is one that receives its support from a small number of individuals or corporations and investment income, rather than from the public at large; and it exists to make grants to public charities. These tax-exempt organizations file an annual Form 990-PF and are subject to several excise taxes for (1) failure to take certain actions (such as distribute a minimum amount to public charities); (2) prohibited behavior (such as speculative investing, self-dealing transactions with disqualified persons, and excess business holdings); and (3) net investment income, which is used to support the costs of auditing tax-exempt organizations. Another disadvantage of private foundation status is that donors are limited in the amount of their charitable deductions. A tax-exempt organization is presumed to be a private foundation unless it meets a specific exclusion allowing it to be considered a public charity.[7]

Public charities receive preferential tax treatment over private foundations because they are funded, operated, and monitored by the public at large, rather than by a limited number of donors. An IRC Sec. 501(c)(3) organization is considered to be a public charity if it notifies the IRS that it meets one of the exclusions to the private foundation definition: For example, it is broadly supported by the public, government, or other public charities; it operates to support another public charity; or it tests products for public safety.

Two parts of the *broad public support test* must be satisfied. The **external support test** is met if at least one-third of the organization's total revenue comes from the

[6]Public disclosure regulations issued in June 1999 now require that tax-exempt organizations provide a copy of their three most recently filed Form 990s and exempt application immediately upon personal request, and within 30 days for a written request. Penalties for not doing so are $20 per day up to a maximum of $10,000, but can be avoided if the organization makes these forms widely available on the Internet [Treas. Reg. §1.6104]. Similar regulations were passed for private foundations and their Form 990–PFs in January 2000.

[7]IRC Sec. 509(a).

Illustration 15–3 Parts of the IRS Form 990

Top of Page 1	Descriptive information: name, address, employer identification number (EIN), type of organization, accounting method
Part I	Statement of Revenue, Expenses, and Changes in Net Assets
Part II	Statement of Functional Expenses with Joint Costs
Part III	Statement of Program Service Accomplishments
Part IV	Balance Sheets (for two years)
Part V	List of officers, directors, trustees, and key employees (with compensation)
Part VI	Other information (e.g., amount of political expenditures, compliance with other regulations, location of the books)
Part VII	Analysis of income-producing activities
Part VIII	Relationship of activities to the accomplishment of exempt purpose
Part IX	Information regarding taxable subsidiaries
Schedule A	
Part I	Compensation of the five highest paid employees other than officers, directors, and trustees
Part II	Compensation of the five highest paid independent contractors for professional services
Part III	Statement about activities (e.g., political activity, leasing, making grants)
Part IV	Reason for nonprivate foundation status (and four-year support schedule)
Part V	Private school questionnaire
Part VI-A	Lobbying expenditures by electing public charities
Part VI-B	Lobbying activity by nonelecting public charities
Part VII	Information regarding transfers to and transactions and relationships with noncharitable exempt organizations
Attachments	Exhibits detailing information from above (e.g., list of all Board members)
990-T	Exempt organization business income tax return

government, general public (e.g., individuals, private foundations, corporations), or other public charities in the form of contributions, grants, membership dues, charges for services, or sales of merchandise.

If gross receipts from any person or governmental agency exceed $5,000 or 1 percent of the organization's support for the taxable year, then the excess is not counted in public support for the purposes of the external support test. Investment income and gains from sales of capital assets are *not* considered public support. Private foundations try not to give a grant to a not-for-profit organization that might cause the public charity to fail the support test and be reclassified as a private foundation. If that happens, the foundation must exercise **expenditure responsibility** and monitor whether the grant was used exclusively for the purpose for which it was made. The private foundation can require the grantee to assure them that the grant will not *tip* the grantee into private foundation status before it is granted. The **internal support test** requires that the NPO *not* receive more than one-third of its total support from investment income and unrelated business income. Classification as a public charity must be redetermined each year.

Unrelated Business Income Tax

Owners of small businesses have long complained that NPOs compete with them in businesslike activities with the unfair advantage of lower costs due to exemption from income taxes. For example, college bookstores sell clothing, credit unions operate travel agencies, YMCAs run health clubs, and universities operate veterinary clinics.[8] In 1950 Congress passed the first unrelated business income tax (UBIT), which assesses tax at corporate rates on income that NPOs derive from activities not substantially related to their charitable or tax-exempt mission.[9] UBIT requirements apply to all not-for-profit organizations and public colleges and universities, except federal corporations and certain charitable trusts.

The IRS is primarily interested in how the unrelated business income was earned, not in how it is used, even if it is used to further the organization's tax-exempt purpose. **Unrelated business income** (UBI) is calculated as the gross income from an unrelated trade or business *regularly* carried on less directly connected expenses, certain net operating losses, and qualified charitable contributions. The first $1,000 of net unrelated business income is excluded from taxation. Unrelated trade or business activities are those that are *substantially* unrelated to carrying out the organization's exempt purpose. The activities that must be carefully examined include sponsorships, advertising, affinity credit card arrangements, sale of mailing lists, travel services, and fund-raising events.

To determine whether the business activity is substantially related to the organization's exempt purpose, the relationship between the business activity and the exempt purpose is examined. Unrelated business income does not include dividends, interest, royalties, fees for use of intangible property, and gains on the sale of property (unless that property was used in an unrelated trade or business), or income from activities in which substantially all of the work is done by volunteers, income from the sale of donated merchandise, income from legally conducted games of chance, rents from real property, or when the trade is conducted primarily for the convenience of its members, such as a laundry in a college dorm. However, rents from debt-financed property, rents based on a percentage of net income rather than gross income, and rents on personal property are considered to be unrelated business income. Excluded from UBI is income from advertising done in the form of corporate sponsorships for particular events if (1) the corporate sponsor does not get any substantial benefit in return for its payment, other than the promotion of its name, (2) the display does not advertise the company's products or services, and (3) the amount of payment is not contingent on the level of attendance at the event.[10] Corporate sponsorships that appear in regularly published periodicals are still UBI. Special rules apply to bingo and distribution of low-cost items, such as pens or stickers.

---

[8]General Accounting Office, *Competition Between Tax-Exempt Organizations and Taxable Businesses*, GGD/T-GGD-88-43 (Washington, DC: Government Printing Office), June 28, 1988.

[9]IRC Secs. 511–513. Unrelated business income is also subject to the alternative minimum tax.

[10]This change came about in the Taxpayer Relief Act of 1997 and was a codification of proposed IRS regulations from three prior years.

Feeder Organizations. NPOs may control a **feeder organization** that is organized to carry on a trade or business for the benefit of the exempt organization and remit its profits to the NPO. The income passed from the feeder to the not-for-profit in the form of interest, rents, royalties, and annuities is subject to unrelated business income tax. In 1997, Congress redefined *control* as more than 50 percent of the voting stock of a feeder organization, down from 80 percent, effectively classifying more income of NPOs as unrelated. Some activities not subject to the feeder organization rules are those that (1) generate rental income that would be excluded from rent for UBIT, (2) use volunteers for substantially all the work, and (3) sell merchandise that was substantially all received as contributions.

Unrelated Debt-Financed Income. If an NPO has income from an asset that is mortgaged or **debt-financed income**, for example, rental of real estate, then that income is UBI. The unrelated business income is the total income times the proportion to which the property is financed by debt. There are many exceptions to this general rule, such as property for which substantially all is used to achieve the organization's exempt purpose.

Political Activity

Early legislative attempts at restricting political activity of public charities were intended to deny a charitable contribution income tax deduction for a selfish contribution made merely to advance the personal interests of the donor. The general rule is that no substantial part of a charity's activities may constitute carrying on propaganda or otherwise attempting to influence legislation. **Propaganda** is information skewed toward a particular belief with a tendency to have little or no factual basis. **Legislation** is generally action by Congress, a state legislative body, or a local council to establish laws, statutes, and ordinances. If any of the activities of the NPO consists of participating in any political campaign on behalf of (or in opposition to) any candidate for public office, the organization will not qualify for tax-exempt status. This includes publishing or distributing political statements. However, the facts and circumstances on the amount of money, time, and energy spent on each case determine whether the organization can be tax-exempt. For example, certain voter education activities or public forums conducted in a nonpartisan manner may not be considered prohibited political activity.

If an organization passes the "no *substantial* amount of propaganda or influencing legislation" hurdle and is granted tax-exempt status, it still faces limitations on the amount of political activity it can conduct. The severest penalty is loss of tax-exempt status. Less extreme is a tax on excessive political expenditures.[11] An exempt organization, other than a church, is allowed to make limited expenditures to influence legislation, if properly elected on Form 5786.[12] A permissible amount of **direct lobbying** (i.e., testifying at legislative hearings, corresponding or conferring with legislators or their staffs, or publishing documents advocating specific legislative action) is allowed, up to a ceiling calculated to allow for **grass-roots**

[11]IRC Sec. 4955.
[12]IRC Sec. 501(h).

lobbying (i.e., an appeal to the general public to contact legislators or to take other action regarding a legislative matter), but not to exceed $1 million in any one year. "Influencing legislation" does not include distributing nonpartisan studies, providing technical advice to a governmental body, opposing legislation that negatively affects the organization, exchanging information among organization members, and communicating on routine matters with governmental officials. The annual Form 990 contains a significant amount of information on legislative and political activities. Federal penalties for excess political activity are in addition to those that might be assessed by a state for lobbying.

Intermediate Sanctions

The preceding sections identified sanctions for specific prohibited or excessive activities by exempt organizations, but until recently, the only sanction for excessive economic benefits received by officers of NPOs was revocation of the organization's tax-exempt status. This drastic measure was seldom used. In 1996 Congress gave the IRS a new weapon in the Taxpayer Bill of Rights 2.[13] **Intermediate sanctions** for private inurement resulting from excess economic benefit transactions are penalties assessed when a transaction confers a substantial benefit on a disqualified person. A **disqualified person** is one who has substantial influence over the organization's affairs. Examples of **excess benefit transactions** include unreasonable compensation, sales of assets at bargain prices, and lease arrangements.[14] The law applies to public charities, but may be extended to other classifications of exempt organizations. The first-tier penalty is a tax of 25 percent of the excess benefit on the disqualified person, in addition to repayment of the excess benefit. If the organization's managers are aware the transaction is improper, then the NPO is assessed a tax of 10 percent of the excess benefit (up to a maximum of $10,000 per transaction). A second-tier penalty of 200 percent of the excess benefit is assessed on the disqualified person if the transaction is not corrected within the taxable period. Careful structuring of management compensation contracts, along with documentation of comparable salaries of similar positions, is critical in avoiding intermediate sanctions.

Reorganization and Dissolution

If an NPO finds that the social needs initially described in the tax-exemption application are met, then they may redefine their mission, merge, or choose to dissolve the organization. Many not-for-profit entities, particularly in the health care industry, are redefining their mission and then merging with other NPOs or associating with for-profit organizations. Mergers may be to achieve optimal **economic size** (i.e., the minimum possible size to be able to provide services without long-term damage to its financial base) or to integrate services. Many grantors fund only pilot programs that result in NPOs looking for financial resources after the start-up phase of the organization.[15] Accounting issues involved in a reorganization include

---

[13]U.S. Congress, H.R. 2337, July 30, 1996.

[14]IRC Sec. 4958.

[15]Thomas A. McLaughlin, *Seven Steps to a Successful Nonprofit Merger* (Washington, DC: National Center for Nonprofit Boards, 1996).

the merging of two information systems, measuring costs and benefits, **due diligence** (i.e., the formal disclosing and discovery of all relevant information, particularly about risks), and the surviving audit firm's reliance on the work of the former auditor. Accountants play a key role, along with legal and financial consultants, in the process of reorganizing or dissolving an NPO.

The accounting issues involved in a dissolution include ensuring that (1) all creditors are paid, (2) all federal, state, and local taxes are paid, and (3) all assets held in trust for the benefit of society are transferred to another public charity or given to a government. If the incorporating documents are silent about the distribution of assets, then state law or IRS regulations dictate. The IRS has said that if an NPO liquidates, dissolves, or terminates, its assets have to be distributed for another exempt purpose or be given to the federal or a state or local government.[16] Involuntary dissolution may come for failure to file an annual report or as a result of a State Attorney General's determination of fraud or unlawful conduct.

Other Issues

The federal government has passed other legislation that impacts NPOs. For example, the Volunteer Protection Act of 1997 holds that a volunteer of a nonprofit organization or governmental entity is relieved of liability for harm in simple negligence cases. An NPO that receives federal grants or contracts must abide by the spending rules found in various OMB Circulars (see Chapter 13 of this text for discussion of cost principles and administrative guidelines for federal assistance recipients). In particular, tax-exempt organizations cannot use federal funds to lobby Congress or state legislatures. Federal legislation also allows tax-exempt entities to apply for reduced postal rates for bulk mailings, as long as mailings do not include excessive for-profit advertising or promotional language describing member benefits, such as affinity credit cards.

Governance

Managers of tax-exempt, not-for-profit organizations are directly accountable to the Board of the organization, which in turn is ultimately responsible to the public and governmental oversight bodies. This relationship is not different from that among corporate managers, Boards of Directors, and stockholders. What is different, however, is the importance of incorporating documents that define the philanthropic or nonprofit mission of the organization and the (sometimes underestimated) responsibilities of Board members who may be invited to serve on the Board more for their fund-raising ability than their financial management expertise.

Incorporating Documents

The incorporating documents include the articles of incorporation, which have an external focus and describe the purpose of the organization without being too

[16]Rev. Proc. 82-2, 1982-1 CB 367 .

restrictive, and the by-laws, which have an internal focus and describe the functional rules of the organization. Other important documents to the accountant include minutes of Board meetings (i.e., the legal history of the organization) and written policies. They establish the charitable or exempt purpose for which the organization was organized and for which it should be held accountable. Expectations of resource providers, such as donors and grantors, as well as federal and state governments requiring reporting on the financial management of assets devoted to the exempt purpose, are revealed in these documents. State laws may govern the type of information that must be included in some of these documents; for example, the articles of incorporation are required to list name, purpose, activities to be engaged in, registered office, and the incorporators.

Nonprofit corporations can take the form of (1) membership, in which there is voting or nonvoting stock (for example, property owners association); or (2) directorship, where the Board is self-perpetuating (i.e., it elects itself). In the case of a directorship there is little threat of removal by the membership at large. The significance of the form of the nonprofit corporation for accountants is that the stakeholders or users of financial information and their needs may differ depending on the organizational form.

Board Membership

Board members are responsible for all authorized activities generating financial support on the organization's behalf.[17] They set policy and provide fiscal guidance and ongoing governance. Characteristics of a quality Board include diversity, leadership, sensitivity, direction, and, probably the most important, the ability of each member to contribute and attract funds. Treasurers of Boards have specific duties articulated in the incorporating documents that require they have custody of corporate funds and securities, keep full and accurate records of all receipts and disbursements, and deposit money and valuables in designated depositories until funds are authorized to be disbursed. Internal Board members, managers, and employees of the organization may have competing objectives from those of external Board members who are outside of the daily operations of the organization and who have no financial stake in the organization. Board members may carry errors and omissions insurance and require that indemnification clauses be included in the articles of incorporation to protect them from lawsuits.

To satisfy its fiduciary responsibilities, the Board should require managers to regularly summarize the activities of administering the entity. It should regularly review the organization's policies, programs, and operations.[18] Incentive performance contracts can be made with managers to encourage certain goals and outcomes. By-laws or policies may call for continuous quality improvement so Boards may assess performance against benchmarks and predetermined performance goals.

---

[17]Richard T. Ingram, *Ten Basic Responsibilities of Nonprofit Boards* (Washington, DC: National Center for Nonprofit Boards, 1996).

[18]Regina E. Herzlinger, "Effective Oversight: A Guide for Nonprofit Directors," *Harvard Business Review*, July–August 1994, pp. 52–60.

Benchmarking and Performance Measures

Oversight bodies, such as Boards of Directors, nonprofit watchdog agencies, and an increasing number of states are tracking performance measures of exempt organizations. Financial and operational outcomes are compared to specified performance targets as well as benchmarked to comparable organizations in the industry. Nonprofit agencies collecting information about entities in the not-for-profit sector include the National Charities Information Bureau (NCIB), Philanthropic Advisory Service (PAS) of the Council of the Better Business Bureau, American Institute of Philanthropy (AIP), Exempt Organizations Division of the Internal Revenue Service (EO), Independent Sector, and Urban Institute.[19]

Generally, financial goals include ensuring that the organization is liquid and can pay its debts, its revenues are sufficient to cover expenses, its expenses are reasonable and primarily spent on the programs rather than supporting the programs, there is intergenerational equity (i.e., future years' revenues are not needed to pay for current services), and there is financial stability and sustained growth in the organization. Donors may incorrectly assume that federal and state laws govern the percentage of annual revenue that a charity must spend on its programs, or that there are limits on the percentage of revenue that is spent on fund-raising.

Specific financial performance objectives that may be stated in Board policies include maintaining a specified current ratio, a balanced budget, spending such that there is neither an excess of expenses over revenues nor a deficit in net assets, program expenses greater than a specified percent of total expenses, a specified ceiling on long-term debt, a targeted balance between current contributions and planned giving or endowment funds, program spending as a specified percentage of current income, fund-raising costs (and efforts) that are never more than a specific percentage of the contributions that result, investment income equal to the market rate, a targeted percent of endowment income spent on the programs (payout rate), and/or that net assets available for the following year are not more than a certain multiple of current year's expenses or next year's budget, whichever is higher.

The watchdog groups mentioned earlier have some published benchmarks, or averages, they use to rank the performance of public charities. For example, the NCIB uses nine basic standards in evaluating charities and specifies that the program/support expense ratio must be greater than 60/40 in order to receive the highest rating.[20] The PAS of the Better Business Bureau's criteria for a similar standard is 50/50. Some states' Attorney General Offices recommend that an organization spend less than 33 percent of total income on fund-raising and administrative support expenses.[21]

---

[19]More information about these groups and the annual reports they produce is available on their Internet websites, which can be reached through the authors' websites (see Preface for address).

[20]National Charities Information Bureau, *Standards in Philanthropy* (New York: NCIB, 1999).

[21]Daniel E. Lungren, *Attorney General's Charity Spending Profiles* (San Francisco: California Department of Justice, April 1995).

Illustration 15–4 Ten Largest NPOs and Selected Performance Measures (1998)

Ranking by Total Revenue		*Size = Total Revenue (in millions)*	*Size = Public Support (in millions)*	*Program Spending as a Percent of Total Income*	*Program Spending as a Percent of Total Expenses*	*Fund-Raising Costs as a Percent of Public Support*
1.	The National Council of YMCAs	$3,249	$ 613	73%	82%	7.62%
2.	Catholic Charities USA	2,309	385	89	91	5.44
3.	Salvation Army	2,078	1,235	73	83	6.32
4.	American Red Cross	2,058	543	87	91	13.52
5.	Goodwill Industries International	1,504	166	84	89	4.27
6.	Shriners Hospitals for Children	1,494	246	24	95	1.03
7.	The Arc	1,262	127	85	88	10.93
8.	Fidelity Investments Charitable Gift Fund	695	572	40	97	0.76
9.	Boy Scouts of America	649	270	71	81	14.31
10.	YWCA of the USA	630	156	78	87	7.39

Source: "NPT100," *The Nonprofit Times*, November 1999, pp. 31–49.

The percentage of total expenses spent on supporting the program as opposed to the program itself is such a publicized measure of effectiveness that organizations are quite careful to allocate as much to the program category as possible. At issue has been the joint costs of advocacy or educational materials that have a fund-raising appeal. As explained in Chapter 14, the AICPA's *SOP 98-2* restricts the amount of such costs that can be classified as program expenses. Another way to increase the proportion of program expenses to total expenses is to recognize the fair value of **gifts in kind** (i.e., contributions of tangible items) and contributed services used in the operations of the program as expenses. Generally accepted accounting principles do require that this type of gift be recognized as both income and expense, if fair value can be objectively determined, expenses would have been incurred even without the donation, nonfinancial assets are enhanced, and amounts are material.[22] At issue is whether fair market value is objective, particularly for corporate contributions of obsolete inventory. If it is overstated, then the public interest is not served.

Form 990 provides a substantial amount of information that can be used in evaluating tax-exempt entities. In addition to financial information, the form asks questions about self-dealing by key officers and for a description of significant program service accomplishments in the charity's own words. Illustration 15–4 provides several performance measures for some of the nation's largest public charities.

As the federal government requires outcome and performance measures of its agencies, we should expect those agencies to require the same information from the

[22]AICPA, Accounting and Audit Guide, *Not-for-Profit Organizations*, pars. 5.39–5.42.

organizations that receive public funds. Many NPOs are voluntarily reporting some type of service efforts and accomplishments in their annual reports. As this practice becomes more widespread, NPOs will report similar statistics to stay competitive for charitable gifts.

Summary

This chapter provides a general description of tax laws and other state and federal regulations so that accountants and decision makers using financial information are familiar with the environment within which tax-exempt organizations operate. It should be clear that a thorough understanding of current case law about exempt organizations is also important, but outside the scope of this text. More specific details are available in Internal Revenue Service literature and books on taxation of tax-exempt organizations. In the future, NPOs can expect increased scrutiny and accountability for performance outcomes as a more well-informed public demands it and as technology enables government agencies, such as the IRS, to audit and monitor tax-exempt organizations.

Key Terms

Charitable solicitation, 697
Debt-financed income, 705
Direct lobbying, 705
Disqualified person, 706
Due diligence, 707
Economic size, 706
Excess benefit transaction, 706
Expenditure responsibility, 703
External support test, 702
Federated fund-raising organization, 701
Feeder organization, 705
Gifts in kind, 710
Grass-roots lobbying, 705
Influencing, 698
Intermediate sanctions, 706
Internal support test, 703
Legislation, 705
Lobbying, 698
Organizational test, 699
Private foundation, 702
Propaganda, 705
Public charity, 702
Unrelated business income, 704

Selected References

Accounting Aid Society. *Michigan Nonprofit Management Manual.* Detroit, MI: Accounting Aid Society, 1999.

Gross, Malvern J. Jr., Richard F. Larkin, Roger S. Bruttomesso, and John J. McNally. *Financial and Accounting Guide for Not-for-Profit Organizations.* 5th ed. with annual Cumulative Supplements. New York: John Wiley & Sons, 1999.

Internal Revenue Service, Department of Treasury. *Application for Recognition of Exemption Under Sec. 501(c)(3) of the Internal Revenue Code.* Package 1023.

———. Pub. 557. *Tax-Exempt Status for Your Organization.*

Oleck, Howard L., and Martha E. Stewart. *Nonprofit Corporations, Organizations, and Associations*. 6th ed. and annual Cumulative Supplements. Englewood Cliffs, NJ: Prentice Hall, 1997.

Perlman, Seth, and Betsy Hills Bush. *A State-by-State Handbook of Registration Forms, Requirements, and Procedures, 2000 Supplement*. New York: John Wiley & Sons, 1999.

Stevenson, David R., Thomas H. Pollak, and Linda M. Lampkin. *State Nonprofit Almanac 1997: Profiles of Charitable Organizations*. Washington, DC: Urban Institute Press, 1997.

Periodicals:

Chronicle of Philanthropy. Washington, DC.

Foundation News. New York: Foundation Center.

The Journal of Taxation of Exempt Organizations. New York: Faulkner & Gray.

Statistics of Income Bulletins. Washington, DC: U.S. Government, Department of Treasury.

Questions

15–1. Why should an auditor understand the laws and regulations that apply to the activities of not-for-profit organizations?

15–2. What are some of the reasons a government has the power and responsibility to regulate a nongovernmental not-for-profit organization?

15–3. Under which statutory authority are these public charities most likely to be exempt from federal income tax?

a. Pine Ridge Cemetery.
b. American Institute of Certified Public Accountants.
c. Elks Lodge.
d. Big Oak Country Club.
e. American Diabetes Association.
f. Parent Teacher Organization.
g. Health Maintenance Organization.
h. Tender Care Child Care Center.
i. League of Women Voters.
j. National Hockey League.

15–4. Why might a not-for-profit organization fail to qualify for exemption from federal income taxes?

15–5. Describe the basic differences between public charities and private foundations. Which status receives the most preferential tax treatment under federal laws? Why?

15–6. Describe the limitations on political activity and lobbying that are placed on tax-exempt organizations by the federal government.

15–7. A museum is considering opening a gift shop to sell novelty items related to the exhibits. A committee has been formed to evaluate the costs and benefits of such an operation. What issues should they consider with respect to unrelated business income?

15–8. Define the term *intermediate sanctions* and explain why this is an important tool for the IRS to use in curbing abuses such as excessive management compensation.

15–9. What types of information must be reported to the IRS annually on Form 990? How can a potential donor get this information and use it for evaluating the organization in making his or her decision to make a contribution?

15–10. Discuss the role of inside and outside Board members. How would an incentive compensation plan help ensure the Board that the manager is accountable for the assets with which the agency is entrusted?

Cases

15–1. Establishing a Nonprofit Organization. John Martinez is a newly elected Representative to the United States Congress. He does not come from a wealthy family, but has a large group of people who supported his candidacy and provided funds for his campaign. In appreciation, he always accepts their invitations to speak to groups back in his home state. He has recently been asked to teach a course by one of these supporters at the local community college. In preparation for this opportunity he prepared a 100-page handout that describes the political system in the United States, and in particular the process that is taken to pass a bill. He uses examples from bills that he cosponsored including his reasons for supporting that legislation. John is aware that other Representatives have recently been under attack by the media and Internal Revenue Service for similar educational activities. He has asked your advice.

Required

a. In general, what type of regulations should John be aware of?

b. Should John establish a not-for-profit corporation to accept the payments he will receive for his speaking and teaching assignments?

15–2. Unrelated Business Income Tax. Linda Brown is a certified internal auditor for the Walnut Hills Country Club, a nonprofit corporation that owns a private members-only country club. The club recently has experienced declining revenues and decided to allow nonmembers to use the restaurant and banquet room facilities. The accountant offset net losses on nonmember sales against the earnings from its investments and reported no unrelated business taxable income. In computing the losses from the unrelated business activities, the club identified two categories of expenses incurred in nonmember sales: (1) variable or direct expenses, such as the cost of food that was exceeded by income from nonmember sales, and (2) fixed overhead expenses, which would have been incurred whether or not sales had been made to nonmembers. Linda is aware that the IRS has recently questioned cost allocation methods used by country clubs in the computation of unrelated business taxable income. She has been asked to make sure the Club is following proper procedures.

Required

a. Is the revenue from sales to nonmembers unrelated business income?

b. Determine a method of allocating indirect costs in computing the net loss from sales to nonmembers and defend your position. (Hint: See the Supreme Court case: *Portland Golf Club* v. *Commissioner of Internal Revenue*, S. Ct. 89-530; 65 AFTR 2d 90-503, June 21, 1990).

Based on a case in "Accounting for the 'Invisible' Nonprofit Sector: Five Mini-Cases," by J. Young and S. Kattelus, *Journal of Accounting Education* 13, no. 3, 1995, pp. 319–42.

15–3. Internet Case. Go to the Internet websites of five of the largest charitable organizations listed in Illustration 15–4. What financial information and performance measures do they disclose? Locate a comparable organization for each of these five NPOs, perhaps a competitor. Calculate the amount that each spent on its program (as a percent of income and as a percent of total expenses) as well as how many dollars were raised for each dollar spent on fund-raising from information provided on their websites. Do you have enough information to compare each pair of organizations? Where could you get other useful information? Prepare a table showing the five charities, their counterparts, and performance measures for each. Which charity would you consider the most efficient and effective? Why?

Exercises and Problems

15–1. Multiple Choice. Choose the best answer.

1. Accountants should be knowledgeable about laws and regulations impacting not-for-profit entities because:
   a. They may be asked by the organization to assist in completing annual compliance reports.
   b. Donors may ask for their help in evaluating a not-for-profit organization.
   c. Auditors are expected to attest to whether the organization complied with all laws and regulations.
   d. All of the above.
2. To qualify as an exempt organization, the applicant:
   a. Need *not* be specifically identified in one of the categories of tax exemption allowed by the Internal Revenue Code, provided that the organization's purposes and activities are of a charitable nature.
   b. Must *not* be classified as a professional organization.
   c. Must *not* be a public charity organized and operated exclusively to influence legislation pertaining to protection of the environment.
   d. May be organized and operated for the primary purpose of carrying on a business for profit, provided that all of the organization's net earnings are turned over to one or more tax-exempt organizations.

3. An organization that tests products for public safety will fail to meet the organizational test to qualify as an exempt organization if:

	The Organization Engages in Insubstantial Nonexempt Activities	*The Organization Directly Participates in Any Political Campaign*
a.	Yes	Yes
b.	Yes	No
c.	No	Yes
d.	No	No

4. Which of the following organizations is most likely to qualify for tax-exempt status as a not-for-profit organization?
   a. Royal Oak Chamber of Commerce.
   b. Disneyland.
   c. Detroit Red Wings.
   d. City of Huron.
5. Which of the following is a characteristic of public charities but *not* private foundations?
   a. They are subject to excise taxes on certain prohibited transactions, such as self-dealing.
   b. They are supported by a broad set of donors organized to meet the common good.
   c. They are exempt from federal income taxes under IRC Sec. 501(c)(3).
   d. They may not participate in any political campaign on behalf of a candidate for public office.
6. Which of the following activities regularly conducted by a tax-exempt organization will result in unrelated business income?
   I. Operating a thrift store staffed by developmentally disabled persons as part of a sheltered workshop program.
   II. Selling goods made by disabled persons as part of their rehabilitation, when the organization is organized exclusively for rehabilitation.
      a. I only.
      b. II only.
      c. Both I and II.
      d. Neither I nor II.
7. New Beginnings, Inc., is an exempt organization that owns an office building and leases it to the Auto Parts Corporation for $120,000 per year. The remaining mortgage on the building is $300,000, and the book value of the building is $500,000. Since the office building is debt-financed property, the unrelated debt-financed income, for purposes of the UBIT, is:
   a. $200,000.
   b. $120,000.
   c. $72,000.
   d. $0.

8. Which of the following statements is correct with regard to unrelated business income of an exempt organization?
   a. An exempt organization that earns any unrelated business income in excess of $100,000 during a particular year will lose its exempt status for that particular year.
   b. An exempt organization is not taxed on the unrelated business income of less than $1,000.
   c. The tax on unrelated business income can be imposed even if the unrelated business activity is intermittent and is carried on once a year.
   d. An unrelated trade or business activity that results in a loss is excluded from the definition of unrelated business.
9. The percentage of total expenses a nonprofit organization spends on its programs as opposed to supporting the programs is a performance measure that can be used in evaluating:
   a. Efficiency or effectiveness.
   b. Liquidity.
   c. Intergenerational equity.
   d. Profitability.
10. Which of the following is an important reason why Board members of a nonprofit agency should be familiar with the laws and regulations that impact the organization?
   a. They have a fiduciary responsibility to ensure that the not-for-profit organization complies with all laws and regulations.
   b. They have a legal responsibility to ensure that the not-for-profit organization complies with all laws and regulations.
   c. They have a responsibility to management to provide on-going fiscal governance, as well as direction.
   d. All of the above.

15–2. Public Charity. The Family Services Agency of Oakville County is a nongovernmental public charity under IRC Sec. 501(c)(3). It had total support last year of the following:

United Way support	$ 70,000
Grant from Oakville County	50,000
Contributions	330,000
Investment income	45,000
	$495,000

Of the $330,000 in contributions, five contributions were each greater than $5,000 and totaled $230,000; the other $100,000 is comprised of small individual contributions.

Required

a. Calculate the total amount of support that qualifies as "public support" in meeting the external support test to escape private foundation status.

b. Is the organization considered a public charity or a private foundation? Why or why not?

c. If the organization received an additional $140,000 grant from one individual during the year, would the NPO still be classified the same as your response to part *b* (assuming that the previous five gifts are still greater than 1 percent of the new total)?

15–3. Lobbying Expenses. LearnMore, Inc., an IRC Sec. 501(c)(3) organization, incurred lobbying expenses of $250,000 and exempt purpose expenditures of $1.1 million in carrying out its exempt mission.

Required

a. What are the tax consequences if the organization *does not* elect to participate in lobbying activities on a limited basis?

b. Discuss the factors involved in the association's decision to elect to participate in lobbying activities under IRC Sec. 501(h).

15–4. Unrelated Business Income Tax. The Lewis and Clark Association has a mailing list of 15,000 members, donors, catalog purchasers, and other supporters of the association and its mission—to educate the public about the historic expedition to the West from the eastern United States in the early 1800s. In prior years, revenue from the sale of this list to for-profit companies for use in their promotional activities averaged $5,000. This year, because of a television special about the historic journey, revenue from sales of the list jumped to $86,000. The accountant recently attended a workshop on tax issues in not-for-profit organizations and learned about unrelated business income tax. She is now concerned that this revenue is subject to that tax.

Required

a. Apply the facts of this case to the unrelated business income tax rules. Is the Association liable for unrelated business income tax?

b. What if next year the revenue from sales of the mailing list increases to $286,000? Would the Association then have unrelated business income?

15–5. Giftshop and UBIT. An exempt organization operates a gift shop and has an operations budget of $2,000,000 for the year. Gift shop sales result in a profit of $50,000. Another $100,000 of endowment income is earned. Both the income from the gift shop and the endowment income are used to support the exempt purpose of the organization. The balance of $1,850,000 required for annual operations is provided through membership dues and charges for services.

Required

a. Calculate the UBIT if the corporate tax rate is 15 percent on the first $50,000 of net income and 25 percent on the next $25,000 of income.

b. Assume that the endowment income is reinvested rather than being used to support annual operations. Calculate the amount of unrelated business income.

15–6. Intermediate Sanctions. For the following independent situations, determine if the organization is at risk for receiving *intermediate sanctions* from the Internal Revenue Service for conferring excess economic benefits on disqualified persons. If so, indicate how the organization can minimize those sanctions.

1. Jane is the president of an IRC Sec. 501(c)(3) public charity and personally owns a building that she has decided to sell to the not-for-profit organization. The appraisal value is $200,000 and the agreed-upon selling price is $250,000.
2. A large public charity is very happy with its president's performance and offers him a new compensation agreement for the coming year. It reads that he will receive a base salary, plus a percentage of the increase in the gross revenues of the organization, with no limitation as to a maximum amount.
3. Ann is a member and director of a symphony association and receives 20 free admission tickets as a member of the organization.
4. The local chapter of the United Way recently hired Joe Curtis as its new president at a salary of $200,000. The outgoing president was paid $150,000. Mr. Curtis had other offers that ranged from $95,000 to $190,000. The minutes of the meeting reflected that he was exceptionally talented and would not have accepted the position for a lower salary.

15–7. Mergers. Two large human service organizations in an urban area have decided to collaborate in order to reduce administrative costs, resulting in more funds available for charitable programs. What financial and accounting issues should they consider in their decision to dissolve one entity or merge the two together?

15–8. Performance Measures. Information from the audited financial statements for the American Heart Association for the fiscal year ending June 30, 1998, is presented on the following pages. Notes to the Financial Statements are not included and some line items have been consolidated to simplify the presentation. Compute the following performance measures and comment on what information they convey to a potential donor, without comparing them to prior years or other comparable agencies.

a. Current ratio—liquidity.
b. Excess of revenues over expenses.
c. Percentage of total expenses spent on the programs as opposed to supporting the programs.
d. Cost of fund-raising.
e. Intergenerational equity: extent to which future generations have to pay for services offered currently.

AMERICAN HEART ASSOCIATION, INC. (NATIONAL CENTER) AND ALL AFFILIATED HEART ASSOCIATIONS COMBINED STATEMENT OF FINANCIAL POSITION AS OF JUNE 30, 1998 (DOLLARS IN THOUSANDS)

	Unrestricted	*Temporarily Restricted*	*Permanently Restricted*	*Total*
Assets				
Current assets:				
Cash and cash equivalents	$ 62,401	$ 2,161		$ 64,562
Short-term investments	153,493			153,493
Accrued investment income	4,909			4,909
Accounts receivable	25,320	36,783	$250	55,151
Materials inventory	8,011			8,011
Prepaid expenses and other assets	5,069			5,069
Total current assets	259,203	38,944	250	298,397
Noncurrent assets:				
Long-term investments	235,011	921	9,798	245,730
Beneficial interest in perpetual trusts			80,996	80,996
Land, buildings, and equipment (net)	69,593	445		70,038
Accounts receivable	852	40,104	87	41,043
Other assets	2,236			2,236
Total noncurrent assets	307,692	41,470	90,881	440,043
Total assets	$566,895	$80,414	$91,131	$738,440
Liabilities and Net Assets				
Current liabilities:				
Accounts payable and accrued expenses	$ 28,528			$ 28,528
Mortgage notes payable	377			377
Research awards payable within one year, net of discount	110,785	3,927		114,712
Deferred revenue and support	7,964			7,964
Other liabilities	3,527			3,527
Total current liabilities	151,181	3,927		155,108
Noncurrent liabilities:				
Other accrued expenses and liabilities	6,533			6,533
Mortgage notes payable	3,317			3,317
Research awards payable after one year, net of discount	96,117	2,346		98,463
Total noncurrent liabilities	105,967	2,346		108,313
Total liabilities	257,148	6,273		263,421
Net assets:				
Net investment in land, buildings, and equipment	65,898	445		66,343
Designated by the governing board or restricted for:				
Programs and operations for the ensuing fiscal year	201,763			201,763
Research designated for future years	16,748			16,748
Bequest stabilization	7,834			7,834
Capital expenditures	1,318			1,318
Specific program and support activities		19,333		19,333
Time restrictions		27,643		27,643
Split interest agreements	1,288	26,720	81,083	109,091
Endowment			10,048	10,048
Unfunded commitments, program supplementation, and operating contingencies	14,898			14,898
Total net assets	309,747	74,141	91,131	475,019
Total liabilities and net assets	$566,895	$80,414	$91,131	$738,440

Note: These statements are adapted from the American Heart Association's audited financial statements.

AMERICAN HEART ASSOCIATION, INC. (NATIONAL CENTER) AND ALL AFFILIATED HEART ASSOCIATIONS
COMBINED STATEMENT OF ACTIVITIES
YEAR ENDED JUNE 30, 1998
(DOLLARS IN THOUSANDS)

	Unrestricted	*Temporarily Restricted*	*Permanently Restricted*	*1998*
Revenue				
Public support:				
Received directly:				
Contributions and capital campaign	$ 76,102	$35,984	$ 361	$112,447
Contributed services	2,152			2,152
Special events	136,945	1,331		138,276
Special events incentives	(26,606)			(26,606)
Net special events	110,339	1,331		111,670
Legacies and bequests	54,452	18,685	458	73,595
Split-interest agreements	354	1,996	1,950	4,300
Total received directly	243,399	57,996	2,769	304,164
Received indirectly:				
Federated fund-raising organizations	7,328	10,375		17,703
Unassociated and nonfederated	2,102	1,938		4,040
Total received indirectly	9,430	12,313		21,743
Total public support	252,829	70,309	2,769	325,907
Other revenue/loss:	90,977	2,368	10,342	103,687
Net assets released from restrictions:				
Satisfaction of research restrictions	20,426	(20,426)		
Satisfaction of program restrictions	22,873	(22,873)		
Expiration of time restrictions	26,424	(26,424)		
Satisfaction of equipment acquisition restrictions	715	(715)		
Satisfaction of geographic restrictions	1,693	(1,693)		
Total net assets released from restrictions	72,131	(72,131)		
Total public support and other revenue	415,937	546	13,111	429,594
Expenses				
Program services:				
Research	127,014			127,014
Public health education	92,291			92,291
Professional education and training	43,097			43,097
Community services	49,463			49,463
Total program services	311,865			311,865
Supporting services:				
Management and general	33,634			33,634
Fund-raising	47,732			47,732
Total supporting services	81,366			81,366
Total program and supporting services	393,231			393,231
Change in net assets	22,706	546	13,111	36,363
Net Assets				
Beginning of year	287,041	73,595	78,020	438,656
End of year	$309,747	$74,141	$91,131	$475,019

AMERICAN HEART ASSOCIATION, INC. (NATIONAL CENTER) AND ALL AFFILIATED HEART ASSOCIATIONS COMBINED STATEMENT OF FUNCTIONAL EXPENSES YEAR ENDED JUNE 30, 1998 (DOLLARS IN THOUSANDS)

	Program Services					Supporting Services			
	Research	*Public Health Education*	*Professional Education and Training*	*Community Services*	*Sub-total*	*Management and General*	*Fund-Raising*	*Sub-total*	*Total 1998*
Salaries	$ 1,960	$35,308	$13,085	$23,375	$ 73,728	$15,727	$17,981	$33,708	$107,436
Payroll taxes	153	2,947	955	1,935	5,990	1,225	1,363	2,588	8,578
Employee benefits	299	4,762	1,803	3,239	10,103	2,420	1,998	4,418	14,521
Occupancy	175	4,132	1,382	2,608	8,297	1,302	1,605	2,907	11,204
Telephone	99	2,303	821	1,448	4,671	1,032	992	2,024	6,695
Supplies	79	1,684	518	951	3,232	569	1,037	1,606	4,838
Rental and maintenance of equipment	143	1,793	803	1,036	3,775	1,365	639	2,004	5,779
Printing and publications	79	12,262	7,943	4,370	24,654	114	7,525	7,639	32,293
Postage and shipping	98	5,042	2,113	1,509	8,762	625	4,788	5,413	14,175
Visual aids, films, and media	3	1,077	153	747	1,980	115	169	284	2,264
Conferences and meetings	664	2,883	6,491	1,664	11,702	2,119	1,392	3,511	15,213
Other travel	111	2,516	778	1,630	5,035	1,130	1,802	2,932	7,967
Professional fees	2,035	10,236	3,500	1,814	17,585	2,943	4,364	7,307	24,892
Awards and grants	120,881	536	471	156	122,044	132	23	155	122,199
Other expenses	58	1,827	1,172	1,202	4,259	1,640	1,055	2,695	6,954
Depreciation and amortization	177	2,983	1,109	1,779	6,048	1,176	999	2,175	8,223
Total functional expenses before special events incentives	127,014	92,291	43,097	49,463	311,865	33,634	47,732	81,366	393,231
Special events incentives					26,606				26,606
Total functional expenses	$127,014	$92,291	$43,097	$49,463	$338,471	$33,634	$47,732	$81,366	$419,837

CHAPTER 16

Accounting for Colleges and Universities

Learning Objectives

After studying this chapter, you should be able to:

- Distinguish between generally accepted accounting principles for public and private colleges and universities.
- Describe financial reporting for governmentally owned colleges and universities.
- Discuss accounting and reporting issues for all colleges and universities, such as
  - Accounting for assets, liabilities, and net assets.
  - Accounting for revenues and expenses.
  - Accounting for cash flows.
- Journalize transactions for governmentally owned colleges and universities following GASB *Statement No. 35*.
- Prepare financial statements for governmentally owned colleges and universities following GASB *Statement No. 35*.
- Prepare financial statements for private colleges and universities following *SFAS No. 117*.
- Discuss managerial, auditing, and reporting issues, such as:
  - Performance measures.
  - Auditing.
  - Federal financial assistance.
  - Related entities.

Institutions of higher learning have long been dichotomized into public colleges and universities, which are governmental in nature, and private colleges and universities, which are nongovernmental not-for-profit organizations. In comparison, public institutions receive a higher share of their total revenues from state appropriations, whereas private institutions depend to a larger extent upon student tuition and fees, private gifts, and research grants. More recently, community colleges have joined the higher education industry, supported in large part by local property tax assessments, as well as a few for-profit corporations that may receive corporate subsidies. The National Center for Education Statistics estimates that in 1998 there were over 3,700 institutions of higher learning with $189 billion of gross revenue and enrollment of 14.7 million students in the United States.[1]

Accounting and Financial Reporting Standards

For most of the twentieth century, the majority of institutions in the higher education industry, without regard to their ownership or sources of financing, followed a single set of accounting and financial reporting standards. This guidance was described in the AICPA Audit Guide *Audits of Colleges and Universities* and included standards set by the American Institute of Certified Public Accountants (AICPA) in cooperation with committees of the National Association of College and University Business Officers (NACUBO) and task forces of groups related to the U.S. Department of Education.[2]

In 1984, the GASB was given jurisdiction over accounting and financial reporting standards for public colleges and universities, as well as state and local governmental units and public schools. The FASB retained jurisdiction over accounting and financial reporting standards for private colleges and universities, and, of course, for for-profit businesses providing higher education. In 1991, the GASB issued a statement that allowed public colleges and universities to continue using the AICPA College Guide model until comprehensive studies of governmental reporting models were completed.[3] The AICPA College Guide model included six fund groups: Current Funds (unrestricted and restricted), Loan Funds, Endowment and Similar Funds, Annuity and Life Income Funds, Plant Funds (comprised of four subgroups), and Agency Funds.

In 1993, FASB issued *Statement Nos. 116* and *117*, which require private colleges and universities to report on the net assets of the entity as a whole, rather than reporting on fund groups as prescribed in the AICPA College Guide model. This change was made to standardize the way all nongovernmental not-for-profit entities report to the public, and make them report more like businesses and less

[1]National Center for Education Statistics (NCES), *Digest of Education Statistics* (Washington, DC: Department of Education, 1999).

[2]American Institute of Certified Public Accountants, Audit and Accounting Guide, *Audits of Colleges and Universities* (New York: AICPA, 1973, reprinted in 1994).

[3]GASB, *Codification*, Sec. Co5.101.

like governments. An important presumption was that decision makers would find this format more useful, even though comparability between public and private universities would be made more difficult.[4] After much due process that included a Research Report (1988), Invitation to Comment (1994), public hearings, user focus groups, task forces, mail surveys, Preliminary Views (1995), and two Exposure Drafts (1997 and 1999), the GASB issued *Statement No. 35*, "Basic Financial Statements—and Management's Discussion and Analysis—for Public Colleges and Universities," in November 1999.[5] This statement amends GASB *Statement No. 34* to include public colleges and universities as special-purpose governments and possibly enterprise funds or component units of another governmental entity. Those who have been concerned about comparability between public and private entities since 1994 (effective date of *SFAS Nos. 116* and *117*) should be reassured as public colleges and universities implement GASB *Statement Nos. 34* and *35*.

Standards applicable to public (governmental) colleges and universities are discussed next, including a presentation of illustrative transactions and financial statements. Standards and financial reporting requirements unique to private colleges and universities are discussed later in this chapter.

Public (Governmentally Owned) Colleges and Universities

GASB *Statement No. 35* requires that all public colleges and universities follow the GASB *Statement No. 34* financial reporting model used by state and local governments (and described in Chapters 2–9) for their separately issued financial statements. Large institutions (i.e., annual revenues of $100 million or more) must implement the standards for periods beginning after June 15, 2001, and institutions that are component units of other governmental units must apply the standards when the primary government does.[6]

In short, GASB *Statement No. 35* permits colleges and universities to use the guidance for special purpose governments engaged only in business-type activities, engaged only in governmental activities, or engaged in both, for their stand-alone reports. A management's discussion and analysis (MD&A) is required, and infrastructure assets must be reported. The accrual basis of accounting must be used and capital assets must be depreciated. A Statement of Cash Flows must be provided using the direct method. The GASB considered many alternative reporting models

---

[4]Rita Hartung Cheng, Ken W. Brown, and Mary L. Fischer, "Response to the GASB Discussion Document 'Invitation to Comment: College and University Financial Reporting Model'," *Accounting Horizons* 9 (September 1995), pp. 104–110; John H. Engstrom and Connie Esmond-Kiger, "Different Formats, Same User Needs: Do the FASB and GASB College and University Reporting Models Meet User Needs?" *Accounting Horizons* 11 (September 1997), pp. 16–34.

[5]See Appendices A and B in GASB *Statement No. 35* for details on the due process and other background information, pars. 13–20.

[6]Mid-size institutions with annual revenues between $10 million and $100 million must apply the standards for periods beginning after June 15, 2002, and small institutions with annual revenues less than $10 million must apply the standards for periods beginning after June 15, 2003.

over the last decade and concluded that there was adequate guidance in existing GASB standards for public colleges and universities, and it did not want to create a precedent of setting standards on an industry-by-industry basis.

Most colleges and universities are expected to follow the model for public institutions engaged only in business-type activities. In this case, the basic financial statements are those required of an enterprise fund in a state or local government, which are:

Statement of Net Assets—Illustration 16–1
Statement of Revenues, Expenses, and Changes in Net Assets—Illustration 16–2
Statement of Cash Flows—Illustration 16–3

Components units, such as university hospitals are discretely presented from the primary institution.

Some public higher education institutions, such as community colleges, have "taxing authority," the power to assess special taxes on local residents. These institutions may elect to report as "engaged in governmental-type activities only" or "engaged in both governmental and business-type activities." The basic financial statements are the same as those discussed for state and local governments in Chapters 1 through 9 and shown in Illustrations 2–1 through 2–10, using revenue and expenditure/expense classifications appropriate to colleges and universities. These institutions would continue to use fund accounting, although the authoritative standing for funds would derive from GASB *Statement No. 34* and no longer from the AICPA College Audit Guide.[7]

Most colleges and universities are expected to continue to use fund accounting for internal purposes, as do many private (nongovernmental) colleges and universities reporting under *SFAS No. 117*, discussed later in this chapter and in Chapter 14. For these institutions, a worksheet can then be used to convert fund accounting information to institution-wide information necessary for the basic financial statements. Of course, GASB *Statement No. 35* prescribes minimum reporting standards, so colleges and universities may choose to report additional fund-based financial information in their annual reports. In this chapter, our focus is on basic external financial reporting for the majority of colleges and universities expected to report as "engaged in business-type activities only"; consequently, there is little discussion of fund accounting in this edition.

Accounting and Reporting Issues

As GASB *Statement No. 35* is relatively new (issued November 1999), we can expect public colleges and universities to continue to rely on industry guidance,

[7]GASB *Statement No. 34* supersedes GASB *Statement No. 15*, "Governmental College and University Accounting and Financial Reporting Models," which allowed public colleges and universities the option of following the AICPA College Guide model; therefore, it is inappropriate to continue using the fund structure provided by that model for external financial reporting.

Illustration 16–1

MIDWEST UNIVERSITY
STATEMENT OF NET ASSETS
JUNE 30, 2002
(IN THOUSANDS)

	Primary Institution	*Component Unit Hospital*
Assets		
Current assets:		
Cash and cash equivalents	$ 1,568	$ 98
Short-term investments	428	225
Accounts receivable, net	110	953
Inventories	95	127
Deposits with bond trustee	373	—
Prepaid expenses	29	47
Total current assets	2,603	1,450
Noncurrent assets:		
Endowment investments	10,450	—
Loans receivable, net	613	—
Long-term investments	7,063	646
Capital assets, net of depreciation	63,440	3,260
Total noncurrent assets	81,566	3,906
Total assets	84,169	5,356
Liabilities		
Current liabilities:		
Accounts payable and accrued liabilities	274	291
Deferred revenue	35	—
Deposits held in custody for others	350	—
Annuities and income payable	1,855	—
Long-term liabilities—current portion	1,050	99
Total current liabilities	3,564	390
Noncurrent liabilities:		
Notes payable	600	
Bonds payable	24,000	220
Total noncurrent liabilities	24,600	220
Total liabilities	28,164	610
Net Assets		
Invested in capital assets, net of related debt	37,790	2,941
Restricted for:		
Nonexpendable:		
Scholarships and fellowships	10,496	—
Expendable:		
Research	1,459	228
Instructional department uses	3,417	—
Loans	756	—
Capital projects	2,185	91
Debt service	430	15
Unrestricted	(528)	1,471
Total net assets	$56,005	$4,746

Source: Adapted from GASB *Statement No. 35*, App. D.

Illustration 16–2

MIDWEST UNIVERSITY
STATEMENT OF REVENUES, EXPENSES,
AND CHANGES IN NET ASSETS
FOR THE YEAR ENDED JUNE 30, 2002
(IN THOUSANDS)

	Primary Institution	*Component Unit Hospital*
Revenues		
Operating revenues:		
Tuition and fees (net)	$ 2,690	
Patient services (net)		$4,629
Federal grants and contracts	35	747
Auxiliary enterprises	2,300	—
Other operating revenues	—	43
Total operating revenues	5,025	5,419
Expenses		
Operating expenses:		
Salaries and wages	5,346	2,699
Benefits	998	775
Scholarships and fellowships	135	—
Utilities	1,211	912
Supplies and other services	215	734
Depreciation	3,000	297
Other operating expenses	302	—
Total operating expenses	11,207	5,417
Operating income (loss)	(6,182)	2
Nonoperating Revenues (Expenses)		
Federal appropriations	438	—
State appropriations	4,170	—
Gifts—unrestricted and restricted	1,621	32
Investment income	975	49
Change in fair value of investments	189	—
Interest expense	(1,850)	(3)
Net nonoperating revenues	5,543	78
Income before changes in capital assets and endowments	(639)	80
Capital grants and gifts	220	71
Additions to permanent endowments	2,186	—
Increase in net assets	1,767	151
Net Assets		
Net assets—beginning of year	54,238	4,595
Net assets—end of year	$56,005	$4,746

Source: Adapted from GASB *Statement No. 35*, App. D.

Illustration 16–3

MIDWEST UNIVERSITY
STATEMENT OF CASH FLOWS
FOR THE YEAR ENDED JUNE 30, 2002
(IN THOUSANDS)

	Primary Institution	*Component Unit Hospital*
Cash Flows from Operating Activities		
Tuition and fees	$ 2,775	—
Research grants and contracts	35	—
Auxiliary enterprise income	2,300	—
Payments from insurance and patients	—	$1,858
Medicaid and Medicare	—	3,164
Payments to suppliers and others	(1,322)	(1,308)
Payments to students—scholarships	(135)	—
Payment to employees	(6,344)	(3,299)
Payment to annuitants	(250)	—
Other receipts (payments)	(447)	(100)
Net cash provided (used) by operating activities	(3,388)	315
Cash Flows from Noncapital Financing Activities		
Federal appropriations	438	—
State appropriations	4,170	—
Gifts and grants received for endowment purposes	4,192	—
Net cash flows provided by noncapital financing activities	8,800	—
Cash Flows from Capital and Related Financing Activities		
Capital grants and gifts received	220	71
Proceeds from capital debt	500	—
Purchase of capital assets	(1,490)	(195)
Principal paid on capital debt	(550)	(13)
Interest paid on capital debt	(1,850)	(3)
Net cash used by capital and related financing activities	(3,170)	(140)
Cash Flows from Investing Activities		
Proceeds from sales and maturities of investments	2,664	284
Investment income	975	7
Loans	(163)	—
Purchase of investments	(4,825)	(454)
Net cash provided (used) by investing activities	(1,349)	(163)
Net increase in cash	893	12
Cash—beginning of year	675	86
Cash—end of year	$ 1,568	$ 98

(Continued)

Illustration 16–3 *(concluded)*

MIDWEST UNIVERSITY
STATEMENT OF CASH FLOWS
FOR THE YEAR ENDED JUNE 30, 2002
(IN THOUSANDS)

	Primary Institution	*Component Unit Hospital*
Reconciliation of net operating revenues (expenses) to net cash provided (used) by operating activities:		
Operating income (loss)	$(6,182)	$ 2
Adjustments to reconcile net income (loss) to net cash provided (used) by operating activities:		
Depreciation expense	3,000	297
Change in assets and liabilities:		
Receivables, net	70	33
Inventories	(15)	(16)
Short-term investments	(128)	—
Deposit with bond trustee	(23)	—
Prepaid expenses	(9)	8
Accounts payable	119	(8)
Deferred revenue	15	—
Deposits held in custody for others	15	—
Annuities payable	(250)	(1)
Net cash provided (used) by operating activities	$(3,388)	$ 315

Source: Adapted from GASB *Statement No. 35*, App. D.

such as NACUBO's *FARM* (*Financial Accounting and Reporting Manual for Higher Education*), and AICPA Audit Guides while implementation guides are developed. Private colleges and universities follow the guidance in *SFAS Nos. 116* and *117*, as described later in this chapter and in Chapter 14. It might be helpful during the following discussion of selected elements of the financial statements to refer periodically to the illustrative financial statements for Midwest University (Illustrations 16–1 through 16–3), a hypothetical public or governmentally owned university, and to those of Valley College (Illustrations 16–4 through 16–6), a hypothetical private college. Differences between generally accepted accounting principles for public and private institutions will be noted where applicable.

Statement of Net Assets

Illustration 16–1 presents a Statement of Net Assets for a public, governmentally owned university, and Illustration 16–4 presents a Statement of Financial Position (or Balance Sheet) for a private college. Some of the accounting issues related to assets, liabilities, and net assets of colleges and universities are discussed next.

Unrestricted and Restricted Assets. Current resources available for use in carrying out operations directly related to the institution's educational objectives arise from the instruction, research, and public service activities of a college or university; as well as from residence halls, food services, intercollegiate athletics, student stores, and other auxiliary enterprises. Assets that are available for all purposes of the institution at the discretion of the governing board are *unrestricted.* Assets that are available for current operating purposes subject to limitations placed on them by persons or organizations outside the institution are *restricted.* Restricted assets arise from federal and other sponsored research grants, scholarship gifts, and other expendable restricted monies. For financial reporting purposes, unrestricted net assets are reported separately from restricted net assets.

Capital Assets. The general sources of capital assets are resources from external agencies, student fees and assessments for plant purposes, borrowings from external sources, investment income, and gifts restricted for plant. Long-lived assets are carried at cost, or at fair value at the date of acquisition in the case of assets acquired by gift. In the absence of historical cost records, the assets may be stated at historically based appraised values. The basis of valuation should be disclosed in the Notes to the Financial Statements.

GASB *Statement No. 35* requires that long-lived assets, including infrastructure assets (e.g., roads, bridges, tunnels, drainage systems, water and sewers, and lighting systems), be capitalized and depreciated. Depreciation of capital assets had been optional under the AICPA Audit Guide model, causing a difference in accounting between public colleges and universities and private colleges and universities that follow FASB *Statement No. 117*. Under GASB *Statement No. 35*, public colleges and universities may elect not to depreciate certain eligible infrastructure assets by adopting the "modified approach." In these cases, if the government uses an asset management system and documents that the eligible assets are being preserved at the level established in that system, then all expenditures incurred to preserve the eligible infrastructure assets at that level are expensed in the period incurred. See Chapter 5 for further discussion on capital assets and depreciation for governmental entities.

Capital assets are very often acquired with long-term debt. Under the AICPA College Guide model being superseded by GASB *Statement No. 35*, Plant Funds were used to account for capital assets, related debt, and debt service. Under *Statement No. 35*, public colleges and universities report capital assets, net of depreciation, in their Statement of Net Assets, as well as long-term debt incurred to acquire capital assets. The difference between capital assets, net, and related long-term debt is reported as Net Assets—Invested in Capital Assets, Net of Related Debt. Disclosures about capital asset activity that should be provided in the Notes to the Financial Statements include a schedule showing additions and retirements of land; infrastructure; buildings; furniture, fixtures, and equipment; library materials; capitalized collections; and related accumulated depreciation.

Collections. Many colleges and universities have historical archives, libraries, and museums containing valuable works of art, historical treasures, and similar assets. Both GASB *Statement No. 34* and FASB *Statement No. 116* provide for note disclosure of such assets rather than reporting them on the Balance Sheet; however, both standards permit nonrecognition only if the donated items are added to **collections** that meet the conditions given below:

a. Are held for public exhibition, education, or research in furtherance of public service rather than financial gain.

b. Are protected, kept unencumbered, cared for, and preserved.

c. Are subject to an organizational policy that requires the proceeds from sales of collection items to be used to acquire other items for collections.

The clear intent of the authoritative guidance is to permit nonrecognition of contributions of valuable collections *only* if the collection is to be maintained to serve the public interest rather than to achieve financial gain from trading in collectible items.

Liabilities. Short-term and long-term liabilities are reported in the Statement of Net Assets for colleges engaged in business-type activities or both business-type and governmental-type activities in their stand-alone reports. Long-term liabilities include leases, bonds payable (revenue bonds and general obligation bonds), compensated absences, and unpaid pension obligations. Disclosures about additions, reductions, the current portion of these long-term liabilities, and segments (identified in part by debt issues) should be provided in the Notes to the Financial Statements.

Net Assets. Three categories of net assets should be reported in the Statement of Net Assets for a public college or university: Invested in capital assets, net of related debt; restricted for nonexpendable and expendable purposes; and unrestricted. Private colleges and universities also report three categories of net assets, but those categories are unrestricted, temporarily restricted, and permanently restricted. Restricted net assets may arise from donors or resource providers stipulating that funds be used for scholarships and fellowships, research, instructional department uses, loans, capital projects, debt service, or other reasons. Some typical examples of restricted net assets are discussed in the following paragraphs.

Loan Assets. Assets that are loanable to students, faculty, and staff of an educational institution are provided by gifts, by grants, by income from endowments, and, in some cases, from loans made to the institution for that purpose. The intent is that the loan activities be operated on a self-sustaining basis: Repayment of loans and interest received on the loans are deposited and are then available for lending to other eligible persons. Interest earned on loans and interest earned on temporary investments of loan assets are expected to offset wholly or partially the cost of administration of loan activities and the loss from uncollectible loans.

Assets may be given to the institution under very specific restrictions as to who may receive loans; other assets may be used in accord with policies set by the governing board of the institution. Assets of the first kind are restricted; assets of the second kind are unrestricted. In each case, accounts and reports must be in detail sufficient to demonstrate that the donor's restrictions and board policies are being adhered to. Accordingly, separate accounts should be kept to show the amounts received from the various sources. Interest on loans should be credited on the full accrual basis to appropriate revenue accounts. Costs of administration of loan activities, losses on investments of loan assets, provision for losses on loans (either estimated or actual), and related expenses and losses serve to reduce loan net asset balances.

Endowments. Gifts whose principal is nonexpendable as of the date of reporting and is invested, or is available for investment, for the purpose of producing income are referred to as "endowments." Pure endowments are gifts for which donors or other external agencies have stipulated, as a condition of the gift, that the principal is to be maintained intact in perpetuity. The principal is invested in order to earn income. The use of the income may be restricted by the donor; if so, the income is considered as an addition to restricted net assets. If the use of the income is unrestricted, the income is considered to increase unrestricted net assets. **Term Endowments** are defined in the same manner as pure endowments, with the exception that the conditions of the gift provide that the assets are released from inviolability to permit all or a part of them to be expended on the happening of a particular event or the passage of a stated period of time. **Quasi-endowments** are assets segregated for endowment by the governing board of the institution to account for assets to be retained and invested. Since they are board-designated, the principal as well as the income may be utilized at the discretion of the board; therefore, quasi-endowments are unrestricted.

Traditionally, the investment objective of most educational institutions has been the preservation of principal and the production of dividend and interest income. More recently, a broadened concept of return on investments has developed that assumes that changes in market value of portfolio securities are also a part of return on assets. This concept is known as **total return,** the sum of net realized and unrealized appreciation or shrinkage in portfolio value plus dividend and interest yield. Total return has another aspect; this is the determination of **spending rate,** the proportion of total return that may prudently be used by an institution for current purposes. The adoption of total return as a policy requires the approval of legal counsel and formal approval of its governing board. The total return concept appears to be used by an increasing number of colleges and universities. In terms of balance sheet valuation, public colleges and universities are required to report investments at fair value, as required by GASB *Statement No. 31*. Private colleges and universities are also required by *SFAS No. 124* to report their investments at fair value.

Split-Interest Agreements. Colleges and universities are often parties to **split-interest agreements,** such as charitable lead and remainder trusts, charitable gift annuities, and pooled life income agreements. In these cases the institution shares either the income from an investment or the investment itself with the donor and sometimes other beneficiaries. These gifts may be established as trusts with the assets held by a third party. If the institution has an interest in an irrevocable split-interest agreement, then the assets received should be recorded at their fair value when received, or the present value of the interest in future income or assets should be recorded. Any liabilities agreed to, such as to pay the donor-stipulated amounts, should also be recorded at the time of the agreement. Chapter 6 of the AICPA Audit and Accounting Guide *Not-for-Profit Organizations* presents more detailed information on accounting for split-interest agreements for private colleges and universities.

Split-interest agreements are common forms of planned giving by donors, who are often alumni, to colleges and universities. **Annuity agreements** are used to account for assets given to an institution under conditions that bind the institution to pay stipulated amounts periodically to the donors, or other designated individuals, for a period of time specified in the agreements, or for the lifetime of the donor or other designated individual. **Life income agreements** are used to account for assets given to an institution under agreements that bind the institution to pay periodically to the donors, or other designated individuals, the total income earned by the donated assets for a period of time, usually the lifetimes of the income beneficiaries.

The acceptance of annuity funds by a nonprofit organization is subject to regulation by the Internal Revenue Service and, in many jurisdictions, by agencies of the appropriate state government. The Internal Revenue Code and Regulations state the conditions under which (for IRS purposes) an annuity trust may be established and administered. State agencies may specify the types of investments in which annuity assets may be invested. Investments received by the institution as a part of the principal of an annuity agreement should be recorded at fair value as of the date of receipt; any assets acquired subsequently by purchase should, of course, be recorded at cost. Liabilities include any indebtedness against the assets and also the present value of all expected annuity payments using appropriate actuarial assumptions.[8] If the liabilities recorded in this manner exceed the initial assets of the annuity agreement, it will start operations with deficit restricted net assets; if the initial assets exceed the liabilities to the annuitants, the annuity will result in positive restricted net assets. Entering into an annuity agreement that has initial deficit Net Assets would not appear to be in the institution's best interests. Agreements with potential donors of annuities should be carefully drawn by competent attorneys in consultation with competent accountants and investment managers in order to protect the interests of the receiving institution as well as the donor. The definition of *income* is one of the matters needing most careful attention. From

[8]NACUBO, *Financial Accounting and Reporting Manual for Higher Education* (FARM), Sec. 366.

the accounting point of view, *income* should be defined in accrual terms. It is also in the interest of the institution that an equitable allocation of indirect administrative expenses be permitted, as well as a deduction for direct expenses of administering each annuity.

Annuity payments are charged to the liability account. Periodically, an adjustment is made between the liability and restricted net assets to record the actuarial gain or loss due to recomputation of the liability based on revised life expectancy and anticipated return on investments. On termination of an annuity agreement, the principal of the annuity is transferred to the net asset category specified in the agreement; if the agreement is silent on the point, the principal of the terminated annuity fund should be transferred to unrestricted net assets and identified so readers of the financial statements will not infer that a new gift has been received.

Life income agreements differ from annuity agreements principally in that the life income fund agreement provides that the income earned by the assets donated will be paid to the donors over the specified period, rather than a stipulated amount. Since the amount to be paid periodically by a life income fund will vary from period to period as the income produced by the life income assets varies, it is not practicable or necessary to compute the present value of the stream of unknown future payments. Accordingly, the liabilities of life income agreements consist of life income payments currently due and any indebtedness against the life income assets. Assets are recorded on the basis of fair market value on the date of receipt of donated assets, or cost, in the case of purchased assets.

The amount credited to restricted net assets initially is, of course, the difference between the amount recorded for the assets and the amount recorded for the liabilities when the fund is established. An expense in the same amount as income from investments, computed as defined in the agreement, should be debited and liability accounts should be credited for any amount of income not yet paid to income beneficiaries. On termination of a life income agreement, the principal of the fund is handled in the manner described for terminated annuities.

The Internal Revenue Code and regulations provide for three variations of the life income "unitrust"—straight, net income, and net plus makeup. The technicalities of income tax law must be complied with by educational institutions with life income agreements in order to qualify for and maintain tax-exempt status. It is not possible in this brief treatment of life income funds to do more than alert the interested reader to the existence of IRS requirements.

Statement of Revenues, Expenses, and Changes in Net Assets

Revenues. Colleges and universities should recognize revenues on the accrual basis. Revenue accounts provided in the NACUBO chart of accounts include:

Tuition and Fees
Federal Appropriations
State Appropriations
Local Appropriations
Federal Grants and Contracts

State Grants and Contracts
Local Grants and Contracts
Private Gifts
Grants and Contracts
Endowment Income
Sales and Services of Educational Activities
Sales and Services of Auxiliary Enterprises
Sales and Services of Hospitals
Other Sources
Independent Operations

All of the account titles listed are control accounts and should be supported by appropriately named subsidiary accounts. For example, Tuition and Fees may be supported by subsidiary accounts for the regular session, summer school, extension, continuing education, and any other accounts providing useful information for a given educational institution. Gross tuition and fees should be recorded as a revenue even though some will be offset by fee remissions, scholarships, and fellowships. Actual refunds should be charged to the Tuition and Fees account. The AICPA Guide *Not-for-Profit Organizations*, which applies to private colleges and universities, requires that tuition revenue be reported net of tuition discounts and scholarships.[9] Public colleges and universities are currently assessing the guidance in footnote 41 of GASB *Statement No. 34* that would have them depart from the current practice of recording remissions, scholarships, and fellowships as Expenses rather than reductions of revenue; and discussing tuition discounting practices.

Also in regard to Tuition and Fees, it should be noted that because college fiscal years and academic years rarely coincide, it is common for tuition and fees collected near the end of a fiscal year to relate in large portion to services to be rendered by the institution during the ensuing fiscal year. Current recommendations of the AICPA and NACUBO indicate that revenues and related expenses that apply to an academic term encompassing two fiscal years should be recognized within the fiscal year in which the term is predominantly conducted.[10] At the end of the year in which revenue is received but not earned, it is reported in the year-end balance sheet as *Deferred Revenue*. As GASB *Statement No. 35* is fully implemented, institutions should use full accrual recognition principles.

Nonexchange Transactions. GASB *Statement No. 33* (discussed in Chapter 3), and *SFAS No. 116* (discussed in Chapter 14) provide guidance to public and private colleges and universities, respectively, when they are the recipients of gifts and grants in nonexchange transactions. Private colleges and universities may depend more on contributions from alumni and other supporters and research grants to

---

[9]AICPA, AAG-NPO, 12.05 and 13.07.
[10]NACUBO, *FARM*, Sec. 311.

keep tuition costs reasonable than do public institutions that receive relatively more state funding. However, this distinction is becoming less evident as public universities recognize the benefits of increasing endowments to decrease reliance on volatile state funding and constrained tuition support. For example, recent capital campaigns have brought the endowment balances at public universities (e.g., University of Texas System, $7.6 billion; and University of California, $3.8 billion) much closer to that of private colleges and universities (e.g., Harvard University, $13.0 billion; and Yale University, $6.6 billion).[11] Endowments are permanently restricted net assets that result from nonexchange transactions.

GASB *Statement No. 33*, *SFAS No. 116*, and the AICPA Audit and Accounting Guide *Not-for-Profit Organizations* distinguish between (1) nonexchange transactions, such as contributions in which the donor does not expect anything of value in return, and (2) exchange transactions in which there is *quid pro quo* or expectation by each party that goods or services will be exchanged between the parties at fair values. Contributions by donors are considered nonexchange transactions as long as the donor does not receive any direct benefits from the donation. Public colleges and universities recognize contributions as revenue when any eligibility requirements and time restrictions have been met. Private colleges and universities recognize contributions as income in the period in which they are made, and report increases as either unrestricted, temporarily restricted, or permanently restricted net assets, depending on the stipulation of the donor. If a contribution to a college or university is contingent upon a future event, such as obtaining matching funds, then the university waits until the condition has been met before recording the contribution revenue. This discussion applies to promises to give, even though they may not be legally enforceable; however, *intentions to give*, such as naming a university in a will, are not recognized as revenue or considered a promise because the potential donor can change the will at any time.

Grants, Awards, and Scholarships. Grants and other assistance given by governments, foundations, or corporations may be nonexchange or exchange transactions, depending upon whether the resource provider directly benefits by receiving something of value through the transaction. For example, a federal research grant given to a university in which the value received by the agency is incidental to the public benefit from using the assets transferred is considered a *nonexchange* transaction; consequently, it is recognized as revenue in the period in which the contribution is made and classified as an increase in expendable restricted net assets by a public college or university or as temporarily restricted net assets by a private college or university. On the other hand, if a federal agency enters into a contract in which the university tests a product and any patent or other results of the activity are retained by the federal agency, then that transaction would be considered an exchange transaction and not a contribution; consequently, this transaction results in an increase in unrestricted net assets because only donors in nonexchange

[11]*NACUBO Endowment Study* (Washington, DC: NACUBO, 1999).

transactions can restrict net assets.[12] Most colleges and universities report grants as exchange transactions, although the terms of the grant are critical in making this distinction.

Gifts in Kind. Contributions of noncash, tangible assets to a college or university are called **gifts in kind.**[13] If these gifts can be used or sold by the institution, they should be recorded in the period received at their fair value. If the donor has stipulated that the assets should be distributed to a third party and the school does not have discretion over the disposition of the assets, then the university is acting as an agent and the gift should not be recorded as a contribution. The university may also receive items, such as tickets or merchandise, that are to be given to the ultimate resource provider at a fund-raising event, for example, an auction for the university's public radio station. In these cases, the value of the contribution to be recognized is initially the fair value of the gift in kind plus any additional amount paid by the ultimate donor (i.e., the listener of the radio station). Of course, if the item is auctioned off for less than the initial fair value, then the contribution revenue should be decreased for the difference between the ultimate amount paid and the fair value at the date of the gift to the university.

Contributed Services. Although contributed service by unpaid volunteers is generally less important for colleges and universities than for other not-for-profit organizations, such as community service organizations and churches, some colleges and universities do utilize volunteers extensively for fund-raising and other activities, and, in the case of religious colleges, for instruction. *Statement No. 116* permits recognition of contributed services at their fair value if the services received create or enhance a nonfinancial asset (e.g., property and equipment); or (1) would need to be purchased by the organization, (2) require specialized skills, and (3) are provided by professionals with those skills. If these criteria are met, then the fair value of the services should be reported as both a contribution and as a salary expense. In any case, reporting the fair value of contributed services is encouraged, if practicable.[14] GASB standards are silent on the issue of reporting revenues and expenses relating to contributed services. Presumably public colleges and universities would also have executives or artists-in-residence who teach courses.

Expenses. Expenses should be recognized on the full accrual basis and can be classified on a natural basis (as seen in Illustration 16–2) or on a functional basis (as seen in Illustration 16–5). Functional classifications provided in the NACUBO chart of accounts for educational and general expenses include:

---

[12]AICPA, Audit and Accounting Guide, *Not-for-Profit Organizations* (AAG-NPO) (New York: AICPA, 1999), 5.16.

[13]Ibid., 5.06–5.08.

[14]Ibid., 5.39–5.40.

Instruction
Research
Public Service
Academic Support
Student Services
Institutional Support
Operation and Maintenance of Plant
Scholarships and Fellowships

Functional expense accounts are also provided for auxiliary enterprises, hospitals, and independent operations.

Within each of the functional expense account categories listed above, accounts are kept by organizational unit, project, or other classification that provides useful information for internal or external users of the financial statements. A third level of analysis of expenses is provided by an object classification—personnel compensation and supplies expense are suggested as object classifications in the NACUBO chart of accounts. Further detail under each of these object classifications is usually kept to facilitate planning and control. For example, "personnel compensation" may be subdivided into "salaries," "other personnel services," and "personnel benefits," with each of these further subdivided as desired by the administrators of a given college or university.

The AICPA Guide *Not-for-Profit Organizations*, pertinent to private colleges and universities, also requires that expenses that relate to more than one function, such as occupancy costs, including operation and maintenance of the plant, repairs and renovations, retirement of the plant, and interest and other expenses, be allocated to the programs or functional expenses to which they pertain.[15] It is not difficult to assign direct expenses, such as travel, to various functions; however, in order to allocate indirect expenses, such as occupancy costs or interest expense, a reasonable allocation basis must be employed. That basis may be square footage of space occupied by each program, or personnel costs. There appears to be a difference of opinion as to whether CPA firms consider the language in the AICPA Audit and Accounting Guide prescriptive or suggestive. For example, some institutions reported plant and interest costs as separate line or object items, rather than allocating them across programs in their audited financial statements.

Statement of Cash Flows

GASB *Statement No. 34*, applicable to public colleges and universities, requires a Statement of Cash Flows to be prepared using the direct method. Private colleges and universities have the option of preparing the statement using either the direct or indirect method, according to *SFAS No. 117*, as described in Chapter 14. Illustration 16–3 shows a Statement of Cash Flows for the sample public university.

---

[15]Ibid., 13.42–13.45.

Note that state appropriations are reported as nonoperating revenues in Illustration 16–2 and as Cash Flows from Noncapital Financing Activities in Illustration 16–3.

Segment Reporting

GASB *Statement Nos.* 34 and 35 require that public institutions that use business-type reporting present segment information in the Notes to the Financial Statements. A segment is an identifiable activity for which one or more revenue bonds or other revenue-backed debt instruments are outstanding; for example, revenue bonds for residence halls or bookstores. Required disclosures include a condensed Statement of Net Assets; Statement of Revenues, Expenses, and Changes in Net Assets; and Statement of Cash Flows. NACUBO initially expressed concern that identifying segments and their revenue pledges may be difficult when many debt issues are outstanding, resulting in a tremendous burden on institutions.[16]

Illustrative Transactions for Public (Governmentally Owned) Colleges and Universities

This section presents journal entries for selected illustrative transactions for Midwest University, a hypothetical public university engaged only in business-type activities and with a component unit hospital. Illustrative transactions for the primary institution are shown in this section; however, transactions for the component unit hospital are omitted for the sake of brevity. This information is then summarized in the financial statements presented earlier in the chapter in Illustrations 16–1 through 16–3. The account balances as of July 1, 2001, the beginning of Midwest University's fiscal year, are provided in the trial balance below.

	Debits	*Credits*
Cash and Cash Equivalents	$ 675,000	
Short-term Investments	300,000	
Accounts Receivable	198,000	
Allowance for Doubtful Accounts		$ 18,000
Loans Receivable	460,000	
Allowance for Doubtful Loans		10,000
Inventories	80,000	
Deposits with Trustees	350,000	
Prepaid Expenses	20,000	
Endowment Investments	8,250,000	
Other Long-Term Investments	6,913,000	
Capital Assets	86,745,000	

[16]NACUBO, Letter of August 20, 1999, to the GASB at http://www.nacubo.org/website/members/letters.

	Debits	Credits
Accumulated Depreciation	$	$ 21,795,000
Accounts Payable		140,000
Accrued Liabilities		15,000
Deposits Held in Custody for Others		335,000
Deferred Revenue		20,000
Annuities and Income Payable		1,720,000
Notes Payable		700,000
Bonds Payable		25,000,000
Net Assets—Invested in Capital Assets, Net of Related Debt		39,250,000
Net Assets—Restricted for Scholarships—Nonexpendable		8,310,000
Net Assets—Restricted for Research		350,000
Net Assets—Restricted for Department Uses		2,990,000
Net Assets—Restricted for Loans		568,000
Net Assets—Restricted for Capital Projects		1,965,000
Net Assets—Restricted for Debt Service		385,000
Net Assets—Unrestricted		420,000
Totals	$103,991,000	$103,991,000

Note: Net Assets—Restricted are expendable unless otherwise noted.

Current Operating Transactions

During the fiscal year ended June 30, 2002, Accounts Receivable were recorded for the following revenue items:

Tuition and Fees	$2,670,000
Federal Appropriations	230,000
State Appropriations	2,150,000
Federal Grants and Contracts	35,000
Gifts	40,000
Investment Income	880,000
Sales and Services of Auxiliary Enterprises	2,300,000
Total	$8,305,000

In addition, Deferred Revenues in the amount of $20,000 reported in the beginning trial balance is reclassified as Revenues—Tuition and Fees, as that amount was collected in the preceding year from students for summer classes offered predominantly in the current year.

Entry 1 records the recognition of this revenue, assuming that the existing balance of Allowance for Doubtful Accounts is adequate to cover the estimated uncollectibles.

	Debits	Credits
1. Accounts Receivable	8,305,000	
Deferred Revenues	20,000	
Revenues—Tuition and Fees		2,690,000
Revenues—Federal Appropriations		230,000
Revenues—State Appropriations		2,150,000
Revenues—Federal Grants and Contracts		35,000
Revenues—Gifts Unrestricted		40,000
Revenues—Investment Income		880,000
Revenues—Auxiliary Enterprises		2,300,000

Entry 2 records the collections of cash for accounts receivable amounting to $8,348,000 during the current year.

	Debits	Credits
2. Cash	8,348,000	
Accounts Receivable		8,348,000

Entry 3 records operating expenses incurred in accomplishing the educational goals of the university: instruction, research, and public service. This university chooses to report expenses by natural (object or line-item) categories, rather than functional categories. One disadvantage to this approach is that Auxiliary Enterprise revenues are separately identified, but not the related expenses.

	Debits	Credits
3. Salaries and Wages Expense	4,321,000	
Benefits Expense	998,000	
Scholarships and Fellowships Expense	135,000	
Utilities Expense	1,160,000	
Supplies and Other Services Expense	508,000	
Accounts Payable		508,000
Accrued Liabilities		6,614,000

Accounts payable and accrued liabilities were paid in the amounts of $456,000 and $6,629,000, respectively. Refunds of students' deposits amounted to $5,000.

	Debits	Credits
4. Accounts Payable	456,000	
Accrued Liabilities	6,629,000	
Deposits Held in Custody for Others	5,000	
Cash		7,090,000

Inventories and prepaid expenses increased during the year in the amounts shown in Entry 5. These increases reduced Expenses as shown.

	Debits	Credits
5. Inventories	15,000	
Prepaid Expenses	9,000	
Supplies and Other Services Expense		24,000

Short-term investments in the amount of $100,000 were purchased during the year. The investments account was increased by an additional $28,000 for interest earnings accrued at June 30, 2002. Note that investment income is reported as nonoperating revenue in the Statement of Revenues, Expenses, and Changes in Net Assets, presented in Illustration 16–2.

	Debits	Credits
6. Short-term Investments	128,000	
Cash		100,000
Revenues—Investment Income		28,000

Entry 7 records the accrual of educational and general expenses relating to university programs at June 30, 2002, in the amounts as shown.

	Debits	Credits
7. Utilities Expense	51,000	
Supplies and Other Services Expense	21,000	
Accounts Payable		65,000
Accrued Liabilities		7,000

Near the end of the current year, the university collected tuition and fees in the amount of $35,000 for classes to be offered in a term to be held predominantly in the following year. In conformity with prevailing practice, the university recognizes a liability of $35,000 and will recognize the entire amount as revenue in the following year.

	Debits	Credits
8. Cash	35,000	
Deferred Revenues		35,000

Entry 9 records private gifts that are fully expendable but restricted for the purpose of research.

	Debits	Credits
9. Cash	1,034,000	
Accounts Receivable	75,000	
Revenues—Gifts Restricted for Research		1,109,000

Expenses for the restricted research purposes described in Entry 9 were incurred during the period in the amount of $1,025,000 as shown in Entry 10.

	Debits	Credits
10. Salaries and Wages Expense	1,025,000	
Accrued Liabilities		10,000
Cash		1,015,000

Cash was received in the amount of $102,000 from various grantors, including the $55,000 billed in the previous year.

	Debits	Credits
11. Cash	102,000	
Accounts Receivable		102,000

Long-term investments were purchased in the amount of $15,000:

	Debits	Credits
12. Long-term Investments	15,000	
Cash		15,000

Loan Transactions

Loan assets consist primarily of cash, investments, and receivables resulting from loans to students, faculty, and staff. Net assets are often received as refundable grants from the federal government, and in other cases, designations by the university of its own unrestricted net assets. Entry 13 records Federal Appropriations that will increase Net Assets—Restricted for Loans.

	Debits	Credits
13. Cash	208,000	
Revenues—Federal Appropriations		208,000

Loans were made during the year in the amount of $260,000, and other loans were repaid in the amount of $95,000 with an additional amount of $7,000 received as interest revenue on these loans, as shown in Entries 14a and b.

	Debits	Credits
14a. Loans Receivable	260,000	
Cash		260,000
14b. Cash	102,000	
Loans Receivable		95,000
Revenues—Investment Income		7,000

Endowment Transactions

Midwest University has endowment funds for which the donors have stipulated that the principal must remain intact in perpetuity, and the investment income is restricted for scholarships and fellowships. Additional endowment gifts were received during the year in the amount of $2,186,000 as shown in Entry 15.

	Debits	Credits
15. Cash	2,186,000	
Revenues—Additions to Permanent Endowments		2,186,000

Long-term investments with a carrying value of $2,000,000 were sold for $2,159,000; the gain on the sale was accounted for as "Change in Fair Value of Investments" which will be reported along with investment revenue in the operating statement. Investments costing $4,200,000 were purchased. Investment income earned on these assets during the year was included in Entry 1.

	Debits	Credits
16a. Cash	2,159,000	
Endowment Investments		2,000,000
Revenues—Change in Fair Value of Investments		159,000
16b. Endowment Investments	4,200,000	
Cash		4,200,000

It should be noted that many public universities maintain separate foundations that have the objective of obtaining contributions and endowments. In those cases, note disclosure should disclose the existence of those foundations, and the amount of investment income or other monies received from them. Related entities are discussed later in this chapter.

Annuity and Life Income Transactions

Midwest University has a large balance in the Annuities and Income Payable account. The amount represents the present value of future payments due under the annuity agreements. For simplicity, we assume that the annuitants of these split interest gifts have restricted the use of these gifts, when conditions are met, for university department use. Split interest agreements are discussed more fully in Chapter 14.

During the fiscal year ended June 30, 2002, cash in the amount of $487,000 was received from new annuity fund contributors. The actuarial annuities payable relating to these annuities were $385,000; the remainder are restricted gifts that will increase Net Assets—Restricted for Department Uses, as shown in Entry 17.

	Debits	Credits
17. Cash	487,000	
Revenues—Gifts Restricted for Department Uses		102,000
Annuities and Income Payable		385,000

Also, during the year, annuitants were paid $250,000 and additional long-term investments were purchased in the amount of $225,000.

	Debits	Credits
18. Annuities and Income Payable	250,000	
Cash		250,000
19. Long-term Investments	225,000	
Cash		225,000

In addition, new Life Income Annuities were received in the amount of $325,000. In these arrangements, all investment income is given to the donor for his or her lifetime (or some specified date), at which time the assets revert to the university. The cash was invested in the amount shown in Entry 21.

	Debits	Credits
20. Cash	325,000	
Revenues—Gifts Restricted for Department Uses		325,000
21. Long-term Investments	325,000	
Cash		325,000

Additional entries would be required for the receipt of investment income and the simultaneous recording of expenses and liabilities for income to be transferred to the life income recipients. Note that these expenses are incurred only during the period income is earned.

Capital Assets Transactions

Midwest University uses one general ledger control account called Capital Assets to record transactions involving Land, Land Improvements, Buildings, Equipment, and Library Books, Construction in Progress, and Infrastructure, as well as another control account for Accumulated Depreciation. Of course, detailed subsidiary ledgers are also maintained.

Cash for construction of a new laboratory building was received from a state grant in the amount of $220,000 and issuance at par of 8 percent term bonds maturing in five years in the amount of $500,000.

	Debits	Credits
22. Cash	720,000	
Bonds Payable		500,000
Revenues—Capital Grants and Gifts		220,000

Long-term investments with a carrying value of $475,000 were sold for $505,000. Realized gains are accounted for as Change in Fair Value of Investments. Other investment income was received in the amount of $60,000.

	Debits	Credits
23a. Cash	505,000	
Long-term Investments		475,000
Revenues—Change in Fair Value of Investments		30,000
23b. Cash	60,000	
Revenues—Investment Income		60,000

During the year, construction costs for the laboratory building and other projects amounted to $1,200,000. The projects were completed by year-end. Other renovations and replacements were made totaling $300,000; however, none of these met the criteria to be capitalized.

	Debits	Credits
24a. Capital Assets	1,200,000	
Cash		1,200,000
24b. Other Operating Expenses	300,000	
Cash		300,000

Cash in the amount of $2,065,000 was received for the service of debt, as detailed in Entry 25.

	Debits	Credits
25. Cash	2,065,000	
Revenues—State Appropriation		2,020,000
Revenues—Gifts Restricted for Debt Service		45,000

Interest and principal payments were made on notes and bonds payable as shown in Entry 26.

	Debits	Credits
26. Interest Expense	1,850,000	
Bonds Payable	500,000	
Notes Payable	50,000	
Cash		2,400,000

During the year, there was an increase in cash deposited with trustees handling debt service in the amount of $23,000.

	Debits	Credits
27. Deposits with Trustees	23,000	
Cash		23,000

A review of capital asset acquisitions revealed that $250,000 of Equipment and $40,000 of Library Books were included in the amount recorded in Entry 3 for Supplies and Other Services Expenses. These expenses meet the criteria established by the Board for capitalization.

	Debits	Credits
28. Capital Assets	290,000	
Supplies and Other Services Expenses		290,000

Certain facilities that were fully depreciated were scrapped.

	Debits	Credits
29. Accumulated Depreciation	210,000	
Capital Assets		210,000

Agency Transactions

Student groups and others deposited $130,000 with the University; $110,000 in withdrawals were made; and $60,000 in cash was invested for the long term.

	Debits	Credits
30. Cash	130,000	
Deposits Held in Custody for Others		130,000
31. Deposits Held in Custody for Others	110,000	
Cash		110,000

	Debits	Credits
32. Long-term Investments	60,000	
Cash		60,000

Detailed records should be kept for each student group and for others for which the college or university is acting as agent.

Adjusting Entries

At the end of the year, a pre-audit review of the accounts receivable indicate that the Allowance for Doubtful Accounts is sufficient. For the sake of simplicity, we assume that the fair value of Endowment and Long-Term Investments is equal to the amount recorded in the accounts; consequently, there is no adjusting journal entry to record a change in fair value, as required by GASB *Statement No. 31*.

Allowance for Uncollectible Loans is increased for expected write-offs in the amount of $2,000.

33. Other Operating Expenses	2,000	
Allowance for Uncollectible Loans		2,000

Capital assets are depreciated as shown in Entry 34.

34. Depreciation Expense	3,000	
Accumulated Depreciation		3,000

The current portion of long-term liabilities is reclassified.

35. Notes Payable	50,000	
Bonds Payable	1,000,000	
Current Portion of Long-term Liabilities		1,050,000

Closing Entries

All revenue and expense accounts were closed to Unrestricted Net Assets.

37. Revenues—Tuition and Fees	2,690,000	
Revenues—Federal Grants and Contracts	35,000	
Revenues—Auxiliary Enterprises	2,300,000	
Revenues—Federal Appropriations	438,000	
Revenues—State Appropriations	4,170,000	
Revenues—Gifts Unrestricted	40,000	
Revenues—Gifts Restricted for Department Uses	427,000	
Revenues—Gifts Restricted for Debt Service	45,000	
Revenues—Gifts Restricted for Research	1,109,000	
Revenues—Investment Income	975,000	
Revenues—Change in Fair Value of Investments	189,000	
Revenues—Capital Grants and Gifts	220,000	
Revenues—Additions to Permanent Endowments	2,186,000	
Salaries and Wages Expense		5,346,000
Benefits Expense		998,000
Scholarships and Fellowships Expense		135,000
Utilities Expense		1,211,000
Supplies and Other Services Expense		215,000
Depreciation Expense		3,000,000
Interest Expense		1,850,000
Other Operating Expense		302,000
Net Assets—Unrestricted		1,767,000

Restricted Net Assets are adjusted to the correct balances.

	Debits	Credits
38. Net Assets—Unrestricted	2,715,000	
Net Assets—Invested in Capital Assets	1,460,000	
Net Assets—Restricted for Capital Projects		220,000
Net Assets—Restricted for Scholarships and Fellowships—Nonexpendable		2,186,000
Net Assets—Restricted for Research		1,109,000
Net Assets—Restricted for Department Uses		427,000
Net Assets—Restricted for Loans		188,000
Net Assets—Restricted for Debt Service		45,000

Private (Nongovernmentally Owned) Colleges and Universities

Setting accounting and financial reporting standards for private colleges and universities, as noted at the beginning of this chapter, is the responsibility of the FASB. Until 1993, with the exception that private colleges and universities were required by FASB *Statement No. 93* to report depreciation of their plant assets, most colleges and universities, both public and private, used the AICPA College Guide model. The issuance of FASB *Statement No. 116*, "Accounting for Contributions Received and Contributions Made," and FASB *Statement No. 117*, "Financial Statements of Not-for-Profit Organizations," in 1993, marked a significant divergence in the accounting and reporting standards applicable to public and private colleges and universities; however, there will be less divergence as public colleges and universities implement GASB *Statement No. 35*.

Private colleges and universities now report on the changes in unrestricted, temporarily restricted, and permanently restricted net assets of the entity as a whole, as do the other nongovernmental not-for-profit organizations described in Chapter 14. The reader is directed back to that chapter for more information on the definitions of net asset classifications and the considerable discretion that is allowed by *SFAS No. 117* in presenting financial information, including optional display of supplementary fund accounting information, if desired. Some of the major differences that now exist between the financial statements of private and public institutions of higher education are in the areas of classification of net assets, format of the operating statement, cash flows statement, investments, pension disclosures, and compensated absences. These differences are similar to those differences between private and public health care organizations described in Illustration 17–2, now that the 1973 AICPA Audit Guide is no longer used for external financial reporting guidance.

Illustrations 16–4, 16–5, and 16–6 present the Statement of Financial Position, Statement of Activities, and Statement of Cash Flows, respectively, for Valley College, a hypothetical private not-for-profit college.

Illustration 16–4

VALLEY COLLEGE
STATEMENT OF FINANCIAL POSITION
JUNE 30, 2002

Assets	
Cash and cash equivalents	$ 1,590,953
Accrued interest on investments	1,344,201
Accounts receivable, less allowance for doubtful accounts of $8,833	588,840
Inventories, at average cost	969,287
Prepaid expenses	415,556
Loans receivable, less allowance for doubtful loans of $52,600	1,906,535
Pledges receivable, less allowance for doubtful pledges of $50,000	5,550,000
Long-term investments, at fair value, cost of $150,645,430	161,785,400
Property, plant, and equipment, net of accumulated depreciation of $10,174,082	23,417,628
Total Assets	$197,568,400
Liabilities and Net Assets	
Liabilities:	
Accounts payable and accrued expenses	$ 1,481,908
Deposits and agency funds	385,476
Annuities payable	1,408,550
Deferred revenue	62,237
Advances from federal government for student loans	124,557
Notes payable	889,934
Bonds payable	5,500,000
Total Liabilities	9,852,662
Net Assets:	
Unrestricted	73,690,687
Temporarily restricted	23,279,442
Permanently restricted	90,745,609
Total Net Assets	187,715,738
Total Liabilities and Net Assets	$197,568,400

Other Accounting Issues

Performance Measures

The performance of the organization is monitored by decision makers, such as internal management (e.g., administrators), oversight bodies (e.g., governing boards, accrediting agencies), funding sources (e.g., governments, donors, grantors, investors), and constituents with a beneficial interest in the school (e.g., students, faculty, alumni). The extent to which these stakeholders use financial information

Illustration 16–5

VALLEY COLLEGE
STATEMENT OF ACTIVITIES
YEAR ENDED JUNE 30, 2002

	Unrestricted	Temporarily Restricted	Permanently Restricted	Total
Operating Revenues and Gains:				
Student tuition and fees (net)	$ 1,348,685	$ —	$—	$ 1,348,685
Government grants for student aid	1,166,566	—	—	1,166,566
Endowment income	6,112,895	—	—	6,112,895
Gifts and donations	2,341,276	—	—	2,341,276
Sales and services of auxiliary enterprises	7,440,722	—	—	7,440,722
Capital gains on investments utilized	258,002	—	—	258,002
Net assets released from restriction	756,194	(756,194)	—	—
Total operating revenues and gains	19,424,340	(756,194)		18,668,146
Operating Expenses and Losses:				
Educational and general expense:				
Instruction	4,581,405	—	—	4,581,405
Public service	1,236,283	—	—	1,236,283
Academic support	149,158	—	—	149,158
Student services	2,830,384	—	—	2,830,384
Institutional support	3,045,734	—	—	3,045,734
Total educational and general expense	11,842,964			11,842,964
Auxiliary enterprises	7,435,036	—	—	7,435,036
Annuity and life income payments	412,648	—	—	412,648
Total operating expenses and losses	19,690,648			19,690,648
Excess of operating expenses and losses over operating revenues and gains	(266,308)	(756,194)		(1,022,502)
Nonoperating Activities:				
Gifts and bequests	2,255,736	1,247,639	882,006	4,385,381
Investment income	587,223	407,481	110,515	1,105,219
Capital gains utilized	3,717,237	173,025	5,389,703	9,279,965
Net assets reclassified from temporarily restricted net assets	—	(28,741)	28,741	—
Matured annuity and life income funds	21,746	(57,346)	35,600	—
Change in net assets from nonoperating activities	6,581,942	1,742,058	6,446,565	14,770,565
Total change in net assets	6,315,634	985,864	6,446,565	13,748,063
Net assets at beginning of year	67,375,053	22,293,578	84,299,044	173,967,675
Net assets at end of year	$73,690,687	$23,279,442	$90,745,609	$187,715,738

to make their decisions, and the most useful form of financial reporting, continue to be accounting research questions. The objective of audited annual financial statements is to assure that statements conform to generally accepted accounting

Illustration 16–6

VALLEY COLLEGE
STATEMENT OF CASH FLOWS
YEAR ENDED JUNE 30, 2002

Cash Flows from Operating Activities:	
Increase in net assets	$ 13,748,063
Adjustments to reconcile increase in net assets to net cash provided by operating activities:	
Depreciation	878,843
Decrease in pledges receivable	207,500
Decrease in accounts receivable	52,701
Increase in accounts payable and accrued expenses	110,987
Increase in deposits and agency funds	22,366
Increase in annuities payable	355,300
Decrease in deferred revenue	(10,621)
Decrease in advances from federal government	(15,177)
Increase in accrued interest receivable	(922,455)
Increase in prepaid expenses	(161,492)
Increase in inventories	(60,534)
Net capital gains used	(9,537,967)
Interest and dividends restricted for long-term investment	(804,467)
Contributions restricted for long-term investment	(4,603,338)
Adjustment of actuarial liability for annuities payable	(25,395)
Net cash used for operating activities	(765,686)
Cash Flows from Investing Activities:	
Proceeds from sale of investments	136,802,105
Purchases of investments	(141,199,838)
Purchases of property, plant, and equipment	(1,380,016)
Loans to students and faculty	(283,781)
Collections of loans to students and faculty	132,725
Net cash used for investing activities	(5,928,805)
Cash Flows from Financing Activities:	
Proceeds from contributions restricted for long-term investment	4,603,338
Issuance of long-term debt	3,000,000
Repayment of long-term debt	(3,021,687)
Interest and dividends restricted for long-term investment	804,467
Increase in long-term loans receivable	(151,043)
Net cash provided by financing activities	5,235,075
Net increase in cash and cash equivalents	(1,459,416)
Cash and cash equivalents, beginning of year	3,050,369
Cash and cash equivalents, end of year	$ 1,590,953

principles, not to document whether the organization performed efficiently. Consequently, other methods of measuring and reporting performance are being developed.

Public colleges and universities are encouraged to present nonfinancial and nonquantitative information, such as service efforts and accomplishments information, that document how well the organization accomplished its mission.[17] However, many accrediting agencies, and a few states, are requiring assessment of student outcomes, sometimes as a determining factor in funding levels. Some states are requiring standardized norm-based objective exams, although more often the institution is allowed to develop its own measure of outcomes based on mission-based objectives. This approach recognizes that the mission of higher education institutions differs in the weight each one places on instruction, research, and service. Outputs, for example, might be faculty productivity, number of graduates, or job placements.[18] Outcomes differ from outputs in that they measure the benefits derived by constituents, such as increased knowledge of students. NACUBO, as well as many universities, have projects on benchmarking for process improvement. The best measures would be those that capture the "value added" to the student through the educational process. Although difficult, many universities are measuring the knowledge and skills of students through pretesting upon entering school, and posttesting as the student reaches graduation.[19] There is more discussion about performance evaluation in Chapter 13.

The financial community, through bond-rating agencies, financial analysts, underwriters, and investors, has always evaluated financial performance and the creditworthiness of public institutions that issue tax-exempt debt. Some key ratios they use to evaluate viability, return, and leverage are (1) expendable resources to debt, (2) unrestricted resources to operations, (3) expendable resources to total net assets, (4) total resources per full-time-equivalent student, and (5) maximum debt service coverage.[20]

Auditing of Colleges and Universities

Most colleges and universities, whether private or public, publish audited financial statements. At a minimum, audits of colleges and universities will be performed in conformity with the generally accepted auditing standards (GAAS) promulgated by the AICPA, as discussed in Chapter 11. Additionally, many colleges and universities, as a condition of accepting federal financial awards, are audited under the auditing standards established by the U.S. General Accounting Office in its publication *Government Auditing Standards* (GAS), also known as the "yellow book," as discussed in Chapter 11. Specifically, if a college or university expends $300,000 or more in federal awards in a given fiscal year, it must have a "single audit" in accordance with the provisions of Office of Management and Budget (OMB) *Circular A-133*, "Audits of States, Local Governments and Nonprofit Organizations." Since

[17]Governmental Accounting Standards Board, *Concepts Statement No. 2*, "Service Efforts and Accomplishments" (Norwalk, CT: GASB, 1994).

[18]Ken Brown and Mary Fischer, "Assessment Measures: Management's Yardstick," *Assessment and Evaluation in Higher Education* 19, no. 3 (1994), pp. 163–74.

[19]J. Gainen and P. Locatelli, *Assessment in the Accounting Curriculum* (Sarasota, FL: AAA, 1995).

[20]See Engstrom and Esmond-Kiger, "Different Formats," pp. 24–25.

the audit requirements for the single audit are described in considerable detail in Chapter 11, they need not be reiterated here.

An item of special emphasis in auditing colleges and universities is to ensure that costs that are unallowable under OMB *Circular A-21*, "Cost Principles for Educational Institutions," are not charged, either as direct costs or indirect costs, to federal grants or contracts. Since 1993, the federal government has devoted an increasing amount of resources to auditing educational institutions that receive federal assistance, in particular their compliance with OMB *Circular A-21*, as well as unrelated business income. The cost principles and administrative requirements under OMB *Circular A-110* are discussed more fully in Chapter 13. Unrelated business income is discussed in Chapter 15. As with single audits of state and local governments, *Circular A-133* audits place heavy emphasis on evaluating the system of internal controls and compliance with applicable laws and regulations, in addition to the traditional audit of the financial statements.

Federal Financial Assistance

The federal government, and sometimes state governments, supports institutions of higher learning in the form of research grants and student loan funds. As mentioned in the previous section on auditing issues, acceptance of federal funds requires reporting back to the grantor and conformance with various cost accounting rules as well as administrative requirements.

Sponsored Research Funds. Research funds received from the federal government are most likely to be in the form of grants in which the government is expecting performance and a report at the end of the grant period as to how the funds were used. In some instances, the organization may contract with the federal government for a specific product for the funds paid. The terms of the grant or contract are critical factors in determining whether it is an exchange or a nonexchange transaction.

Student Grants and Loans. Student assistance takes various forms: loans or grants, subsidized or unsubsidized, held by the institution or given directly to the student. A Pell grant is one in which the federal government provides funds to the institution, which then selects the recipient.[21] Additional guidance is available to the auditor in U.S. Department of Education documents, such as *Compliance Audits (Attestation Engagements) of the Federal Student Financial Assistance Program at Participating Institutions* (1997).

Related Entities

Public and private colleges and universities can be complex in their organizational structure, including majority-owned subsidiaries for intellectual property and businesslike enterprises; medical and research facilities; and controlled affiliates for fund-raising, alumni relations, and management of assets. At issue is whether there is sufficient control of one organization over another to combine their financial information under one reporting entity.

---

[21]Catalog of Federal Domestic Assistance (CFDA) #84.063.

Most institutionally related fund-raising and medical foundations are legally separate organizations independent of the public university they serve and, under the criterion established in GASB standards, would not be reported as a component entity of the university.[22] However, it may be misleading to exclude the foundation from the public university's reports if the foundation operates essentially as an agent of the university and is not fiscally independent. At a minimum, note disclosures should be made in the public university's financial report of the existence of these affiliated organizations. Private colleges and universities, although less likely to have independent fund-raising foundations, often have affiliated organizations that should be disclosed in the Notes to the Financial Statements. The FASB's project on consolidations and related entities applies to nongovernmental nonprofit organizations, such as private schools, as well as for-profit entities. The GASB also has a project on affiliated organizations.

Key Terms

Annuity agreements, 734
Collections, 732
Gifts in kind, 738
Life income agreements, 734
Quasi-endowments, 733
Spending rate, 733
Split-interest agreements, 734
Term endowments, 733
Total return, 733

Selected References

American Institute of Certified Public Accountants. *Audits of Colleges and Universities.* New York: AICPA, 1973, reprinted in 1994.

________. *Statement of Position 74-8.* New York, 1974.

Financial Accounting Standards Board. *Statement of Financial Accounting Standards No. 116.* "Accounting for Contributions Received and Contributions Made." Norwalk, CT, 1993.

________. *Statement of Financial Accounting Standards No. 117.* "Financial Statements of Not-for-Profit Organizations." Norwalk, CT, 1993.

Governmental Accounting Standards Board. *Codification of Governmental Accounting and Financial Reporting Standards as of June 30, 1999.* Norwalk, CT, 1999.

________. *Financial Accounting and Reporting Manual for Higher Education* (FARM). Washington, DC. In loose-leaf form with bimonthly updates.

National Center for Higher Education Management Systems. *Higher Education Finance Manual.* Washington, DC: U.S. Government Printing Office, 1980.

[22] GASB, *Codification*, Sec. 2100.119.

Periodicals:
Business Officer. Washington, DC: NACUBO.
The Chronicle of Higher Education. Washington, DC.
Higher Education Director. Falls Church, VA: Higher Education Publications, Inc.

Questions

16–1. Many colleges and universities are governmentally owned; others are privately supported not-for-profit organizations. What bearing does this situation have on the determination of authoritative financial reporting standards for colleges and universities?

16–2. Explain how restricted gifts and grants are accounted for by a public college or university. How would such restricted gifts and grants be accounted for and reported by a private college or university that follows FASB *Statement Nos. 116* and *117*?

16–3. Explain why a governmentally owned college or university may continue to use the AICPA College Guide fund accounting model for internal purposes.

16–4. Describe typical revenue-generating activities of a college or university.

16–5. "Colleges and universities are deemed to be presenting financial statements in conformity with GAAP if they report short-term investments at fair value and long-term investments of endowments or permanently restricted net assets at cost or amortized cost." Do you agree? Why or why not?

16–6. "Endowments of public colleges and universities should be accounted for in the same manner as permanent trust funds of state and local governments." Do you agree? Why or why not?

16–7. Explain fully accounting for capital assets of a public college or university.

16–8. "Under FASB standards applicable to private colleges and universities, *all* contributions must be recognized as revenues or gains in the period received." Do you agree? Why or why not?

16–9. Explain the conditions that must exist for a public or private college or university to avoid accounting recognition of the value of its collections of art, historical treasures, and similar assets.

16–10. Contrast and compare the financial statements required by the FASB for private colleges and universities with those required for public colleges and universities.

16–11. Describe some measures of performance that can be used in assessing whether a university operates effectively.

Cases

16–1. Component units. The following is a section taken from the Notes to the Comprehensive Annual Financial Report of the State of Michigan for the fiscal year ended September 30, 1999:

Note 1—Summary of Significant Accounting Policies
A. *Reporting Entity* (selected)
Ten of the State's public universities are considered component units because they have boards appointed by the primary government. These universities all follow the American Institute of Certified Public Accountants Industry Audit Guide, *Audits of Colleges and Universities* (the AICPA model). The universities' operating results are reflected in the Combined Statement of Changes in Fund Balances and the Combined Statement of Current Funds Revenues, Expenditures, Transfers, and Changes in Fund Balances. These statements are unique to the AICPA model and only a "Component Units" column appears on these statements because the State has no institutions of higher education which are part of the primary government . . . Michigan State University, the University of Michigan, and Wayne State University are not included in the State's reporting entity because they have separately elected governing boards and are legally separate. The State provides significant funding to support these institutions; however, under the GASB *Statement No. 14* criteria they are considered fiscally independent special purpose governments. All of the State's component units issue their own separately issued audited financial statements.

Required

a. Which criteria under GASB *Statement No. 14* do you expect that the three universities *not* included in the State's CAFR fail to meet? (Hint: Review the GASB *Statement No. 14* criteria in Chapter 9.)

b. What other relationships between states and their public institutions of higher learning might you expect to find (for example, between the State of California and the University of California and California State University systems)?

c. How useful is the *discrete* method of presenting college and university component units (as opposed to *blending* component units with the State's financial information) if the column in the general purpose financial statements entitled "Component Units" includes the 10 institutions of higher learning and authorities for the bridges, state parks, housing development, and higher education student loans?

16–2. Comparison of Public and Private Universities. You have recently been hired as the financial manager of Marywood University, a private university in an urban area. Your previous experience has been with Southern State University, a public university in the area. In order to familiarize yourself with the differences between the audited financial statements of this private university, which follows *SFAS No. 117*, and the public university, which follows GASB *Statement No. 35*, you are comparing Marywood University's Statement of Activities to the Southern State University's Statement of Revenues, Expenses, and Changes in Net Assets shown on the next pages. Student enrollment at the private university is approximately 4,100 and at the public university approximately 23,000.

Required

a. List some of the differences between the format of the two operating statements for the year that are immediately evident.

b. What proportion of the total revenues of Marywood University come from tuition and fees versus state appropriations versus other income? How does that compare to Southern State University?

c. What proportion of all the private gifts, grants, and contracts are in the form of endowments? How does that compare to the public university? Can you tell how much each institution earns on its endowments?

d. What proportion of all of Marywood University's expenses are spent for the educational programs as opposed to that spent on supporting the programs (e.g., general and administrative and fund-raising expenses)? How does that compare with the public university?

e. Which university appears to have had a better year from the perspective of financial activities? Why?

MARYWOOD UNIVERSITY
STATEMENT OF ACTIVITIES
YEAR ENDED JUNE 30, 2002
(IN THOUSANDS)

	Unrestricted	*Temporarily Restricted*	*Permanently Restricted*	*Totals*
Revenues, gains, and other support:				
Tuition and fees (net of scholarships of $805,113)	$15,359	$ —	$ —	$15,359
State appropriation	525	—	—	525
Government grants and contracts	748	—	—	748
Private gifts, grants, and contracts	952	630	257	1,839
Pledges	40	458	63	561
Investment income	1,196	3	—	1,199
Realized gain from investments	3,310	—	—	3,310
Auxiliary enterprises	689	—	—	689
Other sources	384	93	—	477
Net assets released from restrictions	1,643	(1,632)	(11)	—
Total revenues and other support	24,846	(448)	309	24,707
Net appreciation on investments	314	—	—	314
Total revenues, gains, and other support	25,160	(448)	309	25,021
Expenses and losses:				
Instruction	9,391	—	—	9,391
Public service	86	—	—	86
Academic support	2,301	—	—	2,301
Student services	2,056	—	—	2,056
Management and general	2,388	—	—	2,388
Fund-raising	442	—	—	442
Auxiliary enterprises	448	—	—	448
Operations and maintenance of plant	2,768	—	—	2,768
Repairs and renovations	992	—	—	992
Retirement of plant	152	—	—	152
Interest	253	—	—	253
Other	15	—	—	15
Total expenses and losses	21,292	—	—	21,292
Change in net assets	3,868	(448)	309	3,729
Net assets at beginning of year	41,422	891	3,548	45,861
Net assets at end of year	$45,290	$ 443	$3,857	$49,590

SOUTHERN STATE UNIVERSITY
STATEMENT OF REVENUES, EXPENSES, AND CHANGES IN NET ASSETS
FOR THE YEAR ENDED JUNE 30, 2002
(IN THOUSANDS)

	Primary Institution
REVENUES	
Operating revenues:	
Student tuition and fees (net of scholarship allowances)	$ 66,974
Federal grants and contracts	9,068
Auxiliary enterprises	29,074
Other operating revenues	807
Total operating revenues	105,923
EXPENSES	
Instruction	61,498
Research	2,411
Public service	8,005
Academic support	14,930
Student services	14,949
Institutional support	21,048
Scholarships and fellowships	13,303
Operation and maintenance of plant	11,289
Auxiliary activities	24,998
Student loan provision	199
Depreciation	7,837
Other	442
Total operating expenses	180,909
Operating income (loss)	(74,986)
NONOPERATING REVENUES (EXPENSES)	
State grants and contracts	2,129
State appropriations	69,086
Gifts	7,050
Investment income	2,694
Interest expense on capital asset–related debt	(3,428)
Net nonoperating revenues	77,531
Income before other gains	2,545
Additions to permanent endowments	4,787
Increase in net assets	7,332
NET ASSETS	
Net assets—beginning of year	117,718
Net assets—end of year	$125,050

16–3. Internet Case. Assume you are a newly hired accountant in the Office of Financial Operations of a large public university. You will be involved in two major initiatives for the coming year: (1) revising the university's chart of accounts and

(2) assisting in implementing the new financial reporting model for public colleges and universities prescribed by GASB *Statement No. 35*.

Required

a. What type of information is available on the Internet to assist you in understanding the chart of accounts of a public university? For example, look at the Accounting Tutorials at the NACUBO website (http://www.nacubo.org) and search under "university accounting."

b. Use the Internet to identify whether higher education organizations provide guidance on the new financial reporting model. For example, try the AICPA (http://www.aicpa.org), Council for the Advancement of Secondary Education (CASE) (http://www.case.org), NACUBO (http://www.nacubo.org), and other public colleges and universities.

Exercises and Problems

16–1. Multiple Choice. Choose the best answer.

1. Assets that the governing board of a public university, rather than a donor or other outside agency, has determined are to be retained and invested for purposes other than loan or plant would be accounted for as:
   a. An Endowment.
   b. Unrestricted Net Assets.
   c. Deposits Held in Custody for Others.
   d. Restricted Net Assets.
2. Which of the following statements usually will *not* be included in the annual financial report of a governmentally owned public university engaged only in business-type activities?
   a. Statement of Activities.
   b. Statement of Net Assets.
   c. Statement of Cash Flows.
   d. Statement of Revenues, Expenses, and Changes in Net Assets.
3. Oakville College, a public college, has a 10-week summer session that starts on June 25. During the fiscal year ending June 30, 2002, tuition and fees in the amount of $800,000 were collected from students for classes to be conducted in this session. What amount should Oakville College recognize as Unrestricted Revenue in each of the years ended June 30, 2002, and June 30, 2003?

	Year Ended June 30, 2002	*Year Ended June 30, 2003*
a.	$160,000	$640,000
b.	$ 0	$800,000
c.	$800,000	$ 0

   d. Either *a* or *c* is allowed, provided the same pattern of recognition is applied consistently in successive years.

4. Tuition scholarships for which there is *no* intention of collection from the student should be classified by a private university as:
   a. Revenues and Expenditures.
   b. Revenues and Expenses.
   c. A reduction of gross revenue to arrive at net revenue.
   d. Any of the above.
5. An alumnus donates securities to Rex College, a private college, and stipulates that the principal be held in perpetuity and income from the securities be used for faculty travel. Dividends received from the securities should be recognized as increases in:
   a. Endowments.
   b. Unrestricted Net Assets.
   c. Temporarily Restricted Net Assets.
   d. Permanently Restricted Net Assets.
6. During the years ended June 30, 2002, and 2003, Small University, a public university, conducted a cancer research project financed by a $1,000,000 gift from an alumnus. This entire amount was pledged by the donor on July 10, 2001, although she paid only $200,000 at that date. The gift was restricted to the financing of this particular research project. During the two-year research period, Small's related gift receipts and research expenditures were as follows:

	Year Ended June 30	
	2002	*2003*
Gift receipts	$200,000	$800,000
Cancer research expenditures	100,000	900,000

   How much gift revenue should Small report for the year ended June 30, 2003?
   a. $0.
   b. $800,000.
   c. $900,000.
   d. $1,000,000.
7. Assuming full implementation of GASB *Statement No. 35*, are public and private colleges and universities required to report depreciation expense in their financial statements?

	Public	*Private*
a.	Yes	Yes
b.	Yes	No
c.	No	No
d.	No	Yes

8. During the year ended June 30, 2003, Gaudior College, a private college, received a federal government grant of $600,000 for research on the homeless. Expenses for

this research amounted to $200,000 during the same year. Under applicable FASB standards, assuming this is a nonexchange transaction, Gaudior College would report what amount(s) as revenues or support for the year ended June 30, 2003?

	Unrestricted	*Temporarily Restricted*	*Permanently Restricted*
a.	$ 0	$200,000	$ 0
b.	$ 0	$200,000	$100,000
c.	$200,000	$400,000	$ 0
d.	$600,000	$ 0	$ 0

9. Which of the following is *not* a condition that would permit a public or private college or university to avoid accounting recognition of the value of its collections of art, historical treasures, and similar assets?
   a. The assets are held for public exhibition, education, or research in furtherance of public service rather than financial gain.
   b. The assets are protected, kept unencumbered, cared for, and preserved.
   c. The assets are subject to an organizational policy that ensures the proceeds of sales of collectible assets are used for operations of the organization.
   d. None of above; all three items are conditions that will avoid accounting recognition.
10. Which of the following is required as part of a complete set of financial statements for a private college or university?
   a. Statement of Changes in Financial Position.
   b. Statement of Activities.
   c. Statement of Revenues, Expenses, and Changes in Net Assets.
   d. None of these.

16–2. Public College—Operating Activities. The balances of selected accounts for Caribou College, a state-supported institution, as of June 30, 2002, are shown below. Current operating transactions during the year are given. You are required to prepare journal entries for the transactions given and a closing entry as of June 30, 2003.

CARIBOU COLLEGE
TRIAL BALANCE (PARTIAL)
JUNE 30, 2002

	Debits	*Credits*
Cash	$ 73,000	
Accounts Receivable	25,000	
Allowance for Doubtful Accounts		$ 1,000
State Appropriation Receivable	182,000	
Inventory	14,000	
Long-term Investments—Restricted	24,000	
Accounts Payable		20,000
Deferred Revenue		148,000
Net Assets—Unrestricted		130,000
Net Assets—Restricted		19,000
	$318,000	$318,000

1. Fees charged to students for the fall and spring semesters of fiscal 2002–2003 totaled $2,200,000 of which $2,100,000 was collected in cash. The Allowance for Doubtful Accounts was increased by $4,000.
2. Collections of accounts receivable totaled $20,000. Accounts amounting to $1,000 were written off.
3. The Deferred Revenue of $148,000 shown in the Balance Sheet resulted from student fees charged for the summer term, which began in fiscal 2001–2002 but was predominantly conducted in 2002–2003.
4. Fees charged to students for summer school totaled $144,000, all of which was collected in cash. The summer term will be predominantly conducted in fiscal 2003–2004.
5. Long-term investments in the amount of $10,000 held at the beginning of the year were sold for $10,500. Restricted net assets spent for authorized purposes amounted to $2,500.
6. During the year, accounts payable for purchases, salaries and wages, utility bills, and other expenses totaling $1,750,000 were recorded. Accounts payable at the end of the year amounted to $70,000.
7. Supplies inventory at the end of the year amounted to $25,000, according to physical count.
8. During the year, the state appropriation of $182,000 was received. A further appropriation for current general purposes of $192,000 was made by the state but had not been paid to the college by year-end.
9. $500,000 was invested in short-term U.S. Treasury notes.
10. Income received in cash from restricted investments amounted to $1,050; an additional $160 interest was accrued at year-end.
11. All nominal accounts were closed.

16–3. Public University Transactions. The Statement of Net Assets of Rapapo State University, a governmentally owned university, as of the end of its fiscal year ended July 31, 2002, is presented below:

RAPAPO STATE UNIVERSITY
STATEMENT OF NET ASSETS
JULY 31, 2002

Assets:		
Cash		$210,000
Accounts receivable, net		370,000
Prepaid expenses		40,000
Investments		210,000
Capital assets	$1,750,000	
Accumulated depreciation	275,000	1,475,000
Total assets		2,305,000
Liabilities:		
Accounts payable		$105,000
Accrued liabilities		40,000
Deferred revenue		25,000
Bonds payable		600,000
Total liabilities		770,000

Net Assets:	
Invested in capital assets, net of related debt	$ 875,000
Restricted	215,000
Unrestricted	445,000
Total net assets	$1,535,000

The following information pertains to the year ended July 31, 2003:

1. Cash collected from students' tuition totaled $3,000,000. Of this $3,000,000, $362,000 represented accounts receivable outstanding at July 31, 2002; $2,500,000 was for current-year tuition; and $138,000 was for tuition applicable to the semester beginning in August 2003.
2. Deferred revenue at July 31, 2002, was earned during the year ended July 31, 2003.
3. Accounts receivable in the amount of $13,000 were determined uncollectible and were written off against the allowance account. At July 31, 2003, the allowance account was estimated at $10,000.
4. During the year, an unrestricted appropriation of $60,000 was made by the state. This state appropriation was to be paid to Rapapo sometime in August 2003.
5. Equipment was purchased for the student computer labs in the amount of $225,000 for cash.
6. During the year, unrestricted cash gifts of $80,000 were received from alumni. Rapapo's board of trustees allocated $30,000 of these gifts to the students' loans.
7. Interest expense on the bonds payable was paid in the amount of $48,000.
8. During the year, investments with a carrying value of $25,000 were sold for $31,000. Investments were purchased at a cost of $40,000. Investment income of $18,000 was earned and collected during the year.
9. General expenses of $2,500,000 were recorded in the voucher system. At July 31, 2003, the accounts payable balance was $75,000.
10. Accrued liabilities at July 31, 2002, were paid.
11. One-quarter of the prepaid expenses at July 31, 2002, expired during the current year, and pertained to general education expense. There was no addition to prepaid expenses during the year.
12. Depreciation expense on the capital assets was recorded in the amount of $90,000.

Required

a. Prepare journal entries in good form to record the foregoing transactions for the year ended July 31, 2003, including closing the nominal accounts.

b. Prepare a Statement of Net Assets for the year ended July 31, 2003.

16–4. Loan Transactions. Everglades University indicated the following assets restricted for loan activities as of June 30, 2002:

Cash		$61,000	
Investments		30,000	
Loans to Students, Faculty, and Staff	$100,000		
Accrued Interest Receivable	1,000		
	101,000		
Less: Allowance for Doubtful Loans and Interest	2,000	99,000	
Net Assets Restricted for Loans			$190,000

Assume that Everglades University is a public university. Prepare journal entries for the following transactions that occurred in the year 2002–2003. Also prepare a schedule as of June 30, 2003, in the same format as shown above.

1. A bequest of $23,000 in securities was received by Everglades University. The decedent specified that both principal and interest were to be used for student loans.
2. Loans receivable of prior years in the amount of $31,000 were collected during the year. Interest collected on loans receivable in cash during the year amounted to $4,150, $900 of which was accrued at June 30, 2002, and $3,250 of which was earned in 2002–2003.
3. One loan of $600 and accrued interest of $50 (as of balance sheet date) was written off as uncollectible.
4. Loans made to students during the year totaled $42,000. All loans were secured by notes; repayments on these loans during the year amounted to $4,100 ($4,000 principal and $100 interest).
5. Dividends and interest on loan investments collected in cash during the year amounted to $2,150. Accrued interest receivable at the end of the year amounted to $640. The Allowance for Doubtful Loans and Interest was increased to $1,900.
6. Prepare entries to close the loan operating statement accounts to Net Assets Restricted for Loans.

16–5. Endowment Transactions. Selected account balances of Lockhart University as of June 30, 2001, indicated the following with respect to assets restricted by donors or designated by the governing board relating to endowment and quasi-endowments:

Endowment and Quasi-endowment Assets:	
Cash—Restricted by Donors	$ 90,000
Cash—Designated by Board	40,000
Investments—Restricted	730,000
Investments—Designated	70,000
Real Estate	270,000
Cash Held by Trustee	200,000
Total assets	1,400,000
Liabilities:	
Accounts Payable	120,000
Net Assets:	
Net Assets—Invested in Capital Assets (net)	270,000
Net Assets—Restricted	820,000
Net Assets—Unrestricted	190,000
Total Net Assets	$1,280,000

You are required to prepare journal entries to record the following transactions, which relate to the fiscal year 2001–2002. You are also required to prepare a schedule of account balances, as shown above, as of June 30, 2002, assuming Lockhart University is a public university.

1. Cash held by a trustee in the amount of $50,000 was transferred by the trustee to the Endowment Restricted Cash account.
2. Accounts payable on June 30, 2001, were paid.
3. Investments designated by the board and carried at $55,000 were sold for $51,000 and the proceeds reinvested in other securities.
4. Real Estate was purchased for $10,000.
5. Income on Restricted Investments of $80,000 for the year was received.
6. Appropriate accounts were closed at the end of the fiscal year.

16–6. Annuity and Life Income Transactions. Selected account balances of Cougar University as of June 30, 2001, indicated the following with respect to annuity and life income agreements. From the transactions that follow, prepare journal entries and a schedule of selected account balances, in the format shown below, as of June 30, 2002. Assume that Cougar University is a public university.

Assets Restricted for Annuity and Life Income Agreements:		
Cash	$ 30,000	
Investments	135,000	
Total assets		$165,000
Liabilities Payable from Annuity and Life Income Agreements:		
Annuities Payable		62,000
Net Assets Restricted for Annuity and Life Income Agreements:		
Net Assets Restricted for Annuity Agreements	30,000	
Net Assets Restricted for Life Income Agreements	73,000	
Total Net Assets		$103,000

1. On August 1, 2001, a tract of land with fair market value of $600,000 was received under an agreement that Cougar University would pay the donor $30,000 each year on the anniversary date of the agreement as long as the donor lived. No restrictions were placed on the use of the principal of the fund or any income in excess of $30,000 per year. The present value of the liability to the annuitant is $342,000.
2. Cash income received from annuity investments during the year totaled $34,000, of which $11,400 was disbursed to annuitant during the year.
3. During the year, one life income recipient died, her contribution, investments with a fair value of $42,000, was transferred to net assets restricted for loans.

16–7. Capital Assets. The following information is available about the plant assets of Bronco University as of June 30, 2001. From the transactions given below, prepare journal entries and a schedule of account balances in the format shown below as of the end of the year, assuming Bronco University is a public entity that is not yet required to record infrastructure.

Assets Restricted for Acquisition of Capital Assets:		
Cash		$ 25,000
Investments		405,000
Total		430,000
Capital Assets:		
Land	$ 115,000	
Buildings	5,260,000	
Equipment	983,000	
Construction in progress	212,000	
Accumulated depreciation	(2,500,000)	4,070,000
Total		4,500,000
Accounts Payable	82,000	
Bonds Payable	260,000	342,000
Net Assets—Invested in Capital Assets, Net of Related Debt		3,810,000
Net Assets—Restricted for Acquisition of Capital Assets		348,000
Total Capital-Related Net Assets		$4,158,000

Transactions during the fiscal year ended June 30, 2002, were:

1. Investments with a carrying value of $125,000 were sold for $127,000 cash; bonds payable in the amount of $130,000 were retired.
2. A grant of $800,000 was made to Bronco University by the Bronco Foundation to be used for the acquisition of buildings and equipment. The grant was to be paid to the university in equal installments over an eight-year period; the sum for the current year was received in cash.
3. Invoices and payrolls amounting to $50,000 for the construction in progress were recorded as accounts payable. Accounts payable in the amount of $102,000 were paid during the year.
4. The construction in progress, an addition to the School of Business building, was considered completed. It was determined that 80 percent of the total cost was to be charged to Buildings and 20 percent to Equipment.
5. A firm of architects engaged to prepare plans for a new residence hall submitted an invoice for $40,000 for services performed by them this year. (You may credit Accounts Payable.)
6. Depreciation expense on buildings and equipment of $95,000 was recorded on June 30, 2002.
7. Appropriate accounts are closed as of June 30, 2002.

16–8. Private College—Statement of Financial Position. Zenith College had always kept its accounts on a so-called commercial basis and not in the form ordinarily used by educational institutions. Its Balance Sheet as of June 30, 2003, was as follows:

ZENITH COLLEGE
BALANCE SHEET
JUNE 30, 2003

Assets		
Current assets:		
Cash	$ 1,180	
Tuition fees receivable	8,000	
Inventory of supplies	2,000	$11,180
Endowment fund investments:		
Rented real estate—at cost	75,000	
Less: Allowance for depreciation	15,000	
	60,000	
Mortgages, 7 percent—at cost	145,000	
5 percent public utility bonds—at fair value	220,000	425,000
Plant and equipment, net of allowance for depreciation of $166,000		830,000
		$1,266,180
Liabilities		
Current liabilities:		
Bank loans	$ 15,000	
Accounts payable	9,000	$ 24,000
First-mortgage bonds, 7 percent, maturing at the rate of $15,000 semiannually on June 30 and December 31 of each year		300,000
Endowment fund balance		540,000
Capital:		
Balance at July 1, 2002	400,000	
Excess of income over expenses for the year ended June 30, 2003, per annexed statement	2,180	402,180
		$1,266,180

Required

a. Prepare a written report for the Controller of Zenith College to set forth the changes that must be made to bring the College's financial statement into conformity with FASB financial reporting standards for a private college, as described in Chapter 16.

b. Prepare a Statement of Financial Position for Zenith College, as of June 30, 2003, in conformity with FASB financial reporting standards for a private college. Use the format for these statements shown in Illustration 16–4 earlier in this chapter.

(AICPA, adapted)

CHAPTER 17

Accounting for Health Care Organizations

Learning Objectives

After studying this chapter, you should be able to:

- Describe different organizational forms for providing health care services.
- Identify the authoritative accounting literature that governs health care entities.
- Describe financial reporting for health care organizations.
- Explain unique accounting and measurement issues in health care organizations including accounting for revenues, assets, expenses, and liabilities.
- Journalize transactions and prepare the basic financial statements for not-for-profit health care providers.
- Prepare the basic financial statements for governmental health care providers.
- Describe other accounting issues in the health care industry:
  - Budgeting and costs.
  - Auditing.
  - Taxation and regulation.
- Discuss unique issues with certain types of health care organizations, such as prepaid health care services and continuing care retirement communities.
- Explain financial and operational analysis of health care organizations.

Health Care Industry

The health care industry in the United States changed dramatically in the twentieth century. In the early 1900s health care was provided primarily by nonprofit hospitals affiliated with communities or religious organizations; major projects were funded by donations; and hospital managers had little financial expertise and faced few regulations. Today, health care organizations are complex entities that cross the private, public, and not-for-profit sectors; spiraling costs outpace inflation; capital construction requires extensive financing; and professional managers face increasing public scrutiny and governmental oversight. Technological advances brought dramatic changes in the delivery and quality of health care services, but also contributed greatly to rising costs. Health care is now a $1 trillion industry representing 15 percent of gross national product.[1]

There are political, social, and economic factors that explain the tremendous change in the health care industry. For example, in the 1940s and 1950s, health insurance coverage became a common employee fringe benefit, and health care providers began to look to employers and third parties for payment for services. The Hill Burton Program in 1944 encouraged growth in the industry by making federal funds available for the construction of health care facilities.[2] The initiation of entitlement programs, such as Medicare and Medicaid in the 1960s, reflected public policy efforts to make health care a basic right to be regulated at the federal level. In the 1980s employers and insurance companies initiated managed care systems in an attempt to bring down the cost of providing health care coverage. In the 1990s, comprehensive health care reform became a political issue at the federal level. Today, roughly half of *hospital* health care is provided by not-for-profit organizations, although most *providers* of health care are for-profit groups of medical professionals who are associated with governmental or not-for-profit health care organizations.

Illustration 17–1 shows classifications of health care organizations by legal structure as well as by the nature of services they provide. This chapter focuses on the financial reporting and accounting issues of these organizations that charge patients or third parties for the services provided. Voluntary health and welfare organizations, which are nonbusiness-oriented, and which provide more general social services funded primarily by contributions and grants rather than charges for services, are discussed in Chapter 14.

GAAP for Health Care Providers

Generally accepted accounting principles (GAAP) for hospitals and other health care organizations have evolved through the efforts of the American Hospital Association (AHA), the Healthcare Financial Management Association (HFMA),

[1]U.S. Department of Health and Human Services, *Health U.S.*, Pub. No. 96-1232, 1995, Table 114, p. 239.

[2]The Hospital Survey and Construction Act of 1946 (P.L. 79-725).

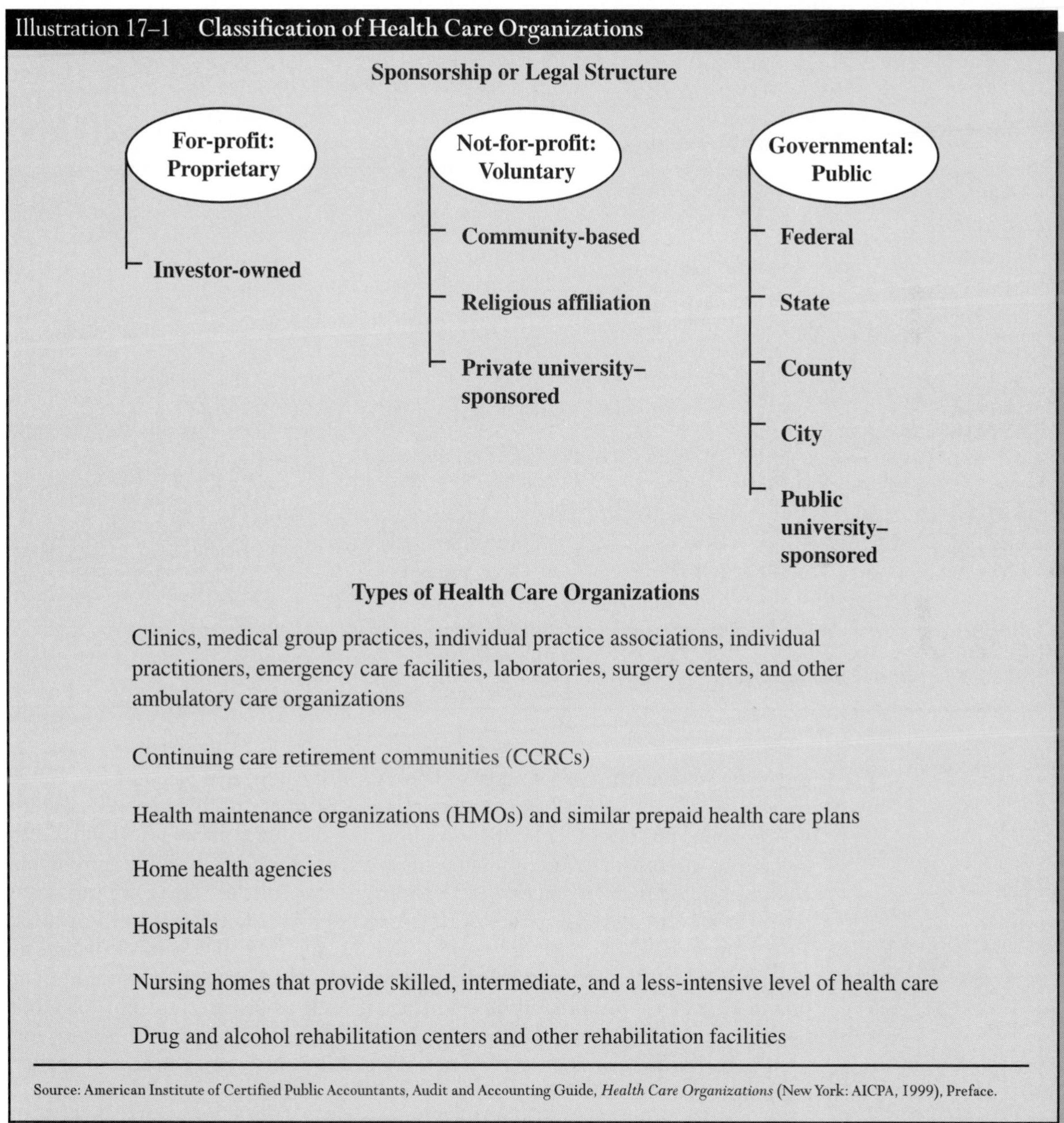

and the American Institute of Certified Public Accountants (AICPA). More recently, Statements of the Financial Accounting Standards Board and the Governmental Accounting Standards Board directly impact accounting and

Illustration 17–2 GAAP for Health Care Entities in Different Sectors

Accounting and Reporting Issue	Health Care Providers		
	Investor-Owned	*Not-for-Profit*	*Governmental**
Reporting entity	APB *Opinion No. 18*, *SFAS No. 94*	AICPA *SOP 94-3*	GASB *Statement No. 14*
Contributions and financial statement display	*SFAS No. 116*	*SFAS Nos. 116* and *117*	GASB *Statement No. 33*
Cash flows	*SFAS No. 95*	*SFAS No. 95*	GASB *Statement No. 9*
Deposits with financial institutions	*SFAS No. 105*	*SFAS No. 105*	GASB *Statement No. 3*
Investments	*SFAS No. 115* and AAG-HCO, Chapter 4	*SFAS No. 124*	GASB *Statement Nos. 3, 28, 31*
Operating leases	*SFAS No. 13*	*SFAS No. 13*	GASB *Statement No. 13*
Prepaid health care arrangements and self-insurance programs	AAG-HCO, Chapters 8 and 14	AAG-HCO, Chapters 8 and 14	GASB *Statement No. 10*
Compensated absences	*SFAS Nos. 43* and *112*	*SFAS Nos. 43* and *112*	GASB *Statement No. 16*
Debt refundings	APB *Opinion No. 26*, *SFAS Nos. 4* and *125*	APB *Opinion No. 26*,	GASB *Statement Nos. 7* and *23* *SFAS Nos. 4* and *125*
Pensions	*SFAS No. 87*	*SFAS No. 87*	GASB *Statement No. 27*
Risks and uncertainties	AICPA *SOP 94–6*	AICPA *SOP 94-6*	GASB *Statement Nos. 10* and *30*
Post retirement benefits	*SFAS No. 106*	*SFAS No. 106*	GASB *Statement Nos. 12* and *27*

*As amended by GASB *Statement No. 34*.

Source: Adapted from AICPA, *Audit Risk Alert, Health Care Industry Developments—1998/99* (New York: AICPA, 1999), par. 121.

reporting for health care providers. The AICPA Audit and Accounting Guide *Health Care Organizations* applies to health care organizations that are either (1) investor-owned businesses, (2) not-for-profit enterprises that, although they have no ownership interests, are essentially business-oriented and self-sustaining from fees charged for goods and services, or (3) governmental entities. These organizations are often classified by the nature of the services provided, as listed in Illustration 17–1. Since 1990, the AICPA Audit and Accounting Guide has covered *all* providers of health care services, not just hospitals. The Guide covers *governmental* providers that use proprietary accounting, as well as private and not-for-profit health care organizations; and it integrates *SFAS Nos. 116* and *117* for not-for-profit organizations, which focus on net assets of the entity as a whole, rather than on fund balances.[3]

Governmental hospitals or health care providers are considered special-purpose governments; that is, legally separate entities that may be either component units of another government or stand-alone governmental entities. GASB

[3]American Institute of Certified Public Accountants, Audit and Accounting Guide, *Health Care Organizations* (AAG-HCO) (New York: AICPA, 1999).

Statement No. 34 provides guidance for these organizations that many be engaged in either governmental or business-type activities or both. The AICPA Audit Guide is considered Category (b) authority for both governmental and nongovernmental entities, which means that GASB and FASB statements take precedence.[4] Consequently, even though there is only one Audit Guide for all health care entities, accounting and reporting rules may differ depending on whether the health care provider is legally structured as an investor-owned, not-for-profit, or governmental organization. Some of the differences relate to accounting and reporting for contributions and financial reporting display, cash flows, and investments, as seen in Illustration 17–2. This chapter illustrates financial accounting and reporting for not-for-profit, nongovernmental health care organizations, the largest segment of the in-patient health care industry, and points out particular differences for investor-owned and governmental health care providers. The reader is directed to Chapter 14 for a more thorough discussion of *SFAS Nos. 116* and *117* for not-for-profit organizations, and to Chapter 7 for a discussion of business-type enterprises of governmental entities.

Financial Reporting

The information needs of users of financial statements differ depending upon whether they are giving, paying, or loaning money to the health care organization. The basic financial statements of a health care entity created to serve a broad set of users include a (1) Balance Sheet, (2) Statement of Operations, (3) Statement of Changes in Equity (net assets/fund balances), and (4) Statement of Cash Flows, as well as Notes to the Financial Statements. The FASB and AICPA allow considerable flexibility in displaying financial information; for example, the Statements of Changes in Equity and Operations may be combined. A health care organization may choose to use fund accounting for internal purposes, in part, to account for revenues and expenses associated with grants (or because it is a governmental entity). For organizations using fund accounting, the fund structure should include general unrestricted funds and donor-restricted funds (e.g., Specific Purpose, Plant Replacement and Expansion, and Endowment). Comparative statements for a hypothetical not-for-profit hospital are presented in Illustrations 17–3 through 17–5. Statements for a governmental entity are discussed later in the chapter.

Balance Sheet

The Balance Sheet presented in Illustration 17–3 shows assets classified into current assets, assets limited as to use, and noncurrent assets, such as property, plant, and equipment. Not-for-profit organizations are required to present information about the liquidity of their assets and liabilities. The equity section of an investor-owned health care provider should show stockholders' equity separated into capital

[4]American Institute of Certified Public Accountants, *SAS No. 69* "The Meaning of 'Present Fairly in Conformity with Generally Accepted Accounting Principles' in the Independent Auditor's Report" (New York: AICPA, 1991).

Illustration 17–3

BLOOMFIELD HOSPITAL
BALANCE SHEET
AS OF SEPTEMBER 30, 2002

Assets	
Current Assets:	
Cash	$ 172,100
Accounts and notes receivable, net of allowance for uncollectibles of $135,000	353,000
Pledges receivable, net of allowance for uncollectibles of $114,300	1,048,700
Accrued interest receivable	44,000
Inventory	160,000
Prepaid expenses	8,000
Short-term investments	1,278,000
Total Current Assets	3,063,800
Assets Limited as to Use:	
By Board for expansion of facilities—cash	6,500
By Board for expansion of facilities—investments	778,000
Total Assets Limited as to Use	784,500
Long-Term Investments	146,000
Property, Plant, and Equipment:	
Land	1,080,000
Buildings, net of accumulated depreciation of $1,365,000	9,685,000
Equipment, net of accumulated depreciation of $1,702,000	3,590,000
Total Property, Plant, and Equipment	14,355,000
Total Assets	$18,349,300

Liabilities and Net Assets	
Current Liabilities:	
Accounts payable	$ 259,000
Accrued expenses payable	173,500
Total Current Liabilities	432,500
Long-Term Debt:	
Mortgages payable	6,000,000
Total Liabilities	6,432,500
Net Assets:	
Unrestricted—Undesignated	8,536,600
Unrestricted—Designated	784,500
Temporarily restricted	2,417,700
Permanently restricted	178,000
Total Net Assets	11,916,800
Total Liabilities and Net Assets	$18,349,300

Illustration 17–4 Illustration of a Two-Part Statement of Operations

BLOOMFIELD HOSPITAL
STATEMENT OF OPERATIONS
YEAR ENDED SEPTEMBER 30, 2002

Unrestricted revenues and gains:		
Net patient service revenue		$ 9,161,000
Other revenue		48,800
Contributions		297,900
Investment income		36,100
Total unrestricted revenues and gains		9,543,800
Net assets released from restrictions:		
Satisfaction of equipment acquisition restrictions		100,000
Total unrestricted revenues, gains, and other support		9,643,800
Unrestricted expenses and losses:		
Nursing services	$4,667,500	
Other professional services	1,311,620	
General services	2,056,260	
Fiscal and administrative services	1,332,320	
Total expenses		9,367,700
Loss on disposal of equipment		1,500
Total unrestricted expenses and losses		9,369,200
Increase in unrestricted net assets		$ 274,600

STATEMENT OF CHANGES IN NET ASSETS
YEAR ENDED SEPTEMBER 30, 2002

Unrestricted net assets (see Part 1)	
Total unrestricted revenues and gains	$ 9,543,800
Net assets released from restrictions	100,000
Total unrestricted expenses and losses	(9,369,200)
Increase in unrestricted net assets	274,600
Temporarily restricted net assets:	
Contributions	25,000
Investment income	77,000
Increase in provision for uncollectible pledges	(66,300)
Loss on sale of investments	(26,000)
Net assets released from restrictions	(100,000)
Decrease in temporarily restricted net assets	(90,300)
Permanently restricted net assets:	
Contributions	24,000
Increase in permanently restricted net assets	24,000
Increase in net assets	208,300
Net assets at beginning of year	11,708,500
Net assets at end of year	$11,916,800

Illustration 17–5 Illustration of Statement of Cash Flows—Not-for-Profit and Investor-Owned Organizations

BLOOMFIELD HOSPITAL
STATEMENT OF CASH FLOWS
YEAR ENDED SEPTEMBER 30, 2002

Cash flows from operating activities:	
Cash received from patients and third-party payors	$ 8,842,000
Other receipts from operations	48,800
Interest received on assets limited as to use	36,100
Receipts from unrestricted gifts	297,900
Cash paid to employees and suppliers	(8,014,200)
Interest paid	(160,000)
Net cash provided by operating activities	1,050,600
Cash flows from investing activities:	
Purchase of property and equipment	(400,000)
Purchase of long-term investments	(737,000)
Proceeds from sale of securities	59,000
Proceeds from sale of equipment	500
Net cash used by investing activities	(1,077,500)
Cash flows from financing activities:	
Proceeds from contributions restricted for:	
Investment in plant	292,000
Future operations	5,000
	297,000
Other financing activities:	
Interest and dividends restricted to endowment	69,000
Repayment of long-term debt	(400,000)
	(331,000)
Net cash used by financing activities	(34,000)
Net increase (decrease) in cash	(60,900)
Cash and cash equivalents, September 30, 2001	239,500
Cash and cash equivalents, September 30, 2002	$ 178,600

RECONCILIATION OF CHANGES IN NET ASSETS TO NET CASH PROVIDED BY OPERATING ACTIVITIES

Changes in net assets	$ 208,300
Adjustments to reconcile change in net assets to net cash provided by operating activities:	
Depreciation	783,000
Loss on disposal of equipment	1,500
Increase in patient accounts receivable, net	(139,000)
Increase in supplies	(80,000)
Increase in accounts payable and accrued expenses	306,500
Decrease in prepaid expenses	4,000
Gifts, grants, and bequests restricted for long-term investment	(49,000)
Interest restricted for long-term investment	(77,000)
Loss on sale of investments	26,000
Increase in provision for uncollectible pledges	66,300
Net cash provided by operating activities	$ 1,050,600

stock and retained earnings. The fund equity section of a nongovernmental not-for-profit organization should classify net assets into unrestricted, temporarily restricted, and permanently restricted in their equity sections. Governmental organizations classify net assets into Invested in Capital Assets, Restricted, and Unrestricted.

Statement of Operations

The principal sources of revenue for a health care organization are (1) patient service revenue; (2) premium revenue derived from **capitation fees,** which are fixed fees per person paid periodically regardless of services provided by a health maintenance organization; (3) resident service revenue, such as maintenance or rental fees in an extended care facility; (4) other revenue; and (5) net assets released from restrictions used for operations. Service revenue is shown net of contractual adjustments, discussed later in this chapter. Other revenue includes sales (e.g., medical supplies and cafeteria meals), fees (e.g., for educational programs or transcripts), rental of facilities other than to residents, investment income and gains, and unrestricted contributions. Some governmental health care organizations may be supported, at least in part, by taxes or intergovernmental revenue. Research grants or contracts may be considered exchange transactions (i.e., sales) or nonexchange transactions (i.e., contributions), as discussed in earlier chapters. Net assets released from temporary restrictions are shown as increases to unrestricted net assets if they were used for operations, otherwise they are reported along with other contributions for property purchases. Bloomfield Hospital, as shown in Illustration 17–4, reports some of these sources of income. Considerable flexibility is allowed in displaying the results of operations, such as classification by operating and nonoperating, expendable and nonexpendable, earned and unearned, or recurring and nonrecurring. FASB Concepts Statements provide guidance on distinguishing operating items (i.e., those arising from ongoing major activities, such as service revenue) from nonoperating items (i.e., those arising from transactions peripheral or incidental to the delivery of health care, such as investment income and unrestricted contributions).[5]

Of course, this not-for-profit hospital reports all expenses as decreases in unrestricted assets. Functional expenses must be displayed or disclosed in the notes and can be as simple as distinguishing between health care services and general/administrative. If functional expenses are displayed, then all natural expenses (e.g., depreciation, interest, and provision for bad debts) must be allocated to the functional expenses.

Health care organizations should include a **performance indicator** to report the results of operations. The principal components of a performance indicator are unrestricted revenues, gains, and other support; expenses; and other income. Examples include excess of revenues over expenses, revenues and gains over expenses and losses, earned income, and performance earnings. Investment income, realized gains and losses, and unrealized gains and losses on trading securities should be

[5]Financial Accounting Standards Board, *Concepts Statement No. 6*, "Elements of Financial Statements" (Norwalk, CT: FASB, 1985).

reported in the performance indicator; however, the following items should be reported separately from the performance indicator:

- Transactions with owners acting in that capacity.
- Equity transfers involving other related entities.
- Receipt of temporarily and permanently restricted contributions.
- Contributions of (and assets released from donor restrictions related to) long-lived assets.
- Unrealized gains and losses on investments not restricted by donors or by law, except for those investments classified as trading securities.
- Investment returns restricted by donors or by law.
- Other items that are required by GAAP to be reported separately, such as extraordinary items, the effect of discontinued operations, or the cumulative effect of accounting changes.[6]

Statement of Changes in Equity

Illustration 17–4 shows increases and decreases in the three classes of net assets for a not-for-profit organization: unrestricted, temporarily restricted, and permanently restricted. Net assets released from restrictions increase unrestricted net assets and decrease temporarily restricted net assets. Net gains on permanently restricted endowments are shown as increases to the permanently restricted net assets in Illustration 17–4; however, the accounting treatment of net gains will depend on donor stipulations, state law, and organizational policy.

Statement of Cash Flows

The Statement of Cash Flows in Illustration 17–5 is that required by *SFAS No. 95* (as amended) for not-for-profit organizations and investor-owned entities.[7] The direct method is presented with a reconciliation of changes in net assets to net cash provided by operating activities, although the indirect method is also acceptable. Note that Illustration 17–6, presented later in this chapter, shows the Statement of Cash Flows required by GASB standards for a governmental health care organization. That statement includes a fourth section called "Cash flows from noncapital financing activities." The FASB statement can be prepared using either the direct method or the indirect method, but under GASB *Statement No. 34*, governmental entities must use the direct method.[8] The statements differ primarily in terms of which cash flows are reported as part of each activity. In the GASB statement, interest paid and interest received are reported as investing activities, whereas the same items are reported as operating activities in the FASB statement, except for investment income added to temporarily or permanently restricted net assets. Such restricted income is reported in the FASB statement as a financing activity. Acquisitions of property and equipment are reported as capital and related financing

---

[6]AAG-HCO, pars. 10.05, 10.16, 10.17.

[7]Financial Accounting Standards Board, *Statement No. 95*, "Statement of Cash Flows" (Norwalk, CT: FASB, 1987), as amended by *SFAS No. 117*, "Financial Statements of Not-for-Profit Organizations" (Norwalk, CT: FASB, 1993).

[8]GASB, *Statement No. 34*, par. 105.

activities in the GASB statement but as investing activities in the FASB statement. Unrestricted gifts are reported as cash flows from noncapital financing activities in the GASB statement but as cash flows from operating activities in the FASB statement. A final, and major, difference is that the reconciliation schedule in the GASB statement reconciles operating income (loss) to cash flows from operating activities, whereas in the FASB statement the schedule reconciles changes in net assets to cash flows from operating activities. In preparing either cash flow statement, the worksheet or T-account approaches explained in most intermediate accounting texts may be useful.

Accounting and Measurement Issues

Revenues

Sources of Revenue. Health care organizations receive the majority of their revenue in the form of fees for services. These fees may come from the patient; the government in the form of Medicare or Medicaid payments; third-party payors, such as Blue Cross/Blue Shield or other private insurance companies; or contracts with other private health care companies. This service revenue is recorded at the gross amount when services are rendered. **Contractual adjustments (or allowances)** are recorded as contra-revenue accounts (i.e., reduction of revenue and receivables) for the difference between the gross patient service revenue and the negotiated payment by third-party payors in arriving at net patient service revenue. Prepaid health care plans that earn revenues from *agreements to provide* services record revenue at the point agreements are made, and not when services are rendered. The variety of payment plans with third-party payors makes accounting for patient service revenue a complicated accounting task. For example, payments can be made on a per case, per service performed, per diem, or per person (capitated) basis. In addition, interim payments are often received with final settlement at a later point in time.

Charity Service. Tax-exempt entities are expected to provide **charity care,** services to persons with a demonstrated inability to pay. Since charity service is never expected to result in cash flows, it is neither recognized as revenue nor receivables nor bad debt expense.[9] In practice, it is often difficult to distinguish bad debt expense from charity service. However, it is important to disclose management's charity care policies and the level of care provided for several reasons. The Hill Burton Act of 1946 requires that hospitals receiving federal assistance for construction projects perform some charity care. The IRS and local tax authorities question the tax-exempt status of some not-for-profit health care providers that do not appear to deliver an adequate amount of charity service to justify their tax exemption, although regulations do not specify levels of adequacy. Some third-party payors reimburse for a portion of bad debts, but not charity service.

[9]AAG-HCO, par. 10.03.

Third-Party Payors. Contracts with Medicare, Medicaid, Blue Cross plans, insurance companies, and state and local welfare agencies customarily provide for payment by **third-party payors** according to allowable costs or a predetermined (prospective) contractual rate rather than paying the service rates billed by the health care provider. For example, under Medicare's **Prospective Payment System** (PPS), payments are based on allowable service costs for medical procedures within the same diagnosis-related group (DRG) rather than on the length of the patient's hospital stay or actual cost of services rendered. Some payment methods, such as capitation fees in prepaid health care plans, shift a considerable amount of risk to the provider. That is, the fixed amount of revenue received per patient may not cover the costs of providing the service.

Other Revenue and Support. Donated services and noncash assets generally are recorded at their fair value when received, if the criteria described in Chapter 14 and the AICPA Audit and Accounting Guide are met.[10] Noncash assets could be supplies used in operations or long-lived items, such as land, buildings, or equipment. Donors may make these gifts-in-kind unrestricted or restricted, either temporarily or permanently.

Assets

Assets Limited as to Use. The phrase **Assets Limited as to Use** refers to assets whose use is limited by contracts or agreements with outside parties other than donors or grantors. Examples include proceeds of debt issues; funds deposited with a trustee; self-insurance funding arrangements, such as medical malpractice funding arrangements; and statutory reserve requirements (i.e., those required under state law for health maintenance organizations). The term can also refer to limitations placed on the assets by the Board of Directors or Trustees, such as for capital acquisition. Information about significant contractual limits should be disclosed in the Notes to the Financial Statements. Internally designated funds should be reported separately from externally designated funds on the Balance Sheet.[11] Assets that are held in trust by other parties are not reported on the Balance Sheet of the health care entity; however, their existence should be disclosed in the Notes.

Investments. Generally, health care organizations report their investments at fair value, although exact treatment of specific assets depends on the legal structure of the organization, as seen in Illustration 17–2. Not-for-profit organizations follow *SFAS No. 124*, which requires that all investments in equity securities with readily determinable values and all debt securities be reported at fair value, with the realized and unrealized gains and losses reported as changes in net assets. Governmental entities follow GASB *Statement No. 31*, which requires that changes in the fair value of certain investments be reported in the Statement of Operations. Investor-owned entities follow *SFAS No. 115*, which is the most complicated set of rules in

[10]Ibid., pars. 10.08–10.12.
[11]Ibid., pars. 1.13–1.14.

that investments are separated into three categories and the accounting treatment differs for each category.[12]

Receivables. Amounts due from patients and third-party payors result in several asset and contra-asset accounts on the Balance Sheet: Accounts Receivable, Allowance for Uncollectible Accounts, Allowance for Contractual Adjustments, Clearing accounts, Interim Payments, and Settlement accounts. **Settlement accounts** are the receivables (or payables) arising from differences between original payment estimates by third-party payors, cash received and paid, and final determinations.

The rate-setting process in the health care industry is complex and beyond the scope of this text. However, an understanding of the relationship between accrual accounting revenue recognition principles and alternative payment methods, such as prospective and retrospective, is critical in properly accounting for revenues and receivables in a health care organization. These organizations may also have pledges receivable that arise from donations and loans receivable that result from loans to employees or physicians' groups.

Expenses

All health care providers use full accrual accounting, and the accrual of expenses is the same as for any business organization. Bad debts is an expense, not a reduction of gross revenue to arrive at net revenue (as it had been in previous Audit Guides). Depreciation is recorded on all capital assets other than land, including donated buildings and equipment. Expenses can be reported using either a natural presentation (e.g., salaries, supplies, and occupancy costs) or a functional presentation (e.g., inpatient services, ancillary outpatient services, and fiscal and administrative services). Functional expenses, if reported, should be based on full cost allocations. Public companies that are registered with the SEC and governmental entities that use proprietary fund accounting must report segment information.[13]

Liabilities

Commitments and Contingencies. Contingencies that are common for health care providers arise from malpractice claims, risk contracting, third-party payor payment programs, obligations to provide uncompensated care, and contractual agreements with physicians. Other commitments and contingencies found in most business enterprises also apply to health care organizations, such as those that arise from construction contracts, pension plans, operating leases, purchase commitments, and loan guarantees. The cost of these claims against the health care organization should be accrued if they can be reasonably estimated, and it is probable

[12]Financial Accounting Standards Board, *Statement No. 115*, "Accounting for Certain Investments in Debt and Equity Securities" (Norwalk, CT: FASB, 1993), and *Statement No. 124*, "Accounting for Certain Investments Held by Not-for-Profit Organizations" (Norwalk, CT: FASB, 1996) 1; GASB, *Statement No. 31*, "Accounting and Financial Reporting for Certain Investments and for External Investment Pools" (Norwalk, CT: GASB, 1996).

[13]AAG-HCO, par. 10.21.

they will have to be paid.[14] Accruals should be made for unasserted claims at the best estimates based on industry experience.

Long-Term Debt. The high cost and critical nature of facilities and equipment in the delivery of health care lead to significant amounts of long-term debt. Very often, health care providers are entitled to financing assistance through tax-exempt debt or governmental financing authorities, such as the federal Health and Education Financing Authority, without regard to their legal structure. Financing agreements often include requirements to set aside funds for repayment of the interest on and principal of the debt. These funds are reported as *Assets Limited as to Use*.

Illustrative Case for a Not-for-Profit Health Care Organization

The illustrative transactions provided in this section are for a hypothetical non-governmentally owned, not-for-profit hospital—the Bloomfield Hospital. Hospitals continue to be the dominant form of health care organization and usually exhibit a greater range of operating activities and transactions than other forms of health care organizations. Typical hospital transactions are illustrated below, for Bloomfield Hospital, following the post-closing trial balance as of September 30, 2001, the end of its fiscal year.

BLOOMFIELD HOSPITAL
(A NOT-FOR-PROFIT ORGANIZATION)
POST-CLOSING TRIAL BALANCE
AS OF SEPTEMBER 30, 2001

	Debits	*Credits*
Cash	$ 233,000	
Short-Term Investments	980,000	
Accrued Interest Receivable	36,000	
Accounts and Notes Receivable	300,000	
Allowance for Uncollectible Receivables		$ 86,000
Pledges Receivable	1,460,000	
Allowance for Uncollectible Pledges		73,000
Inventory	80,000	
Prepaid Expenses	12,000	
Assets Limited as to Use—Cash	6,500	
Assets Limited as to Use—Investments	400,000	
Long-Term Investments	146,000	
Land	1,080,000	
Buildings	11,050,000	
Equipment	4,920,000	

[14]Financial Accounting Standards Board, *SFAS No. 5*, "Accounting for Contingencies" (Norwalk, CT: FASB, 1975); Financial Accounting Standards Board, *Interpretation No. 14*, "Reasonable Estimation of the Amount of a Loss" (Norwalk, CT: FASB, 1976); and GASB, *Codification*, Sec. C50.

	Debits	Credits
Accumulated Depreciation—Buildings		1,050,000
Accumulated Depreciation—Equipment		1,260,000
Accounts Payable		110,000
Accrued Expenses Payable		16,000
Mortgages Payable		6,400,000
Net Assets—Unrestricted, Undesignated		8,640,000
Net Assets—Unrestricted, Designated		406,500
Net Assets—Temporarily Restricted—Plant		2,508,000
Net Assets—Permanently Restricted		154,000
	$20,703,500	$20,703,500

During fiscal year 2002, the gross revenues for patient services from all responsibility centers totaled $9,261,000. It is the practice of Bloomfield Hospital to debit receivable accounts for the gross charges for all services rendered to patients, except for charity care patients; the AICPA Audit and Accounting Guide requires that charity care services be excluded from both receivables and revenues. The following entry should be made:

	Debits	Credits
1. Accounts and Notes Receivable	9,261,000	
Patient Service Revenue		9,261,000

The preceding entry recorded the revenues the hospital would have earned if all services rendered to each patient (other than charity care patients) were to be collected from the patients, or from third-party payors, as billed. Customers of profit-seeking businesses do not all pay their bills in full, and neither do hospital patients nor patients' insurance companies. The variety of third-party payment policies makes estimation of net patient service revenue difficult but obviously necessary for sound financial management and proper financial reporting. For the FY2002, it is assumed the estimated provision for bad debts is $180,000 and actual contractual adjustments from third-party payors is $100,000. The entry to record this information is:

	Debits	Credits
2. Provision for Bad Debts	180,000	
Contractual Adjustments	100,000	
Allowance for Uncollectible Receivables		180,000
Accounts and Notes Receivable		100,000

Provision for Bad Debts is another name for Bad Debts Expense and is reported as an operating expense. Contractual Adjustments, however, is deducted from Patient Service Revenue and only the net amount is reported as revenues of the period.

Examples of other revenues for hospitals include tuition from nursing students, interns, or residents; cafeteria and gift shop revenues; parking fees; fees for copies of medical records; and other activities related to the ongoing major or central operations of the hospital. Similarly, unrestricted gifts, grants, and endowment income restricted by donors to finance charity care would appropriately be classified as other revenue of a hospital. If a total of $48,800 was received in cash during FY2002 from sources classified as other revenue, Entry 3 is appropriate:

	Debits	Credits
3. Cash	48,800	
Other Revenue		48,800

Apart from items previously described, hospitals may receive unrestricted donations of money or services. Ordinarily such donations should be classified as nonoperating gains rather than revenues. Hospitals often receive donated medicines and other materials. If such medicines and materials would otherwise have to be purchased, it is appropriate to record these donations at fair value as other revenue. Hospitals also routinely receive benefits from the services of volunteer workers; however, it is only rarely that the value of such services is recorded as a revenue or gain (and as an expense) since the restrictive conditions required by the AICPA Audit and Accounting Guide for recognition are seldom met. (See related discussions in Chapters 14 and 16.)

Assume total contributions were received in cash in the amount of $297,900 and unrestricted endowment income was $8,100.

	Debits	Credits
4. Cash	306,000	
Contributions—Unrestricted		297,900
Investment Income—Unrestricted		8,100

One piece of capital equipment, which had a historical cost of $28,000 and a book value of $2,000 as of September 30, 2001, was sold early in the 2002 fiscal year for $500 cash. The entry to record the disposal of the asset at a loss is:

	Debits	Credits
5. Cash	500	
Loss on Disposal of Equipment	1,500	
Accumulated Depreciation—Equipment	26,000	
Equipment		28,000

New capital equipment costing $400,000 was purchased during FY2002 by the Bloomfield Hospital; $100,000 with temporarily restricted net assets and $300,000 with unrestricted net assets. The entries should be:

	Debits	Credits
6a. Equipment	400,000	
Cash		400,000
6b. Net Assets Released from Restrictions—Temporarily Restricted	100,000	
Net Assets Released from Restrictions—Unrestricted		100,000

During the year, the following items were recorded as Accounts Payable: the $16,000 accrued expenses payable as of September 30, 2001; nursing services expenses, $4,026,000; other professional services expenses, $947,200; general services expenses, $1,650,000; fiscal and administrative services expenses, $1,124,000; and supplies added to inventory, $400,000. The following entry summarizes that activity:

	Debits	Credits
7. Accrued Expenses Payable	16,000	
Nursing Services Expenses	4,026,000	
Other Professional Services Expenses	947,200	
General Services Expenses	1,650,000	
Fiscal and Administrative Services Expenses	1,124,000	
Inventory	400,000	
Accounts Payable		8,163,200

Collections on accounts and notes receivable during the year amounted to $8,842,000; accounts and notes receivable totaling $131,000 were written off:

	Debits	Credits
8. Cash	8,842,000	
Allowance for Uncollectible Receivables	131,000	
Accounts and Notes Receivable		8,973,000

The following cash disbursements were made during FY2002: Accounts Payable, $8,014,200; a principal payment in the amount of $400,000 was made to reduce the mortgage liability; and interest amounting to $160,000 on mortgages was paid:

	Debits	Credits
9. Accounts Payable	8,014,200	
Mortgages Payable	400,000	
Interest Expense	160,000	
Cash		8,574,200

Supplies issued during the year cost $320,000 ($20,000 of the total was for use by fiscal and administrative services; $120,000 for use by general services; and the remainder by other professional services):

	Debits	Credits
10. Other Professional Services Expenses	180,000	
General Services Expenses	120,000	
Fiscal and Administrative Services Expenses	20,000	
Inventory		320,000

Accrued expenses as of September 30, 2002, included $160,000 interest on mortgages; fiscal and administrative service expenses, $8,700; and other professional services expenses, $4,800. Prepaid expenses, consisting of general services expense items, declined $4,000 during the year:

	Debits	Credits
11. Interest Expense	160,000	
Fiscal and Administrative Service Expenses	8,700	
Other Professional Services Expenses	4,800	
General Services Expenses	4,000	
Accrued Expenses Payable		173,500
Prepaid Expenses		4,000

Depreciation of plant and equipment for FY2002 was in the amounts shown in the following journal entry:

	Debits	Credits
12. Depreciation Expense	783,000	
Accumulated Depreciation—Buildings		315,000
Accumulated Depreciation—Equipment		468,000

The hospital received cash of $28,000 for interest on investments held in the Assets Limited as to Use—Investments account. Entry 13 records the receipt of cash and the corresponding credit.

	Debits	*Credits*
13. Cash	28,000	
Investment Income—Unrestricted		28,000

The $28,000 received in cash for interest (see Entry 13) was reinvested in investments to be held for eventual use for expansion of facilities; the hospital governing board decided to purchase an additional $350,000 of investments for the same purpose. Entries 14a and 14b reflect the purchase of the investments and the increase in unrestricted designated net assets.

14a. Assets Limited as to Use—Investments	378,000	
Cash		378,000
14b. Net Assets—Unrestricted, Undesignated	378,000	
Net Assets—Unrestricted, Designated		378,000

Individual philanthropists and civic and charitable groups have donated money and securities to Bloomfield Hospital subject to the restriction that the assets may be utilized only for plant replacement and expansion. Cash was received during FY2002 from the following sources: Interest on marketable securities (including the amount accrued at the end of the 2001 fiscal year), $69,000; collections of pledges receivable, $292,000;

15. Cash	361,000	
Pledges Receivable		292,000
Accrued Interest Receivable		36,000
Investment Income—Temporarily Restricted		33,000

Marketable securities carried in the accounts at $85,000 were sold for $59,000. The proceeds were reinvested in marketable securities, and $300,000 additional marketable securities were purchased from cash received during the year:

16a. Cash	59,000	
Loss on Sale of Investments	26,000	
Short-Term Investments		85,000
16b. Short-Term Investments	359,000	
Cash		359,000

A review of pledges receivable indicated pledges in the amount of $25,000 should be written off, and the allowance for uncollectible pledges should be increased by $66,300.

17a. Allowance for Uncollectible Pledges	25,000	
Pledges Receivable		25,000
17b. Provision for Uncollectible Pledges	66,300	
Allowance for Uncollectible Pledges		66,300

The fair values of short-term investments and assets limited as to use have not changed during the year. At the end of FY2002, the amount of interest accrued on marketable securities is computed to be $44,000:

	Debits	Credits
18. Accrued Interest Receivable	44,000	
Investment Income—Temporarily Restricted		44,000

Bloomfield Hospital did not have any net assets temporarily restricted for programs as of September 30, 2001. In September 2002, however, a civic organization donated $5,000 to the hospital to be used to augment the physician residency program. The organization pledged an additional sum of $20,000 to be paid at the rate of $5,000 per year for the same purpose.

19. Cash	5,000	
Pledges Receivable	20,000	
Contributions—Temporarily Restricted—Programs		25,000

The governing board and administration of Bloomfield Hospital expect the civic organization to honor its pledge; therefore, no Allowance for Uncollectible Pledges is created. Because the gift was received shortly before the end of FY2002, no expenses for the program were incurred during the year.

The hospital endowment consists of donated assets, the principal of which must be retained intact. The income from hospital endowment assets is expendable as the donor directed—either for general operating purposes or for named items or projects. The discussion in Chapters 8 and 16 concerning problems involved in distinguishing between principal and income are relevant, also, to hospital endowments. In order to be able to show that the terms of each endowment have been complied with, it is desirable to keep records for each separate endowment. As of September 30, 2001, Bloomfield Hospital is assumed to have only one endowment.

During FY2002, the hospital received marketable securities with a market value at the date of the gift of $24,000. The securities are to be held for the production of income; the income from these securities is for unrestricted use. The endowment may be accounted for as shown in the following entry:

20. Short-Term Investments	24,000	
Contributions—Permanently Restricted		24,000

Natural expenses of depreciation, interest, and provision for bad debts were allocated to the functional expenses based on an allocation basis established by the hospital.

21. Nursing Services Expenses	641,500	
Other Professional Services Expenses	179,620	
General Services Expenses	282,260	
Fiscal and Administrative Services Expenses	179,620	
Provision for Bad Debts		180,000
Depreciation Expense		783,000
Interest Expense		320,000

The pre-closing trial balance for Bloomfield Hospital as of September 30, 2002, is shown below. Financial statements reflecting the preceding transactions for Bloomfield Hospital were shown earlier in this chapter as Illustrations 17–3, 17–4, and 17–5.

BLOOMFIELD HOSPITAL
PRE-CLOSING TRIAL BALANCE
AS OF SEPTEMBER 30, 2002

	Debits	*Credits*
Cash	$ 172,100	
Short-Term Investments	1,278,000	
Accrued Interest Receivable	44,000	
Accounts and Notes Receivable	488,000	
Allowance for Uncollectible Receivables		$ 135,000
Pledges Receivable	1,163,000	
Allowance for Uncollectible Pledges		114,300
Inventory	160,000	
Prepaid Expenses	8,000	
Assets Limited as to Use—Cash	6,500	
Assets Limited as to Use—Investments	778,000	
Long-Term Investments	146,000	
Land	1,080,000	
Buildings	11,050,000	
Equipment	5,292,000	
Accumulated Depreciation—Buildings		1,365,000
Accumulated Depreciation—Equipment		1,702,000
Accounts Payable		259,000
Accrued Expenses Payable		173,500
Mortgages Payable		6,000,000
Net Assets—Unrestricted, Undesignated		8,262,000
Net Assets—Unrestricted, Designated		784,500
Net Assets—Temporarily Restricted—Plant		2,508,000
Net Assets—Permanently Restricted		154,000
Patient Service Revenue		9,261,000
Contractual Adjustments	100,000	
Other Revenue		48,800
Contributions—Unrestricted		297,900
Contributions—Temporarily Restricted		25,000
Contributions—Permanently Restricted		24,000
Investment Income—Unrestricted		36,100
Investment Income—Temporarily Restricted		77,000
Net Assets Released from Restrictions—Unrestricted		100,000
Net Assets Released from Restrictions—Temporarily Restricted	100,000	
Nursing Services Expenses	4,667,500	
Other Professional Services Expenses	1,311,620	
General Services Expenses	2,056,260	
Fiscal and Administrative Services Expenses	1,332,320	
Loss on Disposal of Equipment	1,500	
Provision for Uncollectible Pledges	66,300	
Loss on Sale of Investments	26,000	
	$31,327,100	$31,327,100

End-of-the-Year Closing Journal Entries. Unrestricted revenues and expenses that pertain to FY2002 are closed to the Unrestricted, Undesignated Net Asset account as shown below:

	Debits	Credits
22. Patient Service Revenue	9,261,000	
Other Revenue	48,800	
Contributions—Unrestricted	297,900	
Investment Income—Unrestricted	36,100	
Contractual Adjustments		100,000
Nursing Services Expenses		4,667,500
Other Professional Services Expenses		1,311,620
General Services Expenses		2,056,260
Fiscal and Administrative Services Expenses		1,332,320
Loss on Disposal of Equipment		1,500
Net Assets—Unrestricted, Undesignated		174,600

Restricted revenues that pertain to FY2002 are closed to the restricted net asset accounts as shown below:

	Debits	Credits
23. Contributions—Temporarily Restricted—Programs	25,000	
Contributions—Permanently Restricted	24,000	
Investment Income—Temporarily Restricted	77,000	
Net Assets—Temporarily Restricted—Plant	15,300	
Provision for Uncollectible Pledges		66,300
Loss on Sale of Investments		26,000
Net Assets—Temporarily Restricted—Programs		25,000
Net Assets—Permanently Restricted		24,000

Net Assets Released from Restrictions are closed out in the following entry:

	Debits	Credits
24. Net Assets Released from Restrictions—Unrestricted	100,000	
Net Assets—Temporarily Restricted—Plant	100,000	
Net Assets Released from Restrictions—Temporarily Restricted		100,000
Net Assets—Unrestricted, Undesignated		100,000

Financial Reporting of a Governmental Health Care Organization

GASB *Statement No. 34* provides guidance for governmental health care organizations that may be engaged in either governmental activities (i.e., financed through taxes, intergovernmental revenues, and other nonexchange revenues) or business-type activities (i.e., financed in whole or in part by fees charged to external users), or both.[15] Governmental activities are reported in governmental funds and internal service funds, while business-type activities are reported in enterprise funds.

[15]GASB *Statement No. 34*, Appendix D, describes changes that will be codified into Section Ho5 on Hospitals and Other Health Care Providers.

Governmental health care organizations engaged only in business-type activities should present the financial statements required for organizations that use proprietary fund accounting principles. For these governments, basic financial statements and RSI consist of the MD&A, proprietary fund financial statements (Statement of Net Assets or Balance Sheet; Statement of Revenues, Expenses, and Changes in Net Assets; Statement of Cash Flows), notes to the financial statements, and RSI other than MD&A, if applicable.

Governmental health care organizations engaged in more than one governmental program or that have both governmental and business-type activities should provide both fund financial statements and government-wide financial statements. For these governments, all the requirements for basic financial statements and RSI apply. Separately issued financial statements of a component unit hospital or other health care provider should acknowledge that it is a component unit of another government—for example "Sample County Hospital, a component unit of Sample County." In addition, the notes to the financial statements should identify the primary government in whose financial reporting entity it is included and describe its relationship with the primary government.

Fewer differences exist between not-for-profit and governmental health care organizations than did prior to GASB *Statement No. 34*. One difference that remains is that the Statement of Cash Flows prepared by a governmental entity will have four sections, an additional section relating to cash flows from noncapital financial activities, such as unrestricted gifts, investment income, and gifts restricted for future periods, as shown in Illustration 17–6. The Statement of Net Assets (or Balance Sheet) and Statement of Revenue, Expenses, and Changes in Net Assets required for governmental health care organizations that follow proprietary fund accounting—the most common case—are similar to the balance sheet and operating statements illustrated for not-for-profit health care organizations in Illustrations 17–3 and 17–4. Thus, these statements are not illustrated in this chapter. The interested reader should refer to Chapter 7 for illustrations of the formats of proprietary fund statements.

Related Entities

Health care organizations have long been associated with separate fund-raising foundations, medical research foundations, auxiliaries, and guilds. More recently, organizations are networking with other organizations in an effort to integrate health care services, control costs, increase efficiency, and ultimately improve the quality of health care. Some independent organizations combine for a specific purpose, for example, to obtaining financing, in which case they become an **obligated group.** These joint ventures include every combination of legal structure: for-profit, not-for-profit, and governmental organizations. Financial reporting guidance comes from the FASB in existing statements on consolidations and

Illustration 17–6 Illustration of Statement of Cash Flows—GASB Jurisdiction

BLOOMFIELD HOSPITAL
STATEMENT OF CASH FLOWS
YEAR ENDED SEPTEMBER 30, 2002

Cash flows from operating activities:	
Cash received from patients and third-party payors	$8,842,000
Cash paid to employees and suppliers	(8,014,200)
Other receipts from operations	48,800
Net cash provided by operating activities	876,600
Cash flows from noncapital financing activities:	
Unrestricted gifts and income from endowments	306,000
Gifts restricted for future operations	5,000
Net cash provided by noncapital financing activities	311,000
Cash flows from capital and related financing activities:	
Purchase of property and equipment	(400,000)
Principal paid on mortgage	(400,000)
Interest paid	(160,000)
Collection of pledges receivable	292,000
Proceeds from sale of equipment	500
Net cash used for capital and related financing activities	(667,500)
Cash flows from investing activities:	
Proceeds from sale of securities	59,000
Interest received on assets limited as to use	28,000
Interest received on donor-restricted assets	69,000
Cash invested in assets limited as to use	(378,000)
Cash invested in donor-restricted assets	(359,000)
Net cash used by investing activities	(581,000)
Net increase (decrease) in cash	(60,900)
Cash and cash equivalents, September 30, 2001	239,500
Cash and cash equivalents, September 30, 2002	$ 178,600

RECONCILIATION OF OPERATING INCOME TO NET CASH PROVIDED BY OPERATING ACTIVITIES

Operating income (loss)	$ (157,900)
Adjustments:	
Depreciation	783,000
Increase in patient accounts receivable, net	(139,000)
Increase in inventory	(80,000)
Increase in accounts payable	149,000
Increase in accrued expenses	157,500
Decrease in prepaid expenses	4,000
Interest paid in cash (Note 1)	160,000
Net cash provided by operating activities and gains and losses	$ 876,600

Note I: Interest was classified as an operating expense on the income statement but as cash flows from capital and related activities on the cash flows statement prepared in conformity with GASB standards.

affiliated organizations and the GASB in statements on the reporting entity.[16] If one entity controls another, then the financial statements of the two organizations should be consolidated in order to be most useful to the decision maker. At a minimum, any economic interest between the organizations should be disclosed in each other's Notes to the Financial Statements. At issue is a working definition of *control* and *agency*. The FASB is expected to provide further guidance as part of its consolidations project.[17]

Other Accounting Issues

Budgeting and Costs

Governmental and other not-for-profit hospitals and other health care entities, even though they are service institutions, must have an inflow of funds at least equal to their outflow of funds. Since this is the case, prudent management will attempt to forecast the outlays for a definite period and forecast the income for the same period. Most hospitals use comprehensive budgets for managerial purposes but do not incorporate the budgetary provision in the accounts. Other hospitals, principally governmental hospitals, do record their budgets in the ledger. Nevertheless, it is important that every hospital and other health care entity have an annual budget and that the budget be administered intelligently. For a hospital, or for any other enterprise, good financial management requires outlays to be evaluated in terms of results achieved. Insistence on rigid adherence to a budget not related to actual workload (as is the case in some governmental agencies) tends to make the budget useless as a management tool. Generally budgetary accounts are used only if required by law.

Until the 1980s, it was customary for hospitals to determine costs of services rendered during a fiscal year by rearranging financial accounting data generated during that year. Although never satisfactory for financial management purposes, the procedure for cost determination was acceptable for purposes of reporting costs to third-party payors, which reimbursed hospitals on a retrospective (after-the-fact) basis. Since 1983, however, the largest purchaser of hospital services, Medicare, in an attempt to establish better control over hospital costs, has utilized a system of prospective payment. The Medicare system pays health care providers standardized rates for services rendered to patients in each **diagnosis-related group (DRG).** Health care providers, therefore, have an incentive to determine actual costs of services rendered, by DRG, in order to keep their costs commensurate with Medicare's payments for services rendered to Medicare patients. It is now common for most hospitals to have sophisticated systems to capture costs by procedure or DRG.

---

[16]FASB, Exposure Draft, *Consolidated Financial Statements: Purpose and Policy* (Norwalk, CT: FASB, 1999); GASB, *Codification*, Sec. 2100.

[17]When the FASB completes its projects on consolidations and affiliated organizations, the authors will make an Update Bulletin available to adopters of this book.

The DRG is a case-mix classification scheme that is used to determine the payment provided to the hospital for inpatient services, regardless of how much the hospital spends to treat a patient. For example, the DRG for maternity patients may provide payment at 0.8 relative to a norm of 1.0, while the DRG for a heart transplant patient may provide 1.3 times the average payment. These relative numbers are multiplied by the federal standard rate as determined by the Healthcare Financing Administration (HCFA). There are approximately 470 DRGs and the average reimbursement was $6,029 in 1997.

Auditing

Auditing issues of particular significance to the health care industry relate to contingencies, third-party payors, related entities, and restructuring. Renewed efforts on the part of the federal government to curb health care fraud and illegal acts also affect auditors and their clients. Congress instituted new civil and criminal penalties in the Health Insurance Portability and Accountability Act of 1996, False Claims Act, and Stark Laws I and II that are designed to penalize individuals and organizations that contribute to the estimated $100 billion losses due to fraud and abuse in the health care industry. Investigations center on improper billing and coding, improper care, and kickbacks. Health care providers should have written compliance policies and designate a compliance officer who has the authority to implement the compliance program.[18] Another important auditing issue relates to the revision of OMB *Circular A-133* and its application to hospitals and health care organizations, as described in Chapter 11 of this text.

Taxation and Regulatory Issues

Since a large share of health care providers are legally structured as tax-exempt organizations under IRC Sec. 501(c)(3), the regulations and activities of the Internal Revenue Service should be of concern to the accountant working with health care organizations. For example, the penalties for private inurement or excess economic benefits to individuals, introduced in the Taxpayer Bill of Rights 2 of 1996 and Chapter 15 of this text, apply to health care administrators and persons with substantial influence over the organization. The IRS has increased its review of physician recruiting incentives, joint operating agreements for exemption applications, unrelated business income (such as hospital pharmacy sales to the general public), private-activity bonds, and independent contractor (versus employee) status. Congressional and public scrutiny over the distributions of assets of not-for-profit organizations that change legal status and the amount of charity care delivery by tax-exempt hospitals is at its highest point in the century. Sanctions are economically significant and may involve loss of tax-exempt status or eligibility for tax-exempt financing.

---

[18]AICPA, Audit Risk Alert, *Health Care Industry Developments* 1998–99 (New York: AICPA, 1999), p. 10.

Certain Types of Health Care Organizations

Prepaid health care plans, such as **health maintenance organizations (HMOs)** or **preferred provider organizations (PPOs),** function as brokers between the consumer or patient demanding the services and the providers of health care, such as health care professionals or hospitals. Contractual arrangements among these parties, including employers, are complex and varied. If the premium revenue from contracts is not expected to cover the agreed-upon health care costs, then the prepaid plan may transfer some of its risk to an insurance company under *stop-loss insurance*, or a **risk contract.** In any case, the costs of future services to be rendered, net of anticipated revenue, should be recorded as a liability if it meets the criteria of a contingent liability. Certain contract acquisition costs, such as commissions paid to agents based on new enrollments or subscriber contracts, should be expensed as incurred, although there is some theoretical support for deferring these costs.[19]

There are more than 1,000 **continuing care retirement communities** (CCRCs) in the United States that are operated primarily by not-for-profit organizations. CCRCs provide residential care in a facility, along with some level of long-term medical care that is less intensive than hospital care. There are many ways to structure contracts between the patient/resident and the CCRC; however, most plans require advance payment of an entrance fee and periodic fees to cover operating costs in exchange for current use of the facilities and the promise to provide some level of health and residential services in the future. The advance fee may be refundable if certain future events occur, such as the death of the resident. Accounting issues, such as refundable and nonrefundable advance fees, the obligation to provide future services, and the costs of acquiring initial care contracts, are beyond the scope of this text.

Financial and Operational Analysis

The goal of financial and operational analysis depends, of course, on the needs of the decision maker. For example, managers are directly accountable for performance; financial analysts determine the creditworthiness of organizations issuing debt; and third parties determine appropriate payment based on costs. Consumers may want nonfinancial performance and quality measures, such as the success rate for various procedures or the value received for money spent.

Health care entities are evaluated using a variety of ratios and benchmarks, some of which are unique to hospitals and others that are similar to those applied to other businesses. These analyses can be categorized into those that measure:

1. Capacity utilization (e.g., occupancy rate or daily census and average length of stay).

---

[19]AAG-HCO, Sec. 13.10.

2. Profitability (e.g., gross patient service revenue per discharge or operating profit margin or cash flow per bed).
3. Patient and payout mix (e.g., Medicare case-mix index or Medicaid acute care days as a percentage of total acute care days).
4. Pricing strategy (e.g., markup ratio for ancillary or laboratory services).
5. Productivity and efficiency (e.g., full-time-equivalent personnel per average daily census or overhead expenses as a percentage of operating expenses).
6. Capital and liquidity (e.g., plant, property, and equipment per bed or debt per bed and current ratio and number of days in accounts receivable).[20]

Once ratios are computed, they are compared to industry benchmarks. Hospitals are compared based upon bed size, geographic location, and teaching designation. Further analysis is done according to the type of patient care. Organizations that accumulate information about health care norms include the American Hospital Association (AHA); the Institute for Health Care Improvement (IHI); bond-rating agencies, such as Moody's and Standard & Poor's; Health Care Investment Analysts, Inc. (HCIA); and the Center for Health Care Industry Performance Studies (CHIPS).

Conclusion

A single chapter on accounting for health care entities can touch on only the most fundamental features. Variations in the reporting and accounting procedures for individual health care entities exist due to the variety in the type and size of health care providers, the range of services offered, the dependence of these entities on third-party payors, and the financial sophistication of the governing board, administrator, and finance director. For further information, the references cited in the Selected References section are recommended.

Key Terms

Assets limited as to use, 780
Capitation fees, 777
Charity care, 779
Continuing care retirement community (CCRC), 794
Contractual adjustments (or allowances), 779
Diagnosis-related groups (DRGs), 792
Health maintenance organization (HMO), 794
Obligated group, 790
Performance indicator, 777
Preferred provider organization (PPO), 794
Prospective payment system (PPS), 780
Risk contract, 794
Settlement accounts, 781
Third-party payor, 780

[20] Nadia A. Perry, *Introduction to the Health Care Industry* (Englewood, CO: Micromash, 1999).

Selected References

American Institute of Certified Public Accountants. Audit and Accounting Guide, *Health Care Organizations*. New York, 1999.

Financial Accounting Standards Board. *Statement No. 116*. "Accounting for Contributions Received and Contributions Made." Norwalk, CT, 1993.

________. *Statement No. 117*. "Financial Statements of Not-for-Profit Organizations." Norwalk, CT, 1993.

Governmental Accounting Standards Board. *Codification*. "Section Ho5." Norwalk, CT, 1999.

Periodicals

Healthcare Financial Management. The journal of the Healthcare Financial Management Association, Oak Brook, IL.

Hospital Progress. The journal of the Catholic Hospital Association, St. Louis, MO.

Hospitals. The journal of the American Hospital Association, Chicago, IL.

Questions

17–1. "All providers of health care services must use fund accounting." True or false? Explain your answer.

17–2. What are the required financial statements under the provisions of the AICPA Audit and Accounting Guide *Health Care Organizations*?

17–3. What are the major differences between the accounting treatment of hospital property, plant, and equipment used in rendering hospital services and the accounting treatment of general capital assets of state and local governmental units?

17–4. How do the accounting treatments for charity services, patient discounts, contractual adjustments, and provision for bad debts differ in terms of their effects on patient service revenues and related receivables?

17–5. What is the difference in accounting for investments among investor-owned, not-for-profit, and governmental health care organizations?

17–6. Breyer Memorial Hospital received a $100,000 gift that was restricted by the donor for heart research. At fiscal year-end Breyer had incurred $25,000 in expenses related to this project. Explain how these transactions would be reported in Breyer's balance sheet and operating statement under the independent assumptions that (*a*) Breyer is a *governmentally* owned not-for-profit hospital and (*b*) Breyer is a *nongovernmentally* owned not-for-profit hospital.

17–7. "FASB standards applicable to nongovernmentally owned not-for-profit health care entities preclude such entities from distinguishing 'Assets Limited as to Use' from other unrestricted assets." Do you agree? Explain fully.

17–8. What contingent liabilities arise from a health care organization's relations with third-party payors?

17–9. Explain the importance of diagnosis-related groups (DRGs) in the cost accounting systems of a health care provider.

17–10. What are some particular accounting issues in continuing care retirement communities (CCRCs)?

Cases

17–1. Charity Care. The local newspaper of a large urban area printed a story entitled "Charity Care by Hospitals Stirs Debate." The story quotes one legislator who wants "to ensure that the state's nonprofit hospitals are fulfilling their obligation; that is to provide charity care at least equal to the tax exemption they receive as a nonprofit entity." The following chart is provided:

Comparison of Selected Factors in Three Nonprofit Hospitals
(dollars in millions)

	Hope Hospital	*St. Pat's Hospital*	*Capitol Hospital*
Estimated taxes the hospitals would pay if they were not tax-exempt	$6.8	$2.2	$4.5
Charity and other uncompensated care	$17.8 of which $3.8 is bad debts	$3.1 not including bad debts	$6.7
Community service programs*	$1.6	$1.0	n.a.
Unpaid cost of Medicaid and Medicare	$3.4	$0.6	n.a.
Nonreimbursed research and graduate medical education	$2.0	$0.7	n.a.

n.a. = Not available.

*Including such programs as activity sponsorships, playground equipment, neighborhood summits, and scholarships for at-risk students.

Required

a. What are the obligations of nongovernmental IRC Sec. 501(c)(3) organizations to provide charity care?

b. Do you agree that the hospitals are not fulfilling their obligations? Why or why not?

c. What additional information would you like to have? Do you expect to find this information in the audited annual financial statements?

17–2. Purchase of a Health Care Organization. You are an accountant with a large public hospital. The Hospital Board recently decided to horizontally integrate by purchasing other health care organizations that provide specialized services. You have been asked to review Arbor Community Hospital's Statement of Operations (presented on the next page) in order to determine if it is a "profitable" organization. It is a not-for-profit hospital with a self-perpetuating board comprised of community leaders. Arbor Community offers specialized services including an inpatient headache clinic and a substance abuse clinic.

Required

a. Write a concise, professional report to your superior identifying some ratios you find relevant from the Statement of Operations that support your position as to whether the hospital is profitable.

b. What other factors do you consider critical in a decision to purchase an existing health care facility?

c. What other financial information would you like to review in order to form an opinion as to the performance of this hospital?

ARBOR COMMUNITY HOSPITAL
STATEMENTS OF OPERATIONS
YEARS ENDED DECEMBER 31

	2002			2001		
	Unrestricted	*Temporarily Restricted*	*Total*	*Unrestricted*	*Temporarily Restricted*	*Total*
Revenue, gains, and other support:						
Net patient service revenue	$39,408,595	—	$39,408,595	$36,655,677	—	$36,655,677
Other revenue	2,701,284	—	2,701,284	2,411,442	—	2,411,442
Investment income	980,244	$ 32,752	1,012,996	514,844	$ 14,183	529,027
Net assets released from restrictions used for operations	44,034	(44,034)	—	20,086	(20,086)	—
Total revenue, gains, and other support	43,134,157	(11,282)	43,122,875	39,602,049	(5,903)	39,596,146
Expenses:						
Inpatient nursing services	5,035,376	—	5,035,376	5,219,917	—	5,219,917
Outpatient and ancillary services	18,468,238	—	18,468,238	16,236,239	—	16,236,239
Physician offices	1,928,224	—	1,928,224	1,933,725	—	1,933,725
General services	5,692,281	—	5,692,281	5,677,606	—	5,677,606
Fiscal services	1,585,042	—	1,585,042	1,621,436	—	1,621,436
Administrative services	4,967,417	—	4,967,417	4,381,216	—	4,381,216
Interest	809,895	—	809,895	510,008	—	510,008
Depreciation and amortization	2,752,519	—	2,752,519	2,459,604	—	2,459,604
Bad debts	994,506	—	994,506	858,790	—	858,790
Total expenses	42,233,498	—	42,233,498	38,898,541	—	38,898,541
Excess of revenue, gains, and other support over (under) expenses:	900,659	(11,282)	889,377	703,508	(5,903)	697,605
Net gain on investments reported at fair value	48,674	—	48,674	433,446	—	433,446
Contributions	952	158,068	159,020	4,566	135,267	139,833
Net assets released from restrictions used for purchase of property and equipment	36,540	(36,540)	—	488,524	(488,524)	—
Change in net assets before extraordinary item	986,825	110,246	1,097,071	1,630,044	(359,160)	1,270,844
Extraordinary loss on refinancing of debt	—	—	—	(140,129)	—	(140,129)
Increase (decrease) in net assets	$ 986,825	$110,246	$ 1,097,071	$ 1,489,915	$(359,160)	$ 1,130,755

17–3. Internet Case. Many professional associations of health care professionals and providers have published position papers on health care reform. Identify the organizations that have large and/or influential health care constituencies and find their websites on the Internet. See if they have a position paper, publication, or letter to a federal oversight body that articulates their position on proposed changes in the delivery and payment of health care in the United States. List the accounting issues that they discuss (e.g., financial reporting, managerial accounting, taxation, information systems, and auditing) as opposed to financing issues. For example, the American Hospital Association (http://www.aha.org) posted their response to health issues in President Clinton's January 2000 State of the Union Address in the "Press Releases" section of their website. (Note: web pages change frequently, so this letter may not still be on the website when you look at it.)

Exercises and Problems

17–1. Multiple Choice. Choose the best answer.

1. Not-for-profit health care organizations are typically sponsored by:
   a. Community organizations.
   b. Religious organizations.
   c. Universities.
   d. Any of the above.
2. Revenue from the gift shop of a hospital would normally be included in:
   a. Nonoperating gains.
   b. Other revenue.
   c. Patient service revenue.
   d. Professional services revenue.
3. Donated medicine that normally would be purchased by a hospital should be recorded at fair market value and should be credited directly to:
   a. Other Revenue.
   b. Nonoperating Gains.
   c. Unrestricted Net Assets.
   d. Deferred Revenue.
4. A not-for-profit hospital that follows FASB standards and the AICPA Audit and Accounting Guide *Health Care Organizations* should report investment income from endowments that is restricted to a specific operating purpose as:
   a. General Fund revenue.
   b. Endowment Fund revenue.
   c. Unrestricted revenue.
   d. An increase to temporarily restricted net assets.
5. A $50,000 donation is held by a bank in an independent permanent trust with the investment income dedicated for use by a hospital for operating purposes. The $50,000 principal should be:
   a. Reported as assets limited as to use by the hospital.
   b. Reported as nonoperating revenue of the hospital.
   c. Reported as permanently restricted net assets of the hospital.
   d. Disclosed in Notes to the Financial Statements of the hospital.
6. Restricted funds are:
   a. Not available unless the board of directors removes the restrictions.
   b. Restricted as to use by the donor, grantor, or other source of the resources.

c. Not available for current operating use; however, the income earned on the funds is available.

d. Restricted as to use only for board-designated purposes.

7. Depreciation should be recognized in the financial statements of:
   a. Proprietary (for-profit) hospitals only.
   b. Both proprietary (for-profit) and not-for-profit hospitals.
   c. Both proprietary (for-profit) and not-for-profit hospitals, only when they are affiliated with a college or university.
   d. All hospitals, as a memorandum entry not affecting the statement of revenues and expenses.
8. The financial statements of a nongovernmental not-for-profit hospital and its related medical research foundation should be consolidated if:
   a. The hospital "controls" the Foundation by appointing all the directors to its Board.
   b. The hospital has a significant economic interest in the activities and assets of the Foundation.
   c. The assets of the Foundation were contributed by donors who stipulated that they could only be used for the benefit of the Hospital.
   d. All of the above are factors to consider in the determination of whether to consolidate two reporting entities, or merely disclose the existence of each other.
9. Which of the following sets of financial statements is required by GAAP for nongovernmentally owned hospitals?
   a. Balance Sheet, Statement of Revenues and Expenses and Changes in Fund Balances.
   b. Balance Sheet, Statement of Revenues and Expenses, and Statement of Cash Flows.
   c. Balance Sheet, Statement of Changes in Fund Balances, and Statement of Cash Flows.
   d. Balance Sheet, Statement of Operations, and Statement of Cash Flows.
10. A possible contingency that might have to be disclosed in the Notes to the Financial Statements of a health care organization is:
   a. An agreed-upon settlement between a third-party payor and the health care provider.
   b. Premiums received for prepaid health care by a health maintenance organization.
   c. An uncertain result of ongoing negotiations for payment with a third-party payor for services rendered to patients.
   d. None of the above.

17–2. Nongovernmental Hospital. The Clearwater Community Hospital Balance Sheet as of December 31, 2001, is presented on the next page.

CLEARWATER COMMUNITY HOSPITAL
BALANCE SHEET
DECEMBER 31, 2001

Assets			*Liabilities and Fund Balance*	
Current:			Current:	
Cash		$ 65,000	Accounts payable	$ 65,000
Accounts and notes receivable	$ 140,000		Accrued payroll	110,000
Less: Allowance for uncollectibles	12,000	128,000		
Inventory		71,000		
Total Current Assets		264,000	Total Current Liabilities	175,000
Assets Limited as to Use:				
Cash	11,500		Long-Term Debt:	
Investments	210,000		Mortgage payable	3,500,000
Total Assets Limited as to Use		221,500	Total Liabilities	3,675,000
			Net Assets:	
Property, Plant, and Equipment:			Unrestricted, Undesignated	1,782,000
Land		208,000	Unrestricted, Designated for Plant Replacements	221,500
Buildings, at cost	4,516,000			
Less: Accumulated depreciation	1,506,000	3,010,000	Total Net Assets	2,003,500
Equipment, at cost	2,871,000			
Less: Accumulated depreciation	896,000	1,975,000		
Total Property, Plant, and Equipment		5,193,000		
Total Assets		$5,678,500	Total Liabilities and Net Assets	$5,678,500

Required

a. Record in general journal form the effect of the following transactions during the fiscal year ended December 31, 2002, assuming Clearwater Community Hospital is a nongovernmental, not-for-profit hospital.

(1) Summary of revenue journal:

Patient services revenue, gross	$3,497,500
Adjustments and allowances:	
Contracting agencies	122,600

(2) Summary of cash receipts journal:

Interest on Investments in Assets Limited as to Use	20,000
Unrestricted grant from United Fund	160,000
Collections of receivables	3,373,600

(3) Purchases journal:

Administration	163,900
General services expenses	176,800
Nursing services expenses	269,400
Other professional services expenses	256,600

(4) Payroll journal:

Administration	247,600
General services expenses	175,000
Nursing services expenses	540,300
Other professional services expenses	412,200

(5) Summary of cash payments journal:

Interest expense	280,000
Payment on mortgage principal	500,000
Accounts payable for purchases	839,500
Accrued payroll	1,370,000
Transfer to Assets Limited as to Use	30,000

(6) Equipment that cost $6,560, and for which accumulated depreciation totaled $4,920, was traded for similar new equipment costing $9,840; the payment in cash amounted to $8,800 (the cash was paid from Assets Limited as to Use—Cash).

(7) Depreciation charges for the year amounted to $117,000 for the buildings and $128,500 for equipment.

(8) Other information:

(*a*) Provision for uncollectible receivables, $29,000.

(*b*) Supplies inventory:

	12/31/2001	*12/31/2002*
Administration	$ 8,000	$ 7,300
General services expenses	8,700	9,000
Nursing services expenses	17,000	17,200
Other professional services expenses	37,300	40,000
Totals	$71,000	$73,500

(*c*) Portion of Mortgage Payable due within one year, $500,000.

(9) Assume there was no change in fair value of investments at year-end.

(10) Provisions for bad debts, interest expense, and depreciation expense were allocated to functional expense accounts in proportion to their pre-allocation balances. Nominal accounts were closed.

(11) Reflecting the net increase in Assets Limited as to Use of $41,200 (see transactions 2, 5, and 6), record the increase in Net Assets, Unrestricted, Designated for Plant Replacement.

b. Prepare a Balance Sheet as of December 31, 2002.

c. Prepare a Statement of Operations for the year ended December 31, 2002.

17–3. Restricted Contribution. The following transactions occurred in the Jackson Hospital:

1. Under the will of Samuel H. Samuels, a bequest of $100,000 was received for research on gerontology. Because the principal of the bequest, as well as any earnings on investments, are expendable for the specified research purpose, the bequest should be reported as temporarily restricted.
2. Pending the need of the money for the designated purpose, part of it was invested in $95,000 of par value City of Jackson 6 percent bonds, at 103 and accrued interest of $823.
3. An interest payment of $2,850 was received on the City of Jackson bonds.
4. The bonds were sold at 104 and accrued interest of $443.
5. The income from the Samuels gift was used for the stipulated purpose.

Required

Make journal entries for the above transactions assuming this is a nongovernmental, not-for-profit hospital.

17–4. Third-Party Payors. The following transactions took place in the Brady Memorial Hospital during the fiscal year 2002.

1. Gross revenues of $78,000,000 were earned for service to Medicare patients.
2. Expected contractual adjustments with Medicare, a third-party payor, are $36,050,000; an "Allowance for Contractual Adjustments" account is used to record these contractual adjustments.
3. Medicare "cleared charges" of $78,000,000 with payments of $39,608,000 and contractual allowances of $38,392,000.
4. Interim payments received from Medicare amounted to $2,600,000.
5. The Hospital made a lump-sum payment back to Medicare of $1,000,000.

The Hospital uses an Interim Payments account to keep track of the payments made between Medicare and the Hospital until final settlement is determined.

Required

a. Record the transactions in the general journal.
b. Calculate the amount of net patient service revenue.
c. What is the net cash flow from transactions with Medicare?
d. What adjustments must be made at the end of the year to "settle" up with Medicare and properly report the net patient service revenue after this settlement?

17–5. Nongovernmental Hospital Financial Statements. The Dexter Memorial Hospital internal use fund Balance Sheet as of December 31, 2001, is shown on the next page. The Controller asks you to prepare an aggregated balance sheet in accord with current financial reporting standards according to the AICPA Audit and Accounting Guide *Health Care Organizations*. You determine that (1) the cash and investments of the Plant Fund are restricted under the terms of several gifts to use for plant replacement or expansion; income from Plant Fund investments is restricted to the same purposes. (2) Income from Endowment Fund investments may be used at the discretion of the hospital governing board.

DEXTER MEMORIAL HOSPITAL
BALANCE SHEET
AS OF DECEMBER 31, 2001

Assets			*Liabilities and Fund Balances*	
		Operating Fund		
Cash		$ 20,000	Accounts payable	$ 16,000
Accounts receivable	$ 37,000		Accrued expense—payable	6,000
Less: Allowance for uncollectible accounts	7,000	30,000	Total Liabilities	22,000
Inventory of supplies		14,000	Fund balance	42,000
Total		$ 64,000	Total	$ 64,000
		Plant Fund		
Cash		$ 53,800	Mortgage bonds payable	$ 150,000
Investments		71,200		
Land		400,000		
Buildings	$1,750,000			
Less: Accumulated depreciation	430,000	1,320,000	Fund balance: Investment in plant	2,021,000
Equipment	680,000		Reserved for plant improvement and replacement	220,000
Less: Accumulated depreciation	134,000	546,000		2,241,000
Total		$2,391,000	Total	$2,391,000
		Endowment Fund		
Cash		$6,000		
Investments		260,000	Fund balance—income unrestricted	$ 266,000
Total		$ 266,000	Total	$ 266,000

17–6. Governmental Hospital. During 2001, the following events and transactions were recorded by Blackpool City Hospital. Show in general journal form the entries that should be made for each of the 12 transactions and the closing entries in accord with the standards for a governmental health care entity that follows proprietary fund accounting, as discussed in this chapter.

1. Gross charges for hospital services, all charged to accounts and notes receivable, were as follows:

Patient service revenues	$1,086,000

2. Additional information relating to current-year receivables and revenues were as follows:

Contractual adjustments	$30,000
Provision for bad debts	15,000

3. Paid $18,000 to retire mortgage bonds payable with an equivalent face value.
4. During the year, the Hospital received in cash unrestricted contributions of $50,000 and unrestricted income from endowment investments of $6,500.

5. New equipment costing $26,000 was acquired from donor-restricted cash. An X-ray machine that cost $24,000 and had an undepreciated cost of $2,400 was sold for $500 cash.
6. Vouchers totaling $1,191,000 were issued for the following items:

Fiscal and administrative services expenses	$215,000
General services expenses	225,000
Nursing services expenses	520,000
Other professional services expenses	165,000
Inventory	60,000
Expenses accrued at December 31, 2000	6,000

7. Collections of accounts receivable totaled $985,000. Accounts written off as uncollectible amounted to $11,000.
8. Cash payments on vouchers payable (paid to employers and suppliers) during the year were $825,000.
9. Supplies of $37,000 were issued to nursing services.
10. On December 31, 2001, accrued interest income on investments was $800.
11. Depreciation of buildings and equipment was as follows:

Buildings	$44,000
Equipment	73,000

12. On December 31, 2001, an accrual of $6,100 was made for interest on mortgage bonds payable.
13. On December 31, 2001, closing entries were made in the general journal.

17–7. Nongovernmental Hospital. The following selected information was taken from the books and records of Glendora Hospital (a nongovernmental, not-for-profit hospital) as of and for the year ended June 30, 2002.

- Patient service revenue totaled $16,000,000, with the allowance for uncollectible accounts and contractual adjustments amounting to $1,800,000 and $1,600,000, respectively. Other revenue aggregated $346,000 and included $160,000 from specific purpose funds. Revenue of $6,000,000 recognized under cost-reimbursement agreements is subject to audit and retroactive adjustment by third-party payors (other than Medicare). Estimated retroactive adjustments under these agreements have been included in allowances.
- Unrestricted gifts and bequests of $410,000 were received.
- Unrestricted income from endowments totaled $160,000.
- Income from investments aggregated $82,000.
- Operating expenses totaled $13,370,000 and included $500,000 for depreciation computed on the straight-line basis. However, accelerated depreciation is used to determine reimbursable costs under certain third-party reimbursement agreements. Net cost reimbursement revenue amounting to $220,000, resulting from the difference in depreciation methods, was deferred to future years.
- Also included in operating expenses are pension costs of $100,000, in connection with a noncontributory pension plan covering substantially all of Glendora's employees. Accrued pension costs are funded currently. Prior service

cost is being amortized over a period of 20 years. The actuarially computed value of vested and nonvested benefits at year-end amounted to $3,000,000 and $350,000, respectively. The assumed rate of return used in determining the actuarial present value of accumulated plan benefits was 8 percent. The plan's net assets available for benefits at year-end was $3,050,000.

- Gifts and bequests are recorded at fair market values when received.
- Patient service revenue is accounted for at established rates on the accrual basis.

Required

a. Prepare a formal Statement of Operations for Glendora Hospital for the year ended June 30, 2002.

b. Draft the appropriate disclosures in separate notes accompanying the Statement of Operations referencing each note to its respective item in the statement.

(AICPA, adapted)

17–8. Errors in a Nongovernmental Hospital. Esperanza Hospital's post-closing trial balance at December 31, 2001, appears as follows:

ESPERANZA HOSPITAL
TRIAL BALANCE
DECEMBER 31, 2001

	Debits	*Credits*
Cash	$ 60,000	
Investment in U.S. Treasury Bills	400,000	
Investment in Corporate Bonds	500,000	
Interest Receivable	10,000	
Accounts Receivable	50,000	
Inventory	30,000	
Land	100,000	
Building	800,000	
Equipment	170,000	
Allowance for Depreciation		$ 410,000
Accounts Payable		20,000
Notes Payable		70,000
Endowment Fund Balance		520,000
Other Fund Balances		1,100,000
Totals	$2,120,000	$2,120,000

Esperanza, which is a nongovernmentally affiliated not-for-profit hospital, did not maintain its books in conformity with the principles of the AICPA Audit and Accounting Guide *Health Care Organizations*. Effective January 1, 2002, Esperanza's Board of Trustees voted to adjust the December 31, 2002, general ledger balances to conform to the Guide.

Additional Account Information

- *Investment in corporate bonds* pertains to the amount required to be accumulated under a board policy to invest cash equal to accumulated depreciation until the funds are needed for asset replacement. The $500,000 balance at December 31, 2001, is less than the full amount required because of errors in computation of building depreciation for past years. Included in the allowance for depreciation is a correctly computed amount of $90,000 applicable to equipment.

- *Endowment balance* has been credited with the following:

Donor's bequest of cash	$300,000
Gains on sales of securities	100,000
Interest and dividends earned in 1999, 2000, and 2001	120,000
Total	$520,000

The terms of the bequest specify that the principal, plus all gains on sales of investments, is to remain fully invested in U.S. government or corporate securities. At December 31, 2001, $400,000 was invested in U.S. Treasury bills. The bequest further specifies that interest and dividends earned on investments are to be used for payment of current operating expenses.

- *Land* comprises the following:

Donation of land in 1990, at appraised value	$ 40,000
Appreciation in fair value of land as determined by independent appraiser in 2001	60,000
Total	$100,000

- *Building* comprises the following:

Hospital building completed 40 years ago, when operations were started (estimated useful life, 50 years), at cost	$720,000
Installation of elevator 20 years ago (estimated useful life, 20 years), at cost	80,000
Total	$800,000

Required

a. Prepare in general journal form adjusting entries necessary to restate the accounts given in the trial balance properly. Show all supporting computations in good form.

b. Prepare in general journal form entries to reflect account balances that Esperanza Hospital should report in financial statements prepared in conformity with generally accepted accounting principles as set forth in the AICPA Audit and Accounting Guide.

(AICPA, adapted)

Glossary

Some of these definitions were taken with permission from publications of the Government Finance Officers Association. Others were taken from specialized publications cited in the text; the remainder were supplied by the authors. The letters "q.v." signify "which see"; that is, the preceding word is defined elsewhere in the glossary.

Abatement A complete or partial cancellation of a levy imposed by a governmental unit. Abatements usually apply to tax levies, special assessments, and service charges.

Account Group A self-balancing set of accounts, but not a fiscal entity, therefore not a fund. See General Fixed Assets Account Group and General Long-Term Debt Account Group.

Accountability Being obliged to explain one's actions, to justify what one does; the requirement for government to answer to its citizenry—to justify the raising of public resources and expenditure of those resources. Also, in the GASB's view, the obligation to report whether the government operated within appropriate legal constraints; whether resources were used efficiently, economically, and effectively; whether current-year revenues were sufficient to pay for the services provided in the current year; and whether the burden for services previously provided will be shifted to future taxpayers.

Accounting Period A period at the end of which, and for which, financial statements are prepared. See also Fiscal Period.

Accounting System The total structure of records and procedures that discover, record, classify, and report information on the financial position and operations of a governmental unit or any of its funds, account groups, and organizational components.

Accounts Receivable Amounts owing on open account from private persons, firms, or corporations for goods and services furnished by a governmental unit. Taxes Receivable and Special Assessments Receivable are recorded separately. Amounts due from other funds or from other governmental units should be reported separately.

Accrual Basis The basis of accounting under which revenues are recorded when earned and expenditures (or expenses) are recorded as soon as they result in liabilities for benefits received, notwithstanding that the receipt of cash or the payment of cash may take place, in whole or in part, in another accounting period. See also Accrue and Levy.

Accrue To record revenues when earned and to record expenditures (or expenses) as soon as they result in liabilities for benefits received, notwithstanding that the receipt of cash or payment of cash may take place, in whole or in part, in another accounting period. See also Accrual Basis, Accrued Expenses, and Accrued Revenue.

Accrued Expenses Expenses incurred during the current accounting period but not payable until a subsequent accounting period. See also Accrual Basis and Accrue.

Accrued Income See Accrued Revenue.

Accrued Interest on Investments Purchased Interest accrued on investments between the last interest payment date and the date of purchase.

Accrued Interest Payable A liability account that represents the amount of interest expense accrued at the balance sheet date but not due until a later date.

Accrued Revenue Revenue earned during the current accounting period but not to be collected until a subsequent accounting period. See also Accrual Basis and Accrue.

Accrued Taxes Payable A liability for taxes that have accrued since the last payment date.

Accrued Wages Payable A liability for wages earned by employees between the last payment date and the balance sheet date.

Accumulated Depreciation See Allowance for Depreciation.

Acquisition Adjustment Difference between amount paid by a utility for plant assets acquired from another utility and the original cost (q.v.) of those assets less depreciation to date of acquisition.

Activity A specific and distinguishable line of work performed by one or more organizational components of a governmental unit for the purpose of accomplishing a function for which the governmental unit is responsible. For example, Food Inspection is an activity performed in the discharge of the Health function. See also Function, Subfunction, and Subactivity.

Activity-Based Costing (ABC) A cost accounting system that identifies specific factors (cost drivers) that drive the costs of service or production activities, and tracks the consumption of cost drivers in producing outputs of goods or services. See also Cost Determination.

Activity Classification A grouping of expenditures on the basis of specific lines of work performed by organization units. For example, sewage treatment and disposal, solid waste collection, solid waste disposal, and street cleaning are activities performed in carrying out the function of sanitation, and the segregation of the expenditures made for each of these activities constitutes an activity classification.

Actuarial Accrued Liability (AAL) A liability arising from past unfunding and ad hoc changes in pension plan provisions. AAL is determined by using any of several generally accepted actuarial methods, for example, entry age method.

Actuarial Basis A basis used in computing the amount of contributions to be made periodically to a fund so that the total contributions plus the compounded earnings thereon will equal the required payments to be made out of the fund. The factors taken into account in arriving at the amount of these contributions include the length of time over which each contribution is to be held and the rate of return compounded on such contribution over its life. A trust fund for a public employee retirement system is an example of a fund set up on an actuarial basis.

Actuarial Present Value of Total Projected Benefits A component of the annual required contribution that allows for projected salary increases and additional statutory or contractual agreements.

Actuarial Value of Assets The value of a pension plan's assets used by an actuary for purposes of determining annual required contributions and other actuarial aspects of a defined benefit pension plan.

Ad Valorem Property Taxes In proportion to value. A basis for levy of taxes on property.

Advance Refunding The issuance of debt instruments to refund existing debt before the existing debt matures or is callable.

Agency Fund A fund consisting of resources received and held by the governmental unit as an agent for others; for example, taxes collected and held by a municipality for a school district. Note: sometimes resources held by one fund of a governmental unit for other funds of the unit are handled through an agency fund known as a *pass-through agency fund*. An example would be taxes held by an agency fund for redistribution among other funds. See also Allocation.

Allocate To divide a lump-sum appropriation into parts that are designated for expenditure by specific organization units and/or for specific purposes, activities, or objects. See also Allocation.

Allocation A part of a lump-sum appropriation that is designated for expenditure by specific organization units and/or for special purposes, activities, or objects. In federal usage, a transfer of obligational authority from one agency to another. See also Allocate.

Allot To divide an appropriation into amounts that may be encumbered or expended during an allotment period. See also Allotment and Allotment Period.

Allotment A part of an appropriation (or, in federal usage, parts of an apportionment) that may be encumbered (obligated) or expended during an allotment period. See also Allot and Allotment Period.

Allotment Period A period of time less than one fiscal year in length during which an allotment is effective. Bimonthly and quarterly allotment periods are most common. See also Allot and Allotment.

Allotments Available for Commitment/Obligation The portion of a federal agency's allotments not yet obligated by issuance of purchase orders, contracts, or other evidence of commitment.

Allowable Costs Costs that meet specific criteria determined by the resource provider, generally used in the context of federal financial assistance.

Allowance for Amortization The account in which the amounts recorded as amortization of the intangible asset are accumulated.

Allowance for Depreciation The account in which the amounts of cost of the related asset that have been charged to expense are accumulated.

Amortization (1) Gradual reduction, redemption, or liquidation of the balance of an account according to a specified schedule of times and amounts. (2) Provision for the extinguishment of a debt by means of a debt service fund (q.v.).

Annual Pension Cost The annual expense to an employer for a pension plan, which is a function of annual required contribution (ARC), net pension obligation (NPO), interest, and adjustments.

Annual Required Contribution (ARC) An actuarially determined amount that the employer should contribute each year to a defined benefit pension plan to ensure full actuarial funding of the plan.

Annuities Payable A liability account that records the amount of annuities due and payable to retired employees in a public employee retirement system.

Annuity A series of equal money payments made at equal intervals during a designated period of time. In governmental accounting, the most frequent annuities are accumulations of debt service funds for term bonds and payments to retired employees or their beneficiaries under public employee retirement systems.

Annuity, Amount of The total amount of money accumulated or paid during an annuity period from an annuity and compound interest at a designated rate.

Annuity Agreements Funds established to account for assets given to an organization subject to an agreement that binds the organization to pay stipulated amounts periodically to the donor(s).

Annuity Period The designated length of time during which an amount of annuity is accumulated or paid.

Annuity Serial Bonds Bonds for which the amount of annual principal repayments is scheduled to increase each year by approximately the same amount that interest payments decrease.

Apportionment A distribution made of a federal appropriation by the Office of Management and Budget into amounts available for specified time periods.

Appropriation An authorization granted by a legislative body to incur liabilities for purposes specified in the Appropriation Act (q.v.). Note: an appropriation is usually limited in amount and as to the time when it may be expended. See, however, Indeterminate Appropriation.

Appropriation Act, Bill, Ordinance, Resolution, or Order A legal action giving the administration of a governmental unit authorization to incur on behalf of the unit liabilities for the acquisition of goods, services, or facilities to be used for purposes specified in the Act, Ordinance, or so on, in amounts not to exceed those specified for each purpose. The authorization usually expires at the end of a specified term, most often one year.

Appropriation Expenditure See Expenditures.

Appropriations Budget Appropriations requested by departments or by the central administration of a governmental unit for a budget period. When the Appropriations budget has been adopted in accord with procedures specified by relevant law, the budget becomes legally binding on the administration of the governmental unit for which the budget has been adopted.

Appropriations Used An account used in federal government accounting to indicate resources provided by current- or prior-period appropriations that were consumed during the current fiscal period.

Arbitrage Earning a higher interest rate from investing borrowed funds than is applicable to the entity's tax-exempt debt. Federal tax regulations require governments to rebate the investment earnings in excess of that permitted. See also Arbitrage Rebate.

Arbitrage Rebate Required repayment to the federal government arising from the arbitrage rules that prohibit the governmental entity from investing bond proceeds at interest rates higher than that applicable to the entity's tax-exempt debt.

Assess To value property officially for the purpose of taxation. Note: The term is also sometimes used to denote the levy of taxes, but such usage is not correct because it fails to distinguish between the valuation process and the tax levy process.

Assessed Valuation A valuation set on real estate or other property by a government as a basis for levying taxes.

Assessment (1) The process of making the official valuation of property for purposes of taxation. (2) The valuation placed on property as a result of this process.

Assets Probable future economic benefits obtained or controlled by a particular entity as a result of past transactions or events.

Assets Limited as to Use Assets whose use is limited by contracts or agreements with outside parties (such as proceeds of debt issues; funds deposited with a trustee; self-insurance funding arrangements; and statutory reserve requirements) other than donors or grantors. The term also includes limitations placed on assets by the Board of Directors or trustees.

Audit The examination of documents, records, reports, systems of internal control, accounting and financial procedures, and other evidence for one or more of the following purposes:

1. To determine whether the financial statements, or other financial reports and related items, are fairly presented in accordance with generally accepted accounting principles or other established or stated criteria.
2. To determine whether the entity has complied with laws and regulations and other specific financial compliance requirements that may have a material effect on the financial statements, or that may affect other financial reports or the economy, efficiency, or effectiveness of program activities.
3. To determine whether the entity is acquiring, protecting, and using its resources economically and efficiently.
4. To determine whether the desired program results or benefits established by the legislature or other authorizing body are being achieved.

Audit Committee A committee of the governing board whose function it is to help select the auditor, monitor the audit process, review results of the audit, assist the governing board in understanding the results of the audit, and participate with both management and the independent auditor in resolving internal control or other deficiencies identified during the audit.

Audit Findings Items identified by the auditors in the course of the audit, such as internal control weaknesses, instances of noncompliance, questioned costs, fraud, and material misrepresentations (by the auditee).

Auditor's Opinion or Report A statement signed by an auditor stating that he or she has examined the financial statements in accordance with generally accepted auditing standards (with exceptions, if any) and expressing his or her opinion on the financial condition and results of operations of the reporting entity, as appropriate.

Authority A governmental unit or public agency created to perform a single function or a restricted group of related activities. Usually such units are financed from service charges, fees, and tolls, but in some instances they also have taxing powers. An authority may be completely independent of other governmental units, or in some cases it may be partially dependent on other governments for its creation, its financing, or the exercise of certain powers.

Authority Bonds Bonds payable from the revenues of a specific authority. Since such authorities usually have no revenue other than charges for services, their bonds are ordinarily revenue bonds (q.v.).

Auxiliary Enterprises Activities of a college or university that furnish a service to students, faculty, or staff on a user-charge basis. The charge is directly related to, but not necessarily equal to, the cost of the service. Examples include college unions, residence halls, stores, faculty clubs, and intercollegiate athletics.

Available Collectible within the current period or soon enough thereafter to be used to pay liabilities of the current period.

Balance Sheet A statement that reports the balances of assets, liabilities, reserves, and equities of a fund, governmental unit, or nonprofit entity at a specified date, properly classified to exhibit financial position of the fund or unit at that date.

Basic Financial Statements Term used in GASB *Statement No. 34* to describe required government-wide and fund financial statements.

Basis of Accounting The standard (or standards) used to determine the point in time when assets, liabilities, revenues, and expenses (expenditures) should be measured and recorded as such in the accounts of an entity. See Accrual Basis, Cash Basis, and Modified Accrual Basis.

Bearer Bond A bond that requires the holder to present matured interest coupons or matured bonds to the issuer or a designated paying agent for payment. Payments are made to the bearer since the issuer maintains no record of current bond ownership. Note: Federal law requires that all tax-exempt bonds issued since June 15, 1983, must be in registered form (see also Registered Bonds). However, some long-term bearer bonds remain outstanding.

Benchmark A number that represents a target to which actual results are compared, or a basis for comparison; for example, industry averages.

Betterment An addition made to, or change made in, a capital asset that is expected to prolong its life or to increase its efficiency over and above that arising from maintenance (q.v.) and the cost of which is therefore added to the book value of the asset. Note: The term is sometimes applied to sidewalks, sewers, and highways, but these should preferably be designated as "improvements" or "infrastructure assets" (q.v.).

Blending The method of reporting the financial data of a component unit in a manner similar to that in which the financial data of the primary government are presented. Under this method the component unit data are usually combined with the appropriate fund types of the primary government and reported in the same columns as the data for the primary government except general funds. See Discrete Presentation.

Block Grants Federal monies given to state or local governments along with the discretion to administer for many projects and to many recipients, and for which no matching requirement exists.

Board-Designated Funds Funds created to account for assets set aside by the governing board of an organization for specified purposes.

Board-Designated Net Assets Unrestricted net assets that the not-for-profit organization's Board decided to set aside or "designate" for specific purposes.

Bond A written promise to pay a specified sum of money, called the *face value* or *principal* amount, at a specified date or dates in the future, called the *maturity date(s)*, together with periodic interest at a specified rate. Note: The difference between a note and a bond is that the latter runs for a longer period of time and requires greater legal formality.

Bond Anticipation Notes (BANs) Short-term interest-bearing notes issued by a governmental unit in anticipation of bonds to be issued at a later date. The notes are retired from proceeds of the bond issue to which they are related. See also Interim Borrowing.

Bond Discount The excess of the face value of a bond over the price for which it is acquired or sold. Note: The price does not include accrued interest at the date of acquisition or sale.

Bond Fund A fund formerly used to account for the proceeds of general obligation bond issues to be used for construction or acquisition of capital assets. Such proceeds are now accounted for in a capital projects fund (q.v.).

Bond Indenture The contract between a corporation issuing bonds and the trustees or other body representing prospective and actual holders of the bonds.

Bond Ordinance or Resolution An ordinance (q.v.) or resolution (q.v.) authorizing a bond issue.

Bond Premium The excess of the price at which a bond is acquired or sold over its face value. Note: The price does not include accrued interest at the date of acquisition or sale.

Bonded Debt That portion of indebtedness represented by outstanding bonds. See Gross Bonded Debt and Net Bonded Debt.

Bonded Indebtedness See Bonded Debt.

Bonds Authorized and Unissued Bonds that have been legally authorized but not issued and that can be issued and sold without further authorization. Note: This term must not be confused with the terms *margin of borrowing power* or *legal debt margin*, either one of which represents the difference between the legal debt limit of a governmental unit and the debt outstanding against it.

Book Value Value (q.v.) as shown by books of account. Note: In the case of assets subject to reduction by valuation allowances, *book value* refers to cost or stated value less the appropriate allowance. Sometimes a distinction is made between *gross* book value and *net* book value, the former designating value before deduction of related allowances and the latter after their deduction. In the absence of any modifier, however, the term *book value* is understood to be synonymous with net book value.

Budget A plan of financial operation embodying an estimate of proposed expenditures for a given period and the proposed means of financing them. Used without any modifier, the term usually indicates a financial plan for a single fiscal year.

Budget Accounts Accounts used in federal agencies that are broad in scope, for which appropriations are made, and that are not the same as the Standard General Ledger accounts used for accounting purposes. Budget accounts may cover an entire organization or a group of budget accounts may be aggregated to cover an organization.

Budget Calendar A schedule of certain steps to be followed in the budgeting process and the dates by which each step must be completed.

Budget Document The instrument used by the budget-making authority to present a comprehensive financial program to the appropriating body. The budget document usually consists of three parts. The first part contains a message from the budget-making authority, together with a summary of the proposed expenditures and the means of financing them. The second consists of schedules supporting the summary. These schedules show in detail the information as to past years' actual revenues, expenditures, and other data used in making the estimates. The third part is composed of drafts of the appropriation, revenue, and borrowing measures necessary to put the budget into effect.

Budget Message A general discussion of the proposed budget as presented in writing by the budget-making authority to the legislative body. The budget message should contain an explanation of the principal budget items, an outline of the governmental unit's experience during the past period and its financial status at the time of the message, and recommendations regarding the financial policy for the coming period.

Budget Officer A person, usually in the central administrative office, designated to ensure that administrative policies are actually used in budget preparation and that the budget calendar and other legal requirements are met.

Budgetary Accounts Those accounts that reflect budgetary operations and condition, such as estimated revenues, appropriations, and encumbrances, as distinguished from proprietary accounts. See also Proprietary Accounts.

Budgetary Control The control or management of a governmental unit or enterprise in accordance with an approved budget for the purpose of keeping expenditures within the limitations of available appropriations and available revenues.

Budgetary Resources A term that includes new budgetary authority for the period plus unobligated budgetary authority carried over from the prior period and offsetting collections, if any, plus or minus any budgetary adjustments in a federal agency.

Buildings A capital asset account that reflects the acquisition value of permanent structures used to house persons and property owned by a governmental unit. If buildings are purchased or constructed, this account includes the purchase or contract price of all permanent buildings and fixtures attached to and forming a permanent part of such buildings. If buildings are acquired by gift, the account reflects their appraised value at time of acquisition.

Business-Type Activities Commercial-type activities of a government, such as public utilities (e.g., electric, water, gas, and sewer utilities), transportation systems, toll roads, toll bridges, hospitals, parking garages and lots, liquor stores, golf courses, and swimming pools.

Callable Bond A type of bond that permits the issuer to pay the obligation before the stated maturity date by giving notice of redemption in a manner specified in the bond contract. Also called Optional Bond.

Capital Assets Assets of a long-term character that are intended to continue to be held or used, such as land, buildings, machinery, furniture, and other equipment. Note: The term does not indicate the immobility of an asset, which is the distinctive character of "fixture" (q.v.). Also called fixed assets.

Capital Budget A plan of proposed capital outlays and the means of financing them for the current fiscal period. It is usually a part of the current budget. If a Capital Program is in operation, it will be the first year thereof. A Capital Program is sometimes referred to as a Capital Budget. See also Capital Program.

Capital Expenditures See Capital Outlays.

Capital Improvements Fund A fund to accumulate revenues from current taxes levied for major repairs and maintenance to capital assets of a nature not specified at the time the revenues are levied. Appropriations of this fund are made in accord with state law at the time specific projects become necessary.

Capital Lease A lease that substantively transfers the benefits and risks of ownership of property to the lessee. Any lease that meets certain criteria specified in applicable accounting and reporting standards is a capital lease. See also Operating Lease.

Capital Outlays Expenditures that result in the acquisition of or addition to capital assets.

Capital Program A plan for capital expenditures to be incurred each year over a fixed period of years to meet capital needs arising from a long-term work program or otherwise. It sets forth each project or other contemplated expenditure in which the government is to have a part and specifies the full resources estimated to be available to finance the projected expenditures.

Capital Projects Fund (CPF) A fund created to account for all resources to be used for the construction or acquisition of designated capital assets by a governmental unit except those financed by proprietary or fiduciary funds. See also Bond Fund.

Capitation Fee Fixed dollar amount of fees per person paid periodically by a third-party payor to a health care organization, regardless of services provided.

Cash Currency, coin, checks, money orders, and bankers' drafts on hand or on deposit with an official or agent designated as custodian of cash and bank deposits. Note: All cash must be accounted for as a part of the fund to which it belongs. Any restrictions or limitations as to its availability must be indicated in the records and statements. It is not necessary, however, to have a separate bank account for each fund unless required by law.

Cash Basis The basis of accounting under which revenues are recorded when received in cash and expenditures (or expenses) are recorded when cash is disbursed.

Cash Discount An allowance received or given if payment is completed within a stated period of time.

Cash Equivalents Short-term, highly liquid investments that are both readily convertible into known amounts of cash and so near their maturity that they present insignificant risk of changes in value due to changes in interest rates.

Certificate of Participation (COP) A long-term debt instrument authorized for construction of municipal facilities, typically issued by a quasi-independent authority but secured by a long-term lease with a general purpose local government.

Character A basis for distinguishing expenditures according to the periods they are presumed to benefit. See also Character Classification.

Character Classification A grouping of expenditures on the basis of the fiscal periods they are presumed to benefit. The three groupings are: (1) current expenditures, presumed to benefit the current fiscal period; (2) debt service, presumed to benefit prior fiscal periods primarily but also present and future periods; and (3) capital outlays, presumed to benefit the current and future fiscal periods. See also Activity, Activity Classification, Function, Functional Classification, Object, Object Classification, and Expenses.

Charitable Solicitation The direct or indirect request for money, credit, property, financial assistance or other things of value on the representation that these assets will be used for a charitable purpose.

Charity Care Service provided by a health care organization to persons with a demonstrated inability to pay.

Check A bill of exchange drawn on a bank and payable on demand; a written order on a bank to pay on demand a specified sum of money to a named person, to his or her order, or to the bearer, out of money on deposit to the credit of the maker. Note: A check differs from a warrant in that the latter is not necessarily payable on demand and may not be negotiable. It differs from a voucher in that the latter is not an order to pay.

Clearing Account An account used to accumulate total charges or credits for the purpose of distributing them later among the accounts to which they are allocable or for the purpose of transferring the net differences to the proper account. Also called Suspense Account.

Cognizant Agency for Audit Responsibilities The federal awarding agency that provides the predominant amount of direct funding to a nonfederal entity expending more than $25 million in federal awards, as provided by OMB *Circular A-133*, unless the OMB designates a different cognizant agency.

Collateralized Secured with the pledge of assets to minimize the risk of loss. Deposits, investments, or loans are often required to be collateralized.

Collections Works of art, historical treasures, or similar assets that are (1) held for public exhibition, education, or research in furtherance of public service rather than financial gain; (2) protected, kept unencumbered, cared for, and preserved; and (3) subject to an organizational policy that requires the proceeds of items that are sold to be used to acquire other items for collection.

Combined Financial Statement A single financial statement that displays the combined financial data for various fund types and, if applicable, account groups and discretely presented component units in separate adjacent columns. See Combining Financial Statement.

Combining Financial Statement A financial statement that displays the financial data for each of the funds of a given fund type (e.g., special revenue funds) in separate adjacent columns. The totals reported for that fund type should agree with those reported in the column for that fund type in the combined financial statements. See Combined Financial Statement.

Commitment In federal government usage, a reservation of an agency's allotment in the estimated amount of orders for goods or services, prior to actually placing the orders. See also Obligations.

Common Rule Term given to OMB *Circular A-102* that describes administrative requirements that must be met by a state or local government receiving federal financial assistance.

Compliance Audit An audit designed to provide reasonable assurance that a governmental entity has complied with applicable laws and regulations. Required for every audit performed in conformity with generally accepted governmental auditing standards.

Component Unit (CU) A separate governmental unit, agency, or nonprofit corporation that, pursuant to the criteria in the GASB *Codification*, Section 2100, is combined with other component units to constitute the reporting entity (q.v.).

Comprehensive Annual Financial Report (CAFR) A governmental unit's official annual report prepared and published as a matter of public record. In addition to the general purpose external financial statements, the CAFR should contain introductory material, schedules to demonstrate legal compliance, and statistical tables specified in the GASB *Codification*.

Conditional Promise to Give A promise to make a contribution to an organization that depends on the occurrence of a specified future and uncertain event to bind the promisor, such as obtaining matching gifts by the recipient.

Conscience Money Money received by governmental units in payment of previously undisclosed debts, usually based on embezzlement, tax evasion, or theft.

Construction Work in Progress The cost of construction work that has been started but not yet completed.

Consumption Method A method of recording supplies as Inventory when purchased and as Expenditures when used or consumed. The alternative method is called the *purchases method*.

Contingency Fund Assets or other resources set aside to provide for unforeseen expenditures or for anticipated expenditures or uncertain amount.

Contingent Liabilities Items that may become liabilities as a result of conditions undetermined at a given date, such as guarantees, pending lawsuits, judgments under appeal, unsettled disputed claims, unfilled purchase orders, and uncompleted contracts. Contingent liabilities of the latter two types are disclosed in Balance Sheets of governmental funds as Reserve for Encumbrances; other contingent liabilities are disclosed in Notes to the Financial Statements.

Continuing Appropriation An appropriation that, once established, is automatically renewed without further legislative action, period after period, until altered or revoked. Note: The term should not be confused with Indeterminate Appropriation (q.v.).

Continuing Care Retirement Community (CCRC) A facility that provides residential care along with some level of long-term nursing or medical care, generally to elderly or retired persons.

Contractual Adjustments (or allowances) The difference between the gross patient service revenue and the negotiated payment by third-party payors in arriving at net patient service revenue.

Contributions Amounts given to an individual or to an organization for which the donor receives no direct private benefits. Contributions may be in the form of pledges, cash, securities, materials, services, or capital assets.

Control Account An account in the general ledger in which are recorded the aggregate of debit and credit postings to a number of identical or related accounts called *subsidiary accounts*. For example, the Taxes Receivable account is a control account supported by the aggregate of individual balances in individual property taxpayers' accounts.

Cost The amount of money or money's worth exchanged for property or services. Note: Costs may be incurred even before money is paid, that is, as soon as a liability is incurred. Ultimately, however, money or money's worth must be given in exchange. Again, the cost of some property or service may, in turn, become a part of the cost of another property or service. For example, the cost of part or all of the materials purchased at a certain time will be reflected in the cost of articles made from such materials or in the cost of those services in the rendering of which the materials were used.

Cost Accounting The branch of accounting that provides for the assembling and recording of all the elements of cost incurred to accomplish a purpose, to carry on an activity or operation, or to complete a unit of work or a specific job.

Cost Determination The use of statistical procedures to determine or estimate the cost of goods or services, as opposed to accumulating such costs in a formal cost accounting system.

Cost Objective In federal terminology, an organization unit, function, activity, project, cost center, or pool established for the accumulation of costs.

Cost Unit A term used in cost accounting to designate the unit of product or service whose cost is computed. These units are selected for the purpose of comparing the actual cost with a standard cost or with actual costs of units produced under different circumstances or at different places and times. See also Unit Cost and Work Unit.

Coupon Rate The interest rate specified on interest coupons attached to a bond. The term is synonymous with nominal interest rate (q.v.) for coupon bonds.

Credit Risk The risk that a debt issuer will not pay interest and principal when due. See also Default.

Cumulative Results of Operations The net difference between expenses/losses and financing sources, including appropriations, revenues, and gains, since the inception of the activity. A term generally used in federal agencies.

Current A term that, applied to budgeting and accounting, designates the operations of the present fiscal period as opposed to past or future periods.

Current Assets Those assets that are available or can be made readily available to meet the cost of operations or to pay current liabilities. Some examples are cash, temporary investments, and taxes receivable that will be collected within 60 days from the balance sheet date.

Current Financial Resources Cash or items expected to be converted into cash during the current period, or soon enough thereafter to pay current period liabilities.

Current Fund In governmental accounting sometimes used as a synonym for General Fund.

Current Funds Funds the resources of which may be expended for operating purposes during the current fiscal period. Colleges and universities and voluntary health and welfare organizations often use fund types called Current Fund—Unrestricted and Current Funds—Restricted for Internal Purposes.

Current Liabilities Liabilities payable within a relatively short period of time, usually no longer than a year. See also Floating Debt.

Current Resources Resources (q.v.) to which recourse can be had to meet current obligations and expenditures. Examples are estimated revenues of a particular period not yet realized, transfers from other funds authorized but not received, and, in the case of certain funds, bonds authorized and unissued.

Current Revenue Revenues of a governmental unit available to meet expenditures of the current fiscal year. See Revenue.

Current Special Assessments (1) Special assessments levied and becoming due during the current fiscal period, from the date special assessment rolls are approved by the proper authority to the date on which a penalty for nonpayment is attached. (2) Special assessments levied in a prior fiscal period but becoming due in the current fiscal period, from the time they become due to the date on which a penalty for nonpayment is attached.

Current Taxes (1) Taxes levied and becoming due during the current fiscal period, from the time the amount of tax levy is first established to the date on which a penalty for nonpayment is attached. (2) Taxes levied in the preceding fiscal period but becoming due in the current fiscal period, from the time they become due until a penalty for nonpayment is attached.

Current-Year's Tax Levy Taxes levied for the current fiscal period.

Customer Advances for Construction Amounts required to be deposited by a customer for construction projects undertaken by the utility at the request of the customer.

Cycle Billing A practice followed by utilities, retail stores, and other organizations with a large number of credit customers of billing part of the customers each working day during a month, instead of billing all customers as of a certain day of the month.

Data Processing (1) The preparation and handling of information and data from source media through prescribed procedures to obtain such end results as classification, problem solution, summarization, and reports. (2) Preparation and handling of financial information wholly or partially by use of computers.

Debt A liability resulting from the borrowing of money or from the purchase of goods and services. Debts of governmental units include bonds, time warrants, notes, and floating debt. See also Bond, Notes Payable, Time Warrant, Floating Debt, Long-Term Debt, and General Long-Term Debt.

Debt-Financed Income Income from property that is subject to debt, such as rental income from a building that has been financed with a mortgage.

Debt Limit The maximum amount of gross or net debt that is legally permitted.

Debt Margin The difference between the amount of the debt limit (q.v.) and the net amount of outstanding indebtedness subject to the limitation.

Debt Service Fund (DSF) A fund established to finance and account for the payment of interest and principal on all tax-supported debt, serial and term, including that payable from special assessments.

Default Failure of a debtor to pay interest or repay the principal of debt when legally due.

Defeasance A transaction in which the liability for a debt is substantively settled, and the liability is removed from the accounts, even though the debt has not actually been paid. See also Legal Defeasance and In-Substance Defeasance.

Deferred Revenues or Deferred Credits In governmental accounting, items that may not be recognized as revenues of the period in which received because they are not "available" until a subsequent period.

Deferred Serial Bonds Serial bonds (q.v.) in which the first installment does not fall due for two or more years from the date of issue.

Deficiency A general term indicating the amount by which anything falls short of some requirement or expectation. The term should not be used without qualification.

Deficit (1) The excess of liabilities and reserved equity of a fund over its assets. (2) The excess of expenditures over revenues during an accounting period; or in the case of enterprise and internal service funds, the excess of expense over revenue during an accounting period.

Defined Benefit Pension Plan A pension plan that provides a specified amount of benefits based on a formula that may include such factors as age, salary, and years of employment.

Defined Contribution Pension Plan A pension plan that specifies the amount or rate of contribution, often a percentage of covered salary, that the employer and employees must contribute to the members' accounts.

Delinquent Special Assessments Special assessments remaining unpaid on and after the date on which a penalty for nonpayment is attached.

Delinquent Taxes Taxes remaining unpaid on and after the date on which a penalty for nonpayment is attached. Even though the penalty may be subsequently waived and a portion of the taxes may be abated or canceled, the unpaid balances continue to be delinquent taxes until abated, canceled, paid, or converted into tax liens. Note: The term is sometimes limited to taxes levied for the fiscal period or periods preceding the current one, but such usage is not entirely correct. See also Current Taxes, Current-Year's Tax Levy, and Prior-Years' Tax Levies.

Deposit Warrant A financial document prepared by a designated accounting or finance officer authorizing the treasurer of a governmental unit to accept for deposit sums of money collected by various departments and agencies of the governmental unit.

Deposits Money deposited with a financial institution that must be released upon the "demand" of the depositor; for example, demand deposits (checking) and time deposits (savings accounts). These funds are generally insured by the Federal Deposit Insurance Corporation (up to a limit) and are distinguished from investments.

Depreciation (1) Expiration of the service life of capital assets, other than wasting assets, attributable to wear and tear, deterioration, action of the physical elements, inadequacy, and obsolescence. (2) The portion of the cost of a capital asset, other than a wasting asset, that is charged as an expense during a particular period. Note: In accounting for depreciation, the cost of a capital asset, less any salvage value, is prorated over the estimated service life of such an asset, and each period is charged with a portion of such cost. Through this process, the cost of the asset less salvage value is ultimately charged off as an expense.

Derived Tax Revenues A classification of nonexchange transaction, such as income or sales taxes.

Designated Assets, or equity, set aside by action of the governing board are designated; as distinguished from assets or equity set aside in conformity with requirements of donors, grantors, or creditors, which are properly referred to as *restricted*.

Diagnosis-Related Groups (DRGs) A case-mix classification scheme instituted by Congress in 1983 in relation to the Medicare program that is used to determine the reimbursement received by a hospital for inpatient services. Payment is made based on the patient's diagnosis regardless of how much the hospital spends to treat a patient.

Dimension Groupings of expenditure classifications specified by the National Center for Education Statistics (NCES) for public school accounting. Dimensions consist of two main groups: those essential for financial reporting to the federal government and those available optionally for management use.

Direct Cost A cost incurred because of some definite action by or for an organization unit, function, activity, project, cost center, or pool; a cost identified specifically with a cost objective (q.v.).

Direct Debt The debt that a governmental unit has incurred in its own name or assumed through the annexation of territory or consolidation with another governmental unit. See also Overlapping Debt.

Direct Expenses Those expenses that can be charged directly as a part of the cost of a product or service, or of a department or operating unit, as distinguished from overhead and other indirect costs that must be prorated among several products or services, departments, or operating units.

Direct Lobbying Testifying at legislative hearings, corresponding or conferring with legislators or their staffs, and publishing documents advocating specific legislative action.

Disbursements Payments in cash.

Discount on Taxes A cash discount offered to taxpayers to encourage early payment of taxes.

Discrete Presentation The method of reporting financial data of component units in a column(s) separate from the financial data of the primary government.

Disqualified Person A person who has substantial influences over the affairs of a nonprofit organization, such as an officer or manager.

Donated Assets Noncash contributions (q.v.). Donated assets may be in the form of securities, land, buildings, equipment, or materials.

Donated Materials See Donated Assets.

Donated Services The services of volunteer workers who are unpaid, or who are paid less than the market value of their services.

Double Entry A system of bookkeeping that requires, for every entry made to the debit side of an account or accounts, an entry for a corresponding amount or amounts to the credit side of another account or accounts. Note: Double-entry bookkeeping involves the maintaining of a balance between assets on the one hand and liabilities and equities on the other.

Due Diligence Formal disclosure and discovery of all relevant information about a transaction or organization, particularly about risks.

Earnings See Income and Revenue.

Economic Interest An interest in another organization because it holds or utilizes significant resources that must be used for the purposes of the reporting organization, or the reporting organization is responsible for the liabilities of the other entity.

Economic Size The minimum possible size to be able to provide services without long-term damage to the organization's financial base.

Effective Interest Rate The rate of earning on a bond investment based on the actual price paid for the bond, the maturity date, and the length of time between interest dates, in contrast with the nominal interest rate (q.v.).

Eligibility Requirements Specified characteristics that program recipients must possess or reimbursement provisions and contingencies tied to required actions by the recipient.

Encumbrances An account used to record the estimated amount of purchase orders, contracts, or salary commitments chargeable to an appropriation. The account is credited when goods or services are received and the actual expenditure of the appropriation is known.

Endowment A gift whose principal must be maintained inviolate but whose income may be expended.

Engagement Letter Written agreement between an auditor and the audited entity that describes the scope of work to be completed, among other things.

Enterprise Debt Debt that is to be retired primarily from the earnings of governmentally owned and operated enterprises. See also Revenue Bonds.

Enterprise Fund (EF) A fund established to finance and account for the acquisition, operation, and maintenance of governmental facilities and services that are entirely or predominantly self-supporting by user charges; or where the governing body of the governmental unit has decided periodic determination of revenues earned, expenses incurred, and/or net income is appropriate. Governmentally owned utilities and hospitals are ordinarily accounted for by enterprise funds.

Entitlement The amount of payment to which a state or local government is entitled as determined by the federal government pursuant to an allocation formula contained in applicable statutes.

Entity Assets Those assets of a federal agency that the reporting entity has authority to use in its operations, as opposed to holding but not available to spend.

Entitywide Perspective A view of the net assets of the organization as a whole, rather than as a collection of separate funds.

Entry (1) The record of a financial transaction in its appropriate book of account. (2) The act of recording a transaction in the books of account.

Equipment Tangible property of a more or less permanent nature (other than land, buildings, or improvements other than buildings) that is useful in carrying on operations. Examples are machinery, tools, trucks, cars, furniture, and furnishings.

Equity Transfer Nonrecurring or nonroutine transfers of equity between funds. Also referred to as Residual Equity Transfer (q.v.). GASB *Statement No. 34* eliminates this term from usage. See Interfund Transfers.

Escheat Property Private property that reverts to government ownership upon the death of the owner if there are no legal claimants or heirs.

Estimated Expenditures The estimated amounts of expenditures included in budgeted appropriations. See also Appropriations.

Estimated Other Financing Sources Amounts of financial resources estimated to be received or accrued during a period by a governmental or similar type fund from interfund transfers or from the proceeds of noncurrent debt issuance.

Estimated Other Financing Uses Amounts of financial resources estimated to be disbursed or accrued during a period by a governmental or similar type fund for transfer to other funds.

Estimated Revenue For revenue accounts kept on an accrual basis (q.v.), this term designates the amount of revenue estimated to accrue during a given period regardless of whether or not it is all to be collected during the period. For revenue accounts kept on a cash basis (q.v.), the term designates the amount of revenue estimated to be collected during a given period. Under the modified accrual basis (q.v.), estimated revenues include both cash and accrual basis revenues. See also Revenue, Revenue Receipts, Cash Basis, Accrual Basis, and Modified Accrual Basis.

Estimated Revenue Receipts A term used synonymously with estimated revenue (q.v.) by some governmental units reporting their revenues on a cash basis. See also Revenue and Revenue Receipts.

Estimated Uncollectible Accounts Receivable (Credit) That portion of accounts receivable that it is estimated will never be collected. The account is deducted from the Accounts Receivable account on the balance sheet in order to arrive at the net amount of accounts receivable.

Estimated Uncollectible Current Taxes (Credit) A provision out of tax revenues for that portion of current taxes receivable that is estimated will never be collected. The amount is shown on the balance sheet as a deduction from the Taxes Receivable—Current account in order to arrive at the net taxes receivable.

Estimated Uncollectible Delinquent Taxes (Credit) That portion of delinquent taxes receivable that it is estimated will never be collected. The account is shown on the balance sheet as a deduction from the Taxes Receivable—Delinquent account to arrive at the net delinquent taxes receivable.

Estimated Uncollectible Interest and Penalties on Taxes (Credit) That portion of interest and penalties receivable that is estimated will never be collected. The account is shown as a deduction from the Interest and Penalties Receivable account on the balance sheet in order to arrive at the net interest and penalties receivable.

Estimated Uncollectible Tax Liens That portion of tax liens receivable that it is estimated will never be collected. The account is shown as a deduction from the Tax Liens Receivable account on the balance sheet in order to arrive at the net amount of tax liens receivable.

Excess Benefit Transaction A transaction that results in unfair benefits to a person who has substantial influence over a not-for-profit organization, for example, unreasonable compensation, sales of assets at bargain prices, and lease arrangements.

Exchange Transactions Transactions in which each party receives direct tangible benefits commensurate with the resources provided, for example, sales between a buyer and a seller.

Exchange-like Transactions A transaction in which the values exchanged, though related, may not be quite equal or in which the direct benefits may not be exclusively for the parties to the transaction, unlike a "pure" exchange transaction.

Exemption A statutory reduction in the assessed valuation of taxable property accorded to certain taxpayers, such as senior citizens and war veterans.

Exhibit (1) A balance sheet or other principal financial statement. (2) Any statement or other document that accompanies or is a part of a financial or audit report. See also Schedules and Statements.

Expendable Fund A fund whose assets and resources may be converted into cash and used in their entirety for purposes of the fund.

Expendable Trust Fund A trust fund in which the fund balance can be expended for a purpose specified in the trust agreement. Typically used to account for the expendable income of a Nonexpendable Trust Fund (q.v.) (used prior to GASB *Statement No. 34*).

Expended Appropriation A charge against an appropriation for the actual cost of items received; the appropriation is no longer available to acquire additional goods and services.

Expenditure Disbursements A term sometimes used by governmental units operating on a cash basis (q.v.) as a synonym for expenditures (q.v.). It is not recommended terminology.

Expenditure Responsibility The responsibility of one public charity over another to which it has given a grant to ensure that the grant was used exclusively for the purpose for which it was made.

Expenditures Expenditures are recorded when liabilities are incurred pursuant to authority given in an appropriation (q.v.). If the accounts are kept on the accrual basis (q.v.) or the modified accrual basis (q.v.), this term designates the cost of goods delivered or services rendered, whether paid or unpaid, including expenses, provision for debt retirement not reported as a liability of the fund from which retired, and capital outlays. Where the accounts are kept on the cash basis (q.v.), the term designates only actual cash disbursements for these purposes. Note: Encumbrances are not expenditures.

Expenditures Budget See Appropriations Budget.

Expenses Charges incurred, whether paid or unpaid, for operation, maintenance, interest, and other charges presumed to benefit the current fiscal period.

External Investment Pool Centrally managed investment portfolios (pools) that manage the investments of participants (e.g., other governmental units and not-for-profit organizations) outside the reporting entity of the government that administers the pool.

External Support Test One of two parts of the broad public support test to determine if an organization is a public charity, rather than a private foundation. It is met if at least one-third of the organization's total revenue comes from the government or general public in the form of contributions, grants, membership dues, charges for services, or sales of merchandise.

Extraordinary Items Unusual and infrequent material gains or losses.

Face Value As applied to securities, the amount of liability stated in the security document.

Facilities and Administrative Costs (F&A) Costs that are not readily assignable to one program or cost objective in a college or university, but rather are incurred for a joint purpose. These costs are called *indirect costs* in some OMB *Circulars*. See also Indirect Costs.

Fair Value The amount at which a financial instrument could be exchanged in a current transaction between willing parties, other than in a forced or liquidation sale.

Federal Financial Management Improvement Act Act of Congress in 1990 that requires that each federal agency maintain a financial management system that applies federal accounting standards and provides the information necessary to report whether the agency is in compliance with those standards.

Federal Mission, Property, Plant, and Equipment (PPE) PPE of the federal government, such as military weapon systems and space exploration equipment.

Federated Fund-Raising Organization An organization comprised of independent charitable organizations that have voluntarily joined together to raise and distribute money among themselves.

Feeder Organization An organization controlled by a not-for-profit organization and organized to carry on a trade or business for the benefit of an exempt organization and remit its profits to the exempt organization.

Fidelity Bond A written promise to indemnify against losses from theft, defalcation, and misappropriation of public finds by government officers and employees. See also Surety Bond.

Fiduciary Activities Activities in which the government acts in a fiduciary capacity, either as an agent or trustee, for parties outside the government, for example in the collection of taxes, or amounts bequeathed from private citizens, as well as assets held for employee pension plans.

Fiduciary Funds Any fund held by a governmental unit in a fiduciary capacity for an external party, ordinarily as agent or trustee. Also called Trust and Agency Funds.

Financial Accountability The obligation of government to justify the raising of public resources and what those resources were expended for. See Accountability.

Financial Audit One of the two major types of audits defined by the U.S. General Accounting Office (see Performance Audit for the other major type). A financial audit provides an auditor's opinion that financial statements present fairly an entity's financial position and results of operations in conformity with generally accepted accounting principles or that other financial reports comply with specified finance-related criteria.

Financial Condition The probability that a government will meet its financial obligations as they become due and its service obligations to constituencies, both currently and in the future. See Financial Position.

Financial Position The adequacy of cash and short-term claims to cash to meet current obligations and those expected in the near future. See Financial Condition.

Fiscal Accountability Current-period financial position and budgetary compliance reported in fund-type financial statements of governments. See also Financial Accountability.

Fiscal Agent A bank or other corporate fiduciary that performs the function of paying, on behalf of the governmental unit, or other debtor, interest on debt or principal of debt when due.

Fiscal Period Any period at the end of which a governmental unit determines its financial position and the results of its operations.

Fiscal Year A 12-month period of time to which the annual budget applies and at the end of which a governmental unit determines its financial position and the results of its operations. For example, FY99 refers to the year that ends in 1999 (e.g., 7-1-98 to 6-30-99).

Fixed Assets See Capital Assets.

Fixed Charges Expenses (q.v.) the amount of which is set by agreement. Examples are interest, insurance, and contributions to pension funds.

Fixtures Attachments to buildings that are not intended to be removed and that cannot be removed without damage to the latter. Note: Those fixtures with a useful life presumed to be as long as that of the building itself are considered a part of the building; all others are classed as equipment.

Flexible Budgeting Budgeting method that provides for alternative levels of activity, such as separate budgets for high, medium, and low levels of activity.

Floating Debt Liabilities other than bonded debt and time warrants that are payable on demand or at an early date. Examples are accounts payable, notes, and bank loans. See also Current Liabilities.

Force Account Construction of buildings and improvements by some agency of the governmental unit.

Forfeiture The automatic loss of cash or other property as a punishment for not complying with legal provisions and as compensation for the resulting damages or losses. Note: The term should not be confused with confiscation. The latter term designates the actual taking over of the forfeited property by the government. Even after property has been forfeited, it cannot be said to be confiscated until the governmental unit claims it.

Franchise A special privilege granted by a government permitting the continuing use of public property, such as city streets, and usually involving the elements of monopoly and regulation.

Full Accrual Basis See Accrual Basis.

Full Cost The total cost of providing a service or producing a good; the sum of both direct costs (q.v.) and indirect costs (q.v.).

Full Faith and Credit A pledge of the general taxing power for the payment of debt obligations. Note: Bonds carrying such pledges are usually referred to as *general obligation bonds*.

Function A group of related activities aimed at accomplishing a major service or regulatory responsibility for which a governmental unit is responsible. For example, public health is a function. See also Subfunction, Activity, Character, and Object.

Functional Classification A grouping of expenditures on the basis of the principal purposes for which they are made. Examples are public safety, public health, and public welfare. See also Activity, Character, and Object Classification.

Fund A fiscal and accounting entity with a self-balancing set of accounts recording cash and other financial resources, together with all related liabilities, and residual equities or balances, and changes therein, which are segregated for the purpose of carrying on specific activities or attaining certain objectives in accordance with special regulations, restrictions, or limitations.

Fund Accounting An accounting system organized on the basis of funds, each of which is considered a separate accounting entity. The operations of each fund are accounted for with a separate set of self-balancing accounts that comprise its assets, liabilities, fund equity, revenues, and expenditures, or expenses, as appropriate. Resources are allocated to and accounted for in individual funds based upon purposes for which they are to be spent and the means by which spending activities are controlled. Fund accounting is used by states and local governments and internally by not-for-profit organizations that need to account for resources the use of which is restricted by donors or grantors.

Fund Balance The portion of fund equity (q.v.) available for appropriation.

Fund Balance Sheet A Balance Sheet for a single fund. See Fund and Balance Sheet.

Fund Balance with Treasury An asset account of a federal agency representing cash balances held by the U.S. Treasury upon which the agency can draw. The Treasury will disburse cash on behalf of and at the request of the agency to pay for authorized goods and services.

Fund Equity The excess of fund assets and resources over fund liabilities. A portion of the equity of a governmental fund may be reserved (q.v.) or designated (q.v.); the remainder is referred to as *Fund Balance*.

Fund Financial Statements A category of the basic financial statements that assist in assessing fiscal accountability.

Fund Type A classification of funds that are similar in purpose and character.

Funded Debt Same as Bonded Debt, which is the preferred term.

Funded Deficit A deficit eliminated through the sale of bonds issued for that purpose. See also Funding Bonds.

Funded Ratio The ratio of actuarial value of assets to actuarial accrued liability (AAL) of a pension plan.

Funding The conversion of floating debt or time warrants into bonded debt (q.v.).

Funding Bonds See Refunding Bonds.

Funds Functioning as Endowments Funds established by the governing board of an institution, usually college or university, to account for assets to be retained and invested. Also called Quasi-Endowment Funds.

Gains Increases in net assets from peripheral or incidental transactions of an entity.

General Capital Assets Those capital assets of a governmental unit that are not accounted for by a proprietary or fiduciary fund.

General Fixed Assets Account Group (GFAAG) A self-balancing group of accounts set up to account for the general fixed assets of a governmental unit. Eliminated from external financial reporting by GASB *Statement No. 34*.

General Fund (GF) A fund used to account for all transactions of a governmental unit that are not accounted for in another fund. Note: The General Fund is used to account for the ordinary operations of a governmental unit that are financed from taxes and other general revenues.

General Long-Term Debt Account Group (GLTDAG) A self-balancing group of accounts set up to account for the general long-term debt of a governmental unit. See General Long-Term Debt. Eliminated by GASB *Statement No. 34*.

General Long-Term Debt or Liabilities Long-term debt legally payable from general revenues and backed by the full faith and credit of a governmental unit. See Long-Term Debt.

General Obligation (GO) Bonds or Debt Bonds for whose payment the full faith and credit of the issuing body is pledged. More commonly, but not necessarily, general obligation bonds are considered to be those payable from taxes and other general revenues. In some states, these bonds are called *tax-supported bonds*. See also Full Faith and Credit.

General Obligation Special Assessment Bonds See Special Assessment Bonds.

General Property, Plant, and Equipment Property, plant, and equipment used to provide general government goods and services in a federal agency.

General Purpose Financial Statements The term used prior to GASB *Statement No. 34* to describe the five combined financial statements of a reporting entity that are required for conformity with generally accepted accounting principles.

General Purpose Governments Governments that provide many categories of services to their residents, such as states, counties, municipalities, and townships.

Generally Accepted Accounting Principles (GAAP) The body of accounting and financial reporting standards, conventions, and practices that have authoritative support from standards-setting bodies such as the Governmental Accounting Standards Board and the Financial Accounting Standards Board, or for which a degree of consensus exists among accounting professionals at a given point in time. Generally accepted accounting principles are continually evolving as changes occur in the reporting environment.

Generally Accepted Auditing Standards (GAAS) Standards prescribed by the American Institute of Certified Public Accountants to provide guidance for planning, conducting, and reporting on audits by Certified Public Accountants.

Generally Accepted Government Auditing Standards (GAGAS) See Government Auditing Standards.

Gifts in kind Contributions of tangible items to a tax-exempt organization.

Government Auditing Standards (GAS) Auditing standards set forth by the Comptroller General of the United States to provide guidance for federal auditors, state and local governmental auditors, and public accountants who audit federal organizations, programs, activities, and functions. Also referred to as *generally accepted government auditing standards* (GAGAS).

Government-Mandated Nonexchange Transactions A category of nonexchange transactions, such as certain education, social welfare, and transportation services mandated and funded by a higher level of government.

Governmental Accounting The composite activity of analyzing, recording, summarizing, reporting, and interpreting the financial transactions of governmental units and agencies. The term generally is used to refer to accounting for state and local governments, rather than the U.S. federal government.

Governmental Activities Core governmental services, such as protection of life and property (e.g., police and fire protection), public works (e.g., streets and highways, bridges, and public buildings), parks and recreation facilities and programs, and cultural and social services. Also includes general administrative support, such as data processing, finance, and personnel.

Governmental Assets (Liabilities) Assets (or liabilities) that arise from transactions of the federal government, or an entity of the federal government, with nonfederal entities.

Governmental Funds A generic classification used by the GASB to refer to all funds other than proprietary and fiduciary funds. The General Fund, special revenue funds, capital projects funds, debt service funds, and permanent funds are the types of funds referred to as governmental funds.

Government-wide Financial Statements Two statements prescribed by GASB *Statement No. 34* designed to provide a highly aggregated overview of a government's net assets and results of financial activities.

Grant A contribution by one governmental unit to another unit. The contribution is usually made to aid in the support of a specified function (for example, education), but it is sometimes also for general purposes, or for the acquisition or construction of capital assets.

Grants in Aid See Grant.

Grass-Roots Lobbying An appeal to the general public to contact legislators or to take other action regarding a legislative matter.

Gross Bonded Debt The total amount of direct debt of a governmental unit represented by outstanding bonds before deduction of any assets available and earmarked for their retirement. See also Direct Debt.

Gross Revenue See Revenue.

Gross Tax Levy The amount of the tax bill sent to the taxpayer without regard for any estimate of uncollectible taxes.

Health Maintenance Organization (HMO) A prepaid health care plan that functions as a broker of health care between the consumer/patient requiring services and health care providers. HMOs differ depending, in part, on whether or not the health care provider is an employee of the HMO. Also called *preferred provider organizations* (*PPOs*).

Heritage Assets Federal PPE, such as the Washington Monument, that possess educational, cultural, or natural characteristics.

Historical Cost The amount paid, or liability incurred, by an accounting entity to acquire an asset and make it ready to render the services for which it was acquired.

Human Service Organizations See Voluntary Health and Welfare Organizations.

Imposed Nonexchange Revenues A category of nonexchange revenue, such as property taxes and most fines and forfeitures.

Improvements Buildings, other structures, and other attachments or annexations to land that are intended to remain so attached or annexed, such as sidewalks, trees, drives, tunnels, drains, and sewers. Note: Sidewalks, curbing, sewers, and highways are sometimes referred to as *betterments*, but the term *improvements other than buildings* is preferred. *Infrastructure assets* is also a term used.

Improvements Other than Buildings A capital asset account that reflects the acquisition value of permanent improvements, other than buildings, that add value to land. Examples of such improvements are fences, retaining walls, sidewalks, pavements, gutters, tunnels, and bridges. If the improvements are purchased or constructed, this account contains the purchase or contract price. If improvements are obtained by gift, it reflects fair value at time of acquisition.

Income A term used in accounting for governmental enterprises to represent the excess of revenues earned over the expenses incurred in carrying on the enterprise's operations. It should not be used without an appropriate modifier, such as operating, nonoperating, or net. See also Operating Income, Nonoperating Income, and Net Income. Note: The term *income* should not be used in lieu of *revenue* (q.v.) in nonenterprise funds.

Income Bonds See Revenue Bonds.

Incremental Budgeting A budgeting approach that is simply derived from the current-year's budget by multiplying by a factor (i.e., an incremental increase equal to inflation), or by adding amounts expected to be required by salary and other cost increases and deducting expenses not needed when the scope of operations is reduced.

Indenture See Bond Indenture.

Indeterminate Appropriation An appropriation that is not limited either to any definite period of time or to any definite amount, or to both time and amount. Note: A distinction must be made between an indeterminate appropriation and a continuing appropriation. A continuing appropriation is indefinite only as to time, an indeterminate appropriation is indefinite as to both time and amount. Even indeterminate appropriations that are indefinite only as to time are to be distinguished from continuing appropriations in that such indeterminate appropriations may eventually lapse.

Indirect Cost A cost incurred that cannot be identified specifically with a cost objective (q.v.), but rather benefits multiple cost objectives (e.g., a hospital cafeteria, central data processing department, and general management costs).

Indirect Expenses Those expenses that are not directly linked to an identifiable function or program.

Industrial Aid Bonds Bonds issued by governmental units, the proceeds of which are used to construct plant facilities for private industrial concerns. Lease payments made by the industrial concern to the governmental unit are used to service the bonds. Such bonds may be in the form of general obligation bonds (q.v.) or revenue bonds (q.v.). Also called Industrial Development Bonds (IDBs).

Influence Promote, support, affect, modify, oppose, or delay by any means. Often used in the context of "influencing" legislation or political candidates.

Infrastructure Assets Roads, bridges, curbs and gutters, streets, sidewalks, drainage systems, and lighting systems installed for the common good. See also Improvements.

In-Substance Defeasance A transaction in which low-risk U.S. Government securities are placed into an irrevocable trust for the benefit of debtholders, and the liability for the debt is removed from the accounts of the entity even though the debt has not been repaid. See Defeasance and Legal Defeasance.

Interest and Penalties Receivable on Taxes The uncollected portion of interest and penalties receivable on taxes.

Interest Receivable on Investments The amount of interest receivable on investments, exclusive of interest purchased. Interest purchased should be shown in a separate account.

Interest Receivable—Special Assessments The amount of interest receivable on unpaid installments of special assessments.

Interfund Accounts Accounts in which transactions between funds are reflected. See Interfund Transfers.

Interfund Loans Loans made by one fund to another.

Interfund Transfers Amounts transferred from one fund to another. See Equity Transfers and Operating Transfers.

Intergovernmental Revenue Revenue from other governments. Grants, shared revenue, and entitlements are types of intergovernmental revenue.

Interim Borrowing (1) Short-term loans to be repaid from general revenues during the course of a fiscal year. (2) Short-term loans in anticipation of tax collections or bonds issuance. See Bond Anticipation Notes, Tax Anticipation Notes, and Revenue Anticipation Notes.

Interim Statement A financial statement prepared before the end of the current fiscal year and covering only financial transactions during the current year to date. See also Statements.

Intermediate Sanctions Penalties imposed by the IRS in the form of excise taxes on private inurement to disqualified persons resulting from excess economic benefit transactions. For example, excessive salaries paid to a manager of a not-for-profit organization or rents greater than fair market value paid to a Board member who owns the building the organization occupies.

Internal Control A plan of organization under which employees' duties are so arranged and records and procedures so designed as to make it possible to exercise effective accounting control over assets, liabilities, revenues, and expenditures. Under such a system, the work of employees is subdivided so that no single employee performs a complete cycle of operations. Thus, for example, an employee handling cash would not post the accounts receivable records. Moreover, under such a system, the procedures to be followed are definitely laid down and require proper authorizations by designated officials for all actions to be taken.

Internal Exchange Transactions A term (coined by the authors) that captures both the interfund and interactivity nature of reciprocal exchange transactions within an entity (formerly called quasi-external transactions).

Internal Service Fund (ISF) A fund established to finance and account for services and commodities furnished by a designated department or agency to other departments and agencies within a single governmental unit, or to other governmental units. Amounts expended by the fund are restored thereto either from operating earnings or by transfers from other funds, so that the original fund capital is kept intact. Formerly called a *Working Capital Fund* or *Intragovernmental Service Fund*.

Internal Support Test One of two tests of broad public support to determine if an organization is a public charity, rather than a private foundation. The test is met if the not-for-profit organization does not receive more than one-third of its total support from investment income and unrelated business income.

Interperiod Equity A term coined by the Governmental Accounting Standards Board indicating the extent to which current-period revenues are adequate to pay for current-period services.

Intragovernmental assets (liabilities) Claims by, or against, a reporting entity that arise from transactions between that entity and other reporting entities.

Inventory A detailed list showing quantities, descriptions, and values of property and frequently also units of measure and unit prices.

Investment in General Fixed Assets An account in the General Fixed Assets Group of accounts that represents the governmental unit's equity in general fixed assets (q.v.). The balance of this account is subdivided according to the source of funds that financed the asset acquisition, such as general fund revenues and special assessments.

Investment Trust Fund Fund used to account for the assets, liabilities, net assets, and changes in net assets corresponding to the equity of the external participants.

Investments Securities and real estate held for the production of income in the form of interest, dividends, rentals, or lease payments. The term does not include capital assets used in governmental operations.

Irregular Serial Bonds Bonds payable in which the total principal is repayable, but the repayment plan does not fit the definitions of regular serial bonds, deferred serial bonds, or term bonds.

Job Order Cost Cost accounting system most appropriate for recording costs chargeable to specific jobs, grants, programs, projects, activities, or departments.

Judgment An amount to be paid or collected by a governmental unit as the result of a court decision, including a condemnation award in payment for private property taken for public use.

Judgment Bonds Bonds issued to pay judgments (q.v.). See also Funding.

Judgments Payable Amounts due to be paid by a governmental unit as the result of court decisions, including condemnation awards in payment for private property taken for public use.

Land A capital asset account that reflects the carrying value of land owned by a governmental unit. If land is purchased, this account shows the purchase price and costs such as legal fees and filling and excavation costs that are incurred to put the land in condition for its intended use. If land is acquired by gift, the account reflects its appraised value at time of acquisition.

Lapse (Verb) As applied to appropriations, this term denotes the automatic termination of an appropriation. Note: Except for indeterminate appropriations (q.v.) and continuing appropriations (q.v.), an appropriation is made for a certain period of time. At the end of this period, any unexpended and unencumbered balance thereof lapses, unless otherwise provided by law.

Leasehold The right to the use of real estate by virtue of a lease, usually for a specified term of years, for which a consideration is paid.

Legal Defeasance A transaction in which debt is legally satisfied based on certain provisions in the debt instrument (e.g., third-party guarantor assumes the debt) even though the debt has not been repaid. See also Defeasance and In-Substance Defeasance.

Legal Investments (1) Investments that public employee retirement systems, savings banks, insurance companies, trustees, and other fiduciaries (individual or corporate) are permitted to make by the laws of the state in which they are domiciled, or under the jurisdiction of which they operate or serve. The investments that meet the conditions imposed by law constitute the legal investment list. (2) Investments that governmental units are permitted to make by law.

Legal Opinion (1) The opinion of an official authorized to render it, such as an attorney general or city attorney, as to legality. (2) In the case of municipal bonds, the opinion of a specialized bond attorney as to the legality of a bond issue.

Legislation Action by Congress, a state legislative body, or a local council to establish laws, statues, and ordinances.

Levy (Verb) To impose taxes, special assessments, or service charges for the support of governmental activities. (Noun) The total amount of taxes, special assessments, or service charges imposed by a governmental unit.

Liabilities Probable future sacrifices of economic benefits arising from present obligations of a particular entity to transfer assets or provide services to other entities in the future as a result of past transactions or events. Note: The term does not include encumbrances (q.v.).

Life Income Agreements Funds, ordinarily of colleges and universities and other nonprofit organizations, established to account for assets given to the organization subject to an agreement to pay to the donor or designee the income earned by the assets over a specified period of time.

Limited Obligation Debt Debt secured by a pledge of the collections off a certain specified tax (rather than by all general revenues).

Limited Purpose Governments See Special Purpose Governments.

Line Item Budget A detailed expense or expenditure budget, generally classified by object within each organizational unit, and, often, classified within each object as to authorized number of employees at each salary level within each job classification, and so on.

Loans Receivable Amounts that have been loaned to persons or organizations, including notes taken as security for such loans.

Lobbying Communicating directly with a public official in either the executive or legislative branch of the state government for the purpose of influencing legislation.

Local Education Agency (LEA) A broad term that is used to include school districts, public schools, intermediate education agencies, and school systems.

Local Improvement Fund See Special Assessment Fund.

Local Improvement Tax See Special Assessment.

Long-Term Budget A budget prepared for a period longer than a fiscal year, or, in the case of some state governments, a budget prepared for a period longer than a biennium. If the long-term budget is restricted to capital expenditures, it is called a *Capital Program* (q.v.) or a *Capital Improvement Program*.

Long-Term Debt Debt with a maturity of more than one year after the date of issuance.

Losses Decreases in net assets from peripheral or incidental transactions of an entity.

Lump-Sum Appropriation An appropriation made for a stated purpose, or for a named department, without specifying further the amounts that may be spent for specific activities or for particular objects of expenditure. An example of such an appropriation would be one for the police department that does not specify the amount to be spent for uniform patrol, traffic control, and so on, or for salaries and wages, materials and supplies, travel, and so on.

Machinery and Equipment See Equipment.

Macroaccounting Accounting for the economy of the federal government in the aggregate.

Maintenance The upkeep of physical properties in condition for use or occupancy. Examples are the inspection of equipment to detect defects and the making of repairs.

Major Funds A fund is classified as major if it is significantly large with respect to the whole government. A fund is "major" if

(a) total assets, liabilities, revenues, or expenditures/expenses of the individual governmental or enterprise fund are at least 10 percent of the corresponding total of assets, liabilities, revenues, or expenditures/expenses for all funds of that category or type (total governmental or total enterprise funds), and

(b) total assets, liabilities, revenues, or expenditures/expenses of the individual governmental fund or enterprise fund are at lease 5 percent of the corresponding total for all governmental and enterprise funds combined.

Major Programs All federal programs identified by the auditor through a risk-based process that will be audited as part of a Single Audit.

Management's Discussion and Analysis (MD&A) Narrative information, in addition to the basic financial statements, in which management provides a brief, objective, and easily readable analysis of the government's financial performance for the year and its financial position at year-end. An MD&A is required by GASB's *Statement No. 34* for state and local governments and by FASAB's *SFFAC No. 3* for federal agencies.

Market risk The risk of loss arising from increases in market rates of interest or other factors that reduce market value of securities.

Material Weakness A reportable condition of such magnitude that the internal control structure elements do not reduce the risk of material noncompliance to an acceptably low level.

Matured Bonds Payable Bonds that have reached their maturity date but remain unpaid.

Matured Interest Payable Interest on bonds that has matured but remains unpaid.

Measurable Capable of being expressed in monetary terms.

Measurement Focus The nature of the resources, claims against resources, and flows of resources that are measured and reported by a fund or other entity. For example, governmental funds and certain fiduciary funds currently measure and report available financial resources, whereas proprietary and certain other fiduciary funds measure and report economic resources.

Modified Accrual Basis Under the modified accrual basis of accounting, required for use by governmental funds (q.v.), revenues are recognized in the period in which they become available and measurable, and expenditures are recognized at the time a liability is incurred pursuant to appropriation authority.

Modified Approach An approach that allows the government to elect *not* to depreciate certain eligible infrastructure assets provided certain requirements are met.

Modified Cash Basis Sometimes same as Modified Accrual Basis, sometimes a plan under which revenues are recognized on the cash basis, but expenditures are recognized on the accrual basis.

Mortgage Bonds Bonds secured by a mortgage against specific properties of a governmental unit, usually its public utilities or other enterprises. If primarily payable from enterprise revenues, they are also classed as revenue bonds. See also Revenue Bonds.

Municipal In its broadest sense, an adjective that denotes the state and all subordinate units of government. As defined for census statistics, the term denotes a city, town, or village as opposed to other units of local government.

Municipal Bond A bond (q.v.) issued by a state or local governmental unit.

Municipal Corporation A body politic and corporate established pursuant to state authorization for the purpose of providing governmental services and regulations for its inhabitants. A municipal corporation has defined boundaries and a population and is usually organized with the consent of its residents. It usually has a seal and may sue and be sued. Cities and towns are examples of municipal corporations. See also Quasi-Municipal Corporations.

Municipal Improvement Certificates Certificates issued in lieu of bonds for the financing of special improvements. Note: As a rule, these certificates are placed in the contractor's hands for collection from the special assessment payors.

Net Assets The difference between total assets and total liabilities.

Net Bonded Debt Gross bonded debt (q.v.) less cash or other assets available and earmarked for its retirement.

Net Income A term used in accounting for governmental enterprises to designate the excess of total revenues (q.v.) over total expenses (q.v.) for an accounting period. See also Income, Operating Revenues, Operating Expenses, Nonoperating Income, and Nonoperating Expenses.

Net Pension Obligation (NPO) A component of annual pension cost that is comprised of (1) the transition pension liability (or asset), if any, and (2) the cumulative difference from the implementation date of GASB *Statement No. 27* to the current balance sheet date between the annual pension cost and the employer's actual contributions.

Net Position Net assets of a federal agency.

Net Profit See Net Income.

Net Revenue See Net Income.

Net Revenue Available for Debt Service Gross operating revenues of an enterprise less operating and maintenance expenses but exclusive of depreciation and bond interest. *Net revenue* as thus defined is used to compute "coverage" of revenue bond issues. Note: Under the laws of some states and the provisions of some revenue bond indentures, net revenues used for computation of coverage are required to be on a cash basis rather than an accrual basis.

Nominal Interest Rate The contractual interest rate shown on the face and in the body of a bond and representing the amount of interest to be paid, in contrast to the effective interest rate (q.v.). See also Coupon Rate.

Nonentity Assets Those assets of a federal agency that the reporting entity is holding but are not available for the entity to spend.

Nonexchange Revenue See Derived Tax Revenues, Imposed Nonexchange Revenues, Voluntary Nonexchange Transactions, and Government-Mandated Nonexchange Transactions.

Nonexchange Transactions Transactions in which the donor derives no direct tangible benefits from the recipient agency, for example, a contribution to or support for a government or not-for-profit organization.

Nonexpendable Trust Fund A fund, the principal, and sometimes also the earnings, of which may not be expended. See also Endowment Fund.

Nonexpenditure Disbursements Disbursements not chargeable as expenditures; for example, a disbursement made for the purpose of paying a liability previously recorded on the books.

Nonoperating Expenses Expenses (q.v.) incurred for nonoperating properties or in the performance of activities not directly related to supplying the basic service by a governmental enterprise. An example of a nonoperating expense is interest paid on outstanding revenue bonds. See also Nonoperating Properties.

Nonoperating Income Income of governmental enterprises that is not derived from the basic operations of such enterprises. An example is interest on investments or on bank time deposits.

Nonoperating Properties Properties owned by a governmental enterprise but not used in the provision of basic services for which the enterprise exists.

Nonoperating Revenue Revenue arising from transactions peripheral or incidental to the delivery of health care, including investment income, gains and losses, and unrestricted contributions.

Nonrevenue Receipts Collections other than revenue (q.v.), such as receipts from loans where the liability is recorded in the fund in which the proceeds are placed and receipts on account of recoverable expenditures. See also Revenue Receipts.

Normal Cost The present value of benefits allocated to the current year by the actuarial cost method being used.

Not-for-Profit (Nonprofit) Organizations (NPO) An entity that is distinguished from a business enterprise by these characteristics: (1) contributions by providers who do not expect commensurate returns, (2) operating purposes other than to earn a profit, and (3) absence of ownership interests. The AICPA prefers the term *not-for-profit* over *nonprofit*.

Notes Payable In general, an unconditional written promise signed by the maker to pay a certain sum in money on demand or at a fixed or determinable time either to the bearer or to the order of a person designated therein. See also Temporary Loans.

Notes Receivable A note payable held by a governmental unit.

Object As used in expenditure classification, this term applies to the article purchased or the service obtained (as distinguished from the results obtained from expenditures). Examples are personal services, contractual services, materials, and supplies. See also Activity, Character, Function, and Object Classification.

Object Classification A grouping of expenditures on the basis of goods or services purchased, for example, personal services, materials, supplies, and equipment. See also Functional Classification, Activity Classification, and Character Classification.

Objects of Expenditure See Object.

Obligated Group A group of independent organizations that have joined together for a specific purpose, for example, to obtain financing in which case all parties are obligated in some way to repay the debt.

Obligations Generally amounts that a governmental unit may be required legally to meet out of its resources. They include not only actual liabilities but also unliquidated encumbrances. In federal usage, obligation has essentially the same meaning as encumbrance in state and local government accounting.

Obsolescence The decrease in the value of capital assets resulting from economic, social, technological, or legal changes.

Operating Budget A budget that applies to all outlays other than capital outlays. See Budget.

Operating Cycle The cycle of an organization that includes forecasting cash flows; collecting revenues; investing excess cash; tracking the performance and security of investments; making disbursements for various purposes; and monitoring, evaluating, and auditing cash flows.

Operating Expenses (1) As used in the accounts of governmental enterprises, the term means those costs that are necessary to the maintenance of the enterprise, the rendering of services, the sale of merchandise, the production and disposition of commodities produced, and the collection of enterprise revenues. (2) The term is also sometimes used to describe expenses for general governmental purposes.

Operating Fund The fund used to account for all assets and related liabilities used in the routine activities of a hospital. Also sometimes used by governmental units as a synonym for General Fund.

Operating Income Income of a governmental enterprise derived from the sale of its goods and/or services. For example, income from the sale of water by a municipal water utility is operating income. See also Operating Revenues.

Operating Lease A rental-type lease in which the risks and benefits of ownership are substantively retained by the lessor, and that does not meet the criteria defined in applicable accounting and reporting standards as a capital lease. See also Capital Lease.

Operating Revenues Revenues derived from the operation of governmental enterprises of a business character.

Operating Statement A statement summarizing the financial operations of a governmental unit for an accounting period as contrasted with a Balance Sheet (q.v.) that shows financial position at a given moment in time.

Operating Transfers Legally authorized interfund transfers (from a fund receiving revenue to the fund that is to make the expenditures). This term was eliminated by GASB *Statement No. 34*. Instead, operating transfers are now one type of interfund transfers. See also Equity Transfers and Interfund Transfers.

Operational Accountability Information useful in assessing operating results and short- and long-term financial position and the cost of providing services from an economic perspective reported in entitywide financial statements.

Order A formal legislative enactment by the governing body of certain local governmental units that has the full force and effect of law. For example, county governing bodies in some states pass orders rather than laws or ordinances.

Ordinance A formal legislative enactment by the council or governing body of a municipality. If it is not in conflict with any higher form of law, such as a state statute or constitutional provision, it has the full force and effect of law within the boundaries of the municipality to which it applies. Note: The difference between an ordinance and a resolution (q.v.) is that the latter requires less legal formality and has a lower legal status. Ordinarily, the statutes or charter will specify or imply those legislative actions that must be by ordinance and those that must be by resolution. Revenue-raising measures, such as the imposition of taxes, special assessments, and service charges, universally require ordinances.

Organization Unit Units or departments within an entity, such as Police Department or City Attorney Department.

Organizational Test A nonprofit organization meets the organizational test if its articles of incorporation limit the organization's purposes to those described in IRC Sec. 501 and does not empower it to engage in activities that are not in furtherance of those purposes.

Original Cost The total of assets given and/or liabilities assumed to acquire an asset. In utility accounting, the original cost is the cost to the first owner who dedicated the plant to service of the public.

Other Appropriations Realized A budgetary account used in federal government accounting to record an agency's basic operating appropriations for a fiscal period.

Other Financing Sources An operating statement classification in which financial inflows other than revenues are reported, for example, proceeds of long-term debt and operating transfers-in.

Other Financing Uses An operating statement classification in which financial outflows other than expenditures are reported, for example, operating transfers-out.

Outlays Sometimes synonymous with disbursements. See also Capital Outlays.

Overdraft (1) The amount by which checks, drafts, or other demands for payment on the Treasury or on a bank exceed the amount of the credit against which they are drawn. (2) The amount by which requisitions, purchase orders, or audited vouchers exceed the appropriation or other credit to which they are chargeable.

Overhead Those elements of cost necessary in the production of an article or the performance of a service that are of such a nature that the amount applicable to the product or service cannot be determined accurately or readily. Usually they relate to those objects of expenditure that do not become an integral part of the finished product or service, such as rent, heat, light, supplies, management, or supervision.

Overlapping Debt The proportionate share of the debts of local governmental units located wholly or in part within the limits of the government reporting entity that must be borne by property within each governmental unit. Note: Except for special assessment debt, the amount of debt of each unit applicable to the reporting unit is arrived at by (1) determining what percentage of the total assessed value of the overlapping jurisdiction lies within the limits of the reporting unit and (2) applying this percentage to the total debt of the overlapping jurisdiction. Special assessment debt is allocated on the basis of the ratio of assessments receivable in each jurisdiction that will be used wholly or in part to pay off the debt to total assessments receivable that will be used wholly or in part for this purpose.

Oversight Agency The federal agency that makes the predominant amount of direct funding to the nonfederal entity receiving less than $25 million in federal awards. An oversight agency's responsibilities are similar to those of a cognizant agency, but less extensive.

Pay-As-You-Go Basis A term used to describe the financial policy of a governmental unit that finances all of its capital outlays from current revenues rather than by borrowing. A governmental unit that pays for some improvements from current revenues and others by borrowing is said to be on a *partial* or *modified pay-as-you-go basis*.

Pay-In Warrant See Deposit Warrant.

Payment Warrant See Warrant.

Penalty A legally mandated addition to a tax on the day it became delinquent (generally, the day after the day the tax is due).

Pension Trust Fund (PTS) See Public Employee Retirement Systems.

Performance Audit One of the two major types of audits defined by the U.S. General Accounting Office (see Financial Audit for the other type). A performance audit provides an auditor's independent determination (but not an opinion) of the extent to which government officials are efficiently, economically, and effectively carrying out their responsibilities.

Performance Budget A budget format that relates the input of resources and the output of services for each organizational unit individually. Sometimes used synonymously with program budget (q.v.).

Performance Indicator A measure of how well a health care organization "performed." Examples include "excess of revenues over expenses," "revenues and gains over expenses and losses," "earned income," and "performance earnings."

Permanent Fund The governmental-type fund used to account for public-purpose trusts for which the earnings are expendable for a specified purpose, but the principal amount is not expendable (i.e., an endowment).

Permanently Restricted Net Assets A term used in accounting for not-for-profit organizations indicating the amount of net assets whose use is permanently restricted by an external donor. See Endowment and Net Assets.

Perpetual Inventory A system whereby the inventory of units of property at any date may be obtained directly from the records without resorting to an actual physical count. A record is provided for each item or group of items to be inventoried and is so divided as to provide a running record of goods ordered, received, and withdrawn, and the balance on hand, in units and frequently also in value.

Petty Cash A sum of money set aside for the purpose of making change or paying small obligations for which the issuance of a formal voucher and check would be too expensive and time consuming. Sometimes called a *petty cash fund*, with the term *fund* here being used in the commercial sense of earmarked liquid assets.

Planning-Programming-Budgeting System (PPBS) A budgeting approach that integrates planning, programming, and budgeting into one system; most popular in the federal government during the 1960s.

Plant Acquisition Adjustment See Acquisition Adjustment.

Pooled Investments In order to simplify portfolio management, obtain a greater degree of investment diversification for individual endowment or trusts, and reduce brokerage, taxes, and bookkeeping expenses, investments may be merged, or pooled.

Postaudit An audit made after the transactions to be audited have taken place and have been recorded or have been approved for recording by designated officials if such approval is required. See also Preaudit.

Posting The act of transferring to an account in a ledger the data, either detailed or summarized, contained in a book or documentary of original entry.

Preaudit An examination for the purpose of determining the propriety of proposed financial transactions and financial transactions that have already taken place but have not yet been recorded, or, if such approval is required, before the approval of the financial transactions by designated officials for recording.

Preferred Provider Organization (PPO) See Health Maintenance Organization.

Prepaid Expenses Expenses entered in the accounts for benefits not yet received. Prepaid expenses differ from deferred charges in that they are spread over a shorter period of time than deferred charges and are regularly recurring costs of operations. Examples of prepaid expenses are prepaid rent, prepaid interest, and premiums on unexpired insurance.

Prepayment of Taxes The deposit of money with a governmental unit on condition that the amount deposited is to be applied against the tax liability of a designated taxpayer after the taxes have been levied and such liability has been established. See also Taxes Collected in Advance, and Deferred Revenues.

Primary Government A state government or general purpose local government. Also, a special purpose government that has a separately elected governing body, is legally separate, and is fiscally independent of other state or local governments.

Prior-Years' Encumbrances See Reserve for Encumbrances—Prior Year.

Prior-Years' Tax Levies Taxes levied for fiscal periods preceding the current one.

Private Foundation An organization exempt from federal income taxes under IRC Sec. 501(a) that (1) receives its support from a small number of individuals or corporations and investment income, rather than from the public at large, and (2) exists to make grants to public charities.

Private-Purpose Trust Contributions received under a trust agreement in which the investment income of an endowment are intended to benefit an external individual, organization, or government.

Private Trust Fund A trust fund (q.v.) that will ordinarily revert to private individuals or will be used for private purposes, for example, a fund that consists of guarantee deposits.

Pro Forma For form's sake; an indication of form; an example. The term is used in conjunction with a noun to denote merely a sample form, document, statement, certificate, or presentation, the contents of which may be either wholly or partially hypothetical, actual facts, estimates, or proposals.

Process Cost Cost accounting system most appropriate for recording costs of continuous activities or processes, such as governmental services, health care services, or higher education.

Program Budget A budget wherein inputs of resources and outputs of services are identified by programs without regard to the number of organizational units involved in performing various aspects of the program. See also Performance Budget and Traditional Budget.

Program Revenue Revenue linked to a specific function or program and reported separately from general revenues on the government-wide Statement of Activities.

Program-Specific Audit An audit of one specific federal program as opposed to a single audit of the whole entity.

Programs Activities, operations, or organizational units grouped together because they share purposes or objectives.

Project A plan of work, job, assignment, or task. Also refers to a job or task.

Promise to Give A pledge or promise to make a contribution that may be unconditional or conditional.

Propaganda Information that is skewed toward a particular belief with a tendency to have little or no factual basis.

Property Assessment A process by which each parcel of taxable real and personal property owned by each taxpayer is assigned a valuation.

Property Taxes Taxes levied by a legislative body against agricultural, commercial, residential, or personal property pursuant to law and in proportion to the assessed valuation of said property, or other appropriate basis. See Ad Valorem.

Proprietary Accounts Those accounts that show actual financial position and operations, such as actual assets, liabilities, reserves, fund balances, revenues, and expenditures, as distinguished from budgetary accounts (q.v.).

Proprietary Fund Sometimes referred to as *income-determination, business-like*, or *commercial-type* funds of a state or local governmental unit. Examples are enterprise funds and internal service funds.

Prospective Payment System (PPS) Medicare's system in which payments are based on allowed service costs for medical procedures within the same diagnosis-related group, rather than on the length of the patient's hospital stay or actual cost of services rendered.

Public Authority See Authority.

Public Charity An organization exempt from taxes under IRC Sec. 501(a) that receives its support from the public at large, rather than from a limited number of donors. Most often public charities are exempt from federal income taxes under IRC Sec. 501(c)(3).

Public Corporation See Municipal Corporation and Quasi-Municipal Corporation.

Public Employee Retirement Systems (PERS) The organizations that collect retirement and other employee benefit contributions from government employers and employees, manage assets, and make payments to qualified retirants, beneficiaries, and disabled employees.

Public Enterprise Fund See Enterprise Fund.

Public Improvement Fund See Special Assessment Fund.

Public-Purpose Trust Contributions received under a trust agreement in which the investment income or an endowment must be used to benefit a public program or function, or the citizenry.

Public Trust Fund A trust fund (q.v.) whose principal, earnings, or both, must be used for a public purpose, for example, a pension or retirement fund.

Purchase Order A document that authorizes the delivery of specified merchandise or the rendering of certain services and the making of a charge for them.

Purchases Method A method of recording supplies as Expenditures when purchased. If inventory levels have risen at the end of the month, the asset, Supplies Inventory, is debited and Fund Balance—Reserve for Inventory is credited. An alternative method is called the *Consumption Method*.

Purpose Restrictions Specifications by resource providers of the purposes for which resources are required to be used.

Quasi-External Transaction See Internal Exchange Transactions.

Quasi-Municipal Corporation An agency established by the state primarily for the purpose of helping to carry out its functions, for example, a county or school district. Note: Some counties and other agencies ordinarily classified as quasi-municipal corporations have been granted the powers of municipal corporations by the state in which they are located. See also Municipal Corporations.

Questioned Cost A cost identified by an auditor in an audit finding that generally relates to noncompliance with a law, regulation, or agreement, where the costs are either not supported by adequate documentation or appear unreasonable. OMB cost Circulars identify, for different kinds of organizations, which costs are allowable and unallowable.

Rate Base The value of utility property used in computing an authorized rate of return as authorized by law or a regulatory commission.

Realize To convert goods or services into cash or receivables. Also to exchange for property that is a current asset or can be converted immediately into a current asset. Sometimes applied to conversion of noncash assets into cash.

Rebates Abatements (q.v.) or refunds (q.v.).

Receipts This term, unless otherwise qualified, means cash received.

Recoverable Expenditure An expenditure made for or on behalf of another governmental unit, fund, or department, or for a private individual, firm, or corporation, that will subsequently be recovered in cash or its equivalent.

Refund (Noun) An amount paid back or credit allowed because of an overcollection or on account of the return of an object sold. (Verb) To pay back or allow credit for an amount because of an overcollection or because of the return of an object sold. (Verb) To provide for the payment of a loan through cash or credit secured by a new loan.

Refunding Bonds Bonds issued to retire bonds already outstanding. The refunding bonds may be sold for cash and outstanding bonds redeemed in cash, or the refunding bonds may be exchanged with holders of outstanding bonds.

Registered Bond A bond the owner of which is registered with the issuing governmental unit, and that cannot be sold or exchanged without a change of registration.

Registered Warrant A warrant that is registered by the paying officer for future payment on account of present lack of funds and that is to be paid in the order of its registration. In some cases, such warrants are registered when issued; in others, they are registered when first presented to the paying officer by the holders. See also Warrant.

Regular Serial Bonds Bonds payable in which the total principal is repayable in a specified number of equal annual installments.

Regulatory Accounting Principles (RAP) The accounting principles prescribed by federal or state regulatory commissions for investor-owned and some governmentally owned utilities. Also called *statutory accounting principles* (SAP). RAP or some SAP may differ from GAAP.

Reimbursement Cash or other assets received as a repayment of the cost of work or services performed or of other expenditures made for or on behalf of another governmental unit or department or for an individual, firm, or corporation.

Replacement Cost The cost as of a certain date of a property that can render similar service (but need not be of the same structural form) as the property to be replaced. See also Reproduction Cost.

Reportable Condition A significant deficiency in the design or operation of the internal control structure that could adversely affect the entity's ability to administer federal financial assistance programs in accordance with laws and regulations.

Reporting Entity The primary government and all related component units, if any, combined in accordance with GASB *Codification* Section 2100 constitute the governmental reporting entity.

Reproduction Cost The cost as of a certain date of reproducing an exactly similar new property in the same place.

Repurchase Agreement An agreement wherein a governmental unit transfers cash to a financial institution in exchange for securities, and the financial institution agrees to repurchase the same securities at an agreed-upon price.

Required Supplemental Information (RSI) Information that is required by generally accepted accounting principles to be included with the audited annual financial statements, usually directly following the notes to the general purpose external financial statements.

Requisition A written demand or request, usually from one department to the purchasing officer or to another department, for specified articles or services.

Reserve An account that records a portion of the fund equity that must be segregated for some future use and that is, therefore, not available for further appropriation or expenditure. See Reserve for Inventory or Reserve for Encumbrances.

Reserve for Change in Fair Value of Investments An account used by a cash and investment pool to accumulate realized and unrealized gains and losses on sales of investments pending distribution to pool participants. See Undistributed Earnings.

Reserve for Encumbrances A segregation of a portion of fund equity in the amount of encumbrances outstanding. See also Reserve.

Reserve for Encumbrances—Prior Year Encumbrances outstanding at the end of a fiscal year are designated as pertaining to appropriations of a year prior to the current year in order that related expenditures may be matched with the appropriations of the prior year rather than an appropriation of the current year.

Reserve for Inventory A segregation of a portion of fund equity to indicate that assets equal to the amount of the reserve are invested in inventories and are, therefore, not available for appropriation.

Reserve for Noncurrent Interfund Loans Receivable A reserve that represents the segregation of a portion of a fund equity to indicate that assets equal to the amount of the reserve are invested in a long-term loan to another fund and are, therefore, not available for appropriation.

Reserve for Revenue Bond Contingency A reserve in an Enterprise Fund that represents the segregation of a portion of net assets equal to current assets that are restricted for meeting various contingencies, as may be specified and defined in the revenue bond indenture.

Reserve for Revenue Bond Debt Service A reserve in an Enterprise Fund that represents the segregation of a portion of net assets equal to current assets that are restricted to current servicing of revenue bonds in accordance with the terms of a bond indenture.

Reserve for Revenue Bond Retirement A reserve in an Enterprise Fund that represents the segregation of a portion of net assets equal to current assets that are restricted for future servicing of revenue bonds in accordance with the terms of a bond indenture.

Reserve for Uncollected Taxes A reserve equal to the amount of taxes receivable by a fund. The reserve is deducted from Taxes Receivable, thus effectively placing the fund on the cash basis of revenue recognition.

Residual Equity Transfer Nonrecurring or nonroutine transfers of equity between funds (e.g., transfers of residual balances of discontinued funds to the General Fund or a debt service fund). This term was eliminated by GASB *Statement No. 34*. See also Equity Transfer and Interfund Transfers.

Resolution A special or temporary order of a legislative body; an order of a legislative body requiring less legal formality than an ordinance or statute. See also Ordinance.

Resources Legally budgeted revenues of a state or local government that have not been recognized as revenues under the modified accrual basis of accounting as of the date of an interim Balance Sheet.

Restricted Assets Assets (usually of an enterprise fund) that may not be used for normal operating purposes because of the requirements of regulatory authorities, provisions in bond indentures, or other legal agreements, but that need not be accounted for in a separate fund.

Restricted Fund A fund established to account for assets the use of which is limited by the requirements of donors or grantors. Hospitals may use three types of restricted funds for internal purposes: specific purpose funds, endowment funds, and plant replacement and expansion funds. The governing body or administration cannot restrict the use of assets; they may only designate the use of assets. See Board-Designated Funds.

Restricted Net Assets The portion of the residual of assets and liabilities (i.e., net assets) that has been restricted in purpose or time by parties external to the organization.

Retirement Allowances Amounts paid to government employees who have retired from active service or to their survivors. See Annuity.

Retirement Fund A fund out of which retirement annuities and/or other benefits are paid to authorized and designated public employees. A retirement fund is accounted for as a Pension Trust Fund (q.v.).

Revenue The inflow of economic resources resulting from the delivery of services or activities that constitute the organization's major or central operations, rather than from interfund transfers (q.v.) and debt issue proceeds.

Revenue Anticipation Notes (RANS) Notes issued in anticipation of the collection of revenues, usually from specified sources, and to be repaid upon the collection of the revenues.

Revenue Bonds Bonds whose principal and interest are payable exclusively from earnings of a public enterprise. In addition to a pledge of revenues, such bonds sometimes contain a mortgage on the enterprise's property and are then known as *mortgage revenue bonds*.

Revenue Receipts A term used synonymously with *revenue* (q.v.) by some governmental units that account for their revenues on a cash basis (q.v.). See also Nonrevenue Receipts.

Revenues Budget A legally adopted budget authorizing the collection of revenues from specified sources and estimating the amounts to be collected during the period from each source.

Revenues Collected in Advance A liability account that represents revenues collected before they are earned.

Revolving Fund See Internal Service Fund.

Risk-Based Approach This approach, used by auditors to determine which programs will be audited as part of the single audit, is a five-step process designed to select federal programs that are relatively large as well as likely to have problems. The auditors can use their professional judgment to classify programs that have been audited recently without audit findings, have had no significant changes in personnel or systems, or have a high level of oversight by awarding agencies as "low risk."

Risk Contract An insurance policy used to protect a prepaid health care plan from losses arising from excess of actual cost of providing health care over the fixed (capitation) fee.

Schedules (1) The explanatory or supplementary statements that accompany the Balance Sheet or other principal statements periodically prepared from the accounts. (2) The accountant's or auditor's principal work papers covering their examination of the books and accounts. (3) A written enumeration or detailed list in orderly form. See also Exhibit and Statements.

Scrip An evidence of indebtedness, usually in small denomination, secured or unsecured, interest-bearing or noninterest-bearing, stating that the governmental unit, under conditions set forth, will pay the face value of the certificate or accept it in payment of certain obligations.

Securities Bonds, notes, mortgages, or other forms of negotiable or nonnegotiable instruments. See also Investments.

Self-Supporting or Self-Liquidating Debt Debt obligations whose principal and interest are payable solely from the earnings of the enterprise for the construction or improvement of which they were originally issued. See also Revenue Bonds.

Serial Annuity Bonds Serial bonds in which the annual installments of bond principal are so arranged that the combined payments for principal and interest are approximately the same each year.

Serial Bonds Bonds the principal of which is repaid in periodic installments over the life of the issue. See Serial Annuity Bonds and Deferred Serial Bonds.

Service Efforts and Accomplishments (SEA) A conceptualization of the resources consumed (inputs), tasks performed (outputs), and goals attained (outcomes), and the relationship among these items, in providing services in selected areas (e.g., police protection, solid waste garbage collection, and elementary and secondary education).

Shared Revenue Revenue levied by one governmental unit but shared, usually on a predetermined basis, with another unit of government or class of governments.

Shared Tax See Shared Revenue.

Short-Term Debt Debt with a maturity of one year or less after the date of issuance. Short-term debt usually includes floating debt, bond anticipation notes, tax anticipation notes, and interim warrants.

Single Audit An audit prescribed by federal law for state and local governmental units and nonprofit organizations that receive federal financial assistance above a specified amount. Such an audit is to be conducted in conformity with the Office of Management and Budget *Circular A-133*. Such an audit is conducted on an organizationwide basis rather than on the former grant-by-grant basis. The Single Audit Act of 1984, as amended in 1996, and the circular cited above impose uniform, and rigorous, requirements for conducting and reporting on single audits.

Sinking Fund See Debt Service Fund.

Sinking Fund Bonds Bonds issued under an agreement that requires the governmental unit to set aside periodically out of its revenues a sum that, with compound earnings thereon, will be sufficient to redeem the bonds at their stated date of maturity. Sinking fund bonds are usually also term bonds (q.v.).

Special Assessment A compulsory levy made against certain properties to defray part or all of the cost of a specific improvement or service that is presumed to be a general benefit to the public and of special benefit to such properties.

Special Assessment Bonds Bonds payable from the proceeds of special assessments (q.v.). If the bonds are payable only from the collections of special assessments, they are known as *special-special assessment bonds*. If, in addition to the assessments, the full faith and credit of the governmental unit is pledged, they are known as *general obligation special assessment bonds*.

Special Assessment Liens Receivable Claims that a governmental unit has on properties until special assessments (q.v.) levied against them have been paid. The term normally applies to those delinquent special assessments for the collection of which legal action has been taken through the filing of claims.

Special Assessment Roll The official list showing the amount of special assessments (q.v.) levied against each property presumed to be benefited by an improvement or service.

Special District An independent unit of local government organized to perform a single governmental function or a restricted number of related functions. Special districts usually have the power to incur debt and levy taxes; however, certain types of special districts are entirely dependent on enterprise earnings and cannot impose taxes. Examples of special districts are water districts, drainage districts, flood control districts, hospital districts, fire protection districts, transit authorities, port authorities, and electric power authorities.

Special District Bonds Bonds issued by a special district. See Special District.

Special Fund Any fund that must be devoted to some special use in accordance with specific regulations and restrictions. Generally, the term applies to all funds other than the General Fund (q.v.).

Special Purpose Governments Governments that provide only a single function, or a limited number of functions, such as independent school districts and special districts. Formerly called limited purpose governments.

Special Revenue Fund (SRF) A fund used to account for revenues from specific taxes or other earmarked revenue sources that by law are designated to finance particular functions or activities of government. After the fund is established, it usually continues year after year until discontinued or revised by properly legislative authority. An example is a motor fuel tax fund used to finance highway and road construction.

Special-Special Assessment Bonds See Special Assessment Bonds.

Spending Rate The proportion of total return that may prudently be used by an institution for current purposes.

Split Interest Agreements Forms of planned giving by donors who divide the rights to investment income on assets and assets themselves with intended beneficiary organizations in a predetermined manner.

Statements (1) Used in a general sense, statements are all of those formal written presentations that set forth financial information. (2) In technical accounting usage, statements are those presentations of financial data that show the financial position and the results of financial operations of a fund, or an entire governmental reporting entity, or component unit thereof, for a particular accounting period. See also Exhibit and Schedule.

Statute A written law enacted by a duly organized and constituted legislative body. See also Ordinance, Resolution, and Order.

Statutory Accounting Principles See Regulatory Accounting Principles.

Stewardship Investments Beneficial investments of the federal government in such items as nonfederal physical property (property financed by the federal government but owned by state or local governments), human capital, and research and development.

Stewardship Land Federal land other than that included in general property, plant, and equipment (e.g., national parks).

Stewardship Property, Plant, and Equipment Term used to describe three categories of federal PPE: (1) Federal Mission PPE, (2) Heritage assets, and (3) stewardship land.

Stores Materials and supplies on hand in storerooms, subject to requisition and use.

Straight Serial Bonds Serial bonds (q.v.) in which the annual installments of a bond principal are approximately equal.

Subactivity A specific line of work performed in carrying out a governmental activity. For example, replacing defective street lamps would be a subactivity under the activity of street light maintenance.

Subfunction A grouping of related activities within a particular governmental function. For example, "police" is a subfunction of the function "public safety."

Subsidiary Account One of a group of related accounts that support in detail the debit and credit summaries recorded in a control account. An example is the individual property taxpayers' accounts for taxes receivable in the general ledger. See also Control Account and Subsidiary Ledger.

Subsidiary Ledger A group of subsidiary accounts (q.v.) the sum of the balances of which is equal to the balance of the related control account. See also Control Account and Subsidiary Account.

Subvention A grant (q.v.).

Support The increase in net assets arising from contributions of resources or nonexchange transactions and includes only amounts for which the donor receives no direct tangible benefits from the recipient agency.

Surety Bond A written promise to pay damages or to indemnify against losses caused by the party or parties named in the document, through nonperformance or through defalcation. An example is a surety bond given by a contractor or by an official handling cash or securities.

Surplus Now generally obsolete in accounting usage. See Fund Balance.

Surplus Receipts A term sometimes applied to receipts that increase the balance of a fund but are not a part of its normal revenue, for example, collection of accounts previously written off. Sometimes used as an account title.

Suspense Account An account that carries charges or credits temporarily, pending the determination of the proper account or accounts to which they are to be posted. See Suspense Fund and Clearing Account.

Suspense Fund A fund established to account separately for certain receipts pending the distribution or disposal thereof. See also Agency Fund.

Sweep Accounts Arrangements in which a bank automatically "sweeps" cash that exceeds the target balance into short-term cash investments.

Syndicate, Underwriting A group formed for the marketing of a given security issue too large for one member to handle expeditiously, after which the group is dissolved.

Tax Anticipation Notes (TANs) Notes (sometimes called *warrants*) issued in anticipation of collection of taxes, usually retirable only from tax collections, and frequently only from the proceeds of the tax levy whose collection they anticipate.

Tax Anticipation Warrants See Tax Anticipation Notes.

Tax Certificate A certificate issued by a governmental unit as evidence of the conditional transfer of title to tax-delinquent property from the original owner to the holder of the certificate. If the owner does not pay the amount of the tax arrearage and other charges required by law during the special period of redemption, the holder can foreclose to obtain title. Also called *tax sale certificate* and *tax lien certificate* in some jurisdictions. See also Tax Deed.

Tax Deed A written instrument by which title to property sold for taxes is transferred unconditionally to the purchaser. A tax deed is issued on foreclosure of the tax lien (q.v.) obtained by the purchaser at the tax sale. The tax lien cannot be foreclosed until the expiration of the period during which the owner may redeem his property through paying the delinquent taxes and other charges. See also Tax Certificate.

Tax Expenditure A revenue loss attributable to provisions of federal tax laws that allow a special exclusion, exemption, or deduction from gross income, or that provide a special credit, a preferential rate of tax, or a deferral of tax liability.

Tax Increment Debt Debt secured by an incremental tax earmarked for servicing the debt, such as a half-cent sales tax, or payable from taxes derived from incremental growth in the tax base that was financed by the tax increment debt.

Tax Levy See Levy.

Tax Levy Ordinance An ordinance (q.v.) by means of which taxes are levied.

Tax Liens Claims that governmental units have on properties until taxes levied against them have been paid. Note: The term is sometimes limited to those delinquent taxes for the collection of which legal action has been taken through the filing of liens.

Tax Liens Receivable Legal claims against property that have been exercised because of nonpayment of delinquent taxes, interest, and penalties. The account includes delinquent taxes, interest, and penalties receivable up to the date the lien becomes effective, and the cost of holding the sale.

Tax Notes See Tax Anticipation Notes.

Tax Rate The amount of tax stated in terms of a unit of the tax base, for example, 25 mills per dollar of assessed valuation of taxable property.

Tax Rate Limit The maximum rate at which a governmental unit may levy a tax. The limit may apply to taxes raised for a particular purpose, or to taxes imposed for all purposes; and may apply to a single government, to a class of governments, or to all governmental units operating in a particular area. Overall tax rate limits usually restrict levies for all purposes and of all governments, state and local, having jurisdiction in a given area.

Tax Roll The official list showing the amount of taxes levied against each taxpayer or property. Frequently, the tax roll and the assessment roll are combined, but even in these cases the two can be distinguished.

Tax Sale Certificate See Tax Certificate.

Tax Supplement A tax levied by a local unit of government that has the same base as a similar tax levied by a higher level of government, such as a state or province. The local tax supplement is frequently administered by the higher level of government along with its own tax. A locally imposed, state-administered sales tax is an example of a tax supplement.

Tax-Supported Debt All debt secured by pledges of tax revenues.

Tax Title Notes Obligations secured by pledges of the governmental unit's interest in certain tax liens or tax titles.

Taxable Property All property except that which is exempt from taxation—examples are property owned by governmental units and property used by some religious and charitable organizations.

Taxes Compulsory charges levied by a governmental unit for the purpose of financing services performed for the common benefit. Note: The term does not include specific charges made against particular persons or property for current or permanent benefits such as special assessments. Neither does the term include charges for services rendered only to those paying such charges as, for example, sewer service charges.

Taxes Collected in Advance A liability for taxes collected before the tax levy has been made or before the amount of taxpayer liability has been established.

Taxes Levied for Other Governmental Units Taxes levied by the reporting governmental unit for other governmental units, which, when collected, are to be paid over to these units.

Taxes Paid in Advance Same as Taxes Collected in Advance. Also called *Prepaid Taxes*.

Taxes Receivable—Current The uncollected portion of taxes that a governmental unit has levied but that are not yet delinquent.

Taxes Receivable—Delinquent Taxes remaining unpaid on and after the date on which a penalty for nonpayment is attached. Even though the penalty may be subsequently waived and a portion of the taxes may be abated or canceled, the unpaid balances continue to be delinquent taxes until paid, abated, canceled, or converted into tax liens.

Temporarily Restricted Net Assets A term used in accounting for not-for-profit organizations indicating the amount of net assets temporarily restricted by an external donor for use in a future period or for a particular purpose. See Net Assets.

Temporary Loans Short-term obligations representing amounts borrowed for short periods of time and usually evidenced by notes payable (q.v.) or warrants payable (q.v.). They may be unsecured, or secured by specific revenues to be collected. See also Tax Anticipation Notes.

Term Bonds Bonds the entire principal of which matures on one date.

Term Bonds Payable A liability account that records the face value of general obligation term bonds issued and outstanding.

Term Endowment Funds for which donors or other external agencies have stipulated, as a condition of the gift, that the principal is to be maintained intact for a stated period of time (or term).

Third-Party Payor Term used in health care organizations to refer to the entity that pays for services, other than the patient/client, such as an insurance company or federal insurance program.

Time Requirements Requirements that relate to the period when resources are required to be used or when use may begin.

Time Warrant A negotiable obligation of a governmental unit having a term shorter than bonds, and frequently tendered to individuals and firms in exchange for contractual services, capital acquisitions, or equipment purchases.

Time Warrants Payable The amount of time warrants outstanding and unpaid.

Total Quality Management (TQM) A management approach in which an organization seeks to continuously improve its ability to meet or exceed customer demands, where *customer*, in government or not-for-profit organization usage, may be broadly defined to include such parties as taxpayers, service recipients, students, and members.

Total Return A comprehensive measure of rate of investment return in which the sum of net realized and unrealized appreciation or shrinkage in portfolio value is added to dividend and interest yield.

Traditional Budget A term sometimes applied to the budget of a governmental unit wherein appropriations are based entirely or primarily on objects of expenditure. The focus of a traditional budget is on input of resources, rather than on the relationship between input of resources and output of services. For budgets focusing on the latter, see Program Budget and Performance Budget.

Transfers See Interfund Transfers, Operating Transfers, and Residual Equity Transfers.

Trial Balance A list of the balances of the accounts in a ledger kept by double entry (q.v.), with the debit and credit balances shown in separate columns. If the totals of the debit and credit columns are equal or their net balance agrees with a control account, the ledger from which the figures are taken is said to be "in balance."

Trust and Agency Funds See Agency Fund, Trust Fund, and Fiduciary Fund.

Trust Fund A fund consisting of resources received and held by the governmental unit as trustee, to be expended or invested in accordance with the conditions of the trust. See also Endowment Fund, Private-Purpose Trust Fund, and Public-Purpose Trust Fund.

2a7 Pool An external investment pool that is not registered with the Securities and Exchange Commission as an investment company, but has a policy that it will, and does, operate in a manner consistent with the SEC's Rule 2a7 of the Investment Company Act of 1940.

Unallotted Balance of Appropriation An appropriation balance available for allotment (q.v.).

Unamortized Discounts on Bonds Sold That portion of the excess of the face value of bonds over the amount received from their sale that remains to be written off periodically over the life of the bonds.

Unamortized Premiums on Bonds Sold An account that represents that portion of the excess of bond proceeds over par value and that remains to be amortized over the remaining life of such bonds.

Unapportioned Authority The amount of a federal appropriation made by the Congress and approved by the President, but not yet apportioned by the Office of Management and Budget. See Other Appropriations Realized and Apportionments.

Unbilled Accounts Receivable An account that designates the estimated amount of accounts receivable for services or commodities sold but not billed. For example, if a utility bills its customers bimonthly but prepares monthly financial statements, the amount of services rendered or commodities sold during the first month of the bimonthly period would be reflected in the Balance Sheet under this account title.

Unconditional Promise to Give A promise to make contributions to an organization that depends only on the passage of time or demand by the promisee for performance.

Underwriting Syndicate See Syndicate, Underwriting.

Undistributed Earnings An account used by a cash and investment pool to accumulate investment earnings pending distribution to pool participants. See also Reserve for Change in Fair Value of Investments.

Unearned Income See Deferred Revenues.

Unencumbered Allotment That portion of an allotment not yet expended or encumbered.

Unencumbered Appropriation That portion of an appropriation not yet expended or encumbered.

Unexpended Allotment That portion of an allotment that has not been expended.

Unexpended Appropriations The equity of a federal agency provided by an appropriation that has not yet been expended.

Unfunded Actuarial Liability See Actuarial Accrued Liability (AAL).

Unit Cost A term used in cost accounting to denote the cost of producing a unit of product or rendering a unit of service, for example, the cost of treating and purifying a thousand gallons of sewage.

Unliquidated Encumbrances Encumbrances outstanding.

Unrealized Revenue See Accrued Revenue.

Unrelated Business Income (UBI) Gross income from trade or business regularly carried on by a tax-exempt organization less directly connected expenses, certain net operating losses, and qualified charitable contributions that is not related to its exempt purpose. UBI greater than $1,000 is subject to federal income tax at corporate tax rates.

Unrestricted Assets Assets that may be utilized at the discretion of the governing board of a nonprofit entity.

Unrestricted Funds Funds established to account for assets or resources that may be utilized at the discretion of the governing board.

Unrestricted Net Assets The portion of the excess of total assets over total liabilities that may be utilized at the discretion of the governing board of a governmental or not-for-profit entity. See Net Assets, Temporarily Restricted Net Assets, and Permanently Restricted Net Assets.

User Charge A charge levied against users of a service or purchasers of a product of an enterprise fund or an internal service fund.

Utility Fund See Enterprise Fund.

Utility Plant Acquisition Adjustment The premium paid on a utility plant purchased by a governmental unit. Similar to goodwill in that it is the difference between the purchase price and fair value of the assets acquired; however, it is different because utilities do not capitalize the value of excess earnings.

Value As used in governmental accounting, this term designates (1) the act of describing anything in terms of money or (2) the measure of a thing in terms of money. The term should not be used without further qualification. See also Book Value and Face Value.

Variance Power The unilateral power of an organization to redirect donated assets to a beneficiary different than the third party initially indicated by the donor.

Voluntary Health and Welfare Organization Not-for-profit organizations that receive contributions from the public at large and provide health and welfare services for a nominal or no fee. Also known as Human Service Organizations.

Voluntary Nonexchange Transactions A category of nonexchange transaction that includes certain grants and entitlements and most donations.

Voucher A written document that evidences the propriety of transactions and usually indicates the accounts in which they are to be recorded.

Voucher Check A document combining a check and a brief description of the transaction covered by the check.

Voucher System A system that calls for the preparation of vouchers (q.v.) for transactions involving payments and for the recording of such vouchers in a special book of original entry (q.v.), known as a *voucher register,* in the order in which payment is approved.

Vouchers Payable Liabilities for goods and services evidenced by vouchers that have been preaudited and approved for payment but not been paid.

Warrant An order drawn by the legislative body or an officer of a governmental unit on its treasurer, directing the latter to pay a specified amount to the person named or to the bearer. It may be payable on demand, in which case it usually circulates the same as a bank check, or it may be payable only out of certain revenues when and if received, in which case it does not circulate as freely. See also Registered Warrant and Deposit Warrant.

Warrants for Disbursements A formal certification of the validity of the debt, with authorization or direction to a financial agent to pay the debt. One step beyond a voucher in the payment process.

Warrants Payable The amount of warrants outstanding and unpaid.

Work Order A written order authorizing and directing the performance of a certain task and issued to the person who is to direct the work. Among the items of information shown on the order are the nature and location of the job, specifications of the work to be performed, and a job number that is referred to in reporting the amount of labor, materials, and equipment used.

Work Program A plan of work proposed to be done during a particular period by an administrative agency in carrying out its assigned activities.

Work Unit A fixed quantity that will consistently measure work effort expended in the performance of an activity or the production of a commodity.

Working Capital Fund See Internal Service Fund.

Yield Rate See Effective Interest Rate.

Zero-Based Budget (ZBB) A budget based on the concept that the very existence of each activity must be justified each year, as well as the amounts of resources requested to be allocated to each activity.

Governmental and Not-for-Profit Organizations

AAA **American Accounting Association** An organization of accounting educators and practitioners involved in education whose objectives are to contribute to the development of accounting theory, to encourage and sponsor accounting research, and to improve the quality of accounting education.

ACE **American Council on Education** A not-for-profit organization founded in 1918 with members from institutions of all sectors of higher education and other education-related organizations. It provides leadership and advocacy on adult and higher education issues, represents the views of the higher education community to policy makers, and offers services to its members.

AFGI **Association of Financial Guaranty Insurors** The trade association of the insurers and reinsurers of municipal bonds and asset-backed securities.

AGA **Association of Government Accountants** An association formed in 1950 to serve the professional interests of governmental financial managers by providing education, encouraging professional development, influencing governmental financial management policies and practices, and serving as an advocate for the profession.

AHA **American Hospital Association** An association organized in the early 1900s by hospital administrators to promote economy and efficiency in hospital management. It current mission is to take a leadership role in public policy, representation and advocacy, and health services.

AICPA **American Institute of Certified Public Accountants** The professional organization to which certified public accountants (CPAs) belong. In addition to providing educational and lobbying services on behalf of its members, the AICPA is responsible for promulgating auditing standards.

APPA **American Public Power Association** The national trade association representing state and local government-owned electric utilities.

ASBO **Association of School Business Officials International** A professional association that provides programs and services to employees of public and private schools (including community and junior colleges and state departments of education) that promote the highest standards of school business management practices, professional growth, and the effective use of educational resources.

BMA **Bond Market Association** An association that represents securities firms and banks that underwrite, trade, and sell debt securities, including municipal bonds, U.S. Treasury securities, Federal Agency securities, and other asset-backed securities.

CBO **Congressional Budget Office** An office of the legislative branch of the federal government established in 1974 that gathers information for the House and Senate budget committees with respect to the budget submitted to the executive branch, appropriations bills, other bills providing budget authority, tax expenditures, and other analysis.

CSG **Council of State Governments** An association of state financial officers formed in 1933 to assist states with multistate and regional solutions to problems.

FAF **Financial Accounting Foundation** The organization that finances and appoints members of the Financial Accounting Standards Board and Governmental Accounting Standards Board.

FASAB **Federal Accounting Standards Advisory Board** The nine-member standards-setting body that recommends federal governmental accounting and financial reporting standards to the U.S. Comptroller General, Secretary of the Treasury, and Director of the Office of Management and Budget.

FASAC **Financial Accounting Standards Advisory Council** The council that advises the Financial Accounting Standards Board on policy matters, agenda items, project priorities, technical issues, and task forces.

FASB **Financial Accounting Standards Board** An independent, nongovernmental, privately funded entity that is responsible to the public at large and the public accounting profession for developing concepts, standards, and guidance on financial accounting and reporting for commercial entities as well as nongovernmental, not-for-profit organizations. The organization was established in 1973 and replaced the Accounting Principles Board.

GAO **General Accounting Office** An agency of the legislative branch of the federal government responsible for prescribing accounting principles for federal agencies. The auditing arm of Congress.

GASAC **Governmental Accounting Standards Advisory Council** The council that advises the Governmental Accounting Standards Board on policy matters, agenda items, project priorities, technical issues, and task forces. Its members are broadly representative of preparers, attestors, and users of financial information.

GASB **Governmental Accounting Standards Board** The independent agency established under the Financial Accounting Foundation in 1984 as the official body designated to set accounting and financial reporting standards for state and local governments.

GFOA **Government Finance Officers Association** A professional association of government finance managers founded in 1906 (formerly the Municipal Finance Officers Association) to help establish uniformity in state and local government accounting practices. The GFOA administers the Certificate of Achievement program to reward excellence in financial reporting, budgeting, and other areas.

GRA **Governmental Research Association** A national organization, founded in 1914, of individuals professionally engaged in governmental research.

HFMA **Healthcare Financial Management Association** A nonprofit organization of financial management professionals employed by hospitals and other health care providers established in 1946 to provide professional development opportunities, influence health care policy, and communicate information and technical data.

ICMA **International City/County Management Association** An organization founded in 1914 (formerly International City Management Association) that is the professional and educational association of appointed administrators serving cities, counties, other local governments, and regional entities around the world.

NACo **National Association of Counties** An organization created in 1935 by county officials to provide legislative, research, technical, and public affairs assistance to members, and ensure that the concerns of over 3,000 counties in the United States are heard at the federal level of government.

NACUBO **National Association of College & University Business Officers** A nonprofit professional organization founded in 1962 representing chief administrative and financial officers at colleges and universities whose mission is to promote sound management and financial practices at institutions of higher education.

NASACT **National Association of State Auditors, Comptrollers, and Treasurers** An organization formed in 1915 to represent the states' views on financial management issues and to provide leadership and training in meeting state fiscal and financial management challenges in order to improve the financial management of state government.

NASBO **National Association of State Budget Officers** The professional membership organization for state finance officers through which the states have collectively advanced state budget practices for more than 50 years.

NASRA **National Association of State Retirement Administrators** An organization comprised of the administrators of the state retirement systems for the 50 states, the District of Columbia, and U.S. territories.

NCGA **National Council on Governmental Accounting** The body that established accounting and financial reporting standards for state and local governments prior to the formation of the Governmental Accounting Standards Board.

NCSL **National Conference of State Legislatures** A national association of state legislatures that includes many sections offering services to member legislatures, such as the NCSL Leadership Staff Section for leaders and party caucuses and the National Legislative Services and Security Association, which produces a manual to enable legislatures to cope with the problems of maintaining order and normal operations.

NFMA **National Federation of Municipal Analysts** An association chartered in 1983 to promote professionalism in municipal credit analysis and furthering the skill level of its members through educational programs and industry communication.

NGA **National Governors' Association** A bipartisan national organization of the nations' governors founded in 1908 through which the governors identify priority issues and deal collectively with issues of public policy and governance at both the national and state levels.

NLC **National League of Cities** An organization founded in 1924 (formerly the American Municipal Association) by state municipal leagues to serve and represent municipal governments by establishing unified policy positions, advocating these policies, and sharing information that strengthens municipal government throughout the nation.

OMB **Office of Management and Budget** An office of the executive branch of the federal government that has responsibility for establishing policies and procedures for approving and publishing financial accounting principles and standards to be followed by executive branch agencies. It also has the authority to control the size and nature of appropriations requested of each Congress.

PCIE **President's Council on Integrity and Efficiency** A federal agency established by executive order that is comprised of all presidentially appointed Inspectors General, as well as other federal agency members. Its charge is to conduct interagency and interentity audits, and inspection and investigation projects in order to effectively and efficiently deal with government-wide issues of fraud, waste, and abuse.

SEC **Securities and Exchange Commission** An independent, quasi-judicial federal agency formed in 1934 to protect investors in publicly traded securities by ensuring that there is full and fair disclosure of all material facts concerning securities offered for sale across state lines.

USCM **U.S. Conference of Mayors** A nonpartisan organization established in 1932 representing U.S. cities with populations of 30,000 or more. The conference aids the development of effective national urban policy, strengthens federal–city relationships, ensures that federal policy meets urban needs, and provides mayors with leadership and management tools of value in their cities.

For the address, phone number, fax number, Internet address, and journal of each of these organizations, see one of the authors' websites: http://www.online.emich.edu/~acc_kattelus under "Government and Nonprofit Resources."

Index